MEDITATION:

CLASSIC AND CONTEMPORARY PERSPECTIVES

MEDITATION:

CLASSIC AND CONTEMPORARY PERSPECTIVES

Deane H. Shapiro, Jr.

Roger N. Walsh

Editors

ALDINE
Publishing Company
New York

About the Editors

DEANE H. SHAPIRO, JR. is currently a faculty member in the Department of Psychiatry and Human Behavior, University of California Irvine Medical Center, California College of Medicine. Dr. Shapiro, a Diplomate of the American Board of Professional Psychology (Clinical), served for several years on the clinical faculty of the Department of Psychiatry and Behavioral Sciences, Stanford University Medical School and as Dean of Academic Affairs at the Pacific Graduate School of Psychology. He is author of the critically acclaimed *Meditation: Self-Regulation Strategy and Altered State of Consciousness,* as well as *Precision Nirvana,* and co-editor (with Roger Walsh) of *Beyond Health and Normality: Explorations of Exceptional Psychological Well Being.*

ROGER N. WALSH is a psychiatrist on the Faculty of the School of Medicine at the University of California at Irvine. Though initially skeptical, his own experiences with meditation led him to conclude that it was a potentially valuable discipline, and has now been a student of meditation practice and research for many years. His current interests include the integration of Eastern and Western science and the understanding which mental health professionals might bring to the solution of the global problems which currently threaten human welfare and survival. He is the author of *Toward an Ecology of Brain and Beyond Ego: Readings in Transpersonal Psychology.*

Aldine Publishing Company
200 Saw Mill River Road
Hawthorne, New York 10532

Library of Congress Cataloging in Publication Data
Main entry under title:

Meditation, classic and contemporary perspectives.

    Bibliography: p.
    Includes index.
    1. Meditation—Therapeutic use. I. Shapiro, Deane H.
II. Walsh, Roger N.
RC489.M43M43 1984   615.8'51   84-300
ISBN 0-202-25136-5

Printed in the United States
10 9 8 7 6 5 4 3 2 1

DEDICATION

To those individuals who, through whatever path and means—from science to the arts—dedicate themselves to the building and preservation of a world filled with peace and caring (DHS)

Dedicated to Jack Kornfield, Joseph Goldstein, and the staff and teachers of the Insight Meditation Center at Barre, Massachusetts, who through selfless service have done so much to aid the spread of meditation in the West. And to all those who have committed themselves to meditation practice as a means of self-awakening and of contributing to the welfare of us all (RNW)

TABLE OF CONTENTS

III PHYSIOLOGY OF MEDITATION

Contents   ix

IV ADDITIONAL DEVELOPMENTS IN CLINICAL AND RESEARCH ASPECTS OF MEDITATION

V VIEWS OF THE STATE-OF-THE-ART

VI EPILOGUE

LIST OF PERMISSIONS

We give thanks to the following journals and authors for permission to reprint articles:

Psychological Bulletin for permission to reprint Smith, J., Meditation as psychotherapy: A review of the literature.

Archives of General Psychiatry for permission to reprint Shapiro, D. and Giber, D., Meditation and psychotherapeutic effects: Self-regulation strategy and altered state of consciousness.

Journal of Clinical and Consulting Psychology for permission to reprint Goleman, D. and Schwartz, G., Meditation as an intervention in stress reactivity.

Journal of Clinical and Consulting Psychology for permission to reprint Linden, W., Practicing of meditation by school children and their levels of field dependence—independence, test anxiety, and reading achievement.

Lea and Febiger for permission to reprint Benson, H. and Wallace, R. K., Decreased drug abuse with transcendental meditation: A study of 1,862 subjects.

Journal of Chronic Disease for permission to reprint Benson, H., et al., Decreased blood pressure in pharmacologically treated hypertensive subjects who regularly elicited the relaxation response.

The New England Journal of Medicine for permission to reprint Stone, R. A. and De Leo, J., Psychotherapeutic control of hypertension.

Indian Journal of Psychiatry for permission to reprint Vahia, N. S., et al., Further experience with therapy based on concepts of Patanjali in the treatment of psychiatric disorders.

Comprehensive Psychiatry and Springer Publishing Co. for permission to reprint Glueck, B. and Stroebel, C., Meditation in the treatment of psychiatric illness.

Journal of Humanistic Psychology for permission to reprint Lesh, T., Zen meditation and the development of empathy in counselors.

Journal of Counseling Psychology for permission to reprint Leung, P., Comparative effects of training in external and internal concentration of counseling behaviors.

Journal of Transpersonal Psychology for permission to reprint Bono, J., Psychological assessment of transcendental meditation.

Perceptual and Motor Skills for permission to reprint Pelletier, K., Influence of transcendental meditation upon autokinetic perception.

Journal of Abnormal Psychology for permission to reprint Davidson, R., Goleman, D. and Schwartz, G., Attentional and affective concomitants of meditation: A cross-sectional study.

Journal of Transpersonal Psychology for permission to reprint Walsh, R., Initial meditative experiences.

Journal of Transpersonal Psychology for permission to reprint Kohr, R., Dimensionality in meditative experience: A replication.

The International Journal of Clinical and Experimental Hypnosis for permission to reprint Brown, D., A model for the levels of concentrative meditation.

Journal of Transpersonal Psychology for permission to reprint Goleman, D., The Buddha on meditation and states of consciousness.

Archives of General Psychiatry for permission to reprint Woolfolk, R., Physiological correlates of meditation.

Perspectives in Biology and Medicine for permission to reprint Davidson, J., The physiology of meditation and mystical states of consciousness.

American Journal of Physiology for permission to reprint Wallace, R. K., Benson, H. and Wilson A. F., A wakeful hypometabolic physiologic state.

Psychosomatic Medicine for permission to reprint Orme-Johnson, D., Autonomic Stability and transcendental meditation.

Biological Psychology for permission to reprint Fenwick, P. B., et al., Metabolic and EEG changes during transcendental meditation: An explanation.

Archives of General Psychiatry for permission to reprint Corby, J., et al., Psychophysiological correlates of the practice of tantric yoga meditation.

Electroencephalography and Clinical Neurophysiology for permission to reprint Anand, B. K., et al., Some aspects of electroencephalographic studies in yogis.

Folia Psychiatrica et Neurologica Japonica for permission to reprint Kasamatsu, A. and Hirai, T., An electroencephalographic study of the Zen meditation (zazen).

Electroencephalography and Clinical Neurophysiology for permission to reprint Banquet, J. P., A spectral analysis of the EEG in meditation.

Electroencephalography and Clinical Neurophysiology for permission to reprint Williams, P. and West, N., EEG responses to photic stimulation in persons experienced at meditation.

Psychophysiology for permission to reprint Bennett, J. and Trinder, J., Hemispheric laterality and cognitive style associated with transcendental meditation.

Psychosomatic Medicine for permission to reprint Pagano, R. and Frumkin, L. R., The effect of transcendental meditation and right hemispheric functioning.

Comprehensive Psychiatry and Springer Publishing Co. for permission to reprint Glueck, B. and Stroebel, C., Psychophysiological correlates of meditation: EEG changes during meditation.

Science for permission to reprint Pagano, R., et al., Sleep during transcendental meditation.

Journal of Consulting and Clinical Psychology for permission to reprint Smith, J., Psychotherapeutic effects of transcendental meditation with controls for expectation of relief and daily sitting.

Journal of Consulting and Clinical Psychology for permission to reprint Malec, J. and Sipprelle, C., Physiological and subjective effects of Zen meditation and demand characteristics.

Journal of Consulting and Clinical Psychology for permission to reprint Smith, J., Personality correlates of continuation and outcome in meditation and erect sitting control treatments.

Psychosomatic Medicine for permission to reprint Schwartz, G. E., Davidson, R. J., and Goleman, D., Patterning of cognitive and somatic processes in the self-regulation of anxiety: Effects of meditation versus exercise.

American Psychologist for permission to reprint Shapiro, D. H. and Zifferblatt, S., Zen meditation and behavioral self-control: Similarities, differences, and clinical applications.

International Journal of Clinical and Experimental Hypnosis for permission to reprint Davidson, R. J. and Goleman, D., The role of attention in meditation and hypnosis: A psychobiological perspective on transformations of consciousness.

Prentice-Hall for permission to reprint Davidson, R. J. and Schwartz, G. E., Matching relaxation therapies to types of anxiety: A patterning approach.

Plenum Publishing Co. for permission to reprint Glueck, B. and Stroebel, C., Passive meditation: Subjective, clinical comparison with biofeedback.

The American Journal of Clinical Hypnosis, Walrath, L. and Hamilton, D., Autonomic correlates of meditation and hypnosis.

Psychosomatic Medicine, Morse, D. R., et al., A physiological and subjective evaluation of meditation, hypnosis, and relaxation.

We would like to give special thanks to the following authors who contributed original material to this book:

C. A. Marlatt, R. Pagano, R. Rose and J. K. Marques, Effects of meditation and relaxation upon alcohol use in male social drinkers.

L. Otis, Adverse effects of transcendental meditation.

J. Bono, Psychological assessment of transcendental meditation.

D. Brown and J. Engler, A Rorschach study of the stages of mindfulness meditation.

D. Giber for his help on the tables in Part I.

R. Jevning and J. P. O'Halloran, Metabolic effects of transcendental meditation: Toward a new paradigm of neurobiology.

R. Woolfolk, Self-control meditation and the treatment of chronic anger.

I. Beiman, S. Johnson, A. Puente, H. Majestic, L. E. Graham, The relationship of client characteristics to outcome for transcendental meditation, behavior therapy, and self-relaxation.

A. Ellis, The place of meditation in cognitive-behavior therapy and rational-emotive therapy.

R. Woolfolk and C. Franks, Meditation and behavior therapy.

J. Smith, Meditation Research: Three observations on the state-of-the-art.

A. Deikman, The state-of-the-art of meditation.

G. Globus, Potential contributions of meditation to neuroscience.

A. Akishige, The principles of the psychology of Zen.

A. Lazarus, Meditation: The problems of any unimodal technique.

PREFACE

There are many popular self-help books on the market; books about "how to" do meditation certainly make up a fair proportion. In addition, in the popular media and elsewhere, there are claims and counterclaims suggesting that meditation may be either an incredibly effective technique or sheer quackery. This book is not intended to be a popular book, but rather an academic one, which takes these claims, counterclaims, and debate to a deeper level of analysis, providing a fuller, more well reasoned account of the science of meditation. It provides a collection of theory and empirical studies from such diverse fields as clinical psychology and psychiatry, the neurosciences, psychophysiology, biochemistry, and also includes descriptions of classical meditation texts and phenomenological studies of advanced meditators.

The articles included in this book were selected because they have made a substantial contribution to the field, either by being an original classic piece of research, methodologically elegant, or heuristically interesting and creative. By gathering these articles in one source, the book provides an opportunity to read the original articles from which the themes discussed in the volume, *Meditation: Self-Regulation Strategy and Altered State of Consciousness* were drawn. These themes cover such topics as the effects of meditation in dealing with stress, hypertension, the addictions; comparison of meditation with other self-regulation strategies; the adverse effects of meditation; refinement of subject variables; components and mediating mechanisms of meditation; and meditation-induced altered states of consciousness.

It is our hope that such a collection of readings will help deepen sophisticated, scholarly debate within the field. To that end, we invited recognized experts in the clinical health sciences to comment on the field of meditation research. In addition, we hope that this collection of readings and commentary by recognized experts will stimulate further improved and relevant research, and will ultimately provide more precision on the clinical efficacy of meditation for a particular person with a particular clinical problem.

In keeping with the guiding principles presented in the volume, *Meditation: Self-Regulation Strategy and Altered State of Consciousness,* this book contains articles which represent a broad overview of the field and which illustrate several different methodological approaches. It is our feeling that the juxtaposition of these different approaches, drawing from both the phenomenological experiences reported in the Eastern classical texts and from data measured by the most technologically advanced scientific equipment, may ultimately be the most fruitful in helping us illuminate both the art and the science of meditation.

Deane H. Shapiro, Jr.
Roger N. Walsh

ACKNOWLEDGMENTS

We would like to acknowledge those individuals whose pioneering efforts make up the pages of this book. It is only because of their important work that a scientific field of meditation research has come into being—thereby making this book possible. We also wish to acknowledge those masters whose practice of meditation, at the very least, aroused our curiosity to explore this technique further, and perhaps gave us a partial vision of something more that we wished to seek in our own lives.

The editor (DS) would like to thank Ann Reeder for her help in securing permissions, typing and persisting throughout the early and mid rounds; to Sybil Carrere for her technical assistance, and to Susan Fontana for her typing assistance in the final stages of this manuscript. In addition, I would like to thank Beverly Sommer and Sheila Heller for their exceptionally careful help and diligence in the final stages of proofreading and review of the manuscript. Finally, my thanks to Larry Sporty, Gordon Globus, and the Department of Psychiatry for their support and help in the preparation of this multiyear project.

The editor (RW) would like to acknowledge the contribution and efforts of Deane Shapiro, whose interpersonal skills assisted us through the difficulties inherent in collaborative writing. Frances Vaughan continued in her multiple roles as guide, sage, therapist, teacher, and friend. In the Department of Psychiatry, Larry Sporty and Gordon Globus supported a leave of absence during which part of this book was prepared, while Sonja Hays continued her threefold function of secretary, administrator, and preserver of order and sanity. As always, my family continued to offer unconditional love and support.

LIST OF CONTRIBUTORS

Akishige, Yoshiharu,* *Zen Institute, Komazawa University, Japan*

Anand, B. K., *Department of Physiology, All India Institute of Medical Sciences, New Delhi, India*

Banquet, J. P., *Centre National de la Recherche Scientifique, Laboratoire d'Electrophysiologie et d' Neurophysiologie, Hospital de la Salpetriere, France*

Beiman, Irving H., *Department of Psychology, University of Georgia, Athens, Georgia*

Bennett, James E., *Department of Psychiatry, University of Virginia Medical Center, Charlottesville, Virginia*

Benson, Herbert, *Department of Medicine, Beth Israel Hospital, Harvard Medical School, Boston, Massachusetts*

Bono, Joseph Jr., *Dearborn, Michigan*

Brown, Daniel P., *Department of Psychiatry, Cambridge Hospital, Harvard Medical School, Boston, Massachusetts*

Corby, James C., *Department of Psychiatry and Behavioral Sciences, Stanford University School of Medicine, Stanford, California.*

Davidson, Julian M., *Department of Physiology, Stanford University School of Medicine, Stanford, California*

Davidson, Richard J., *Department of Psychology, State University of New York, Purchase, New York*

Deikman, Arthur J., *University of California, San Francisco, San Francisco, California*

De Leo, James, *Division of Nephrology, Department of Medicine, University of California, San Diego, California*

Ellis, Albert, *Institute for Advanced Study in Rational Psychotherapy, New York, New York*

Engler, Jack, *Board of Religious Studies, University of California, Santa Cruz, California*

Fenwick, P. B. C., *Department of Clinical Neurophysiology, St. Thomas Hospital, London, Great Britain*

Franks, Cyril M., *Graduate School of Applied and Professional Psychology, Rutgers University, New Brunswick, New Jersey*

Friedman, Meyer, *Meyer Friedman Institute, Mount Zion Hospital and Medical Center, San Francisco, California*

Frumpkin, Lynn R., *Department of Psychology, University of Washington, Seattle, Washington*

Giber, David, *Department of Psychology, Duke University, Durham, North Carolina*

Globus, Gordon G., *Department of Psychiatry and Human Behavior, Medical School, University of California, Irvine, Irvine, California*

Glueck, Bernard C., *Institute for the Living, Hartford, Connecticut*

Goleman, Daniel J., New York Times, *New York, New York*

Hamilton, David W., *Eastern Washington State College, Cheney, Washington*

Hirai, Tomio, *Faculty of Medicine, Tokyo University, Branch Hospital, University of Tokyo, Tokyo, Japan*

Jevning, Roland A., *School of Medicine, University of California at Irvine, Irvine, California*

Kasamatsu, Akira, *Department of Neuropsychiatry, School of Medicine, University of Tokyo, Tokyo, Japan*

Kohr, Richard L., *State Department of Education, Harrisburg, Pennsylvania*

Lazarus, Arnold, *Multimodal Therapy Institute, Kingston, New Jersey*

Lesh, Terry, V., *Student Counseling Services, University of Lethbridge, Alberta, Canada*

Leung, Paul, *Rehabilitation Psychiatry, University of Arizona, Tucson, Arizona*

Linden, William, *Bureau of Child Guidance, Brooklyn, New York*

Malec, James, *Rehabilitation Medicine, Rehabilitation Center, University of Wisconsin, Madison, Wisconsin*

Marlatt, Alan, C., *Department of Psychology, University of Washington, Seattle, Washington*

Morse, Donald R., *Department of Endontology, Temple University School of Medicine, Philadelphia, Pennsylvania*

O'Halloran, James, P., *School of Medicine, University of California at Irvine, Irvine, California*

Orme-Johnson, David, *Maharishi Institute, Iowa*

*Deceased.

Otis, Leon, S., *Stanford Research Institute, Menlo Park, California*

Pagano, Robert R., *Department of Psychology, University of Washington, Seattle, Washington*

Pelletier, Kenneth R., *Langley Porter Neuropsychiatric Institute, University of California, San Francisco, San Francisco, California*

Schwartz, Gary E., *Department of Psychology and Psychiatry, Yale University, New Haven, Connecticut*

Shapiro, Deane H., Jr., *Department of Psychiatry and Human Behavior, University of California Irvine Medical Center, California College of Medicine, Irvine, California*

Singer, Jerome L., *Department of Psychology, Clinical Psychology Program, Yale University, New Haven, Connecticut*

Sipprelle, Carl N., *Department of Psychology, University of South Dakota, Vermillion, South Dakota*

Smith, Jonathan C., *Department of Psychology, Roosevelt University, Chicago, Illinois*

Stone, Richard A., *Division of Nephrology, Department of Medicine, University of California at San Diego, San Diego, California*

Stroebel, Charles F., *Institute for the Living, Hartford, Connecticut*

Trinder, John, *Department of Psychology, University of Tasmania, Hobart, Tasmania, Australia*

Vahia, N. S., *Dr. Balabhai Nanavati Hospital, Bombay, India*

Wallace, R. Keith, *Maharishi International University, Fairfield, Iowa*

Walrath, Larry C., *Department of Psychology, Washington University, St. Louis, Missouri*

Walsh, Roger N., *Department of Psychiatry and Human Behavior, School of Medicine, University of California at Irvine, Irvine, California*

West, Michael, *Social Psychology Research Unit, University of Kent at Canterbury, Canterbury, Great Britain*

Williams, Paul, *Department of Psychological Medicine, University Hospital of Wales, Wales*

Wilson, Archie F., *Department of Pulmonary Disease, School of Medicine, University of California at Irvine, Irvine, California*

Wolpe, Joseph, *Department of Psychiatry, Temple University, Philadelphia, Pennsylvania*

Woolfolk, Robert L., *Department of Psychology, University College, Rutgers University, New Brunswick, New Jersey*

Zifferblatt, Steven, M., *National Institutes of Health, National Heart, Lung, and Blood Institute, Bethesda, Maryland*

I

INTRODUCTION

Research Overviews: Classic and Contemporary Perspectives

Meditation is a technique which has been used for thousands of years within the religious and philosophical traditions of the East and only within the last 30 years within the medical, health care, scientific, and psychotherapeutic traditions of the West. As would be expected, the goals for which meditation is used often differ markedly depending upon the cultural context in which it is practiced, and the specific orientation of the person teaching and/or learning it.

The first two articles (1 and 2) in this introductory part look at the empirical literature as it relates to both the classic and contemporary perspectives. The first article reviews studies comparing meditation on both clinical and physiological dimensions with other self-control strategies. These clinical and physiological dimensions are the primary concerns for which contemporary, scientific, medical, and health care scholars and professionals utilize meditation. However, meditation has classically been utilized by religious traditions to produce profound phenomenological changes in which individual perceives self, other, and the world in a radically new way. The second article explores research bearing on ways to understand this classic perspective of meditation: as an altered state of consciousness.

The final two articles (3 and 4) in this introductory part look at empirical models which may help give us better understanding of meditation research: both an historical and evolutionary overview (Article No. 3) as well as a systems model for clarifying and refining future efforts in meditation research (Article No. 4).

OVERVIEW: CLINICAL AND PHYSIOLOGICAL COMPARISON OF MEDITATION WITH OTHER SELF-CONTROL STRATEGIES

Deane H. Shapiro, Jr.

In 1977 the American Psychiatric Association called for a critical examination of the clinical effectiveness of meditation. The author provides a review of the literature bearing on clinical and physiological comparisons of meditation with other self-control strategies. He begins by providing a definition of meditation and then cites the literature comparing meditation with such self-regulation strategies as biofeedback, hypnosis, and progressive relaxation. He pays particular attention to the "uniqueness" of meditation as a clinical intervention strategy as well as the adverse effects of meditation. Finally, he offers suggestions and guidelines for future research.

To my knowledge, there have been four major reviews of the meditation literature. Woolfolk (1) and Davidson (2) reviewed the physiological effects of meditation, and Smith (3) and Giber and I (4) reviewed the psychotherapeutic and clinical effects. All four of these reviews are substantial and provide a thorough discussion of the literature available at the time they were written. However, in the past few years there has been a dramatic increase in the empirical literature. This new literature is methodologically more sophisticated and goes beyond comparing the effects of meditation with baseline observations or comparing a group trained in meditation with a control group. Instead, the newer studies compare meditation with other self-regulation strategies such as biofeedback, hypnosis, and progressive relaxation. These more recent studies are in keeping with the following recommendation of the American Psychiatric Association (5):

The Association strongly recommends that research be undertaken in the form of well-controlled studies to evaluate the specific usefulness, indications, contraindications, and dangers of meditative techniques. The research should compare the various forms of meditation with one another and with psychotherapeutic and psychopharmacologic modalities.

Received Aug. 18, 1980; accepted Nov. 12, 1980.

From the California College of Medicine, University of California, Irvine. Address correspondence to Dr. Shapiro, Department of Psychiatry and Human Behavior, University of California, Irvine, Medical Center, Orange, CA 92668.

In a previous paper (4) Giber and I reviewed the literature to determine whether meditation might be a clinically effective strategy for certain clinical problems, such as stress and tension management, the addictions, and hypertension. We reviewed "first-round studies," which generally consisted of anecdotal single case studies or a comparison between a meditation group and a control group rather than between groups given different self-regulation strategies. The more sophisticated question that clinicians and psychotherapists now need to ask is not just whether a technique "works" but when that technique is the treatment of choice for which particular patient with what type of clinical problem.

In order to help clinicians make that determination, and following the recommendation of APA's position statement, in this paper I review the literature comparing meditation physiologically and clinically with other self-regulation strategies. I then comment on the adverse effects of meditation so that clinicians might be sensitive to indications and contraindications. Finally, I offer guidelines and suggestions for future research.

MEDITATION: TOWARD A WORKING DEFINITION

One of the problems in studying meditation is the lack of a clear definition. Because of its effects, some have tried to define it as a relaxation technique (6). This raises problems similar to those encountered in the literature on relaxation (7), in which a relaxation technique is defined as one producing certain effects—decreased skeletal muscular tension and decreased sympathetic arousal, for example. However, defining the independent variable by its dependent variable—its effects—is tautological and unsatisfactory as a complete definition.

Another problem with defining meditation is that there are so many different types of meditation techniques. Some involve sitting quietly and produce a state of quiescence and restfulness (8). Some involve sitting quietly and produce a state of excitement and arousal (9, 10). Some, such as the Sufi whirling dervish, tai chi, hatha yoga, and Isiguro Zen, involve physical movement to a greater or lesser degree (11, 12). Sometimes these "movement meditations" result in a state of excitement, sometimes a state of relaxation (2, 13).

Accordingly, depending on the type of meditation, the body may be active and moving or relatively motionless and passive. Attention may be actively focused on one object of concentration to the exclusion of the other objects (14). Attention may be focused on one object, but as other objects, thoughts, or feelings occur, they too may be noticed and then attention returned to the original focal object (Vipassana and transcendental meditation, for example). Attention may not be focused exclusively on any particular object (Zen's shikan-taza, for example) (15, 16). However, there seem to be three broad general groupings of attentional strategies in meditation: a focus on the field (mindfulness meditation), a focus on a specific object within the field (concentrative meditation), and a shifting back and forth between the two. This fits in nicely with brain attentional mechanisms, which Pribram (17) described as similar to a camera and of two types. The first type is a focus similar to a wide-angle lens—a broad, sweeping awareness taking in the entire field (mindfulness meditation). The second type is a focus similar to a zoom lens—a specific focusing on a restricted segment of the field (concentrative meditation).

Using attentional mechanisms as the basis for the definition, therefore, we may state that *meditation refers to a family of techniques which have in common a conscious attempt to focus attention in a nonanalytical way and an attempt not to dwell on discursive, ruminating thought.*

There are several important factors in this definition. First, the word "conscious" is used. Meditation involves intention: the intention to focus attention either on a particular object in the field or on whatever arises. Second, the definition is noncultic. It does not depend on any religious framework or orientation to understand it. I do not mean to imply that meditation does not or cannot occur within a religious framework. However, what meditation is and the framework within which it is practiced, although they are interactive, are two separate issues and need to be viewed as such. Therefore, although there may be overlap in terms of the concentration on a particular object or repetition of a sound or phrase, we should not a priori equate meditation with prayer. This is particularly true when the intent of the prayer has a goal-directed focus outside oneself (e.g., asking a higher power to absolve one of one's sins).

Third, the word "attempt" is used throughout. This allows us to deal with the process of meditation. Because meditation is an effort to focus attention, it also involves how we respond when our attention wanders, or how we respond when a thought arises. There is a continuum of instructions from very strong to very mild in terms of how to deal with thoughts (18). For example, Benson (6) instructed students to ignore thoughts, Deikman (19) said to exclude them, and a 5th-century Buddhist treatise said, "With teeth clenched and tongue pressed against the gums, . . . by means of sheer mental effort hold back, crush and burn out the thought" (20). The Vipassana tradition instructs one to merely notice and label the thought (thinking thinking) and Zen to merely notice, observe with equanimity, and, when weary of watching, let go (21).

Fourth, there is an important "metamessage" implicit in the definition: namely, the *content* of thoughts is not so important. They should be allowed to come and go. Consciousness, or awareness of the *process* of thoughts coming and going, is more important. The context—conscious attention—is the most important variable. Although cognitions and images may arise, they are not the end goal of meditation. Thus, although there may be overlap in content, we should not a priori equate meditation with techniques of guided imagery (22), daydreaming (23), covert self-instructional training (24), hetero-hypnosis (25), self-hypnosis (26), or other cognitive strategies (27).

By describing meditation techniques precisely and by having experimenters report accurately all procedures used, meditation techniques are described behaviorally and may be compared both clinically and physiologically with other cognition-focusing, relaxation, and self-regulation strategies.

PHYSIOLOGICAL COMPARISONS

There was initial enthusiasm that meditation might be a unique self-regulation strategy (28). This position was based on certain first-round clinical studies and physiological findings. However, Benson (6, 29) argued that the physiological response pattern found in meditation was not unique to meditation per se but common to any passive relaxation strategy. This view has been supported and replicated by a number of studies that suggest no physiological differences between meditation and other self-regulation strategies and, often, no differences between meditation and "just sitting."

For example, early first-round studies suggested that skin resistance significantly increased within subjects (8, 30) and in a transcendental meditation group compared with a control group (31). Recent studies (32–37), however, showed no significant differences in galvanic skin response between meditation and other self-regulation strategies, including self-hypnosis, progressive relaxation, and other modes of instructional relaxation. Further, the studies cited also showed no difference between meditation and other self-regulation strategies in heart rate or respiration rate.

Morse and associates (32), in a rather complex study, noted that neither respiration rate, pulse rate, nor systolic and diastolic blood pressure differentiated experimental conditions. These authors noted that the physiological responses to transcendental meditation and simple word meditation were similar and concluded that "relaxation, meditation, and relaxation hypnosis yield similar physiological responses suggestive of deep relaxation." Other studies found no difference in effect on respiratory rate between meditation and progressive relaxation (unpublished data of Pagano and associates) or between meditation and listening to music (38). Fenwick and associates (38) noted that subjects who were tense to begin with showed greater relaxation in response to both meditation and listening to music than subjects who were not and suggested that Wallace and associates' findings of increased skin resistance in meditators (8) may have been due to high initial levels of metabolism and tension.

Glueck and Stroebel (39) also suggested that meditation might be characterized by a unique EEG pattern—the synchronization of slow alpha. However, Travis and associates (37) noted that a striking effect was the *lack* of alpha EEG during transcendental meditation, and Morse and associates (32) noted that when synchronization of slow alpha occurred it was not unique to transcendental meditation but was found in all the relaxation conditions they studied.

A similar lack of metabolic uniqueness has been found by other investigators. Michaels and associates (40) attempted to differentiate meditators from resting control subjects biochemically. Because stress increases blood catecholamines, the experimenters looked at plasma epinephrine and norepinephrine as well as plasma lactate. Twelve experienced meditators (more than 12 months' experience) were compared with control subjects matched for sex and age who rested instead of meditating. There were no significant fluctuations of plasma epinephrine during meditation. No significant differences were observed between control subjects and meditators. The same held true for plasma lactic acid concentration. These findings failed to replicate Wallace's earlier findings on transcendental meditation (30).

More recent studies further call into question the uniqueness of meditation's effects. In 1976, Goleman and Schwartz (41) showed increased responsiveness of meditators to an upcoming stressful event on a film and a quicker recovery time in comparison with a relaxing control group. However, from a cognitive standpoint, in terms of number of poststress intrusive thoughts, significant differences between meditators and control subjects have not been detected (42). Further, theories suggesting that transcendental meditation is unrelated to sleep have recently been called into question by Pagano and Frumkin (43) and Younger and associates (44), who noted that at least beginning meditators may spend an appreciable part of their time in sleep stages two, three, and four.

Thus it appears that the original belief that we would be able to discriminate meditation as a unique physiological state has not been confirmed—on either an autonomic or a metabolic level or in terms of EEG

pattern. Although it seems clear that meditation can bring about a generalized reduction in many physiological systems, thereby creating a state of relaxation (2, 4), it is not yet clear from the available data that this state is differentiated from the effects of other relaxation techniques, whether they be hypnosis (33) or deep muscle relaxation (32, 34, 35, 37). Most studies have found that the constellation of changes is significantly different between meditation groups and placebo control groups but not between meditation and other self-regulation treatments.

In fairness, it should be noted that although the results thus far seem quite convincing that there is no physiological difference between the effects of meditation and other self-regulation strategies, they are not unequivocal. For example, Elson and associates (45) compared a "wakefully relaxed" group and a group of ĀnandaMarga meditators. They noted that the meditators experienced an increase in basal skin resistance and a decrease in respiratory rate, changes which were not observed in the control subjects. Further, 6 of the 11 control subjects fell asleep, but none of the meditators fell asleep. The alpha and theta EEG activity of the meditators remained in a relatively stable state. In addition, Jevning and O'Halloran (46) suggested that there might be changes in blood flow that are unique to meditation.

Some authors would disagree with the way in which I have interpreted the literature. For example, Jevning and O'Halloran (46) stated that additional unique physiological response patterns will be found in meditators and that current findings do not reflect this simply because we do not have physiological measures sensitive enough to ferret out the unique aspects of meditation compared with other self-regulation strategies. They also noted that one must be careful in generalizing from beginning meditators, who may in fact fall asleep and whose physiological changes may not be different from individuals practicing other self-regulation strategies. There is no assurance, they correctly noted, that beginning practitioners will have anything like the dramatic physiological changes of advanced meditators who have spent decades perfecting their practice. However, they also pointed out that in order to determine if meditation is truly unique, these advanced practitioners would have to be compared with advanced practitioners of other self-regulation strategies.

CLINICAL COMPARISONS

Findings of meditation's nonuniqueness are also being reported on a clinical level. Meditation appears to be equally but no more effective than other self-regulation strategies for such problems as anxiety (36, 47–52), anxiety in alcoholics (53), alcohol consumption (54), insomnia (55), and borderline hypertension (56).

The self-regulation strategies compared with meditation included progressive relaxation (36, 45, 48, 54, 55), Benson's relaxation response (47, 54), a pseudo-meditation treatment (49), antimeditation treatments (36, 49, 50), self-administered systematic desensitization (51), and cardiovascular and neuromuscular biofeedback (56, 57).

Two studies involving clinical comparison of self-regulation techniques seem representative (51, 54). First, Marlatt and associates (54) described a nicely designed study of heavy social drinkers during a 2-week pretreatment baseline phase, a 6-week treatment phase, and a 7-week follow-up. There were four groups: a meditation group (using Benson's method) (6), a progressive relaxation group, a group practicing bibliotherapy (called an "attention placebo group"), and a no-treatment control group that was monitored and took all the tests. This study is one of the first in which there was a specific, clearly spelled-out theoretical rationale between the independent variables (relaxation procedures) and the dependent variable (decrease in alcohol consumption). Results suggested that relaxation training, whether it was meditation, progressive relaxation, or "attention placebo," had a significant effect on the consumption of ethanol compared with no treatment. However, there were no significant differences between the three different relaxation training groups.

Second, Kirsch and Henry (51) assigned 38 "highly motivated" subjects who had a great deal of anxiety about public speaking to four groups: 1) a desensitization-relaxation group, which was given instructions for relaxation training, hierarchy contruction, and imagery-relaxation pairing, 2) a desensitization-meditation group, which was identical to the first group except that instructions in meditation similar to Benson's (6) replaced instructions in relaxation training, 3) a meditation-only group, which was given instructions in meditation and in relaxation training but not in hierarchy construction or imagery-relaxation pairing, and 4) a no-treatment group. The treatment phase lasted 3 weeks, and pre- and posttreatment assessments of pulse rate and performance anxiety were made. Results showed that improvement occurred in all three treatment groups according to self-report and behavioral measures and that this improvement was significantly greater than improvement in the no-treatment control group. However, there were no significant differences in improvement between the three treatment groups.

The data from these clinical studies seem to indicate that meditation is no more effective than other self-regulation strategies on a wide variety of clinically relevant variables. It should be noted, however, that my interpretation of the data is not without its critics. The critics point to the studies of Vahia and associates (58, 59) and Glueck and Stroebel (39), which found that meditation was more effective than pseudo-yoga (58, 59) and biofeedback (39). However, I believe it could be argued that therapists' belief in the efficacy of the treatment (3) may have been a critical confounding factor in the studies of Vahia and associates. Further, the fact that Glueck and Stroebel's study was conducted at the Institute for Living, where a great deal of research on transcendental meditation was being conducted, could have caused strong demand characteristics, possibly accounting for subjects' continuing to adhere to the transcendental meditation program while dropping out of the biofeedback treatment group.

ADVERSE EFFECTS AND CONTRAINDICATIONS

Carrington and Ephron (60) as well as Stroebel and Glueck (61) pointed out the importance of the therapist's availability to psychiatric patients to aid with any material that comes into the patient's awareness. Therefore, Carrington (18) noted that meditation should not be prescribed for borderline psychotic or psychotic patients unless their practice of it can be supervised by a psychotherapist familiar with meditation. In this regard, almost all meditation researchers and those who use it in their clinical practice caution that the therapist should provide careful instruction, training, and follow-up observation. This is especially true as we become more sensitive to unpleasant and adverse experiences patients sometimes have during meditation (62–68). These feelings may include occasional dizziness, feelings of dissociation, and other adverse feelings produced by the release of images, thoughts, and other material that they had not been sensitive to. In addition to anecdotal reports, to my knowledge there have been three case reports in the literature suggesting that meditation has negative effects (63, 67, 68). There is also one study with a large number of subjects (64) that discussed potential adverse effects of meditation.

Otis (64) reanalyzed data he had collected previously and examined particular subjects who had reported a considerable increase (51% or over) of negative feelings. He found that the longer an individual meditated, the more likely it was that adverse effects would occur. These adverse effects included increased anxiety, boredom, confusion, depression, restlessness, and withdrawal. Otis also noted that teacher trainees who were long-term meditators reported more adverse effects than long-term meditators who had not made a commitment to become teachers. Although there are many ways to analyze these data, it seems that there is a subgroup of people for whom meditation will have negative effects.

For example, certain individuals seem to be attracted to meditation for inappropriate reasons, seeing it as a powerful cognitive avoidance strategy. Some are attracted to the technique of concentrative meditation as a way of blocking out unpleasant areas of their lives. Similarly, many individuals who lack basic social skills (i.e., those who are shy or withdrawn) may be attracted to meditation. For all of these individuals meditation may not be a useful therapeutic intervention (certainly not as a sole intervention strategy). Rather, it may be more appropriate for them to have some kind of social skill or assertiveness training, either in place of or in addition to meditation treatment (68).

Meditation may not be a useful therapeutic intervention for chronically depressed individuals, who may need to have their arousal level activated (this might also be the case for hypotensive adults and hyperactive children). Many therapists consider arousal one of the prime conditions facilitating therapeutic change (69); therefore, meditation would not be considered a treatment of choice if used as a strategy to calm or relax a person. In addition, it may not be a useful strategy for individuals with high somatic but low cognitive activity (7). Meditation may not be the treatment of choice for individuals whose locus of control is very external (47) or those with clinical problems such as migraine headaches or Raynaud's disease, which Stroebel and Glueck (61) noted might be better treated with temperature and EMG biofeedback to elicit vasodilation and muscle relaxation.

There are additional issues to be considered regarding negative effects. Is the individual meditating for too long a time, thereby impairing reality testing (63, 67)? Is the person spending too much time letting go of thoughts (not analyzing them) and therefore not gaining pinpointed cause-and-effect awareness? If so, then, even though an inappropriate affect may be reduced, has the person learned the antecedent conditions that caused the inappropriate maladaptive behaviors? Has he or she learned, in addition to skills of letting go of thoughts and goals, the skills of setting goals—existentially choosing who he or she wants to be and how he or she wants to act.

There is also the important issue of preparation. Negative effects may occur if the individual has not been given sufficient preparation for meditation. For example, a self-critical, perfectionistic, Western-goal-oriented individual who learns meditation will probably bring that same cognitive orientation to the task of meditation. He or she may, therefore, be highly critical (e.g., I am not doing it right); each thought may be seen as defeat, and an internal fight might ensue to stop "thoughts." As one patient said to me, "I became distracted by thoughts, then worried about being distracted; but I couldn't stop the flood of thoughts; I started crying; it was almost impossible for me to then return to breathing."

My hope in presenting this discussion of adverse effects is twofold. On the one hand I would like to insert a note of caution into the "hosannahs" with which many greet meditation. The transpersonal or spiritual perspective gives an answer elegant in its simplicity for dealing with adverse effects: "Watch the process. Don't get caught up in it. Let it be a learning experience for yourself, a new awareness of your resistance and defenses. Keep the context." The answer to every dilemma becomes, "Adverse effects are only part of the path. Stay centered. It takes years of practice." Eastern philosophy, with a world view espousing acceptance, says that all things, good and bad, should be accepted with equanimity. Philosophically and theoretically, once a person can do that, life becomes free from suffering, as the Buddha noted in his Four Noble Truths. On the one hand I subscribe to this advice. On the other hand I find it too absolute; it strikes me as similar to the classic psychoanalytic dictum: insight causes cure. If you are not cured, by definition you need more insight. Similarly, if you are not keeping the context, practice keeping it more.

As clinicians, I feel we need to exercise extreme caution in using a technique like meditation; we need to be sensitive to some of the adverse effects that may occur with patients for whom we prescribe it. On the other hand, I believe meditation is an extremely powerful technique that can bring a great deal of good to many patients. I do not want it to be too readily dismissed by the scientific community just because the initial global claims of its effectiveness do not appear to be warranted. My hope is that we can develop a cautious approach to the use of meditation, neither overstating its worth nor arbitrarily dismissing it.

FUTURE DIRECTIONS

There are five different directions that I feel clinically oriented research could profitably pursue. First, I believe we need to look more carefully at the context of meditation. In particular, this would involve an understanding of individuals' expectations in learning meditation as well as some assessment of the demand characteristics of the teacher/training organization (70, 71). Most religious traditions have a series of preparations that must be made before an individual is thought to be ready to begin the spiritual practice of meditation (72, 73). These preparations range from the highly structured and complex—changing dietary habits, cultivating feelings of love and compassion, decreasing thoughts of selfishness and greed—to much less complex—preparatory lectures and instructional training. Additional contextual variables would include motivation and the role of individual responsibility (74, 75).

A second issue that must be addressed is a component analysis of meditation to separate the active from the inert aspects. In other words, how much of meditation's effects is due to antecedent variables of preparation, environmental planning, and components of the behavior itself—physical posture, attentional focus and style, and breathing? By breaking meditation into its various components, it might be possible to determine which aspects of meditation might be profitably combined with other self-regulation strategies (76–79).

A third area that might be profitably pursued involves a refinement of the dependent variable. For example, as noted, Davidson and Schwartz (7) suggested that anxiety has both a cognitive and somatic component, and meditation may be more effective for reducing cognitive anxiety while doing relatively little for somatic anxiety.

A fourth approach involves examining subject variables (47, 80). This approach attempts, on the basis of certain pretest indicators, to develop a subject profile of those for whom meditation is likely to provide a successful clinical intervention and those for whom there may be adverse effects (81).

All four of these refinements would enable us to become more precise in choosing the correct clinical intervention (or combination of interventions) for a specific individual with a specific clinical problem.

A final approach involves looking at the phenomenology of meditation. This approach, valued by the Eastern tradition for centuries, is just beginning to gain favor within the Western scientific community. Despite methodological and conceptual problems (82), researchers are beginning to note its importance. For example, although Morse and associates (32) found that there were no significant differences in physiological responses to three relaxation states, they pointed out that there were significant differences in the subjects' evaluations of these states, as did Gilbert and associates (83). Therefore, Morse and associates cited and concurred with Charles Tart's remark that "in [the] subject's own estimate of his behavior, an internal state is a rich and promising source of data which some experimenters tend to ignore in their passionate search for objectivity." Similarly, Curtis and Wessberg (35) noted that more subjective positive changes were reported by the meditation group than by the control relaxation group even though there was no difference on physiological measures. They suggested that if meditation has a unique effect, it seems to be different from a visceral or neuromuscular effect.

If meditation is a unique technique, its uniqueness may not be as a self-regulation strategy, and therefore it will not differ from other self-regulation strategies clinically or physiologically. Its uniqueness may be seen, however, in the way the individual experiences it. The phenomenological or subjective experiences of meditation—meditation as an altered state of consciousness (2, 4, 68)—may be an important and critical area for future scientific examination.

Setting aside the question of meditation's uniqueness, however, we are now confronted by the issue of developing more precision as to when to use meditation rather than other self-regulation strategies. Although meditation seems to be no more effective as a clinical intervention than other self-regulation strategies, this is not a reason either to use or not to use

meditation. It appears that we now have several self-regulation strategies which are more effective than controls in the alleviation of certain clinical problems. We are now faced with the task presented at the start of this paper—to design more sophisticated and precise research strategies in order to help clarify which self-regulation strategy is the treatment of choice for which patient with what clinical problem.

I hope that the definition developed at the start of this paper, the update of the literature on clinical and physiological studies that has been provided, and the guidelines and suggestions presented here will help researchers evolve that necessary next step of methodological sophistication.

REFERENCES

1. Woolfolk R: Psychophysiological correlates of meditation. Arch Gen Psychiatry 32:1326–1333, 1975
2. Davidson J: Physiology of meditation and mystical states of consciousness. Perspect Biol Med 19:345–380, 1976
3. Smith J: Meditation and psychotherapy: a review of the literature. Psychol Bull 32:553–564, 1975
4. Shapiro DH, Giber D: Meditation and psychotherapeutic effects: self-regulation strategy and altered states of consciousness. Arch Gen Psychiatry 35:294–302, 1978
5. American Psychiatric Association: Position statement on meditation. Am J Psychiatry 134:720, 1977
6. Benson H: The relaxation response. New York, William Morrow & Co, 1975
7. Davidson R, Schwartz G: The psychobiology of relaxation and related states: a multi-process theory, in Behavior Control and the Modification of Physiological Activity. Edited by Mostofsky DI. Englewood Cliffs, NJ, Prentice-Hall, 1976
8. Wallace R, Benson H, Wilson A: A wakeful hypometabolic physiologic state. Am J Physiol 221:795–799, 1971
9. Das H, Gastaut H: Variations de l'activité electrique du cerveau, du coeur, et des muscles squelettiques au cours de la méditation et de l'extase yogique. Electroencephalogr Clin Neurophysiol Suppl 6:211–219, 1955
10. Corby JC, Roth WT, Zarzone VP, et al: Psychophysiological correlates of the practice of tantric yoga meditation. Arch Gen Psychiatry 35:571–580, 1978
11. Hirai T: Psychophysiology of Zen. Tokyo, Igaku Shin, 1974
12. Naranjo C, Ornstein R: On the Psychology of Meditation. New York, Viking Press, 1971
13. Fischer R: A cartography of the ecstatic and meditative states. Science 174:897–904, 1971
14. Anand B, Chinna G, Singh B: Some aspects of electroencephalographic studies in yogis. Electroencephalogr Clin Neurophysiol 13:452–456, 1961
15. Kasamatsu A, Hirai T: An electroencephalographic study of the Zen meditation (zazen). Folia Psychiatr Neurol Jpn 20:315–336, 1966
16. Krishnamurti J: Meditation. Ojai, Calif, Krishnamurti Foundation, 1979
17. Pribram K: Languages of the Brain: Experimental Paradoxes and Principles in Neuropsychology. Englewood Cliffs, NJ, Prentice-Hall, 1971
18. Carrington P: Freedom in Meditation. New York, Anchor Press/Doubleday, 1978
19. Deikman AJ: Deautomatization and the mystic experience. Psychiatry 29:324–338, 1966
20. Conze E: Buddhist Meditation. New York, Harper & Row, 1969, p 83
21. Herrigel E: Zen in the Art of Archery. New York, McGraw-Hill Book Co, 1953
22. Kretschmer W: Meditative techniques in psychotherapy, in Altered States of Consciousness. Edited by Tart C. New York,

John Wiley & Sons, 1969

23. Singer JL: Navigating the stream of consciousness: research in daydreaming and related inner experience. Am Psychol 30:727–738, 1975

24. Michenbaum D, Cameron R: The clinical potential of modifying what clients say to themselves, in Self-Control: Power to the Person. Edited by Mahoney MJ, Thoresen CE. Monterey, Calif, Brooks/Cole, 1974

25. Paul G: Physiological effects of relaxation training and hypnotic suggestion. J Abnorm Psychol 74:425–437, 1969

26. Fromm E: Self-hypnosis. Psychotherapy: Theory, Research and Practice 12(3):295–301, 1975

27. Tart C (ed): Altered States of Consciousness. New York, John Wiley & Sons, 1969

28. Muehlman M: Transcendental meditation (ltr to ed). N Engl J Med 297:513, 1977

29. Benson H: Reply to M Muehlman: Transcendental meditation (ltr to ed). N Engl J Med 297:513, 1977

30. Wallace R: The physiological effects of transcendental meditation. Science 167:1751–1754, 1970

31. Orme-Johnson DW: Autonomic stability and transcendental meditation. Psychosom Med 35:341–349, 1973

32. Morse DR, Martin S, Furst ML, et al: A physiological and subjective evaluation of meditation, hypnosis, and relaxation. Psychosom Med 39:304–324, 1977

33. Walrath L, Hamilton D: Autonomic correlates of meditation and hypnosis. Am J Clin Hypn 17:190–197, 1975

34. Cauthen N, Prymak C: Meditation versus relaxation. J Consult Clin Psychol 45:496–497, 1977

35. Curtis WD, Wessberg HW: A comparison of heart rate, respiration, and galvanic skin response among meditators, relaxers, and controls. Journal of Altered States of Consciousness 2:319–324, 1975/1976

36. Boswell PC, Murray GJ: Effects of meditation on psychological and physiological measures of anxiety. J Consult Clin Psychol 47:606–607, 1979

37. Travis T, Kondo C, Knott J: Heart rate, muscle tension, and alpha production of transcendental meditation and relaxation controls. Biofeedback Self Regul 1:387–394, 1976

38. Fenwick PB, Donaldson S, Gillis L, et al: Metabolic and EEG changes during transcendental meditation: an explanation. Biol Psychol 5:101–118, 1977

39. Glueck BC, Stroebel CF: Biofeedback and meditation in the treatment of psychiatric illness. Compr Psychiatry 16:303–321, 1975

40. Michaels R, Huber M, McCann D: Evaluation of transcendental meditation as a method of reducing stress. Science 192:1242–1244, 1976

41. Goleman D, Schwartz G: Meditation as an intervention in stress reactivity. J Consult Clin Psychol 44:456–466, 1976

42. Kanas N, Horowitz MJ: Reactions of transcendental meditators and nonmeditators to stress films: a cognitive study. Arch Gen Psychiatry 34:1431–1436, 1977

43. Pagano R, Frumkin L: Effect of TM in right hemispheric functioning. Biofeedback Self Regul 2:407–415, 1977

44. Younger J, Adrianne W, Berger R: Sleep during transcendental meditation. Perceptual Mot Skills 40:953–954, 1975

45. Elson B, Hauri P, Cunis D: Physiological changes in yoga meditation. Psychophysiology 14:52–57, 1977

46. Jevning R, O'Halloran JP: Metabolic effects of transcendental meditation, in The Science of Meditation. Edited by Shapiro DH, Walsh RN. Hawthorne, NY, Aldine Publishing Co (in press)

47. Beiman IH, Johnson SA, Puente AE, et al: Client characteristics and success in TM. Ibid

48. Thomas D, Abbas KA: Comparison of transcendental meditation and progressive relaxation in reducing anxiety. Br Med J 2:1749, 1978

49. Smith JC: Psychotherapeutic effects of transcendental meditation with controls for expectation of relief and daily sitting. J Consult Clin Psychol 44:630–637, 1976

50. Goldman BL, Domitor PJ, Murray EF: Effects of Zen meditation on anxiety reduction and perceptual functioning. J Consult Clin Psychol 47:551–556, 1979

51. Kirsch I, Henry D: Self-desensitization and meditation in the reduction of public speaking anxiety. J Consult Clin Psychol 47:536–541, 1979

52. Zuroff DC, Schwarz JC: Effects of transcendental meditation and muscle relaxation on trait anxiety, maladjustment, locus of control, and drug use. J Consult Clin Psychol 46:264–271, 1978

53. Parker JC, Gilbert AS, Thoreson RW: Reduction of autonomic arousal in alcoholics. J Consult Clin Psychol 46:879–886, 1978

54. Marlatt G, Pagano R, Rose R, et al: Effect of meditation and relaxation training upon alcohol use in male social drinkers, in The Science of Meditation. Edited by Shapiro DH, Walsh RN. Hawthorne, NY, Aldine Publishing Co (in press)

55. Woolfolk R, Carr-Kaffeshan L, McNulty TF: Meditation training as a treatment for insomnia. Behavior Therapy 7(3):359–365, 1976

56. Sururt RS, Shapiro D, Good MI: Comparison of cardiovascular biofeedback, neuromuscular feedback, and meditation in the treatment of borderline hypertension. J Consult Clin Psychol 46:252–263, 1978

57. Hager JL, Sururt RS: Hypertension self-control with a portable feedback unit or meditation-relaxation. Biofeedback Self Regul 3:269–275, 1978

58. Vahia HS, Doengaji DR, Jeste DV, et al: A deconditioning therapy based upon concepts of Patanjali. Int J Soc Psychiatry 18:61–66, 1972

59. Vahia HS, Doengaji DR, Jeste DV, et al: Psychophysiologic therapy based on the concepts of Patanjali. Am J Psychother 27:557–565, 1973

60. Carrington P, Ephron HS: Meditation as an adjunct to psychotherapy, in New Dimensions in Psychiatry: A World View. Edited by Arieti S, Chrzanowski G. New York, John Wiley & Sons, 1975

61. Stroebel C, Glueck B: Passive meditation: subjective and clinical comparison with biofeedback, in Consciousness and Self-Regulation. Edited by Schwartz G, Shapiro D. New York, Plenum Press, 1977

62. Van Nuys D: Meditation, attention, and hypnotic susceptibility: a correlational study. Int J Clin Exp Hypn 21:59–69, 1973

63. Lazarus AA: Psychiatric problems precipitated by transcendental meditation. Psychol Rep 10:39–74, 1976

64. Otis LS: Adverse effects of meditation, in The Science of Meditation. Edited by Shapiro DH, Walsh RN. Hawthorne, NY, Aldine Publishing Co (in press)

65. Kohr E: Dimensionality in the meditative experience: a replication. Journal of Transpersonal Psychology 9(2):193–203, 1977

66. Osis K, Bokert E, Carlon ML: Dimensions of the meditative experience. Journal of Transpersonal Psychology 5(1):109–135, 1973

67. French AP, Schmid AC, Ingalls E: Transcendental meditation, altered reality testing, and behavioral change: a case report. J Nerv Ment Dis 161:55–58, 1975

68. Shapiro DH: Meditation: Self-Regulation and Altered States of Consciousness. Hawthorne, NY, Aldine Publishing Co, 1980

69. Yalom I, Bend D, Bloch S, et al: The impact of a weekend group experience on individual therapy. Arch Gen Psychiatry 34:399–415, 1977

70. Malec J, Sipprelle C: Physiological and subjective effects of Zen meditation and demand characteristics. J Consult Clin Psychol 44:339–340, 1977

71. Orne MT: On the social psychology of the psychological experiment with particular reference to demand characteristics and their implications. Am Psychol 17:776–783, 1962

72. Brown D: A model for the levels of concentrative meditation. Int J Clin Exp Hypn 25:236–273, 1977

73. Deikman AJ: The state of the art of meditation, in The Science of Meditation. Edited by Shapiro DH, Walsh RN. Hawthorne, NY, Aldine Publishing Co (in press)

74. Shapiro J, Shapiro DH: The psychology of responsibility. N Engl J Med 301:211–212, 1979

75. Globus GG: On "I": the conceptual foundations of responsibility. Am J Psychiatry 137:417–422, 1980

76. Woolfolk R: Self-control, meditation, and the treatment of chronic anger, in The Science of Meditation. Edited by Shapiro DH, Walsh RN. Hawthorne, NY, Aldine Publishing Co (in

Meditation: Clinical/Physiological Comparison 11

press)

77. Shapiro DH, Zifferblatt SM: Zen meditation and behavioral self-control: similarities, differences, and clinical applications. Am Psychol 31:519–532, 1976

78. Shapiro DH, Zifferblatt SM: An applied clinical combination of Zen meditation and behavioral self-management techniques: reducing methadone dosage in drug addiction. Behav Ther 7:694–695, 1976

79. Shapiro D: Precision Nirvana. Englewood Cliffs, NJ, Prentice-Hall, 1978

80. Smith J: Personality correlates of continuation and outcome in meditation and erect sitting controlled treatments. J Consult Clin Psychol 46:272–279, 1978

81. Walsh R, Roche L: The precipitation of acute psychotic episodes by intensive meditation in individuals with a history of schizophrenia. Am J Psychiatry 136:1085–1086, 1979

82. Walsh R: The consciousness disciplines and the behavioral sciences: questions of comparison and assessment. Am J Psychiatry 137:663–673, 1980

83. Gilbert GS, Parker JS, Claiborn CD: Differential mood changes in alcoholics as a function of anxiety management strategies. J Clin Psychol 34:229–332, 1978

2

CLASSIC PERSPECTIVES OF MEDITATION: TOWARD AN EMPIRICAL UNDERSTANDING OF MEDITATION AS AN ALTERED STATE OF CONSCIOUSNESS

Deane H. Shapiro, Jr.

In our modern world it has always been assumed . . . that in order to observe oneself all that is required is for a person to "look within." No one ever imagines that self-observation may be a highly disciplined skill which requires longer training than any other skill we know. . . . The . . . bad reputation of "introspection" . . . results from the particular notion that all by himself and without guidance and training, a man can come to accurate and unmixed observations of his own thought and perception. In contrast to this one could very well say that the heart of the psychological disciplines in the East and the ancient Western world consists of training at self-study.

Jacob Needleman

As noted in the previous chapter, most research on meditation carried out in Western laboratory and field settings has focused on physiological and overt behavioral changes: meditation as a self-regulation strategy. Recently, however, Western investigators have begun to call for a more detailed phenomenology of the meditation experience in order to assess subjective changes during meditation more precisely (Tart, 1975; Shapiro & Giber, 1978; Shapiro, 1980; Walsh, 1980): meditation as an altered state of consciousness.

There are three primary reasons for this. First, from a social learning or cognitive psychology standpoint, the role of internal events, thoughts, and images has become an increasingly important area of study (Homme, 1965; Mahoney & Thoresen, 1974; Meichenbaum & Cameron, 1974; Ellis, 1962; Shapiro & Zifferblatt, 1976). Since meditation is a technique purported to bring about strong subjective experiences in practitioners, experiences which involve radically new perceptions of their relationship with themselves, others, and the world around them, it becomes crucial to understand what goes on "internally."

Second, several research studies which have focused primarily on the physiological and overt behavior changes resulting from meditation have found no differences between meditation and other self-regulation strategies (e.g., Michaels, Huber, & McCann, 1976; see also articles by Beiman *et al.* and Marlatt *et al.*, in this volume). However, in some cases, although there have been no physiological or overt behavioral differences between meditation and other self-regulation strategies, subjects have reported their experiences of meditation as more profound, deeper, and/or more enjoyable than the comparative control groups (Morse *et al.*, 1977; Cauthen & Prymak, 1977; Travis *et al.*, 1976; Curtis & Wessberg, 1975–1976). Thus, even though there may not be overt behavioral and/or physiological differences between meditation and other self-regulation strategies, subjective differences occur, and from a clinical or research standpoint these may be critical.

Third, although there are many different conceptual definitions of meditation, it seems important to attempt to identify what "covert behaviors" actually occur during meditation. In other words, what kinds of thoughts and images does a person have while meditating? What kinds of statements does a person make prior to and after meditating? By investigating these questions, the "internal behaviors" of meditation may be compared with the "covert behaviors" of other cognitive self-regulation strategies to determine where similarities and differences exist.

The Phenomenology of Meditation

Those involved with the psychology of religion (Smith, 1965; Stace, 1960) and those who have studied spontaneous religious experiences (e.g., William James, 1901) note that often during times of meditation there are powerful subjective experiences which individuals claim have radically altered their lives, given them a new sense of meaning and purpose, new values, and a new relationship not only with themselves, but with other people and the world around them. In Eastern traditions some of these are referred to as satori, kensho, and samadhi. Many of the phenomenological qualities of these of these meditation-induced religious experiences are described in the classical texts such as the *Abhidhamma* and the *Visuddhimagga,* and are summarized and discussed in this book in articles by Brown and Goleman.

These experiences, although of high salience for the individual, are sometimes spoken of as ineffable. Those who experience them have difficulty communicating these experiences to others (Frank, 1977), which presents a dilemma to the researcher who needs some kind of verbal or symbolic representation to help quantify, label, and describe them. Often the task of experimentally validating these experiences has seemed so difficult that some researchers have dismissed the experiences themselves as epiphenomena at best or at worst artificial schizophrenia with complete withdrawal of libidinal interest from the outside world (e.g., Alexander, 1931; GAP Report, 1977). Dismissing the experiences as epiphenomena is based not only on the difficulty of describing the phenomena, but also involves a paradigm clash between the Western model of physicalistic science and the internal, experiential nature of the altered state phenomena (Walsh, 1980). As Tart has noted (1975:21, 24–25), "The philosophy of physicalism is a belief system stating that physical reality—physical data are the only data that are ultimately 'real.' Therefore, internal or experiential phenomena, being inherently unreliable and unreal, must be reduced to physiological data to become reliable. If they cannot be so reduced, they are generally ignored."

The second attitude—that these experiences are like psychotic episodes or schizophrenia—can again be a function of a paradigm clash, overlaying a Western paradigm on an experience within a different context and value system. Just as it may be a mistake to assume *a priori* that all altered state of consciousness (ASC) experiences are unilaterally examples of higher or enlightened consciousness, it may similarly be a mistake to dismiss them *a priori* as delusional. What truly is needed is a precise study of these so-called altered-state phenomena. Again, as Tart noted (1975:21), "Given the great complexity of spiritual phenomena and discrete altered states of consciousness phenomena and their significance, the need for replication by trained observers to form a data base for future research is of exceptional importance." How might we go about this? First, we need a definition.

Altered State: Toward a Working Definition, Problems in Studying, and Available Approaches

As a basis for our discussion, we will use the general definition of altered states proposed by Tart (1975:24):

> Our ordinary discrete state of consciousness is a *construction* built up in accordance with biological and cultural imperatives for the purpose of dealing with our physical, intrapersonal, and interpersonal environments. A discrete altered state of consciousness is a radically different way of handling information from the physical, intrapersonal, and interpersonal environments, yet the discrete altered state of consciousness may be as arbitrary as our ordinary discrete state of consciousness (p. 24).

Note that this definition is value free. It allows us to study a discrete altered state of consciousness without *a priori* judgment.

At this point, further clarification should be made about my use of the phrase "altered state of consciousness.'' There are some problems with this phrase which merit comment. First, the problem of defining meditation by its effects needs to be considered. As noted in a previous work (Shapiro and Giber, 1978), we need to distinguish whether meditation as an altered state is conceptualized as an independent variable (causing certain subsequent behavioral changes in a person) or a dependent variable (what are the altered-state effects of meditation). The phrase "meditation as an altered state" does not make that distinction.

Second, the phrase seems to imply a uniform "altered state" unique to meditation. Although there may be certain experiences common to meditation practice (Osis *et al.*, 1973; Kohr, 1977), there are certainly many different types of altered-state experiences which may occur as a result of a specific meditation technique, as well as across different techniques. Further, there are many different methods to attain ASC experiences similar to those which occur in meditation. I have tried to be as precise as possible in discussing these issues throughout the text. As noted earlier (Shapiro & Giber, 1978), the phrase "meditation as an altered state of consciousness" is intended primarily to help researchers differentiate what aspect of meditation they are studying—i.e., its self-regulation qualities or altered-state qualities.

Given the above definition and discussion, how might we go about studying these altered state phenomena? What are the problems inherent in this undertaking? Tart's comments on this issue are the best to date and are summarized here. The first two problems relate to the nature of the state itself: its ineffability and the problem of state-dependent learning. Another problem is that the person doing the investigation must often be subject, observer, and experimenter.

The first problem, as noted above, is the fact that many of the experiences of an ASC are described as ineffable and therefore beyond conceptualization. Second, there is a problem, seldom mentioned in the literature, of the generalizability of an ASC. We know from research on the state-dependent learning that what is learned in one state, say inebriation (Fischer, 1971), *is not always recalled in the uninebriated state* although it may be *stored* and recallable when once again drunk; learning, therefore, does not necessarily generalize to other states of consciousness. Again, as Tart noted, for reasons we know almost nothing about, the experiences of discrete altered states of consciousness eventually may be transferable to a different state of consciousness.

> So some people may have a spiritual experience occuring only in a particular discrete altered state of consciousness for a while, but then find it becomes part of their ordinary discrete state of consciousness. We know almost nothing scientifically about the degree to which such transfer can take place, the conditions favoring or hindering it, or the fullness of the transfer. (1975:25).

Here we may need to look to the social learning theorist for the laws of generalization and discrimination training (Bandura, 1977).

Additional problems derive from the need for individuals to sometimes be subject, observer, and experimenter. Tart suggested that this requires special training in order to develop a true phenomenology of the spiritual experience. Even such trained observers need to be cautious of experimenter bias (Rosenthal *et al.*, 1962). They need to be aware of the demand characteristics of the training experimental situation (Orne, 1962). Further, Tart noted that the "individual who follows a spiritual path or tries to reach truth in a discrete altered state of consciousness may settle for the feeling of certainty rather than pressing on with his investigations" (1975, p. 48). In other words, the person may feel that they have an obvious perception of the truth and therefore not want to question that perception.* In fact, as Tart noted, the individual may be building fantasy worlds that seem real to that person, and therefore they create a reality which they believe to be a truthful *a priori* reality, without questioning the belief systems they brought to the situation.

In summary, Tart noted that state-specific sciences are possible, although difficult, and would involve, in the true scientific tradition, (a) observing, (b) making public the nature of the observation: consensual validation, (c) forming logical hypotheses based on the material, (d) testability: the search for testable consequences.

Given these problems, as well as the importance of the phenomena, what approaches might be available to us?

---

*It should be noted that this phenomenon is not at all unique to altered-state-of-consciousness research.

Overview of Approaches to Studying the Phenomenology of Meditation: Advantages and Problems

There have been several ways that researchers have tried to gather information about the phenomenology of meditation. One way to gather information is by looking at the classical texts, such as the *Abhidhamma* and its summary by Buddhaghosa, the *Visuddhimagga* (Goleman, 1972, 1977), and the classical root texts of the Mahamudra tradition (Brown, 1977). These texts provide phenomenological reports of the experience of advanced meditators.

A second experimental methodology is to have individuals meditate and then to give them the opportunity to describe their meditation experience. In this approach the meditator and the experimenter/investigator are different individuals. This methodology has been used by several investigators (VanNuys, 1973; Kubose, 1976). They had individuals push a button during the meditation experience to determine frequency of thought intrusion, and later asked subjects about the nature of their thoughts. Corby *et al.* (1978) looked at physiological changes and compared those changes with the subjects' accounts of their subjective experiences. Banquet (1973) had subjects push buttons signaling different types of subjective experience and tried to correlate that with EEG data.

Other techniques used to understand phenomenological content include a retrospective content analysis of the meditation experience in terms of thought intrusions (Kanas & Horowitz, 1977), rater coding of the meditation experience (Maupin, 1965; Kornfield, 1979; Lesh, 1970), a factor analysis of self-reports about the meditation experience (Osis *et al.*, 1973; Kohr, 1977), and verbal report from the client after meditation focus (Deikman, 1966).

A third approach involves having the subject be both the meditator and the experimenter. This approach, suggested by Tart (1971), involves training individuals in behavioral science skills and then having them be their own subjects in an experiment to look at internal experiences. Tart himself has utilized this approach (Tart, 1971), describing a one-year experience with Transcendental Meditation, and Walsh (1977, 1978) has utilized this approach describing a two-year meditation experience.

Each of these approaches has advantages and disadvantages. The experience of long-term, proficient meditators described in the classical texts is useful because it provides first-hand accounts of individuals who have had extensive meditation experience. However, one of the potential limitations of this approach is these individuals' lack of behavioral science skills and the resultant inattention to nonspecific placebo effects such as expectation effects and demand characteristics.

The second approach—with the experimenter and subjects separate—gives some useful information about subjective experiences, but those experiences are susceptible to certain contaminating variables. First, they are retrospective accounts (except in Banquet, 1973) and thus subject to the vagaries of *post hoc* subject "memory." Second, the subjects' experiences are filtered through hypotheses generated by different individual experimenters who may or may not be sensitive to subtle nuances of meditation experience. Further, as with factor analytic research (Osis *et al.*, 1973: Kohr, 1977), the factors are an artifact of and are limited by the experimenter's initial coding questionnaire.

The third approach, having an individual subject/experimenter, has the advantage of allowing for immediate access of material between subject and experimenter, although it presents a greater potential for problems of experimenter bias (Rosenthal, 1962) and demand characteristics (Orne, 1962). This is the primary reason Tart recommends that the experimenter be someone well trained in the behavioral sciences.

Findings from the Different Approaches

Subjective Experiences During Meditation

As noted, one approach to gaining information about subjective experiences during meditation involves only slight variations on the traditional scientific experiment in which the experimenter tries to gather information from the subjects. The first group of these studies to be completed are interesting primarily from a heuristic standpoint.

Maupin (1965) had ordinary subjects focus on breathing for nine sessions. These subjects' meditation experiences were rated on a five-point scale by "blind" judges. Based on their self-report data, described after each session, six of the twenty-eight subjects were rated as high experiencers. A high experiencer was one who reported at least one Type Five experience (concentration and detachment). Ten subjects were rated as having moderate responses to meditation: i.e., no Type Five experience but at least one Type Three or Type Four experience (pleasant body sensations or vivid breathing). Twelve subjects were rated "low response" because they reported nothing more than relaxation (Stage Two) or dizziness (Stage One). Maupin (1965: 145) notes that his five-point response scale does not register all observed responses.

Subjectively felt benefits similar to those resulting from relaxation therapies were reported by several subjects. Subjects in the high and moderate response group occasionally mentioned the emergence of very specific and vivid effects other than anxiety while they were practicing. These included hallucinoid feelings, muscle tension, sexual excitement, and intense sadness.

Lesh (1970) also had subjects practice Zen breath meditation; he slightly modified Maupin's five-point scale but found essentially the same results.

In a study using external concentration, Deikman (1966) had subjects focus on a blue vase, and he also found strong subjective changes in ordinary subjects' phenomenological perceptions. Every subject noted an alteration in perception of the vase, a shift to a deeper and more intense blue: brighter, more vivid, luminous. Further, subjects noted instability in the vase's shape or size: a loss of the third dimension, a diffusion or loss of perceptual boundaries. One subject noted feelings of merging with the vase, as though "it were almost part of me." Another subject noted complete loss of body feelings (Deikman, 1966).

Kanas and Horowitz (1977) used a content analysis questionnaire devised by Horowitz (1969, 1970) to gain information about subjective experiences during meditation. Subjects were shown a stress film and then asked to estimate the percentage of time spent thinking about the stress film, the experimental task, life issues, fantasies, mantra (where appropriate), other thoughts, and no thoughts, during the ten minutes they meditated or rested.

Kornfield (1979) gathered extensive data from meditators at five 2-week and one 3-month retreats for intensive insight meditation (Vipassana). Kornfield's data came from reports which the meditators gave their teachers every 2 or 3 days and from answers to a series of three questions about (1) sleep/food intake; (2) changes in clarity of perception, concentration, mindfulness; (3) what was currently predominant in meditation experience; any unusual experiences. Although Kornfield's study generated an enormous amount of rich information, the interpretation of these data must be tentative, since the coding instrument was made *post hoc* as a way of sorting the data, rather than prior to the experiment to test the hypotheses. However, this type of heuristic study is necessary initially to give us information about the phenomenology of meditation experience.

These five studies involve having subjects report on their experiences at the completion of the meditation session or in Kornfield's case, at intervals. In Deikman's (1966) and Kornfield's (1979) studies, the reports were made directly to the experimenters/teachers, who grouped and reported the data; in the Maupin (1965) and Lesh (1970) studies, raters coded the experiences on a five-part scale, a methodological improvement, *after* sufficient heuristic information has been accumulated via previous studies.

A second group of studies to obtain reports of meditators' experiences involved having subjects push buttons *during* the meditation session whenever certain thoughts or feelings occurred (Van Nuys, 1973; Banquet, 1973; Kubose, 1976).

Van Nuys had subjects push a button every time they became aware of an intrusive thought. The nature of intrusions reported by subjects in the postmeditation interview included: itches, aches, and other bodily feelings of discomfort; thoughts about the nature and purpose of the experiment; and thoughts about roommates, girlfriends, courses, and other current concerns. In addition, many subjects reported such subjective responses as vivid visual experiences, feelings of paranoia, feelings of being "turned on," dreamlike experiences, temporary loss of orientation in time or space, primary-process perceptual distortions (Van Nuys, 1973, p. 67).

Kubose (1976) debriefed meditators after their experience with a questionnaire asking them to divide the thoughts they had into the following categories: (a) thoughts about bodily sensations; (b) thoughts relating themselves to the present situation; (c) thoughts relating themselves to past events; (d) thoughts about the future; (e) thoughts about ideas and things that did not have a strong time component. His data revealed that subjects in the meditation group categorized most of their thoughts along a present-time dimension, whereas subjects in the control group categorized their thoughts as past and future. As Kubose noted, meditation seemed to minimize the intrusion of distracting thoughts, and relative to a control group, when thoughts did occur, they tended to be categorized as oriented toward the present rather than the past or future.

Banquet (1973) had individuals push buttons to signal thoughts or feelings. He refined the technique of Kubose and had five different buttons for the individuals to push, depending on the category of events during the meditation experience; bodily sensations, involuntary movement, visual images, deep meditation, and transcendence (deepest part of meditation). However, as with any intrusive procedure, there may be difficulties in having a person push a button while in a state of transcendence and attempting to maintain that state.

Finally, two other studies, still within the same scientific tradition of an experimenter trying to gain information from subjects, was undertaken by Osis *et al.* (1973) and later repeated by Kohr (1977). These studies involved asking meditators to respond to a questionnaire after their sessions, and then performing a factor analysis. The research by Osis *et al.* (1973) is described in some detail here because it is an interesting application of multivariate statistical analysis to the issue of meditation experience. He gave subjects a premeditation mood questionnaire and a postmeditation questionnaire before and after four different sittings. Both questionnaires were used in the same factor analysis to determine how closely the subjects' meditation and premeditation states were related. Subjects came from a variety of different religious traditions, including Unitarian, Zen, Raja Yoga, Hassidic Judaism, and Catholicism. There was an attempt to determine the extent to which meditation experience would cut across different disciplines and different orientations. Osis posited that in most religions the central concept is a belief in a spiritual reality felt to be larger and more valuable than (and often inclusive of) the personal self. The issue of self-selection was mentioned and even maximized; experimenters then tried to select subjects ''to whom meditation was a kind of quest for meaning and growth in their lives'' (Osis *et al.*, 1973, p. 113). It was found in both the Osis and later the Kohr studies that there was almost no correlation between initial mood and meditation experience, suggesting that meditation did produce a state of consciousness different from the state of consciousness which the person brought to the practice of meditation.

Six factors were replicated in at least three of the meditation experiences: self-transcendence and openness; mood brought to the session (both appeared in all four experiments); intensification and change of consciousness; meaning dimension; forceful exclusion of images; and general success of meditation. Self-transcendence and openness involved the following core items: a feeling of merging with others, unity with the group, and oneness with the external. For mood brought to the session the core items were elation, freedom from anxiety, content with self, and greater vitality. The next factor, intensification and change of consciousness, seemed to be the most central and complex. Thirteen core items, one-half of the items in the post-session questionnaire, are contained in this factor. They include: intensification of consciousness, ways of experiencing change, love and joy, perceptual enrichment, refreshment after session, depth of insight, unity with group, and the feeling that it was a good session. There often seemed to be an organismic arousal during this intensification and change of consciousness. Another factor, the meaning dimension, included core items such as relevant visual images, relevant thoughts, deep insights, alertness, and sense of presence. The next factor, what Osis called ''forceful exclusion of images,'' included negative items. As the authors stated, ''The predominant note is one of tension: negative loadings on relaxation, serenity, and affirmation of the external'' (Osis *et al.*, 1973, p. 122). In the fourth experiment, they introduced a negative experience factor. It expresses ''the opposites of affirmation and deep acceptance of self and others. It appears to express the feeling that the meditation was interfered with'' (p. 130).

In the Kohr experiment (1977), which tried to extend and replicate the Osis experiment, again there was strong bias in the subjects selected: a sampling from members of the Association for Research and Enlightenment agreeing to participate in meditation research and answer questionnaires. Some of the refinements that occurred in the questionnaire were breaking the subjects into various subgroups of high and low categories on five variables: anxiety level as measured by the IPAT Anxiety Scale Questionnaire; incidents of perceived personal problems as indicated by the total score on the Mooney Problem Check List (Mooney & Gordon, 1951); the length of time previously spent engaged in meditation on a fairly regular basis; the amount of previous meditation experience combined with whether a consistent schedule had been maintained in the month prior to the study, and the degree to which the participants adhered to the procedures (low anxiety, high anxiety, low problems, high problems, low regular schedule, high regular schedule, low prior experience, high prior experience, low adherence, high adherence).

The meditators in Kohr's study meditated alone, based on a manual, whereas the subjects in the Osis experiment meditated and discussed their experiences in a small group context. The major factor was intensification and change of consciousness. Kohr found, ''This factor conveys the impression of a heightened sense of fullness, deep positive emotion, and intensification of awareness, perceptual change and enhancement, a presence of religious significance and a sense of satisfaction with the session'' (1977: 200). The authors noted that this factor seemed a blend of the factors of self-transcendence and openness as well as the intensification factor. The ''psychological state prior to session'' was also a consistent factor, similar to Osis's mood-brought-to-session factor. Importantly, this factor was independent of the other factors except for the tendency for the freedom-from-anxiety item to load with the ''negative experience factor'' in a majority of the subgroup analysis. This suggests that anxiety can often impair the meditation experience unless one is successful in reducing its effects prior to the session. Kohr noted, ''Overall, the cohesiveness of this factor suggests that one's mood and functioning during the day represented a different state of consciousness than the altered state as measured by the post-session questionnaire'' (1977:200). The negative experience factor was based on those items added in Osis's fourth experiment plus some additional items. These included sessions characterized by an inability to relax, compounded by the intrusion of unwanted thoughts, some of them anxious residues from the day's experience or anticipations of future events. The mental clarity factor, reflecting retention of awareness and sense of alertness was not observed in the Osis experiment. The physical effects factor, including various physical sensations like an increase in bodily warmth and sensations around the ''seven spiritual centers'' of Oriental and occult religions, was also weak.

The independence of the psychological-state-prior-to-session factor seems important, both in the Kohr and Osis experiments. As Osis (1973:130) noted, ''The items of everyday mood as measured in the pre-meditation questionnaire did not appreciably load on any other factors of the meditation experience and formed a strong common compact factor by themselves. The subjects' free comments support the view that successful meditation leads to altered states of consciousness.'' Similarly, in the Kohr experiment, the independence of states arises from the fact that ''Good sessions frequently occurred regardless of feeling tired or depressed prior to the session. In these sessions there seemed to be an ability to let go of a negative emotion or to move beyond fatigue'' (1977:202). The only area where a prior psychological state demonstrated leakage into a meditation period was anxiety associated with having negative experiences. The author noted, ''negative experience is not uncommon among individuals who resolve to meditate on a daily basis, especially the novice.''

As noted, the above studies involve only a slight variation on the traditional scientific experiment in which an experimenter gathers information from subjects. But there is also a different approach to gathering information on the phenomenology of meditation—one in which the subject and experimenter are the same person. The roots of this approach go back to the classical texts, such as the *Adhidhamma* (Goleman, 1972, 1977) and the classical texts of Mahamudra tradition (Brown, 1977). These texts attempt to develop a scientific phenomenology of meditation, a cartography of the ''inner voyage.'' The scientists are the meditators who use themselves as subjects and through a process of introspective psychology try to chart which experiences and thoughts are helpful in moving toward enlightened experiences, and which are harmful. Their texts provide us with one model derived from long-term experienced meditators. They may or may not be a state-specific science in the sense that we do not know how much the practitioners' own belief systems were looked at carefully as part of the ''outcome'' success.

The reports in the classical texts give us information from long-term meditators who were presumably not trained in the behavioral sciences. Three studies have been done by behavioral scientists who are also meditators of intermediate, one to several years, experience (Tart, 1971; Walsh, 1977, 1978; Shapiro, 1980). Theoretically, those trained in the behavioral sciences should have more acute and accurate discrimination skills, should be less biased and more willing to admit where the technique of meditation is or is not useful, and should try to communicate those subjective experiences to others in accessible terms. For example, Tart (1971) practiced TM meditation for a year and Walsh (1977, 1978) described his experiences during 2 years of Vipassana (insight meditation). In a similar vein, Shapiro (1980) recorded thoughts and images during several meditation sessions, and subsequently analyzed data for number and type of thoughts and cognitions, and percentage of time when there did not appear to be thoughts.

This approach, using behavioral scientists as subject, observer, and experimenter, has several potential

Classic Perspectives of Meditation   **19**

pitfalls. However, it does have the advantage of direct experience and reporting by the same person, without the intervening hypotheses and interpretations of another experimenter. At the very least, observing one's own meditation experience should be a rich source of gaining experiential understanding of relevant concepts and of generating hypotheses and refining dependent variables for subsequent research.

Concurrent Validity for Subjective Experience during Meditation

Because of the subjective nature of the meditation experience, it is difficult to obtain concurrent validity on subjects' self-report. Maupin (1965) attempted to correlate attention measures (digit span, continuous additions, size estimation) with response to meditation. However, Van Nuys (1973) has suggested that these measures were not relevant to the type of attention involved in meditation (see also Galin, 1974). Van Nuys notes that alterations in consciousness occur when attention is relatively fixed and sustained, whereas the tests Maupin used involved tasks that require a constant and rapid shifting of the focus of attention; furthermore, "they invite discursive, analytic thought that is actively restricted in meditation" (Boals, 1978, p. 165).

Van Nuys (1973) developed a simple technique for studying attention during the latter stages of meditation. He had his subjects push a button to report intrusion of "off-task" thoughts that distracted them from the task of meditation. He found that the reports of these intrusions correlated with hypnotizability. Other promising methods of obtaining concurrent validity may be the use of experimenter-controlled buttons to signal physiological values of the meditator to the meditator, requesting a continuing experimenter-subjective report (Herbert & Lehmann, 1977), the signal detection format employed in the daydreaming studies of Singer (1975) to obtain reports of occurrence of "task-irrelevant thoughts," and monitoring hemispheric laterality and synchrony to determine brain wave patterns within and between hemispheres during meditation (Davidson, 1976; Galin, 1974).

Subjective Reports of Changes in
Attitudes and Perceptions After Meditation

The studies reported above have tested short-term, mostly in-state effects of meditation. Other researchers have tried to document perceptual and/or behavioral changes that occur at times other than during meditation. These studies, which look at self-concept and perceived behavior change, have gathered data primarily by use of pencil and paper tests, including Shostrom's Personal Orientation Inventory (Hjelle, 1974; Nidich, Seeman & Dreskin, 1973; Seeman, Nidich & Banta, 1972); the Northridge Development Scale (Ferguson & Gowan, 1976); and the Otis Descriptive Personality List and Otis Physical and Behavioral Inventory (Otis, 1974). All of these studies report that meditators change more than control groups in the direction of positive mental health, positive personality change, and "self-actualization." (Studies that used self-report data, but that focused primarily on anxiety, are not included here.) These changes include such items as self-perceived increase in capacity for intimate contact, increased spontaneity, self-regard, acceptance of aggression, and inner directedness.

There are, however, several methodological problems with the above studies. First, none of the studies, except Hjelle's (1974), controls for expectations and demand characteristics, and Hjelle's study, as already noted, does not control for commitment (long-term practice). The commitment or motivation of the subjects may be quite important. For example, it appears that five of the original twenty subjects in the experimental condition in Seeman, Nidich, and Banta's (1972) study dropped out, a fact that could have biased the experiment in a direction favoring meditation. A second methodological problem of the above studies is that they do not show, aside from paper and pencil test scores, whether the meditating subjects demonstrated behavior changes.

In an attempt to learn more about daily changes in behavior, Shapiro (1978a), in addition to pre- and post-tests, had subjects self-monitor nine variables daily: Feelings of anger, seeing beauty in nature, positive self-thoughts, negative self-thoughts, feelings of anxiety, feelings of creativity. The experimental group (informal and formal Zen meditation) daily reported data significantly more in a favorable direction:

less feelings of anxiety, more feelings of creativity, etc. This longitudinal study was useful because it provided self-report of feelings rather than simply before and after pencil and paper test data of global feeling change. However, it is unclear from the study which parts of the treatment intervention were responsible for what percentage of the variance of the successful outcome. Further, no concurrent covarying overt variables were involved in the study, which still leaves us with the problems of self-reported data.

Summary

What can we make of these studies? First, it clearly seems important to distinguish between short- and long-term meditation experience. Compared to "Eastern" standards most Western meditators are at a "beginning level" in terms of length of time spent in meditation practice. The classical texts give us a cartography—a context for clarifying different types of long-term meditation experience. Second, it seems a useful scientific strategy to have those trained in the behavioral sciences who also meditate be both experimenters, subjects, and observers, although certain conditions must be observed. Third, it does seem possible to gain useful and precise information about the phenomenology of the meditation experiences. As Osis *et al.* noted, "in spite of the almost universal claim that the meditation experience is ineffable, clear dimensionalities emerge" (1973:130). Fourth, it appears that even in short-term meditators, relatively strong experiences occur (Deikman, 1966; Maupin, 1965). Further, as the work of Osis and Kohr suggest, meditation experiences, with the exception of anxiety, were different from the mood brought to the session—evidence for the view of meditation as an altered state of consciousness. Fifth, both Osis and Deikman argue that although belief systems may be part of the variance accounting for the effect of the altered state, more than simply belief systems are at work in meditation because "different beliefs of different subjects will on the whole cancel each other out . . . whereas meditation seems to tap more universal dimensions" (Osis *et al.*, 1973, p. 130). Deikman noted that "hypnotic experiences do not appear to have the ineffable, profoundly uplifting, highly valued quality of the mystic state and are not remembered as such" (1963, p. 340). He noted that there may be strong belief systems, suggestion, and demand characteristics operating but then suggests that the hypothesis of demand characteristics is not consistent with the fact that the highest mystic experiences are similar in their basic content despite wide differences in cultural backgrounds and expectations: (a) feeling of incommunicability, (b) transcendence of sense modalities, (c) absence of specific content, such as images and ideas, and (d) feelings of unity with the ultimate. Sixth, not all altered states are pleasant and uplifting. For example, in his final experiment, Osis put in questions to tap these negative experiences, and Kohr found a negative experience factor to be a clear dimension. As noted, these negative experiences can also be seen in the earlier reports of Van Nuys, and in an article by French, Schmid and Ingalls (1975) on altered reality testing resulting from too much meditation. Further, an article by Otis (this volume, No. 17) describes the adverse effects of meditation, presumably some of which resulted from experiences during meditation.

Therefore, in conclusion, greater clarity and precision seem necessary in describing altered states. Rather than, on the one hand, shying away from this area as epiphenomena or dismissing it *a priori* as "psychotic and delusional," or, on the other hand, calling it "enlightened and higher consciousness," we need to gather more precise information to see when these powerful experiences may in fact be psychotic and when they may be truly enlightened and spiritual. Further, with this kind of precise information, in addition to being able to compare meditation with other self-regulation strategies, we also may be able to learn more about meditation as an altered state of consciousness, and thereafter compare it to other altered states such as dreaming (Faber *et al.*, 1978), hypnotic trance, psychosis, sleep, and others.

References

Alexander, F. Buddhistic training as an artificial catatonia. *Psychoanalytic Review*, 1931, *18*, 129–45.

Bandura, A. *Social learning theory*. Englewood Cliffs, NJ: Prentice Hall, 1977.

Banquet, J. P. EEG and meditation. *Electroencephalography & Clinical Neurophysiology*, 1973, *33*, 454. a.

Banquet, J. P. Spectral analysis of the EEG in meditation. *Electroencephalography & Clinical Neurophysiology*, 1973, *35*, 143–51. b.

Boals, G. Toward a cognitive reconceptualization of meditation. *Journal of Transpersonal Psychology,* 1978, *10* (2), 143–182.

Brown, D. A model for the levels of concentrative meditation. *International Journal of Clinical & Experimental Hypnosis,* 1977, *25,* 236–73.

Cauthen, N. and Prymak, C. Meditation versus relaxation. *Journal of Consulting & Clinical Psychology,* 1977, Jun, *45* (3), 496–7.

Corby, J. C., Roth, W. T., Zarcone, V. P., and Kopell, B. S. Psychophysiological correlates of the practice of Tantric Yoga meditation. *Archives of General Psychiatry,* 1978, *35,* 571–80.

Curtis, W. D. and Wessberg, H. W. A comparison of heart rate, respiration, and galvanic skin response among meditators, relaxers, and controls. *Journal of Altered States of Consciousness,* 1975/6, *2,* 319–24.

Davidson, J. Physiology of meditation and mystical states of consciousness. *Perspectives in Biology and Medicine,* 1976, *19,* 345–80.

Deikman, A. J. Deautomatization and the mystic experience. *Psychiatry,* 1966, *29,* 324–38.

Ellis, A. *Reason and emotion in psychotherapy.* New York: Lyle Stuart and Citadel Press, 1962.

Faber, P. A., Saayman, G. S., and Touyz, W. Meditation and archetypal content of nocturnal dreams. *Journal of Analytic Psychology,* 1978, *23* (1), 1–22.

Ferguson, P. O. and Gowan, J. C. Transcendental meditation: Some preliminary findings. *Journal of Humanistic Psychology,* 1976, *16* (3), 51–60.

Fischer, R. A cartography of the ecstatic and meditative states. *Science,* 1971, *174,* 897–904.

Frank, J. D. Nature and functions of belief systems: Humanism and transcendental religion. *American Psychologist,* 1977, *32* (7), 555–9.

French, A. P., Schmid, A. C., and Ingalls, E. Transcendental meditation, altered reality testing, and behavioral change: A case report. *Journal of Nervous & Mental Disease,* 1975, *161,* 55–8.

Galin, D. Implications for psychiatry of left and right cerebral specialization. *Archives of General Psychiatry,* 1974, *31,* 572–83.

Goleman, D. The Buddha on meditation and states of consciousness, part II. A typology of meditation techniques. *Journal of Transpersonal Psychology,* 1972, *4* (2), 151–210.

Goleman, D. *The varieties of the meditative experience.* New York: E. P. Dutton, 1977.

Group for the Advancement of Psychiatry. *Mysticism: Spiritual quest or psychic disorder?* Washington, D.C.: Group for the Advancement of Psychiatry, 1977.

Herbert, R. and Lehmann, D. Theta bursts: An EEG pattern in normal subjects practicing the transcendental meditation technique. *Electroencephalography & Clinical Neurophysiology,* 1977, *42,* 387–405.

Hjelle, L. A. Transcendental meditation and psychological health. *Perceptual & Motor Skills,* 1974, *39,* 623–8.

Homme, L. Control of covenants: The operants of the mind. *Psychological Record,* 1965, *15,* (4), 501–11.

Horowitz, M. J. Psychic trauma: Return of images after a stress film. *Archives of General Psychiatry,* 1969, *20,* 552–559.

Horowitz, M. J. *Image formation and cognition.* New York: Appleton-Century-Crofts, 1970.

James, W. *The varieties of religious experience.* New York: Longmans, 1901.

Kanas, N. and Horowitz, M. Reactions of TMers and non-meditators to stress films. *Archives of General Psychiatry,* 1977, *34* (12), 1431–36.

Kohr, E. Dimensionality in the meditative experience: A replication. *Journal of Transpersonal Psychology,* 1977, *9* (2), 193–203.

Kornfield, J. Intensive insight meditation: A phenomenological study. *Journal of Transpersonal Psychology,* 1979, *11,* (1), 41–58.

Kubose, S. K. An experimental investigation of psychological aspects of meditation. *Psychologia,* 1976, *19* (1), 1–10.

Lesh, T. Zen meditation and the development of empathy in counselors. *Journal of Humanistic Psychology,* 1970, *10* (1), 39–74.

Mahoney, M. J. and Thoresen, C. E. *Self-control: Power to the person.* Monterey, CA: Brooks/Cole, 1974.

Marlatt, G., Pagano, R., Rose, R., and Margues, J. K. Effects of meditation and relaxation training upon alcohol use in male social drinkers. This book, Article 10.

Maupin, E. Individual differences in response to a Zen meditation exercise. *Journal of Consulting Psychology,* 1965, *29,* 139–45.

Meichenbaum, D. and Cameron, R. The clinical potential of modifying what clients say to themselves. In M. J. Mahoney & C. E. Thoresen. *Self-control: Power to the person.* Monterey, CA: Brooks/Cole, 1974.

Michaels, R., Huber, M., and McCann, D. Evaluation of transcendental meditation as a method of reducing stress. *Science,* 1976, *192* (4245), 1242–4.

Mooney, R. L. and Gordon, L. *Mooney problems checklist.* New York: Psychological Corp., 1951.

Morse, D. R., Martin, S., Furst, M. L., and Dubin, L. L. A physiological and subjective evaluation of meditation, hypnosis, and relaxation. *Psychosomatic Medicine,* 1977, *39,* 304–24.

Nidich, S., Seeman, W., and Dreskin, T. Influence of transcendental meditation on a measure of self-actualization: A replication. *Journal of Counseling Psychology,* 1973, *20,* 565–6.

Orne, M. T. On the social psychology of the psychological experiment: With particular reference to demand characteristics and their implications. *American Psychologist,* 1962, *17,* (10), 776–83.

Osis, K., Bokert, E., and Carlson, M. L. Dimensions of the meditative experience. *Journal of Transpersonal Psychology,* 1973, *5,* (1), 109–135.

Otis, L. S. If well-integrated but anxious, try TM. *Psychology Today,* 1974, *7,* 45–46.

Rosenthal, R., Persinger, G., and Fode, K. Experimenter bias, anxiety and social desirability. *Perceptual & Motor Skills,* 1962, *15* (1), 73–4.

Seeman, W., Nidich, S., and Banta, T. Influence of TM on a measure of self-actualization. *Journal of Counseling Psychology,* 1972, *19* (3), 184–7.

Shapiro, D. H. Behavioral and attitudinal changes resulting from a Zen experience workshop in Zen meditation. *Journal of Humanistic Psychology,* 1978, *18* (3), 21–9.

Shapiro, D. H. *Meditation: Self-regulation strategy and altered state of consciousness.* New York: Aldine, 1980.

Shapiro, D. H. and Giber, D. Meditation and psychotherapeutic effects. *Archives of General Psychiatry,* 1978, *35,* 294–302.

Shapiro, D. H. and Zifferblatt, S. M. An applied clinical combination of Zen meditation and behavioral self-management techniques: Reducing methadone dosage in drug addiction. *Behavior Therapy,* 1976, *7,* 694–5.

Singer, J. L. Navigating the stream of consciousness: Research in daydreaming and related inner experience. *American Psychologist,* 1975, *30,* 727–38.

Smith, H. *The religions of man.* New York: Harper, 1965.

Stace, W. T. *Mysticism & philosophy.* 1st. Ed. Phil: Lippincott, 1960.

Tart, C. A psychologist's experience with T.M. *Journal of Transpersonal Psychology,* 1971, *3* (2), 135–40.

Tart, C. *Transpersonal psychologies.* New York: Harper & Row, 1975.

Travis, T., Kondo, C., and Knott, J. Heart rate, muscle tension, and alpha production of transcendental meditation and relaxation controls. *Biofeedback & self-regulation,* 1976, *1,* (4) 387–94.

VanNuys, D. Meditation, attention, and hypnotic susceptibility: A correlation study. *International Journal of Clinical & Experimental Hypnosis,* 1973, *21,* 59–69.

Walsh, R. Initial meditative experiences: Part I. *Journal of Transpersonal Psychology,* 1977, *9,* (2), 151–92.

Walsh, R. Initial meditative experiences: Part II. *Journal of Transpersonal Psychology,* 1978, *10* (1), 1–28.

Walsh, R. Behavioral sciences and the consciousness disciplines. *American Journal of Psychiatry,* 1980, *137,* (6), 663–673.

3

AN EVOLUTIONARY MODEL OF
MEDITATION RESEARCH

Roger Walsh

Despite the fact that it has a longer history than almost any other psychotherapeutic endeavor, it is only within the last few years that meditation has attracted significant scientific attention. Meditation of one type or another can be found in a wide variety of cultures and traced back for at least two and a half thousand years. Its ultimate aim is said to be to enable its practitioners to attain control of their minds and develop levels of psychological well being and states of consciousness beyond those recognized in traditional Western psychological models.

Until recently, the typical Western reaction to these claims tended to be one of cynicism. At first sight, many of the claimed effects seem to run counter to traditional Western psychological assumptions. Indeed, some of the reported experiences appear as reminiscent of psychopathology as of extreme health, e.g., claims of the loss of ego boundaries and of a sense of merging with the universe.

However, closer examination, personal experience of these disciplines, and a recognition of the limitations imposed by paradigm clash and communication across different states of consciousness has made these claims appear more coherent and comprehensible (Tart, 1975, 1976; Shapiro, 1980; Walsh, 1980; Walsh and Vaughan, 1980). Furthermore, the generally favorable findings of empirical research have now established this as a respectable area for scientific inquiry. Indeed, research in this area appears to be expanding rapidly, a fact which can be traced to several roots. In part, it is a reaction to popular interest and practice of these disciplines. In addition, a number of behavioral scientists have themselves undertaken meditative practice, and several have described positive results including an expanded comprehension of meditative claims once they had some experiential basis for understanding (e.g., Tart, 1972; Walsh, 1977, 1978; Shapiro, 1979, 1980). The wide spread of popularity of transcendental meditation has also been helpful since it comprises a simple, rapid, highly standardized training procedure which readily lends itself to experimental investigation.

The aim of this article is not to perform a detailed analysis and review of individual studies, since this has been done elsewhere (Carrington, 1978; Shapiro, 1980). Rather, it aims at providing an evolutionary model of meditation research which provides a context from which to view and understand it.

This model represents a specific application of a more general stimulus response model of the evolution of research (Walsh, 1981). In this case, the stimulus represents the meditative practice and the responses are considered to be mediated by a variety of psychological, physiological, and chemical mechanisms (Fig. 1).

This model has five major divisions based on the sequence in which specific aspects of meditation tend to be examined. The first of these is the response side of the paradigm, i.e., just what are the qualitative and quantitative changes which occur as a result of meditation? Historically, this is the first division to be investigated and in fact the first demonstration of a significant response can be considered to represent the founding of this research area. As is appropriate for a young field, most studies today have been concerned with this division.

After responses have been demonstrated, interest tends to turn toward the temporal aspects. Research at this level tends to ask questions such as what the time course of the development, and sometimes regression, of these changes is, how long they will persist under various conditions, and what the minimum duration in which effects can be detected is.

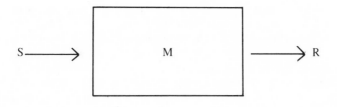

Fig. 1

Fig. 1

When a research field begins to feel more secure in its demonstration of a respectable range of responses, interest begins to turn toward the stimulus side of the paradigm. It is then appreciated that the sensory stimulus employed, in this case the meditative practice, actually represents a multidimensional array of stimulus components. The question is then posed, what are the precise stimulus attributes which elicit which effects? This stage is essentially one of component analysis.

In the fourth stage, the effects of additional independent variables are investigated. Whereas initial studies were concerned only with the effects of meditation per se, more complex experimental designs are now employed in which the interaction between the stimulus and other factors such as drugs, biological rhythms, genetic and experiential background of the subject are investigated.

The fifth level is concerned with the mechanisms which mediate the production of the observed findings. Ideally, such a consideration should be a multi-level one which takes into account mechanisms at a variety of levels from the psychological through the physiological to the chemical.

Since research tends to evolve across these five levels, the maturity of the field can to some extent be judged by the relative amounts of work at each stage. For meditation, the major emphasis has been on the first level. Each of these divisions will now be considered in more detail.

Responses

The responses to meditation are most readily subdivided into psychological, physiological, and chemical. As might be expected, the general trend has been one of moving from initial fairly gross parameters to finer, more subtle, and more discrete ones, and from those parameters which are most easy to measure to more difficult ones. For example, the first physiological measures examined parameters such as respiratory rate and rhythm, which have subsequently largely given way to electrophysiological investigations, including spectral analyses and interhemispheric comparisons.

Psychological Parameters

Turning first to the psychological arena, studies in this area fall readily into behavioral and phenomenological subdivisions. In accordance with Western research paradigms, most work has focused on the more easily and objectively measured behavioral parameters even though the aim of meditation is primarily phenomenological. In normals, such trait variables as intelligence, personality factors, self-actualization, and field dependence have been examined.

Perceptual studies have looked at both external and internal stimuli. Studies of extroceptive perception have examined such factors as sensory thresholds, which are lowered, and empathy, which is increased (Lesh, 1970; Leung, 1973).

Phenomenological changes are of special interest since they represent the very raison d'etre for meditation. Two different approaches have been used here which essentially represent both sides of the old nomothetic versus idiographic debate. The nomothetic approach has used groups of subjects and check lists or rating scales of predetermined experiences. The other approach has been one of intensive single case study using a participant-experimenter, usually one who is trained in the Western behavioral sciences (Tart, 1972; Shapiro, 1980; Walsh, 1977, 1978). Such an approach obviously suffers from all the limitations inherent in a self-report single case approach. On the other hand, it must also be acknowledged that single case designs are now recognized as valuable and, at times, irreplaceable clinical research strategies. For studies of meditation, they have the advantage of allowing an examination of process and the evolution of effects, and they also allow greater room for serendipity, the fortuitous finding of unexpected phenomena.

Participant-experimenters have provided novel information on a number of processes including perception, identification, and psychodynamics. They have also reported a progressive experientially based increase in intellectual understanding of the statements and claims made by more advanced meditators. It thus appears that intellectual understanding in this area demands an experiential basis and that what was incomprehensible at one stage may subsequently become understandable once an individual has sufficient experience of the meditative process. In part, this may reflect state-dependent learning, a suggestion made by Western scientists as well as Eastern yogis (e.g., Rajneesh, 1975). ''(This) is a learning in which a basic requirement is: First change your consciousness.''

It is this area of phenomenology which is currently the most subtle and difficult for Western science and hence the one which has been most avoided. In part, this avoidance is based on a general anti-phenomenological bias. It should be noted that this bias is partly based on uncertain assumptions concerning scientific ''objectivity'' and may be without solid philosophical justification (Tart, 1976).

Another factor is the ''means-oriented'' rather than ''problem-oriented'' nature of most research. These are terms introduced by Maslow (1966) to suggest that what tends to be measured is what is easy to measure, rather than what is especially important. In many cases, the phenomenological responses lie outside Western measurement technologies and in some cases outside the realm of traditional Western psychology itself, since they represent alternate states of consciousness. The very existence of such states has only recently been acknowledged in the West (Tart, 1975). It is here that the ''East-West'' split is largest, for the meditative disciplines have provided millenia old exquisitely articulated phenomenological maps of altered states, and some of these states are held to be *sine qua nons* of advanced meditation (Goleman, 1977; Goldstein, 1976). These hold far-reaching implications for Western psychology, and the difficulty of measuring and conceptualizing them should not deter their investigation. Indeed, as Maslow (1966) noted, it is the responsibility of science to confront all areas of knowledge irrespective of the difficulty involved and not to shirk investigation because the areas in question do not readily lend themselves to the best-honed experimental tools presently at hand. ''Most psychological problems do and should start with phenomenology rather than with experimental, behavioral laboratory techniques. We must press on from phenomenological beginnings *toward* objective experimental, behavioral laboratory methods. . . . It is easy for the laboratory scientist to criticize all this. But in the end, these criticisms come down to an accusation that the final state of knowledge has not yet been achieved'' (Maslow, 1966, pp. 47, 130).

Relatively few studies measure the types of effects that meditation was designed to produce, e.g., altered states of consciousness, perceptual enhancement, concentration, increase in certain ''mental factors'' such as mindfulness, equanimity, tranquility, and reduction in others, e.g., anger, fear, aversion. Indeed, meditative practitioners sometimes laugh at our current scientific investigations and tell the story of the two thieves who went to one of the Buddha's talks. One of them used the rapt attention of the crowd to his advantage by picking pockets while the other listened to the talk and became enlightened. At the end of the lecture, the pickpocket chastised his friend for coming away with nothing concrete to show for his time.

The suggestion is being made that we are investigating epiphenomena. The information we are collecting may be of interest and value from our traditional Western perspective. On the other hand, it may be of less relevance to meditation, and ultimately of less significance than an examination of the effects which yogis describe as the goals for which meditation was introduced.

Physiological Parameters

One dimension of the evolution of physiological research has already been described as a movement from gross to more sensitive parameters. Early studies employed such parameters as respiration and heart rate. More recent ones have used a range of sophisticated electrophysiological, metabolic, and chemical measures. These are not only more sensitive but allow greater specificity. Thus, for example, spectral analyses and precise regional mapping of EEG's are beginning to point to meditation-induced regionally specific spectral patterns (e.g., Banquet, 1975). Regionally specific intra- and interhemispheric synchronicities are also becoming apparent (Glueck and Stroebel, 1977) as are responses to one hemisphere which presumably reflect hemispheric specialization (e.g., Pagano and Franklin, 1978).

A Systems Approach

Obviously, a research field can go on indefinitely investigating a single or a few parameters at a time. However, treating variables in isolation sets obvious limits to the information which can be derived from them. Moreover, the inherently holistic nature of systems has become increasingly apparent in a variety of disciplines and levels (Capra, 1975; Walsh, 1981). Therefore, as a research area starts to develop a respectable number and range of variables under investigation, there is an increasing recognition of the need to adopt an organismic (holistic, general systems, integrative) approach. Thus, variables begin to be considered in relationship to other parameters and in the context of the functioning of the whole organism and it is recognized that a change in one variable affects all others.

The first such attempt to consider variables in relationship to one another usually involves simple correlations. For meditation, such attempts to date have been few in number, e.g., attempts to correlate anxiety with GSR. This type of comparison usually makes overly simplifying assumptions about the nature and complexity of the underlying constructs being correlated, and it is not surprising that successes to date have been few.

A more sophisticated approach employs multivariate studies and statistics. These provide more accurate and valid measures of underlying constructs, e.g., anxiety, as well as of correlations between constructs, e.g., by canonical correlation. Their added complexity is probably a necessary price to pay for the advancement of the field beyond a certain point, but to date, only a few such studies have appeared in the meditation literature (e.g., Osis et al., 1973; Kohr, 1977).

The interrelated organismic nature of systems holds further implications. If changes in one variable produce changes in all, then it follows that any intervention such as meditation will affect the whole organism. This provides a very different research perspective from the one usually employed and suggests that negative findings may be due to a lack of experimental and measurement sensitivity rather than to a lack of meditative effects. The question now becomes one, not of "Does meditation produce an effect?", but rather "Is the meditative effect of any practical significance and if so, what proportion of the variance does it account for?" This shift from asking simple "yes or no" questions to more quantitative, correlative, and ecological approaches represents an evolutionary stage which is appropriate for developing research fields once responses have been clearly demonstrated but is also one which is often unnecessarily delayed.

The question of the sensitivity, appropriateness, reliability, and validity of response measures is an extremely important one for the evolution of any research field, and this is especially true for meditation. For what will subsequently become apparent is that limitations at any one stage of research become limiting factors for the evolution of subsequent stages. As the demonstration of responses is the first of the five stages, it will be apparent that measurement limitations at this stage will act as limiting factors for all subsequent research.

Temporal Factors

The study of the temporal characteristics of meditation involves several dimensions. The first of these is the effect of varying durations of practice and thus looks at the time course or evolution of effects. As yet, we have very little information on this. Not surprisingly, the trend seems to be for greater practice to produce more marked effects. However, the nature of the learning curve is quite unclear and with few exceptions, subjects have had amounts of experience which would be considered only beginning level by most meditative systems. On the other hand, a study of Goleman and Schwartz (1976) suggested that even first-timers might show detectable GSR effects.

The second dimension concerns the permanence and reversibility of meditation-induced effects, a question of obvious therapeutic importance. Here, there are actually several subquestions, such as "Will the effects be maintained after practice ceases?" "If so, for what parameters?" "Can the extent of this maintenance be increased or decreased (reversed) by various means including other therapeutic practices?" "What is the optimum scheduling of practice to maximize gains?" To date, these questions remain untested and unanswered.

The problem may actually be more complex. This is suggested by other fields such as research on effects of psychotherapy or sensory environments which have found interactions among various temporal factors and between these factors and other dimensions (Walsh, 1981). Thus, for example, the effects of meditation in young individuals might differ not only in magnitude, but also in time course from those in older ones. Furthermore, different parameters may exhibit different temporal profiles. It therefore seems prudent to be very cautious in drawing general conclusions from the few facts currently available to us.

The Stimulus

Research on the stimulus side of the stimulus-response paradigm tends to be a type of component analysis. Initial studies of any stimulus input tend to consider the stimulus as a whole and are not too concerned with its individual components. However, after the stimulus complex has been demonstrated to be effective, then the question arises as to precisely which component stimuli are responsible for which effects. That is, the initial approach is a unidimensional one where the total stimulus impact alone is considered, whereas later studies begin to recognize the multidimensional nature of this complex and to question the contribution of various stimulus dimensions to it. When sufficient work has been done at this level, then the question arises as to the nature of the interactions between stimulus components. Related questions include "Are stimuli additive, inhibitory, or synergistic?" and "What is the optimum (most effective) combination of stimuli for which effect?" To date, there appears to have been little in the way of attempts to conceptualize these stimulus dimensions.

A question which arises during this phase is the basic one of "What is meditation?" For, on closer examination, most meditative practices are seen to consist of an array of behaviors ranging from the focusing of awareness to somatic posturing, and to be couched within a philosophical, ethical, and life style context. A precise definition of meditation becomes essential so as to differentiate between those behaviors which are inherent or essential to the practice and those which can be regarded as ancillary.

Meditation is defined here as the conscious training of attention aimed at modifying mental processes so as to elicit enhanced states of consciousness and well being. It should be noted that this definition avoids saying anything about the nature of the object(s) of awareness, which may be single and fixed as in concentration meditation or multiple and varied as in "open" meditation. It also recognizes that meditation may be independent of posture or behavior and is not restricted to sitting meditation, a confusion which is not infrequently made by people who assume that all meditation is a function of awareness and not necessarily of overt behavior, then it becomes obvious that it may be impossible to tell whether meditation is occurring by behavioral measures alone. Any, and in some practices all, behavior may thus provide an opportunity for meditation. Furthermore, within a single session, there may be wide fluctuations in the degree to which attention is successfully controlled. Thus, for research purposes, it is necessary not only to differentiate meditation from nonmediation, but also usually to limit investigation to one specific type of meditation, e.g., sitting meditation. It is also important to be aware of the probable occurrence of considerable within-trials variability, even where the overt behavior remains stable.

Initially research fields tend to assume a certain degree of equality between different stimuli. However, as component analysis proceeds, it is usually recognized that stimulus complexes vary, and at this stage, it becomes possible to begin categorizing different complexes. Thus, initial studies of meditation tended to make implicit assumptions about the uniformity of meditation traditions and rarely furnished precise details of the practices being studied.

One ancient division has been between three categories of meditation: concentrative, receptive, and combined. Concentrative practices aim at focusing awareness on a single object only, whereas receptive meditations open awareness in a nondiscriminative manner to any and all stimuli: combined practices follow both approaches, alternating between fixed and open awareness. This division is not absolute and there is some overlap in effects (Goleman, 1977).

While this categorization represents a considerable advance over assumptions of equivalence, it represents only an initial stage of stimulus analysis. The next stage moves toward the simultaneous examination of greater numbers of stimulus dimensions. In view of the multidimensional nature of the meditative stimulus complex, an adequate description and conceptualization must necessarily entail description and measurement of as many as possible of these dimensions, effectively necessitating a multidimensional descriptive grid. Development of this aspect of research, which is a form of progressive component analysis, thus tends to consist of moving from a unidimensional to an increasingly multidimensional conceptualization, toward increasing specificity of description of component stimuli, and to more precise control such that experimental and control subjects differ on fewer stimulus dimensions.

As yet, there has been almost no research on meditation at this level of sophistication, a fact which is not surprising in view of the field's recent history. However, the importance of an appreciation of this potential level of analysis is essential if adequate controls are to be employed. Thus, for example, in a study (Smith, 1976) designed to determine whether meditation effects were due to expectancy, the experiment employed a control group who sat repeating a specific phrase. The study concluded that since there were no detectable differences between experimental and control groups, the meditative effects were indeed due to expectation. However, this type of repetition might be viewed as a mantra, so that in point of fact the control group might be considered to also be doing a form of meditation, though a different type than the experimental group.

Other Independent Variables

The fourth stage investigates the interactions between independent variables. When other independent variables go unrecognized or uncontrolled, they then function as confounding variables which reduce the sensitivity, reliability, and validity of experimental findings. On the other hand, when they are recognized and appropriately manipulated and controlled, they provide information on their interactive nature on meditative effects.

These variables can be divided into two major categories: those associated with the experimental subjects and those independent of the subjects. The major subject variables can be subsumed under the headings of genetic, sex, age, intellectual, experiential, and personality factors. Non-subject variables are limitless in number but common significant ones include such things as demand characteristics of the experimental situation, experimenter expectancy (Rosenthal effect), other forms of training given simultaneously, etc. Subject variables can be examined from two perspectives, employing them as either independent or dependent variables. Where they are used as independents, then the response of preselected groups differing in these characteristics, e.g., extraversion-intraversion, can be determined. In the other case, then, individuals manifesting differential responsivity, e.g., people who persist in meditation versus those who drop out, are examined and the role of subject variables in accounting for these differential responses can be determined. By experiments such as these, it is possible to determine the characteristics most likely to facilitate or hinder successful outcome. As might be predicted, there has as yet been little work done at this level. However, Otis (1974) and Smith (1978) found, that compared with those who drop out, individuals who persist with the practice of transcendental meditation are likely to be less psychologically disturbed, to have low psychoticism scores, and to be more open to recognizing and acknowledging unfavorable personal characteristics. Future research in this area is likely to focus especially on defining those subjects who will respond optimally, those at risk for negative effects, and be possible means of enhancing favorable responses, e.g., matching subjects to type of practice, manipulating expectancy, provision of previous training and information.

Mediating Mechanisms

This stage comprises the study of mechanisms which mediate the production of the observed effects. In most research areas, mechanisms tend to be viewed overly simplistically and to be advanced singly and in competition with one another. Unfortunately, meditation has been no exception to his principle. However, a moment's thought suggests that there will be many mechanisms involved at all levels from the psychological to the molecular biological. A more useful approach may employ a multidimensional hierarchical model which acknowledges mechanisms at all levels: psychological, physiological, and chemical. From this perspective, what is viewed as a response at one level may be seen as a mechanism at another. Indeed, it may be that forms of reciprocal feedback exist such that, for example, chemical responses may mediate phenomenological changes which, in turn, may themselves affect physiology and chemistry. In any event, the search for *the* single mechanism is clearly an anachronistic approach reflecting an atomistic nonholistic nonorganismic model of the universe, in general, and biological systems, in particular. A considerable body of data is now available to support the organismic model at all levels from quantum physics to neuroscience (e.g., Capra, 1975; Walsh and Vaughan, 1980). The recognition of this model serves as a useful antidote for the common tendency toward reductionism which attempts to explain (away) meditation only in terms of lower order processes, e.g., relaxation or reduced blood lactate, and to sometimes suggest that it is nothing but these lower order processes.

Suggested psychological mechanisms include relaxation and global desensitization (Goleman, 1971), deconditioning, behavioral reactivity, heightened awareness (Walsh, 1977), dehypnosis (Walsh, 1982), behavioral self-control skills (Shapiro, 1980), and facilitation of psychological development and maturation (Wilber, 1982). At the physiological level, suggested mechanisms include reduced arousal, hemispheric-lateralization (Pagano and Franklin, 1978) and electroencephalographic resonance and coherence (Glueck and Stroebel, 1976). To date, no chemical mechanisms seem to have been advanced, although a number of relevant responses have been identified, e.g., reduced serum cortisol (Jevning *et al.,* this volume). As data accumulates, the multiply overdetermined nature of any response becomes apparent and, ultimately, one is forced to a viewpoint of "omnideterminism" in which it is recognized that every component influences every other and the very concept of mediating mechanisms becomes meaningless (Walsh, 1981; Walsh and Vaughan, 1980).

Overview

In overview, then, this model provides a context in which the evolution of research on meditation can be viewed. In addition, current and future problems and limiting factors can be identified and an overview of this field as a whole can be obtained.

It can be seen that this field has met the criteria for acceptance as a serious area of investigation in that a broad range of significant responses have now been identified. On the other hand, a major limitation is set by the phenomenological nature of many of the most significant variables since traditionally Western science has been hesitant to tackle these areas. Not surprisingly, research at subsequent levels has as yet been limited. However, an examination of the second level, i.e., temporal factors, suggests a further major limitation, namely, that most experimental subjects have practiced amounts of meditation which would be considered miniscule by most meditative disciplines. The complex multidimensional nature of the stimuli which comprise meditation has as yet been little recognized, a situation which must be remedied to allow for more sophisticated controls and the identification of the effective components. Studies of other independent variables may improve meditation results by such procedures as selecting and matching subjects, providing pretrainings, expectation setting, social support, etc.

Finally, I would like to add two personal pleas based on my own experience as a meditator, researcher, and journal editor. The first is for researchers to begin to acquaint themselves with the Asian literature on meditation. Some of these practices span thousands of years and some of humankind's best minds have devoted themselves to their study. The result has been a voluminous literature, as yet largely untapped by Western researchers, by people with far greater experience and knowledge of meditation than most of us who are now beginning research on it. Their understanding may be valuable, despite their derivation from different cultures and centuries.

My second plea is for researchers to have some personal experience of meditation practice. The meditative traditions almost invariably state the intellectual understanding of the nature of the meditative process is dependent on an adequate base of personal experience. This seems to be borne out by the personal experience of researchers who have themselves undertaken the practice and also in some cases by the quality of research. In my role as a journal editor, it is sometimes painfully apparent that researchers lack direct experience when statements are made and conclusions drawn that are markedly at variance with even a basic experiential understanding.

To give an example of a problem which could have been avoided by either personal experience or familiarity with the traditional literature, I will cite the case of the controversy around the role of sleep in meditation. When EEG patterns consistent with certain stages of sleep were found in some meditators, some researchers concluded that this was the major mechanism mediating any beneficial effects or dismissed meditation entirely. Certainly, sleepiness can occur in the initial stages of meditation as even a small amount of personal experience will show. But greater experience and the Asian literature both suggest that this is a largely transient phenomenon which is one of the major traps for the beginner. Incidentally, subjects with 1 or 2 years' experience of 20 to 40 minutes daily practice would be regarded as beginners by most traditions. Indeed, many traditions contain detailed discussions and instructions on the need and means for overcoming what the Buddhists picturesquely call "sloth and torpor" (Goldstein, 1976). Thus, some Western researchers dismissed meditation on the basis of an epiphenomenon which meditation traditions explicitly warn against. Personal acquaintance with both the practice and its traditional literature may thus deepen our understanding of this millenia old discipline which we are beginning to explore.

References

Banquet, J. P. Spectoral analysis of the EEG in meditation. *Electroencephalography & Clinical Neurophysiology,* 1973, *35,* 143–151.

Brown, D. and Engler, J. This volume, article 21.

Carrington, P. *Freedom in Meditation.* New York: Doubleday, 1982.

Glueck, B. C. and Stroebel, C. F. Biofeedback and meditation in the treatment of psychiatric illness. *Comprehensive Psychiatry,* 1975, *16,* 303–321.

Goldstein, J. *The Experience of Insight.* Santa Cruz, CA: Unity Press, 1976.

Goleman, D. Meditation as a meta-therapy: Hypotheses toward a proposed fifth state of consciousness. *Journal of Transpersonal Psychology,* 1971, *3,* 1–25.

Goleman, D. *The Varieties of the Meditative Experience.* New York: EP Dutton, 1977.

Goleman, D. and Schwartz, G. Meditation as an intervention in stress reactivity. *Journal of Consulting and Clinical Psychology,* 1976, *44,* 456–466.

Jevning, R. and O'Halloran, J. P. This volume, article 33.

Kohr, R. L. Dimensionality in the meditative experience: A replication. *Journal of Transpersonal Psychology,* 1977, *9,* 193–203.

Lesh, T. Zen meditation and the development of empathy in counselors. *Journal of Humanistic Psychology,* 1970, *10,* 39–74.

Leung, P. Comparative effects of training in external and internal concentration on two counseling behaviors. *Journal of Counseling Psychology,* 1973, *20,* 227–234.

Maslow, A. *The Psychology of Science.* Chicago: Gateway, 1966.

Osis, K., Bokert, E., and Carlson, M. L. Dimensions of the meditative experience. *Journal of Transpersonal Psychology,* 1973, *5,* 109–135.

Pagano, R. and Frumkin, L. Effects of Transcendental Meditation in right hemispheric functioning. *Biofeedback and Self-Regulation,* 1977, *2,* 407–415.

Rajneesh. *The Way of the White Cloud.* Poona, India: Rajneesh Foundation, 1975.

Shapiro, D. H. *Precision Nirvana.* Englewood Cliffs, NJ: Prentice-Hall, 1978.

Shapiro, D. H. *Meditation: Self-Regulation Strategy and Altered State of Consciousness.* New York: Aldine, 1980.

Smith, J. Psychotherapeutic effects of Transcendental Meditation with controls for expectations of relief and daily sitting. *Journal of Consulting and Clinical Psychology,* 1976, *44,* 630–637.

Smith, J. Personality correlates of continuation and outcome in meditation and erect sitting control treatments. *Journal of Consulting and Clinical Psychology,* 1978, *46,* 272–279.

Tart, C. States of consciousness and state specific sciences. *Science,* 1972, *186,* 1203–1210.

Tart, C. *States of Consciousness.* New York: EP Dutton, 1975(a).

Tart, C. *Transpersonal Psychologies.* New York: Harper and Row, 1975(b).

Walsh, R. Initial meditative experiences: Part I. *Journal of Transpersonal Psychology,* 1977, *9,* 151–192.

Walsh, R. Initial meditative experiences: Part II. *Journal of Transpersonal Psychology,* 1978, *10,* 1–28.

Walsh, R. The consciousness disciplines and the behavioral sciences: Questions of comparison and assessment. *American Journal of Psychiatry,* 1980, *137,* 663–673.

Walsh, R. Meditation practice and research. *Journal of Humanistic Psychology,* 1983, *23,* 18–50.

Walsh, R. and Vaughan, F. *Beyond Ego: Transpersonal Dimensions in Psychology.* Los Angeles: JP Tarcher, 1980.

Wilber, K. The evolution of consciousness. In R. Walsh & D. H. Shapiro (eds.) *Beyond Health and Normality: Explorations of Exceptional Psychological Well Being.* pp. 338–369. New York: Van Nostrand Reinhold, 1983.

4

A SYSTEM'S APPROACH TO MEDITATION RESEARCH: GUIDELINES AND SUGGESTIONS

Deane H. Shapiro, Jr.

Most of the empirical research on meditation in Western settings has been concerned with looking at physiological and/or behavioral measures related to its use as a self-regulation strategy. As noted in Article 2, less attention has been paid to the classical perspective of meditation–phenomenological aspects of meditative-induced altered states of consciousness. Articles 1 and 2 in this volume offered several suggestions and guidelines for future meditation research in each of these two respective areas. This article provides one additional perspective: a systems framework, involving six dimensions, which may be helpful in providing further clarity and precision when researching meditation, whether as a self-regulation strategy or as an altered state of consciousness.

Before describing the dimensions of this model, it should be clear that this model is not considered to be the one and only exclusive avenue toward future meditation research. For example, there are several additional areas, discussed previously, which this approach does not directly address, including: (1) Efforts toward understanding the cultural context and vision of psychological health for which meditation might be utilized (Shapiro, 1978a; Walsh & Shapiro, 1983; Shapiro, 1984, in press); (2) understanding the components of meditation which could help us determine inert from active variables, and percentage of variance accountable for treatment success (Shapiro, 1980, Chapter 8; Walsh, Chapter 3); and (3) mediating mechanisms which may account for the effects of meditation—from a biochemical to an attentional level (Shapiro, 1980, Chapter 9; Earle, 1981). However, this model may help us ground clinical, health care, and therapeutic research involving meditation, may help provide a unification for understanding seemingly isolated studies, and may be useful for refining research even when meditation is being taught as as a ''spiritual'' intervention within a religious organization.

Dimensions of the Model

There are six different dimensions discussed in this model. These include, on the input side of the equation: (1) *a therapist, health provider, physician, teacher, trainer*. Issues here include the variables of expectation and demand characteristics, and therapeutic orientation; and (2) *client, patient, student*—the person who wishes to learn (or may be taught) the meditative technique. Relevant variables here include motivation, expectation effects, beliefs about ability to learn a meditative technique, individual responsibility, and personality profile (prediction for treatment success, dropout variables, and adverse effects). Initially the above two dimensions are independent inputs into the system, but their interaction forms the third dimension: (3) *relationship*, including issues of nontechnical definitions of transference and countertransference, resistance, trust, and empathy. Further, (4) both therapist and patient (teacher/pupil) initially have independent views that they bring to the clinical problem, or, in therapeutic terms, the goal of the technique, the *assessment of clinical concern* or reason for learning the technique. This may be formally or informally assessed depending on the context. The fifth dimension, involves the (5) *selection of a specific meditative technique*. This should include theoretical and clinically based rationale between the technique of independent variable and the clinical concern as dependent variable: i.e., matching strategy to person. The sixth dimension includes (6) *method of teaching the strategy* with particular reference to issues of *adherence and compliance*.

Additional factors in the total use of meditation should include evaluation and follow-up. These are not considered as dimensions of the system, but are relevant to any research and clinical effort and, therefore, are included as part of the systemic model. This allows for an interactive approach in which the multiple dimensions are tied together following general systems theory, providing feedback and information at each successive stage of the intervention process.

The Input Sides of the Model:
Dimensions One and Two

The term input sides of the equation is used because perceptions of the (1) health care provider/teacher/ training organization, and (2) patient/student are the filters through which all subsequent information is determined. By using dotted arrows (Fig. 1) from the patient to the clinical concern and intervention selection, I do not mean to abnegate their responsibility for assessing clinical concern and intervention selection. They are used to point out the importance of the patient's perception in helping to understand and formulate both assessment and interventions.

The Therapist/Teacher: Orientation, Beliefs, and "Demand"

At least one aspect of the question of whether meditation is effective seems to depend upon the therapist's or researcher's theoretical orientation, and what s/he decides to measure as the criteria for "successful outcome." Therefore, we as therapists, researchers, and educators, when we use meditation, need to be as aware as possible of our own professional and personal preconceptions, values, and biases toward therapeutic treatment. In particular, it has been argued elsewhere (Shapiro, 1983) that all of us have implicitly or explicitly, a vision of positive health, a view of normality, a view of the person's possibility of changing, a view of disease etiology, and interventions utilized to reach that goal. These views will determine how the health care provider assesses the patient's concern and what interventions are deemed appropriate (evidenced by the dotted lines from Dimension One—the therapist—to Dimensions Four and Five in Fig. 1). These views, which are really a loosely constructed theoretical orientation, create a certain demand on the client (Orne, 1962). This "demand" postulates implicitly or explicitly the following: (a) belief in a vision of positive physical and/or mental health; (b) belief in a procedure, set of values, or series of techniques which can enable an individual to reach that vision; (c) the belief that if the patient believes as the therapist believes, practices as the therapist practices and/or advocates, s/he will achieve the desired vision. This demand has an effect on treatment outcome, moving it, as we would suspect, toward the effect postulated by the therapist (Smith, 1976; Rosenthal, *et al.,* 1962; Meehl, 1960;).*

The importance of differences of focus of dimension one becomes clearer when we look at how individuals from different theoretical orientations utilize the technique of meditation. From a psychoanalytic standpoint, meditation has been conceptualized as an "evocative" strategy which allows repressed material to come from the unconscious (e.g., Carrington and Ephron, 1975) and facilitates controlled

*The creation of demand characteristics is not "wrong," for belief in the efficacy of one's treatment strategy or orientation appears to be an important factor in therapeutic success (e.g., McReynolds *et al.,* 1973). The transmission of this belief to the client, and the client's belief in its credibility, are also important factors. The only possible adverse effect of these "demands" is when the therapist or organization holds them so strongly as to be unwilling to question them, and/or have them altered by invalidating evidence. Then the orientation, rather than being a useful method for organizing information and hypotheses about the world, becomes a blinder to new information and may cause a type of evangelical fervor to convince others of the rightness of one's view. From a clinical standpoint, we are faced with an interesting philosophical and ethical dilemma. On the one hand, we are aware of the power of belief systems and the self-fulfilling nature of these belief systems (Frank, 1963; Pelletier & Peper, 1977; Benson, 1978). Thus, as clinicians, we would want to *maximize* expectations and beliefs in the client; however we would want to do this only within the limitations of honesty and integrity.

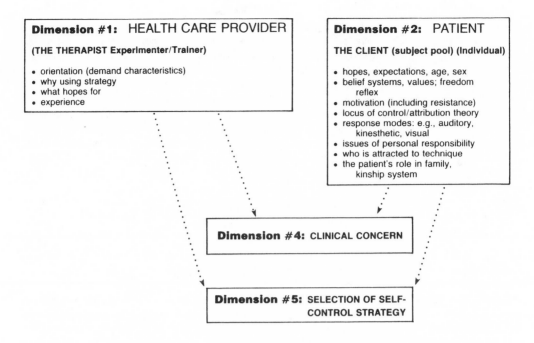

Fig. 1. Input sides of the systems model—the health care provider and the patient.

regression in the service of the ego (e.g., Shafii, 1973). Those individuals when utilizing meditation with their patients see it as a positive vehicle for inducing primary process thinking, for avoiding or bypassing rational defense mechanisms, and for recollecting memories of traumatic events. These are all criteria which Freud himself has posited as necessary for developing psychological health and overcoming pathology (Breuer and Freud, 1893; Freud, 1936; Greenson, 1968).

Others have conceptualized meditation as useful in humanistic psychotherapy* for clients and therapists (e.g., Keefe, 1975; Schuster, 1979; Lesh, 1970). Those humanistically oriented psychologists who use meditation in their practice view it as a technique for helping a person become sensitive to his/her innate self-actualizing nature (as posited by Maslow, 1968; Rogers, 1961) and for helping an individual turn from an external to an internal orientation. From the perspective of holistic medicine (Hastings *et al.*, 1980, Pelletier, 1979), meditation is viewed as a way of enhancing individual client responsibility and of teaching the client to develop nonpharmacological approaches to self-care. Meditation is considered to be a successful strategy if the client is able to become more in touch with his/her ''true'' self; become more inner-directed; to take more self-responsibility; and to be more psychologically and physically centered.

Behaviorally oriented individuals who use meditation in their research or practice view it primarily as a self-regulation strategy for dealing with clinical, health-related, and stress-related concerns. Thus it has been conceptualized as a self-regulation strategy with potential applications in behavioral medicine (Stroebel & Glueck, 1977; Schwartz & Weiss, 1977; Pomerleau, 1979) or as a clinical tool for the management of anxiety and the addictions within a behavioral framework (Shapiro & Zifferblatt, 1976a; Shapiro, 1978b; Berwick & Oziel, 1973; Woolfolk & Franks, this volume). From this perspective, meditation is considered to be a successful treatment if it proves effective in significantly reducing the target behavior problem (Skinner, 1953; Bandura, 1969, 1977; Wolpe, 1969; Lazarus, 1971).

A fourth school of therapy which utilizes meditation is the transpersonal approach. This approach is probably most clearly aligned with the original spiritual intent of meditation practices of the East. it

*I am utilizing humanistic psychology, as represented by Rogers (1961), as a summary term for the ego psychologies. This lumping together, although convenient, obscures some of the differences between the neo-Freudian psychoanalytic ego developmental psychologists and the humanistic psychologist (cf. Shapiro, 1983 for a refinement of this distinction). However, for the purposes of this chapter, the similarities seem sufficient to warrant the lack of differentiation.

includes many of the qualities associated with the humanistic tradition (i.e., developing inner-directedness, strong sense of oneself), but also goes beyond them. From a transpersonal perspective, meditation is conceptualized as a technique that helps individuals let go of thoughts, become relatively egoless, yielding, present-centered (Weide, 1973; Goleman, 1971; Clark, 1977; Shapiro, 1978b; Walsh & Vaughan, 1980). The individual learns how not only to build a strong sense of self, but as Maslow (1968) pointed out, how to surrender the ego.

According to the transpersonal viewpoint, what constitutes successful meditation is simultaneously illusive and all-encompassing. Pleasant and unpleasant experiences, even wandering mind, all occur in "correct" meditation. The goal is to keep as sensitively mindful as possible to one's experiences, to cultivate an attitude of compassionate acceptance and to utilize each experience as "grist for the mill," new learning to be observed, new objects of awareness. One needs to develop a high degree of perceptual clarity about one's thought patterns, habits, and behaviors without the accompanying affect—a mindfulness of each moment (Goleman, 1971). Effective or successful meditation becomes therefore a misnomer. It is not an end state, but a path, a vehicle for "transcending" the personal boundaries of the self, and for feeling a sense of spiritual harmony.

The Patient/Student: Dimension Two

By careful attention to the "patient" side of the equation, we can develop a greater sensitivity to what has loosely been termed the "whole person" described in both psychosomatic medicine (Gottschalk, 1975) as well as in behavioral (Benson, 1978) and holistic medicine (Pelletier, 1979). Attention to the whole person, rather than attention just to manifest disease represented by the clinical concern, is more than a philosophical or abstract statement. In terms of health care treatment, it is a functional question and influences treatment outcome as evidenced in the following discussion of the third-round literature on patient variables. There are several major issues which we need to address with respect to the patient.

Belief in Ability to Change, Responsibility, and Attitude Toward a Self-Control Technique

The first area involves the patients' belief in their ability to change. The second issue is individual responsibility, and the third is the belief in the efficacy of a particular treatment technique (Benson, 1978; Franks, 1963; Shapiro, 1971).

Since the literature is quite convincing that expectation effects, as a placebo, can influence treatment outcome (Smith, 1976; Benson, 1978; Franks, 1963), before teaching meditation we would want to assess the individual's beliefs about the possibility of learning the technique and thereby changing their behavior, attitudes, images, and cognitions. This would include general locus of control issues (Rotter, 1966; DiNardo, 1979; Bugental & Whalen, 1978), but become more precise and domain specific.

A second issue implicit in the area of meditation is the one of individual responsibility. In order for an individual to learn a strategy, he or she must be willing to take responsibility for the practice of it (Knowles, 1977; Globus, 1980; Shapiro & Shapiro, 1979). Again, it would seem important to assess the client's "level" of individual responsibility as one important antecedent context for the eventual teaching of the self-control strategy itself.*

We would also want to assess the client's view of meditation. For example, Barber and Calverly (1964) noted that calling a technique hypnosis improved the likelihood of successful outcome. In the selection of meditation, it is important that we look closely at the client's affect toward the verbalization which describes our technique, whether that word be hypnosis, meditation, biofeedback, etc.

Initial Motivation and Expectation

If an individual requests to learn a particular self-control technique, we need to assess carefully why they wish to learn that technique. If we look at meditation, in particular, we might theorize that many of

---

*The very words "teaching of the self-control strategy" may be considered paradoxical because the therapist is in effect, teaching the strategy to the client. However, in utilizing this term, I use it in the sense of a continuum in which throughout the course of therapy more of the "control" is given to the client. Further, the actual practice of the technique rests solely with the client.

the individuals in our culture who want to learn meditation wish to do so for its self-regulation qualities. For example, they may wish to learn meditation as a strategy for stress management, relaxation, reducing blood pressure, etc. based on the "demand characteristics" of the data in our scientific journals (as well as the promotional literature of some organizations). Others may be attracted to meditation for "spiritual reasons," i.e., meditation as an altered state of consciousness, based on the "demand characteristics" of reports in classical meditation texts. For those who want self-regulation, perhaps the mystical garb (e.g., Katz and Crawford 1978) and even the label itself may be a hinderance. For those looking for "new meaning," perhaps the "mysticism" surrounding the technique is important to successful outcome.

Although several studies have attempted to control for expectation effects (Smith, 1976, 1978; Malec & Sipprelle, 1977), to my knowledge no article has been published which assesses subject's expectations prior to meditation (Shapiro, 1980). It may be critical to determine why people meditate: what they perceive this "technique" as being able to do for them. For example, if they meditate for "relaxation" do they ever have an altered state experience? If they meditate for "spiritual meaning" do they relax as well as those who are meditating just for relaxation?

An issue related to expectation effects is motivation. How much does a person "want to learn to relax" to find "new meaning"? For example, Maupin (1965) noted that those who entered his study had a strong "therapy-seeking motivation." Are individuals who begin to meditate looking for "personal growth," self-actualization, relief from painful stress and tension, or seeking a cognitive avoidance strategy with which to escape from problems? How much do they want to change or grow? How intensely committed do they perceive themselves as being to work for this change? The studies of Kubose (1976), Goleman, Domitor, & Murray (1979) provide preliminary evidence that motivation—the subject's initial desire to learn the technique—is an important issue with respect to meditation outcome.

These above questions are as yet unanswered, but are empirically testable. Thus, it would be useful to administer a brief subject questionnaire to measure the subject's expectation and motivation level prior to beginning the practice of a self-control strategy. It would then have to be determined, however, how well initial motivation translates into long-term commitment as evidenced by adherence and compliance (Shapiro, 1980).*

Client Profile

The first question regarding client "profile" is to determine which individuals seem to seek out which type of self-control strategies. With respect to meditation, there has only been one study in the literature which has assessed this (Stek & Bass, 1973) and, unfortunately, the results were equivocal. A second question in need of investigation is the subject profile of those who continue to practice a self-control strategy. Here we could look at adherence and compliance to determine whether certain people are more likely over time to practice one self-control strategy than another.

Further, we would also want to develop a profile on people who drop out and those who continue. With respect to meditation research, the profile of those who drop out of meditation is a rather negative one. Dropouts were highly defensive (Otis, 1974; Smith, 1978), scored higher on the psychosis scale of the Tennessee Self-Control Scale (TSCS) (Smith, 1978), had serious problems (Otis, 1974), and were emotionally disturbed (Kanas & Horowitz, 1977). However, clinical experience suggests that there are psychologically healthy individuals who drop out of meditation just as in any other self-regulation strategy, including medication adherence, dental floss adherence, etc. In any case, the profile for meditation drop-outs is not specific enough and requires further research and refinement.

A third question involves the profile of individuals who continue with a self-control strategy, and have a successful outcome. With respect to meditation, the profile that emerges is based on small numbers and

*It should be noted that the studies cited in the discussion on expectation and motivation as well as in the section on subject variables all pertain to Western meditators. Another interesting question, and one which has not yet received attention, is what is the psychological profile of "Eastern" people who meditate? Of those in the East who really commit themselves? Of those who drop out? And of those who have positive outcome? We are just beginning to investigate these cross-cultural issues with The Shapiro Self-Control Inventory (SSCI), which consists of the following scales: (1) personal beliefs about self-control; (2) motivation; (3) individual responsibility; (4) expectations and adherence; (5) prior history and experience; (6) assertiveness/yielding profile; (7) intimacy profile; (8) overcontrol profile; (9) general questions.

with a wide range of variability between subjects. However, some interesting trends emerge about the "type" of individual who might be most successful at meditation. This person already has a high "internal locus of control" (Beiman *et al.*, this volume), is enthusiastic (Anand, Chinna & Singh, 1961), has high base-line alpha to begin with (Anand, Chinna & Singh, 1961), is more interested in internal subjective experiences, has flatter, less labile affect (Smith, 1978), has better ability to maintain attentional focus (Vahia *et al.*, 1972), and is more able to be open to and tolerant of "unrealistic" altered state experiences (Maupin, 1965; Lesh, 1977). Another subject variable which is worth noting in this profile is what Pelletier & Peper (1977) describe as the "chutzpah factor"—the importance of believing in the possibility of one's success (Bandura, 1977).

Within the context of the above profile, even seemingly contradictory findings may be understandable. For example, Smith (1978) noted that high anxiety was correlated with positive outcome and Bono (this volume) showed that prior to TM, subjects had lower real/ideal correlation. However, high anxiety, willingness to be self-critical, and the belief of one's own internal locus of control may all be part of the profile of the successful meditator. Again, these issues need to be approached with respect to other self-control strategies in order to best determine the subject profile which will best predict successful outcome.

One final subject population on which there has been almost no research is comprised of those individuals who continue practice of meditation, but report adverse effects (Otis, this volume). Why do they continue? Are these "pain-dependent" people? Do they believe that "adverse" effects are a stage (necessary and sufficient; necessary, but not sufficient) after which more learning will take place, i.e., a higher sensitivity to formerly defended material?

The only report to date on subject profile (Walsh & Rauche, 1979) cited case reports of psychotic breaks during intensive meditation in individuals with a prior history of schizophrenia. Thus subjects prior clinical history may be important as a means of screening patients to determine their appropriateness for learning meditation. For example, psychotic patients with strong paranoid systems or a poor sense of reality testing may not be appropriate subjects. Further, people experiencing acute anxiety and trauma may be overwhelmed with the emotionally charged material that might present itself during meditation (Patel, 1975a,b). To deal with any overwhelming emotional reactions that may develop in their patients, Glueck & Stroebel (1975) had experienced teachers check the patient's meditation process on a daily basis during the first 3 weeks. They note, as did French *et al.* (1975), that overt psychotic episodes may be precipitated in individuals with psychiatric disorders who meditate more than the prescribed 20 minutes a day. Clearly, this area is a critical one for further investigation.

Finally, it should be noted in this discussion on subject profile that most of the "predictors" of meditation's success have involved "trait" and personality descriptions. Given the rather convincing review of the situational specificity of behavior (Mischel, 1968), it might be important to define nontrait skills (attentional skills, ability to sit quietly) and/or cognitive beliefs, and their ability to predict successful outcome. Further, successful outcome has most often been measured by variables relating to anxiety. However, it is quite possible that some introverted, shy individuals may turn to meditation because it fits their temperament. They may show a reduction of anxiety, and therefore be "successful meditators." However, from a therapeutic standpoint, meditation may not be a sufficient intervention for them. They may need for example, assertiveness training, social skills training, and training in risk-taking behavior (Shapiro, 1980).

Relationship and Issues of Resistance

Self-control strategies are generally taught within a context involving two individuals (physician and patient; therapist and client; researcher and individual). However, different orientations place varying emphasis upon the importance of the relationship context. For example, classical Rogerian client-centered therapy (Rogers, 1961) views the relationship as the critical variable in successful therapeutic outcome, whereas a behaviorist would argue that taped instructions on the self-control strategy could be equally successful in effecting the desired therapeutic outcome. Thus, depending upon the orientation, the relative emphasis on relationship ranges from unimportant (e.g., taped instructions of meditation) to the critical variable (e.g., Rogers' client-centered therapy).

From a humanistic psychology standpoint, the necessary and sufficient variables for therapeutic personality change to occur must be two people in close interpersonal contact, the therapist's empathetic understanding of the client's frame of reference, and unconditional positive regard for the client (both of which the client perceives). Truax and Carkhuff developed scales for measuring congruence and genuineness, nonpossessive warmth, and nonjudgmental accurate empathy and concluded from their research that these three variables are characteristics of human encounters that change people for the better (Truax & Carkhuff, 1967, p. 41).

The analytic perspective also views the relationship as an important variable, particularly in the area of transference and countertransference. Technically, transference is defined as the experiencing of feelings, drives, attitudes, fantasies, and defenses toward a person in the present which do not benefit that person but are a repetition of reactions originating in regard to significant persons of early childhood, unconsciously displaced onto figures in the present (cf. Freud, 1912). The problem with transference, as Greenson (1968, p. 155) noted, is that it is repetitious and inappropriate. In the context of this article, the terms refer (nontechnically) to the relationship between the client and therapist: how the client perceives the therapist (transference), e.g., does the client want an authority figure, male or female therapist, warm individual, etc.? And how the therapist perceives the client (countertransference), e.g., can s/he work with this client? Does s/he dislike the client? These are variables which may clearly effect the therapist's ability to teach the client a self-regulation technique.

The transpersonal, or spiritual perspective, has two different views with regard to the role of the teacher/therapist and relationship. Initially it is seen as critical in the therapeutic process to have someone as a guide. Much as in classical psychoanalysis, this person should be someone who has undergone the practice—the spiritual discipline. However, ultimately, in many traditions, although the role of the teacher is acknowledged, eventually the individual must leave the teacher and experience for him/herself. As Watts (1961) noted, the basic position of the Zen master is that s/he has nothing to teach. In Hesse's *Siddhartha*, Siddhartha met Buddha but left him, "for Siddhartha had . . . become distrustful of teachings and learning . . . I have little faith in words that come to us from teachers" (Hesse, 1951, p. 28).

The role of the therapist and therapeutic relationship is emphasized much less in the behavioral tradition. The emphasis is on the utility of the strategy, and therefore tape-recorded or other semiautomated methods of disseminating techniques to individuals are considered appropriate and useful.

Implicit in the above discussion of relationships is the issue of trust. Is the client willing to trust the therapist? How important is this as a variable in positive therapeutic outcome? Even from a behavioral perspective, it has been noted that to have an individual close his or her eyes can be a frightening experience, and therefore important that the client trust the therapist enough to do that (Davison, 1973).

Resistance

Resistance is a technical term first used by Freud and refers to the two aspects of the person warring between life (eros) and death (thanatos). Freud saw this as a battle the person under treatment must fight every step of the way, between that part striving toward recovery and the opposing forces, urging destruction and chaos. Freud, as therapist, felt he too had to fight against the patient's resistance. He did this by representing himself as infallible, as in the case of Frau Elizabeth Von R. and with Lucy R. in which he pitted his will and efforts against her contrary insistence and desires (Freud, 1959).

In teaching an individual meditation, the therapist needs to be sensitive to several potential resistances, as well as how s/he will deal with resistance within the framework of their chosen therapeutic orientation.

Why do some people resist meditating? Carrington and Ephron (1975) made several useful comments on why there is refusal to learn to continue to meditate: (1) incompatibility with the individual's lifestyle or belief system, (2) a fear of loss of control, (3) difficulty in giving up the parent/child roles of transference, (4) misconceived "shoulds" about how one should meditate, (5) reluctance to give up symptoms useful to the patient. In addition, a person may feel "pressured" to learn a technique by a spouse or intimate who recently learned meditation. Thus we need to look at the general family (significant-other) system of a person who wishes to begin, or thinks s/he might want to begin learning meditation. Finally, learning an essentially nonanalytical technique may be frightening to individuals who have been brought up in a culture such as our own which places such a high value on the analytical skills.

In utilizing any self-control strategy, an additional area of potential resistance which is important to consider is the question of "What happens if the technique works successfully and helps the individual change?" Although we are discussing *self*-control strategies, in which an individual may wish to exert change over his or her own attitude and behavior, people generally live within some kind of interpersonal context. Therefore, the change of one person will inevitably effect others. Clinical experience suggests that often resistance to utilizing a technique can be addressed by trying to understand the consequences if the technique is successful (Minuchin *et al.*, 1978).

Effects of Meditation as a Clinical Intervention for a Particular Concern: Dimensions Four and Five

Most of the literature, as noted in Article 1 in this volume, has focused on the effects of meditation on specific clinical concerns. Although meditation per se is discussed here, a comparison with other self-control strategies is also made in order to help highlight when meditation might be the self-control strategy of choice.

Dimension #4 CLINICAL CONCERN:

ASSESSMENT OF DEPENDENT VARIABLE

- View of Disease "Etiology"
- Refinement of Clinical Problem

  Focus: historical/current
  Brain: attention, cognition, imagery
  Body: somatic, physiological
  Behavior: excess, deficit, new skill
  Environment: family, physical, social

Dimension #5 SELECTION OF
SELF-CONTROL STRATEGY
(INDEPENDENT VARIABLE)

- Theoretical/clinically based rationale
  between independent/dependent variable
- Definition of Technique
- Components

  Cognitions
  Imagery
  Attention
  Body
    Breathing
    Physical Posture
  Physical (environmental) planning
  Behavioral skills (rehearsals)
  Lifestyle modification
  Social Network Support

- Assessment of utility in combining techniques

Fig. 2. The self-control strategy and the clinical concern—independent and dependent variables.

The first round literature suggested that meditation may be a promising strategy both for treating stress-related disorders—including hypertension, the addictions, fears, and phobias (meditation as a self-regulation strategy)—as well as for helping individuals create new ways of perceiving the world and understanding themselves (meditation as an altered state of consciousness) (Shapiro & Giber, 1978). Based on these clinical findings, as well as certain physiological findings (Woolfolk, 1975; Davidson, 1976), some individuals suggested that meditation was a unique strategy different from all other self-control strategies (Mulchman, 1977).

In terms of its self-regulation effects, meditation's uniqueness has not been borne out in the second-round literature (Shapiro, 1980). There are several studies which suggest meditation to be equally effective but no more effective than other self-regulation strategies whether they be progressive relaxation (Elson et al., 1977; Marlatt et al., this volume; Woolfolk et al., 1976; Boswell and Murray, 1979; Thomas & Abbas, 1978), Benson's relaxation response (Beiman et al., this volume; Marlatt et al., this volume), a pseudo-meditation treatment (Smith, 1976), anti-meditation treatments (Boswell and Murray, 1979; Smith, 1976; Kirsch & Henry, 1979), self-administered systematic desensitization (Kirsch & Henry, 1979), or cardiovascular and neuromuscular biofeedback (Sururt et al., 1978; Hager & Sururt, 1978). This is true whether the dependent variable is anxiety (Beiman et al., this volume; Boswell & Murray, 1979; Thomas & Abbas, 1978; Smith, 1976; Goldman, Domitor & Murray, 1979; Kirsch & Henry, 1979; Zuroff & Schwartz, 1978), anxiety in alcoholics (Parker et al., 1978), alcohol consumption (Marlatt et al., this volume), insomnia (Woolfolk et al., 1976), or borderline hypertension (Stuart et al., 1978).

The third-round literature on clinical effects tries to become more precise about the nature of the dependent variable. An example of this is the work done by Schwartz et al. (1978; Davidson & Schwartz, 1976) suggesting that stress may be primarily cognitive or primarily somatic. They argue that actual differences between the technique of meditation and other self-regulation strategies do exist and that it is the imprecise measuring of the dependent variable that is lumping the results together. One study which attempts to detect this difference (Schwartz et al., 1978), gave a group of meditators and a group of individuals who exercised an anxiety questionnaire involving both somatic and cognitive components. Somatic anxiety refers to butterflies in the stomach, sweaty palms, tight jaw, etc., and cognitive anxiety involves what a person says, e.g., I feel out of control, helpless, tense, a warring mind. Subjects who practiced physical exercise reported relatively less somatic and more cognitive anxiety than meditators. Meditators conversely reported less cognitive and more somatic anxiety than the exercisers. This study suggests the potential clinical promise of refinement of the dependent variable. Since the study was not a longitudinal design the results are somewhat difficult to interpret definitively. However, if further research bears out this experimental hypothesis, matching meditation technique to cognitively anxious people and exercise to somatically anxious people, has clear clinical relevance. Additional examples of matching strategy to clinical problem are discussed in the next section.

Dimension Five: The Selection of the Type of Meditation (The Intervention Strategy)

The selection of meditation as an intervention should involve as clear a theoretical rationale as possible between the independent and the dependent variable. This rationale necessitates having a precise definition of the technique, a difficulty which has heretofore hampered research in meditation. If we examine the independent variable side of the equation, we need to consider three different areas. First, we need to come up with a precise definition; second, we need to make distinctions between different levels of experiencing of the technique (Tellegen & Atkinson, 1974); and third, we need to develop a component analysis of the technique in order to determine what are the active and what are the inert criteria which may be effecting treatment outcome (cf. Mahoney & Thoreson, 1974; Thoreson & Mahoney with respect to behavioral self-management; and Meichenbaum, 1977, with respect to cognitive factors in biofeedback training). In order to eventually be able to compare self-regulation strategies as independent variables, this kind of precision in describing them needs to be undertaken.

As noted in article 1 of this book, there are a plethora of techniques subsumed under the label meditation. In order to deal with the problems of unclarity with regard to what constitutes meditation, we have offered the definition in article 1 as follows:

> Meditation refers to a family of techniques which have in common a conscious attempt to focus attention in a nonanalytical way, and an attempt not to dwell on discursive, ruminating thought.

The implications of this definition have been discussed elsewhere, and are therefore only briefly summarized here: the definition is noncultic, and separates out the framework within which the technique is taught from the technique itself. Thus, although meditation may have aspects in common with prayer as a technique (e.g., conscious attempt to focus attention), one should not assume an *a priori* overlap because of the different contexts in which the technique may be practiced. Similarly, there is an important meta-message in this definition—that the content of the thought is not important; rather that awareness of the context—conscious attention—is the most important criterion. Thus, cognitions and images are not the end goal of meditation; although there may be overlapping content, one should not *a priori* equate meditation with techniques of guided imagery, covert self-instructional training, heterohypnosis, self-hypnosis, or other cognitive strategies.

Meditation as an independent variable has often been conceptualized as a self-regulation strategy effective for certain psychosomatic and stress-related disorders. This is particularly true of Western research. However, meditation is a technique developed within an Eastern philosophical/religious framework in order to induce altered states of consciousness and provide a new way of perceiving oneself, others, and the world around—meditation as an altered state of consciousness. Therefore, in describing the independent variable, the distinction between meditation as a self-regulation strategy and meditation as an altered state of consciousness may be an important one (Shapiro & Giber, 1978; Shapiro, 1980). This distinction may reflect different levels of depth of experience during meditation (Shapiro & Zifferblatt, 1976), and these different levels of experience may influence different outcome measures (Shapiro, 1978b).

The third area which needs to be looked at with respect to a self-control strategy is the component analysis. With respect to meditation, it is important to examine its different components and how they may be interacting with each other to produce treatment effects. For example, components of meditation which need to be analyzed include the required preparatory ritual (change of eating habits, lectures) (Smith, 1979); the physical postures, whether movement or stabilized; and if stabilized, lotus, half-lotus, or sitting (Ikegami, 1973); the attentional focus (i.e., a specific object—a mantra) (Smith, 1976) and whether it is a meaningful or meaningless word (Elson *et al.*, 1977); whether intention is choiceless awareness (Kasamatsu & Hirai, 1969); whether the attentional style is active or receptive; and finally the issue of regulation of breathing—whether breathing is ignored, attended to actively, and if actively attended to, is there an attempt to control the breathing or simply to attentively observe its automaticity.

By breaking meditation down into its various components, it may be possible to determine which are active and which inert. Further, by breaking other self-regulation strategies down into their components, it may be possible to determine why there are actual differences between techniques and where differences are only semantic distinctions. In so doing, it may then be possible to determine whether a single technique or combination of techniques might be useful in treating a particular clinical problem. In this respect, meditation has been compared with several different self-regulation strategies: hypnosis (Davidson & Goleman, 1977), biofeedback (Glueck & Stroebel, 1975), behavioral self-control (Shapiro & Zifferblatt, 1976; Shapiro, 1978b), autogenic training (Onda, 1965), as well as generally with other self-regulation strategies (Davidson & Schwartz, 1976). Harai & Watanabe (1977) tried to determine whether previous meditation experience enhanced biofeedback training, and Solomon & Bumpus (1978) have investigated combining meditation with running.

Once we have a more complete understanding of what the independent variable actually consists of (e.g., a definition and components), we are then in a better position to determine when it is the treatment of choice. For example, on a research level, as we have noted, Schwartz, Davidson, and Goleman (1978) suggest differentiating between meditation and exercise dependent upon the subject's level of cognitive and somatic anxiety. Further, based on the research with subject variables, meditation may not be the treatment of choice for individuals with high external locus of control, or with clinical problems such as migraine headaches or Reynaud's disease which, as Glueck & Stroebel (1975) note, are not as amenable to amelioration by meditation as by temperature and EMG biofeedback for eliciting vasodilation and muscle relaxation. On the other hand, it appears for ''general relaxation'' meditation is the treatment of choice; and for a specific stress area, biofeedback (Schwartz, 1973).

If a person's stress is caused by lack of basic social skills (e.g., those shy or withdrawn), meditation may not be a useful therapeutic intervention (certainly not as a sole intervention strategy). Rather it may be more appropriate for them to undergo some kind of social skill or assertiveness training either in place of or in addition to the meditation treatment. Also, it appears that meditation may not be useful for chronically depressed individuals who may need to have their arousal level activated (cf. also hypotensives, hyperactive children).

Further, meditation may not provide as much information as other strategies about cause and effect (i.e., a functional analysis of the person's behavior and the environment). Therefore, a strategy such as behavioral self-observation and some of the behavioral self-management skills may be useful as an additional treatment of choice. Here we may consider a combination of independent variables as is often done with biofeedback and autogenic training. Some researchers have also attempted to combine the independent variable of meditation with other self-regulation strategies (Woolfolk, this volume; Shapiro, 1978b) in order to make it a more powerful clinical intervention. These results, though promising, await further investigation (cf. Shapiro & Shapiro, 1980).

A final promising literature may involve the matching of a person's perceptual response mode to a cognitive focusing strategy. For example, if a person's response mode is primarily auditory, then when using biofeedback, a visual stimulus may be preferable (Branstrom, 1979). When using meditation or hypnosis, an auditory stimulus may be preferable (Davidson & Schwartz, 1976).

These refinements are only a beginning step in matching treatment to person to clinical problem. However they are at least a start in the right direction, and provide a beginning framework for additional research refinement and sophistication.

Other efforts may involve looking at the classical literature which suggests beginning with concentrative meditation and then eventually teaching a person mindfulness meditation (Goleman, 1971).

Teaching of the Technique—Skill Acquisition Plus Issues of Practice, Adherence, and Compliance; Dimension Six

In addition to the interactive dimension of relationship (between therapist, patient and/or teacher/student) as can be seen from Fig. 3, the other important interactive dimension is the means by which the self-control technique is taught—what are the best methods of communicating techniques between health care provider and patient in such a way that skill leaning is maximized and adherence and compliance facilitated.

Adherence to treatment is an important aspect of any self-regulation strategy, whether that strategy be for assertiveness training, relaxation, or medication compliance (Dunbar & Stunkard, 1977). With respect to meditation, these issues include the following: Is there an optimal maximum amount of time per day for practice? Can one practice too much (French, Schmid & Ingalls, 1975)? What is the relationship between length of experience and effectiveness (Benson & Wallace, 1972; Shafii, Lavely & Jaffe, 1974; Otis, 1974)? Recent studies, for example, suggest that the effectiveness of meditation as a treatment depends on both steady and prolonged practice of the technique (Lazar *et al.*, 1977; Marcus, 1975; Kasamatsu and Hirai, 1969); that the longer the practice, the greater the increase in concentration (Davidson, Goleman & Schwartz, 1976); and that the more experienced the meditator, the more physically stable the posture (Ikegami, 1968).

Past studies, however, have shown that a large percentage of meditators (ranging from 25 to 50% and sometimes higher) do not continue to practice the technique. For example, Kanas & Horowitz (1977) note that within 4 months of beginning, three out of eight subjects had already dropped out of the meditation group. Similarly, Glueck and Stroebel (1975) noted that the greatest difficulty was in getting patients with significant depression or younger teenage patients to meditate regularly. Marlatt *et al.* (this volume) monitored adherence to different relaxation strategies and noted that after the intervention phase, when given a choice, individuals, almost without exception, chose to discontinue all types of treatment, ranging from pleasurable reading to meditation (Benson's method) and progressive relaxation. Glueck and Stroebel (1975) noted that all subjects in their biofeedback and autogenic training groups dropped out, as well as, at a later time, a sizable number of their meditation group.

There are three critical issues with respect to adherence and compliance: (a) whether subjects say they

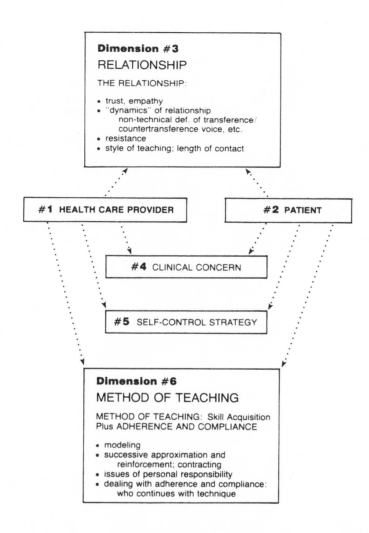

Fig. 3. Relationship and method of teaching—interaction of patient and health care provider.

practiced, (b) whether they, in fact, practiced, and (c) how to maintain adherence. Goldman, Domitor & Murray (1979), to ensure practice, had subjects meditate in a laboratory setting and debriefed them after each session to determine the nature of their experience to see if they were meditating "correctly." This certainly ensures practice during the intervention phase, a point about which experimenters cannot always be sure. However, it is cumbersome and expensive, and thereby usually results in a short experiment [e.g., Goldman, Domitor & Murray's (1979) lasted only 5 days], making it hard to evaluate meditation's effectiveness against reported claims—i.e., much of the research which has been done in the West has been done with relatively short-term meditators as subjects, whereas claims from the Orient are based on experiences of subjects who were skilled masters and have spent decades perfecting the discipline through intense practice.

Ways of increasing adherence and compliance involve providing preparation before the teaching of the technique (Smith, 1979) as well as providing follow-up checking after the technique has been taught (Glueck & Stroebel, 1975). Other ideas include having the client develop a self-contract, working with the client to determine time and place of practice, building in an initial reinforcement, providing for successive approximations to the desired time limit, carefully understanding the client's initial motivation and desire to learn meditation, and using positive images of desired consequences as ways of facilitating and increasing motivation to continue the practice.

System's Approach to Meditation

Evaluation: The Interactive System

Evaluation of clinical efficacy is a standard part of any good psychotherapeutic and health care treatment, regardless of orientation. And it is at this point where a systems model, involving feedback loops between our different dimensions, becomes critical (see heavy dark lines, Fig. 4). The systems model that we have described and the various dimensions which we have explicated can now be put within an overall framework illustrated by Fig. 4.

If evaluation is positive (therapeutic success) then termination and follow-up are again appropriate standard aspects of treatment. However if not, feedback loops from the evaluation to each of the various dimensions can help us determine very precisely which ones may be facilitating treatment outcome and which not.

If the technique does not appear to be successful for the client, a reassessment of the clinical concern, the therapist "teaching" style, and/or the strategy itself may be in order. An additional strategy or combination of strategies may be indicated. By following this feedback model in an intensive case study approach, clinicians can contribute invaluable information toward helping generate more sophisticated hypotheses for future research.

Unfortunately, given the state of our current art, in many cases we do not know which treatment strategy is the most effective for a particular client. Therefore, at this stage, clinicians often have to use

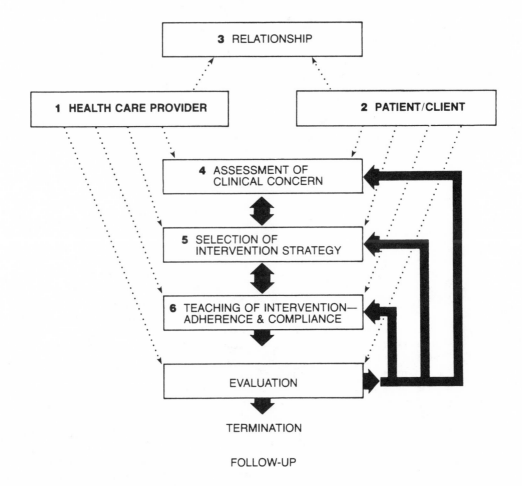

Fig. 4. Dimensions relevant to the clinical use of a self-control strategy—an interactive systems theory model.

their "intuition" in making a decision. Insofar as possible, this decision should be based on the research literature, but where the literature is not yet adequate, the clinician should try to evaluate as honestly and accurately as possible the effects of the intervention, including how effectively the technique(s) utilized generalize to nonpractice times.

The systems model as illustrated, in addition to providing clinical utility in intensive design studies, should also help us more clearly indicate directions in which future research needs to go. Using more complex multivariate designs, and specifying replicable components within each of the dimensions as described in this article, we can design more precise and sophisticated studies to determine relative variances from each related dimension contributing to treatment success. Further, through multiple regression techniques, we may determine potential predictors of treatment success (level of motivation, responsibility, self-efficacy, etc.). By building up our information base within the dimensions of this framework, we should develop the requisite knowledge about patient, intervention, and clinical concern. Further in the case of meditation, the "clinical concern" may range from stress management and relaxation to spiritual growth and "personal transformation." This knowledge should, in turn, help us be in a much more sophisticated position to understand our own biases as health care providers, and can subsequently contribute to optimal utilization of meditation as an intervention in order to maximize treatment success for our patients and clients.

References

Anand, B., Chinna, G., and Singh, B. Some aspects of electroencephalographic studies in yogis. *Electroencephalography & Clinical Neurophysiology*, 1961, *13*, 452–6.

Bandura, A. *Principles of behavior modification*, New York: Holt, Rinehart, Winston, 1969.

Bandura, A. *Social learning theory*. Englewood Cliffs, NJ: Prentice Hall, 1977.

Barber, T. X. and Ca.verly, D. S. Toward a theory of hypnotic behavior. Effects of suggestability on defining the situation as hypnosis and defining response to suggestions as easy. *Journal of Abnormal and Social Psychology*, 1964, *68*, 585–592.

Beiman, I. H., Johnson, S. A., Puente, A. E., Majestic, H. W., Graham, L. E. This volume, article 46.

Benson, H., *The mind/body effect*. New York: Simon and Schuster, 1978.

Benson, H. & Wallace, R. Decreased blood pressure in hypertensive subjects who practice meditation. *Circulation*, 1972, Suppl. No. 2, 516.

Berwick, P. & Oziel, L. J. The use of meditation as a behavioral technique. *Behavioral Therapy*, 1973, *4*, 743–5.

Boswell, P. C. and Murray, G. J. Effects of meditation on psychological and physiological measures of anxiety. *Journal of Consulting and Clinical Psychology*, 1979, *47* (3), 606–607.

Branstrom, M. Preferred perceptual mode and biofeedback training. Unpublished doctoral dissertation. Pacific Graduate School of Psychology. 1979.

Breuer, J. and Freud, S. (1893), *Studies in Hysteria*. In the standard edition of the complete psychological works of Freud. J. Strachey (ed.), Vol. 2. London: Hogarth, 1955.

Bugental, D. B. & Whalen, C. Attributional and behavior changes following two behavior management interventions with hyperactive boys. *Child Development*, 1978, *49*, 247–250.

Carrington, P. and Ephron, H. Meditation as an adjunct to psychotherapy. In S. Arieti & G. Chrzanowski (eds.) *The world biennial of psychotherapy and psychiatry* (III). New York: J. Wiley, 1975.

Clark, F. V. Transpersonal perspectives in psychotherapy. *Journal of Humanistic Psychology*, 1977, *17* (2), 69–81.

Davidson, J. Physiology of meditation and mystical states of consciousness. *Perspectives in Biology and Medicine*, 1976, *19*, 345–80.

Davidson, R. and Goleman, D. The role of attention in meditation and hypnosis: A psychobiological perspective on transformations of consciousness. *International Journal of Clinical & Experimental Hypnosis*, 1977, 25 (4), 291–308.

Davidson, R. and Schwartz, G. The psychobiology of relaxation and related states: A multi-process theory. In D. I. Mostofsky (Ed.), *Behavior control and the modification of physiological activity*. New York: Prentice-Hall, 1976.

Davidson, R., Goleman, D., and Schwartz, G. Attentional and affective concomitants of meditation: A cross-sectional study. *Journal of Abnormal Psychology*, 1976, 85, 235–38.

Davison, G. C. Counter control and behavior modification. In Hammerlynck, L. A. et al. (Eds.), *Behavior change: Methodology, concepts, practice*. Champaign, IL: Research Press, 1973.

DiNardo, R. Locus of control and attention during meditation. *Journal of Consulting and Clinical Psychology*, 1979, *47* (6), 1136–1137.

Dunbar, J. and Stunkard, A. J., Adherence to diet and drug regimens. In R. Levy, B. Rifkink, B. Dennis, & N. Ernst (Eds.), *Nutrition, lipids, and coronary heart disease*. New York: Raven Press, 1977.

Earle, J. B. B. Meditation and cerebral laterality. *Journal of Transpersonal Psychology*, 1981, *2*.

Elson, B., Hauri, P., and Cunis, D. Physiological changes in Yoga meditation. *Psychophysiology*, 1977, *14*, 52–7.

Franks, J. *Persuasion and healing*, New York: Schocken Books, 1963.

French, A. P., Schmid, A. C., and Ingalls, E. Transcendental Meditation, altered reality testing, and behavioral change: A case report. *Journal of Nervous & Mental Disease*, 1975, 161, 55–8.

Freud, S. Dynamics of transferences, (1912). *Standard edition of the complete psychological works of Freud*, J. Strachey (Ed.), Vol. 2. London: Hogarth, 1955, Vol. 12. 97–98.

Freud, S. *The problem of anxiety*. New York: W. W. Norton, 1936.

Freud, S. *Studies in hysteria*, Collected Papers, New York: Basic Books, 1959.

Globus, G. On I: The conceptual foundations of responsibility. *American Journal of Psychiatry*, 1980, 137, *4*, 417–422.

Glueck, B. and Stroebel, C. Biofeedback and meditation in the treatment of psychiatric illness. *Comprehensive Psychiatry*, 1975, 16 (4), 303–21.

Goldman, B. L., Domitor, P. J., and Murray, E. J. Effects of Zen meditation on anxiety reduction and perceptual functioning. *Journal of Consulting and Clinical Psychology*, 1979, 47 (3), 551–56.

Goleman, D. Meditation as metatherapy: Hypotheses toward a proposed fifth state of consciousness. *Journal of Transpersonal Psychology*, 1971, 3 (1), 1–25.

Gottschalk, L. Psychosomatic medicine: Past, present and future. *Psychiatry*, 1975, *38*, 334–345.

Greenson, R. *The technique and practice of psychoanalysis*, Vol. 1. New York: International University Press, 1968.

Hager, J. L., and Surwit, R. S. Hypertension self-control with a portable feedback unit or meditation-relaxation. *Biofeedback and Self-Regulation*, 1978, 3(3), 269–275.

Hastings, A. Fadiman, J., and Gordon, J. S. (Eds.), *Holistic Medicine*. Rockville, MD: NIMH, 1980.

Hesse, H. *Siddhartha*, New York: New Directions Books, 1951.

Hirai, T. and Watanabe, T. Biofeedback and electrodermal self-regulation in a Zen meditator. *Psychophysiology*, 1977, 14, 103 (abstr.).

Ikegami, R. Psychological study of Zen posture. *Bulletin of the Faculty of Literature of Kyushu University*, 1968, 5, 105–35.

Kanas, N. and Horowitz, M. Reactions of TMers and non-meditators to stress films. *Archives of General Psychiatry*, 1977, 34(12), 1431–36.

Kasamatsu, A. and Hirai, T. An electroencephalographic study of the Zen meditation (zazen). *Psychologia*, 1969, 12, 205–25.

Katz, N. W. & Crawford, C. L. A little trance and a little skill. Paper presented at the meeting of the Society for Clinical and experimental hypnosis, Chapel Hill, N.C., October, 1978.

Keefe, T. Meditation and the psychotherapist. *American Journal of Orthopsychiatry*, 1975, 45(3), 484–9.

Kirsch, I. and Henry, I. Self-desensitization and meditation in the reduction of public speaking anxiety. *Journal of Consulting & Clinical Psychology*, 1979, 47(3), 536–41.

Knowles, J. H., The responsibility of the individual, *Daedalus*, 1977, *106* (1), 57–80.

Kubose, S. K. An experimental investigation of psychological aspects of meditation. *Psychologia*, 1976, *19* (1), 1–10.

Lazar, Z., Farwell, L., and Farrow, J. Effects of transcendental meditation program on anxiety, drug abuse, cigarette smoking, and alcohol consumption. In Orme-Johnson, D., Farrow, J. (eds.) *Scientific research on the transcendental meditation program*. 2nd ed., Vol. 1. Maharishi European Research University Press, 1977.

Lazarus, A. A., *Behavior therapy and beyond*, New York: McGraw Hill, 1971.

Lesh, T. Zen meditation and the development of empathy in counselors. *Journal of Humanistic Psychology*, 1970, *10* (1), 39–74.

McReynolds, W. T. The role of attention placebo influences in the efficacy of systematic desensitization. *Journal of Consulting and Clinical Psychology*, 1973, *41*, 86–92.

Mahoney, M. J. and Thoresen, C. E. *Self-control: Power to the person*. Monterey, CA: Brooks/Cole, 1974.

Malec, J. and Sipprelle, C. Physiological and subjective effects of Zen meditation and demand characteristics. *Journal of Consulting & Clinical Psychology*, 1977, *44*, 339-340.

Marcus, J. B. Transcendental meditation: Consciousness expansion as a rehabilitation technique. *Journal of Psychedelic Drugs*, 1975, *7* (2), 169–179.

Marlatt, G., Pagano, R., Rose, R., and Marques, J. K. This volume, article 10.

Maslow, A. *Toward a psychology of being*. New York: Van Nostrand, 1968.

Maupin, E. Individual differences in response to a Zen meditation exercise. *Journal of Consulting Psychology*, 1965, *29*, 139–45.

Meehl, P. E. The cognitive activity of the clinician. *American Psychologist*, 1960, *15*, 19–27.

Meichenbaum, D. *Cognitive behavior modification: An integrative approach*. New York: Plenum, 1977.

Minuchin, S., Rosman, B. L., and Barker, L. *Psychosomatic families: Anorexia nervosa in context*. Cambridge, MA: Harvard University Press, 1978.

Mischel, W. *Personality and assessment*, New York: J. Wiley, 1968.

Mulchman, M. Transcendental Meditation. *New England Journal of Medicine*, 1977, *297* (9), 513.

Onda, A. Autogenic training and Zen. In W. Luthe (Ed.), *Autogenic Training*. New York: Grune & Stratton, 1965.

Orne, M. T. On the social psychology of the psychological experiment with particular reference to demand characteristics and their implications. *American Psychologist*, 1962, 17 (10), 776–83.

Otis, L. S. If well-integrated but anxious, try TM. *Psychology Today*, 1974, 7, 45–46.

Otis, L. S. This volume, article 17.

Parker, J. C., Gilbert, A. S., and Thoreson, R. W. Reduction of autonomic arousal in alcoholics. *Journal of Consulting and Clinical Psychology*, 1978, 46 (5), 879–886.

Patel, C. Randomized control trial of Yoga and biofeedback in management of hypertension. *Lancet*. 1975, 11, 93–4. a.

Patel, C. Twelve-month follow-up of Yoga and biofeedback in the management of hypertension. *Lancet*, 1975, 1, 62–5. b.

Pelletier, K. *Holistic Medicine*, New York: Delacourte, 1979.

Pelletier, K. and Peper, E. The chutzpah factor in altered states of consciousness. *Journal of Humanistic Psychology*, 1977, *17* (1) 63–73.

Pomerleau, O. F. Behavioral medicine. *American Psychologist*, 1979, *34*, 654–663.

Rogers, C. *On becoming a person*. Boston: Houghton Mifflin, 1961.

Rosenthal, R., Persinger, G., Fode, K. Experimenter bias, anxiety, and social desirability. *Perceptual and Motor Skills*, 1962, *15*, 73–74.

Rotter, J. B. Generalized expectancies for internal versus external control of reinforcement. *Psychological Monographs*, 1966, *80*, (1) (Whole No. 609).

Schuster, R. Empathy and mindfulness. *Journal of Humanistic Psychology*, 1979, *19*, (1) 71–77.

Schwartz, G. Biofeedback as therapy: Some theoretical and practical issues. *American Psychologist,* 1973, *28,* 666–673.

Schwartz, G. and Weiss, S. What is behavioral medicine? *Psychosomatic Medicine,* 1977, *36,* 377–381.

Schwartz, G., Davidson, R., and Goleman, D. Patterning of cognitive and somatic processes in the self-regulation of anxiety: Effects of meditation versus exercise. *Psychosomatic Medicine,* 1978, *40,* 321–328.

Shafii, M. Silence in the service of ego: Psychoanalytic study of meditation. *International Journal of Psychoanalysis,* 1973, *54* (4) 431–43.

Shafii, M., Lavely, R., and Jaffe, R. Meditation and marijuana. *American Journal of Psychology,* 1974, *131,* 60–63.

Shapiro, A. K. Placebo effects in medicine, psychotherapy, and psychoanalysis. In Bergin, A. and Garfield, S. (eds.), *Handbook of psychotherapy and behavior change.* New York: Wiley, 1971.

Shapiro, D. H. *Precision Nirvana.* Englewood Cliffs, New Jersey: Prentice Hall, 1978. (a).

Shapiro, D. H. Instructions for a training package combining Zen meditation and behavioral self-management strategies. *Psychologia,* 1978, *21* (2), 70–76. (b).

Shapiro, D. H. Motivation, expectation effects and ''vision'' in meditation research. Invited participant in Meditation: Aspects of research and practice. *Journal of Transpersonal Psychology,* 1978, *2,* 126–129. c.

Shapiro, D. H. *Meditation: Self-regulation strategy and altered state of consciousness,* New York: Aldine, 1980.

Shapiro, D. H. A content analysis of Eastern and Western, traditional and new age approaches to therapy, health, and healing. In Walsh, R. N. & Shapiro, D. H. (Eds.) *Beyond Health and Normality.* New York: Van Nordstrom, 1983. (a).

Shapiro, D. H., The construct of self-control: Toward a unifying theory. Manuscript in preparation. 1983. (b).

Shapiro, D. H. Psychological health. In Corsini, R. (ed.) *The Handbook of Psychology.* New York: Wiley, 1984.

Shapiro, D. H. and Giber, D. Meditation and psychotherapeutic effects. *Archives of General Psychiatry,* 1978, 35, 294–302.

Shapiro, D. H. and Shapiro, J. The clinical management of stress: Nonpharmacological approaches, *Family Practice Recertification,* 1980, *2*(10), 55–63.

Shapiro, D. H. and Zifferblatt, S. M. An applied clinical combination of Zen meditation and behavioral self-management techniques: Reducing methadone dosage in drug addiction. *Behavior Therapy,* 1976, 7, 694–5. (a).

Shapiro, D. H. and Zifferblatt, S. M. Zen meditation and behavioral self-control: Similarities, differences and clinical applications. *American Psychologist,* 1976, 31, 519–32. (b).

Shapiro, J. and Shapiro, D. H. The psychology of responsibility. *New England Journal of Medicine,* 1979, 301 (4), 211–212.

Skinner, B. F. *Science and human behavior.* New York: MacMillan, 1953.

Smith, J. Meditation and psychotherapy: A review of the literature. *Psychological Bulletin,* 1975, 32 (4), 553–64.

Smith, J. Psychotherapeutic effects of TM with controls for expectations of relief and daily sitting. *Journal of Consulting and Clinical Psychology,* 1976, 44 (4), 630–7.

Smith, J. Personality correlates of continuation and outcome in meditation and erect sitting control treatments. *Journal of Consulting & Clinical Psychology,* 1978, 46 (2), 272–9.

Smith, J. Meditation and preparatory variables. Unpublished manuscript, Roosevelt University, 1979.

Solomon, G. G., and Bumpus, A. K. The running meditation response: An adjunct to psychotherapy. *American Journal of Psychotherapy,* 1978, 32 (4), 583–592.

Stek, R. and Bass, B. Personal adjustment and perceived locus of control among students interested in meditation. *Psychological Reports,* 1973, 32, 1019–22.

Stroebel, C. and Glueck, B. Passive meditation: Subjective and clinical comparison with biofeedback. In G. Schwartz & D. Shapiro (Eds.), *Consciousness and self-regulation.* New York: Plenum, 1977.

Sururt, R. S., Shapiro, D., and Good, M. I. Comparison of cardiovascular biofeedback, neuromuscular feedback, and meditation in the treatment of borderline hypertension. *Journal of Consulting and Clinical Psychology,* 1978, 46 (2), 252–263.

Tellegen, A. and Atkinson, G. Openness to absorbing and self-altering experiences. *Journal of Abnormal Psychology,* 1974, 83 (3), 268–77.

Thomas, D. and Abbas, K. A. Comparison of Transcendental Meditation and progressive relaxation in reducing anxiety. *British Medical Journal,* 1978, 2 (6154), 17.

Truax, C. B. and Carkuff, R. R. *Toward effective counseling and psychotherapy.* Aldine: New York, 1967.

Vahia, H. S., Doengaji, D. R., Jeste, D. V., *et al.* A deconditioning therapy based upon concepts of Patanjali. *International Journal of Social Psychiatry,* 1972, 18 (1), 61–66.

Walsh, R. and Rauche, L. The precipitation of acute psychoses by intensive meditation in individuals with a history of schizophrenia. *American Journal of Psychiatry,* 1979, 138 (8), 1085–6.

Walsh, R. N. and Shapiro, D. H. *Beyond health and normality: Toward a vision of exceptional psychological health.* New York: Van Nostrand, 1983 in press.

Walsh, R. and Vaughan, F. *Beyond ego: Readings in transpersonal psychology.* Los Angeles: J. B. Tarcher, 1980.

Watts, A. *Psychotherapy East and West.* New York: Ballantine Books, 1961.

Weide, T. Varieties of transpersonal therapy. *Journal of Transpersonal Psychology,* 1973, *5* (1), 7–14.

Woolfolk, R. Psychophysiological correlates of meditation. *Archives of General Psychiatry,* 1975, 32 (10), 1326–33.

Woolfolk, R. Self-control, meditation and the treatment of chronic anger. In Shapiro, D. H. & Walsh, R. N. This volume, article 44.

Woolfolk, R. and Franks, C. Meditation and behavior therapy. In Shapiro, D. H. & Walsh, R. N. This volume, article 55.

Woolfolk, R., Carr-Kaffeshan, L., and McNulty, T. F. Meditation training as a treatment for insomnia. *Behavior Therapy,* 1976, 7 (3), 359–65.

Wolpe, J. *The practice of behavior therapy.* New York: Pergamon Press, 1969.

Zuroff, D. & Schwartz, J. Effects of TM and muscle relaxation on trait anxiety, maladjustment, locus of control, and drug use. *Journal of Consulting & Clinical Psychology,* 1978, 46 (2), 264–71.

II

THE PSYCHOLOGY OF MEDITATION

An Introduction to Part II: Psychology of Meditation

In order to obtain an overview of the multiple areas subsumed under the label the psychology of meditation, we have divided Part II into three sections. Section A contains two review articles (5 and 6). These two articles are currently the only major critical review articles of the psychotherapeutic effects of meditation.*

Based on the distinction put forth in article 6 between meditation viewed as a self-regulation strategy, and meditation viewed as a means of inducing altered states of consciousness, this part of the book is divided accordingly. Section B reviews articles relevant to meditation as a clinical self-regulation strategy, including both stress management and stress-related disorders; the addictions; hypertension; general psychotherapeutic applications both for the client and for the therapist; and additional effects with normal subjects, both adverse and positive. Section C discusses meditation as an altered state of consciousness, concerning both attentional training issues and experiences during meditation.

---

*These two review articles provided the soil for the major review of the clinical literature undertaken in Volume One: *Meditation: self-regulation strategy and altered state of consciousness* (New York: Aldine, 1980), Chapter 5 (Meditation as a self-regulation strategy) and Chapter 7 (Meditation as an altered state of consciousness).

A. On Therapeutic Effects of Meditation

This section contains the only major critical review articles of the psychotherapeutic effects of meditation to date. The article by Smith (5) is a seminal article in that it was the first critical review of the lieterature looking at alternative explanations for the effects of meditation. Smith suggests that even though the effects of meditation are real and seem well documented, it is unclear whether these are due primarily to meditation or to expectation effects and just sitting. Although the article may err on the side of too conservative an estimation of meditation's effectiveness, it is an important in that it provided a balance for many of the claims that were being made by meditation adherents.

The article by Shapiro and Giber (6) refined Smith's article in three ways. First, the dependent variable of "psychotherapeutic effects" is refined into more specific dependent variables—stress management; the addictions; hypertension. Second, the independent variable of meditation is looked at more precisely and is broadened to include such areas as amount of subject practice, nature and length of training, therapist contact, and description of techniques. Third, meditation can be conceptualized both as a self-regulation strategy and also as an altered state of consciousness. The authors describe specific research strategies which may be appropriate depending upon the nature of the dependent variable investigated.

5

MEDITATION AS PSYCHOTHERAPY:
A REVIEW OF THE LITERATURE

Jonathan C. Smith

It has been widely argued that meditation has psychotherapeutic potential. Research on meditation has yielded three sets of findings: (a) Experienced meditators who are willing to participate without pay in meditation research appear happier and healthier than nonmeditators; (b) beginning meditators who practice meditation for 4–10 weeks show more improvement on a variety of tests than nonmeditators tested at the same time; and (c) persons who are randomly assigned to learn and practice meditation show more improvement over 4–10 weeks than control subjects assigned to some form of alternate treatment. However, this is not conclusive evidence that meditation is therapeutic. The therapeutic benefits found could be the result of expectation of relief or of simply sitting on a regular basis.

The term *meditation* refers to a family of mental exercises that generally involve calmly limiting thought and attention. Such exercises vary widely and can involve sitting still and counting breaths, attending to a repeated thought, or focusing on virtually any simple external or internal stimulus.

To the casual observer it may seem implausible that a simple mental exercise could have any effect on widespread problems of neurosis and anxiety. However, since 1936 at least 100 scholarly books and journal articles have argued that meditation does have psychotherapeutic potential (most of these references appear in the bibliographies of Haimes, 1972; Kanellakos & Ferguson, 1973; Lesh, 1970a; Timmons & Kamiya, 1970; and Timmons & Kanellakos, 1974). Numerous versions of this claim have appeared, including the idea that mystical experiences associated with meditation are therapeutic and that meditation can supplement or even take the place of psychotherapy. Virtually every school of psychological thought has been invoked to support these claims, including psychoanalytic, neo-Freudian, Jungian, client-centered, gestalt, Maslovian, existential, logotherapy, bioenergetic, and learning theory. Perhaps the essence of what has been written is conveyed by Goleman (1971):

I conceptualize meditation as a "meta-therapy": a procedure that accomplishes the major goals of conventional therapy and yet has as its end-state a change far beyond the scope of therapies . . . an altered state of consciousness. (p. 4)

In light of this exhilarating display of speculation, it is surprising that serious research on the therapeutic effects of meditation began only recently. This research has yielded

Requests for reprints should be sent to Jonathan C. Smith, who is now at the Department of Psychology, Roosevelt University, 430 South Michigan Avenue, Chicago, Illinois 60605.

three sets of findings: (a) Experienced meditators who are willing to participate without pay in meditation research typically praise meditation and indeed appear happier and healthier than the beginning meditator, the average college student or the everyday man in the street; (b) beginning meditators who practice meditation for 4–10 weeks show more improvement on a variety of tests than nonmeditators tested at the same time; and (c) persons who are randomly assigned to learn and practice meditation show more improvement over 4–10 weeks than control subjects assigned to some form of alternate treatment. I examine each of these findings in detail and evaluate what they show about the therapeutic potential of meditation.

REVIEW

Studies using mail-in questionnaires consistently yielded results that appeared to speak favorably for meditation. Wallace and Benson (cited in Gattozzi & Luce, 1971) found that of 400 transcendental meditators who completed a questionnaire regarding changes in mental and physical health, 84% judged that their mental health had improved significantly since learning meditation. Similarly, Otis (Note 1) sent questionnaires to 1,900 randomly selected transcendental meditators and 800 transcendental meditation (TM) practitioners attending a TM teacher training course. The questionnaire in part asked what problems the respondent had before learning TM and which of these problems had changed since learning TM. The 1,095 who responded generally claimed some improvement after learning TM (the actual number claiming improvement was not reported).

In addition, transcendental meditators who were willing to be tested in the laboratory appeared healthier than nonmeditators on the Freiburger Personality Inventory (Fehr, Nerstheimer, & Torber, 1973), the Personal Orientation Inventory (POI) (Hjelle, 1973), and tests of "autonomic stability" measuring the rate of galvanic skin response (GSR) habituation to a series of loud tones and the number of spontaneous GSR fluctuations during a period of quiet inactivity (Orme-Johnson, 1973).

The major weakness of these studies is that they relied on data resembling solicited testimonials. A meditator asked to participate in a study investigating the beneficial effects of meditation might view this as a calling or opportunity to "step forth for meditation" somewhat analogous to the evangelist's call to "step forth for Jesus." In both cases we are left wondering about those who remained seated. Put technically, the sample of those who volunteered to participate in meditation research was perhaps not representative of the population of those who learned to meditate. We cannot conclude from such studies that the practice of meditation is therapeutic.

One way around the ambiguities present in testimonial data is to test a sample of meditators before learning meditation and then after practicing meditation for a period of weeks or months. Using such a design Benson and Wallace (1972) found that 22 hypertension patients showed a significant reduction in blood pressure after 4–63 weeks of meditation. Of course, one might ask if such a decrease could be the result of simple passage of time rather than meditation. In order to answer this question we need a control group of nonmeditators tested during the same time period. Six studies, all using TM, have incorporated such a control and have found that over 4–10 weeks, meditators showed a significantly greater decrease in spontaneous GSRs (Orme-Johnson, Kiehlbauch, Moore, & Bristol, 1973) as well as significantly greater improvement on the State–Trait Anxiety Inventory (Ballou, 1973; Ferguson & Gowan, 1973), the POI (Nidich, Seeman, & Dreskin, 1973; Seeman, Nidich, & Banta, 1972), the IPAT Anxiety Scale Questionnaire and Northridge Depression, Neuroticism, and Self-Actualization scales (Ferguson & Gowan, 1973), and the Hypochondria, Psychasthenia, Social Introversion, Schizophrenia, and Taylor Anxiety scales of the Minnesota Multiphasic Personality Inventory (MMPI) (Orme-Johnson, Author Franklin, O'Connell, & Zold, 1973; Orme-Johnson et al., 1973).

Unfortunately, studies that compare changes experienced by meditators and nonmeditators are faulted because the two populations may not be comparable. At the very least, meditators, by their decision to learn meditation, demonstrate some motivation for self-improvement not demonstrated by nonmeditator controls. Such motivated subjects may be ripe for growth and may display reductions in pathology regardless of what they choose to do.

One study clearly illustrates this problem. Lesh (1970b) selected 16 counseling graduate students interested in learning meditation and 23 other graduate students, half of whom were interested in and half "definitely against" learning meditation. The first group was taught a form of Zen meditation, while the second served as a nonmeditation control. All subjects were given the Affective Sensitivity Scale (a measure of empathy) and the Fitzgerald experience inquiry (a measure of tolerance to and openness to regressive, irrational, and nonordinary experiences). After four weeks the meditators improved significantly more than the controls on the Affective Sensitivity Scale but not on the experience inquiry.

Lesh himself pointed to the problem of initial group differences:

The criticism might be raised that the experimental group was indeed an exceptional group of people in that they volunteered for such an unusual experiment in the first place. This is a cogent argument since the pretest scores for the experimental group on the tests measuring openness to experience and self-actualization are significantly higher than for either of the control groups. The same is true for the scales on the ASS_{ua} [the empathy measure] at pretest. That is, the experimental group was significantly higher in empathy before the experiment had begun. (p. 59)

However, the most rigorous studies on the therapeutic effects of meditation have controlled for the problem of initial group differences by randomly assigning subjects to meditation and alternative treatment conditions and testing before and after several weeks of treatment.

Otis (1974, Note 1) randomly assigned 62 employees of the Stanford Research Institute to a TM treatment group (in which the TM initiation fee was paid by the Institute) or to one of three control treatment conditions: a no-treatment condition, in which the subjects simply took pretests and posttests; a nonmeditation treatment condition, which involved sitting quietly for 15–20 minutes twice daily; and a meditative treatment (not TM) condition, which involved sitting quietly and restfully while repeating the phrase "I am a witness only" 15–20 minutes twice daily. All subjects were given a self-image pretreatment questionnaire. After a 3-month treatment period, the subjects were again given the self-image questionnaire, plus a problem checklist that requested estimates of the degree of improvement on a variety of physical and behavioral problems over the treatment period. In addition, the subjects were interviewed and the control subjects were offered TM or financial remuneration equivalent to the TM initiation fee.

Numerous lapses in methodological rigor seriously weaken what is otherwise an ambitious and creative design. First, Otis himself admitted that the treatment conditions were not matched for expectation of relief. The TM treatment, more than the control treatments, promoted the belief on the part of the subjects that they would benefit. This was clearly evidenced in the posttreatment interview and by the fact that after the 3-month treatment period, all but five of the control subjects chose to learn TM. Considerable research indicates that the expectation of relief can render potent even the lowliest of sugar pills, and its absence can render impotent treatments that are ordinarily respected and accepted (Borkovec, 1972; Goldstein, 1962; Lazarus, 1968; Leitenberg, Agras, Barlow, & Oliveau, 1969; Marcia, Rubin, & Efran, 1969; Shapiro, 1971). Second, the questionnaires Otis used were new, homemade tests of questionable validity and reliability. Otis reported that the variability of the data from the questionnaires was high, a problem one would expect of weak measures of low reliability. Finally, and most seriously, Otis chose to pool the three control groups—the no-treatment group, the group that sat and rested twice daily, and the group that meditated upon the phrase "I am a witness only" twice daily. The reasons he gave for pooling were the high variability of his questionnaire data and the small size of his samples. All major comparisons were between the TM group and the pooled control group. Obviously this unusual pooling procedure defeats the purpose of having control groups in the first place.

One would expect a confused set of results from these deficiencies. And this is exactly what Otis obtained. After 3 months the TM and pooled control group did not differ significantly in the degree of improvement in self-image. Yet, the TM group displayed a greater degree of estimated improvement on several items of the problem checklist, specifically "enjoyment of life, restfulness of sleep, energy level, sexual adjustment, and creativity." And in posttreatment interviews the TM group claimed more benefits than the pooled control group.

Other studies have fared considerably better. Brautigam (Note 2) sent letters to 19 drug abusers inviting them and their friends to attend an information lecture on TM. As a result, 20 people signed up for TM and agreed to participate in the project. The subjects were given a questionnaire and interview on drug habits and a questionnaire testing self-confidence, stability, adjustment, anxiety, and extroversion. In addition, each subject was observed and rated by a psychologist and a psychiatrist on a checklist of pathological behaviors. The subjects were then divided into two groups of 10 each, equated for frequency of drug use. For 3 months one group practiced TM twice daily, while the other was offered group counseling 4 hours every 2 weeks. At the end of the project all subjects were tested again. Brautigam found that the meditators displayed a significant reduction in drug abuse, pathological behaviors, and anxiety, as well as a significant increase in adjustment. The group counseling subjects improved on none of these measures.

For several reasons these results are not clear evidence for the therapeutic effects of meditation. First, all 20 subjects signed up for the experiment wanting and expecting to get TM. Some got group counseling every other week instead. The disappointment among these subjects must have been considerable. Indeed 30% did not attend any of the counseling sessions, and most, according to Brautigam, exerted "strong pressure" on the experimenter to teach them TM. The impact of attitude on the effectiveness of therapy is well documented (Luborsky, Chandler, Auerbach, Cohen, & Bachrach, 1971). The attitudes of these control subjects toward their treatment probably interfered, if anything, with its effectiveness. Also, the TM subjects received much more than meditation. In addition to four 2-hour training sessions, they received weekly individual checking to evaluate how well they were practicing, and participated in an 8-day trip for group meditation.

Appropriately, in interpreting her findings, Brautigam did not claim that the TM meditation exercise was the only, or even the crucial, therapeutic agent. Instead, she suggested: "Meditation opened up new opportunities for social contact without drugs," and "meditation offered an opportunity to break with previous role expectations and find a new role—that of a mediator" (p. 9).

In the first study involving teaching meditation to children, Linden (1973) randomly assigned 90 third-grade students to three groups of 30 each. One group met with a guidance counselor 45 minutes a day for 18 weeks; counseling focused on study skills. A second group was taught meditation, and these students practiced 25 minutes a day, twice weekly for 18 weeks. A third group received no treatment. As compared with the guidance and no-treatment controls, the meditators became more field independent, as measured by the Children's Embedded Figures Test, and less test anxious, as measured by the Test Anxiety Scale for Children. Unfortunately the results of this well-designed study are limited to test anxiety and field dependence among children and should not be generalized to adult psychopathology.

One study stands out for its methodological elegance. Vahia, Doongaji, Jeste, Kapoor, Ardhapurkar, and Ravindranath (1973) wished to isolate the essential components of psychophysiological therapy, a yoga-meditation therapy used at King Edward VI Memorial Hospital in Bombay, India. This therapy is based on ancient Hindu yoga teachings and incorporates physical yoga stretching exercises as well as meditation.

Ninety-five psychoneurotic patients who displayed no improvement in response to previous therapy were randomly divided into two groups matched for age, sex, diagnosis, and duration of illness. One group was given total psychophysiological therapy (i.e., yoga exercises plus meditation), while the other group was given partial psychophysiological therapy (i.e., a control treatment consisting of exercises resembling yoga exercises and no meditation). Both groups practiced 1 hour each weekday for 4–6 weeks and were given support, reassurance, and placebo tablets.

The measurements included: (a) blind clinical assessment before, after, and every week of the project based on target symptom relief and work efficiency on the job as reported by the patients themselves, their relatives, friends, and colleagues; (b) daily notebooks written by all subjects on thoughts that came to mind while practicing; (c) the MMPI and Rorschach tests given before and after the project; and (d) the Taylor Manifest Anxiety Scale given before, after, and every week of the project.

These results were obtained: (a) 73% of the subjects in the total therapy treatment showed significant improvement (an improvement of at least 50%) on the basis of clinical assessment, while 42% in the partial therapy treatment showed significant improvement; (b) the total therapy group showed significantly greater reduction in anxiety as measured by the Taylor scale than the group receiving partial therapy ($p < .05$); (c) those receiving total therapy showed a consistent reduction in anxiety as measured by the Taylor scale in each of the 6 weeks of the project, while those receiving partial therapy showed no consistent reduction; (d) the MMPI results showed a greater overall improvement for the subjects receiving total therapy than for those receiving partial therapy; and (e) those who displayed greater ability to meditate in the total therapy group displayed more clinically assessed improvement than those who did not.

One simple flaw mars this otherwise impressive study. Both the control and experimental treatments were taught by the same person, a physiotherapist with 11 years of experience in yoga. Probably this therapist knew, or at least suspected, that the partial treatment was in fact a control treatment. And since the partial treatment did not involve true yoga exercises, but "exercises resembling yoga exercises," one wonders about the therapist's belief in their effectiveness and about what theoretical rationale, if any, he gave for practicing. Recent research on classical desensitization points to the importance of the credibility and perceived authenticity of control treatments and of the therapists who administer them. For example, McReynolds, Barnes, Brooks, & Rehagen (1973) found that a placebo treatment taught by a therapist who was blind to its placebo nature and accompanied by a highly credible, yet contrived, theoretical rationale, is just as effective in reducing minor phobias as systematic desensitization. Moreover, such a placebo is significantly more effective than an attention placebo not accompanied by a theoretical rationale and taught by a therapist aware of its placebo nature.

CONCLUSIONS

Without exception the studies reviewed show the regular practice of meditation to be associated with decrements in psychopathology, particularly anxiety, over a period of time usually ranging from 4–10 weeks. The effects of meditation persist when controls are included for initial group differences, passage of time, therapist support and reassurance, individual contact with therapist, and interpersonal contact with practicing peers.

However, this general finding is not clear evidence that meditation is in and of itself therapeutic. The critical therapeutic variables underlying meditation could be something other than the meditation exercise. Two main possibilities not controlled for in the studies reviewed are (a) expectation of relief and (b) the regular practice of sitting quietly.

As mentioned earlier, McReynolds et al. (1973) found that the therapeutic effectiveness of a placebo treatment can be increased when it is presented in such a way as to nurture the expectation of relief. Two crucial variables contributing to the expectation of relief appear to be the therapist's belief (or lack of disbelief) in the treatment and the theoretical rationale presented for the treatment. In all the studies reviewed here, either the meditation instructors or the subjects demonstrated some initial belief (or absence of disbelief) in the therapeutic potential of meditation. And the most frequently cited form of meditation, TM, is not only taught by believing, practicing meditators but is introduced by two mandatory lectures that present a plausible psychophysiological theory of the technique's effectiveness as well as summaries of numerous "verifying" scientific studies.

Second, all forms of meditation reviewed here are practiced while sitting quietly. Perhaps the practice of regular sitting, and not the meditation exercise, is the crucial therapeutic variable. This possibility was hinted at (and rejected) in 1936 by Bagchi in one of the first published psychologically based arguments for the therapeutic potential of meditation:

> If some critic . . . contends that it is not so much the intention to relax [as is present in meditation] as the physical quietness and lying still that have the recuperative effect, at the present we can only point to clinical cases as a practical counterargument, waiting for further neurological evidence to support our belief. (p. 433)

This criticism is still valid 39 years later and the therapeutic potential of meditation remains to be demonstrated.

REFERENCE NOTES

1. Otis, L. S. Meditation or simulated meditation by nonpredisposed volunteers: Some psychological changes. In E. Taub (Chair), *The psychobiology of meditation*. Symposium presented at the meeting of the American Psychological Association, Montreal, August 1973.

2. Brautigam, E. *The effect of transcendental meditation on drug abusers*. Unpublished manuscript, City Hospital of Malmö, Sweden, 1971.

REFERENCES

Bagchi, B. K. Mental Hygiene and the Hindu doctrine of relaxation. *Mental Hygiene*, 1936, *20*, 424–440.

Ballou, D. Transcendental meditation research: Minnesota State Prison. In D. P. Kanellakos & P. C. Ferguson (Eds.), *The psychobiology of transcendental meditation*. Los Angeles: MIU Press, 1973. (Abstract)

Benson, H., & Wallace, R. K. Decreased blood pressure in hypertensive subjects who practiced meditation. *Circulation*, 1972, *46* (Suppl. 2), 130. (Abstract No. 516)

Borkovec, T. D. Effects of expectancy on the outcome of systematic desensitization and implosive treatments for analogue anxiety. *Behavior Therapy*, 1972, *3*, 29–40.

Fehr, T., Nerstheimer, U., & Torber, S. Untersuchung von 49 praktizierenden der Transzendentalen Meditation mit dem Freiburger Personlich Keitsinventar. In D. P. Kanellakos & P. C. Ferguson (Eds.), *The psychobiology of transcendental meditation*. Los Angeles: MIU Press, 1973. (Abstract)

Ferguson, P. D., & Gowan, J. The influence of transcendental meditation on anxiety, depression, aggression, neuroticism, and self-actualization. In D. P. Kanellakos & P. C. Ferguson (Eds.), *The psychobiology of transcendental meditation*. Los Angeles: MIU Press, 1973. (Abstract)

Gattozzi, A. A., & Luce, G. Physiological effects of a meditation technique and a suggestion for curbing drug abuse. In J. Segal (Ed.), *Mental Health Program Reports—5* (DHEW Publication No. (HSM) 72-9042). Washington, D.C.: U.S. Government Printing Office, 1971.

Goldstein, A. P. *Therapist-patient expectancies in psychotherapy*. New York: Pergamon Press, 1962.

Goleman, D. Meditation as meta-therapy: Hypotheses toward a proposed fifth state of consciousness. *Journal of Transpersonal Psychology*, 1971, *3*, 1–25.

Haimes, N. Zen Buddhism and psychoanalysis. *Psychologia*, 1972, *15*, 22–30.

Hjelle, L. A. Transcendental meditation and psychological health. In D. P. Kanellakos & P. C.

Ferguson (Eds.), *The psychobiology of transcendental meditation*. Los Angeles: MIU Press, 1973. (Abstract)

Kanellakos, D. P., & Ferguson, P. C. (Eds.) *The psychobiology of transcendental meditation*. Los Angeles: MIU Press, 1973.

Lazarus, A. A. Behavior therapy and graded structure. In R. Porter (Ed.), *The role of learning in psychotherapy*. London: Churchill, 1968.

Leitenberg, H., Agras, W. S., Barlow, D. H., & Oliveau, D. C. Contribution of selective positive reinforcement and therapeutic instructions to systematic desensitization therapy. *Journal of Abnormal Psychology*, 1969, *74*, 113–118.

Lesh, T. V. Zen and psychotherapy: A partially annotated bibliography. *Journal of Humanistic Psychology*, 1970, *10*, 75–83. (a)

Lesh, T. V. Zen meditation and the development of empathy in counselors. *Journal of Humanistic Psychology*, 1970, *10*, 39–74. (b)

Linden, W. Practicing of meditation by school children and their levels of field dependence–independence, test anxiety, and reading achievement. *Journal of Consulting and Clinical Psychology*, 1973, *41*, 139–143.

Luborsky, L., Chandler, M., Auerbach, A. H., Cohen, J., & Bachrach, H. M. Factors influencing the outcome of psychotherapy: A review of the quantitative research. *Psychological Bulletin*, 1971, *75*, 145–185.

Marcia, J. E., Rubin, B. M., & Efran, J. S. Systematic desensitization: Expectancy change or counterconditioning? *Journal of Abnormal Psychology*, 1969, *74*, 382–387.

McReynolds, W. T., Barnes, A. R., Brooks, S., & Rehagen, N. J. The role of attention–placebo influences in the efficacy of systematic desensitization. *Journal of Consulting and Clinical Psychology*, 1973, *41*, 86–92.

Nidich, S., Seeman, W., & Dreskin, T. Influence of transcendental meditation: A replication. *Journal of Counseling Psychology*, 1973, *70*, 556–566.

Orme-Johnson, D. W. Autonomic stability and transcendental meditation. *Psychosomatic Medicine*, 1973, *35*, 341–349.

Orme-Johnson, D. W., Authur, G., Franklin, L., O'Connell, J., & Zold, T. Transcendental meditation and drug abuse counselors. In D. P. Kanellakos & P. C. Ferguson (Eds.), *The psychobiology of transcendental meditation*. Los Angeles: MIU Press, 1973. (Abstract)

Orme-Johnson, D. W., Kiehlbauch, J., Moore, R., & Bristol, J. Personality and autonomic changes in meditating prisoners. In D. P. Kanellakos & P. C. Ferguson (Eds.), *The psychobiology of transcendental meditation*. Los Angeles: MIU Press, 1973. (Abstract)

Otis, L. S. If well-integrated but anxious, try TM. *Psychology Today*, November 1974, pp. 45–46.

Seeman, W., Nidich, S., & Banta, T. Influence of transcendental meditation on a measure of self-actualization. *Journal of Counseling Psychology*, 1972, *19*, 184–187.

Shapiro, A. K. Placebo effects in medicine, psychotherapy, and psychoanalysis. In A. E. Bergin &

S. L. Garfield (Eds.), *Handbook of psychotherapy and behavior change: An empirical analysis.* New York: Wiley, 1971.

Timmons, B., & Kamiya, J. The psychology and physiology of meditation and related phenomena: A bibliography. *Journal of Transpersonal Psychology,* 1970, *2,* 41–59.

Timmons, B., & Kanellakos, D. P. The psychology and physiology of meditation: Bibliography II. *Journal of Transpersonal Psychology,* 1974, *6,* 32–38.

Vahia, N. S., Doongaji, D. R., Jeste, D. V., Kapoor, S. N., Ardhapurkar, I., & Ravindranath, S. Further experience with the therapy based upon concepts of Patanjali in the treatment of psychiatric disorders. *Indian Journal of Psychiatry,* 1973, *15,* 32–37.

6

MEDITATION AND PSYCHOTHERAPEUTIC EFFECTS: SELF-REGULATION STRATEGY AND ALTERED STATE OF CONSCIOUSNESS

Deane H. Shapiro, Jr. and David Giber

● We review the research literature dealing with the psycho-therapeutic effects of meditation. The first part of the article reviews studies in which meditation is viewed as a self-regulation strategy. In the second part, studies in which meditation is viewed as a technique for inducing altered states of conscious-ness are reviewed. We conclude by giving guidelines and suggestions for future research.

There is a great deal of literature investigating the relationship among meditation, psychotherapy, and states of consciousness. Some articles deal with ways in which the practice of meditation could aid the patient.[1-10] Others concern ways in which meditation could benefit the therapist[11-12] or provide a paradigm for the therapeutic relationship.[13] There have been claims for the efficacy of meditation in educational settings[14-16] and in health prob-lems such as drug and alcohol abuse, hypertension, stress, and tension management. Although there are several annotated bibliographies of the meditation literature,[17-20] there have been only three major critical reviews of the meditation research literature.[21-23] Two of these reviews have attempted to assess and document the physiological changes and subjective experiences that occur during the practice of meditation.

Woolfolk's[21] review gave a systematic basis for (1) comparing physiological changes (eg, oxygen consumption, skin response, blood pressure, heart rate, EEG) resulting from different independent variables (yoga, Zen, transcen-dental meditation [TM]) and (2) looking at methodological

Accepted for publication June 20, 1977.

From the Pacific Graduate School of Psychiatry (Dr Shapiro), Palo Alto, Calif; Clinical Instructor, Department of Psychiatry and Behavioral Sciences (Dr Shapiro), Stanford University Medical School; and Department of Psychology (Mr Giber), Stanford University, Palo Alto, Calif. Mr Giber is currently with the Department of Psychology, Duke University, Durham, NC.

Read before the American Association for the Advancement of Science, Pacific Regional Meeting, Missoula, Mo, June 1976.

Reprint requests to PO Box 2084, Stanford, CA 94305 (Dr Shapiro).

issues within each study (ie, experience of meditators, type of design, and quality of control procedure). Davidson[1] attempted to specify the physiological correlates that may be associated with the strong subjective changes during meditation: the so-called altered states of consciousness.

From a clinical standpoint, however, it is important to document if and how the physiological changes and subjec-tive experiences during meditation generalize to other settings and times in the patient's life. Smith's[23] article is the only review of meditation as a type of psychotherapy. After a cogent and carefully reasoned methodological critique of the literature, Smith noted that there is not "conclusive evidence that meditation is therapeutic. The therapeutic benefits could be the result of expectation of relief or of simply sitting on a regular basis."[23] The only limitations of Smith's review are that he never defined specifically what is meant by psychotherapy, or what is meant by meditation. Studies involving different medita-tion techniques measuring different dependent variables are contrasted with one another.

This article attempts to build on Smith's review by placing the clinical research literature within the same general framework as Woolfolk's[21] article. Particular attention is paid to descriptions of the independent variables (therapist contact, length of training, description of techniques), method of subject selection, description of the dependent variable (the clinical problem), method of data collection and nature of data collected (physiological, behavioral, subjective, overt concurrent), the type of fol-low up, and the quality of control procedures. (This infor-mation is summarized in detail in five tables available from the first author on request: stress and tension management, fears and phobias [Table 1], the addictions [Table 2], hypertension [Table 3], subjective and other changes during and following meditation [Table 4], studies on attention and perception [Table 5].)

The first part of the article reviews studies in which meditation is viewed as a self-regulatory strategy for clinical problems: treatment of the addictions–alcohol, cigarettes, drugs; hypertension; stress and tension management; and the reduction of fears and phobias. The second part of the article reviews studies in which meditation is viewed as a technique for inducing "altered states of consciousness," including studies showing subjective and other changes during and following meditation. Because of space limitations, these first two sections do not attempt to review in detail the outcome data (see tables available from first author). Rather, they attempt to review, in broad perspective, trends from the different clinical areas and to point out, where appropriate, methodological concerns. The final section of the article provides guidelines and suggestions for future research.

MEDITATION AS A SELF-REGULATION TECHNIQUE
Addiction and Drug Use

There have been seven studies evaluating meditation's effectiveness in treating various types of addictions and drug use.[26-31] The research design of these studies falls into two categories: retrospective sampling and longitudinal design. In general, these seven studies indicate that meditation may be a promising preventive and/or rehabilitative strategy in decreasing the use of addictive substances. It is hard to make more definitive claims at this point because of a number of methodological problems. For example, the retrospective questionnaires in the first group of studies[26-28,42] are subject to a number of criticisms. Subjects were asked to recall daily drug use patterns as far back as two years. There are three possible problems with this type of questionnaire: (1) subject's report on a paper and pencil questionnaire may be inadvertently inaccurate (ie, we may not be aware of how we in fact act); (2) subject's memory of two years ago may be faulty;[27] and (3) subjects may try to deceive the experimenters to gain experimenter approval (eg, demand characteristics). With regard to demand characteristics, the most experienced meditators noted that they had "strong positive feelings about the experience of meditation."[32] This positive feeling about meditation, coupled with the instructions in the TM initiation that drug use adversely affects TM performance, may have contributed to an exaggeration on the retrospective questionnaire about the decrease in drug use and the magnitude of prior drug use patterns. As Shafii et al[12] noted, meditators retrospectively reported using twice as much marijuana prior to their TM initiation as non-meditators. A second problem with the retrospective questionnaires is one of sample bias.[11] In the above studies, the questionnaire was only given to long term meditators. The TM initiates who stopped meditating (30% of the original sample) were not considered.[12] Therefore, there may have been a subject selection bias in that the surveyed group had a commitment to meditation. Finally, the earliest two studies[26,27] had no control group. Shafii et al's later studies on marijuana[12] and alcohol abuse[28] added a control group (TM meditators provided their own matched control). However, the control group does not effectively control for possible variance of treatment due to subject's motivation and/or expectations.

Because of the methodological problems inherent in retrospective sampling, the three most recent drug studies have employed longitudinal designs.[29-31] In these studies, self-report of drug use was obtained on a daily, ongoing basis. Although there is still the possibility of deception in two of the studies,[30,31] there is minimization of the possibilities of inadvertent inaccurate reporting and of memory lapses. The most effective means of data gathering thus far have combined drug use information from self-report with concurrent validity on the self-report through random urinalysis checks.[29] Thus, these longitudinal within subject[29] and group designs[30,31] are improvements on previous studies. However, they are not definitive because of methodological problems of their own, including self-report without concurrent validity[30,31]; combination treatments[29]; and lack of control for demand characteristics, expectation effects, and subject's motivation.[29-31]

Further, the studies often suffer from a lack of clear theoretical rationale between the independent and the dependent variable. For example, Brautigam[31] divided the dependent variable into two groupings: light drugs (hashish) and heavy drugs (LSD, amphetamines, opiates). This lumping of LSD, amphetamines, and opiates together as "heavy drugs" clouds several issues. First, amphetamines and LSD do not produce physical addiction, whereas opiates do. Second, possible reasons for using LSD and amphetamines—eg, self-knowledge, creativeness, spiritual enlightenment, expansion of consciousness,[14] could be quite different from the reasons for opiate use, such as social pressure, rebellion against authority, primary reinforcement, escape from social and emotional problems, relief of withdrawal symptoms.[29] As Brautigam's report now stands, it is impossible to tell who stopped taking which "heavy drugs" for what reasons.

Hypertension

There are seven studies that have involved the use of meditation in reducing blood pressure.[35-42] Certainly, from a research standpoint, blood pressure is one of the "cleanest" dependent variables to measure. These studies consistently indicate a reduction in blood pressure in the treatment group,[35-42] a reduction in the use of hypertensive medication,[38,42] and a reduction in reports of somatic symptoms.[42] Follow-up data have shown that treatment gains were maintained during a 12-month period.[38]

Although the treatment effect seems relatively clear, there are still several unanswered questions as to what is causing that effect. The treatment interventions have ranged from a combination of yoga breathing, concentration, and muscle relaxation,[42] the "relaxation response" technique,[35-38] a combination of yoga, breath meditation, muscle relaxation, concentration, and biofeedback,[39] to a Buddhist meditation procedure.[41] Future research should attempt to isolate the variance of treatment success due to different aspects of the intervention. For a more detailed discussion of possible variables influencing treatment outcome, readers are referred to an excellent review of the literature by Jacob and associates.[43]

Fears, Phobias, Stress and Tension Management

There have been 13 studies concerned with the reduction of fears and phobias and stress and tension management.[10,44-56] These studies suggest that meditation may be a promising clinical intervention technique for stress-related dependent variables. All studies reported successful outcomes on dependent variables ranging from fear of enclosed places, examinations, elevators, being alone[45] to "generalized anxiety,"[46] anxiety neurosis,[47] pain due to bullet wounds, back pain[57] and fear of heart attack,[57] rehabilitation after myocardial infarct,[55] and bronchial asthma.[56] Of the 13 studies, four have involved within subject design[45,47,57] and all four involved a combination of meditation and other techniques; sometimes meditation came first[47]; sometimes second[45]; sometimes concurrently.[46] These four reports gathered data using subjective measures (patient verbal self-report). Girodo[47] also used an anxiety system questionnaire and Shapiro[46] had the patient monitor daily feelings of anxiety using a wrist counter.

The study by Vahia et al,[48] the first to use control groups, reported a consistent and greater reduction in anxiety for the treatment group. The control groups consisted of a "pseudo treatment" with superficial postures and breathing exercises. Data were gathered from patient notebooks, from Taylor's Manifest Anxiety Scale, and from relatives, friends, and colleagues.

Other studies, using control group designs, have also reported a consistent reduction in anxiety for the meditating treatment group. The data has been gathered primarily by pre-test and post-test questionnaires, including the Speigelberg trait/state anxiety scale,[50,51,58,59] the IPAT anxiety questionnaire[30,59] and the Bendig anxiety scale,[52] and the Test Anxiety Scale for Children.[53] Other data measuring anxiety-related behaviors include heart rate and phasic skin conductance (meditators recover more quickly after viewing a stressful film)[51] and insomnia (meditators showed substantial improvement on variables of sleep onset and rated difficulty of falling asleep).[54]

Possible Mechanisms Mediating Therapeutic Effects

The above studies suggest that meditation may be a promising therapeutic intervention strategy for several different clinical areas. One hypothesis that attempts to explain meditation's effectiveness in these clinical areas is that meditation helps relax an individual. There seems general agreement that meditation does, in fact, produce a state of relaxation.[25,60] This type of relaxation produced by meditation has variously been described as an activity (effortless breathing)[61]; a "state" (the hypometabolic state)[62]; and a response (the relaxation response).[60] During the act of meditation itself, certain physiological changes have been rather consistently reported: reduced heart rate,[61-70] decreased oxygen consumption,[62,63,65-67,71-75] decreased blood pressure,[62,63,67,70] increased skin resistance,[62,63,65,67,70,76,77] and increased regularity and amplitude of alpha activity.[62,63,68-70,72,75,76,78-81] It has been hypothesized that these physiological changes during meditation produce a "hypometabolic state,"[62] a state of relaxation.

However, there are still many methodological problems and unanswered questions that need to be addressed. For example, is meditation responsible for, or a manifestation of, this hypometabolic state? Are the physiological changes attributable to the act of meditation; or, as Smith suggests, are the changes attributable to "just sitting" or to the expectation effects of the subject or the therapist?[50,82-85]

Hjelle's study[52] attempted to control for expectation effects, but did not take into account the fact that a certain percentage of the meditators dropped out, and thus does not control for commitment (as evidenced by long term practice). Other research also raises the question of whether the relaxation effect among transcendental meditators may not be due to falling asleep during meditation.[86,87]

A second hypothesis that attempts to explain meditation's effectiveness in reduction of fears and phobias was proposed by Goleman[6] in a seminal article in 1971. Goleman described meditation as a type of global desensitization: first, an individual learns to achieve a relaxed state; and then, as new thoughts arise, the individual learns to witness the random flow of thoughts from this relaxed state, thereby reciprocally inhibiting the anxiety normally elicited by those thoughts. Although plausible, there are many questions that this hypothesis leaves unanswered. For example, there is some question as to whether reciprocal inhibition offers the most parsimonious explanation for systematic desensitization.[88-91] Yulie et al[88] and Wilkins[89] suggest that perhaps the important variables are attention shifts and cognitive refocusing.[90] Further, there is no research that yet supports the hypothesis that the "global desensitization hierarchy is inherently self-regulating" and "optimal salience is guaranteed."[6] In fact, clinical experience suggests that the original assumptions of Goleman,[6] Otis,[44] Shapiro and Zifferblatt[61] regarding meditation as global desensitization may be too simplistic. An individual may not attain a state of sufficient relaxation to deal with unpleasant experiences that arise during meditation. For example, French and co-workers,[72] Carrington and Ephron,[10] Kanellakos and Lukas[22] described complaints from transcendental meditators who felt themselves overwhelmed by negative and unpleasant thoughts during meditation. In addition, Otis[44] noted that transcendental meditators who dropped out had more negative self-images before beginning the practice than those who didn't drop out. It may be that the meditators who dropped out did so because the unpleasant images that arose during meditation were too unpleasant to deal with. Further, anecdotal accounts of meditators suggest that the thoughts during meditation, rather than being the most important in their life, are often trivial and irrelevant. Based on this latter assumption, Yalom et al[41] even used meditators as a control group in a clinical study testing the impact of a weekend group experience on individual therapy. Therefore, in order to more substantially document this second hypothesis, future research would have to determine whether the meditator's thoughts are (1) self-paced so that they are never more overwhelming than the individual can deal with; and (2) are necessarily concerned with the most important variables in the individual's life.

MEDITATION AS AN ALTERED STATE

Davidson[24] has suggested the term "mystical states" for those experiences that occur during meditation and involve an alteration in consciousness. Stace,[94] after reviewing the literature, described certain qualities associated with this state: such as "deeply felt positive mood"; "unity" or "union"; "a oneness with all things"; "sense of ineffability"; "enhanced sense of reality"; "alteration of time and space." Davidson[24] points out that these mystical experiences are unique, and not common to most meditative experiences.

Altered state, as we are using the term in this study, needs to be seen along a continuum. On one end of the continuum are "full blown" mystical and spiritual experiences (eg, nirvana, satori, kensho, samadhi) at the other end of the continuum are profound, intense, but more common alterations of perception.[93] This section looks at research literature dealing with issues related to meditation and altered states: (1) subjective experiences during meditation, (2) attempts to obtain concurrent validity of these experiences, (3) subjective reports of changes in attitude and perceptions after meditation, and (4) non-self-reported changes in attitudes and perceptions after meditation.

Subjective Experiences During Meditation

Two studies have focused primarily on the subjective experiences during meditation[96,97] and two studies have focused tangentially on these experiences.[98,99] These studies are valuable primarily from a heuristic standpoint, as they attempt to precisely describe the subjects' phenomenological perceptions during breath meditation[96,99] and external focusing meditation.[97] Because of the private, internal nature of the meditative experience, all data were based on self-report information. Maupin's[96] study showed that strong subjective feelings could be evoked in ordinary subjects after only two weeks of Zen breath meditation. These subjects' meditative experiences were rated on a five-point scale by blind judges. Based on their self-report data, six of the 28 subjects were rated as high experiencers. A high experiencer was one who reported at least one type five experience (concentration and detachment). Ten subjects were rated as having "moderate responses" to meditation: ie, no type five experience, but at least one type three or type four experience (pleasant body sensations or vivid breathing). Twelve subjects were rated "low response" because they reported nothing more than relaxation (stage two) or dizziness (stage one).[96] Deikman's[97] study using the concentrative technique of focusing on a blue vase, also found strong subjective changes in ordinary subjects' phenomenological perceptions. (It should be noted that in Zen meditation, these hallucinations and perceptual changes, called makyo, are considered diabolical enticements. The meditator is instructed not to become attached to them, but rather to note them, then to let them go, and continue to focus on breathing.) Every subject noted an alteration in perception of the vase: a shift to a deeper and more intense blue; "brighter, more vivid"; "luminous"; further, subjects noted an instability in the shape of the vase: eg, a felt change in size or shape, a loss of the third dimension, a diffusion or loss of perceptual boundaries. One subject noted feelings of merging with the vase, as though "it were almost part of me." Another subject noted complete loss of body feelings.[54]

Concurrent Validity for Subjective Experience During Meditation

Because of the subjective nature of the meditative experience, it is difficult to obtain concurrent validity on subjects' self-report. Maupin[96] attempted to correlate attention measures (digit span, continuous additions, size estimation) with response to meditation. However, Van Nuys[100] has suggested that these measures were not relevant to the type of attention involved in meditation (Galin[101]). Van Nuys notes that alterations in consciousness occur when attention is relatively fixed and sustained, whereas the tests Maupin used involved tasks that take a constant and rapid shifting of the focus of attention; furthermore, "they invite discursive, analytic thought that is actively restricted in meditation."[101]

Van Nuys[102] developed a simple technique for studying attention during the latter stages of meditation. He had his subjects push a button to report intrusion of "off-task" thoughts that distracted them from the task of meditation. He found that the reports of these intrusions correlated with hypnotizability. Other promising methods of obtaining concurrent validity may be the use of signal detection format employed in the daydreaming studies of Singer[103] to obtain reports of occurrence of "task irrelevant thoughts," and the hemispheric laterality literature, to determine brain wave shifts within and between hemispheres during meditation.[24,101]

Subjective Reports of Changes in Attitudes and Perceptions After Meditation

The studies reported above have tested short-term, mostly in-state effects of meditation. Other researchers have tried to document perceptual and/or behavioral changes that occur at times other than during meditation. These studies, which look at self-concept and perceived behavior change, have gathered data primarily by use of paper and pencil tests, including Shostrom's Personality Orientation Inventory[52,104,105]; the Northridge Developmental Scale[106]; Otis Descriptive Personality List and Otis Physical and Behavioral Inventory.[44] All of these studies report that meditators change more than control groups in the direction of positive mental health, positive personality change, and "self-actualization." (Studies that used self-report data, but that focused primarily on anxiety, are not included here because they have already been discussed in a previous section.) These changes include such things as self-perceived increase in capacity for intimate contact, increased spontaneity, increased self-regard, increased acceptance of aggression, and increased inner directedness.

There are, however, several methodological problems with the above studies. First, none of the studies, except Hjelle's,[52] control for expectations and demand characteristics; and Hjelle's study, as already noted, does not control for commitment (long term practice). The commitment, or motivation of the subjects may be quite important. For example, it appears that five of the original 20 subjects in the experimental condition in Seeman, Nidich, and Banta's[104] study dropped out, a fact that could have biased the experiment in a direction favoring meditation. A second methodological problem of the above studies is that they do not show whether the meditation subjects demonstrated any other behavior change, aside from answering questions on the paper and pencil tests.

In an attempt to learn more about daily changes in

behavior, Shapiro,[107] in addition to pre-tests and post-tests, had subjects self-monitor on a daily basis nine variables (eg, feelings of anger; seeing beauty in nature; positive self-thoughts; negative self-thoughts; feelings of anxiety; feelings of creativity). The experimental group (informal and formal Zen meditation) reported daily data that were significantly more in a favorable direction (ie, less feelings of anxiety, more feelings of creativity, etc). This longitudinal study was useful because it provided daily self-report of feelings rather than simply before and after paper and pencil test data of global feeling change. However, it is unclear from the study which parts of the treatment intervention were responsible for what percentage of the variance of the successful outcome. Further, no concurrent covarying overt variables were involved in the study, which still leaves us with the problems of self-reported data.

Non-self-reported Indices of Attitude and Perceptual Change After Meditation

Several studies have looked at behavioral indices of attitude and perceptual change.[58,103,108-112] Some studies[53,108,111] have noted that meditators seemed to have better auditory receptivity and perceptual discrimination than controls, as well as improved reaction times and increased capacity to attend. Linden[53] and Pelletier,[108] using the Witkin Embedded Figures Test, found differences between meditators and non-meditators in field dependence and independence. The above studies provide useful information about the relationship between meditation and perceptual changes. Two studies that attempt to measure clinically the effects of perceptual changes were done by Lesh[110] and Leung.[111]

Lesh[110] found that counselors who had practiced Zen meditation for one-half hour per day for one month had substantially increased accurate empathy, while those in two control groups did not change. Accurate empathy was measured by an "affective sensitivity" videotape showing a client telling about his/her problem. Subjects were to formulate what they thought the client's problem was. Lesh hypothesized that meditation helped the counselors by giving them an openness to their own inner experience. The counselor, by knowing what he/she was feeling, was less likely to project those feelings and judgments onto what the client was saying.

In one of the few studies to compare the efficacy of different meditation techniques, Leung[111] taught counselors a deep breathing (internal focus) technique and an external concentration technique. He randomly assigned subjects to treatment groups that reversed the order of teaching the techniques. Outcome criteria were accurate empathy on a task similar to the one used by Lesh, and also having the subjects count the number of "notice authority" statements made by client-actors on a simulated client situation videotape. Regardless of the order in which the techniques were taught, both groups showed more accurate empathy and heard more notice authority statements than controls.

Guidelines for Future Research

Meditation, if it is to be considered an empirically effective clinical strategy, needs to be subjected to the same scientific scrutiny as any other psychotherapeutic strategy. Further, it should be apparent from the methodological issues raised in our review, that many of the research concerns with meditation are similar to those encountered in psychotherapeutic outcome studies. This section attempts to suggest ways of tightening future research in order to ensure more clinically reliable and valid results.

One of the primary weaknesses in meditation studies thus far has been the lack of a clear theoretical rationale between the independent variable and the selection of the dependent variable. Future research should attempt to clarify precisely the theoretical rationale between the independent and dependent variables. This relationship should be the foundation of a proposed research design, not an afterthought; and it should make future researchers decide whether they are conceptualizing meditation as a self-regulation strategy, or as an altered state of consciousness.

Further, careful consideration should be given to the nature of the independent variable. It is crucial that experimenters report accurately all procedures used. In this way meditation techniques are described behaviorally, and may be compared for clinical efficacy with other cognitive focusing, relaxation, and self-regulatory strategies. (As Woolfolk[21] has noted, meditation is normally associated with a philosophical-religious framework and has certain social-cultural variables [eg, peer pressure] accompanying it. Therefore, even if the techniques are accurately described, it is difficult, if not impossible to precisely account for the treatment variance due to these religious and sociocultural variables.) Second, experimenter contact should be more precisely described as part of the treatment. This description should include both length and frequency of contact, and, if possible, the actual monitoring of positive verbal and non-verbal statements the experimenter makes to the client. This monitoring of differential reinforcement of client behavior may give experimenters a method of operationalizing one aspect of the concept of demand characteristics. These authors would suggest that demand characteristics are an important part of any therapeutic treatment strategy in a clinical or educational setting. Therefore, rather than have no demand characteristics (eg, use a tape recorder or some mechanical means of training), we would suggest that these demand characteristics be explicitly stated and maximized for clinical success. Third, experimenters should try to standardize expectation effects. Although the media and cultural milieu cannot be controlled, standard written introductory expectations could be read to all groups participating in the experiment.[100,113] In this way, there can be a systematic effort to take into account subjects' expectations as part of the treatment variable.[21] (In certain studies,[47,50] as well as in the introductory and preparatory lectures of TM, this expectation effect is maximized by explicitly stating the benefits of the treatments.) In addition, other nonspecific effects, such as (a) being in a structured treatment/training framework, or (b) the need to reorganize and replan one's life in order to find the time to practice meditation two times a day may also be factors in therapeutic efficacy of the techniques.[100]

When the technique involves practice at home, the experimenter should make a concerted effort to determine how much the subjects have in fact practiced. This "practice effect" should be reported as part of the intervention.

Fourth, it may be important to evaluate the quality of the meditative experience. For example, how do we know that the subjects have meditated rather than just sat? How do we know which subjects have learned to focus attention most effectively? (Vahia et al[45,46] for example, noted that psychoneurotic patients with psychosomatic disorders showed significantly more improvement depending on their differential ability to concentrate.) Possible methods for concurrent validity of the meditative experience are suggested by the perceptual studies,[100] by physiological criteria[20,24,36] and/or rater coding of subjective responses.[96,99]

Fifth, it may be important to look at the length of treatment. This would include both time per day (eg, Is there a maximum amount of time per day that is optimal? Can one practice too much?[42]) and the relationship between length of experience and effectiveness.[27,28,44] Recent studies, for example, suggest that the effectiveness of meditation as a treatment depends on both steady and prolonged practice of the technique.[10,44]

In summary, future research should begin to pinpoint answers to the following questions about the independent variable: what are the inert and what are the active variables of the treatment strategy (eg, attention focusing, muscular relaxation, just sitting with eyes closed); what is the role of demand characteristics; what are the effects of subject's motivation, expectation; therapist's expectation; the structured "non-specific" variables of the research design itself. In so far as we can begin to precisely specify the above aspects of the independent variable, appropriate research designs may be undertaken, and answers to the variance of treatment success attributable to various aspects of the independent variable may be determined.

It should be emphasized, however, that from a clinical standpoint, the above questions are of a second order importance. Questions of the first order importance include the following: for which clinical populations, under what conditions, for what clinical problem, is the treatment effective?

In order to answer these questions, a few additional comments about subject selection, data gathering and research design are in order. Although standard scientific procedures do not need to be reiterated here, some caveats particular to meditation research may be useful. Regarding subject selection, in addition to subject motivation, expectations, and commitment (ie, history of prior meditation), it is important to obtain detailed information about subject's prior clinical history. For example, Girodo[47] in his study of anxiety neurosis, found that yoga treatment was effective only for those with a short prior history (average 14.2 months), and that those with a longer history of illness (average 44.2 months) achieved successful remission of symptoms only with the addition of imaginal flooding.[47] Prior length and severity of illness may also be important in determining the effectiveness of meditation with related problems such as hypertension, insomnia, and asthma.

Subject's prior clinical history may also be important as a means of screening patients to determine their appropriateness for learning meditation. For example, patients who are psychotic, who have strong paranoid systems, or who have a poor sense of reality testing may not be appropriate subjects. Further, people experiencing acute anxiety and trauma may be overwhelmed with the emotionally charged material that might present itself during meditation.[10] (To deal with any "overwhelming" emotional reactions that may develop in their patients, Glueck and Stroebel[117] had experienced teachers check the patient's meditation process on a daily basis during the first three weeks. They note, as did French et al,[52] that overt psychotic episodes may be precipitated in individuals with psychiatric disorders who meditate more than the prescribed 20 minutes twice a day.)

Future research should also investigate differences between subjects who enter meditation, and those who don't[10,118] as well as differences between those who continue meditation and those who quit.

Regarding data gathering strategies, future research should attempt to corroborate self-report data with other overt behavior or physiological measure. This should involve the issue of how do self-report measures on global paper and pencil tests translate into actual behavior in the patient's life. Clinically oriented studies also need to determine whether statistical significance on a pre-post test (eg, of anxiety) is of clinical significance to the patient.[119]

Type of Research Design

When meditation is conceptualized as a self-regulation strategy for anxiety reduction, stress and tension management, reduction of fears and phobias, certain research methodologies are necessary. To support its effectiveness as a treatment of choice, control group designs involving other self-regulatory strategies need to be employed.[8,9,10] These control group designs should address questions of if, how, and to what extent does the state of relaxation during meditation generalize to non-meditating times; is meditation as effective as other self-regulation techniques, such as progressive relaxation, in the management of stress and tension; or as effective as systematic desensitization in the reduction of fears and phobias. Additional studies may then be necessary to determine relative variance of the different components of meditation: eg, the use of the mantra[30]; the role of expectations[30,42]; as well as to determine other aspects of meditation that may account for clinical change following meditation (eg, muscular relaxation, just sitting, reciprocal inhibition, cognitive refocusing, interruption of threat-arousal-threat spiral).

When meditation is conceptualized as an altered state of consciousness, a different research methodology may be necessary. As Tart[120] has pointed out, there is a need for detailed mapping of internal states of consciousness. However, since these internal states are subjective phenomena, the subject also needs to be the experimenter. This raises several methodological problems, including experimenter bias and reactive effects of observation.[120] For mapping the subjective experiences of altered states, well-documented intensive research designs seem necessary.[121-132] This is especially true until we have more accurate knowledge about the dependent variables associated with altered states. In addition, we need to continue to search for physiological correlates of these "altered states," such as the promising literature on hemispheric laterality.[24-36]

Finally, in researching states of consciousness, it is important to determine whether consciousness is an independent or dependent variable: that is, is a researcher interested in looking at how meditation techniques produce different states of consciousness (dependent variable) or how altered states of consciousness (independent variable) affects subsequent self-referential attitudes and/or behavior.

COMMENTS ON THE PHILOSOPHY OF SCIENCE

The above discussion on research design suggests an interesting observation: that the philosophy of science necessitates a two-step process. The first step involves forming intuitive hypotheses based on past data, anecdotal reports, and subjective experiences. This is most clearly seen with the early clinical studies and with the research on subjective experiences during meditation. These studies are almost exclusively case studies involving within subject designs. These case studies cause us to rethink our models, and pose questions that cannot be answered with existing paradigms.[112] They help us gain specific information about the independent variable, about possible dependent variables, about data gathering strategies and possible methodological problems.[121-132]

The second step in the process involves control group designs to determine treatment variance within the independent variable (eg, expectation effects, nonspecific variables, demand characteristics, etc). Although we believe strongly in the importance of control procedures, we also believe that there are limitations to control group designs in which clinical inferences are based only on statistical significance of group averages as measured by pre-tests and post-tests. Further, even when control group designs are necessary for pinpointing variance of treatment success, it is important to point out that we can only take this posture because case studies and the testing of intuitive hypotheses were previously undertaken. One cannot have a tight, well-controlled research design without a clear dependent variable. The connection between the independent and dependent variable, however, is part of the simultaneous process of theory testing and theory building, and does not spring forth without some prior hypothesis testing.

We may now be at a point in meditation research where, when meditation is conceptualized as a self-regulation strategy, control group designs are useful and even necessary. However, when meditation is conceptualized as an altered state of consciousness, a different methodology may be required. The dependent variables are not as clear, are more delicate, and more difficult to ferret out. Therefore, there may still be a need to use a well-documented intensive design approach to gain specific information about the dependent variables, data gathering strategies, and possible methodological problems.

Future researchers need to clarify which dependent variables are being investigated and then determine appropriate methodologies. Both types of methodologies—intensive design and control group designs—can represent scientific injury at its best. Both can complement each other and add to our knowledge so that science truly serves the promotion of human welfare.

CONCLUSION

We have reviewed several dependent variables in this study, ranging from clinically oriented rehabilitative studies (the addictions, stress and tension management, fears and phobias, hypertension, insomnia) to self-reported personality change (creativity, heightened consciousness, "self-actualization").

This article has pointed out several methodological weaknesses with past studies and suggested guidelines for future meditation research. These suggestions include the need for precise descriptions of the independent variable; controlling for expectation effects and subject motivation (and where clinically appropriate, demand characteristics); care in subject selection; specification of dependent variable; a rationale between the dependent and independent variable; data gathering strategies that provide precise information and, where possible, concurrent validity; follow-up data; and finally, research designs appropriate to the dependent variable investigated.

On the one hand, meditation may be conceptualized as a self-regulation strategy. When thus conceptualized, it needs to be compared in control group designs with other self-regulation strategies to determine the treatment of choice for the clinical problems such as stress and tension, the addictions, and hypertension. On the other hand, meditation may be conceptualized as an altered state of consciousness. When thus conceptualized, it may be necessary, at this state of our knowledge, to use within subject designs in order to further obtain precise information to detail "maps of consciousness."

Because of the excitement and aura of mystery currently surrounding the technique of meditation, there is a tendency to let enthusiasm replace methodology. However, we believe that by taking into account the above methodological concerns, it is possible to design clinically oriented research studies that provide relevant information about the efficacy of different types of meditation strategies, for specific types of populations, with specific concerns. It is this type of research that can truly be of use to fellow researchers, clinicians, and ultimately to the patients themselves.

Julian Davidson, Miles Vich, Robert Kantor, Roger Walsh, Johanna Shapiro, and the psychiatric residents participating in Dr Shapiro's seminar, "Psychotherapy and Self-Control: An East-West Approach" provided comments and suggestions in the preparation of this manuscript.

References

1. Kondo A: Zen in psychotherapy: The virtue of sitting. *Chicago Rev* 12:57-64, 1958.
2. Kretschmer W: Meditative techniques in psychotherapy. *Psychologia* 5:76-83, 1962.
3. Malhotra JC: Yoga and psychiatry: A review. *J Neuropsychiatry* 4:375-385, 1963.
4. Candelent T, Candelent G: Teaching transcendental meditation in a psychiatric setting. *Hosp Community Psychiatry* 26(3):156-159, 1975.
5. Shafii M: Adaptive and therapeutic aspects of meditation. *Int J Psychoanal Psychother* 2:(3)364-382, 1973.

6. Goleman D: Meditation as metatherapy: Hypothesis toward a proposed fifth state of consciousness. *J Trspl Psychol* 3:1-25, 1971.

7. Hirai T: *Zen Meditation Therapy.* Tokyo, Japan Publications, 1975.

8. Bloomfield H, Cain MP, Jaffe D, et al: *TM. Discovering Inner Energy and Overcoming Stress,* New York, Dell Publishing Co, 1975.

9. Deathridge G: The clinical use of "mindfulness" meditation techniques in short-term psychotherapy. *J Trspl Psych* 2:133-144, 1975.

10. Carrington P, Ephron HS: Meditation as an adjunct to psychotherapy, in Arieti S, Chrzanowski G (eds): *New Dimensions in Psychiatry: A World View,* New York, John Wiley & Sons Inc, 1975.

11. Keefe T: Meditation and the psychotherapist. *Am J Orthopsychiatry* 45:3, 484-489 (April 1975).

12. Shafii, M: Silence in service of the ego: Psychoanalytic study of meditation. *Int J Psychoanal Psychother* 54:441-443, 1973.

13. Neki J: Guru-chela: The possibility of a therapeutic paradigm. *Am J Orthopsychiatry* 43:5, 1973.

14. Schechter H: The Transcendental Meditation program in the classroom: A psychological evaluation, in Orme-Johnson D, Domash L, Farrow J (eds): *Scientific Research on the Transcendental Meditation Program, Collected Papers.* Geneva, MIU Press, 1975.

15. Rubottom AE: Transcendental meditation and its potential uses in schools. *Soc Ed* 36(4):851-857, 1972.

16. Peerbolte M: Meditation for school children. *Main Currents Mod Thought* 24:19-21, 1967.

17. Timmons B, Kamiya J: The psychology and physiology of meditation and related phenomena: A bibliography. *J Trspl Psych* 2(1):41-59, 1970.

18. Timmons B, Kanellakos D: The psychology and physiology of meditation and related phenomena: Bibliography II. *J Trspl Psych* 6(1):32-38, 1974.

19. Lesh TV: Zen and psychotherapy: A partially annotated bibliography. *J Hum Psych* 10:75-83, 1970.

20. Griffith F: Meditation research; its personal and social implications, in White J (ed): *Frontiers of Consciousness.* New York, The Julian Press Inc, 1974, pp 119-138.

21. Emerson V: Research on meditation, in White J (ed): *What Is Meditation?* New York, Anchor Books, 1974, pp 225-244.

22. Kanellakos D, Lukas J: *The Psychobiology of Transcendental Meditation: A Literature Review.* Menlo Park, Calif, WA Benjamin Inc, 1974.

23. Woolfolk RL: Psychophysiological correlates of meditation. *Arch Gen Psychiatry* 32:1326-1333, 1975.

24. Davidson JM: The physiology of meditation and mystical states of consciousness. *Perspect Biol Med* 19:345-380, 1976.

25. Smith J: Meditation as psychotherapy: A review of the literature. *Psychol Bull* 82(4):558-564, 1975.

26. Benson H: Yoga for drug abuse. *N Engl J Med* 281(10):1133, 1969.

27. Benson H, Wallace RK: Decreased drug abuse with Transcendental Meditation: A study of 1,862 subjects, in Zarafonetis CTD (ed): *Proceedings of the International Symposium on Drug Abuse.* Philadelphia, Lea & Febiger Publishers, 1972, pp 369-376.

28. Shafii M, Lavely R, Jaffe R: Meditation and the prevention of alcohol abuse. *Am J Psychiatry* 132(9):942-945, 1975.

29. Shapiro DH, Zifferblatt SM: An applied clinical combination of Zen meditation and behavioral self control strategies: Reducing methadone dosage in drug abuse. *Behav Ther,* to be published.

30. Lazar Z: The effects of the Transcendental Meditation program on anxiety drug abuse, cigarette smoking and alcoholic consumption, in Orme-Johnson D, Domash L, Farrow J (eds): *Scientific Research on the Transcendental Meditation Program, Collected Papers.* Geneva, MIU Press, 1975, vol 1.

31. Brautigam E: The effect of transcendental meditation on drug abusers. Research Report, City Hospital of Malmo, Sweden, 1971.

32. Shafii M, Lavely R, Jaffe R: Meditation and marijuana. *Am J Psychiatry* 131(1):60-63, 1974.

33. Marcus J: Transcendental meditation: Consciousness expansion as a rehabilitation technique. *J Psychedelic Drugs* 7:2, 1975.

34. Cohen Y: Inside what's happening: Sociological, psychological, and spiritual perspectives on the contemporary drug scene. *Am J Pub Health* 59:2092-2097, 1969.

35. Benson H, Wallace RK: Decreased blood pressure in hypertensive subjects who practiced meditation. *Circulation* 46(4):131, 1972.

36. Benson H, Rosner BA, Marzetta BR, et al: Decreased blood pressure in borderline hypertensive subjects who practiced meditation. *J Chron Dis* 17:163-169, 1974.

37. Benson H, Rosner BA, Marzetta BR, et al: Decreased blood pressure in pharmacologically treated hypertensive patients who regularly elicited the relaxation response. *Lancet* 1:289-291, 1974.

38. Patel CH: Yoga and biofeedback in the management of hypertension. *Lancet* 2:1053-1055, 1973.

39. Patel CH: Twelve-month followup of yoga and biofeedback in the management of hypertension. *Lancet* 2:62-64, 1975.

40. Patel CH: Randomized controlled trial of yoga and biofeedback in management of hypertension. *Lancet* 2:93-95, 1975.

41. Stone RA, DeLeo J: Psychotherapeutic control of hypertension. *N Engl J Med* 295:80-84, 1976.

42. Datey KK, Deshmukh SN, Dalvi CP, et al: "Shavasan": a yogic exercise in the management of hypertension. *Angiology* 20:325-333, 1969.

43. Jacob RG, Kraemer HC, Agras WS: Relaxation therapy in the treatment of hypertension: A Review. *Arch Gen Psychiatry* 34:1417-1427, 1977.

44. Otis LS: If well-integrated but anxious, try TM. *Psych Today* 7(11):45-46, 1974.

45. Boudreau L: TM and yoga as reciprocal inhibitors. *J Behav Ther Exp Psychiatry* 3:97-98, 1972.

46. Shapiro DH: Zen meditation and behavioral self-management applied to a case of generalized anxiety. *Psychologia* 9(3):134-138, 1976.

47. Girodo M: Yoga meditation and flooding in the treatment of anxiety neurosis. *J Behav Ther Exp Psychiatry* 5:157-160, 1974.

48. Vahia NS, Doongaji DR, Jeste DV, et al: Psychophysiologic therapy based on the concepts of Patanjal. *Am J Psychother* 27:557-565, 1972.

49. Vahia NS, Doongaji DR, Jeste DV, et al: Further explorations with the therapy based upon concepts of Patanjali in the treatment of psychiatric disorders. *Indian J Psychiatry* 15:32-37, 1973.

50. Smith JC: The psychotherapeutic effects of transcendental meditation with controls for expectation of relief and daily sitting. *J Consult Clin Psychol* 44:456-467, 1976.

51. Goleman D, Schwartz GE: Meditation as an intervention in stress reactivity. *J Clin Consult Psychol* 44(3):456-466, 1976.

52. Hjelle LA: Transcendental meditation and psychological health. *Percept Mot Skills* 39:623-638, 1974.

53. Linden W: The relation between the practice of meditation by schoolchildren and their levels of field dependence–independence, test anxiety, and reading achievement. *J Consult Clin Psychol* 41(1):139-143, 1973.

54. Woolfolk R, Carr-Kaffashan L, McNulty TF: Meditation training as a treatment for insomnia. *Behav Ther* 7(3):359-366, 1976.

55. Tulpule TH: Yogic exercises in the management of ischaemic heart disease. *Indian Heart J* 23(4):259-264, 1971.

56. Honsberger R: The effect of transcendental meditation upon bronchial asthma. *Clin Res* 21:368, 1973.

57. French AP, Tupin JP: Therapeutic application of a simple relaxation method. *Am J Psychother* 28:282-287, 1974.

58. Davidson R, Goleman D, Schwartz GE: Attentional and affective concomitants of meditation. *J Abnorm Psychol* 85:235-238, 1976.

59. Ferguson P, Gowan J: TM: Some preliminary findings. *J Hum Psych* 16(3):51-59, 1977.

60. Benson H, Beary JF, Carol MP: The relaxation response. *Psychiatry* 37:37-46, 1974.

61. Shapiro DH, Zifferblatt SM: Zen meditation and behavioral self-control: Similarities, differences, and clinical applications. *Am Psychol* 31(7):519-532, July 1976.

62. Wallace RK, Benson H, Wilson AF: A wakeful hypometabolic physiologic state. *Am J Physiol* 221(3):795-799, 1971.

63. Wallace RK: Physiological effects of transcendental meditation. *Science* 167:1751-1754, 1970.

64. Anand BK, Chhina GS: Investigations on Yogis claiming to stop their heart beats. *Indian J Med Res* 49:90-94, 1961.

65. Wegner MA, Bagchi BK: Studies of autonomic functions in practitioners of yoga in India. *Behav Sci* 6:312-323, 1961.

66. Goyeche JRM, Chihara T, Shimizu H: Two concentration methods: A preliminary comparison. *Psychologia* 15:110-111, 1972.

67. Karambelkar PV, Vinekar SL, Bhole MV: Studies on human subjects staying in an airtight pit. *Indian J Med Res* 56:1281-1288, 1968.

68. Anand BK, Chhina GS, Singh B: Some aspects of electroencephalographic studies in Yogis. *Electroencephalogr Clin Neurophysiol* 13:452-456, 1961.

69. Das NN, Gastaut H: Variations de l'activite electrique du cerveau, du coeur au cours de la meditation et de l'extase Yogique. *Electroencephalogr Clin Neurophysiol* 6(suppl):211-219, 1955.

70. Bagchi BK, Wenger MA: Electrophysiological correlates of some Yogi exercises. *Electroencephalogr Clin Neurophysiol* 7(suppl):132-149, 1957.

71. Sugi Y, Akutsu K: Studies on respiration and energy metabolism during sitting in Zazen. *Res J Physiol El* 12:190-206, 1968.

72. Watanabe T, Shapiro D, Schwartz GE: Meditation as an anoxic state: A critical review and theory. *Psychophysiol* 9:279, 1972.

73. Allison J: Respiratory changes during transcendental meditation. *Lancet* 7651:832-834, 1970.

74. Treichel M, Clinch N, Cran M: The metabolic effects of trancendental meditation. *Physiologist* 16:471, 1973.

75. Hirai T: *The Psychophysiology of Zen.* Tokyo, Igaku Shoin Ltd, 1974.

76. Akishige Y (ed): *Psychological Studies on Zen.* Tokyo, Zen Institute Komazawa Univ, 1970.

77. Orme-Johnson DW: Autonomic stability and transcendental meditation. *Psychosom Med* 35(4):341-349, 1973.

78. Kasamatsu A, Hirai T: An electron encephalographic study on Zen meditation (Zazen). *Folia Psychiatr Neurol Jpn* 20:315-336, 1966.

79. Banquet JP: EEG and meditation. *Electroencephalogr Clin Neurophysiol* 33:454, 1972.

80. Banquet JP: Spectral analysis of the EEG in meditation. *Electroen-*

B. Meditation as a Clinical Self-Regulation Strategy

In this section we are going to look at studies in which meditation is viewed as a potential clinically useful self-regulation strategy for stress and stress disorders (B1, Articles 7 and 8) for addictive behaviors (B2, Articles 9 and 10), and for hypertension (B3, Articles 11 and 12). In addition we will examine the way meditation has been conceptualized and the research supporting its utility for general psychotherapeutic applications both for the client (B4, Articles 13 and 14) and for the therapist (B4, Articles 15 and 16). Finally, we will look at literature bearing on additional general effects with normal subjects including both adverse effects and benefits (B5, Articles 17 and 18).

When meditation is conceptualized as a clinical self-regulation strategy for stress, the addictions, and hypertension, it seems that clinical and research investigators are primarily conceptualizing and using it as a type of relaxation response. What we find is that when meditation is so conceptualized, it appears to be effective as a clinical self-regulation strategy. The studies included in this section are primarily useful in illustrating the promise of meditation in its self-regulation capacity. As noted in article 1, it is then necessary to look at possible methods of refining the independent variable, and becoming more specific about for which subject population and which clinical problem it is most effective (see Part IV). Thus, articles in this section are useful primarily to point out the general effectiveness of a broadly conceived independent variable, "meditation" on certain broadly conceived, clinically relevant dependent variables.

B1. Meditation and Stress Management

For a general review of the literature on meditation and stress management, the reader is referred to the appropriate sections in the Chapter by Shapiro and Giber (Article 6) as well as the table which is included summarizing the literature on meditation and its effectiveness in the treatment of stress, phobias, and fears.

The two articles included in this subsection, by Goleman and Schwartz (7) and Linden (8) are clear, well-designed studies which show the effects of meditation for stress reduction. In the Goleman and Schwartz study, the authors found that meditators exhibited greater autonomic responses in anticipation of the stressful scene during a film, but recovered quicker. This finding is consistent with the work on autonomic stability and meditators (see Article 30 by Orme-Johnson). Linden's study suggests that, even with children in the third grade, changes in test anxiety can occur with a relatively short 5 week intervention.

It should be noted that both of these studies were performed with normal subjects and are included here as examples of studies which show that meditation is an effective strategy in reducing stress in normal subjects. Generalizing to a clinical population seems plausible, but there are some considerations which need to be made (see Article 13 by Vahia *et al.,* and Article 14 by Glueck and Stroebel). For example, with a clinical population there should be additional checking to ensure that meditation is practiced correctly, an assessment of appropriate attentional skills, and assurance that the possible anxiety-arousing stimuli that might be accessed during meditation are not too overwhelming for the individual.

All of the articles point out the potential promise of meditation as a stress management strategy. Whether it is more effective than other self-control strategies, or equally effective with all types of stress, or with all types of subject population is not clear.

Additional developments which elaborate and refine the aforementioned expectations are presented elsewhere in this volume: (1) see Part III, Article 27 by Davidson and by Orme-Johnson (Article 30) for possible explanations of the physiological effects of meditation; (2) Article 52 by Walrath and Hamilton and by Morse *et al.* (Article 53) which suggest that meditation may not be the only way to attain physiological relaxation, or any more effective than other self-regulation strategies for gross physiological parameters; (3) Article 47 by Schwartz *et al.* which refines stress into both cognitive and somatic dimensions and suggests that meditation may be more effective with cognitive than with somatic stress; (4) Article 46 by Beiman *et al.* for client characteristics that may be relevant in determining effectiveness; (5) Article 42 by Smith for some of the component analyses which may contribute to the variance of treatment success.

Table 1. Studies on Fears and Phobias, Stress, and Tension Management

| | | | INDEPENDENT VARIABLE | | DEPENDENT VARIABLE | | | | | |
Investigator(s)	Clinical Problem	S's (N, age, sex, prior experience)	Type and Length of Treatment/Training	Frequency of Therapist (E) Contact	Subjective Effects	Behavioral	Physiological	Overt, Concurrent (e.g. medical)	Follow-up	Type of Design, Quality of Control, Methodological Problems
Boudreau 1972	Case One: fear of enclosed places, examinations, elevators, being alone. Duration of problem 5 years.	N=1, 18 yrs. male, not stated specifically "adept at TM"	Systematic desensitization and massed desens. first (3 days x 3 hrs.), then since no improvement Transcendental Mediation (one month) TM practiced both non-contingently, and contingent upon imagining phobic scenes.	Sys. dens. and massed desens. done with tape recorder	Self-reported tension decrease	Avoidance behavior had disappeared.	None	None	None	N=1 case report, an in-vivo assessment pre and post of fears would have been useful.
	Case Two: excessive perspiration. Duration of problem 35 years.	N=1, 40 yrs. female, took summer course in Yoga	Intervention #1: Relaxation practice w/paired anxiety/arousing imagery (6 months) provided partial symptom alleviation. Intervention #2: Yoga practice (3 mos. x ½ hr. daily) plus additional practice during tense moments.	Not stated	Not reported	None	None	Daily Perspiration: mild/excessive. Intervention #1: mild perspiration decreased from 12 hrs. to 5 hrs. on average; excessive from 3 to 1 hr. Intervention #2: excessive disappeared, mild is below 1 hr. per day.	6 months: perspiration maintained at below 1 hr. daily	N=1 case report, relative effects of relaxation and Yoga not clear. Operationalizing of mild and excessive perspiration good and follow-up admirable.
French and Tupin 1974	Case One: esophagitis. Duration of problem: 20 years.	N=1, 65 yrs. male, not stated	3 phases: (1) slowed breathing and (2) muscle relaxation followed by (3) focusing on pleasant images. (In this case for 10-15 min.)	Not stated	Self-reported decrease in pain and relief of sleep disturbance	None	None	None	Patient reported successful use of method for 6 months	N=1, within subj. case report, pre and post ratings of pain severity and sleep disturbance would have been useful.
	Case Two: severe pain due to bullet wounds, anxiety and depression during 3 mos. hospitalization, poor eating, weight loss.	N=1, 22 yrs. male, not stated	Same method as above (in this case, used for 30 min. according to patient self report)	Not stated	Self-report of improved ability to manage pain and sleep, also improvement in general mood and eating.	None	None	None	None	Same as above
	Case Three: widely disseminated oatcell carcinoma of the lung, sleep disturbance, pain, relief through narcotic use.	N=1, 53 yrs. male, not stated	Same method as above	Not stated	Found focusing technique "frightening and distressing," used only muscle relaxation. if pain controlled by relaxation, patient could sleep without use of hypnotic.	None	None	None	None	Same as above
	Case Four: referred for psychiatric sucs. panic, neurotic fear of heart attack, used 120 mg. diazepam per day, severe sleep disturbance.	N=1, 50 yrs. male, not stated	Same method as above	Not stated	Used method to monitor heart beat and control fear of heart attack. however, fear resumed after other patient's died of myocardial infarction. patient returned to use of technique 10 min./daily for "relaxing," no soporific effect.	None	None	None	None	Pre and post ratings of fear would have been useful.
	Case Five: hospitalized for chronic back pain.	N=1, 45 yrs. male, failed at hypnotic induction	Same method as above	Not stated	Method unsuccessful in inducing relaxation, subsequent surgery revealed herniated disc at L4-5.	None	None	None	None	Case report.
Vahia, et al 1972-1973	Psychoneurosis and psychosomatic disorders that failed to respond to conventional treatment.	Stage One: N=165 Stage Two: N=37 Stage Three: treatment: N=21, controls: N=18, age range for all S's 15-50 yrs. experience not stated	Nine year study Stage One: psychophysiologic therapy based on concepts of Patanjali (yoga). (1) postures, (2) breathing exercises, (3) withdrawal from senses, (4) concentration on object, (5) identification with object) practiced one hr. 6 days/week for 6 weeks Stage Two: treatment compared with controls receives similar pseudotreatment with "superficial" postures, breathing exercises, and no interpretation or insight for steps 3-5 practiced one hr. each weekday for 4-6 weeks.	Not stated	Stage One: clinical assessment at 3 and 6 weeks for target relief symptom (final) 70% of patients rated for anxiety depression, hysteria and bronchial asthma showed improvement. Stage Two patients self-reported improvement. Taylor's Anxiety Rating Scale given pretreatment, and at 3 and 6 weeks showed greater and consistent anxiety reduction for treatment group. MMPI and	Self-reported increase in work efficiency on the job and objective global improvement reported by patient's as friends, spouse, other relations, and colleagues.	None	Bronchial asthma assessed	None	Double blind used: stage two groups matched for age, sex, diagnosis and duration of illness. Same therapist used for total treatment and pseudotreatment introducing possible experimenter effect (Smith, 1975).

		INDEPENDENT VARIABLE			DEPENDENT VARIABLE					Type of Design, Quality of Control, Methodological Problems
Investigator(s)	Clinical Problem	S's (N: age: sex, prior experience)	Type and Length of Treatment/Training	Frequency of Therapist (E) Contact	Subjective Effects	Behavioral	Physiological	Overt, Concurrent (e.g. medical)	Follow-up	
(Vahia et al. 1972-1973 continued)			both groups given placebo tablets, support and reassurance. Stage Three: treatment compared with controls using anxiolytic and antidepressant drugs (e.g. Amitriptyline and chlordiazepoxide).			Rorschach tests given pre and post-treatment. 73% of S's in total therapy showed improvement of at least 50% on basis of clinical assessment, while 42% of S's in "pseudo-treatment" showed significant improvement. MMPI showed greater overall improvement for total therapy group. Those who showed greater ability to meditate to total therapy group displayed more clinical improvement than those who did not. Stage Three: pre-treatment, 3 and 6 week assessment with Taylor's Anxiety Rating Scale, Hamilton's Depression Rating Scale, and Bell's Social Adjustment Scale. treatments equally effective on depression rating; psycho-physiologic therapy showed greater reduction than drug therapy on anxiety scale, and psychophysiologic therapy patients showed reduction on social adjustment scale.				
Girodo 1974	Patients diagnosed as "anxious," "neurotic," length of illness: 5-71 months.	N=9, 7 male, 2 female, ages 18-42 years, not stated	"TM like" meditation on mantric sound used 20 min., twice per day used for all patients; combined with imaginal flooding procedure and relaxation for 4 patients who failed to show anxiety decrement after 8 sessions with meditation alone (total length of treatment: 6-8 months)	Patients seen every 7-14 days	Anxiety-symptom question-naire (administered every 2 weeks) showed reduction in anxiety symptomatology by 8th session of meditation. 4 patients found meditation unbeneficial, but experienced relief of symptoms with flooding. Note: later analysis showed difference in group successful with meditation treatment (mean group dura-tion of symptoms—14.2 months and mean "cognitive" symptom severity of 9.5) and group successful with flooding (mean group duration of symptoms—44.2 months and mean "cognitive" symptom severity of 16.4)	None	Degrees of somatic symptoms reported in questionnaire	None	6 month mailed follow-up questionnaire	Patients as own controls, patients told to expect "calm relaxation", etc. from technique introducing expectation effect, no control group.
Shapiro 1976	Complaining of "free-floating anxiety".	N=1 female college stu-dent, no prior experience	(1) 2 weeks: monitoring of anxiety with counter. (2) weekend Zen workshop teaching anxiety contingent Zen breath meditation plus covert self modeling (3) 3 weeks with instructions to meditate 10 min., 2x per day, to continue anxiety monitoring and practice informal breath meditation when anxious	Therapist (E) did not contact patient during 3 week meditation period.	Significant decrease in feel-ings of anxiety during inter-vention phase (3 weeks) and positive self perception change on semantic differential	Wrist counter used as anxiety monitor	None	None	None	N=1 design, relative effect of formal vs. informal medi-tation in relief of anxiety not clear. also possible reactive effect from initial self monitoring.
Smith 1976	Anxiety (Isolating effect of TM from expectation of relief and daily sitting.)	Exp. 1: N=139, college students, mean age 22 yrs., 70 male, 69 female, no prior meditation experience	Exp. 1: 1) Pretreatment: Elaborate placebo procedure with con-trol treatment. Rationale given. Assessment included STAI A-Trait Inventory, Epstein-Fenz Manifest Anxiety Scale, and other supplementary measures including test of skin conductance reactivity. 2) Random assignment of S's to: 1) Standar/ TM training (N=49) 2) Control treatment called (PSI) "Periodic Somatic Inactivity" (sitting, eyes closed) (N=51) 3) No treatment - (waiting list) (N=39)	Exp. 1: Placebo treatment matched with TM procedure for similar amount of therapist contact and treatment credibility.	Subjective Exp. 1: TM and PSI groups did not differ significantly on post-test STAI-A Trait Scale (trait anxiety) scores; symptoms of striated muscle tension and autonomic arousal (Epstein-Fenz Manifest anxiety scale). Both TM and PSI post-test means significantly lower than No Treatment on all dep. var.	None	None	None	Exp. 1: No treatment S's post-tested at 3.5 mos.; TM and PSI S's post-tested at 6 mos. including assessment on drug use. and subjective reponses to treatment.	Useful study is beginning to isolate aspects of treatment variance.
		Exp. 2: N=54, college students, mean age 21.5 yrs. 27 male, 27 female.	Exp. 2 1) No treatment controls. Exp. 1 (N=24) and others (N=30) given similar pretreatment assessment (cf. Exp. 1) placebo procedure 2) Random assignt. of S's to: 1) TM-like meditation called "Cortically Mediated Stabilization" 2) "Anti-meditation" exercise involving sitting with eyes closed, actively generating pos. thoughts	Exp. 2: Both treatments taught in similar fashion by experimenter with elaborate treatment rationales given.	Exp. 2: Groups did not differ significantly on dep. var. measures. T-test of within group differences reveal signifi-cant impact. on STAI-A Trait and symptoms of autonomic arousal for both groups.				Exp. 2: Same post-tests (Exp. 1) given at 11 weeks	

Table 1. Studies on Fears and Phobias, Stress, and Tension Management (cont'd.)

Investigator(s)	Clinical Problem	DEPENDENT VARIABLE — S's (N, age, sex, prior experience)	Type and Length of Treatment/Training	Frequency of Therapist (E) Contact	INDEPENDENT VARIABLE — Subjective Effects	Behavioral	Physiological	Overt, Concurrent (e.g. medical)	Follow-up	Type of Design, Quality of Control, Methodological Problems
Goleman and Schwartz 1976	Ability to reduce stress in lab situation in response to stressful film.	Group One: N=30, avg. age approx. 25 yrs. more than 2 years TM experience. Group Two: N=30, avg. age approx. 23 yrs. non-meditators interested in TM or Yoga. Note: Difference in "life-style" found meditators reported reduced usage of licit and illicit drugs, alcohol, cigarettes and coffee, and dietary changes (e.g. less meat and candy).	Experimental Procedure – Note: S's assigned serially to 1 of 3 experimental conditions 1) 4 min. baseline 2) 20 min. treatment – 3 conditions a) Meditation: eyes closed (not using mantra) b) Relaxation, eyes open c) Relaxation, eyes closed 3) 5 min. rest 4) 12 min. exposure to stressful film	None	Pre and post treatment testing on State-Trait Anxiety Inventory A State Form (Spielberger, 1970) showed meditators reported less state and trait anxiety before and after treatment Affective Adjective Checklist (Zuckerman, 1960) showed meditators reported feeling more positive upon entering lab and throughout treatment. Activity Preference questionnaire (Lykken & Katzenmeer, 1960) administered post treatment found S's in meditation condition were less anxiety prone after leaving lab though no between group differences. Post treatment testing on Eysenck Personality Inventory showed meditators significantly less neurotic and more stable than non-meditators.	None	Meditators' heart rate less than controls during treatment, increase heart rate more in response to anticipation of stress or impact, then recover more quickly post impact. On phasic skin conductance–all groups decrease equally in response frequency during treatment; meditators increase more in anticipatory minute prior to stressor impact and decrease more during post impact minute. Meditators compared to controls had higher skin conductance freq peaks and lower troughs.	None	None	Treatment conditions randomized and controlled; eyes open/closed factor. "Life-style" differences between groups suggest importance of other factors besides meditation in stress response.
Linden 1973	Test anxiety, field independence, and reading ability.	N=15 male and 15 female randomly assigned to each treatment condition. S's drawn from upper half (in reading ability) of third grade classes of school in disadvantaged urban areas.	Group One: Taught Zen breath meditation (Maupin, 1965) and visual fixation task (Dekeman, 1963), practiced 2x per week x 13 weeks for 20-25 min. Group Two: Given guidance counseling focusing on improving study skills; met 45 min. per week for 18 weeks in 3 groups of 10 S's. Controls: Controlled for by guidance condition	None	Pre and Post Treatment Test Results. Meditating group showed gain in field independence (Children's Embedded Figures Test) and decrease in test anxiety (Test Anxiety Scale for Children over controls. There was no effect on reading achievement.	None	None	None	Follow-up to be reported.	Well designed study, between groups design.
Lazar, Farwell and Farrow 1977	Anxiety	Group A: N=12, 7 male, 5 female, mean age 23.66 yrs. 4 weeks meditation experience. Group B: N=11, 5 male, 6 female, mean age 24.10, prospective meditators.	Standard TM training	Same as above	IPAT anxiety scale questionnaire administered pre and post–after 2 weeks) meditation instruction found mean group average reduction from 80th to 66th pop. percentile (Group B). Mean postest score of Group A (50th percentile) was significantly lower than pretest score of Group B and insignificantly different from their postest score	None	None	None	None reported	Employed recurrent Institutional Design (Campbell & Stanley, 1963).
Woolfolk et al. 1976	Chronic insomnia	N=24, mean age approx. 44.3 yrs. 6 male, 18 female. Avg. duration of trouble with insomnia – 14.1 yrs.	All S's suspended sleep medication Group One: N=8. Taught meditation technique involving immobility, closed eyes and a passive focus on breathing. Breathing focus shifted (session 2) to mantra and then. to focus on a specific image (session 3) Group Two: N=8. Taught in 4 weekly 1 hr. sessions in groups S's instructed to practice 30 min. /2x daily at home. Group Three: Waiting list controls, asked to keep records of sleep patterns for 4 more weeks with promise of treatment at end of experiment	4 wks. x 1 hr treatment	S's retrospective rating reflect "belief in treatment effectiveness" of treatments revealed no significant differences in treatment groups. College students asked to rate credibility of treatment procedures and rationale on same scale showed no significant differences between treatments.	Behavioral Treatments reported on– (1) Latency of Sleep Onset: Means (in minutes) Meditation 74.08 Progressive Relaxation 65.01 Control 67.21 Treatments equally effective. Both meditation and Progressive Relaxation groups showed significant improvement over pretreatment, while pretreatment and follow-up means for control group did not differ. (2) Rated Difficulty of Falling Asleep (10 – extremely difficult) Meditation 5.92 Progressive Relaxation 6.35 Control 5.38	Pretest Post-test Follow-up / 34.19 24.51 / 29.20 26.73 / 66.61 — / Pretest Post-test Follow-up / 2.91 2.94 / 3.48 3.28 / 5.79 —	None	6 month in form of 1 week of daily sleep records.	Techniques called "self-control" skills protecting against meditation placebo effect. Excellent study
Tupule et al. 1971	Ischemic Heart disease Group One: all but 2 patients with history of myocardial infarct. Period from infarction to time of study ranged from 1 to 10 yrs. avg 3.9 yrs. no relief from antianginal drugs. Group Two: all except 1 belonged to a sedentary occupation.	Group One: N=23, avg. age=48.5 yrs, male, "all of high economic class with sedentary habits except 1 farmer." Group Two: N=21, avg. age=32.4 yrs., 19 male, 2 female, "all except 1 belonged to a sedentary occupation.	11 Hatha Yogic positions (asana) practiced until patient was symptom free (e.g. stable heart rate, and blood pressure, and absence of complications of E.C.G.) Positions practiced daily	Not stated specifically	Group One: Patients who performed exercises regularly expressed "feeling of physical well-being" and ability to work without fatigue. Group Two: Similar subjective feelings reported. Ambulation achieved during 2nd week in 10 cases and 3rd week in 10 cases. Rehabilitation effected during 5th week in 8 cases and before 9th week in others	None	Physiological Group Two: 150 observations made before & after exercise on heart rate, B.P. & respiration Behavioral Group One: Report states: "Patients unable to return to their full occupation, ever, after a year from infarct. could be rehabilitated after about a month of starting these exercises.	None	One month to 7 years	Patients in group one had been treated by one of experimenters in past; measure of "well-being" not reported; no controls; no statistical data reported.
Honsberger and Wilson 1973	Bronchial asthma	N=22 no prior experience with TM	Treatment Group (N=11) Practiced Transcendental Meditation for 3 months Control Group (N=11) read related material daily x 3 months	Not reported	74% of patients reported "self has benefitted their asthma. 69% thought TM had helped their emotional life. None reported worsening on these parameters	None Reported	Pulmonary function data obtained at baseline, 3, 6 months. GSR showed 79% of patients effectively meditated 55% of patients better with TM 27% of patients had improved airway resistance after TM in comparison to control values	None	At 6 months 80% of patients still meditating only 60% thought it was helping their asthma.	Parameters of "general health" and emotional assistance from TM vague

Journal of Consulting and Clinical Psychology
1976, Vol. 44, No. 3, 456–466

7

MEDITATION AS AN INTERVENTION IN STRESS REACTIVITY

Daniel J. Goleman and Gary E. Schwartz

Although records and phenomenologic accounts of meditation date back to the Vedic period of India, only in very recent years have there been empirical studies of meditation. The changes in psychophysiological state accompanying passive forms of meditation (see Davidson & Schwartz, in press) constitute a configuration opposite to that of a hyperarousal reaction to stress (Gellhorn & Kiely, 1972; Wallace & Benson, 1972). The implications of meditation as an "antidote" for stress reactions (Goleman, 1971) have been tested inferentially in terms of habituation rate (Orme-Johnson, 1973), but thus far there has been no direct assessment of the interaction of the effects of meditation in a stress situation using complex emotional stimuli. This study sought to determine the efficacy of meditation as an intervention in stress, using a laboratory film as stressor in an analogue of emotional arousal to complex stimuli (Lazarus, 1966), in a design systematically varying both experience as a meditator and meditation itself with appropriate control treatments.

From early studies of Indian yogis (Anand, Chhinna, & Singh, 1961; Wenger & Bagchi, 1961) and Zen monks (Kasamatsu & Hirai, 1966) to more recent studies of meditators in America (Banquet, 1973; Wallace, Benson, & Wilson, 1971), a consistent pattern of characteristic state concomitants of passive meditation practices has emerged. Major dependable autonomic trends include slowing of breath and heart rate, decrease in oxygen consumption, lowering or stabilization of blood pressure, decrease in skin conductance, and fewer spontaneous skin conductance responses—a pattern of responses suggesting generalized sympathetic inhibition. Electroencephalogram recording during meditation tends toward a steady decrease in initial beta level and an increase in alpha and then theta as the session progresses, but the progression halts short of sleep, has a pattern of response to external stimuli more like that of waking, and is seldom accompanied by drowsiness. This pattern of response is opposite to Cannon's "fight or flight" defense-alarm syndrome arousal.

Meditation may have clinical application in stress-related disorders or it may alleviate the adverse effects of normal daily stress, depending on the resiliency of demonstrated state effects. The significance of meditation as a stress intervention appropriate for daily life might prove major if these meditation state effects carry over and transform the meditator in a more permanent way, becoming traits. Initial evidence supports this possibility: Meditators as a group have been found to be less anxious (Ferguson & Gowan, in press; Linden, 1973; Nidich, Seeman, & Dreskin, 1973) and more self-actualizing (Seeman, Nidich, & Banta, 1972). The relationship of meditation to stress has been tested inferentially in terms of habituation of skin conductance responses to tones, and meditators have been found to habituate more quickly, implying a more rapid recovery from stress-related arousal (Orme-Johnson, 1973).

Stoyva and Budzynski (1973) suggested that with sufficient training the beneficial effects of a low-arousal state in a stressful situation can become habitual, with hyperreactivity to stress being supplanted by a new pattern marked by a lessening of sympathetic arousal in the face of threat. Meditation shares with certain relaxation procedures the induction of a generalized low arousal pattern of responses characterized by sympathetic inhibition, which may prove to inhibit the autonomic activation seen in the stress response. In view of the demonstrated efficacy of relaxation techniques in lessening a stress reaction, and in line with the observed state effects of meditation, the present study was designed to determine whether meditation might be an effective procedure for reducing reactivity to a stressor.

The meditation technique employed was transcendental meditation, though the results are seen as generalizable to other passive meditation techniques (Davidson & Schwartz, in press) that meet our proposed definition for "meditation": the systematic and continued focusing of the attention on a single target percept—for example, a mantra or sound—or persistently holding a specific attentional set toward all percepts or mental contents as they spontaneously arise in the field of awareness. Meditation as defined here is different from popular usages that denote contemplation or rumination, as in thinking about a conceptual theme. Meditation per se is the self-regulation of attention, not of belief or other cognitive processes.

The design of this study is based on the stress research of Lazarus (1966) and his colleagues, who have provided content-specific reorientations of cognitive set toward a stressor film as effective means for coping with threat. In the present study meditation—an attentional manipulation—was interposed between an initial threat cue and the stressor confrontation in order to alleviate stress reactivity. The predictions were that (a) subjects in a meditation condition would display less autonomic arousal and experience less subjective anxiety in response to a film stressor than would subjects in a relaxation condition and (b) experienced meditators compared with controls would have autonomic response patterns and personality traits more consistent with the expected meditation state effects.

Method

Subjects

Sixty subjects were recruited from among two groups: 30 meditators with more than 2 years' experience with transcendental meditation and 30 nonmeditators who were interested in meditation or yoga but practiced neither. Meditators' average age was 25 years, nonmeditators, 23 years; ages ranged from 18 to 31. All subjects were paid for participation. The two sample groups differed on certain background variables in a manner consistent with patterns found in a study of meditator lifestyles (Schwartz, Note 1); significantly reduced usage of licit and illicit drugs, alcohol, cigarettes, and coffee, and dietary changes such as eating less meat and candy.

Apparatus

The experimental chamber was a sound-attenuated room containing a comfortable chair for the subject facing a videomonitor 4 feet (1.2 m) away, equipment for attaching electrodes, and an intercom system over which instructions were given. The recording equipment was located in an adjacent room.

Skin conductance was monitored via Beckman silver-silver-chloride cup electrodes placed approximately 1½ inches (3.8 cm) apart, on the palm of the left hand. Surface oils were removed from the skin by swabbing electrode sites with acetone, and Beckman electrode paste was used as the electrolyte. The signal was directed through a skin conductance coupler (designed by Lykken & Venables, 1971), to a preamplifier and then to two channels of a Grass Model 7 polygraph. One channel provided an alternating current measure of fluctuations in conductance; the time constant of a direct current preamplifier was set at .8, and the sensitivity was set at .2 μ V/cm, displaying skin conductance responses. Heart rate was recorded using metal plate electrocardiogram (EKG) electrodes with Sanborn Redux paste as the electrolyte. The electrodes were placed on the left and right upper arms; the raw EKG signal was transmitted through an alternating current preamplifier and displayed on a polygraph channel.

Experimental Procedure

Subjects were run individually and were assigned serially to one of three experimental conditions. As each subject came to the laboratory, he was asked to sign a consent form warning of the nature of the stressor film he was to see and the nature of the measurements to be made. The consent form constituted an initial threat cue (Lazarus, 1966). The subject also filled out the State-Trait Anxiety Inventory A-State form (Spielberger, Gorsuch, & Lushene, 1970). After each subject was conducted to the experimental chamber and seated facing the videomonitor he filled out the Affect Adjective Check List (Zuckerman, 1960) in the "Now" form. The experimental procedure was then explained to him, and electrodes were attached. The experiment was divided into four periods, throughout which autonomic activity was monitored continuously: 4 minutes of baseline, 20 minutes of treatment (with a warning after Minute 18 that treatment would end in 2 minutes), a 5-minute posttreatment rest ending with a warning that a film would begin in 1 minute, and a 12-minute film. After electrodes were detached postfilm, subjects filled out the Affect Adjective Check List for feelings during the treatment and during the accidents portrayed in the film, the Activity Preference Questionnaire (Lykken & Katzenmeyer, 1960), the State-Trait Anxiety Inventory A-State and A-Trait scales, and the Eysenck Personality Inventory (Eysenck & Eysenck (1968). Specifics of the experimental periods are as follows.

Baseline

Baseline began shortly after the experimenter left the experimental room, having affixed electrodes to the subject and explained the procedure. The subject then was instructed via intercom simply to sit quietly and relax while looking at the blank videoscreen. This period allowed the subject to become accustomed to the experimental setting and provided a baseline of autonomic activity.

Treatment

After baseline, the subject was given the instructional set for one of three treatment conditions. Subjects within each sample group (meditators and controls) were assigned in serial order to one of three random conditions: meditation, relaxation with eyes open, and relaxation with eyes closed. Subjects in the meditation condition were asked to do transcendental meditation if they were from the experienced meditator group, and the controls were instructed in a simple meditation technique modeled on transcendental meditation. Subjects in the eyes-open condition were told to continue to keep their eyes on the screen without actively staring at it, sit relatively still, and relax. Subjects in the eyes-closed condition received similar instructions, except that they were told to relax with their eyes closed, letting their thoughts wander but not dozing off. The experienced meditators were told not to use their mantra in this condition. Meditation was with eyes closed, and the two relaxation conditions were designed to control for this factor. All treatments lasted for 18 minutes, at which point there was a warning that treatment would end in 2 minutes, during which those in the eyes-open condition were told to close their eyes in order to control for the transition from closed to open eyes at the end of the other treatments. Verbatim instructions are given in Goleman (1973).

Posttreatment rest

After the 20-minute treatment all subjects were told to open their eyes, keeping them oriented toward the videoscreen, and were reminded that the film would begin in 5 minutes. After 4 minutes, subjects were told that the videoscreen was about to go on and that the film would start in 1 minute. They were reminded that the film would be about woodworking shop accidents and were told to watch it as they would any other movie.

Film

The film was shown on the videomonitor and lasted approximately 12 minutes. The film *It Didn't Have to Happen* has been used as a stressor in many studies of autonomic reactions to stress. Originally designed to impress the need for safety practices on wood-mill workers, the film uses actors in a dramatic scenario depicting three shop accidents, all caused by poor safety habits: the fingers of a worker are lacerated, a finger of another is cut off, and an innocent bystander is killed by a wooden plank driven through his midsection as a result of carelessness by a circle-saw operator. These three episodes are invariably marked by both autonomic reactivity and affective disturbance in most subjects; Lazarus, Opton, Nomikos, and Rankin (1965) reported that for every subject the maximum point of skin conductance level and heart rate always occurred within two 10-sec intervals prior to or following the points of impact in the accident scenes. At the end of the film all subjects were told to continue watching the screen for 2 min.

Results

Within groups, the treatment conditions consistently tended to be ranked similarly to those in the other subject group, both throughout the experimental period and across measures. For this reason only the main effects are reported, by group and by condition, with the exception of the single significant interaction effect.

Autonomic Measures

The experimental periods were divided into 1-min segments for purposes of scoring. All measures were adjusted for each subject on the basis of mean values for the baseline period. Segments of minutes during instructions to subjects were not scored, and the treatment period was scored at intervals selected to pick up major trends. Scoring during the film was oriented around the accidents so that the minute immediately before and the minute following the accident impact would be scored. Using accidents as primary division points meant that some of the remaining time blocks were in unscorable segments of less than 60 sec. Analyses of variance were performed on all measures using Data-Text programs in a repeated-measures design on the dependent variable with treatment condition and sample group as the independent factors (Armor & Couch, 1971).

Phasic Skin Conductance Activity

A skin conductance response was defined as an upward needle deflection corresponding to at least .04 μV in the absence of any known stimulus (other than the stressor film). Skin conductance responses were scored using values from the base of the pen deflection to the maximum amplitude change before the pen return. The sum of all such responses for each minute was taken as the skin conductance response frequency, the basic measure for analysis of phasic activity.

Although there were no significant effects during baseline, there was, as expected, a major trend for all subjects to show a decline in skin conductance response frequency during the treatment period, for time, $F(9, 486) = 3.43$, $p < .001$, leveling off halfway through treatment and rising abruptly with the announcement that treatment would end in 2 minutes.

Analyzing results from midway through treatment until the minute prior to the film the meditation condition had the largest posttreatment skin conductance response frequency increase and stayed at the highest frequency throughout most of the posttreatment, prefilm rest: for the Condition $\times$ Time interaction, $F(22, 594) = 2.39$, $p < .001$. These trends are shown in Figs. 1 and 2.

On the average, during the film all cells tended to have response frequency peaks at the accident impact points and troughs before and after impacts: for time, $F(11, 594) = 32.73$, $p < .001$. Meditators compared to controls had both higher skin conductance response frequency peaks and lower troughs: for the Group $\times$ Time interaction, $F(11, 594) = 3.97$, $p < .001$. Combining values across accidents into a single composite, the meditator group across all accidents showed a greater increase in skin conductance response frequency during the preimpact minute than did controls, for group, $F(1, 54) = 16.32$, $p < .001$, but also showed a greater average decrease during the postimpact minute than did controls, for group, $F(1, 54) = 26.04$, $p < .001$, pointing to a more rapid habituation from stress arousal. Taking the difference between

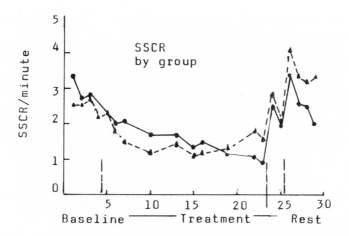

Fig. 1. Skin conductance response frequency during baseline, treatment, and rest by group. Solid triangle, meditator; Solid circle, nonmeditator.

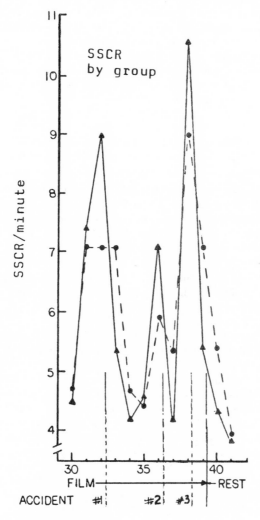

Fig. 2. Skin conductance response frequency during film by group. Symbols as in Fig. 1.

Meditation as an Intervention   **81**

preimpact and postimpact values for all accidents, the meditator group on the average showed a greater decrease than controls, for group, $F(1, 54) = 6.37$, $p < .05$.

Because the meditators had higher skin conductance response frequency on the average than controls during the preimpact minute, the significantly larger decrease during recovery may have been a regression to the mean artifact or due to rebound from an initially higher value. If this difference between anticipatory and postimpact response frequency levels were simply an artifact of the law of initial values, one would predict that there would be no between-group differences in the rate of change. In order to test for an effect due to the law of initial values, 14 subjects from each group were matched with corresponding values from the other group according to anticipatory values and then compared on recovery values. A t test comparing the subjects selected for matching with the remaining subjects in each group showed there to be no significant difference; subjects selected for matching were representative of their respective groups. There was a significant difference between matched groups, with the meditators recovering significantly more than controls from anticipatory arousal levels, $t(13) = 2.73$, $p < .02$. Thus, the larger recovery among meditators from anticipatory arousal, rather than merely being an artifact of higher preimpact response levels, is attributable to characteristics of this group.

Skin conductance response effects during the film for controls meditating for the first time tended to be congruent with patterns seen in meditators as a group, but they were not nearly as strong. During recovery from the first accident impact the meditation condition among control subjects decreased in response frequency, whereas subjects in the eyes-open condition increased and subjects in the eyes-closed condition did not change: for condition, $F(2, 54) = 3.46$, $p < .05$. This recovery pattern did not hold for the second and third accidents.

To summarize, the main results were for all groups to decrease equally in response frequency during treatment and for the meditator group to increase more in the anticipatory minute prior to stressor impact and then decrease even more postimpact. The meditator group's recovery pattern was duplicated by the meditation condition, though less strongly.

Heart Rate

Heart rate was scored as beats per minute and adjusted for values during the first minute of baseline. There was a general trend for all subjects to decelerate in heart rate from the final baseline minute throughout the treatment until the announcement that treatment would end and an increase after this low point until the first posttreatment minute: for time, $F(4, 229) = 6.34$, $p < .001$. Deceleration during treatment was greater for controls than for meditators: for group, $F(1, 54) = 3.35$, $p < .05$.

During the stressor film on the average all subjects increased in heart rate during the minute prior to the accident impacts and decreased during the postimpact minute: for time, $F(4, 229) = 20.74$, $p < .001$. There was a significant group difference in heart rate changes preaccidents and postaccidents; combining values into a composite accident, meditators decelerated from a preimpact mean above the controls to a postimpact level below: for group, $F(1, 54) = 6.326$, $p < .02$.

As with the skin conductance measure, the possibility was tested that the meditators' greater postimpact recovery was an artifact of the law of initial values rather than an intrinsic group difference in response to stress. Ten meditators and 10 controls matched on preimpact heart rate were compared on recovery values; the meditators' recovery was significantly greater than for controls, $t(18) = 4.78$, $p < .001$. As was the case with the parallel skin conductance effect, the meditators' greater recovery from anticipatory arousal is a group characteristic rather than an artifact due to initially higher levels (see Fig. 3).

The only treatment effect for heart rate was an interaction with subject group for postimpact recovery rate (see Fig. 4): Meditators in the meditation condition had the largest recovery decrease, controls in the same condition slightly increased heart rate postimpact, and subjects in the remaining cells had a moderate recovery decrease: for the Group $\times$ Condition interaction, $F(2, 54) = 5.262$, $p < .009$. The recovery magnitude for the meditator/meditation cell was approximately four times that of the meditator/eyes-closed cell, $t(18) = 2.76$, $p < .05$, and of the control/eyes-closed cell, $t(18) = 3.17$, $p < .01$, and in the opposite direction of the control/meditation cell, $t(18) = 4.37$, $p < .001$.

To summarize, the main results were for the meditator group to decrease heart rate less than controls during treatment and, in response to the stressor impact, to increase heart rate more in anticipation and then

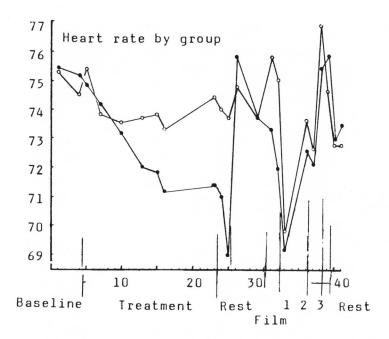

Fig. 3. Heart rate during baseline, treatment, rest and film by group. Symbols as in Fig. 1.

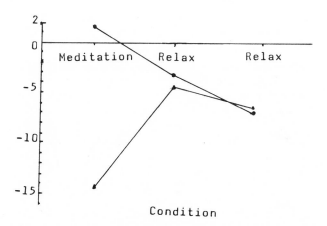

Fig. 4. Change in heart rate during stressor impact recovery by group and by condition. Symbols as in Fig. 1.

recover more strongly postimpact (see Fig. 3.) Stressor recovery was greater for meditators in the meditation condition and least for controls in the same condition.

Personality Variables

Affect Adjective Check List

This state measure of affect showed that as expected meditators as a group reported feeling more positive than nonmeditators on entering the laboratory, even after knowing that they were to see a stressful film: for group, $F(1, 54) = 8.55, p < .01$. These between-group differences tended to weaken during the treatments: for group, $F(1, 54) = 2.87, p < .10$, the meditators being only slightly more positive, since all subjects' mean scores on the average reflected a ceiling effect of a more positive feeling state during treatments. The between-group difference became enhanced once again during the film accidents, with the meditators continuing to report more positive affect: for group, $F(1, 54) = 5.14, p < .05$. Means for all personality measures are displayed in Table 1.

Activity Preference Questionnaire

Even though there were no between-group differences on this measure of anxiety proneness, there was an apparent treatment effect; subjects in the meditation condition were significantly less anxiety prone as indicated by this measure after leaving the laboratory: for condition, $F(1, 54) = 4.54, p < .05$. The mean for the meditation condition was 15.4, in the normal range and well below the 19.0 criterion applied by Dichter (Note 2) to identify "psychopaths" using the identical Activity Preference Questionnaire form among subjects drawn from the same student community.

State—Trait Anxiety Inventory

Another index of anxiety level, this inventory showed meditators compared to controls reporting less state anxiety both before entering the laboratory, for group, $F(1, 54) = 26.15, p < .001$, and after leaving: for group, $F(1, 54) = 34.06, p < .001$. Meditators also were lower on trait anxiety than controls, $F(1, 54) = 39.67, p < .001$: both state and trait findings met expectations.

Table 1. Means for Personality Measures

Measure	By group			By condition			
	Meditators	Controls	p	Meditation	Eyes closed	Eyes open	p
AACL[a]							
Before M	15.0	12.7	.01	13.8	16.9	14.2	ns
Treatment M	14.8	13.7	ns	14.5	14.5	13.7	—
Stressor M	8.1	6.0	.05	7.1	7.5	6.6	ns
APQ[b] M	12.9	14.0	ns	15.4	11.7	13.4	.05
STAI[c]							
Baseline M	27.2	36.4	.001	31.3	32.1	31.3	ns
Poststressor M	25.3	36.0	.001	30.6	30.2	31.4	ns
Trait M	29.2	41.9	.001	37.2	34.1	35.3	ns
EPI							
Neuroticism[d] M	5.3	11.8	.001	9.8	7.7	8.2	ns
Extraversion[e] M	11.4	11.7	ns	12.6	11.1	11.5	ns
Lie[f] M	2.5	1.8	ns	2.3	2.1	2.1	ns

[a]Higher score indicates positive affect.
[b]High score indicates low anxiety.
[c]Lower score indicates less anxiety.
[d]High score indicates neuroticism; low score indicates stability.
[e]High score indicates extraversion; low score indicates introversion.
[f]Score of 5 or above indicates "lie."

The Neuroticism scale showed that meditators compared to controls were significantly less neurotic and more stable, for group, $F(1, 54) = 32.59$, $p < .001$, as expected. There were no significant differences between groups on the Lie scale, for group, $F(1, 54) = 2.12$, $p < .152$, and the overall means were below the "lie" range, signifying that the positive halo effect for the meditators across scales reflects genuine differences rather than the attempt to appear good, as they might alternatively have been interpreted.

Discussion

During the meditation and relaxation treatments, autonomic measures showed lowered levels, reflecting a successful "relaxation response" (Benson, Beary, & Carol, 1974) despite the anticipated stressor. During the stressor film autonomic measures rose, indicating a pattern of autonomic arousal typical of a stress reaction (Lazarus, 1966), peaking in direct response to accident impacts and falling postimpact. Evidence for both trait and state effects of meditation were obtained, though the latter were much stronger than the former.

Meditator Trait Effects

During the treatment period, meditators' heart rates decreased less than that of controls, although both subject groups had similar treatment decreases in phasic skin conductance. The major effect for both heart rate and skin conductance response during the stressor film was, in reaction to each accident, a consistent pattern of greater increase in meditators during the anticipatory preimpact minute, a greater postimpact decrease, and a greater overall decrease from preaccident response frequency rate to that postaccident. On first analysis this pattern would seem to suggest that meditators had greater autonomic stress arousal than nonmeditators; therefore, meditation might have little potential as a means of mitigating the adverse effects of stress. However, this seemingly parsimonious interpretation ignores the complexity of the configuration of autonomic, affective, and personality variables found here, most of which support an alternative interpretation.

The meditator's response pattern can be interpreted in terms of dual components in autonomic response to stress impact, as was seen on the average for all subjects—an *anticipatory* increase in activation and a *recovery* phase decrease, or inhibition, indicating habituation of the anticipatory response—with both components more pronounced for meditators than nonmeditators. Many studies of stress reactivity have used anticipatory arousal as an index of the efficacy of different intervention strategies (e.g., Folkins, 1970: Lazarus et al., 1965). By this single criterion, meditation would seem to have negative potential as a stress intervention. This conclusion does not seem fully justified, however, when one takes into account the paradoxical autonomic patterning of meditators in this stress situation with the anticipatory rise being offset by an even greater postimpact habituation. Importantly, this large recovery effect was not simply an artifact of the law of initial values: It also was significantly greater among a subgroup of meditators than for controls matched for anticipatory arousal. The more rapid skin conductance response decrease during postimpact recovery replicates Orme-Johnson's (1973) finding that meditators habituate more rapidly to tones of differing intensities and extends it to a situation of emotionally complex stimuli. The net effect for meditators appears to be greater recovery from anticipatory arousal, a pattern consistent with their more positive affect and lower situational and trait anxiety levels.

The larger anticipatory arousal among meditators may respresent a defensive reaction that combines both a set to respond and a sensitization to incipient stimuli. Lazarus and Averill (1972) made the point that in a threat situation anxiety, and accompanying physiological arousal, is adaptive insofar as it mobilizes the organism for vigilance in order to facilitate appropriate coping reactions. The anxiety gradient tends to peak in anticipation of the stressor confrontation as the organism makes maximal preparations to defend against the impending threat (Epstein, 1962). This defensive reaction becomes maladaptive, however, when it is maintained after the threat has passed, failing to habituate. The sense in which meditation can be seen from this study as "adaptive" is principally in terms of recovery from stress arousal, not in terms of coping actions while under stress: The experimental situation did not call for any activity in response to the stressor other than a passive defensive reaction. Although anticipatory stress arousal could be interpreted as maladaptive, there is as yet no systematic data on the actual performance of meditators under stress.

Even though other attempts to intervene in stress coping have manipulated cognitions of threat (e.g., Lazarus et al., 1965), an equally significant phase of stress reactivity is recovery. During threat, the orienting response represents an optimal coping strategy, preparing and focusing the organism for accurate perception of both the stimulus complex and whatever situational change may follow (Koepke & Pribram, 1966). However, the maintenance of an orienting response, or more appropriately, a defensive arousal to threat, beyond the time required for coping responses—that is, the failure to habituate—represents a dysfunctional mode. Mackworth (1970), reviewing studies of habituation, suggested that when the set to respond to an event diminishes the organism is free to consider other novel (and potentially dangerous) events.

Habituation of stress-induced physiological, psychological, and behavioral arousal is a direct index of the extent of recovery. Slower autonomic habituation has been found to be associated with anxiety symptoms and poorer prognosis among psychiatric patients (Stern, Surphlis, & Koff, 1965). Martin (1971), in reviewing findings on physiological responses in anxiety, concluded that patients diagnosed as having an "anxiety reaction" or with prominent anxiety symptoms show greater physiological arousal to stress, slower habituation to repeated stresses, and slower recovery from stress. The stress reactivity pattern found here in meditators is in partial contrast to that of chronically anxious individuals, particularly the meditators' rapid stress recovery and lower state and trait anxiety levels.

Meditation State Effects

Treatment effects were not as ample as the between-group findings, but they partially support the predictions made for the meditation condition. The posttreatment increase in skin conductance frequency for the meditation conduction may reflect a rebound from a low to a high activation level; this pattern replicates a postmeditation increase in phasic responses found by Orme-Johnson (1973) in experienced meditators. The electrodermal effects of the meditation condition persisted into the middle of the stressor film: Subjects in this group recovered more rapidly from the first stressor confrontation although this effect disappeared by the third stressor. Stress recovery benefits of meditation for heart rate were strongest for the experienced meditators but negligible for the novices. On the self-report measures, meditation proved more potent than simple relaxation in reducing poststressor anxiety.

Significant effects for the meditation treatment for the most part duplicate the patterns found among meditators. The major exception is heart rate, which failed to recover arousal levels poststressor for controls in the meditation condition. The fractionation of heart rate stressor recovery from electrodermal and affective measures likely reflects functional differences between electrodermal and cardiovascular measures. The difference in heart rate pattern poststressor between experienced meditators and novices also suggests that meditator trait effects are not quickly inculcated, though the electrodermal and affective measures suggest that meditation state effects could in time become traits.

Since the meditator sample in the present study differed in life-style from controls, it is possible that meditator group differences are due to factors other than the practice of meditation. On the other hand, the meditation condition, even among naive subjects meditating for the first time, produced a pattern of autonomic and anxiety-reducing effects largely consistent with those found among experienced meditators. These results tentatively support the contention that cultivation of meditation state effects through daily meditation could account for at least some of the stress-reactivity pattern seen as traits of meditators. An alternative possibility is that the meditator traits were due to a bias in the meditator sample, perhaps due to a self-selection in staying with regular meditation over a long period. However, other studies using longitudinal designs premeditator and postmeditator have found significant changes on anxiety measures in the direction found here for meditators (e.g., Linden, 1973; Ferguson & Gowan, in press) as well as in what are usually considered developmentally invariate perceptual processes (Pelletier, 1974). In order to be more certain that the meditator traits found here are due to meditation per se rather than to other factors such as self-selection in either becoming a meditator or continuing as a meditator for a protracted period, longitudinal studies are indicated to determine if these patterns develop over time. Should meditation prove to be an effective means for inculcating an improved resistance to stress, controlled basic and clinical research would be required to determine the extent and appropriate domain of any possible psychological and medical use of meditation and related relaxation procedures.

Acknowledgments

This study is based on a doctoral dissertation by the first author, directed by the second author. The research was supported in part by a grant to the first author from the Stouffer Fund, and in part by a subcontract to the second author from the Army Research Projects Agency of the Department of Defense and monitored by the Office of Naval Research under Contract N 0014-70-C-0350 to the San Diego State Research University Foundation and by the General Service Foundation.

Reference Notes

1. Schwartz, G. E. *Pros and cons of meditation: Current findings on physiology and anxiety, self-control, drug abuse, and creativity.* Paper presented at the meeting of the American Psychological Association, Montreal, September 1973.
2. Dichter, B. *The relationship between psychopathy and empathy.* Undergraduate honors' thesis, Harvard University, 1972.

References

Anand, B. K., Chhinna, G. S., & Singh, B. Some aspects of EEG studies in yogis. *Electroencephalography and Clinical Neurophysiology,* 1961, *13,* 452–456.

Armor, D. J., & Couch, A. S. *The Data-Text primer.* New York: Free Press, 1971.

Banquet, J. P. Spectral analysis of the EEG in meditation. *Electroencephalography and Clinical Neurophysiology,* 1973, *35,* 143–151.

Benson, H., Beary, J. F., & Carol, M. P. The relaxation response. *Psychiatry,* 1974, *37,* 37–46.

Davidson, R. J., & Schwartz, G. E. The psychobiology of relaxation and related states: A multiprocess theory. In D. Mastofsky (Ed.), *Behavior control and motivation of physiological activity.* New York: Prentice-Hall, in press.

Epstein, S. The measurement of drive and conflict in humans: Theory and experiment. In M. R. Jones (Ed.), *Nebraska Symposium on Motivation* (Vol. 10). Lincoln: University of Nebraska Press, 1962.

Eysenck, H. J., & Eysenck, S. B. G. *Manual for the Eysenck Personality Inventory.* San Diego. Calif.: Educational and Industrial Testing Service, 1968.

Ferguson, P. C., & Gowan. J. Transcendental meditation: Some preliminary findings. *Journal of Humanistic Psychology,* in press.

Folkins, C. H. Temporal factors and the cognitive mediators of stress reactions. *Journal of Personality and Social Psychology,* 1970, *14,* 173–184.

Gellhorn. E., & Kiely, W. F. Mystical states of consciousness: Neurophysiological and clinical aspects. *Journal of Nervous and Mental Disease* 1972, *154,* 399–405.

Goleman, D. Meditation as meta-therapy. *Journal of Transpersonal Psychology,* 1971, *3,* 1–27.

Goleman. D. *Meditation and stress reactivity.* Unpublished doctoral dissertation, Harvard University, 1973.

Karess reactions. *Journal of Personality and Social Psychology,* 1970, *14,* 173–184.

Gellhorn. E., & Kiely, W. F. Mystical states of consciousness: Neurophysiological and clinical aspects. *JGSR as a function of stimulus duration and spontaneous activity. Journal of Comparative and Physiological Psychology,* 1966, *61,* 442–448.

Lazarus, R. S. *Psychological stress and the coping process.* New York: McGraw-Hill, 1966.

Lazarus, R. S., & Averill, J. R. Emotion and cognition: With special reference to anxiety. In C. D. Spielberger (Ed.), *Anxiety: Current trends in theory and research.* New York: Academic Press, 1972.

Lazarus, R., Opton, E. M., Nomikos, M. S., & Rankin, N. O. The principle of short-circuiting of threat: Further evidence. *Journal of Personality,* 1965, *33,* 622–635.

Linden, W. Practicing of meditation by school children and their levels of field independence-dependence, test anxiety, and reading achievement. *Journal of Consulting and Clinical Psychology,* 1973, *41,* 139–143.

Lykken, D. T., & Katzenmeyer, C. *Manual for the Activity Preference Questionnaire.* Minneapolis: University of Minnesota Press, 1960.

Lykken, D. T., & Venables, P. H. Direct measure of skin conductance: A proposal for standardization. *Psychophysiology,* 1971, *8,* 656–672.

Mackworth, J. F. *Vigilance and habituation.* Baltimore: Penguin, 1970.

Martin, B. *Anxiety and neurotic disorders.* New York: Wiley, 1971.

Nidich, S., Seeman, W., & Dreskin, T. Influence of transcendental meditation: A replication. *Journal of Counseling Psychology,* 1973, *20,* 565–566.

Orme-Johnson, D. W. Autonomic stability and transcendental meditation. *Psychosomatic Medicine,* 1973, *35,* 341–349.

Pelletier, K. Influence of transcendental meditation upon autokinetic perception. *Perceptual and Motor Skills,* 1974, *39,* 1031–1034.

Seeman, W., Nidich, S., & Banta, T. A study of the influence of transcendental meditation on a measure of self-actualization. *Journal of Counseling Psychology,* 1972, *19,* 184–187.

Spielberger, C. D., Gorsuch, R. L., & Lushene, R. E. *STAI manual.* Palo Alto, Calif.: Psychosomatic Medicine, 1973, *35,* 341–349.

Pelletier, K. Influence of transcendental meditation upon autokinetic perception. *Perceptual and Motor Skills,* 1974, *39,* 1031–1034.

Seeman, Wtoyva, J., & Budzynski, T. Cultivated low arousal—An anti-stress response? In L. V. DiCara (Ed.), *Recent advances in limbic and autonomic nervous system research.* New York: Plenum, 1973.

Wallace, R. K., & Benson, H. The physiology of meditation. *Scientific American,* 1972, *226,* 84–90.

Wallace, R. K., Benson, H., & Wilson, A. F. A wakeful hypometabolic state. *American Journal of Physiology,* 1971, *221,* 795–799.

Wenger, M., & Bagchi, B. Studies of autonomic function in practitioners of yoga in India. *Behavioral Science,* 1961, *6,* 312–323.

Zuckerman, M. The development of an affect adjective check list for the measurement of anxiety. *Journal of Consulting Psychology,* 1960, *24,* 457–462.

Journal of Consulting and Clinical Psychology
1973, Vol. 41, No. 1, 139–143

8

PRACTICING OF MEDITATION BY SCHOOL CHILDREN AND THEIR LEVELS OF FIELD DEPENDENCE-INDEPENDENCE, TEST ANXIETY, AND READING ACHIEVEMENT*

William Linden[†]

Meditiation may be viewed as essentially a method of training attention. The aim is to suspend the flow of ordinary thought and thereby bring the practitioner more fully "into the present." The training intensifies the individual's alertness to certain environmental sensory data normally masked by automatized cognition (Deikman, 1963). It also heightens awareness of subjective components of experience (Berger, 1962).

Electroencephalogram (EEG) alpha wave production, usually associated with a state of relaxed alertness in ordinary Ss, increases markedly during meditation (Wallace, 1970). In a study of Zen disciples, four stages of EEG change were classified, and the patterns of change were highly correlated with meditator adeptness; this in turn was a function of the length of time practicing meditation (Kasamatsu & Hirai, 1969). Adept Yogis also displayed prominent alpha activity during meditation and were able to sustain this state even while distracting stimuli were introduced (Anand, Chhina, & Singh, 1969).

Maupin (1962) has suggested that Zen training procedures are analogous in some respects to Western insight-oriented psychotherapy. He proposed that the practice of meditation guides the *S* through a series of stages of adaptive regression ("regression in the service of the ego") to a stage at which the individual can accept his observations in a nondefensive, "mirrorlike" way (Maupin, 1965). Recently, Lesh (1970) found that counseling psychology students who practiced meditation significantly increased their empathic ability (to detect and describe the affective states of others) and their openness to experience.

"Field independence" reflects a general disposition to perceive and think in an articulated as opposed to a nonanalytic fashion (Witkin, Dyk, Faterson, Goodenough, & Karp, 1962). One measure of this ability is the Children's Embedded Figures Test (CEFT) which requires the *S* to discern a given form within the context of a distracting stimulus background. Meditation practice trains the individual to focus his attention on an object or process ("figure") and to resist distraction from other sources of stimulation ("background"). Therefore, meditation practice may be expected to enhance field independence, as measured by the CEFT (Hypothesis 1).

Anxiety and relaxation are incompatible feeling states. Meditation practice trains the individual to relax. It does this by teaching him to stay "in the present" and detach himself from distractions. This

*This study is based on a dissertation submitted to the School of Education of New York University in partial fulfillment of the requirements for the PhD degree.

[†]Requests for reprints should be sent to William Linden, Bureau of Child Guidance, 362 Schermerhorn Street, Brooklyn, New York 11217.

results in the ability to volitionally decrease his level of anxiety. Therefore, meditation practice may be expected to decrease test anxiety, as measured by the Test Anxiety Scale for Children (TASC; Hypothesis 2).

Through its postulated effects on the *S*s ability to focus attention and to lower test anxiety, meditation practice may also be expected to enhance reading achievement, as measured by the Metropolitan Achievement Test (Hypothesis 3).

Method

Subjects

The study was performed in a school in an economically disadvantaged neighborhood composed of blacks and Puerto Ricans in approximately a 50:50 ratio.

The school administration placed children in the third-grade classes mainly on the basis of their reading scores at the end of the second grade. The sample was drawn from the top 5 of 10 classes on the third grade. The sample was restricted to these classes in order to eliminate from the *S* pool any child who had been held over (and was therefore older than the rest), who was actually or functionally retarded, or who was an outstanding behavior problem.

From separate lists of the boys and girls in each class, nine boys and nine girls were picked at random. Of these, three boys and three girls from each class were randomly assigned to one of the three treatment conditions: meditation group, guidance group, and a group remaining with the rest of the class and receiving no special attention outside of the classroom. This selection method yielded an initial pool of 90 *S*s: 15 boys and 15 girls for each of the three treatment conditions.

Instruments

The CEFT was used to measure level of field independence. Scores on the CEFT range from 0 to 25. The TASC was used to measure level of test anxiety. Scores on the TASC range from 0 to 30. The Metropolitan Achievement Test, Primary II, Battery was used to obtain reading grade levels. Reading grade scores were the mean of the scores on the Word Knowledge Test and the Reading (Comprehension) Test. All measures were administered before and after the course of the experiment.

Collection and Treatment of Data

Reading achievement scores from the previous year were available from inspection of the cumulative record cards. Posttest scores were obtained after routine grade-wide and school-wide testing was performed. In the few cases where an *S* was absent, the missing score was assigned the mean value of that particular treatment group.

The TASC scores were obtained by administering the test to the entire class. The teacher was present on pretesting and posttesting occasions, and the *E* read the questions to the class.

To obtain pretest CEFT scores, the *S*s were assigned by means of a random number table to the *E*, the guidance counselor conducting the guidance group, or to the school's other guidance counselor. Posttest scores were obtained in the same manner. In order to be able to refer the obtained scores to age norms, approximately 12% of the *S*s were posttested before the experiment was over. Those *S*s whose birthday fell before the termination date were tested within three days prior to their ninth birthday.

Procedure

The *S*s assigned to the guidance group were divided into three groups of 10. These *S*s met with the guidance counselor for 45 minutes once per week for 18 weeks. The group was guidance oriented, that is, of an information-giving nature, rather than process oriented. The leader focused on study skills and the problems that children have in developing or using them.

The *S*s assigned to the meditation group were divided into two groups of 15. These groups met separately with the *E* twice per week for 20 to 25 minutes. Thirty-six meditation training sessions were conducted. Both the meditation and the guidance groups began and ended during the same weeks. The two treatment groups could not be identical with respect to duration of each session and number of members due to administrative and practical considerations. However, the groups provided equal total time outside the classroom. (Parental permission was obtained for the *S*s in the experimental group.)

The setting of the experimental room conformed as much as possible to the recommendations of Deikman (1963), that there be minimal distractions, and of Maupin (1965), that the room be dimly lit and sparsely furnished. The meditation group practiced two exercises: one for 10 to 15 minutes, the other, for 5 to 10 minutes. A pause was scheduled between the exercises to allow for stretching, yawning, standing, etc. At this time the *S*s were encouraged to share their experiences if they wished to.

The E began each session by saying:

> We're now beginning our exercises. Get into a comfortable position, one which you can hold without moving for a number of minutes. When we are together in this room, we all have the same job to do. All of us are paying attention to one thing, to ourselves. Your job is to just sit quietly. Try to keep your full attention within yourself. You will be paying attention only to yourself and a little to me as I give you the instructions. Remember, do not be concerned with your neighbor during the exercises. If he should cough, or move, or whatever, you pay no attention to it. The same with outside noises. Your job is to learn about yourselves and how you work, and the way to do it is to just sit and keep your mind within yourself. This is one place where nobody will tell you what to feel or what to think. Just watch; just keep your mind on whatever you are experiencing as you do the exercise. If your mind should go off the track and you find yourself watching or thinking something else, gently let go of what you're seeing or hearing and bring your attention back to yourself breathing.

Then Maupin's (1965) instructions for the breathing exercise were recited.

During the pause between exercises, the *E* tried to elicit a discussion of any experience the *S*s might have had. Within his inquiry, the *E* usually included a reformulation of the instructions so that, for example, the following type of questions were frequently asked: "Were you observing yourself breathing while you also notice *x*?" or "Where was your attention as you felt *x*?" In these discussions the *S* was reassured that he had control over the experience, and its general significance was mentioned.

Then Deikman's (1963) instructions for the visual fixation exercise were recited.

The *E* participated with the *S*s after the instructions were given. Sometimes a portion was repeated. The *E* used the child who was having the most difficulty settling into the exercise on a given day as a base line. When this *S* succeeded in relinquishing his fidgeting and otherwise seemed to be complying with the instructions, the *E* told the *S*s that he too was going to be quiet and do the exercise with them.

A few clinical observations need to be mentioned as qualitative evidence that the independent variable "took." Many of the *S*s were unaccepting of the instructions at first or seemed to fear being judged "silly" if they accepted them. The *E* maintained the expectation, stated verbally, that they would all do nothing to prevent their neighbor from doing the exercise if they were unable to do it on a given day. Gradually the groups' norm shifted from curiosity and hesitancy to approval and anticipation of the instructions. As the sessions continued, the *S*s seemed to do the exercises more readily. It is likely that in addition to the *E*'s demand, the *S*s sensed that their neighbors really were engaged in something they wished to continue doing undisturbed. Had the new group norm not become operative, the effectiveness of the meditation practice would have been nil or severely limited.

Results

Mean pretest and adjusted posttest scores on the three dependent variables are presented in Table 1. A comparison of pretest scores revealed no significant difference among the groups on any measure.

As Table 1 shows, the meditation group gained on the measure of field independence and reduced on the measure of text anxiety. Analyses of covariance were performed to evaluate posttest differences among the groups. The analyses revealed significant differences among the groups on the CEFT ($F = 4.58$, $df =$

Table 1. Mean Pretest and Adjusted Posttest Scores on Dependent Variable Measures[a]

| | Dependent variable measure | | | | | |
| | CEFT | | TASC | | MAT | |
Treatment group	Pre	Post	Pre	Post	Pre	Post
Meditation	9.15	16.82	17.73	11.71	3.57	4.28
Guidance	12.27	14.53	16.31	16.09	3.49	4.14
No outside attention	9.93	13.90	16.07	16.19	3.51	3.72

[a]Posttest scores are the scores after adjustment from the analysis of covariance. MAT = Metropolitan Achievement Test.

Table 2. Neuman-Keuls Multiple-Comparison Test of Mean Differences on the CEFT and the TASC

| | Treatment group | |
Variable	Guidance	No outside attention
CEFT		
Meditation	2.28*	2.92*
Guidance	—	4.44
TASC		
Meditation	4.38**	4.48**
Guidance	—	.10

*$p < .05$.
**$p < .01$.

2/80, $p < .05$) and on the TASC ($F = 7.86$, $df = 2/80$, $p < .01$). There was no significant difference among groups on the measure of reading achievement.

In order to determine where most of the difference was located, a multiple-comparison test was done. Table 2 presents these data.

It is apparent from Table 2 that there was a difference between the meditation group and the two control groups. There was no difference between the other two groups. These results indicate that the meditation group was significantly different from the other two groups on the CEFT and the TASC.

Discussion

The central aim of this study was to determine whether children could be trained in the practice of meditation and to examine the effects that such training might have on selected aspects of their cognitive and affective functioning. The results confirm that children can be taught this discipline and apparently with beneficial results.

The data supporting Hypothesis 1 suggest that the Ss had learned to focus and refocus their attention and to disregard intrusions by distracting stimuli. The instructions for meditating, particularly for the breathing exercise, require the S to form the habit of asking himself, "Where am I (attentionally)?" If his attention is not "here," he must let go of the current object and return his attention to a designated "target" within the ongoing present. Learning to fix attention in this manner demands the maintenance of a clear referent amid a background of "noise." These skills parallel those required for performing effectively on tests of field independence such as the CEFT.

The results also support Hypothesis 2. From these data it may be inferred that the Ss had learned to relax by meditating. Equally important, it seems to indicate that the Ss had been alerted to various subjective feeling states and that they learned to cope with some anxiety responses in testing situations by voluntarily changing their feeling state. They may have done this by meditating briefly, that is, by shifting attention from anticipated dangers associated with failures of achievement to the moment by moment flow of ongoing and primarily bodily experience.

Thus, although there is ample correlational evidence to suggest that meditating Ss shift into an "alpha state," the salient point is that on the behavioral and subjective levels S can learn to volitionally alter his state of consciousness to one characterized by relaxed alertness.

A few methodological issues may be raised at this point. It has been suggested (Lynch & Paskewitz, 1971) that in previous research the Ss, typically college students, may have entered the experiment hoping to experience a change of mood or perhaps a "high." In the present study, the age and circumstances of the Ss make the possibility of such motivation very remote.

Another facet to be considered is the Ss' rapport with the E and the hypnoidal-like quality of the situation. The E sought to mitigate these factors by having the Ss train in a group, by the E's inclusion of himself as a participant in the practicing and, by his occasional reminders that the Ss could control the intensity and duration of whatever effects they were experiencing.

The negative finding for Hypothesis 3 may be attributed to the fact that CEFT scores correlated only .37 with reading achievement, with IQ held constant (Bruininks, 1969). Therefore, as Ss improve on measures of field independence, only some of the aspects involved in reading achievement should improve concomitantly. Another explanation might be that the Ss were sampled from classes in which they were already relatively efficient in reading performance, and therefore the meditation-induced improvements in the emotional and attentional factors measured by the TASC and CEFT, respectively, might have more noticeable effects in third graders in different ranges of the reading achievement distribution. An alternative explanation is that meditation is a skill that requires practice over a long period of time, and only after a certain level of adeptness has been attained, fairly consistently, do the effects of the practice ramify.

Conclusions from this study should be limited to the population studied. However, the results encourage further investigation of meditation as a training method of self-discovery and self-mastery.

References

Anand, B. K., Chhina, G. S., & Singh, S. Some aspects of electroencephalographic studies of Yogies. In C. T. Tart (Ed.), *Altered states of consciousness.* New York: Wiley, 1969.

Berger, E. Zen Buddhism, general psychology and counseling psychology. *Journal of Counseling Psychology,* 1962, *9,* 122–127.

Bruininks, R. H. Auditory and visual perceptual skills related to the reading performance of disadvantaged boys. *Perceptual and Motor Skills,* 1969, *29,* 179–186.

Deikman, A. J. Experimental meditation. *Journal of Nervous and Mental Disease,* 1963, *136,* 329–343.

Kasamatsu, A., & Hirai, T. An electroencephalographic study of the Zen meditation (zazen). In C. T. Tart (Ed.), *Altered states of consciousness.* New York: Wiley, 1969.

Lesh, T. V. *The relationship between Zen meditation and the development of accurate empathy.* (Doctoral dissertation, University of Oregon) Ann Arbor, Mich.: University Microfilms, 1970, No. 70-9450.

Lynch, J. J., & Paskewitz, D. A. On the mechanisms of the feedback control of human brain wave activity. *Journal of Nervous and Mental Disease,* 1971, *153,* 205–218.

Maupin, E. W. Zen Buddhism: A psychological review. *Journal of Counseling Psychology,* 1962, *26,* 362–378.

Maupin, E. W. Individual differences in response to a Zen meditation exercise. *Journal of Consulting Psychology,* 1965, *29,* 139–145.

Wallace, R. K. Physiological effects of transcendental meditation. *Science,* 1970, *167,* 1751–1754.

Witkin, H. A., Dyk, R. B., Faterson, H. F., Goodenough, D. R., & Karp, S. A. *Psychological differentiation.* New York: Wiley, 1962.

B2. Addictions

The literature on meditation and the addictions is reviewed in Article 6 by Shapiro and Giber and in the accompanying table.

The two studies included in this subsection were selected for entirely different reasons. The Benson *et al.* study (Article 9) is a classic in the field. It is one of the first large-scale studies to show the potential effect of meditation in reducing drug usage for a variety of different types of drugs ranging from marijuana to heroin. The study by Marlatt *et al.* (Article 10), is one of the best designed drug studies currently available in the literature. Furthermore, it is one of the only drug studies that has a clear theoretical rationale between the dependent and the independent variable. Marlatt *et al.* suggest that it is really the relaxation effect of meditation that is having the primary influence upon alcohol consumption.

The table which is provided summarizes the studies which can be found in the literature on a variety of addictions including drugs, cigarettes, and alcohol.

Table 2. Studies on Addictions: Drugs/Cigarettes/Alcohol

Investigator(s)	Clinical Problem	INDEPENDENT VARIABLE S's (N. age, sex, prior experience)	Type and Length of Treatment/Training	Frequency of Therapist (E) Contact	DEPENDENT VARIABLE Subjective Effects (unless otherwise noted)	Follow-up	Type of Design, Quality of Controls, Methodological Problems
Benson, 1969	Drug abuse	N=20. male. age 21-38	Standard TM training	None. study done by retrospective survey	19 claimed to have stopped drug abuse ranging from marijuana to LSD. heroin. amphetamines. and barbiturates. S's reported drug induced feelings became "extremely distasteful" compared with those during TM	None reported	No control group. subject self selection bias: subject were only those who had continued to meditate more than 3 months; and were motivated to attend a one-month training session. no concurrent validity. retrospective questionnaire.
Benson and Wallace. 1972b	Drug abuse. alcohol and cigarette consumption.	N=1950 (original sample) N=1862 (final no. of respondents). 50% between 19-23 yrs. 1080 men. 781 women. Avg. experience: 20 months. Minimum: 3 months	Standard TM training. S's were attending one month TM teacher training course	Same as above	With three mos. TM. S's reported marked decrease in abuse of all categories of drugs (marijuana. LSD. narcotics. amphetamines. tobacco and liquor). With continued TM. S's report progressive decrease of drug use. After 21 mos. most S's completely stopped using drugs. In 6-mo. period pre-TM 90% of S's reported marijuana use. 28% heavy use (once a day or more). After 6 mos. TM. 37% reported marijuana use. 6.8% heavy use. Marked decreases in LSD and narcotic abuse. Also. S's reported stopping former drug selling and discouraging others from drug use. after TM. Most S's felt TM important in curbing their drug abuse.	None reported	Same as above
Brautigam 1971	Drug abuse. pathological behavior and anxiety.	N=20. 6 light drug users (e.g. hashish) and 4 heavy drug users (e.g. amphetamines. LSD. opiates) in each group: no prior meditation experience	Group One N=10. TM instruction 2 hrs. per day x 4 days. Checking one a week for first month Group Two N=10. controls group counseling 4 hrs. per week	Not stated specifically	Hashish use dropped from approx. 20x/mo to 3x/mo. among experimental group and meditation. After 3 mo. hashish use during first 3 mos. post TM 18.2x/mo. among controls. Reduction in pathological behaviors and anxiety self-reported by meditators. Behavioral Data Tension-restlessness. flaccidity. psychomotor retardation reported improved by outside observers. Ratings and S's self-estimate.	None reported	Possible expectation effect. S's informed of probable subjective benefits. effect of motivation. In experimental group. only 6 S's meditated regularly. Dependent variables lumped together: hashish. LSD. and opiates. These should be treated as separates. Other effects— e.g.. meeting a new group of non-drug using peers" may be part of treatment variance.
Shafii. Lavely and Jaffe 1974	Marijuana use	S's provided their own matched control N=90. S's placed in 5 groups according to length of TM practice (range from 1-39 mos). N=125 (original sample) N=115 (final no. respondents)	Standard TM training	None. study done by retrospective survey	1) 92% of meditators (2 yrs. or more exp.) reported significant decreased marijuana use. 77% reported stopping of usage. 2) In above group. 69% reported stopping marijuana use during first 3 mos. post TM in contrast to 15% stoppage among controls. 3) In Group I (1-3 mos. TM) a 46% decrease and a 23% stoppage reported in marijuana use during first 3 mos. post TM instruction. Controls reported 15% stoppage. 4) In Groups II (4-6 mos. TM). III (7-12 mos. TM) and IV (13-24 mos. TM) reported significant decrease and stoppage marijuana use during first 3 mos. post TM instruction. 5) The longer group practiced meditation. the more they reported a decrease or discontinuation of marijuana use. 6) Mean frequency marijuana use per month for meditators pre TM was 7.3. The control group's mean was 3.6. Following TM. mean of the meditators dropped to 2.8. whereas the control group's mean stayed the same.	None reported	Control group does not control for possible variance of treatment due to S's motivation. Margin same.
Shafii. Lavely and Jaffe 1975	Alcohol abuse	Same as above	Standard TM training	Same as above	No control S's reported discontinuation of beer and wine use. 40% of S's meditating for more than 2 yrs. reported discontinuation of wine and beer use within first 6 mos. After 25-34 mos. of meditation. 60% reported discontinuation. with 54% discontinuing hard liquor use. 6-20% of S reported discontinuation of beer and wine in first 3 mos. 11-40% of S reported discontinuation of beer and wine in second 3 mos.	None reported	Control group picked by the meditators. This control group. however. does not control for possible variance of treatment due to S's motivation. Also. dependent variables gathered by retrospective questionnaire.
Lazar. Farwell and Farrow 1975	Anxiety. drug abuse. cigarette smoking and alcohol consumption.	Study Two: Group 1: N=24. 8 male. 16 female. mean age 25.29 yrs.. (S.D. 7.37). Controls Meditators Group 2: N=13. 9 male. 4 female. mean age 20.85 yrs.. (S.D. 4.41) Group 3: N=9. 2 male. 7 female. mean age 29.11 yrs.. (S.D. 10.75) Group 4: N=14. 6 male. 8 female. mean age 23.5 yrs. (S.D. 7.88)			Study Two: IPAT anxiety scale and questionnaire concerning drug abuse. alcohol and cigarette and alcohol consumption. Group one controls administered a few days prior to TM instruction. and 4 weeks (group 2). eight weeks (group 3). or twelve weeks (group 4) after instruction. Showed progressive decreases in anxiety among meditators and use of drugs. cigarettes and alcohol. drug use showed initial rapid decrement then continuing gradual decline.		
Shapiro and Zifferblatt 1976	Methadone addiction	N=2 Case One 25 yrs. male no prior experience Case Two 29 yrs. male no prior experience	Clients taught behavioral functional analysis to monitor drug abuse. covert behavioral rehearsal and formal Zen breath meditation. Practiced one month	Not stated specifically	Overt. Concurrent Case One. Drop in dosage from 30 milligrams methadone to complete detoxification. Case Two. Drop in dosage from 40 milligrams methadone to complete detoxification. Concurrent validity random urinalyses to monitor possible drug use.	Case One 2 yrs. S's self-report free of all opioid use. Case Two 6 mos. + 2 yrs. S's self-report free of all opioid use.	Within subject design relative effects of varying treatments unclear.

Reprinted by permission. From "Drug Abuse: Proceedings of the International Conference" (C.J.D. Zarafonetis, ed.). Lea E. Febiger, Philadelphia, PA., 1972.

9

*DECREASED DRUG ABUSE WITH TRANSCENDENTAL MEDITATION— A STUDY OF 1,862 SUBJECTS**

Herbert Benson, and R. Keith Wallace, with the Technical Assistance of Eric C. Dahl, and Donald F. Cooke

The abuse of drugs of all kinds is widespread in the United States and the extent of abuse, particularly of marihuana and hallucinogenic drugs, is growing.[1-3] It is estimated that in the United States 35 to 50% of high school and college students have tried marihuana at least once, and of these about 35% have tried marihuana more than ten times.[2] A conservative estimate of persons in the United States, both juvenile and adult, who have used marihuana is about five million and may be as high as 20 million.[1] In surveys of d-lysergic acid diethylamide (LSD) use in college populations, 5% of the students polled admitted to using LSD, with about 30% of the sample being classified as "serious" users and the remaining 70% as "experimenters."[2] Law enforcement agencies report there are approximately 65,000 active "hard" narcotic addicts in the United States. Other estimates indicate

* Supported in part by grants from the National Heart and Lung Institute (HE 10539-05), the National Institutes of Health (SF 57-111), and from Hoffmann-LaRoche, Inc., Nutley, New Jersey, 07110.

that there are 100,000 active narcotic abusers.[2] The abuse of amphetamines and barbiturates is widespread, but difficult to estimate. College surveys have indicated that more than 20% of the students have abused these drugs.[3] Stanley F. Yolles, M.D., Director of the National Institute of Mental Health summed up the situation as follows:

> The spreading of the abuse pattern into unusual and exotic drugs and the involvement of increased numbers of people have serious implications. It seems that today if a chemical can be abused, it will be. Further, it appears that stronger and more dangerous drugs tend to displace weaker drugs during this period of excessive preoccupation with mind-altering chemicals. One further identifiable ominous trend is the indulgence in drugs of abuse by younger and younger age groups.
> It is to be expected that the use of all sorts of drugs in the next 10 years will increase a hundred fold. It is necessary, therefore, to develop effective processes to control their abuse today.[3]

Few programs or treatments have been reported which reduce drug abuse. One apparently successful program for the rehabilitation of persons abusing narcotics involves the substitution of methadone.[4,5] Existing programs for the alleviation of other drug abuse usually involve education concerning the dangerous effects of drugs and sometimes provide personal counseling or psychiatric care.[6-9] The efficacy of these programs has yet to be established.

A preliminary observation suggested that the practice of Transcendental Meditation, as taught by Maharishi Mahesh Yogi, may be effective in alleviation of drug abuse.[10] The present report confirms and expands the earlier observation.

METHODS

The technique of Transcendental Meditation is reported to be an easily learned mental technique which originated in ancient Vedic tradition of India.[11,12] Practitioners are personally instructed by a teacher qualified by Maharishi Mahesh Yogi. The technique is claimed to be a spontaneous natural process, and, unlike many techniques of meditation or self-improvement, does not employ mental control, physical control, belief, suggestion, or any change in life style. It is also claimed that anyone can learn the technique in four or five instructional sessions. Practitioners are asked to abstain from drug abuse for a 15-day period prior to starting Meditation. Following instruction in Transcendental Meditation, the program involves practicing the technique twice a day for periods of 15 to 20 minutes. The program does not provide any type of personal counseling or advice about personal problems. Individuals practice the technique on their own. The only additional contact between the individual and the instructors or organization is concerned with ensuring correct practice of the technique and providing further knowledge about it.

Questionnaires were given to approximately 1,950 subjects who had been practicing Transcendental Meditation for three months or more and who were attending one

of two Meditation training courses offered by the Students' International Meditation Society* in the summer of 1970. Of these, 1,862 subjects completed the questionnaire, giving information concerning age, sex, educational status, and length of time that Transcendental Meditation had been practiced. Frequency of drug use, drug-selling activity, and attitudes towards drug abuse were assessed for each of five separate time periods: (1) 6 months before starting Meditation; (2) 0 to 3 months after starting; (3) 4 to 9 months after starting; (4) 10 to 21 months after starting; and (5) 22 months or more after starting. The separate drugs and categories of drugs included in the questionnaire were (1) marihuana; (2) LSD; (3) other hallucinogens (2,5-dimethyloxy-4-methyl amphetamine [STP], N,N-dimethyl-tryptamine [DMT], peyote, and mescaline); (4) narcotics (heroin, opium, morphine and cocaine); (5) amphetamines; and (6) barbiturates.

Additional information was requested concerning the frequency of use of "hard liquor" and the number of packs of cigarettes smoked. Hard liquor was defined as "alcoholic beverages stronger than wine or beer."

The information on the questionnaires was analyzed on an IBM 360-65 computer. The CROSSTABS† multivariant data analysis program was utilized and all processing was done by Urban Data Processing, Inc.‡ The subjects were classified into four categories depending on the frequency of drug use: (1) non-users; (2) light users; (3) medium users; and (4) heavy users. For the subjects using marihuana, narcotics, amphetamines, barbiturates, hard liquor, and cigarettes, a "light user" indicated a frequency of three times a month or less; "medium user," once a week to six times a week; and "heavy user," once a day or more. For LSD

* National Headquarters, 1015 Gayley Avenue, Los Angeles, California 90024.

† Cambridge Computer Associates, 22 Alewife Brook Parkway, Cambridge, Massachusetts, 02138.

‡ Urban Data Processing, 552 Massachusetts Avenue, Cambridge, Massachusetts, 02139.

and other hallucinogens, "light user" indicated a frequency of less than once a month; "medium user," from one to three times a month; and "heavy user," once a week or more.

RESULTS

A total of 1,862 subjects responded to the questionnaire. There were 1,081 male subjects and 781 female subjects (Table 1). The age of the subjects ranged from 14 to 78 years and approximately half of the subjects were between the ages of 19 and 23. Most had attended college and many had college degrees (Table 2). The average length of time they had been practicing Transcendental Meditation was approximately 20 months.

Following the start of the practice of Transcendental Meditation, there was a marked decrease in the number of drug abusers for all drug categories (Tables 3 to 8). As the practice of Meditation continued,

Table 1 Age and sex of the respondents to the questionnaire

Sex		Age					
		14–18 years	19–23 years	24–28 years	29–38 years	39 years and older	Totals
Male	No.	61	574	322	82	42	1081
	%	3.3	30.8	17.3	4.4	2.3	58.1
Female	No.	71	363	167	81	99	781
	%	3.8	19.5	8.9	4.4	5.3	41.9
Totals	No.	132	937	489	163	141	1862
	%	7.1	50.3	26.2	8.8	7.6	100.0

Table 2 Education of the respondents to the questionnaire

Educational experience	Less than high school	High school graduate	Some college	College graduate	Advanced college degree	Totals
Number	100	183	971	460	148	1862
Percent	5.4	9.8	52.2	24.7	7.9	100.0

Table 3 Use of marihuana and hashish before and after starting the practice of Transcendental Meditation

Usage*	Before (time in months) 6–0		After (time in months)							
			0–3		4–9		10–21		22–33	
	n	%	n	%	n	%	n	%	n	%
Heavy	417	22.4	47	2.5	39	2.1	18	1.3	1	0.1
Medium	618	33.2	190	10.2	137	7.5	65	4.6	18	2.1
Light	422	22.7	613	32.9	500	27.3	264	18.6	85	10.0
Non-user	405	21.7	1012	54.4	1154	63.1	1070	75.5	748	87.8
Totals	1862	100.0	1862	100.0	1830	100.0	1417	100.0	852	100.0

* See text for definitions.

13

Decreased Drug Abuse with TM

Table 4 Use of LSD before and after starting the practice of Transcendental Meditation

Usage*	Before (time in months) 6–0		After (time in months) 0–3		4–9		10–21		22–33	
	n	%	n	%	n	%	n	%	n	%
Heavy	132	7.1	14	0.7	13	0.7	6	0.4	0	0.0
Medium	301	16.1	60	3.3	36	1.9	23	1.7	3	0.3
Light	467	25.1	159	8.5	151	8.3	72	5.1	23	2.7
Non-user	962	51.7	1629	87.5	1630	89.1	1316	92.8	826	97.0
Totals	1862	100.0	1862	100.0	1830	100.0	1417	100.0	852	100.0

* See text for definitions.

Table 5 Use of other hallucinogens before and after starting the practice of Transcendental Meditation

Usage*	Before (time in months) 6–0		After (time in months) 0–3		4–9		10–21		22–23	
	n	%	n	%	n	%	n	%	n	%
Heavy	5	0.3	4	0.2	5	0.3	3	0.2	0	0.0
Medium	56	3.0	32	1.7	30	1.7	19	1.4	0	0.0
Light	665	35.7	143	7.7	130	7.0	90	6.4	34	4.0
Non-user	1136	61.0	1683	90.4	1665	91.0	1305	92.0	818	96.0
Totals	1862	100.0	1862	100.0	1830	100.0	1417	100.0	852	100.0

* See text for definitions.

Table 6 Use of narcotics before and after starting the practice of Transcendental Meditation

Usage*	Before (time in months) 6–0		After (time in months) 0–3		4–9		10–21		22–33	
	n	%	n	%	n	%	n	%	n	%
Heavy	12	0.6	1	0.1	1	0.1	1	0.1	0	0.0
Medium	17	0.9	2	0.2	2	0.2	2	0.2	0	0.0
Light	286	15.4	47	2.5	39	2.1	30	2.1	10	1.2
Non-User	1547	83.1	1812	97.2	1788	97.6	1384	97.6	842	98.8
Totals	1862	100.0	1862	100.0	1830	100.0	1417	100.0	852	100.0

* See text for definitions.

Table 7 Use of amphetamines before and after starting the practice of Transcendental Meditation

Usage*	Before (time in months) 6–0		After (time in months) 0–3		4–9		10–21		22–33	
	n	%	n	%	n	%	n	%	n	%
Heavy	30	1.6	7	0.4	3	0.2	2	0.1	0	0.0
Medium	96	5.2	11	0.6	9	0.5	2	0.2	0	0.0
Light	470	25.2	104	5.6	79	4.3	49	3.4	10	1.2
Non-User	1266	68.0	1740	93.4	1739	95.0	1364	96.3	842	98.8
Totals	1862	100.0	1862	100.0	1830	100.0	1417	100.0	852	100.0

* See text for definitions.

Table 8 Use of barbiturates before and after starting the practice of Transcendental Meditation

Usage*	Before (time in months) 6–0		After (time in months) 0–3		4–9		10–21		22–33	
	n	%	n	%	n	%	n	%	n	%
Heavy	19	1.0	1	0.1	3	0.2	1	0.1	0	0.0
Medium	43	2.3	7	0.4	3	0.2	2	0.1	1	0.1
Light	258	13.9	56	2.9	37	2.0	27	1.9	8	1.0
Non-User	1542	82.8	1798	96.6	1787	97.6	1387	97.9	843	98.9
Totals	1862	100.0	1862	100.0	1830	100.0	1417	100.0	852	100.0

* See text for definitions.

Table 9 Use of "hard liquor" before and after starting the practice of Transcendental Meditation

Usage*	Before (time in months) 6–0		After (time in months) 0–3		4–9		10–21		22–33	
	n	%	n	%	n	%	n	%	n	%
Heavy	50	2.7	21	1.2	16	0.9	8	0.6	3	0.4
Medium	295	15.8	149	8.0	100	5.5	52	3.7	22	2.6
Light	770	41.4	646	34.7	551	30.1	365	25.8	187	21.9
Non-User	747	40.1	1046	56.1	1161	63.5	992	69.9	640	75.1
Totals	1862	100.0	1862	100.0	1830	100.0	1417	100.0	852	100.0

* See text for definitions.

the subjects progressively decreased their drug abuse until after practicing 21 months of Meditation most subjects had completely stopped abusing drugs. For example, in the six-month period before starting the practice of Meditation, about 80% of the subjects used marihuana and of those about 28% were heavy users. After practicing Transcendental Meditation six months, 37% used marihuana and of those only 6.5% were heavy users. After 21 months of the practice, only 12% continued to use marihuana and of those most were light users; only one individual was a heavy user. The decrease in abuse of LSD was even more marked. Before starting the practice of Transcendental Meditation, 48% of the subjects had used LSD, and of these subjects about 14% were heavy users. In the three months following the start of the practice of Meditation, 11% of the subjects took LSD, while

after 21 months of the practice only 3% took LSD. The increase in the number of non-users after starting the practice of Meditation was similar for the other drugs: non-users of the other hallucinogens after 21 months of the practice rose from 61 to 96%; for the narcotics from 83 to 99% for the amphetamines from 70 to 99%; and for the barbiturates from 83 to 99%.

In the six-month period before starting the practice of Meditation, 60% of the subjects took hard liquor and, of these, about 4% were heavy users (Table 9). After 21 months of the practice of Meditation, approximately 25% took hard liquor and only 0.1% were heavy users. Approximately 48% smoked cigarettes before starting Meditation and 27% were heavy users (Table 10). After 21 months of practicing Meditation, 16% smoked cigarettes and only 5.8% were heavy users.

Decreased Drug Abuse with TM

Table 10 Use of cigarettes (number of packs) before and after starting the practice of Transcendental Meditation

Usage*	Before (time in months) 6–0		After (time in months) 0–3		4–9		10–21		22–33	
	n	%	n	%	n	%	n	%	n	%
Heavy	503	27.0	314	16.9	222	12.2	118	8.4	49	5.7
Medium	180	9.7	165	8.9	136	7.4	86	6.0	34	4.0
Light	203	10.9	186	10.0	163	8.9	105	7.4	55	6.4
Non-User	976	52.4	1197	64.2	1309	71.5	1108	78.2	714	83.9
Totals	1862	100.0	1862	100.0	1830	100.0	1417	100.0	852	100.0

* See text for definitions.

Most subjects felt that Transcendental Meditation was instrumental in their decreasing or stopping abuse of drugs: 61.1% stated that it was extremely important; 22.8% that it was very important; 12.0% somewhat important; and 3.6% not important. Of those individuals who continued the use of drugs following starting Transcendental Meditation, 55.9% had been irregular in Meditation and 24.8% had stopped for a week or more.

Three hundred seventy-four subjects (20.1%) sold drugs before starting Meditation. Of these, 71.9% stopped and 12.5% decreased drug selling during the period 0-3 months after instruction. Among the subjects who practiced Meditation 21 months or longer and who at one time were actively involved in selling drugs, 95.9% stopped selling drugs. In addition, 997 (65.5%) had either encouraged or condoned drug abuse before starting Meditation. Over 95% of these subjects discouraged drug abuse in others after beginning the practice of Meditation.

DISCUSSION

Individuals who regularly practiced Transcendental Meditation (1) decreased or stopped abusing drugs, (2) decreased or stopped engaging in drug-selling activity, and (3) changed their attitudes in the direction of discouraging others from abusing drugs.

The magnitude of these changes increased with the length of time that the individual practiced the technique. Similar decreases were noted in the use of "hard" alcoholic beverages and cigarette smoking. A high percentage of the individuals who did change their habits felt that Transcendental Meditation was very or extremely important in influencing them to change.

During Transcendental Meditation, oxygen consumption and heart rate significantly decrease, skin resistance significantly increases, and the electroencephalogram shows predominantly slow alpha wave activity with occasional theta wave activity.[13] Thus, the practice of Transcendental Meditation is physiologically distinguished from sitting quietly with eyes open or closed, from sleeping or dreaming, and from the relaxation or rest suggested by hypnosis. During Transcendental Meditation subjects report that their awareness is spontaneously drawn to "finer" or "more abstract" levels of the thinking process.

There are no simple explanations of the factors which lead to drug abuse. The types of motives which initiate and prolong drug abuse range from such things as social pressure, curiosity, desire for "kicks," rebellion against authority, escape from social and emotional problems to more philosophical motives such as self-knowledge, creativeness, spiritual enlightenment, or expansion of consciousness.[14] Student drug users are, as a group, knowledgeable about the undesirable effects of drug abuse. In general, it is not difficult for most student drug abusers to stop; the problem is to get them to want to stop. For a drug abuse program to be effective it must provide a non-chemical alternative which can fulfill at least some of the basic motivations behind student drug abuse.

Transcendental Meditation is acceptable among youthful drug abusers. It is offered as a program for personal development and is not specifically intended to be a treatment for drug abuse; the alleviation of the problems of drug abuse is merely a side effect of the practice. Thus, it may not threaten the beliefs of the committed abuser who condones the use of drugs. Since the introduction of Transcendental Meditation into the student community five years ago, more than 40,000 individuals have allegedly begun the practice.[15] Furthermore, the movement continues to grow. It is presently being presented through campus organizations at some 300 colleges and universities and is offered in the context of an accredited course at several universities.

Involvement in other kinds of self-improvement activities may also lead to decreased drug abuse. The motivation to start Meditation may have influenced the subjects to stop drug abuse. The subjects in the present study may have spontaneously stopped, continued, or increased taking drugs independently of Transcendental Meditation. However, since there are few effective programs which reduce drug abuse, Transcendental Meditation should be investigated as an alternative to drugs by a controlled, prospective study.

SUMMARY

Drug abuse is widespread and increasing in the United States, especially in student populations. However, few effective programs exist for the alleviation of drug abuse. Transcendental Meditation, a popular and easily learned mental technique which allegedly originated from the ancient Vedic tradition of India, was investigated as a possible means of decreasing drug abuse. Eighteen hundred sixty-two subjects who had practiced Transcendental Meditation at least three months formed the basis of this study. In these subjects, after starting Transcendental Meditation there was a significant decrease in the amount of drugs used or discontinuance of drug use; a decrease or cessation in engaging in drug-selling activity; and changed attitudes in the direction of discouraging others from abusing drugs. Further, the subjects decreased their consumption of "hard" alcoholic beverages and smoked fewer cigarettes. The magnitude of these changes increased with the length of time that the subject practiced Transcendental Meditation. Involvement in other types of self-improving activities may also lead to decreased drug abuse. However, since there are few effective programs which decrease drug abuse, Transcendental Meditation should be investigated as an alternative to drugs by a controlled, prospective study.

ACKNOWLEDGEMENT

We thank Miss Barbara R. Marzetta and Miss Lyne Heppner for their help in the preparation of the manuscript.

REFERENCES

1. *Resource Book for Drug Abuse Education.* National Clearinghouse for Mental Health Information, United States Department of Health Education and Welfare. Public Health Service, Health Service and Mental Health Administration, National Institute of Mental Health: 1969. Washington, D.C., Government Printing Office, 1969 (PHS Publication No. 1964), p. 25.
2. *Recent Research on Narcotics, LSD, Marijuana and Other Dangerous Drugs.* National Clearinghouse for Mental Health Information, U. S. Department of Health, Education and Welfare. Public Health Service, Health Service and Mental Health Administration, National Institute of Mental Health, 1969. Washington, D.C., Government Printing Office, 1969 (PHS Publication No. 1961), pp. 1, 2, 7, 11, 18.

3. Yolles, S. F.: Statement for Stanley F. Yolles, M.D., Director, National Institute of Mental Health, before the Subcommittee on Public Health and Welfare of the Interstate and Foreign Commerce Committee on H.R. 11701 and H.R. 13743, 1969, loose leaf, pp. 13–16.

4. Byrd, O. E.: *Medical Readings on Drug Abuse.* Reading, Mass., Addison-Wesley Publishing Co., 1970, pp. 255–257.

5. Eddy, N. B.: Methadone maintenance for the management of persons with drug dependence of the morphine type. *Drug Dependence 3*:17–26, 1970.

6. Wiesen, R. L., Wang, I. H., and Stensper, T. J.: The drug abuse program at Milwaukee County Institutions. *Wisconsin Med J 69*:141–150, 1970.

7. Murphy, B. W., Leventhal, A. M., and Balter, M. B.: Drug use on the campus: A survey of university health services and counseling centers. *J Amer Coll Health Assoc 17*:389–402, 1969.

8. Pollock, M. B.: The drug abuse problem: Some implications for health education.

9. Hickox, J. R.: Drug abuse education. *Texas Med 65*:31–33, 1969.

10. Benson, H.: Yoga for drug abuse. *New Eng J Med 281*:1133, 1969.

11. Maharishi Mahesh Yogi: *The Science of Being and Art of Living,* rev. ed. London, International S.R.M., 1966, pp. 50–59.

12. Maharishi Mahesh Yogi: *Maharishi Mahesh Yogi on the Bhagavad Gita: A New Translation and Commentary.* Baltimore, Penguin, 1969. (Originally published by International S.R.M., London, 1967, pp. 10–17.)

13. Wallace, R. K.: Physiological effects of transcendental meditation. *Science 167*:1751–1754, 1970.

14. Cohen, A. Y.: Inside what's happening: Sociological, psychological, and spiritual perspectives on the contemporary drug scene. *Amer J Publ Health 59*:2092–2097, 1969.

15. Jarvis, J.: Personal communication from the Students' International Meditation Society, 1015 Gayley Avenue, Los Angeles, California, 90024.

J Amer Coll Health Assoc 17:403–411, 1969.

10

EFFECTS OF MEDITATION AND RELAXATION TRAINING UPON ALCOHOL USE IN MALE SOCIAL DRINKERS

C. Alan Marlatt, Robert R. Pagano, Richard M. Rose,
and Janice K. Marques

Introduction

The practice of meditation has recently been suggested as a potential treatment technique for the problems of alcoholism and drug abuse (e.g., Carrington & Ephron, 1975; Swinyard, Chaube, & Sutton, 1974). Evidence in support of this recommendation can be found in several survey studies which have reported dramatic reductions in alcohol and drug use by individuals practicing Transcendental Meditation (TM). In the first major survey, Benson & Wallace (1972) analyzed questionnaire data returned from 1862 subjects who had practiced TM for periods ranging from 3 to 33 months. Based on retrospective self-report data, the majority of subjects showed a notable decrease in drug and alcohol use after beginning the regular practice of TM. In terms of alcohol use, for example, the percentage of subjects describing themselves as "heavy drinkers" (drinking once a day or more) dropped from 2.7% of the sample, prior to regular TM practice, to 0.4%, after 22 to 33 months of practice (Benson, 1974). Because the data were based entirely on retrospective accounts of drinking, with the absence of appropriate control groups, the results of this study are open to criticism on methodological grounds.

Shafii, Lavely, and Jaffe (1975) report the results of a questionnaire study comparing the frequency of alcohol use for subjects who had practiced TM, for periods up to 39 months, with that of a nonmeditation control group. Most of the subjects ($N = 216$) were young adults, with a college-level education. All subjects were asked to give retrospective estimates of their drinking behavior, dating back to the year preceding initiation into TM for the meditators, or an equivalent time period for the control subjects. The authors report that 40% of the subjects who had been meditating for more than two years claimed that they had discontinued the use of wine and beer in the first 6 months following initiation; none of the control subjects reported this effect during an equivalent time period. In addition, 54% of this meditating group had stopped drinking hard liquor, compared with only 1% of the control subjects. The results are subject to caution, however, as all the findings were based on retrospective reports spanning up to a 4-year period.

Despite the methodological shortcomings of these survey studies, the results are impressive enough to indicate the need for a prospective controlled experiment to assess the effects of meditation on alcohol use. There are a number of theoretical assumptions which suggest that the regular practice of meditation or a similar relaxation technique may lead to a reduction in alcohol consumption. If excessive drinking is viewed as a learned coping response to stress and anxiety (cf., Marlatt, 1976), then the practice of an alternative coping response as a successful antedote to stress should decrease the probability of subsequent drinking. Recent research has shown that the regular practice of meditation is associated with a reduction in general stress, as measured by a wide variety of psychological, behavioral, and physiological measures (summarized in Bloomfield, Cain, Jaffe, & Kory 1975). In one series of experiments, for example, it was found that physiological indices of stress (skin conductance fluctuations) were lower in subjects who regularly practiced meditation than in nonmeditating control subjects (Orme-Johnson, 1973).

Although a simple tension-reduction explanation of drinking behavior has been seriously challenged (Cappell, 1975; Cappell & Herman, 1972), there is some evidence to suggest that alcohol consumption increases as a response to stress, particularly when it arises from social and interpersonal sources (Higgins & Marlatt, 1975; Miller, Hersen, Eisler, & Hilsman, 1974). Rather than acting as a kind of tranquilizer for anxiety, alcohol may serve to increase the drinker's sense of perceived control in stressful situations. In a review of the literature bearing on this hypothesis, Marlatt (1976) has argued that the probability of drinking will vary in a particular situation as a function of (1) the degree of perceived stress in the situation, (2) the degree of perceived personal control the individual experiences, (3) the availability of an adequate coping response to the stressful situation, and (4) the individual's expectations about the effectiveness of alcohol as a coping response. In one test of this hypothesis, it was shown that if subjects who were exposed to an interpersonally stressful situation (being criticized and angered by a confederate subject) were then given the opportunity to engage in an alternative coping response (retaliation against the confederate), they showed a significant decrease in alcohol consumption in an analog drinking test (Marlatt, Kosturn, & Lang, 1975). Similarly, the practice of meditation may serve as an alternative coping response to drinking, perhaps because it increases the subject's actual or perceived ability to cope with stress. Several recent studies have indicated, for example, that the practice of meditation leads to significant positive changes in personality test scores associated with perceived control. Hjelle (1974) found that experienced meditators were classified as significantly more "internal" on Rotter's Locus of Control scale compared with a nonmeditating control group. Other research has also shown that the practice of meditation leads to significant positive changes associated with measures of internal control and self-actualization on Shostron's Personal Orientation Inventory (Nidich, Seeman, & Dreskin, 1972; Seeman, Nidich, & Banta, 1972).

In a recent survey of studies which have assessed the therapeutic effects of meditation on a variety of psychological and behavioral problems, Smith (1975) concluded that almost all of the reports reviewed lacked appropriate attention-placebo and no-treatment control groups. In addition, several problems were discussed concerning the difficulties of investigating TM in a control group design. It is particularly difficult to devise comparison groups which control for such factors as biased subject selection and expectation effects which are associated with the TM movement (subjects must pay a substantial fee for initiation into TM; the initiation ceremony has religious overtones; introductory lectures are designed to build up strong positive expectancies for the technique, etc.). TM, however, is not the only form of meditation available (see White, 1974, for descriptions of other techniques). Recently, Benson (1975) has argued that all forms of meditation and other relaxation procedures are similar in their effects. He posits a mediating "relaxation response" which is associated with the beneficial effects of meditation, including TM. In his own research, Benson has outlined a simple meditative-like technique which can be taught to any subject, and yet is free from the religious and mystical overtones of TM. Because of its advantages from a research standpoint, and its similarity to TM (repetition of a mantra-like word in a quiet and relaxed setting), the present investigation employed Benson's exercise as the meditation treatment condition.

The subjects, male college students classified as heavy social drinkers, monitored their drinking behavior for a 2-week baseline period prior to treatment, a 6-week treatment period, and a 7-week follow-up period. In addition to the self-monitored reports of drinking, subjects also took part in a pre- and posttreatment assessment procedure in which their alcohol consumption was measured in an analog drinking task. Personality measures of state and trait anxiety, and locus of control were also obtained before and after treatment. Because of the exploratory nature of this research, no specific hypotheses were advanced concerning the relative effectiveness of the two main relaxation procedures.

Method

Subjects

Potential subjects were recruited by administering a Drinking Habits Questionnaire to 1200 students in undergraduate classes at the University of Washington. This questionnaire, adapted from Cahalan's national drinking habits survey (Cahalan, Cisin, and Crossley, 1969), is a computer-scored, multiple-choice instrument, which classifies respondents according to the quantity, frequency, and variability of alcoholic beverages consumed. The Volume Variability index devised by Cahalan and Room (1974), was used to select high-volume drinkers (averaging at least one and a half drinks per day) for the present experiment. Heavy social drinkers were selected in order to explore the usefulness of meditation and relaxation training in the prevention and treatment of problem drinking.

From the original pool, 130 males between 21 and 35 years of age who qualified as high-volume drinkers were invited to attend a meeting at which the procedures and purpose of the study were presented. At this time, potential subjects who were currently practicing meditation or similar relaxation procedures, receiving treatment for drinking problems, or had previously participated in drinking experiments on the campus were eliminated. The study was described as a preliminary investigation of the effects of practicing relaxation techniques on drinking of alcoholic beverages. Care was taken to emphasize the experimenters' uncertainty about what those effects would be, to avoid creating an expectation or demand that drinking would decrease after relaxation training. Subjects were informed about the relaxation techniques and dependent measures to be used in the study, and were told that they would receive payments of $4.00 for their participation. A total of 44 qualified heavy drinkers agreed to participate, and were asked at that time to indicate whether or not they considered themselves "problem drinkers." Four of the subjects, who indicated that they did have a drinking problem, were included in the sample and were each assigned to one of the four experimental conditions. Of the original sample, 41 subjects (93%) completed the treatment phase of the study; their mean age was 23.5 years.

Overview of Procedures

The study was divided into three phases: a baseline period (2 weeks), a treatment period (6 weeks), and a follow-up period (7 weeks). During baseline, all subjects reported their daily alcohol consumption on detailed recording forms. At the end of this period, each subject was scheduled for a laboratory session in which he completed the pretreatment personality measures and participated in the taste-rating task as a further measure of his alcohol consumption rate. Following these tests, subjects were randomly divided into four groups, with the restriction that groups would be matched based on their alcohol consumption during the first week of the baseline period. The four groups were: meditation, progressive relaxation, attention-placebo control (bibliotherapy), and a no-treatment control.

Subjects in the first three groups were taught a relaxation technique, and instructed to practice it for two 20-minute sessions each day during the 6-week treatment period. Daily records of the time spent in relaxation sessions and the subjective level of relaxation experienced after each session were completed by these subjects throughout the treatment period. All groups, including the no-treatment control groups, continued to keep daily records of alcohol consumption. At the end of the treatment period, the personality measures and taste-rating task were again administered.

During the follow-up period, the daily record-keeping procedures were continued, but practice of the relaxation techniques was optional for the trained subjects. At the end of this period, subjects were asked to complete a follow-up questionnaire, which assessed their personal observations and conclusions about the study. A $4.00 weekly payment was made to each subject throughout the study, contingent upon receipt of his daily records of alcohol consumption. Confidentiality was maximized by having all subjects identify their records with a randomly assigned subject number.

Measures

Consumption Diaries

Recording forms were distributed weekly to all subjects, with instructions to supply on a daily basis the following information: (1) exact type and brand of alcoholic beverage consumed (proof or percentage alcohol if known), (2) amount consumed (exact number and size of glasses or bottles, ratios of mixer to alcoholic beverages in mixed drinks), (3) the period of time spent drinking, (4) drinking situation (location and presence of others), and (5) total cost of the alcoholic beverages consumed that day. Subjects were also instructed to indicate any extenuating circumstances, particularly illness, which may have affected their consumption that day. When subjects were unable to supply all of the information requested (e.g., exact size of a pitcher at a tavern), efforts were made to obtain it from the establishment where the drinking occurred; in other cases, standard estimates were used (e.g., for mixed drinks in private settings).

The consumption diary data were transformed into standard units of consumption (milliliters of ethanol), and a score was assigned each week indicating each subject's consumption. The only adjustments in this procedure were made when a subject reported an illness which kept him from drinking for a period of 4 days or more. A correction was made in these cases by substituting the subject's mean consumption score from the previous week for the illness-related abstinent days.

Taste-Rating Task

This task is a standardized laboratory procedure developed as an unobtrusive measure of alcohol consumption (Marlatt, in press). Subjects were given individual laboratory appointments for a "wine-tasting test," with the following explanation:

> The overall purpose of this study is to investigate the effects of practicing a relaxation technique on the drinking of alcoholic beverages. In addition to possible changes in daily drinking habits, we are interested in whether relaxation training affects other aspects of drinking behavior, such as the perception of alcoholic beverages. In the wine-tasting sessions, we will be measuring your ability to discriminate taste differences among several wines before and after the 6-week period of relaxation practice.

Subjects were asked to refrain from all food and drugs (including alcohol) for a period of 4 hours prior to their appointments, which were set in the afternoon and early evening. When the subject arrived at the laboratory, the experimenter (a female undergraduate student) administered a breathalyzer test to determine his blood alcohol level. If the reading indicated the presence of alcohol, the subject was rescheduled for a later appointment.

After checking each subject's indentification to assure that he was at least 21 years of age, the experimenter left the room for 10 minutes while the subject completed the personality tests described in the following section. The experimenter returned with the bottles of wine, and seated the subject at a table with three decanters, three empty glasses, a memory drum, and taste-rating forms. The task instructions then read to the subjects were similar to those described in previous papers (Higgins & Marlatt, 1975; Marlatt, Kosturn & Lang, 1975). The experimenter poured each of the 3700-ml bottles of wine into a separate decanter and labeled each with a code letter as the subject averted his eyes. The subject was asked to pour some wine from each decanter into a separate glass, and to rate and compare them on a list of 65 adjectives that appeared one at a time on the memory drum. For each adjective (e.g., "sweet," "mellow"), the subject was told to sample the wines and record which wine the adjective applied to best, and which it applied to least. The subject was instructed to repeat this procedure for each adjective presented, working at his own pace. Ad-lib consumption was encouraged by including the instruction, "Feel free to sample as much of each wine as you need in order to arrive at a decision." Subjects were not told the length of the adjective list or the time limit for the task (15 minutes). Following the task, the amount of wine consumed by the subject during the task period was subsequently determined by subtracting the amount left from the total 2100 ml presented to the subject.

Personality Measures

Two self-report personality scales were administered pre- and posttreatment to determine the effects of relaxation procedures on anxiety and perceived locus of control. The Spielberger State-Trait Anxiety Inventory (STAI) contains two separate scales for measuring state and trait anxiety (Spielberger, Gorsuch, and Lushene, 1970). The 20-item A-State scale asks respondents to rate how they feel at the moment, yielding a measure of their transitory level of anxiety. The A-Trait Scale (also 20 items) requires respondents to rate how they generally feel, yielding a dispositional measure of anxiety proneness. The Locus of Control scale developed by Rotter (1966), was also administered.

Relaxation Records

Relaxation recording forms were distributed to subjects in the three relaxation groups during the treatment and follow-up periods. The subject was instructed to indicate, immediately after each relaxation session, the period of time spent in that session, and his rating of the level of relaxation achieved. These subjective ratings were based on a seven-point scale, extending from "very tense" (-3), to "very relaxed" ($+3$). The subject was told to consider the "0" point on the scale equal to the level of relaxation he normally experiences while just sitting quietly. A weekly mean relaxation score was computed by dividing the sum of the subject's ratings by the number of sessions recorded.

Follow-up Questionnaire

This questionnaire, administered at the end of the follow-up period, was designed to assess the subject's personal observations and conclusions about the study. The 34 items were grouped into three main topics: (1) drinking patterns, asking the subject to describe his reasons for drinking, effects of keeping daily records of consumption, and changes noted in drinking habits over the course of the study, (2) purpose of the study, assessing the subject's awareness of the experimenters' hypotheses and the basis for his selection as a subject; and (3) relaxation procedure, requesting the relaxation subjects' opinions about the techniques they learned, daily practice, and perceived effects of relaxation.

Training Procedure

Subjects in each of the three relaxation groups (meditation, progressive relaxation, and attention-placebo control) were trained as a group in a 1-hour session with one of the experimenters. The trainers were all faculty members in the department of psychology. All relaxation subjects were told to practice their respective techniques for two 20-minute periods each day, with the following instructions regarding the timing of sessions:

> Ideally, you should have one session in the morning before eating breakfast and one session in the late afternoon before eating dinner. Occasionally, you might find this inconvenient, and will want to chose some other time. When this is the case please try to space your two sessions so that one is in the morning and one in the afternoon. In addition, please try not to schedule a session within two hours after eating, nor directly before going to bed.

During the week after the training meeting, each relaxation subject was contacted individually by his trainer, who checked to see that the subject was following the instructions, and offered to answer any questions the subject had about the procedure. After this point, the subject had no further contact with the experimenter who trained him.

Treatment Conditions

Meditation (n = 10)

This group received instruction in a meditative technique developed by Benson (1975) as an analog to Transcendental Meditation. The trainer in this condition (R.R.P.) was an experienced practitioner of TM.

As in TM, the basic components of Benson's technique were: (1) subvocal repetition of a constant sound, (2) a passive attitude, (3) decreased muscle tonus, and (4) regular practice. During the training session, the components of the procedure were explained, specific instructions were given, and a trial session was conducted by the trainer. The instructions used were those published by Benson, Rosner, Marzetta, and Klemchuk (1974):

1. Sit quietly in a comfortable position.
2. Close your eyes.
3. Deeply relax all your muscles, beginning at your feet and progressing up to your face. Keep them deeply relaxed.
4. Breathe through your nose. Become aware of your breathing. As you breathe out, say the word, "ONE," silently to yourself. For example, breathe IN . . . OUT, "ONE," IN . . . OUT, "ONE,"; etc.
5. Continue for 20 minutes. Occasionally open your eyes to check the time. When you finish, sit quietly for several minutes, at first with closed eyes and later with opened eyes.
6. Do not worry about whether you are successfully achieving a deep level of relaxation. Maintain a passive attitude and permit relaxation to occur at its own pace. When distracting thoughts occur, ignore them and continue repeating "ONE." With practice, the response should come with little effort. Practice the technique once or twice daily, and not within two hours after any meal, since the digestive processes seem to interfere with the elicitation of anticipated changes.

Subjects were further advised to practice the technique in a straight-backed chair, in a quiet, dimly lit room. When interruptions occurred, such as the telephone ringing or a knock at the door, they were instructed not to respond, except in emergencies. They were told instead to attend to the distracting sound "lightly and passively," returning their awareness to their breathing and the word "ONE" when the sound ended.

Progressive Relaxation (n = 8)

Subjects in this condition were trained in the relaxation technique originally developed by Jacobson (1938) as a method for reducing muscular tension. In this procedure, the subject initially practices muscle relaxation while lying down in a quiet room. By alternatively tensing and relaxing selected muscle groups, the subject learns to recognize the sensations associated with muscular tension and practices eliminating the tension. In daily sessions, the subject practices making the discrimination of muscle tension and reducing that tension, as he cycles through about fifteen different muscle groups. Over time, a progressively larger portion of the time in each session is spent relaxing the muscle groups, rather than discriminating tension in them. Finally, the subject practices progressive relaxation while sitting and then attempts to incorporate his skill, as appropriate, into his daily activities.

The trainer for this group (R.M.R.), was experienced in practicing this technique, and introduced it as a skill the subjects could teach themselves by following a systematic program. After describing the basic steps in the progressive relaxation program, the trainer had the subjects practice alternatively tensing and relaxing muscles while listening to standard relaxation instructions presented on tape. A programmed text for self-administration of progressive relaxation training (Rosen, in press) was then given to each subject to follow during the treatment period. This text provided a description of the activities to be followed each day. On two days of each week, these subjects were told to practice for just one 40-minute session instead of two 20-minute sessions. During the 40-minute periods, subjects made progress either by introducing additional muscle groups into their practice routine or by combining several such groups into one relaxation drill.

Attention-Placebo Control (n = 9)

This group was included to control for possible nonspecific effects of relaxation training, including: (1) contact with the experimenters during training, (2) demand characteristics, (3) expectations of subjects about the effects of relaxation on drinking, (4) daily periods of rest or quiet activities, and (5) daily monitoring of relaxation levels (completion of relaxation records). A technique was therefore chosen which would be credible to the subjects as a relaxation procedure and would involve sitting quietly for two periods a day, but which had not been shown to produce any specific relaxation effects (e.g. physiological changes) associated with the other two relaxation techniques. The procedure selected for the attention-placebo control condition was called "bibliotherapy," and involved having the subject engage in quiet, restful reading activities twice a day. The trainer (G.A.M.), an experienced clinician, presented the following rationale to the subjects during the training session:

> People often complain that they have no time to engage in "recreational" reading, because of the flow of normal obligations and commitments. The opportunity to engage in quiet reading of material the person has chosen for its restful and relaxing effect is thought to produce a state of quietness and calmness which is very relaxing in its overall effects. There is a sense of, "I am doing *what I want to do* during these reading periods," rather than the sense of obligation one feels in reading assignment materials.

The subjects were instructed to select a quiet room and a comfortable chair, away from other people and any distractions, for their reading sessions. Specific instructions regarding the selection of reading material (to be read only during the bibliotherapy sessions) were presented as follows:

> Your reading should be limited to either: (a) fiction—including novels, collections of short stories, poetry, and other such material; or (b) reading associated with a hobby or special interest of yours, such as sailing, stamp-collecting, and photography. It should not include newsmagazines or other reading of a nonfiction kind, including textbooks or other assigned school work. In addition, try to pick reading material which is relaxing to you, rather than accounts of violence or material of a particularly erotic nature.

No-Treatment Control ($n = 14$)

This group participated in the pretreatment and posttreatment assessment procedures (personality measures and taste-rating task), and recorded their daily alcohol consumption throughout the study, but did not practice any relaxation technique. This condition was included to assess the effects of: (1) self-monitoring of alcohol consumption, (2) repeated administration of the assessment procedures, and (3) environmental influences on alcohol consumption (particularly the effects of the academic schedule, such as examination periods).

Results

Table 1 presents a summary of the means for the major dependent measures to be described below. Separate two-way analyses of variance (treatment groups × trials) were performed for each of the dependent measures. Where appropriate, nonparametric tests were also conducted. All t tests reported are one-tailed.

Treatment Period

Alcohol Consumption

Based on the daily consumption data provided in the drinking diaries, changes in alcohol consumption were determined by comparing the mean daily consumption during the 2-week baseline period ("pre") with that during the last two weeks of the 6-week treatment period ("post"). These data, for each treatment group, are plotted in Fig. 1.* The repeated-measures analysis revealed no significant effect for treatment conditions, $F (3, 37) = 1.32, p > .20$. However, there was a significant trials effect (baseline versus treatment) $F (1, 37) = 9.08, p > .005$; and the treatments × trials interaction attained borderline

*Both a 12-oz bottle of beer, and 1.2 oz of 80-proof liquor (for example) contain 14.2 ml of ethanol.

Table 1. Group Means on the Major Dependent Measures

	Meditation ($n=10$)	Progressive relaxation ($n=8$)	Attention-placebo control ($n=9$)	No-treatment control ($n=14$)
Daily Ethanol consumption (ml)				
Pre	51.9	39.1	35.9	48.3
Post	26.6	26.7	23.7	48.6
Taste-rating task consumption (ml of wine)				
Pre	199	115	157	158
Post	204	129	156	263
Locus of control				
Pre	11.9	11.6	10.8	9.5
Post	9.9	9.5	7.1	10.2
Trait anxiety				
Pre	34.5	35.5	36.6	34.8
Post	33.6	35.4	35.6	34.5
State anxiety				
Pre	36.5	34.4	33.9	32.8
Post	32.1	32.7	33.7	34.2
Relaxation ratings				
Pre	0.80	1.10	0.54	—
Post	1.64	1.41	0.66	—

significance, $F (3, 37) = 2.31$, $p < .09$. Individual t tests revealed that the trials effect was due to significant decrements in alcohol consumption in the meditation group, $t (9) = 2.07$, $p < .05$; the progressive relaxation group, $t (7) = 2.37$, $p < .025$; and the attention-placebo control group, $t (8) = 2.83$, $p < .03$. No significant effect was found for the no-treatment control group.

Although the pretreatment means for alcohol consumption are not perfectly matched, the analysis of variance revealed no significant differences among groups during the baseline period, $F (3,37) = < 1$. Analysis of the posttreatment means did reveal a significant effect for treatment conditions, $F (3,37) = 3.97$, $p < .025$. Subsequent tests showed that all three relaxation groups (including the bibliotherapy control condition) were significantly lower in alcohol consumption than the no-treatment control group. The t tests comparing each group with the no-treatment control condition yielded $t (37) = 2.39$, $p < .025$ for the progressive relaxation group; $t (37) = 2.40$, $p < .025$ for the meditation group; and $t (37) = 2.72$, $p < .01$ for the attention-placebo group. Individual comparisons yielded no significant differences, however, among the three relaxation groups. Thus, subjects who were regularly practicing a relaxation technique showed similar decreases in alcohol consumption, whether they practiced meditation, progressive relaxation, or the attention-placebo control technique of bibliotherapy. Analyses with nonparametric tests revealed the same pattern of findings.

The results for the taste-rating task (the analog drinking task) are shown in Fig. 2. Analysis of these data yielded a similar, although less striking, pattern. Again, there was no main effect for treatment conditions in the repeated measures analysis, $F (3,35) = 1.58$, $p > .20$. As in the self-monitoring data, there was a significant trials effect, $F (1,35) = 3.47$, $p = .07$. In this case, however, the trials effect was due to a significant increase in wine consumption for the no-treatment control group, $t (11) = 2.74$, $p < .01$. There were no significant trial effects for any of the three relaxation groups ($p > .20$ for each comparison). As with the daily consumption data, there were no significant differences in consumption on the taste-rating task among groups prior to treatment, $F (3,35) = 1.22$, $p > .20$. Thus, in the taste-rating task, the three relaxation groups again differed in consumption from the no-treatment control group, although in this case the no-treatment control group showed an increase while the other groups showed no change. In considering this pattern of results, it should be noted that the posttreatment taste-rating task

Psychology of Meditation

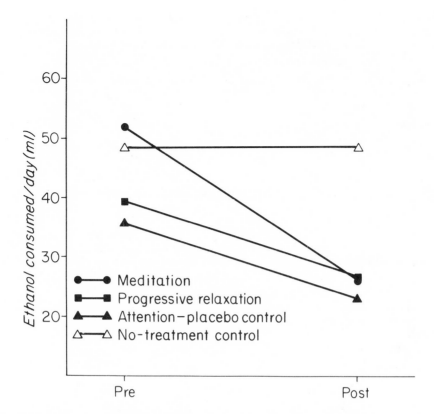

Fig. 1. Mean daily ethanol consumption in experimental and control groups during the 2 weeks of baseline ("pre") and the last 2 weeks of treatment ("post"), as reported on consumption diaries.

occurred just prior to the final examination period, when subjects could be expected to be most concerned or anxious. This speculation is strengthened by the finding that subjects in the no-treatment group were the only ones who showed a mean increase in state anxiety, administered just prior to the taste-rating task.

Personality Measures

The most interesting results for the personality measures were the changes observed in the locus of control scores, presented in Fig. 3. The analysis revealed a pattern of results similar to that found for the alcohol consumption data. There was no significant overall effect for treatment conditions, $F(3,35) < 1$, in the repeated measures analysis. Significant effects were found for the trials factor, $F(3,35) = 10.92$, $p < .005$; and the treatments × trials interaction, $F(1,35) = 3.84$, $p < .025$. Subsequent t tests showed significant decreases in test scores (indicating a shift toward internal locus) for the progressive relaxation group, $t(7) = 2.55$, $p < .025$; the attention-placebo control group, $t(8) = 4.38$, $p < .005$; and a decrease of borderline significance in the meditation group, $t(9) = 1.62$, $p = .07$. The no-treatment control group showed a nonsignificant increase in test scores. The results show, then, that the regular practice of a relaxation technique, including the attention-placebo control procedure, was associated with shifts toward a more internal locus of control.

There were no significant changes in either trait or state anxiety, based on the analysis of Spielberger's STAI scores (all F's < 1). The state anxiety scores did show a similar pattern to the locus of control scores: decreases in the three relaxation groups and an increase in the no-treatment control group. However, due to large within-group variances, these differences did not reach significance. Group means for the STAI scores are presented in Table 1.

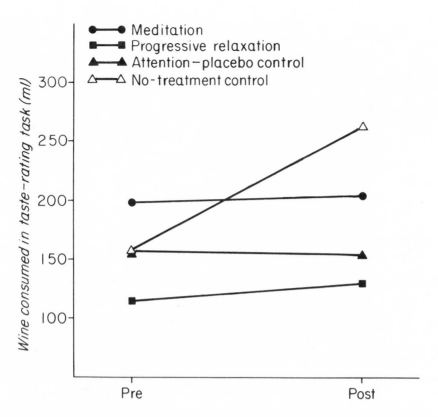

Fig. 2. Wine consumed by experimental and control groups in pretreatment and posttreatment taste-rating tasks.

Relaxation Ratings

Subjects in the three relaxation groups were asked to provide daily ratings of how relaxed they felt after practicing the technique. Figure 4 shows the group means for the relaxation ratings and corresponding alcohol consumption data across the 6 weeks of the treatment period. Although there is a clear correspondence between weekly levels of relaxation ratings and consumption in the meditation group, this relationship is not so apparent in the other two groups. In the repeated-measures analysis, the means of the first week of treatment period were compared with the mean ratings for the last week of the treatment period. The analysis revealed a significant trials effect, $F(1, 24) = 10.14$, $p < .005$, and a borderline treatments effect, $F(2,24) = 2.65$, $p = .09$. There were no significant differences among the groups in the first week of practice, $F(2,24) = 2.14$, $p > .10$. By the end of the treatment period, however, the ratings for the meditation group increased significantly, $t(9) = 3.36$, $p < .005$. The t values for the progressive relaxation and attention-placebo control groups did not show a significant effect. The number of relaxation sessions subjects reported they engaged in for the three groups did not differ significantly, $F(2,24) < 1$. The meditation subjects reported completing 88% of their assigned sessions, with the progressive relaxation subjects reporting 92% and the attention-placebo control subjects 91%.

Follow-Up Period

Of the subjects who completed the treatment phase of the study, 82% also agreed to complete the 7-week follow-up phase. There was one drop-out in the meditation group, one in the progressive relaxation

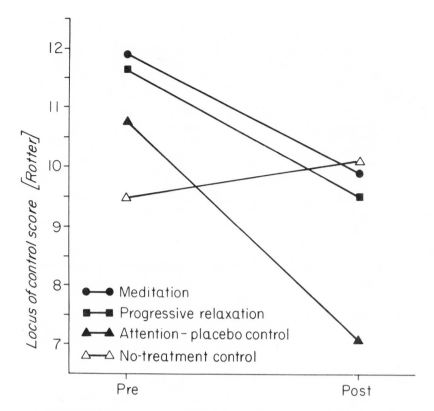

Fig. 3. Pretreatment and posttreatment scores for experimental and control groups on Rotter's Internal-External Locus of Control Scale. Lower scores indicate a more internal locus of control.

group, two in the attention-placebo group, and three in the no-treatment group. The daily consumption means at pretreatment, posttreatment, and follow-up for subjects completing the entire study ($N = 34$) are shown in Fig. 5. As in the other phases of the study, reported means are based on the last 2 weeks of the follow-up period. During the last 2 weeks of the follow-up period, consumption in each of the three relaxation groups increased from the posttreatment level, but was still below the pretreatment consumption level. The no-treatment control group showed a slight decrease in consumption at follow-up, compared to their prior stable levels. Although these trends appear fairly clear in Fig. 5, none of the groups had a consumption level at follow-up that was significantly different from either its pretreatment or posttreatment level. The pre–post changes, however, were still significant for the relaxation groups, even in this reduced sample.

The interpretation of these follow-up data is difficult because of the optional nature of relaxation practice during this period. Most of the relaxation group subjects either stopped practicing their assigned techniques, or practiced sporadically during follow-up. Seven subjects in the meditation group reported some continued practice after treatment, as did two subjects in the progressive relaxation groups and three in the attention-placebo control group. By the last 2 weeks of the follow-up period, however, only three meditators, two progressive relaxers, and two attention-placebo controls recorded any relaxation sessions, and only one subject (who was in the progressive relaxation group) was practicing twice daily. Perhaps the most important information from the follow-up data, then, is that nearly all subjects chose to discontinue regular practice of their assigned techniques when given the option to do so.

In this study, regular practice of a relaxation technique was associated with significantly decreased alcohol consumption. When regular practice was discontinued, consumption tended to increase. The major question regarding the interpretation of these findings is: "What is mediating this effect?" Since the attention-placebo controls showed the same consumption patterns as the other relaxation groups, we

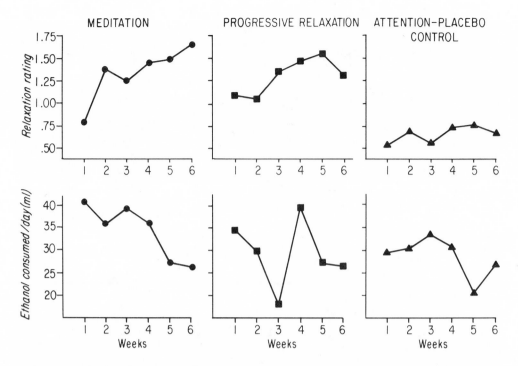

Fig. 4. Mean relaxation ratings and mean daily ethanol consumption across the 6 treatment weeks in the meditation, progressive relaxation, and attention-placebo control groups, as reported on daily records.

looked first for possible "nonspecific" factors common to all three groups which might answer this question.

Expectancy Factors

We first explored the possibility that expectancy factors accounted for the similar consumption decrements in the meditation, progressive relaxation, and attention-placebo control groups. Although we had attempted to avoid creating an expectation or demand that drinking would decrease after relaxation training, the subjects may have assumed that we were looking for this effect, or may have expected the effect themselves, based on their own experiences or the popular "common-sense" notion that people drink more when tense. Since all of the subjects who participated in the follow-up period of our study returned the follow-up questionnaire, we had some data on expectancy factors for all but four of our 27 relaxation subjects. Of these 23 relaxation subjects, only five indicated that they had expected regular practice of their assigned technique to produce decreased alcohol consumption. Three of these five were attention-placebo control subjects; the other two were meditation subjects. Although these data suggest that expectation may have played a greater role in our attention-placebo condition, they do not support the hypothesis that a positive expectation produced the consumption decrements in our groups. In fact, as can be seen in Table 2, we found no evidence for a relationship between subjects' expectations and their consumption change scores. Fishers exact test reveals no significant effects of expectation on consumption ($p > .20$).

Demand Characteristics

To assess possible demand characteristics of this study, each subject was asked to indicate what he thought was the purpose of the study, and what results the experimenters were hoping to find. On the basis

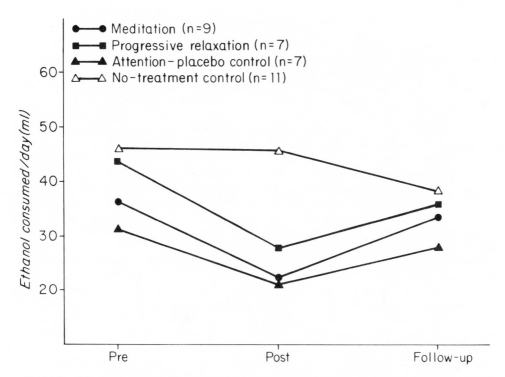

Fig. 5. Mean daily ethanol consumption in experimental and control groups during the 2 weeks of baseline ("pre"), the last 2 weeks of treatment ("post"), and the last 2 weeks of follow-up, as reported on consumption diaries. Only data from subjects completing the follow-up period are included in the group means.

Table 2. Relationship between Awareness Level and Consumption Change Scores

	Subjects with change scores > median Greater decreases in consumption	Subjects with change scores ≤ median Smaller or no decreases in consumption
Aware	7	6
Partially aware	3	4
Unaware	1	2

of their responses to those items, subjects were divided into two levels of awareness: (1) "aware" subjects, who indicated that the experimenters were looking for a decrease in alcohol consumption after relaxation training; and (2) "unaware" subjects who stated either that the experimenters were hoping to find effects of relaxation on consumption but did not indicate the expected direction of these effects, or stated that they did not know the purpose of the study or that the experimenters expected drinking to increase as a result of relaxation. There were 13 subjects who fell into the aware category and 10 subjects in the unaware category. Mean consumption decreases pre-post for the aware group was 14.18 ml; for the unaware group it was 12.58 ml. The difference between groups was not significant, $t(21) = .27, p > .20$.

Discussion

The results of this study show that the regular practice of a relaxation technique, whether it is Benson's meditation procedure, progressive relaxation, or just sitting quietly and reading for two short time periods each day, leads to a significant reduction in alcohol consumption for subjects who are heavy social drinkers. The possibility that this decrease is due simply to a reactive effect, stimulated by participation in a study on drinking behavior in which subjects monitored their consumption on an ongoing daily basis, seems unlikely as subjects in the no-treatment group (who also monitored intake and completed the pre- and posttreatment measures) failed to show a similar decrement. Our follow-up questionnaire data, presented above, also call into question whether the obtained effects are mediated solely by subjects' expectancies or response to the experimental demand characteristics. Thus, although the attention-placebo group subjects did not differ significantly in alcohol consumption from the meditation and relaxation groups, it is possible that this control group (bibliotherapy) contained some "active ingredients" (other than expectation and attention factors) which were common to the two other treatment conditions. No studies of the psychophysiological effects of "bibliotherapy" as practiced by our subjects have been reported in the literature.

What is there about taking time out for two 20-minute periods a day that may be associated with decreased drinking behavior? Of all the personality measures we administered which might give us some clue to this question, only one showed a significant change which was consistent with changes in alcohol consumption shown in three treatment conditions. The locus of control measure (Fig. 3) showed that there was a significant shift toward the internal side of the scale for subjects in all three relaxation groups. Subjects in the no-treatment group, on the other hand, actually showed a slight increase in externality on the locus of control scale. It seems unlikely that the shift toward internality in the meditation, progressive relaxation, and bibliotherapy groups was mediated by expectancy or demand effects. How can we then explain the finding that decreased consumption is associated with increased internal control?

It may be that our three treatment groups practiced techniques which all elicited a common "relaxation response" in our subjects (cf., Benson, 1975). While the exact nature of this response cannot be determined from our findings, the three treatment groups would seem to have the following characteristics in common: (1) daily "time-out" periods, in which subjects sit quietly in a calm and relaxed environment, providing an opportunity for them to reflect on the day's activities (perhaps a form of self-regulated desensitization); (2) a feeling of taking time out for oneself, to be alone for short periods, uninterrupted by the demands and stresses of daily living (this "doing something for yourself" attitude was also stressed in the bibliotherapy procedure, as subjects were told to choose their own reading materials and avoid reading any assigned materials). It is possible, therefore, that subjects felt an increased sense of personal control as they continued to engage in these procedures over a 6-week period. If heavy drinkers use alcohol to increase their sense of perceived control (Marlatt, 1976), these relaxation techniques may have provided an alternative "self-control" procedure which led to a decrease in alcohol consumption. This feeling of increased self-control may have mediated the shift toward internal locus of control. It is possible that other programs or activities that might mediate a shift of this sort on the I-E scale would also lead to a decrease in alcohol consumption. For example, perhaps a regular daily activity such as calisthenics would offer the same feelings of taking time out for oneself and lead to a decrease in alcohol consumption. It may also be the case, of course, that subjects who are drinking less may describe themselves as having more control over their lives. Our data do not tell us which is cause and which is effect in the relationship between locus and control and alcohol consumption.

Given that all three relaxation procedures were equally effective in terms of reduced alcohol consumption, is there any reason to recommend one procedure over the others? This question assumes considerable significance if any of these techniques are to be applied as treatment procedures for problem drinkers or alcoholics. In the context of treatment, we would like to recommend a technique which would be readily accepted by our clients, and one that they would continue to practice over long periods of time. It is clear from our data that although all three techniques were equally effective during the 6-week treatment period, the majority of subjects discontinued their practice of the technique during the follow-up period. There is, however, some reason to believe that the meditation group subjects were more "hooked" on the technique than subjects in the other two conditions. As reported earlier, more meditation subjects continued some practice of the procedure of their own volition during follow-up than in any other group.

Second, as is evident from inspection of Fig. 4, the subjects in the meditation group were the only ones who reported a linear increase in daily relaxation reports over the 6-week treatment period (associated with a linear decrease in consumption). These data suggest that the meditation subjects were becoming more and more "relaxed" as the treatment period continued. If these findings are representative of meditation techniques, in general, it would appear that this procedure is more intrinsically reinforcing or satisfying than the other techniques we investigated. In support of this hypothesis, Glueck and Stroebel (1975) have reported that psychiatric patients who were taught progressive relaxation discontinued practice of the technique soon after instruction because it was considered to be rather laborious and a more difficult procedure than meditating. Based on these observations, meditation may be a more effective technique because it is easy to do and intrinsically more satisfying, and thus would be practiced over a longer period of time than the other relaxation methods.

We included four subjects who described themselves as problem drinkers in our sample. Each of these was assigned to a different treatment condition in our study. Examination of the findings for these few subjects may illustrate the relative effectiveness of the different relaxation techniques as potential treatment procedures for alcoholism. The subject assigned to the meditation condition showed the largest drop in daily consumption of all four subjects: a decrease of 66% in daily consumption (absolute drop of 126 ml of pure alcohol a day, from baseline to the treatment period). The other problem drinkers showed drops of 29 (progressive relaxation), 32 (bibliotherapy), and 34% (no-treatment control). Of these four, the only subjects who continued practice of their technique during the follow-up period were the ones assigned to the meditation and progressive relaxation groups Although these results are certainly speculative, they suggest that meditation may be the best option for alcoholism treatment among the relaxation procedures we evaluated in our study.

There is one additional reason why meditation may be the relaxation treatment method of choice with problem drinkers or alcoholics. Much of the research literature in this area (reviewed by Marlatt and Marques, 1976) suggests that meditation produces an altered state of consciousness which is qualitatively different from other conscious states, although recent studies have questioned this finding (e.g., Pagano, Rose, Stevens, and Warrenburg, 1976). Numerous reports from meditators describe this altered state as a kind of "high" or pleasant affective experience. It is also clear that most problem drinkers consume alcohol to alter their own consciousness, to get "stoned" or "high" on booze. In the search for alternatives to alcohol, meditation seems to offer the drinker a non-drug "high" which offers none of the drawbacks of excessive drinking. Some alcoholics may, in fact, be searching for a sense of new meaning in their lives by altering their consciousness through ingestion of a drug: the "spirits" in the bottle. The fact that Alcoholics Anonymous (AA) is so effective with many alcoholics, may be due in part to the spiritual orientation and underpinnings of the AA philosophy. Meditation may offer a similar experience.

Which form of meditation should be recommended? While research may eventually show that the various forms are equivalent in terms of their overall effectiveness, at this stage of development it would seem that TM has the most to offer the problem drinker. The nonspecific effects of TM, which we tried to control for in our own design by employing the relatively neutral Benson technique, may serve to increase the likelihood that the alcoholic would benefit from the meditation experience. The positive expectancies engendered by the introductory lectures and the initiation ceremony, the commitment incurred by paying the course fee, the mutual enthusiasm and group support which the TM instruction offers (not unlike the enthusiasm and social reinforcement which characterize AA), and the availability of follow-up and "checking" provided, all combine to increase the probability that the alcoholic will continue the practice of the technique. Whether or not this form of meditation will prove itself to be an effective substitute for drinking remains to be empirically demonstrated.

Acknowledgment

This research was supported, in part, by grants from the University of Washington Alcoholism and Drug Abuse Institute and the National Institute of Alcoholism and Alcohol Abuse (Grant No. 1 RO3 AA 01868-01).

References

Benson, H.: Decreased alcohol intake associated with the practice of meditation: A retrospective investigation. *Annals of the New York Academy of Sciences,* 1974, **233**, 174–177.

Benson, H. *The relaxation response.* New York: William Morrow & Co., 1975.

Benson, H., and Wallace, R. K. Decreased drug abuse with Transcendental Meditation: A study of 1,862 subjects. In C. J. D. Zarafonetis (Ed.), *Drug abuse: Proceedings of the International Conference.* Philadelphia, Pa.: Lea and Febiger, 1972.

Benson, H., Rosner, B. A., Marzetta, B. R., and Klemchuk, H. M. Decreased blood pressure in pharmacologically treated hypertensive patients who regularly elicited the relaxation response. *Lancet,* 1974, **i**, 289–291.

Bloomfield, H. H., Cain, M. P., Jaffe, D. T., and Kory, R. B. *TM: Discovering inner energy and overcoming stress.* New York: Dell, 1975.

Cahalan, D., and Room, R. *Problem drinking among American men.* New Brunswick, N.J.: Rutgers Center of Alcohol Studies, Monograph No. 7, 1974.

Cahalan, D., Cisin, I. H., and Crossley, H. M. *American drinking practices: A national study of drinking behavior and patterns.* New Brunswick, N.J.: Rutgers Center of Alcohol Studies, Monograph No. 6, 1969.

Cappell, H. An evaluation of tension models of alcohol consumption. In R. J. Gibbins, Y. Israel, H. Kalant, R. E. Popham, W. Schmidt, and R. G. Smart (Eds.), *Research advances in alcohol and drug problems,* Vol. 2. New York: Wiley, 1975.

Cappell, H., and Herman, C. P. Alcohol and tension reduction: a review. *Quarterly Journal of Studies on Alcohol,* 1972, **33**, 33–64.

Carrington, P., and Ephron, H. S. Meditation as an adjunct to psychotherapy. In S. Arieti (Ed.), *New dimensions in psychiatry: A world view.* New York: Wiley, 1975.

Glueck, B. C., and Stroebel, C. F. Biofeedback and meditation in the treatment of psychiatric illness. *Comprehensive Psychiatry,* 1975, **16**, 303–321.

Higgins, R. L., and Marlatt, G. A. Fear of interpersonal evaluation as a determinant of alcohol consumption in male social drinkers. *Journal of Abnormal Psychology,* 1975, **84**, 644–651.

Hjelle, L. A. Transcendental Meditation and psychological health. *Perceptual and Motor Skills,* 1974, **39**, 623–628.

Jacobson, E. *Progressive relaxation.* Chicago: University of Chicago Press, 1938.

Marlatt, G. A. Alcohol, stress, and cognitive control. In I. G. Sarason & C. D. Spielberger (Eds.), *Stress and anxiety* (Vol. 3). Washington, D.C.: Hemisphere Publishing Co., 1976.

Marlatt, G. A. Behavioral assessment of social drinking and alcoholism. In G. A. Marlatt and P. E. Nathan (Eds.), *Behavioral approaches to alcoholism.* New Brunswick, N.J.: Center for Alcohol Studies, in press.

Marlatt, G. A., and Marques, J. K.: *Meditation, Self-control and Alcohol Use.* Presented at the 8th Banff International Conference on Behavior Modification, Banff, Alberta, March, 1976.

Marlatt, G. A., Kosturn, C. F., and Lang, A. R. Provocation to anger and opportunity for retaliation as determinants of alcohol consumption in social drinkers. *Journal of Abnormal Psychology,* 1975, **84**, 652–659.

Miller, P. M., Hersen, M., Eisler, R. M., and Hilsman, G. Effects of social stress on operant drinking of alcoholics and social drinkers. *Behavior Research and Therapy,* 1974, **12**, 67–72.

Nidich, S., Seeman, W., and Dreskin, T. Influence of Transcendental Meditation: A replication. *Journal of Counseling Psychology,* 1972, **20**, 656–666.

Orme-Johnson, D. W. Autonomic stability and Transcendental Meditation. *Psychosomatic Medicine,* 1973, **35**, 341–349.

Pagano, R. R., Rose, R. M., Stevens, R. M., and Warrenburg, S. Sleep during Transcendental Meditation. *Science,* 1976, **191**, 308–309.

Rosen, G. M. Self-administered progressive relaxation training. In J. G. Flanders, *Practical Psychology.* New York: Harper & Row, (in press).

Rotter, J. B. Generalized expectancies for internal versus external control of reinforcement. *Psychological Monographs, 1966,* **80**, No. 1 (Whole No. 609).

Seeman, W., Niditch, S., and Banta, T. Influence of Transcendental Meditation on a measure of self-actualization. *Journal of Counseling Psychology,* 1972, **19**, 184–187.

Shafii, M., Lavely, R., and Jaffe, R. Meditation and the prevention of alcohol abuse. *American Journal of Psychiatry,* 1975, **132**, 942–945.

Smith, J. C. Meditation as psychotherapy: A review of the literature. *Psychological Bulletin,* 1975, **82**, 558–564.

Spielberger, C. D., Gorsuch, R. L., and Lushene, R. E. *Manual for the state-trait anxiety inventory.* Palo Alto, California: Consulting Psychologist Press, 1970.

Swinyard, C. A., Chaube, S., and Sutton, D. B. Neurological and behavioral aspects of Transcendental Meditation relevant to alcoholism: A review. *Annals of the New York Academy of Science,* 1974, **233**, 162–173.

White, J. *What is meditation?* Garden City, N.Y.: Anchor Books, 1974.

B3. Hypertension

For a review of the hypertension studies, readers are referred to the summary in the Article by Shapiro and Giber (Article 6) and to the accompanying table.

The studies included in this section are representative of the hypertension literature and were chosen because they used meditation as the primary treatment variable. In the Benson *et al.* study (Article 11), there was a definite reduction of systemic arterial pressure in hypertensive and borderline hypertensive subjects who practiced transcendental meditation and did not take any drugs. Stone and DeLeo's study (Article 12) used a meditation procedure of counting breaths. The experimental group showed a reduction of mean arterial pressure which averaged 12 mm. Stone and DeLeo also measured dopamine β-hydroxylase under the assumption that it provided an index of sympathetic nervous system function, and was more sensitive than catecholamines. They found that there was, in fact, a significant reduction in dopamine β-hydroxylase in the experimental group.

Both of these studies suffer from a limitation of not having a randomized placebo control group. However, the results are suggestive and promising. One excellent study (not included here for reasons of space), is by Patel (1975). Although Patel's study is a more elegant experimental design, it is difficult to ferret out the effects of treatment due to the combination of meditation and biofeedback.

Table 3. Studies on Hypertension

Investigator(s)	Clinical Problem	S's (N, age, sex, prior experience)	INDEPENDENT VARIABLE Type and Length of Treatment/Training	Frequency of Therapist (T) Contact	Subjective Effects	DEPENDENT VARIABLE Physiological (Note BP measures given systolic/diastolic unless otherwise noted)	Follow-up	Type of Design; Quality of Controls; Methodological Problems
Benson and Wallace, 1972a	Hypertension	N=22, no prior experience	Standard TM training by Student's International Society—8½ hrs. S's instructed practice technique 2x20 min/daily	Not stated	None reported	Found decreased resting systemic arterial blood pressure levels. Mean BP levels prior to meditation—150±17/94±9mmHg (mean ± one S.D.) Mean BP levels post meditation—141±11/87±7mmHg (mean ± one S.D.)	4-63 weeks	N=1, S's as own control pre, during, and post meditation.
Benson et al., 1974a	Borderline hypertension with S's not using anti-hypertensive drugs	N=22, avg. age approx. 43.1 + 12.9 yr. (mean 1 one S.D.) 10 male, 12 female volunteers from introductory TM lecture group	Same as above	Not stated	None reported	Found decreased resting blood pressure levels. Mean BP levels prior to meditation—146.5±13.7/6.1±6.96mmHg Mean BP levels post meditation—139.5±12.6/90.7±± 8.76mmHg	Post meditation instruction measurement every 2-3 weeks x 25 weeks	N=1, S's as own control 6 weeks prior to meditation instruction baseline measurement
Benson et al., 1974b	Hypertension with S's using anti-hypertensive drugs	N=14, avg. age approx. 53.3 yrs. (S.D 9.1/9.6 female. No prior experience. volunteers from introductory TM lecture.	Same as above	Not stated	None reported	Found decreased resting blood pressure levels. Mean BP levels prior to meditation—145.6±/38.9/1.9± 11.9mmHg Mean BP levels post meditation—135.0±8.37/87.0±11.34mmHg S's diet and antihypertensive drug use (mean 1 one S.D.) monitored by questionnaire	Post instruction measurement 10 days x 20 weeks	1 x 6 weeks prior to meditation instruction measurements taken. study unbiased in regard to alterations in antihypertensive agents or significantly altered diet
Patel 1973, 1975a follow-up	Hypertension with S's using anti-hypertensive drugs. Duration of hypertension from 1-20 years (avg. 6.8 years) Symptomatology ± tiredness (14 patients) headache (13), dyspnoea on exertion (11), dizziness (a), irritability (8), chest pain (6), angina (2), palpitation (6), and nervousness and depression in (5).	N=20, avg. age 57.35 yrs. 9 males, 11 females Group Two N=20 controls matched for age and sex	Patients instructed to practice Yogic breath meditation, muscle relaxation, and concentration meditation on an idea also biofeedback of GSR through audio signal of 'relaxometer' given continuously. Patients also told pre and post session BP levels.	3x per week x 3 months for ½ hr. relaxation training	Report stated "patients responded favourably, criteria of subjective effects not stated	1) Alteration in BP over 3 months of Relaxation Training "Pre-trial" BP Treatment Group 159.1±15.9/100.1±12.8 Control Group 163.1±20.9/9.99±12.8 "End of trial" BP Treatment Group 138.7±16.0/85.9±8.7 Control Group 162.6±24.4/97.0±12.0 2) Follow-up Results End of trial annual BP Treatment Group 144.6±11.0/86.0±5.74 Control Group 167.7±9.73/97.1±6.54 Final follow-up measured BP Treatment Group 144.4±5.83/86.7±3.33 Control Group 163.5±42/98.1±7.83 (12 month)/(9 month)	3, 6, 9 and 12 months	Variance of treatment effect attributable to Yoga, biofeedback and role of therapist not clear with 42% drop in total drug requirement among patients. 5 patients ended use of drugs, of four patients who did not control BP one achieved control of migraine and stopped antidepressant drug therapy. BP respiration rates recorded and given to patient pre and post session. also biofeedback of GSR given continuously during treatment
Patel 1975b	Hypertension with S's using anti-hypertensive drugs	Phase One (N=34) Group One: (treatment) N=17, mean age 59.5 yrs. 6 male, 11 female Group Two (control) N=17, mean age 58.6 yrs. 7 male, 10 female. Phase Two former control group (2) given treatment	Treatment procedure (2 sessions per week x 6 weeks) 1) Educational discussion about hypertension, physiology of relaxation, etc. and patients 2) Instruction in methodical (yogic) relaxation and slowed breathing 3) After mastery of Step 2: Transcendental meditation-like technique taught 4) Biofeedback (e.g., audio signal of GSR level) given continuously by "relaxometer" during steps 2 and 3 5) S's urged to practice informal relaxation and meditation outside of treatment when tense (e.g. each patient had a red disc on his watch as a reminder to relax when he looked at the time	Extensive doctor patient interaction between doctor	None reported	1) BP before trial Treatment Group 167.5±23.6/99.6±9.3mmHg Control Group 168.9±20.0/100.6±11.4mmHg 2) Mean final BP Phase I Treatment Group 141.4/84.4mmHg Control Group 160.0/96.4mmHg 3) Mean Phase 2 Mean initial BP Treatment (formerly control) 176.6/104.3 Control (formerly control) 148.6/89.3 Mean final BP Treatment (formerly control) 148.81/87.8 Control (formerly control) 146.21/86.2	2 wks. x 3 months after phase one, then 2 month interval prior to phase two. Phase two; single used follow-up examination	Same criticism as above
Datey et al., 1969	Hypertension with chronic hypertensive (essential hypertension — 32 patients; renal — 12, arteriosclerotic — 3) Symptomatology: dizziness (30 patients) headache (28), chest pain in 12 (angina 7), palpitation in 12, breathlessness on exertion in 10, exhaustion in 10, insomnia in 8, irritability and nervousness in 8	N=47, avg age 46 yrs. 37 male, 10 female Group One N=10, not using antihypertensive drugs. Group Two N=22, BP well controlled with antihypertensive drugs. Group Three N=15, BP inadequately controlled with antihypertensive drugs.	"Shavasana" Yogic breathing concentration and muscle relaxation done 30 min. daily for approx. 30 weeks. EMG feedback of frontalis muscle tension used as check of muscle relaxation	Not stated specifically "experienced supervisor" checks exercising patients for correctness in breathing exercise	Report states, "patients experienced a sense of well-being after exercise. Improvement reported among almost all patients in somatic symptoms (e.g. headaches, giddiness, nervousness, irritability, and insomnia)	Decreases in avg. mean blood pressure Group One: 134mmHg to 107mmHg (reduction 27mmHg) Group Two: 102/100mmHg unchanged (since patient's BP well controlled by drugs. therapy aimed at reducing drug dosages for 13 S's (59%). avg. drug requirement was reduced to 32% of original dosage. for 9 patients. dosage could not be reduced. however, 6 of these S's performed Yogic exercise irregularly Group Three: 120mmHg to 110mmHg drug requirement reduced to 29% of original in 6 patients (40% dosage unchanged in 7 patients (of these 2 were irregular and 2 could not perform exercise correctly). does had to be increased in 2 patients (regular with exercise). Essential (62.5%), Renal (47%), not statistically significant. arteriosclerotic (not favorable response)	to 40 weeks	Placebo tablets given S's not using anti-hypertensive drugs one month prior to treatment, data substantiating report of improvement in somatic symptoms needed; also follow-up needed.
Stone and DeLeo 1976	Mild or moderate hypertension (defined as mean arterial BP greater than 105mmHg during at least 50% of 14 pretreatment examination) with S's who had never received antihypertensive therapy	N=19 Group One (controls) N=5, avg. age 28, all male Group Two (treatment) N=14, avg. age 28, (±1 yrs.) (mean ± s.e.m.) Baseline BP for both groups similar	"Buddhist" meditation taught (e.g. count- ing breathing in fine 20 min. training sessions S's told to repeat technique 2x daily for 10-15 min.	Not stated specifically	None reported	Effect of Physiologic Relaxation on Arterial Blood Pressure (mean ± Standard error mean systolic/diastolic BP in mmHg) Group One (controls) Baseline—Supine 144±6/90±2 Upright 147±7/93±2 6 mos.—Supine 145±7/92±3 Upright 145±3/93±2 Group Two (treatment) Baseline—Supine 141±3/90±3 Upright 132±3/82±2 6 mos.—Supine 146±/95±3 Upright 131±4/85±2 Found lowered mean (by 12mmHg) BP for treatment group over controls. Changes in dopamine betahydroxylase activity in blood plasma elevated; showed decrease among treatment group which correlated with BP reduction. Also reduction in furosemide-stimulated renin activity (PRA) uncorrelated with BP changes. No significant changes in blood volume.	6 months	Effect of possible dietary salt restriction, assessed by measuring urinary sodium excretion, controls nonrandomized with small % reduction in adrenergic activity (DPH) may be statistically significant but not a physiologically important alteration

11

DECREASED BLOOD-PRESSURE IN PHARMACOLOGICALLY TREATED HYPERTENSIVE PATIENTS WHO REGULARLY ELICITED THE RELAXATION RESPONSE

Herbert Benson, Bernard A. Rosner,
Barbara R. Marzetta, and Helen M. Klemchuk

Summary A wakeful hypometabolic state may be induced by simple, non-cultic mental techniques or by traditional meditational practices. The hypometabolic state seems to represent an integrated hypothalamic response ("relaxation response") which is consistent with a state of decreased sympathetic-nervous-system activity. A prospective investigation was designed to test whether regular elicitation of the relaxation response might lower blood-pressures in hypertensive patients who were maintained on constant antihypertensive therapy. Fourteen people were investigated. During the control period of 5.6 weeks, blood-pressures did not change significantly from day to day and averaged 145.6 mm.Hg systolic and 91.9 mm.Hg diastolic. During the experimental period of 20 weeks, systolic blood-pressures decreased to 135.0 mm.Hg ($p < 0.01$) and diastolic blood-pressures fell to 87.0 mm.Hg ($p < 0.05$). The regular elicitation of the relaxation response may, therefore, have usefulness in the management of hypertensive subjects who are already on drug therapy. The use of the relaxation response may influence the economics of the therapy of hypertension since it is practised at no cost other than time.

Introduction

A WAKEFUL hypometabolic state may be induced by the use of simple, non-cultic mental techniques or by traditional meditational practices.[1-4] The hypometabolic state is characterised by decreased oxygen consumption, carbon-dioxide elimination, respiratory-rate, and minute ventilation with no change in respiratory quotient. There is a marked decrease in arterial-blood lactate and a slight decrease in arterial-

Reprinted with permission from *The Lancet*, 1974, 289-291.

blood pH and base excess. In subjects experienced in the elicitation of the hypometabolic state, intra-arterial blood-pressures are low before, during, and after its practice. The hypometabolic state seems to represent an integrated hypothalamic response, termed the "relaxation response," which is consistent with a state of decreased sympathetic-nervous-system activity.[5] The relaxation response is suggested to be the counterpart of another hypothalamic response—the emergency reaction of Cannon,[6,7] which is popularly called the fight or flight response.

Continual elicitation of the emergency reaction with its resultant increased sympathetic-nervous-system activity has been implicated in the pathogenesis of systemic arterial hypertension.[8,9] The relaxation response may serve to counteract the effects of the fight or flight response, therefore we investigated the therapeutic usefulness of the relaxation response in hypertensive individuals. In a prospective study of twenty-two patients with untreated borderline hypertension, blood-pressures averaged 146.5 mm.Hg systolic and 94.6 mm.Hg diastolic during the control period, which averaged 6 weeks.[10] During the subsequent 25-week experimental period when the patients regularly elicited the relaxation response, blood-pressures fell to 139.5 mm.Hg systolic ($p <$ 0.001) and to 90.8 mm.Hg diastolic ($p < 0.002$). Measurements were made at random times of the day, but never during meditation.

We have extended the investigation to patients taking antihypertensive medications. Significant decreases in both systolic and diastolic blood-pressures were noted after beginning the regular elicitation of this hypometabolic response.

Methods

The technique used to elicit the relaxation response was transcendental meditation. Transcendental meditation is individually taught by a teacher trained in this Indian yogic technique by Maharishi Mahesh Yogi. The instruction is given by a non-profit organisation, the International Meditation Society, and costs $75 for the four consecutive daily lessons required. The technique involves:

A mental device.—There is a constant stimulus of a silently repeated secret sound or word called a mantra. The purpose of this repetition is to free one's self from logical, externally oriented thought. The eyes remain closed throughout the practice.

A passive attitude.—If distracting thoughts do occur during repetition, they should be disregarded and one's attention should be redirected to the mantra. One should not worry about how well one is performing the technique.

Decreased muscle tonus.—The subject should sit in a comfortable position so that minimal muscular work is required.

Regular practice.—The subject is instructed to practise the technique for two daily 20-minute periods, usually before breakfast and before dinner.

No contact with the International Meditation Society is required after initiation, although it is encouraged. Emphasis is placed upon having a trained teacher both to initiate the subject and to "check" the meditation periodically.

The fourteen subjects volunteered to take part in this investigation while at introductory lectures on transcendental meditation given by the Students International Meditation Society in Cambridge, Massachusetts, in Berkeley and Los Angeles, California, and in Minneapolis, Minnesota. At these lectures, an offer was made to waive the regular instruction fee for those individuals who knew they had hypertension, and who would postpone learning the technique for approximately 6 weeks during which control blood-pressure measurements were made. The fee was either waived by the Society or paid from research-grant funds. The subjects also agreed to return every 2–3 weeks for at least a year after learning the technique to have their blood-pressures measured. Before the subject was accepted in the investigation, blood-pressures were measured three or four times over a period of 15–20 minutes and had to be either greater than 140 mm.Hg systolic or 90 mm.Hg diastolic, or both, on the last measurement. These arbitrary levels are higher than those considered to be normotensive.[11]

On each day of measurement, before the blood-pressures were recorded, each subject filled out a questionnaire. The questionnaire assessed the amount and type of medication, including antihypertensive medication, which was being used. It also established the frequency of meditation and the dietary habits of the subjects. Each subject was instructed to adhere to the medication schedule prescribed by his physician. In this investigation, all of the fourteen subjects remained on constant antihypertensive medications during both the premeditation (control) and postmeditation (experimental) periods. One was taking diazepam; seven were taking chlordiazepoxide or diazepam and one of either a benzothiadiazine derivative, one of the rauwolfia alkaloids, or spironolactone; three were taking chlordiazepoxide or diazepam and two or three of the following drugs: a benzothiadiazine derivative, one of the rauwolfia alkaloids, and spironolactone; and three were taking methyldopa and a benzothiadiazine derivative. Sixty-four people volunteered for the study, but fifty had either altered their antihypertensive medication or diet and therefore were excluded from the study due to the uncontrolled effects of these changes.

Blood-pressure was measured by means of a random-zero sphygmomanometer.[12] This device consists of a standard blood-pressure cuff and air-inflation system with a visible calibrated mercury column. The random-zero sphygmomanometer varies the zero position of the mercury column in a random manner, adding 0–60 mm.Hg to the column before each reading. Only at the end of each measurement is the actual "zero" for the column of mercury known to the person measuring the blood-pressure. Thus, observer bias is eliminated. The disappearance of the Korotkoff sounds (phase v) was used as the criterion for determining diastolic blood pressure. Recordings were taken with the subject in the sitting position.

During the first 5.6 weeks of the premeditation-control period, 279 measurements of blood-pressure were obtained. These control measurements were made on an average of 7 separate days. On each day, measurements were repeated every 5 minutes until both systolic and diastolic pressures did not change more than 5 mm.Hg from the preceding measurements. After each subject was trained in the practice of transcendental meditation, he or she returned on an average of 10 separate days over a period averaging 20 weeks for similar blood-pressure measurements. During the postmeditation-experimental period, 340 measurements were obtained. They were made during non-meditational periods of the day and bore no consistent relation to the meditational period. Attempts were made to have all of a given subject's measurements at the same time of day. The average systolic and diastolic blood-pressures were calculated for each patient at each visit. The premeditation-control period was divided into three intervals: 7 days or less after the initial blood-pressure reading, 8–14 days afterwards, and more than 14 days after the initial reading. The average blood-pressures for each patient within each of these three time intervals were computed. A two-way analysis of variance[13] was performed, yielding comparisons of blood-pressure levels between the three time intervals using each subject as his own control. For the postmeditation-experimental period, paired t tests were done, comparing the average blood-pressure levels within two time intervals. These two intervals were 30 days or less and more than 30 days after the first day blood-pressures were measured after the start of the regular practice of meditation. There were no significant changes of blood-pressure levels between the three premeditation-control period time intervals and between the two postmeditation-experimental period intervals. Therefore, the average blood pressure levels for the entire premeditation-control and postmeditation-experimental periods were computed and compared by paired t tests.

COMPARISON OF BLOOD PRESSURE LEVELS (mm. Hg) DURING THE PREMEDITATION-CONTROL PERIOD TO THOSE OF THE POSTMEDITATION-EXPERIMENTAL PERIOD

Blood-pressure	Premeditation control period	Postmeditation experimental period	Difference
Systolic			
Mean............	145.6	135.0	−10.6
S.D..............	7.38	11.19	12.45
S.E.M...........	1.97	2.99	3.33
Diastolic			
Mean...........	91.9	87.0	−4.85
S.D.,...........	8.32	11.34	7:69
S.E.M...........	2.22	3.03	2.05

Results

The mean age of the participants was 53.3 years (s.d. 9.9). There were eight females and six males.

During the premeditation-control period, the systolic blood-pressures averaged 145.6 mm.Hg and the diastolic pressures 91.9 mm.Hg (table). During the postmeditation-experimental period, the systolic pressures averaged 135.0 mm.Hg and the diastolic pressures averaged 87.0 mm.Hg. Comparisons of the blood-pressures of the premeditation-control period to those of the postmeditation-experimental period yielded significant differences for both systolic ($p < 0.01$) and diastolic ($p < 0.05$) pressures.

Discussion

The results show that the regular practice of a technique which elicits the relaxation response is associated with decreased blood-pressures in pharmacologically treated hypertensive patients. The investigation is unbiased with regard to the alteration of antihypertensive agents, significantly altered diet, observer error, and subject familiarity with blood-pressure measurement. In this study and in the previously cited study of untreated hypertensive subjects,[10] blood-pressures were decreased by a behavioral intervention, and these data support the theory that behavioral factors play an important role in both the development and therapy of hypertension.[9]

We believe that results similar to those reported here would be obtained with other techniques which elicit the relaxation response. The basic components of the elicitation of the relaxation response (a mental device, a passive attitude, decreased muscle tonus, and regular practice) are present in a technique now employed in this laboratory.[1] The instructions for this technique are:

(1) Sit quietly in a comfortable position.

(2) Close your eyes.

(3) Deeply relax all your muscles, beginning at your feet and progressing up to your face. Keep them deeply relaxed.

(4) Breathe through your nose. Become aware of your breathing. As you breathe out, say the word "one" silently to yourself—e.g., breathe in . . . out, "one;" in . . . out, "one", and so on.

(5) Continue for 20 minutes. Occasionally open your eyes to check the time. When you finish, sit quietly for several minutes at first with closed eyes and later with opened eyes.

(6) Do not worry about whether you are successfully achieving a deep level of relaxation. Maintain a passive attitude and permit relaxation to occur at its own pace.

When distracting thoughts occur, ignore them and continue repeating "one." With practice, the response should come with little effort. Practice the technique once or twice daily, and not within 2 hours after any meal, since the digestive processes seem to interfere with the elicitation of anticipated changes.

Investigations employing this technique have demonstrated the same hypometabolic changes elicited by transcendental mediation.[1] This non-cultic technique is easily learned and costs nothing.

Other investigators have also reported decreased blood-pressures in hypertensive subjects who practised a yogic technique called shavasan[14] and a yogic technique combined with biofeedback.[15] We suggest that a passive attitude is essential to the elicitation of the relaxation response, and therefore, the concentration and the attention to external stimuli required in biofeedback training[16] may actually interfere with the elicitation of the response. In addition, biofeedback requires costly physiological monitoring equipment, and this would seriously hinder its widespread application.

When the relaxation response has been elicited for two limited daily periods of 20–30 minutes, no adverse side-effects have been reported or observed. However, the side-effects of the extensive practice of the relaxation response have not been well documented.[17] When transcendental meditation has been practised for several hours daily over a period of several days, some individuals have experienced feelings of withdrawal from life and symptoms which range in severity from insomnia and uncontrolled movements of the limbs to hallucinatory experiences. These side-effects are difficult to evaluate on a retrospective basis because individuals with emotional problems might be drawn to any technique such as transcendental meditation which evangelistically promises relief from tension and stress.

No data are available in the present investigation regarding the aetiology of the subjects' hypertension. It is likely that most of the participants had essential hypertension.[18] The long-term effects and the relative preventive and therapeutic value of the relaxation response in hypertension and hypertensive disease remain to be established. If the response does have value, it will have a profound effect on the economics of the therapy of hypertension and its sequelae since it is practised at no cost other than time.

For his review of the manuscript and helpful comments, we thank Dr Walter H. Abelmann. We thank the Students International Meditation Society, National Headquarters, 10145 Gayley Avenue, Los Angeles, California, 90024, for their cooperation. For their technical assistance, we thank Robert K. Wallace, James F. Calvert, Geoffrey Curran, Bohdan P. Diakiwski, Ruth Baker, Ralph C. Burger, Mitchell J. Posser, Marsha Stowell, Ann Beth Hefley, and Martha M. Greenwood. For her secretarial assistance, we thank Nancy E. MacKinson.

This work was supported in part by grants from the U.S. Public Health Service (HL 14486-02, RR-76 from the General Clinical Research Centers Program of the Division of Research Resources, HL 10539-07, HD 03693, and TO1 AI 00068) and the General Service Foundation.

Requests for reprints should be addressed to H. B., Thorndike Memorial Laboratory, Boston City Hospital, Boston, Massachusetts 02118, U.S.A.

REFERENCES

1. Beary, J. F., Benson, H. *Psychosom. Med.* 1974, **36** (in the press).
2. Wallace, R. K. *Science*, 1970, **167**, 1751.
3. Wallace, R. K., Benson, H., Wilson, A. F. *Am. J. Physiol.* 1971, **221**, 795.
4. Wallace, R. K., Benson, H. *Sci. Am.* 1972, **226**, 84.
5. Benson, H., Beary, J. F., Carol, M. P. *Psychiatry*, 1974, **37**, 37.
6. Cannon, W. B. *Am. J. Physiol.* 1914, **33**, 356.
7. Hess, W. R. The Functional Organization of the Diencephalon. New York, 1957.
8. Folkow, B., Rubinstein, E. H. *Acta physiol. scand.* 1966, **68**, 48.
9. Gutmann, M. C., Benson, H. *Medicine, Baltimore*, 1971, **50**, 543.
10. Benson, H., Rosner, B. A., Marzetta, B. R. *J. chron. Dis.* (in the press).
11. Kannel, W. B., Schwartz, M. J., McNamara, P. M. *Dis. Chest.* 1969, **56**, 43.
12. Wright, B. M., Dore, C. F. *Lancet*, 1970, i, 337.
13. Snedecor, G. W., Cochran, W. C. Statistical Methods. Ames, Iowa, 1967.
14. Datey, K. K., Deshmukh, S. N., Dalvi, C. L., Vinekar, S. L. *Angiology*, 1969, **20**, 325.
15. Patel, C. H. *Lancet*, 1973, ii, 1053.
16. Benson, H., Shapiro, D., Tursky, B., Schwartz, G. E. *Science*, 1971, **173**, 740.
17. *Lancet*, 1972, i, 1058.
18. Laragh, J. H. *Am. J. Med.* 1965, **39**, 616.

12

PSYCHOTHERAPEUTIC CONTROL
OF HYPERTENSION

Richard A. Stone and James De Leo

Abstract We conducted a six-month trial to determine the effect of psychologic relaxation on blood pressure. Alterations of peripheral sympathetic-nervous-system activity, as reflected by changes of dopamine-beta-hydroxylase in plasma, were evaluated, and plasma volume and plasma renin activity were measured. Treated patients exhibited significant (P < 0.05) reductions of blood pressure when supine and upright, and of plasma dopamine-beta-hydroxylase activity, and furosemide-stimulated renin activity when upright. Blood-pressure changes after six months correlated best with differences in plasma activity of dopamine-beta-hydroxylase with patients supine (r = 0.54; P < 0.05) and upright (r = 0.62; P <0.05). These results suggest that a reduction of peripheral adrenergic activity contributes importantly to the improvement of hypertension observed with this form of therapy. Furthermore, the decrease of furosemide-stimulated plasma renin activity suggests that alterations of the renin-angiotensin system may help lower blood pressure in certain patients. (N Engl J Med 294:80-84, 1976)

PREVIOUS studies have indicated that psychotherapy may ameliorate hypertension. Investigators using a variety of technics, including yoga, Transcendental Meditation, and biofeedback, have observed blood-pressure reductions in many patients.[1-3] Most of these studies report that patients continued drug therapy at reduced dosages, and they do not completely rule out the possibility of increased compliance with prescribed medications. Benson et al. observed a definite reduction of systemic arterial pressure in borderline hypertensive subjects who used meditation and received no drugs.[4] However, the possible contribution of an alteration of dietary salt intake was not eliminated. In the present investigation of a well defined group of hypertensive subjects, we have attempted to determine the affect of a psychologic relaxation technic on blood pressure. The patients received no medications, and possible dietary salt restriction was assessed by the measurement of urinary sodium excretion.

Considerable evidence is accumulating that psychotherapeutic reduction of blood pressure may result from a decrement of neuronal activity.[5-7] The measurement of the enzyme, dopamine-beta-hydroxylase (DβH) in plas-

ma appears to be a useful way to investigate adrenergic function.[8,9] DβH is the enzyme that converts dopamine to norepinephrine within the synaptic vesicles of sympathetic neurons.[10] A neurogenic stimulus is accompanied by the release of norepinephrine through exocytosis and is associated with the simultaneous discharge of the soluble portion of DβH.[11] There is no established pathway of DβH excretion, and the enzyme appears to have a longer metabolic half-life than catecholamines.[12] The proposal of Weinshilboum and Axelrod that plasma DβH activity provides an index of sympathetic-nervous-system function supports the theoretical framework of this study.[9]

METHODS

Patients

Nineteen hypertensive patients from the Veterans Administration Hospital of San Diego were studied. None of them had been evaluated or treated previously for elevated blood pressure. Selection was performed arbitrarily by one of us (R.A.S.) who used the criteria of apparent ability to comprehend instructions, motivation, willingness to adhere to the experimental protocol and blood-pressure criteria listed below. Although 15 subjects were hospitalized for selected diagnostic evaluations, all the reported laboratory determinations and blood-pressure measurements were obtained on an outpatient basis. All patients gave their informed written consent, and the Committee on Human Experimentation of the University of California, San Diego, approved the protocol.

From the Division of Nephrology, departments of Medicine, University of California, San Diego, School of Medicine, and Veterans Administration Hospital (address reprint requests to Dr. Stone at the Division of Nephrology, Veterans Administration Hospital, San Diego, CA 92161).

Supported by a grant (HL 18095) from the National Institutes of Health and by the Veterans Administration.

Diagnostic Procedures

The evaluation of each patient included a complete history and physical examination, multiple determinations of blood pressure (arm-cuff method), measurements of plasma DβH and renin activity (PRA), ^{131}I albumin plasma volume, blood chemical studies including determinations of the blood urea nitrogen concentration and the plasma concentrations of sodium, potassium, chloride, bicarbonate, creatinine, and total protein, a hemogram, a complete urinalysis (including microscopical examination of the urinary sediment), urinary excretion of 17-hydroxycorticosteroids and catecholamines, a roentgenogram of the chest, and an intravenous urogram. In most (15) patients, selective renal arteriography and measurements of PRA in the renal venous effluent from the two kidneys were obtained. The results of all the above studies were normal in all subjects but one (Group 2, Case 5), who exhibited a unilateral atrophic kidney on both the urogram and the arteriogram.

The blood-pressure criterion for entry into the study was a mean arterial pressure (diastolic blood pressure plus one-third pulse pressure) greater than 105 mm Hg (with the subject either supine or upright) during at least 50 per cent of 14 pretreatment determinations. All measurements (arm-cuff method were performed by an independent observer (technician or nurse), who possessed no knowledge of the assigned study groups. Systolic blood pressure was measured by palpation, and diastolic blood pressure represents the disappearance of all Korotkov sounds. Pretreatment and post-treatment (six-month) average blood-pressure and pulse measurements reflect the mean of 14 determinations (seven in the supine and seven in the upright position) over 10 to 14 days between 10 a.m. and 2 p.m.

All patients maintained an unrestricted dietary salt intake documented by urinary sodium excretions of 124 to 235 mEq per 24 hours. Peripheral blood samples were collected in chilled vacuum tubes containing either EDTA (for PRA) or heparin (for DβH). The blood for assay was placed on ice, separated in a refrigerated centrifuge (4°C), and stored at −20°C for subsequent assay. Blood samples for determination of DβH and PRA were obtained between 11 a.m. and noon after four to five hours of upright position and ambulation. Patients were then placed in the supine posture for 45 to 60 minutes, and peripheral venous blood was collected for measurement of DβH, PRA, and protein concentration. Plasma volume was determined while the patients maintained the recumbent position. The patients then received 80 mg of furosemide by mouth, and PRA was measured a third time between 4 and 6 p.m. after four hours of upright position and ambulation.

All patients were followed for a six-month interval. For further analysis, subjects were placed in the following categories (Table 1): Group 1, five controls subjects, who were seen for blood-pressure determinations only once a month throughout the six-month period of observation; and Group 2, 14 patients treated with psychologic relaxation.

Psychologic-Relaxation Technic

All procedures were performed by one of us (J.D.). The subjects attended five 20-minute training sessions and were instructed in a technic based on Buddhist meditation exercises designed to elicit a relaxation response.

They were advised to find a comfortable chair in an area that was relatively quiet and free from distractions. They were then told to loosen tight clothing, sit in an upright position, and relax their muscles.

The subjects were then asked to count their breaths subvocally. The count was to be a continuous arithmetic progression. When distractions occurred, they were told simply to return to counting their breaths.

Finally, the patients were told to repeat the technic twice daily for intervals of 10 to 15 minutes, preferably before breakfast and before retiring.

All patients practiced the technic during the instruction period. Any questions regarding the technic were answered after the exercise.

Chemical Assays

Determinations of PRA were performed with the method of Haber, Koerner, and Page,[13] by means of the radioimmunoassay of angiotensin I generated after incubation at pH 5.5 for one hour at 37°C. Simultaneous blanks were determined at 4°C. Reagents were purchased from New England Nuclear, Boston, Massachusetts. All assays were performed in duplicate, and the values were required to fall within ±15 per cent of the mean. Reproducibility was established by replicate analyses of single plasma samples (20 in number) with "high" and "low" PRA. The inter-assay coefficients of variation (expressed as one standard deviation per mean) was 12 and 14.6 per cent for the "high" and "low" samples respectively. All results are expressed as nanograms of angiotensin I generated per milliliter per hour.

The measurement of plasma DβH activity was performed with the procedure of Nagatsu and Udenfriend.[14] All determinations were done in duplicate on 50-μl aliquots of plasma, and the results were required to fall within ±2 units of the mean. The inter-assay coefficient of variation (for 40 assays) of a single sample was 4.5 per cent. N-ethyl-maleimide provided an effective way of inactivating endogenous inhibitors as previously described.[15] Results are expressed as International Units (μmoles per minute)/liter of plasma at 37°C, μmoles of octopamine formed (Units per liter). Other blood and urine chemical determinations were performed in the routine hospital laboratories.

Plasma volume was measured in the supine position with the injection of radioiodine labeled serum albumin. The dose was calculated to exceed background count by a factor of four. The isotope was injected intravenously, and plasma samples were obtained at 10 and 20 minutes.

Statistics

Paired and unpaired t-tests were used to determine differences within groups and between groups respectively. Linear regression analysis was performed with standard technics.[16] All values are expressed as the mean ± standard error of the mean (± S.E.M.), unless otherwise stated.

RESULTS

The two groups were similar in age and race. The average age of the five control patients (Group 1) was 28 years (range of 21 to 32 years), and the 14 treatment patients (Group 2) ranged in age from 23 to 36 years (mean of 28 ± 1.1 years). All patients were white; there were only two women, who were both in the treatment group.

The base-line blood pressures were similar in the two groups. Before therapy, mean arterial pressure in the supine and upright positions in Group 2 subjects was 110 ± 3 mm Hg and 112 ± 2 mm Hg respectively. These pressures did not differ (P > 0.05) from those of the control patients (Table 1). The two groups were also similar (P > 0.05) in average systolic and diastolic blood pressures (Fig. 1). After six months of psychologic relaxation measurements of mean arterial pressure in the supine and upright positions in Group 2 were significantly (P < 0.05) less than both their own base-line values and those of the control subjects. Both the systolic and diastolic blood pressures were significantly less (P < 0.05) than their previous pre-

Table 1. Mean Arterial Pressure (MAP) and Plasma-Volume Data before and after Psychologic Relaxation (PR). *

Group	Age (Yr)	MAP[1] (Mm Hg)		Volume/BSA[2] (Ml/M[2])
		Supine	Upright	
1:	28 ± 3.0			
Before PR		108	111	1380
		±3	±3	±327
After PR:		110	110	1409
		±3	±1	±265
2:	28 ± 1.1			
Before PR		110	112	1796
		±3	±2	±126
After PR		98	100	1879
		±3[3][4]	±3[3][4]	±99

*Data are means ± SEM.
[1]Diastolic + 1/3 pulse pressure.
[2]Body-surface area (calculated from height & weight).
[3]P <0.05 as compared to control patients (by unpaired t-test).
[4]P <0.05 compared to pretreatment (by paired t-test).

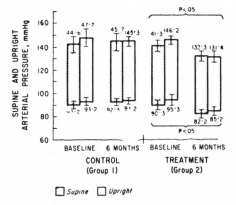

Figure 1. Effect of Psychologic Relaxation on Arterial-Blood Pressure.
Each column represents an average of systolic and diastolic pressures, taken initially and after six months, in the supine and upright positions (expressed as mean ± S.E.M). The treatment group (Group 2) exhibited significant (P < 0.05) declines of both systolic and diastolic pressures as compared to pretreatment measurements (paired t-test). Treated patients, in both supine and upright positions, also had diastolic and systolic pressures significantly (P < 0.05) less than those of control subjects (by unpaired t-test).

treatment measurements but differed from control patients only in that the diastolic and systolic blood pressures with subjects both upright and supine were lower (P < 0.05, Fig. 1).

Pretreatment measurements of PRA with subjects supine, upright, and furosemide stimulated were similar, (P > 0.05) in both groups (Table 2). Determinations in the supine and upright positions did not differ significantly (P > 0.05) within or between groups at six months. Furosemide-stimulated PRA measurements were significantly less (P < 0.05) than pretreatment values in Group 2 subjects (Table 2).

Pretreatment determinations of plasma DβH activity did not differ (P > 0.05) between the two groups. After six months, patients in the treatment group (Group 2) exhibited an average plasma DβH activity in the upright position of 47 ± 5 Units per liter, which was significantly less (P < 0.05) than both that of the control group and their own base-line measurements (Table 2).

Table 2. Plasma Renin Activity (PRA) and Dopamine Beta-Hydroxylase (DβH) Activity before and after Psychologic Relaxation (PR).*

Group	DβH (U/Liter)		PRA (Ng of Angiotensin I/Ml/Hr)		
	SUPINE	UPRIGHT	SUPINE	UPRIGHT	FUROSEMIDE STIMULATED
1:					
Before PR	59	61	1.38	3.77	8.6
	±3	±2	±0.3	±1.0	±1.6
After PR	58	61	1.74	4.12	6.3
	±3	±3	±0.6	±0.9	±1.4
2:					
Before PR	51	54	2.76	5.3	8.7
	±5	±6	±1.2	±1.4	±2.2
After PR	47	47	1.98	4.4	7.1
	±5	±5†‡	±0.4	±1.3	±2.3

*All values are means ±SEM.
†P <0.05 as compared to control patients (by unpaired t-test).
‡P <0.05 as compared to pretreatment (by paired t-test).

Base-line radioiodinated plasma-volume measurements (standardized for body-surface area) averaged 1796 ± 126 ml per square meter in Group 2. Volume changes were not significant (P > 0.05, Table 1) in either group.

Plasma protein concentration averaged 7.3 ± .4 g per 100 ml in Group 1 and 7.4 ± 0.6 g per 100 ml in Group 2 before therapy. At six months, Group 1 patients exhibited an average plasma protein concentration of 7.2 ± .5 g per 100 ml, and Group 2 subjects an average of 7.5 ± .4 g per 100 ml. None of these determinations differed (P > 0.05) from the others.

In an attempt to determine the mechanism of blood-pressure alteration, linear-regression analysis was applied to the changes of mean arterial pressure versus the changes of DβH, PRA, and volume determinations (Table 3). Significant correlation was observed for changes of DβH activity in the supine and upright positions in the treatment group and DβH activity in the supine position in the control patients. A significant negative correlation was observed between mean arterial pressure and furosemide-stimulated renin in control subjects, an observation that remains unexplained. Although there was a significant decrement of furosemide-stimulated PRA after treatment, these alterations did not show significant correlation with mean arterial pressure.

DISCUSSION

The present investigation suggests that at least one form of psychologic relaxation is an effective method of therapy for selected young white men with mild or moderate hypertension. Nineteen patients with modest blood-pressure elevation, who had never received antihypertensive therapy, were studied for six months. Fourteen of these subjects (Group 2) were taught a psychologic relaxation exercise, which they were instructed to perform twice a day (morning and evening). This group exhibited a significant reduction of mean arterial pressure, which averaged 12 mm Hg in both the supine and upright positions. As in other investigations,[3,17] there was no significant change of blood pressure in subjects who did not receive any psychotherapeutic instruction. Although interpretation of these findings must be tempered with caution because of the pitfalls of a nonrandomized study, the reduction in the mean arterial pressure of at least 14 mm Hg (range of 14 to 30 mm Hg) in 57 per cent (eight of 14) of patients given psychotherapeutic instruction attests to the efficacy of a rather simple technic.

Although biochemical indexes of peripheral sympathetic-nervous-system activity after psychotherapeutic blood-pressure reduction have not been reported, adrenergic function has been studied in many forms of human hypertension.[18] Chemical measurements of neuronal activity have included the determinations of plasma and urinary catecholamines or metabolites,[19-21] but any potential meaning of these observations had been lessened by the recognition of the concept that urinary and plasma concentrations of catecholamines may be effected by variables other than adrenergic function — i.e., alterations of neuronal reuptake and storage, tissue metabolism, and renal clearance.

We believe that the activity of DβH in plasma may provide a better index of chronic adrenergic activity than assays of catecholamines or metabolites. DβH, a catecholamine-synthesizing enzyme, is released with norepinephrine from the storage granules of sympathetic neurons. There is no known excretion, and no reuptake, and plasma half-life appears to be much longer than that of catecholamines.[12,22] Many animal and human studies support the hypothesis that plasma DβH activity provides a good index of sympathetic-nervous-system activity.[23-25] From the long plasma half-life of DβH[12] and the small amount of soluble enzyme in vesicles in relation to the large circulating pool of DβH, one may propose that DβH activity in plasma will best reflect catecholamine release during a prolonged period.[26-28]

Possible reasons for differing values of plasma DβH activity in human beings have not been established, and some investigators have suggested the DβH in plasma does not represent adrenergic function.[29] Alternative hypotheses include individual variations in plasma enzyme clearance and differences within the storage vesicle of the ratio between soluble DβH and catecholamines.[29] Consequently, one group of investigators has suggested that directional changes of DβH in plasma represent alterations of adrenergic activity better than the determination of absolute amounts of enzyme.[30] Studies in laboratory animals that were not given drugs suggest that enzyme half-life and the ratio of soluble DβH to catecholamines remain constant.[9-12] Previous studies, which indicated individual variability in the relation between enzymatic and immunologic activities,[12] have not been confirmed,[31] and investigations in man continue to suggest that plasma DβH activity is useful as an index of peripheral sympathetic-nervous-system function.[32] However, further human studies will be required to establish the relation of adrenergic function and measurements of DβH activity in plasma.

In the present investigation, plasma DβH activity remained unchanged in control subjects (Group 1), and the stability observed confirms several previous reports of this phenomenon.[15,24,33] On the other hand, there was a significant reduction of plasma DβH activity in treated patients in the upright position. If one analyzes only subjects who exhibited blood-pressure reductions of at least 14 mm Hg, there was a significant decrease of plasma DβH activity in both supine and upright positions. Furthermore, there was a significant correlation of change in mean arterial pressure in both positions with alterations of activities of DβH in plasma in supine and upright positions. The observed relation of changes of DβH and blood pressure suggests that a reduction in peripheral adrenergic activity contributes importantly to the observed amelioration of hypertension with this form of therapy. In addition, these results, in conjunction with previous physiologic studies,[5] support the proposal that changes of DβH in plasma provide an index of alterations of adrenergic function.

Measurements of plasma volume and peripheral venous renin activity were performed in all subjects before and after therapy. No significant alterations of plasma vol-

Table 3. Correlation of Changes in Mean Arterial Pressure (MAP) with Alterations of Renin (PRA), Dopamine-Beta-Hydroxylase (DβH), and Plasma Volume (PV). *

Datum	Group 1		Group 2	
	Correlation Coefficient	Probability	Correlation Coefficient	Probability
Δ Supine MAP (mm Hg):				
Vs Δsupine DβH (U/liter)	0.902	<0.05	0.536	<0.05
Vs Δsupine PRA (ng of angiotensin/ml/hr)	0.415	NS†	0.264	NS
Vs Δsupine PV (ml/m²)	0.089	NS	0.386	NS
Δ Upright MAP (mm Hg):				
Vs Δupright DβH (U/liter)	0.405	NS	0.615	<0.05
Vs Δupright PRA (ng of angiotensin/ml/hr)	0.02	NS	0.194	NS
Vs Δfurosemide-stimulated PRA (ng of angiotensin/ml/hr)	−0.90	<0.05	−0.149	NS

*Standardized for body-surface area. †No significant correlation.

ume were detected and, therefore, would not provide an explanation for the blood-pressure changes observed. On the other hand, there was a significant decrement of furosemide-stimulated PRA in the treatment group. Since it has been proposed that adrenergic activity influences renin secretory rate,[34] it is attractive to hypothesize that a decrement of sympathetic tone was responsible for the changes of PRA observed. The decrease in PRA is not likely to have been due to changes in blood volume since this measurement did not differ significantly. Furthermore, the decrease of PRA may have contributed to the blood-pressure reduction in certain patients, but the lack of correlation of PRA and mean arterial pressure suggests that a change in the rate of renin release was not the primary mechanism of blood-pressure reduction.

In conclusion, we have demonstrated that at least one psychotherapeutic method can provide improved blood-pressure control in certain patients with mild or moderate hypertension. In addition, we have provided evidence that this blood-pressure reduction is associated with biochemical evidence of reduced peripheral adrenergic activity. We have also detected alterations in the renin angiotensin system that may contribute to the observed amelioration of hypertension in certain patients.

We are indebted to Darrell D. Fanestil, M.D., for advice on the manuscript, to Ms. Rachel Rubin and Mr. James Converse for technical assistance, to Mr. Bryan Tucker for statistical assistance and to Mrs. Linda Brandt for assistance.

References

1. Benson H, Rosner BA, Marzetta BR, et al: Decreased blood-pressure in pharmacologically treated hypertensive patients who regularly elicited the relaxation response. Lancet 1:289-291, 1974
2. Kristt DA, Engel BT: Learned control of blood pressure in patients with high blood pressure. Circulation 51:370-378, 1975
3. Patel C: Randomized controlled trial of yoga and biofeedback in management of hypertension. Lancet 2:93-95, 1975
4. Benson H, Rosner BA, Marzetta BR, et al: Decreased blood pressure in borderline hypertensive subjects who practiced meditation. J Chronic Dis 27:163-169, 1974
5. Wallace RK: Physiological effects of transcendental meditation. Science 167:1751-1754, 1970
6. Henry JP, Stephens PM, Axelrod J, et al: Effect of psychosocial stimulation on the enzymes involved in the biosynthesis and metabo-

lism of noradrenaline and adrenaline. Psychosomat Med 33:227-237, 1971

7. Henry JP, Stephens PM, Santisteban GA: A model of psychosocial hypertension showing reversibility and progression of cardiovascular complications. Circulation Res 36:156-164, 1975

8. Geffen L: Serum dopamine-beta-hydroxylase as an index of sympathetic function. Life Sci 14:1593-1604, 1974

9. Weinshilboum K, Axelrod J: Serum dopamine-beta-hydroxylase activity. Circulation Res 28:307-315, 1971

10. Gewirtz GP, Kopin IJ: Release of dopamine-beta-hydroxylase with norepinephrine during cat splenic nerve stimulation. Nature 277:406-407, 1970

11. Depotter WP, de Schaepdryver AF, Moerman EJ, et al: Evidence for release of vesicle proteins together with nor-adrenaline upon stimulation of the splenic nerve. J Physiol (Lond) 204:102p-104p, 1969

12. Rush RA, Geffen LB: Radioimmunoassay and clearance of circulating dopamine-β-hydroxylase. Circulation Res 31:444-452, 1972

13. Haber E, Koerner T, Page LB: Application of a radioimmunoassay for angiotensin I to the physiologic measurements of plasma renin activity in normal human subjects. J Clin Endocrinol Metab 29:1349-1355, 1969

14. Nagatsu T, Udenfriend S: Photometric assay of dopamine-β-hydroxylase activity in human blood. Clin Chem 18:980-983, 1972

15. Stone RA, Gunnells JC, Robinson RR, et al: Dopamine-beta-hydroxylase in primary and secondary hypertension. Circulation Res: Suppl 1:34 and 35:1-47, 1974

16. Bliss EI: Statistics in Biology. New York, McGraw-Hill Book Company, 1970

17. Patel C: 12-month follow-up of yoga and bio-feedback in the management of hypertension. Lancet 1:62-64, 1975

18. DeQuattro V, Miura Y: Neurogenic factors in human hypertension: mechanism or myth. Am J Med 55:362-378, 1973

19. Nestel PJ, Esler MD: Patterns of catecholamine excretion in urine in hypertension. Circulation Res: Suppl 2: 26 and 27:75-81, 1970

20. Engelman K, Portnoy B, Sjoerdsma A: Plasma catecholamine concentrations in patients with hypertension. Circulation Res 27:Suppl 1:141-146, 1970

21. Louis WJ, Doyle AE, Anavekar S: Plasma norephinephrine levels in essential hypertension. N Engl J Med 288:599-601, 1973

22. Molinoff PB, Brimijoin S, Weinshilboum R, et al: Neurally mediated increase in dopamine-β-hydroxylase activity. Proc Natl Acad Sci USA 66:453-458, 1970

23. Lamprecht F, Williams RB, Kopin IJ: Serum dopamine-beta-hydroxylase during development of immobilization-induced hypertension. Endocrinology 92:953-956, 1973

24. Schanberg S, Stone RA, Kirshner N, et al: Dopamine-beta-hydroxylase: a diagnostic aid in the evaluation of hypertension. Science 183:523-525, 1974

25. Rockson S, Stone RA, Van Der Weyden M, et al: Lesch-Nyhan syndrome: evidence for abnormal adrenergic function. Science 184:934-935, 1974

26. Stone RA, Kirshner N, Reynolds J, et al: Purification and properties of dopamine-β-hydroxylase from human pheochromocytoma. Mol Pharmacol 10:1009-1015, 1974

27. Stone RA, Kirshner N, Gunnells JC, et al: Changes of plasma dopamine-β-hydroxylase activity and other plasma constituents during the cold pressor test. Life Sci 14:1797-1805, 1974

28. Ross SB, Eriksson HE, Hellstrom W: On the fate of dopamine-B-hydroxylase after release from the peripheral sympathetic nerves in the cat. Acta Physiol Scand 92:578-580, 1974

29. Horowitz D, Alexander RW, Lovenberg W, et al: Human serum dopamine-B-hydroxylase: relationship to hypertension and sympathetic activity. Circulation Res 28:594-599, 1973

30. Alexander RW, Gill JR Jr, Yamabe H, et al: Effects of dietary sodium and of acute saline infusion on the interrelationship between dopamine excretion and adrenergic activity in man. J Clin Invest 54:194-200, 1974

31. Rush RA, Thomas PE, Udenfriend S: Measurement of human dopamine-β-hydroxylase in serum by homologous radioimmunoassay. Proc Natl Acad Sci USA 72:750-752, 1975

32. Naftchi EN, Wooten FG, Lowman EW, et al: Relationship between serum dopamine-β-hydroxylase activity, catecholamine metabolism and hemodynamic changes during paroxysmal hypertension in quadriplegia. Circulation Res 35:850-861, 1974

33. Rockson SG, Stone RA, Gunnells JC, et al: Plasma dopamine-β-hydroxylase activity in oral contraceptive hypertension. Circulation 51:916-923, 1975

34. Ganong WF: Biogenic amines, sympathetic nerves, and renin secretion. Fed Proc 32:1782-1784, 1973

B4. General Psychotherapeutic Applications for the Client and the Therapist

The section has been divided into two different areas. The first area deals with psychotherapeutic applications of meditation for clients. There are two studies reported. The second area deals with the possible application of meditation for the therapist.

Other than a few anecdotal case studies and intensive design research studies, there has been very little work done on the effectiveness of meditation with clinically disturbed populations. Most of the research has been done with normal subjects. In this section we present the only two studies which attempted controlled designs. Vahia's study (Article 13) was done with patients with the diagnosis of psychoneurosis or psychosomatic disorder. The treatment was based on the concepts of Patanjali. The techniques are a graded series of five yoga-meditation exercises. The first attempts to gain voluntary control over the musculature (asana exercises—selected postures for relaxation). The second is an attempt to gain voluntary control over the autonomic nervous system (e.g., pranayama exercises—breathing exercises). The third is pratyahara—restraint of the senses by voluntary withdrawal from the external environment, and still later over the thought processes themselves (e.g., four, dharana—selection of an object for concentration; and five, dhyana—development of total concentration on the selected object and eventually union with it). The theory behind these graded exercises is that one has to learn to develop internal standards and to rely less on the views of others about one's functioning. As long as we are vulnerable to external standards or internalized "conscience" standards we will be vulnerable to stress. Therefore, stress is seen as the mediating variable which these exercises help to correct.

Vahia divided the groups in two, one which practiced all five steps of the exercise and one which practiced "pseudo-exercises." The results are quite impressive.

The second study by Glueck and Strobel (Article 14) has much the same rationale as the Vahia study. Glueck and Stroebel note that meditation or meditation-like procedures help patients to reduce tension and anxiety, and therefore represent a useful addition to other psychotherapeutic modalities. The dependent variable of Glueck and Stroebel's study—condition on discharge from the hospital (though crude, as the authors note) does provide a useful indication of the effectiveness of the meditation strategies. What also is of interest in Glueck and Stroebel's article is the effectiveness of the meditation-like strategies over a wide range of diagnostic categories. Other issues which they raise include the issues of adherence in the population, and guidelines for the therapist who wishes to use meditation with the clients, e.g., telling the clients not to free-associate to the material that arises but merely return to breathing, and later after the meditative session to deal with whatever material came up. They also note the importance of regular checking and assessment of the client, especially clients in the clinical population.

Two studies are cited which have implications for therapy and counseling. Lesh's study (Article 15) took counselor trainees and found that they were more empathic, based on the ability to perceive a client's concern, than a control group who did not meditate. Lesh offers several explanations including the therapist's developing a greater openness and sensitivity to those around him or her, being more centered and less overwhelmed by client problems, and being more aware of his or her own needs, and therefore less projective of feelings onto the client.

Leung's study (Article 16) is interesting because it looks at both internal and external concentration and the effects of these two types of concentration on two different counseling behaviors: (1) sensitivity (similar to the study of Lesh) and (2) the ability to discriminate certain verbal statements which are worthy of reinforcement. Leung notes that "good counselors" have the ability to be both open and sensitive, and also the ability to discriminate selectively important issues that clients bring up.

13

FURTHER EXPERIENCE WITH THE THERAPY BASED UPON CONCEPTS OF PATANJALI IN THE TREATMENT OF PSYCHIATRIC DISORDERS

N. S. Vahia, D. R. Doongaji, D. V. Jeste,
S. N. Kapoor, Indubala Ardhapurkar, and S. Ravindra Nath

Introduction

A review of literature shows that the present methods of psychiatric treatment for neuroses are unsatisfactory. After a survey of the result of psychotherapeutic treatment of over 70,000 cases, Eysenck (1952, 1965) came to the conclusion that these "fail to prove that psychotherapy, Freudian or otherwise, facilitates the recovery of neurotic patients." According to Wolberg (1967), "Neither clinical studies nor ordered observation and experiment have established beyond reasonable doubt the virtuosity of psychotherapy." Click (1967) stated that "while conditioning therapy appears to be of greater value than psychotherapy in the treatment of phobias, neither is exactly what the world is waiting for." Regarding drugs, Caffey *et al.* (1970) noted that "drug therapy's greatest value is in the treatment of schizophrenias. Drug therapy for the treatment of depressions has been less impressive. Anti-anxiety agents offer little that is new. Similarly, Wainwright (1971) held the view that "E. C. T. in the depressions of psychoneuroses and the personality disorders is of negligible aid. Probably the same is true of the antidepressants."

This paper presents some of the results of therapy based on the concepts of Patanjali, the value of which is being studied in the K. E. M. Hospital, Bombay. The concepts of the therapy and the technique have been presented in our previous publication (Vahia, *et al.* 1972).

Material and Method

The patients were selected from the out-patient department of K. E. M. Hospital, Bombay. The criteria for selection were:

1. Diagnosis—Psychoneurosis.
2. Age—15 to 50 years.
3. No concomitant serious physical illness.
4. No improvement with treatment in the past.

Details of the technique have been presented in a previous paper (Vahia *et al.*, 1972). There are five steps in the treatment,—Asana, Pranayama, Pratyahara, Dharana and Dhyana. The patients took this treatment for one hour daily on all week days for at least four weeks. A physiotherapist trained by a physician of 11 years' experience in Yoga, gave the treatment.

All patients were assessed clinically before, during (at weekly intervals), and after the treatment. This assessment was based on target symptom relief and work-efficiency in the job, as reported by the patients themselves, their relatives, friends and colleagues.

In 1970–1971, a double-blind study of psychophysiological treatment *versus* pseudo-treatment was carried out. Patients were assigned randomly to one of the two treatments. Both therapies were given by the same physiotherapist. In pseudo-treatment, the patients were asked to relax and do some postures resembling Asanas, and breathing practices resembling Pranayama. They were also asked to write all the thoughts that came to their mind during the treatment (similar to Dharana and Dhyana). They had to do this for one hour daily on all week days for at least four weeks. They were given same support, reassurance, and placebo tablets (calcium lactate) as the psychophysiological treatment group. All patients were assessed clinically (as described above) and by psychological testing (Rorschach, M. M. P. I., and Taylor's Anxiety scale), before and after the treatment. Taylor's Anxiety scale was administered every week during the therapy. Both the assessors were blind to the type of treatment given to the patient.

Results

Table 1 shows the comparison of the results of psychophysiological therapy in 1963–1964 and 1970–1971. The two groups were matched for age, sex, diagnosis, and duration of illness. The therapist remained same for both the groups though the assessors had changed.

Statistician's Comments

The difference between the groups (1963–1964 and 1970–1971) is not significant.

Table 2 shows the comparison of the results of the total therapy and *partial* therapy. Both the groups were matched for age, sex, diagnosis, and duration of illness. The mean duration of illness was 2 years and 7 months.

Table 1. Comparison of Results of Psychophysiological Therapy in 1963–1964 and 1970–1971

Year	Total number of patients	No. of patients improved 50% and more	No. of patients improved less than 50%	Percentage of cases showing significant improvement
1963–1964	52	37	15	71.15
1970–1971	46	35	11	73.9

Table 2. Comparison of Results of Total Therapy and Partial Therapy

	Total number of patients	No. of patients improved 50% and more	No. of patients improved less than 50%	Percentage of cases showing significant improvement
First three steps only	49	21	28	42.87
All five steps	46	35	11	73.9

Statistician's Comments

Chi square between the two groups is 8 which is higher than the table values. So there is a significant difference between the two groups. The group who took total treatment has improved more than those who took only the first three steps of the treatment.

Table 3 shows the comparison of patients who concentrated well as observed from their writings. The patients were asked to write in a notebook all the thoughts that disturbed their concentration during Dharana and Dhyana. These notebooks were studied months after the treatment was over by two psychiatrists who had no knowledge of the patient's clinical improvement with the treatment. From the daily writings, the assessors noted improvement or otherwise in concentration during the treatment. This was then compared with clinical improvement.

Statistician's Comments

The Chi square calculated is 4. This is greater than the critical value for Chi square with 1 degree of freedom at 5% level. We reject the hypothesis that clinical improvement is independent of improvement in concentration. We conclude that the patients who showed improvement in concentration have definitely improved clinically more than those who did not show improvement in concentration.

Table 4 shows the report of the psychologist based upon Taylor's Anxiety scale before and at the end of the treatment among patients treated with "A" (regular treatment) compared with patients treated with "B" (pseudotreatment).

Statistician's Comments

A comparison of the final scores shows there is a significant difference between the two groups. As there is no reduction in the scores for group B, and there is no significant difference between the initial scores of groups A and B. We can conclude that the effect of the treatment is significant at 5% level.

Table 3. Improvement in Patient Concentration

Improvement in concentration	No. of patients showing clinical improvement more than 50%	No. of patients who did not show clinical improvement	Total
Present	20	3	23
Absent	20	12	32
	40	15	55

Table 4. Pre- and Post-Comparison of Change of Anxiety in Group A and B

Treatment	Mean of T. A. score	
	Group "A" ($N = 15$)	Group "B" ($N = 12$)
Before	25.53 ± 8.8	29.83 ± 6.4
After	18.87 ± 6.9	30.33 ± 7.2

Table 5 shows the two groups with their initial scores and improvement after every week of the treatment.

Statistician's Comments

In group A we can observe a consistent reduction in score week after week, whereas in group B the scores are more or less same at every instant. We do not draw any conclusion on the basis of this data as there are only 7 cases in group A and 5 in B. The downward trend in group A is obvious even though for a valid result we have to study more cases.

Table 6 shows the results of Rorschach test given before and after the treatment in groups A and B.

Statistician's Comments

There is a marked improvement in the total number of responses. The group "A" shows a higher rate of improvement. The response time has been significantly reduced in group A. A detailed statistical analysis is not attempted at this stage. But the trend of improvement is clearly brought out from this data.

Table 7 shows the results of M. M. P. I. given before and after the treatment.

Statistician's Comments

The mean values of the scores for the different factors were compared for signifying the differences between the two groups. Even though we are not able to give a significance test to prove the difference between the two groups, the data suggests a better rate of improvement in group A. We will be studying more cases for an absolute finding. In scales "D" and "P" the difference between the groups were more marked.

Table 5.   Weekly Improvements

	Mean of T. A. score	
	Group A (N = 7)	Group B (N = 5)
After 1 week	22.28	29.4
After 2 weeks	20.28	30
After 3 weeks	19.7	30
After 4 weeks	17.4	31
After 5 weeks	15.0	29.6
After 6 weeks	14.28	29.6

Table 6.   Results of Rorschach Test

	Total number of responses		Reaction time in scores	
	A (N = 15)	B (N = 12)	A (N = 15)	B (N = 12)
Before	13.9	13.7	23	25.1
After	22.2	18.9	15.7	20.5

Table 7. Mean Scores Before and After Treatment in Group A and B

Group		L	F	K	Ma	D	Hy	Pd	Mf	Pa	Pt	Se	Ma	Si
A	Before	51.1	65.7	47.8	74.3	64.6	57.4	60.3	66.8	57.9	79.8	74.5	57.2	45
(N = 15)	After	55.7	63.7	47.4	70.5	56.8	53.1	59.3	63.2	53.1	68.8	69.5	57.2	44
B	Before	43.6	75.6	41	77.1	68.1	59.4	66.6	55.6	70.1	86.8	83	63	49
(N = 12)	After	45.1	73.2	41.2	74.1	65.8	56	63	54.7	64.4	80.2	77.8	62.4	47

Discussion

It may be stressed that the psychophysiological therapy represents a new approach to the treatment of psychiatric disorders. Most of the current psychotherapeutic methods aim at adjustment to society, i.e., the interaction with the environment should be such as to result in getting pleasure and avoiding pain. According to Patanjali (Vivekananda, 1966), it is this preoccupation with the environmental gratifications and frustrations that is the root cause of many psychiatric disorders. In this therapy, the object is to remove or at least reduce this preoccupation. The aim is self-realization, a better integration of personality resulting in actualization of one's creative potentialities.

An assessor's bias for a particular therapy as well as the initial enthusiasm over its efficacy have been frequently blamed for good results with any new treatment. However, as seen from Table 1, there is no significant difference in the results with this treatment though the evaluators had changed over a period of 7 years.

Table 2 suggests that the total psychophysiological therapy is more useful than the first three steps which mainly consist of physiological part only. Jacobson (1938) and Wolpe (1958) have stressed the value of physical relaxation. Many Yoga centers too concentrate on achieving control over voluntary and autonomic nervous system. Our study shows that this part is not sufficient for the improvement of majority of patients. Whether it is necessary for this, or whether only the psychological part is enough can be judged only by comparing three groups of patients—one group given only the physical part, another group only psychological part, and yet one other group both. We plan to do this at a subsequent date.

However, it may be pointed out that in our series the mean duration of illness was 2 years and 7 months and the patients had not responded to other treatments in the past. So improvement even in 42.87% of the patients given only the physical therapy might be considered significant.

As seen from Table 3, there is a positive correlation between concentration during therapy and clinical improvement as judged by target symptom relief and work-efficiency in outside life. In other words, improved concentration during the therapy period results in "generalization" as the term is used by behaviorists (Wolpe, 1958), so that the person can concentrate better outside the treatment situation too.

A noteworthy finding is that 20 out of 23 patients (87%) who took all the five steps of the treatment and who could concentrate well during the therapy showed significant clinical improvement. This suggests that in properly selected patients who have taken the total treatment in a correct way, the improvement rate is very high.

Tables 4 to 7 show that this therapy is significantly superior to placebo as shown by psychological testing. Thus the value of the therapy is better than can be explained on the basis of time, suggestion and milieu. Table 5 shows that the fall in anxiety score on Taylor's scale is progressive, suggesting that longer the therapy is taken, the greater the improvement. Whether this means that continuation of the therapy beyond six weeks would lead to even greater improvement needs further study.

It may thus be suggested that this therapy is of definite value in the treatment of neuroses. This finding is significant in view of the fact that the value of most of the current therapeutic procedures for neuroses remains to be proved beyond reasonable doubt.

It will be interesting to find the value of this therapy in other parts of the country and to compare these results with ours. We will therefore welcome if others try this therapy, using the same technique, in their regions.

Summary

1. A change in assessors over a period of 7 years did not affect the results.

2. When the patients took all the five steps of the treatment, the improvement rate was significantly higher than among those who took the first three steps of the treatment.

3. Among those that could concentrate better, the improvement rate was significantly higher than among those that could not concentrate satisfactorily in the treatment.

4. The regular treatment was better than the pseudo-treatment as judged by psychological testing.

Thus the therapy is of definite value in the treatment of psychoneuroses.

Acknowledgment

We are thankful to the Dean, King Edward Memorial Hospital and Seth G. S. Medical College, Parel, Bombay 12, for allowing us to use the case materials for publishing this paper.

References

Caffey, Eugene M., Hollister, Leo E., Kaim, Samuel, C., and Pokorny, Alex D. Drug Treatment in Psychiatry. *Inter. J. Psychiat.*, 1970–1971, **9**, 429.

Eysenck, H. J. The Effects of Psychotherapy: An Evaluation. *J. Consult. Psychol.*, 1952, **16**, 319.

Eysenck, H. J. The Effects of Psychotherapy. *Inter. J. Psychiat.*, 1965, **1**, 99.

Glick, Burton, S. Conditioning: A Partial Success Story—Critical Evaluation. *Inter. J. Psychiat.*, 1969, 493.

Jacobson, E. Progressive Relaxation. Chicago: University Chicago Press, 1938.

Vahia, N. S., Doongaji, D.R., Deshmukh, D. K., Vinekar, S. L., Parekh, H. C. & Kapoor, S. N. A Deconditioning Therapy Based Upon Concepts of Patanjali. Vivekanand, Swamy (1966) Patanjali's yoga Sutra (Apoorisms) in Raja yoga. Advaita Ashram, Calcutta. *Inter. J. Soc. Psychiat.*, 1972, **17**, 61.

Wainwright, W. H. Discussion on—'Are Antidepressants better than Placebo?' *Amer. J. Psychiat.*, 1971, **127**, 1605.

Volberg, Lewis R. The Technique of Psychotherapy. 2nd Ed. New York: Grune and Stratton, 1967.

Wolpe, J. Psychotherapy by reciprocal inhibition. Stanford: Stanford University Press, 1958.

14

MEDITATION IN THE TREATMENT
OF PSYCHIATRIC ILLNESS

Bernard C. Glueck and Charles F. Stroebel

In the past six years we have been studying, both in the research laboratory and in clinical settings, techniques directed toward the general goal of inducing a more relaxed state in research subjects and in patients with a variety of illnesses. We have tended to subsume all of these efforts under the general heading of "relaxation techniques." We are not, however, using "relaxation" in the very specific way that Dr. Herbert Benson (1) does, since not everyone agrees with his contention that humans have both an emergency response and a relaxation response system. Benson argues that the built-in response systems that are designed to produce a more relaxed state within the organism are triggered by all of the relaxation techniques, be it his particular technique, Transcendental Meditation, other forms of yoga, or the increasingly sophisticated electronic approaches, using various biofeedback techniques, that are proliferating rapidly.

Interestingly, Benson's argument that there is a natural tendency within the organism to produce a more relaxed state that can be triggered by a variety of techniques, is quite similar to the contention of one of the leading exponents of the meditational approaches, Maharishi Mahesh Yogi, that the organism moves naturally toward a state of lessened tension and greater pleasure (2). This also is the thesis of one of the foremost psychoanalytic thinkers of recent times, Sandor Rado (3), who states that for a healthy adaptation man must be motivated by the experience of, and desire for, pleasurable gratification, as well as seeking to avoid or escape from painful situations. Whether the pleasure response capabilities are inherent in the organism, or need to be learned, or can be evoked by specific techniques, is still open to debate. There seems to be little doubt, however, that the various techniques used to produce relaxation all have an impact on the emergency response systems. This may be perceived by the individual as a reduction in the subjective feelings of anxiety, or it may be measured by the observer as a drop in pulse rate, a fall in blood pressure, an increase in the galvanic skin response (GSR), or in significant changes in the patterns of electrical activity of the brain.

We began investigating the patterns of brain wave activity using scalp electrodes and the traditional electroencephalographic (EEG) recordings six years ago, starting at a time when alpha wave EEG biofeedback was the primary biofeedback technique. Our first two studies used volunteer subjects who were interested in enhancing relaxation in order to relieve some of the tensions and stresses that they felt were interfering with their daily patterns of living. In these experiments we utilized the EEG signals coming from the occipital cortex, analyzed by a computer, and fed back to the individual as either a tone or a light. Changes in the amount of alpha waves produced would cause corresponding changes in the loudness of the sound or the intensity of the light.

The brain waves in the 8–12 hertz frequency band, the alpha waves, were utilized in these early experiments because of the observations made by some of the early investigators (4,5) who were able to study individuals who had spent their lives learning and practicing various yogic and meditational techniques. They found that these men, who appeared to be very well integrated, calm, relaxed individuals, were able to produce alpha, and the even slower theta wave forms, almost at will. The argument was made that alpha wave production was somehow directly associated with the relatively calm and relaxed state in these individuals. Therefore, if we could teach our subjects to increase the amount of alpha that they were producing, they would feel a greater degree of calmness and tranquility.

These expectations were met only partially, in general by subjects who were both good spontaneous alpha producers initially, and who seemed to be fairly well integrated, healthy people. Other subjects, who showed a greater degree of anxiety and tension, ranging in two cases to fairly severe overt psychiatric symptoms, showed little or no spontaneous alpha wave production, and seemed to have considerable difficulty in learning to enhance their alpha wave production. There was enough enhancement of the alpha density in most of our subjects, however, accompanied by a drop in skin conductance, in pulse rate, and in the respiratory rate, all presumed to be indicators of a more relaxed psychophysiologic internal steady state, and described subjectively as an awareness of a reduction in inner tensions, for a decision to continue the studies with our psychiatric inpatient population. Our general hypothesis was that if we could teach the patient techniques which he could employ on his own, that would reduce tension and anxiety, and improve the patient's general level of adaptation, this would be a useful addition to the other treatments being utilized in the hospital setting.

To briefly summarize our results, which have been reported elsewhere (6,7), two of our patient groups—those doing a general relaxation exercise modeled on Luthe's techniques (8), and the patients doing alpha biofeedback training—soon dropped out of the experiment because of their inability to subjectively perceive any significant changes in their tension and anxiety levels. This was reflected in our objective measures, such as changes in the EEG patterns, in the GSR, blood pressure, and pulse rate. By contrast, patients who were practicing the passive type of meditation known as Transcendental Meditation (TM) seemed to be subjectively aware of a drop in their inner tensions and anxieties following the very first meditation. Initially this tended to be of fairly short duration. However, as meditation continued, the feeling of reduced tension seemed to persist for longer periods.

Because we had lost our two comparison groups of patients, we selected a group of patients from the remainder of the hospital population to compare with patients doing TM. The comparison group was matched for sex, age within three years, and level and kind of psychopathology as reported by the patient using the Minnesota Multiphasic Personality Inventory (MMPI) at the time of admission to the Institute of Living. The mean MMPI profiles for the male and female TM patients, and the matched comparison groups, are shown in Figs. 1 and 2. From these profiles it would appear that, at least on their self-appraisal, the groups were well matched at the time of admission.

By contrast, it is interesting to note that only 18% of the pairs were diagnosed identically on admission, 26% were diagnosed within the same general group, e.g., schizophrenia or neurosis, and 56% carried quite different diagnoses. This same general discrepancy in diagnostic classification existed at the time of discharge, with 18% of the pairs having identical diagnoses, 24% being within the same general group, and 58% having quite different diagnoses. Since the treating psychiatrist's assessment of his patient, which is summed up in the shorthand of the diagnostic label, determined the treatment of all patients in the study, except for the addition of TM for the experimental group, the sizeable discrepancy in the diagnoses on admission to the hospital explains, at least in part, the rather wide variation in treatment patterns observed in the two groups.

While condition on discharge is an admittedly crude measure of change in a patient, it does represent a global judgment on the part of the treating psychiatrist that can be used for comparison purposes. Patients doing TM showed a statistically significant greater degree of improvement than was seen for the hospital in general ($\chi_2 = 37.75$, $df = 2$, $p = <.0001$). They also showed a significantly better level of improvement than their comparison twins ($\chi_2 = 13.93$, $df = 2$, $p = <.001$). That both groups of patients, those practicing and the comparison group, may have been somewhat different from the total group of hospital patients, e.g., better candidates for any sort of treatment, cannot be refuted from the condition on discharge figures since the matched comparison group also showed significantly better levels of improvement than the total hospital group ($\chi_2 = 11.13$, $df = 2$, $p = <.01$). These figures would seem to indicate, however, that even if both the TM and the comparison patients started from a somewhat better level of adustment upon admission to the hospital, the addition of TM to the hospital treatment program appears to have had a positive effect, since the patients doing TM appear to have achieved significantly better levels of improvement at the time of discharge than either the comparison group or the total hospital population.

The subjectively perceived changes in both groups of patients, as expressed through the MMPI, show an even closer level of improvement at the time of discharge from the hospital, and very similar degress of

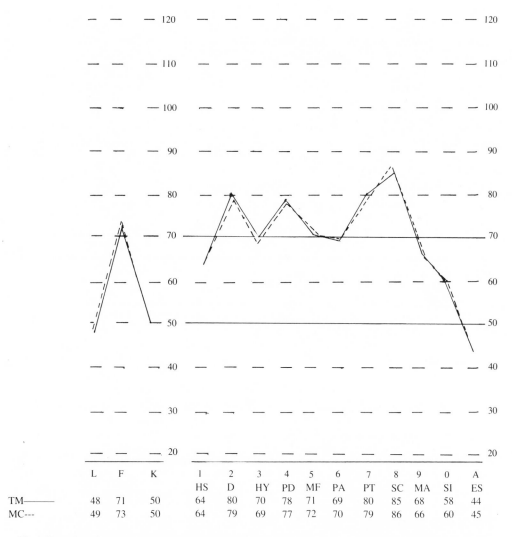

		L	F	K		1	2	3	4	5	6	7	8	9	0	A
						HS	D	HY	PD	MF	PA	PT	SC	MA	SI	ES
TM———		48	71	50		64	80	70	78	71	69	80	85	68	58	44
MC---		49	73	50		64	79	69	77	72	70	79	86	66	60	45

Fig. 1. Comparison of mean admission MMPI profiles for male patients doing TM and the matched comparison group. The solid line shows the mean admission MMPI profile for the patients (males, $N = 68$ for both groups) who were taught TM, while the broken line shows the mean admission profile for the comparison group of patients.

change from admission, as illustrated in Figs. 3 and 4. The somewhat greater degree of improvement reported by the treating psychiatrist is reflected to a lesser extent in the comparison of the admission and discharge profiles, both in the number of scales showing significant differences for the two groups, and perhaps in the quantity of change.

It was our intent to try to cover as many of the diagnostic entities that are treated in our hospital as possible, in order to test the effectiveness of the relaxation techniques across a broad range of diagnoses. The distribution of our patient sample, the matched group, and the total hospital population, by major diagnostic categories, is shown in Table I. The distribution by diagnoses is fairly similar for the TM group and the total hospital population. There is a sizeable discrepancy, however, mainly in the number of patients diagnosed as suffering from a schizophrenic illness, between the TM patients and the comparison group.

The different diagnostic distributions may have influenced the outcome figures for the TM and the comparison group, as shown in Table II where the distribution of the two groups by diagnosis and by level

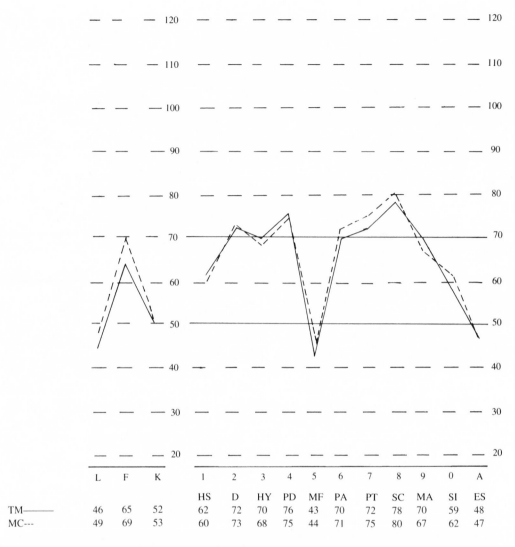

	L	F	K	1	2	3	4	5	6	7	8	9	0	A
				HS	D	HY	PD	MF	PA	PT	SC	MA	SI	ES
TM———	46	65	52	62	72	70	76	43	70	72	78	70	59	48
MC---	49	69	53	60	73	68	75	44	71	75	80	67	62	47

Fig. 2. Comparison of mean admission MMPI profiles for the female patients doing TM and the female matched comparison group. The solid line shows the mean admission MMPI profile for the patients (females, $N = 40$ for both groups) who were taught TM, while the broken line shows the mean admission profile for the comparison group of patients.

Table I. Distribution of Diagnoses for Patients Doing TM, the Matched Comparison Patients, and Overall Hospital Figures for 1973–1974

Diagnosis	TM		MC		HP[a]	
	N	%	N	%	N	%
Schizophrenia	43	39	69	62	240	38
Neuroses	26	24	11	10	129	20
Personality disorders	18	16	12	11	64	10
Alcoholism	4	4	5	5	44	7
Drug dependence	11	10	4	4	21	3
Adjustment reactions	8	7	9	8	39	6
Other	—	—	—	—	100	16
Totals	110	100	110	100	637	100

[a]Hospital percentage, 1973–1974.

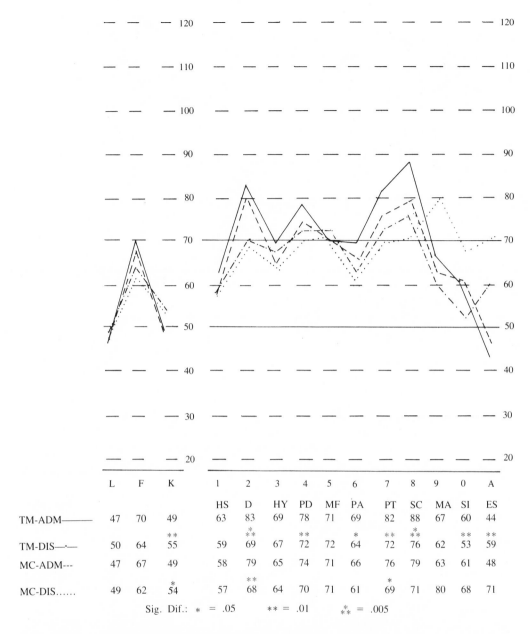

	L	F	K	1	2	3	4	5	6	7	8	9	0	A
				HS	D	HY	PD	MF	PA	PT	SC	MA	SI	ES
TM-ADM———	47	70	49	63	83	69	78	71	69	82	88	67	60	44
TM-DIS—·—	50	64	55**	59	69*/**	67	72**	72*	64	72**	76*/**	62	53**	59**
MC-ADM---	47	67	49	58	79	65	74	71	66	76	79	63	61	48
MC-DIS......	49	62	54*	57	68**	64	70	71	61	69*	71	80	68	71

Sig. Dif.: * = .05   ** = .01   *⁄** = .005

Fig. 3. The admission and discharge profiles for male TM patients and the male comparison group. The mean admission and discharge profiles, shown by the solid line and the dash-dot-dash line, for 36 male patients (TM–N = 36; MC–N = 35) doing TM are compared with the mean admission and discharge profiles, shown by the dashed and the dotted line, for 35 male comparison patients. Eight scales show significant differences for the TM patients between admission and discharge, while only three scales show significant differences for the comparison group.

of improvement is given. Comparing the outcome figures for the schizophrenic patients shows a significant difference in level of improvement in favor of the patients doing TM ($\chi_2 = 15.814$, $df = 2$, $p = <.0002$). By comparison, the remainder of the sample, comprising the other diagnostic groupings, shows no significant difference in the outcome levels between the two groups ($\chi_2 = 1,638$, $df = 2$, $p = $ n.s.).

The fact that 40% of our sample had a diagnosis of a schizophrenic illness demonstrates, we believe, that even quite seriously ill hospitalized psychiatric patients can learn the meditation technique if they are

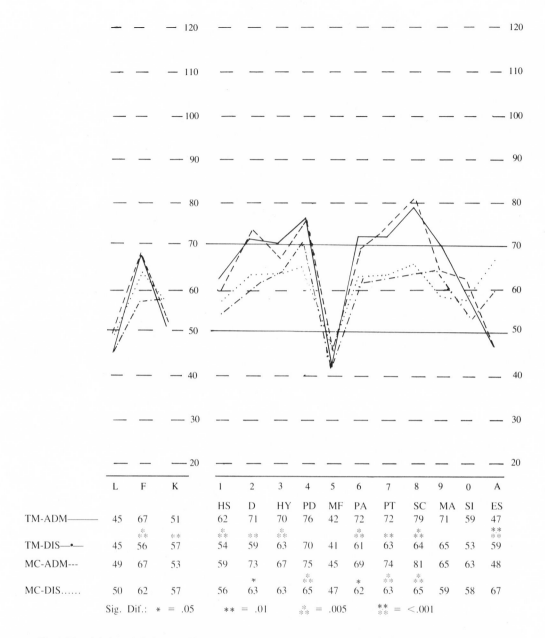

	L	F	K	1	2	3	4	5	6	7	8	9	0	A
				HS	D	HY	PD	MF	PA	PT	SC	MA	SI	ES
TM-ADM———	45	67	51	62	71	70	76	42	72	72	79	71	59	47
		*	**	*	**	*			*	**	*			**
TM-DIS—•—	45	56	57	54	59	63	70	41	61	63	64	65	53	59
MC-ADM---	49	67	53	59	73	67	75	45	69	74	81	65	63	48
					*		**		*	**	**			
MC-DIS......	50	62	57	56	63	63	65	47	62	63	65	59	58	67

Sig. Dif.:   * = .05   ** = .01   *̲*̲ = .005   **̲ = <.001

Fig. 4. The admission and discharge profiles for female TM patients and the female comparison group. The mean admission and discharge profiles, shown by the solid line and the dash-dot-dash line, for 23 female patients (TM–N = 23; MC–N = 22) doing TM are compared with the mean admission and discharge profiles shown by the dashed line and the dotted line for 22 female comparison patients. Nine scales show significant differences for the TM patients between admission and discharge, while five scales show significant differences for the comparison patients.

able to comprehend the instructions. Because of the immediate awareness of a drop in the levels of anxiety and tension, most of our patients were willing to continue practicing the technique on a regular, twice daily, basis. We experienced the greatest difficulty in getting patients to meditate regularly in those individuals with a significant amount of depression, and in our younger, teenage patients. Even in these individuals it was more a matter of reminding them to practice the meditation regularly, rather than any

Table II. TM Versus Matched Comparison Group Condition on Discharge by Diagnosis[a]

Condition	Group 1		Group II		Group III		Totals	
	TM	MC	TM	MC	TM	MC	TM	MC
Schizophrenia	20	18	22	28	1	23	43	69
Neuroses	17	5	5	4	4	2	26	11
Personality disorders	5	3	9	8	4	1	18	12
Alcoholism	1	2	3	1	0	1	4	5
Drug dependence	4	1	6	3	1	0	11	4
Adjustment reaction adolescence	5	2	3	6	0	1	8	9
Totals	52	31	48	51	10	28	110	110

[a]$N = 220$. TM = 110; MC = 110. Group I, recovered or much improved; Group II, moderately improved; Group III, slightly improved or unimproved.

resistance or unwillingness to do so. In fact, less than 10% of the total number of patients taught to meditate stopped meditating within the first six weeks of learning the technique.

While the patients remained in the hospital most attempted to meditate quite regularly during the period of time that they were in the research project. After termination of their participation in the project, there was a gradual attrition in the regularity of meditation which continued after discharge from the hospital. At the time of our first follow-up inquiry, approximately three months after discharge, 42% of the respondents were continuing regular twice daily meditation. Another 22% were meditating somewhat irregularly, and 36% had stopped entirely for one or another reason. Many of these patients indicated that they planned to resume meditation at some point in the future. In a somewhat smaller sample, followed up at one year, 43% of the respondents were continuing to meditate regularly, but the number of patients who had stopped had risen to 42%, with the remainder reporting irregular or infrequent meditation.

There are no precise figures available from the TM organization as to the number of individuals in the general community who stop meditating after going through the learning process. Estimates from several sources seem to agree on about a 50% attrition rate. If this is, in fact, correct, then our patients are continuing to meditate in about the same percentage as individuals learning the TM technique who do not have psychiatric problems.

It is interesting that Benson reports the major difficulty with the use of his technique is the failure of individuals taught the technique to continue to use it regularly. This is true in spite of the fact that most of the individuals with whom he deals have significant problems with their blood pressure, coronary artery disease, etc. We have seen the same phenomenon in the patients in our Biofeedback Clinic where we are teaching people to trigger a general relaxation through vasodilation of the vessels in the hand, and through relaxation of the striated muscle. These patients have seriously incapacitating, painful headaches (vascular and tension headaches) or Raynaud's disease of the fingers and sometimes the toes. In spite of the extreme pain that these conditions can cause, of pain which is either completely relieved or significantly improved through the use of the relaxation techniques, approximately 50% of these individuals complain of a recurrence of symptoms at four to six months. In addition to whatever else may have changed, the universal finding is that they have stopped doing their daily relaxation exercises entirely or do them only very sporadically. Usually, if they come back into the Clinic for a refresher course in the relaxation techniques, their symptoms are again brought under good control.

Over and above the general human tendency to become careless or sloppy about doing anything regularly and consistently that takes some time and effort, we are concerned with the possibility of significant psychodynamic factors in these individuals that may make it very difficult or impossible for them to lead comfortable, pain-free lives. One can construe this as a reflection of the puritan ethic (life should be hard, difficult, uncomfortable), or one can label these individuals masochistic, or, in a more recent terminology, pain-dependent. Unfortunately, due to the limitations of personnel time, we have not been able to investigate the detailed psychodynamic patterns in these patients in sufficient detail to arrive at any conclusions on these points.

An additional factor in individuals learning TM may be the very common experience that the initial relief of tension and anxiety feelings, which may be quite dramatic, tends to become less and less noticeable as the individual continues to meditate over the first two or three months. Since it is extremely difficult for us to remember, with any precision, exactly how tense and anxious we may have been at some previous point in time, even fairly recently, the degrees of difference from day to day as the general levels of tension subside become increasingly difficult to distinguish. It is at this point, we feel, that many individuals, if they are not reinforced in some way to continue the daily meditation or relaxation techniques, may conclude that nothing of significance is occurring and that the sessions are really a waste of time.

In addition, in many individuals, at about the same point in time, the meditation process appears to release memories that have previously been quite thoroughly repressed. For individuals, and this includes some of our psychiatric patients, who have had little or no contact with their unconscious processes, this can be quite a disturbing experience. The appearance in a fully conscious, alert state, of intense affects and ideation that are usually quite completely repressed, can be a very disturbing experience, especially if there is no one to help the individual to understand what is happening. Even though the TM teachers try to deal with this experience by stating that these thoughts represent stress being released from the nervous system, that this is a good experience, and that the thoughts should simply be allowed to float through the mind and disappear, this may not be sufficiently convincing or reassuring for many individuals who become troubled by both the content and the intensity of the ideation. We are convinced that many individuals stop meditating at this point because of their conviction that meditation is harming them and may perhaps be causing some sort of mental disturbance.

While we had some awareness of this phenomenon when we began our research project, we were not prepared for the intensity and rapidity with which these repressed memories can arise. We are quite certain that several of the patients who stopped meditating within the first two to three weeks early in the project did so because we were not dealing with the ideation adequately. Once we became aware of the significance of the above events, and alerted the psychotherapist to this possibility, we found that we could turn the experience to a distinct advantage for our patients. We feel that there is little question that meditation can speed up the entire psychotherapeutic process by virtue of the release of previously completely repressed material. This has been the experience of other therapists using TM with their patients, as reported by Drs. Carrington and Ephron, and by Dr. Bloomfield (9–11).

If one does attempt to use techiques like TM in an effort to mobilize the release of material that has been previously repressed, it is extremely important that the patient understand and carefully follow the instructions about how to deal with the thoughts as they arise in meditation. We gave patients very specific instructions to follow the meditation rules while they were meditating. In general, these rules state that one should not attempt to understand, associate to, or otherwise deal with ideas that come up while meditating; that one should simply let the ideas pass through the mind and if they seem to be too bothersome, to return to the mantra. We believe this is an essential instruction since the meditation would be seriously interferred with otherwise. We also instruct our patients, however, that following the meditation, if they can recall specific ideas, events, situations that have come into their mind while meditating, to utilize these in their psychotherapeutic activity. Once we understood this general process and had conveyed the information to the therapists in the hospital, many of them utilized this phenomenon to great advantage in the treatment of their patients. Carrington carries this process several steps further by timing the meditation to occur just before the therapeutic session, or, at times, having the patient meditate during the session, so that any idea that comes up will be quite fresh and available for the psychotherapeutic process. While we do not understand how this phenomenon occurs, we do have some ideas about what may be involved in the central nervous system. (This is discussed in this volume in Part II in the article Psychophysiological Correlates of Meditation, where we talk about the electrophysiologic phenomena that accompany the meditation process.)

Up to this point I have been reporting primarily subjective responses to these relaxation techniques. To be sure, a change in symptoms, such as the loss of intense tension and anxiety feelings, the disappearance of migraine headaches, the normalization of the blood supply in the fingers in Raynaud's disease, are all fairly important indicators that something significant may be happening. We are fortunate, however, in that there is accumulating a wealth of more objective evidence, primarily psychophysiologic data, that tends to support the subjective, anecdotal type of reports. It was the finding of significant changes in basic psychophysiologic mechanisms, such as the galvanic skin response (GSR), the electroencephalographic (EEG) wave forms, changes in heart rate, and in blood pressure that first excited the interest of psychophysiologists in exploring these various relaxation techniques. Since there is such a wide variety of relaxation techniques, including all of the various forms of yoga, the meditational techniques, such as TM and Zen meditation, similar derivations of these, such as Carrington's Clinically Standardized Meditation, and Benson's Relaxation Response technique, one must ask what the similarities are in these various techniques, and do they, in fact, produce the same end point as their proponents insist. Competition in this area is very keen, with the adherents of each technique insisting that theirs is the best technique to use in the attempt to achieve the results desired. In the oriental yogic and meditation techniques this usually is the state of exaltation, or bliss, given various names, such as Nirvana, Sahmedi, etc. With the Western variations that have been developed, the end point tends to be more specifically targeted; for example, relief of psychic tension and symptoms; relief of specific psychophysiological difficulties, such as hypertension, migraine, and Raynaud's disease, as well as achieving a general state of relaxation. At this point in time, with an as yet incomplete understanding of the specific details of the impact of all of these various approaches, we are inclined toward the idea that all of these techniques represent different paths toward the same general end. We are also quite certain that they vary in effectiveness with different individuals, perhaps different basic personality types, and also vary in their impact on specific pathologic processes. One good example is the generally acknowledged failure of TM to significantly effect migraine headaches and Raynaud's disease. We would add a caution here that the individuals we have studied have been practicing TM for six months to several years. It is entirely possible that with long-term use of the TM technique, significant improvement might occur in these somatic illnesses. By contrast however, the same individuals, after three to six hours of training in the specific biofeedback techniques of vasodilation and muscle relaxation, obtain either complete relief or marked improvement in their somatic complaints in approximatly 80% of cases.*

References

1. Benson, H. *The relaxation response.* New York: Wm. Morrow, 1975.
2. Maharishi Mahesh Yogi. *The science of being and the art of living.* London, SRM Publications, 1966, p. 251.
3. Rado, S. *Adaptational psychodynamics: motivation and control.* New York: Science House, 1969.
4. Green, E. E., Green, A. M., and Walters, E. D. Voluntary control of internal states: Psychological and physiological. *J. Transpersonal Psychol.,* 1972, **1**, 1–26.
5. Kamiya, J. Operant control of EEG alpha rhythm and some of its reported effects on consciousness. In C. T. Tart (ed.) *Altered states of consciousness.* New York: John Wiley and Sons, 1969, pp. 507–517.
6. Glueck, B. C. and Stroebel, C. F. Biofeedback and meditation in the treatment of psychiatric illnesses. *Compr. Psychiatry,* 1975, **16**, 303–321.
7. Glueck, B. C. and Stroebel, C. F. Biofeedback and meditation in the treatment of psychiatric illnesses. In J. Masserman (ed.) *Current psychiatric therapies*, Vol. 15, 1975, pp. 109–116. New York: Grune & Stratton.
8. Luthe, W. *Autogenic training.* New York: Grune & Stratton, 1965.
9. Carrington, P. and Ephron, H. S. Meditation as an adjunct to psychotherapy. In Arieti, S. and Chrzanowski, G. (eds.) *New dimensions in psychiatry: a world view.* New York: John Wiley and Sons, 1975.
10. Carrington, P. *Freedom in meditation.* New York: Anchor Press-Doubleday, 1977.
11. Bloomfield, H. H. and Kory, R. B. *Happiness: the TM program, psychiatry and enlightenment.* New York: Dawn Press/Simon and Schuster, 1976.

Editor's note: The second half of this article appears in Part II of this volume, Article 40 and is entitled Psychophysiology Correlates of Meditation.

ZEN MEDITATION AND THE
DEVELOPMENT OF EMPATHY
IN COUNSELORS[1,2]

Terry V. Lesh

BACKGROUND AND RATIONALE

The experience of counseling supervisors and researchers of the counseling process has suggested that student counselors, as well as experienced counselors, frequently do not demonstrate adequate sensitivity to the client's feelings (Rogers *et al.*, 1967). Yet these same counselors often are quite sophisticated in psychological and counseling theory. If it is true that the ability of the counselor to demonstrate his sense of what the client is communicating through his feelings is an important dimension of the counseling relationship, then it is necessary to look deeper at what constitutes the more subtle nuances between human beings.

It has been very difficult to determine through the process of the experimental method the conditions that allow positive growth in the client. Carl Rogers points out that at the present time research in psychotherapy is in a state of chaos. He refers to the volumes of data of research on counseling as "an ocean of confusion" (Stollak, 1966).

Some of the most consistent findings suggest, however, that the counselor's use of accurate empathy is directly related to the positive growth of the client (Stollak, 1966; Rogers, 1962-67; Van Buren, 1963; Truax, 1961 & 1966; Truax & Carkhuff, 1963; Rogers *et al.*, 1967;

1 Based on a doctoral dissertation submitted to the University of Oregon. The author wishes to express his special appreciation to his wife Patricia, Barton E. Clements, Gordon A. Dudley and Philip Runkle.

2 Requests for reprints should be addressed to Terry V. Lesh, Student Counselling Services, University of Lethbridge, Lethbridge, Alberta, Canada.

Kagan, 1967). While the studies that have been done on empathy do show its importance in the counseling process, there still exists some debate on the exact meaning of this concept.

Rogers (1964, 1967) probably comes closest to an ideal description of what empathy means in counseling. He defines it as a twofold process: (1) The capacity of the counselor to sense or feel what the client is feeling and (2) the ability to communicate this sensitivity to the client at a level that is attuned to the client's current emotional state.

While the studies cited above have shown the importance of the counselor's ability to empathize with the client, there has been little success in increasing this ability in counselors (Matthes, 1967; Albright, 1967; Mellow, 1964). Some studies have shown that graduate students in counseling do not demonstrate any more empathic ability than a random selection of high school students (Truax & Carkhuff, 1963). These findings suggest that either researchers are not looking deeply enough at the intrapsychic processes within the counselor that allow his empathic abilities to develop, or they do not fully understand the process of empathy itself. More elaboration about empathy and its concomitant intrapsychic components is required. Why do counselors in training programs gain little or nothing in their empathic capacities? What are the psychological processes within an individual that allow him to be empathic or open to the feelings of another? It is necessary to turn to another conceptual framework in order to answer some of these questions.

The concept of *regression-in-the-service-of-the-ego* (hereinafter called "adaptive regression") may aid in understanding the deeper intrapsychic processes involved in the human capacity for relating. Shafer (1954) considers adaptive regression to be the essential process, insofar as it is adaptive, involved in direct interpersonal relations such as empathy, intimacy, orgasm, therapeutic understanding, and communication. He suggests that adaptive regression depends on certain facilitative conditions. These conditions are very much like those we would hold for the growth-producing counseling relationship (Shafer, 1954; Mellow, 1964; Rogers, 1958).

If the capacity to be empathic is related to adaptive regression, how is a person taught to utilize this deeper potentiality, to "regress in the service of his ego?" How do we teach someone (counselor, therapist, etc.) to "modify his level of psychic awareness and functioning to more basic primary processes within himself?"

The underlying assumption in this study is that a form of Zen meditation, *zazen,* is a way an individual learns to control and to be aware of these internal psychic processes.

Empathy

Accurate empathy is defined, as has been mentioned in the introduction of this study, by Rogers and others (Rogers *et al.*, 1967) as a twofold process. The first component is the counselor's capacity to sense or feel what the client is feeling. The second component is the ability of the counselor to communicate this sensitivity to the client at a level that is attuned to the client's current feeling state. Truax also refers to these two aspects of empathy:

> Accurate empathy involves more than just the ability of the therapist to sense the patient's "private world" as if it were his own. It also involves more than just the ability of the therapist to know what the patient means. Accurate empathy involves *both* the sensitivity to *current feelings* and the *verbal facility to communicate* this understanding in a language attuned to the client's current feelings [Truax, 1967, p. 555, emphasis added].

Accurate empathy has been difficult to measure with any degree of reliability. Truax (1963, 1966, 1967) and others (Matthes, 1967; Albright, 1967) have reported high reliability and validity using the Truax Scale of Accurate Empathy with counselors in various settings. However, Albright found that intra-judge ratings of accurate empathy were not of acceptable reliability. Truax does not report test-retest reliability on the Scale of Accurate Empathy in his studies.

In another very comprehensive study of empathy (Kagan, 1967), it was decided that the most clear-cut way of measuring empathy was by some kind of situational test; namely, objective observation of client and counselor interaction. After a formidable review of the literature on empathy and empathy studies, Kagan concluded that there are not just two, but at least three components to the empathy process. These are, in his classification, (1) the ability to perceive the client's feelings; (2) the interpretation to oneself of the client's feelings; and (3) the communication of this final personal interpretation of the perceived feelings back to the client.

When the psychoanalytic explanation (Reik, 1948; Fenichel, 1945) of empathy is included, two more components are added to the process; the objectification of one's own feelings from the client's feelings, and the identification of the client's preconscious feelings, in addition to his stated feelings. Fenichel (1945) explains the objectification phase

> . . . empathy consists of two acts: (a) An identification with the other person, and (b) an awareness of one's own feelings after the identification, and in this way an awareness of the object's feelings [p. 511].

Rogers (1964) himself incorporates the psychoanalytic view of empathy when he states that accurate empathy touches on that which is just emerging in the client, but is not yet fully conscious.

Through this maze of attempts to define, operationalize, and measure accurate empathy, one realizes that: (1) It is an important concept in human interaction, and as such has been the subject of extensive research; and (2) rather than being a simple single component, accurate empathy is a complex process of interaction between human beings involving at least six major components. These could be described as: (1) The *perception* of two levels of feeling in the client, those that are stated or conscious and those that are not stated but are present—preconscious; (2) the *identification* of the feelings of the client; (3) the *differentiation* between the client's feelings and the counselor's feelings; (4) the *objectification* or separation of the client's feelings; (5) the *interpretation* of the client's feelings; and (6) the *articulation* of the client's feelings, both stated and preconscious.

The disagreement and lack of reliability resulting from attempts to measure this process reflect the substantial subjective judgment required to rate samples of client-counselor interactions which occur at different phases of the process. This study, therefore, will attempt measurement of only the first phase of the empathic process; that is, ". . . the ability to detect (perceive) and describe the immediate affective state of another . . . (Kagan, 1967, p. 463)." In terms of communication theory this is ". . . the ability to receive and decode affective communication (Kagan, Krathwohl, & Farquhar, 1965)." This definition of empathy is called "affective sensitivity."

Admittedly this definition does not, at face value, appear to be different than the initial definition of empathy. However, as the later discussion of instruments will show, the measurement of affective sensitivity is considerably different than the measurement of accurate empathy as reported by Truax and others.

Zen Meditation or Zazen

Zazen means sitting Zen meditation. "The student [of Zen] sets aside a portion of the day to sit motionless and concentrate" (Maupin, 1962). The object of the concentration is one's own breathing. The aim of this concentration is to suspend the flow of ordinary thoughts without falling asleep or going into a trance. As Wienpahl (1964) explains it:

"Zen" means meditation. *This cannot be repeated too often.* "Meditation" in this context means sitting quietly, more specifically sitting a certain way and breathing in a certain manner. It may mean more, for meditation has layers; but basically "Zen" means meditation and that is sitting quietly and breathing quietly [p. 3].

But, as Wienpahl suggests, there is another way of describing *zazen.* "It is learning to listen. It is learning to accept [p. 122]."

In the author's experience, observing counseling sessions of both beginning and experienced counselors, it seemed that many of the counselors frequently were not relating to the reality of the person in front of them. It seemed as though the counselors were responding to something in their own minds—some image or idea, but certainly not to the person that was talking to them. It seemed that the counselors were more concerned about their role as a counselor than listening to the client. It seemed they were more interested in their own need to be the "problem solver" than to accept the feelings the client was pouring out. There was a marked change from the person of the counselor to the "counselor" who was now "being a counselor."

What was desired was to bring the counselor to be himself; to be open to the experiences of the client. One cannot be empathic with another if he does not even know what his own experience is. This is the identification-differentiation-objectification phase in empathy referred to above. The counselor was urged to be in tune with himself, i.e., in tune with his own feelings as well as the feelings of the client. As Rogers has put it, "This new way of being with the client or patient requires a heightened awareness on the part of the therapist of the shifting flow of felt experiencing within himself (Rogers, 1964)." There can be discussion about this, students can read about it, but still they are not "there." Note now the similarity of what is being said to counseling students and the following passage about Zen from Wienpahl (1964).

The Zen student is told to feel the force of the universe behind him. One day he does. His intense concentration in *zazen* leads him to this step, for it is a concentration of his energies. From here he goes on to sense more and more deeply that pillow on which he sits for *zazen* is helping him, that *it* is part of *his* work. Eventually he merges with the pillow. Other distinctions between subjective and objective disappear. He feels at one with the things and people around him, ultimately with the whole world. *His growing strength is not dissipated by this realization of identity. It is rather freed thereby: to bring him out of the past and future of his memories and plans into the immediate present.* The Zen student then increasingly has a sensation as of awakening abruptly from a daydream. The world about him is suddenly sharply in focus at these moments. During them he feels the blinding effect of the illusion from which he ordinarily suffers. He may describe this in various ways. "I am in touch with reality." "I have got beneath the idea of self." "I and reality are one." "There is no self. There is only reality. Appearance and emptiness are the same; the relative and the absolute." At other times he may see that this experience is none other than a feeling of calm. Indeed, it is calmness itself. He finds himself simply and fully in the workaday and matter-of-fact world, the world of common sense in which he had always lived but with which he now sees, he had been strangely out of touch [pp. 137-38, emphasis added].

The above quotation points out the emphasis of "being present" in Zen philosophy. Essentially *zazen* is the conscious attempt to loosen oneself from all the thoughts one has about oneself in the past and in the future. To free oneself from the past and the future (in thought), and to enter the present fully, is the aim of Zen in terms of its attentional dimension. To be "in the present," or to be aware or conscious of all that is "present" in the present includes the awareness of what is "inside" one's mind (Berger, 1962). In order to move from the present in the outer environment to the present in the inner environment one must speak in terms of "mental states."

There are various terms used to describe different mental states: e.g., awake, sleeping, dreaming, unconscious, entranced, etc. (Singer, 1966; Kubie, 1967; Neisser, 1967). The attentional process of *zazen* is one of allowing one's conscious attention to open inward to one's own mental processes.

The following passage by a man who went through Zen training from a Zen master describes the sequence of experiences that occur during meditation.

The demand that the door of the senses be closed is not meant by turning energetically away from a sensible world, but rather by a readiness to yield without resistance. In order that this actionless activity may be accomplished instinctively, the soul needs an inner hold, and it wins it by concentrating on breathing. This is performed consciously with a conscientiousness that borders on the pedantic. The breathing in, like the breathing out, is practiced again and again by itself with the utmost care. One does not have to wait long for results. The more one concentrates on breathing, the more the external stimuli fade into the background. They sink away in a kind of muffled roar which one hears with only half an ear at first and in the end one finds it no more disturbing than the distant roar of the sea, which, once one has grown accustomed to it, is no longer perceived. In due course one even grows immune to larger stimuli and at the same time detachment from them comes easier and quicker. Care has only to be taken that the body is relaxed whether standing, sitting, or lying, and if one then concentrates on breathing one soon feels oneself shut in by impermeable layers of silence. One only knows and feels that one breathes. And to detach oneself from this feeling and knowing, no fresh decision is required for the breath slows down of its own accord, becomes more and more economical in the use of breath, and finally, slipping by degrees into a blurred monotone, escapes one's attention altogether.

This exquisite state of unconcerned immersion in oneself is not, unfortunately, of long duration. It is liable to be disturbed from the inside.

As though sprung from nowhere, moods, feelings, desires, worries and even thoughts incontingently rise up, in a meaningless jumble. . . . The only successful way of rendering this disturbance inoperative is to keep on breathing, quietly and unconcernedly, to enter into friendly relations with whatever appears on the scene, to accustom oneself to it, to look at it equably and at last grow weary of looking. In this way one gradually gets into a state which resembles the melting drowsiness of sleep.

To slip into it [sleep] finally is a danger which has to be avoided. It [this drowsy stage] is met by a peculiar leap of concentration, comparable perhaps to the jolt which a man who has stayed up all night gives himself when he knows that his life depends on all his senses being alert; and if this leap has been successful but a single time it can be repeated with certainty. With its help the soul is brought to a point where it vibrates of itself in itself—a serene pulsation which can be heightened into the feeling, otherwise experienced only in rare dreams, of extraordinary lightness, and rapturous certainty of being able to summon up energies in any direction, to intensify or to release tensions graded to a nicety.

This state, in which nothing definite is thought, planned, striven for, desired, or expected, which aims in no particular direction and yet knows itself capable alike of the possible and the impossible, so unswerving in its power—this state, which is at the bottom purposeless and egoless, was called by the master truly "spiritual." It is in fact charged with spiritual awareness and is therefore called "right presence of mind." This means that the mind or spirit is present everywhere because it is nowhere attached to any particular place. And it can remain present because, even when related to this or that object, it does not cling to it by reflection and thus lose its original mobility. Like water filling a pond, which is always ready to flow off again, it can work its inexhaustive power because it is free, and be open to everything because it is empty. *This state is essentially a primordial state* . . . [Herrigel, 1953, pp. 56 ff., emphasis added].

The primordial state referred to in the above passage is conceptualized as being below or underneath normal waking thought. Speaking in psychoanalytic terms, we may think of the usual intellectual, rational thought processes as being at the top (of consciousness) and the more basic, primitive mental functions at the bottom. The leap spoken of by Herrigel is a shift at once to a vertical downward movement, or direction of attention, while maintaining a state of mental alertness.

Kubie (1967) describes how education has served to overemphasize the conscious control of thinking which acts to inhibit one's capacity for "fully functioning" thinking. This in turn inhibits preconscious processes. Kubie continues with some suggestions for the direction research in mental functioning might take. Continuing with the above line of thought:

This premature introduction of conscious sampling, through the repetitive emphasis on drill and grill, is precisely what makes jailers out of the processes of conscious sampling and conscious symbolic representation. Conscious processes thereby become inhibiting and paralyzing forces which restrict the free play of preconscious function. Therefore the goal of basic research in education must be to find better substitutes, to find better ways of tapping what is going on, and finding out what is being taken in subliminally and what is being processed preconsciously. We must find out how to dip a tin cup into the rushing preconscious stream without damming it up or diverting it [Kubie, 1967, p. 88].

This taking of larger samples of the "other than conscious processes" is precisely what *zazen* is. The attentional aspects of *zazen* may be considered (for the purpose of describing the conscious *process* of meditation) as directional. Starting with the assumption that "other than conscious processes" lie underneath (e.g., subliminal = below awareness) normal waking thought, the attention is turned (or opened) to the next most immediate level of awareness, the preconscious processes. Continuing with the intense concentration, the attention is opened to the next level of consciousness underlying the preconscious, the unconscious processes. This is as far as Western thought goes. Herrigel (1953), in the passage quoted previously, suggests yet another level of consciousness, which shall be referred to here as "pure consciousness."

The object of *zazen* is the allowing of all these processes to surface to one's awareness until there is no splitting-up of consciousness. There is no cognition, no dreaming, no hallucinations, no data input, (via normal sensory modalities), no information processing, no conscious activity at all, just full waking attention.

Adaptive Regression or Regression in the Service of the Ego

The meditation process, as outlined above, parallels Maupin's suggestion (1962) that "meditation brings about a sequence of more or less regressive states." This is taken to mean a conscious regression of attention to more primitive mental processes than one is normally aware of in the daily waking state. In his study of individual differences in response to Zen meditation, Maupin found a significant (tau = .49, P = < .001) correlation between responses to meditation and adaptive regression as measured by the Rorschach, and a test of visual imagery in free association. In psychoanalytic terms (Kris, 1952), "regression-in-the-service-of-the-ego" is synonymous with adaptive regression. As Maupin reported in his study, "structurally the process implies suspension of some ego functions such as defensive or logical functions and sometimes emphasis on genetically primitive mechanisms."

Shafer (1958) has expanded on the concept of regression in the service of the ego to account for the ability of individuals to make use of increased access to pre-conscious mental content, and its organization, without being overwhelmed by this pre-conscious material. The enlarged concept has been used to promote understanding of sleeping, dreaming, empathy, capacity for orgastic experience, hypnosis, free association, etc. The pre-conscious refers to "material, which though at the moment unconscious, is available and ready to become conscious; also topographically of a region, as it were, in the mind, intermediate between consciousness and the unconsciousness as such (Drever, 1952, p. 215)."

A body of literature (Freud, 1900, 1911; Drever, 1952; Fitzgerald, 1966; Kris, 1952; Pine & Holt, 1960; Holt & Havel, 1960) has focused on the "regression to primitive mode functioning" with the return to secondary process functioning. One gets the idea that adaptive regression is a uni-directional process where the attention of the individual is either at the secondary process level *or* the primary process level. Such may be the case in certain instances; however, as Kubi (1967) and Neisser (1967) have suggested, it is more likely that adaptive regression is actually more of an "opening" to inner experience, while still being entirely conscious and operating quite adequately at the secondary process level. This conception of adaptive regression is suggested by Schachtel (1959). Openness to experience, as defined by Fitzgerald (1966), means an openness to *all* experience, both inner and outer. This openness does not necessarily mean a regression to primitive modes of thought and behavior, but a progressive encountering of inner and outer experience with a sensing of all their possibilities and nuances.

The following phases of the empathic process show the similarity in the process to the function of *zazen*—the oscillation of ego-involvement-detachment that occurs in adaptive regression.

a. Identification. . . . Partly through an instinctive, imitative activity and partly through relaxation of our conscious controls, we allow ourselves to become absorbed in contemplating the other person and his experiences. It is an indulgence in fantasy which makes us lose our self-awareness. It is essential if we are to become engaged in an experience of others.

b. Incorporation. By this term we mean the act of taking the experience of the other person into ourselves. . . . When we identify, we experience what the other person feels; when we incorporate or take in, we feel his experience as if it were our own.

c. Reverberation. . . . What we have taken into ourselves now echoes upon some part of our own experience and awakens a new appreciation. . . . We allow for an interplay between two sets of experience, the internalized feelings of others and our own experience and fantasy. . . .

Our self-knowledge is therefore sharpened or reawakened. With this deepening of our self-appreciation comes an understanding of what others feel.

d. Detachment. In this phase of empathic understanding we withdraw from our subjective involvement and use the methods of reason and scrutiny. We break our identification and deliberately move away to gain social and psychic distance necessary for objective analysis [Katz, 1963, pp. 41-45, 47].

Moving then, from the concept of adaptive regression, focusing primarily on the oscillation between secondary and primary thought processes, to the concept of openness to experience, it can be seen that openness to experience includes inner experiences as well as outer experiences. From the standpoint of research it will be much easier to discriminate among those who are open to experience and those who are not, than to discriminate on the basis of "regression in the service of the ego" in terms of primary-and-secondary process operation.

HYPOTHESES

The purpose of this study is to determine if there is a relationship between the practice of *zazen* and the development of empathy in counseling students.

Hypothesis 1

Counselors who practice *zazen* regularly over a prescribed length of time will develop a higher degree of empathy as measured by the Affective Sensitivity Scale than counselors who do not practice *zazen* over the same time span.

Hypothesis 2

There will be a positive correlation between the individual response to meditation and scores on the Affective Sensitivity Scale.

Hypothesis 3

Response to meditation will be positively correlated with openness to experience as measured by the Experience Inquiry.

Hypothesis 4

Individual scores in openness to experience will be positively correlated with individual scores in affective sensitivity (from low to high).

Hypothesis 5

Those individuals scoring high in affective sensitivity will score high in each of 12 categories of the Personal Orientation Inventory (Shostrom, 1966):

DESIGN AND SAMPLE

The Solomon Four-Group Design (Kerlinger, 1964; Runkle and McGrath, in press) was originally intended to be used in the study. However, when the subjects (all of the first-year students in the 1968-69 Master's degree program in counseling psychology at the University of Oregon) were presented with the idea of the study, they expressed considerable fear and anxiety about being required to participate in the meditation experience. These students were involved in other research projects at the same time; consequently, they resisted the meditation study so that all hopes of randomization had to be given up.

The alternative was to ask for volunteers to participate in the study. The resulting design was of a three-group nature. The first group (N = 16) were those students in the Master's degree program (regardless of level) who volunteered to participate in the study and who actually did the meditation. The result was that only one of these subjects was not a first-year student, but one who was finishing his second year in the Master's program.

The second group (N = 12) were all Master's degree students *taking* counseling courses, but who were not necessarily in the counseling department. This group volunteered to do the meditation, but, in fact, did not actually do it. This group served as the first control group.

The third group (N = 11) were again Master's degree students taking counseling courses, but were not necessarily students under the counseling department. Again all levels of progress in the degree program were represented. (One doctoral candidate was in this group.) These were people who definitely were against participating in the meditation exercise, but did complete all of the criterion measures, as did groups one and two.

PROCEDURES

All of the subjects in the three groups were given a pretest (on the same day) for empathy or affective sensitivity, openness to experience (for adaptive regression), and a measure of self-actualization. Exactly 4 weeks later, at the same time during the day, all the subjects in all three groups were given the same measures again. A detailed description of the criterion measures will follow the report of the experimental group below.

In the intervening 4 weeks, the people in all groups continued with their regular studies in the counseling program. The subjects in the experimental group, however, participated in the meditation exercise. The other two groups did not. A room was selected in the music listening section of the library where all the subjects could do the meditation together. They practiced the meditation exercise for 30 minutes each week day for 4 weeks, from 12:30 to 1:00 p.m.

The experimenter met with the 16 subjects who were to do the meditation and informed them of the time, location and length of the experience. They were told of the importance of keeping to the schedule. It was explained that in order for the study to maintain its "tightness," i.e., reduce experimenter effect, personal contact with them, by the experimenter, would have to be kept to an absolute minimum. To accomplish this, it was explained that the instructions for the exercise would be on a prerecorded tape that would be turned on after they arrived for the sessions. In order to alleviate any fears, they were told that the experimenter would be in the immediate vicinity of the meditation room if anyone felt it was absolutely essential to talk to him. The following are the actual instructions for the meditation exercise.

INSTRUCTIONS FOR MEDITATION EXERCISE

Keep your back straight and erect; your hands in your lap, the left hand palm facing inward on the right palm, with the tips of the thumbs touching. Your head too is erect, the ears on the plane of the shoulders, and the nose in line with the navel. You may keep your eyes closed or open as you prefer. If you have them open fix them, unfocused, on the floor at a point about two or three feet in front of you. Now raise your whole body slowly and quietly, move it repeatedly to the left and to the right, forward and around, until you feel the best position.

Breath through your nose, inhaling as much as you need, letting the air come in by distending the diaphragm. Don't draw it in, rather let it come to you. Exhale slowly and completely, getting all the air out of your lungs. As you exhale slowly, count "one." Now inhale again, then exhale to the count of "two." And so on up to ten. Then start over again with "one" and repeat up to ten again, etc.

You will find the counting difficult as your mind will wander. Keep at it though, keep bringing your mind back to the process of counting your breath. As you become able to do the counting with reasonable success start playing the following game with the counting. As you count "one" and are slowly exhaling, pretend that the "one" is going down, down, down, into your stomach. Then think of its being down there as you inhale, and begin to count "two." As you exhale bring the "two" down and place it in your stomach beside the "one." Eventually you will find that your mind itself, so to speak, will descend into your stomach. Gradually it will become possible for you to concentrate with more and more success on the numbers. Your mind will wander, and you will find yourself carried away on trains of thought, but it will become easier and easier to bring your mind back to the counting of your breath. Don't try to keep the "alien" thoughts out. Instead just try to concentrate on the counting. You may take note of the thoughts as they come in, if necessary, and then return to the counting. Get rid of the thoughts not by pushing them out of your mind, but by concentrating on the counting.

You may find that you become anxious or uncomfortable. This is because sitting still and concentrating like this restricts the usual ways we have of avoiding discomfort. If you feel uncomfortable, just accept it. If you feel pleasant, accept that with the same indifference. Eventually you will be able to be quiet in both body and mind [adapted from Wienpahl (1964) and Maupin, 1962].

The tape then ran silently for exactly 30 minutes, after which the experimenter's voice again became audible: "OK, the time is up, now without talking to anyone, please record your experience."

As the subjects arrived for the exercises, they were handed a 4 by 6 card with their name and the session number on it. After the session was over and they had recorded their experience on the cards, the cards were collected by the experimenter. There was no discussion of the experience with the experimenter.

At the end of the 4 weeks, after the posttests were given, all of the session reports were rated by three judges. The cards were all coded by number, so that the individuals could not be recognized. The rating system is reproduced below:

INSTRUCTIONS FOR RATING RESPONSE PATTERNS TO MEDITATION

The material you are to rate consists of reports given by subjects after thirty minutes of practice in a breath concentration exercise.

There are a number of patterns which seem to recur in these reports. You are to identify those session reports which seem to express these patterns. This is a task which must often rely heavily on your clinical judgment. Different subjects have different ways of expressing themselves; so it will be necessary for you to try to "get behind" the words they use to describe the experience they are trying to communicate. The context of all session reports given by one subject should be of help to you in rating single sessions.

The following are the patterns you are trying to identify.

Type 0: The subject reports difficulty in concentration and his remarks indicate that little else has occurred.

Type 1: The identifying characteristic of these sessions is dizziness, some type of "befogged" consciousness, which occurs when some subjects begin to concentrate. Typically, subjects report feeling dizzy or having sensations "like going under anaesthetic" or "like being hypnotized." These feelings are experienced as somewhat unpleasant, and it is common to find the subject retreating from the task of concentration into increased thinking.

Type 2: These are sessions in which the subject reports feeling quite calm and relaxed. His concentration need not have been very sustained. Be fairly cautious in applying this score when the subject reports only "I was pretty relaxed," or "It was easier today."

Type 3: In this pattern relaxation seems to take the form of pleasant body sensations. These are often reminiscent of hypnotic phenomena and sometimes involve feelings which would be strange in the ordinary states of waking consciousness. They may be rather erotic-sounding as they are described. Sensations like "vibrations" or "waves" are often reported, or the subject feels his body is "suspended" or "light." Typically, concentration is somewhat more sustained in these sessions, although a subject's estimate of how well he concentrated is probably so unreliable that ratings could not be based on this alone.

Type 4: The distinguishing feature of this pattern is that the breathing is experienced very vividly. Often the belly movements seem larger or the subject feels "filled with air." The concentration seems almost effortless in these sessions, and sometimes you will want to scrutinize comments about especially intense concentration to see if the breathing has become a vivid experience during that session.

Type 5: This is the experience described by Herrigel in the passage you read. It appears to be a very lucid state of consciousness which is deeply satisfying. There is a "non-striving" attitude, and the subject appears able to take a calmly detached view of any thoughts and feelings which happen to emerge. Concentration seems to be easy and fairly complete. A frequent accompaniment of this pattern is extensive loss of body feelings. This should help in alerting you to the possibility that this pattern is being expressed, but do not place much weight on the word "detached" when a subject uses it. Often subjects use this word when they talk about letting their breathing become uncontrolled. The "calm" which characterizes this pattern must be distinguished carefully from that which is reported in pattern "2." Usually this can be done on the basis of the concentration involved, plus an attention to signs of altered consciousness, which are generally lacking in the other patterns.

Score "X": When you feel that a session report clearly indicates more response than a score of 0 would cover, but none of the other patterns seem to apply. Included in this score would be such session responses that might be called a "satori" experience. This means that a completely new insight or experience of oneself or the universe has occurred. Usually the response is full of emotional description. Sometimes the subject will report the vision of an "eye" that approaches his attentional field.

When more than one pattern applies: Score both. Any questions about scoring may be discussed with the experimenter who can be located at ———.

To summarize the scoring:

SCORE	Prevailing Experience
0 =	Difficulty in concentration
1 =	Dizziness, unpleasantness → increased or dreaming

thinking ↗

↘

      parapsychological

2 =	Definite calmness, childhood scenes
3 =	Pleasant "erotic" sensations, floating, waves, lightness, better concentration
4 =	*Very* vivid breathing, effortless concentration, filled with air
5 =	Deeply satisfying, lucid consciousness, intense alertness, extreme calm, altered consciousness
X =	Not 0, but not 1-5, "satori," eye, great emotional experience, insight [Rating system adapted from Maupin, 1962]

The judges were: the experimenter, a doctoral student in counseling psychology who was quite familiar with Zen literature, and a Master's degree student in counseling psychology who had just finished the degree, who was also familiar with the literature in Zen.

Two separate X^2 tests for judge bias significantly supported the assumption that the ratings did in fact depend on the individual session reports of the subjects. The judges' function was to translate those reports to the pre-described scoring criteria for the levels of consciousness described in the instructions above. The subjects were then ranked according to their response to meditation in the following manner. Since there were six (0, 1, 2, 3, 4, 5, and X) levels, a total score was obtained for each subject based on the sum of the levels he had experienced. The number of times any subject achieved any one level was ignored. For example, one subject may have achieved only levels 1, 2, and 3. His total score is therefore $1 + 2 + 3 = 6$, even though he may have achieved level 2 or 3 a number of times. The subject who achieved all levels (0, 1, 2, 3, 4, 5, and X) received the score $1 + 2 + 3 + 4 + 5 + 6 = 21$, again regardless of the number of times he achieved any one level. The individual response to meditation is later used to examine correlational relationships with the criterion measures. The findings here, relative to the ratings of the judges, suggest that there was very good agreement, and that subsequent use of any individual's meditation response score is sound.

CRITERION MEASURES

Affective Sensitivity Scale

This instrument is a situational test designed to measure that aspect of empathy called affective sensitivity. The test consists of a video tape of client-counselor interactions with an attending answer sheet on which the subject being tested marks the feeling he thinks the client is expressing on the video tape. The original form (Form B) of this test was being used in another study prior to the start of this study. Form B requires that the subject choose among several possibilities on the answer sheet after watching the video tape. The following is a sample item.

CLIENT I

Scene I

Item 1
1. This exploring of my feelings is good. It makes me feel good.
2. I feel very sad and unhappy.
3. I'm groping and confused; I can't bring it all together.

The subject has about 20 seconds to answer. According to the authors of this test:

> The test is made up of video taped sequences from actual counseling sessions accompanied by items which describe various affective states which the client may be expressing. The procedure requires that the subject [empathizer] be able to detect and identify the feelings experienced by the client. It provides a highly realistic yet standardized mode of presenting the total stimuli from a real-life situation to subjects in a manner which should differentiate between those sensitive and those not sensitive to the affective state of another [Kagan *et al.*, 1967, p. 136].

In order to determine the "right" answers for the scenes in the construction of the test the "right" answers were determined by doing an item analysis on the results of (1) four "qualified" judges giving their answers to the client's feeling; (2) three 'informed' judges who had full clinical data on each of the clients, giving their responses to the client's feelings; and (3) the clients themselves viewing the scenes and "recalling" their feelings.

While test-retest reliability (Spearman's rho, $R_s = .75$), stability ($R_s = .58$ and $.67$), concurrent validity and construct validity checks yield relatively impressive figures, it was felt by the experimenter that Form B of the ASS_s was not realistic enough in its present form.

To eliminate this problem with Form B, another answering method was developed. It consisted merely of an unstructured answer sheet, where after every scene, the subject had 30 seconds to write in, in his own words, the feelings the client was expressing, and the feelings the client had about the counselor. This seemed much more like the real conditions of facing the client, where one must depend only on oneself to find the words that can express the feelings the client seems to be revealing. This form of the Affective Sensitivity Scale shall be referred to from here on as the ASS_{us} (Affective Sensitivity Scale, unstructured). Form B shall be referred to as ASS_s (structured).

Test-retest reliability with the ASS_{us} on control group one and control group two (eliminating the experimental group) over the 4-week period shows an r_s of .94. Correlation by the rational equivalence method (which uses all groups) shows an R_{11} of .84 on the pretest, and an R_{11} of .80 on the posttest.

Validity was demonstrated by correlating scores on the ASS_{us} with scores on the ASS_s (Spearman's rho = .67). The Interpersonal Sensitivity scale of Shostrom's (1966) Personal Orientation Inventory correlated significantly (rho = .45) with the ASS_{us} but nonsignificantly (rho = .29) with the ASS_s. "Empathy" scores on the Truax scales (1961) and "empathic understanding," as measured by the Barrett-Leonard Scales (1962) produced essentially low, nonsignificant correlations with ASS_{us} and ASS_s scores.

It can be seen, therefore, that the ASS_{us} appears to be reliable and valid in measuring the subject's ability to detect and describe the feelings of another person. It is clear that all the attempts to measure empathy or affective sensitivity are not in fact measuring the same things. The ASS_{us} has such high face validity, that when the above correlations are taken into consideration, it must be the most valid measure among the ones shown.

Experience Inquiry

The Experience Inquiry was developed (Fitzgerald, 1966) to measure adaptive regression by tapping the subjects' openness to inner and outer experience. This test samples the person's experience with life in terms of the way he approaches, perceives and experiences life. A total score is obtained that gives an overall openness to experience rating. The test is made up of items designed to tap each of the following categories: Tolerance for Regressive Experience; Tolerance for Logical Inconsistencies; Constructive Use of Regression; Capacity for Regressive Experiences; Altered States; Peak Experiences; Tolerance for the Irrational.

According to Fitzgerald's research, the Experience Inquiry does discriminate quite adequately between the person who is more open to experience and the person who is not. He is satisfied (on the basis of other measures used in his study) that Schachtel's (1959) description of the person who is open to experience fits the characteristics of those subjects who scored highly on the Experience Inquiry. Namely, that they are not bound by the conventional modes of thought, memory and perception; they are sensitive to the possibilities and subtle nuances of experience which elude others; they are at home in the midst of conceptual disorder and complexity; and that they seek change and novelty. Fitzgerald found significant differences between males and females in the nature of their openness to experience. High-scoring males were more open to inner experiences and were involved in some role conflict, while high-scoring females were more open to outer experience. Another study (Pine & Holt, 1960) showed that males were more controlled in their regressive experiences, while females were "expressively regressive." The author of the Experience Inquiry reports reliability figures of r = .80 (*Kuder-Richardson 20*) and r = .85 (split-half) in a study with an N of 143 (Fitzgerald, 1966).

In this study the Experience Inquiry test is combined with Shostrom's Personal Orientation Inventory (1966), which measures, "self-actualization." The resulting 206 statements are presented with the instructions, "Please read each statement and decide whether it is true or false as applied to you."

Personal Orientation Inventory (POI)

This inventory attempts to measure, by the use of 12 subscales, the individual's degree of self-actualization. The subscales are titled: Time competence, inner support, self-actualizing value, existentiality, feeling reactivity, spontaneity, self-regard, self-acceptance, nature of man, synergy, acceptance of aggression, and capacity for intimate contact.

Results of one of several validity studies reported by Shostrom (1966) show that every subscale (except nature of man) on the test has a score significantly higher for a group rated clinically as "relatively self-actualized," as compared to a group clinically rated "relatively nonself-actualized."

Shostrom reports another validation study by Murry in which the POI successfully discriminated between those teachers who were rated high and those who were rated low on "teacher concern for students," by the students (2,333 students, 26 teachers, grades 7-12). The implication being that the more self-actualized the teacher the more the students sense that he or she is concerned for them.

One-week test-retest reliability has also been demonstrated with 48 college undergraduates. Correlations of .55 — .85 were produced on the 12 subscales, nine of them above .71.

RESULTS

Table 1 shows the increases in ASS_{us} scores for the experimental group after the meditation experience. After adjustment of means within and between the groups for variability, the experimental group shows a net mean gain of 7.23—significant beyond the .001 level.

TABLE 1 CHANGES IN ASS_{us} MEAN DIFFERENCE (MD) SCORES
AFTER MEDITATION

Group	Post Treatment MD	Adjusted MD*	Adjusted S_EMD	Adjusted t**
Experimental	+6.000	+8.5894	1.0870	7.23***
Control 1	+1.667	+0.3459	1.0618	0.29†
Control 2	+0.500	−2.3711	1.2794	−1.82†

* After analysis of covariance[3]
** Required t's; df = 35; .001 = 3.291
*** P = < .001; † nonsignificant

The hypothesis that the practice of *zazen* is an effective means of increasing empathy *is confirmed*.

The second hypothesis is: There will be a positive correlation between the individual response to meditation and scores on the Affective Sensitivity Scale. Correlations between the subjects' meditation responses in the experimental group and their scores on the ASS_{us} are Tau = .034 at pretest and .086 at posttest. *The hypothesis is rejected.*

The third hypothesis is: Response to meditation will be positively correlated with openness to experience as measured by the Experience Inquiry. Correlations between the subjects' meditation responses in the experimental group and their scores on the Experience Inquiry are: Tau = .560 at pretest (significant at the .01 level) and Tau = .412 at posttest (significant at the .05 level). *The hypothesis is confirmed.*

The fourth hypothesis, that individual scores in openness to experience will be positively correlated with individual scores in Affective Sensitivity, *is also confirmed.* Table 2 shows that when the groups are combined and the data are treated in a manner allowing the test-

---

[3] The final three groups in the study turned out to be of unequal sizes, and had unequal means on both pre- and posttesting, therefore program BMDO4V, analysis of covariance with multiple covariates, modified for IBM 360/50 at the University of Oregon Computing Center, and revised May 14, 1968, by the Health Sciences Computing Facility at UCLA, was used to analyze the data for this hypothesis. The analysis of covariance is used when due to actual working conditions in an experiment it is impossible to equate the experimental and control groups at the start. The test allows for adjustments in posttest scores on criterion measures.

ing of this hypothesis across all groups, the relationship between openness to experience and affective sensitivity is highly significant.

TABLE 2   CORRELATIONS BETWEEN OPENNESS TO EXPERIENCE AND
AFFECTIVE SENSITIVITY WITHIN AND ACROSS GROUPS
(REPORTED IN TERMS OF Z)

		Experimental Group	Control Group 1	Control Group 2	All Comb.
ASS_{us}	Pretest	2.09*	1.13	1.21	3.88***
	Posttest	0.19	0.70	0.48	3.99***

* P = < .05 level (Tau)
*** P = < .001 level (Tau)

The fifth and last hypothesis [that those individuals scoring high in Affective Sensitivity will score high in self-actualization, as measured by the Personal Orientation Inventory (Shostrom, 1966)], *is also confirmed*. Table 3 shows that when the data for all three groups are combined a highly significant relationship exists between self-actualization and affective sensitivity.

TABLE 3   CORRELATIONS BETWEEN SELF-ACTUALIZATION AND
AFFECTIVE SENSITIVITY WITHIN AND ACROSS GROUPS
(REPORTED IN TERMS OF Z)

POI

		Experimental Group	Control Group 1	Control Group 2	All Comb.
ASS_{us}	Pretest	2.51*	0.27	1.44	2.63**
	Posttest	0.19	1.10	0.48	3.37***

* P = < .05 level (Tau)
** P = < .01 level (Tau)
*** P = < .001 level (Tau)

DISCUSSION

ZAZEN AND COUNSELOR EMPATHY

The interpretation of the data in support of the first hypothesis, (a highly positive relationship between the practice of *zazen* and the development of empathy or affective sensitivity) is still a limited one. The least we can say is that with this group of counselor trainees, the practice of *zazen* did, in fact, seem to contribute significantly to an increase in their ability to accurately detect and describe the affective states of others under less than ideal conditions. That is, the ability to perform this function while watching a video tape of relatively poor technical quality would possibly be demonstrated to a higher degree under the actual conditions of facing a live client, factors of anxiety and role conflict notwithstanding.

The criticism might be raised that the experimental group was indeed an exceptional group of people in that they volunteered for such an unusual experiment in the first place. This is a cogent argument since the pretest scores for the experimental group on tests measuring openness to experience and self-actualization are significantly higher than for either of the control groups. The same is true for the scores on the ASS_{us} at pretest. That is, the experimental group was significantly higher in empathy before the experiment had even begun.

Further analysis of the data reveals that the experimental group increased in openness to experience after the meditation, but not significantly so. Control group one apparently decreased on the dimension of openness to experience, but again not significantly so. However, control group two decreased in openness to experience between pre- and posttesting 3.38 points (adjusted for variance), which is significant at the .01 level.

The tests of openness to experience and self-actualization were administered in an effort to try to describe some of the psychodynamics of the people in the study during the intervening experimental time in all three of the groups.

Keeping this in mind, one explanation for the decrease in the openness to experience scores in the two control groups may be indicated by data in Table 4 which show that there were three specific areas in which control group two went down: tolerance for logical inconsistency, capacity for regressive experience, and capacity for peak experience. All of these are significant decreases. Control group one decreased significantly on the subscale measuring tolerance for the illogical. This one depressed subscale did not, however, pull the total score of the test down enough to warrant a significant change between pre- and posttesting.

TABLE 4 ADJUSTED MEAN DIFFERENCES ON OPENNESS TO EXPERIENCE AFTER TREATMENT (SUBSCALE ANALYSIS)

Group	TRE	TLI	CUR	CRE	AS	PE	TFI
Experimental	.46	.63	−.37	.32	.34	.63	.45
Control 1	.09	−.22	−.14	−.51	−.70	.48	−.64*
Control 2	−.77	−.86*	.14	−1.45**	−.01	−.99*	.41

* P = < .05 level
** P = < .01 level

SE_{MD} for each value not shown, but used in the determination of significance levels.

The table shows that the experimental group did not have any significant decreases. In view of the fact that all of these people were actively engaged in a primarily didactic counseling program during the experiment, the data suggest that, as the term wore on, the rational intellect took a firmer and firmer hold on these people and tolerance for nonrational or affective experience generally decreased; that is, *except* for the people who were doing the meditation. Whether or not this would have still been the case for this same group of people without the meditation is still open to question; however, it does not stand alone that the experimental group was so unusual. Admittedly, they were exceptional people from the start. It appears they were introduced to means whereby they could at least maintain that uniqueness and openness in the face of a formal didactic training program.

For the writer, the above findings emphasize a point made by Kubie (1967):

> Psychologists, psychiatrists, neurologists, neurophysiologists have erred together in their undue emphasis on the conscious components of mentation. This has led the educator into neglecting the *preconscious* instrument of learning, which is the effective instrument of recording, processing and of creating [Kubie, 1967, p. 78].

This is particularly relevant to a counselor training program. Are counselors being trained to "go into their heads," and "get up tight?" Is the result of a heavily didactic program that a "trained" counselor has no tolerance for the irrational and illogical in his client?

These findings, while not conclusive, are certainly suggestive; they are consistent with Traux and Carkhuff's (1963) and Mellow's (1964) findings that accurate empathy tends to stay the same or decrease among counselor trainees in formal counseling training programs.

LEVEL OF CONCENTRATION AND EMPATHY

The rejection of the second hypothesis (the predicted relationship between the *individual's* response to the meditation experience and his affective sensitivity scores) seems to indicate that the levels of concentration one achieves in meditation appears not to have any effect on an increase or decrease in empathic ability. This is contrary to what would have been expected. The only speculation that can be offered here is that with the instrument used to detect an individual's empathic ability, and under the conditions it was administered, the scores achieved by the experimental group began to approach the maximum possible and further score changes could not be detectable.

Another consideration is that those people achieving the deepest levels of concentration found that this in itself was a very significant and somewhat upsetting (upsetting in terms of their having to reorient their previous views of themselves) experience. The explanation of the findings on hypothesis three will clarify the nature of the influence of the meditation experiences. It is suggested that these people were still in a state of personal or psychic flux and reorientation during the time of posttesting (which was done on the afternoon of the last meditation session). Followup testing in a study such as this is almost mandatory, but nearly impossible with such a mobile population.

The data indicate that the meditation was most effective in helping those who scored relatively low in the pretest on the ASS_{us}. Only one of the six lowest ASS_{us} scorers in the experimental group at pretest did not improve above the mean upon posttesting. This suggests that meditation might be most useful for those people who have the most difficulty in empathizing with others. It is truly unfortunate that the lowest scoring people on all of the criterion measures, namely the second control group, could not have been mixed with the experimental group. Yet, these were the people who wanted no part of such a study. One cannot force people who are rather closed to experience to engage in such an unfamiliar experience even if it might help them to become better counselors.

ZAZEN AND OPENNESS TO EXPERIENCE

The testing of the third hypothesis was found to confirm the idea that response to meditation is related to openness to experience. The interpretation here is that people who are normally open to experience will be interested in meditation and have significant experience in the practice of it. The kind of experiences one encounters in the practice of *zazen* ranges from extreme difficulty in even sitting still, through dream-like states, to experiences that border on the religious, mystical and parapsychological.

An example of the kind of difficulties encountered in *zazen* is conveyed by excerpts from comments written by some meditators immediately after their sessions.

> I feel like a real failure as far as meditating goes. My mind is awash with thoughts—I am holding in, holding on, holding out; and there is no change. I hated sitting still, and had to force myself to concentrate. I'm confused about my goal because I think what I was doing for meditation earlier is not right for me now. I still feel too vulnerable to let go.

It's clear that the form of concentration required in *zazen* quickly reveals to one how unrelated people usually are to their innermost thoughts, fears, feelings, and desires. All forms of resistance to facing oneself emerge during such intense concentration.

The two session reports below show how one's attention is brought to one's own mental and physical condition.

> I feel as if I started noticing how things are inside me—sensorywise. Like how I felt—then I went beyond the senses—then I almost went to sleep.

If this person could have managed, at the point of going beyond his senses and not falling asleep, to make the leap Herrigel refers to in the passage quoted earlier in the introduction, he may well have learned something very significant.

Meditation apparently precipitates an acute awareness first of one's immediate outer environment (provided one can concentrate at all), then an awareness of one's immediate innermost environment, and then an awareness of something beyond any of these. The next report to be given here demonstrates the awareness of the immediate inner environment.

> I was anxious when I started this time, but soon fell into a pattern of breathing. Then the breathing fell into the background and there began a building up of anxieties with reference to sexual capabilities and all associated with a client I was working with. I felt alone and inside of myself and a tremendous feeling of awareness of things within me.

Resistance seems to occur at three main points in the practice of *zazen:* first at the point of even sitting still and facing oneself, secondly at the point of allowing into one's consciousness the inner conflicts that are going on, and thirdly at the point of realizing one is a part of something "not self."

Resistance to inner conflict is second in frequency to the initial facing of oneself. This is demonstrated in the report below.

> After I went into it I got a vague image of some people holding a puppy and discussing it. I immediately snapped out of it—with a very sudden jerk of my head and tried to remember some of the words, but couldn't. It seemed to upset me and I couldn't understand why. I ended up feeling shaky and with a headache. The whole thing makes very little sense to me.

Sleepiness, dizziness, crying without knowing why, feeling angry, upset, etc., all occurred in many of the subjects during or right after the meditation. It becomes quite easy to understand or at least to see what the cues are for one's resistances when he meets frightening or unacceptable material in his own head. The session reports clearly show where a person is "hung up" and what forms the resistance takes to avoid facing the encounter and resolution of these problems.

On the other hand, a few people managed to break through all these barriers and "see" further. The following report is the most dramatic of these.

> I hate to try and put this into words—it's mine and I don't feel like sharing it. But I'll try. I had cotton in my ears and my breathing was loud in my head. I stayed in my head—seemed as if I flipped my eyeballs backward

and up. Kind of a big void—then it seemed like I was looking in a long tunnel with a pinpoint of light at the very end. My eyelids were flickering, trying to pull open, but I kept pulling them shut because I didn't want to lose whatever I was drawn to. I felt like I was one with God—I was aware I was crying—I felt like I'd come home at last—an end to all loneliness and struggle—and I wanted to stay there forever. I didn't but kept going back *up* into my head anytime I felt anything intruding—all the while my breathing was kind of a comforting background rhythm. My head stayed erect—time went quickly—I feel very peaceful and quiet inside.

Other people mentioned "touching on something enormous and frightening," and then drawing back. One person, after having such an experience, stopped meditating for 2 days. At the next session she again became fearful, and reported that she still felt like she was avoiding facing "the full encounter."

The probability of the occurrence of any of the levels of consciousness being achieved is reported below. (These figures are, of course, relative to this group only, but it would be interesting to replicate this part of the study elsewhere to find out more about these probabilities.)

TABLE 5 PROBABILITY OF OCCURRENCE OF THE DIFFERENT LEVELS OF CONSCIOUSNESS (EXPERIMENTAL GROUP)

Level		Probability
0	(Difficulty in concentration)	20.50%
1	(Befogged consciousness)	26.60
2	(Definite calmness)	26.50
3	(Floating, waves, better concentration)	13.57
4	(Very vivid breathing)	2.97
5	(Deeply satisfying, intense alertness)	1.67
X	(Great emotional experience, insight)	1.22

There were a number of unusual phenomena that occurred during the meditation sessions. An incident was described by a subject who said during the meditation he felt like the back of his head was burning and moving. He then got an image of the man behind him getting up and coming over to say something to him; he couldn't remember what it was the other subject wanted to say. (Most of the subjects went through the meditation exercise with their eyes closed.) The subject sitting immediately behind the one mentioned above, reported during this same session that he had an image of this man getting up and coming over to say something to him. It seems unusual that two separate persons sitting relatively near each other would have comparable images and sensations. It's difficult to accept this type of thing as being merely coincidental. After the study these two subjects were asked if they had been talking together prior to the session, or in any way felt they had any unresolved conflicts between each other. Neither one had seen each other that day, or within the previous week, except during the time they came for the meditation. Neither felt they had had any previous unresolved feelings about each other, except the man in front felt he was a bit self-conscious around the one sitting behind him.

The explanation of these phenomena are difficult without going over into the area of extra-sensory perception, or at least budding beginnings of it (Barron and Mordkoff, 1968). It's quite likely, in the opinion of the author, that very highly developed empathy touches on extra-sensory perception of a sort. It appears as though one person can sense from another his feelings, even though the other person has not mentioned them. The transference of images between individuals without using language is suggested in incidences such as the one above. Just how far accurate empathy reaches, or what the human potential for empathy may be, are unexplored questions. It appears to offer extremely interesting possibilities.

The relevance of meditation, specifically a form of Zen meditation as defined in this study, to the interpersonal process of counseling offers some material for speculation. Since meditation appears to train the subjects to delve into more primitive or primary process ways of thinking, this would allow a therapist (provided he could achieve this level during the counseling session) to more fully understand and appreciate what the client is saying and feeling. The primary process modes of thinking and conflict resolution employ symbols and meanings foreign to the more rational, secondary process modes of thought. The counselor relying entirely on his intellect during a session in which the client is exploring the tensions arising from misunderstood or dimly perceived primary material, could hardly understand or tolerate what the client was going through. This leads to some further insight as to why those who scored low on openness to experience, which is a measure of tolerance for adaptive regression, also scored quite low on the ASS_{us}.

Further support for this comes from the fact that of all the sub-scales on the Experience Inquiry, Capacity for Regressive Experience correlates most highly with the meditation response of the subjects in the experimental group. (Tau = .53, which is significant at the .01 level, at pretest time, and .51 at the posttest time, also significant at the .01 level.) This supports the original notion introduced at the beginning of the study—that adaptive regression (CRE) is a significant process employed in accurate empathy. The question as to whether meditation increases this ability still remains unanswered since (as can be seen from Table 4) the only change that took place in the capacity for regressive experience between pre- and posttesting was that the two control groups went down on the scale, while the meditation group improved negligibly. The answer in this seems to be that adaptive regression is a potential mode of functioning innate in everyone, but only some people have learned to use it. However, it may be more correct to say that it is an ability that they have been able to maintain, whereas most people lose it through education's overemphasis on the rational processes. Meditation may act more as means of maintaining this ability in people who already have it than developing or recovering it in people who have lost it. A study would need to be done with people who are low in this ability to decide whether meditation could help them regain it. The ideal situation in terms of this study would have been to have the experimental and control groups reversed. This would mean putting those people scoring high on openness to experience and self-actualization in the control groups, and those scoring low would be in the experimental group (doing the meditation).

OPENNESS TO EXPERIENCE AND EMPATHY

The acceptance of the fourth hypothesis (that there is a relationship between openness to experience and empathic ability) lends support to the idea that in order for one to be able to sense or feel what another person is experiencing he must be open to what is going on in himself as well. Openness to experience, as measured by the Experience Inquiry, means that the person is open to both his inner and outer experiences. Openness to experience means that one is able to enter into many different situations and allow himself to experience these situations without placing any judgment on the experience. It might be said that such a person understands because he *feels* what it is like. Much of human experience, especially at the deeper levels of feeling and emotion, is irrational and nonlogical. These experiences cannot be denied just because they don't make sense to us. The client's experience of what he is trying to communicate to us cannot be denied because it doesn't make any sense to us.

Zen meditation may be looked upon as an exercise in learning to listen to one's own inner experience. Reference to the quotes of the meditators' experiences show how difficult this really is. The therapeutic process is one wherein the people involved flow and move in each others' and their own experience of life and the immediate relationship they are in. Blindness and judgment come when one person says something of an emotional nature to another that sets up in him an emotional reaction that he does not recognize or cannot deal with in himself. An example might be a situation wherein the counselor has not dealt openly with his fears of his own sexuality. This counselor is susceptible to seductive actions on the part of the client. He is not able to see through to the person who is using this seduction. He therefore is apt to be judgmental, never really allowing the client to work through the meaning of this behavior.

Certain kinds of experiences are *not* acceptable, or are threatening to any therapist who is not able to sense and bring out his own feelings about these experiences. The low scores in empathy correlating with the low scores in openness to experience support the notion that the less open to experience, the more judgmental the person is.

Going over the responses given on the ASS_{us} show that all of the wrong answers given by the subjects are judgments about what the client was trying to say, rather an accurate perception and understanding of what the client was saying and feeling. Knowing what one's own experience is or at least being somehow secure enough in one's self not to deny experience in others is crucial for empathic understanding. The deeper levels of Zen meditation are those wherein experiences can occur, but their occurrence requires no action on the part of the experiencer.

To summarize what is being said here, the first requirement for perceiving what someone else is feeling is that one have some idea what his own experiences are as opposed or in relation to the experiences the other person is having. If this requirement is not met, projection occurs; and the supposed perceiver sees in the other person what he, the perceiver is feeling, but is unaware of in himself. This point is made quite clear by examining the answers that some of the low-scoring people on the ASS_{us} gave. Looking at these answers shows first that the answers are in no way related to what the client is saying, secondly that there is constant theme in the respondent's answers throughout the entire test, and thirdly that this theme is the respondent himself. In other words, the unstructured form of the ASS has turned out to be a projective test as well. Those scenes where the emotion of the client is the strongest, *or* the vaguest, what appears on the respondent's answer sheet are feelings that the respondent has, *not* the feelings the client is trying to express.

In this sense, it seems that the ASS_{us} could be a very useful tool in the training of counselors, especially in the development of empathic understanding. The use of such a situational test would give immediate feedback to the counselor about what he is seeing in others. This, of course, would precipitate the necessity of his examining himself to learn more about his own feelings.

The second requirement of accurate empathy, following the differentiation of the client's feelings from the counselor's feelings, is the ability to enter into the flow of mutual experience without having to act on it. To be able to experience fully what is going on, in both the other person and in oneself, but not react to this experience, is one of the highest levels of accomplishment in Zen meditation. The goal is to calm the mind so that it is as undisturbed as a smooth lake. When something enters the mind, it does so and passes through leaving no more disturbance than the ripples a pebble leaves after having been dropped into a quiet lake.

This degree of inner peace and quiet allows the therapist to experience the deepest and strongest emotions that human beings have without becoming fearful or feeling he must do something about the thing he is experiencing. This is the level at which B-Love occurs between human beings, and the level at which healing may begin (Maslow, 1962).

SELF-ACTUALIZATION AND EMPATHY

The fifth hypothesis (that there is a relationship between self-actualization and affective sensitivity) was accepted. The Personal Orientation Inventory (Shostrom, 1966) measures self-actualization through the use of a number of subscales described previously. Generally, the acceptance of this hypothesis means that people who are more self-actualizing, who have realized their own potentials more than others, are also more able to exercise greater empathic understanding for others. This finding is consistent with Foulds' (1969) study on counselor interpersonal functioning. Subscale correlations (Kendall's Tau) of the POI and the ASS_{us} show that the following subscales are most contributory to the overall correlation of self-actualization and empathy; Self Regard ($p = < .05$); Self-Actualizing Value ($p = < .01$); Feeling Reactivity ($p = < .01$); Spontaneity ($p = < .01$); Inner Directedness ($p = < .01$).

These findings indicate that apparently the most important personal characteristics required in empathic ability are: a high personal self regard, a value system that sees developing one's own potential as important, a high degree of awareness and acceptance of one's feelings, a sense of personal freedom and willingness to be one's self, and a high degree of *acting* out of one's own feelings rather than *reacting* to others.

Examining the data for individual scores shows that those people who went down in empathic ability also went down in the above areas, but they also went down in their ability to express and receive negative feelings such as anger. No measures of anxiety were administered, but it seems likely that as anxiety became higher during the term, and as there became less and less opportunity for the expression of this frustration, that there soon arose an inner conflict between the way these people were feeling about what was happening to them, and a sense of inappropriateness, or futility in expressing their feelings.[4]

CONCLUSIONS AND SUGGESTIONS FOR FURTHER RESEARCH

Younger people are expressing a growing interest in Eastern psychology and philosophy (Lapham, 1968; Horn, 1968). The behavioral scientist, especially in the rapidly expanding humanistic movement in psychology, is becoming more and more interested in utilizing Eastern methods in psychotherapy and in education (Berger, 1962; Kretschmer, 1951). Zen meditation has held increasing interest for scientific study both in the psychological and physiological sciences (e.g., Deikman, 1966; Kamiya, 1968; Platt, 1969).

The primary conclusion the experimenter has reached as a result of the present study is that Zen meditation holds far more potential for personal growth and scientific investigation than we have previously supposed. Meditation does appear to have a significant effect in the psychological and interpersonal domains of our experience. The psychic dynamics of the mind during the concentration required by *zazen* holds almost unlimited potential for investigation and further understanding of the functioning of consciousness.

The writer has long held that there is more hope for discovery in anomalous experience than there is in the already known and accepted. If there are questions about the meaning of our existence, the place to look for the answers seems to be in those odd and infrequent experiences that exist but cannot be explained. What we call mystical, cultish, and parapsychological, are no doubt just unexplored and undeveloped areas of our own potential. The taboo of exploring these areas, of experiencing them, is a holdover from the times of witch-burning. Fear and superstition about things that seem to be super-

---

[4] Several of the low scoring people were interviewed after the data were collected in order to make some verification between the data and the human experience. These interviews were held in order to give the subjects feedback on their performance as well. The results of these interviews verified that there was a tremendous amount of hostility being aroused in most of the subjects as a result of one class in particular. Many of the people were very angry with the instructor in this class, and felt that there was no communication possible between themselves and the instructor. One student said he came as close as he ever had to feeling like a failure and leaving school.

To the experimenter, who did the interviewing, these expressions of what had happened during the term recalled to mind that many of the subjects who did the meditation frequently came to the meditation sessions looking very tense and angry. Further followup after the study was completed revealed that the class that was so upsetting to many of the students immediately preceded the meditation sessions. All of the subjects were students in this class.

natural are understandable in the sense that we all fear knowing something new about ourselves.

Perception is a function of belief and need as well as a function of how we utilize our neurophysiological systems. There is enough evidence now accumulated (Deikman, 1966; Platt, 1969; Asimov, 1966) to substantiate the fact that there is a reality of time, space, and matter beyond that which has been thought real and fixed. The suggestion is that the way we perceive our world and its objects is morphologically bound. That is, we cannot see through solid objects because our mass is unable to move through them. Under different physical properties of our own existence, undoubtedly our perception of the environment would also be different. Even though our present mode of perceiving the world is physiologically functional (though perhaps increasingly less psychologically functional), we do have the potential of seeing greater aspects of reality.

Accordingly, further studies in empathy, as well as further studies in meditation, should be geared to that end. Studies of the type that Deikman (1966) has done would offer greater knowledge in this area. He has employed the individual-longitudinal design in order to demonstrate and attempt to isolate the dynamics of the perception of a different reality than the one we normally experience.

Relevant to the study that has been presented here, further work with the first hypothesis (the relationship between *zazen* and the development of accurate empathy) would need to overcome a number of obstacles encountered in this study. First, the difficulty of assuring randomization; all potential subjects should be required to participate in the study. The assignments for the experimental and control groups should be matched for sex, sensitivity group experience, and scores on the EI and POI, factors which have been shown to have an effect in this, as well as other studies using these concepts and measures.

Secondly, the video tape of the ASS needs to be improved in quality. Previous work done in the development of the ASS has shown that video and audio quality do have an effect on the scores achieved on the test.

Thirdly, the meditation practice needs to be of longer duration (i.e., over more weeks) to allow the subjects to go through the unsettled times resulting from the meditation experience. Along with the practice of the meditation should be the opportunity for group discussion of the experiences, as well as discussion with someone who is quite familiar with the practice of *zazen*.

Fourth, there should be incorporated followup testing with all the criterion measures in order to detect further score changes in both positive and negative directions. Such followup testing done 4 to 6 months after treatment would give more stable data that could be compared with the pre- and posttreatment findings.

Lastly, the unstructured form of the ASS needs to be standardized in its scoring procedure. The correct answers as indicated on the answer key of the ASS$_s$ could be condensed into key words by a set of judges, and a standardized scoring criterion list of answers, much like those used with the "information" part of the Wechsler Adult Intelligence Scale, could be developed. This would simplify and speed the scoring of the ASS$_{us}$.

Along with such studies should come work that would help the understanding of how to utilize this new knowledge in aiding the development of potentials and to help people overcome difficulties in their lives. Frequently it is the gifted person (i.e., that person whom, for whatever reasons yet to be understood, seems to have talents or abilities or senses that others do not seem to understand) who has the most trouble living an unburdened life. In his review of the mystical literature and after having worked with several "unusual" people, William James (1963) concluded that unexplainable experiences do happen, that they are valid, they are real, they are frequently ineffable, and they are unpredictable. However, he also concluded that these experiences seem to happen to people who are in some kind of conflict or who might be called more neurotic than most.

The writer is coming to the conclusion that this is an intrapsychical conflict that arises out of the person's inability to understand his gift or potential and to integrate the use of his potential with what the culture calls a normal life. It is not that the neurosis causes unusual experiences, but that the different way of seeing things seems unacceptable to the culture, and the person comes to feel as if the way he feels about life is so unacceptable that he must be wrong. He therefore "puts himself down," becomes inhibited, tense, closed to experience, judgmental, unhappy, etc.

To apply the findings of this study to everyday life and the educational process, one could use Zen meditation in a counseling training program. Practice must be done daily, and the students should be required to keep a log of the experiences. The ideal condition would be that they also meet in encounter groups to discuss their experiences with the meditation as well as their experiences in life. This combination of "getting with oneself," and then being able to manifest the self in relation to others may be the most potent catalyst for growth yet discovered.

SUMMARY

Three groups of people participated in this study, the purpose of which was to determine if practicing *zazen* could aid counselors in developing their empathic abilities. Previous studies have been relatively unsuccessful in demonstrating any significant improvement in empathic abilities among counseling trainees. For the large part, these studies have shown the reverse to be true. Namely that after they have been in a formal training program, empathic ability tends to decrease among the trainees.

The vehicle for developing empathic ability in this study was a form of Zen meditation called *zazen*. The first group of subjects, called the experimental group, volunteered to participate in the meditation experience and did, in fact, follow through with the experience.

The first control group also volunteered to do the meditation, but in fact did not actually practice it.

The third group, called the second control group, did not want any part of the meditation experience, but agreed to take the tests that were used as criterion measures.

The study had two aspects. The first and most important part was to determine whether the practice of *zazen* could be effective in improving empathic ability. The second aspect was to attempt to describe some of the psycho-dynamics of the people in all the groups as the study progressed.

The main criterion measure was a test of affective sensitivity, which was modified to more closely measure what the operational definition of empathy calls for. The other criterion measures were two tests, one to measure the degree of openness to experience and capacity for adaptive regression for all subjects, and the other to measure the degree of self-actualization of the subjects.

The treatment (Zen meditation) lasted for 4 weeks, after which all subjects were retested. The following is a summary of the findings.

a. The group who practiced *zazen* over the 4-week period improved significantly in their empathic ability. The two control groups did not.
b. The level of concentration reached in *zazen* does not appear to be related to the degree of accurate empathy achieved by any one individual. However, there is reason to question this finding.
c. Related to the above findings, evidence exists that *zazen* is most effective in improving empathic ability in those people who start out rather low in this ability.
d. Response to meditation, that is the depth of concentration achieved in the practice of meditation, is related to an individual's openness to experience and his ability to regress in the service of the ego.

e. Openness to experience is also related to empathic ability. The more open to experience a person is the more empathic he seems to be.

f. Empathic ability is related to the degree of self-actualization a person has achieved in himself. The more self-actualizing (the more one depends on his own feelings and value system), the more he is willing to be himself, the more empathic he is.

g. Meditation appears to be an effective means of assisting people in self-actualization.

h. Meditation appears to be an effective means of maintaining one's unique experiencing of life under conditions that might tend to repress individual growth.

i. Certain experiences occur during the practice of meditation that seem to be either unexplainable or indicative of a higher potential of perception, bordering on the extra-sensory or para-psychological.

j. People who are less open to experience seem to be unwilling to partake of the practice of *zazen*. These people also are far less empathic than those who are more open to experience.

REFERENCES

ALBRIGHT, D. R. An application of a theory of process in client-centered psychotherapy in counseling. Unpublished doctoral dissertation, Indiana University, 1967.

ASIMOV, I. *The universe: From flat earth to quasar.* New York: Walker & Co., 1966.

BARRETT-LEONARD, G. T. Dimensions of therapist responses as causal factors in therapeutic change. *Psychological Monographs,* 1962, *76* (43, Whole No. 562).

BARRON, F. & MORDKOFF, A. M. An attempt to relate creativity to possible extrasensory empathy as measured by physiological arousal in identical twins. *Journal of the American Society for Psychical Research,* 1968, *62* (1), 73-79.

BERGER, E. Zen Buddhism, general psychology and counseling psychology. *Journal of Counseling Psychology,* 1962, *9* (2), 122-127.

DEIKMAN, A. J. Implications of experimentally induced contemplative meditation. *The Journal of Nervous and Mental Disease, 142* (2), 1966.

DREVER, J. *A dictionary of psychology.* Baltimore: Penguin Books Ltd., 1952.

FENICHEL, O. *The psychoanalytic theory of neurosis.* New York: W. W. Norton, 1945.

FITZGERALD, E. T. The measurement of openness to experience: A study of regression in the service of the ego. Unpublished doctoral dissertation, University of California, 1966.

FOULDS, M. L. Self Actualization and Level of Counselor Interpersonal Functioning. *Journal of Humanistic Psychology,* Spring 1969, *9* (1), 87.

FREUD, S. The Interpretation of Dreams. (1900) In *The basic writings of Sigmund Freud.* New York: Modern Library, 1938.

FREUD, S. Formulations Regarding the Two Principles in Mental Functioning. (1911) In *Collected papers.* Vol. 4. London: Hogarth, 1946.

HERRIGEL, E. *Zen in the art of archery.* New York: Pantheon, 1953.

HOLT, R. R. & HAVEL, J. A method for assessing primary and secondary process in the rorschach. In M. Rickers-Ovsiankina (Ed.), *Rorschach psychology.* New York: Wiley, 1960.

HORN, P. A visit with India's high-powered new prophet. *Look,* Feb. 6, 1968.

JAMES, W. The varieties of religious experience. In W. P. Alston, *Religious beliefs and philosophical thought.* New York: Harcourt, Brace & World, Inc., 1963.

KAGAN, N. & KRATHWOHL, D. R. *et al. Studies in human interaction.* Educational Publication Services: Michigan State University, Lansing, Mich. Project No.5-0800) 1967.

KAGAN, N., KRATHWOHL, D. R. & FARQUHAR, W. W. Developing a scale to measure affective sensitivity. *Educational Research Series,* March 1965, Michigan State University, No. 30.

KAMIYA, J. Conscious control of brain waves. *Psychology Today, 1* (11), April 1968.

KATZ, R. L. *Empathy: Its nature and uses.* Glencoe, Illinois: The Free Press of Glencoe, 1963.

KERLINGER, F. N. *Foundations of behavioral research.* New York: Holt, Rinehart and Winston, Inc., 1964.

KRETSCHMER, W. JR. Meditative techniques in psychotherapy. *Zeitschrift Für Psychotherapie und Medizinische Psychologie,* May 1951, *1* (3). (Available from Psychosynthesis Research Foundation, 527 Lexington Ave., New York, New York 10017.)

KRIS, E. *Psychoanalytic explorations in art.* New York: International Universities Press, 1952.

KUBIE, L. S. Research in protecting preconscious functions in education. In R. M. Jones (Ed.), *Contemporary educational psychology.* New York: Harper Torch Books, 1967.

LAPHAM, L. H. There once was a guru from rishikesh. *Saturday Evening Post,* May 4, 1968.

MASLOW, A. H. *Toward a psychology of being.* Princeton: D. Van Nostrand Company, Inc., 1962.

MATTHES, W. A. The relationship between conditions in counseling and selected outcome variables. Unpublished doctoral dissertation, Indiana University, 1967.

MAUPIN, E. W. An exploratory study of individual differences in response to a Zen meditation exercise. Unpublished doctoral dissertation, University of Michigan, 1962.

MELLOW, R. A. Accurate empathy and counselor effectiveness. Unpublished doctoral dissertation, The University of Florida, 1964.

NEISSER, U. The Multiplicity of Thought. In R. M. Jones (Ed.), *Contemporary educational psychology.* New York: Harper Torch Books, 1967.

PINE, F. & HOLT, R. R. Creativity and primary process: A study of adaptive regression. *Journal of Abnormal and Social Psychology,* 1960, *61,* 370-379.

PLATT, J. R. The two faces of perception. In B. Rothblatt (Ed.), *Changing perspectives on man.* Chicago: University of Chicago Press, 1969.

REIK, T. *Listening with the third ear.* (1948) New York: Pyramid Books, 1964.

ROGERS, C. R. The characteristics of a helping relationship. *The Personnel and Guidance Journal, 37* (1), 1958.

ROGERS, C. R. The interpersonal relationship: The core of guidance. *Harvard Educational Review,* 1962, *32,* 416-429.

ROGERS, C. R. *Client centered therapy: A changing approach to psychotherapy.* Western Behavioral Sciences Institute, 1964 (Mimeo.).

ROGERS, C. R., GENDLIN, E. T., KIESLER, D. & TRUAX, C. G. *The therapeutic relationship and its impact: A study of psychotherapy with schizophrenics.* Madison: University of Wisconsin Press, 1967.

RUNKLE, P. & McGRATH, J. E. *Studying human behavior.* New York: Holt, Rinehart and Winston, in press.

SCHACHTEL, E. *Metamorphosis.* New York: Basic Books, Inc., 1959.

SHAFER, R. *Psychoanalytic interpretation in Rorschach testing.* New York: Grune and Stratton, 1954.

SHAFER, R. Regression in the service of the ego: The relevance of a psychoanalytic concept for personality assessment. In G. Lindzey (Ed.), *Assessment of human motives.* New York: Rinehart, 1958.

SHOSTROM, E. L. *Manual, personal orientation inventory.* San Diego: Educational and Industrial Testing Service, 1966.

SINGER, J. L. *Daydreaming: An introduction to the experimental study of inner experience.* New York: Random House, 1966.

STOLLAK, G. E., GURRNEY, JR., B. G. & ROTHBERG, M. (Eds.) *Psychotherapy research.* Chicago: Rand McNally, 1966.

TRUAX, C. B. Therapist empathy, warmth, and genuineness and patient personality changes: A comparison between interaction unit measures, time sample measures, and patient perception measures. *Journal of Clinical Psychology,* 1966, *22,* 225-229.

TRUAX, C. B. A scale for the measurement of accurate empathy. *Discussion Paper #20,* Wisconsin Psychiatric Institute, University of Wisconsin, September 26, 1961.

TRUAX, C. B. & CARKHUFF, R. R. For better or worse: The process of psychotherapeutic personality change. In *Recent advances in the study of behavior change.* Montreal: McGill University Press, 1963.

TRUAX, C. B. In C. R. Rogers, (Ed.) *The therapeutic relationship and its impact.* Madison: University of Wisconsin Press, 1967.

VAN BUREN, J. D. An assessment of the relationship between the capacity to empathize and the emotional maturity of a group of counselor trainees. Unpublished doctoral dissertation, Boston University, 1963.

WIENPAHL, P. *The matter of zen: A brief account of zazen.* New York: New York University Press, 1964.

16

COMPARATIVE EFFECTS OF TRAINING IN EXTERNAL AND INTERNAL CONCENTRATION ON TWO COUNSELING BEHAVIORS

Paul Leung[1]

Two behaviors variously stressed by different counselors are the ability to have empathic understanding of the client and the ability to respond selectively to client statements during a counseling interview. A training procedure that appears to contain elements for facilitating training in these two techniques is one built around the training of Zen Buddhist monks. Subjects trained in Zen techniques of external and internal concentration were found to increase their ability in these two counseling behaviors.

The ability to have empathic understanding is characteristic of the relational approach to counseling and involves the sensing by the counselor of the client's inner world (Rogers, 1962). It is partially a perceptual task in which the counselor attempts to be as accurate as possible. Inasmuch as he is able, he is more empathic.

The second behavior of responding selectively is characteristic of the behaviorally oriented counselor (Krasner, 1966). For example, the reinforcing of specified verbal classes was found functional and effective for group counseling (Daane, Gold, McGreevy, Maes, & Kenoyer, 1969). The implementation of such a technique requires the concentration or attention of the counselor toward that class of statements that he wants to reinforce.

A training procedure that contains elements for facilitating training in these two techniques is one built around the training of Zen Buddhist monks. Zen Buddhism, because of its varied psychological implications, has been a subject of interest to psychiatrists and psychologists for many years. Berger (1962) suggested its use in counseling psychology and counselor education almost a decade ago.

The results of Zen training have been useful not only in the monastery setting but also in the daily life of the individual; Zen is not intended to be out of reach for the ordinary person. Maupin (1962) in a psychological review of Zen Buddhism alluded to Tokyo bus drivers who, having received Zen training, had fewer accidents than before. Physiological as well as psychological changes have been found to occur in the practice of Zen concepts (Deikman, 1963; Kasamatsu & Hirai, 1963, 1966; Maupin, 1965; Sakamoto, 1961).

Required behaviors of counselors parallels the results of Zen training. A counselor working with a client having a crisis must be able to empathize or understand what is happening to the client and at the same time must be able to concentrate on those aspects of the interview that are relevant for that client.

PROBLEM

The purpose of this study was to determine whether training following Zen concepts of external and internal concentration (meditative deep breathing) could be accomplished and what effects it would have on individuals in terms of their facility to (*a*) hear accurately and consistently a specified class of verbal stimuli considered desirable for reinforcement and (*b*) be able

[1] Requests for reprints should be sent to Paul Leung. Rehabilitation Center, University of Arizona. Tucson. Arizona 85721.

to predict accurately and consistently the self-attitudes of another individual.

Definition of Terms

External concentration is a condition where an individual focuses his attention on one specific object or stimulus. In this study concentration is measured by the ability to hear accurately and consistently specified verbal material.

Internal concentration (meditative deep breathing) is a technique whereby an individual consciously forms a rhythm and also slows down his breathing or respiratory rate following a technique described by practitioners of Zen.

Analytical empathy refers to the prediction of self attitudes of one individual as he meets with another individual (Daane & Rhum, 1962).

Material desirable for reinforcement is that material that a counselor using a reinforcement technique decides is desirable for reinforcement. In this study, the specified materials considered desirable were statements that an individual used to describe the behavior he has noticed in authority figures.

The Hypotheses

The following four null hypotheses, were tested: (a) Individuals trained in the internal concentration (meditative deep breathing) technique show no difference in analytical empathy score from individuals who experience no special training, (b) individuals trained first in internal concentration (meditative deep breathing) show no difference in analytical empathy score from individuals trained in internal concentration following external concentration training, (c) individuals trained in external concentration show no difference in ability to hear accurately and consistently materials deemed desirable for reinforcement than those individuals who experience no special training, and (d) individuals trained first in external concentration show no difference in ability to hear accurately and consistently material deemed desirable for reinforcement than those individuals trained first in internal concentration (meditative deep breathing) followed by training in external concentration.

METHOD

The posttest-only control group design described by Campbell and Stanley (1963) was used with three groups. One experimental group (E-1) received the treatment sequence of deep breathing training first and then external concentration training. The second experimental group (E-2) received the treatment sequence of concentration training first and then deep breathing training. A third group (C-1) used as the control group received no training.

Subjects

The subjects were 67 volunteers, 45 women and 22 men, recruited from undergraduate classes in the College of Education, Arizona State University. The age range was from 18 to 48 with the average age for the group being 22.75 years. Of those assigned to the experimental groups, 37 of 40 completed the full sequence of training in both concentration and meditative deep breathing. Twenty were assigned to the control group.

Treatment

The treatment for the experimental groups consisted of a total of 14 hours divided into 7 hours of training in meditative deep breathing and 7 hours of training in external concentration.

Meditative deep breathing. An essential part of the study was to produce what Maupin (1969) termed a "special combination of suspended action and waking attention" by training in meditative deep breathing. The exercise used in this study followed that described by Chang (1963), and the procedures used were adapted from Maupin (1965) and Deikman (1969).

The subjects received instructions in a room in which the lighting was dimmed. To provide a minimum of distraction, the subjects were seated facing a blank wall. The exercise was demonstrated, and the subjects were then asked to practice the exercise. When the exercise was done correctly, subjects were given social verbal reinforcement in the form of "good" and "very good."

Concentration. Zen participants deal with mental functioning in specific ways (Maupin, 1965). This study attempted to adopt those specific ways of maintaining attention to external stimuli. The treatment sequence for external concentration specified certain conditions under which the subjects were able to convey to the experimenter that the mental exercise of focusing attention toward a specific object was occurring. Verbal stimuli were used since a major portion of counseling involves verbal cues. Again, as in the breathing training, social reinforcement techniques were incorporated into the treatment.

Subjects in the study were asked to focus or concentrate on particular verbal stimuli recorded on audio tape. Subjects would indicate by recording on paper that they had heard the specified material. The assumption was that if the subjects heard the specified material, then they had to be concentrating on that specified stimuli. This method provided the observable behavioral cue that the subject was concentrating.

Evaluation. After completion of each treatment phase, subjects were shown a videotaped sequence consisting of four actor clients talking about themselves and their environment. Of the four actor clients, two were men and two were women; two were also drama students and two were graduate students in counseling and educational psychology. They were instructed to talk about themselves, describe how they saw their surroundings, and, in particular, discuss authority figures for 10 minutes. This videotape, 40 minutes in total length, was used for two purposes in the evaluation: first, as verbal stimuli in which subjects were asked to listen to specified statements and second, as verbal and nonverbal stimuli for subjects who were asked to predict how the actor clients completed a scale descriptive of attitudes toward self, ideal self, best friend, ideal teacher, and ideal employer. A videotape recording was utilized because it provided a uniform situation each time and was consistent with the definition of analytical empathy.

Subjects who had just completed the meditative deep breathing treatment were instructed to breathe as trained during the treatment. After each 10 minute portion, the videotape was stopped, and the subjects were given the scale to complete as the individual they had just viewed would complete it. This was repeated for the four actor clients on the videotape.

Subjects who had received the external concentration training were instructed to indicate to the experimenter each time they heard a statement in which the actor clients indicated that he or she had noticed authority acting. The experimenter kept a tally of the number of statements indicated on a typescript made of the videotaped sequence.

The Criterion Measures

Measurement took place at the conclusion of each treatment for the experimental groups. The criterion included an accuracy of prediction scale for analytical empathy and a quantitative count of the number of "notice authority" statements indicated.

Analytical empathy measurement. Daane and Rhum (1962), in a review of empathy measurement, found that most investigators agreed that "at least one form of empathy can be thought of as predictive ability, a process whereby one predicts the self-feelings and attitudes of another." An estimate of this ability can be obtained through the matching of predictions with the testimony of the individual being judged.

The scale used in this study was devised following two models: (a) The Role Construct Repertory Test, REP (Kelly, 1965), was used to formulate the concepts used in the prediction scale and (b) the use of the concepts elicited by the REP followed that of Daane and Rhum (1962). Stimulus words were used to formulate a prediction scale for the measurement of analytical empathy; that is, the predictive ability of the subjects with regard to the client actors on videotape.

Prediction scale construction. After formation of the constructs for the four actor clients from the REP test, the concepts were placed on a bipolar summative scale from 1 to 7. Each actor client rated himself using the scale with respect to the topic areas of self, ideal self, best friend, ideal employer, and ideal teacher. These concepts were chosen because they indicate an individual's concept and attitude toward himself, his ideal self or what he would like to be, his view or attitude toward someone close to him, his ideal role in terms of occupation, and the authority role related to occupation.

The subjects in this study were asked after viewing each 10 minute segment of the videotape to complete the prediction scale as the individual they just viewed would complete the scale. A difference or discrepancy score was computed between the actual score as completed by the actor client and the predicted score as given by the subject.

Hearing of "notice authority" statements. A second criterion measure was the ability to hear selected material considered desirable for reinforcement. The emphasis of this study was on how consistently and accurately an individual was able to focus or attend to a particular category of statements and whether improvement was possible through training.

The statement category in the study was a category that generally occurs in counseling situations and is considered desirable for reinforcement. The category chosen was used in the development of group counseling models for the Neighborhood Youth Corps (Daane et al., 1969). A statement category of that model was the client noticing authority behaving in some manner. These "notice authority" statements had reference by the speaker to authority behaving or showed awareness of it. Actor clients were used in this study because of the uniformity possible in evaluation.

Instructions were given the actor clients prior to making the videotape to include as much information as possible with regard to their noticing authority figures such as parents and employers behaving. The final typescript of the four client actors contained a total number of 115 "notice authority" statements.

Subjects were given instructions prior to viewing the videotape to indicate to the experimenter by lifting their finger each time they heard a "notice authority" statement. A score was computed for each subject consisting of the number of correct indications minus those statements that were wrongly indicated.

RESULTS

Self–Other Attitude Prediction

The comparison related to the first hypothesis was accomplished by the application of a one-way analysis of variance statistic for unequal groups. Difference or discrepancy scores were calculated for each of the experimental groups (E–1 and E–2) and compared with similarly computed scores for the control group (C–1) with respect to each topic. These areas included self, ideal self, best friend, ideal teacher, and ideal employer (Tables 1 and 2). While the null hypotheses were rejected at the .25 level, the findings are reported also at the .05 level of significance when such a level was reached to indicate the relationship of the present findings to the more traditional levels of statistical significance. The .25 level was chosen in order to increase the probability of detecting significant effects as this study was exploratory in nature with Type 1 and Type 2 errors being of equal importance.

The mean discrepancy scores for group E–1 were lower on all 20 topic areas than the discrepancy scores for group C–1. Eighteen out of 20 differences were significant at the .25 level significance. The mean discrepancy scores of group E–2 were also generally lower than the mean discrepancy scores of group C–1. Seventeen of 20 were lower for E–2 than C–1. Six of these were found to be significantly different at the .25 level of significance. The three mean discrepancy scores of C–1 which were lower than E–2 were not significantly different.

TABLE 1

EXPERIMENTAL GROUP E–1 AND CONTROL GROUP C–1 TOPIC AREAS (MEANS, STANDARD DEVIATIONS, AND F-RATIOS ON DISCREPANCY SCORES)

Group	Group E-1 N = 19		Group C-1 N = 20		F-ratios
	$\bar{X}$	SD	$\bar{X}$	SD	
First actor-client					
Self	24.00	3.10	31.40	3.51	2.90*
Ideal self	13.94	2.81	22.45	3.01	5.36**
Best friend	26.00	3.16	33.90	3.73	9.93**
Ideal teacher	45.94	6.08	66.35	7.00	11.10**
Ideal employer	21.10	2.01	28.01	2.90	2.07*
Second actor-client					
Self	12.94	2.13	21.20	2.40	1.83*
Ideal self	13.36	2.11	21.15	2.54	2.51*
Best friend	16.42	1.87	22.70	2.80	2.09*
Ideal teacher	17.63	2.95	22.65	2.91	1.30
Ideal employer	18.47	2.89	27.00	3.12	3.20*
Third actor-client					
Self	14.78	1.98	26.70	2.54	8.62*
Ideal self	7.63	1.73	10.35	1.10	1.79*
Best friend	10.10	2.03	17.10	2.00	3.46*
Ideal teacher	06.57	.89	11.55	1.00	6.71*
Ideal employer	7.42	1.69	12.60	1.98	6.34*
Fourth actor-client					
Self	14.36	2.31	16.20	2.68	.55
Ideal self	15.52	1.97	22.80	2.31	3.43*
Best friend	13.64	1.98	19.55	2.05	10.39**
Ideal teacher	13.78	1.98	18.00	2.41	6.35**
Ideal employer	12.36	2.01	15.30	2.55	5.15**

* $p < .25$.
** $p < .05$.

TABLE 2

EXPERIMENTAL GROUP E-2 AND CONTROL GROUP C-1 TOPIC AREAS (MEANS, STANDARD DEVIATIONS, AND F-RATIOS ON DISCREPANCY SCORES)

Group	Group E-2 N = 18		Group C-1 N = 20		F-ratios
	$\bar{X}$	SD	$\bar{X}$	SD	
First actor-client					
Self	27.33	2.91	31.40	3.51	.95
Ideal self	19.05	2.54	22.45	3.01	.84
Best friend	33.94	3.34	33.90	3.73	.00
Ideal teacher	54.33	3.49	66.35	7.00	4.70**
Ideal employer	30.20	2.93	28.01	2.90	.20
Second actor-client					
Self	20.11	2.13	21.20	2.40	.03
Ideal self	20.72	2.45	21.15	2.54	.00
Best friend	24.89	2.83	22.70	2.80	.13
Ideal teacher	21.27	1.85	22.65	2.91	.05
Ideal employer	25.05	2.68	27.00	3.12	.10
Third actor-client					
Self	19.50	2.31	26.70	2.54	3.20*
Ideal self	8.83	2.10	10.35	1.10	.68
Best friend	16.11	1.88	17.10	2.00	.04
Ideal teacher	7.94	.89	11.55	1.00	3.68*
Ideal employer	12.11	2.31	12.60	1.98	.05
Fourth actor-client					
Self	15.50	2.10	16.20	2.68	.17
Ideal self	19.50	1.91	22.80	2.31	6.10**
Best friend	16.83	2.38	19.55	2.05	4.19**
Ideal teacher	17.00	2.19	18.00	2.41	.34
Ideal employer	13.38	1.39	15.30	2.55	4.50**

* $p < .25$.
** $p < .05$.

This hypothesis was rejected, as the experimental groups had significantly lower mean discrepancy scores on the self-other prediction scale.

The second null hypothesis comparison was accomplished by the application of a one-way analysis of variance statistic to the data obtained during the testing period following the treatment sequence of internal concentration. Difference or discrepancy scores were calculated for each of the experimental groups (E-1 and E-2) and compared with each other. Group E-1 received external concentration training first before training in internal concentration. Group E-2 received internal concentration first before training in external concentration. Discrepancy scores were calculated on each

topic used to rate themselves by the actor clients (Table 3).

All 20 of the mean discrepancy scores were lower for Group E-1 than the mean discrepancy scores for Group E-2. Twelve of these lower mean discrepancy scores were significantly different from the mean discrepancy scores of Group E-2 at the .25 level of significance.

This hypothesis was rejected, as the experimental group (E-1) had significantly lower mean discrepancy scores and thus more accurate predictive skill on the self–other attitude scale than the experimental group (E-2).

"Notice Authority" Statements

The comparison for the third hypothesis was accomplished using data obtained in

TABLE 3

EXPERIMENTAL GROUP E–1 AND EXPERIMENTAL GROUP E–2 TOPIC AREAS (MEANS, STANDARD DEVIATIONS, AND F-RATIOS ON DISCREPANCY SCORES)

Group	Group E-1 N = 19		Group E-2 N = 18		F-ratios
	$\bar{X}$	SD	$\bar{X}$	SD	
First actor-client					
Self	24.00	3.10	27.33	2.91	.65
Ideal self	13.94	2.81	19.05	2.54	7.36**
Best friend	26.00	3.16	33.94	3.34	6.48**
Ideal teacher	45.94	6.08	54.33	3.49	1.50*
Ideal employer	21.10	2.01	30.27	2.93	3.83*
Second actor-client					
Self	12.94	2.13	20.11	2.13	2.12*
Ideal self	13.36	2.11	20.72	2.45	1.34
Best friend	16.42	1.87	24.28	2.83	3.10*
Ideal teacher	17.63	2.95	21.27	1.85	.35
Ideal employer	18.47	2.89	25.05	2.68	1.22
Third actor-client					
Self	14.78	1.98	19.50	2.31	2.77*
Ideal self	7.63	1.73	8.83	2.10	.37
Best friend	10.10	2.03	16.11	1.88	3.78*
Ideal teacher	6.57	0.89	7.94	0.89	.84
Ideal employer	7.42	1.69	12.11	2.31	7.45**
Fourth actor-client					
Self	14.36	2.31	15.50	2.10	.18
Ideal self	15.52	1.97	19.55	1.91	6.00**
Best friend	13.64	1.98	16.83	2.38	3.19*
Ideal teacher	13.78	1.98	17.00	2.14	2.60*
Ideal employer	12.36	2.01	13.38	1.37	.51

* $p < .25$.
** $p < .05$.

the testing period following the external concentration training sequence. Subjects were instructed during the viewing of the videotape to indicate to the experimenter each time they heard a statement in which the actor client showed an awareness of authority acting. The resulting number was calculated by subtracting statements wrongly indicated by the subject. The one-way analysis of variance statistic was applied to these data (Table 4).

The mean number of statements reported was higher for both the experimental groups than for the control group. The mean for E–1 was 92.57 and for the E–2, 98.38. The control group mean was 79.15. The F obtained in comparison of E–1 and E–2 with C–1 was significant at the .25 level of significance.

This hypothesis was rejected since the experimental groups had a siginficantly higher number of "notice authority" statements indicated as being heard than the control group.

The comparison for the fourth hypothesis also was accomplished by the analysis of variance technique applied to data collected following the treatment sequence in external concentration. The data consisted of the number of statements indicating an awareness of authority acting heard by the subjects (Table 5).

This hypothesis was considered rejected since the experimental group receiving prior

Effects of Training on Concentration

TABLE 4

Experimental Groups E-1, E-2, and Control Group C-1 (Means, Standard Deviations, and F-Ratios) and Number of "Notice Authority" Statements Accurately Heard

Group E-1 N = 19		Group C-1 N = 20		F-ratios
$\bar{X}$	SD	$\bar{X}$	SD	
92.57	4.81	79.15	3.79	3.79**

Group E-2 N = 18		Group C-1 N = 20		
$\bar{X}$	SD	$\bar{X}$	SD	
98.38	5.23	79.15	3.79	19.56**

* $p < .25$.
** $p < .05$.

training in internal concentration heard more accurately and consistently the "notice authority" statements than the experimental group receiving external concentration first.

DISCUSSION

The results suggest that training applied here is feasible for increasing awareness of verbal and nonverbal cues and for increasing the ability to concentrate on specified material.

A number of questions were raised by the results. Can a counselor adopt the breathing posture during an actual situation without interfering with the client? A similar question was raised with regard to external concentration training. Was time spent with one class of specified cues transferable to another? Both of these questions center on the transfer effects of training to actual counseling situations. Exploration is needed toward application of training in other than experimental conditions.

Training in one kind of concentration brought about significant gains in the other kind of concentration. This is consonant with the literature on Zen training. However, further research is needed to define the nature of this interaction.

Another question raised was what are the significant differences between experimental groups when one group received prior training? Better scores may be attributed to the "Hawthorne" effect where longer time was spent with the experimenter. Further work should control for this variable. The results of this study suggest rich areas for future investigation in the application of Zen concepts to counseling training.

TABLE 5

Experimental Groups E-1, E-2, and Control Group C-1 (Means, Standard Deviations, and F-Ratios) and Number of "Notice Authority" Statements Accurately Heard

Group E-1 N = 19		Group E-2 N = 18		F-ratios
$\bar{X}$	SD	$\bar{X}$	SD	
92.57	4.81	98.38	5.23	2.89*

* $p < .25$.

REFERENCES

BERGER, E. M. Zen buddhism, general psychology, and counseling psychology (1962). In C. Beck (Ed.), *Guidelines for guidance*. Dubuque, Iowa: William C. Brown, 1966.

CAMPBELL, D. T., & STANLEY, J. C. Experimental and quasi-experimental designs for research on teaching. In N. L. Gage (Ed.), *Handbook of research on teaching*. Chicago: Rand McNally, 1963.

CHANG, CHUNG-YUAN. *Creativity and Taoism*. New York: Julian Press, 1963.

DAANE, C. J., GOLD, R., McGREEVEY, P., MAES, W., & KENOYER, D. *Final report on developing group counseling models for the neighborhood youth corps*. Tempe: Arizona State University, 1969.

DAANE, C. J., & RHUM, G. Explorations in the measurement of empathy as analytical predictive ability. *Iowa Academy of Science*, 1962, **69,** 502–512.

DEIKMAN, A. J. Experimental meditation (1963). In C. Tart (Ed.), *Altered states of consciousness*. New York: Wiley, 1969.

KASAMATSU, A., & HIRAI, T. Science of Zazen. *Psychologia*, 1963, **6,** 86–89.

KASAMATSU, A., & HIRAI, T. An electroencephalographic study on the Zen meditation (1966). In C. Tart (Ed.), *Altered states of consciousness*. New York: Wiley, 1969.

KELLY, G. A. *The psychology of personal constructs*. New York: Norton, 1955.

KRASNER, L. The reinforcement machine (1966). In B. Berenson & R. Carkhuff (Eds.), *Sources of gain in counseling and psychotherapy*. New York: Holt, Rinehart & Winston, 1967.

MAUPIN, E. W. Zen buddhism: A psychological review. *Journal of Consulting Psychology*, 1962, **26,** 363–378.

MAUPIN, E. W. Individual differences in response to a zen meditation exercise. *Journal of Consulting Psychology*, 1965, **29,** 139–165.

MAUPIN, E. W. On meditation. In C. Tart (Ed.), *Altered states of consciousness*. New York: Wiley, 1969.

ROGERS, C. R. The interpersonal relationship: The core of guidance (1962). In R. Mosher, R. Carle, & C. Kehas (Eds.), *Guidance: An examination*. New York: Harcourt, Brace & World, 1965.

SAKAMOTO, A. A study of the acid-base balance in neurosis. *Psychologia*, 1961, **4,** 17–23.

(Received July 6, 1971)

B5. Additional Findings: Normal Subjects

The vast majority of the studies which have been conducted on meditation show its effectiveness along a variety of dimensions. This literature is summarized in Article 6 by Shapiro and Giber and in the table included here. These include such measures as decrease of psychosomatic complaints, increase in measures of "self-actualization," increase in self-concept and self-esteem, increased feelings of internal locus of control, as well as the other areas discussed in previous sections (e.g., decrease in anxiety, decreased use of addictive drugs).

In light of the above findings, the Otis article (17) included here comes as somewhat of an unexpected shock. It is included here, not because it in any way invalidates the above findings, but because it does throw a note of caution in the field. Otis, on reanalyzing some of his previous data, found that there may be dysphoric effects in meditators, and that these effects seem to increase with the length of practice. There is some question of how to interpret Otis's data. For example, if one takes a long-term perspective of meditation or psychotherapy in general, the dysphoric effects may occur and be part of the process, which is not necessarily a bad thing. Further, it may be suggested that as one becomes more sensitive, one finds increased layers of areas where one is not totally centered, totally calm. On an overall level, the individual may be less anxious, but he or she may be more sensitive to anxiety. This may or may not be a problem. On the other hand, it supports previous literature (e.g., Article 19 by Pelletier) that meditators become more field independent as a result of the practice of meditation. However, it also points out that they do not seem to become any more field independent than a group of controls who "just sit," a result differing from and extending Pelletier's observations. Second, there is an interesting result. Although meditators had a lower "self-regard" (defined as congruence between "real" and "ideal" self) than the control group, after six months of meditation, there was a significantly increased correlation between real and ideal self. Their perception of their real self moved closer to their ideal. The third interesting point raised in Bono's study (Article 18) has to do with meditators' ability to operantly control their autonomic learning aptitude, e.g., to raise their heart rate. He found that long-term meditators were slightly more effective than control subjects in changing their heart rate, but not significantly different than short-term meditators; he also found that long-term (5-year) meditators were significantly better than control subjects and 6-month meditators in ability to control phasic electrodermal responses. What is admirable in this study is Bono's attempt to correlate perceptual style (measured by field independence and dependence), self-concept, and operant learning. This type of integrated research seems critical for a complete understanding of meditation.

Table 4. Additional Findings: Normal Subjects

Investigator(s)	Focus of Investigation	S's (N, age, sex, prior experience)	Type and Length of Treatment/Training	Frequency of Therapist (E) Contact	Subjective Effects (unless otherwise noted)	Follow-up	Type of Design, Quality of Controls, Methodological Problems
		INDEPENDENT VARIABLE			**DEPENDENT VARIABLE**		
Seeman, Nidich and Banta 1972	"Self Actualization"	Group One control N=20, 10 male 10 female. Group Two meditation N=15, 8 male, 7 female. Prior experience not stated	Standard Transcendental Meditation training, 30-60 min. initial instruction 3 days, verification + further instruction. then S's instructed to meditate 2x daily for 15-20 min.	Not stated	Shostrom's Personal Orientation Inventory, 1966 (POI) tested 2 days prior to and 2 months post TM instruction showed meditators moved in positive "Self actualizing" direction compared to controls.	None reported	Group selection and/or matching procedures not stated. Need behavioral measures of such items as spontaneity, capacity for intimate contact, tolerance for verbal aggression, willingness to self disclose.
Nidich, Seeman and Dreskin 1973	"Self Actualization"	Group One N=9 non-meditating controls. Group Two N=9 meditation	Same as above	Not stated	Shostrom's POI measured pre and post (10 weeks) TM instruction showed meditators moved in direction of "self actualization." Controls showed no significant differences in testing.	None reported	Same as above
Stek and Bass 1973	Tested differences between those interested and not interested in meditation in "perceived locus of control" and "personal adjustment"	Group One N=17 median age 20 yrs. 12 male, 5 female attended free meditation lectures, paid TM initiation fee. Group Two N=32 median age 18 yrs. 14 M, 20 F. Group Three N=32, median age 19 yrs. 12 M, 15 F, uninterested in meditation. Group Four N=30 median age 19 yrs. 18 M, 12 F controls.	Tests given pre-meditation training	Not stated	Administration of Rotter's I-E Locus of Control Scale (1966) and Shostrom's POI (time competence + internal support) found no significant difference between test scores for all 4 groups and common scores for college students	None reported	Study might indicate that initial group differences between meditators and non-meditators are insignificant; however, group differences may exist in willingness to change, etc.
Hjelle 1974	"Anxiety," "Locus of control" and "Self Actualization"	Group One N=15 7 M 8 F meditating experience = 22.63 mo. Group Two N=21 11 M 10 F tested 1 week prior to receiving meditation instruction	Standard TM training	Not stated	Regular meditators (group one) scored significantly lower than beginners on Bendig's Anxiety Scale (1956) and Rotter's Internal-External Locus of Control (1966) and significantly higher on 7 of 12 POI scales (Shostrom, 1966).	None reported	Possible demand characteristics in testing; study supports Seeman, Nidich & Banta.
Otis 1974	Self concept change, improvement in physical and/or behavioral problems	Group One (N=30) Transcendental Meditation. Group Two (N=15) Passive Controls; took pre and post tests. Group Three Active Controls. A sitting quietly 15-20 min./2x daily. B "meditative" treatment, repeating "I am a witness only" 15-20 min./2x daily	Group One standard TM training for 3 months. All S's baseline physiological measurements for 3 months	Not stated	Psychological tests. Questionnaire on self-concept (Otis Descriptive Personality List) and checklist on variety of behavioral and physical problems (Otis Physical and Behavioral Inventory) found no overall differences between TM and pooled control S's. However, item analysis revealed TM S's claimed more specific benefits than passive controls. Interview conducted 3 months post-training indicated that specific benefit claims of active controls and TM S's did not differ. Author suggests that simply resting may account for benefits.	To 18 months	Treatment conditions not matched for expectation of relief.
Udupa et al. 1973	Performance, Intelligence, and Memory Quotient(s), Neuroticism and Psychological Health assessed. Plasma Acetycholine and Serum Cholinesterase monitored	N=12, avg. age 23.0 ± 3.36 yrs. "from a uniform socioeconomic class"	Hatha Yoga exercises (done in group) for 1 hour daily x 6 months. Exercises involved graduated sequence of muscle coordination exercises, postures (asanas), breathing (prānāyāma) meditation, etc.	One hour daily x 6 months with trained Yoga instructor	*See Table I below*	None reported	Within subject design. S's served as own controls.

Table I. Certain Psychological Changes Induced by the Practice of Yoga

Observations	Test Used	Initial (baseline)	3rd month	6th month	Direction
Performance quotient (PQ)	Alexander's Passalong Test	93.15±12.50	102.6±16.40	108.2±14.70	Increased significantly
Intelligence quotient (IQ)	Koh's Block Design Test	92.17±18.60	100.3±6.40	106.2±16.70	
Memory quotient (MQ)	Wechsler Memory Scale	89.75±9.15	97.3±13.20	100.8±9.60	Increased significantly
Neuroticism index (MPI) N	Mursley Personality Inven.	19.50±9.95	11.40±10.70	9.82±8.40	Decreased
E		27.10±5.60	28.40±6.80	26.54±8.40	
Q		2.66±5.53	1.00±2.19	2.58±5.57	
Mental fatiguability	Digit Cancellation Test				
Time taken		3.52±0.68	3.31±0.90	3.03±0.41	
Mistake score		5.54±4.69	1.31±1.73	3.64±3.30	Lowered
Fatigue index		1.59	0.40	1.20	
Health Index	Cornell Medical Index				
Physiological complaints		125	83	64	
Psychological complaints		67	31	30	Lowered

Note: Significant values in decreased complaints on Cornell Medical Index include gastrointestinal, psychoneurological, and respiratory complaints (physiological), and anxiety, tension, and inadequacy complaints (psychological).

		INDEPENDENT VARIABLE			DEPENDENT VARIABLE		
Investigator(s)	Focus of Investigation	S's (N, age, sex, prior experience)	Type and Length of Treatment/Training	Frequency of Therapist (E) Contact	Subjective Effects (unless otherwise noted)	Follow up	Type of Design, Quality of Controls, Methodological Problems

Table II Certain Biochemical Response to the Practice of Yoga

Physiological Data

Observations	Mean±S.D. and comparison with initial		
	Initial (baseline)	3rd month	6th month
Plasma Acetylcholine in μg/100 ml	181.7±149.3	101.1±34.3 $t = 1.825$ $p < 0.1$	58.7±18.05 $t = 2.83$ $p < 0.01$
Serum Cholinesterase in pH units/hour	1.17±0.309	0.894±0.313 $t = 2.177$ $p < 0.05$	0.95±0.087 $t = 2.095$ $p < 0.05$

Note: Both show statistically significant decreases, also found increase in urinary excretion of testosterone and 17-hydroxy corticosteroid, increase in serum proteins and reduction of blood sugar. EEG showed more prominent alpha with less spikes.

Shapiro 1978a — Daily overt behavior and "Global" self perception — N=15, college students in class on "Zen Buddhism and Self Management"; no prior meditation experience. — Experimental Group (N=9) 1) 2 weeks behavioral observation on 9 variables 2) weekend Zen experience workshop 3) formal Zen breath meditation practiced 2x daily plus contingent informal breath meditation and continued behavioral observation for 3 weeks. Control Group (N=6) 1) 5 weeks behavioral observation 2) weekend Zen experience workshop — During intervention phase (weeks 3-5) experimenter had no contact with either group — Data from pre and post testing on Semantic Differential, Rotter's I-E Locus of Control showed no significant group differences but moved in hypothesized (positive) direction. Stanford Hypnotic Susceptibility Scale (Form C, Group Variant) showed increase in susceptibility for experimental group and decrease for controls. Behavioral Data: Self monitoring of frequency of behaviors with questionnaire (e.g. positive self statements, negative self statements, feelings of creativity, feelings of self-control feeling anxious, becoming angry, noting positive things in nature relating to only part of a person, and not living in the moment). Combined index of behavioral self-observation data showed greater movement in a more favorable (hypothesized) direction for experimental group than controls. — None reported — Modified multiple time series design (c.f. Campbell & Stanley 1963, pp. 55-57). Positive direction looked at daily change as well as global pre/post. Weakness: need overt covarying variables with daily self-reported change of feelings.

Lesh 1970 — Counselors measured on empathy and openness to experience — All S's were college students taking counseling courses. Group One N=16, taught Zen breath meditation. Group Two N=12, controls. Group Three N=11, group "definitely against" meditation exercise. — Group One Zen breath meditation practiced 30 min./day x 4 weeks. — Meditation instructions given by tape to avoid bias — Pre and Post Treatment Measures: 1) Increased empathy among meditating group on Affective Sensitivity Scale (ASS) responses to videotaped client situation. Both control groups did not show improvement in empathic ability. 2) No correlation found between ASS and blind ratings of subjective response to meditation (Maupin 1965). 3) Positive correlation found between openness to experience (Experience Inquiry Fitzgerald 1966) and response to meditation. 4) Positive correlation between individual scores on openness to experience and ASS. 5) Correlation found between high scores on ASS and "self-actualization" measure (Shostrom's POI). — None reported — Between subjects design; possible selection bias.

Leung 1973 — Counselors measured on empathic ability and ability to respond selectively to clients (e.g. hearing of "notice authority" statements) — N=57, avg. age 22.75 yrs. 22 male, 45 female, prior experience not stated. Group E-1: Deep breathing training first + external concentration training. Group E-2: External concentration training first + deep breathing training (E-1 + E-2, N=37). Group 3: N=20, controls; given no training. — Training for groups 1 + 2: 7 hrs training in meditative deep breathing. 7 hrs training in external concentration on a specific verbal stimuli on tape. Social verbal reinforcement given S's for correct performance of exercises. — Not stated — Criterion Measures: Group E-1 — Measured S's predictive analytical empathy in response to videotaped sequences of acted client situations (40 min. total). Analytic empathy measurement taken after 10 minute portions of videotape. Group E-2 — indicated to E number of "notice authority" statements made by actor "clients" in videotape. In second part of training the criterion measures were reversed. Both (E) groups showed more accurate analytic empathy and heard more notice authority statements by clients than controls. E-1 showed more predictive ability on self-other attitude scale and heard more notice authority statements than E-2. — None reported — Post-test only control group design.

17

ADVERSE EFFECTS OF TRANSCENDENTAL MEDITATION

Leon S. Otis

Currently there is a large and increasing literature suggesting the positive effects of meditation, its applications to health care, psychotherapy, and education. When one reads the literature, there are only two studies reported which suggest possible negative effects (1,2). Unfortunately, most journals do not report negative effects because of lack of statistical significance due to small sample size. However, from a clinical perspective, negative effects are quite important. This article describes a study done at SRI to determine what, if any, are the negative effects of transcendental meditation.

Our investigation came about as a result of reader reaction to an article that the author published in *Psychology Today* (3) in 1974. The article summarized an experiment conducted at SRI to determine whether people who adopted the practice of Transcendental Meditation (TM) were a self-selected population or whether a relatively disinterested random sample of volunteers could realize the benefits claimed to accrue to practitioners. In the article, the author briefly mentioned that the SRI findings suggested TM may not be a suitable practice for everyone, and he cautioned that it might even be harmful for some. After the article was published, the author began to receive unsolicited letters, telephone calls, and some visits from people complaining about adverse effects from TM.[1]

In the research, we used a relatively neutral population of 60 volunteer SRI employees; half were randomly assigned to learn TM and the other half were assigned to learn and practice one of three control conditions.[2] The TM group received the standard training at a local chapter of the Students International Meditation Society (SIMS), the parent organization of TM. After training, they were instructed to meditate twice daily for 15 to 20 minutes for the next 3 months. Two groups of control subjects received mock "meditation" training and subsequently practiced sitting quietly twice daily. One group was instructed to relax as best they could. The other group was given a "mock" mantra and was told to mentally repeat the phrase "I am a witness only" during their meditation periods. In contrast to these two "active" control groups, the subjects in a third "passive" control group did not change their life style in any way. They simply reported for the baseline and the subsequent psychological and physiological tests that were given to all subjects.

Well before the 3-month period of daily practice was over, we began to receive complaints during weekly meetings about physical or mental distress (headaches, insomnia, anxiety, gastrointestinal upset, etc.) from both the TM and active control subjects. The problems the TM subjects experienced were interpreted by the SIMS organization as being caused by "unstressing"—a phenomenon claimed to be a natural consequence of the initial stages of TM. We could not explain the problems reported by control

---

[1]SIMS, the parent organization of TM, circulated a "rebuttal" to the article to all its teachers in the United States without giving the author an opportunity to respond. A disillusioned teacher informed the author that teachers were provided with "standard answers" to the points raised in the article, especially those concerning the possibility of adverse effects.

[2]The initiation fee was covered by research project funds. The controls were given an equivalent amount for their participation in the experiment.

subjects but assumed that they were transient and need not overly concern us. We were wrong, at least with respect to a few of the subjects. Two of the controls were advised by their physicians to terminate their participation in the experiment because of the reoccurrence of previously quiescent medical problems. Three of the TM subjects quit because of medical or other problems.

Because the percentage of dropouts in the TM group was low and because subjects in the control groups also experienced problems, we believed that uncontrolled variables probably accounted for the adverse effects. Also, in the light of the glowing reports of the effects of TM appearing in the literature (4), the author simply mentioned these unexpected results in the *Psychology Today* article and cautioned that further research might be needed.

Unlike other investigators (5,6), we found no differences in EEG, alpha frequency, heart rate, blood pressure, peripheral blood pulse volume, respiration rate, skin temperature, or personality measures between the TM and the combined control groups. The absence of differences between the TM and control groups, however, may have been due to the short (i.e., 3 month) period of practice of our TM subjects. Interestingly, the TM subjects showed significantly more Sleep Stage 1 than control subjects. TM subjects tended to vacillate between light sleep and wakefulness more than controls (7)—results that have since been corroborated by others (8,9).

During the period between 1972 and 1974 when the *Psychology Today* article appeared, other factors developed that kept the question of possible adverse effects alive for this investigator. Conversations with colleagues at national meetings where the SRI experimental results were presented indicated that they also had noted adverse effects in some people, especially in subjects from a psychiatric population. We also compared dropout rates, which varied from 35 to 70% over a year. The question of why people dropped out was intriguing, but the press of other demands precluded the author's pursuing this question.

The totally unexpected response to the few brief lines about possible adverse effects that he had included in his article rekindled the author's interest. The people who wrote, called, or visited him were everyday folks—housewives, students, tradesmen, professionals—and their distress was real. Many reported adverse effects that continued even though they had stopped meditating. A few reported that they felt addicted to TM. That is, they said that quitting had exacerbated their symptoms, and they had started again to keep from feeling worse. Some of these people had been in meditation for years before their problems arose, and some had quit without their problems disappearing. Therefore, this researcher believed that there were some important unknowns regarding the possible effects of TM that merited further investigation.

He reexamined the results of a survey SRI had sent to every twentieth person on the SIMS mailing list in 1971 (approximately 40,000 individuals were on the mailing list then).[3] Approximately 47% of the 1900 people surveyed responded to the survey, which included two instruments developed by the author that were intended for use in the SRI experiment. One was a self-concept word list (Descriptive Personality List) and the other was a check list of physical and behavioral symptoms (Physical and Behavioral Inventory). The SIMS sample was used to validate the tests before they were used at SRI. Both tests proved to be valid in that each discriminated significantly between dropouts and those practicing TM for 6 months or less as well as those practicing TM for 18 months or more. The tests also discriminated between the latter two TM groups.

Relevant to the present discussion is the symptom check list, which consisted of three parts. Part I requested information about the subject's TM history. Included were such items as when the subject was instructed, how long he or she had been practicing, how regularly the subject had practiced, and whether he or she was still practicing. Part II was a list of behavioral symptoms, culled from the literature on TM, that practitioners most frequently reported had changed for the better (see Fig. 1). The subject was asked to indicate in Column 1 whether the category was a problem before he or she started TM and to check Columns 2, 3, 4, or 5 to indicate the extent and kind of change (positive or negative) noted since starting TM. Part III mirrored Part II, except that symptoms related to physical health were used.

The responses of all members of three subgroups of the SIMS sample were analyzed. The subgroups consisted of 121 people who had discontinued the practice (average time in TM was 7.4 months), 156 "novice" meditators (those who had been practicing for 3 to 6 months; average was 4.2 months), and 78

[3]The mailing of the questionnaires was undertaken by the SIMS Headquarters in Los Angeles. The sample was instructed to return the completed forms to SRI. Stamped, self-addressed envelopes were provided.

Before TM		Since Starting TM							
1	Category	2 Little or no change (0–25%)		3 Some change (26–50%)		4 Considerable change (51–90%)		5 Complete change (91–100%)	
Was a problem for me		Incr	Decr	Incr	Decr	Incr	Decr	Incr	Decr
	Ability to relax								
	Academic performance								
	Antisocial behavior								
	Anxiety								
	Awareness								
	Boredom								
	Confusion								
	Creativity								
	Depression								
	Emotional stability								
	(30 Items)								

Fig. 1. Symptom check list.

"experienced" meditators (those who had been practicing TM for 18 months or more; average was 22.7 months).

Initially, we compared dropouts with experienced meditators because we expected that considerably more dropouts would claim adverse effects than experienced meditators. Surprisingly, and totally unexpectedly, the reverse was true. Dropouts reported fewer complaints than experienced meditators, and to a statistically significant extent.[4] To evaluate the reliability of this unexpected finding, we also analyzed the data for the novice meditators. Novice meditators fell between dropouts and experienced meditators in terms of the number of complaints.

Table I summarizes these data and presents data from a similar analysis of identical questionnaires returned by a group of novice (3–6 months TM) and experienced (18+ months) meditators who were being trained to become teachers of TM.[5] The latter data were examined to test the generalizability of the SIMS data to another TM population. Approximately 71% of this sample of 832 returned the survey questionnaires.

Although the original expectations were that the number of adverse effects reported would be negatively correlated with the length of time in meditation and that dropouts would report the greatest number of adverse effects, Table 1 shows that the opposite was the case. The number and severity of complaints were *positively* related to duration of meditation. That is, people who had been meditating for the longest period of time reported the most adverse effects. Of considerable interest is the finding that the specific adverse effects reported were remarkably consistent between groups and formed a pattern suggestive of people who had become anxious, confused, frustrated, depressed, and/or withdrawn (or more so) since starting TM.

[4]All references to statistical significance in this paper are at the 0.05 level of significance or better. In all cases two-tailed *t* tests for independent groups were used.

[5]This group also included a number of teachers. The number is indeterminant from the survey data, but they would most likely be included within the group of experienced meditators.

Adverse Effects of TM   **203**

Table 1. Percentage of TM Dropouts and Meditators Reporting Adverse Effects[a]

| | Percentage reporting adverse changes | | | | |
| | SIMS random sample | | | Teacher trainees | |
Symptom	Dropouts ($N = 121$)	3–6 Month TM ($N = 156$)	18+ Month TM ($N = 78$)	3–6 Month TM ($N = 77$)	18+ Month TM ($N = 142$)
Antisocial behavior	—	—	5.2	—	9.2
Anxiety	—	5.8	11.5	—	12.7
Boredom	—	—	9.0	—	6.3
Confusion	—	—	6.4	—	11.3
Depression	—	—	6.4	9.1	9.9
Frustration	—	—	5.1	7.8	7.7
Impulsiveness	—	—	—	9.1	—
Physical and mental tension	—	—	9.0	9.1	7.0
Procrastination	—	—	5.1	—	5.6
Restlessness	—	—	7.7	—	5.6
Suspiciousness	—	—	—	7.8	—
Withdrawal	—	—	6.4	—	6.3

[a]Only symptoms for which at least 5% of the subjects of one or more subgroups reported an increase of 51% or more are tabulated.

Several other aspects of the table are of interest. In the SIMS sample, none of the adverse effects were reported to have increased by 51% or more by at least 5% of those who had dropped out of TM, and only one item (anxiety) was so reported by the naive meditators. In contrast, at least 5% of the experienced meditators reported that 10 of the 12 adverse effects listed had increased by 51% or more since they started practicing TM. A similar pattern was seen for the teacher trainees. The naive meditators in the teacher trainee group reported that 5 of the 12 adverse effects had increased by 51% or more since starting TM, whereas those who had practiced TM for 18 months or longer identified the same 10 adverse effects reported by the experienced SIMS meditators as having increased by 51% or more.[6]

These data suggest that the longer a person stays in TM and the more committed a person becomes to TM as a way of life (as indicated by the teacher trainee group), the greater the likelihood that he or she will experience adverse effects. This contrasts sharply with the promotional statements promulgated widely by the SIMS, IMS, WPEC,[7] and related TM organizations that TM is a simple, innocuous procedure.

Two hypotheses, alone or in combination, may be advanced to explain these data. The first is that the practice of meditation makes a person more aware of his or her problems and/or more willing to report them. A comparison of the two groups of naive meditators from the SIMS and the teacher trainee samples, however, does not support this hypothesis. Although both groups had been meditating for approximately the same length of time, the SIMS group reported that only *one* adverse effect had increased by 51% or more, whereas the trainee group reported that *five* adverse effects had increased by this percentage. This finding suggests that differences between people in their commitment to TM as a way of life may be a more critical variable. More of the naive meditators who had decided to become teachers of TM reported becoming depressed, frustrated, impulsive, and/or as experiencing greater physical and mental tension and suspiciousness since starting TM than did the naive meditators in the SIMS random sample. Of considerable interest is the finding that this trend was magnified the longer that individuals practiced TM. The experienced meditators in both samples reported considerably more adverse effects than the dropouts or naive meditators in either sample.

The second hypothesis is that the adverse effects reported are a manifestation of "unstressing," a term used by the SIMS organization to describe an initial, transient process whereby the problem areas in one's life are solved or "normalized." This could, presumably, include experiencing all the adverse effects listed in Table 1, and perhaps others. If the adverse effects we found were due to unstressing, however, it would

[6]Since this paper was written, similar data were analyzed for individuals who had been meditating for between 6 and 12 months in both the SIMS and teacher trainee groups. The SIMS sample ($N = 92$) reported increased antisocial behavior (8.7%), anxiety (7.6%), and decreased restfulness of sleep (6.5%). The teacher trainee sample ($N = 152$) reported increased anxiety (5.9%) and depression (5.3%).

[7]WPEC is the acronym for World Plan Executive Council.

seem reasonable to expect that those who had practiced TM for 18 months or more would experience fewer problems in their lives and therefore less unstressing than naive meditators. Our results were the exact opposite. The experienced meditators (and not the naive ones) reported the most adverse effects.

It could be argued, however, that the longer an individual practices TM the more willing he or she becomes to allow problems to surface and that this could account for the greater number of adverse effects reported by experienced meditators. Should this be the case, one might legitimately question how long it takes before unstressing results in the normalization of the problem areas in one's life. In an attempt to follow up on this question, we reanalyzed the responses of individuals in our SIMS and teacher trainee samples that had been practicing TM for 3 years or more (average, 46.7 months). Table 2 shows that these very long-term meditators continued to report the same type of adverse effects. Consistent with differences previously noted between the SIMS and teacher trainee groups, the seasoned meditators in the trainee group reported that all 12 of the symptoms listed had increased in severity, where the SIMS group identified only 7 as becoming more of a problem since they started TM. Also, in every case but one (physical and mental tension), a greater percentage of the seasoned trainees reported a worsening of symptoms than did the seasoned SIMS group. Accordingly, we may conclude from these data that if adverse effects are due to unstressing, unstressing may continue for at least four years and that adverse effects are more poignantly experienced by teacher trainees than by those less committed to the TM way of life. These data do not support the contention that unstressing (if unstressing accounts for our data) is an initial, transient process.

The number of subjects in each sample who contributed the data used in constructing Tables 1 and 2 was determined by tabulating the number of individuals in each of the subgroups that identified one or more adverse effects as having increased by at least 51% after starting TM. The results are shown in Table 3. As Table 3 shows, the percentage of TM practitioners (including dropouts) reporting one or more adverse effects included a sizable portion of the sample (range was 19.8–48.6%).

Two alternative hypotheses are suggested that may account for the consistent increase in adverse effects reported by long-term practitioners. The first is that the practice of meditation per se engenders adverse effects and/or exacerbates prior symptoms. A corollary is that the longer one practices TM the more exacerbated his symptoms become.

The occurrence of marked physiological and psychological changes which may adversely affect the individual when meditational or related techniques are attempted is not a new phenomenon. Benson (10) has cautioned that adverse effects may be expected in some people who practice his relatively new

Table 2. Percentage of Long-Term Meditators Reporting Adverse Effects[a]

Symptom	Percentage reporting adverse effects		
	SIMS (N = 34)	Teacher trainees (N = 77)	Both groups (N = 111)
Antisocial behavior	11.8	14.3	13.5
Anxiety	8.8	9.1	9.0
Confusion	—	9.1	7.2
Depression	5.9	9.1	8.1
Emotional stability[b]	—	5.2	4.5
Frustration	5.9	10.4	9.0
Physical and mental tension	8.8	7.8	8.1
Procrastination	—	9.1	7.2
Restlessness	5.9	10.4	9.0
Suspiciousness	—	7.8	6.3
Tolerance of others[b]	—	5.2	4.5
Withdrawal	5.9	7.8	7.2

[a]Only symptoms for which at least 5% of the subjects reported an adverse change of 51% or more are tabulated.
[b]A decrease of 51% or more for these items was reported.

Table 3. Percentage of Practitioners that Reported that One or More Adverse Effects Had Increased 51% or More Since Starting TM

Months of TM practice	SIMS random sample	Teacher trainees
Dropouts	19.8	—
3–6	35.3	37.7
18+	46.1	48.6

relaxation technique modeled after TM but lacking its mystical underpinnings. In a recent note (11), he warned that insulin and propranolol doses prescribed for diabetic and hypertensive practitioners, respectively, may have to be scaled down to avoid overdosing, presumably because of changes induced in the individual's physiology by the practice and the resulting increased sensitivity to drugs. Similarly, Carrington (12) and Glueck and Stroebel (13) have noted that psychiatric patients require careful monitoring to minimize and manage the occurrence of adverse effects. Practitioners of Kundalini yoga are warned that "the release of the serpent" may be extremely traumatic (14) and that they require continuous instruction by an experienced teacher if they are to benefit from this practice. Those interested in learning Autogenic Training, a technique that emphasizes offsetting stress and preventing illness by systematically training the body to achieve homeostasis, are carefully screened for a wide variety of medical and psychological conditions because the training has been shown empirically to be contraindicated for some people (15). Finally, biofeedback training may result in adverse effects. Wesch (16) reported recently that a thyroidectomized patient on replacement therapy being treated with thermal and EMG feedback for migraine headaches began showing recurrent signs of hyperthyroid symptomatology. Her dose of thyroxine had to be lowered to compensate for the effects of the feedback training on her general physiology. Although the reasons for such effects are poorly understood at present, their occurrence testifies to the powerful psychophysiological changes that may be induced, at least in some people, by meditational and related techniques.

The second hypothesis is that dropouts and those that continue the practice of TM may differ in some fundamental way(s) *prior* to learning TM. In the SIMS sample the dropouts reported significantly fewer symptoms as "problems" in the Physical and Behavioral Inventory before starting TM than did either the naive or experienced meditators (see Column 1, Fig. 1). Naive meditators also reported significantly fewer problems than the experienced meditators. However, since the experienced meditators were asked to recall problems that may have existed 2 years earlier (average time in TM for the experienced meditators was 22.7 months), an argument could be that they had poorer recall and therefore erred in claiming more problems than the other two groups. This argument may be valid for the experienced meditators. However, it cannot explain the significantly larger number of problems claimed by the naive meditators as compared with dropouts; the latter had meditated 7.4 months, on the average, before discontinuing the practice whereas the naive meditators had been meditating an average of only 4.2 months at the time of the survey. Dropouts had to recall events that occurred almost twice as long ago as did the naive meditators. Yet they claimed significantly fewer problems before starting TM. Thus, the hypothesis that recall errors accounted for the differences in the number of problems claimed by the different groups before they started TM is not supported. A more likely hypothesis is that fundamental differences existed between dropouts and those that continued the practice of TM. The latter appeared to have more problems before starting TM than the former.[8]

Further evidence of fundamental differences between dropouts and those that stayed in TM comes from an analysis of the Descriptive Personality List which measured the individual's self-concept. As mentioned earlier the Descriptive Personality List was also circulated to SRI subjects and survey respondents. Analysis of this test indicated that both the SRI subjects and the SIMS sample that dropped out of TM admitted to more negative traits (were realistically more self-critical?) than did those that stayed in TM.

[8]Our experience has suggested that among the naive meditators approximately 50% drop out before the end of the first year Thus, this group included both potential dropouts and potential experienced meditators. It would be interestng to determine whether those who eventually dropped out had fewer presenting problems than those who remained in TM long enough to fit our criterion of "experienced" meditators.

Within the SIMS sample the dropouts claimed significantly more negative traits than the naive or the experienced meditators. The difference between the SRI dropouts and those that continued in TM was of borderline significance ($p < .10$). Of considerable interest, however, is the finding that this difference was evident in the SRI group during baseline (i.e., pretraining) tests as well as during tests given 3 and 12 months after training. These findings support the supposition that the differences between the dropouts, naive and experienced SIMS meditators in the number of negative traits claimed also may have been evident before these groups had started meditating.

Irrespective of which of these hypotheses, if either, is correct, our data raise serious doubts about the innocuous nature of TM. In fact, they suggest that TM may be hazardous to the mental health of a sizable proportion of the people who take up TM.

The writer has formulated a tentative theory to explain the occurrence of adverse effects associated with TM. The theory suggests that there are two major interacting variables operating. The first is physical and the second is mental. The physical variable relates to the sitting posture assumed by the meditator and the loss of support (which may be experienced as frightening) that invariably occurs if the individual enters a sleep pattern during the meditational period (7,8,9). The person's head may fall forward and be snapped to the upright position forcefully or he may catch himself falling from his chair. Both of these events may be experienced as an acute anxiety episode and the associated physiological state may be adversely conditioned to the practice of TM, per se. Thus, the frequent (most likely, aperiodic) occurrence of this sequence of events over a period of months or years of practice could lead to meditation, per se, becoming the occasion for the arousal of emotional disturbance. Such disturbance could generalize to thoughts about meditation during nonmeditational periods of the day so that the person could experience an increase in his or her overall level of emotional upset—variously interpreted as increased anxiety, depression, confusion, etc.—since starting the practice of TM.

The mental variable relates to the possible release of repressed material during the meditation period, especially during the period when the individual hovers between light sleep and wakefulness. While the individual is thinking his mantra, other thoughts typically displace the mantra. Some of these thoughts may represent previously repressed material which are sufficiently disturbing to abruptly shift the level of arousal from a low level (i.e., from a level of relaxation and/or light sleep) to a high level (i.e., fully awake). If the individual returns to thinking his mantra when this occurs, a self-regulated desensitization of the disturbing thought(s) could occur. If, however, the emotional disturbance occasioned by the release of the previously repressed material is too great, or if he does not return to thinking the mantra but perseveres in thinking the aroused anxiety-provoking thoughts, he may experience a high level of emotional disturbance or even loss of control. Such loss of control by TM practitioners has been witnessed by neutral observers invited as guests to rounding sessions (17).

A curious question remains: Why do people who experience adverse effects continue the practice? At this stage, we can only speculate about the reasons. One may be that the benefits received outweigh the negative effects. However, it is difficult to imagine a benefit that would outweigh the pervasive anxiety and depression reported by some of the correspondents. Another reason may be that, like all well-learned habits, TM is difficult to extinguish. Many people have written that they continue meditating because they feel worse if they do not. Some have even compared meditation to a drug addiction and complain about feeling trapped—not wishing to continue but unable to stop.

Particularly curious is the desire of very long-term meditators who have experienced or are experiencing adverse effects to become teachers, that is, to pass on the practice to others. It may be that such individuals have, in fact, had a number of positive experiences and have been told that their current complaints will eventually disappear. The strong social reinforcement and encouragement offered by practitioners who do not experience adverse effects and the TM organizational representatives are undoubtedly difficult to set aside.

We hope that the data reported here will not discourage people from taking up TM or clinicians from using TM as an adjunct to traditional therapeutic interventions. It is clearly of benefit to many people. In our survey samples approximately 52–64% of the subjects who continued the practice did not list a single adverse effect as defined in our study (i.e., a change of 51% or more for the worse). Nevertheless, adverse effects do occur in a sizable percentage of those that take up the practice. Furthermore, the probability of occurrence of adverse effects is higher among psychiatric populations (10,12,13). Accordingly, clinicians that incorporate TM, and possibly other relaxation or meditational techniques into their practice, should be vigilant about the possible occurrence of adverse effects and be prepared to deal with them. Experience indicates that frequent, if not daily, monitoring of psychiatric patients trained to meditate is advisable (12,13).

A final word appears justified regarding SIMS promotional efforts. SIMS advertises that TM results in beneficial effects for anyone who takes up the practice and learns to perform it "correctly." Our data raise serious doubts about the validity of this position. It is hoped that SIMS will publicly recognize that problems may be engendered by meditation and so instruct potential initiates as well as offer guidelines to both the general public and the psychotherapeutic profession for their amelioration. Most needed in this field are reliable instruments and considerably more rigorous, well-controlled studies to determine who may profit from meditation and who may not.

References

1. French, A. T., Snid, A. C., and Ingalls, E. Transcendental Meditation, altered reality testing and behavioral change: A case report. *Journal of Nervous and Mental Diseases*, 1975, **161**, 55–58.
2. Lazarus, A. A. Psychiatric problems precipitated by Transcendental Meditation. *Psychological Reports*, 1976, **39**, 601–602.
3. Otis, L. The facts on Transcendental Meditation: Part III. If well-integrated but anxious, try TM. *Psychology Today*, 45–46 (April, 1974).
4. Bloomfield, H. H., Cain, M. P., Jaffee, D. T., and Kory, R. B. *TM: discovering inner energy and overcoming stress*. New York: Dell Publishing Co., 1975. (A favorable summary of many of the positive claims and research results.)
5. Wallace, R. K., Benson, H., and Wilson, A. F. A wakeful hypometabolic state. *American Journal of Physiology*, 1971, **221**, 795–799.
6. Hjelle, L. A. Transcendental Meditation and psychological health. *Perception and Motor Skills*, 1974, **39**, 623–628.
7. Otis, L. TM and Sleep. Paper presented at the American Psychological Association Convention, New Orleans, 1974.
8. Younger, J., Adriance, W., and Berger, R. J. Sleep during Transcendental Meditation. *Perception and Motor Skills*, 1975, **46**, 953–954.
9. Pagano, R. P., Rose, R. M., Stiver, R. M., and Warrenburg, S. Sleep during Transcendental Meditation. *Science*, 1976, **191**, 308–310.
10. Benson, H. *The relaxation response*. New York: William Morrow & Co., Inc., 1975.
11. Benson, H. Systemic hypertension and the relaxation response. *New England Journal of Medicine*, 1978, **296**, 1152–1155.
12. Carrington, P. *Freedom in meditation*. Garden City, New York: Anchor Press/Doubleday, 1977.
13. Glueck, B. C. and Stroebel, C. F. Biofeedback and meditation in the treatment of psychiatric illness. *Comprehensive Psychiatry*, 1975, **16**, 303–321.
14. Gopi Krisna. *Kundalini. The evolutionary energy in man*. Boulder Colorado: Shanbhala Publications, 1971.
15. Luthe, W. Autogenic Standard Therapy: Non-Indications, Contraindications and Relative Contraindications. Basic Training Course in Autogenic Therapy, Hospital St.-Jean-de-Dieu, Montreal, Canada, 1974. See also W. Luthe and J. H. Schultz. *Autogenic therapy*. Vol. II: Medical Appplications. New York: Grune & Stratton, 1969.
16. Wesch, J. E. Clinical Comments Section. *Newsletter of the Biofeedback Society*, 1977, **5**(3), July.
17. Benson, H., Personal communication.

18

PSYCHOLOGICAL ASSESSMENT OF
TRANSCENDENTAL MEDITATION

Joseph Bono, Jr.

The scientific investigation of the popular technique of Transcendental Meditation (TM) has generated equivocation about whether it has a unique effect. While Wallace and Benson (1972) in a study of the physiology of TM suggest that the physiological correlates of the meditative state are unlike other resting states such as sleep or hypnosis, especially in terms of changes in blood metabolism, Michaels, Huber, and McCann (1976) in a study of catecholamine secretion in practitioners of TM found that "meditation does not induce a unique metabolic state but is seen biochemically as a resting state" (p. 1242). Subsequent to his initial (1972) findings, Benson and Klipper (1975) asserts that TM merely promotes a "relaxation response" that can be easily achieved without TM. On the other hand, Glueck and Stroebel (1975) report that individuals with 6 months or more of TM practice show that "changes in the EEG patterns appear more consistently, with greater rapidity, and to greater degree . . . than in individuals using other types of meditation and in nonmeditating resting subjects" (p. 313). Such equivocation suggests the need for continued research to more clearly describe the process of TM and how its practitioners are different from other people.

Other less ambiguous research findings suggest that TM promotes mental health (Orme-Johnson *et al.*, 1974; Seeman, Nidich, and Banta, 1972). Truly a plethora of studies has emerged to suggest that TM has manifold positive effects on the personality (Orme-Johnson, Domash, & Farrow, 1974; Shaffi *et al.*, 1974; LeDain, Campbell, Stein, Moore, Lehman & Bertrand, 1974). However, a critical review of some of the studies reveals that the TM program's push for publications supporting their claims (via the Maharishi International University Press) has resulted, at times, in an uncritical interpretation of the results. Some of the research has been used prematurely to promote TM, not having been passed by an editorial review board, but only having been submitted for publication. Ornstein (1976) views this trend as "ideologically based research, done almost exclusively by believers, proving that Transcendental Meditation is Good for You" (p. 64).

The present study is concerned with clarifying what TM is and does through psychological assessment of individuals practicing TM. This multidimensional psychological study integrates learning, perceptual, personality, and psychophysiological variables, including evaluation of personality adjustment and differentiation, autonomic learning aptitude, and physiologic response patterns during the TM state. Personality adjustment was assessed using a measure of self-regard, an adjective Q-set with a specified 7-point distribution ($N = 70$) with 10 adjectives in each category (Block, 1961). Within this measure, self-concept is regarded as the *relationship* between one's real and ideal self, with a higher correlation indicating higher self-regard. Personality differentiation was accomplished with the rod and frame test (Witkin, Lewis, Hertzman, Machover, Meiser, Wapner, 1974), and with a test of autokinesis (Voth & Mayman, 1963; Cancro & Voth, 1969). Autonomic or "limbic" learning aptitude (LLA) was assessed in accordance with the procedures defined by Ax and Bamford (1968), and Ax, Bamford, Beckett, Fretz, and Gottlieb (1970). In both the test of autonomic learning aptitude and during the experimental meditation session heart rate, peripheral vascular response, skin conductance, and spontaneous electrodermal responses were the physiologic variables of interest.

The rationale for selecting these particular variables derives from an interest in assessing core psychological phenomenon, involving personality, perception, learning, and psychophysiology. Inasmuch as the purported benefits of TM effect the whole person in multifaceted ways, this article attempts to be sensitive to the major psychological systems within the person. Self-concept was selected as a measure of adjustment as it permits a study of the phenomenology of TM practitioners. The rod and frame and autokinesis tests were selected to help differentiate the TM personality because they reliably determine scientifically validated bipolar personality dimensions. Their respective field dependence/independence and ego closeness/distance continuums integrate personality characteristics with perceptual/cognitive style. The need to further evaluate psychophysiological processes during TM stems from earlier research; however, an assessment of the aptitude for autonomic self-regulation was made as a natural extension of the interest in the psychophysiology of TM practitioners. A reasonable inference from the description of the TM process (i.e., turning one's attention inward and attuning oneself to subjective nuance) is that it would facilitate or improve an aptitude for consciously controlled autonomic behavior. The test of limbic learning aptitude (LLA) is essentially an operant conditioning paradigm.

Isolation of the TM condition was attempted with a pre-/posttreatment design, using a 6-month control period in both a meditating and nonmeditating control group. However, the subjective nature of the TM state remained an uncontrolled problem leading to a rejection of any causal relation in the apparent treatment effect. To illustrate, ordinary sleep may well be a confounding variable during TM, even to the extent that the sleeping meditator may feel as if he were meditating as usual. Furthermore, attendance at advanced lectures and residence courses, and frequency of TM remained uncontrolled for variables that may have influenced the data. And so at best, the appreciable differences from the control group or over time are regarded as multidetermined in association with the entire TM program.

Method

Subjects

It was necessary to enlist the support of the International Center for Scientific Research, Maharishi International University, in order to solicit subjects from introductory lectures at local TM centers. Twenty-nine prospective TM subjects were tested before meditation instruction. By the end of the 6-month control period, 13 of the 29 were eliminated from the study. Eight of the 13 attrition subjects never learned TM; 2 had changed residences and left no forwarding address; 2 were too busy to schedule the last testing session; and 1 subject discontinued meditation within several weeks of beginning. The remaining 16 subjects consisted of a rather heterogeneous group of 6 men and 10 women with a mean age of 30.18, who reported that they had been regular and consistent in their meditations for the 6-month control period. This group of 16 subjects was the first experimental group. A more homogeneous group of control subjects was selected from volunteer psychology students at the University of Detroit, consisting of 10 men and 10 women with a mean age of 22.35. In addition, a group of 5-year meditators was included in the study. This second experimental group consisted of 7 men and 2 women with a mean age of 22.44.

Apparatus

Part of the testing was done in the absence of a structured visual surround, necessitating a light-tight cubicle. The experimental room in the University of Detroit Psychophysiology Laboratory served this purpose. A Grass Model 7 polygraph with accouterments was used for the recording of the physiological variables in determining limbic learning aptitude. For determining space orientation a luminescent rod and frame (24 in.^{2}) on independent axes was necessary. A small beam of light (.028 mm diameter) was needed to measure autokinesis, along with paper and pencil (18 × 24 in.).

Procedure

The total testing sequence consisted of 2 full batteries and 1 abbreviated battery. (1) At the outset the control group and first experimental group were given a full battery of tests. (2) After the 6-month control period, during which time the first experimental group began practicing TM, the control group, first, and second experimental groups were given another full battery. (3) Upon completion of the second full battery, the control group was asked to sit quietly with their eyes closed while both experimental groups were asked to meditate for 20 minutes—all physiologic variables were recorded at this time. (4) Immediately following the experimental meditation (or eyes-closed session in the control group), all subjects were given an abbreviated battery, consisting of the rod and frame and autokinesis tests. By giving subjects the perceptual tests before and after the control meditation session, it was possible to detect any immediate effects on those scales.

The procedure to determine space orientation or field dependence involved eight trials with four-position arrangements of the rod and frame presented twice. The four-position arrangements always entailed a tilt of 28 degress on both the rod *and* the frame; however, they were not always tilted in the same direction. On each trial the subject was asked to turn the rod until it seemed in the vertical upright position. The specifications of this procedure were in accordance with those developed by Witkin, Lewis, Hertzman, Machover, Meiser, and Wapner (1974).

Before measurement of the autokinetic effect could be made, subjects sat in total darkness for 20 minutes. After 20 minutes of dark adapting, they were asked to trace with a pencil on a piece of paper the direction and extent of perceived movement of light. This recording procedure was in accordance with those of Voth and Mayman (1963), and Cancro and Voth (1969).

Three physiologic variables (heart rate, peripheral vascular response, and skin conductance) were of interest in assessing limbic learning aptitude. These variables were selected on the basis of their being significantly associated with this aptitude (A. F. Ax, personal communication). During the recording of these variables, three experimental conditions were introduced, and comparisons were made from one condition to another. The three conditions were: (1) resting, (2) raising (trying to consciously arouse the autonomic nervous system, ANS), and (3) lowering (trying to relax the ANS). The parameter of interest in the peripheral vascular response was the average level of blood flow. A larger finger pulse was expected during the lowering session when subjects strived for greater sympathetic enervation, effecting peripheral vasodilation. The method of measuring the peripheral vascular response was the back-scattered technique of optical plethysmography with the transducer attached to the distal phalange of the index finger of the right hand. The relevant phasic and tonic skin conductance parameters were the number of spontaneous electrodermal responses (EDR) and the amount of microhms per square centimeter. The microhm is a measure of conductance, with its reciprocal being a microhm. The electrodermal parameters were expected to be less during the lowering trials. The electrodes used for the recording of skin conductance were made of nonpolarized silver-silver chloride 4 or 9 mm in diameter, filled with Redux electrode paste, and attached to the volar surface of the distal phlange of the third and fourth fingers of the left hand. Electrodes used to record heart rate were attached to the legs and right arm with the ground electrode on the right leg. Heart rate was expected to increase during the raising sessions.

Autonomic learning aptitude was determined according to an operant conditioning paradigm. Subjects were instructed to raise their heart rate for one minute when a light on the right side of a meter went on. This light was labeled "R" for raise. Then when the light on the left side of the meter labeled "L" for lower was lit, subjects attempted to lower their heart rate. They were told how others have managed to control their heart rate by thinking of scenes of situations that actually produce change in heart rate, such as dying scenes or running a race. The total testing procedure consisted of five 1-minute trials of lowering HR and five 1-minute trials of raising HR randomly ordered with 1-minute rest periods interspersed between each trial.

Aside from the Q-sort, the three other tests were administered in random order. Two of the three randomly ordered tests involved a dark-adapted room, requiring the dark-adapted block of testing to be randomly interspersed from subject to subject with the LLA test. Furthermore, in the dark-adapted block the test of autokinesis and space orientation were given in random order. Any sequence effect should have been eliminated by random presentation of the tests.

Results

Cognitive Style

The observed data from the rod and frame test suggests meditators to be less field-dependent than controls. Although the TM group was slightly less field-dependent than control subjects before instruction in TM, the difference was not significant. After the 6-month control period, however, the meditation group made a significant shift toward field independence [t (15) = 1.86, $p < .05$]; and although the control group made a shift in the same direction, the difference was not significant [t (19) = 1.61, $p < .12$]. While both groups moved in the predicted direction, the difference between groups was not significant. The long-term meditation group was significantly less field-dependent than controls [t (22) = 2.43, $p < .02$], but not different from 6-month meditators. Meditators did not show any immediate change in their rod and frame test performance following a 20-minute control meditation; however, control subjects made a significant shift toward field independence after a 20-minute eyes-closed rest period [t (19) = 2.87, $p < .01$].

As reported in the literature (Voth & Mayman, 1963; Cancro & Voth, 1969) the log of the length of the autokinetic line was used for statistical purposes. Control subjects demonstrated greater autokinetic effect than meditators when observed before and after the 6-month control period. Although meditators showed a slight shift toward greater perceived autokinesis after the two control periods, as predicted, while control subjects moved slightly in the opposite direction, no significant differences were found. Five-year meditators were not found to be appreciably different from control subjects in reported autokinetic effect; however, the difference between long- and short-term meditators approached significance [t (20) = 1.38, $p < .10$], with long-term meditators perceiving more autokinesis.

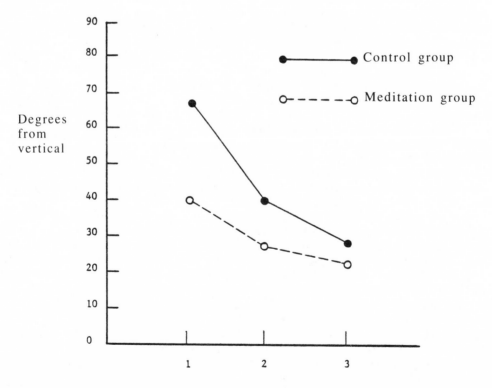

Fig. 1. The meditation group made a significant shift ($p < 0.05$) toward field independence after 6 months of TM practice. However, control subjects moved significantly ($p < 0.01$) toward field independence after merely sitting quietly with eyes closed for 20 minutes. (1) Before 6-month control period; (2) after 6-month control period; (3) after experimental meditation.

Table 1. Summary of Means and Standard Deviations

Variables	Test A		Control period	Test B		Control meditation	Test C	
	X	SD		X	SD		X	SD
Field dependence								
Experimental (E)	39.19	54.3	6 mo.	25.53	26.96	20 min.	24.25	19.89
Control (C)	54.9	65.3	6 mo.	37.15	31.59	20 min.	28.8	27.62
Autokinesis								
E	0.66	1.48	6 mo.	0.55	1.45	20 min.	0.16	1.34
C	1.22	0.43	6 mo.	0.78	1.32	20 min.	0.75	1.33
Self-concept								
E	0.43	0.26	6 mo.	0.71	0.12	—	—	—
C	0.61	0.21	6 mo.	0.67	0.20	—	—	—
Heart rate[a]								
E	3.82	2.23	6 mo.	2.51	1.74	—	—	—
C	3.15	2.20	6 mo.	2.03	2.27	—	—	—
Skin conductance[b]								
E	5.11	14.9	6 mo.	2.91	8.20	—	—	—
C	-1.75	43.0	6 mo.	1.03	5.39	—	—	—
Spontaneous EDR								
E	2.18	8.23	6 mo.	0.23	0.71	—	—	—
C	0.74	1.62	6 mo.	0.30	0.59	—	—	—
Peripheral vascular response[c]								
E	0.03	0.15	6 mo.	0.003	0.12	—	—	—
C	0.05	0.09	6 mo.	-0.01	0.11	—	—	—

[a]Change in beats/minute, raising–lowering trials.

[b]Change in micromhos/square centimeer, raising–lowering trials.

[c]Percentage greater finger pulse during lowering trials.

Self-Concept

Assessment of self-concept reveals a dramatic increase in self-regard in those subjects practicing Transcendental Meditation for 6 months. Prior to TM instruction, experimental subjects had significantly lower real/ideal self correlations than control subjects [t (34) = 2.23, $p < .03$]. Following the 6-month control meditation period, meditators had significantly raised their mean self-concept from $r = .44$ to $r = .71$ [t (15) = 5.02, $p < .0001$], while control subjects moved from $r = 0.61$ to $r = 0.67$ [t (19) = 2.18, $p < .04$]. Although short-term meditators' scores were higher than those of control subjects, there was no significant difference between scores after the 6-month control period. However, the difference in magnitude of increase in self-regard was significantly greater for meditators than for controls [t (34) = 3.61, $p < .001$]. Although self/ideal correlations in long-term meditators were higher than in control subjects, there was no meaningful difference between those groups or between long- and short-term meditators.

Inasmuch as the short-term meditation group meaningfully increased their self-regard, further analysis of the data shows that their perception of their real self changed more than their ideal. The mean correlation between meditators' real self-concept before and after the 6-month control period was $r = .65$, whereas the mean correlation of their ideal self-concept before and after TM was $r = .84$. The difference between the mean ideal/ideal and real/real self correlations before and after was found to be significant [t (15) = 3.96, $p < .01$].

Psychological Assessment of TM

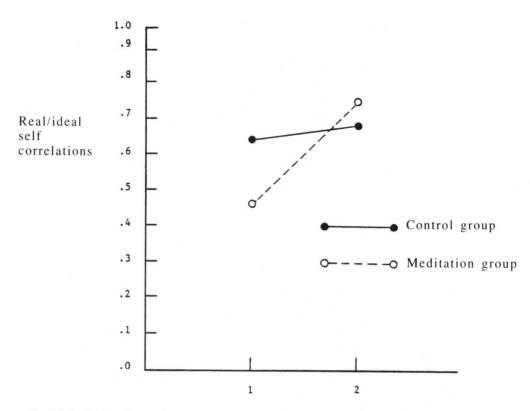

Fig. 2. Before TM instruction experimental subjects had significantly ($p < 0.03$) lower real/ideal self correlations than controls. Following 6 months of TM, meditators dramatically increased their self-concept ($p < 0.001$). Although both groups increased in self-regard after the 6-month control period, the TM group made a significantly larger increase ($p < 0.001$). (1) Before 6-month control period; (2) after 6-month control period.

Autonomic Learning Aptitude

Analysis of heart rate data suggests a slight relationship between Transcendental Meditation and aptitude for consciously meditated operant autonomic conditioning; however, statistics are not appreciable. Long-term meditators were slightly more effective than control subjects in changing their heart rate [t (9) = 1.53, $p < .10$], but not significantly different than short-term meditators. And while the short-term meditation group was slightly better than the control group in modifying heart rate, the difference was not statistically significant.

The change in skin conductance in micromhos per square centimeter was slightly greater in the control group before the 6-month control period, however, not statistically significant. After the 6-month control period, meditators showed more change than control subjects in skin conductance, but again there was no appreciable difference. There were no noticeable differences found between or within groups before and after the 6-month control period. Long-term meditators were more effective than short-term meditators in altering skin conductance, but not beyond chance expectation. Long-term meditators were, however, significantly better than control subjects in changing absolute skin conductance [t (11) = 1.88, $p < .05$].

Before the 6-month control period slightly, but not significantly, more phasic electrodermal responses were observed in the meditation group. After the 6-month control period there were no appreciable differences found between or within groups in ability to modify spontaneous EDR's. When considering long-term meditators, however, there is a suggested relationship between autonomic learning aptitude and Transcendental Meditation. Five-year meditators were significantly better than control subjects [t (8) = 2.07, $p < .01$] and 6-month meditators [t (8) = 3.15, $p < .01$] in ability to control phasic EDR's.

Psychology of Meditation

Reduction of heart rate during TM was greater than the reduction resulting from sitting quietly with eyes closed, but the difference was not beyond change expectancy between the control group and short- or long-term meditators.

Six-month meditators showed a slightly, but not significantly, greater reduction in skin conductance during TM, compared to control subjects sitting with eyes closed [t (33) = 1.4, $p < .10$]. Skin conductance in 5-year meditators decreased more during TM than in short-term meditators or control subjects, but the differences were not significant.

Short-term meditators show somewhat but not significantly fewer electrodermal responses during meditation when compared to the control group sitting with eyes closed. However, the 5-year meditation group demonstrated a significant attenuation of spontaneous EDR's during meditation when compared to control subjects [t (27) = 4.74, $p < .0001$] and 6-month meditators [t (23) = 4.03, $p < .001$].

No meaningful differences were found between or within groups in changes in the peripheral vascular response from baseline to meditation conditions.

Discussion

As Pelletier (1974) found in people practicing TM, increased field independence can be attributed to the effect of regular meditation. It seems reasonable to conclude that a generalized result of the regular inward deployment of attention required by the practice of TM is an increased sensitivity to subjective nuances. When confronted with an ambiguous, novel, and misleading problem, the field articulate/independent perceptual style leads to a more accurate resolution of the problem partly, one can assume, as a function of this sensitivity to and trust in one's subjective experience. Although there seems to be a clear relationship between TM practice and the field-independent cognitive style, merely sitting quietly with eyes closed can produce a shift toward greater field independence. Relaxation and calmness seem to be crucial factors involved in the fluctuation of this perceptual style, along with perhaps a practice effect. And while meditation is a sufficient cause of these quieting responses, it is not a necessary one.

Unlike Pelletier's (1974) findings, this group of both long- and short-term meditators did not demonstrate a relationship between TM and the ego/closeness, distance personality dimension. The discrepancy could possibly be accounted for by the differences in technique used to measure autokinesis. While Pelletier's subjects used a 2-foot tabular apparatus 6 inches in diameter, the method used in our lab was according to the specification of Cancro and Voth (1969), and consisted of a light-tight cubicle with a light source .028 inch diameter placed 9 feet from the subject. Also, while Pelletier considers the amount of autokinetic effect as a measure of field independence, Cancro and Voth (1969) found that, "despite the similarity in personality trait description we were unable to demonstrate any relationship—linear or curvilinear—between differentiation (i.e. field dependence) and autokinesis" (p. 102). Statistically insignificant intercorrelations were found in this study between autokinesis and field dependence in control subjects and meditators, and confirm the findings of Cancro and Voth that no demonstrable relationship exists between these two bipolar personality dimensions. Thus, while it is reasonable to infer that increased field independence goes with the TM program, the extent of ego-distance/closeness is a factor independent of both.

The most dramatic result observed in this study is the change in self-concept. The significantly lower scores in the meditation group before TM instructions suggest greater dissatisfaction with self, neuroticism, and readiness for change. This low self-esteem condition before meditation is similar to those individuals seeking psychotherapy and other forms of self-help. The impetus to engage in systematic self-improvement may well stem from these dark feelings about oneself. Given a low level of self-esteem, the TM program appears to be a clearly demonstrable therapeutic agent. However, the observed increase in self-regard may well be explained in terms of an increased sense of self-discipline and mastery competence. As the individual achieves integration of systematic self-improvement in his daily routine, he begins to feel more positively about himself with a concomitant sense of increased self-control and responsibility. However, one may assume that other forms of disciplined self improvement may work as well to improve self-concept.

The findings that the TM subjects real self-concept changed more than their ideal suggests that they may have actually reduced the maladaptive elements within themselves that caused them to perceive such a large discrepancy between their real and ideal selves before learning TM. Further research into the relationship between meditation and self-concept may well help to clarify the particular personality attributes which are subject to change with the practice of meditation. Such a project will be subsequently undertaken by this investigator.

The suggested sense of increased self-control is also evidenced in the results of the operant autonomic conditioning paradigm. Although the hypothesis has only modest support, the meditation groups tended to be consistently across parameters slightly better at operant autonomic learning. Although it seems fair to conclude that 6 months of TM practice does not appreciably improve autonomic learning aptitude, long-range practice is definitely associated with this aptitude, if only in terms of electrodermal activity.

While the TM groups were slightly more effective in reducing physiological arousal than increasing it, control subjects were slightly better at increasing electrodermal activity above baseline. On the basis of this suggested finding, there appears to be a lowered range of physiological arousal potential in meditators, suggesting a relationship between TM practice and parasympathetic dominance. One may therefore postulate greater facilitation of excitatory potentials in the parasympathetic nervous system with more inhibitory potentials in the sympathetic branch in meditators. The suggested parasympathetic dominance in meditators is interpreted as a learned phenomena resulting from the systematic repetition of the relaxation response. During acquisition, the mantra of conditioned stimulus becomes associated with the relaxation response. The pleasurable subjective experience associated with deep relaxation may serve to reinforce the habit strength of that conditioned response. Successive reinforcements over months or years of TM practice heightens the reaction potentiality of that response, and through generalization the response becomes more or less dominant. This seems to support the Orme-Johnson (1971) hypothesis of greater autonomic stability in people who practice TM.

As autonomic stability is taken to refer to a general reduction in autonomic arousal potential, the maintenance of physiological equilibrium is enhanced. But inasmuch as the results only modestly suggest greater reduction in physiological arousal during TM when compared to just sitting quietly with eyes closed (except in the case of long-term meditators who emit significantly fewer spontaneous EDR's), the hypothesis of a fourth major state of consciousness involving a unique "wakeful physiologic hypometabolism" (Wallace, Benson, & Wilson, 1971) remains uncertain. The postulate of increased parasympathetic dominance resulting from TM practice merely implies improved physiological homeostasis, perhaps the chief physiological advantage in meditators, but not necessarily a unique function of TM.

References

Ax, A. F., and Bamford, J. L. Validation of a Psychophysiological Test of Aptitude for Learning Social Motives. *Psychophysiology*, 1968, **5**, 316–332.

Ax, A. F., Bamford, J. L., Beckett, P. G. S., Fretz, N. P., and Gottlieb, J. S. Autonomic Conditioning in Chronic Schizophrenia. *Journal of Abnormal Psychology*, 1970, **76**, 140–154.

Benson, H., and Klipper, M. Z. *The Relaxation Response*. New York: Avon Books, 1975.

Block, J. *The Q-Sort Method in Personality Assessment and Psychiatric Research*. Springfield, Illinois: Charles C. Thomas, 1961.

Cancro, R., and Voth, H. Autokinesis and Psychological Differentiation. *Perception and Motor Skills*, 1969, **28**, 99–103.

Glueck, B. C., and Stroebel, C. F. Biofeedback and Meditation in the Treatment of Psychiatric Illness. *Comprehensive Psychiatry*, 1975, **11**, 303–321.

LeDain, G., Campbell, I. L., Stein, J. P., Moore, J. J., Lehman, H. E., and Bertrand, M. A. A Report of the Commission of Inquiry into the Non-Medical Use of Drugs. In D. W. Orme-Johnson, L. H. Domash, & J. T. Farrow (Eds.), *Scientific research on transcendental meditation: collected papers*, Vol. 1, 34–39, Los Angeles, California: MIU Press, 1974.

Michaels, R. R., Huber, M. J., and McCann, D. S. Evaluation of Transcendental Meditation as a Method of Reducing Stress. *Science*, 1976, **192**, 1242–1244.

Orme-Johnson, D. W., Domash, L. H., and Farrow, J. T., (Eds.) *Scientific research on transcendental meditation: collected papers*, Vol. 1. Los Angeles, California: MIU Press, 1974.

Ornstein, R. E. *The mind field*. New York: Viking Press, 1976.

Pelletier, K. R. Influence of Transcendental Meditation Upon Autokinetic Perception. *Perceptual and Motor Skills*, 1974, **39**, 1031–1034.

Seeman, W., Nichich, S., and Banta, T. The Influence of Transcendental Meditation on a Measure of Self-Actualization. *Journal of Counseling Psychology*, 1972, **19**, 184–187.

Schaffi, M., Lavely, R., and Jaffee, R. Meditation and Marijuana. *American Journal of Psychiatry*, 1974, **131**, 60–63.

Voth, H., & Mayman, M. A dimension of Personality Organization. *Archives of General Psychiatry*, 1963, **8**, 36–41.

Wallace, R. K., Benson, H., and Wilson, A. F. A Wakeful Hypometabolic Physiologic State. *American Journal of Physiology*, 1971, **221**, 795–799.

Witkin, H. A., Lewis, H. B., Hertzman, M., Machover, K., Meiser, P., Bretnal, and Wapner, S. *Personality through perception.* New York: Harper & Row, 1974.

C. Meditation as Altered States of Consciousness

In this section we are going to look primarily at two different issues. In the first part we are going to look at studies which involve attentional training issues (C1) and the training of consciousness. In the second part we are going to look at studies which deal with experiences that individuals have during meditation itself (C2).

C1. Attentional/Perceptual Issues

There is an old Zen saying that if one wants to understand the true meaning of Zen, one needs only to follow the prescription of the following three words: *attention, attention, attention*. There are two well-designed studies in this section which relate to the issues of attention and perception. The first article by Pelletier (19) is a clear, well-designed study that shows that over a course of 3 months, meditators become more field-independent than a control group which just sits. The correlations and interpretations between this increased perceptual sensitivity and personality style is still open to much interpretation and debate. However, there can be little debate that, in fact, there is an increased perceptual acuity following meditation. The second study by Davidson, Goleman, and Schwartz (20), uses the Tellegan absorption scale and shows that attentional absorption increases in direct proportion to the length of meditative practicing experience.

For discussion of the importance of the issue of attention and a summary of recent findings, see Article 6 by Shapiro and Giber. The accompanying table summarizes other related studies on perception and attention.

The third article in this section, by Brown and Engler (21), is a Rorschach study of the stages of mindfulness meditation—a quite innovative and creative study. Rorschach protocols were given to individuals who were rated as either a beginners' group, a samadhi group, an advanced insight group, and a masters' group. Individuals in this study were meditators who had attended a 3-month meditation retreat, an advanced study of meditation, or a South Asian study. Although only a preliminary study, it illustrates the importance of utilizing experienced long-term meditators. As such, it provides a counterpoint to many of the articles in this collection, whose data is based upon individuals who have engaged in comparatively short practice of meditation.

Table 5. Studies on Attention and Perception

Investigator(s)	Clinical Problem	Independent Variable: S's (N, age, sex, prior experience)	Type and Length of Treatment/Training	Frequency of Therapist (T) Contact	Dependent Variable: Subjective Effects	Behavioral, Physiological, Overt, Concurrent Data	Type of Design, Quality of Controls, Methodological Problems
Van Nuys 1973	Meditation attention and hypnotic susceptibility	N=47 males, prior experience not reported	Task: Concentration on doorstep and flame breath meditation. Session One: Individual tests of 15 min focused attention on each object. Session Two: Same	Not reported	Tests given post-task. Session One: Embedded Figures Test. Session Two: Stroop Color Word Test. A's Experience Inquiry Harvard Scale of Hypnotic Susceptibility Field Depth of Hypnosis Test. Found correlation between 2 measures of hypnotic susceptibility and number of intrusions reported during meditation	Behavioral: Self-report of intrusions of thought during attention task	Within subject. S's served as own controls
Pelletier 1974	Autokinetic perception ("perceptual style")	N=40 avg age 24.7 yrs. 20 male 20 female. Group One Meditators, volunteers from intro TM meeting. Group Two Sitting controls	Group One Standard TM instruction. 3 mos. practice. Group Two Instructed to sit quietly 20 min morning (x 3 mos)	Not reported	Pre and post tests of autokinetic effect shifted towards field indep. On Rod and Frame Test (Cancro & Voch, Witkin et al.) meditators showed increased accuracy. On Embedded Figures Test (Gardner et al.) meditators showed shorter latency time	None reported	Half of S's in each group not pretested to control for possible interaction effects of perceptual measures and meditation
Shaw and Kolb 1977	Simple reaction time	Group One N=9 meditators, one mo or more experience. Group Two N=9 non-meditators	1) Learning trials 2) 100 trials with reaction device 3) Rest or meditation (20 min) 4) 100 more trials	Not reported	Report states: "Meditators brighter in mood and more responsive in conversation after meditating"	Behavioral: Meditators had shorter reaction than non-meditators in first test. After resting, meditators improved, non-meditators were slower in reacting	Test of statistical significance not reported. Matching of groups not reported.
Brown, Stuart & Blodgett 1974	1) 2 point threshold determination of skin sensitivity 2) visual brightness discrimination 3) simple reaction time 4) complex reaction time	Group One N=11, 18-22 yrs. female meditators with experience from few weeks to few mos. Group Two N=11, 18-22 yrs. female non-meditating controls	1) Pre-state performance measurement 2) Pre-state resting (eyes open) 3 min. 3) Group One Transcendental Meditation (15 min.) Group Two resting, eyes closed (15 min.) 4) Post-state resting (eyes open) Note: meditators took 3 min. avg to open eyes 5) Post-state performance measures	Not reported	Not reported	Behavioral: Tests given pre and post meditation or sitting for 3 meditators meeting physiological criteria performance improved on all measures. One control also met meditative criteria. Performance of all controls worsened. Physiological: Note heart and respiration rates, presence of frontal EEG alpha and kappa rhythms used to define 'meditation state' - only 3 S's met this criteria	Small N. short meditation time used (15 min.) and only 1 trial reported. Experimenter anecdotes suggest meditators may have been sleeping
Graham 1975	Frequency and amplitude discrimination of auditory threshold	Study Group N=8 experience with TM not reported	Condition One 20 minutes meditation. Condition Two 20 minutes rest with 3 to 10 days interval between conditions	Not reported	Not reported	Behavioral: Pre and post tests showed greater percentage improvement after meditating (+25.4%) than after reading (−3.2%) in auditory discrimination and +37.0% and −15.1% respectively for frequency discrimination. Meditators seem to evidence lower perceptual thresholds after practice.	S's divided into 2 groups. AB, BA design. Study does not report S's selection procedures.
Pirot 1973	Perceptual auditory discrimination of tones	N=32, 8 in each cell; prior experience not stated	Stimuli: 40 pairs of tones; one 2,000 milliseconds and one 2,225 milliseconds in length (1,000 Hz 30 dB). S's had to discriminate longest tone after TM or relaxation	Not reported	Not reported	Behavioral: Meditators performed better post-meditation than relaxation, despite in which order they had meditated. Physiological: GSR, EMG, finger pulse volume and EKG measures to be reported.	Four groups with all possible orders of meditation and relaxation represented. Repeated measured and one-way between groups analysis performed.
Davidson, Goleman & Schwartz 1976	Differences in attentional absorption and trait anxiety	N=58 mean age 20.81 yrs. (S.D. 2.77). 36 male 23 female.	Meditation practice ranged from TM to Zen breath meditation. Group One (N=11) Controls expressing interest in meditation. Group Two (N=14) Beginners: one month's meditation exp. or less. Group Three (N=18) Regular practice of meditation for 1-24 months. Group Four (N=15) Long-term meditators (greater than 24 month's exp.)	Tests given as "take home" among battery of other personality and attitude questionnaires.	S's tested on Shor Personal Experience Questionnaire (PEQ), Tellegen Absorption Scale (TAS), and Spielberger State Trait Anxiety Inventory (STAI). Reliable increment in PEQ and TAS (e.g. increase in capacity to attend) and reliable decrement in STAI (train anxiety) observed across groups from controls through long-term meditators.	None reported	Cross-sectional design.

19

INFLUENCE OF TRANSCENDENTAL MEDITATION UPON AUTOKINETIC PERCEPTION

Kenneth R. Pelletier

Summary.—Unpaid, normal volunteers (20 men and 20 women) were administered the autokinetic test, the embedded-figures test (EFT), and the rod-and-frame test (RFT) prior to meditation instruction. After 3 mo. of instruction in Transcendental Meditation, Ss were retested and demonstrated increased ego distance and field independence on all of the above tests. These variations in an autonomic, enduring response clarify several issues in research on perceptual style and meditation.

A basic assumption inherent in research on perceptual style is that the form and quality of deployment of attention will be manifested in particular perceptual styles or enduring response-dispositions. Out of this assumption arose the construct of ego closeness versus ego distance (Voth, 1962). Ego-close individuals tend to invest attention in the immediate external environment and are receptive to external stimuli, while ego-distant Ss tend to be detached from the external environment and are more aware of internal stimuli than external stimuli. Several personality variables have been demonstrated to be associated with these two dimensions such as: (1) ego close with projection and repression (Voth, Cancro, & Kissen, 1968) and field dependence (Witkin, Dyk, Faterson, Goodenough, & Karp, 1962); and (2) ego distant with need for solitude (Cancro, Voth, & Voth, 1968), and field independence (Witkin, *et al.*, 1962). These systematic differences fall upon two ends of a continuum and any significant change in deployment of attention from external toward internal stimuli should be exhibited by a concomitant shift in manifest perceptual style. This study was designed to test for such a shift from ego-close to ego-distant or field-dependent to field-independent in a group of meditation students since the explicit goal of all meditative systems is for the individual to gain more reliance upon internal stimuli and to increase his focus of attention upon a given task.

Transcendental Meditation is defined as "turning the attention inwards towards the subtler state and arrives at the source of the thought" (Mahesh Yogi, 1969). Such a clear mandate of turning the attention inward would be expected to be indicated according to indices of perceptual style. If such a shift was observed, it would clarify several issues in research on perceptual style and meditation.

METHOD

Subjects

Ss were 40 unpaid, normal volunteers selected from a group of people in attendance at an introductory lecture concerning Transcendental Meditation. There were 20 men and 20 women with a mean age of 24.7 yr. ($SD = 7.2$ yr.).

Procedure

Ss were randomly assigned to a group of meditators and a control group of nonmeditators with an equal number of males and females in each group. Each S served as his own control in a pretest-posttest design with 3 mo. between testing. In order to control for a possible interaction effect of the perceptual measures and meditation, half of the Ss in the control and experimental groups were not pretested with the perceptual indices. Meditators were permitted to undergo 3 mo. of practice of meditation while the nonmeditator-controls were instructed to simply "sit quietly" for 20 min. each morning.

Administered perceptual style measures were the autokinetic effect, the embedded-figures test, and the rod-and-frame test (Cancro & Voth, 1969) which were given in that invariate sequence. All Ss were individually tested in a double-blind procedure in an evenly lit quiet room. For the autokinetic testing, S was asked to look into a 2-ft. tube, 6 in. in diameter and mounted on supports above a 25-in. square drawing board. S was told to place a pencil at the center of the paper and to look into the tube at a small point of light. He was instructed to look steadily at the light and that it might appear to move. If the light moved, he was to trace its movement on the paper. Three aspects of the autokinetic phenomena were recorded: (1) autokinetic latency time which was recorded from when the light was first turned on until task completion at 3 min.; (2) autokinetic length of the line which was determined by a map distance reader; and (3) the radius of the tracings which was determined as the farthest point of movement from the center of the paper.

A 12-item embedded-figures test (Gardner, et al., 1959) was used and consisted of the first 12 of the standard 24 figures. Standard administration was followed with the complex figure exposed for 15 sec. and then turned over. The complex figure was turned over again, and S instructed to trace the outline of the simple figure in the complex one. Individual performance on the embedded-figures test was recorded as the average seconds of elapsed time over the 12 trials. Lastly, the rod-and-frame test (Witkin, et al., 1954) was administered and the average absolute deviation from the true vertical for 8 trials was utilized as the rod-and-frame score. On each of the 8 rod-and-frame trials, the frame was tilted either right or left according to a table of random numbers.

RESULTS AND DISCUSSION

Meditators and nonmeditators were compared on each of the 5 perceptual variables by means of the three-way analysis of variance of the least square method, equal Ns, fixed-effects model (Winer, 1962). No correlation between perceptual tests was observed which affirmed their independence. There were no significant interactions between meditation and the perceptual measures at pretest or on any of the variables between pretest and posttest for the non-meditators.

All meditators demonstrated a shift toward increased field independence. On posttest male meditators tended to shift from an autokinetic latency time mean of 15.5 sec. to 7.6 and females tended to shift from 33.2 sec. to 21.8. Analysis of variance indicated meditation ($F = 75.13, P < .001$) and duration ($F = 273.51, P < .001$) were significant effects. The men also demonstrated an increased autokinetic length of line from a mean of 16.1 cm to 24.8 and the women an increase from 15.3 cm to 25.4. Analysis of variance indicated meditation was an effect ($F = 53.12, P < .001$). The women demonstrated an increased autokinetic distance away from center from a mean of 6.16 cm to 7.01 cm and men from 5.94 cm to 7.68. There was some effect of meditation ($F = 5.52, P < .05$). Three indices of autokinetic perception demonstrated a shift toward increased field-independence following 3 mo. of meditative practice.

On the embedded-figures test, the male meditators in posttest tended to shift toward a shorter latency time from a mean of 48.2 sec. to 41.2 and female meditators from 69.6 sec. to 60.8. Variance analysis gave a main effect of meditation ($F = 48.76, P < .001$). More accurate performance on the embedded-figures test indicates a shift toward field-independence.

On the rod-and-frame test male practitioners showed increased accuracy, from a mean of 3.30° to 2.00 and women from 3.70° to 2.14. Analysis showed meditation was a significant main effect ($F = 35.91, P < .001$). More accurate performance on the rod-and-frame test indicates a shift toward field-independence.

Practitioners of Transcendental Meditation demonstrated a shift toward increased field-independence on 5 indices of perceptual style following 3 mo. of meditative practice. Since deployment of attention is the critical factor in determining performance on these perceptual tasks and since it is the expressed goal of meditation to achieve an inward, focused attention, it is suggested that these observed differences can be attributed to an alteration in the individual's deployment of attention due to meditative practice.

REFERENCES

CANCRO, R., & VOTH, H. M. Autokinesis and psychological differentiation. *Perceptual and Motor Skills*, 1969, 28, 99-103.

CANCRO, R., VOTH, H. M., & VOTH, A. C. Character organization and the style of hospital treatment. *Archives of General Psychiatry*, 1968, 19, 161-164.

GARDNER, R., HOLZMAN, P. S., KLEIN, G. S., LINTON, A., & SPENCE, D. P. Cognitive control: a study of individual consistencies in cognitive behavior. *Psychological Issues*, 1959, 2, No. 4.

MAHESH YOGI, M. *The science and art of living.* London: International SRM, 1966.

VOTH, H. M. Choice of illness. *Archives of General Psychiatry*, 1962, 6, 149-156.

VOTH, H. M., CANCRO, R., & KISSEN, M. Choice of defense. *Archives of General Psychiatry*, 1968, 18, 36-41.

WINER, B. J. *Statistical principles in experimental design.* New York: McGraw-Hill, 1962.

WITKIN, H. A., DYK, R. B., FATERSON, H. F., GOODENOUGH, D. R., & KARP, S. A. *Psychological differentiation.* New York: Wiley, 1962.

WITKIN, H. A., LEWIS, H. B., HERTZMAN, M., MACHOVER, K., MEISSNER, P., & WAPNER, S. *Personality through perception.* New York: Harper, 1954.

Accepted August 27, 1974.

20

ATTENTIONAL AND AFFECTIVE CONCOMITANTS OF MEDITATION: A CROSS-SECTIONAL STUDY

Richard J. Davidson, Daniel J. Goleman, and Gary E. Schwartz

Recent research has begun to systematically define a personality trait, moderately correlated with hypnotizability, which represents a disposition for having episodes of "total" attention, termed absorption (Roberts, Schuler, Bacon, Zimmerman, & Patterson, 1975; Shor, 1960; Shor, Orne, & O'Connell, 1962; Tellegen & Atkinson, 1974). Although attempts to modify hypnotizability have been only partially successful (see Diamond, 1974), with test-retest reliabilities over a 10-year span found to be .60 (Morgan, Johnson, & Hilgard, 1974), the plasticity of absorption has never been explored.

Recent prospective longitudinal research on certain forms of meditation has indicated that their regular practice is associated with significant enhancement in attentive ability, as assessed by the Embedded Figures and Rod and Frame Tests (Linden, 1973; Pelletier, 1974), as well as significant decrements in trait anxiety (Linden, 1973). The purpose of the present study was to explore the association between these practices of relatively passive, sitting meditation (see Davidson & Schwartz, in press) and absorption and anxiety using a cross-sectional design.

Although the contributions of self-selection and differential drop-out rates among the three groups of meditators could not be unambiguously assessed with this design, we believed that the present study might provide a foundation for more systematic longitudinal research with these variables in the future. It was hypothesized that a linear increment in measures of absorption concomitant with a linear decrement in a measure of trait anxiety would be observed across four groups of subjects representing nonmeditating controls, beginners, and short-term and long-term meditators, respectively.

Method

Subjects

A total of 58 Harvard undergraduates served as subjects. The subjects were divided into four groups on the basis of their responses to questionnaires asking whether they meditate regularly and, if so, for how many months. The groups included (a) controls ($n = 11$) who expressed an interest in meditating although they did not practice; (b) beginners ($n = 14$) who indicated that they meditated for 1 month or less; (c) short-term meditators ($n = 18$) who regularly practiced for 1–24 months; and (d) long-term meditators ($n = 15$) who have regularly practiced for greater than 24 months.[1] The mean age for the total sample was 20.81 years ($SD = 2.77$) and did not differ between groups. There were 36 males and 23 females in the

---

[1]Beginners and short-term and long-term meditators were enrolled in a class on the psychology of consciousness while controls were students in a physiological psychology course.

total sample and the sex ratio was comparable between groups. All subjects were solicited, unpaid volunteers.

The type of meditation practiced by the subjects was varied and ranged from transcendental meditation (see Kanellakos & Lukas, 1974) to Zen and traditional Buddhist practices such as focusing attention on breathing (see Goleman, 1972). All were relatively passive in nature and performed while sitting quietly (Davidson & Schwartz, in press).

Measures

Shor Personal Experience Questionnaire (PEQ)

The PEQ is a 45-item scale developed by Shor et al. (1962) through cross-validated studies designed to assess personality variables which predict hypnotizability. Subjects are required to indicate whether or not they have experienced the particular event described by each item and to rate the intensity of their experience on a scale from 0 to 2. Two representative items are: "Have you ever become so absorbed in listening to music that you almost forgot where you were?" and "Have you ever remembered events in your past life so vividly that it felt like living it again?" In their validation and cross-validation studies, Shor et al. (1962) found a significant positive association between hypnotizability and intensity (for the validation study, the phi coefficient = .22; for the cross-validation study, $r = .46$) with no significant association observed between the frequency of occurrence of such experiences and hypnotizability. On the basis of these data, it was predicted that greater changes over time would be observed in the intensity versus frequency measures.

Tellegen Absorption Scale (TAS)

The TAS is a 32-item scale developed by Tellegen and Atkinson (1974) through a series of replicated, cross-validated factor analytic studies. Roberts et al. (1975) report alpha coefficient reliabilities over .80. The TAS has been found to correlate consistently with hypnotizability in the range of .40 (Roberts et al., 1975; Tellegen & Atkinson, 1974). Absorption is interpreted as a disposition for having episodes of total attention "during which the available representational apparatus seems to be entirely dedicated to experiencing and modeling the attentional object, be it a landscape, a human being, a sound, a remembered incident, or an aspect of one's self" (Tellegen & Atkinson,1974, p. 274). Importantly, Tellegen and Atkinson show absorption to be fully independent of stability-neuroticism and introversion-extroversion. The following two representative items, if answered true, would be indicative of absorption: "If I wish, I can imagine some things so vividly that they hold my attention in the way a good movie or story does" and "It gives me—or would give me—deep satisfaction to devote myself to someone I care about."

State-Trait Anxiety Inventory (STAI)

The STAI, in the trait form, was employed (Spielberger, Gorsuch, & Lushene, 1970). This 20-item scale distinguishes among subjects on the basis of the degree to which they respond to perceived threat or stress with different intensities of anxiety and reflects relatively stable differences in anxiety proneness.

Procedure

All subjects were administered the scales in the context of other personality and attitude questionnaires. The test battery was given to subjects at the end of a class period. Subjects were told that this was a study on the "medical and physical correlates of behavior" and were requested to answer the questionnaires as honestly as possible. Subjects' social security numbers rather than names were employed for identification. Subjects were requested to return the questionnaires at the next class meeting (in 4 days).

Results

One-way analyses of variance with groups (controls, beginners, short-, and long-term meditators) as a factor were computed separately for the three dependent measures.

On the PEQ frequency measure, no significant differences were observed between the four groups, $F(3,54) = 2.35, p < .08$. As predicted, however, differences did emerge on an intensity measure. The groups were compared on the number of "2" (most intense) ratings given. Analysis of variance revealed a significant main effect for groups, $F(3,54) = 3.47, p < .03$. These data are illustrated in the top panel of Fig. 1 and indicate a reliable, relatively linear increase in PEQ intensity from controls to long-term meditators. The significant main effect for groups is primarily a function of the significant differences between long-term meditators and the remaining three groups: for long-term versus controls, $t(22) = 4.13$, $p < .001$;[2] for long-term versus beginners, $t(27) = 3.41, p < .01$; for long-term versus short-term, $t(31) = 3.30, p < .01$. None of the remaining individual group comparisons were significant on this measure.

The group means on the TAS are illustrated in the middle panel of Fig. 1. A highly significant main effect for groups was obtained, $F(3,54) = 6.24, p < .002$, indicating a reliable linear increase in TAS score from controls to long-term meditators. Unlike the PEQ intensity findings, the TAS data reveal a significant difference between controls and beginners, $t(23) = 3.02, p < .01$, and between controls and short-term meditators, $t(27) = 5.04, p < .001$. The difference between controls and long-term meditators was also highly significant, $t(24) = 5.35, p < .001$. In contrast to the PEQ data, no significant difference was obtained on the TAS between long- versus short-term meditators. Finally, the long-term versus beginners comparison was significant, $t(27) = 2.40, p < .05$, while the short-term versus beginner comparison failed to reach significance.

The group means on the STAI trait scale are illustrated in the bottom panel of Fig. 1 and reveal a highly significant linear decrement in trait anxiety from controls to long-term meditators, $F(3,53) = 5.16$, $p < .004$.[3] There were no significant differences between controls and beginners or between long- versus short-term meditators. Significant differences were obtained between controls and short-term meditators, $t(23) = 4.77, p < .001$. Finally, beginners had significantly more trait anxiety than both long-term, $t(27) = 4.25, p < .001$, and short-term meditators, $t(30) = 2.61, p < .02$.

Correlational data across groups revealed a highly significant correlation between the PEQ intensity measure (number of "2" ratings) and TAS score ($r = .53, p < .001$). Moreover, neither the PEQ intensity measure nor the TAS correlated significantly with the STAI trait scale. Correlations between number of months meditating and scores on the three dependent variables revealed, as predicted, positive correlations with the PEQ and TAS and negative correlations with the STAI (for PEQ, $r = .37, p < .01$; for TAS $r = .27, p = ns$; for STAI, $r = -.35, p < .05$).

Discussion

The data from the present study reveal reliable increases in measures of attentional absorption in conjunction with a reliable decrement in trait anxiety across groups as a function of length of time meditating. Interestingly, these differences (i.e., increases in absorption and decrements in trait anxiety) appear to be independent of one another as shown by the lack of significant correlation between the STAI and the two absorption measures. That these dimensions are *orthogonal* is consistent with the factor analytic findings of Tellegen and Atkinson (1974).

One limitation of the present study should be noted in interpreting these data. Since this study employed a cross-sectional design, the contributions of predispositional influences could not be assessed (see Smith,

---

[2] All p values are based on two-tailed tests.
[3] One control subject failed to complete the STAI.

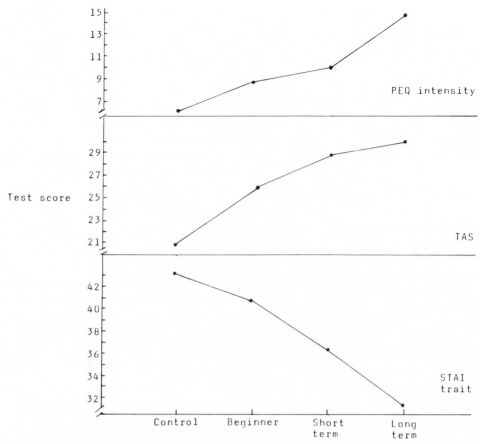

Fig. 1. Mean test score on each of the three dependent variables by group. [PEQ intensity = number of "2" ratings on the Shore Personal Experiences Inventory; TAS = Tellegen Absorption Scale; STAI Trait = Spielberger State-Trait Anxiety Inventory in trait form. Controls (n = 11) were nonmeditators interested in meditation; beginners (n = 14) meditated 1 month or less; short-term meditators (n = 15) practiced more than 2 years.]

1975). However, the linear changes obtained across groups in conjunction with the correlational data seem to be more parsimoniously consistent with a training effect. This interpretation is further supported by the lack of any differences between control and beginners on two out of the three dependent measures. If predispositional effects were strongly influencing the data, one would expect differences between controls and subjects who actually began the practice of meditation. However, it should be noted that the contributions of differential drop-out rates among the groups employed could not be assessed with the present design and could conceivably have contributed to the pattern of results obtained. Future studies on this topic might fruitfully employ a longitudinal design where these variables may be unambiguously disentangled. Also, different forms of meditation might be compared so that the generality of these findings could be ascertained (e.g., Schwartz, Davidson, & Goleman, Note 1).

Finally, the pattern found to be associated with the practice of meditation in the present data—decrements in trait anxiety and increments in the capacity to attend—is consistent with a large body of physiological data (e.g., Banquet, 1973; Davidson & Schwartz, in press; Goleman & Schwartz, in press; Hirai, 1974; Orme-Johnson, 1973) indicating that these practices of meditation are associated with decrements in autonomic arousal and increments in cortical responsivity.

Psychology of Meditation

Reference Note

1. Schwartz, G. E., Davidson, R. J., & Goleman, D. J. *Meditation and exercise in the reduction of cognitive and somatic anxiety.* Manuscript in preparation.

References

Banquet, J. P. Spectral analysis of EEG in meditation. *Electroencephalography and Clinical Neurophysiology*, 1973, **35**, 143–157.

Davidson, R. J., & Schwartz, G. E. The psychobiology of relaxation and related states: A multiprocess theory. In D. I. Mostofsky (Ed.), *Behavior control and the modification of physiological activity.* New York: Prentice-Hall, in press.

Diamond, M. J. Modification of hypnotizability: A review. *Psychological Bulletin*, 1974, **81**, 180–198.

Goleman, D. J. The buddha on meditation and states of consciousness, Part II: A typology of meditation techniques. *Journal of Transpersonal Psychology*, 1972, **4**, 151–210.

Goleman, D. J., & Schwartz, G. E. Meditation as an intervention in stress reactivity. *Journal of Consulting and Clinical Psychology*, 1976, in press.

Hirai, T. *Psychophysiology of Zen.* Tokyo: Igaku Shoin, 1974.

Kanellakos, D. P., & Lukas, J. S. *The psychobiology of transcendental meditation: A literature review.* Menlo Park, Calif.: W. A. Benjamin, 1974.

Linden, W. Practicing of meditation by school children and their levels of field dependence-independence, test anxiety and reading achievement. *Journal of Consulting and Clinical Psychology*, 1973, **41**, 139–143.

Morgan, A. H., Johnson, D. L., & Hilgard, E. R. The stability of hypnotic susceptibility: A longitudinal study. *Inernational Journal of Clinical and Experimental Hypnosis*, 1974, **22**, 249–257.

Orme-Johnson, D. W. Autonomic stability and transcendental meditation. *Psychosomatic Medicine*, 1973, **35**, 341–349.

Pelletier, K. R. Influence of transcendental meditation upon autokinetic perception. *Perceptual and Motor Skills*, 1974, **39**, 1031–1034.

Roberts, A. H., Schuler, J., Bacon, J. G., Zimmerman, R. L., & Patterson, R. Individual differences and autonomic control: Absorption, hypnotic susceptibility and the unilateral control of skin temperature. *Journal of Abnormal Psychology*, 1975, **84**, 272–279.

Shor, R. E. The frequency of naturally occurring 'hypnotic-like' experiences in the normal college population. *International Journal of Clinical and Experimental Hypnosis*, 1960, **8**, 151–163.

Shor, R. E., Orne, M. T., & O'Connell, D. H. Validation and cross-validation of a scale of self-reported personal experiences which predicts hypnotizability. *Journal of Psychology*, 1962, **53**, 55–75.

Smith, J. C. Meditation as psychotherapy: A review of the literature. *Psychological Bulletin,*, 1975, **83**, 558–564.

Spielberger, C. D., Gorsuch, R. L., & Lushene, R. E. *Manual for the State-Trait Anxiety Inventory.* Palo Alto, Calif.: Consulting Psychologists Press, 1970.

Tellegen, A., & Atkinson, G. Openness to absorbing and self-altering experiences ("Absorption"), a trait related to hypnotic susceptibility. *Journal of Abnormal Psychology*, 1974, **83**, 268–277.

21

A RORSCHACH STUDY OF THE STAGES
OF MINDFULNESS MEDITATION

Daniel P. Brown[1,2] and Jack Engler[3,4]

Defining Meditation

In a previous article (Brown, 1977) it was pointed out that the trend of current research is to define meditation primarily according to the model of stress reduction. Such a model is a likely consequence of psychophysiological investigations of meditation. Another trend is to define meditation according to models of psychotherapy (Goleman, 1976; Goleman & Schwartz, 1976). Such studies may tell us useful information about the applicability of meditation to Western-defined systems of mental health. These

[1]Department of Psychiatry, Harvard Medical School at The Cambridge Hospital, Boston, Massachusetts.

[2]Rorschach data on the American meditators was collected under a Post-doctoral Training Grant in Social-Behavioral Sciences (NIMH-5T32MH14246-04) through Harvard Medical School under the supervision of Elliot Mishler, Ph.D. The author wishes to acknowledge the inspiration of Dr. Charles Ducey, Director of Psychological Services, the Cambridge Hospital, who supervised the data collection, as well as contributing greatly to an understanding of Rorschach scoring and interpretation. The author also wishes to thank the staff of the Insight Meditation Society, especially Michael Grady and James Roy, for not only allowing this data to be collected at IMS but dedicating themselves to organizing and ensuring the data collection. The author would also like to thank all of the teachers at IMS for their cooperation in this study, especially Dr. Jack Kornfield, whose training as both a meditation teacher and a psychologist allowed him to be a model for the integration of eastern and western psychologies, thereby making the project of collecting research data in a quasi-monastic setting credible to the meditation students. He would also like to thank Joseph Goldstein, resident teacher at IMS, who was kind and patient enough to read a draft of this paper and offer corrections so that the final draft presented an understanding of Buddhist practice that was free of serious distortion and misunderstandings. The author would also like to thank the following people for their careful reading of the paper and their offering of helpful suggestions: Drs. Roger Walsh & Deane Shapiro, the editors of this volume; Charles Ducey, Ph.D., Bennett Simon, M.D., Gerald Epstein, M.D., Paul Fulton, M.A.

[3]Board of Religious Studies, University of California, Santa Cruz, California.

[4]Interview and test data on the South Asian meditators was collected under a Fulbright Research Fellowship to India in 1976–1977, through the University of Chicago. The author wishes to thank first of all Prof. Don Browning and Prof. Frank Reynolds of the Divinity School, The University of Chicago, who supervised the planning of this research and have kept faith through its many vicissitudes; also Ven. Dr. U Jagara Bhivamsa, Prof. of Pali at the Nalanda Pali Institute of Post-Graduate Buddhist Studies, Nalanda, who supervised the actual execution of the project in the field. The author would also like to acknowledge Ven. Nyanaponika Mahathera of Sri Lanka, who first introduced him to this tradition and suggested the site for research; and Dr. Jack Kornfield and Mr. Joseph Goldstein, resident teachers at IMS, who ensured that the proper foundation for the research was laid before leaving and who suggested the only approach by which the author was able to gain access to this group of subjects. The many friends and colleagues in Asia to whom the author is indebted are too numerous to mention. He would like to thank two in particular who contributed directly to the data collection as test consultants: Dr. Manas Raychaudhari, Prof. of Clinical Psychology at Rabindra Bharati University, Calcutta, for the Rorschach; and Dr. Uma Chowdhury, Prof. of Clinical Psychology at the All-India Institute for Public Hygiene, Calcutta, for the TAT. Dr. Chowdhury is herself the author of the Indian adaptation of the TAT used in this study. The author also wants to acknowledge the Ven. Mahasi Sayadaw, the head of this teaching lineage, for his invitation to study at Thathana Yeiktha and for his active support of this research. Most of all, the author wants to thank the subjects of this study who volunteered several months of their time during the hottest months of the hot season, under conditions which are too difficult to imagine at this distance and under the press of family and professional lives, without complaint. Two especially deserve his thanks: the teacher who represents the Masters Group in this paper and who made her home available for the bulk of the interviewing and testing; and her teacher, who was the author's own mentor and main "informant" throughout his stay in Asia and who first identified the Ss for this study and then solicited their cooperation on the author's behalf. Last, he would like to acknowledge and thank his wife, Ms. Jellemieke Stauthamer of The Wright Institute in Berkeley, who collaborated in every phase of this study, especially the data collection. In the interviewing and testing, she opened the study in a unique way to the lives of women which are not shared with men, especially in Asia.

studies do not, however, tell us much about the essential phenomena of meditation as conceived in the East, or about an Eastern understanding of meditation's role in mental health.

The assumptions underlying this study are very different. As noted in that chapter, we have been studying indigenous Buddhist meditation practitioners and the authoritative textual traditions in which their practices have been recorded. The outstanding feature of meditation in most of these textual traditions is a conception of meditation in terms of a stage model. Each major tradition we have studied in their original languages presents an unfolding of meditation experience in terms of a stage model: for example, the *Mahamudra* from the Tibetan Mahayana Buddhist tradition (Brown, 1977); the *Visuddhimagga* from the Pali Theravadin Buddhist tradition (Nyanamoli, 1976); and the *Yoga Sutras* from the Sanskrit Hindu tradition (Mishra, 1963). One is struck by great similarities in these three stage models. The models are sufficiently close to suggest an underlying common invariant sequence of stages, despite vast cultural and linguistic differences as well as different styles of practice (Brown, 1979). Although such convergence remains to be established on empirical grounds, the idea of conceiving meditation in terms of a stage model is intuitively appealing. The traditions themselves, like Theravada Buddhism, expresses the practice with metaphors of "path" (magga) and "development" (bhavana).

The current study is about one such stage model, the Theravadin Buddhist tradition. We have had the fortune to conduct extensive investigations on contemporary practitioners of this tradition. According to this tradition, there are three major divisions of the entire system of meditation. Preliminary training, sometimes called Moral Training; Concentration Training; and Insight Training. The former is recommended for beginners; the latter two comprise meditation in its more restricted sense of formal sitting practice.

Each of these divisions represents a very different set of practices and leads to a distinct goal. Each involves a very different kind of psychological transformation. The preliminary practices include the study of the teachings, following the ethical precepts, and training in basic awareness of one's daily activities as well as the flow of one's internal experience. These preliminaries may also include learning meditative postures, learning to sit quietly in order to observe and, thereby, calm one's thoughts, and learning to observe the flow of one's internal experience free from distraction. Concentration practice is defined in terms of one-pointed attention, the ability to hold attention steady on an object without distraction. This is said to result in a relative reduction in thinking and higher perceptual processes. The fully concentrated meditator has learned to develop a deep concentrated state called samadhi in which awareness is held continuously and steadily upon very subtle activities of the mind, at a level simpler than that of thinking or perceptual pattern recognition. Insight practice is the most important. All earlier stages are preparations. The meditator has trained his awareness to observe the subtle workings of his mind and is now in a position to genuinely know how the mind works at its most refined levels. There are a number of individual stages of insight, all of which are quite technically defined. The yogi is said to learn fundamental truths regarding the operations of the mind. His awareness is said to become so refined that he begins to explore the interface of mind/universe. He explores how events come into existence and how they pass away. In so doing, he learns that there is no real boundary between the mind-inside and the universe-outside. Eventually a fundamental non-dual awareness will intuitively and experientially understand the operations of the mind/universe, leading to a radical transformation of experience called enlightenment. Moreover, there may be several such transformations, more than one such enlightenment. Those readers who wish to study translations of the classical accounts of the stages of meditation in Theravdin Buddhism are referred elsewhere (Nyanomali, 1976; Mahasi Sayadaw, 1965; Mishra, 1963).

The Problem of Validation

The problem with the traditional Buddhist accounts of the stages of meditation is their status as subjective reports. These texts may contain archaic historical artifacts which have no validity in terms of describing the experience of contemporary meditators. Or, the texts may represent experiences very similar to those of present-day meditators, but both descriptions of experience may be the consequences of rigid belief systems, i.e., merely expectation effects. Then again, the texts may be descriptions of stages of meditation experience that have external validity. The task of our current research is to determine just what sort of validity these textual accounts have.

In order to approach the issue of validity, interviews were first conducted with contemporary indigenous practitioners to see if their experiences were consistent with those in the classical texts

(Kornfield, 1976; Engler, 1980). Questionnaires were also designed to quantify these descriptions (Brown, Twemlow, Engler, Maliszewski, & Stauthamer, 1978). Second, an attempt was made to compare the textual accounts to constructs drawn from specific traditions of western psychology, particularly cognitive psychology. A previous article (Brown, 1977) is an example of some of our efforts. In the article, learning meditation was likened to the acquisition of a cognitive skill, specifically, skill in attention deployment and awareness training. Those who persist in the attention and awareness training seem to undergo a set of meditation experiences which unfold in a very orderly manner, perhaps in discernable stages. The stages were viewed according to a cognitive/developmental stage model, i.e., one in which more complex thinking and perceptual processes are deconstructed during meditation so that more subtle levels of information-processing could be observed. Although the article was theoretical and not empirical, a case was made that the traditional textual accounts may depict a sequence of cognitive changes that could indeed have construct validity.

Such theoretical work is only a preliminary step toward validation. Does the yogi "really" alter his attitudes, behavior, and awareness during the preliminary stages of practice? Does he "really" reduce thinking and perceptual processes during concentration practice? Does he "really" become aware of the most subtle workings of his mind and the universe during insight practice? What "really" changes during and following enlightenment? The objective of a validation study is to establish independent empirical measures of the alleged cognitive changes described in the traditional texts and in the subjective reports and questionnaires of contemporary practitioners. The Rorschach may not seem to be a likely choice for such a validation study. In fact, the Rorschach was originally used as a personality measure. However, we began to notice that practitioners at different levels of the practice gave records that looked very distinct. In fact, the Rorschach records seemed to correlate with particular stages of meditation. Common features were more outstanding than individual differences at each level of practice. This unexpected observation raised the further question whether perhaps there were qualitative features (and quantitive variables) on the Rorschach that discriminated between the major divisions or stages of the practice. If so, this would be an initial step toward establishing the possible validity of the stage-model of meditation. In the current study, the Rorschach is used as a stage-sensitive instrument by administering it to criterion groups defined according to their level of practice. The main reason that the Rorschach was useful as a validating instrument was that we used it as a measure of cognitive and perceptual change, not as a personality measure, as it is so often used.

The Population of Meditators

Finding a proper instrument to test the validity of the textual accounts of the stages of meditation is insufficient unless the research is able to select a sample of meditators who indeed have experiences comparable to those in the traditional texts. A fundamental problem with contemporary meditation research is the failure to use subjects who have acquired sufficient training in the cognitive skills specific to meditation. Most experiments use naive subjects, often college students, sometimes experienced meditators of a given discipline, e.g., zen or Transcendental Meditation. Even these experienced meditators, by traditional criteria, are beginners. For example, Maupin (1951) conducted a Rorschach study of zen meditators. He used naive college students who were given ten 45-minute sessions in breath concentration. It is very doubtful that these Ss perfected concentrative skills in ten sessions. Nevertheless, Maupin concluded that these Ss experienced an increase in primary process thinking along with a greater capacity to tolerate it. While this may indeed be an effect of meditation, it may very well be a beginner's effect. Inexperienced Ss manifest the general effects of a hypoaroused state of consciousness (Brown, 1977). Similar reports of increased primary process thinking have been reported for another hypoaroused state, hypnotic trance (Fromm, Oberlander & Grunewald, 1970). Effects such as increased primary process may have little to do with effects of meditation in more experienced Ss as defined by the tradition.

In one cross-sectional study which attempted to control for *level of experience*, Davidson, Goleman & Schwartz (1976) segregated their Ss into beginning, short- and long-term meditation groups. The criterion for the long-term group was two or more years of regular practice in either TM or Buddhist breath concentration. The problem, of course, is that *length of practice* need not strongly correlate with *acquisition of skill*. Such cross-sectional studies attempted across criterion groups typically employ a purely temporal factor, length of time meditating, as a means to discriminate beginning, intermediate, and advanced subjects. As all teachers of meditation and most students are painfully aware, however, length of time one has practiced is no index to depth of practice. This relationship is highly variable and indeterminate. This kind of global and rather artificial tripartite grouping on the basis of time has been resorted to in the absence of more appropriate criterion measures derived from the practice itself.

The current study does not rely on length of practice as the sole criterion of selection, although it does not abandon this. Initially, Ss were selected who had sufficient experience in intensive meditation in a well-defined tradition. Intensive practice served as the initial criterion. Moreover, teacher ratings and self-reports on questionnaires were used as primary criteria to further delineate the level of experience of Ss from among this group of intensive meditators according to the textual model of stages of meditation. Goleman (1971) already pointed to the need for a cartography of meditation a decade ago. Without it, as he pointed out, the researcher cannot know what he is comparing to what: what variables he is actually measuring, whether they are relevant, and what their interrelationship is. By cartography, however, Goleman largely meant a typology of techniques (Goleman, 1972). By cartography we mean instead the textual model of the stages of meditation. Presumably, the teachers are cognizant of the traditional accounts of the stages of meditation, on the one hand, and are alleged to be capable of discerning through interview the type of experiences and level of skill a given Ss has achieved. Certain responses to questionnaire items also disclose the level of skill.

The present study in both its Asian and American components draws upon meditators in the context of a well-defined tradition, not a college population. It utilizes meditators who attend intensive retreats of several weeks or months duration. The daily routine involves a continuous alternation between periods of sitting and periods of walking meditation, usually 1 hour in length to start, over a span of 18 hours. There are two meals before noon and a one hour discourse in the evening. Subjects practice from 14 to 16 hours/day, continuously for the length of the retreat. They adopt traditional Buddhist precepts, such as, silence and abstinence from sex or substance use. They do not interact with other meditators. There is no eye contact. They do not write or talk except for a 15-minute interview with one of the teachers on alternate days. This routine is defined as *intensive meditation* and is the basic structure for both short- and long-term retreats. During this time practitioners have the opportunity to work uninterruptedly toward the acquisition of meditative skills and to cultivate the kind of stage-specific training and mental development (bhavana) which this tradition of meditation aims at.

The instructions for formal periods of sitting and walking meditation follow the traditional mindfulness instructions of one of the major Burmese teaching lineages, that of the Venerable Mahasi Sayadaw (Mahasi Sayadaw, 1972; Goldstein, 1976). The practice begins with an initial concentration exercise. Attention is focused on the in/out movement of the breath at the tip of the nostrils or the rise and fall of the abdomen. After an initial period, when some degree of concentration is developed, new classes of objects are then added in a series: bodily sensations, emotions, thoughts, images, memories, perceptions, and the pleasant, unpleasant or neutral quality of each moment of expeience. The meditator is instructed to become aware of any of these objects at the exact moment it occurs, for as long as it occurs, in his stream of consciousness. When no other object presents itself to awareness, attention is returned to the basic meditation object, the breath. It is mainly this extension of the range of attention to a variety of objects in their momentary arising and passing away that now converts this exercise from a concentrative to a mindfulness technique. The second care instruction in this tradition of practice is that attention should be "bare." Objects are to be attended to without reaction: without evaluation, judgment, selection, comment or any kind of cognitive or emotional elaboration. If any of these types of mental reaction occur over and above mere perception of the object, the student is instructed to make them in turn the object of "bare attention" or "choiceless awareness." The specific object chosen is not nearly as important as this quality of detached observation with which it is registered in awareness. *Bare attention,* then, denotes a noninterpretive, nonjudgmental awareness of one's predominant experience, moment by moment. Emphasis is on the *process* by which a particular event occurs, not on the individual content itself. Walking meditation is done in the same way, with the movement of the feet taken as the basic meditation object, with awareness expanded to include all other events which occur, as they occur, during the walking. Equally important, the student is instructed to remain mindful of each and every other activity he engages in throughout the day, as he does it. In effect then meditation is continuous and is ideally carried on without a break from rising to sleeping. This continuity in practice is the single most important factor in developing and maintaining that high degree of concentration which facilitates the development of insight.

The present study combines data from three independent projects: a *Three-Month Study* of intensive meditation; data collection on *Advanced Western Students*; and a *South Asian Study* of enlightened masters. Through combining the data, we hoped to have Rorschachs that represented all the major stages

Meditation: A Rorschach Study   **235**

of practice, from beginners to enlightened masters. The first project used Western students. The research site was the Insight Meditation Society (IMS) center in Barre, Massachusetts. This center offers a series of 2-week courses throughout the year and a 3-month fall retreat annually. Data was collected at one of these 3-month retreats. The second project also took place at IMS. In addition to the 3-month meditators, data was also collected from the staff and teachers of the retreat center and from advanced meditators who visited the center throughout the year. The third project took place in South Asia. The subjects of this independent study included a number of well-known meditation masters in the same teaching lineage. Thus, data is available from meditators at nearly all levels of practice, from beginners to enlightened masters. Primary emphasis is given here to the longitudinal data from the Three-Month Study with some illustrations of very advanced practice drawn from the data of the Advanced IMS meditators and the South Asian masters. However, because data was combined from three independent projects some mention must be made of the different assumptions made and designs used in each of these projects as they affect the conclusions of this paper.

The Three-Month Study

A total of 30 Ss on the same 3-month retreat from mid-September to mid-December, 1978, were used. Of the 30 tested, only one dropped out. Six had attended a previous 3-month retreat. For 24, it was their first intensive retreat of this length. The design was intended to distinguish between expectation effects and meditation effects. In an excellent study, Smith (1976) demonstrated that most of the enthusiastic claims about meditation outcomes were largely instances of *expectation of change* and not due to the specific meditation skills, e.g., concentration on a mantra. In order to distinguish between meditation and expectation effects, the staff of the IMS center served as a control. The staff live in the same setting for the same length of time as the retreat meditators. They adopt the same belief system and attend each of the evening discourses. They expect the meditation to work and devote a minimum of 2 hours a day to meditation along with the retreat meditators. The main difference between the staff and retreat meditators is the amount of daily practice (2 versus 14–16 hours). Differences between the groups presumably are suggestive of the treatment effect (intensive meditation) and not simply of expectation, assuming that both groups expect that the meditation they are practicing will result in some positive change. The unusual Rorschach findings reported in this study were found only in the meditation, not in the control group thereby suggesting that the findings are not entirely attributable to expectation.

The instruments used in the study were primarily the "Profile of Meditation Experience" (POME) and the Rorschach. The POME is a 600-item questionnaire designed to discriminate different types of meditation as well as different levels within the same type of meditation. It was administered together with a Social Desirability Scale (Crowne & Marowe, 1960) and a demographic sheet. The Rorschach was administered individually in the traditional manner by a half-dozen Rorschach clinicians, only one of whom was familiar with the hypotheses of the experiment to minimize experimenter bias.

The original design of the experiment called for a comparison of types of individuals, as measured by factor analytic ratings of a personality rating scale for the Rorschach, with patterns of response on the POME. The intention was to find out whether different types of individuals had different experiences with the same instructions after the course of the 3-month retreat. Post-Rorschach measures were included more out of curiosity. Much to our surprise, the post-Rorschach measures looked dramatically different. The Rorschachs were collected at the beginning and end of the 3-month retreat. Since the meditators had not talked for the entire period, the concluding phase of the retreat was a 5-day transition period in which they were allowed to talk and interact with other meditators and staff, but were also expected to continue their meditation. The post-Rorschachs were collected between the first and second day of the transition period, i.e., after the retreatants became used to talking again, but before the state of consciousness accumulated from 3 months of continuous practice had been disrupted. Only the post-Rorschachs are reported for the current study.

The Advanced Western Meditators

The teachers at IMS nominated a small group of Western students whom they felt had a "deep" practice. Whenever these Ss visited IMS, data was collected in the same manner as in the Three-Month Study.

No such longitudinal pre/post-design was possible in the South Asian study, or was it possible to employ control groups. The study was conducted on the basis of two different assumptions from the Three-Month Study. First, meditation research, including the Three-Month Study, had not had access to the more advanced Ss as classically defined by the experience of enlightenment. Second, the experience of enlightenment was used as the sole criterion of selection, a criterion which superceded length of practice or even teacher ratings of practice as in the Three-Month Study. An experience of enlightenment was based on consensual teacher nomination. According to the tradition of mindfulness meditation, enlightenment is said to result in permanent and irreversible changes in perception and experience. The tradition distinguishes between what in Western psychology might be called state and trait changes (Davidson, Goleman & Schwartz, 1976). In the tradition, trait effects are said to be the result *only* of enlightenment and not of prior stages of practice. Meditation can produce both state and trait changes but these are not to be confounded. The tradition itself makes this distinction and forcibly emphasizes it in warning of the dangers of self-delusion. The yogi may mistake state effects for trait effects and suffer subsequent disillusionment and discouragement to the detriment of his/her practice (*Yoga Sutras* IV.27; *Visuddhimagga*, IV, 86f.xxiii.2). Likewise, if the researcher accepts this assumption, then enlightenment must be used as a criterion independent of level of skill or stage or practice. The changes alleged to occur as a result of enlightenment must be studied in their own right.

In this Theravadian Buddhist tradition there are four distinct stages of enlightenment. Since irreversible trait effects are said to occur at *each* of these four stages and only there, experience of one or more of the subsequent stages of enlightenment became a secondary criterion. As can be appreciated, this required a rather special group of subjects. At the time this study was conceived, such a group could only be found in Asia. These were understandably individuals who had already completed a certain course of training. No pre-test measures were available for them, or were they tested just after a period of intensive meditation as in the Three-Month Study. In fact, this was the first time any such group of yogis had agreed to be subjects for research at all, in South Asia as well as in the West.

Because a longitudinal design was not possible under the circumstances, an individual case study approach was taken instead, based on precedents in ethnographic research using similar research instruments (Boyer *et al.*, 1964). By an "ideographic" case study method as it has been employed in studies of child development (Flavell, 1970; Mahler *et al.*, 1975), it was hoped to discover in the individual case examples of nomothetic principles. Eight subjects, including two teachers, were nominated by two masters. The masters themselves also agreed to participate in the study, making a total of $n = 10$: eight women, mostly mothers and housewives, and two men. All were middle-aged. All practiced the same type of Burmese Satipatthana-vipassana or mindfulness meditation in the lineage of the Ven. Mahasi Sayadaw of Rangoon (Kornfield, 1977) on which the subsequent 3-month study of western meditators at IMS was also based. According to teacher-rating, 5 subjects had attained first enlightenment, 4 had attained second, and 1 had attained third. In interesting contrast to the western group of meditators, most of these Asian yogis had a minimum of prior retreat experience. Most of their practice was done at home in the context of daily family and vocational activities. In all but one case, the actual experience of enlightenment did occur during a retreat, but a retreat of short duration and often the only retreat the individual had done. The length of time from first beginning practice to the experience of enlightenment ranged from 6 days to 3 years. This contrasts again with the relatively slow rate of progress experienced by most of the western meditators in our larger study.

The instruments used in the South Asian Study included the same instruments used in the study of American meditators at IMS with some additions. First, a case history was obtained from each practitioner. Because married women in Asia will discuss certain subjects only with another married woman, to ensure completeness of data collection the case history interviews with the female subjects were conducted by the wife of the author, Ms. Jellemieke Stauthamer, a clinical psychologist. For the same reason, a trilingual married woman, Ms. Maitri Chatterjee, was chosen from among many interviewed as interpreter. Next a series of semi-structured interviews were conducted with each individual on their meditative experience. The attempt was made to obtain separate protocols of the meditative process and its experienced outcomes in the form of self-reports. The Rorschach was then administered by a colleague and Rorschach clinician from the host culture who was neither a Buddhist, nor familiar with this system of meditation and its claims, nor known to the subjects. This was followed by administration of the TAT in its Indian form

(Chowdhury, 1960) in a separate session.[5] The interviewing and testing were carried out over a 4-month period either in the rooms of two of the teachers or in the hall adjoining the nearby Buddhist temple. All interviews and tests were tape recorded and translation subsequently checked for accuracy by an independent interpreter. Finally, the POME was translated into the language of the host culture, independently checked for accuracy, and administered.

The Current Study: Criterion Grouping

An attempt was made to establish clear criterion groups in order to see if the pattern of responses on the Rorschach were different in each of the criterion groups. The five groups that were established followed the traditional divisions of the stages of practice: (1) beginners; (2) samadhi group; (3) insight group; (4) advanced insight group (attainment of at least first enlightenment); (5) masters (attainment of the higher stages of enlightenment as defined in Theravadin Buddhism, e.g., Nanamoli, 1975). The criterion groups were established by two independent modes of assessment: objective ratings by four teachers for the western group and by two masters for the Asian group; and patterns of response on the POME. The four teachers rated each of the 30 western Ss on the 3-month retreat along three different scales:[6] (1) use of the practice to work on emotional problems; (2) depth of concentration (proficiency in samadhi); (3) depth of insight. The scale end points were 1 and 10. A rating of 1 meant "little" and 10 meant "great." Anchor points were given a specific meaning. For example, 1 meant very little concentration, very little insight, and very little evidence for working on emotional problems. A rating of 5 meant moderate concentration (beginner's samadhi), moderate insight ("easy" insights such as perception of the constant change of mental events), and moderate evidence of working on emotional problems. A rating of 10 meant deep concentration (Access Samadhi), deep insight (realization of the stages of Arising and Passing Away, or the stage of Equanimity), and considerable evidence of working on emotional problems.[7] In addition, certain key questions on the POME were used as an independent means to differentiate groups. The POME contains certain questions regarding types of insight. Several of these latter questions are sorted such that they are only intelligible to those who have had the direct experience of the stage, such as the experience of the state called "Access" or the stage called "Arising and Passing Away." Those students who answered these questions as "sometimes, often, usually or always" characteristic of their current practice (post-retreat) were sorted into groups. A given S had to meet *both* teacher rating and questionnaire criteria in order to be placed within a given group.

The *beginners group* consisted of 15 Ss who received a mean rating of 6 or more by the teachers on the scale of Emotional Problems. The *samadhi group* consisted of 13 Ss who met the dual criteria of receiving a mean rating of 6 or more by the teachers and a minimum self-report of "sometimes" or more on the POME questions concerning concentration and samadhi. These 13 Ss were defined as having accomplished some level of samadhi, from Beginner's samadhi to Access/Samadhi, but no attempt was made to ascertain the exact level of samadhi. Likewise, the *insight group* consisted of 3 Ss who met the dual criteria of a mean rating of 6 or more by the teachers and a minimum self-report of "sometimes" or more on the POME questions regarding levels of insight. There were some differences between the teacher and self-ratings of insight. The teachers were more liberal in their ratings. They included relatively "easy" insights, such as perception of the constant change of events, in their high ratings. A total of 11 Ss were given a mean rating of 6 or more by the teachers. However, according to the POME, 8 of these Ss had only the "easier" insights. Only three had actually progressed to the more advanced Insight stages, as classically defined.

---

[5]The Indian version of the TAT was selected over the Murray set after considerable consultation with clinicians of the host country who had worked with both; and after a small pilot study confirmed the appropriateness of the Indian version for this subject population.

[6]The effective reliability for the ratings by the four teachers was 0.98. This does not necessarily mean that the teachers are highly reliable independent judges of the students' meditation progress. This high correlation may be an artifact of the fact that the four teachers probably talked among each other about each student's progress daily during the 3 months of the retreat and had probably reached some informal consensus as to their progress prior to the ratings.

[7]Technical terms like "Access Samadhi," "Arising and Passing Away" and "Equanimity" refer to stages recognized by tradition (Nanamoli, 1975) and adopted by the teachers (Mahasi Sayadaw, 1965) in their assessment of the student's progress. They will be discussed in some detail later in the text.

Thus, in the Three-Month Study, using the very same instructions, Ss varied markedly at the end of their 3 months of practice. The great majority were still working through the problems of the beginning stage. About half had progressed to the next major stage of practice, the samadhi stage. These Ss had become genuine meditators by traditional standards. Some of these same Ss also began to experience pre-access levels of insight. Others, though relatively weak in their concentration, developed stronger mindfulness and insight. The reason for this variation is due at least in part to the dual set of instructions used: concentration on the breath and mindfulness of any or all categories of objects. It may also be partly due to the fact that a given meditation object like the breath can be used to develop either concentration or insight. Ss differed in their use of these instructions over the 3 months. Those who felt scattered tended to practice more concentration. Those who desired insight practiced mindfulness more. The reason why so many meditators achieved samadhi is explained by tradition: both concentrative skills and mindfulness skills can lead to the attainment of at least beginner's samadhi, although concentrative skills are necessary to deepen the samadhi state. The reasons why so few reached the Insight Series of meditations are also explained. These require considerable time to master. In addition, they follow after attainment of Access samadhi. This is supported by the strong positive correlations between concentration and insight on the POME. All 3 Ss in the Insight Group had at least five years of previous experience with the same instructions. All 3 had also received very high ratings on concentration by the teachers. Thus, it seems that those who practice mindfulness without achieving optimal concentration reach a plateau at the pre-access levels of insight, while those who practice concentration without sufficient mindfulness tend to lose their "state effects" after the retreat ends. It is difficult for each student to find the optimal balance so the variation after 3 months is great.

Nevertheless, it was possible to establish strict criterion groups for the traditionally defined levels of samadhi and insight. Because of the small number of Ss in the insight group, these data were pooled with data from advanced Ss collected outside the retreat, yet meeting the same strict criteria. This still only brought the total n to 7, which suggests the difficulty of attaining the classical or post-Access stages where the fundamental insights into the very workings of the mind are perceived during meditation in the Theravadin tradition.

A fourth group was designated the *advanced insight group*. It consisted of advanced western meditators who had reached at least the first of the 4 stages of enlightenment as recognized by their Asian teachers. A fifth group was designated the *master's group*. The tradition recognizes a fundamental difference between the first two and the last two "Paths" or stages of enlightenment. This is based on qualitative differences in degree of difficulty in attainment, extent of trait change, expressed in terms of the "fetters" or "defilements" permanently eliminated from the personality, all of which are claimed to radically differentiate the second from the third Path. In accordance with this principle, the master's group is defined in this study as those who have attained either the third or fourth Path, either the penultimate or ultimate stage of enlightenment. This group is represented in the present study by a single individual. Contemporary Theravadin Buddhists recognize a number of such "ariyas" or "ones worthy of praise" but data is available for only one, an individual residing in South Asia and a subject in the South Asian Study. The following table summarizes the data:

	Criterion group				
Source	Beginner's	Samadhi	Insight	Advanced Insight	Master's
Three-Month Study	15[a]	13	3[b]	—	—
Advanced IMS Study	—	—	4	4	—
South Asian Study	—	—	—	(9)[c]	1

[a]There is some overlap between the Beginner's and Samadhi groups (5 Ss).

[b]There is some overlap between the Samadhi and Insight groups (3 Ss). All 3 Ss in the Insight group also meet the criteria for the Samadhi Group, but are included only in the latter. This means that a total of 7 Ss did not meet the dual criteria for *any* group and are not included in this study.

[c]The enlightened Ss in the Advanced Insight Group are derived from the Advanced IMS and South Asian groups, pooled. A total of 9 more such Rorschachs have been collected. These have not been included, however. Only Rorschachs from Westerners are included in order to circumvent the difficulties of cross-cultural Rorschach interpretation.

Data Analysis

A number of traditional and nontraditional procedures were used for scoring the Rorschach. These included scoring of: *determinants* [a version of the Exner system (Exner, 1974), modified in that it uses the Mayman system (Mayman, 1970) for scoring form-level and the Binder system (Binder, 1932) for shading]; *formal variables* (Holt and Havel, 1960; Watkins & Stauffacher, 1975); and the *fabulization scale* (Mayman, 1960). Because of the unusualness of the post-Rorschachs, a nontraditional scoring manual was developed by the senior author, the Manual of Feature-Dominated Responses. The blind scoring and quantitative analysis of nearly 80 such Rorschachs according to all the stated scoring systems is time consuming and complicated. As it is far from completed, what follows is only a preliminary report based on the work completed to date. The data reported are representative of the outstanding features on the Rorschachs in the respective criterion groups. By outstanding features is meant those *qualitative features* of Rorschachs which are characteristic of a given criterion group and relatively uncharacteristic of the remaining pool of Rorschachs. Clear-cut qualitative features are readily apparent for each group so that in a pilot study clinicians and experimentalists were able to blindly sort these Rorschachs into the appropriate a priori groupings. What follows is a summary of these qualitative features.

The value of a purely qualitative analysis of these Rorschachs may be questioned. Quantitative analysis may indeed inspire more confidence in deciding the question of validity. However, quantification alone will not render the unusual features of these Rorschachs interpretable. Therefore, the first approach to analyzing the data is felt to be properly qualitative. Those who put confidence only in formal experimental designs and statistical methods to the neglect of qualitative evidence are reminded of the recent warnings against overconfidence in experimentation and statistics by none other than Donald Campbell (1979). Campbell has reconsidered the value of qualitative evidence, such as case studies, especially when an investigator has "superior acquaintance" with the context in which the data is collected. That, in fact, is exactly the situation in the present case. The authors are familiar with the cultural context of the practice, know the languages, have read or translated the authoritative texts, and have engaged in actual practice. In addition, the senior author is also a practicing clinical psychologist with extensive experience using the Rorschach as both an experimental and clinical instrument. In addition to his academic position, the junior author is also a teacher in the Theravadin Buddhist tradition on which this study is based, though he was not then on the IMS teaching staff during the period when data for this study was collected. This is exactly the kind of "acquaintance" with the phenomena that Campbell says may lead to more valid interpretations as long as the investigator remains critical of his own interpretive processes. At any rate, it is hoped that such an approach will help to make sense out of this very unusual Rorschach data.

Results

Beginners Group

The Beginners group consisted of 15 Rorschachs collected immediately after 3 months of intensive meditation. These Rorschachs were not especially different from the respective Rorschachs collected from the same subject just prior to the meditation retreat. The only differences were a slight decrease in productivity across subjects and a noticeable increase in drive-dominated responses for some subjects (Holt & Havell, 1960).

Samadhi Group

The most outstanding characteristic of the samadhi Rorschach is its seeming *unproductivity* and *paucity of associative elaborations*. Recall that the test instruction are for the S to describe what the inkblot "looks like." Meditators in deep samadhi experience these instructions as being somewhat incongruous with the functioning of their altered state of consciousness. Many complained that it "took too much energy" to produce images and associations while perceiving the inkblot. One S said: "I just lack the kind of motivation or interest to look for stuff . . . I could force things, but that's about it . . . (3 months of meditation) really wiped out my interest in trying to find things. If I decided to engage it more, it just sends off all these associations, but I'm just not interested in these . . . it's as if cognitive layering and motivation are connected somehow (I)."[8] When asked it he could say what the inkblot "looked like" if he tried, he said that he could produce images; and indeed, he was able to produce a record not significantly less productive than his pre-test Rorschach. He added, however, that to generate such images required "go(ing) into the various levels of perceptual layering," that is, "break(ing) down (perception) into its (perceptual) patterns and concepts." Like this S, all the Ss in the Samadhi group showed a decrease in their overall productivity. Since the task demand was presumably contrary to the actual organization of their perceptual experience, their very accommodation to the instruction biased the results so that even this degree of productivity is probably inflated, a response to task requirements rather than to perceptual functioning.

What does the S experience? Subjects in the Samadhi group distinguished between three levels of their perceptual processes: the *perceptual features* of the inkblot, *internal images* given in response to these features, i.e., the content applied to the inkblot, and *associative elaborations* of these images. During the samadhi state, Ss' focus of attention was primarily on the perceptual features of the inkblot and only secondarily on the images and associations that might follow from these features. Each Rorschach in the Samadhi group was characterized by a mixture of responses in each of the three categories, though the overall tendency was to comment on the pure perceptual features of the inkblot. To them, the inkblot "looked like" an inkblot. The same subject says:

> . . . the meditation has wiped out all the interpretive stuff on top of the raw perception . . . like, there's this thing out here, but then (when asked to make it look like something) I go into it, into the various levels of perceptual layering. (I)

Those units of perception involving images and associations were often given some qualification, the kind of qualification not usually found in normal and pathological Rorschachs. For example, Ss were careful to distinguish images and associations from the raw perceptual features. Some distinguished their memory from perception with comments, such as: "I remember it from last time, but I don't *really* see it there." Some distinguished their associative processes from perception with comments like: "My association to it is a bat, that was my first thought, and then I elaborated it." Many adopted a critical attitude toward their own image. They felt the image was nonveridical. Percepts, even those of good form-level, were often qualified with statements, such as: "It doesn't *really* look like that . . . I'm just projecting." At times, Ss were unable to find words to label or describe a particular unit of an inkblot's features, even when their attention was fixed on it. Comments in such cases were similar: "I know what it is, but I can't put a name on it;" or, "It's real interesting but it's like nothing I've seen before."

Nevertheless, Ss were able to report specific images for the majority of the cards, although not for all of them. These images, however, were quite *fluidly perceived*. Ss complained, for instance, that the images "kept changing." While describing a particular image, it was not unusual for it to change into something else. Sometimes the image seemed to change so rapidly that it was difficult to specify a single image: "It's becoming so many different things so quickly, they go before the words come out" (II). Or Ss reported simultaneous images for the same areas of the blot: "It's a lot of things at once—could be a bat, a butterfly, a flying man" (I). The focus of attention was less on the actual image and more on the *process* by which the image manifested itself in their stream of consciousness. For example, one S said, "It's just beginning to become something . . . (pause) . . . a bat."

The most unusual finding, yet characteristic of the entire Samadhi group, is the high incidence of comments on the *pure perceptual features* of the inkblot. In traditional scoring language, these Ss used a lot of pure determinants: pure form, pure color (chromatic and achromatic), pure shading, and pure inanimate movement. Pure form responses were those in which the Ss became fascinated with the various shapes and configurations of a given inkblot in their own right, without attempting to associate to them. They spent as much time commenting on the shapes, edges, and outlines of the blot in the post-test as they did producing images in the pre-test. For example:

---

[8]The notation following each student response indicates the card number and the specific location of the response on the card (following Exner, 1974).

Meditation: A Rorschach Study

One of the things I focus upon is the outline of the blot, the different variations, up and down, the little patterns, the little ridges of the blot . . . then, I see um . . . ah . . . a human pelvis. (I)

Comments on chromatic colors as colors were equally common: "It's as though more, more comes from the color . . . it's a remarkably stronger input, an incredible set of impressions (from each color on card IX)." And on achromatic color as well: "Most about this one is the color, the shades, the heaviness of the dark with the contrast to the white, and the shades of grey" (IV).

Among the pure perceptual responses, the most unusual finding was the high incidence of pure shade responses and color-shading responses, often in combination with pure inanimate movement:

So many quick changes . . . my focus was somewhere else (than the images) . . . it's easier to look at the movement . . . the vibration, the texture and the movement . . . occasionally more obvious forms come up, but what comes up is the ones I remember I saw (in the pre-test) . . . but within the ink itself, there's so much movement . . . like sometimes there were these faces and eyes, but they changed so quickly that when I tried to say something it was no longer there. (X)

Another subject gives a similar report:

One of the things that's real striking about the picture is just the variations in shading. It just keeps sort of moving (laughs), with the grays. . . . There's sort of these pink blotches (red in black area) like it's sort of full of motion, um, sort of like it makes my eyes move around so it's hard to focus . . . my attention keeps shifting to the different variations of the light gray, the dark gray . . . the outlines are really fascinating, especially in the center where there's a space. (II)

This subject actually became fascinated with the stipple effect which made up the printing of the card!

Each S varied in the relative production of specific images, fluid patterns, and pure perceptual features over all ten cards. Some Ss commented that some cards favored "obvious" images while others did not. As an example of such variation, the entire passage—the actual test response and the inquiry—are given for cards VIII–IX for a single subject. This subject saw "two rats and a woman's dress" on card VIII and "two eyes and a rabbit" on card IX in the pre-test. Post-test responses—pure perceptual features—are not clearly related to pre-test responses, but rather are a function of samadhi effects:

VIII 23″ 52″	Well the color, all of it . . . colors against the white color, they're striking . . . (form?) all the different forms of the color, each shading of color has a certain form to it (what might it look like?) Nothing, nothing at all . . . last time I was struck very much with this one . . . I tried to find something, and turned it around and around . . . once somebody told me that you were real bright if you turned it around . . . I never forgot that, so I did (this time?). This time the colors were enough . . . very pleasant, pretty, doesn't look like a thing to me . . . but there is part of it that takes on a very distinct form . . .
2. rodents climbing	They look exactly like rodents (how so?) The shape . . . the feeling I get of the way they're climbing, moving their feet, tail, faces. . . .
IX. 8″ 50″	
1. hazy color . . . movement	The shadings make it hazy . . . very, very light color here . . . and it gets darker or clearer . . . there's a movement to it . . . very fast movement (?) the lines . . . the shading gives the illusion of it moving very quickly. (Did it suggest anything to you? No, not at all, other than a moving form. (Does it look like anything?) No.

This illustration is again intended to emphasize the main feature of this group of protocols: the unproductivity and relative paucity of associative process which characterizes the samadhi state. The "animals" on card VIII are one of the easiest and most popular responses on the entire test because the features of the card are closely representative of an animal form. Despite the strong stimulus-pull, the immediate impact of the card on this S is *not* the obvious pattern, but rather the pure perceptual features of color and form.

The Insight Group

The Rorschachs of the Insight group point in a direction nearly opposite to that of the Samadhi group. They are primarily characterized by *increased productivity* and *richness of associative elaborations*. These meditators experienced the test instructions as an opportunity to exercise the apparently increased availability of their associative and imaginal processes, while keeping these closely and realistically attuned to the perceptual features of the inkblot.

The average response/card was 10, but only because the cut-off point was also 10. Whereas repeated measures of normal and clinical Rorschachs evidence many of the same responses, the post-test responses in this group showed little overlap with pre-test responses. These meditators claimed that their productivity per card was unlimited, that their mind was constantly turning over. One said: "When I can't see anything else I hang out with it for a while . . . allow space . . . I stay with my awareness of not seeing anything . . . then, more images come. . . ." This openness to the flow of internal associations and images is characteristic of the Insight Rorschach. The experience may be likened to the extemporaneous music of a jazz musician.

Moreover, most of the associations are richly fabulized, with a great variability and intensity of affect. Color symbolism, or better, metaphoric use of color, abounds. The content shows great cultural diversity. One of the more unusual features of these long, elaborate associations, in light of their richness, is the relative absence of looseness. Subjects employ one of the two styles of elaboration, the empathetic and the creative. In the *empathetic style*, the S puts himself fully into his percept, especially the human movement percept. Note, for example, not only the attention to subtle perceptual detail but also the successful construction of a scene with its own affective quality:

I see . . . um the head of someone who's sitting at a piano . . . it's funny, I don't really see the piano . . . it's almost like the posture of the head reminds me of someone who's intently playing the piano . . . his shoulders and the arms feel like they're in the position of someone playing the piano . . . and I see some little tiny dots, shapes, of ink above the head that remind me of musical notes . . . and it's like a visual image of the music that's being played . . . the person has kind of unkempt hair as musicians sometimes do . . . scraggly hair . . . and a short beard . . . and I just get the sense of someone who's just playing ah . . . a real intense, basically fairly happy um . . . kind of music, probably jazz, or possibly classical. (I)

Actually on this side it's a bit more distance (D6 V). Really couldn't see the piano (?), general physical shape . . . couple of things, one a certain postural attitude, that reminded me of somebody intensely playing the piano, postural attitude, the shoulders, mainly . . . kind of like the neck and head is what I saw and then the outline of the head suggesting hair that's kind of flying in a lot of different directions . . . like I tend to associate with musicians or players that really put a lot of energy into their music, and with a beard that kind of suggested the same things . . . so these little dots up here . . . these spots kind of struck me as being musical notes, and then that became a visual image of what was happening . . .

This illustrates the slow unfolding of a single perception until the S gets a certain "feel" for it. In the *creative style*, the S also slowly unfolds his elaboration of a single percept but changes his perspective on the same image one or more times during the response. Often, the S ascribes several very different affective states to the same image:

First, I see a woman in the middle with her hands raised in supplication, a very aspiring movement. It's either in supplication or in praise, maybe both . . . it's not to God, it's not to anyone or anything out there, it's more an inner movement of the heart with the feeling of great joy, great tenderness, great longing . . . it started off as a very chaste image and it's becoming more sensual now, as I look at it, but it still has that, that quality and the person is still in that position I described. . . . (I)

It's a combination of shape and shading . . . the transparency here (?) (D4), shape, her hips here, thighs and hips. I don't associate to this other gray area here, just the inner form (supplication?), the erect posture and the hands raised to the heavens. I don't mean heaven and hearth in the traditional sense (becomes more central?). I was more aware of the shape of the form, the hips, and the breasts, the figure of the woman as a very ideal figure.

Note that in each case, the S never departs from the original percept. Note also that the original percept is a classic example of a qualitatively distinct mode of reality testing that Mayman (1970) has called the F+ in which:

the subject maintains an objective, realistic, appropriately critical attitude toward a given response. He stays close to the determining influence of the blots and maximizes the fit between the associated idea and the blot outline. His associations, however rich, will form themselves around the outline he finds in the inkblots.

These protocols also contain a high incidence of original responses. Thus, the Ss are able to manifest a high degree of congruency between the flow of their internal world, moment-by-moment, and the changing demands of external reality. This *enhanced reality attunement* is clearly illustrated in the following response:

> This is a wonderful one, too . . . sideways this is again, the red figure is a 4-legged animal, like a mountain lion and now he's running, leaping over a real rocky and difficult terrain . . . there's a sense of great energy and power in him, but the most wonderful thing of all is how sure-footed he is . . . a great sense of flight . . . he always lands on just the right crop of rock . . . never misses . . . always instinctively sure of his footing so he'll be able to go on like that, wonderful mastery and wonderful fit between the animal and his world, kind of perfect harmony between them, even though it's very dynamic, leaping, he always does it . . . here, he's in flight . . . just landed with the front paw and the back paw is still in the air and he's feeling, not very reflective, just doing it spontaneously. He's feeling the great energy and lightness and challenge. He loves the challenge because he's equal to it, but it's always keeping him out there on his limit . . . with this is another wonderful thing. It has to do with the colors again, a progression in his progress from warm wonderful colors to colder, finally very cold colors; in other words, he started from a place of warmth and security and as he started from there, he can carry it out and conquer the cold, insecure place because he himself is the pink, the color of the heat, light, energy, warmth . . . and so he can go out and master the cold of the world again. . . . (VIII, without inquiry D1)

There are also some remarkably life-affirming insights contained within these fabulized human movement percepts:

> I see 2, I see 2 heads. It's like a large being, a tall person and a shorter person . . . a tall rather massive person and a smaller . . . could be an adult and a child . . . a father and a son or . . . probably a father and a son . . . that's what it reminds me of . . . and they're just sitting quietly together looking off into the distance . . . very at ease with each other . . . and there's a lot of real warmth between them, just a real feeling of connectedness . . . the feeling of knowing the limitations of the communication that can come between them . . . accepting those limits, not finding them painful, and just being real happy with what is there . . . and the limits are really the limits that are . . . not like generational, but the limits like that are there between any two people whatever their relationship might be . . . the limits of two people trying to communicate to each other . . . .there's a certain place where that breaks down and you just can't get any closer, where you can't bridge the gap anymore, and yet you can come to a real deep acceptance of that limitation. (IV, without inquiry, Dd at base of D2)

Nevertheless, these insight Rorschachs are not without conflicts, such as the fusion of sexual and aggressive impulses in this response by the same S who gave the mountain lion:

> and this which I first saw as just the two trunks of the elephant, this I see as a circumscribed penis; at first I saw it very solitary, just sort of proud of itself to be there, but now I'm beginning to see it in connection with the two red spaces above as though it's thrusting up through, between them, but they seem a little threatened as though they could damage it, could hurt it, as though they were two twin creatures with little paws, little legs outstretched wanting to pounce on it, maybe claw it . . . the feeling it seems to have, flinches a little anticipating that but it's going to keep on moving, thrusting, moving upward anyway and finally the two little creatures will withdraw their paws and snuggle against it because their shapes will fit right down in here, see the contours match here, and this will come up and it will fit snug and come together (fits red into white spaces) and it will be alright, it will be a very nice experience and a feeling of real union and sharing and closeness. (II, without inquiry, D4)

The reader may wish to compare the mountain lion to the previous excerpt from the Samadhi Rorschach, both of which are responses to Card VIII. The difference in elaboration between this and the previous example of a samadhi response to the same card is obvious.

Advanced Insight Group

The advanced insight group consisted of four Rorschachs collected from western-born students of mindfulness meditation. These advanced practitioners are alleged to have achieved at least the first stage of enlightenment as defined by the tradition. Unlike the previous groups, these Rorschachs were *not* collected after a period of intensive meditation. One might think that few valid statements could be made from only four such protocols. Nevertheless, three of the four Rorschach protocols[9] showed remarkable consistency, enough consistency to warrant a preliminary statement regarding Rorschachs from enlightened practitioners.

These Rorschachs do not evidence the same outstanding qualitative features as found in the Samadhi and Insight groups. They appear, at first glance, to be more like the Rorschachs of the Beginners group. The range of content is quite varied. Responses are nearly always images with brief associative elaborations. Responses are seldom dominated by the pure perceptual features of the inkblots, as was true for the Samadhi group. Responses also lack the richness of associative elaboration so characteristic of the Insight group.

Nevertheless, there do appear to be certain qualitative features which distinguish this group of protocols which we are calling "residual effects." We hypothesize them to be the consequences of having previously mastered both the samadhi and insight practices. Like the Rorschachs of the Samadhi group, these Rorschachs contain occasional but less frequent references to the perceptual features of the inkblots, notably the shapes, symmetry, color, and variation in shading. Responsivity to achromatic color and shading variations is also quite high, as was true for the Samadhi group. Such responses are, however, seldom pure shading responses. Instead, the shading is more likely to be interpreted as a certain *quality* or *state of mind* such as "pain . . . beauty," "dark and heavy," "unpleasantness," to draw examples from Rorschachs of the respective advanced practitioners. The use of inanimate movement responses, alone and in conjunction with color and shading, is also quite high, much higher, in fact, than in any other group. At least 10–20% of the total responses were inanimate movement responses for each of the four Ss. No S's record contained less than a raw count of 8 such responses. Compared to norms, this is extraordinarily high. Furthermore, these Rorschachs evidence residual effects akin to the effects in the Insight group. Productivity was high for each of the Ss (total number of responses ranged from 55 to over 100). These responses, in contrast to those of the Insight group, showed less variation in subsequent testing.

If these Rorschachs are not so strikingly different from those of the previous criterion groups, especially the Beginners group, what then is distinctive about them? The most unusual feature, clearly present in a number of responses on three of the four Rorschachs, is the degree to which they perceive the inkblots as an *interaction of form and energy* or *form and space*. That is, *each* of the Ss, in several responses, perceived the inkblot primarily as *energy-in-motion* or as *empty space*. Such responses were, of course, distributed among the variety of specific images on all the cards. However, the Ss saw the specific images (content) and the energy-in-motion (process) as distinct but interrelated "levels" of perception.

A range of 5 to 20% of the content for each of the protocols referred specifically to various perceptions of energy. For example: "movies that I saw in science class which were talked about . . . let's see . . . talked about organism . . . um . . . atoms and molecules, and kind of a changing energy, changing energy" (IX).

Most often content was given in conjunction with inanimate movement or inanimate movement/shading responses. In this respect, the S's sensitivity to inanimate movement and shading was somewhat different from comparable responses in the Samadhi group. Whereas meditators during samadhi are likely to see the shapes themselves (in shading itself) moving on the card, these Ss seldom saw this. Instead, the movement and shading was usually "interpreted," i.e., it was given content, and usually the content referred to some manifestation of energy.

These energy responses might best be seen as representing various "levels" of energy organization. On the simplest level are responses referring to pure space from which energy unfolded. For example:

the space between each form serves a purpose, not too compressed, and yet gives enough space for each quality to be its own and yet have enough room to exchange its own individual energy; however, it's a natural source of energy, unfolding and extending to take certain forms, um . . . almost feels more explo . . . I don't know if explosive is the right word. Let's say, such a strong source that it could come from that center core, that central orange, and go up into the blue and just push off just a little so that it could have its definite, um, shape and function. . . . (VIII)

On the next level are responses depicting the activity of the molecules of the universe or the primal elements within the body.[10]

---

[9]The fourth Rorschach was very different. It contained over 100 responses. The responses were specific in their content with very little evidence of either feature-dominated responses (pure shapes, colors, and shading) or rich associative elaboration, as was true for the Samadhi and Insight groups, respectively. There was, however, an unusually high number of aggression-dominated responses.

[10]Extension, cohesion, heat, and motion—traditionally symbolized as earth, water, fire and air (cf. Narada, 1975).

and the pink and the orange add to the beauty of the skeleton and it almost indicates evolution like to top, the blue, the gray, seems to indicate a step on the evolutionary scale and the orange and pinks seem to indicate more of the beginning, um, I just got the image of when there w s fire, but not fire like bright red, but say, the *heat element* and more of the beginnings . . . prehuman . . . prehuman qualities, when the elements were just doing their dance . . . fire wasn't quite the right word, but it being indicative of primary elements just forming . . . kind of like when, when all of the elements are in a huge interplay and then that linking between the orange of this division, at the very core say of this picture; and then also the orange kind of feeding into the blue color, right, the orange root into the blue, um, color. It feeds into the blue like evolution . . . it's becoming skeletal features, and then here the bear . . . it's like the evolutionary force is feeding into them and their back foot is on the primary elements . . . just one foot as if having that as a link . . . it's like that primary element on either side is making a circle so that the elements feeding into the skeletal, feeding into the animal and with the animal's foot back into its primary source. . . . (VIII)

At still another level are responses indicating the types of energy organization within the human body, as conceptualized by any one of traditional eastern systems of energy yoga (Dasgupta, 1946; Eliade, 1969; Varenne, 1976; Avalon, 1931). Such responses include diffuse body energies such as a "life-force" (X), as well as energies that have specific directions to the body (III). According to the yogic physiology, the body is said to contain both diffuse and specific energy. The latter is said to flow through invisible channels. Note that the organization of energy into specific currents represents a more complex form of energy than that of the primal elements. *All* of the Ss also made reference to the main "centers" of energy within the body. Again according to yogic physiology, the body energies are said to be concentrated in specific centers called "chakras" within the body. Here we note an even further organization of energy, now into specific, quasi-stable locations: "I see the different colors . . . going up the different energy centers of the body, starting with the whole pelvic region . . . the abdomen, chest, and head, and each color representing the different energy in that part of the body (VIII).

In addition to these more common references to internal "yogic" anatomy, two of the Ss also made reference to a type of energy more akin to western physiological processes, such as the energy of cell division (VI) or that of chromosomes dividing: "It looks like a chromosome splitting in half . . . creating itself" (VI). Even more common were responses akin to what in western psychology has been called drive energy:

I see a vagina and ovaries or some kind of organs, internal organs . . . internal organs . . . I see (something) very phallic . . . a lot of thrusting energy I get from it . . . I see like an energy flow between like, ah, the vagina and the penis . . . it's like one continuum, the flow of energy between them, sexual energy. . . . (VI)

Such direct references to sexual energy were found on all four protocols; one also made comparable references to aggressive energy. Finally, there were a number of responses depicting the type of energy that is bound up within inanimate objects, thereby causing them to move. Typical responses were spinning tops (II) or airplanes (II). Note, however, that these responses, in which form predominates over movement, are quite rare in each of the four protocols. By way of summary, all of these energy responses can be represented along an energy/form continuum, with pure empty space at one end, form-dominated energy at the other, and the various intermediate levels of energy organization in between.

	Elemental			Body-energy				External energy
Empty space	Diffuse primal energy	Primal elements molecules	Life force energy currents	Chakras	Cell energy	Drive energy		Form dominated energy

What is implicit in such responses is an understanding of the *interrelationship of form and energy/space*. The most striking feature of *all* these Ss' Rorschachs is the extent to which they view their own internal imagery, in response to the shapes on the inkblots, as merely manifestations or *emanations of energy/space*. Here is a typical but especially clear example: "I feel the energy coming from that, the whole energy of the picture . . . there's an intensity, a certain power of it, and everything else is just a dancing manifestation of that energy coming out" (V).

Here we see that the advanced practitioners have a perspective that is quite unlike that of the previous groups. They see all of their percepts as merely emanations of energy, as part of the "dance of the mind."

In fact, the Ss sometimes reported that such a transformation from energy/space into form actually took place before their eyes during the test. Recall the response about the evolutionary force. That S saw the primal elements transform into skeletal forms, and then into full animals (bears). Here is an example from another S:

> seems like there's a whole vortex of energy swirling around that central core, that's um, more stable, that's just spinning around it (motions) now it looks like um some sort of beings sort of dancing around, um, this blob in the center (laughs, amused at response). Um . . . something that is just pure energy, not a figure, the figures are sort of dancing around it . . . so somehow it feels more like the center, then becomes these dancing creatures, dancing around the center, and then when it gets to be just energy again, it's dizzy, spinning and um very strong. . . . (VIII)

Here, the energy-in-motion becomes immediately organized into external appearances, in this case, dancing creatures (lions). Another S gave a very similar response to the same card. That S added that the animals (bears in that case) on the side (D 1) were not exactly "solid." The latter S, along with another, also gave responses which illustrate an interesting variation of the same theme. For these, the energy became organized into quasi-stable mind states rather than external forms:

> I see a face now. It's hard to describe . . . the eyes are very clear and exposed, the eyelids go verticle, not sideways . . . tongue, uvula, shoulders . . . it's like an X-ray scene. He's looking with X-ray vision . . . these are clouds happening in his head, forces of the kinds of energies in his mind, some dark, some light, like a chakra is opening and a lot of energy is pouring in, a lot of light. He's talking, saying something important, but it's also already clear and doesn't need to be said . . . now he's laughing at himself. (IX, 10)

Sometimes particular qualities of mind were specified. Here is an example from another:

> that um dark part, and the red at the top seem more painful, and the red at the bottom . . . an element of pain, but also an element of beauty [inquiry: it's more of the planetary sufferings and like ecology and the things man does to man (beauty?)]. The red seemed to balance out and be a statement of beauty or truth. (II, 5)

Although responses pertaining to mind states are rare, it is important to point out that they hardly ever occur in the records of the beginner's samadhi or insight groups. They occur occasionally in the protocols of these advanced practitioners and will become even more important in records of the master's group.

While the Ss more often comment on the actual process by which forms and images come into existence, they also often comment, though less often, on the reverse process, namely, how forms and images dissolve into space. For example, one S saw a number of typical images on Card X, such as dancing insects. Then there followed a distinct shift of perception. She began to see the card as mere color and form and noticed that the colors and forms seemed to move inward, concentrating themselves at the center blue region of the card. She explained that all the forms and colors were connected by a "unifying force" by which the seemingly separate images on the card tended to "flow" back into the center region of "localized energy." Upon their return, the S subject noted another perceptual shift, namely, a figure-ground reversal. She ended up seeing only the white (former background) of the card, as if all the colors and forms had become absorbed into it. Such figure-ground reversals and movement toward the central unifying point were other distinctive features of these Rorschachs.

In summary, the most distinctive feature of these Ss' Rorschachs is their unique perspective in which they actually witness energy/space in the moment-by-moment process of arising and organizing into forms and images; and conversely, witness the forms and images becoming absorbed back into energy/space. Here is one response which stands out as a particularly clear example of an advanced practitioner's perception of the momentary arising and passing away of phenomena:

> sort of like just energy forces and um like molecules . . . something like the energy of molecules . . . very much like a microscopic view . . . in some way there are more patterns of energy . . . there are different energies in the different colors . . . it looks like it's a view into the body where there's energy, there's movement, but it's steady because it's guided by a life-force . . . there is arising and passing away of these different elements. Inquiry: the colors seemed very alive and suggested life and they seemed very basic or elemental—both the shapes and size. They don't have heavy substance, you know; they each, um, are relatively fragile (different colors suggested different elements?) yeah . . . and then it started to seem just like a vibration, really not a swelling movement but a pulsation, just a coming and going of um kind of elemental bits

(laughs because of word choice) of life (laughs) (arising and passing away of elements?) It was very far out when it happened . . . I can't um . . . some of that was because of the suggestion of the spinal column (previous response) . . . um it reminded me somewhat of those electron microscope pictures of the body and I just had this sense of movement of it all. (X,15)

One might expect certain consequences from seeing form as a manifestation of energy, from seeing the world as not particularly solid and durable. Some evidence for this may be found in the form-level scores on these Rorschachs. Using the Mayman criteria for scoring form-level (Mayman, 1970), the Rorschachs of the advanced practitioners evidence a high percentage of vaguely and amorphously perceived forms; while the number of weak, spoiled or poor forms is quite low (from 20 to 25% vague, amorphous responses on each of the 4 records). The reason, of course, is due to the high number of energy responses and qualities of mind, all of which get a vague or amorphous form-level score. According to Mayman, vaguely and amorphously perceived responses are interpreted as a noncommittal hold on reality. These data suggest a rather different interpretation, what might be called the *relativization of perception*. No particular feature on an inkblot, or aspect of external reality, is compelling enough to suggest perception of solid and durable forms.

The way this unique perspective is developed seems to be related to awareness of one's bodily and mental processes. For example, the number of references to bodily parts and internal organs (especially the spinal column and sex organs) and the psychic energy centers within the body is very high. Examining the flow of associations in each Rorschach, one discovers something interesting. In one Rorschach, every response involving the unfolding and transformation of energy/space into form was immediately preceded by an image of a bodily part or internal organ. One possible interpretation of this contiguity between body and energy responses is that insight into bodily (and mental) processes becomes a vehicle through which to observe the fundamental energy transformations of body/mind/universe.

While emphasizing the distinctive features of these Rorschachs, it is important to keep in mind that the responses discussed above constitute only a small proportion of the total Rorschach record for each advanced practitioner. The remainder of the imagery is quite varied. Examination of this imagery reveals that these allegedly enlightened advanced practitioners are not without intrapsychic conflict. Using the Holt system for scoring drive-dominated content, there is a consistently low but scorable number of aggression-related responses in the protocols of 3 of the 4 advanced practitioners. Overall, however, there appears to be an intensification of other drive states, e.g., sexual, relative to beginners and insight practitioners, even though the experience of aggression seems to diminish for most. Concerns with the awareness and management of impulses was characteristic for all the advanced practitioners to some degree.

In addition, each of these Rorschachs evidenced idiosyncratic conflictual themes, such as, fear of rejection, struggles with dependency and needs for nurturance, fear and doubt regarding heterosexual relationships, and fear of destructiveness. All of these issues are related to intimacy. They may reflect the peculiar role of an enlightened person in the context of modern western culture. In any case, the unusual feature of these Rorschachs is *not* that these people are without conflict, but rather their *nondefensiveness in experiencing such conflicts*. Vivid drive-dominated content was often present while employing minimal or no defense against it (using Holt defense scoring criteria). This empirical finding is supported by the directness and matter-of-factness with which these advanced practitioners talked about personal problems during a follow-up interview. They tended to see their own sexual and aggressive drives, as well as their individual dynamics, as intense mind states which could be experienced and acted on with awareness, but not necessarily invested in to any great degree.

The Master's Group

The single Rorschach in this group is included because it is so unusual. It is the only data available on the final stages of "development" (bhavana), that is, from someone who attained all or all but one of the four levels of enlightenment and has allegedly undergone a cognitive-emotional restructuring that has completely or almost completely eliminated suffering from their human experience. It should not be necessary to emphasize the extraordinary uniqueness and potential significance of data from this range of experience. This Rorschach was collected in South Asia, and for reasons of confidentiality cannot be further identified. Analysis of this Rorschach reopens all the complicated problems of cross-cultural Rorschach interpretation. Nevertheless, several features are so striking that they are worthy of comment. First is its notable *shift in perspective*. Of the 32 total number of responses, 13 pertain to specific states of mind (41%) and 3 to states of the ordinary and nonordinary world (9%). Whereas most "normal" Rorschach subjects unquestioningly accept the physical "reality" of an inkblot and then project their imagings onto it; this master sees an inkblot itself as a projection of the mind. All the various stages of the mind and the world that might be articulated are themselves a kind of immediate reality. So also, the testing situation is a projection of the mind in a certain sense. The master, therefore, uses the situation as an occasion to teach about the various states of the mind and cosmos, especially those that enable others to alleviate their suffering.

The second unusual feature of the protocol is its *integrative style*. Each of the 10 cards, as it is presented, is utilized in the service of a systematic discourse on the Buddhist teachings pertaining to the alleviation of human suffering. Thus, Card I sets the stage with four images of humans and beasts in their everyday life of suffering. Card II depicts a picture of the mind in its angered state, and Card III depicts the creatures of hell, the hellish state of mind produced by anger in this life, or the plane on which an angry person is believed to take birth in a future life, both in accordance with the Buddhist teachings on karmic action based on hatred. Cards IV–V depict the ignorance and craving of the mind, believed to be the two-root causes of suffering in Buddhist psychology. So far, the master has set forth the traditional doctrine of the Three Poisons: anger, craving, and ignorance. Card VI illustrates how the same mind and body can be used to gain liberation:

1. A pillar. It has taken the form of truth. This pillar reminds me of a process of getting at or discovering the human mind. (D 5)
2. Inside there is envy   disease   sorrow   hatred in the form of black shapes. (W)
3. A human torso. (Dd 25)
4. After conquering truth, the mind has become clean and white. (D 11)

Card VII gives the results of the practice:

1. I see a body (here, which reminds me of) a temple. The mind, here, like a cavern. I can also call this (with the portion identified as "mind" inside it) the physical body (term used implies a sense of lack of respect in the original language).
2. From it, wings have spread—the impulses. (D 10)
3. Ultimately, this body has gone up to the temple (identifies a second temple, D 8). At the end of spiritual practice, the mind can travel in two temples (i.e., the first is the human body, once the source of the impulses but now the master of them; the second is the temple at the end of spiritual practice).

The remainder of the cards depict the enjoyment of the perfected practice, as well as the consequences of not perfecting practice.

Integrating all ten cards into a single associative theme is an extremely rare finding. Note that the master achieves this without any significant departure from reality testing and without ignoring the realistic features of the inkblot, although there is considerable reliance on shading responses and vague and amorphously perceived form.

Discussion

In each of the criterion groups, there are unique qualitative features in the Rorschachs which are distinctly different from those of the other groups. This finding in itself suggests that there are indeed different stages of the practice. Even more interesting is the fact that the specific qualitative features of the Rorschachs for each group are consistent with the classical descriptions of the psychological changes most characteristic of that stage of practice. Thus, the Beginners Rorschach is understandable in light of the classical descriptions of the preliminary stage of moral training; the Samadhi Rorschach, in terms of the classical descriptions of the stages of concentration leading to access concentration and samadhi; the Insight Rorschachs, in terms of the classical stages of insight; and the Advanced and Masters Rorschachs in terms of enduring trait changes upon attainment of the classical stages of enlightenment. The classical descriptions used in this study are those found in the *Visuddhimagga* (Nyanamoli, 1975) and in the *Progress of Insight* (Mahasi Sayadaw, 1965). Such convergence of the Rorschach qualitative features, on the one hand, and the classical descriptions, on the other, may be an important step toward establishing the cross-cultural validation of the psychological changes at each major stage of the practice. What follows is a brief discussion of the convergence in each instance.

The Beginner's Group

The qualitative features of the post-Rorschachs of the 15 Ss in the Beginners Group were not especially different from the pre-Rorschachs, with one important exception. The Rorschachs of a significant number of these Ss manifested an increased incidence of drive-dominated content as well as significant changes in the formal aspects of their verbalizations (Holt & Havel, 1960; Watkins and Stauffacher, 1975).

These findings are consistent with those of Maupin (1965). Using the Rorschach, Maupin reported an increase in primary process thinking and tolerance for unrealistic experience for beginning zen students. Maupin also found that such an increase in primary process thinking and tolerance predicted successful response to meditation while attentional measures did not. Maupin concludes:

Capacity for regression and tolerance for unrealistic experience significantly predicted response to meditation, while attention measures did not. Once issues related to comfort in the face of strange inner experience are resolved, attention functions necessary to the exercise probably become available.

Thus, at the start of meditation practice, the naive S is introduced, perhaps for the first time, to the vast world of his internal experience. Maupin correctly points out that, whereas the beginning meditator's task may be to train attention, most are readily distracted from that task by the very strangeness of their internal world.

There is a characteristic storminess to the beginner's experience. Subjective reports of an increased awareness of fantasy and daydreaming, of incessant thinking, and of lability of affect about in the literature (Mahasi Sayadaw, 1965; Walsh, 1977, 1978). Objective measures such as primary process scores on the Rorschach lend some validity to these reports. Likewise, Davidson, Goleman & Schwartz (1976) have reported an increase in state-anxiety for the beginning meditator, in contrast to a decrease for the advanced meditator. Overall, the beginner's experience is largely a matter of *adaptation to the flow of internal experience*, an adaptation perhaps understandably necessary and anxiety-producing in a culture that lays so much stress on external adaptation and reality-boundness at the expense of imaginative involvement (Hilgard, 1970). What is necessary to keep in mind is that this phase of adaptation, though necessary, has very little to do directly with meditation in the formal sense.

The beginning meditator's introduction to his internal world is not essentially different from the naive Ss who begins exploratiin of other hypoaroused states, e.g., self-hypnosis, reverie, and free-association. For example, using the Rorschach, a similar increase in primary process thinking has been reported for hypnotized Ss (Fromm, Oberlander & Gruenewald, 1970) and for patients who had undergone psychoanalysis (Rehyer, 1969). Using questionnaires, an increased awareness of imagery was reported for self-hypnosis (Brown *et al.*, 1980). According to these findings, adaptation to the internal milieu may be a common feature of *any* hypoaroused state of consciousness and may have little to do with the "specificity" of meditation per se (Tart, 1975).

The implication is that beginners, in a strict sense, are not necessarily "meditating" even when they appear to be sitting in a meditation posture for some period of time. What, then, are they doing? This question was recently put to an esteemed Asian Buddhist teacher of this practice. He was asked why only a very few of the, say, 60 students who meditate intensively for 3 months in this country reach the more advanced stages of concentration and insight according to classical criteria; whereas the majority of students who meditate the same way for a comparable length of time in certain meditation centers in South

Asia are alleged to reach these advanced stages.[11] He attributed the difference in part to a difference in cultural beliefs and to the degree of conviction and understanding the students bring to the practice. In addition, he said, "Many western students do not meditate. They do therapy . . . they do not go deep with the mindfulness." The answer is to the point. It suggests a difference between adaptation and attentional training, mindfulness in this case. Much in line with Maupin's findings, it seems that many westerners become so fascinated with the content of their internal world, understandably perhaps since it is often their first real conscious encounter with it—fantasies, personal problems, emotional reactions, thoughts—that they become preoccupied with an exploration of this content. In effect, they fail to go beyond the content and proceed to the necessary task of training concentration, mindfulness, and related processes of attention. This form of *self-exploratory therapy* often gets confounded in both practice and in the theoretical and research literature with *formal meditation,* defined in terms of the specific training of attentional skills.

In order to avoid such confusion, many eastern systems have devised a more or less elaborate system of "preliminary practices" to be done before formal meditation. These practices are often referred to as the stage of Moral Training.[12] They consist of an often elaborate set of instructions for: changing attitudes about self and world; thorough exploration of internal states; and the regulation of external behavior through precepts. They demand nothing less than a radical change in one's view of oneself, an exploration of the working through of qualities of one's internal milieu, and a thorough behavioral change. Considerable time may be spent in these practices—several years is not uncommon in some traditional systems—before formal training in meditation is begun.

It is indeed remarkable that formal meditation has become so popular in this country while the preliminary moral training has been largely ignored. The psychological changes characteristic of the preliminary practices are the necessary precondition to formal meditation. What happens when they are skipped over? One can predict that the beginner is destined to "work through" these changes during meditation itself. Consequently, the preliminary therapeutic change and the stages of formal meditation become confounded. In this country, meditation is indeed a form of "therapy" for many.

Unfortunately, this makes it more difficult for even the most sincere students of meditation to advance in the more formal practice. Outcome studies have shown that expectations play a significant role, whether in therapeutic outcomes (Frank, 1962) or meditation outcomes (Smith, 1976). Once the cultural belief that formal meditation is a form of therapy is firmly entrenched, students are likely to engage the content of their internal milieu at the expense of attentional training, even during intensive practice. Such students are unlikely to advance in the more characteristic features of formal meditation at a very rapid rate. This is perhaps one reason why over one-half of the experimental Ss were still exploring emotional issues after 3 months of continuous 16 hour/day practice. Some, however, who become less distracted by the content and proceed to train their attention may advance. The self-reports and Rorschach of the Samadhi group are illustrative of such advance.

The Samadhi Group

The Rorschach data of the Samadhi group might be considered in light of the classical descriptions of the psychological changes occurring in the first set of formal meditations: the stages of concentration. These classical stages have been described in detail elsewhere, along with comparisons to constructs from western cognitive and perceptual psychology (Brown, 1977). Briefly, according to the tradition, the formal meditation begins when the yogi trains his posture and learns to quiet his mind so that internal events, such as thoughts and imagery, and external events such as sights and sounds, no longer distract the meditator from an ongoing awareness of the internal milieu. The meditator begins by concentrating on some object, such as the breath. As his concentration becomes more steady, with fewer lapses in attention,

---

[11]This was confirmed in the South Asian study, for example, for Thathana Yeiktha in Rangoon, Burma, the major teaching center of this tradition of practice and the residence of the Ven. Mahasi Sayadaw.

[12]Cp. the Yamas and Niyamas, the first two "limbs" or stages of "eight-limbed" astanga or raj yoga (*Yoga Sutras*, II.27–43); and the cultivation of sila as the first of the threefold division of training or mental culture (bhavana) in the standard structure of Buddhist practice (*Visuddhimagga*, Section I).

the meditator slowly and systematically expands the range of his awareness to the moment-by-moment recognition of the changing events in the internal milieu. As he becomes more skilled, he is able to become aware of events very quickly, so quickly that he is aware not so much of the content but of the very *process* of moment-by-moment change itself. At times he may experience a relative cessation of specific visual, auditory, and other perceptual patterns during the meditation while remaining uninterruptedly aware of the process of moment-by-moment change in the flux of stimuli prior to their coalescence into particular patterns of objects. These changes mark the onset of samadhi.[13]

There are different stages or refinements of samadhi. A *Beginner's Samadhi* is here defined according to two criteria: the object of awareness and the quality of that awareness. With respect to the object of awareness, a Beginner's Samadhi is characterized by relative freedom from distracting thoughts. If thoughts occur, they are recognized immediately after their occurrence and subside upon being noticed. As with thoughts, the yogi is struck by the immediate awareness of all forms of sense data. Though specific gross perceptual patterns may occur, e.g., a sight or sound, emphasis is on registration of the impact, not on the pattern. For example, in glancing at a specific object like one's hand or hearing a specific sound like a bell, the yogi is more aware that he has glanced at something or that a sound has occurred than he is of the content of the sight or sound. Nevertheless, in Beginner's Samadhi there is a strong tendency to become lost in a given thought or in the interpretation of a moment of sense data and to thereby lose awareness of the immediate sensory impact. Second, with respect to the quality of awareness, Beginner's Samadhi is characterized by a relative steadiness. The yogi's awareness is relatively continuous. During each sitting period, there are fewer periods of nonawareness, that is, of becoming distracted by or lost in the content.

The next stage of samadhi in this system is *Access Samadhi*. With respect to the object of awareness, Access is characterized by a distinct lack of thinking and recognizable perceptual patterns. The yogi has "stopped the mind," at least in the sense of its so-called "higher operations": thinking and pattern recognition. The yogi keeps his awareness at the more subtle level of the *actual* moment *of occurrence* or *immediate impact* of a thought or of a sensory stimulus. Thus, instead of recognizing specific thoughts, images or perceptual patterns (as still occurs in Beginner's Samadhi), the yogi is more aware of their moment of impact only. Each discrete event is experienced more as a subtle movement, vibration, at the very onset of its occurrence. Although the yogi is aware of a myriad of discrete events, happening moment-by-moment, he no longer elaborates the cognitive on perceptual content of such events. The meditation period is experienced as a succession of discrete events: pulses, flashes, vibrations, or movements without specific pattern or form. With respect to awareness itself, Access is now characterized by completely stable and steady attention. Though mental and bodily events occur moment-by-moment in uninterrupted succession, attention remains fixed on each discrete moment. Awareness of one event is immediately followed by awareness of another without break for the duration of the sitting period, or for as long as this level of concentration remains. This succession of moments of awareness is called "momentary concentration" (Mahasi Sayadaw, 1965).

The essential distinction between these levels of Samadhi, however, is the grossness or subtleness of the object of awareness, on the one hand, and the degree of uninterrupted awareness, on the other. Steadiness is most important. Once stabilized, the more advanced yogi can hold his samadhi at different levels, from gross to subtle, for the purpose of insight at each level. He may, for example, purposely allow the gross content of the mind to return in full force, especially thoughts, feelings, and meaningful perceptual patterns, in order to deepen insight into the nature of mental and bodily processes. However, this skilled yogi's steady awareness continues in the midst of the various content. Now, there is little problem with the distraction which was such a problem for the beginning meditator.

The Rorschach data from the samadhi group are consistent with these classical descriptions of samadhi. Recall that these Rorschachs were characterized by: (a) a paucity of associative elaborations; (b) a significant decrease in the production of internal images; (c) a concentration on the pure perceptual features of the inkblot. Despite the experimenter demand to produce image and associations, the Ss are believed to have partially maintained their state of samadhi during the testing. This is hypothesized to account for the

---

[13]In some systems, these stages are kept relatively distinct. In some Mahayana Buddhist systems, such as Mahamudra, the postural and thought changes are described separately in a set of Exercises called the "Three Isolations." The succeeding perceptual changes are described in another set of exercises called "Concentration on Gross Objects." In the Theravadin Buddhist *Visuddhimagga*, the preliminary postural and thought changes are merely implied and assumed. In the Burmese style of mindfulness that the meditators of this study employed, all of the respective changes are collapsed into a single set of instructions consisting of concentration on the breath followed by mindfulness of all types of events, moment-by-moment.

marked reduction in the availability of ideational and pattern recognition components of perception, concomitant with an increased awareness of the immediate impact of the inkblot. Thus, the yogis were primarily attentive to, and occasionally absorbed in, the pure perceptual features, e.g., outlines, colors, shades, and inanimate movement.

Although the data analysis is not yet complete, an attempt will be made to correlate the level of samadhi (as measured by teacher ratings and discriminatory items on the POME) with the pure determinant scores on the Rorschachs of the samadhi group. It is hypothesized that the Rorschachs from those in Beginners Samadhi are likely to produce more internal images and less pure determinant responses, while those of the more advanced Access Samadhi will produce less internal images and more pure determinant responses. In addition, it is hypothesized that the pure inanimate movement response, or inanimate movement in combination with shading, is a specific predictor of Access Samadhi. A high incidence of such responses was found only in a few Ss and only the post-Rorschachs of the samadhi group. Shading and inanimate movement responses are the least understood of all the Rorschach determinants, no doubt because of their rarity of occurrence. It has been pointed out that shading responses may indicate a sensitivity to subtle perceptual nuances (Schachtel, 1966). According to the data from the samadhi group, we might interpret these findings in terms of an increased sensitivity to the subtle undercurrents of perception, namely, awareness of a perceptual field in constant but subtle change. Thus, yogis at the level of Access Samadhi may "see" the inkblots merely as a field of continuous changing events, a pulsing swirling mass. They do not "see" bats, butterflies or other specific perceptual patterns.

Whether such fine distinctions can be made empirically remains to be established. Nevertheless, it is at least clear from the data that the yogis' awareness in this group is at the level of the immediate perceptual impact of the inkblot, not at the level of an elaboration or interpretation of that sensory impact. Because such pure determinant Rorschach responses are highly atypical of either normal or clinical Rorschachs, and are uncharacteristic of both the pre-test Rorschachs of the same Ss and the Rorschachs of the control group as well, these Rorschach responses may be seen as evidence validating the classical description and existence of the state of samadhi as a definite kind of perceptual event or level of perceptual experience.

The Insight Group

In the classical stages of meditation, Access Samadhi is merely a prerequisite for Insight Meditation. Just as a scientist may painstakingly construct a sensitive electronic instrument to measure some process, likewise the meditator has carefully prepared himself through the refinement and steadying of attention with its accompanying shifts in levels of perception in order to gain insight into the fundamental workings of the mind. The meditator is now ready to proceed to the Stages of Insight. Because the descriptions of these stages are technical, the reader is referred elsewhere (Nyanamoli, 1976; Mahasi Sayadaw, 1965). Suffice it to say that the foundation of all insight in Buddhism is understanding of the three "laksanas" or "marks" of existence: impermanence, suffering and selflessness or nonsubstantiality. According to the tradition, a genuine experimental understanding of these is possible only after having achieved Access Samadhi.

In each discrete moment of awareness the meditator concomitantly notices both the mental or bodily event and his awareness of that event. In a single meditation session he is likely to experience thousands of such discrete moments of awareness because his attention is now refined enough to perceive increasingly discrete and rapidly changing mind-moments. When this level of moment-to-moment change is actually experienced, the meditator is led to a profound and radical understanding of the impermanence (anicca) of all events. He may also notice a tendency to react to the events, to prefer some or to reject others. This reactive tendency disrupts the clear perception of the moment-by-moment flow and, in fact, has the effect of blocking the flow itself in an attempt to resist it—to hold on, or push away. The continual experience of this with clear awareness eventually leads to an understanding of the suffering (dukkha) inherent in the normal reactive mind and its relationship to its experience in terms of liking and disliking, attraction, and aversion. Furthermore, as discrete events/moments of awareness arise and cease in rapid succession, the yogi finds it increasingly difficult to locate anything or anyone that could be either the agent of these events or the recipient of their effects. He cannot find any enduring or substantial agent behind the events to which they could be attributed. The only observable reality at this level is the flow of events themselves. From

Meditation: A Rorschach Study 253

this perspective of constant change, what was once a solid body, a durable perceptual object such as a tree, a fixed idea, or even a fixed point of observation, no longer appear substantial, durable or existent in their own right. By viewing this changing process, the yogi comes to understand the lack of intrinsic durable nature or the selflessness (anatta) of mind, body, and external perceptions. These insights into the fundamental operations of the mind and its "marks" result in a profound reorganization of the meditator's experience called, in the *Visuddhimagga*, "Purification of View."

At first it is easier to obtain these insights by holding awareness at the level of Access, i.e., at the level of the subtle moment-by-moment pulsation of events. Eventually, the meditator is able to sustain the same insights even when allowing his awareness to return to the ordinary gross content of experience such as specific thoughts, bodily sensations, or perceptual patterns. With perfectly uninterrupted and steady awareness, he observes this various content moment-by-moment and thereby deepens his insight into the three characteristics of all mental and bodily processes. This is called, again in the terminology of the *Visuddhimagga*, "Overcoming Doubt." Eventually, the very way that these events are perceived to arise undergoes a series of significant shifts, both in duration as well as in vividness. Regardless of the content, the events flash very quickly, like pulses of light, moment-by-moment. The beginning and ending of each event is clearly perceived. This is called "Knowledge of the Arising and Passing Away" of events and is a key stage in Insight Meditation (Nyanamoli, 1975).

The moment-by-moment arising and passing away of bodily and mental events and their concomitant awareness eventually "break up." This is called the experience of "Dissolution." Only the rapid and successive passing away of discrete events and their awareness are perceived. Their arising is no longer noticeable. Events and awareness of them seem to vanish and disappear together moment-by-moment. The net effect of this level of perception is either to experience reality as a state of continual and ongoing dissolution, moment-by-moment, or to experience forms and percepts as literally void—to have no perception, for instance, of a form like one's arm or leg or even entire body, or of an external object like a tree in front of one, at all.

The first reaction to this experience is often one of exhilaration or ecstasy. If so, it is usually short-lived. It is soon followed in subsequent stages of practice by states of fear and terror, misery and disgust, as the implications of this discovery become apparent and sink in. These are affective reactions to the experience of reality as a condition of continual dissolution or radical impermanence, but they are not affective states in the normal sense. The yogi's awareness remains steady and balanced behind these affects. They are experienced fully and observed as mind-states, but without further reaction. They, in turn, become objects of bare attention and continue to be observed with uninterrupted mindfulness toward further insight. They are technically described as "knowledges" (nanas) rather than affects and are considered separate stages in the insight series.

In subsequent meditation, events reoccur. The yogi is not only aware of each event which occurs within consciousness but is also aware of its context, i.e., he is aware that each event is located within the entire fabric of a cosmos comprised of infinite potential interactions. From this wider perspective called "dependent origination" all potential events are again seen to break up rapidly. The yogi, however, has changed his attitude toward these dissolving events. He has come to realize that no event could possibly serve as an object of satisfaction or fulfillment. Precisely for this reason, he experiences a profound desire for deliverance from them, from which this stage derives its technical name, "Desire For Deliverance." He subsequently begins to reexamine these events with renewed effort and dedication: the stage of "Re-Observation For the Purpose of Deliverance." With continued practice he next realizes what is called "Equanimity About Formations": a perfectly balanced, *effortless* and *nonreactive awareness* of each rapidly changing and vanishing event moment-by-moment, with a clear perception of their impermanence, unsatisfactoriness, and nonsubstantiality. Despite great individual variation at the level of gross content, there is no difference at the subtlest level of awareness or reaction to any events. Awareness proceeds spontaneously, without any referent to any individual self or personal history. A fundamental shift in time/space organization has occurred so that the yogi is now aware of the continuous occurrence of all the potential events of the mind/cosmos.

These classical descriptions of the stages of insight in Theravadin Buddhism can be compared to the Rorschachs produced by the Insight group. Recall that the insight Rorschachs were characterized by: (a) increased productivity; (b) richness of associative elaboration with shifts in affect; (c) realistic attunement of the image and the blot. These Rorschachs are strikingly different from those of the Samadhi group. In fact in some respects they are nearly opposite. In interpreting these data, we assume that a meditator skilled in insight is likely to allow a very great variety of content to pass through his mind during a single meditation session. With uninterrupted and steady awareness and without reaction he simply notices the great richness of the unfolding mind states. He notices the play of mental events from all the sensory and cognitive modes moment-by-moment, all dependently arising according to their respective causes and conditions.[14] In a test situation like the Rorschach, one would predict this state of nonreactive moment-to-moment awareness to affect Rorschach performance. According to our understanding of the insight stages, the striking increase in productivity as well as its richness is not at all surprising. In response to a given inkblot one would expect a great richness of content arises moment-by-moment. The unfolding of such rich content would be seemingly endless with nothing experienced as especially durable or lasting. Nevertheless, just as the Buddhist texts claim that such events arise by causes and conditions, so also the meditators were sensitive to and aware of the relative stimulus-pull of each Rorschach card. In the same way, they were finely attuned to the reality features of the blots. Moreover, during the Insight Stages the yogi is less likely to be restricted by any form of reaction to these subtle events, by any selection or rejection of them. Thus it is not surprising to find a distinct *quality of nondefensiveness* in Rorschachs of such practitioners. There is a distinct acceptance and matter-of-factness even of what would normally be conflictual sexual and aggressive material. Furthermore, the experienced absence of any solid or durable self behind the flow of mental and physical events is consistent with these yogis' flexibility in switching perspectives on the same response, a pattern atypical of normal and clinical Rorschachs. Nevertheless, despite the impersonal nature of the experience of insights such as insubstantiality, these Rorschachs, contrary to the stereotypical and erroneous notions of insubstantiality as a void stage, are deeply human and fraught with the richness of the living process. One need only quickly gloss the Rorschachs of these Ss to see that we are dealing with a very unusual quality and richness of life experience.

Advanced Insight Group

At a specifiable point—when the mind is perfectly balanced, insight into the three marks is clear in each moment of perception and all forms of desire consequently cease—the most fundamental shift of all occurs. Awareness, previously tied to each momentary event, now passes beyond these events. During this moment all conceptual distinctions and ordinary understandings of the "mind" fall away. All objects of awareness and individual acts of awareness cease. There is only stillness and vastness, "the Supreme Silence" as one Asian teacher described it, without disturbance by any event whatsoever but with pure awareness. This profound shift is called the Cessation Experience (nirodha) and is the First or Basic Moment of Enlightenment. It is immediately followed by another shift, also a Cessation Experience, technically called "Entering the Path (magga)" or Stream (to Nirvana). When this Path-Moment (lit. Sotapatti or "stream-entry") is experienced certain erroneous conceptions about the nature of reality and certain emotional defilements are eradicated. This moment is followed by yet another shift, called Fruition (phala), in which the "fruit" of Path-Entry is experienced; mind remains silent and at peace. This is followed in quick succession by a moment of Reviewing in which awareness of the content of the meditator's individual experience returns and he becomes reflexively aware of the extraordinary thing that has happened to him. As ordinary mental events pass through awareness, the meditator simply lets this relative content run its own course while his awareness is no longer bound to it. The state immediately following Path-Fruition-Reviewing is typically one of great lightness and joy which may last several days. The important fact, however, is that enduring trait changes are said to occur upon enlightenment.

Several options are available to the meditator at this point. He may simply return to his daily affairs. If he does, he may or may not continue formal practice.[15] Whether he does or not, however, the gains of this experience of First Path are thought to be permanent. If the meditator continues practice, on the other hand, either in the context of his daily life or in further intensive retreat settings, two courses are open to him. He may remain on the level attained at First Path and practice to develop what is technically termed the "Maturity of Fruition." This refers to the ability to enter into the state of awareness he experienced at

[14]This is the central doctrine, common to all Buddhist schools, of Dependent Origination and has its origin and confirmation at this level of practice.

[15]We encountered a number of practitioners in South and Southeast Asia who did not feel the need to pursue the practice further after attaining First Path or first enlightenment. This is not considered unusual or unacceptable.

the initial moments of both Path and Fruition. Both these moments are moments of Cessation in which all ordinary perceptual, cognitive, affective and motivational activity ceases. They last only a brief moment each before ordinary consciousness and mental activity resumes. Phenomenologically they are both experienced as a state of supreme silence. The difference between them lies in the power of the Path-Moment preceding Fruition. It is at that moment that the fundamental and irreversible shift or change in the meditator takes place. This is expressed as a "change-of-lineage" (gotrabhu) and is traditionally defined in terms of the specific "fetters" (samyojanas) or perceptual-cognitive and affective modalities that are permanently eliminated at that stage of enlightenement. (Nyanamoli, 1975).[16] The experience of Path and the changes associated with it are accordingly said to occur only once at each stage of enlightenment, four times in all. The silent and peaceful mental state of Fruition, on the other hand, can be reexperienced, in principle, indefinitely. This is termed "Entering the Fruition State." With practice, the meditator can learn to reexperience the Fruition State at will for extended periods of time.[17]

The other course open to the individual who wants to continue meditation is to practice for a subsequent Path experience, which defines the advanced enlightenment experiences. There are three further Paths or stages of enlightenment in this tradition. Each is attained in the same way. If the yogi chooses to work for Second Path, for instance, he must begin by formally and deliberately renouncing the Fruition State of the First Path. This is a consequential decision. According to tradition and confirmed by self-reports in the South Asian study, once having made this renunciation he will never experience the Fruition of First Path again, whether or not he is successful in attaining Second Path. Attainment of a prior Path does not guarantee attainment of the succeeding Path. After making this renunciation, he returns to the stage of Arising and Passing Away. He must then pass through all the subsequent stages of insight a second time until he once more experiences a Path-Moment at their conclusion. Again stage-specific changes will occur, additional and different emotional defilements permanently disappear from his psychic organization. Again this Path-Moment will be followed by moments of Fruition and Reviewing and again he may discontinue practice or, choosing to continue, either cultivate Fruition or practice for the Third and, finally, the Fourth Path which is said to produce a final state of perfect wisdom and compassion and freedom from any kind of suffering. Each stage of enlightenment is more difficult to attain than the previous one. The yogi passes through the same stages of practice prior to the experience of Path each time; but each time the experience is more intense, the suffering greater, as more deeply rooted fetters are extinguished and insight into the nature of reality grows.[18] Though possible in principle, as all the advanced practitioners and masters in this study maintain, our research in the Buddhist cultures of Asia, where a higher incidence of such attainments is still to be expected, disclosed that few meditators attain all four Paths.

The Rorschachs of the Advanced Insight group can be interpreted by considering the consequences of enlightenment specified by the tradition. Enlightenment is said to be followed by a return to ordinary mental experience, though one's perspective is radically altered. One might expect such Rorschachs to reflect the idiosyncrasies of character and mental content for each of the respective practitioners. One would also expect such Rorschachs to retain some of the features of enlightenment specified by tradition. These features are: (a) changes in the conception of reality, following the Cessation experience; (b) eradication of certain defilements upon Path experience. The four Rorschachs, though a small sample, are consistent with the classical accounts of the trait change said to follow the enlightenment experience.

Recall that these enlightenment Rorschachs did not evidence a high degree of the unusual qualitative features of the samadhi and insight Rorschachs. They are not especially distinct from the Rorschachs of the pre-test population of the Three-Month Study. Their lack of immediate distinctiveness poses some interesting issues for interpretation. One might conclude either that the outcomes of long-term meditation are psychologically insignificant or a function of unstable state changes. Or, one might conclude that the Rorschach is unable to measure those psychological outcomes, whatever they may be. From another

[16]The experience of Path is also thought to affect one's rebirth status in specific ways as well, but this consideration lies outside the perspective of this study (cf. Nanamoli, 1975, XIII; Narada, 1975).

[17]According to his degree of "mastery," the meditator can enter Fruition when he wants, where he wants, for as long as he wants (subject to an upper limit of 7 days), leaving it at the time he resolves on prior to entering it (Nanamoli, 1975, XXIII). This claim was confirmed in the self-reports of a number of the subjects in the South Asian study.

[18]There appears to be some similarity between this repetitive process at deeper and deeper levels of meditation and a similar phenomenon sometimes encountered in psychoanalytically oriented psychotherapy where, for example, a given problem such as oedipal guilt may be worked through in successive treatments at different phases of an individual's life history under qualitatively more severe forms of stress (personal communication, Dr. Richard Weiser, California School of Professional Psychology).

standpoint, the very mundaneness of these Rorschachs could be interpreted as a highly significant finding. Consistent with the classical descriptions of enlightenment, especially the Review following enlightenment, the practitioner is said to retain his ordinary mind. Though his perspective is radically different, nevertheless, the content of his experience is just as it was prior to meditation, though he may no longer react to it with the usual emotional attitudes of attraction, aversion or indifference. There is a famous Zen saying which speaks directly to this point:

> Before I began meditating, mountains were mountains and rivers were rivers. After I began meditating, mountains were no longer mountains and rivers were no longer rivers. Once I finished meditating, mountains were once again mountains and rivers were once again rivers.

In the language of the present tests from the advanced practitioners, "Rorschachs are once again Rorschachs." The advanced practitioner lives out his or her idiosyncratic life history, though in the context of a relativized perception of self and object world.

Though, for the most part, these are seemingly mundane Rorschachs, each contains evidence that the enlightened practitioner perceives reality differently. An enlightened person is said to manifest awareness on different levels. On the mundane level, such a person continues to perceive solid and enduring forms in the external world as well as habitual mind-states such as emotions and attitudes. To the extent that perception has been relativized by enlightenment, on an absolute level these external forms and mental states are no longer viewed as solid and durable. They exist only in a relative sense.

These alleged changes may be reflected in the Rorschachs. For enlightened subjects, the inkblots do indeed "look like" specific images such as butterflies, bats, etc., and yet these images as well as mind-states like pain and pleasure are perceived as merely manifestations of energy/space. Such Ss perceive content but also energy processes in the inkblots. One possible interpretation is that the enlightened practitioner has come to understand something fundamental about the process by which this perceived world comes into existence in our ordinary awareness.

While retaining an ability to perceive external forms and ordinary mental experience on both these levels—as relatively real but ultimately mere configurations of changing energy/space—the enlightened practitioner becomes free of the constraints of nonveridical perception or attainment to external forms or internal mind-states. One alleged outcome is that the enlightened person sees that man's place in the universe is not self-contained but is located within a fabric of many other modes of existence and potential interactions, all of which are interrelated, and mutually conditioned. He comes to understand, experientially, the doctrine of dependent origination.[19] Life becomes multidimensional and multidetermined in its dynamism and manifestation. This mode of perception leads to a deeper acceptance of human life and death, now set within the context of an unfolding universe in which there is both form and emptiness. Here is an example of a Rorschach response which illustrates this *nonattached, contextualist* mode of perception:

> It looks like a combination caterpillar-butterfly. It seems to be in motion. It gives me the feeling of this creature, this being, walking through the meadow or through a field of grass. It has the feeling of being at home with what it's doing . . . simple and right, at one with what it's doing. It's just its movement. (I, W)

Human life in its most ordinary form is now perceived as precious.

The Rorschachs also contain evidence that the enlightened practitioner may experience conflict differently. One very important discovery from these Rorschachs is that the enlightened practitioners are

---

[19]This perception that each individual form is ultimately void of substance and, further, that the uniqueness of each form arises from the fact that it exists in relation to every other form is systematically formulated in the most central of all Buddhist teachings in both Theravada and Mahavana, the doctrine of Dependent Origination. In the work which probably represents the culmination of Indian Mahayana, the *Avatsamsaka Sutra*, it is expressed metaphorically in the image of a vast network of gems or crystals, like a spider's web at dawn, in which each gem reflects all the others and in which a touch at any point vibrates through the entire network and affects every other point. This net of gems is the Dharmadhatu, the universe, the realm of ennumerable "dharmas" or "events," individual configurations empty of substance and continually in process. The same perception underlies Whitehead's notion of "actual occasion," the nearest equivalent in contemporary philosophical thought. This is also the quantum mechanical vision of the universe which underlies modern physics.

Meditation: A Rorschach Study

not without conflict, in a clinical sense.[20] They show evidence for the experience of drive states and conflictual themes such as fears, dependency struggles, etc. They are, however, less defensive in their awareness of and presentation of such conflicts. Enlightenment does not mean a person becomes conflict-free.[21]

According to the tradition, only certain defilements are removed upon the experience of First Path. What changes is not so much the amount or nature of conflict but the awareness of it. During enlightenment, the locus of awareness, in a manner of speaking, transcends conflict. Awareness "goes to the other shore" so that it is no longer influenced by any mental content. After enlightenment, the content, including conflictual issues, returns. In this sense, enlightenment provides sufficient distance, or better, a vastly different perspective, while one continues to play out the repetitive dynamic themes of life history. There is greater awareness of and openness to conflict but paradoxically less reaction at the same time in an impulsive, identificatory, and, therefore, painful way. Awareness is less caught up in the relative play of conflictual content or indeed any kind of content at this stage. For example, problems concerning sexual intimacy are more likely to be seen as "states of mind." The individual may observe these clearly for what they are and thereby have more freedom in his/her possible reactions to such states. He/she may note the intense desire until it passes, like every other transient mental state, or he/she may act on it, but with full awareness.[22]

One reported effect of first enlightenment is said to be immediate awareness of any "unwholesome" mental state. Mindfulness is said to automatically intervene between impulse or thought and action in such cases. This mechanism of delay, combined with clear and impartial observation, allows a new freedom from drive and a new freedom for well-considered and appropriate action. In this sense, suffering diminishes while conflictual content nevertheless recurs as long as one is alive and has not yet attained the subsequent enlightenments.

If these traditional accounts of the effects of enlightenment are considered in dynamic terms, one might say that such enlightened individuals exhibit a loosening of defense with a decreased susceptibility to the usual effects of unbound drive energy or the lifting of repression because they no longer have the power to compel reaction, i.e., to produce an affective or drive state which must be acted upon or defended against. The model of defense seems, then, not well suited to explain these processes. Likewise, the notion of insight. Enlightened practitioners do not necessarily have greater psychological insight into the specific nature of conflicts. Many may tolerate and naturally let conflictual mind states pass. The degree to which enlightened persons achieve psychological insight varies according to the degree of psychological sophistication of the individual (cf. also Carrington & Ephron, 1975). There is apparently less need to "see through" on the level of content what can be "let go of" on the level of process.

Our finding for this group then is complex. On the one hand, enlightenment at this level at least does not necessarily eliminate intrapsychic and interpersonal conflict, though the possibility of this occurring at higher levels of enlightenment is not foreclosed. On the other hand, enlightenment does enable the individual to suffer less from its effects. This suggests a rethinking of current models of the relative position of meditation and normal adult development, or meditation and psychotherapy insofar as therapy reinstitutes the normal developmental process (Blanck & Blanck, 1974). First, meditation is both different from normal development and/or psychotherapy and something more. While meditation apparently parallels some of the processes and accomplishes some of the goals of conventional therapies in alleviating intrapsychic conflict and facilitating mature object relations, it aims at a perceptual shift and a goal-state which is not aimed at or even envisaged in most psychotherapeutic models of mental health and development. However, meditation and psychotherapy cannot be positioned on a "spectrum" (Wilbur, 1977) in any mutually exclusive way as though both simply pointed to a different range of human

[20]This may explain why some of the more controversial and allegedly enlightened teachers and gurus currently in the United States seem to have rather active sexual involvements, problems with aggression, etc.

[21]According to the tradition, personal conflicts are actually likely to intensify between the second and third experience of enlightenment. This contradicts one major misconception in both western and eastern cultures. It is often mistakenly assumed by western students of meditation that enlightenment solves all of one's problems. Asian teachers know this is not so. But they in turn point almost exclusively to the remaining "fetters" of "defilements" that will be eliminated only with the attainment of further degrees of enlightenment. They are often unaware of the extent to which psychodynamic conflicts continue in at least the earlier enlightenment stages; though, as pointed out, individuals at these stages may manage the effects of such conflicts better, even without specific psychological insight into their nature.

[22]There are no dictates in terms of social role with respect to such passions. One may be monk, lay person or tantric adept. The only dictate is clear awareness.

development (Rama *et al.*, 1976). Not only do postenlightenment stages of meditation apparently affect the manifestation and management of neurotic and even borderline conditions, but this type of conflict continues to be experienced after enlightenment.[23] This suggests either that psychological maturity and the path to enlightenment are perhaps two complementary but not entirely unrelated lines of growth; or that indeed they do represent different "levels" or ranges of health/growth along a continuum, but with much more complex relationships between them than have previously been imagined. It may be, for instance, that still higher stages of enlightenment may indirectly affect the intrapsychic structural foundations of neurotic or borderline level conflict and so resolve it, even though this is not their main intent.[24] This will be an issue for the next group of protocols. It is also one of the most important issues for future empirical research.

The Masters Group

Masters at the third stage of enlightenment are alleged to no longer be subject to sexual or aggressive impulses and painful affects. The fully enlightened master (Fourth Path) is alleged to have perfected the mind and to be free of any kind of conflict or suffering. These two types of "ariyas" or "worthy ones" constitute a unique group according to past tradition and current practice.[25] The single Rorschach of the master representing this group[26] is certainly unusual. The interpretive question, however, is whether this protocol can be distinguished from the dogmatic opinions of a religious fundamentalist or the fixed delusions of the paranoid schizophrenic where one might also expect attempts to relate the various test cards into a single theme. There are differences. The decision to use the testing situation as an occasion to teach stands in direct contrast to the guardedness and constrictedness of a paranoid record. The personalized nature of paranoid delusion contrasts with the systematic presentation of a consensual body of teaching established by the cultural tradition. These are culture-dominated, not drive-dominated, percepts. The associations are consistent and integrated across all ten cards rather than being loosely related from card to card. We know of no paranoid record that compares with its level of consistency and integration. It is a considerable feat to integrate all ten cards into a single body of teaching over and against the varied stimulus-pull of ten very different cards, and to do so without significant departure in reality testing.

[23]There is an analogous situation perhaps on the border between neurotic and psychotic levels of organization. Recent exploration of the borderline and narcissistic conditions has led to a recognition that different "developmental lines" (A. Freud,1963) can be simultaneously structured at different levels of organization so that, e.g., a personality generally organized at a neurotic level can be seriously impaired and infiltrated by developmental deficits in specific psychic functions (Blanck & Blanck, 1979). The potential relevance of this finding and of this kind of thinking to meditation development has not yet been explored.

[24]A similar suggestion has been made by Wilbur (1977) in his cross-cultural integration of many of these same traditions into a unified spectrum model of consciousness, though he does not develop the point or analyze the mechanism by which this comes about. He states: (1977:272f): "In undercutting these dualisms (persona vs shadow, psyche vs soma), one simultaneously undercuts the support of the individual neuroses. . . . In recognizing a depth of one's identity that goes beyond one's individual and separate being, a person can more easily go beyond his individual and separate neuroses. . . . Once this process quickens, the individual is no longer exclusively identified with just his separate self sense and hence is no longer exclusively tied to his purely personal problems. He can start to let go of his fears and anxieties, depression and obsessions, and begin to view them with some clarity and impartiality." Again, the situation on lower levels of personality integration is apparently similar according to the most advanced clinical thinking. In discussing impairments in certain "developmental lines" which could ordinarily be expected to lead to borderline pathology, Blanck & Blanck (1979) point out, following Mahler (1975), that "Affront at a given phase or subphase does not result in cessation of development. Although fixation and regression may occur in one of several developmental lines, the forward march of the totality of development and organization proceeds nonetheless. Sometimes, with favorable subsequent experience, the sweep of organization carries with it and may even repair the damage of an earlier process by subsuming it favorably" (1979: 134).

[25]While collecting data in the South Asian component of this study, the second author was interrupted by the master when he began to ask an advanced subject to describe their practice for Third Path. He was told the question about attainment of higher Paths was not appropriate and was not generally asked. This happened only this once and contrasts with the rather extraordinary openness and frankness which all the subjects had shown throughout the study. This cooperation was itself extraordinary in light of the fact that traditionally these experiences are never discussed with anyone but one's teacher. To the best knowledge of the authors, no Asian practitioners at any stage of enlightenment have agreed to be subjects of research before or since this study. This was the only question the author was not permitted to ask—or was not answered—in 6 months of interviewing and testing. No such prohibition applied to questions about first or second Path experiences and the author obtained extensive autobiographical accounts of these moments of enlightenment. These are being incorporated in a subsequent study (in preparation).

[26]Though the author was not allowed to ask the question of attainment directly, data from the case history interview, corroborated by the Rorschach and the additional TAT protocols which were administered in the South Asian study, permits this classification.

Meditation: A Rorschach Study

One additional piece of evidence that might speak to the validity of the integrative style is its documentation in other field work. Though to our knowledge there are no other Rorschachs reported for meditation masters, Rorschachs have been reported for advanced teachers from other spiritual traditions. For example, Boyer *et al.* (1964) administered the Rorschach to Apache shamans. He also collected indigenous ratings on the authenticity of the shamans by having the Indians themselves rate whether they felt a given shaman was real or fake. The Rorschachs of the pseudoshamans looked like pathological records. The records of the shamans rated authentic were atypical. In a separate paper, Klopfer & Boyer (1961) published the protocol of a "real" shaman. It is surprisingly similar to our master's Rorschach. There also the shaman used the ten cards as an occasion to teach the examiner about his lived world-view; in that case, about his ecstatic flights through the universe. There also the shaman relied heavily upon shading and amorphously used form. Boyer was unclear as to the significance of the shading and saw it as pathological. We are not so sure, especially in light of the high use of shading by our Ss during samadhi. Shading in very high incidence for practitioners of altered states may be a valid indicator of the awareness of subtle internal and external nuances in stimuli that is a result of disciplined exploration of these states. The integrative style is perhaps an additional feature of those individuals who have carried their skill to its completion. One possible implication of such cross-cultural similarities is that this style may be suggestive of a "master's Rorschach" regardless of the spiritual tradition. The master is not at all interested in expressing the individual content of his/her mind to an examiner. Out of compassion, the master is only interested in pointing a way for others to "see" reality more clearly in such a way that it alleviates their suffering. The test situation becomes a teaching situation whereby the examiner becomes a witness to a guided exploration of the transpersonal level of the mind/universe.

A second possible inference from the master's protocol is that intrapsychic structure has undergone a radical enduring reorganization. The protocol shows no evidence of sexual or aggressive drive conflicts, or indeed any evidence of instinctually based drive at all. Remarkable though it may seem, there may be no endopsychic structure in the sense of permanently opposed drives and controls. We assume that "a perfectly mature person" would be "a whole unified person whose internal psychic differentiation and organization would simply represent his diversified interests and abilities, within an overall good ego development and good object-relationships" (Guntrip, 1969).[27]

Summary

The purpose of this study has been to illustrate an approach to the empirical validation of the classical scriptural accounts and current reports of meditation attainments using a single instrument, the Rorschach. The Rorschachs in the respective criterion groups were so obviously different as to merit this preliminary report, even without completion of the quantitative data analysis. These Rorschachs illustrate that the classical subjective reports of meditation stages are more than religious belief systems; they are valid accounts of the perceptual changes that occur with intensive meditation toward the goal of understanding perception and alleviating suffering.

As it happens, the Rorschach, in addition to being a personality test, is an excellent measure of perception for such an investigation. Ducey (1975) has argued that the Rorschach is a measure of "self-created reality." The task requires a subject to attribute meaning to a set of ambiguous stimuli. In so doing, the experimenter learns something of how the subject constructs an inner representation of the world. This task is congruent with the meditator's own practice, namely, to analyze the process by which his mind works in creating the internal and external world. Much to our surprise, the unusual performance on these Rorschachs for most subjects seemed to give a clear indication of the most important changes in mental functioning that occur during the major stages of the meditative path.

To the extent that these findings are valid, the prospect of quick advance along the path of meditation is not realistic. Note that after 3 months of continuous intensive daily practice about one-half the Ss have shown very little change, at least as defined in terms of formal meditation. The other half achieved some proficiency in concentration. Only three perfected Access concentration and began to have insights similar

---

[27]Guntrip (1969: 428) himself however goes on to say that, "We cannot, however, hope for such perfection." The Masters Group in this study suggests that such hope may actually not be misplaced.

to those described in the classical accounts of the insight series of meditations. Only one of these, in turn, advanced in the insight series to the stage of Equanimity, a stage short of enlightenment. This slow rate of progress, at least for western students, is humbling, but it is also consistent with general patterns of growth. It should also inspire confidence. Such unusual and far-reaching transformations of perceptual organization and character structure could not possibly be the work of 3 months or a year, or could they be attained by short-cuts without an adequate foundation being laid first. Patience, forebearance, and a long-enduring mind, or what one master has called "constancy" (Suzuki Roshi, 1970), is listed among the traditional "paramis" or perfections required of practitioners. On the other hand, both the self-reports as well as the test data from both the South Asian and the American study seem to validate the hypothesis that meditation is something very much more than stress-reduction and psychotherapy; and that its apparent goal-states are commensurate with the effort and perseverence they undoubtedly require.

Meditation, then, is not exactly a form of therapy but a soteriology,i.e., a means of liberation. It is said to be an extensive path of development that leads to a particular end: total liberation from the experience of ordinary human suffering and genuine wisdom that comes from true perception of the nature of mind and its construction of reality. Western therapy utilizes ideational and affective processes as its vehicle of treatment toward the end of behavioral and affective change. This is *not* so of formal meditation. As seen in the Rorschachs, ideational and affective processes do not even occur to any significant extent in the initial development of samadhi, though they reoccur much later as objects of, not vehicles for, insight. Though meditation concerns itself with a thorough analysis of all mental operations—ideational, affective, and perceptual—yet meditation is primarily an analysis of perception of the world and how ignorance of peceptual processes contributes to human suffering. Trait transformations are indeed very difficult to achieve. Meditation may provide enduring and radical trait benefits only to a very few who attempt to practice. Yet, for those of us who have had occasion to come in contact with and study the few masters, like the one whose Rorschach is given here, they are indeed unusual and deeply compassionate individuals who stand as rare living examples of an ideal: civilization beyond discontent.

References

Avalon, A. *The serpent power*, Madras: Ganesh & Co., 1931.

Binder, H. *Die Helldunkeldeutungen im Psychodiagnostischem Experiment von Rorschach*. Zurich: Urell Fussli, 1932.

Boyer, L. B., Klopfer, B., Brawer, F. B. and Kawai, H. "Comparison of the shamans and pseudoshamans of the Apache of the Mescalero Indian Reservation: A Rorschach Study." *J. Proj. Techn. Person. Assessment*, 1964, **28**, 173–180.

Blanck, G. and Blanck, R. *Ego psychology: theory and practice*. New York: Columbia Univ. Press, 1974.

Blanck, G. and Blanck, R. *Ego psychology II: psychoanalytic developmental psychology*. New York: Columbia University Press, 1979.

Brown, D. P. "A Model for the levels of concentrative meditation." *Int. J. Clin. Exper. Hypnosis*, 1977, **25**(4), 236–273 (Oct.).

Brown, D. P. "Mahamudra meditation-stages and contemporary cognitive psychology: a study in comparative hermaneutics." Unpublished Doctoral Dissertation, The University of Chicago, 1979.

Brown, D. P., Twemlo, S., Engler, J., Maliszewski, M., and Stauthamer, J. "The Profile of Meditation Experience (POME)," Form II, Psychological Test Copyright, Washington, D.C., 1978.

Brown, D. P., Hurt, S., Oberlander, J., Pfeiffer, G., Boxer, A., and Fromm, E. "The Phenomena of Self-Hypnosis." *Int. J. Clin. Exptl. Hypnosis*, 1980.

Campbell, D. "Degrees of freedom and the case study." In T. Cook & C. Reichardt (Eds.), *Qualitative and quantitative methods in evaluation research*. Beverly Hills, California: Sage Publications, 1975.

Carrington, P. and Ephron, H. S. "Meditation as an Adjunct to Psychotherapy." In S. Arieti & G. Chrazanowski (Eds.), *The world biennial of psychotherapy and psychiatry*, 262–291, 1975.

Chowdhury, U. *An Indian modification of the thematic appreciation test*. Calcutta: Sree Saraswaty Press Ltd., 1960.

Crowne, D. P. and Marlowe, D. A. "A new scale of social desirability independent of psychopathology." *J. Consult. Psychol.*, 1960, **24**, 349–354.

Dasgupta, S. *Obscure religious cults*. Calcutta, F. K. Mukhopadhyay, 1946.

Davidson, R. J., Goleman, D. and Schwartz, G. E. "Attentional and affective concomitants of meditation: a cross-sectional study." *J. Abnormal Psychol.*, 1976, **85**, 235–238.

Ducey, C. "Rorschach experimental and representational dimensions of object relations: a longitudinal study." Unpublished Doctoral Dissertation, Harvard University, 1975.

Eliade, M. *Yoga: immortality and freedom*. New York: Bollingen Foundation, Inc., 1969.

Engler, J. "The Undivided Self: Clinical Case Studies of Object Relations in Buddhist Mindfulness Meditation." 1980.

Exner, J. E. The Rorschach: a comprehensive system. New York: John Wiley & Sons, 1974.

Flavell, J. H. *The developmental psychology of Jean Piaget*, Princeton, New Jersey: Van Nostrand, 1963.

Frank, J. *Persuasion and healing*. New York: Schocken Books, Inc., 1962.

Freud, A. "The concept of developmental lines." *The psychoanalytical study of the Chi.*, Vol. 8, 245–265. New York: International Univ. Press, 1963.

Fromm, E. F., Oberlander, M. I. & Grunewald, D. "Perception and cognitive processes in different states of consciousness: the waking state and hypnosis." *J. Proj. Tech. Pers. Assessment*, 1970, **34**, 375–387.

Goldstein, J. *The experience of insight: a natural unfolding.* Santa Cruz: Unity Press, 1976.

Goleman, D. "Meditation as Metatherapy." *J. Transper. Psychol.*, 1971, **3**, 1–15.

Goleman, D. "The Buddha on Meditation and States of Consciousness, Part I: The Teachings." *J. Transper. Psychol.* 1972, 4.

Goleman, D. "Meditation and consciousness: an Asian approach to mental health." *Am. J. Psychother.*, 1976, **30**, 41–54.

Goleman, D. and Schwartz, G. E. "Meditation as an intervention in stress reactivity." *J. Consult. Clin. Psychol.*, 1976, **44**, 456–466.

Guntrip, H. *Schizoid phenomena, object relations and the self.* New York: International Univ. Press, 1969.

Hilgard, E.R. "Issues bearing on recommendations from the behavioral and social sciences study committee." *Am. Psychol.*, 1970, **25**(5), 456–463.

Holt, R. and Havel, J. "A method for assessing primary and secondary process in the Rorschach." In M. A. Rickers-Ovsiankina (Ed.), *Rorschach psychology.* New York: John Wiley & Sons, Inc., 1960.

Klopfer, B. and Boyer, L. B. "Notes on the personality structure of a North American Indian shaman: Rorschach interpretation." *J. Proj. Tech. Pers. Assess.*, 1961, **25**, 170–178.

Kornfield, J. M. "The Psychology of Mindfulness Meditation." Unpublished Doctoral Dissertation, The Humanistic Psychology Institute, 1976.

Kornfield, J. M. *Living buddhist masters.* Santa Cruz: Unity Press, 1977.

Mahasi Sayadaw, *Progress of insight.* Kandy: Buddhist Publication Society, 1965.

Mahasi Sayadaw, *Practical insight meditation.* Santa Cruz: Unity Press, 1972.

Mahler, M., Pine, F., and Bergman, A. *The psychological birth of the human infant.* New York: Basic Books, 1975.

Maupin, E. W. "Individual differences in response to a zen meditation exercise." *J. Consult. Psychol.*, 1965, **29**, 139–145.

Mayman, M. Measuring introversiveness on the Rorschach Test: the fabulization scale." Unpublished, Aug., 1960.

Mayman, M. "Reality contact, defense effectiveness and psychopathology in Rorschach form-level scores." In Klopfer, B., Meyer, M. & Brawer, F. (Eds.), *Developments in the Rorschach Technique III: Aspects of Personality Structure*, New York: Harcourt, Brace, Jovanovich, 1970, pp. 11–46.

Mishra, R. M. *Yoga sutras: the textbook of yoga psychology.* Garden City: Anchor Press, 1963.

Narada, *A manual of abhidhamma.* Kandy: Buddhist Publication Society, 1975.

Nyanomoli, B. (Translatr) *Visuddimagga [The path of purification.] Buddhaghosa.* 2 Vol. Boulder, CO: Shambhala Publications, 1976.

Rama, S., Ballentine, R., and Ajaya, S. *Yoga and psychotherapy.* Glenview: Himalayan Institute, 1976.

Reyher, J. 1969. Electroencephalogram and rapid eye movements during free imagery and dream recall. *J. Abnormal Psychol.*, 1969, **74**, 574–582.

Schachtel, E. G. *Experiential Foundations of Rorschach's test.* New York: Basic Books, Inc., 1966.

Smith, J. C. "Psychotherapeutic effects of TM with controls for expectation of relief and daily sitting." *J. Consult. Clin. Psychol.*, 1976, **44**, 630–637.

Suzuki Roshi, *Zen mind, beginners mind.* New York: Weatherhill, 1970.

Tart, C. *States of consciousness.* New York: E. P. Dutton, 1975.

Varenne, J. *Yoga and the hindu tradition.* Chicago: Univ. of Chicago Press, 1976.

Walsh, R. "Initial meditative experiences." *J. Transper. Psychol.*, 1977, **9**, 151–192; *ibid.*, 1978, **10**, 1–28.

Watkins, J. G. and Stauffacher, J. C. "An Index of Pathological Thinking in the Rorschach." In P. M. Lerner, (Ed.), *Handbook of Rorschach scales.* New York: International Univ. Press, 1975.

Wilbur, K. *The spectrum of consciousness.* Wheaton: Theosophical Publ. House, 1977.

C2. Experiences During Meditation

One of the most important and least researched aspects of meditation is the experiences that occur during meditation. This area is quite difficult to research because of the often nonverbal quality, the "ineffable" quality of the experience.

The articles included here give different perspectives and methodologies for dealing with the phenomenology of meditation. Walsh (22), based on Charles Tart's earlier attempt (1971), utilized his training in the behavioral sciences and described, as a participant-observer, his meditative experiences, including both daily meditation as well as experiences during a 3-month long retreat. Although titled, "Initial Meditative Experiences," Walsh's 2-year account covers a considerably longer time frame than most reports, which involve only a few weeks (e.g., Deikman, 1966; Maupin, 1965).

Kohr's article (23) trying to replicate an earlier study by Osis (1973; reviewed in some depth in article 2) takes a look at what factors are common to more intermediate long-term meditators. Of major importance in Kohr's findings is that the experiences during meditation are qualitatively different than the experiences premeditation. The exact nature of these experiences and the various factors give us one clue as to the nature of this altered state of consciousness.

Finally, Brown's (24) and Goleman's (25) articles, based on classical texts, give us an in-depth look at some of the experiences that occur in long-term meditators. Brown's article, based on classical root texts of the Mahamudra tradition, describes in depth the stages of concentrative meditation. Goleman's article provides us a discussion of both concentrative and mindfulness meditation. These articles round out this particular section in that they are based on the phenomenological experiences of masters as recorded in their texts. Thus, we progress from initial experiences of meditators of a few weeks (summarized in the accompanying table) to the intermediate experiences of meditators of several years (e.g., Walsh, Kohr) to analysis of the phenomenology of the classic meditative texts.

22

INITIAL MEDITATIVE EXPERIENCES

Roger Walsh

The following is a condensed description of the first 2 years of my own meditative experiences. Such an account was written in the belief that it may give some sense, however partial and inadequate, of the powerful and personally meaningful nature of the practice. There is a huge gap between a theoretical paper on meditation and the direct experience. Hopefully such a report by a fellow mental health professional may be of personal interest to readers who are considering the possibility of trying meditation for themselves. A more detailed account of these experiences is available elsewhere (Walsh, 1977, 1978), and for those readers who wish to see a detailed case study of meditation employed for a specific clinical disorder an excellent account is available in Shapiro (1980).

Because parts of this account describe experiences which occurred during very intensive continuous meditation in retreats, many of the experiences are far more intense and difficult than those usually encountered by people practicing for brief daily periods.

This is an account of the subjective experiences of some 2 years of Vipassana or Insight meditation. During the first year this comprised an average of approximately 1 hour per day. During the second year, this was increased to about 2 hours, as well as some 6 weeks of intensive meditation retreats, usually of 2 weeks duration. These retreats comprised about 18 to 20 hours daily of continuous walking and sitting meditation performed in total silence and without eye contact, reading, or writing. While this amount of practice may be vastly less than that of more experienced practitioners, it has certainly proved sufficient to elicit a range of experiences beyond the ken of day-to-day nonmeditative living.

I began meditation with one-half hour each day and during the first 3–6 months there were few times during which I could honestly say with complete certainty that I was definitely experiencing benefits from it. Except for the painfully obvious stiff back and sore knees, the psychological effects other than occasional relaxation felt so subtle and ephemeral that I could never be sure that they were more than a figment of my wishes and expectations. The nature of meditation seems to be, especially at first, a slow but cumulative process, a fact which may be useful for beginners to be aware of.

However, with continued perseverance, subtle effects just at the limit of my perceptual threshold began to become apparent. I had expected the eruption into awareness of powerful, concrete experiences, if not flashes of lightening and pealing of bells, then at least something of sufficient intensity to make it very clear that I had "gotten it," whatever "it" was. What "it" actually turned out to be was not the appearance of formerly nonexistent mental phenomena, but rather a gradual incremental increase in perceptual sensitivity to the formerly subliminal portions of my own inner stream of consciousness.

When one sits down with eyes closed to silence the mind, one is at first submerged by a torrent of thoughts—they crop up everywhere like frightened, nay, aggressive rats" (Satprem, 1968, p. 33). The more sensitive I became, the more I was forced to recognize that what I had formerly believed to be my rational mind preoccupied with cognition, planning, problem solving, etc., actually comprised a frantic torrent of forceful, demanding, loud, and often unrelated thoughts and fantasies which filled an unbelievable proportion of consciousness even during purposive behavior. The incredible proportion of consciousness which this fantasy world occupied, my powerlessness to remove it for more than a few seconds, and my former state of mindlessness or ignorance of its existence staggered me. Interestingly, this "mindlessness" seemed much more intense and difficult to deal with than in psychotherapy (Walsh, 1976), where the depth and sensitivity of inner awareness seemed less, and where the therapest provided a perceptual focus and was available to pull me back if I started to get lost in fantasy.

The subtlety, complexity, infinite range and number, and entrapping power of the fantasies which the mind creates seems impossible to comprehend, to differentiate from reality while in them, and even more so to describe to one who has not experienced them. Layer upon layer of imagery and quasilogic open up at any point to which attention is directed. Indeed, it gradually becomes apparent that it is impossible to question and reason one's way out of this all-encompassing fantasy since the very process of questioning, thinking, and seeking only creates further fantasy.

The power and pervasiveness of these inner dialogues and fantasies left me amazed that we could be so unaware of them during our normal waking life and reminded me of the Eastern concept of maya of all-consuming illusion.

The First Meditation Retreat

The first meditation retreat, begun about 1 year after commencing sitting, was a very painful and difficult 2-week affair. A marked hypersensitivity to all stimuli both internal and external rapidly developed, resulting in intense arousal, agitation, discomfort, and multiple chronic muscle contractions, especially around the shoulders.

One of the most amazing rediscoveries during this first retreat was the incredible proportion of time, well over 90%, which I spent lost in fantasy. Most of these were of the ego self-aggrandizing type, so that when eventually I realized I was in them, it proved quite a struggle to decide to give them up and return to the breath, but with practice this decision became slightly easier, faster, and more automatic. This by no means happened quickly since over the first 4 or 5 days the proportion of time spent in fantasy actually increased as the meditation deepened. During this period, each time I sat and closed my eyes I would be immediately swept away by vivid hallucinations, losing all contact with where I was or what I was doing until after an unknown period of time a thought would creep in such as, "Am I really swimming, lying on the beach?" etc., and then I would either get lost back into the fantasy or another thought would come: "Wait a moment, I thought I was meditating." If the latter, then I would be left with the difficult problem of trying to ground myself, i.e., of differentiating between stimulus-produced percepts ("reality") and entirely endogenous ones ("hallucinations"). The only way this seemed possible was to try finding the breath, and so I would begin frantically searching around in this hypnagogic universe for the sensations of the breath. Such was the power of the hallucinations that sometimes I would be literally unable to find it and would fall back into the fantasy. If successful, I would recognize it and be reassured that I was in fact meditating. Then in the next moment I would be lost again in yet another fantasy. The clarity, power, persuasiveness, and continuity of these hallucinations is difficult to express adequately. However, the effect of living through 3 days during which time to close my eyes meant losing contact almost immediately with ordinary reality was extraordinarily draining, to say the least. Interestingly enough while this experience was uncomfortable and quite beyond my control, it was not particularly frightening; if anything the opposite was true. For many years I had feared losing control if I let down defenses and voyaged too far along the road of self-investigation and discovery. This appears to be a common fear in most growth traditions and seems to serve a major defensive function. Having experienced this once feared outcome, it now no longer seems so terrifying. Of course, the paradox is that what we usually call control is actually exactly the opposite, a lack of ability to let go of defenses.

While a good 90% or more of this first retreat was taken up with mindless fantasy and agitation, there did occur during the second week occasional short-lived periods of intense peace and tranquility. These were so satisfying that, while I would not be willing to sign up for a life-time in a monastery, I could begin to comprehend the possibility of the truth of the Buddhist saying that "peace is the highest form of happiness." Affective lability was also extreme. There were not infrequently sudden apparently un-precipitated wide mood swings to completely polar emotions. Shorn of all my props and distractions, it became clear that I had little more than the faintest inkling of self-control over either thoughts or feelings and that my mind had a mind of its own.

This recognition is commonly described as one of the earliest, strongest, and most surprising insights which confronts people who begin intensive meditation practice, who are always amazed that they had not recognized it previously (Goldstein, 1976).

Attachments and Needs

It soon became apparent that the type of material which forceably erupted into awareness and disrupted concentration was most often material—ideas, fantasies, thoughts, etc.—to which I was attached (addicted) and around which there was considerable affective charge. There was a definite sense that attachments reduced the flexibility and power of the mind, since whenever I was preoccupied with a stimulus to which I was attached, then I had difficulty in withdrawing my attention from it to observe other stimuli which passed through awareness.

Paradoxically it seems that a need or attachment to be rid of certain experience or state may lead to its perpetuation. The clearest example of this has been with anxiety. Some months ago I suddenly began to experience mild anxiety attacks of unknown origin which, curiously enough, seemed to occur most often when I was feeling really good and in the presence of a particular person who I loved. At such times I would try all my various psychological gymnastics to eradicate it since it was clearly not okay with me to feel anxious. However, these episodes continued for some 5 months inspite of, or as it actually turned out because of, my resistance to them. During this time my practice deepened and I was able to examine more and more of the process during meditation. What I found was that I had considerable fear of fear and my mind therefore surveyed in a radarlike fashion all endogenous and exogenous stimuli for their fear-evoking potential and all reactions for any fear component. Thus there was a continuous mental radarlike scanning process preset in an exquisitely sensitive fashion for the detection of anything resembling fear. Consequently, there were a considerable number of false positives, i.e., non-fearful stimuli and reactions which were interpreted as being fearful or potentially fear-provoking. Since the reactions to the false positives themselves comprised fear and fear components, there was, of course, an immediate chain reaction set up with one fear response acting as the stimulus for the next. It thus became very clear that my fear of, and resistance to, fear was exactly what was perpetuating it.

This insight and the further application of meditative awareness to the process certainly reduced but did not eradicate these episodes entirely. Paradaoxically they still tended to recur when I felt very calm and peaceful. It was not until the middle of the next meditation retreat that the reasons for this became clear. After the first few days of pain and agitation I began to feel more and more peaceful and there came a sitting in which I could feel my meditation deepen perceptibly and the restless mental scanning slow more and more. Then as the process continued to deepend and slow, I was literally jolted by a flash of agitation and anxiety accompanying a thought—"But what do I do now if there's no more anxiety to look for?" It was apparent that if I continued to quieten, there would be neither anxiety to scan for nor a scanning process itself, and my need to get rid of anxiety demanded that I have a continuous scanning mechanism, and the presence of the mechanism, in turn, created the presence of anxiety. My "but what do I do now?" fear had very effectively removed the possibility of the dissipation of both, and its occurrence at a time when I was feeling most peaceful, relaxed and safe, of course explained why I had been subject to these anxiety episodes at the apparently paradoxical times when I felt best. Paradoxically then it appears that within the mind, if you need to be rid of certain experiences, then not only are you likely to experience a number of false positives but you may also need to have them around continuously so you can keep getting rid of them. Thus within the province of the mind, what you resist is what you get.

Perception

With continued practice the speed, power, loudness, and continuity of thoughts and fantasies began to slowly diminish, leaving subtle sensations of greater peace and quiet. After a period of about 4 or 5 months here occurred episodes in which I would open my eyes at the end of meditation and look at the outside world without the presence of concomitant internal dialogue. This state would be rapidly terminated by a rising sense of anxiety and anomie accompanied by the thought, "I don't know what anything means." Thus, I could be looking at something completely familiar, such as a tree, a building, or the sky, and yet without an accompanying internal dialogue to label and categorize it, it felt totally strange and devoid of meaning. It seems that what made something familiar and hence secure was not simply its recognition, but the actual cognitive process of matching, categorizing and labeling it, and that once this was done, then more attention and reactivity was focused on the label and labeling process rather than on the stimulus itself. Thus the initial fantasy and thought-free periods may feel both strange and distinctly unpleasant so that we are at first punished by their unfamiliarity. We have created an unseen prison for ourselves whose bars are comprised of thoughts and fantasies of which we remain largely unaware unless we undertake intensive perceptual training. Moreover, if they are removed we may be frightened by the unfamiliarity of the experience and rapidly reinstate them.

We uphold the world with our internal dialogue. (Castaneda, 1974)

Presumably this labeling process must modify our perception in many ways, including reducing our ability to experience each stimulus fully, richly, and newly, by reducing its multidimensional nature into a lesser dimensional cognitive labeling framework. This must necessarily derive from the past, be less tolerant of ambiguity, less here now, and perpetuative of a sense of sameness and continuity to the world. This process may represent the phenomenological and cognitive mediational basis of Dikman's (1966) concept of automatization and Don Juan's "maintaining the world as we know it" (Castaneda, 1971, 1974).

Interestingly, the extent of reaction to the stimulus itself as opposed to the label seems to be a direct function of the degree of mindfulness or meditative awareness. If I am mindful, then I tend to be focused on the primary sensations themselves, to label less, and to react to these labels less. For example, there was a period of about six weeks during which I felt mildly depressed. I was not incapacitated, but was uncomfortable, dysphoric, and confused about what was happening to me throughout most of the waking day. However, during daily meditation this experience and its affective quality changed markedly. The experience then felt somewhat like being on sensory overload, with many vague ill-defined somatic sensations and a large number of rapidly appearing and disappearing unclear visual images. However, to my surprise, nowhere could I find stimuli which were actually painful. Rather there was just a large input of vague stimuli of uncertain significance and meaning. I would therefore emerge from each sitting with the recognition that I was actually not experiencing any pain and feeling considerably better. This is analogous to Tarthang Tulku's (1974) statement that "The more you go into the disturbance—when you really get there—the emotional characteristics no longer exist." . . .

However, within a very short time I would lapse once more into my habitual non-mindful state and when I next became mindful once again I would find that I had been automatically labeling the stimulus complex as depression and then reacting to this label with thoughts and feelings such as "I'm depressed. I feel awful, what have I done to deserve this?", etc. A couple of moments of relaxed mindfulness would be sufficient to switch the focus back to the primary sensations and the recognition once again that I was actually not experiencing discomfort. This process repeated itself endlessly during each day. This effect of mindfulness or phenomenology and reactivity should lend itself to experimental neurophysiological investigation. It is also an interesting example of one difference in the therapeutic processes of meditation and traditional western therapies. Where the latter attempt to change the content of experience, meditation is also interested in changing the perceptual-cognitive processes by which the mind produces such experiences.

Perceptual Sensitivity

One of the most fundamental changes has been an increase in perceptual sensitivity which seems to include both absolute and discrimination thresholds. Examples of this include both a more subtle awareness of previously known precepts and a novel identification of previously unrecognized phenomena.

Sensitivity and clarity frequently seem enhanced following a meditation sitting or retreat. Thus, for example, at these times it seems that I can discriminate visual forms and outlines more clearly. It also feels as though empathy is significantly increased and that I am more aware of other people's subtle behaviors, vocal intonations, etc., as well as my own affective responses to them. The experience feels like having a faint but discernible veil removed from my eyes, and that the veil is comprised of hundreds of subtle thoughts and feelings. Each one of these thoughts and feelings seems to act as a competing stimulus or "noise" which thus reduces sensitivity to any one object. Thus after meditation any specific stimulus appears stronger and clearer, presumably because the signal:noise ratio is increased. These observations provide a phenomenological basis and possible perceptual mechanism to explain the findings that meditators in general tend to exhibit heightened perceptual sensitivity and empathy.

One unexpected demonstration of greater sensitivity has been the occurrence of the synesthetic perception of thoughts. Synesthesia, or cross-modality perception, is the phenomenon in which stimulation of one sensory modality is perceived in several, as for example, when sound is seen and felt as well as heard (Marks, 1975). Following the enhanced perceptual sensitivity which occurred during my prior psychotherapy, I began to experience this phenomenon not infrequently, suggesting that it may well occur within all of us, though usually below our thresholds (Walsh, 1976). Now during moments of greater meditative sensitivity I have begun to experience this cross-modality perception with purely mental stimuli, e.g., thoughts. Thus, for example, I may initially experience a thought as a feeling and subsequently become aware of a visual image before finally recognizing the more familiar cognitive information components.

Another novel type of perception seems to have occurred with continued practice, since I have begun to find myself gradually able to recognize increasingly subtle mental phenomena when I am not meditating, but rather am involved in my daily activity. This has resulted in an increased recognition of affects, motivations, and subtle defensive maneuvers and manipulations. Indeed, these latter recognitions seem to now constitute the sensitivity limiting factor since the discomfort which attends their more frequent perception is often sufficient to result in a defensive contraction of awareness.

Trust and Surrender

These experiences have led to a greater understanding of, and willingness to surrender to, the meditative process. In the West surrender has connotations of succumbing or being overwhelmed but here it is employed more in line with its use in the meditative traditions. Thus with increasing experience I have begun to surrender to the process in the sense of trusting, following, and allowing it to unfold without attempting to change, coerce, or manipulate it and without necessarily requiring prior understanding of what I may be about to go through or predicting the outcome. Thus, for example, one of my major fears has been the threat of losing certain psychological and intellectual abilities, e.g., of losing control, intellectual skills, and scientific capacities. This seems reminiscent of the idea that one of the major barriers to moving on to the next level is always the fear of losing that which we have.

Thus although I need to make it very clear that this surrender is far from complete for me, it has come a long way since first beginning. The experiences which seem to have contributed to this are as follows. First of all, to the best of my knowledge the feared catastrophes have not eventuated. Thus, for example, my intellectual and scientific skills seem to have remained intact. In addition, meditation seems to have provided a range of experiences, insights, and developments formerly totally unknown to me. Thus, to expect, demand, and limit that which is novel to extensions of that which is already known can prove a major limitation. This is similar to the statement by Bugental (1956) that growth is always a voyage into the unknown.

Furthermore, it now seems clear that allowing experiences to be as they are, and experiencing them without forcibly trying to change them, is effective. This is especially true when viewed with the recognition that any experience can be used for growth even to the point of perceiving the experience as necessary and perfect for the process. Indeed, recognizing the perfection and functionality of each experience appears to be a highly productive perspective for several reasons. First, it reduces the deleterious agitation, resistance, and eruption of defenses and manipulation which occur secondary to judgment and negative perspectives. Second, contrary to my previous beliefs, acceptance and a nonjudgmental attitude toward an experience or situation does not necessarily remove either the motivation or capacity to deal with it in the most effective manner. Thus my prior beliefs were that I *needed* my judgments, aversions, and negative reactions in order to power my motivation to modify the situations and stimuli eliciting them. It should be noted here that the experience of perfection is just that, an experience, which may say more about the psychological state of the individual perceiving it than about the stimulus per se, and may not necessarily in any way vitiate the perceiver's perception of the need to modify it. Finally, there has been the recognition that the great meditation teachers really knew what they were talking about. Time and time again I have read descriptions, explanations, and predictions about meditation, the normal psychological state, the states that arise with more and more meditation, latent capacities, etc., and have scoffed and argued against them feeling that they were just so removed from my prior experiences and beliefs that they could not possibly be true. However, by now I have had a variety of experiences which I formerly would have believed to be impossible and have gained the experiential background with which to understand more of what is being taught. Thus I now have to acknowledge that these people know vastly more than I do and that it is certainly worth my while to pay careful attention to their suggestions. Thus experiential knowledge may be a major limiting factor for intellectual understanding of psychological processes and consciousness, and unfortunately even highly intellectually sophisticated nonpractitioners may not fully understand such phenomena. Indeed, my experiences lead me to believe that the scope of the mind, its range of experiences, its capacity for producing encompassing and absorbing illusions which we take for reality, the extent to which it is usually out of control, and its nature and potentials when fully trained may not only be more than we believe, but may also be more than we can believe.

References

Bugental, J. *The search for authenticity*. New York: Holt, Rinehart, and Winston, 1965.

Castaneda, C. *A separate reality: further conversations with don Juan*. New York: Simon and Schuster, 1971.

Castaneda, C. *Tales of power*. New York: Simon and Schuster, 1974.

Deikman, A. Deautomatization and the mystic experience. *Psychiatry*, 1966, **29**, 324–338.

Goldstein, J. *The experience of insight*. Santa Cruz, California: Unity Press, 1976.

Marks, L. On colored-hearing synesthesia: Cross modal translations of sensory dimensions. *Psychol. Bull.*, 1975, **82**, 303–331.

Maslow, A. H. *The farther reaches of human nature*. New York: Viking Press, 1971.

Sataprem. *Sri Aurobindo or the adventure of consciousness*. New York: Harper and Row, 1968.

Shapiro, D. *Meditation: self-regulation strategy and altered state of consciousness*. New York: Aldine, 1980.

Tarthang Talku. On thoughts. *Crystal Mirror*, 1974, **3**, 7–20.

Walsh, R. N. Reflection on psychotherapy. *J. Transpers. Psychol.*, 1976, **8**, 100–111.

Walsh, R. Initial meditative experiences: I. *J. Transpers. Psychol.*, 1977, **9**, 151–192.

Walsh, R. Initial meditative experiences: II. *J. Transpers. Psychol.*, 1978, **10**, 1–28.

23

DIMENSIONALITY IN MEDITATIVE EXPERIENCE: A REPLICATION

Richard L. Kohr

Meditation is considered by some to lead the persistent seeker to an altered state of consciousness, characterized by a sense of expansiveness, unity, joy, of contact with the infinite (i.e., Naranjo and Ornstein, 1971; Puryear and Thurston, 1975). The "spiritual" quality of the experience is one which meditators emphasize in their descriptions. Such states have also been termed peak experiences by Maslow (1962). Edward Carpenter, the English poet-scientist, testified to the universal quality of the experience when he wrote (1912, p. 79–80):

> Of all the hard facts of science, . . . I know of none more solid and fundamental than the fact that if you inhibit thought (and persevere) you come at length to a region of consciousness below or behind thought, and different from ordinary thought in its nature and character—a consciousness of quasi-universal quality, and a realization of an altogether vaster self than that to which we are accustomed. And since the ordinary consciousness, with which we are concerned in ordinary life, is before all things founded on the little local self, and is in fact self-consciousness in the little local sense, it follows that to pass out of that is to die to the ordinary self and the ordinary world.
>
> It is to die in the ordinary sense, but in another sense it is to wake up and find that the "I," one's real, lost intimate self, pervades the universe and all other beings—that the mountains and the sea and the stars are a part of one's body and that one's soul is in touch with the souls of all creatures.

This grandiose view of the potential of meditation is not shared by all. Others would suggest that meditation is simply a form of relaxation induced by autosuggestion or perhaps by self-hypnosis. Certainly, a "relaxation response" (Benson, 1975) is generally regarded as beneficial from the standpoint of relieving stress. In his review of the therapeutic effect of meditation, Smith (1975, p. 562) wonders whether "the practice of regular sitting, and not the meditation exercise, is the crucial theraputic variable." Obviously experiences while practicing meditation vary widely, some mild and some profound, but are there some common characteristics which might be described?

Efforts to identify common experimental components from a study of individual cases and available mystical and occult literature produced evidence of certain recurrent patterns (e.g., James, 1958; Johnson, 1959; Stace, 1960). A systematic effort to examine the subjective experience of "ordinary" people meditating in small semi-structured groups was reported by Osis and Bokert (1971) and Osis, Bokert and Carlson (1973) who found certain stable patterns emerging from factor analyses of questionnaire data. They identified five dimensions which appeared in at least three of their experiments. Furthermore, certain "core items" persistently clustered together giving a clarity and stability to each of the replicated dimensions. The authors point out that despite universal claims that meditation experience is ineffable, clear dimensions were obtained. And these experiential dimensions did not reflect everyday states of consciousness. Rather, they mirrored a change in the manner of experiencing. These replicated factors were called, Self-Transcendence and Openness, Intensification and Change in Consciousness, Meaning, Forceful Exclusion of Images, and General Success of Meditation. A Negative Experience factor also appeared in their final experiment apparently as a result of the inclusion of items tapping negative experience. This factor was regarded as a probable pseudo-dimension which had little to do with successful meditation, but instead was expressive of disruptive influences. While this may be so, many individuals, especially beginning meditators, find their efforts to be counterproductive. Hence, such a factor is quite probably indicative of some people's experience in meditation, albeit an unsuccessful one.

The present study reports on an effort to replicate the findings of Osis and his associates under conditions which were quite different from the small group context. This study was part of a larger investigation which sought to test the utility of a meditation technique described by Edgar Cayce (Puryear and Thurston, 1975). The effects which accrued from this approach over a 28-day experimental period, such as reduction in anxiety for experimental subjects while controls demonstrated no change in anxiety, was reported in a previous article (Puryear, Cayce and Thurston, 1976). An examination of changes in subjective meditation experience for groups differing on characteristics such as anxiety level or degree of adherence to meditation guidelines was reported by Kohr (1978).

Method

Selection and Characteristics of Participants

A multi-stage process best characterizes the selection of the participants for this project. Initially, the ARE membership was surveyed regarding personal psychic experience, dreaming, practice of meditation, etc. A pool of potential subjects was formed by those who indicated a desire to participate in future meditation research. Subsequently, invitations were sent to a sample from the pool. The invitation stated that the participants would have to agree to spend (a) approximately three hours studying a specially prepared meditation manual, (b) approximately two hours completing psychological inventories prior to the experimental period, (c) 20 minutes daily in meditation for 28 days, following the method outlined in the manual, (d) about two hours completing psychological scales after the experimental period. Of the 218 who registered 145 completed all phases of the project including pre and post psychological tests and a special daily meditation questionnaire. The participants were obviously self-selected. About two-thirds were married, two-thirds were female and the average age was 38. The participants were well disbursed geographically with each region of the country amply represented. Educationally, the sample was well above the national average. The average years of education was 15.5 where 16.0 is equivalent to a bachelors degree. Their religious orientation was also quite varied, ranging from practitioners of various forms of yoga, Rosicrusian, Unity, New Thought to the more conventional church affiliations. Except for the broad geographical distribution, the sample appears to be rather similar to the subjects who were involved in the meditation-ESP study reported by Osis and Bokert (1971).

Instruments

Instruments completed before and after the experimental period included the IPAT Anxiety Scale Questionnaire (Cattell, 1957), which yields "covert" and "overt" anxiety scales in addition to a total score, and the Mooney Problem Checklist (Mooney and Gordon, 1950) which provides an index of perceived problems in the respondent's life. A special background questionnaire provided indices of prior meditation experience and the degree to which the participant adhered to the procedures outlined in the meditation manual. In order to ascertain the nature of their experience during each of the 28 meditation sessions each participant responded to a questionnaire developed by Osis and his associates (Osis & Bokert, 1971 and Osis, Bokert & Carlson, 1973) and modified by the ARE staff.

All items on the modified Osis questionnaire[1] represent a nine point continuum ranging from one extreme to the opposite. Ten items consist of pre-meditation session scales. The first four items are original Osis items which measure the general mood prior to the session. The remaining six items were new and dealt with mental, physical and emotional functioning during the day. Thirty items pertain to the

---

[1]The 40 items comprising the pre- and post-session questionnaire are available from the author.

meditation experience. Of these, 23 are taken directly from the Osis scale which also consisted of 30 items. Seven items are new ones and were developed by Mark Thurston of the ARE staff. The following pre-session illustrates the format of the pre- and post-session questionnaire.

I feel very happy and   :___:___:___:___:___:___: I feel greatly dissatisfied
content with myself   with myself

Subgroups

To introduce greater depth in a present study, the data was subdivided into various subgroups. These groups were "low" and "high" categories on five variables which appeared promising based on a visual inspection of preliminary correlational analyses. These variables included anxiety level as measured by the IPAT, incidence of perceived personal problems as indicated by the total Mooney score, the length of time one had previously engaged in meditation on a fairly regular basis, the amount of previous meditation experience combined with whether a consistent schedule had been maintained during the month prior to the study and the degree to which the paticipants adhered to the procedures detailed in the meditation manual. Table 1 describes the decision rule for each classification. The "N" column refers to the number of participants in the respective group while the "sessions" column denotes the number of meditation sessions comprising the analysis for that group.

Meditation Procedure

Although the participants had varying degrees of previous meditation experience, and from a variety of orientations, there was an effort to obtain some uniformity during the 28-day experimental period. A 31-page manual served as a guide for this activity. Incorporating the approach first described by Edgar Cayce (Puryear & Thurston, 1975), the manual guided the participant in (a) formulating a clear definition of meditation, (b) establishing ideals and purposes, (c) understanding mind/body relationships, (d) choosing a regular time, place, and position for meditation, (e) carrying out preparatory activities, (f) employing aids for attunement, and (g) engaging in a period of silent, focused attention on a short, self-composed statement of one's ideal for spiritual growth.

Table 1. Summary of Subgroups for Which Analyses Were Performed

Group	N	Sessions	Definition
1. Total sample	145	4060	All cases
2. Low anxiety	55	1540	Total IPAT score of 1–25
3. High anxiety	90	2520	Total IPAT score of 26+
4. Low problems	54	1512	Total Mooney score of 1-28
5. High problems	91	2548	Total Mooney score of 29+
6. Low regular schedule	34	952	No previous meditation experience up to one month of prior experience
7. High regular schedule	76	2128	One or more years of meditation experience
8. Low prior experience	30	840	Up to 1 month prior meditation experience with up to 3 meditation periods per week during preceding month
9. High prior experience	36	1008	One or more years of meditation experience with 4 or more meditation periods per week during preceding month
10. Low adherence	38	1064	Those who indicated they followed only "somewhat" or "very little" the steps in the meditation manual
11. High adherence	107	2996	Those who indicated they followed "very closely" the steps in the meditation manual

Factor Analysis

Consistent with the analysis conducted by Osis and his associates the present study subjected questionnaire data to a principle components analysis followed by orthogonal rotation using the varimax criterion. To guard against possible distortion due to skewed item distributions Osis first performed a log transformation. In the present study data for the total group were first analyzed in both the raw and log transformed state. A comparison of the two analyses revealed the same factor structure, the essential difference being somewhat lower loadings when log transformed data were used. Since the results did not seem to differ in a material way all the remaining analyses were carried out on raw data and all tabled results are shown for raw data analyses.

Results

Of initial interest is a comparison of mean item scores obtained by the participants of the present study, who meditated alone in accordance with manual specified guidelines, and for the subjects in the Osis experiments who meditated and discussed their experiences in a small group context. There were 23 items common to both questionnaires for which mean data was available. Shown in Table 2 are the 10 pre-session items followed by the 30 postmeditation session items. The sequence number of the item as it appeared in the ARE questionnaire and in the Osis *et al.* (1973) questionnaires is also given. Parentheses around an item number signifies that the ARE item is very similar to, but not identical to, the corresponding Osis item. Mean scores are presented for a 1968 and 1969 experiment as reported in the Osis & Bokert (1971) article.

Despite the difference in methodology the mean item scores appear remarkably similar. Since the Osis investigation did not report standard deviations, statistical significance tests are not possible; however, some observations can still be made. Of the 23 items which can be compared, 16 were within ±0.5 points of one another. Particularly close are the mean scores of the four mood prior to session items (items 1–4). Of the seven items demonstrating a discrepancy of greater than ±0.5 points, the ARE group reported less visual imagery, a greater sense of relevance when images were experienced, a greater sense of mental alertness during meditation, greater relaxation, greater sense of relevance regarding thoughts, a greater sense of joy and less often experienced a sense of presence.

Of the 11 factor analyses conducted, one was based on the total sample and the remaining 10 were based on the subgroups as defined in Table 1. The factor analyses yielded five identifiable factors which were consistent for the total sample and most of the ten subgroups. Three of the factors, "Intensification and Change of Consciousness," "Psychological State Prior to Session" (termed "Mood Prior to Session" by Osis), and "Negative Experience" were replications of factors identified by Osis *et al.* These factors were generally the first, second, and third extracted and usually accounted for about 28, 10, and 5% of the variance, respectively. Two weak, but consistent and coherent factors also emerged in the present study. These factors, called "Mental Clarity" and "Physical Effects" typically accounted for about 4 and 3.5% additional variance. Together, the five factors account for about 50% of the total variance.

In the description which follows occasional reference will be made to certain items called "core items" by Osis *et al.* Core items were so called because they consistently exhibited loadings in excess of 0.30 on a given factor. Such items were used to define the basic nature of the factor. In the tables showing the three replicated factors the Osis core items are designated by an asterisk.

The first factor extracted in most of the 11 analyses and, of course, the dominant one, consists of 18 items, 11 of which are core items as identified by Osis *et al.* Displayed in Table 3 are the items consistently loading on this factor which, following Osis, is named "Intensification and Change of Consciousness." This factor conveys the impression of a heightened sense of connectedness with the world and with others, a sense of purpose and meaningfulness, deep positive emotion, an intensification of awareness, perceptual change and enhancement, a presence of religious significance, and a sense of satisfaction with the session. The quality of transcendence (item 15) and oneness (items 10 and 11) which is so prominent in the present data suggests a blend of two factors found in the Osis study, namely, "Self-Transcendence and Openness" as well as the "Intensification" factor.

Table 4 shows the items comprising the "Psychological State Prior to Session factor. This factor is

Sequence		Descriptive phrase	Mean scores		
ARE	Osis		ARE	Osis 1968	Osis 1969
Pre-session Items					
1	1	Content with self	6.1	6.4	6.1
2	3	Elation	5.8	5.8	5.7
3	2	Feeling of vitality	5.0	5.0	5.3
4	4	Freedom from anxiety	6.2	6.6	6.2
5	—	Slept soundly last night	7.3	—	—
6	—	Awoke easily this morning	6.3	—	—
7	—	Energetic today	5.8	—	—
8	—	Good mental focus today	6.2	—	—
9	—	Memory excellent today	6.3	—	—
10	—	Positive mood today	5.8	—	—
Post-session Items					
1	1	Feeling it was a good session	5.6	5.8	5.8
2	2	Absence of visual images	6.8	5.3	5.1
3	3	Visual images relevant	5.0	3.9	4.2
4	4	Alertness	5.8	4.9	5.3
5	5	Serenity	5.7	6.2	5.9
6	6	Relaxation	6.9	5.8	6.1
7	9	Few thoughts	4.7	4.4	4.4
8	10	Thoughts relevant	5.5	4.3	4.4
9	(16)	Affirmation with external	5.0	5.0	4.0
10	12	Oneness with external	5.4	5.6	5.2
11	(8)	Merging with others	4.6	4.5	4.5
12	—	Experience of light	3.5	—	—
13	—	Consciousness maintained	7.4	—	—
14	—	Sensed order in universe	4.0	—	—
15	—	Transcendence of space/time	3.9	—	—
16	(11)	Love and joy	5.6	5.0	4.8
17	—	Body felt warmer	3.6	—	—
18	—	Sensed endocrine activity	4.0	—	—
19	—	Spinal sensations	3.2	—	—
20	14	Absence of frustration	6.9	—	—
21	15	Deep insights	4.0	3.6	3.5
22	17	Sense of presence	3.6	4.4	—
23	19	Security	5.0	5.5	—
24	20	Refreshed after session	6.2	6.0	6.2
25	22	Perceptual enrichment	3.3	2.9	—
26	24	Inner resources available	5.5	5.7	5.4
27	25	Free of anxiety during session	6.7	—	—
28	27	No feeling of anger	8.2	—	—
29	28	Awareness directed inward	6.0	—	—
30	29	Intensification of consciousness	4.6	5.1	—

essentially like the Osis *et al.* "Mood Brought to Session" factor with the four core items marked with an asterisk. In the present scale six additional items pertaining to mood and psychological functioning complete this factor. The items comprising this factor were the most consistent in appearing together as a solid factor. The compactness of this factor is also demonstrated by the nonappearance of the items in other factors. The lone exception to this rule was the tendency for the freedom from anxiety item to load with the "Negative Experience" factor in a majority of the subgroup analyses. This suggests that anxiety can often impair the meditation experience unless one is successful in reducing its effects prior to the session. Overall, the cohesiveness of this factor suggests that one's mood and functioning during the day represent a different state of consciousness than the altered state as measured by the post-session questionnaire.

Dimensionality in Meditation

Table 3. Intensification of Consciousness Factor

Item/description	Osis IV	Total group	Low anx	High anx	Low prob	High prob	Low reg sh	High reg sh	Low exper	High exper	Low adher	High adher
1. Feeling it was a good session[a]	0.53	0.65	0.67	0.64	0.43	0.69	0.74	0.71	0.32	0.68	0.60	0.68
3. Visual images relevant	—	0.52	0.51	0.50	0.44	0.44	0.47	0.53	0.47	0.58	0.51	0.52
5. Serenity	0.53	0.67	0.63	0.69	0.45	0.71	0.72	0.70	0.38	0.67	0.64	0.69
8. Thoughts relevant	—	0.55	0.59	0.53	0.43	0.51	0.63	0.51	0.46	0.62	0.61	0.53
9. Affirmation with external[a]	0.52	0.78	0.48	0.79	0.74	0.78	0.77	0.81	0.59	0.84	0.72	0.79
10. Oneness with the external[a]	0.36	0.69	0.51	0.69	0.71	0.67	0.68	0.69	0.53	0.69	0.72	0.69
11. Merging with others[a]	0.32	0.59	—	0.61	0.63	0.60	0.64	0.61	0.52	0.63	0.69	0.58
12. Experience of light	—	0.44	—	0.45	0.33	0.53	0.42	0.53	0.53	0.38	0.31	0.48
14. Sensed order in universe	—	0.78	0.36	0.80	0.81	0.76	0.70	0.78	0.75	0.77	0.76	0.77
15. Transcendence of space/time	—	0.62	0.47	0.60	0.66	0.62	0.64	0.69	—	0.65	0.60	0.62
16. Love and joy[a]	0.59	0.67	0.48	0.71	0.48	0.72	0.76	0.69	0.50	0.62	0.72	0.67
22. Deep insights[a]	0.57	0.74	0.38	0.72	0.65	0.76	0.71	0.75	0.70	0.73	0.67	0.74
22. Sense of presence[a]	0.54	0.66	—	0.67	0.67	0.71	0.63	0.70	0.69	0.67	0.70	0.67
23. Security	—	0.59	0.73	0.56	0.40	0.59	0.65	0.63	—	0.63	0.44	0.62
24. Refreshed after session[a]	0.44	0.43	0.47	0.41	—	0.49	0.53	0.44	—	0.42	0.45	0.45
25. Perceptual enrichment[a]	0.60	0.47	—	0.48	0.43	0.59	0.40	0.60	0.70	0.49	0.44	0.50
26. Inner resources available[a]	0.41	0.61	0.58	0.56	0.48	0.64	0.63	0.64	0.43	0.59	0.67	0.60
30. Intensification of consciousness[a]	0.62	0.67	0.59	0.67	0.54	0.69	0.78	0.72	—	0.55	0.55	0.71

[a]Osis core items.

Table 4. Psychological State Prior to Session

Item/description	Osis IV	Total group	Low anx	High anx	Low prob	High prob	Low reg sh	High reg sh	Low exper	High exper	Low adher	High adher
1. Content with self[a]	0.79	0.71	0.77	0.73	0.72	0.76	0.68	0.76	0.70	0.68	0.76	0.66
2. Elation[a]	0.86	0.74	0.79	0.76	0.75	0.80	0.68	0.80	0.69	0.72	0.78	0.70
3. Feeling of vitality[a]	0.53	0.64	0.56	0.62	0.65	0.55	0.62	0.64	0.60	0.71	0.55	0.62
4. Freedom from anxiety[a]	0.76	0.67	0.76	0.69	0.68	0.70	0.56	0.71	0.57	0.64	0.74	0.61
5. Slept soundly last night	NA[b]	0.38	—	0.42	0.35	—	0.41	—	0.44	0.30	—	0.44
6. Awoke easily this morning	NA	0.43	—	0.44	0.32	—	0.61	0.32	0.62	0.44	—	0.49
7. Energetic today	NA	0.67	0.64	0.65	0.68	0.39	0.68	0.63	0.67	0.66	0.58	0.68
8. Good mental focus today	NA	0.64	0.45	0.62	0.61	—	0.65	0.51	0.66	0.59	0.57	0.63
9. Memory excellent today	NA	0.62	0.43	0.61	0.60	—	0.60	0.51	0.61	0.57	0.54	0.66
10. Positive mood today	NA	0.73	0.74	0.75	0.75	0.67	0.63	0.75	0.63	0.68	0.75	0.70

[a]Osis core items.
[b]NA denotes not applicable since they are unique to the ARE questionnaire.

Table 5. Negative Experience Factor

Item/description	Osis IV	Total group	Low anx	High anx	Low prob	High prob	Low reg sh	High reg sh	Low exper	High exper	Low adher	High adher
4. Freedom from anxiety	—	-0.39	—	-0.37	-0.38	-0.37	-0.56	-0.37	-0.56	-0.41	—	-0.44
6. Relaxation	—	-0.64	-0.51	-0.64	-0.64	-0.65	-0.65	-0.62	-0.64	-0.65	-0.61	-0.64
7. Few thoughts	—	-0.49	-0.51	-0.54	-0.52	-0.48	-0.51	-0.37	-0.58	—	-0.64	-0.44
8. Thoughts relevant	—	-0.40	-0.59	-0.44	-0.57	-0.40	-0.33	-0.42	-0.36	-0.33	-0.40	-0.40
20. Absence of frustration[a]	-0.53	-0.72	-0.68	-0.73	-0.74	-0.73	-0.67	-0.75	-0.58	-0.72	-0.72	-0.72
23. Security	—	-0.47	-0.73	-0.49	-0.64	-0.44	-0.36	-0.40	—	-0.40	-0.62	-0.43
24. Refreshed after session	—	-0.37	-0.47	-0.38	-0.52	-0.35	—	-0.39	-0.35	-0.44	-0.42	-0.37
27. Free of anxiety during session[a]	-0.59	-0.71	-0.60	-0.71	-0.70	-0.71	-0.75	-0.71	-0.70	-0.72	-0.70	-0.72
28. No feeling of anger[a]	-0.55	-0.56	-0.43	-0.53	-0.49	-0.59	-0.60	-0.55	-0.60	-0.58	-0.54	-0.57
29. Awareness directed inward[a]	-0.42	-0.40	-0.46	-0.42	-0.47	-0.38	-0.49	-0.31	-0.48	-0.41	-0.38	-0.41

[a]Osis core items.
[b]The low anxiety group did not exhibit a clean factor that was clearly indicative of negative experience.

Of additional interest is Osis *et al.*'s comment that in each of their four experiments the items were ordered, in terms of relative size of the loadings, with elation first, followed by content with self, freedom from anxiety and vitality. This order was also confirmed in seven of the eleven analyses with the present data.

The "Negative Experience" factor is composed of nine items, four of which appeared in the fourth experiment of Osis *et al.* when the items were introduced for the first time. These items, displayed in Table 5, seem to offer the individual an opportunity to endorse feelings experienced during the session but which are antithetical to a positive, satisfying meditation. Certainly some sessions have been characterized by an inability to relax, compounded by the intrusion of unwanted thoughts, some of them anxious residues from the day experience or in anticipation of a future event. A mounting sense of frustration and resultant tenseness can easily lead to fatigue from the session rather than being refreshed. The appearance of the freedom from anxiety item (prior to session) suggests that anxiety is often a persistent emotion which can impair one's ability to "let go" both physically and mentally. This factor is hardly descriptive of the highly valued, positive, transcendent experience described by the first factor. Rather, it seems descriptive of some efforts at meditation and the occasional difficulty in breaking the grip of interferring emotions.

A "Mental Clarity" factor, composed of two and sometimes three items appeared in each of the analyses. Although a rather weak factor, its persistence in occurrence, together with similar loadings across groups seemed to warrant its inclusion. This factor seems to reflect a retention to awareness and a sense of alertness that, for certain groups, was also associated with a feeling of having transcended time and space. The loadings on this factor are presented on Table 6. This factor was not observed in the Osis experiments.

Table 7 presents the loadings for the items which define the "Physical Effects" factor. This factor was also weak, appearing in seven of the 11 analyses. Three of the items in this factor were new, appearing only in the ARE version of the questionnaire. These items depict various physical sensations often reported by meditators. These include an increase in bodily warmth, sensations around the "seven spiritual centers" of occult and oriental religious lore which are situated in the proximity of various endocrine glands, and spinal sensations presumably related to energy movement sometimes referred to as Kundalini. Perceptual enrichment was sometimes associated with this factor.

Discussion

Despite the different methods employed, the meditative experience observed in the present study bear some important similarities with the Osis studies. These similarities would seem to testify to their generalizability. Perhaps the most important findings is that the meditation experience is more than just an intensified day residue and more than merely physical relaxation. Both sets of data suggest a distinct change in the way of experiencing. Often there seems to be a sense of having transcended the limitation of three-dimensional reality; a melting of the psychological barriers between oneself and others. A sense of the sacred frequently occurred in this highly valued state of awareness. The experiential properties expressed in the items comprising the "Intensification and Change of Consciousness" factor were separate from the "Psychological State Prior to Session" factor. This independence of states arises from the fact that "good" sessions frequently occurred regardless of feeling tired or depressed prior to the session. In these sessions there seemed to be an ability to "let go" of a negative emotion or to move beyond fatigue. Interestingly, the only area where a prior psychological state demonstrated leakage into a meditation period was anxiety which was associated with having a negative experience. Thus, anxiety exerts a disruptive influence on meditation.

Negative experience is not uncommon among individuals who resolve to meditate on a daily basis, especially the novice. An important concern for future research is the clarification of reasons for negative experience and a determination of what physical and mental preparations might be effective in counteracting anxiety and other deterents to a satisfactory experience.

In their discussion of the "Intensification" factor, Osis *et al.* (1973) refer to another characteristic historically found during meditation. Many people have reported a sense of coming into contact with an energy field, force or power. Subjects in the Osis studies also reported physical sensations which were subjectively interpreted as a sign that something important was happening to them. The Osis scale had a

Table 6. Mental Clarity Factor

Item/description	Osis IV	Total group	Low anx	High anx	Low prob	High prob	Low reg sh	High reg sh	Low exper	High exper	Low adher	High adher
4. Alertness	—	0.67	0.67	0.67	0.68	0.61	0.58	0.72	0.55	0.68	0.66	0.64
13. Consciousness maintained	—	0.72	0.77	0.71	0.61	0.76	0.70	0.77	0.63	0.74	0.38	0.79
15. Transcendence of space/time	—	0.30	—	0.31	—	0.38	—	—	—	0.32	—	0.31

Table 7. Physical Effects Factor

Item/description	Osis IV	Total group	Low anx	High anx	Low prob	High prob	Low reg sh	High reg sh	Low exper	High exper	Low adher	High adher
17. Body felt warmer	—	-0.57	a	-0.55	-0.49	b	b	-0.45	b	-0.54	-0.44	-0.48
18. Sensed endocrine activity	—	-0.60	a	-0.71	-0.69	b	b	-0.45	b	-0.61	-0.63	-0.46
19. Spinal sensations	—	-0.65	a	-0.73	-0.66	b	b	-0.53	b	-0.65	-0.47	-0.53
25. Perceptual enrichment	—	-0.39	a	-0.36	-0.34	b	—	—	b	-0.36	-0.48	-0.30

[a] Items embedded in Negative Experience Factor.
[b] Items embedded in Intensification of Consciousness Factor.

single item concerning the sensation of a surge of energy in or around oneself which loaded with the "Intensification" factor. In the present study this item was replaced by three such items and not surprisingly, they did cluster together as the "Physical Effects" factor.

It is unclear why other factors such as "Meaning" and "Self-Transcendence" failed to replicate. Obvious partial reasons are the different methodology and alterations made in the questionnaire itself.

Overall, the results of this investigation support the notion that the meditative state is susceptible to measurement and that certain regularities can be observed in the experiences of people who are engaging in meditation under quite different conditions.

Researchers interested in conducting analyses with this data base may obtain the data along with documentation by writing to the author. This is made possible by the policy established by the ARE Research Advisory Committee to share project data with other researchers.

References

Benson, H. *The relaxation response*. New York: Morrow, 1975.

Carpenter, E. *The drama of life and death*. London: Allen, 1912.

Cattell, R. B. *IPAT anxiety scale questionnaire (self analysis form)*. Champaign, IL: Institute for Personality & Ability Testing, 1957.

James, W. *The varieties of religious experience*. New York: Mentor, 1958.

Johnson, R. C. *Watcher on the hills*. New York: Harper, 1959.

Kohr, R. L. Changes in subjective meditation experience during a short term project. *J. Altered States of Consciousness*, 1978, **3**, 221–234.

Maslow, A. H. *Toward a psychology of being*. Princeton: Van Nostrand, 1962.

Mooney, R. L. and Gordon, L. V. *The Mooney problem checklist (Adult Form)*. New York: Psychological Corporation, 1950.

Naranjo, C. and Ornstein, R. *On the psychology of meditation*. New York: Viking, 1971.

Osis, K., Bokert, E. ESP and Changed states of consciousness induced by meditation. *J. American Society for Psychical Research*, 1971, **65**, 17–65.

Osis, K., Bokert E., and Carlson, M. L. Dimensions of the meditative experience. *J. Transpersonal Psychology*, 1973, **5**, 109–135.

Puryear, H., Thurston, M. *Meditation and the mind of man*. Virginia Beach, VA: A.R.E. Press, 1975.

Puryear, H., Cayce, C., Thurston, M. Anxiety reduction associated with meditation: home study. *Perceptual and Motor Skills*, 1976, **43**, 527–531.

Smith, J. C. Meditation as psychotherapy: a review of the literature. *Psychological Bulletin*, 1975, **82**, 558–564.

Stace, W. T. *Mysticism and philosophy*. New York: Lippincott, 1960.

The International Journal of Clinical and Experimental Hypnosis
1977, Vol. XXV, No. 4, 236–273

24

A MODEL FOR THE LEVELS OF CONCENTRATIVE MEDITATION[1]

Daniel P. Brown[2, 3]

Abstract: Classical Tibetan meditation texts are used to specify the most important variables in meditation that can be subjected to empirical test. There are 3 kinds of variables: (a) nonspecific variables, common to all meditation systems; (b) specific variables, limited to specific types of meditation practice; and (c) time-dependent variables, changing over the course of meditation practice. The latter, time-dependent variables, comprise the majority of meditation variables. One set of time-dependent variables for classical concentrative meditation is explored. Using the semantic-field method of translating, technical terms most important in each level of the entire phenomenology of concentrative meditation are discussed. These terms are translated into hypotheses, which are worded in terms of traditional constructs from cognitive psychology. Supporting empirical research is presented and suggestions for further research are made. Certain similarities are noted between the Yogic texts and the constructivist theories of perception, information-processing, and affect. The overall direction of change in concentrative meditation follows an invariant sequence of levels of consciousness.

In the experimental literature, meditation has many meanings. It has been largely defined in terms of certain physiological variables, for example, as a certain mentation pattern, measured by EEG (Akishige, 1973; Anand, Chhina, & Singh, 1961; Banquet, 1973; Kasa-

Manuscript submitted January 22, 1976; final revision received August 23, 1976.

[1] This paper is based on a dissertation submitted to the field of Religion and Psychological Studies, Divinity School, The University of Chicago. It is a modified version of a paper presented in Erika Fromm (Chm.), Altered states of consciousness and hypnosis. Symposium presented at the 27th annual meeting of the Society for Clinical and Experimental Hypnosis, Chicago, October 1975.

[2] The author would like to thank Erika Fromm for clarifying many of the stages in this paper's preparation. The author would also like to thank Ven. Geshe Wangyal, under whose auspices he was able to learn the Tibetan language; as well as Stuart W. Twemlow, under whose assistance this manuscript was prepared and reviewed; Richard G. Davis, who helped clarify several of the technical points on information-processing; and the secretarial staff at the Veterans Administration Hospital, Topeka, Kansas, who provided support. The author is now at McLean Hospital, Belmont, Massachusetts.

[3] Reprint requests should be addressed to Daniel P. Brown, Department of Psychology, McLean Hospital, 115 Mill Street, Belmont, Massachusetts 02179.

matsu & Hirai, 1966); by certain changes in arousal (Fischer, 1971); by more specific autonomic variables (Wallace, 1970; Walrath & Hamilton, 1975); and, by a certain pattern of muscular tension/relaxation (Ikegami, 1973). Others have defined meditation more in terms of attention deployment (Davidson & Schwartz, 1976; Deikman, 1966; Van Nuys, 1973), related cognitive control mechanisms (Silverman, 1968), or ego control mechanisms (Maupin, 1965). Still others have defined meditation more as a process of therapy, with resultant significant changes in affective and trait variables (Davidson & Goleman, 1975; Davidson, Goleman, & Schwartz, 1976; Goleman, 1971).

There is little agreement on: how to define meditation, what should be measured, and what the most useful measuring instruments may be. Research on meditation is still in an embryonic state. No doubt, the slow process of data accretion will advance our knowledge of meditation so that some day we may better know what sort of data to collect. Yet, the present state of meditation research is largely wasteful; some consensual criteria must be used to establish which kinds of data are most useful to collect. The two most fundamental questions in meditation research should be: (a) What are the most important variables of meditation and how may they be operationally defined and measured? (b) How are these variables related to each other?

One practical way to approach these questions is to research the important variables of meditation as defined by the classical meditation literature. For example, the Tibetan Buddhist tradition alone contains thousands of volumes written on the meditative experience. The phenomenologies of meditative experiences are reasonably consistent across texts, with consensus on the most important subjective experiences of meditation. These texts have a sophisticated technical language for most aspects of the meditative experience; beginning yogis are required to learn this language much in the same way an apprentice to a modern scientific discipline must learn the language of his research trade. The terminology for the major variables in the meditative experience is quite precise. There are technical categories, reasonably comparable with the psychological categories of attention, thinking processes, perception, information-processing, physiological parameters, affect, and time. The texts specify the major items in these categories which are most important in meditation. To the extent that these items can be translated into hypotheses, testable by the standards of modern empirical psychology, they may serve as one possible set of criteria to establish aspects of meditation most important to research.

The most obvious theme in all the classical meditation literature is a longitudinal emphasis. The texts illustrate which variables of meditation are most likely to undergo change at certain definable stages of practice over time. In fact, the texts mention relatively few stable meditation variables across all stages of practice. It is difficult to speak of a single meditative state apart from the level of experience. Viewing the empirical research on meditation against the longitudinal emphasis in the classical meditation literature, one must seriously question whether physiological and cognitive measures of meditation, taken without careful specification of the level of practice, will ever be of great consequence. The obvious implication is that meditation needs to be researched over time with the same Ss. To approach the question concerning how the variables of meditation relate to each other, it is important to consider how they interact over time, since no longitudinal studies of meditation are presently available. This paper illustrates one of the Tibetan phenomenological cartographies of a meditative path.

Method of Analysis

In translating classical meditation texts, it is important to consider the technical language used to describe the meditative experience. Contrary to popular opinion, meditative and mystical states are rarely ineffable. Ineffability is largely a function of inadequate data sources, inadequate methods of analyzing the texts, and lack of verbal skills. For example, the meditation system in this paper contains several hundred technical terms of varying degrees of importance. When appropriate sources and methods of analysis are used, a sophisticated phenomenology of meditation emerges in which its technical terms are organized around distinct levels of attainment.

A cartography of meditation is presented for a single meditative tradition called *Mahāmudra*, which is within Tibetan Buddhism. The *Mahāmudra* texts have refined their technical language over many decades and centuries and are therefore intelligible to only a very specialized audience of yogis. Such texts are written in a highly condensed style and are called root texts. Root texts assume that the yogi already knows the technical language for the practice and therefore summarize it in only the briefest mnemonic outline (Evans-Wentz, 1935; Kồn-sprul Blo-gros-mthá-yas, 1971).

A number of lengthy commentaries explain the subjective experiences of the root texts. Five root texts and two of the most widely used commentaries were analyzed in order to reconstruct the consensual phenomenological accounts within the *Mahāmudra* tradition (Bkra-śis-rnam-rgyal, 1974; 'Jam-dpal-dpa'-bo, 1969).

Translating in such a way that the technical language of meditation was preserved, was accomplished by the semantic field method which is used in cultural anthropology (Bahr, Gregorio, Lopez, & Alvarez, 1974). Each technical term within the text was scored. The exact context was recorded for each term, so that it was possible to construct a semantic field for each technical term, and also to discern the relationship between technical terms within the entire system of usage. The result is a fabric of terms, or linguistic cartography, for the subjective aspects of the meditative path. (Translated technical terms appear in quotation marks in the paper; the italicized Tibetan word follows in brackets.)

One additional feature of the *Mahāmudra* texts is their subdivision of the entire practice into discrete levels of attainment. The root text[1] and commentaries in question for the most part agree in their method of subdividing the levels and the technical terms for each level, but they may use different meditation exercises to effect the same end.

One assumption guiding the research is that there is a common psychophysiological basis behind each stage of the meditative path, despite wide cross-cultural variation in the phenomenological cartographies of meditation (Goleman, 1972). This does not mean that *Mahāmudra* is the best template for the common psychophysiological stages until it is further known how culture-bound or valid these stages are. Initial efforts to work with Buddhist, Hindu, and Christian meditation texts within their original languages – Sanskrit, Tibetan, Pali, Greek, and Latin – have been encouraging. There may be more than superficial commonalities between these stages of meditation which, when studied cross-culturally, may justify pursuing the question of possible cross-cultural analysis of these texts by statistical means. Until the more difficult cross-cultural statistical task is carried out, any initial findings are better couched within a single consistent and highly refined tradition of meditation. However, the usefulness of a single-template approach is quickly exhausted beyond its purpose of generating hypotheses to guide meditation researchers.

Non-Specific Meditation Factors

Mahāmudra meditation, as many other meditation systems within Tibet, presupposes certain universal psychological operations, or what are called "mental factors" [*sems'byung*]. Chapters on the "mind" and the "mental factors" in the *Abhidharma* literature outline the basic theory of attention/perception in Buddhism (Guenther & Kawamura, 1975). Certain of these mental factors are essential for

[1] The reader may also want to refer to the only previously available translation into English of a root text from the *Mahāmudra* system of meditation: Book II of *Tibetan yoga and secret doctrines* (Evans-Wentz, 1935).

the practice of meditation, irrespective of the type of meditation. First are five "always present" [*kun'gro*] mental factors: "sense contact" [*reg pa*]; two attentional components, "directing the mind" [*sems pa*] and "holding the mind" [*yid la byed pa*]; "categorizing" [*'du shes*]; and "perceiving" [*tshor ba*]. Of these five mental factors which are present in every operation of the mind, the two attentional factors, directing and holding the mind, are particularly important in meditation. The yogi must learn to cultivate these two mental factors. The former, directing the mind, is defined as general movement of the mind toward any sense object. The latter, holding the mind, is defined as holding the mind to a particular object.

In cognitive terms, enhanced discriminatory functions of attention may be important in the initial training of the yogi. Schachtel's (1954) construct of focal attention is reasonably similar: directing attention to a particular object at the exclusion of the rest of the field, and involving an active mental grasp, in which the same object can be perceived from a variety of subtly different perspectives upon many renewed applications. Initial Yoga training seems to require an ability to isolate out central from peripheral stimuli. The construct of field articulation, and its empirical measures, may be a way of testing this hypothesis. The Embedded Figures Test (Witkin, 1969) given to naive meditators yielded insignificant results (Van Nuys, 1973). This one empirical finding should not militate against the near universal Yoga claim for "one-pointed" [*rtse gcig*] concentration (i.e., the ability to finely discriminate a point of concentration and hold the mind to it). The texts see one-pointedness as an enhancement of the normal function of holding the mind. Further tests of discriminatory ability, given to more experienced meditators, have shown significant increases in field-articulation over time (Pelletier, 1974).

In addition, there are five mental factors which make the object "definite" [*yul nges*]. The yogi must train these. The five are gradations along a continuum, and have as their root the process of "recollection" [*dran pa*]. Recollection is standardly defined by three attributes: "interest" in the meditative object (breath, *mantra,* visual object); "staying with" the meditation object; and "not losing track of" the meditation object. Recollection is said to "establish the foundation" for meditation practice and is so basic to meditation that comparable terms are found in Hindu Yoga [Sanskrit *smrti*] and in early Christian contemplation (uninterrupted prayer). The fact that recollection and its associated mental factors are put in a separate class suggests that they are more important than discriminatory factors at the beginning of meditation practice.

Van Nuys (1973) used a key-press to measure the number of distractions reported by naive meditators. Low scores on distraction correlated with high scores on hypnotic susceptibility. The measure for *un-distraction* failed to correlate with the Stroop Color Word Test (Messick & Fritzky, 1963) and the Embedded Figures Test (Witkin, 1969) reputed to measure attentional discrimination. Davidson et al. (1976) has reported a correlation between the absorption factor in the Tellegen Absorption Scale (Tellegen & Atkinson, 1974) and a similar factor in the Personal Experiences Questionnaire (Shor, 1960) for beginning meditators as well as an increase in the scores with meditation practice. Davidson et al.'s finding of greater absorption and Van Nuys' finding of undistraction are similar to the adjectives used to describe recollection. That Van Nuys' distraction measure failed to correlate with the attentional-discrimination measures is also similar to a tendency in the meditation texts to put "recollection" and "holding the mind" in separate classes. Their exact usage in the texts suggests that recollection is trained first and the enhanced discriminatory ability follows in consequence, much as the empirical findings confirm.

One of the immediate results of recollection is the ability to discern the mind as a "continuum" [*rgyun*], i.e., as a flow of discrete mental events with gaps between them, what the texts call an alternation between "movement" [*gyo*] and "rest" [*gnas*]. With greater training, the gaps become wider so that it is easier to discriminate whatever events occur in the mind. Though no empirical evidence is available, the hypothesis for a subjectively sensed slowing of information-processing could be tested by such methods as tachistoscopic recognition time.

A second consequence is "isolating" [*dben-ba*]. One use for the term refers to enhanced segregation of information from the different sense modalities. In practical terms, it becomes more difficult for the yogi to concentrate on an object utilizing more than one sense channel. For example, it is more difficult to integrate the act of attending to a *mantra* and a visual meditation object at the same time. Since the Yogic texts see thinking processes as a sixth sense modality, it is difficult to perceive a meditative object and think about it at the same time. Consistent with this hypothesis is the evidence for "cortical specification" in meditation. Certain systems of meditation utilize different areas of the cortex more than others. For example, *S*s monitored during Transcendental Meditation show greater activity in the sensory/motor regions of the brain relative to *S*s in Zen meditation, who show greater activity in the other areas.[5]

---

[5] Davidson, personal communication, 1975.

A third consequence is called "clarity" [*gsal ba*]. Clarity is used to describe a heightened awareness of "perception" [*snang ba*], "thought" [*rtog pa*], and "emotional disturbances" [*nyon mong*]. One likely hypothesis is a lowered threshold to internal stimuli so that the yogi becomes more sensitive to the thought, sensations, affects, and perceptions exactly as they occur. It would be interesting to measure changes in stimulus modulation for experienced yogis in order to test this hypothesis.

Another consequence is captured by two terms: "suppleness" [*shin sbyangs*] and "balance" [*btang snyoms*]. "Suppleness" is a mental factor which refers to the efficient, alert, and nonsluggish use of the mind achieved through great practice. The same word is used for an athlete who trains his body to move quickly and agilely. "Balance" is a term used to describe a state achieved after many oscillations between "drowsiness" [*bying*] and "excitedness" [*rgod*]. Suppleness and balance appear to be descriptions of an alert-integrated mentation and autonomic state. EEG synchronization has been well-documented for several meditation systems: Zen (Kasamatsu & Hirai, 1966; Yamaoka, 1973), Hindu Yoga (Anand et al., 1961), and Transcendental Meditation (Banquet, 1973). Most of these studies agree that meditation results in progressive synchronization of EEG with the possibility of dominant theta rhythms in more advanced practice. Progressive reduction in autonomic arousal has been reported for self-hypnosis, Transcendental Meditation, and relaxation (Walrath & Hamilton, 1975). Irregular autonomic changes during meditation have been postulated, but with subsequent predominance of parasympathetic nervous system (Gellhorn, 1967). The cortical and autonomic changes accompanying meditation have been described as a stable pattern (Akishige, 1973).

In summary, these changes have been called nonspecific because they are found in most meditation systems independent of the type of meditation practiced.

Specific Factors of Meditation

Beyond the preliminary nonspecific meditative training, the texts make two main divisions of meditation — concentration and mindfulness. "Concentration" [*sems gzung*], an enhancement of the discriminatory function, holding in the mind, is the restriction of attention to a single point — *mantra*, breath, visual object — and holding it in the mind for long periods. Any other mental activity is subjectively perceived as "distraction" [*gyeng ba*] from the point of concentration. "Mindfulness" [*lhag mthong*], an enhancement of the recollective function, is nearly the opposite. Mindfulness expands awareness to as many possible mental events—sensations, thought, memory, emotions, perceptions—exactly as they occur over time. Any new event that arises is taken as the meditative object; nothing is considered to be a distraction.

Different styles of meditation have been reported in the experimental literature. Ornstein (Naranjo & Ornstein, 1971) has reported three types of meditation: restriction, opening up, and negative meditation. That different meditation systems may train different attentional functions is given some support in the neurobiological literature. Two major cortical control mechanisms for the subcortical mechanisms involved in selecting and processing information have been reported: a frontal system associated with restrictive processing and a posterior-temporal system associated with more wide-range processing of information (Pribram, 1971; Pribram & McGuiness, 1975). The brain may be likened to a camera that can use either a wide-angle lens or a zoom lens. Or, in cognitive terms, attention can be directed to the more dominant details in a stimulus field or to the entire field. To train either concentration or mindfulness presupposes some common factor which is hypothesized to be enhanced segregation of the functions involved in information-processing.

Concentrative and mindfulness meditations also involve different kinds of effort. Initial concentration is said to require great effort. It also takes effort to "cut-off" [bcod pa] thoughts, sensations, and perceptions so that they do not persist in certain kinds of mindfulness practice. That is, thoughts, sensations, and other mental events pass quicker and quicker when effort is used to cut them off. Furthermore, effortless-receptive concentration and effortless-receptive mindfulness are also reported in the texts—usually at higher stages. Deikman (1971) has reported an active and a receptive mode of consciousness. Davidson and Schwartz (1976) have classified meditation into more active and more passive types. The exact correlations between the degree of effort and the discriminatory functions involved in concentration and mindfulness are yet to be researched.

There is one other very important question raised by the division of concentration and mindfulness in the texts. In concentrative meditation, the yogi is reported to go through distinct levels of practice, each level being some major alteration in cognitive organization and functioning. These levels appear to have a logical order much in the same way that child development has been conceptualized. They appear to demonstrate an invariant sequence. Mindfulness meditations, on the other hand, do not have well-defined levels. After many years of practice, there is a sudden and dramatic reorganization of cognition. Classically, a distinction is made between the quick and gradual meditative paths. Exactly why the practice of restrictive attention correlates with distinct levels of practice and why expansive meditation does not have clear levels needs to be researched.

One approach would be to examine what the classical meditation texts say about the longitudinal progression of mindfulness and concentrative practice. Results of the research on concentration are given below. According to the analysis, *Mahāmudra* meditation has five levels of attainment, each level having a fundamentally different cognitive organization from the previous, but following each other in invariant sequence. Each of the five divisions also has three subjectively distinct sublevels. Four of these levels are summarized in Figure 1. Eventually, the exact number and sequence of the levels of concentrative meditation will be put to cross-cultural tests. The changes in mindfulness meditation are currently being researched by a colleague.[6]

The Path of Concentration

Level 1: Preliminaries – The Virtuous Mind; Affective and Intellectual Change

The preliminary training for the yogi is divided into ordinary and extraordinary training. The ordinary training consists of cultivating recollection. The standard classes of objects to be recollected are: sensations; hedonic tone (pleasant, unpleasant, neutral); emotions; and states of consciousness. The yogi is instructed to contemplate each of these four classes as they arise during meditation. This is the "inner" [*nang du*] limb or ordinary practice. The "outer" [*mngon du*] limb consists of taking the same classes of objects as a point of observation in everyday activity and is called "vigilance" [*shes bzhin*]. The yogi cannot advance to the fundamental concentrative meditations until he can uninterruptedly maintain awareness of all his inner experience and outer actions 24-hours per day.

The extraordinary preliminaries consist of two parts: "advanced recollection" [*khad bar dran pa*] and "isolation" [*dben ba*]. Advanced recollection is prayerful visualization, called "Guru Yoga," [*bla ma'i rnal'byor*]. To help others, the yogi reflects upon the defiled and virtuous aspects of his current experience. He "confesses," or more accurately "lets go of" [*stang ba*], any defilements (e.g., craving, anger, pride, doubt). Then, he visualizes a *mandala* and the image of his guru within it. He reflects upon all of the virtuous qualities of his guru, and prays for "empowerment" [*byin gyis brlabs*]. Through empowerment, he exchanges the guru's virtuous, perfected mind for

[6] J. Engler, personal communication, September 6, 1975 and J. M. Kornfield, personal communication, September 25, 1976.

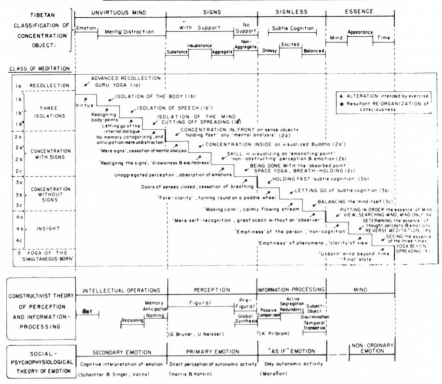

FIG. 1. Levels of concentrative meditation in the *Mahāmudra* lineage.

his own. Then, he dissolves the visualized form into clear light. He completes the meditation by praying that his insight be used for others' gain and not for his own. Guru Yoga cultivates the corresponding virtues, detachment, patience, and so forth. In addition to altering the internal emotional state, there are corresponding behavioral and attitudinal changes, if Guru Yoga is practiced over time.

The process of Guru Yoga is like an analytic therapy, accomplished through projective visualization of a guru/therapist. The beginning yogi analyzes the emotional factors in his experience and visualizes an identificatory figure towards the end of an emotionally corrective experience. Much like analytic therapy, the results are described in terms of affective change, insight, and behavioral change. Likewise, these changes take place slowly; it takes years of such preliminary training before the yogi can attempt the more advanced concentrative meditations. These initial affective and behavioral changes, so very important in the Yogic literature, have not been adequately appreciated by meditation researchers. To see meditation largely in terms of cognitive or psychophysiological change is to miss the therapeutic, or better, soteriological, thrust of meditation. Of notable exception is

Goleman's (1971) construct of "unstressing" in which he views beginning meditation experience in terms of emotional and physiological stress reduction. Davidson et al. (1976) have more recently reported empirical evidence for a significant reduction in anxiety, as measured by the State-Trait Anxiety Inventory (Spielberger, Gorsuch, & Lushene, 1970), and also increased absorption as measured by the Tellegen Absorption Scale (Tellegen & Atkinson, 1974). Absorption and anxiety reduction failed to correlate. The Buddhists' division of the preliminaries into ordinary recollection-training and extraordinary training toward the end of affective and behavioral change may likewise indicate some recognition that changes in awareness and affect within the same stage of practice are largely independent of each other.

The second of the extraordinary preliminaries, "isolation," is the initial step in concentrative meditation. The first of the "three isolations" is called "the isolation of the body" [lus dben]. The yogi is told to "re-align his body" [rten'brell ba] according to the perfect posture of the god, Vairocana. There are seven "main points" [lus gnad] of the body to be re-aligned: crossed-legs; hands flat, one on the other, below the navel; straight spine; shoulders back and chest out; neck slightly hooked; tongue rolled up; and eyes gazing straight forward. The yogi must "hold fast" [sgrim ba] all of the "main body-points" for long sitting periods without even the very slightest movement from perfect re-alignment; any slight movement greatly increases thought, distraction, and dizziness.

There are several important factors to be considered in "the isolation of the body." First, the yogi is able to "stay for a long time and his body does not become tired." The body is composed of subtle energy currents. By keeping perfect alignment over a long period, each of these currents is "held fast." These currents are said to mediate between the gross physiological processes of the body and mental operations. Therefore, the most important effect of simply holding the body fast is described in terms of a great reduction in normal thinking processes which distract meditation.

The essential elements of the body isolation exercise are: re-alignment and holding fast the main body-points, keeping the body alert, changes in subtle energy, and reduction in thought. Empirical research on Zen meditation postures sheds some light on the meaning of re-alignment and holding fast. Holding rigid meditation postures was not found to cause global relaxation in muscular activity, but rather, to maintain a regularly distributed pattern of muscular activity. Further, the most geometrically stable posture, in which the crossed-feet and straight spine approximated two perpendicular equilateral triangles, were found to yield the most even distribution of muscular activity and the least random muscle noise (Ikegami, 1973). In direct contrast to deep relaxation effects of EMG biofeedback and hypnosis, where global muscle tension can be significantly reduced (Green, Green, & Walters, 1970), re-aligning and holding fast a meditation posture is not technically relaxing in the sense of reduced muscle activity.

Furthermore, deep relaxation through EMG biofeedback or hypnosis is often accompanied by subjective reports of changes in the body image (e.g., tingling sensations, heaviness of limbs, dissociations, and distortions in size). In contrast, rigidly held meditation postures are seldom accompanied by such changes and, if anything, the experienced yogi is able to "isolate" himself from all distracting bodily sensations. Also, the effort needed to keep the posture stable keeps the yogi alert. It is difficult to comprehend, let alone operationalize, what the yogi calls "subtle energy" [rlung]. Ikegami (1973) found a strong correlation between postural and mental stability. At the beginning of practice, postural factors predominate; with greater experience, posture becomes automatized and attentional factors dominate. No data is available on the subjective sense of thought reduction associated with postural rigidity.

The second factor, "isolation of speech" [ngag dben], deepens the reduction of thought. The very name of the exercise indicates a meditation designed for thought process in which bodily distractions have become relatively unimportant. The yogi isolates himself from speech by switching from an attitude opposite to that of "holding fast" [sgrim ba] the body, namely "letting go" [glod ba]. The yogi "lets go" and continues his meditation period. By "not investing" [ma brtshon] in speech, he is able to "isolate" himself from it. The term, speech isolation, has a highly technical double meaning. Speech means the gross sound or noise of thought and, therefore, speech isolation is the first sign of achieving a "noncognitive mind" [mi rtog]. Not only the sporadic moments of distraction, but the entire background-noise of thought – the internal dialogue – become calm [gyo med]. Also, as speech is homologous to breath, the breath likewise becomes "immobile."

The essential items of speech isolation are: "letting go," "noncognition," and slowing the breath. A number of studies have documented decreased respiration rate during meditation (Kasamatsu & Hirai, 1966; Wallace, 1970). The slow stable respiratory pattern is also correlated with stable, synchronous mentation during meditation (Akishige, 1973). The texts further suggest that cognitive-noise reduction may be the subjective component to synchronous mentation and, likewise, "letting go" may be the subjective dimension accompanying the reduced metabolic-energy expenditures.

The third exercise is called "isolation of the mind" [sems dben]. Now that the background-noise of thought has receded, the yogi is better able to discern specific moments of thought as they arise. The interval in which a thought arises, adds other thoughts by accretion, and builds itself into a fantasy or concept is technically called "spreading" ['phro ba]. There are three kinds of spreading: spreading to the past, present, and future; these are roughly equivalent to memory, categorizing, and anticipation respectively. The yogi uninterruptedly watches, or "recollects," each kind of spreading from his new vantage point. The meditation is called "Cutting Off Yoga" [bcod pa]. Some fundamental change has taken place. By simply being aware of spreading, its duration becomes shorter and shorter. Four adjectives are used to illustrate the attainment: "uninterrupted" [lhun par], "letting go" [glod], "fresh" [so mar], and "alone" [rang gar]. These are summarized by the technical term, "undistraction" [ma gyeng ba]. In sum, the yogi is no longer distracted by thought.

In the previous speech isolation, higher intellectual operations, such as reasoning, ceased. In this exercise, other intellectual operations, though occurring, "become calm of themselves" [rang zhi]. That thinking operations are reduced during meditation is a near universal claim in the classical literature – what has been called the "progressive simplification of thought." Empirical studies have not been devised to adequately test this hypothesis. Based on Rapaport's (1967b) theory of attention-cathexis, Deikman (1966) has advanced the concept of "de-automatization." In meditation, higher thinking processes are decathected, while simple perceptual events are recathected with attention. As a result, complex behavior patterns and thinking processes become de-automatized which in turn results in a variety of cognitive and perceptual changes (Deikman, 1966). The claim of the Yogic texts is more extreme. Higher cognitive operations cease to be an important part of the experience during meditation and, in fact, until the cognition ceases, the yogi has not sufficiently prepared his mind for the concentrative exercises.

Level 2: Concentration with Signs; Perceptual Change

Level 2a: Concentration on substance; categorizing. When the mind does not wander excessively into any of the various classes of thought – reasoning, memory, anticipating, and categorizing – nor into emotions, it is quiet enough to begin concentrative training. Concentration is not possible unless the object is "definite" [nges bar]. Thought, having no correlation to external stimuli, is not a suitable object for beginning concentration. Only a definite perceptual object can be used. Any "substance" [*dngos po*] of the five main sense systems is considered to be a definite object. The technical term, "substance," is any object taken to exist in its own right such as a stone, a sound, etc. To an ordinary person, substances appear to be durable, real, and nameable. To an advanced yogi, these same substances are less real, impermanent, and nameable only hypothetically. However, at the beginning of concentrative practice, it is useful to fix the mind upon seemingly solid and durable objects. The actual class of sense object — visual object, *mantra* — is much less important at the beginning of practice than the act of concentration upon it. The texts are practical; they recommend that the yogi use "whatever works." Many Tibetan systems emphasize visual objects, whereas Hindu systems emphasize sound objects [*mantras*]. The present system exemplifies concentrative stages only for visual objects.

The purpose of the meditation is to concentrate the mind. First, the yogi "directs his mind" [*sems gtan*] to the supporting stone. He "perceives the object outwardly" [*kha phyin bltas*]. He sits in a stable posture, keeps his eyes half open, and stares undistractedly. All the texts emphasize a straight "gaze" [*blta stangs*] that "never changes" [*mi'gyur ba*] and "closely examines" [*btsir'bzin*] the stone. Then, the yogi "concentrates" [*sems bzung*]. The word, "concentrate," literally means to "have grasped with the mind." The act of losing track, no matter how momentary, is called "distraction" [*gyeng ba*]; it means the yogi is thinking about the stone instead of seeing it. Distraction is the main "enemy" to concentration. Two factors control concentration: the first factor is the "straight gaze"; the second factor is the five-object determiners.

After many sessions over an extended period, the yogi attains the first real proof of concentration called the "partially resting mind" [*sems gnas cha*]. Upon attaining the partially resting mind for visual objects, he repeats concentration on each of the other sense objects — sounds, tastes, etc. The resultant state is described as: (*a*) "mere undistraction" [*ma gyeng tsam*], or never losing track of the stone due to thinking anything; (*b*) "mere signs" [*mtshan ma tsam*]; and (*c*) cessation of "mental analysis" [*yid shes*] of the sense object.

Before initial, concentrative training, thinking and perceptual processes were well integrated in the same perceptual event. After much practice, the links between thought and perception are severed. Henceforth, the yogi perceives two distinct types of mental content within the "continuum" of a single meditation session. Two distinct terms are used: cognitive content [*rtog ba*], e.g., thought, emotion, and perceptual content [*snang ba*]. The latter is pure perception without any higher cognitive elaboration. Perceptual content has become "insubstantial" [*dngos med*]. Without higher cognitive discrimination of the stone, it is no longer possible to establish, with any certainty, the reality, solidity, durability, class of object, or meaning. "Signs," such as roundness, brightness, etc. still remain. As little more is known than the simple perceptual signs, perceptual objects are less convincing and less substantial than normal perception.

The essential items of concentration on "substantial" objects are: (*a*) two attentional items, "effort" and "indistraction"; (*b*) a physiological manipulation, the "gaze"; and (*c*) two perceptual changes, "simple perception" free from thinking processes and derealization of the object—what the texts call "insubstantiality." One is thus reminded of the New Perception research. According to Bruner (1973), perception is a constructive act which involves the higher intellectual operation of categorizing. On the basis of certain minimally defining perceptual features, higher intellectual operations are used to sort the perceptual information into one category or another. These "perceptual hypotheses" are subsequently tested by scanning the perceptual stimuli, and they are either confirmed or modified. Perception is a constructive act which makes a more or less veridical model for the world (Bruner, 1973). The phenomenology of concentrative meditation is much like perceptual categorization in reverse; the yogi stops categorizing perceptual objects and is left only with the "mere signs."

The shift from substantial to insubstantial perception of the object is also quite similar to the classical problem of the "stimulus-error" in introspective psychology. An introspective S strives to be free of stimulus-error as the yogi, through concentration, strives to no longer confuse the solid, durable world he perceives with the raw information coming to his senses—shapes, brightness, and magnitude. Or, in New Perception language, he no longer makes the mistake of absolute veridicality.

Level 2a': Concentration with insubstantial signs; object constancy. When concentration becomes very keen, the yogi is given a much more difficult object of awareness, namely a series of very intricate "reflected images" [*gzugs brnyan*] to "visualize" [*dmigs pa*]. For example, he may look at a statue or painting or a Buddha and subsequently visualize it as a reflected image with his eyes closed. The standard icon has 32 major "signs" and 80 minor signs to be visualized—signs such as facial features, ornaments, etc. Each sign has a highly specified location, depth in a visual field, color, brightness, size, etc. The yogi perfects his concentration until he can visualize *all* the signs at once without letting any fade, even a little. Visualization meditation is said to be very difficult unless all "spreading thought" has ceased so that the meditation session remains largely "noncognitive."

Reflected images are a class of "insubstantial" objects which are created through effortful visualization, but are not thought to be existing in themselves. Visualization continues the process of derealization, but is differentiated from fantasy production. Intensive-visualization practice creates reflected images seemingly as "real" as external objects, because the mind is said to "take the shape of" its object [yid la byed pa]. It is as if the visualized Buddha, himself, becomes a "close friend" and identificatory ideal for all the virtuous qualities, much like the seeming reality of a child's imaginary playmate. However, insubstantiality is not the main purpose of the meditation. Visualization of a Buddha serves to "re-align the signs in one's own mental continuum" [rten 'brel rgyud la bsgrig]. The mind takes the shape of the Buddha. The main result is affective. There are also problems with "drowsiness" [bying] and "excitedness" [rgod] throughout the meditation. Upon perfecting visualization, the yogi "washes away defilements" and transforms himself into the "virtuous qualities" of the sacred object.

When concentration is so strong that the yogi can hold all 112 signs of the Buddha for long periods without distraction, he is given even more subtle signs with which to re-align himself (e.g., light rays as fine as hair). The consequence of many re-alignment meditations is reduction of perception to "simple aggregates" ['du byed] or what is called a "point" [thig le].

The essential items of the meditation appear to be: (a) a perceptual change, "re-aligning the signs" and (b) an affective change, "re-aligning with virtue." One plausible hypothesis is that the yogi is dismantling object constancy in a controlled and systematic way. Loss of object constancy has been reported for sensory deprivation Ss (Zubek, 1969), and the analogy has been extended to meditation (Naranjo & Ornstein, 1971). Hochberg (1970) has reported changes in reversal-perspective figures with prolonged fixation by normal Ss, though not by meditators. It is of interest that the Yogic texts, like the experimental literature, recognize some correlation between the "gaze" and perceptual constancy (Kahneman, 1973). Reduction in microsaccadic eye movements have been reported for hypo-aroused states (Fischer, 1971; Fischer, 1975). Correlations between long fixations of eye movements and lack of fine visual discriminations have also been reported (Furst, 1971). The reputed correlation between altered object constancy and positive, affective factors is unclear. That prolonged concentration can result in autonomic disturbances leading to arousal or drowsiness is suggested by research on sustained vigilance to near-threshold tones, which resulted in alternate periods of alertness and falling asleep (Oswald, 1959). Likewise, Gellhorn (1967) and Gellhorn and Kiely (1972) have suggested that prolonged monotonous stimuli can produce a reduction in reticular and cortical discharge as well as autonomic activation during meditation.

Level 2b: Skill of supporting signs; pattern recognition. After many "re-alignments of signs," only a "point" [*thig le*] remains. This point may be used as an object of awareness. Although highly condensed, it still "appears" [*snang ba*]. The point has two conditions. In its "condensed form" [*bsdus ba*], it is the potential unity behind all particular perceptions in which all information from the various sense systems is condensed into a single aggregate, similar to "space." In its "emanating form" [*'char ba*], particular simple and complex appearances—rays of light, sounds, complex visual patterns—arise from the vibrating point. The verb structure indicates that an emanating point is thought to be a dynamic perceptual event in which things "continually arise and have arisen." The dual nature of the point is likened to the seed from which roots, trunk, branches, and leaves sprout.

Once the point is "set up" [*bzhag*] in the mind, the yogi is able to capitalize on his achieved concentration. Now he is told to stop concentrating and practice "skill" [*rtsal*]. Skill is a quality of practice in which the mind is able to stay "rested" [*gnas*] even in the midst of cognitive activity. Instead of getting lost, the yogi sees cognitive activity clearly for what it is. Because of his sustained awareness, the word "clarity" [*gsal*] is used in place of the technical term for the previous level, namely, "spreading." To practice skill, he must "not obstruct" [*ma'gag pa*] cognition and perception. The yogi sets up the point and, without interfering, witnesses the particular colored light rays, specific visions, and the entire worlds which emanate from it. He is also told to make the point and its emanations as large as an ocean; and at other times he is told to make them as small as a sesame seed. He should also vary the location and color as well as the size. The point always remains, but its emanations vary. The yogi should see each specific emanation in clarity, note how long it remains, and watch it recede and re-emanate again. At first, "various" [*sna tshags*] patterns arise. After great practice, they arise less often and recede more quickly when arisen. The yogi practices until only the fully "absorbed point" [*thim ba*] remains, like empty space. Then, he repeats skill-training for the "emotional disturbances." He watches, in clarity, any hatred, sexual desire, pride, and doubt that may arise in his mind, how it is associated with particular thought patterns, and how it recedes again. He continues until all the emotional disturbances melt into a mass of light and cease to arise again. When only the absorbed condition remains, particular perceptual, cognitive, and emotional factors cease to arise. Since they can no longer serve as supporting objects of concentration, the yogi enters a state called "non-support" [rten med] or "non-visualization" [dmigs med]. The absorbed point is called "unaggregated" ['du ma byed]. Nothing is left but empty space.

The essential items in the skill of meditation are: (a) a perceptual change, aggregation/unaggregation, as depicted in the phenomenological description of the emanating and absorbed point and (b) an affective change, absorption of emotional disturbances. The Yogic attainment of unaggregated empty space suggests the stabilized-image research (Pritchard, Heron, & Hebb, 1960) and the Ganzfeld experiments (cited in Naranjo & Ornstein, 1971). It has been well-established that particular perceptual images disappear under excessive stimulus-constancy, but the research fails to specify the exact mechanisms by which it occurs. In this regard, the Yogic texts may say a great deal. A reasonable hypothesis is that the Tibetan item, aggregation/unaggregation, is analogous to the process of pattern recognition in cognitive psychology, but in reverse. The constructivist theories of perception maintain that perception is by no means an exact model of the external stimuli, but an active synthesis — what has been called "figural synthesis" (Neisser, 1967), "figure-formation" (Dember, 1960), and "structural organization" (Allport, 1955). Pattern recognition is an important component of figure-formation. It is the process by which a definite pattern is constructed out of more limited information, (i.e., or how fleeting discontinuous perceptual information is recognized in terms of similar and dissimilar features and constructed into a particular recognizable pattern, and also how changes in these featural relations affect the type of pattern recognized).

Trace theories of perception (e.g., Hebb, 1949) and constructivist theories (e.g., Neisser, 1967) though fundamentally different, agree that figure-formation occurs in at least two steps. For Hebb (1949), "figural unity" is the simpler of two processes which merely detects the existence of a figure; and "figural identity," the more complex of the two processes through which the figure is recognized as similar to one class of figures or dissimilar to another class. Likewise, figural synthesis occurs in two steps in constructivist theories such as Neisser's (1967) a global, nonspecific, "preattentive synthesis," and a more selective "feature-analysis-and-synthesis" of specific recognizable patterns. Likewise, Allport's (1955) constructivist theory of perception sees "perceptual aggregates" as the foundation of higher perceptual operations. Allport regrets that perceptual theories give no phenomenological data to clarify the process of aggregate-formation.

However, some phenomenological evidence is available. Surgical restoration of sight to patients born with cataracts (Senden, 1932) and restoration of sight to visually deprived chimpanzees (Reisen, 1950) resulted in two stages of recovery: sensing the appearance of objects without recognition of patterns; and subsequent recognition of specific patterns.

These two components of figure-formation parallel the two conditions of the Yogic point: (*a*) a more absorbed condition akin to Hebb's (1949) figural unity and Neisser's (1967), parallel, global synthesis, in which the object merely appears and (*b*) an emanating condition akin to Hebb's (1949) figural identity and Neisser's (1967) feature-analysis-and-synthesis, in which specific patterns can be recognized. One might use these traditional cognitive paradigms and their experiments to test whether the yogi is indeed witnessing the very process of pattern recognition in reverse. The Yogic instructions to vary the size, color, and location of the point call to mind experiments which investigate changes in pattern recognition accompanying experimentally manipulated feature and context alterations (Dember, 1960).

If it were possible to test the hypothesis that skill meditation reverses the process of pattern recognition, there would be a way of demonstrating whether the descriptions of the Point Meditations indeed represent an accurate phenomenology for pattern recognition in reverse. Utilizing more recent advances in cognitive psychology, it would be possible to construct test stimuli more congruent with the phenomenological descriptions of the Yogic "point." For example, complex, free-formed figures much like the descriptions of the Yogic "point," have been generated by computer Fourier synthesis to study nonverbal recognition tasks, such as the magnitude of perceived difference in a series of free-formed figures (Shepard & Cermack, 1973).

Level 2c: Being done with; perceptual synthesis. When only the fully absorbed point remains so that emanations no longer occur, there is "no support" [*rten med*] for concentration. Therefore, the yogi stares blankly into empty "space" [*rnam mkha'*], or he focuses upon his own breath, which is said to be "like space." Still space is said to have a sense of "presence" [*snang ba*] and therefore has "signs." The signs of the absorbed point are described in terms of its "roaming toward various sense objects" [*yul la 'phyan pa*]. The yogi has taken a new object of awareness, mental processes rather than specific mental content, in this case, the very process by which the "mind perceiver" [yid shes] organizes sense data into a point. It is the first meditation on mental processes, of which several follow.

In order to sharpen mental processes as the object of concentration, the remaining organizational tendencies with respect to sense data must be terminated. The meditation is entitled "being done with" [zad pa] or "stopping the mind" [sems med]. The easiest method by which this is accomplished is through a traditional Yogic technique, "breath-holding" [bum ba can] (i.e., holding the breath as long as possible, staring into space once the breath is held, and holding the mind continually at "rest" so that it cannot "move" toward any sense stimuli). A more difficult meditation is called a "Space Yoga" [rnam mkha'i rnal 'byor], namely staring blankly into space and refusing to "hold the mind" [yid la ma byed pa] on any sense or cognitive object. The latter is essentially the same without the crutch of physiological manipulation. In either case, the ratio of exhalation to inhalation is said to get smaller and smaller until the breath "stays inside" [sems kong glod]. As the breath is said to have an intricate relation to the mind perceiver, the mind perceiver likewise stays inside. More precisely, the exercise "closes the sense gates of the mind" [yid kyi kha sbyor du byas] so that it no longer responds to sense stimuli. The outer world stops.

"Gross cognition" [rtog rtags], the generic term for thought, emotional disturbances, and percepts, is "done with." For the first time, the yogi "intuits" [rig pa] the mind's subtle process behind all its content. Only "subtle cognitions" [rtog 'phra] remain. Subtle cognitions are described in terms of fleeting movements, as quick as a meteor, fluctuating between equally short moments of stillness. They are called subtle cognitions because they are not "built up" [bcos ba] into cognition and perception. The resultant state, described as "non-cognition" [mi rtog], does not mean that gross cognitions completely cease, but simply that the mind "continually rests" in its concentration on its new object, subtle mental processes, irrespective of whether gross cognitions "happen to arise" or not. Thus, the new object of the "done with" meditation is technically called the "indifferent mind" [rang lugs], in that it no longer is bothered by higher cognitive processes.

The essential items in the "done with" meditation are: (a) a perceptual item, aggregation/nonaggregation of the sense data making up the absorbed point; (b) an attentional item, holding in the mind/indifference; and (c) a physiological item, fundamental changes in the subjective sense of breathing. Yogic disintegration of the absorbed point into subtle cognition bears some analogy to figural unity in Hebb's (1949) trace theory and to preattentive synthesis in Neisser's

(1967) constructive theory of perception, but in reverse. Viewing the Yogic meditation backwards, fluctuations in "subtle cognition" become organized into an absorbed point—a point which combines information from all the sense systems. Similarly, preattentive synthesis is a fast, crude, holistic synthesis of sense data from different sense systems. Neisser (1967) calls the process "preattentive" because it utilizes "wholistic operations which form the units to which attention may then be directed [p. 86]" in the later feature-analysis-synthesis stage of perceptual construction. The yogi's shifts from active "holding in the mind" to "indifference," viewed in reverse, is inconsistent with Neisser's claim that the process of synthesis is preattentive. For the yogi, synthesis involves an active attentional process—"holding in the mind." Again, such an hypothesis is testable by traditional cognitive experiments.

Exactly how the breath may be correlated to the process is unclear. That the breath "stops" is a claim most psychologists would question. The notion that breath tends to "stay inside," however, has some empirical support. Studies on breathing during Zen meditation indicate that the time of inhalation relative to exhalation greatly increased with meditative practice (Nakamizo, 1973).

Level 3: Signless Concentration; Information-Processing

Level 3a: Holding fast. As the mind has stopped, no perceptible events are left to serve as an object for concentration, yet subtle "events" [*'byung*] still occur. These events are described as a fluctuations between fleeting "movements" [*gyo*] and periods of "rest" [*gnas*]. Yet, fluctuations can be "grasped" [*'dzin pa*] and in this sense can serve as an object of concentration. The first meditation is designed to bring the "subtle cognition" into focus due to the problem of "subtle drowsiness" [*bying'phra ba*] (i.e., concentration tends to "slip away from" [*gyeng ba*] the less tangible subtle mental process and to try to once again "build up" gross cognitions—perceptions, thoughts, and emotions as more tangible objects for concentration). The technique is called "holding fast" [*sgrim*], which is described as a single-minded intent to "keep the resting mind every single moment" and also described as actively "cutting off" (i.e., turning over any mental event very quickly before it spreads into a gross cognition). As a result, since the movement of subtle cognition comes faster and faster [*'phral 'phral*] there is an increasingly rapid oscillation of subtle cognition "like a ball rolling down a steep incline." Perception of subtle cognition is described as "turning round and round on a paddlewheel." Upon completion of the exercise, the yogi sees subtle cognition in "fore-clarity" [*gsal-ngar*] that is at a stage *before* it is built up into higher cognitive events. Adjectives such as clarity, brightness, and clear light are commonly used; the mind is seen in terms of light rays.

Level 3b: Letting go. The second meditation is designed to slow the perception of a fluctuating stream by reversing the strategy. The mind is said to be "subtly excited." That is, it is difficult to find a subtle perspective from which to observe the fluctuating stream of subtle cognition. The technique used is called "letting go" [*glod*], the opposite of holding fast. Letting go is necessary because the mind subtly acts to discriminate subtle cognition. The technical term for this subtle action is called "abandoning and carrying out" [*dgags-grub*] and is described as a subtle form of attachment. By cultivating the attitude of letting go, similar to the skill-exercise, the fluctuating stream is "made calm." Making calm is given the technical term, "one pointedness," because a profound leap in concentrative ability has occurred so that the mind is not the slightest bit distracted. Concentration does not require the slightest bit of effort and any "events" [*'byung*] that occur in the mind "calm themselves" [*rang zhi*], remain in their lowered energy states.

One problem in these subtle meditations is that letting go tends to produce drowsiness, while holding fast tends to produce subtle excitedness. The very meditation exercise itself tends to result in a flip-flop back and forth between subtle drowsiness and subtle excitedness, so that the cycle is repeated endlessly. Therefore, the yogi is given a new object for concentration, namely the "mind itself" observing the subtle fluctuating conditions, and the cycle tends to "balance itself out." The remaining problem is "the agent who meditates" [*sgom mkhan*] – the "doer" [*sgom byed*] and "observer" [*tam khan*] of the subtle cognition. By focusing on the mind that is acting upon and observing subtle cognition, the yogi realizes that there is no spreading construct – a doer or an observer – aside from subtle cognition itself. In the same way that he reduced gross cognitions such as thought, perception, and feeling to their most rudimentary subtle fluctuations, likewise, by this fine shift in meditative strategy, he reduces the doing and observing component of meditation to the same level. Everything gets "balanced out" [*btangsnyoms*].

A new technical term, "mere self-recognizing" [*rang ngo shes tsam*], is introduced for the quality of knowledge attained. In Tibetan texts, the participle, "recognizing," defines the act of knowing any gross or subtle cognitions that occur in the mind. The prefix, "self," has been added to indicate that there is no "entity" [*ngo bo*], namely an observer, to recognize the mind and its processes. The adverb, "mere," has also been added to indicate that there is nothing other than self-recognizing in every instance of the mental continuum. In sum, all aspects of the mind itself are clear; it is all process. The yogi has attained the final state of concentration called "*samādhi*" [*mnyam bzhags*]. *Samādhi* is defined in the texts as: "all the subtle discriminations tend to calm themselves because their very moment of arising and self-recognition occur concomitantly from the perspective of the mind itself." "Calm" in no way means cessation; it simply means that whatever arises is not discriminated nor acted upon.

The essential items in signless concentration are: (*a*) recognition of subtle cognition and (*b*) associated autonomic changes, such as subtle drowsiness [*bying*] and excitedness [*rgod*]. The level is hypothesized to be a description of information-processing. There are three sublevels to the meditation: a passive, drowsy stage in which effort must be supplied for recognition; an active-excited stage in which effort must be taken away from the system for its recognition; and a balanced stage in which there is rudimentary discrimination expressed largely in temporal terms.

A very interesting, though far-fetched hypothesis, is that the yogi, upon stopping his mind, is able to become aware of and gain insight into the very stages of information-processing within the mind. Certain neurobiological theories of information-processing are suggested by the text. In different kinds of information-processing theories, the problem is the same: What are the mechanisms for coding similarities and differences in the recognition of specific patterns in the perceptual world? The template theories postulate that the mind is able to recognize "features" existing in the physical objects themselves, in the real world (Gibson, 1966; Hebb, 1949). The spatial distribution of the features of objects themselves, matched by retinal and cortical components of the information-processing system, are necessary for perception. A different kind of approach is taken by the constructivist theories which propose that matching and identifying similarities and differences occur not by the special features of the object itself, but through discrimination of the temporal fluctuations within the input system over time. Such a theory, until recently, was supported by questionable evidence. For example, Lindsley (1960, 1961) postulated a temporal discrimination process for information-processing based largely on gross EEG evidence (i.e., the fluctuation in synchronous and desynchronous EEG measures). Although the gross EEG evidence has tended to throw Lindsley's theory into disfavor, a temporal discrimination model for information-processing has recently gained popularity in the work of Pribram. According to Pribram's (1975) holonomic theory of perception, perception is constructed largely in terms of the information-processing system itself, and not in terms of the features of objects in the physical world. For example, incoming visual stimuli are segregated into the light frequencies and incoming auditory stimuli into respective-sound frequencies. Information is processed by temporally discriminating the interference patterns caused by the fluctuations of these frequencies over time and the patterns are constructed into an image or sound for the stimuli.

If our hypothesis is plausible, and the Buddhist texts illustrate a phenomenology for information-processing, they strongly favor the constructivists' temporal-analyzing model over the template feature-analyzing model. The description of subtle cognition in terms of rapid oscillation between movement and stillness is a temporal description. The phenomenological accounts given in the signless meditations leave open the possibility that the texts describe stages in information-processing in reverse. Viewing the three Yogic exercises backwards:

1. In the preliminary stage, some rudimentary form of subject/object discrimination takes place. Sensory stimuli are translated into temporal units. The metaphor of a "calmly flowing river" suggests a wave-pattern.

2. The second stage is an active stage, and it is called "subtle attachment" in the texts. One might hypothesize active selection and segregation of temporal components. The compound "abandon and carry out" [dgag sgrub] suggests a segregation process. The metaphor of "being turned round and round on a paddle-wheel" further suggests redundant processing of a temporal component.

3. The third stage is a passive stage. It is called "slipping away" in the texts. The yogi is able to recognize some difference between the subtle cognition he has held his focus upon and other fluctuations of subtle cognition that slip away. One might hypothesize some comparison between the processed unit of information to ongoing fluctuation much like that described in the constructivist theories, and also some filtration of other information. This comparison becomes the basis of subsequent perceptual synthesis. The reader will recall that the main problem for the yogi in Level 3a (Holding Fast) was to prevent subtle cognition from "building" [bcos ba] into gross cognition.

In contrast, the higher stages of concentration in Hindu Yoga, e.g., the *Yogasutras* (Woods, 1914), differ significantly from comparable Buddhist stages. The essential differences are threefold: (*a*) classical Indian Yoga says that the subtle fluctuations of the mind [*vrtti*] cease; an *unbroken* awareness remains. The *Yogasutras* contest the Buddhist position of *discrete temporal units*. (*b*) The Hindu Yoga analyzes "*subtle matter*" [*prakrti*], and the forces which govern its transformation [*gunas*], not subtle cognitive flux. (*c*) Indian Yoga posits a universal "observer" [*purusha*] while the Buddhist Yoga admits the observer may be an artifact (Eliade, 1970). The classical Hindu Yogic position favors a feature-analyzing model of information-processing, in which the "mind-stuff" [*cittam*] derives from recognized similarities and differences between the states of subtle matter.

The debates between the Hindu and Buddhist views of "form-*samādhi*" parallel the debates between the constructivist and template views of information-processing. The debate is famous in physics: is light a particle or a wave? Experiments in quantum mechanics and X-ray defraction lend support to both positions. The issue is largely a problem of the "observer" and, also, from which level of the cosmic system the observation is made.

Both the Hindu and Buddhist texts are aware of some connection between subtle cognition and "drowsiness" and "excitedness." They are aware of some correlation between information-processing and arousal. The literature on the role of arousal in information-processing is massive and need not be reviewed here.

Constructivist theories of information processing have been criticized for reintroducing the problem of mind back into psychology. In the words of Pribram (1975), "when a neurohologram constructs an image, who is the observer [p. 176]?" Pribram answers the question by saying that there need be no observer nor is the image constructed for the world veridical. His position is interestingly enough quite close to the central philosophy of Buddhism, which is, namely, emptiness. There are two kinds of emptiness: emptiness of the self and emptiness of phenomena. The former means that there may not be any observer, and the latter means that there may not be any phenomena truly existing "out there." It does *not* mean that the "stuff" of the world does not exist; emptiness simply means you cannot know for certain whether it exists or not. The only thing that you can know for certain is the workings of your own mind. The present meditative exercises, as the previous, are a practical method of achieving this knowledge. Any other knowledge about the self or the world is not genuinely knowable or, in the terms of constructivist perception, it is simply more or less veridical.

The yogi has now successfully attained *samādhi* and has finished the process of concentration. Next, he begins a second series of insight meditations. There are two more major levels of practice, each level having three subdivisions. The meditations are subtle and complex and far beyond the purposes of this paper. Let it suffice to mention that they concern themselves largely with the problem of emptiness of the self and the world (i.e., the likelihood of its veridicalness). They also concern themselves with an analysis of the temporal processes within the mind itself. According to the text, the attainment of *samādhi* is simply the starting point of meditative insight. All of the stages described so far are merely preparatory. They have little to do with subtler meditations and the insights the yogi derives about himself and his world.

If we are to define the critical variables of meditation, the *samādhi* state (level 3c – Balancing) is perhaps the most central. The longitudinal analysis of each stage towards the attainment of *samādhi* has attempted to lay the proper conceptual foundations for understanding this state. Depending on the level of analysis, *samādhi* can be used for very different insights in different traditions. Yet, a thoughtless, perception-less, self-less state is the common starting point of insight whether it be the Buddhist "concentrative *samādhi*" [Tibetan, *zhi gnas*], the Hindu "form-*samādhi*" [Sanskrit, *rupasamādhi*], or the Christian "prayer of quiet."

DISCUSSION

The Stages of Information-Processing

A classical meditation tradition has been used as one set of criteria to answer the question: "What are the most important variables of meditation?" The following variables have been found to be most important: attention, intellectual processes, perception, information-processing, and affect. It is no doubt true that these classes of variables are best researched by convergent operations; that is, researched by using a combination of phenomenological, psychophysiological, and cognitive-task measures. However, because the texts greatly emphasize attention deployment and thought/perceptual change, they suggest that empirical investigation of cognitive-task performance is more likely to yield interpretable "hard" data on the essential variables in meditation, relative to the rapid accretion of psychophysiological data.

The classical cartography further suggests, that except for a small number of non-specific and specific variables, the greater number of variables that are important in meditation are variables dependent over time. For example, the quality of affective experience and also specific physiological indices – EEG, eye movement, breathing, and autonomic activity – vary with specific cognitive changes over time. Thus, it is unlikely that affective and physiological measures will be useful without taking the time-dimension of measurement into consideration.

The texts offer a phenomenological model for information-processing much like that found in the constructivist theories of perception (e.g., Allport, 1955; Bruner, 1973; Neisser, 1967) and the constructivist theories of information-processing (e.g., Pribram, 1975). In fact, the Yogic model is comprehensive and ties these various theories — each with differing emphasis — into a unitary model with greater explanatory value. Figure 1 summarizes this comprehensive model. The center portion of the chart summarizes the meditation exercises and the specific attainment for each level and sublevel of the entire path of concentration. The top horizontal line gives the Tibetan technical terms for the respective objects of concentration for each sublevel. One of the bottom horizontal lines sets out the constructs from the psychology of cognition and information-processing hypothesized to correspond to each of the Tibetan technical terms.

The meditators appear to repeat the stages of information-processing in reverse: information-processing — rudimentary subject/object discrimination and sorting information temporally (level 3c), active segregation of the temporal fluctuations (level 3b), comparison of a selected frequency (level 3a); perception — global synthesis of an "appearance" from the temporal fluctuation (level 2c), recognition of similarities and differences to detect a specific pattern (level 2b), pattern constancy despite further fluctuations in the stimulus-input (level 2a'), categorizing the constructed sensory pattern (level 2a); higher intellectual operations — perceptual sets associated with affect, needs, motivations, attitudes, judgments, memories, and intellectual understanding of the constructed pattern. To the extent that the phenomenologies are valid, it appears that the yogi, through concentration, learns to discern each stage in information-processing in the construction of his world. One might wonder how the yogi is able to discern components of information-processing that happen very quickly for the normal person. The reader will recall that one of the nonspecific effects of meditation is a subjectively sensed slowing down of mental operations over time. That the yogi is able to observe the stages in the workings of his own mind is at least plausible and can be subject to empirical tests.

Psychophysiological Measurement and Meditation

The present model of concentrative meditation challenges a tendency in the experimental literature to reduce the complexities of meditation to simple, gross, psychophysiological measures. The model suggests that physiological measurements will be crude and impractical without specific hypotheses to guide measurement and without a means to longitudinally evaluate the measurements. Though physiological measurement is yet not greatly refined, it may still be useful. In fact, the texts specify which physiological indices are likely to yield useful measures, and at which level of practice they are most likely to change: eye movements (levels 1-2a), breath (level 2c), and autonomic changes (levels 1, 2a–c, 3a–b).

Also, the texts illustrate serious problems of interpretation when physiological measures are interpreted independent of the level of experience. The data collected by Das and Gastaut (1957) are interesting in this respect. Yogis at the onset of *samādhi* had synchronized EEG, as is the case in other experimental studies with meditators. However, the yogis in this particular study were all found to yield fast-EEG rhythm with high amplitude for the duration of most of the *samādhi* state. This experimental finding has been replicated for the transcendental phase of Transcendental Meditation (Banquet, 1973). In level 4b of the *Mahāmudra* path, the yogi is given the instructions for a "reverse meditation" in which he allows the mind to "build up" [*bcos ba*] at any level from subtle cognition to gross cognition such as perception, emotion, and thought. He maintains a paradoxical state in which he sees the world exactly as it appears to an ordinary person in the waking state concomitant to seeing all of its stages as a mere mental construction, as "empty" [*stong ba*]. In light of this paradoxical perceptual state, EEG data are understandable. During the special *samādhi* of "reverse meditation," one might expect EEG desynchronization comparable to the waking state, whereas in earlier *samādhi* states (levels 3c–4a) – those *samādhi* states tending toward dismantling of information-processing – one might expect the opposite – EEG synchronization. It may be premature to dismiss Das and Gastaut's (1957) and Banquet's (1973) data as artifacts when they may yield valuable data on differential *samādhi* states.

Affective Change in Meditation

The importance of affective change in meditation has been appreciated by only a small number of investigators. With one exception (Davidson et al., 1976), no attempt has been made to systematically study affective changes in meditation longitudinally. This is highly unfortunate since the Yogic texts emphasize affect as the central variable. Unlike the level-specific changes in thought, perception, and information-processing, there are affective changes at each level of practice. One of the main results of concentration (levels 1–3c) is that "gross emotional disturbances" [*nyon mong*] are "done with." There are affective changes at each level of concentration leading to this final goal: virtuous mind and behavior (level 1); re-aligning the virtues, autonomic disturbances (level 2a); absorption of emotional disturbances (level 2b); being done with the emotional disturbances (level 2c); subtle autonomic shifts (levels 3a–b); and no gross emotions nor autonomic disturbances (level 3c). Further, a main result of insight (levels 4a–4c) is that the "subtle propensities" [*bag chags*] of the emotions are permanently removed but, paradoxically, the gross emotional disturbances are reinstated (level 4b). A common passage from the texts summarizes the approach: "Emotional mistakes arise as wisdom; this is called great bliss." As a result, the yogi is able to purposefully and detachedly express "as if" emotions such as anger when they might be useful as compassionate devices for communication with others. However, the yogi is said to be completely free of any compelling emotional drive. As such claims are far beyond the normal conception of therapeutic change, Eastern systems are more accurately termed soteriological rather than therapeutic and they lead to complete liberation from emotional disturbances. It is noteworthy to mention that the technical word for emotional disturbance [*nyon mong*] literally means "fetter" or "bondage." Final liberation from bondage is usually described in terms of an affect qualitatively different from ordinary affect (e.g., bliss, playfulness, equanimity). Western therapeutic systems stress the relationship between thought and affect in the form of rational clarification. Concentrative meditation emphasizes the relationship between perception, information-processing, and affect. This is the essential difference between Western therapy and Eastern soteriology. Few Western therapists would admit that a healthy individual could eliminate drives, though one may develop a rational awareness of them. The Yogic texts have a more optimistic, thorough-going and socialized view of drive-mastery. One difference is that the yogi has carried his analysis of affect beyond thought to their very base, "wrong view" [*blta ldog*], which is rooted in perception and information-processing.

The Yogic theory of emotions is not without its counterpart in Western empirical psychology. The main debate in the theories of emotion is whether or not autonomic arousal is a necessary component of emotional experience. The social-psychological theories emphasize cognitive evaluation of autonomic activity as being at least equally important as autonomic activity itself (Schachter & Singer, 1962). In defined instances, autonomic activity is unnecessary to emotional experience (Valins, 1967). The psychophysiological theories contest that autonomic activity must always be a necessary component of emotional experience (Katkin & Murray, 1968). Harris and Katkin (1975) have recently reviewed the theories in order to clarify discrepancies in the data and integrate them into a single theory. The main problem in the research has been a failure to distinguish between two different uses of the word, "emotion." The sociopsychological theories equate emotion with certain nameable behavioral consequences which are more complex than the simple subjective experience of the emotion. Harris and Katkin distinguish between two types of emotion: "primary emotion," in which autonomic activity is necessary, and which includes the veridical, direct subjective experience of that autonomic activity; and "secondary emotions," in which autonomic activity may not be necessary, and in which cognitive sets, situational contexts, and false physiological feedback may result in nonveridical experience of autonomic activity. A third possibility is Marañon's (1924) research on "as if" emotions in which autonomic arousal can be induced by drugs independent of emotional experience.

The Yogic texts also acknowledge the importance of autonomic arousal, "drowsiness and excitedness" throughout the stages of concentration. As longitudinal data, the Yogic texts present a model for stages of affect not accounted for in the Harris and Katkin (1975) theory alone. When affective change is considered in relationship to major cognitive changes along the concentration path, a distinct model appears: in level 1 the yogi attains a virtuous mind. Reduction in thought processes accompanies the affective change. One might hypothesize that the yogi is less influenced by perceptual sets or situational context concomitant to the changes in thought. Thus, the yogi would be expected to be less reactive in his everyday behavior and set towards more veridical, emotional experience. This stage is comparable to the construct of "secondary emotion" in Harris and Katkin (1975) and in the sociopsychological work of Schachter and Singer (1962) and Valins (1967). In level 2a', the yogi "re-aligns" with the virtues of the Buddha and "cleanses away defilements" concomitant to changes in categorization and constancy of perception. This is the first stage during which the autonomic disturbances of drowsiness and excitedness occur. This change in affect is comparable to Harris and Katkin's (1975) "primary emotion" (i.e., veridical emotional experience based directly on autonomic activity). As a result of the perceptual changes, the yogi has removed any biasing set to his emotional experience. In level 2b, the emotions are "absorbed"; in level 2c they are "done with." In levels 3a–b, only pure autonomic activity – "subtle drowsiness and excitedness" – remains. This is comparable to the "as if" emotions of Marañon (1924). Reduction of the simpler stages of perception and information-processing is concomitant to cessation of specific emotions, and their subsequent reduction to "as if" emotions. In level 3c, the yogi "balances out" autonomic activity and thereby removes the basis from which specific emotions are constructed. Figure 1 summarizes the stages. Essentially, the

Yogic model is a constructivist model of emotion based on interpretation of fluctuating autonomic activity.

A constructivist theory of emotion has certain consequences for therapeutic change. The yogi repeats *in reverse* the stages in affective construction. At the end-point of concentration, when all thought and perception has ceased, emotions are said to be "empty" of reality. To paraphrase in cognitive terms, all specific emotions are mere constructs, more or less veridical as the case may be. Such an insight, if stable and enduring, has certain behavioral consequences not envisioned in Western therapies. The yogi is less likely to get angry at or feel sexual impulses toward persons or objects, which are mere "empty" constructs of varying veridicality. He is less likely to feel anxiety, alienation, or depression when his perception of self and body is likewise an "empty" construct. Still, the yogi can willfully express "as if" emotions, "empty" emotions, in appropriate interpersonal situations so as to be helpful to others. A variety of adjectives are also used to describe the enduring, nonordinary, positive quality of the yogi's state (e.g., bliss, equanimity).

Affective and concomitant behavioral change are the more practical variables to be researched in meditation. The importance of longitudinal specificity of affective change is indicated by the Yogic map. It may also be important to study subjectively reported affective change concomitant to specific autonomic changes within a longitudinal framework.

It is of interest that the Buddhist material has anticipated a current trend within wide areas of psychology, namely constructivist theories of perception, and information-processing, and constructivist theory of emotion that could be read into currently debated theories of emotion. Yet, whereas the constructivist theories of perception have been known for some time, they have not been practically applied to therapy or to everyday experience; this is precisely what the Buddhist material emphasizes. What are the intellectual, affective, perceptual, and behavioral consequences of viewing each of these dimensions of one's experience as "empty" constructs with only some probability of veridicality?

Levels of Consciousness

Another way to view the levels of concentrative meditation is as an orderly progression of alterations in consciousness. Many intellectual and perceptual measurements have been made on changes accompanying sensory deprivation in naive Ss. The sensory deprivation research fails to take into account whether or not the intellectual and perceptual changes associated with sensory deprivation occur in any logical progression. In contrast, concentrative meditation, viewed cross-culturally, always proceeds as a logical progression of alterations in consciousness.

An altered state of consciousness has been defined as a subjectively experienced, qualitative shift in consciousness associated with an alteration in the configuration of cognitive structures such as thought, perception, and time/space (Ludwig, 1966; Rapaport, 1967a, b; Tart, 1975). According to Tart (1971), "induction techniques" can disrupt the stability of the structures of normal waking consciousness and can produce a stable alteration in consciousness. Each stable alteration in consciousness has its own unique organization of structures. Thought, perception, reality, and time/space may be quite different from the waking state. He has called this "state-specificity." Dreams, psychedelic drug-induced states, psychoses, possession states, and meditative states each have their own "state-specificity." Learning, knowledge, and perception of self and world are "state-bound" and not necessarily continuous with normal waking, learning, knowledge, and perception (Fischer & Landon, 1972). Furthermore, certain states of consciousness, experienced over time, result in subjectively different levels, each with different cognitive organization, for the same state of consciousness—what Tart (1971) has called the "level-specificity." For example, four levels of consciousness have been reported for LSD-induced states of consciousness, yet all four levels are heuristically similar enough to retain their "state-specificity" as "psychedelic" states (Grof, 1975; Masters & Houston, 1966).

Concentrative meditation is a specific type of meditation; in Tart's (1971) terms, it exhibits "state-specificity." There are also five subjectively distinct levels and a number of sublevels experienced along the path of concentrative meditation. These are hypothesized to be associated with definable cognitive changes. The central part of Figure 1 illustrates the levels of consciousness along the concentrative path. Each specific meditation exercise, like Tart's induction mechanisms, is designed to disrupt some aspect of the habitual, stable structures of normal waking cognition (marked ▲ in Figure 1). As a result, a distinct reorganization of the cognitive structure in question occurs, which is subjectively felt as a shift in consciousness (marked ● in Figure 1). Then a new technique is used to induce another alteration resulting in other reorganization and so on. The subjective world of the yogi is different at each level of practice; it is state-bound. For example: a world of perception without thought (level 2), a world without perception (level 3), and a world without self (level 4). Structural changes in concentrative meditation appear to follow an invariant sequence. The overall direction of change in concentrative meditation is toward temporary or complete destructuring of single structures – thought structures, perceptual structures – and towards *de-differentiation* concerning the interrelationship between these structures. Cognitive organization becomes progressively simpler in the more advanced levels of concentration.

Structural theories of child development, notably Piaget (see Flavell, 1963), assume an invariant sequence of structural variations over the course of child development. Piaget also assumes certain invariant functions across the variant stages of development, namely assimilation and accommodation. Structural change – generalization and differentiation – is dependent upon constant interaction between the organism and novel stimuli in the environment. Concentrative meditation reverses the fundamental interactive proposition in Piaget's theory. The yogi minimizes his interaction with the environment and disrupts stimulus-novelty by restricting his concentration to a single object for long periods. An invariant sequence of structural changes and levels of meditation likewise occurs, but in the opposite direction: decreased generalization and de-differentiation of structures. Thus, the yogi claims, "To understand the true nature of mind and reality, you must make the mind simple."

References

AKISHIGE, Y. (Ed.) *Psychological studies on Zen*. Tokyo: Zen Institute of Komazawa Univer., 1973.

ALLPORT, F. H. *Theories of perception and the concept of structure: A review and critical analysis with an introduction to a dynamic-structural theory of behavior*. New York: Wiley & Sons, 1955.

ANAND, B. K., CHHINA, G. S., & SINGH, B. Some aspects of electroencephalographic studies in yogis. *Electroenceph. clin. Neurophysiol.*, 1961, *13*, 452–456.

BAHR, D. M., GREGORIO, J., LOPEZ, D. I., & ALVAREZ, A. *Piman shamanism and staying sickness*. Tucson: Univer. of Arizona Press, 1974.

BANQUET, J. P. Spectral analysis of the EEG in meditation. *Electroenceph. clin. Neurophysiol.*, 1973, *35*, 143–151.

BKRA-ŚIS-RNAM-RGYAL, DWAGS-PO PAN-CHEN. *Ñes don Phyag rgya chen po'i sgom rim gsal bar byed pa'i legs bśad zla ba'i'od zer*. [*A detailed study of the practices of Mahāmudra meditation*.] Delhi, India: block print, 1974.

BRUNER, J. S. *Beyond the information given: Studies in the psychology of knowing*. (J. Anglin, Ed.) New York: Norton, 1973.

DAS, N. N., & GASTAUT, H. Variations de l'activité électrique du cerveau, du coeur et des muscles squelettiques au cours de la méditation et de l'extase yogique. [Variations in electrical activity of the brain, heart, and skeletal muscles during meditation and yogic ecstasy.] *Electroenceph. clin. Neurophysiol.*, 1957, *6*, 211–219.

DAVIDSON, R. J., & GOLEMAN, D. J. The role of attention in meditation and hypnosis: A psychobiological model of transformations of consciousness. In E. Fromm (Chm.), Altered states of consciousness and hypnosis. A symposium presented at the 27th annual meeting of the Society for Clinical and Experimental Hypnosis, Chicago, October 1975.

DAVIDSON, R. J., GOLEMAN, D. J., & SCHWARTZ, G. E. Attentional and affective concomitants of meditation: A cross-sectional study. *J. abnorm. Psychol.*, 1976, *85*, 235–238.

DAVIDSON, R. J., & SCHWARTZ, G. E. The psychobiology of relaxation and related states: A multi-process theory. In D. I. Mostofsky (Ed.), *Behavior control and modification of physiological activity.* Englewood Cliffs, N. J.: Prentice-Hall, 1976. Pp. 399–442.

DEIKMAN, A. J. De-automatization and the mystic experience. *Psychiatry*, 1966, *29*, 324–338.

DEIKMAN, A. J. Bimodal consciousness. *Arch. gen. Psychiat.*, 1971, *25*, 481–489.

DEMBER, W. N. *The psychology of perception.* New York: Holt, Rinehart & Winston, 1960.

ELIADE, M. *Yoga: Immortality and freedom.* (2nd ed.) (W. R. Trask, Trans.) New York: Bollingen, 1970.

EVANS-WENTZ, W. Y. (Ed.) *Tibetan yoga and secret doctrines.* (Lāma Kazi Dawa-Samdup, Trans.) New York: Oxford Univer. Press, 1935.

FISCHER, R. A cartography of the ecstatic and meditative states: The experimental and experiential feature of a perception-hallucination continuum are considered. *Science*, 1971, *174*, 897–904.

FISCHER, R. Cartography of conscious states: Evolution and transformations of self-awareness. In E. Fromm (Chm.), Altered states of consciousness and hypnosis. A symposium presented at the 27th annual meeting of the Society for Clinical and Experimental Hypnosis, Chicago, October 1975.

FISCHER, R., & LANDON, G. M. On the arousal state-dependent recall of 'subconscious' experience: Stateboundness. *Brit. J. Psychiat.*, 1972, *120*, 159–172.

FLAVELL, J. H. *The developmental psychology of Jean Piaget.* Princeton, N. J.: Van Nostrand, 1963.

FURST, C. J. Automatizing of visual attention. *Percept. Psychophys.*, 1971, *10*, 65–70.

GELLHORN, E. *Principles of autonomic-somatic integrations: Physiological basis and psychological and clinical implications.* Minneapolis: Univer. of Minnesota Press, 1967.

GELLHORN, E., & KIELY, W. F. Mystical states of consciousness: Neurophysiological and clinical aspects. *J. nerv. ment. Dis.*, 1972, *154*, 399–405.

GIBSON, J. J. *The senses considered as perceptual systems.* Boston: Houghton Mifflin, 1966.

GOLEMAN, D. Meditation as meta-therapy: Hypotheses toward a proposed fifth state of consciousness. *J. transpers. Psychol.*, 1971, *3*, 1–25.

GOLEMAN, D. The Buddha on meditation and states of consciousness. Part I, II. *J. transpers. Psychol.*, 1972, *4*, 1–44; 151–210.

GREEN, E. E., GREEN, A. M., & WALTERS, E. D. Voluntary control of internal states: Psychological and physiological. *J. transpers. Psychol.*, 1970, *2*, 1–26.

GROF, S. *Realms of the human unconscious: Observations from LSD research.* New York: Viking, 1975.

GUENTHER, H. V., & KAWAMURA, L. S. (Trans.) *Mind in Buddhist psychology.* Emeryville, Calif.: Dharma, 1975.

HARRIS, V. A., & KATKIN, E. S. Primary and secondary emotional behavior: An analysis of the role of autonomic feedback on affect, arousal, and attribution. *Psychol. Bull.*, 1975, *82*, 904–916.

HEBB, D. O. *The organization of behavior: A neuropsychological theory.* New York: Wiley & Sons, 1949.

HOCHBERG, J. Attention, organization, and consciousness. In D. Mostofsky (Ed.), *Attention: Contemporary theory and analysis.* New York: Appleton-Century-

Crofts, 1970. Pp. 99–124.

IKEGAMI, R. Psychological study of Zen posture. In Y. Akishige (Ed.), *Psychological studies on Zen*. Tokyo: Zen Institute of Komazawa Univer., 1973. Pp. 105–133.

'JAM-DPAL-DPA'-BO. *Phyag chen lhan cig skyes sbyor dnos gźi'i khrid yig cun zad spros pa sems kyi rdo rje'i nes gnas gsal bar byed pa*. [*Explanatory induction into the praxis of Mahāmudra focussing on the union of the tutelaries, Chakrasamvara and Varahi, according to the Cakrasamvara Tantra*.] Chemre, India: block print, 1969.

KAHNEMAN, D. *Attention and effort*. Englewood Cliffs, N. J.: Prentice-Hall, 1973.

KASAMATSU, A., & HIRAI, T. An electroencephalographic study on the Zen meditation (Zazen). *Folia psychiat. neurol. jap.*, 1966, *20*, 315–336.

KATKIN, E. S., & MURRAY, E. N. Instrumental conditioning of autonomically mediated behavior: Theoretical and methodological issues. *Psychol. Bull.*, 1968, *70*, 52–68.

KOŇ-SPRUL BLO-GROS-MTHA'-YAS. *Gdams nag mdzod*. [*A treasury of instructions and techniques for spiritual realization*.] Delhi, India: Lungtok & Gyaltsan, 1971.

LINDSLEY, D. B. Attention, consciousness, sleep and wakefulness. In J. Field (Ed.), *Handbook of physiology: A critical, comprehensive presentation of physiological knowledge and concepts. Section 1: Neurophysiology. Vol. III*. Washington, D. C.: American Physiological Society, 1960. Pp. 1553–1593.

LINDSLEY, D. B. The reticular activating system and perceptual integration. In D. E. Sheer (Ed.), *Electrical stimulation of the brain: An interdisciplinary survey of neurobehavioral integrative systems*. Austin: Univer. of Texas Press, 1961. Pp. 331–349.

LUDWIG, A. M. Altered states of consciousness. *Arch. gen. Psychiat.*, 1966, *15*, 225–234.

MARAÑON, G. Contribution a l'étude de l'action émotive de l'adrénalin. [Contribution to the study of emotional arousal of adrenalin.] *Rev. franç. Endocr.*, 1924, *2*, 301–325.

MASTERS, R. E. L., & HOUSTON, J. *The varieties of psychedelic experience*. New York: Holt, Rinehart & Winston, 1966.

MAUPIN, E. W. Individual differences in response to a Zen meditation exercise. *J. consult. Psychol.*, 1965, *29*, 139–145.

MESSICK, S. J., & FRITZKY, F. J. Dimensions of analytic attitude in cognition and personality. *J. Pers.*, 1963, *31*, 346–370.

NAKAMIZO, S. Psycho-physiological studies on respiratory pattern. In Y. Akishige (Ed.), *Psychological studies on Zen*. Tokyo: Zen Institute of Komazawa Univer., 1973. Pp. 135–166.

NARANJO, C., & ORNSTEIN, R. E. *On the psychology of meditation*. New York: Viking, 1971.

NEISSER, U. *Cognitive psychology*. New York: Appleton-Century-Crofts, 1967.

OSWALD, I. Experimental studies of rhythm, anxiety and cerebral vigilance. *J. ment. Sci.*, 1959, *105*, 269–295.

PELLETIER, K. R. Influence of transcendental meditation upon autokinetic perception. *Percept. mot. Skills*, 1974, *39*, 1031–1034.

PRIBRAM, K. H. *Languages of the brain: Experimental paradoxes and principles in neuropsychology*. Englewood Cliffs, N. J.: Prentice-Hall, 1971.

PRIBRAM, K. H. Toward a holonomic theory of perception. In S. Ertel, L. Kemmler, & M. Stadler (Eds.), *Gestalttheorie in der Modern Psychologie*. [*Gestalt theory in modern psychology*.] Köln: Erich Wergenroth, 1974. Pp. 161–184.

PRIBRAM, K. H., & McGUINNESS, D. Arousal, activation, and effort in the control of attention. *Psychol. Rev.*, 1975, *82*, 116–149.

PRITCHARD, R. M., HERON, W., & HEBB, D. O. Visual perception approached by the method of stabilized images. *Canad. J. Psychol.*, 1960, *14*, 67–77.

RAPAPORT, D. Cognitive structures (1957). In M. M. Gill (Ed.), *The collected papers of David Rapaport*. New York: Basic Books, 1967. Pp. 631–664. (a)

RAPAPORT, D. The theory of attention cathexis: An economic and structural attempt at the explanation of cognitive processes (1959). In M. M. Gill (Ed.), *The collected papers of David Rapaport*. New York: Basic Books, 1967. Pp. 778–794. (b)

REISEN, A. H. Arrested vision: In which chimpanzees raised in the dark shed light on the relationship between visual experience and visual development. *Sci. Amer.*, 1950, *183*, 16–19.

SCHACHTEL, E. G. The development of focal attention and the emergence of reality. *Psychiatry*, 1954, *17*, 309–324.

SCHACHTER, S., & SINGER, J. E. Cognitive, social, and physiological determinants of emotional state. *Psychol. Rev.*, 1962, *69*, 379–399.

SENDEN, M. V. *Raum-und Gestaltauffassung bei operierten Blindgeborenen vor und nach der operation.* [Space and form conception before and after surgery in persons born blind and operated on.] Leipzig: Barth, 1932.

SHEPARD, R. N., & CERMAK, G. W. Perceptual-cognitive explorations of a toroidal set of free-form stimuli. *Cognitive Psychol.*, 1973, *4*, 351–377.

SHOR, R. E. The frequency of naturally occuring "hypnotic-like" experiences in the normal college population. *Int. J. clin. exp. Hypnosis*, 1960, *8*, 151–163.

SILVERMAN, J. A paradigm for the study of altered states of consciousness. *Brit. J. Psychiat.*, 1968, *114*, 1201–1218.

SPIELBERGER, C. D., GORSUCH, R. L., & LUSHENE, R. E. *Manual for the State-Trait Anxiety Inventory ("Self-Evaluation Questionnaire")*. Palo Alto, Calif.: Consulting Psychologists Press, 1970.

TART, C. T. Scientific foundations for the study of altered states of consciousness. *J. transpers. Psychol.*, 1971, *3*, 93–124.

TART, C. T. *States of consciousness.* New York: Dutton, 1975.

TELLEGEN, A., & ATKINSON, G. Openness to absorbing and self-altering experiences ("absorption"), a trait related to hypnotic susceptibility. *J. abnorm. Psychol.*, 1974, *83*, 268–277.

VALINS, S. Emotionality and autonomic reactivity. *J. exp. Res. Person.*, 1967, *2*, 41–48.

VAN NUYS, D. Meditation, attention, and hypnotic susceptibility: A correlational study. *Int. J. clin. exp. Hypnosis*, 1973, *21*, 59–69.

WALLACE, R. K. Physiological effects of transcendental meditation. *Science*, 1970, *167*, 1751–1754.

WALRATH, L. C., & HAMILTON, D. W. Autonomic correlates of meditation and hypnosis. *Amer. J. clin. Hypnosis*, 1975, *17*, 190–197.

WITKIN, H. A. *Embedded Figures Test, Form A.* Palo Alto, Calif.: Consulting Psychologists Press, 1969.

WOODS, J. H. (Trans.) *The yoga-system of Patanjali* (Vol. 17). In C. R. Lanman (Ed.), *Harvard Oriental Series*. Cambridge, Mass.: Harvard Univer. Press, 1914.

YAMAOKA, T. Psychological study of mental self-control. In Y. Akishige (Ed.), *Psychological studies on Zen*. Tokyo: Zen Institute of Komazawa Univer., 1973. Pp. 225–270.

ZUBEK, J. P. (Ed.) *Sensory deprivation: Fifteen years of research*. New York: Appleton-Century-Crofts, 1969.

THE BUDDHA ON MEDITATION AND
STATES OF CONSCIOUSNESS

Daniel J. Goleman

Manifestation is mind;
And so is Voidness too.
Enlightenment is mind;
And so is blindness too.
The emergence and extinction
Of things are also in one's mind.
May I understand that all and everything
Inhere only in the mind.

—Tilopa, *The Vow of Mahamudra*

INTRODUCTION

The predicament of Westerners setting out to explore those
states of consciousness discontinuous with the normal is like
that of the early sixteenth century European cartographers
who pieced together maps from explorers' reports of the New
World they had not themselves seen. Just as Pizarro's report of
the New World would have emphasized Peru and South
America and underplayed North America, while Hudson's
would be biased toward Canada and North America to the
detriment of South America, so with explorers in psychic
space: each report of states of consciousness is a unique
configuration specific to the experiences of the voyager who
sets it down. That the reports overlap and agree makes us
more sure that the terrain within has its own topography,
independent of and reflected in the mapping of it. The differences in maps show us that there are many routes to these
states, and that they can be reached in distinct ways and

*problems of
exploration*

[1]To Acharya Anagarika Munindra of the International Meditation Center, Bodh
Gaya, India, for his instrumental instruction in the teachings of the *Visuddhimagga*; to Baba Ram Dass for our conversations during the preparation of
this paper; to Joseph Goldstein for his seminal comments on the mathematics of
higher states of consciousness; and to Maharaj-ji for arranging my stay in India
so as to make possible this work; I am deeply and humbly grateful. Any errors
are my own.

Buddha on Meditation

told of within disparate systems of language, metaphor, and symbol.

extending the framework of modern Western psychology

Perhaps the most thorough maps of the realms of consciousness today are among the teachings of the religious systems of the East. The Tibetan *bardo* or the *loca* of the Vedas and Buddhism are in their esoteric sense metaphors for those mental states traditionally dealt with by Western psychology, as well as for a range of states not yet widely acknowledged by psychology in the West. Buddhadasa Bhikku (1968), for example, gives the esoteric meaning in Theravadan scriptures for these terms: "hell" means anxiety; *preta loca,* the "realm of hungry ghosts," refers to motivation based on craving or deficiency; *asura loca,* the "realm of frightened ghosts," is irrational fear; and "heaven" is sensual bliss of the highest order. All these states exist here and now. Beyond these more familiar states the Eastern systems go on to describe realms of mind that have only recently begun to be recognized and investigated by psychologists in the West. What has for ages constituted a fundamental transcendental religious experience, and so been described in the terminology of religious belief systems, is on the verge of being translated into the framework of modern psychology, itself a belief system, as "altered" or "higher states of consciousness" (ASC and HSC, respectively).

meditation-specific states of consciousness

This paper is concerned with a subcategory of ASC: meditation-specific states of consciousness, or MSC. Meditation states are distinct from ASC in that they include only those states attained through meditation that transcend normal conditions of sensory awareness and cognition. ASC subsumes a wider range than does MSC: altered states include, e.g., those induced by hypnosis and psychedelics (topics beyond the scope of this paper) as well as MSC. In their effects on the three normal states of waking, dreaming, and sleeping, MSCs produce a higher state, in accord with Tart's (1971) criterian for HSC: (1) all functions of "lower" states are available—i.e., waking, dreaming, sleeping—and (2) some new functions derivative of meditative states are present in addition. What I have called elsewhere (1971) the "fifth state" has by definition the attributes of an HSC; the meditation-specific states to be discussed here are not HSC within Tart's formulation.

As systematic investigation of states of consciousness comes to fruition, seeming differences among traditional sources in descriptions and delimitations of meditation and higher states may prove to be due to the individual idiosyncracies of those who have experienced and told of them, rather than to the innate nature of the states themselves. Since most of the teachings about MSC and HSC are within a religious framework, the particular belief system in terms of which the experiences of an HSC are interpreted also must be seen as accounting for some of the variance. Here, as elsewhere, the Schachter (1962) effect prevails: cognitive predispositions determine the interpretation and labeling of internal stimuli. Ramana Maharshi, for example, a being who has experienced higher states himself, says of St. Paul's great experience on the Damascus road that, when he returned to normal consciousness, he interpreted it in terms of Christ and the Christians because at the time he was preoccupied with the thought of them; St. Paul then identified his realization with this predominant thought (Chadwick, 1966). A more recent example is R. M. Bucke (1961), who spontaneously entered a high state while riding home after an evening of reading Whitman's Vedantic poetry, and subsequently saw his experience in terms of "cosmic consciousness." As Suzuki (1958) points out, in every religion it has been the core experience of an altered state which has preceded and been foundation for the subsequent structures of institution and theology. Too often it is the latter that have survived rather than the former; thus the modern crisis of the established churches might be seen in terms of the disappearance in our age of personally experienced transcendental states, the "living spirit" which is the common base of all religions. Still, for each being who enters these states without a guide, it is as though he were discovering them for all the world for the first time. A biographer of Sri Aurobindo, for example, notes (Satprem, 1970, p. 256):

the Schachter effect

> One may imagine that Sri Aurobindo was the first to be baffled by his own experience and that it took him some years to understand exactly what had happened. We have described the . . . experience . . . as though the stages had been linked very carefully, each with its explanatory label, but the explanations came long afterwards, at that moment he had no guiding landmarks.

This paper begins in Part I with a detailed discussion of the *Visuddhimagga* account of Gotama Buddha's teachings on meditation and higher states of consciousness—perhaps the most detailed and extensive report extant of one being's explorations within the mind. On the basis of these teachings, implications are discussed for research in the psychophysiology of meditation, and a framework of landmarks are proposed for methodical laboratory tests of meditation and meditative states of consciousness. In Part II, a three fold dynamic

organization of Part I and Part II

typology is generated, using the Buddha's account and map as reference point: concentration on a single object versus contemplation of the workings of the mind itself, plus the integrated combination of the two. This typology is used as a template in a survey of many of the meditation systems currently coming into popularity in the West.

VISUDDHIMAGGA: THE BUDDHA'S MAP OF HIGHER STATES OF CONSCIOUSNESS

> In the Buddhist doctrine, mind is the starting point, the focal point, and also, as the liberated and purified mind of the Saint, the culminating point.
> —Nyanaponika, *Heart of Buddhist Meditation*

Perhaps the broadest and most detailed treatment of higher states of consciousness is the encyclopedic *Abhidhamma,* attributed to the disciples' rendition of more than forty years of Gotama Buddha's discourses. The *Abhidhamma* was summarized in the fifth century by Buddhaghosa in his voluminous *Visuddhimagga,* the "path to purification."[2] Buddhaghosa explains that "purification" should be understood as *nirvana.* In the course of delineating this path virtually every other path to meditative states is touched on; the Buddha, it is said, traversed them all before attaining the nirvanic state. Indeed, the system of paths and their respective states given in the *Visuddhimagga* encompasses or intersects the major practical teachings of most all the Eastern schools newly transplanted to the West.

three major divisions of the Buddha's system of training

The Buddha's system begins with *sila*—virtue or moral purity —the systematic cultivation of thought, word, and deed, converting energies spent unprofitably into profitable or wholesome directions. "Wholesome" is understood in its dharma language sense as that which leads one toward meditative states of consciousness, to nirvana. In the process that culminates in nirvana, sila is the essential foundation, the "cool-headedness" which serves as the basis for attaining MSC. Sila is one of three major divisions of training in the Buddha's schema, the other two being *samadhi* or concentration and *prajna* or insight. There is a psychological interaction effect between sila, samadhi, and prajna. Effortful sila facilitates initial concentration, which enables sustained insight. Established in either samadhi or prajna, sila, formerly an act of the will,

---

[2]In addition to the translation by Bhikku Nanamoli, I have also consulted contemporay commentaries on the Visuddhimagga by: Bhikku Soma (1949), Conze (1956), Dhammaratana (1964), Kashyap (1954), Lama Govinda (1969), Ledi Sayadaw (1965), Mahasi Sayadaw (1965, 1970), Narada Thera (1956), Nyanaponika Thera (1949, 1962, 1968), Nyanatiloka (1952a,b), and Mahathera (1962).

becomes effortless and natural. Prajna can reinforce purity while aiding concentration; strong concentration can have both insight and purity as byproducts. The dynamic of interaction is not linear; the development of any one of the three facilitates the other two. There is no necessary progression, but rather a simultaneity and spiral of interactions in the course of traversing any given meditation path. Though the presentation here is of necessity linear, it should be kept in mind that in actuality there is a complex interrelation in an individual's development of moral purity, concentration, and insight. These are three facets of a single process.

To attain effortless sila, ego must "die"—i.e., desires originating from thoughts of self cease to be the primary determinants of behavior. According to the *Visuddhimagga*, if this "death" comes about through development of samadhi, ego will remain in the form of latent tendencies which will remain inoperative so long as mind is concentrated and will bloom again when concentration wanes. If ego death is due to maturing of prajna, ego will cease to exist as an operative force in behavior, though it may continue in thought as old habits of mind; with full insight mind remains disenchanted with ego desires which are now realized to be impermanent, unsatisfactory, and non-self. On full attainment of nirvana, sila is perfected, the potential for impure acts having been utterly relinquished. From the Eastern viewpoint, this end-state is *vairagya*, choiceless sila. Sila is not merely abstention from acting in proscribed ways, but also involves restraint from even thinking in those ways, for thought is seen as the root of action. Thus, e.g., the *Visuddhimagga* urges the meditator, should lustful thoughts arise, immediately to counter those thoughts by contemplating the loathsomeness of the body. The object of the practice of moral purity is to free the meditator from thoughts of remorse, guilt, or shame.

ego "death" and effortless virtue

What was initially effortful practice facilitates a change in consciousness to higher states where the attitudes embodied in sila are an effortless and natural by product of the state itself. In these states the laws of thought and behavior are determined by the experiences of bliss, contentment, and detachment that prevail there. The old psychologies of the West, based on fundamental assumptions such as sexual dynamisms and the urge to power, cease to apply in these new realms of the mind, just as Newtonian physics was found to be inadequate for understanding physics within the atom.[3]

[3]One exception is the late Abraham Maslow's (1970) "Theory Z," which could, along with the work of R. Assagioli and C. G. Jung, become for the West the cornerstone for a psychological understanding of HSC.

Meditative and higher states are from the perspective of most Western psychology "transcendental" in that they are a realm beyond that particular body of thought, but MSCs and HSCs are not without laws and rules of their own.

sila, or virtue and the psychological preconditions for meditation

Sila in the Visuddhimagga tradition begins with the observance of the codes of discipline for laity, novices, and fully ordained monks. The precepts for laity are but five: abstaining from killing, stealing, unlawful sexual intercourse, lying, and intoxicants. For novices the list expands to ten; for monks it mushrooms to 227 prohibitions and observances regulating monastic life. While the practice of sila varies in accord with one's mode of life, its intent is the same: it is the necessary preparation for meditation. On one level these are codes for proper social behavior; in this Buddhist tradition, that level is secondary in importance to the life of motivational purity proper behavior foreshadows. Sila is to be understood not only in the ordinary external sense of propriety, but also as mental attitudes or as psychological preconditions out of which right speech, action, and thought arise. Behavior is to be controlled insofar as it affects consciousness. Sila is conscious and intentional restraint of action designed to produce a calmed and subdued mind. Purity of morality has only the purity of mind as its goal.

satipatthana, or mindfulness

Because a controlled mind is the goal of sila, its practices include restraint of the senses. The means for doing so is *satipatthana,* or mindfulness. Control is exercised over the sense organs through cultivation of the habit of simply noticing sensory perceptions, and not allowing them to stimulate the mind into thought-chains of reaction to them. This attitude of paying sensory stimuli bare attention, when systematically developed into *vipassana,* seeing things as they are, becomes the avenue to the nirvanic state. In daily practice it facilitates detachment toward one's internal universe of perception and thought. One becomes an onlooker to his own stream of consciousness, preparing the way to those states that transcend normal consciousness.

optimum life setting

In the initial stages, before becoming firmly grounded in mindfulness, one is vulnerable to distractions from external circumstances. Accordingly the *Visuddhimagga* gives instructions to the would-be meditator for what constitutes an optimum life setting. One must engage in "right livelihood" so that the source of financial support will not be cause for misgivings. In the case of monks, professions such as astrology, palm-reading, and dream interpretation are expressly forbidden, while the life of a mendicant is recommended.

Psychology of Meditation

Possessions should be kept to a minimum. A monk is to possess only eight articles: three robes, a belt, a begging bowl, a razor, a sewing needle, and sandals. Food should be taken in moderation, enough to ensure physical comfort but less than would make for drowsiness. One's dwelling should be aloof from the world, a place of solitude; for householders who cannot live in isolation, a room should be set aside solely for meditation. Undue concern for the body should be avoided, but in case of sickness appropriate medicine should be obtained. The four requisites of possessions, food, dwelling, and medicine are to be acquired only insofar as they are necessary to well-being, and without greed, so that even one's material necessities will be pure and untainted.

Since the state of one's mind is seen to be affected by the state of mind of one's associates, it is recommended that the meditator surround himself with likeminded people. This is one of the advantages of a *sangha* (Sanskrit: *satsang*), narrowly defined as those who have attained the nirvanic state and, applied in its widest sense, the community of people on the path. Meditation is facilitated by the company of mindful or concentrated persons, and is impeded by "hanging out" with those who are agitated, distracted, and immersed in worldly concerns. The latter are likely to engage in talk which does not lead to detachment, dispassion, or tranquility. The sort of topics typical of such unprofitable talk are enumerated by the Buddha as (from Mahasi Sayadaw, 1965, p. 232): *community of people on the path*

> Talk about kings, thieves, ministers, armies, famine, and war; about eating, drinking, clothing, and lodging; about garlands, perfumes, relatives, vehicles, cities and countries; about women and wine, the gossip of the street and well; about ancestors and various trifles; tales about the origin of the world, talk about things being so or otherwise, and similar matters. *unprofitable talk*

Having gained the advantages and encouragement to be found in a sangha and become firmly set in meditation, the determined meditator at a later stage may find to be obstacles what once were aids. The *Visuddhimagga* lists ten categories of potential attachments or hindrances to progress in meditation: (1) any fixed dwelling place if its upkeep is the cause of worry, (2) family, if their welfare causes concern, (3) accruing gifts or reputation which involves spending time with admirers, (4) a following of students or being occupied with teaching, (5) activities or projects, having "something to do," (6) traveling about, (7) people dear to one whose needs demand attention, (8) illness involving treatment, (9) theoretical studies unaccompanied by practice, and (10) su- *ten hindrances to progress in meditation* pernormal psychic powers, the practice of which becomes more interesting than meditation. The principle underlying this list is that release from worldly obligations frees one for single-minded pursuit of meditation. This is purification in the sense of freeing the mind from affairs that might disturb it.

optional ascetic practices

There is a further set of thirteen practices of self-purification treated in the *Visuddhimagga* apart from sila. These ascetic practices are optional in the "middle way" of the Buddha. If someone set on a contemplative life should find any of them conducive to that aim, he may practice them but in their observance must be discreet, preferably doing them without anyone noticing. These ascetic means to purification include wearing robes made only of rags; begging for food; eating only one bowl of food, and just once a day; living in the forest under a tree; dwelling in a cemetery or in the open; sitting up throughout the night. Though optional, the Buddha praises those who follow these modes of living "for the sake of frugality, contentedness, austerity, detachment," while crit-

criticism of spiritual pride

icizing those who pride themselves on practicing austerities and look down on others. In all facets of sila, spiritual pride mars purity. The goal of sila is a mind unconcerned with externals, calm and ripe for the inward turning of attention that is meditation.

SAMADHI: THE PATH OF CONCENTRATION

With the development of sila a psychological base is prepared for training in samadhi, concentration. The essence of concentration is nondistractedness; sila is the systematic prun-

essence of concentration; nondistracted-ness

ing away of sources of distraction. Now the meditator's work is to attain unification of mind, one-pointedness. The stream-of-thought normally contains myriad concomitants. The goal of samadhi is to break and steady the thought continuum by fixing the mind on a single thought. That one thought is the subject of meditation. In samadhi the mind is not only directed toward the subject, but penetrates it, is absorbed in it, and becomes one with it. The concomitants of the thought-stream are prevented from dissipation by being firmly fixed on that one point.

Anything that can be the object of attention can be the subject for samadhi meditation. Samadhi is simply sustained attention to a single point. But the character of the object attended to has definite consequences for the outcome of meditation. The compilation of sutras known as the *Nikayas* gives the fullest list of subjects of meditation recommended by the Buddha, elaborating 101. The *Visuddhimagga* enumerates 40 meditation subjects:

ten *kasinas,* contemplation devices: earth, water, fire, air, dark-blue, yellow, blood-red, white, light, bounded space;

*meditation
subjects*

ten *asubhas,* loathsome and decaying corpses: e.g., a bloated corpse, a gnawed corpse, a worm-infested corpse, a skeleton;

ten reflections: on the attributes of the Buddha, his Teaching, the sangha, one's own sila, one's own liberality, one's own possession of godly qualities, or on the inevitability of death; contemplation on the 32 parts of the body, or on in-and-out breathing;

four sublime states: lovingkindness, compassion, joy in the joy of others, and equanimity;

four formless states: contemplation of infinite space, infinite consciousness, the realm of no-thing-ness, and the realm of neither-perception-nor-nonperception;

the loathsomeness of food; and

the four physical elements (earth, air, fire, water) as abstract forces.

Each of these subjects has characteristic consequences for the nature, depth, and by-products of concentration. All of them can serve as bases for developing concentration to the depth necessary for attaining the nirvanic state. The concentration produced by those of a complicated nature—e.g., the attributes of the Buddha—will be less unified than that produced by a simple object—e.g., the earth kasina, a clay-colored wheel. Apart from the quality of concentration produced by a given meditation subject, each has distinct psychological by products. The meditation on lovingkindness, for example, has among its fruits: the meditator sleeps and wakes in comfort, dreams no evil dreams, is dear to all beings, his mind is easily concentrated, his expression serene, and he dies unconfused. Perhaps the most important consequence of a subject is the depth of absorption—*jhana*—it will produce.

MEDITATION SUBJECT	HIGHEST JHANA LEVEL ATTAINABLE
Kasinas; Mindfulness of breath; Neither-perception-nor-nonperception	Eighth
No-thing-ness	Seventh
Infinite consciousness	Sixth
Infinite space	Fifth
Equanimity	Fourth
Lovingkindness; Selfless joy; Compassion	Third
Body parts; Corpses	First
Reflections; Elements; Loathsomeness of food	Access

meditation sub-jects for different temperaments

The Buddha recognized that persons of different tempera-ments would be more suited to some meditation subjects than to others. The typology of temperaments he set down as guidelines for advising which person should be given which subject has four main types: (1) one disposed to hatred, (2) the lustful, deluded, or excitable, (3) one prone to faith, (4) the intelligent.[4] Subjects suitable for type (1) are the four sublime states and the four color kasinas; for type (2) the 10 asubhas, body parts, and respiration; for type (3) the first six reflections; for type (4) reflection on death, the loathsomeness of food, and the physical elements. The remaining subjects are suitable for all cognitive dispo-sitions.

role of teacher

The ideal meditation teacher was the Buddha, who, it is said, had developed the power to know the mind and heart of others, and so could match perfectly each person with the appropriate subject for concentration. In lieu of the Buddha, the *Visuddhimagga* advises the would-be meditator to seek out a teacher according to his level of attainment in medita-tion, the most highly accomplished being the best teacher. His support and advice are critical in making one's way through unfamiliar mental terrain. The pupil "takes refuge" in his teacher, and must enter a contract of surrender to him. What is surrendered is the propensities of ego—"hindrances" —which might prevent the student from purposefully pur-suing meditation to the point where those ego propensities

responsibility of student

are transcended. But the responsibility for salvation is laid squarely on the student's shoulders, not on the teacher's; the teacher is not a traditional Eastern guru, but a "good friend" on the path. The teacher will point the way, the student must walk for himself. The essence of the role of teacher in this tradition is given in the lines from the *Zenrin*:

If you wish to know the road up the mountain,
You must ask the man who goes back and forth on it.

Jhana: Levels of Absorption

Having found a suitable teacher and been instructed in an appropriate subject, and established to some degree in sila, the meditator begins in earnest. This first stage is marked by an internal psychological tension between concentration

---

[4]This typology parallels a psychoanalytic scheme of character types based on cognitive styles; in the same order (Shapiro, 1961): (1) the "paranoid," who sees others as separate and suspect, (2) the "hysteric," who judges and acts on the first impulse, (3) the "obsessive-compulsive," who looks to others for direction, and (4) the "psychopath," who perceives accurately but restructures reality as he wishes.

Psychology of Meditation

on the primary object of attention—the meditation subject—and distracting thoughts, which hinder concentration. These hindrances mainly take the form of: desires; ill will, despair, and anger; sloth and torpor; agitation and worry; and doubt and skepticism. With sustained effort there comes the first moment when these hindrances are wholly subdued, marked by a quickening of concentration. At this moment those concomitants of consciousness that will mature into full absorption come into dominance. This is the first noteworthy attainment of samadhi; because it is the state verging on full absorption, it is called "access" concentration.

description of "access" concentration

This state of concentration is comparable to a child not yet able to stand steady but always trying to do so. The factors of mind characteristic of full absorption are not strong at the access level; their emergence is precarious, and the mind fluctuates between them and "inner speech," the usual ruminations and wandering thoughts. The meditator is still receptive to sensory input and remains aware of environmental noises and body states. The primary object is a dominant thought, but it does not yet fully occupy the mind. At this stage there may emerge (though not always) any of the following: strong feelings of zest or rapture, happiness and pleasure, equanimity, initial application to the primary object as though striking at it, or sustained application to the primary object as though repeatedly noting it. Sometimes there are luminous shapes or flashes of bright light, especially if the meditation subject is a kasina or respiration. Visionary experiences associated with MSC occur at this level, where mind is purified but still can be occupied with name and form. There may also be a sensation of bodily lightness, as though floating in the air. Access concentration is a precarious attainment, and if not solidified into full absorption at the same sitting, it must be guarded between sessions by avoiding distracting endeavors or encounters.

With continued application of mind to the primary object comes the first moment marking a total break with normal consciousness. This is full absorption, or jhana. The mind suddenly seems to sink into the object and remains fixed in it. Hindering thoughts totally cease. There is neither sensory perception nor the usual awareness of one's body; bodily pain cannot be felt. Apart from the initial and sustained attention to the primary object, there are only rapture, bliss, and one-pointedness. There is a subtle distinction between "rapture" and "bliss": rapture at the level of this first jhana is likened to the initial pleasure and excitement of getting a long-sought object; bliss is the enjoyment of that object.

description of full absorption and first jhana

Rapture may be experienced as raising of the hairs on the body, as momentary joy flashing and disappearing like lightning, as showering through the body again and again in waves, as the sensation of levitation, or as the pervasive suffusion of thrilling happiness. Bliss is a more subdued state of continued ecstasy. One-pointedness is the property of mind that centers it in the jhanic state. The first experience of jhana lasts but a single moment of consciousness. With continued practice the jhanic state can be maintained for progressively longer intervals. Until the jhana is mastered, it *mastery* is an unstable attainment which might be lost. Full mastery is stabilized when the meditator can attain this first jhana whenever, wherever, as soon as, and for as long as he wishes.

PATH OF CONCENTRATION

FORMLESS STATES	Eighth	Neither-perception-nor-nonperception. Equanimity and one-pointedness.
	Seventh	Awareness of no-thing-ness. Equanimity and one-pointedness.
	Sixth	Objectless infinite consciousness. Equanimity and one-pointedness.
	Fifth	Consciousness of infinite space. Equanimity and one-pointedness.
MATERIAL STATES	Fourth	Equanimity and one-pointedness. Bliss and all feelings of bodily pleasure cease. Concentration imperturbable. Breath ceases.
	Third	Feelings of bliss, one-pointedness, and equanimity. Rapture ceases.
	Second	Feelings of rapture, bliss, and one-pointedness. No thought of primary object.
	First Jhana	Hindering thoughts, sensory perception, and awareness of painful body states all cease. Initial and unbroken, sustained attention to primary object. Feelings of rapture, bliss, and one-pointedness.
	Access	Hindering thoughts overcome; other thoughts remain—awareness of sensory inputs and body states. Primary object dominant thought. Feelings of rapture, happiness, equanimity; initial and sustained thoughts of primary object; flashes of light; or bodily lightness.

In the further course of meditation of one-pointed-ness will become more and more intensified by the successive elimination of rapture, bliss, and attention; the energy invested in the eliminated factors becomes absorbed by one-pointedness at each higher jhanic level (see above). The process of becoming totally one-pointed proceeds, after mastery of the first jhana, with the systematic elimination of initial and sustained attention to the primary object, which, on reflection after emerging from the jhanic state, seems gross relative to the other mental factors. Just as the hindrances were overcome in attaining access, and all thoughts were stilled in attaining *second jhana* the first jhana, applied and sustained attention to the primary object are abandoned at the threshold of this second jhana.

Psychology of Meditation

The procedure for this requires entering the first level of absorption on the basis of the primary object, and then, having previously so resolved, turning the mind toward the feelings of rapture, bliss, and one-pointedness, free of any idea of the primary object. This level of absorption is both more subtle and more stable than the first; mind is now totally free of any verbal formations or ideas of form embodied in the primary object. This jhana is to be mastered as before.

After mastery, on emerging from and reviewing the second jhana, the meditator sees the factor of rapture—a form of excitement—as gross compared to bliss and one-pointedness. The third level of jhana can be attained by again contemplating the primary object, and abandoning sequentially thoughts of the object, and then rapture. The third level of absorption is marked by a feeling of equanimity and impartiality toward even the highest rapture, which manifests with the fading away of rapture. This jhana is extremely subtle, and the mind would be pulled back to rapture without this newly emergent equanimity. An exceedingly sweet bliss fills the meditator, and on emerging from this state he is aware of bliss throughout his body. Because the bliss of this level is accompanied by equanimity, mind is kept one-pointed in these subtle dimensions, resisting the pull of rapture. Having mastered the third jhana as before, and on reviewing it, the meditator sees bliss as gross and disturbing compared to one-pointedness and equanimity.

third level of jhana

Proceeding again through the jhanic sequence, with the abandonment of all forms of mental pleasure, the meditator attains the fourth level. With the total cessation of bliss, the factors of equanimity and one-pointedness achieve full strength and clarity. All mental states that might oppose these remaining two factors have been overcome. Feelings of bodily pleasure are fully abandoned; feelings of pain ceased at the first jhana. There is not a single sensation or thought. Mind rests with one-pointedness in equanimity at this extremely subtle level. Just as mind has become progressively more still at each level of absorption, breath has become more calm. At this fourth level breath, it is said, ceases altogether. Concentration here is imperturbable; the meditator will emerge after a time limit set before entering this state.

fourth level of jhana

Each jhana rests on that below. In entering any jhana, mind traverses successively each lower level, eliminating its constituents one by one. With practice the traversal of jhanic levels becomes almost instantaneous, the mind residing at each level on the way for but a few moments of consciousness. As mental factors are eliminated, concentration is intensified.

the "formless" jhanas

The next step in development of concentration culminates in the four states called "formless." While the first four jhanas are attained by concentration on a material form or some concept derived therefrom, the formless states are attained by passing beyond all perception of form. While the first four jhanas are attained by removing mental factors, with the formless jhanas the complete removal of one stage constitutes the next attainment. All the formless jhanas share the factors of one-pointedness and equanimity, but at each level these factors are progressively refined.

the fifth jhana: first of the formless absorptions

The first formless absorption—the fifth jhana—is attained by first entering the fourth jhana through any of the kasinas. Mentally extending the limits of the kasina to the largest extent imaginable, the meditator turns his attention to the space touched by it. With this infinite space as the object of contemplation, and with the full maturity of equanimity and one-pointedness, mind now abides in a sphere where all perceptions of form have ceased. Mind is so firmly set in this level of sublime consciousness that no external sensory input can perturb or disrupt it. Still, the tendencies of the mechanisms associated with sensory perception exist in the fifth jhana, though they are not attended to: the absorption would be broken should attention turn to them.

sixth jhana

seventh jhana

The next level is attained (fifth jhana having been mastered) by achieving the consciousness of infinite space, and then turning attention to the element of infinite awareness. Thus the thought of infinite space is abandoned, while objectless infinite consciousness remains. This marks the sixth jhana. Having mastered the sixth, the meditator attains the seventh jhana by first entering the sixth and then turning contemplation to the nonexistence of infinite consciousness. The seventh jhana is thus absorption with no-thing-ness, or the void, as its object. That is, consciousness has as its object the awareness of absence of any object. Mastering this jhana, the meditator then reviews it and finds any perception at all a disadvantage, its absence being more sublime.

So motivated, the meditator can attain the eighth jhana by first entering the seventh, and then turning attention to the aspect of peacefulness, and away from perception of the void. The delicacy of this operation is suggested by the stipulation that there must be no hint of desire to attain this peacefulness, nor to avoid perception of no-thing-ness.

Attending to the peacefulness, he reaches the ultrasubtle state where there are only residual mental formations. There is no gross perception here at all: thus "no-perception"; there is ultrasubtle perception: thus "not-nonperception." This eighth jhana is called the sphere of "neither-perception-nor-nonperception." The same degree of subtlety of existence is here true of all concomitants of consciousness. No mental states are decisively present, yet residuals remain in a degree of near-absence. The *Visuddhimagga* says of mental states in the eighth jhana, "not having been, they come to be; having come to be they vanish." Lama Govinda (1969) describes it as the ultimate limit of perception. As with mind, so with body: metabolism becomes progressively more still through the formless jhanas until the eighth, where Kashyup's (1954) characterization of cognition applies, too, to physiological processes: it is a state "so extremely subtle that it cannot be said whether it is or is not."

eighth jhana

The states of consciousness embodied in the jhanas are characteristic of what are called in the Visuddhimagga system the "Brahma realms," the "planes of illumination," and the "pure abodes." Just as the jhanas are out of the relative world of sense-perception, thought, time, and space, are permeated with bliss and/or equanimity, embody infinite consciousness, and so on, so these other planes of existence are seen as existing solely in those jhanic dimensions. Beings may be born into an existence on one or another of these planes according to karmas of past lifetimes, especially the degree to which one has mastered jhanas in a human birth.[5] Thus, for example, developing the second jhana and practicing it to the highest degree is said to bring rebirth in the realm of "radiant Brahmas," from whose bodies rays of light are emitted like flashes of lightning.

discussion of jhanic dimensions

The section on supernormal powers is the one part of the *Visuddhimagga* most dubious from the standpoint of the West, since it treats as real, events that overleap the bounds of even the most advanced physical sciences. The *Visuddhimagga* enumerates among these supernormal accomplishments: knowing the minds of others, knowing any past or future event, materialization of objects, seeing and hearing at great distances, walking on water, flying through the air, and so on. More interesting, the *Visuddhimagga* describes in technical detail how these feats are performed, while Western science at present cannot reconcile their possibility.[6]

the Visuddhimugga on supernormal powers

caution regarding misuse of supernormal powers

[5]These "kingdoms of heaven" are sometimes called in other cosmological teachings "astral planes," *deva locas, bardos,* and the like.
[6]Tart (1971) describes as a "state-specific science" one where a group of practitioners are able to achieve a certain state of consciousness and agree with one

Yet every school of meditation acknowledges them as by-products of advanced stages of mastery, if only to caution against their misuse. The *Visuddhimagga* sees them as fruits of concentration but a hindrance to full insight, and sets down stiff provisos as prerequisites for supernormal powers, warning that they are hard to maintain and the slightest thing breaks them. The required degree of mind-mastery for their use is formidable. One must first have full proficiency in fourteen methods of mind-control, beginning with achievement of all eight jhanas, using as a base each of the eight kasinas up to the white one, and including such feats as skipping both alternate kasinas and alternate jhanas—i.e., attaining first jhana on the earth kasina, then third jhana on the fire kasina, etc.—in both forward and reverse order. The *Visuddhimagga* estimates that of those who try, only one person in 100,000 or one million will achieve the prerequisite level of mastery. It further marks as a "blemish" wanting it to be known one can practice these things (little wonder that Western parapsychological researchers have yet to encounter a subject capable of the supernormal feats of mind—e.g., telekinesis and supernormal hearing—described).

powers of no value in themselves for progress toward liberation

From the Buddhist point of view, the attainment of powers is a minor advantage, of no value in itself for progress toward liberation. Powers in one who has not yet attained the nirvanic state are seen as an impediment, for they may endanger progress by enhancing his sense of self-esteem, thus strengthening attachment to self. In Buddhist tradition powers are to be used only in circumstances where their use will be of benefit to others. It is an offense against the community of monks for a Buddhist monk to display before laity any psychic powers that are beyond the capacity of ordinary men; a false claim to their possession would mean expulsion from the Order.

PRAJNA: THE PATH OF INSIGHT

the crux of training: "prajna" or discriminating wisdom

From the standpoint of the *Visuddhimagga,* mastery of the jhanas, and the sublime bliss and supernormal powers that may accrue therefrom, is of secondary importance to the cultivation of *prajna,* discriminating wisdom. Jhana mastery is part of a fully rounded training, but the advantages are seen in terms of making the mind wieldy and pliable for

another on their common attainment of that state, and then investigate further areas of interest—e.g., the interaction of that state with "reality." By these criteria, the Buddha and his meditating disciples are analogous to a principle investigator and coinvestigators in the science of MSC, the *Visuddhimagga* and other Buddhist teachings are their findings, and the supernormal powers described here are a representative body of technology generated by their research efforts.

Psychology of Meditation

speeding the training in prajna. Indeed, the deeper stages of samadhi are sometimes referred to in Pali, the language of the *Visuddhimagga,* as concentration-games, the "play" of those well advanced in the practice. But the crux of this training is the path that begins with mindfulness (*satipatthana*), proceeds through insight (*vipassana*), and ends in nirvana.

The first phase, mindfulness, entails breaking through habits of stereotyped perception. The natural tendency is to "habituate" to the world surrounding one, to substitute abstract cognitive patterns or perceptual preconceptions for the raw sensory experience. The practice of mindfulness is purposeful de-habituation: to face the bare facts of experience, seeing each event as though occurring for the first time. The means for de-habituating is continual observation of the first phase of perception when the mind is in a *receptive,* rather than reactive, state. Attention is restricted to bare noticing of objects. Facts of perception are attended to as they arise at any of the five sense-doors or in the mind, which in the *Visuddhimagga* constitutes a sixth sense. While the meditator attends to sense impressions, reaction is kept to a bare registering of the facts of impression observed. If further mental comment, judgment, or reflection should arise in one's mind, these are themselves made objects of bare attention; they are neither repudiated nor pursued, but dismissed after their noting. The essence of mindfulness is, in the words of Nyanaponika Thera (1962), "the clear and single-minded awareness of what actually happens *to* us and *in* us, at the successive moments of perception."

purposeful de-habituation through mindfulness

bare attention

It is in the thorough pursuit of mindfulness that the concentration developed previously finds its utility. In adopting and applying this new habit of bare perception, one-pointedness and the concomitant factors of concentration are essential. The optimal level of concentration in practicing mindfulness is, however, the lowest: access. Mindfulness is to be applied to the perceptual process of normal consciousness, and from the first jhana on, those processes cease. A level of concentration less than that of access, on the other hand, would be overshadowed by hindering thoughts and mental wandering, and so be dysfunctional for practicing mindfulness. It is only at the access level that there is a perfect balance: perception and thought retain their full strength, but concentration is powerful enough to keep the mind from being diverted from steadily noting the processes of perception and thought.

The preferred method for cultivating mindfulness is to precede it with training in the jhanas. Having some degree of mastery in samadhi, the meditator then applies his power of concentration to the task of mindfulness. There is, however, a method of "bare insight," where these practices are undertaken without any previous attainment in absorption. With bare insight the prerequisite level of absorption is attained through the practice of mindfulness itself. During the first stages of bare insight, the meditator's mind will be intermittently interrupted by wandering, hindering thoughts which will arise between moments of noticing. Sometimes they will be perceived, sometimes not. Gradually the momentary concentration of mind in noticing will strengthen until virtually all stray thoughts are noted; such thoughts will then subside as soon as noticed, and the practice will resume immediately afterwards. Finally the point will be reached where the mind will be unhindered by straying. Then the noticing of perceptual and cognitive processes will proceed without break; this is functionally equivalent to access concentration.

the method of "bare insight"

In practice there are four varieties of mindfulness, identical in function but distinguishable by virtue of their point of focus. Contemplation can focus on the body, on feelings, on the mind, or on mind-objects. Any one of these serves as a fixed point for bare attention to the processes of experience. Mindfulness of the body entails attending to each moment of bodily activity, such as posture and movement of limbs, regardless of the nature of the activity engaged in. All functions of the body in daily experience are to be clearly comprehended by simply registering their occurrence; the aim of action is to be disregarded—the focus is on the bodily act itself. Mindfulness of feeling involves focusing on internal sensations, disregarding whether pleasant or unpleasant. All proprioceptive stimuli are simply noted as they come to attention. Some will originate as the initial reaction to sensory input, some as physiological concomitants of psychological states, some as by-products of physiological life processes; whatever the source, the sensation itself is registered.

four points of focus: body, feelings, mind or mind objects

body

feeling

In mindfulness of the mind, it is mental states as they come to awareness that are objects. Whatever mood, mode of thought, or psychological state presents itself, it is simply to be registered as such. If, for instance, there is anger at a disturbing noise, at that moment one simply notes, "anger." The fourth technique, mindfulness of mind-objects, is virtually the same as the one just described save for the level

mind

mind-objects

at which the mind's workings are observed. Rather than noting the quality of mental states as they arise, the meditator notes the objects of the thoughts which occupy those states—e.g., "disturbing noise." When a thought arises it is noted in terms of a schema for classifying mental contents which broadly categorizes all thought forms as either hindrances to, or factors of, enlightenment.

The Stages of Insight

As any of these four techniques of mindfulness are persistently pursued, they break through the normal illusions of continuity and reasonableness that sustain cognitive and perceptual processes. The mind begins to witness the random and discrete units of stuff from which a reality is continually being structured. There emerge a series of realizations concerning the true nature of these processes, and mindfulness matures into insight. The practice of insight begins when contemplation continues without lag; mind is fixed on its object so that contemplating mind and its object always arise together in unbroken succession. This marks the beginning of a chain of insights—mind knowing itself—culminating in the nirvanic state (see following table).

emergence of series of realizations concerning true nature of these processes

The first cognitive realization is that the phenomena contemplated are distinct from mind contemplating them. The faculty whereby mind witnesses its own workings is experienced as different from what is witnessed. As with all the stages of insight, this realization is not at all on the level of verbalization at which it is expressed here, but rather at the level of raw experience. The understanding arises, but not necessarily an articulation of that understanding.

first cognitive realization

Once the two-fold nature of mind and its objects is realized, there arises in the meditator a clear understanding that these dual processes are devoid of self. They are seen to arise as effects of their respective causes, not as the result of direction by any individual agent. All come and go according to their own nature, regardless of "one's will." It becomes a certainty to the meditator that nowhere in the mind's functioning can any abiding entity be detected. This is direct experience of the Buddhist doctrine of *anatta,* literally "not-self," that all phenomena are devoid of an indwelling personality, including "one's self." All one's past and future life is understood as merely a conditioned cause-effect process. Doubts whether "I" might really exist have gone: "I am" is known to be a misconception. The truth of these words of the Buddha (*Samyutta-Nikaya,* 135) are realized:

realization of absence of in-dwelling personality

Just as when the parts are set together
There arises the word "chariot,"
So does the notion of a being
When the aggregates are present.

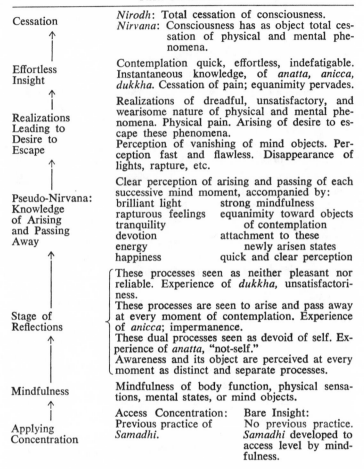

PATH OF INSIGHT

Cessation ↑	*Nirodh*: Total cessation of consciousness. *Nirvana*: Consciousness has as object total cessation of physical and mental phenomena.
Effortless Insight ↑	Contemplation quick, effortless, indefatigable. Instantaneous knowledge, of *anatta, anicca, dukkha*. Cessation of pain; equanimity pervades.
Realizations Leading to Desire to Escape ↑	Realizations of dreadful, unsatisfactory, and wearisome nature of physical and mental phenomena. Physical pain. Arising of desire to escape these phenomena. Perception of vanishing of mind objects. Perception fast and flawless. Disappearance of lights, rapture, etc.
Pseudo-Nirvana: Knowledge of Arising and Passing Away ↑	Clear perception of arising and passing of each successive mind moment, accompanied by: brilliant light strong mindfulness rapturous feelings equanimity toward objects tranquility of contemplation devotion attachment to these energy newly arisen states happiness quick and clear perception
Stage of Reflections ↑	These processes seen as neither pleasant nor reliable. Experience of *dukkha*, unsatisfactoriness. These processes are seen to arise and pass away at every moment of contemplation. Experience of *anicca*; impermanence. These dual processes seen as devoid of self. Experience of *anatta*, "not-self." Awareness and its object are perceived at every moment as distinct and separate processes.
Mindfulness ↑	Mindfulness of body function, physical sensations, mental states, or mind objects.
Applying Concentration	Access Concentration: Bare Insight: Previous practice of No previous practice. *Samadhi*. *Samadhi* developed to access level by mindfulness.

flux and change seen to characterize whole field of consciousness

Further contemplation reveals that witnessing mind and the phenomena it takes as objects arise and pass away at a frequency beyond the meditator's ken. Flux and change are seen to characterize the whole field of consciousness. The realization strikes the meditator that his world of reality is continually renewed every mind-moment in a seemingly endless chain of experiences. The fact of impermanence (Pali: *anicca*) is known in the depths of his being. Seeing that these phenomena arise and pass away at every moment, the meditator comes to see them as neither pleasant nor reliable. Disenchantment sets in: what is constantly changing cannot be the source of lasting satisfaction. The psycho-

Psychology of Meditation

logical process, begun with the realizations of reality as devoid of self and ever-changing, culminates in a state of detachment from one's world of experience to the point where it can be seen as a source of suffering (Pali: *dukkha*).

detachment from one's world of experience

Without any such further reflections, contemplation continues. A stage follows where the beginning and end of each successive object of contemplation is clearly perceived. With this clarity of perception there arise:

Stage of "Knowledge of Arising and Passing Away"; a pseudo-nirvana

the vision of a *brilliant light* or other form of illumination, which may last for just one moment or longer;

rapturous feelings causing goose-flesh, tremor in the limbs, the sensation of levitation, and so on (as described above in the factors of the first jhana);

a calm *tranquility* of mind and body, making them light, plastic, and easily wielded;

devotional feelings and faith, which may take as their object the meditation teacher, the Buddha, his Teachings —including the method of insight itself—and the *Sangha,* accompanied by joyous confidence in the virtues of meditation and the desire to advise friends and relatives to practice it;

ten signs of pseudo-nirvana

vigorous and steady *energy* in contemplation, neither too lax nor too tense;

sublime feelings of *happiness* suffusing the whole body, a wholly unprecedented bliss which seems never-ending and motivates the meditator to tell others of this extraordinary experience;

quick and clear perception of the phenomena noticed: noticing is keen, strong and lucid, and the characteristics of impermanence, non-self, and unsatisfactoriness is understood quite clearly and at once;

strong mindfulness in practicing insight so that all successive moments of phenomena present themselves effortlessly to noticing mind;

equanimity toward all mental formations: neutral feelings prevail toward the objects of insight, which proceeds of itself without effort;

a subtle *attachment* to the lights and other factors listed here, and to pleasure in contemplation.

The meditator is elated at the emergence of these ten signs, and may speak out his experiences thinking he has attained enlightenment and finished the task of meditation. Even if he does not think they mark his liberation, he may pause from the task of insight to bask in their enjoyment. For this reason this stage, called "Knowledge of Arising and Passing Away," is subtitled in the *Visuddhimagga* "The Ten Corruptions of Insight"; it is a pseudo-nirvana. The great danger here is in "mistaking what is not the Path for the Path," or, in lieu of that, faltering in the pursuit of insight because of attachment to these phenomena. When the meditator, either by himself or through advice from his teacher, realizes these experiences to be a landmark along the way rather than his final destination, he turns his focus of contemplation on them, including his own attachment to them.

attachment to "The Ten Corruptions of Insight"

Proceeding, the meditator finds that these experiences gradually diminish and the perceiving of objects becomes clearer. The discrimination of successive phenomena becomes increasingly finer; perception is flawless. The perception of objects becomes faster, and their ending or vanishing is more clearly perceived than their arising. Only their vanishing comes to be perceived at every moment of contemplation: contemplating mind and its object are experienced as vanishing in pairs at every moment. The meditator's world of reality seems to be in a constant state of dissolution. A series of realizations flow from this experience. The mind becomes gripped with fear and dread; all mental formations are seen to be dreadful in nature. Becoming—i.e., the coming into being of thoughts—is regarded as a state of terror. The occurrence of mental phenomena—ordinarily reckoned a source of pleasure—is seen only as a state of being continuously oppressed, which mind is helpless to avoid.

insights into "dissolution"

Then arises realization of the faults and unsatisfactoriness of all phenomena. All mental formations are seen as utterly destitute of any core or satisfaction. In them is nothing but danger. The meditator comes to feel that in all the kinds of becoming there is not a single thing that he can place his hopes in or hold on to. All mental formations—whether the objects noticed or the consciousness engaged in noticing, or in any kind of existence brought to mind—appear insipid. In all the meditator perceives, he sees only suffering and misery.

realization of the unsatisfactoriness of all phenomena

Having known the misery in all phenomena, the meditator becomes entirely disgusted with them. Though he continues with the practice of insight, his mind is dominated by feelings of discontent and listlessness toward all mental formations. Even the thought of the happiest sort of life or the most desirable objects will seem unattractive and boring. He has become absolutely dispassionate and adverse toward the multitudinous field of mental formations, and to any kind of becoming, destiny, or state of consciousness.

dispassionate attitude toward mental formations

Between the moments of noticing, the thought will arise that only in the ceasing of all mental formations is there relief. Now mind no longer fastens on to formations; the meditator becomes desirous of escape from suffering on account of these phenomena. Painful feelings may arise throughout his body, and he may be unwilling to remain long in one posture. The comfortless nature of mind-stuff becomes more evident than ever; motivation for deliverance from it emerges at the root of his being. With this strong motivation for surcease from mental formations, the meditator intensifies his efforts of noticing these formations for the very purpose of escaping them. Then the nature of these phenomena—their impermanence, the element of suffering, and their voidness of self—will become clearly evident. Also at this stage the meditator's body will usually undergo severe, sharp pains of growing intensity. His whole body and mind will seem a mass of suffering; restlessness may overwhelm his application to insight. But by applying the practice of noticing to these pains, they will come to cease. At this point noticing becomes strong and lucid. At every moment he knows quite clearly the three characteristics of these phenomena, and one of the three will come to dominate his understanding.

comfortless nature of mind stuff evident

Now contemplation proceeds automatically, without special effort, as if borne onward of itself. The feelings of dread, despair, misery, etc. which formerly arose cease. Bodily pains are absent entirely. Both dread and delight in mental objects have been thoroughly abandoned. Exceedingly sublime clarity of mind and pervasive equanimity toward all mental formations emerge. The meditator need make no further deliberate effort; noticing continues in a steady flow for hours without interruption or tiredness. Contemplation proceeds by its own momentum, and insight becomes especially quick and active.

both dread and delight in mental objects thoroughly abandoned

Insight is now on the verge of its culmination; noticing is keen, strong, and lucid. All mental formations are instantly known to be impermanent, painful, or without self just by seeing their dissolution. All formations are seen either as

*cessation of
physical and
mental phe-
nomena and
the "signless,
no-occurrence,
no-formation":
nirvana*

limited and circumscribed or as devoid of desirability, or
as alien. Detachment from them is at a peak. Noticing no
longer enters into or settles down on any formations at all.
Then consciousness arises that takes as its object the "signless, no-occurrence, no-formation": nirvana. Physical and
mental phenomena cease entirely. This moment of realization
of nirvana does not, in its first attainment, last even for a
second. Immediately following, mind reflects on the experience of nirvana just past.

NIRVANA

The experience of nirvana is a cognitive shock of deepest
psychological consequence. Its nature is of a realm beyond
that of the consensual phenomenal reality from which our
language is generated, and so nirvana, the unconditioned
state, is describable only in terms of what it is not. It is the
"Unborn, Unoriginated, Uncreated, Unformed." The word
itself is derived from the negative prefix "nir" and the root
"vana," to burn, a metaphorical expression for the extinction
of all forms of becoming: desire, attachment, and ego.
Decisive behavior change follows from this change in consciousness. With the realization of nirvana, aspects of ego,
or normal consciousness, are abandoned, never to arise
again. The path of insight differs significantly from the path
of samadhi on this point: nirvana destroys "defiling" aspects

of ego—hatred, greed, delusion, etc.—whereas jhana suppresses them. Nirvana makes sila effortless; in fact, sila
becomes the only possible behavior. Jhana supplants defilements, but their seeds remain latent in personality as potentialities; on emergence from the jhanic state these acts again
become possible as appropriate situations arise.

There are four levels of realization of nirvana, contingent
upon the depth of insight attained in approaching it. Persons
who have achieved nirvana are distinguished according to
their level of attainment. The number of times one enters
the nirvanic state determines his degree of mastery—i.e.,
the ability to attain nirvana whenever, wherever, as soon as,
and for as long as he wants—but is not related to the level
of attainment. One can enter nirvana with a given level of
insight countless times without any change of level. The
deeper the development of insight prior to entering nirvana,

the higher the level of attainment, and the more pervasive
the consequent personality changes. The experience of nirvana itself is identical at each level of attainment; the differ-

ence between levels is reckoned in terms of the consequent permanent loss of ego on emergence from nirvana. Entering the nirvanic state is one's "awakening"; subsequent ego loss is one's "deliverance" from bondage to personality. D. T. Suzuki (1957, p. 55) says of the Buddha's prototypic experiences of enlightenment:

> The enlightenment feeling affects the whole personality, his attitude toward life and the world. . . .Buddha's experience was not just a matter of feeling which moves on the periphery of consciousness, but something awakened in the deepest recesses of a human being.

The first level is that of *Sotapanna,* "Stream Enterer." One becomes a Stream Enterer at the first moment of the first experience of nirvana, and remains so until insight deepens to the degree necessary to mark the next level of attainment. The "stream" entered is that leading to the total loss of ego, the cessation of all becoming. This final liberation, it is said, is sure to occur "within seven more lifetimes." At this first level the following strata of personality traits and attitudes drop away: greed for sense desires and resentments strong enough to produce anxiety; greed for one's own gain, possessions, or praise strong enough to cause inability to share with others; failure to perceive the relative and illusive nature of what seems pleasurable or beautiful; the misapprehension of permanence in what is impermanent (*anicca*); and of self in what is devoid of self (*anatta*); adherence to mere rites and rituals, and the belief that this or that is "the Truth"; doubt or uncertainty in the utility of the path of vipassana; lying, stealing, sexual misconduct, physically harming others, or earning a livelihood at the expense of others.

personality traits and attitudes dropped at first level of "Stream Enterer."

When insight deepens so that the realizations of dukkha (suffering), anatta, or anicca more fully pervade one's being, there comes a quantum-level intensification of insight: nirvana is now attained at a level where both greed for sense desires and ill-will become attenuated. One is now a *sakadgami,* "Once-Returner," who will be fully liberated in this lifetime or the next. Added to the elements of ego abandoned with Stream Entry are gross feelings of desire for sense objects, and strong resentment. The intensity of experiences of attraction and aversion undergoes a diminution: one can no longer be strongly impelled toward or put off by any phenomena; sex, for example, loses its appeal, though it might still be engaged in for procreation. An impartial attitude toward any and all stimuli is typical.

elements of ego abandoned at level of "Once-Returner"

At the next quantum-level intensification of insight, both greed for sense desires and ill-will are abandoned without remainder. What was diminished on attaining to Once Returner is now wholly extinguished. One's status becomes *anagami,* "Non-Returner" and one is bound to become totally liberated from the wheel of becoming in the present lifetime. In addition to previously abandoned ego elements, the last remaining residual propensities for greed or resentment drop away. All aversion to worldly states such as loss, disgrace, pain, or blame ceases. Malicious motivation, volition, or speech becomes impossible—one can no longer even have a thought of ill-will toward anyone; the category of "enemy" vanishes from thinking, along with that of "dislike." Similarly, even the subtlest desire for sense objects disappears. Sexual activity, for example, is now extremely unlikely, because feelings of craving or lust are extinguished. Equanimity prevails toward all external objects; their valence to the Non-Returner is absolutely neutral.

*level of
"Fully-Realized
Being"*

The final and full maturity of insight results in overcoming all fetters of ego, and the dissolution of any subjective meaning in the consensual conceptual universe. One is now an *arahant,* a "Fully-Realized Being" or saint. He is absolutely free from suffering and from the generation of any new karma. Having no feelings of "self," any acts will be purely functional, either for maintenance of the body or for the good of others. There remains not a single unabandoned internal state from one's past owing to which thoughts of greed, hatred, etc. could come to mind. All past deeds are erased, as is all future becoming; only pure being remains. The last vestiges of ego relinquished in this final

*last vestiges
of ego
relinquished in
final stage*

stage include: all feelings of approval for or desire to seek the worldly states of gain, fame, pleasure, or praise; any desire for even the bliss of the material or formless jhanas; mental stiffness or agitation, covetousness of anything whatsoever. The least inherent tendency toward an unvirtuous thought or deed is literally inconceivable.

From the level of arahant the validity of the noble truths of impermanence, suffering, and non-selfhood is evident at every moment. Wei Wu Wei (1968, p. 61) says of the meaning of suffering from this level of consciousness:

"Awake"

When the Buddha found that he was Awake . . . it may be assumed that he observed that what hitherto he had regarded as happiness, as compared to suffering, was such no longer. His only standard henceforward was *ananda* or what we try to think of as bliss. Suffering he saw as the negative form of happiness, happiness as the positive form of suffering, respectively the negative and positive aspects of experience. But relative to the noumenal state which now alone he knew, both could be described . . . as *dukkha* (suffering). *Dukkha* was the counterpart of *sukha* which implied "ease and well-being," . . . to the Buddha nothing phenomenal could appear to be *sukha* although in phenomenality it might so *appear* in contrast to *dukkha*.

Understanding the truth of non-self for an arahant is more straightforward. Suzuki (1958, p. 293) puts it simply: when one attains that level he finds "by immediate knowledge that when one's heart was cleansed of the defilements of the ordinary ego-centered impulses and desires, nothing was left there to claim itself as ego-residuum." Impermanence is perceived at the primary stage of cognition. For an arahant, perception in vipassana is perfected: he is a witness of the most minute segments of the mind's working, the chain of mind-moments. According to this tradition, the Buddha witnessed 17×10^{21} mind-moments in "the wink of an eye," each one distinct and different from the one preceding and the one following it. Like him, the arahant sees that elementary constituents of the flow of consciousness are changing at every moment. Nothing in the universe of one's mind is constant, and one's external reality follows from one's internal universe. Nowhere, then, is there any stability or permanence.

the truth of non-self

NIRODH

There is a state apart from nirvana, little known in the West, called *nirodh*, cessation. In nirvana, awareness has as its object the cessation of consciousness: in nirodh, awareness ceases altogether. It is the absolute cessation of consciousness and its concomitants. Nirodh is accessible only to a Non-Returner or an arahant who has also mastered all eight jhanas. Neither a Stream Enterer nor a Once-Returner has relinquished enough strata of ego to muster the superconcentration required for nirodh—in the access process to this state of total non-occurrence even the slightest residuum of sense desire will be an obstruction.

the state of "nirodh"

The path to nirodh entails the practice of vipassana using as a base each jhana in succession up to the eighth, neither-perception-nor-nonperception. With the cessation of this last state of ultrasubtle consciousness, one enters nirodh. Cessation is "differently real," all the data of our experience of reality, even the most sublime states, being absent. Although nirodh can last for up to seven days of the human time-rhythm, there is no time sequence in the state itself: the moment immediately preceding it and that immediately following it are experienced as of immediate succession. The limit of seven days given for the duration of nirodh may be due to its unique physiology: heart-beat and normal metabolism, it is said, cease along with consciousness, though metabolic processes continue at a residual level so that the meditator's body can be distinguished from a corpse. Prior to entering this state the meditator must set a pre-determined length of time for staying in it. On emergence, he will go through the jhanas in reverse order to normal consciousness. At the eighth jhana, awareness resumes; at the third, normal bodily function; at the first, discursive thought and sense perception.

THE TWO PATHS: THEIR HIGHEST EXTREMES

At their highest extremes, the path of samadhi through the jhanas and the path of insight to nirvana tend to meet. But between these ultimate states of rarefied consciousness there remain extremely subtle but crucial differences. The seventh jhana is a state of awareness of consciousness that has no object: no-thing-ness. In the eighth jhana the consciousness of no-thing-ness cannot even be said to be operative, but yet remains as a latent function, and so cannot be said not to exist: this is the realm of neither-perception-nor-non-perception. At nirvana the final extinguishing of consciousness begins, with a state that is the awareness of no consciousness at all. This process of extinguishing culminates in nirodh, where there is no awareness whatsoever. The attainment of even the highest jhanas does not on emergence necessarily affect normal ego function, while the experience of nirvana irrevocably alters ego function.

jhana, nirvana and ego function

two paths

These different paths mark two extremes on a continuum of exploration and control of mind. One who could marshall enough one-pointedness to attain, say, the formless jhanas might easily attain the nirvanic state should he choose to turn his powerful concentration ability to watching his own mind. And, conversely, one who had entered the nirvanic state might well possess a mind so indifferent to hindrances and distractions that should he choose to focus on a single object of awareness, he would readily enter and proceed through the jhanic levels. Thus those beings who have traversed these distinctly different paths to their highest extremes may no longer belong solely to one, but rather to both. With full mastery of either samadhi or insight, the other is readily attainable, the distinction between meditation avenues melts. As the *Zenrin* puts it:

From of old there were not two paths   *one way*
"Those who have arrived" all walked the same road.

THE BUDDHA'S MAP: IMPLICATIONS FOR RESEARCH

In an earlier article (1971) I proposed a comparative study of meditation techniques to see whether differences in technique are psychophysiologically consequential. This elaboration of the Buddha's ancient system can be a step toward that investigation, by serving as the framework for a grid and gradient in psychophysiological studies of those techniques. Dalal & Barber (1969), in reviewing studies of yogis, concluded that "yogic samadhi" is an hypothesized ASC as yet inadequately denoted and without objectively verifiable criteria; the Buddha's map of MSC can be seen as a model for research meeting Barber's methodological requirements. The *Visuddhimagga* is unique in the orderly fashion in which it delineates MSC along both psychological and physiological parameters (see Table 1); the distinct levels of MSC shown can be conceptualized as the ledges of a psychophysiological step-function (see Ashby 1970). Though this psychophysiological cartography of MSC is by no means complete, it gives enough key landmarks in these realms of mind to serve as a skeleton on which might hang amplifications. *value of psycho-physiological cartography for research*

The initial stage in either path is access concentration. The major psychological indicators of the access level are an initial stilling of the mind, qualitatively distinct from normal consciousness though thoughts and sensory perceptions remain; visions and bright lights; feelings of rapture, happiness, and bodily lightness. It may be that the bulk of EEG studies of meditation have been of subjects at this level, and that the state most often produced by alpha-wave feedback devices with normal subjects resembles access concentration: Kamiya (1969) describes the "alpha state" as "a general calming down of the mind." My own experience as a subject in an alpha-feedback experiment at Harvard Medical School was that when I was emitting a more or less sustained train of alpha my consciousness was at a level of "access to access concentration." That is, my mind was not so stilled as to be at the level of access concentration, but it was qualitatively more calm compared to its normal state; there were feelings of bliss, quiet rapture, and contentment *access concentration as the initial stage in both paths*

access and alpha-feedback

TABLE 1
PSYCHOPHYSIOLOGICAL LANDMARKS OF HSC

PATH OF JHANA Subjective Landmarks	Objective Measures	PATH OF INSIGHT Subjective Landmarks
	Shut-down of metabolic function; "near-death" metabolism	*Nirvana:* cessation of awareness as primary object; no awareness of physical/mental phenomena.
Jhana 8. Neither-perception-nor-nonperception		*Nirodh:* total cessation of experience; neither knower nor object.
Jhana 7 Awareness of No-thing-ness	Metabolism bare minimum	*Effortless insight.* Instantaneous awareness of mind-moments; fatigueless energy; equanimity; cessation of pain.
Jhana 6. Awareness of Infinite Consciousness		*Desire to escape physical/mental phenomena.* Realization of dreadfulness of mind-moments; physical pain.
Jhana 5. Awareness of Infinite Space		*Pseudo-nirvana rejected.* Clear perception of *end* of mind-moments; lights, rapture, etc. vanish.
Jhana 4. Equanimity and one-pointedness; cessation of feelings of pleasure, bliss.	*Jhana 4:* Cessation of breath Concentration impervious to any and all distractions	*Pseudo-nirvana.* Clear perception of arising and passing of mind-moments; accompanied by: bright light(s) rapture, happiness,
Jhana 3. Feelings of bliss, one-pointedness, and equanimity; rapture ceases.		

TABLE 1 (con't)

Jhana 2. Feelings of bliss, one-pointedness, and rapture; no thoughts of primary object.			tranquility, devotion energy, strong mindfulness equanimity toward mind-objects attachment to these states.
Jhana 1. Continuous, sustained concentration on primary object; accompanied by feelings of rapture and bliss, one-pointedness; thoughts hindering concentration, sensory perception, and awareness of pain all cease.	Decreasing metabolic indicators: heart rate, cardiac output, respiration rate, etc. *Jhana 1:* No response to external inputs; habituation.		*Reflections.* Awareness and its objects seen as distinct processes; experience of impermanence, unsatisfactoriness, and impersonality of mental functions.
Access concentration. Primary object dominant thought interspersed with other thoughts, hindrances to concentration tentatively overcome; awareness of sensory inputs and body states remains; feelings of rapture, happiness; flashes of lights and visions; sensation of body lightness.	Mindfulness: non-habituation to external stimulus. Alpha, theta states		*Mindfulness.* All sensory stimulus and thoughts (mind-moments) register in awareness. *Access concentration.*

while thoughts floated by. Had I entered full access, the alpha perhaps would have gotten stronger. In a study of the subjective states associated with alpha activity, Brown (1970) found greatest enhanced alpha to be related to narrowing of perceptual awareness and pleasant feeling states—two fundamental components of access concentration. Both yogis practicing samadhi and zazen meditators produce alpha and sometimes theta (Anand et al. 1961, Kasamatsu & Hirai 1969), but in no study thus far has there been a scale used for judging the level of absorption the subject had attained.

discussion of psychophysio-logical measures

When appropriate studies are done, alpha giving way to theta may be found associated with jhanas above the level of access as well as with skilled practice of insight techniques like zazen, where mastery of concentration at the access level seems to be an adjunct. Theta may be associated both with the higher jhanas and the later stages of insight; delta may accompany the higher jhanas and nirvana, and nirodh may even be marked by a subdelta EEG. One might anticipate a discrepant pattern of measures like brain-wave changes comparing concentration and insight techniques, the former becoming slower through the jhanas, the latter leveling off at access level with a quantum leap at nirvana. Within the jhanas and the stages to nirvana, there may be unique and distinct shifts in patterns of psychophysiological measures at any given stage—e.g., excitation due to rapture at the access level may produce an increase in heart rate while EEG shows alpha or even theta waves. But generally speaking, metabolic indicators such as oxygen consumption, cardiac output, heart rate, and respiration rate should decrease as mind becomes progressively stiller, as is suggested by Elmer Green's (Green, Green & Walters 1970) "psychophysiological principle":

> Every change in the physiological state is accompanied by an appropriate change in the mental–emotional state, and conversely, every change in the mental–emotional state, conscious or unconscious, is accompanied by an appropriate change in the physiological state.

On attaining the first jhana, the meditator should experience cessation of all discursive thoughts other than that of the primary object; loss of awareness of all sensory stimuli; intense rapture, bliss, and fixity of mind in the state itself. Behaviorally this internal state should be verifiable to investigators in the meditator's failure to react in any way to external sensory inputs. Orme-Johnson found that TM meditators habituated more quickly than nonmeditating controls. Tests of habituation in Indian yogis practicing samadhi have shown that they fail to respond to external sounds at all (Anand et al. 1961)—an indication that the subjects were at least at the first level of jhana.

The successive transitions upward from first jhana until the fourth are difficult to discriminate. Subjectively the change undergone in transition from first to second is primarily the disappearance from awareness of the primary object or any discursive thinking whatever. From second to third the feelings of rapture fall away, replaced by an attitude of equanimity. On ascending to the fourth jhana all feelings of bliss cease, leaving only equanimity and one-pointedness; breath is said to cease, and the meditator is utterly impervious to any distraction. Just as the mind becomes more still at each higher jhana, so with respiration, until at the fourth jhana breath is said to cease altogether. Whether or not breath actually ceases remains an empirical question; it may be found that breath in the higher jhanas actually becomes very shallow and slows, say, to a rate of one every minute, and so might *seem* to cease. One of the few studies to date of yogis practicing samadhi meditation found an extreme slowing of respiration rate to 4 to 6 per minute in some subjects (Bagchi et al. 1971). The jhanas with their accompanying progressive respiratory quiescence constitute what Wallace (1970, 1971) calls the "fourth state of consciousness," and describes as "a wakeful hypometabolic physiologic state." On the basis of physiological studies of practitioners of "transcendental meditation"—a concentration technique—he postulates a shift in the cellular metabolization of oxygen which would allow breathing to become still, perhaps ultimately to the point of cessation. The formless jhanas—i.e., fifth through eighth—differ from the fourth not in factors of consciousness but in the degree of refinement of those factors as well as in primary object. At the eighth jhana mind function is stilled to its most subtle extreme. The same can be expected from metabolism.

The path of insight is distinguishable at inception from concentration techniques: at its initial stages the insight meditator is mindful of each successive thought or sensation and so does *not* habituate (see, e.g., the study of zazen—an insight technique—by Kasamatzu & Hirai 1969). The next major landmark is the stage of "Knowledge of Arising and Passing Away" of mind-moments, the pseudonirvana. The insight meditator will experience at this point any or all of these signs: visions of brilliant lights, feelings of rapture,

psychophysiological measures and the jhanas

tranquility, devotion, energy, and happiness; quick, clear perception, strong mindfulness and equanimity in the practice itself; and attachment to this state. There are no necessary physiological concomitants of this stage, though some may be discovered such as alpha or a quickened heartbeat. Nor are there any in the following phases of realization, where the dissolution of each mind moment is clearly perceived, and the indicators of the previous stage fade. But accompanying the ensuing series of realizations about the wearisome and dreadful nature of these phenomena and the arising of the desire to escape them, sharp pains frequently rack the meditator's body. These pains cease only at the next phase, where equanimity prevails. At this point contemplation is effortless, and the meditator can continue for hours or days without fatigue.

*psychophysio-
logical measures
and the path
of insight*

Not until the end of the path of insight is it likely to be most fruitful for psychophysiologic studies. On entering the nirvanic state awareness takes as its object nonawareness. This blackout of consciousness entails all the metabolic shutdowns of the eighth jhana, perhaps to an even more marked degree. On ascension to nirodh, awareness ceases totally, as does metabolic functioning.[7] Heartbeat is said to stop as well as all organic systems; according to the *Visuddhimagga,* the only distinctions between a corpse and the body of one in nirodh is that the latter remains warm and does not decompose. As with the breath rate, the actual degree of slowing of heart rate awaits empirical verification.[8] The "seven days" traditionally set for the duration of this state suggest a metabolically determined limit in nirodh for bodily maintenance. Similarly phenomena of a "survived death" under rare circumstances have been reported in patients clinically dead on the operating table, and in some persons struck by lightning, who have revived and recovered fully (Taussig 1969).

In almost every school and tradition the specifics of these higher states are not regarded as suitable subjects for teaching. As realities they transcend words; being inexpressible,

[7] The ascension through insight into nirvana can be seen as the psychophysiological analog of Heisenberg's Uncertainty Principle, that consciousness mediates and affects the object it observes. Nirodh is the penultimate case: when consciousness observes itself, the process culminates in the cessation of consciousness.

[8] Investigations of "heart stoppage" thus far have studied hatha yogis using effortful breath and muscle manipulation, not meditators (e.g., Wenger et al. 1961). One patient in California reportedly slowed his heart to a standstill for approximately 5 seconds—his method was merely relaxing (McClure 1959). When Swami Rama demonstrated a 17-second fibrillation of his heart for Elmer Green (Green, Green & Walters 1971) through a "solar plexus lock," the Swami commented that he knew another way to stop his heart which involved a "hibernation-like" state, though he wasn't prepared to demonstrate it at the time.

Psychology of Meditation

they are to be experienced rather than discussed: thinking mind hinders realization. Detailed maps of the psychophysiology of these states can take their major landmarks from traditional sources like the *Visuddhimagga,* but data on the intricacies of mind-body topography in MSC and HSC will have to come from thoroughgoing research.[9]

the problem of suitable subjects for studies

There is a paradox in seeking suitable subjects for the studies that might develop in this area; those nations with the required affluence and technological sophistication generally lack the traditions and schools that produce people developed enough in meditation to be worthwhile testing. One exception is Japan, where the Zen Institutes have pioneered in psychophysiological studies of zazen (see, e.g., Akishige 1970). But the largest untapped pool of potential subjects extends from the Middle East eastward throughout Asia outside the Communist nations, among Sufis or Muslim fakirs, the yogis of India, Tibetan lamas, and Buddhist monks. A further complication is that those who have developed greatest familiarity with MSC are the least likely to speak of their own attainments, except with deprecation. If they are to be tested in psychophysiological labs, they must be approached with the utmost discretion. In the West, for the most fruitful studies of MSC it is not the students of the numerous rapidly proliferating techniques who should be tested, but rather their masters.

MAPS OF CONSCIOUSNESS IN PERSPECTIVE

This exposition, based on Buddha's map of MSC, may be an aid to those who seek to formulate theories or conceptualize and design research in this area. This was my intent.

[9]The jhanas from first to eighth have been characterized as a fourth major state of consciousness (Wallace 1971), and the effects in waking consciousness of meditation I have called a fifth state (1971). Both nirvana and nirodh are by description discontinuous with both the fourth and fifth states, and may well come to be seen with their psychophysiological concomitants as constituting a sixth major state—that of the near-total, or total, absence of any consciousness whatever, accompanied by a "near-death" metabolism. On the other hand, research may show there to be no distinction between these states and the higher jhanas. It may be that the path of insight and the path of jhana are on the same continuum, the Buddha having articulated a variant of the access-level approach to MSC. Fischer (1971) posits what he calls "zazen"—i.e., access concentration in insight practice—as a prior level to samadhi (i.e., jhana), and suggests that as one enters a hypoactive, meditative state, "the separateness of object and subject gradually disappear and their interaction becomes the principal content of the experience." It is precisely this subject-object *interaction* that the stages of insight articulate in such detail. If it is indeed the case that the path of insight is an artifact of a hyperdescription of the journey from normal awareness to MSC, and of a consequent misidentification of insight as an angle of entry to MSC distinct from that of concentration, then jhana and nirvana/nirodh will be two appellations for an identical state, and the path of insight simply a clarification of the dynamics of access.

Those who through personal practice are themselves exploring these states may or may not find these thoughts or this map helpful. The work of *sadhana* is often amorphous, its delimitation fluid, and the stages of progress as intricate as one's life experience. There is as much variety in paths to higher states of being as there are persons on the path; any one map does not necessarily apply to a given person's situation. There is a Sufi saying, "He who tastes knows." In the words of Meher Baba (1967, p. 191):

> In the spiritual life it is not necessary to have a complete map of the Path in order to begin traveling. On the contrary, insistence upon having such complete knowledge may actually hinder rather than help the onward march. . . . He who speculates from the shore about the ocean shall know only its surface, but he who would know the depths of the ocean must be willing to plunge into it.

Editor's Note: The systems to which the template is applied in Part II will include those of: Hindu Bhakti, Sufism, The Christian Prayer of the Heart, Meher Baba, Sri Aurobindo, Pantanjali's Ashtanga Yoga, Ramana Maharshi, Maharishi Mahesh Yogi, Swami Muktananda, Kirpal Singh, Tantra Yoga, Tibetan Vajrayana, Zen, Gurdjieff, and J. Krishnamurti.

GLOSSARY[10]

Abhidhamma—lit., "the nature of now," a lengthy treatise on consciousness attributed to Gotama Buddha and included among the oldest of Buddhist scriptures in the Pali language.

anagami—lit., "non-returner," the third of four levels at which nirvana can be realized.

ananda—subtle and exquisite feelings of bliss.

anatta—lit., "not-self," the Buddhist doctrine that all phenomena, including "one's self," are devoid of any indwelling personality; the realization that there is no abiding entity within one's mind or being.

anicca—lit., "impermanence," the Buddhist doctrine that all phenomena are transitory; the realization that one's world of reality is continually arising and disappearing every mind-moment.

[10]The meanings given are for the terms as used in the context of this paper and are not to be considered definitive.

arahant—lit., "saint," the final of four stages of realizing nirvana, at which the last vestige of selfish motivation has disappeared; the end of the path in the Visuddhimagga system of psychospiritual development.

asubhas—decaying corpses used as objects for meditation in their natural state in burial or burning grounds, classified according to their state of decomposition and including a skeleton.

Dharma language—the esoteric, spiritually oriented, or symbolic sense of ordinary words and their meanings.

dukkha—lit., "suffering," the Buddhist doctrine that the world of consensual reality is the source of all woe; the realization of the unsatisfactory nature of all mental phenomena.

bardos—intermediate states between life and death; realms of reality representing mind states.

HSC—Higher states of consciousness; a state where functions of "lower" states are available in addition to new functions of other, altered states of consciousness.

jhana—a degree of absorption on a continuum beginning with a full break with normal consciousness marked by one-pointed concentration on a meditation object to the exclusion of all other thoughts or awareness of external sensory inputs, and ending in a state of ultrasubtle residual perception.

kasina—a visual meditation object, usually a foot or so in diameter, circular or square, consisting of a single color or light, which may be concrete or imagined.

loca—a realm of reality existing in mental or supramental dimensions, spoken of as a "world" as real as our own, and typifying a distinct mental state.

MSC—meditation-specific states of consciousness; a state attained through meditation which transcends normal sensory awareness and cognition.

Nikaya—lit., "collection," a compilation of Southern Buddhist sutras.

nirodh—the state of total cessation of awareness attained through meditation.

nirvana—the state in meditation of awareness of no consciousness at all, the experience of which diminishes the ego as a subsequent effect; the unconditioned state.

Pali—the North Indian dialect spoken by Gotama Buddha in preference to Sanskrit, and the sacred language of scriptures in Southern Buddhism (as Latin is used in Catholicism).

prajna—lit., "insight," also, "wisdom," the ability to perceive phenomena simply as they exist rather than in terms of a meaning derived from a learned personal, group, or cultural belief system or other consensual notion of reality.

sadhana—any system of spiritual practice; a path for psychospiritual evolution.

sakadgami—lit., "once-returner," the second of four levels of realizing nirvana.

sangha (Pali) or *satsang* (Sanskrit)—technically, those who have attained the nirvanic state, and generally speaking, the community of seekers on a spiritual path.

samadhi—the technique of one-pointed concentration in meditation; also, in Sanskrit sources, a psychophysiological state of absorption in a single object of concentration to the exclusion of all awareness of any other sensory inputs or thoughts (see *jhana*).

satipatthana—lit., "mindfulness," a technique of constant bare attention to all sensory perceptions or thoughts, so that the mind is not stimulated by them into thought chains, but witnesses them all without reaction; when mastered, satipatthana develops into vipassana.

sila—lit., "virtue," the practice of moral precepts for the purpose of clearing the mind of preoccupations which would distract one from spiritual practice, especially concentration in meditation.

sotapanna—lit., "stream-enterer," the first of four levels of attainment of nirvana.

sukha—a state of intense pleasure and well-being.

sutra—a literary form used for most Hindu and Buddhist sacred scriptures.

varagya—the falling away of desires as a side-effect of spiritual growth.

vipassana—lit., "seeing things as they are," a meditation technique where attention is turned to constant scrutiny of each successive unit in the thought-continuum.

Visuddhimagga—a summary of the Abhidhamma sections on meditation and consciousness, done in the fifth century A.D. by Bhuddaghosa.

REFERENCES

AKISHIGE, Y. (ED.). *Psychological studies on Zen*. Tokyo: Zen Institute of Komazawa Univ., 1970.

AMMA. *Dhyan-yoga and kundalini yoga*. Ganeshpuri, India: Shree Gurudev Ashram, 1969.

ANAND, B., CHHINA, G., SINGH, B. Some aspects of EEG studies in Yogis, EEG *Clin. Neurophysiol.*, 1961, *13*, 452–56. Also in C. Tart (Ed.), *Altered states of consciousness*. New York: Wiley, 1969.

ANDERSON, M. *The unknowable Gurdjieff*. London: Routledge & Kegan Paul, 1962.

ASHBY, W. R. *Design for a brain*. London: Science Paperbacks, 1970.

AUROBINDO, SRI. *The life divine*. New York: Sri Aurobindo Library, 1949.

AUROBINDO, SRI. *The synthesis of yoga*. Pondicherry, India: Sri Aurobindo Ashram Press, 1955.

AUROBINDO, SRI. *On yoga II, tome two*. Pondicherry, India: Sri Aurobindo Ashram Press, 1958.

BABA RAM DASS. *Be here now*. New York: Crown, 1971.

BAGCHI, B. K., WENGER, M. A. Electro-physiological correlates of some Yogi exercises. Reprinted in T. X. Barber et al. (Eds.), *Biofeedback and Self-Control*. Chicago: Aldine-Atherton, 1971.

BHIKKU SOMA. *The way of mindfulness*. Colombo, Ceylon: Vajirama, 1949.

BLAKNEY, R. B. *Meister Eckhart*. New York: Harper & Row, 1941.

BLOFELD, J. *The Zen teaching of Hui Hai*. London: Rider, 1962.

BROWN, B. B. Recognition of aspects of consciousness through association with EEG alpha activity represented by a light signal. *Psychophysiology*, 1970, *6*, 442-52.

BUCKE, R. M. *Cosmic consciousness*. New Hyde Park, NY: University Books, 1961.

BUDDHADASA, BHIKKU (Ariyananda Bhikku, Transl.). *Two kinds of language*. Bangkok, Thailand: Sublime Life Mission, 1968.

CASTAÑEDA, C. *A separate reality*. New York: Simon & Schuster, 1971.

CHADWICK, A. W. *A sadhu's reminiscences of Ramana Maharshi*. Tiruvannamali, India: Sri Ramanasram, 1966.

CHANG, G. C. C. *Teachings of Tibetan yoga*. New York: New York Univ. Press, 1963.

CHANG, G. C. C. *The hundred thousand songs of Milarepa*. New York: Harper Colophon Books, 1970.

CHOGYAM TRUNGPA. *Meditation in action*. London: Stuart & Watkins, 1969.

CHOGYAM TRUNGPA. *Garuda*, 1971, *I*:1.

COLEMAN, J. E. *The quiet mind*. London: Rider & Co., 1971.

CONZE, E. *Buddhist meditation*. London: Allen & Unwin, 1956.

DALAI LAMA, THE FOURTEENTH. *An introduction to Buddhism*. New Delhi: Tibet House, 1965.

DALAI LAMA, THE FOURTEENTH. *Short essays on Buddhist thought and practice*. New Delhi: Tibet House, n.d.

DALAL, A. S., BARBER, T. X. Yoga, "yogic feats," and hypnosis in the light of empirical research. *Amer. J. Clin. Hypnosis*, 1969, *11*, 155-66.

DHAMMARATANA. *Guide through Visuddhimagga*. Varanasi, India: Mahabodhi Society, 1964.

DONKIN, W. *The wayfarers*. New York: Dodd, Mead, & Co., 1954.

DOUGLAS, N. *Tantra yoga*. New Delhi: Munshiram Manoharlal, 1971.

ELIADE, M. *Yoga: immortality and freedom*. Princeton, N.J.: Princeton Univ. Press, 1970.

EVANS-WENTZ, W. Y. *Tibetan yoga and secret doctrines*. London: Oxford Univ. Press, 1968.

EVANS-WENTZ, W. Y. *The Tibetan book of the great liberation*. London: Oxford Univ. Press, 1969.

FISHER, R. A cartography of the ecstatic and meditative states. *Science*, 1971, *4012*, 897-904.

GOLEMAN, D. Meditation as meta-therapy: hypotheses toward a proposed fifth state of consciousness. *J. Transpersonal Psychol.*, 1971, *3*(1), 1-25.

GOVINDA, LAMA ANAGARIKA. *The psychological attitude of early Buddhist philosophy*. London: Rider, 1969.

GOVINDA, LAMA ANAGARIKA. *Foundations of Tibetan mysticism*. London: Rider, 1970.

GREEN, E. E., GREEN, A. M., WALTERS, E. D. Voluntary control of internal states: psychological and physiological. *J. Transpersonal Psychol.*, 1970, 2(1), 1-26.

GREEN, E. E., GREEN, A. M., WALTERS, E. D. Biofeedback for mind-body self-regulation: healing and creativity. Paper delivered at symposium on "The Varieties of Healing Experience," Cupertino, California, October, 1971.

GUENTHER, H. V. *The life and teaching of Naropa*. London: Oxford Univ. Press, 1963.

GURDJIEFF, G. I. *Meetings with remarkable men*. New York: Dutton, 1969.

GURDJIEFF, G. I. *The herald of coming good*. New York: Samuel Weiser, 1971.

KABIR (R. Tagore, Transl.). *Poems of Kabir*. Calcutta: Macmillan, 1970.

KADLOUBOUSKY, E., PALMER, G. E. H. *Writings from the philokalia on prayer of the heart*. London: Faber & Faber, 1971.

KAMIYA, J. Operant control of the EEG alpha rhythm and some of its reported effects on consciousness. In C. T. Tart (Ed.), *Altered states of consciousness*. New York: Wiley, 1969, 507-17.

KAPLEAU, P. *The three pillars of Zen*. Boston: Beacon Press, 1967.

KASAMATSU, A., HIRAI, T. An EEG study of Zen meditation, *Folia Psychiat. Neurol. Jap.*, 1966, *20*, 315-36. Also in C. Tart (Ed.), *Altered states of consciousness*. New York: Wiley, 1969.

KASHYAP, J. *The Abhidhamma philosophy*, Vol. I. Nalanda, India: Buddha Vihara, 1954.

KRISHNA PREM. *Yoga of the Katopanishad*. Allahabad, India: Ananda Publ. House, 1958.

KRISHNAMURTI, J. (D. Rajagopal, Ed.). *Commentaries on living: Third series*. London: Victor Gollancz Ltd., 1962.

LAO TZU (D. C. Lau, Transl.). *Tao te ching*. Baltimore: Penguin Books, 1968.

LEDI SAYADAW. *The manuals of Buddhism*. Rangoon, Burma: Union Buddha Sasana Council, 1965.

LUK, C. *Ch'an and Zen teaching, third series*. London: Rider, 1962.

LUK, C. *Secrets of Chinese meditation*. London: Rider, 1966.

LUK, C. *Practical Buddhism*. London: Rider, 1971.

M. *Gospel of Sri Ramakrishna*. Mylapore, India: Sri Ramakrishna Math, 1928.

MAHADEVAN, T. M. P. (Transl.). *Self-inquiry of Bhagavan Sri Ramana Maharshi*. Tiruvannamalai, India, 1965.

MAHARISHI MAHESH YOGI. *On the Bhagavad Gita*. Baltimore: Penguin Books, 1971.

MAHASI SAYADAW (Nyanaponika Thera, Transl.). *The process of insight*. Kandy, Ceylon: The Forest Hermitage, 1965.

MAHASI SAYADAW. *Buddhist meditation and its forty subjects.* Buddha-gaya, India: International Meditation Center, 1970.

MAHATHERA, P. V. *Buddhist meditation in theory and practice.* Colombo, Ceylon: Gunasena, 1962.

MANZANI, R. P. *The conference of the birds: a Sufi allegory.* London: Oxford Univ. Press, 1924.

MASLOW, A. Theory Z. *J. Transpersonal Psychol.,* 1970, *2*(1), 31-47.

MASLOW, A. New introduction: Religions, values, and peak experiences (New Edition), *J. Transpersonal Psychol.* 1970, *2*(2), 83-90.

McCLURE, C. Cardiac arrest through volition. *California Med.,* 1959, *90,* 440-41.

MEHER, BABA. *Discourses I, II, III.* San Francisco: Sufism Reoriented, 1967.

MERTON, T. *The wisdom of the desert.* New York: New Directions, 1960.

MERTON, T. *Mystics and Zen masters.* New York: Farrar, Straus & Giroux, 1967.

MERTON, T. *The way of Chuang Tzu.* London: Unwin, 1965.

MIURA, I., SASAKI, R. F. *The Zen koan.* New York: Harcourt, Brace & World, 1965.

MUDALIAR, A. D. *Day by day with Bhagavan.* Tiruvannamalai, India: Sri Ramanasram, 1968.

MUKTANANDA PARAMAHANSA, SWAMI. *Soham-japa.* New Delhi: Siddha Yoga Dham, 1969.

MUKTANANDA PARAMAHANSA, SWAMI. *Gurukripa.* Ganeshpuri, India: Shree Gurudev Ashram, 1970.

MUKTANANDA PARAMAHANSA, SWAMI. *Guruvani Magazine.* Ganeshpuri, India: Shree Gurudev Ashram, 1971.

MUKTANANDA PARAMAHANSA, SWAMI. *Guru.* New York: Harper & Row, 1972.

NARADA THERA. *A manual of abhidhamma, I & II.* Colombo, Ceylon: Vajirarama, 1956.

NIKHILANANDA, SWAMI. *Drg-drysa-viveka: an inquiry into the nature of the 'seer' and the 'seen.'* Mysore, India: Sri Ramakrishna Ashram, 1964.

NYANAPONIKA THERA. *Abhidhamma studies.* Colombo, Ceylon: Frewin, 1949.

NYANAPONIKA THERA. *The heart of Buddhist meditation.* London: Rider, 1962.

NYANAPONIKA THERA. *The power of mindfulness.* Kandy, Ceylon: Buddhist Publication Society, 1968.

NYANATILOKA. *The word of the Buddha.* Colombo, Ceylon: Buddha Publishing Committee, 1952(a).

NYANATILOKA. *Path to deliverance.* Colombo, Ceylon: Buddha Sahitya Sabha, 1952(b).

Osborne, A. *Sri Ramanasramam*. Tiruvannamalai, India: Sri Ramanasram, 1964.

Orme-Johnson, D. Autonomic stability and transcendental meditation. Unpublished manuscript.

Ouspensky, P. D. *The fourth way*. New York: Vintage, 1971.

Poddar, H. P. *The divine name and its practice*. Gorakhpur, India: Gita Press, 1965.

Poddar, H. P. *The philosophy of love: Bhakti sutras of Devarsi Narada*. Gorakhpur, India: Gita Press, 1968.

Prabhavananda, Swami. *Srimad Bhagavatam*. Mylapore, India: Sri Ramakrishna Math, 1964.

Prabhavananda, Swami, Isherwood, C. *How to know God: Yoga aphorisms of Patanjali*. New York: Signet, 1969.

Prabhavananda, Swami, Isherwood, C. *Crest-jewel of discrimination*. New York: Mentor, 1970.

Ramana Maharshi. *Maharshi's gospel, I & II*. Tiruvannamalai, India: Sri Ramanasram, 1962.

Rice, C. *The Persian Sufis*. London: Allen & Unwin, 1964.

Reps, P. *Zen flesh, Zen bones*. New York: Doubleday, 1961.

Saradananda, Swami. *Ramakrishna the Great Master*. Mylapore, India: Sri Ramakrishna Math, 1963.

Satprem (Tehmi, Transl.). *Sri Aurobindo: The adventure of consciousness*. Pondicherry, India: Sri Aurobindo Society, 1970.

Schachter, S., Singer, J. Cognitive, social, and physiological determinants of emotional state, *Psychol. Rev.* 1962, *69,* 379.

Shah, I. *The Sufis*. London: Jonathan Cape, 1970.

Shah, I. *Wisdom of the idiots*. New York: Dutton, 1971.

Shapiro, D. *Neurotic styles*. New York: Basic Books, 1961.

Shastri, H. P. *Yoga-vasistha: the world within the mind*. London: Shanti Sadan, 1969.

Singh, K. *The crown of life*. Delhi: Ruhani Satsang, 1971.

Sivananda, Swami. *Kundalini yoga*. Sivanandagar, India: The Divine Life Society, 1971.

Sullivan, H. S. *The interpersonal theory of psychiatry*. New York: Norton, 1953.

Suzuki, D. T. *The Zen doctrine of no-mind*. London: Rider, 1949.

Suzuki, D. T. *Mysticism: Christian and Buddhist*. New York: Macmillan, 1957.

Suzuki, D. T. *Essays in Zen Buddhism (second series)*. London: Rider, 1958.

SUZUKI, D. T. In C. Humphreys (Ed.), The field of Zen. *Contributions to the Middle Way, the Journal of the Buddhist Society.* London: The Buddhist Society, 1969.

TART, C. Scientific foundations for the study of altered states of consciousness. *J. Transpersonal Psychol.* 1971, *3*(2), 93-124.

TAUSSIG, H. B. "Death" from lightning and the possibility of living again. *Amer. Sci.* 1969, *57*(3), 306-16.

THOMAS À KEMPIS (R. Whitford, Transl.). *The imitation of Christ.* Garden City, New York: Image Books, 1955.

TULSI DASS (M. Growse, Transl.). *Ramayana.* Gorakhpur, India: Gita Press, n.d.

VENKATARAMIAH, M. (Transl.). *Advaita Bodha Deepika: Lamp of non-dual knowledge.* Tiruvannamalai, India: Sri Ramanasram, 1967.

VIMUKTANANDA, SWAMI. *Aparokshanubhuti: Self-realization of Sri Sankaracharya.* Calcutta: Advaita Ashrama, 1966.

VIVEKANANDA, SWAMI. *Bhakti-yoga.* Calcutta: Advaita Ashrama, 1964.

VIVEKANANDA, SWAMI. *Raja-yoga.* Calcutta: Advaita Ashrama, 1970.

VYAS DEV, SWAMI. *First steps to higher yoga.* Gangotri, India: Yoga Niketan Trust, 1970.

WALKER, K. *A study of Gurdjieff's teaching.* London: Jonathan Cape, 1969.

WALLACE, R. K. *Physiological effects of TM: A proposed fourth major state of consciousness.* Los Angeles: Students International Meditation Society, 1970.

WALLACE, R. K., BENSON, H., WILSON, A. E. A wakeful hypometabolic state. *Amer. J. Physiol.,* 1971, *224*(3), 795-99.

WEI WU WEI. *Posthumous pieces.* Hong Kong: Hong Kong Univ. Press, 1968.

WENGER, A. M., BAGCHI, B. K., ANAND, B. K. Experiments in India on "voluntary" control of the heart and pulse. *Circulation,* 1961, *204.*

WOODROFFE, J. *Hymn to Kali.* Madras, India: Ganesh, 1965.

YOGANANDA. *Autobiography of a yogi.* Los Angeles: SRF Publishers, 1946.

III

PHYSIOLOGY OF MEDITATION

An Introduction to Part III:
Physiology of Meditation

This part is divided into four sections. Section A presents the two major review articles. Section B comprises major studies of the general metabolic and autonomic changes which occur during meditation, while Section C contains the major EEG findings. Section D comprises a specific section on the relationship between sleep and meditation.

The evolution of research on the physiology of meditation parallels in many ways the evolution of research on other meditation effects (see Article 3 by Walsh in the Introduction of this volume). It began with sporadic investigations of some of the more spectacular feats allegedly performed by certain yogis, such as, the ability to alter cardiac rate, and even to stop the heart temporarily (e.g., Wenger, 1961; Wenger et al., 1961). Initially the reports of spectacular findings were either ignored or discounted. However, with replication and increasing interest they were accepted as valid phenomena and more systematic investigation was begun. The introduction of better controls led to the appearance of the next phase in which it was found that many of the physiological effects initially assumed to be unique to meditation could actually be induced by a number of self-regulation strategies such as relaxation or self-hypnosis. This, in turn, has led to a reductionistic nihilism in which it is commonly assumed that there is little that is unique to meditation or its effects and its status as a distinct practice is doubtful.

Thus, for example, in the field of metabolism, the initial reports of Wallace (1970; Wallace et al., 1971) were met with a combination of enthusiasm and skepticism. Wallace reported marked reductions in metabolic rate as measured by oxygen consumption, CO_2 production, and blood lactate levels, and suggested that transcendental meditation led to a unique hypometabolic state. Subsequent studies have, in fact, confirmed a reduced metabolic rate (e.g., Akishige, 1968; Sugi and Akutsu, 1968), but better controls such as by Fenwick et al. (1977) and Pagano et al. (1978) revealed that the effects could be accounted for by normal physiological mechanisms once an adequate baseline measure was obtained.

At this stage some researchers felt that the uniqueness of meditation as a metabolic state had been disproved but recent studies of blood hormone levels and blood flow by Jevning et al. (see this part, Section B, Article 33) suggest that more refined measures may yet reveal unique metabolic patterns. Jevning and his co-workers have found changes in regional blood flow and in blood levels of cortisone, prolactin, and phenylalanine without concomitant changes in other hormones and amino acids. This response patterning is different from that occurring during rest or sleep.

Studies of autonomic nervous system function have followed a similar pattern. The original reports of findings which lay outside the normally accepted range of autonomic capacities such as changing cardiac rate, were greeted with initial skepticism. This was especially so since it was widely assumed at that time that voluntary control of the autonomic nervous system was impossible. However, as this belief system changed and interest in meditation expanded, a spate of studies appeared examining meditative effects on autonomic function, most commonly respiration, heart rate, and GSR (galvanic skin response). By far the majority of these studies reported reduced autonomic activity (Orme-Johnson, 1973) and this was generally accepted as a pattern typical of meditation. More recent studies, however, comparing meditation to other self-regulation strategies as self-hypnosis or progressive relaxation have failed to differentiate between these techniques (e.g., Walrach and Hamilton, 1975; Curtis and Wessberg, 1975; Cauthen and Pyrmak, 1977; Travis et al., 1977; Morse et al., 1977). However, almost all of these comparative studies have employed very few parameters and it is questionable whether they would be sensitive enough to discriminate between subtle states of consciousness and physiology.

Indeed, this raises a number of conceptual and methodological questions of considerable importance. The aim of meditation is an increasing subtlety of perception and awarensss in which the meditator intends to move between states of consciousness which differ only in subtle ways (see Goleman, Article 25 and by

Brown, Article 24). However, physiological studies have, in general, employed relatively gross measures and then only with small numbers of parameters. It seems doubtful that this approach is adequate since in addition to the subtlety of expected effects, it is well known that there are marked inter- and intraindividual differences in the patternings of autonomic responses. Individual autonomic parameters may provide some information, but it is clear that the patterning of responses among autonomic parameters is more sensitive to both individual and state-specific effects.

Such response patterns are best analyzed and examined by multivariate statistical approaches, which, with rare exceptions (e.g., Fenwick *et al.* 1978), have not been employed in meditation studies. In addition there have been premature assumptions about the probable uniformity of different meditation practices. Thus, for example, whereas most studies, the majority of which are on transcendental meditation, report autonomic quiescence, a study by Corby *et al.* (1978) of an Indian Yogic meditation revealed marked activation especially in one practitioner who reached extremely high levels of concentration. It is also well to remember that the effects for which meditation was initially intended were not relaxation, but rather for reaching changes in consciousness. These require years of very intense practice and yet, with rare exceptions (e.g., Corby *et al.*, 1978), all studies have employed subjects who have practiced less than an hour per day for 2 or 3 years at most.

As in other meditation research areas, there has been a degree of confusion about controls. Most studies have employed control subjects who rest with eyes closed, although some have employed subjects who focus their attention on a specific word or phrase. However, upon closer inspection of the nature of meditation, it seems that this latter control is actually doing a form of meditation (see Article 42 by Smith in Part IV). As previously discussed, meditation is clearly a complex multidimensional process and these multiple dimensions need to be taken into account when considering the appropriateness of any control procedure. Certainly it seems apparent that some of the failures to detect effects may represent the use of controls who were thought to be neutral but were actually performing a variety of meditative practices.

In view of these conceptual and methodological considerations it seems premature to make sweeping statements about the specificity and uniqueness of the physiological response to meditation. If we assume a holistic interconnectedness system model of meditation (Shapiro, 1979; Walsh, see Introduction, Article 3) then it is apparent that all components of the organism will show some response of some degree. The question which remains is whether these responses will be of sufficient magnitude to detect and what percentage of variance they account for. Thus, it may be more sensitive controls and multivariate investigation will in fact reveal a number of unique and discrete metabolic patterns. The question is whether they differ significantly enough from states induced by other self-regulation strategies to be considered informative in illuminating the mechanisms underlying the psychological and phenomenological changes which are the goal of meditation.

Table 6. Summary of Studies Comparing Meditation with Other Self-Regulation Strategies: Physiological Measures

Roger N. Walsh

Reference	Type of Meditation	Amount of Meditation	Changes During Meditation	Type of Design	Quality of Control Procedures
Walrath & Hamilton, 1975	TM	> 6 months practice	Meditators, autohypnotizers and con[t]... showed decreases in heart and resp... rates and GSR activity but did not ... between groups.		
Curtis & Wessburg, 1975/76	TM	~ 2 years practice	No effects across trials or between ...tion, progressive relaxation and con... in GSR, heart or respiration rate.		
Cauthen & Prymak, 1977	TM	7 days, 14 months, or 5 years	2 more experienced groups of me[d]... showed ↓ heart rate during medita... Relaxers and least experienced me...		
Travis, Kondo, & Knott, 1977	TM	5-30 months	No differences between meditators... relaxation controls on EEG, alpha, and frontal EMG. Both groups sho... showed less EEG sleep patterns t...		
Morse et al., 1977	TM	2 months - 8 years	Measures of pulse rate, respirator... blood pressure, GSR, EEG and muscle acti-vity all suggested significantly greater relaxation in experimental sub-jects trained in TM, self-hypnosis or both, than in controls. However experimental groups did not differ between themselves except for lower muscle activity in TM.		...analysis.
Pagano et al., (Note 14)	TM	Experienced average = 3.4 years	Both TM and progressive muscle relaxation subjects showed similar small (2-5%) decrements in 0₂ consumption from a resting baseline, which did not differ from eyes closed controls.	Between-subjects	Adequate. Good statistical analysis.

Table 6. Summary of Studies Comparing Meditation with Other Self-Regulation Strategies: Physiological Measures (cont'd.)
Roger N. Walsh

Reference	Type of Meditation	Amount of Meditation	Changes During Meditation	Type of Design	Quality of Control Procedures
Glueck & Stroebel, 1977	TM	Intermediate	Showed heart and respiration rates ↑ GSR. ↑ EEG alpha. Intrahemispheric alpha and theta synchrony even in inexperienced meditators. Greater intrahemispheric synchrony in thermal and EMG biofeedback subjects than in TM or relaxation response subjects. Evidence of interhemispheric synchrony in TM and relaxation response subjects but not in biofeedback subjects.	Between and within subjects	Adequate.
Boswell & Murray, 1979	Zen	2 weeks	No significant differences between groups in Spiegelberger Trait-State Anxiety inventory, GSR, skin conductance, and heart rate.	Between-subjects	Good. Three control groups: Relaxation, placebo, and no treatment.
Beiman et al., 1980	TM	Seven 1½ hour sessions	No significant differences in effectiveness of TM, behavior therapy, or self relaxation. were detected for self report measures (locus of control, regression sensitization, autonomic perception, trait anxiety, or fear survey schedule), or physiological measures (skin resistance, skin response, pulse rate, EMG). Locus of control accounted for a major proportion of variance in the response to TM.	Between-subjects	Adequate. Good use of multivariate analyses, especially multiple regression to determine amounts of variance accounted for by subject variables.

A. Physiology of Meditation: Review Articles

There have been two major reviews of the physiology of meditation, and one of the hemispheric laterality literature. The first article by Woolfolk (26) is a useful introduction to the physiology of meditation in that it divides the different types of meditation into major groupings—Zen, Yoga, TM—and provides initial information about physiological changes of both an electrocortical nature—EEG; electrodermal (skin conductance); metabolic—respiration, and cardiovascular changes. The tables in Woolfolk's article have been updated by Roger Walsh and are included as a useful summary for the subsequent sections [The reader is also referred to Part II, Section C2, (Tables 4 and 5) for additional tables describing comparisons between different types of meditative procedures.] The second article by Davidson (27) reviews the physiology of meditation and offers a theoretical discussion for possible physiological parameters which may mediate and be representative of subjective and phenomenological experiences of a mystical state of consciousness.

The third by Earle (28), reviews the conflicting literature on cerebral laterality and meditation regarding whether meditation produces activation in the nondominant (right) hemisphere and, in addition, in the dominant (left) hemisphere. Studies of hemispheric lateralization, EEG synchronization, and attentional issues are addressed.

PSYCHOPHYSIOLOGICAL CORRELATES
OF MEDITATION: A REVIEW

Robert L. Woolfolk

● The scientific research that has investigated the physiological changes associated with meditation as it is practiced by adherents of Indian Yoga, Transcendental Meditation, and Zen Buddhism has not yielded a thoroughly consistent, easily replicable pattern of responses. The majority of studies show meditation to be a wakeful state accompanied by a lowering of cortical and autonomic arousal. The investigations of Zen and Transcendental Meditation have thus far produced the most consistent findings.

Additional research into the mechanisms underlying the phenomena of meditation will require a shifting from old to new methodological perspectives that allow for adequate experimental control and the testing of theoretically relevant hypotheses.

(Arch Gen Psychiatry 32:1326-1333, 1975)

For many centuries, individuals in the East have practiced different forms of meditation and alleged salutary effects on physical and psychological functioning. Numerous similarities have been noted among methods of meditation and such Western therapeutic devices as progressive relaxation and autogenic training.[1] Meditation has been successfully substituted for relaxation as a counter-conditioning agent in systematic desensitization[2] and has been theorized to operate as a kind of "global desensitization procedure."[3] As an adjunct to psychotherapy, meditation has been employed with neurotic populations[4] and with inpatient groups classified as psychotic.[5] The practice of meditation has been found to be associated with lowered trait anxiety,[6] decreased drug abuse,[7,8] and gains on a measure of self-actualization.[9,10] Some research has shown that regular practice of meditation can lead to improvement in bronchial asthma[11] and decreased systolic blood pressure in hypertensive patients.[12]

The evidence cited above is largely suggestive, some arising from uncontrolled research and some based on conclusions from paper-and-pencil psychometric data rather than more salient behavioral or physiological data.

Accepted for publication Jan 3, 1975.
From the Department of Psychology, University College, Rutgers University, New Brunswick, NJ.
Reprints not available.

Clinical outcome studies can suggest that *something* involved in the rather complex "package" of training in and practice of meditation (usually Transcendental Meditation) may possibly produce therapeutic benefits. But what remains unknown is *which* aspects of the package are the active ingredients and *what* mechanisms underlie their purported efficacy. The increasingly widespread use of meditation procedures requires both an adequate scientific understanding of these phenomena as well as controlled studies of efficacy. This review, in bringing together the basic psychophysiological research on meditation, will attempt to clarify what is known about the effects of meditation, to indicate what sorts of questions are as yet unanswered, and to specify methods for obtaining answers to those questions. It does not specifically focus on the issues of methodology relating to efficacy.

The search for psychophysiological correlates of meditation has centered essentially on three groups: Yogis and students of Yoga in India, adherents of Transcendental Meditation in the United States, and practitioners of Zen Buddhism in Japan. These studies have typically measured various physiological indexes (electroencephalogram [EEG], galvanic skin response [GSR]) of individuals "accomplished" at meditation and have made comparisons either with control groups or in a within-subject design. What actually has been investigated is the effects of some rather specific meditative procedures practiced by individuals within a complex framework of philosophical commitment and social influence. The experimental designs reviewed do not allow us to draw inferences concerning the relative effects of these technical and "extratechnical" factors. Thus, the findings reported here pertain to the effects of very complex sets of independent variables, rather than the influences of variables specifiable and manipulatable under normal laboratory conditions.

YOGA

Yoga has been an integral feature of the Hindu culture for over 2,000 years. The term itself refers to the set of practices and beliefs whose goal is the attainment of *samadhi*, or "union" with the "Universal Self." The different sects of Yoga vary greatly in their use of such tech-

Table 1.—Summary of Studies of Indian Yogic Meditation				
References	Experience of Meditators	Changes During Meditation*	Type of Design	Quality of Control Procedures
Das & Gastaut[13]	Highly experienced	Faster EEG, increase in HR	Within-subject	Poor, measurements taken in field under highly variable conditions
Anand et al[14]	Highly experienced	Faster EEG, decrease in O_2 consumption, decrease in HR	Within-subject	Excellent, laboratory study
Bagchi & Wegner[15]	Highly experienced	No change in EEG, increase in SR level, no change in HR, no change in BP	Within-subject	Poor, measurements taken in field under highly variable conditions
Kasamatsu et al[18]	Highly experienced	Slower EEG	Within-subject	Adequate, laboratory study, meditation period too short
Anand et al[19]	Highly experienced	Slower EEG	Within-subject	Excellent, laboratory conditions
Wegner & Bagchi[20]	Moderately experienced	Decrease in SR level, decrease in respiration rate, increase in HR, increase in BP	Within-subject	Poor, initial readings not comparable before meditation & relaxation periods
Karambelkar et al[21]	Moderately experienced	No change in SR level, increase in O_2 consumption, no change in HR, no change in BP	Between-subjects	Poor, no control over duration of meditation, sketchy reporting

* Electroencephalogram indicated by EEG; heart rate, HR; oxygen, O_2; skin resistance, SR; and blood pressure, BP.

niques as physical postures (*asana*), breath control (*pranayama*), fixed attention on an idea or image (*dharana*), and extended contemplation or meditation (*dhyana*). Sects also vary in their degree of mysticism from Hatha Yoga, which primarily emphasizes different bodily postures and exercises as a means of achieving physical health and psychological well-being, to the esoteric schools and their decidedly more spiritual orientations. These divergences in belief and practice are, in all likelihood, responsible for the dissimilarity of findings produced by the following research into the physiological correlates of Indian Yoga (see Table 1).

Electrocortical Activity

Das and Gastaut[13] measured the EEGs of seven practitioners of Yoga during 20 meditative sessions. During meditation, high-frequency electrocortical activity replaced slower premeditation rhythms and remained until meditation was terminated. The one subject who reported achieving *samadhi* evidenced considerable increases in the amplitude of the beta waves recorded during this state. During this period, his EEG was not affected by the presentation of auditory or visual stimulation, indicating an insensibility to external events. In research that examined the responses of a highly regarded Indian Yogi during two periods of prolonged meditation in an airtight box, Anand et al[14] also found meditation to be associated with beta activity. Prior to his entry into the box, the EEG of the subject showed a predominance of alpha waves. This pattern was quickly replaced by higher-frequency beta activity with occasional runs of alpha waves interspersed, suggestive of drowsiness or light sleep. Bagchi and Wegner[15] found no change in the EEG patterns of 14 Yogis when comparisons were made between readings taken during meditation and readings taken during control periods of quiet rest in the lotus position. Although the predominant electrocortical activity observed during meditation was in the alpha frequency range, this was also the case during control periods. An increase in the slower frequencies that some writers[16,17] have considered to be a defining characteristic of meditation was not observed. In the following two studies on Indian Yoga, however, this slowing of the EEG was demonstrated.

Kasamatsu et al[18] compared the EEGs taken during meditation of an experienced Yogi and a control subject whose resting EEG was similar to that of the Yogi. After

eight minutes the Yogi demonstrated a substantial increase in alpha activity, while the pattern of the resting control remained unchanged. There was no blocking of the meditator's alpha rhythm on the sudden presentation of auditory stimuli.

In a well-controlled study, Anand et al[19] made within-subject comparisons of the electrocortical activity of four experienced Yogis during rest and during meditation. All the subjects displayed considerable alpha activity during periods of rest. This activity became more prominent and increased in amplitude during meditation. Two Yogis were exposed to auditory, haptic, and visual stimuli before and during meditation. During the control period, all stimulation blocked the alpha rhythm, converting it to low-voltage fast activity. This blocking pattern failed to habituate on repetition of the same stimuli. When the Yogis were in meditation, however, no blocking of the alpha rhythm occurred. Failure of alpha blocking to habituate has been hypothesized to reflect both heightened perceptual sensitivity and some degree of cortical excitation.[17]

Electrodermal Activity

Bagchi and Wegner[15] found that palmar skin resistance (SR) increased during meditation, with a median increase of 56% during control periods. When these same authors[20] compared the responses of four Yoga students during meditation in the lotus position with responses from an equivalent period of reclining relaxation, SR was found to be greater during meditation.

The interpretation of this last finding is unclear not only because of the postural differences but also because the conditions were not comparable with respect to initial readings. The picture regarding Indian Yogic meditation and electrodermal activity is also complicated by a third study that found no consistent differences between two practitioners of Yoga and two control subjects on measures of SR.[21] In considering this finding, criticism must be directed both at the small sample size for a between-subjects design and the lack of clarity of the authors' report, from which it is not clear whether the Yogis were involved in meditation throughout the entire experiment.

Respiration

Bagchi and Wegner[15] found that during meditation the rate of respiration tended to decline relative to levels set

Physiology of Meditation

Table 2.—Summary of Studies of Transcendental Meditation

References	Experience of Meditators	Changes During Meditation*	Type of Design	Quality of Control Procedures
Wallace[22]	Moderately experienced	Slower EEG, increase in SR level, decrease in O_2 consumption, decrease in HR	Within-subject	Excellent, laboratory study, statistical comparisons made
Wallace et al[23]	Moderately experienced	Slower EEG, increase in SR level, decrease in O_2 consumption, decrease in BP	Within-subject	Excellent, laboratory study, statistical comparisons made
Schwartz[24]	Moderately experienced	Slower EEG, increase in SR level (these changes not significantly from those found in controls)	Between-subjects	Excellent, laboratory study, statistical comparisons made, appropriate control group
Banquet[25]	Moderately experienced	Slower EEG (stages I & II), in some individuals faster EEG observed during third stage	Within-subject	Excellent, laboratory study, statistical comparisons made
Orme-Johnson[26]	Moderately experienced	Galvanic skin response more stable	Between-subjects	Excellent, laboratory study, statistical comparisons made, appropriate control group
Allison[30]	Not reported	Decrease in rate of respiration	Within-subject	Adequate, laboratory study, sketchy reporting

* See footnote to Table 1.

during control periods. Wegner and Bagchi[20] found the rate of respiration to be slower during meditation than during reclining relaxation. The Anand et al[14] study found dramatic decreases in oxygen consumption during meditation in an airtight box, while a study that attempted to replicate these results[21] found that the oxygen consumption of Yogis, relative to basal levels, was greater than that of controls exposed to the same environment.

Cardiovascular Responses

Das and Gastaut[14] found that heart rate increased during meditation. Their findings were supported by Wegner and Bagchi[20] who recorded faster heart rate and higher systolic and diastolic blood pressure during meditation. Anand et al[14] observed a decrease in heart rate during meditation, while two studies[15,21] failed to find meditation associated with consistent changes in any cardiovascular response.

Despite the presence of many obvious inconsistencies, one clear commonality does emerge from the research on physiological concomitants of Indian Yogic meditation. The failure of meditator's EEGs to be affected by sensory input was a clear finding in three studies.[15,18,19] This evidence suggests that a "turning off" of awareness or a "shutting down" of input processing occurred in these subjects. Methodologically speaking, the research on Yoga leaves much to be desired. Many of the studies were conducted in the field under adverse circumstances. Yogis willing to submit to psychophysiological measurement often were not readily available. Thus, consequent small numbers and the considerable variability among subjects likely contributed to the incompatible findings reported. Some Yoga states[15,20] are associated with patterns of electrocortical excitation, while others[15,18,19] produce a predominance of slow wave activity. Findings with respect to other variables, eg, heart rate, show a similar inconsistency. These divergences, in large part, result from the lack of uniformity both among the experimental procedures employed and in the goals, beliefs, and practices of Indian Yoga.

TRANSCENDENTAL MEDITATION

A variety of Yoga known as Transcendental Meditation (TM) was adapted from the Indian Yogic tradition by the Maharishi Mahesh Yogi. As an object of scientific study, it offers many advantages over more traditional forms of Yoga. It is a much less rigorous and demanding discipline, apparently easily learned, and widely practiced in the United States. Essentially, it is a streamlined form of Mantram Yoga in which practitioners meditate in any comfortable position on a specific *mantram*, or set of words. Meditators, in two daily 20-minute sessions, silently repeat the words of a particular mantram again and again throughout each session, returning focus to the words whenever attention wanders.

Although less esoteric than its Hindu precursors, TM is not without its own brand of arcane practices that include delivery of an "individualized" secret mantram to every student. The additional presence of philosophical teachings and strong expectations of salutary derivative effects precludes drawing any inferences from the following research (see Table 2) concerning effects of the meditative techniques per se.

Electrocortical Activity

Wallace[22] recorded the EEGs of 15 college-aged students of TM during meditation and made within-subjects comparisons with base lines taken during periods of quiet rest. The EEGs of subjects showed that alpha activity present prior to meditation increased in regularity and amplitude. Some of the subjects demonstrated periods of low-voltage theta wave predominance. In most subjects, alpha activity was blocked by both auditory and visual stimuli. This blocking failed to habituate on repeated presentation of the stimuli.

A similar pattern of electrocortical activity was observed in the 36 meditators studies by Wallace et al.[23] The EEG pattern during TM showed increases in alpha activity. In some subjects, the increases in alpha activity were accompanied by occasional trains of theta waves.

Schwartz[24] reported two experiments that obtained results that can be interpreted as being at variance with those of Wallace and his co-workers. First, occipital alpha activity was recorded from 12 experienced meditators during three brief meditations separated by brief periods of relaxation with eyes open. The investigation employed a control group matched on age and sex who relaxed with eyes closed during the meditation periods. Increases in alpha activity were recorded for both groups during periods when eyes were closed relative to times when eyes were open. However, alpha activity declined during the periods of meditation, the decrease in alpha being somewhat less for the meditators. An interesting finding reported was what appeared to be a postmeditation "cortical sensitization effect." Although pre-experimental measurements of both groups taken with eyes open disclosed more alpha activity in meditator's EEGs, during the post-meditation phase meditators evidenced less alpha activity than did the controls. In a second experiment that attempted to replicate this effect, Schwartz[24] recorded the EEGs of 16 meditators during one 22-minute meditation session. The findings were consistent with those of the earlier experiment. When compared with data from the control group, the electrocortical readings did suggest a sensitization effect in meditators following meditation.

A recent study of electrocortical activity during TM[25] found for all meditators an initial slowing of the EEG, indicative of lowered cortical arousal. Alpha activity present at the beginning of meditation became predominant, yielding to a dominant theta pattern as the meditation progressed. However, subsequent to the period of theta predominance, some subjects displayed a pattern of generalized fast beta frequencies similar to those recorded by Das and Gastaut.[11] As in this earlier research on Indian Yoga, these periods of beta activity were associated with subjects' reports of very deep meditation. In response to click-and-flash stimulation, alpha activity, when present, was usually not blocked; but the theta pattern was blocked by stimuli. The beta activity associated with "profound meditation" was not affected by auditory or visual stimulation.

Electrodermal Activity

Wallace[22] reported a substantial increase in palmar SR during TM. This increase was not sustained in the rest period following meditation. Wallace et al[24] observed a substantial increase of approximately 60% during meditation. Schwartz[24] reported very slight increases in SR during meditation. However, increases in SR observed in meditators were comparable to those found in a group of matched controls who rested with eyes closed. Following meditation, SR levels fell below those of controls, suggesting heightened arousal in the meditators following meditation.

Orme-Johnson[26] reported two studies that sought to determine if stability of SR results from the practice of TM. Fluctuations in SR have been associated in the literature both with individual stress levels and with various environmental stressors.[27-29] In the first study, GSR habituation to noxious tones was observed in eight practitioners of TM and eight controls after both groups had been instructed to relax in a comfortable sitting position. It was found that GSR habituated faster for meditators than for controls. In a subsequent test of GSR stability, meditators made fewer spontaneous GSR fluctuations during meditation than did controls during an equal period of rest.

In the second experiment, which attempted to control for differences between individuals who chose to learn TM and randomly selected controls, Orme-Johnson studied spontaneous GSR in eight meditators and eight nonmeditators who planned to begin TM training in two weeks. The findings of the earlier study were replicated. The GSR of meditators was demonstrated to be more stable during meditation than that of the resting controls. Some support of Wallace's findings was generated in that a substantial decrease of basal SR was observed for meditators during meditation but not found in the resting controls.

Respiration

Allison,[30] in a one-subject study, found that the subject's rate of respiration during meditation decreased by approximately 50% relative to a base rate achieved while the subject watched television. Breathing became somewhat shallower, returning to control levels during the period following meditation. Wallace[22] observed that for his subjects, oxygen consumption showed a mean decrease of 20%, rising to control levels following meditation. Wallace et al[23] reported measures of respiration on five meditators that indicated a decrease in both rate of respiration and in oxygen consumption during meditation.

Cardiovascular Responses

Wallace and his co-workers,[22,23] to my knowledge, are the only investigators to have reported cardiovascular data on TM. They reported a decrease in heart rate during TM and no substantial change in systolic or diastolic blood pressure.

When compared to the variegated corpus of Indian Yoga, the methods of TM are highly consistent. As one might expect, the data on physiological concomitants also evidence greater consistency. All studies that measured rate of respiration found decreases on this variable during TM. All studies showed initial increases in alpha activity during meditation, with other frequencies often appearing during the latter stages of meditation. In some cases theta rhythms were observed,[22,23,25] while in one study,[25] beta frequencies were recorded. In Schwartz studies,[24] equipment settings did not allow a determination of which frequencies increased as alpha diminished.

During TM there appears to be both an increase and stabilization of SR, although Schwartz[24] demonstrated only minimal changes in GSR. Procedural differences involving sequencing and duration of meditation and control periods may account for some of the disparity in the data. However, Schwartz[24] suggests that the differences in findings may have stemmed from the fact that Wallace et al[22,23] maintained a personal relationship with their subjects and were able to put them at ease, allowing them to attain a deeper and more natural state of meditation. As support for this contention that situational factors may interact with meditation procedures, Schwartz[24] presents some compelling evidence. Skin resistances of 30 meditators and 30 nonmeditators were compared as they anticipated the viewing of a stressful film. Meditators showed a mean *decrease* in SR while meditating. This decrease was greater than that observed in the controls who simply rested. These findings serve again to highlight the necessity for rigorous experimental controls. The pattern or hypometabolism seen in some studies may indeed be an elusive one, obtained with great difficulty under less than optimum experimental conditions.

ZEN

Zazen, or Zen meditation is an integral part of both the Soto and Rinzai sects of Zen Buddhism. It is the primary method by which the enlightened or transcendent state known as *satori* is achieved. The practice of Zazen itself is much more highly standardized than are the various Yogic techniques of meditation. Zazen is practiced in the lotus or half-lotus position with eyes open. An initiate begins by focusing all attention on his breathing. After some period of time, when he has learned to rivet attention on the process of breathing, the student is given a *koan*, or riddle to meditate on. The aim is not for the student to generate a solution through rational proceses, but rather to provide a more difficult exercise in concentration. Serious practitioners of Zen lead very austere and disciplined lives, no small part of which is the attempt to emulate the style and attitudes of the Zen master.

Physiological studies of Zen meditation suggest that it may be a state quite similar to that achieved through forms of Yogic meditation (see Table 3).

	Experience	Changes During	Type of	Quality of
References	of Meditators	Meditation*	Design	Control Procedures
Kasamatsu et al[18]	Highly experienced	Slower EEG	Within-subject	Adequate, laboratory study, meditation period too short
Kasamatsu & Hirai[31]	Moderately experienced & highly recommended	Slower EEG	Within-subject	Excellent, laboratory conditions
Akishige[32]	Highly experienced	Slower EEG, galvanic skin response more stable, decrease in O_2 consumption, decrease in respiration rate	Within-subject	Excellent, laboratory conditions
Hirai[33]	Highly experienced	Slower EEG, decrease in respiration rate	Within-subject	Adequate, laboratory conditions
Sugi & Akutsu[34]	Highly experienced	Decrease in O_2 consumption	Within-subject	Excellent, laboratory conditions
Goyeche et al[35]	Minimally experienced	Decrease in respiration rate, decrease in HR	Within-subject	Excellent, laboratory conditions, order of meditation & control periods randomized

Table 3.—Summary of Studies of Zen Meditation

* See footnote to Table 1.

Electrocortical Activity

Kasamatsu et al[18] report substantial increases in alpha activity during the Zazen of an experienced practitioner of Zen. These changes were analogous to changes in the EEG of a Yogi who meditated under the same conditions. Blocking of alpha activity by external stimuli was not observed. Kasamatsu and Hirai,[31] in a rather intensive study, measured the electrocortical activity of 48 priests and disciples during Zazen. All subjects showed an increase in alpha activity immediately subsequent to beginning meditation. Less experienced subjects tended to maintain high-amplitude alpha throughout the meditative session, whereas the EEGs of those with more years in Zen training showed rhythmical theta wave patterns during latter stages of Zazen. Whether or not these differences are the result of their greater experience itself or other differences between subjects, eg, age, is not clear. These findings are consistent with those of Akishige[32] and Hirai[33] who found a similar slowing of the EEG during Zazen. Kasamatsu and Hirai[31] observed that both alpha and theta activity were blocked by the presentation of auditory stimuli. This blocking failed to habituate. In control subjects habituation of alpha occurred quite rapidly.

Electrodermal Activity

In his study of experienced practitioners of Zen, Akishige[32] reports a decrease in spontaneous skin conductance responses during Zazen. This tendency for GSR to stabilize was similar to that reported in research on TM.[26]

Respiration

Sugi and Akutsu[34] observed a 20% decrease in oxygen consumption associated with the meditation of ten Zen monks with many years of experience. Hirai[33] discovered that the respiratory rate decreased during Zazen. Still more studies of skilled practitioners of Zen[32] showed both a decrease of oxygen consumption and rate of respiration. In another study,[33] the rate of respiration associated with Zen meditation was found to be slower than during control periods.

Cardiovascular Responses

Goyeche and others[35] compared Zen meditation with relaxation. In their within-subject design the order of treatment was randomly assigned to each of the eight subjects. It was found that heart rate decreased during Zen meditation.

The available research on Zen shows a pattern of physiological correlates that are analogous to those reported in some of the studies of Indian Yogic meditation and TM.

Oxygen consumption, rate of respiration, and frequency of electrocortical activity were all found to diminish during Zazen. The observed changes were in the direction of hypometabolism and suggest a lowered state of arousal of the autonomic and central nervous systems.

COMMENT

The studies reported thus far have sought to bring the precision of laboratory measurement to bear on the study of individuals schooled in various meditation techniques. In these studies, relatively great control was exercised over the selection and collection of dependent measures. These were not, however, investigations of the influences of easily specified and highly refined independent variables. The inference of precise causal relationships is not possible from the data.

From the perspective of one seeking scientific understanding of the mechanisms that underlie the various forms of meditation, the research reviewed is only suggestive. Findings reflect the influences of very complex sets of social, cognitive, perceptual, and physiological variables. New methodologies will be required to specify and tease out the effects of these variables. The early research does suggest three areas whose exploration might provide us with added refinement of variables and tentative hypotheses concerning the relationships of these variables. These areas are the phenomenological reports of meditators, the techniques of meditation themselves, and the physiological correlates.

An examination of phenomenology is of great potential import. For example, if some technique of meditation consistently produced reports of pleasurable affect from all who used it, the technique would be of great interest for this reason alone. However, all the severe problems of introspective research that caused scientific inquiry to turn away from subjective data are present in the research on meditation. These problems are particularly acute in the study of disciplines whose vocabularies are highly esoteric and mystical. The variability of practices within the sects and practitioners of Indian Yoga leave the investigator in a quandary when attempting to understand such issues as the difference between a period of meditation that yields *samadhi* and one in which the experience approximates but does not achieve the sought-after state. Although *samadhi* is universally described by terms such as "transcendence" and "bliss" and characterized as a "turning off" of the external world, one Yogi shows cortical excitation in very "deep" meditation while another clearly evidences greater synchronization and slowing of the EEG. Thus consistent reports of the phenomenology of meditation may simply reflect similarly shaped verbal sets, rather than any regularities along other dimensions.

On conducting an inspection of the meditative techniques themselves employed by the different disciplines, we find many interesting similarities. Virtually all forms of meditation require physical immobility. All require some form of perceptual concentration. This concentration may be on an object, idea, image, or mantram, as in many forms of Yoga. In Zazen, attention is focused on the breathing or on a *koan*. The net result of this concentration of awareness is a limitation of one or more of the visual, auditory, or haptic sensory modes to a single invariate stimulus configuration.

When we turn to the physiological data of the research literature on meditation in a search for commonalities, we find what seems to be a somewhat inconsistent picture. Studies have thus far failed to verify an easily replicable, special "state" of meditation with physiological concomitants that are consistent across the various esoteric traditions. This is not surprising in view of the fact that extratechnical factors inherent in the training of meditators and laboratory situational factors have tended to be quite diverse. These problems are particularly evident in studies of Indian Yoga, while the research on TM and Zen has yielded a much more consistent picture. This research indicates meditation to be associated with a slowing and increased synchronization of electrocortical rhythms, an increased or more stable SR, and slower rate of respiration. These changes are all in the direction of lowered arousal and suggest a diminishing of energy metabolism. The results of several studies, however, demonstrate a profile unlike that arising from simple relaxation. For example, Banquet[25] found high-frequency electrocortical activity to be evidenced by some meditators during the latter stages of a meditative period. It should also be recalled that the majority of studies used control periods of nonmeditative rest in comparison with meditation and found differences between the two conditions. Several authors[17-31] have concluded that the failure of habituation of blocking of alpha activity by sensory input indicates some substantial degree of cortical excitation to be present during meditation. This dishabituation, however, is not consistent across all studies. For example, Anand et al[1a] found that, in Yogis, alpha blocking failed to habituate in control periods, but that during meditation sensory input did not alter their subjects' EEGs. Naranjo and Ornstein[16] have suggested that the data on alpha blocking reflect:

... two basic types of meditation exercises ... those which "turn off" input processing for a period of time to achieve an *after-effect* of "opening up" of awareness, and those which consist of the active practice of "opening up" during the period of the exercise.[16(p198)]

Any future investigations that attempt to ascertain what, if any, are the effects of the meditative procedures removed from their religious contexts will likely begin to grapple with the question of underlying mechanisms. Two theories have thus far been put forth that address this issue.

Kasamatsu and Hirai[11] noted similarities between the EEG of Zen meditation and that produced by other situations that reduce the consumption of oxygen. When air is breathed at high altitudes under reduced pressure, oxygen intake is lowered and an increase of alpha activity is observed.[1a] Watanabe et al[15] proposed the reduction of oxygen consumption common to all forms of meditation to be the single most important factor in producing the physiological changes associated with meditation. The potential utility of this theory is very great as it is quite amenable to empirical confirmation. Its fundamental proposition could be tested quite easily by holding oxygen consump-

tion constant across meditative and control sessions by use of a breathing apparatus that would allow the experimenter to systematically vary the oxygen-nitrogen mixture. If changes associated with meditation do not occur when oxygen consumption is held constant, then powerful support for the theory is generated. Conversely, if psychophysiological correlates of meditation are observed, it would suggest a role of limited importance for anoxia in the production of meditative phenomena. It should be noted that there is evidence indicating that for Zen meditation the observed reduction in respiratory rate per se does not account for decreases in oxygen consumption.[34] The oxygen consumption of controls who had assumed meditative postures *increased* slightly when breathing frequencies were lowered to levels found in Zazen.

Deikman[38,39] and Ornstein[40] have proposed that similarities existing among the correlates of different types of meditation are due to their common procedural feature, the focusing of perception on invariate sources of stimulation. Ornstein contends that the central nervous system is so constructed that concentration of awareness on an unchanging stimulus produces a cessation of awareness of the external world. This theory finds some support in the experimental literature. Cohen[41] studied the effects of an unchanging, homogeneous visual field of low illumination (*Ganzfeld*) on perception. Five of 16 subjects reported a total "cessation" of visual experience:

This was a unique experience which involved a complete disappearance of the sense of vision for short periods of time, and not simply the presence of a dark, undifferentiated visual field.[41(p407)]

In a subsequent experiment the phenomenon was replicated.[42] Bursts of alpha activity were associated with visual cessation, and subjects whose EEGs showed high levels of alpha activity were more likely to experience the visual termination. Cohen hypothesized that perceptual mechanisms may have evolved to process differentiated fields and that unchanging stimulation may cause a temporary disruption of these mechanisms.

Lehmann et al[43] produced a "stabilized" image on subjects' retinas by means of a tiny projector mounted on a contact lens. Subjects reported disappearance of the image after a few seconds of continuous viewing. The authors reported that electrocortical activity was low-voltage beta during periods of visibility as contrasted with predominant alpha after a fading out of the image.

These studies do suggest that restriction and repetition of sensory input may be a very important ingredient in meditative procedures. This perceptual theory of meditation is likely to prove of great heuristic value for the more carefully controlled studies required to demonstrate what are the contributions of technical factors to the correlative phenomena of meditation. More specifically, to pursue its implications investigators would attempt to isolate the effects on psychophysiological variables of stimulus consistency across one or more modes of sensation.

The methodologies of such studies would of necessity require better control over the influences of independent variables than has been exercised in the research on the esoteric schools of meditation. For the major task of any future research on meditation is that of developing experimental designs enabling the teasing out of variables active in producing the effects associated with the meditative practices of the mystical traditions. The study of individuals who meditate in conjunction with religious practices is highly inappropriate because of the impossibility of separating the effects of techniques per se from the multiple additional factors comprising the context within which the techniques are practiced. Furthermore, the use of such individuals often requires relationships of a more personal nature between subjects and experimenters (resulting from the exigencies of recruitment and preparation of subjects) than is optimal in research seeking to limit uncontrolled sources of variation.

When naive subjects are employed and specific, repeatable procedures tested, the important questions are more readily answered. The effects of various techniques potentially can be examined without the contaminating influence of expectations and demand characteristics. Furthermore, these extratechnical factors can be experimentally manipulated while techniques are held constant to permit systematic investigation of set and setting variables.

These recommended changes in methodology are necessary not only to achieve a scientifically acceptable explanation of meditation, but also if effective meditative procedures are likely ever to achieve appropriate clinical availability. All who have investigated this area believe that meditation may be, at the very least, of great potential utility to members of stressful, high-speed Western societies. The average citizen has not the time to study for years in Japan or India, nor often the inclination to become an acolyte of the Maharishi. As long as the mechanisms that underlie meditation remain shrouded in mystery, whatever benefits it may hold will be for most of us unrealized.

CONCLUSIONS

Various practices of Yoga, Zen Buddhism, and other esoteric disciplines share the common label "meditation."

Scientific investigation of these practices has failed to demonstrate an integrated, clearly defined set of responses common to all forms of meditation. The studies of Zen and TM have thus far yielded the most consistent pattern of responses associated with meditation. The pattern most frequently observed is indicative of a reduction in arousal and a slowing of energy metabolism. However, some Yoga states have been found to be associated with electrocortical excitation and increases in oxygen consumption.

Although the preponderance of evidence on the various forms of meditation suggests that meditative procedures can produce under some circumstances a lowering of cortical and autonomic arousal, variables of set and setting have been shown to determine to some extent the kind of state produced. The research thus far has not generated an adequate scientific understanding of the specific independent variables and causal relationships that account for meditative phenomena. This is largely because research has thus far investigated the effects of rather specific techniques practiced within a complex framework of expectation, philosophical belief, and social influence. To develop acceptable scientific explanations of meditative phenomena, future research must address itself to the development of new methodologies that allow for the systematic isolation and investigation of technical and extratechnical factors that are active in producing psychophysiological change.

References

1. Benson H, Beary JF, Carol MP: The relaxation response. *Psychiatry* 37:37-46, 1974.
2. Boudreau L: Transcendental Meditation and Yoga as reciprocal inhibitors. *J Behav Ther Exp Psychiatry* 3:97-98, 1972.
3. Coleman D: Meditation as a meta-therapy: Hypotheses toward a proposed fifth state of consciousness. *J Transpers Psychol* 3:1-25, 1971.
4. Carrington P, Ephron HS: Meditation as an adjunct to psychotherapy, in Arieti S, Chrzanowski G (eds): *New Dimensions in Psychiatry: A World View.* New York, John Wiley & Sons Inc, 1975.
5. Glueck B: Current research on Transcendental Meditation. Read at the Rensselaer Polytechnic Institute, Hartford, Conn, 1973.
6. Nidich S, Seeman W, Siebert M: Influence of Transcendental Meditation on state anxiety. *J Clin Consult Psychol*, to be published.
7. Benson H, Wallace RK: Decreased drug abuse with Transcendental Meditation: A study of 1,862 subjects, in Arafonetis CJD (ed): *Drug Abuse: Proceedings of the International Conference.* Philadelphia, Lea & Febiger, 1972, pp 369-376.
8. Shafii M, Lavely R, Jaffe R: Meditation and marijuana. *Am J Psychiatry* 131:60-63, 1974.
9. Seeman W, Nidich S, Banta T: Influence of Transcendental Meditation on a measure of self-actualization. *J Counsel Psychol* 19:184-187, 1972.
10. Nidich S, Seeman W, Dreskin T: Influence of Transcendental Meditation: A replication. *J Counsel Psychol* 20:565-566, 1973.
11. Wilson AF, Honsberger R: The effects of Transcendental Meditation upon bronchial asthma. *Clin Res* 21:278, 1973.
12. Benson H, Rosner BA, Marzetta BR: Decreased systolic blood pressure in hypertensive subjects who practiced meditation. *J Clin Invest* 52:8a, 1973.
13. Das NN, Gastaut H: Variations de l'activité electrique due cerveau, du coeur et des muscles squelletiques au cours de la meditation et de l'extase Yogique. *Electroencephalogr Clin Neurophysiol Suppl* 6:211-219, 1955.
14. Anand BK, Chhina GS, Singh B: Studies on Shri Ramanand Yogi during his stay in an air-tight box. *Indian J Med Res* 49:82-89, 1961.
15. Bagchi BK, Wegner MA: Electrophysiological correlates of some Yogi exercises. *Electroencephalogr Clin Neurophysiol Suppl* 7:132-149, 1957.
16. Naranjo C, Ornstein R: *On the Psychology of Meditation.* New York, The Viking Press, 1971.
17. Gellhorn E, Kiely WF: Mystical states of consciousness: Neurophysiological and clinical aspects. *J Nerv Ment Dis* 154:399-405, 1972.
18. Kasamatsu A, Okuma T, Takenaka S, et al: The EEG of Zen and Yoga practitioners. *Electroencephalogr Clin Neurophysiol Suppl* 9:51-52, 1957.
19. Anand BK, Chhina GS, Singh B: Some aspects of electroencephalographic studies in Yogis. *Electroencephalogr Clin Neurophysiol* 13:452-456, 1961.
20. Wegner MA, Bagchi BK: Studies of autonomic functions in practitioners of Yoga in India. *Behav Sci* 6:312-323, 1961.
21. Karambelkar PV, Vinekar SL, Bhole MV: Studies on human subjects staying in an air-tight pit. *Indian J Med Res* 56:1282-1288, 1968.

22. Wallace RK: Physiological effects of Transcendental Meditation. *Science* 167:1751-1754, 1970.
23. Wallace RK, Benson H, Wilson AF: A wakeful hypometabolic physiological state. *Am J Physiol* 221:795-799, 1971.
24. Schwartz GE: Pros and cons of meditation: Current findings on physiology and anxiety, self-control, drug abuse and creativity. Read before the 81st annual convention of the American Psychological Association, Montreal, 1973.
25. Banquet JP: Spectral analysis of the EEG in meditation. *Electroencephalogr Clin Neurophysiol* 35:143-151, 1973.
26. Orme-Johnson DW: Autonomic stability and Transcendental Meditation. *Psychosom Med* 35:341-349, 1973.
27. Mundy-Castle AC, McKiever BL: The psychophysiological significance of the galvanic skin response. *J Exp Psychol* 46:15-24, 1953.
28. Katkin ES: Relationship between manifest anxiety and two indices of autonomic response to stress. *J Pers Soc Psychol* 2:324-333, 1965.
29. Katkin ES, McCubbin RJ: Habituation of the orienting response as a function of individual differences in anxiety and autonomic lability. *J Abnorm Psychol* 74:54-60, 1969.
30. Allison J: Respiration changes during Transcendental Meditation. *Lancet* 1:833-834, 1970.
31. Kasamatsu A, Hirai T: An electroencephalographic study on the Zen meditation (Zazen). *Psychologia* 12:205-225, 1969.
32. Akishige Y: A historical survey of the psychological studies in Zen. *Kyushu Psychol Stud* 11:1-56, 1968.
33. Hirai T: Electroencephalographic study on the Zen Meditation. *Psychiatr Neurol Japon* 62:76-105, 1960.
34. Sugi Y, Akutsu K: Studies on respiration and energy-metabolism during sitting in Zazen. *Res J Physiol El* 12:190-206, 1968.
35. Goyeche JRM, Chihara T, Shimizu H: Two concentration methods: A preliminary comparison. *Psychologia* 15:110-111, 1972.
36. Gibbs FA, Williams D, Gibbs EL: Modification of the cortical frequency spectrum by changes in CO_2, blood sugar, and O_2. *J Neurophysiol* 3:49-58, 1940.
37. Watanabe T, Shapiro D, Schwartz GE: Meditation as an anoxic state: A critical review and theory. *Psychophysiologia* 9:279, 1972.
38. Deikman AJ: Experimental meditation. *J Nerv Ment Dis* 136:329-343, 1963.
39. Deikman AJ: Implications of experimental meditation. *J Nerv Ment Dis* 142:101-116, 1966.
40. Ornstein R: *The Psychology of Consciousness.* San Francisco, WH Freeman, 1972.
41. Cohen W: Spatial and textural characteristics of the Ganzfeld. *Am J Psychol* 70:403-410, 1957.
42. Cohen W, Cadwallader TC: Cessation of visual experience under prolonged uniform visual stimulation. *Am Psychol* 13:410, 1958.
43. Lehmann D, Beeler GW, Fender DH: EEG responses during the observation of stabilized and normal retinal images. *Electroencephalogr Clin Neurophysiol* 22:136-142, 1967.

27

THE PHYSIOLOGY OF MEDITATION
AND MYSTICAL STATES OF CONSCIOUSNESS

Julian M. Davidson*

If the proper study of mankind is man, it is a paradox worth pondering that consciousness, the receptacle of all that is truly human, has not yet found a place in the life sciences. This is not to imply that neuroscientists are uninterested in physiological correlates and mechanisms of sleep and wakefulness, or that psychopharmacologists are not intensively investigating psychoactive drugs, and so forth. Rather, the experimentalist feels compelled to limit himself to considering physical or behavioral variables in order to comply with the dominant physicalist-reductionist paradigm of modern science. As far as scientific practice is concerned, consciousness is still regarded, at best, as an epiphenomenon. Similarly, if we had a science of consciousness, biochemical, physiological, and behavioral data might appear to it to be epiphenomena, for we have not even an inkling of how physical phenomena are linked to the "subjectively" manifested activity of consciousness.

There is no denying the very real philosophical and practical difficulties impeding the scientific investigation of psycho-physical interactions. But despite these difficulties and the past neglect of the subject, the current unprecedented public interest in the varieties of conscious experience is reflected in a number of research papers and theoretical analyses attempting to deal with physiological correlates of altered states of consciousness (ASCs). This survey is primarily concerned with one subset of this group: studies directed at physiological events during meditation. The specific questions on which I hope to shed some light are: (1) What conclusions can be drawn from existing physiological studies on meditating subjects? (2) How do these findings and other current concepts relate to mystical experience? (3) What, if any, reasonable approaches can be suggested for the future scientific study of these states of consciousness, given the currently available methodologies? Before engaging these issues, however, it is necessary to devote some attention to the nature and purposes of meditation and the claims of its proponents.

The Psychology of Meditation

"Meditation" is a term applied to a diverse group of practices having the common goal of producing in the short-term desired mental states, and in the long term the promotion of personality growth and mental health (traditionally referred to as "enlightenment"). These practices extend far back in recorded history and were previously most often taught within the context of religious (but not necessarily theistic) disciplines, so that the expected benefits have often been described in terms of spiritual progress. In the last few years, there has been an explosive increase of interest in meditation in the Western world, spearheaded

*Department of Physiology, Stanford University School of Medicine, Stanford, California 94305. I am grateful to my friend John Sundsten of the University of Washington Medical School for many discussions and helpful suggestions; to the Battelle Seattle Research Center for a year of study during which this paper was written; and to Richard J. Davidson and the members of an informal discussion group on consciousness which met in Seattle in 1975 for having read and discussed the manuscript.

by a variety of organizations operating within, or derived from the Hindu and Buddhist traditions. The most (numerically) successful of these is the (Students) International Meditation Society. While headed by a rather traditional Hindu guru, Maharishi Mahesh Yogi, and resting on ancient Vedic traditions, this organization disclaims any direct religious objective, preferring instead to represent its teachings as scientific [1]. Its professed aims are the transformation of man and the resulting solution of the world's problems [2]. Advocating a brand of meditation which it calls transcendental meditation (TM), it has had phenomenal success in many countries. Between 1968 and May 1974, 360,000 initiates were claimed in the United States alone [3, p. vi]. These include prominent public figures, including scientists, and resolutions of support have been introduced in Congress as well as in several state legislatures.

Since, particularly in the Hindu tradition, the pursuit of consciousness alteration is sought through postural and breathing exercises as well as through the mental practice of meditation, and since experienced yogis have often claimed unusual physical powers, there have been several investigations of physiological events in meditating yogis, as well as in Zen practitioners. The available published reports of these studies are few in number and preliminary in nature. Due to the active encouragement of the TM movement, however, several more authoritative reports have recently appeared in the scientific literature, and this trickle of studies together with others on the lasting effects of TM on psychological variables seems to be growing into a flood [3]. In a series of scientific [3, 4] and other publications [1, 2, 5], it has been proposed that the practice of TM leads to the experience of a fourth major state of consciousness (the first three being waking, dreaming, and nondreaming sleep states). This claim is extensively used in the publicizing and teaching of TM.

Perhaps because of Maharishi's scientific education and perhaps as a device to attract followers in Western technologically oriented countries, the TM movement has placed great stress on physiological responses in meditation and on scientific research on its psychological and medical effects. As a direct result of this, most of the relevant current research on meditation uses TM practitioners, and much of it enjoys the support if not sponsorship of the movement.

The unique value of TM for purposes of research is stated to be the uniformity of training and technique (e.g., [4]). This advantage may, however, be more apparent than real. There is nothing unique about the method itself, which is a simple *mantra* meditation technique involving relaxed sitting with upright spine, and the subvocal repetition of a traditional Hindu word (the *mantra*) with eyes closed in a quiet environment. No active attempt is made by the meditator to direct his experience, but he is encouraged to resist the intrusion of thoughts, albeit with minimum expenditure of effort. These techniques are used in many Eastern (and other) disciplines. Although the *mantra* is supposedly tailor-made for each initiate, it is difficult to check the validity of this claim, since the individual *mantras* and the method of choosing them are kept secret. However, personal contact between teacher and initiate is extremely brief prior to presentation of the *mantra*, and no overt testing procedures are involved.[1]

Beyond the unremarkable nature of the training of initiates and the procedures used in meditation, there is no reason to suspect anything unique or uniform about the *experiential* state resulting from the practice of TM. In addition, resemblances undoubtedly exist between the meditative experience and that induced in various relaxation therapies (such as self-hypnosis, progressive relaxation[7], autogenic therapy [8], and perhaps biofeedback training, particularly where electroencephalographic [EEG] alpha or theta rhythm training is involved [9]).

Proponents of meditation throughout history have aimed to induce certain peak experiences in which consciousness is profoundly altered. The attainability and importance of these experiences (*Satori, Samadhi, Kensho, Nirvana*, Cosmic Consciousness, etc.) is attested by a vast literature from many if not all of the major cultures [10-15], and both religious mystics and others have reported lasting positive effects on their lives (e.g., [16–18]). In fact, the psychiatric application of these experiences (including their usefulness in suicide prevention!) is being discussed [19–21]. Since meditation is recognized as an important (though neither necessary nor sufficient) gateway to the expanded states of consciousness described by the mystics of many traditions, one cannot ignore them in a discussion of meditation. However, any attempt to define these alterations in consciousness (which for want of a better term, I call

---

[1]The presentation of a *mantra* by guru to aspirant is an event of considerable significance in the Hindu tradition [6]. Regardless of any explicit or implicit assumptions about extraordinary powers of the *mantra*, however, it is an effective device for suppressing thoughts and producing inner-directed attention. It should be noted that the *mantra* is meaningless to the meditator, although in Christian meditation, phrases with religious content are similarly used.

"mystical experiences") quickly encounters a language barrier. The many descriptions of mystical experience are generally couched in literary-poetic and/or religious terms which are outside the framework of current scientific discourse.

Recent psychological evaluations [22–24] agree in describing certain common elements of mystical consciousness. These seem to be based generally on the list derived from careful analysis of the mystic literature by the philosopher Stace [13]: (a) deeply felt positive mood, described as "bliss," "peace," "love," etc.; (b) the essential experience of "unity," or "unison," which can be expressed as the oneness of all things, or decreased experience of the separateness of self from others or the outside world; (c) a sense of ineffability; (d) an enhanced sense of reality, authenticity, meaning; (e) alteration of time and space perception, experienced as transcendence of time and space; (f) paradoxicality, that is, the acceptance of propositions which in normal consciousness seem contradictory. Another characteristic stressed by some authors is a sense of sacredness [13, 23]. Between this and other items in the typology there may be overlap [15], but it would be a mistake to expect categorical uniqueness or precise psychological definition from a list such as this. These characteristics of mystical experience can be present to some extent in ASCs induced by psychopathology or other means [25] and particularly by psychedelic drugs [23]. Other characteristics of nonmystical ASCs would include a variety of alterations in thinking and in emotional expression, the experience of loss of psychological control, changes in body image, perceptual distortion, and hypersuggestibility [25]. Some of these are also present to some extent in "true" mystical experience.

Now, full-blown mystical experiences are clearly not common occurrences [17], apparently not even for full-time "mystics." Furthermore, the experiences are transient, often lasting only for minutes or seconds [17, 23, 24]. Clear, to catch such an occurrence red-handed, as it were, during an experimental study of meditation in normal subjects, would be a rather improbable happenstance. It is a point often glossed over in the literature on meditation that it deals *primarily* with a less profound alteration of consciousness than that of the full mystical experience, although some shared characteristics are presumably often present [22]. To avoid the resulting confusion, the term "mystical" should be reserved for those unique experiences some of whose psychologic characteristics have just been described, and whose putative physiologic correlates may differ greatly from those of "common" meditation, as we shall see.

A major difficulty in meditation research is that were is no way to validate objectively that a subject is indeed in the presumed meditative state. The problem is not merely the relatively trivial one of deception but, rather, arises from the fact that even practiced meditators are "successful" (in their own terms) only part of the time. Clearly, an important goal of this research should be to establish the kind of criteria which exist for sleep states (EEG, etc.) For the present, however, the only way to validate "successful meditation" is by the statement of the subject himself that he clearly recognizes having experienced the desired change in consciousness. Perception by the subject of qualitative alteration in his normal conscious experience is the description adopted by several authors for defining the term "altered state" [25, 26]. Painful though the reliance on subjective reports is to the scientist for whom all data must be "objective," that is, physically measurable, it cannot be avoided in any consideration of conscious states.

Notwithstanding the growing psychological literature on meditation, there is no agreement on an accepted core of psychological features, perhaps due to the many varieties of meditative practice. Certainly, however, a prominent feature of most, if not all, forms of meditation is a more or less profound sensory detachment from the external environment. This is also true of forms of meditation which involve concentration on a specific visual image (*mandala*) and, I believe, even of those Zen exercises wherein the reception of stimuli may be encouraged but without emotional impact or perhaps any effect except that of awareness itself. In all cases, a common result seems to be the achievement of a state in which the normal relationship between subject and internal or external environmental stimuli is abolished such that the latter do not operate in the normal way to control behavior of thought processes. In this sense, meditation departs from the normal waking state of consciousness which Hilgard defines as one in which we "can report accurately what is happening in the environment about us, and can use this information to control our behavior"[27]. To avoid the question of violation in meditation, the term "can" should be ignored, for our purposes.

Clearly, the sensory detachment in meditation is not related to a clouding of consciousness but, rather, to a prominent inner-directedness of attention. Yet a vital characteristic of successful meditation (particularly where concentrative practices are employed) is the active, or more often passive, suppression of thinking. This statement is valid using the most inclusive definition of thinking to comprise all such cognitive activities as daydreaming, dreaming, imagining, guessing, remembering, understanding, and especially problem solving; it refers particularly to verbal thinking (the "internal dialogue") but also, to a certain extent, to various nonverbal thinking processes. These cognitions are ubiquitous in the normal waking state but greatly reduced in successful meditation, and the many different exercises all seem primarily aimed at this end.

Physiological Changes in Meditation

Accepting that the successful practice of meditation may lead to a condition of consciousness whose distinctiveness and intensity vary to the extent that full-blown mystic experience is approached, what is the evidence for physical correlates of this state of consciousness which has led to the claims of psycho-physiological uniqueness [3, 4]? I shall discuss the available published data separately under the headings of autonomic-metabolic and of electrophysiologic variables. Studies on TM and those on Yoga and Zen will be considered together. The literature is at the moment sparse, but TM research is growing rapidly as attested, for example, by the number of these and unpublished reports listed in a recent annotated bibliography [3]. Most of the original studies on Zen meditation are only generally available through Akishige's book [28].[2]

Autonomic-Metabolic Effects

Studies on practitioners of TM have recorded the occurrence during meditation of significant decreases in heart rate, respiration rate, oxygen consumption and carbon dioxide elimination, arterial blood lactate titer, and minute ventilation, as well as significant decreases in skin conductance. No significant effects were obtained on systolic and diastolic blood pressures[3] and rectal temperature[3]. The findings are based primarily on the work of Wallace and collaborators [4, 31]. It is important to note that in these original studies the subjects served as their own controls, that is, the experimental session (one per subject) was sandwiched between two periods of control observation when he sat quietly without attempting to meditate; findings were related to the measurements in the preexperimental period. The question to be dealt with is whether these changes are, in fact, connected with the actual practice of meditation rather than being a byproduct of the experimental situation, and, if so, are they related specifically to the state or condition of consciousness during meditation?

First, let us look at the cardiovascular variables. Decreased heart rate has not been consistently found; for instance, a recent unpublished report on TM failed to find a decrease compared to a control group [32]. In the published reports, the changes were either not analyzed statistically [31, 33] or were marginally (if at all) significant [4]. A decrease in cardiac output was reported in the first TM study, but no data were given [33].

Since TM is derived from the Hindu tradition of yogic meditation, it is appropriate at this point to ask what physiological changes are found in meditating yogis. Unfortunately, properly controlled experiments with adequate numbers of subjects are not to be found in the literature. In one widely quoted study, Bagchi and Wenger [34] could find no consistent changes in heart rate. Relevant to this discussion, however, is the well-known claim of yogis to be able to slow or even stop the heart, the evidence for which is mostly anecdotal [35]. There is no proof that the heart can be stopped in this manner, although there seems little doubt that it can be slowed, a phenomenon which Bagchi and Wenger suggested was mediated (in three cases) by a Valsalva maneuver (expiratory movement with closed glottis, which decreases venous return to the heart) or (in one case) some other mechanism involving striated muscle [36]. The recent biofeedback literature is, however, replete with evidence of conscious control of heart rate (as well as blood pressure) and the interpretation by biofeedback researchers is that the effect is obtained by operant conditioning of autonomic nervous control of cardiac function [37]. When subjects are experienced in directly controlling

---

[2]This unique monograph unfortunately presents little "hard" data, and the physiological conclusions are mostly equivocal or uninterpretable. A recent book by Hirai [29] is more clearly written but describes in detail only the author's studies.

[3]But a chronic decrease in systolic blood pressure resulting from meditation has been reported in hypertensive patients [30].

the physiological function being measured, it is not logical to use measurements of that variable in establishing physiological correlates of the state of consciousness under study.

Changes in respiration are another case in point. Marked decreases in respiration rate are reported for Zen practitioners [28] and yogis [34]. It should be noted, however, that both these traditions place great stress on breathing: The breaths may be counted or merely observed and concentrated upon, and in some sects hyperventilation is practiced. Thus, it is again difficult to regard this measure as a dependent variable resulting from the practice of meditation since, in this case, it may be part of the technique used. In TM studies, total ventilation has often decreased, either due to decreased rate or tidal volume [4, 31, 33]. Again, the change (not so great as that cited in some studies of yogic [34] and Zen meditation [28]), was found to be significant in relation to a preexperimental control period in the same subjects. However, in a recent briefly reported study, minute volume (but not respiration rate) was decreased, both during TM and also in a control group instructed merely to sit quietly with eyes closed [38].

A similar situation applies to studies on metabolic rate. Much anecdotal evidence indicates the ability of trained yogis to exist under conditions of restricted oxygen supply—one trick being the incarceration of the yogi in a box or pit for prolonged periods. In one study, a very marked reduction of oxygen consumption (up to 40–50% at one point) was reported from a yogi incarcerated in an air-tight box (6 × 4 × 4 feet) for 8 hours [39]. Decreased oxygen consumption is also reported in Zen meditators [28, p. 19; 29].

The decreased oxygen consumption reported for TM subjects was accompanied by the decrease in CO_2 production as well as in blood lactate,[4] with no change in respiratory quotient. The differences were significant in relation to the preexperimental control observations on the same subjects. These results were recently replicated, using an improved continuous recording technique, although the magnitude of change found was considerably less [42]. Although unpublished work (cited in [3, pp. 75, 76]) suggested that control groups did not show the oxygen consumption effect, Treichel et al. [38] have reported decreased CO_2 elimination both in the experimental (TM) and in a separate control group. They concluded that the decreased metablism "was not necessarily related to the practice of the technique."

There is one recently reported finding which may modify the force of what has just been said. Beary and Benson [43] trained volunteers with a meditative procedure, which produces what they call the "relaxation response." The essentials of the training (which lasted no more than 1 hour in any of the subjects) were: sitting quietly, relaxing deeply, maintaining a passive attitude, and the use of a modified *mantra* procedure in which the breaths were followed and the word "one" was repeated subvocally on each expiration. In this study, a 13% decrease in oxygen consumption, a 12% decrease in carbon dioxide elimination, and a decrease in respiration rate from 16 to 11 breaths per minute were reported. These differences were statistically significant, and the experiment was well controlled. For the reasons discussed, no great significance can be attached to changes in respiration frequency, which are also not uniformly found in meditation studies. The work of Beary and Benson does, however, indicate that meditative techniques, even when very newly learned, can result in a greater change in metabolic rate than that found in control periods when subjects merely sat and relaxed. The fact that similar effects were reported by Treichel et al. [38] in separate control groups and that changes in the same direction are found in relaxation, sleep, and meditation do nevertheless suggest that judgment be suspended as to any claim for the uniqueness of reduced metabolism in meditation.

Like the other autonomic changes discussed, increases in skin resistance, or reductions in its fluctuations, known as galvanic skin reflexes (GSR), have been related to low levels of anxiety or "arousal," and are, therefore, of special interest. This effect has also been reported for Yogic [32] and Zen [26] meditators. The large increases in resistance found in the studies of Wallace and co-workers [4, 29] were impressive, especially since restoration of the control levels was found in the postmeditation period. In a more systematic study, specifically devoted to electrodermal response, Orme-Johnson [41] did not find such striking effects on basal skin resistance, and the study on experienced Yogis [32] showed less effect than that found by Wallace. Although Bagchi and Wenger [32] mentioned the occurrence of large spontaneous oscillations of the GSR, Orme-Johnson's study demonstrated fewer spontaneous GSR's in TM practitioners. Spontaneous GSR's were also low in practiced meditators outside of meditation and they

---

[4]The finding of decreased blood lactate during TM has been tied to the hypothesis that increased blood lactate is a, or the, cause of anxiety [40]. However, the "lactate theory of anxiety" has recently been subjected to serve critical analysis [41] in a review which pointed out inadequacies in experimental evidence and interpretation. Thus, in the experimental stimulation of anxiety by infusions of lactate, the nonnatural (racemic) form was used, and conditions were described in which the postulated correlation between anxiety and elevated blood lactate was absent.

Physiology of Meditation

showed faster habitation and fewer multiple responses during habituation. These findings were taken to imply greater "behavioral stability."

Recently, studies on circulating levels of hormones and various metabolites before, during, and after TM have been initiated by Jevning and collaborators [41a, 41b]. No striking changes have been found although preliminary reports indicate that there is a small decline in plasma cortisol in long-term (3–5 years) practitioners, but no change in prolactin level [41a]. Phenylalanine concentration increased significantly by 20% in the same subjects, but not other amino acids [41b]. In a collaborative unpublished study with the author's laboratory, Jevning found no change in plasma testosterone, another hormone known to respond to "stress," although the meditators did not show the decline during the postmeditation period which was found in controls.

How are we to evaluate the significance of these changes in terms of the postulated physiological uniqueness of meditation? As pointed out by Kanellakos and Lukas [3], the autonomic-metabolic changes reported to occur in TM are also found during sleep, although obviously other changes occur during sleep which are not found in meditation. The implication is that the changes in TM are more rapid and, in some cases, more profound than attained with sleep [4, 2—p. 343]. This is not clearly established, at least for the respiratory, cardiovascular, and other autonomic-metabolic functions which have been studied. Of course, considerable variation in these kinds of measures is found in relationship to stages of sleep, and sufficiently extensive and controlled studies comparing sleep and meditation have not yet been published.

A new development is the demonstration in several recent unpublished studies [42, 43, 44] that even experienced TM meditators may pass a considerable portion of the session in EEG-validated sleep. In a carefully controlled study [49] with subjects who had 2.5 or more years' experience (including some teachers of TM), blind scoring of the EEG records showed that 23 percent of the time was spent in stage II sleep and 17 percent in stages III and IV. Overall, sleep times did not differ significantly between periods of meditation and other periods when the subjects were asked to nap. It should be noted that these findings are not relative to the question of the benefits of TM and that trainees are in fact taught not to resist sleep. They are, however, highly relevant to the contention that the experimental findings provide important support for meditation as a unique psycho-physiological state.

In summary, all that is clearly established by the data on autonomic-metabolic measurements during meditation is the hardly surprising conclusion that meditators are in a state of relaxation. The somatic component of this state—muscular relaxation—has been documented in several studies showing very low electromyographic activity [3, p. 11; 28; 50; 51]. The lack of nonmeditating control subjects in the most authoritative (and widely publicized) experiments of Wallace was a serious defect, and it is still highly questionable whether some or all of the changes noted might not be regularly present in nonmeditating individuals sitting relaxedly with their eyes closed and occasionally napping. This conclusion is amply confirmed by a study on subjects selected for hypnotic suggestability, published while this manuscript was being prepared [52]. Autonomic measures were compared during meditation (TM) or autohypnosis or in controls simply instructed to relax and "reduce autonomic function." All groups showed significant decreases in heart and respiration rates and GSR (basal and discrete responses). There were no significant differences between the groups, although the decline in heart rate persisted after meditation for at least 10 min, an effect which was not found in the other groups or with the other measures. At any rate, the claims that (a) TM represents a state of profound physiological rest, greater than that attainable with sleep of much longer duration; and (b) the specific changes in consciousness and the unique (and, in my opinion, unquestionable) benefits of meditation are somehow linked to the physiologic changes discussed above still seem to lack a solid basis in experimental fact.

Cerebral Electrophysiologic Effects

EEG changes in meditation have been very scantily reported in earlier studies on four yogis by Anand et al. [53], on seven Kundalini Yoga practitioners by Das and Gastaut [51], on 48 Zen monks by Kasematsu and Hirai [54], and in a variety of other studies apparently accessible to the non-Japanese reader only through the rather unclear and inconsistently documented compendium of Akishige [28]. Some EEG data on TM meditators were sketchily presented by Wallace [31] and Wallace et al. [4], and a study with spectral analysis has been reported by Banquet [55], the latter being the most detailed study devoted specifically to EEG measurements. A survey of the results of these studies follows.

The most common findings are of changes in incidence and/or properties of the alpha rhythm (8–13 Hz). While considering them, it should be borne in mind that the highest incidence of this rhythm is found in the normal waking state when recordings are made from occipital leads with eyes closed. The case made by Lynch and co-workers [56] that increases above this base line cannot be obtained even during biofeedback training of the alpha rhythm has not been disproven at the time of writing. Thus the commonly reported high alpha densities in meditation may well result from the same process apparently operating in biofeedback studies: the disinhibition of stimuli (oculomotor, attentional, etc.) which block alpha frequencies. Banquet [55] reports topographical extension of alpha during meditation from posterior to frontal leads and its maintenance into the postexperimental eyes-open condition. The studies of Zen subjects almost invariably report increased alpha density [28, 54] through all regions of the scalp from which EEG is recorded. Zen meditation is conducted with the eyes open, while in TM the eyes are closed. Increases in amplitude of alpha waves were also reported in Zen and TM [28, 31, 55]. Another finding common to various studies is a decrease in alpha *frequency* (i.e., shift to lower end of frequency band) during the course of meditation [28, 31, 54, 55]

These findings on the alpha rhythm are probably reliable, but more because of the frequency with which they have been reported than because of the convincing nature of the individual studies. Although the data of Banquet were quantitatively processed (by spectral analysis), the tendency in all of these studies was merely to report conclusions or samples of the data, and in no case were experimental groups statistically compared to controls. In fairness to the investigators, one notes that until recently this mode of data presentation was the norm for EEG studies. Nevertheless, these weaknesses must affect our judgments of the other EEG findings which, unlike the above changes in alpha, have not been repeatedly observed.

Several investigators have studied the alpha blocking response to clicks or visual stimuli (orientation response). Anand et al. [53] reported the absence of alpha blocking during meditation when a variety of stimuli were presented to a small group of yogis,[5] and Banquet [55] obtained similar findings in TM subjects presented with clicks or flashes. On the other hand, Kasematsu and Hirai [54] reported absence of habituation of the response following repeated presentation of click stimuli in three Zen masters, and extensions of this study were recently reported [29]. These diametrically opposed findings on Zen and yogic meditators have been interpreted as reflecting differences in the two types of disciplines. It is said that the yogic meditator develops an inner-directed awareness in which external stimuli are excluded, while an objective of Zen is to retain full awareness of the outside world, although remaining "unaffected" by it [57, 58]. The implication is that in the former case afferent stimuli are blocked at below the cortical level, while in the latter case attention is somehow deployed in such a fashion that environmental input is received but without emotional impact [54].

How meaningful this interpretation may be is not the major point at issue but, rather, the need for replication, since none of the reports presented adequate support for their striking findings. Apart from the small number and the absence of statistical validation, there is the question of how to evaluate alpha blocking in Zen meditation with eyes open [54]. The comparison to controls where eyes were closed and whose initial blocking time (before habituation) was longer than in the meditators seems questionable. It should be noted parenthetically that Wallace [31] mentioned finding absence of habituation of alpha, which does not support the above interpretation, since his TM meditators "should" have been in a state of environmental detachment more like that of the yogic than the Zen practitioners.

Another finding in EEG studies on meditation is the occasional appearance of trains of theta waves (4–7 Hz) [4, 31, 54, 55]. In Banquet's experiment these could be blocked by click stimulation, with reappearance of theta within a few seconds in Zen monks, "the rhythmical theta train (6 to 7 cycles per second 70–100 μV)" was found only in subjects having spent more than 20 years in Zen training and rated as highly proficient in meditation by the Zen master [54].

If the EEG record can indeed reflect simultaneous shifts in conscious experience, it is important that the electrophysiological data be correlated with whatever subjective changes are found during the recording session. In the two best studies [54, 55], account was taken of different "levels" or "depths" of meditation. Banquet asked his subjects to signal major changes in consciousness by pressing a button, using a five-signal code to distinguish occurrence of "body sensations, involuntary movements, visual imagery,

---

[5]Subjects were also reported to maintain alpha with hands immersed in ice cold water for 45 min.

deep meditation and transcendence (deepest point of meditation)." Presentation of the last two signals by the subjects was correlated with appearance of generalized fast frequencies of the dominant beta rhythm. The frequency was "almost constant" at about 20 cycles per second, and high-voltage patterns were present in anterior channels. Similar high-frequency patterns were found in yogis in deep meditation in a brief report by Das and Gastaut [51], and these were of high amplitude in the one subject stated to have attained the state of *Samadhi* during the experiment.

From the perspective of this paper, the important question is whether the reported EEG changes are significantly different from those one would expect to find in various conditions of sleep and wakefulness. If meditation were not unique, one might expect initially a background of high alpha (as in a relaxed state with eyes closed) shifting to increasingly slower frequencies when the subject becomes drowsy and sleepy and to faster ones when focused cognitive activity occurs. Banquet [55] argues that the patterns in meditation do indeed differ from the normal drowsy or alert states. Thus, in drowsiness one sees mixed frequencies—alpha, low delta, and discontinuous theta—whereas his meditating subjects (like those of Kasematsu and Hirai [54]) showed continuous trends of dominant theta rhythm at constant frequency, which persisted when the eyes were opened postexperimentally. The low voltage fast activity (in spindle-like amplitude modulation) appeared on a background of slow frequencies, whereas activated EEG's in the control group were found "without any rhythmicity or regularity." In favor of the uniqueness of the EEG findings, he also states that they were accompanied by (*a*) absence or decrease of EEG response to click or light stimulation and (*b*) persistence of alertness which allowed the subject to respond to questions of the experimenter and to push buttons to signal his internal state. In addition, he stresses the topographical alterations, specifically synchronization of brainwaves from anterior and posterior regions: spread of alpha from occipito-parietal to anterior channels and of theta and beta from frontal to more posterior regions.

Banquet's claim of unique electrophysiological phenomena merits serious consideration if the findings are indeed statistically significant. Quantitative comparisons with controls in various stages of wakefulness, relaxation, and sleep are essential, especially in view of the recent findings on sleep during TM.

The scientific importance of such validation goes beyond the need for elucidating the nature of changes in meditation. In the half-century since Hans Berger, establishment of the EEG correlates of behavior and conscious experience has been a will-o'-the-wisp chased frequently and generally fruitlessly. What successes have been obtained are in the area of evoked potential measurements in relation to attention and reactions to stimuli [59] but not to conscious experience per se. If the history of failure is now being reversed, this is an event of sufficient significance to justify attempts at adequate replication of the findings under the most rigorous conditions and with the fullest possible reporting of data.

Résumé

We have seen that, although physiological changes do occur during meditation, it is not yet established that these changes are unique or that they reveal a "fourth major state of consciousness" as has been claimed. What then do these changes mean? How do they relate to alterations of conscious experience? In particular, what is their relationship to the more intense and unique mystical experience to which meditation can lead? Since, as should be obvious by now, the existing data are not sufficient to generate definitive answers to these questions, the rest of this paper will be largely speculative, depending as it does on a meager data base and the few relevant conceptual approaches available in the literature. Although such poorly based speculation is distasteful to most experimental scientists, it is justified by the need for further research in this area whose importance and interest I shall briefly reiterate: (1) Reportedly, hundreds of thousands of individuals have recently begun to practice meditation in the United States alone, and there is a widespread belief based on reasonable evidence that beneficial medical and/or psychological effects result [3, 60–62]. (2) The occurrence of mystical experience in people of many cultures, religions, and historical periods, though presumably rare, is extensively documented, as are its potential profound beneficial effects [10–21]. (3) Despite its undoubted diversity, there are enough common characteristics to allow us to look at mysticism as a definite category of experience [13].

Autonomic-Somatic Integration

The established physiologic changes in meditation are indicative of a level of activation or arousal[6] which is low, but not so low as to preclude maintenance of the waking state. This is manifested (*a*) in various functions related to sympathetic activity (or the presence of a low sympathetic/parasympathetic activity ratio), for example, heart rate, respiration, sweating; (*b*) in function of cerebral cortex (slowing and synchronization of EEG); and (*c*) in skeletal muscle which is maximally relaxed consistent only with maintenance of upright posture.

That this triad of cerebral, peripheral-autonomic, and skeletal muscle functions is far from a random assembly has been amply demonstrated in the extensive and fascinating, but neglected, work of the neurophysiologist Gellhorn [65, 66], who elaborated the concepts of autonomic-somatic relationships organized by Hess [67]. Based on Hess's pioneering investigation on hypothalmic stimulation in freely moving cats, it was shown that conditions leading to increased sympathetic nervous discharges (environmental, visceral, or brain stimulation) are accompanied by cerebral cortical activation. To characterize this coordinated complex of sympathetic-visceral, cerebral, behavioral, and skeletal muscle reactions (which are adaptive for emergency situations), Hess [67] coined the term "ergotropic activation." Rage induced by hypothalamic stimulation represents an extreme point on the ergotropic continuum. In contrast, stimuli which increase parasympathetic activation are associated with effects (presumed to be adaptive for cellular restitution) which include sleep-like EEG activity, decreased muscle tone, and behavioral quiescence. This complex of events, the mirror image of ergotropic activation, was termed "trophotropic." The two sets of events were presumed to depend on the activity of two anatomically separate systems represented at all levels of the nervous system.

Gellhorn made a major contribution to the neurophysiological validation of this scheme. He also devoted much effort to working out presumed relationships between ergotropic and trophotropic activation under a variety of circumstances and applying these concepts of emotional behavior in animals as well as (more speculatively) to human emotions. Admittedly, his attempt to show that wide areas of behavior and consciousness depend closely on the balance between activation of the two systems remains speculative, and the applications of specific situations are often vague. Nevertheless, Gellhorn's thinking on these problems, often heavily documental by data from his and other laboratories [65, 66], remains unique, and there seems to be no other comparable framework from which to consider the psychophysiology of meditative and mystic experience.

Gellhorn's concept of ergotropic-trophotropic "tuning" assumed that peripheral or central ergotropic or trophotropic stimulation alters the reactivity of the central nervous system. During ergotropic or trophotropic activation within a moderate range, a principle of reciprocity between the two systems is manifested, such that activation of one tends to suppress activity in the other. Furthermore, there is congruence between the cerebral or peripheral-autonomic and somatic components of the system, that is, in normal circumstances they are activated in concert. However, at more intense levels of activation (or in "stressful" circumstances), there is a breakdown of reciprocity and congruence. The resulting "imbalances" result in paradoxical responses to stimuli (with high ergotropic activation, trophotropic stimuli may have ergotropic effects and vice versa), and finally simultaneous ergotropic and trophotropic discharges occur. These breakdowns of reciprocity and congruence form, in Gellhorn's opinion, the physiological basis for many types of psychopathology and altered states of consciousness (see examples below). The changes which Gellhorn presents as resulting from noxious stimuli are fitted to Pavlov's behavioral description of experimental neurosis [68], although he replaced emphasis on the cortex with a more hypothalamically centered mechanism. Thus Pavlov's "equivalent," "paradoxical," and "ultraparadoxical" phases of experimental neurosis correspond to changes in hypothalamic "tuning," with corticopetal discharges influencing behavior and "downward discharges" affecting somatic-visceral functions. The common theme is that, in stressful situations producing aberrant behavioral-conscious states, there are major shifts in responses to stimuli, and Gellhorn has documented this for many situations such as anoxia, hypoglycemia, fever, pain, sleep deprivation, sensory deprivation, and narcolepsy, wherein departures from ergotropic-trophotropic reciprocity and congruence occur [65, 66].

---

[6]I prefer to avoid the term "arousal." This concept, so widely used in psychology, is of dubious ontological status [63] and explanatory value [64]. Both it and "activation" are too often applied to systems (e.g., the whole organism) which seldom, if ever, respond globally.

Meditation and the Ergotropic-Trophotropic Systems

Procedures used in meditation are well adapted to elicitation of trophotropic reactions. Common to many meditative disciplines are sensory isolation and physical immobility with maximal relaxation of the skeletal muscles consistent with an upright spine. In the Hindu-Buddhist traditions, this is obtained by sitting in the lotus or similar positions[7] in a nondisturbing environment. However, the advanced practitioner can dispense with the need for maximal environment isolation, presumably due to skillful application of selective attention.

Based on various lines of evidence from his own and other laboratories, Gellhorn demonstrated rather convincingly the central role of proprioceptive input from muscle spindles in maintaining ergotropic activation. Thus, stimulation of these afferents increase heart rate, while curare-like drugs, which immobilize skeletal muscle, inhibit ergotropic responsiveness [65, 70]. A positive feedback loop appears to be operating here in that increased muscle tone produces diffuse ergotropic activation, while the latter, induced by other means, results in increased muscle tone. According to Gellhorn, the ergotropic-trophotropic balance may be determined to a considerable extent by the intensity of proprioceptive discharges.[8] It should be pointed out parenthetically that the resulting low level of muscular activity in meditation may be the cause of the reported decrease in oxygen consumption. This suppression of muscular activity, widely used in meditation as well as in a variety of relaxation therapies (autogenic, hypnosis, progressive relaxation, systematic desensitization, etc.), is thus viewed as facilitating a state of trophotropic dominance, with result in cerebral, metabolic, and visceral changes. The same end is served by restriction of other sensory inputs in meditation, for example, environmental isolation, avoidance of the postprandial period, and eye closing. Attending to the respirations or a *mantra*, etc., blocks normal cognitive activity, incidentally preventing the intrusion of emotionally arousing thoughts, which again reinforces the trophotropic state.

In a rather sketchy and somewhat confusing paper published shortly before his death, Gellhorn, in fact, attempted to apply his concepts to meditation and mystical states of consciousness [19]. Apart from pointing out the generally trophotropic nature of the meditative state, it was suggested that "some degree of ergotropic excitation exists" in meditation. This mention of a measure of ergotropic drive in the face of a predominantly trophotropic situation was said to be reflected in the nonhabituation of EEG alpha block [54]. On the other hand, the mystical state of yogic ecstasy was characterized as predominantly ergotropic, based on the findings of Das and Gastaut [51]. However, the low EMG with desynchronized EEG and increased heart rate reported by these authors was interpreted [19, 65] as an example of "imbalance" in the two systems, very similar to that existing in REM sleep.

The article by Gellhorn and Kiely [19] was sharply criticized by Mills and Campbell [58] on the following bases: (1) The concepts of ergotropic and trophotropic activation are vague, difficult to validate experimentally in man, and therefore not experimentally testable. In general, the inadequacy of current scientific data on this subject was stressed. (2) There was a failure to recognize the difference between different forms of Yoga and Zen. Particular stress was placed on the extrapolation of the nonhabituation of alpha block in Zen subjects to all forms of meditation, ignoring the very different reports on yogis showing absence of alpha block [53]. (3) It was pointed out that the report of Das and Gastaut [51] was the only one in which "acceleration" of the EEG was found during meditation. In the absence of replication, Mills and Campbell reject the evidence of ergotropic activation in *Samadhi*.

Clearly the first point of Mills and Campbell is well taken. But the inadequacy of available data is a two-edged sword in this debate, for the authors also support their contentions with an uncritical acceptance of poor data. As to the differences among various meditative disciplines, the interpretation [11, 29, 57, 58] that the discrepant findings of Kasematsu and Hirai [54] and Anand et al. [53] reflect differences in philosophy practice, and goals of Yoga and Zen is a premature conclusion in terms of the existing data, as we have discussed earlier.

---

[7]Though Westerners most often meditate while sitting in chairs, the skilled lotus sitter is presumably at an advantage in being able to sit with maximum stability for prolonged periods of time. The importance of the stable, balanced, relaxed posture is often stressed (e.g., [28, pp. 26–27, 105–134]). It prevents sleep as well as supposedly having other desirable effects on respiration and physiologic functions [69].

[8]Apart from the general effects, the possibility was discussed that proprioceptive input from facial muscles may have a specifically important role in emotional experience [66], a sugestion supported by recent psychophysiologic work (see n. 10).

More so, however, this kind of interpretation implies that we are dealing with well-defined differences in psychological state, to which physiological mechanisms can be applied. But rather than supplying precise descriptions of the nature of meditative or mystical experience, the writings of the mystics are clothed in metaphor and symbolism. Traditional Zen literature particularly shies away from psychological descriptions of mystic experience. Even the writings of modern academic scholars of Zen (e.g., [28, 71]) are not easily translatable into the terms of modern scientific discourse. This literature is often more concerned with the desirable characteristics of the enlightened individual than with the psychological phenomenology of the *Satori* experience. The many different Hindu, Buddhist, and other disciplines certainly differ in their philosophies, and no doubt there are psychological differences in the experiential results obtained. But as pointed out by Kiely [72] in his rebuttal to Mills and Campbell [58], there is no acceptable evidence of parallel physiological differences.

That mystical states are experientially and presumably physiologically quite different from meditative ones is often not sufficiently recognized. Mills and Campbell [58] make much of the difference between the usual EEG findings in studies on meditation and those of Das and Gastaut [51]. But the latter is the only experimental report in which it was frankly claimed that data were obtained during actual mystical experience (*Samadhi*), though similar claims are tentatively advanced for some of the findings of Hirai [29, 54]. Certainly, the brief report of Das and Gastaut on increased heart rate, hyperaroused EEG, and flat EMG, though striking, is rather insufficient evidence on which to base the conclusion that yogic *Samadhi* shows (*a*) a strong ergotropic component and (*b*) noncongruence between the different components of the system reflecting the breakdown of ergotropic-trophotropic balance [19, 65]. However, other lines of evidence can be found to support this thesis, and these will now be discussed.

As mentioned earlier, Banquet [55] also reported desynchronized EEG in advanced meditators during very deep meditation. Second, from a large variety of first-hand descriptions of enlightenment experiences from Buddhist, Hindu, or other sources, the subject appears to be in a state of great excitement [16–18, 73]. The assumption seems reasonable that their autonomic-somatic condition is ergotropic. The suggested progression from trophotropic meditation to ergotropic ecstacy quite possibly involves mechanisms of the type described by Gellhorn: either "imbalance" resulting from intense prolonged trophotropic activation, or the postulated "rebound" of the ergotropic system, whereby after *cessation* of trophotropic excitation, strong ergotropic activation supervenes.

Unfortunately, this "model" of the induction of mystical expeiences does not by any means cover all the known situations. Thus, among the many practices of the many mystical sects are some which certainly induce ergotropic rather than trophotropic conditions in the subject. Two examples will suffice: the circling dances of the Sufi Whirling Dervishes [11, p. 155] and the practice of *Ishiguro* Zen, which includes prolonged shouting and violent abdominal contractions [28]. In these cases, the *approach* to the mystical experience would be ergotropic, although we know little if anything about physiological conditions *during* the experiences induced by such means. They may well be trophotropic; at least, this is suggested by analogy with a variety of situations described in a recent interesting semi-scientific book by Sargant [74] which merits some discussion.

Based on Pavlov's descriptions of experimental neurosis in dogs and his own experiences with abreaction therapy for treating battle neuroses, Sargant proposes a succession of events which, among other effects, leads to profoundly altered states of consciousness. When people undergo extreme excitation, induced either by psychologic or intense sensory stimuli, a stage is reached when the subject collapses, and extreme changes of mental and physical state supervene involving altered states of consciousness and greatly heightened suggestibility. Sargant points out that similar techniques have been used in many cultures for thousands of years in the successful treatment of psychosomatic or mental illness (as in exorcism) or to induce altered states of consciousness for religious or other purposes.

The relationship of these events to hypnotic suggestion is stressed, and Sargant draws an interesting analogy to sexual activity (a temporary state of extreme "brain excitation" leading to collapse and transient inhibition). His major concern, however, is the religious-type conversion. In a survey of shamanistic rites in many tribal cultures, he shows the ubiquity of such methods as dancing, chanting, and hyperventilating leading to frenzied states which result in collapse and "trance" states. In our own culture, preachers (or pop music heroes!) may whip people into a frenzy of excitement by charismatic evangelistic oratory, singing, dancing, etc. In the resulting organismic switch into a state of mental and physical collapse, the subjects may be in a hypersuggestible condition and may also experience extreme alteration of consciousness, which can be interpreted in a religious context. Both of these are conducive to religious conversions or changes in belief systems. Other authors have described the important role of altered states of consciousness in shamanistic healing [75]. A recent example is seen in the current revival of shamanistic rites among the Salish Indians of British Columbia which reportedly is achieving therapeutic success in cases where Western psychiatry has failed [76].

The points of resemblance between the Pavlovian phenomena and those described by Gellhorn and by Sargant are certainly sufficient to indicate that all were describing essentially similar *physiologic* states although interpreted in different terms. A point of commonality is sudden shifts in organismic state related to prolonged or intense autonomic activation or other "stressful" forms of stimulation. I would postulate that such conditions in general tend to be correlated with experience of altered states of consciousness and that they may be approached either from the ergotropic or trophotropic side. For instance, a rapid ergotropic to trophotropic shift is found in orgasm, which can be regarded as an altered state of consciousness, albeit short-lived. The opposite switch from trophotropic to (relative) ergotropic dominance is seen in the transition from slow wave to REM sleep, which is accompanied by a profound alteration in consciousness, and in sensory deprivation experiments [77, 78] where hallucinogenic activity is correlated with increased ergotropic activation (increased heart rate, EEG arousal, etc.). A shift in the same direction can be induced by raising and then rapidly lowering body temperature. Unpublished experiments by R. Crist have demonstrated that when the oral temperature is raised to about 103°F by immersion in a hot bath and then the subject is immediately transferred to a cold bath, a major alteration of consciousness occurs, including kinesthetic sensations (tumbling) and perceptual alterations.[9]

Now it is not being argued that the circumstances described by these workers necessarily involve mystical experiences but only that profound altered states of consciousness may result, leading to equally profound effects on the individual's behavior and future belief system. That similar physiological phenomena may be common to mystical and other forms of altered states of consciousness is a major theme of this essay that I shall develop further in due course. Sargant himself extends his analysis to traditional mystical states, but to fit them into his Pavlovian scheme he has to create a rather strained analogy between concentrative meditation and focal excitation of one area of the cortex in the experiments of Pavlov [68]. But Sargant's work is not helpful to us in terms of specific or up-to-date physiologic thinking.

To return to the major question under consideration, it appears that mystical states may be experienced (or approached) during either ergotropic- or trophotropic-dominated conditions; at least where is no adequate rationale for limiting it to either condition. In a rather fanciful though interesting article, Fischer [79] in fact claims that the mystic may switch between extreme ergotropic and extreme trophotropic forms of mystical experience. This is equated to the rebound phenomenon concept which Gellhorn developed; it is basically Pavlov's mechanism of protective inhibition which is conceived as a homeostatic device encountered in experimental neurosis. Unfortunately, Fischer presents no direct evidence for what he calls the "loop connecting the two extreme exalted states." But the important question at this point is: How is it possible for mystical experiences (which we know to have important common features regardless of when, where, and by whom experienced) to be related to such diverse physiological circumstances? The next section deals with considerations bearing on this issue.

The Psychology of Emotions

In order to appreciate the likely constraints on the relevance of physiological variables to conscious experience in meditative and mystical states, it will be helpful to note how psychologists have dealt with similar problems in the context of emotions. A tradition dating back through Cannon to William James has attempted to "explain" feelings and emotions in terms of the commonly observed, concomitant activation of autonomic nervous activity. The ubiquity of these visceral phenomena in affective states suggests a role in humans beyond Cannon's and Hess's characterizations of sympathetic/parasympathetic events as preparatory for fight-and-flight or for restitution of bodily functions. However, the general nonspecificity of autonomic changes makes them unlikely candidates as specific mediators for the great variety of

---

[9]This phenomenon is enhanced by (and may require?) small doses of sympathomimetic drugs. It may not be irrelevant to mention the recent tragic death of Crist from drowning while experimenting with this procedure.

emotional experience. In fact, despite many attempts [80, 81], there is no satisfactory classification of emotion in terms of visceral events [82], that is, no known physiological event(s) is (are) diagnostic for a given type of conscious experience or of emotional behavior.

The way in which psychophysiology has dealt with this problem in the last decade or so has been to postulate an interaction between visceral phenomena and cognitive variables in the determination of affective state and emotional behavior. The key experiment is that of Shachter and Singer [83]. These investigators injected epinephrine (adrenalin) or a placebo into groups of subjects who expected vitamin injections. The subjects were then exposed to a confederate who feigned either anger or euphoria about the experiment and the investigator. Some of the subjects were told to expect sympathomimetic effects of the "vitamin." Subjects not receiving the epinephrine *or* warned about the physiological effects did not become emotional. Those receiving epinephrine *and* exposed to the angry confederate felt angry and behaved accordingly, while those injected *and* exposed to the euphoric confederate became euphoric. The conclusion was that the presence of physiological-autonomic responses influence the extent to which emotion in general is felt, while social influences can determine the type of emotional response accompanying the physiological changes. A considerable body of literature (see [84]) has grown up around this now classic study. Emotions depend on a large variety of real and imagined internal and external cues[10] interacting in a complex evaluative process. The emotional experience "is particularly affected by a person's attributions of the casuality, intent and extent of those factors" [88].

The (conscious or potentially conscious) attitudes, expectations, and desires (which shall be referred to collectively as cognitive variables) play an important role in emotional experience and behavior in normal waking consciousness. Can we expect similar effects in conditions of profound alterations of consciousness such as are seen in mystical states? To support the positive answer which I would give to this question, the following are examples of experimentally demonstrated situations in which altered states of consciousness, presumably dependent on physiological changes, are profoundly affected by such cognitive variables.

The crucial importance of psychological set and environmental setting in determining the nature of the experience of major and minor psychedelic drugs is well known [26, 89–91]. Conscious experience and behavior under hypnosis are largely determined by cognitive variables, so much so that there are no demonstrated specific physiologic correlates of hypnosis [90]. Investigations on the experimental control of dream content show that the setting of the experiment and the relationship between experimenter and subject have important effects on the dream experience [92]. Other areas where the conscious or quasiconscious attribution of meaning or significance importantly affects experiential (and physiological) aspects of emotion are sexual arousal [93], anxiety [41], pain [69], and, most dramatically, collective psychoses [94].

At this point, I feel the need to respond to the anticipated criticism of those who believe that all psychological phenomena will ultimately be explained in neurophysiological terms (as probably do the great majority of biologists). To these, the distinction between physiological and cognitive variables may appear artificial, since the latter can be thought of as phenomena which have simply not yet been reduced to physiologic terms. A slowly increasing number of philosophically inclined biologists seem to be arriving at a position which lies somewhere between the classical reductionist viewpoint and the old vitalism [95, 96]. Without taking a stand on this issue. I would simply point out that since we have no concept of what might be the physiological counterpart of the cognitive variables under discussion, it is of no consequence, in the present context, how this class of variables is labeled. For those who will be more comfortable with such a formulation, however, we can speak of "overt physiological variables" for these physiological correlates which have been identified, and "covert physiological" can be substituted for the word "cognitive."

Finally, there are some experimental observations which might be thought of as providing an animal model for these phenomena. The identical electrical stimulation of a single brain locus can be shown to have very different effects on behavior depending on the "motivational" state of the animal at the time of experimentation [97]. This is equivalent to the "set" mentioned in the above examples; "setting" (concurrent environmental influences) also plays an important role in the outcome of intracerebral stimulation in animals [98]. This kind of observation may be regarded as a starting point for research which

---

[10]These may include the individual's behavioral responses themselves [85]; *false* information on his autonomic responses [86]; and his facial expression: arranging a person's features in a happy position will tend to make him feel happy [87]!

might begin to convert some of the covert physiological variables to overt ones, without regard for the (philosophic) issue of whether such conversion could ever be total.

Cognitive Variables and the Mystical Experience

If identical autonomic changes are consistent with such different experiences as anger and euphoria [83], but the threshold for either experience is lessened in the absence of those changes, then what is the role of the physiological events? We may assume that they supply some level of nonspecific activation (often referred to as "arousal"), although the specific nature of the experience is determined by cognitive variables. It seems likely that this is what is happening in meditation. Thus, the physiologic variables (which can be described in terms of ergotropic-trophotropic balance) are unlikely to be the determining factor in the "success" of meditation. In this regard, the TM movement is seriously misled when it attaches importance to the known physiological changes in relation to successful attainment of meditational states. The extent to which the TM movement is confused on this point is seen when they propose to use physiological measures as indices of educational-spiritual progress in students of meditation. Thus, in the Maharishi International University it is proposed to use metabolic rate, oxygen consumption, blood chemistry, EEG recordings, etc., "to objectively validate" the student's "subjectively experienced improvement in physical health, the stability of his intellect and emotions, his inventiveness, intelligence and breadth of awareness" [2, pp. 6, 7].

As to mystical experience, whatever physiological correlates may finally be established, it is a reasonable assumption that they will only supply a backdrop on which the cognitive set and the setting superimpose direction, quality, meaning, and effects. Cognitive variables presumably determine both the content of the mystic experience and, at a higher level, its interpretation in terms of different religious or philosophical beliefs (see [13, p. 37]). Included, too, would be the ultimate effect of the experience on the individual's life-style, personality, and behavior. We also have to consider that an identical set of overt physiological events may in different subjects or at different times lead either to mystical experience or to quite different altered states of consciousness. A relevant example is the psychedelic experience, whose relationship to mystical states will be discussed later. Here the same physical stimulus in the form of, say, LSD can induce a psychotic state or an experience which, in the opinion of various authorities, is remarkably close if not indistinguishable from the mystical state [99–102]. Finally, there is ample evidence for "spontaneous" mystical experiences [14, 17], and it seems not unlikely that these, and the experiences of the great mystics whom one might (facetiously!) describe as chronically enlightened, need not be preceded by unusual physiological conditions. If so, this merely reaffirms the argument that conditions of altered ergotropic-trophotropic balance, though conducive to these experiences, are not crucial or necessary for their occurrence.

Too little is known to attempt to detail the specific cognitive variables of importance in meditative and mystical experiences. However, I might mention two factors. First, there is the religious and philosophical framework within which mystic experience is sought. Particularly relevant also is the emphasis in many mystic disciplines on the dependence on a teacher or guru [6, 16] in whom the subject vests his trust and hopes for enlightenment. There is certainly reason to believe that the capacity for psychological surrender ("letting go"), which is somehow paradoxically linked with personal realization and autonomy [103] is a major factor in attainment of mystical states. But it is not clear that either of these factors plays a role in spontaneous "unsolicited" experiences of "everyday mysticism" [14] whose etiology is indeed mysterious.

Finally, there is one point which emerges from this discussion of cognitive variables which has immediate relevance to the interpretation of studies on physiological correlates of transcendental meditation. All TM practitioners receive detailed instruction which includes rather heavy emphasis on the physiological changes to be expected in meditation. The possible effects of "demand characteristics" of this sort on experimental results merit consideration.

Mystical Experience and Hemispheric Lateralization

The thesis which has been presented is that ergotropic-trophotropic shifts may be conductive to various kinds of altered states of consciousness, that these may include meditative and mystical experience, and that the *specific* determining factors of the conscious experience are cognitive set (and to a lesser extent setting) rather than specific (overt) physiologic events. From the physiological point of view, this model is unsatisfyingly vague in that virtually nothing has been said about possible mechanisms relating to the switch from normal to altered consciousness. I shall, therefore, now explore one such hypothesis: that during mystical experience cerebral function is dominated by the right ("minor") cerebral hemisphere.

The realization that the use of language is a function for which the left hemisphere is specialized originated from early observation of the effects of brain lesions [104]. More recently, Sperry's work with epileptics subjected to therapeutic commissurotomy ("split brain") provided a basis for the concept that each hemisphere has "its own private sensations, perceptions, thought, feelings and memories" [105]. Though the concept of two minds in one body is difficult to digest,[11] it is now well established that each hemisphere is specialized for a different form of cognition. Current views indicate that the left is better qualified to deal with verbal, arithmetic, sequential, conceptual, analytic thinking and is the side primarily involved in directing motor function. The right hemisphere, on the other hand, seems specialized to deal with spatial relationships: relating parts to wholes—nonverbal, holistic thinking, based on direct perceptual, "intuitive" experience [105, 107, 108]. On the information-processing model, hemispheric specialization may be conceived as involving sequential processing for the left and simultaneous for the right. If the latter is in a sense the "nonrational" hemisphere, it is likely the one which seems to dominate in creative activity of various kinds, as well as aesthetic, artistic, and musical appreciation. Undoubtedly, under normal conditions (in healthy individuals), both hemispheres function together continuously, either by rapidly alternating or simultaneous operation [105, 107, 108]. Nevertheless, one can demonstrate by several methods the *relative* hemispheric dominance in normal subjects in verbal-analytic versus spatial holistic cognition or musical perception. These methods include dichotic listening experiments and observation of lateral differences in the ongoing EEG or evoked electrical activity in normal subjects presented with appropriate tasks (reviewed in [107]).

Reports of mystical experience invariably include reference to its ineffability. Even highly literate individuals sense a large discrepancy between the experience and their capacity to verbalize it. In considering this problem, we may distinguish among four possible elements: (*a*) amnesia for the details of the experience; (*b*) the simple absence of linguistic terms adequate to describe it; (*c*) a basic inarticulateness of the individual *during* the experience; and (*d*) a post hoc inability to express the remembered experience in words. Although experiences during many altered states of consciousness are frequently not remembered, mystical experiences are in fact often vividly remembered and may have a permanent influence throughout life [16–18, 73]. As to the poverty of language, this may seem to be particularly applicable to our culture. In the East, however, these states of consciousness have been widely pursued for thousands of years, presumably enough time for appropriate language to develop (see [26, p. 3]). Nevertheless, Eastern mystics make the same complaint of ineffability as do the Westerners. It therefore appears that mystical ineffability cannot be accounted for by the factors of amnesia or language but that it depends, rather, upon a real difficulty with verbal expression during and/or after the experiences.

If a careful analysis of this problem, Stace [13] argues that the use of language is inconceivable during mystical states, simply because the mode of experiencing at that time differs from normal consciousness in ways that make verbalization impossible. Specifically, the experience of "undifferentiated unity" is inherently contradictory to the function of language, which is the conveying of discrete concepts in words. As to the remembered experience, the subject is then in his normal state of consciousness, and Stace sees no reason why the mystic should not be able to describe it at least by comparing the difference between the mystic experience and his normal conscious experience at the time of reporting. In fact, he does describe it—albeit often metaphorically or poetically. But he has the *conviction* of its ineffability because he is attempting to describe an experience that defies the logical structure which underlies language; it paradoxically eliminates dualities; it sees opposites as identical.

Such arguments are not easy to follow, since the "advanced" mystical state which Stace describes—that of "undifferentiated unity" or the "void"—is so far from the experience of most people. Perhaps easier to grasp is the account of Deikman [22], who describes mystical experience as taking the form of a "vertical organization of concepts." By this he apparently means an enhanced capacity for simultaneous perceptions

---

[11]The philosophical difficulties which arise from conclusions based on "split brain" work are ably discussed by Nagel [106]. He argues, however, that though there is presumably more than one mind per individual, there is no reason to limit the number to two!

Physiology of Meditation

or understandings, as opposed to the normal mode of sequential (i.e., horizontal) organization of cognitions. Thus whole sets of relationships may be simultaneously grasped—an experience not translatable into language, which deals in the orderly succession of single concepts.

But whether the stress is on departures from logic, independence of space and time, simultaneous (holistic) versus sequential processing, or nonverbalizable perceptions, the resemblance to current concepts of right-hemispheric functioning is apparent. I should pause to reiterate the speculative nature of these arguments, while emphasizing one clear correlation: there is no disagreement that most of the language function is "in" the left hemisphere and that mystical states are invariably described as ineffable.

Now since the proposed model suggests that common physiological mechanisms may precipitate a variety of altered states of consciousness, it is relevant that other altered states have been linked to right-hemisphere function. Thus lesions which disrupt or destroy right-brain function seem to interfere with dreaming, and there is other evidence which suggests the possibility of right-hemisphere dominance in dreaming [107]. But dreaming is only one manifestation of the type of mental function described by Freud as primary process, that is, that type of cognition which characterizes the so called sub- or unconscious mind [109]. Avoiding psychoanalytic terminology, this mode may be described as extralogical, independent of normal rules of causality, of spatial and temporal sequence, and uses nonverbal representation by multimodality images. These features of the primary process are in fact those which are believed to characterize right-hemisphere function [107].

The right hemisphere most likely functions continuously in the normal state of consciousness, and right-hemisphere specialized functions, such as perception of part-whole relations, are certainly necessary for normal mental function. So also primary process thinking has a role in our normal waking consciousness. Apart from daydreaming and fantasy, it is a fair assumption, for instance, that intuition (decision making on the basis of "inadequate" information) is an essential component of all normal thought processes and particularly of symbolizing. However, the validation of intuitions requires logical analysis [110], that is, secondary process cognition. The importance of the primary processes in creativity is well recognized, although again it requires integration with secondary processes for expression in a work of art or science. This is described by Arieti [111] as the "tertiary process."

The mystic element in creative art or science is well described by Scharfstein [14], and Ehrenzweig [112] demonstrates the role of primary process in musical comprehension, for which the right hemisphere is apparently specialized [104, 113]. Ehrenzweig describes a form of scanning common to the artist looking at a canvas and the musician listening to polyphonic music, in which one may "grasp in a single act of comprehension several mutually incompatible constellations" [112, p. 386]. This mental act is said to be "unconscious"; perhaps the essence of mystical experience is to become aware of such processes. At any rate, the element of experiential *simultaneity* or holistic perception is a common feature connecting artistic and mystical consciousness to current notions of right-hemisphere function.

It remains to attempt to link the hypothesis of right-hemisphere dominance in mystical experience to the conclusions about the etiology of these states arrived at in our previous discussion. The consciousness of the psychotic is dominated by the primary process; and experiences which approach the mystical in nature may be more common in the psychotic than the sane [14, 114]. This being so, we may ask two questions about the psychotic-mystical analogy. What differentiates the two experiences, and what relationships can we find in the etiology of the two conditions?

The model which I am developing postulates the overt physiological variables predispose to altered states of consciousness, but the nature of the individual experience is determined by such cognitive variables as beliefs and attitudes resulting from experience and training. These factors (and the presence of brain dysfunction, mental disorder, etc.) would decide whether a right hemisphere-dominated experience would be classified as hallucinatory or psychotic or mystical, etc. As to etiology, the conditions leading to acute schizophrenic episodes, whose onset is characterized by "psychedelic" or mystical experience, will sound familiar. As described by Bowers [115], these psychoses often arise acutely out of a desperate struggle resulting in impasse, hopelessness, and the despairing abandonment of the struggle. This is reminiscent of the experiences of mystics emerging from "the dark night of the soul" into "ecstatic union" [22]. And the model fits well with the sequence defined by Sargant as common to conversion, shamanistic, and other similar experiences resulting in altered states of consciousness. It corresponds to the conditions precipitating Pavlovian experimental neurosis, that is, in physiologic terms, ergotropic activation leading to trophotropic collapse.

Conclusions and Research Prospects

The several lines of circumstantial evidence supporting the link between right-hemisphere function and primary process cognition supply a basis for the hypothesis that links the right hemisphere to mystic experience. Conditions which predispose to the dissolution of normal waking consciousness and the predominance of primary process thinking can lead—depending on the psychological status of the individual and the circumstances in which he finds himself—to dreaming, hallucinations, frank psychosis, meditative states, or (rarely) to mystical experience. The precipitation conditions include switches or unusual combinations of ergotropic-trophotropic activation, which may switch hemispheric function by affecting neural conduction in the corpus callosum or by other means. This hypothesis is frankly speculative, and such speculations earn a well-deserved fate on the refuse heap of sterile ideas unless they are amenable to research capable of examining their validity. I believe such experimental validation to be feasible and will not attempt to substantiate this within the framework of a brief consideration of experimental prospects in the field of meditation research in general.

The major objectives facing this area of endeavor in its present essentially neonatal stage of development are the elucidation of (a) possible medical-psychological benefits of meditative experience, (b) its physiological correlates, and (c) the relationship between physiological variables, on the one hand, and conscious experience as well as lasting effects in the meditation, on the other.

As to the benefits, it is to be expected that further examination of changes in personality, life style, psychosomatic health, etc., will continue to show positive effects of meditation. These results are predictable mostly on the basis of traditional knowledge and of recent research findings [3, 30, 60–62]. Since true mystical experience is rare, the evidence for lasting benefits in this area will remain largely anecdotal, unless the present surge of interest in meditation leads to a whole new generation of experimentally available mystics! One area of considerable interest is the application of meditation in psychotherapy [20]. The extent to which meditation can be used in a traditional Western psychotherapeutic context, and the implication for the role of the therapist need to be clarified. The lasting effects of traditional meditative practices should be compared with relaxation therapies, such as autogenic training. The variables of age, sex or personality characteristics, and organizational, philosophical, or religious affiliations should also be investigated.

As to physiology, the first requirement is to determine whether the various results already obtained can be replicated and statistically validated in quantitative experiments under well-controlled conditions. Second, we need to know if the autonomic–metabolic-EMG findings differ from those in relaxation and what, if any, is the role of intermittent napping in their production. This will involve comparisons within and between subjects in the presence and absence of sleep. The *mantra* variant should be compared with other forms of meditation, especially Zen. Of particular interest would be comparative studies within one laboratory of various Zen and yogic meditations, in terms of responses to sensory stimuli. In addition to EEG-orienting reflexes from different baseline conditions, evoked potentials should also be measured. To determine whether meditators showing EEG signs of sleep are indeed behaviorally asleep, thresholds of arousal to sensory stimuli and subjective reports on "awakening" may be investigated. Among the variables of blood chemistry which merit study, biogenic amine metabolism may be of particular interest.

Temporal correlations between ongoing measurements of different physiological variables in meditation have hardly ever been reported. Simultaneous measures of EMG, heart and respiration rates, GSR, etc., can indicate whether the departures from congruence among autonomic, somatic, and EEG variables are correlated with changes in conscious experience. This will allow conclusions as to the proposed triggering role of "switches" in autonomic-somatic integration. In addition, Schwartz [116] has recently contended that the patterning of physiologic responses is the important dimension for identification of psychophysical states in relation to biofeedback regulation and its application to psychosomatic problems and meditation.

The extent to which the various physiological variables may have bearing on conscious experience cannot be understood without attempting to obtain reports as complete as possible of experiences during (and after) meditation and to correlate these with physiological events. It will be necessary to identify common experiential effects and to score meditations within and between sessions in terms of these criteria. The problem of interference by the experimenter in the process of meditation is real but not insuperable, as shown by Banquet [55], who used button pressing to score categories of experience, albeit crudely. Retrospective reporting can also be used, if done immediately after the experiment. From studies involving these types of observation it may be possible to separate the experiential effects of relaxation, posture, lack of thinking, and sensory detachment.

To elucidate the role of cognitive variables in meditative and mystic experience, it would be of initial interest to compare the conscious experience of "traditional" meditators with that of subjects in relaxation therapies and Benson's technique [43], which resembles meditation but lacks a philosophical-religious set. To the extent that physiologic differences between these techniques are less than the differences in reports of conscious experience of the lasting effects, the role of cognitive variables will become apparent. Such studies will, of course, require careful investigation of subjects' attitudes if we are to understand the nature of the "attributions" involved.

As to true mystical experience, the prospects for scientific investigation are poor, to the extent that it requires the availability and cooperation of individuals who can predictably experience these unusual states of consciousness. In the circumstances, the best strategy may be to study effects of psychedelic drugs such as LSD, mescaline, and psilocybin, which provide the best available experimental models. While most psychedelic "trips" certainly do not result in mystical experience, the probability of precipitating something which approaches or approximates it [99–102] can be greatly increased by using predisposed subjects and optimizing the environmental situation, that is, by making maximal use of set and setting. This is exemplified by the unique experiments of Pahnke in which seminarians ingested psilocybin while listening to a Good Friday service piped in from an adjoining chapel [23]. Similar situations could be designed in different religious and other contexts.

Without underestimating the difficulties, under such circumstances, of obtaining physiologic measurements which could be correlated with subjective report, experiments of this kind would be of such major interest as to justify considerable effort. For instance, small transmitters could be employed to obtain measurements of lateral differences in cerebral activity, with minimal disturbance to the subject. Such a set-up could be used for studying on-going EEG, evoked potentials, etc., as well as for the monitoring of extracerebral physiologic events. Present noninvasive techniques of measuring relative hemispheric dominance (see [107]) may be unsatisfactory, but new ones will surely evolve as a result of the considerable current interest in this topic. The problem of eliminating irrelevant drug effects when psychedelic experiences are used as models can be dealt with by careful cataloging and temporal correlation of the physiologic data with reports of mystic-like experiences, which will only occur during a small portion of the session. This simple appoach should permit confirmation or denial of hypotheses, such as the one proposed here of a link between certain extracerebral physiologic events, right-hemisphere dominance, and mystical experience.

In conclusion it remains only to express the hope that the past opposition to this kind of psychopharmacologic investigation on the part of those who control biomedical research will not remain an insuperable barrier to the study of the physical correlates of man's most unique and treasured experiences.

Dr. Gordon Globus has suggested in a personal communication that, since the mystical experience is "acognitive at its core," it is misguided to suggest that it can be determined by cognitive variables, though he concedes that they do determine the way people talk about these experiences. This criticism would not affect the point that the initiation of the mystical experience (or other altered states) may be determined by preexisting cognitive variables. In addition, however, the descriptions of the mystics show that the contentless experience of the "void" may be accompanied by a variety of hallucinatory phenomena whose content is undoubtedly influenced by the factors we have discussed.

References

1. Maharishi Mahesh Yogi. *The science of being and art of living.* London: Unwin, 1963.
2. Maharishi International University Catalog. Los Angeles: MIU Press, 1974/75.
3. D. P. Kanellakos and J.S. Lukas. *The psychobiology of transcendental meditation: a literature review.* Menlo Park, Calif.: Benjamin, 1974.
4. R. K. Wallace, H. Benson, and A. F. Wilson. *Am. J. Physiol., 221*:795, 1971.
5. A Campbell, *Seven states of consciousness: a vision of possibilities suggested by the teaching of Maharishi Mahesh Yogi.* New York: Harper & Row, 1974.
6. P. Brent. *The godmen of India.* Harmondsworth: Penguin, 1972.
7. E. Jacobson. *Progressive relaxation.* Chicago: Univ. Chicago Press, 1938.
8. J. W. Schultz and L. Luthe. *Autogenic training.* New York: Grune & Stratton, 1969.
9. B. B. Brown, *New mind, new body: bio-feedback: new directions for the mind.* New York: Harper & Row, 1974.

10. W. James. *The varieties of religious experience*. New York: Modern Library, 1929.
11. C. Naranjo and R. E. Ornstein. *On the psychology of meditation*. New York: Viking, 1971.
12. A. Huxley. *The perennial philosophy*. New York: Harper & Row, 1944.
13. W. T. Stace. *Mysticism and philosophy*. Philadelphia: Lippincott, 1960.
14. B-A Scharfstein. *Mystical experience*. New York: Bobbs-Merrill, 1973.
15. R. C. Zaehner. *Zen, drugs and mysticism*. New York: Random House, 1972.
16. P. Kapleau (ed.). *The three pillars of Zen: teaching, practice and enlightenment*. Boston: Beacon, 1965.
17. R. M. Bucke. *Cosmic consciousness*. Philadelphia: Dutton,1901.
18. G. Krishna. *Kundalini*. Berkeley: Shambhala, 1971.
19. E. Gellhorn and W. F. Keily. *J. Nerv. Ment. Dis.*, *154*:399, 172.
20. W. Kretschmer. *Psychologia, 5*:76, 1962.
21. P. C. Horton. *Am. J. Psychiatry, 130*:294, 1973.
22. A. J. Deikman. *Psychiatry, 29*:324, 1966.
23. W. Pahnke. *Int. J. Parapsychol., 8*:295, 1966.
24. R. Prince and C. Savage. *Psychedelic Rev.*, no. 8, p. 59, 1966.
25. A. M. Ludwig. *Arch. Gen. Psychiatry, 15*:225, 1966.
26. C. T. Tart (ed.). *Altered states of consciousness*. New York: Wiley, 1969.
27. E. R. Hilgard. *J. Nerv. Ment. Dis.,149*:68, 1969.
28. Y. Akishige. In: Y. Akishige (ed.). *Psychological studies on Zen*. Kyushu psychol. studies, no. 5, p. 1, 1968.
29. T. Hirai. *Psychophysiology of Zen*. Tokyo: Igaku Shoin, 1974.
30. H. Benson, B. A. Rosner, B. R. Marzetta, and H. M. Klemchuk. *Lancet*, p. 289, February 23, 1974.
31. R. K. Wallace. *Science, 167*:1751, 1970.
32. A. Vassiliadis. Unpublished report, 1972 (cited in [3]).
33. J. Allison. *Lancet, 1*:833, 1970.
34. B. Bagghi and M. Wenger. *Electroencephalogr. Clin. Neurophysiol., 7*:132, 1957.
35. B. K. Bagghi. *J. Am. Soc. Psychosom. Dent. Med., 16*:1, 1969.
36. M. Wenger, B. Bagghi, and H. Anand. *Circulation*, 24:1319, 1961.
37. P. A. Obrist, R. A. Webb, J. R. Sutterer, and J. L. Howard. *Psychophysiology, 6*:569, 1970.
38. M. Treichel et al. *Physiologist, 3*:472, 1923 (abstr.).
39. B. K. Arnand, G.. Chhina and B. Singh. *Indian J. Med. Res., 49*:82, 1961.
40. F. N. Pitts, Jr. *Sci. Am., 220*:59, 1969.
41. S. H. Ackerman and E. J. Sachar. *Psychosom. Med., 36*:69, 1974.
42. A. H. Benson, R. F. Steinart, M. M. Greenwood, H. M. Klemchuk, and N. H. Peterson, *J. Hum. Stress, 1*:37, 1975.
43. J. F. Beary and H. Benson. *Psychosom. Med., 36*:115, 1974.
44. D. W. Orme-Johnson. *Psychosom. Med., 35*:341, 1973.
45. R. Jevning, A. Wilson, E. Vanderlaan, and S. Levine. Program, 57th annual meeting, Endocrine Soc., p. 257, 1975 (abstr.).
46. R. Jevning, A. F. Wilson, and W. R. Smith. Paper presented at Int.Conf. Psychophysiol. of Sleep, Edinburgh, Scotland, June 1975 (abstr.).
47. J. A. Wada and E. A. Hamm. Am. Electroencephalogr. Soc. 27th annual meeting, 1973 (abstr.).
48. J. Younger, W. Adriance, and R. Berger. Program, 13th annual meeting, Assoc. for Psychophysiol. Study of Sleep, San Diego, Calif., May 1973.
49. R. R. Pagano, R. M. Rose, R. M. Stivers, and W. S. Warrenburg. *Science, 191*:308, 1975.
50. K. K. Datey, S. N. Deshmuckh, C. P. Dalvi, and S. L. Vinekar. *Angiology, 20*:325, 1969.
51. N. N. Das and H. Gastaut. *Electroencephalogr. Clin. Neurophysiol., 6*(suppl.): 211, 1955.
52. L. C. Walrath and D. W. Hamilton. *Am. J. Clin. Hypn. 17*:190, 1975.
53. B. K. Anand, G. S. Chhina, and B. Singh. *Electroencephalogr. Clin. Neurophysiol., 13*:452, 1961.
54. A. Kasamatsu and T. Hirari. *Folia Psychiatr. Neurol. Jpn., 20*:314, 1966.
55. J. P. Banquet. *Electroencephalogr. Clin. Neurophysiol., 35*:143, 1973.
56. J. J. Lynch, A. Paskewitz, and M. T. Orne. *Psychosom. Med. 36*:399, 1974.
57. L. C. Johnson. *Psychophysiology, 6*:501, 1970.
58. G. K. Mills and K. Campbell. *J. Nerv. Ment. Dis., 159*:191, 1974.
59. W. C. McCallum and J. R. Knott (eds.). *Electroencephalogr. Clin. Neurophysiol.*, suppl. 33, 1973.
60. L. A. Hielle. *Percept. Mot. Skills, 39*:623, 1974.
61. K. R. Pelletier. *Percept. Mot. Skills, 39*:1031, 1974.
62. R. Honsberger and A. F. Wilson. *Respir. Ther., 3*:79, 1973.
63. L. Henderson. *Br. J. Psychol., 63*:1, 1972.
64. R. J. Andrew, *Behavior, 51*:135, 1974.
65. E. Gellhorn. *Principles of autonomic somatic integrations*. Minneapolis: Univ. Minnesota Press, 1967.
66. E. Gellhorn. *Psychol. Forsch., 34*:48, 1970.
67. W. R. Hess. *Functional organization of the diencephalon*. New York: Grune & Stratton, 1957.
68. I. P. Pavlov. *Conditioned reflexes and psychiatry*. London: Lawrence & Wishart, 1961.
69. S. Brena. *Pain and religion*. Washington, D.C.: Thomas, 1972.
70. E. Gellhorn. In: E. Gellhorn (ed) *Biological foundations of emotions*, p. 56. Glenview, Ill.: Scott Foresman, 1968.
71. D. T. Suzuki, E. Fromm, and R. DeMartino. *Zen Buddhism and psychoanalysis*. New York: Grove, 1963.
72. W. F. Kiely. *J. Nerv. Ment. Dis., 159*:196, 1974.
73. J. T. Huber. *Through an eastern window*. Boston: Houghton Mifflin, 1965.
74. W. Sargant. *The mind possessed*. New York: Lippincott, 1974.

75. A. Ludwig. *Int. J. Clin. Exp. Hypn.*, *12*:205, 1964.

76. W. G. Jilek and N. Todd. *Can. Psychiatr. Assoc. J.*, *19*:351, 1974.

77. W. Keup (ed.). *Origin and mechanisms of hallucinations.* New York: Plenum, 1970.

78. J. P. Zubek (ed.). *Sensory deprivation: fifteen years of research.* New York: Irvington, 1969.

79. R. Fisher. *Science, 174*:897, 1971.

80. D. H. Funkenstein, S. H. King, and M. E. Drolette. *Mastery of stress.* Cambridge, Mass.: Harvard Univ. Press, 1957.

81. M. B. Arnold. *Emotion and personality.* New York: Columbia Univ. Press, 1960.

82. D. Bindra. In: P. Black (ed.). *Physiologic correlates of emotion.* New York: Academic Press, 1970.

83. S. Schachter and J. E. Singer. *Psychol. Rev., 69*:379, 1962.

84. H. London and R. E. Nisbett (eds.). *Thought and feeling: cognitive alteration of feeling states.* Chicago: Aldine,1974.

85. D. J. Bem. In: ref. [84], p. 211, 1974.

86. S. Valins. *J. Pers. Soc. Psychol., 4*:400, 1966.

87. J. Laird and M. Crosby. In: ref. [84], p. 44, 1974.

88. J. E. Singer. In: ref. [84], p. 3, 1974.

89. C. T. Tart. *On being stoned: a psychological study of marijuana intoxication.* Palo Alto, Calif.: Science and Behavior Books, 1971.

90. T. X. Barber. *LSD, marijuana, yoga, and hypnosis.* Chicago: Aldine, 1970.

91. A. Weil. *The natural mind: a new way of looking at drugs and the higher consciousness.* Boston: Houghton Mifflin. 1973.

92. P. C. Walker and R. F. Q. Johnson. *Psychol. Bull., 81*:362, 1974.

93. M. Zuckerman. *Psychol. Bull., 75*:297, 1971.

94. S. Arieti and J. M. Meth In: S. Arieti (ed.). *Handbook of psychiatry*, p. 546. New York: Basic, 1959.

95. A. Koestler and J. R. Smthies (eds.). *Beyond reductionism.* Phoenix: Hutchinson, 1969.

96. F. J. Ayala and T. Dobzhansky (eds.). *Studies in the philosophy of biology.* Berkeley: Univ. California Press, 1974.

97. J. Kopa, I. Szabo, and E. Arastyan. *Acta Physiol. Acad. Sci. Hung., 21*:207, 1962.

98. E. Valenstein. *Brain control.* New York: Wiley, 1973.

99. A. Huxley. *The doors of perception.* London: Chatto & Windus, 1954.

100. A Watts. In: A. Watts (ed.). *What does it matter?* New York: Pantheon, 1968.

101. H. Smith. *J. Philos., 61*:517, 1964.

102. R. E. L. Masters and J. Houston. *The varieties of psychedelic experience.* New York: Holt, Rinehart & Winston, 1966.

103. G. Bermant. *A psychological perspetive on autonomy.* Unpublished manuscript, 1975.

104. R. J. Joynt and M. N. Goldstein. In: W. J. Friedlander (ed.). *Adv. Neurol., 7*:147, 1974.

105. R. W. Sperry. In: F. J. McGuigan and R. A. Schoonover (eds.). *The psychophysiology of thinking.* New York: Academic Press, 1973.

106. T. Nagel. *Synthese, 22*:396, 1971.

107. D. Galin. *Arch. Gen. Psychiatry,* 31:572, 1974.

108. R. D. Nebes. *Psychol. Bull., 81*:1, 1974.

109. S. Freud, *The interpretation of dreams.* (1900) Westminster, Md.: Modern Library, 1938.

110. J. R. Royce. In: E. C. Carterette and M. P. Friedman (eds.). *Handbook of Perception*, p. 149. New York: Academic Press, 1974.

111. S. Arieti. In: S. Arieti (ed.). *Handbook of psychiatry*, vol. 3, p. 712. New York: Basic, 1966.

112. A. Ehrenzweig. In: W. Neusterberger and S. Axelrob (eds.). *The psychoanalytic study of society*, p. 373. New York: International Universities Press, 1964.

113. J. E. Bogen. *Los Angeles Neurol. Soc. Bull., 34*:135, 1969.

114. M. B. Bowers and D. X. Freedman. *Arch. Gen. Psychiatry, 15*:240, 1966.

115. M. B. Bowers. *Arch. Gen. Psychiatry, 19*:348, 1968.

116. G. E. Schwartz. *Am. Sci., 63*:314, 1975.

28

CEREBRAL LATERALITY AND MEDITATION:
A REVIEW OF THE LITERATURE

Jonathan B. B. Earle

Within the last decade, Western psychologists have begun to investigate the processes by which meditation may induce changes in mental experience. Most recently, several authors have hypothesized that through the manipulation of attention, most systems of meditation alter consciousness by inhibiting cognitive functions associated with the dominant or left cortical hemisphere. Ornstein (1975), for example, has suggested that meditation can be considered a method of "turning off" the verbal, linear and analytic style of processing associated with the normal waking state. Similarly, Prince (1979) has proposed that meditation interferes with the functioning of the dominant lobe such that the sense of time, logic and verbal processing no longer dominate consciousness. In association with this proposed left hemisphere inhibition is a hypothesized shift to a non-dominant or right hemisphere specific mode of experience which has been described as holistic, receptive and beyond language or logic (Bakan, 1971; Fischer, 1975). Indeed, Davidson (1976) has even argued that meditation may lead to the development of dormant right hemisphere associated abilities. Support for the right hemisphere theory of meditation is derived principally from descriptions of the phenomenology of meditative experience, comparisons of cognitive task performance of meditators and non-meditators, and electrophysiological investigations. However, consideration of data from similar sources suggests that the cortical hemispheres are affected similarly by meditation and that inhibitory and excitatory influences within each hemisphere may be generated and evolve as meditation practice progresses. In the following discussion, a review of these data will be presented with the aim of delineating the role both hemispheres may play in the production of meditative states of consciousness.

meditation and changes in mental experience

Verbal activity and meditation

*support
for
right
hemisphere
theory of
meditation*

Evidence in support of the right hemisphere theory of meditation may be found in the descriptions of meditative experiences and in discussions of the impediments to successful practice. In the literature of yoga, the antithetical nature of verbal analytical thought to the meditation process is often expressed in the form of a warning. For example, Blofeld (1977, pp. 38-9) in commenting on the symbolic aspects of mantra meditation, has written,

> Successful contemplation does not, however, require careful reflection upon the symbolism ... Such interpretations are naturally of interest, but it is necessary to stress that reflection upon the symbolism forms no part of the contemplative practice. The mantric syllables cannot produce their full effect upon the deepest levels of the adept's consciousness if his mind is cluttered with verbal concepts. Reflective thought must be transcended, abandoned.

*abandoning
the
intellect*

Statements regarding the importance of abandoning the intellect may also be found in the Buddhist literature. Humphreys (1968, p. 159), for instance, has asserted,

> Until the student can overcome this 'cocoon of discrimination' in thought and speech he will never attain that self-realization of which the Sutra speaks at a later stage. 'Self-realization is an exalted state of inner attainment which transcends all dualistic thinking and is above the mind system with its logic, reasoning, theorizing and illustrations'.

Indeed, the techniques of meditation seem to be designed purposely to avoid logical, verbal and rational reactions to perceived events. Sustaining attention on one object as in one-pointed concentration, naming or noting stimuli successively as they enter consciousness as in Buddhist mindfulness, and maintaining a visual mode of imagery combined with concentration as in tantric practice, all appear to reduce abstract thought and verbal associations.

*concentration
practice
and
verbal
activity*

It is clear, however, from the descriptions of these techniques that the extent to which meditators engage in verbal activity may vary across the types of meditation practice and according to how successful any particular meditation may be. During the practice of one-pointed concentration, verbal thoughts may arise in several forms—verbal association to perceived events unrelated to meditation, verbal reactions to meditation-induced experiences, and verbal recognition and discrimination of changes in the direction and quality of attention. While thoughts of the first category are easily avoidable given adequate motivation, thoughts associated with the meditation process are more difficult to escape. For example, because the early phase of this type of meditation involves discrimination of proper from improper meditation, it is likely that meditators initially utilize a verbal recognition strategy to monitor their progress. Specifically, the meditator may use a method by which he identifies the condition of "attending to the meditation support" and discriminates it from "not attending to the support." After a certain amount of experience or upon instruction from a teacher, the meditator relinquishes the use of this inner voice in his meditation efforts. Ironically, it is acquisition of the logical concept that thinking about meditation interferes with the very process of meditation that leads to a reduction of dualistic and verbal thought.

thoughts associated with meditation process

For the more advanced meditator, the problem is of a slightly different nature. Changes in the state of consciousness induced by meditation may include the evocation of images, emotions and an increased feeling of power. Such changes not only disturb attention, but may alter the motivational state of the meditator. Involvement in these phenomena may lead to increased verbal reflection upon their nature and a lessening in the will to overcome their attractive qualities. Like the initiate, the experienced meditator is taught or comes to realize that involvement with these phenomena may lead to a slowing of meditation progress. Thus, the meditator once more abandons a habitual way of reacting to perceived events.

problems in advanced concentration practice

While similar considerations are relevant to the practice of Buddhist mindfulness, verbal notation and the development of discrimination describes both the technique and major consequence of the practice. Mindfulness entails the successive labeling of the objects of consciousness as they appear without further elaboration. Thus, while a verbal-analytic style of processing information is avoided, the technique cannot be described as a holistic non-verbal process. While automatization of this cognitive strategy probably leads to less and not more dominant lobe activation (Earle & Pikus, 1981)*, the practice may lead to finer and finer discriminations of mental and behavioral phenomena suggesting that left hemisphere abilities may be facilitated as meditation experience is gained.

mindfulness practice and verbal activity

---

*Automatized tasks, such as counting, for example, appear to be associated with large amplitude EEG alpha activity indicative of cortical inactivation, while other types of arithmetic tasks induce attenuation of alpha activity. The ability to carry out such well learned tasks also appear to be spared in most cases of cortical brain damage suggesting that sub-cortical processes may control such functions (Lezak, 1976; Brain, 1969).

*tantric
meditation
and
verbal
activity*

In tantric meditation, in which visual imagery is utilized, the limited role of verbal activity appears obvious. However, in the initial development and manipulation of the complex and ritualized meditation imagery support, it is likely that a verbal-visual strategy is chosen. Furthermore, in many traditional mantram meditations, the initiate is directed to imagine both ideographic and representational images.

MENTAL ACTIVITY AND MEDITATION

*inhibiting
mental
activity*

While it is possible that meditation is designed to reduce verbal-analytical thought, most manuals of meditation emphasize that the intention of practice is to inhibit all mental phenomena. Obviously, this includes day dreams, internal and external perceptions and somatic feelings which may have a right hemisphere basis. Verbal thoughts may be inhibited initially because their existence may be tied directly to an active mode involving the shifting of attention or strategies of discrimination. As meditation becomes a learned process, however, passively experienced phenomena such as hypnogogic hallucinations may become more prevalent. The meditator, at this point, is usually instructed to ignore such phenomena and to maintain his/her attentional focus on the meditation support. Alternatively, if distracting thoughts seem too overwhelming, they are at least briefly incorporated as an object of meditation. In most systems of meditation, the meditation leads to a state in which all mental constructions disappear from consciousness. In commenting upon yoga, the Indian philosopher Behanan (1964, p. 214) has written

> The objective that the yogin lays before himself in practicing the exercises is the complete elimination of thoughts, or rather that of getting behind thoughts, *i.e.*, transcending the activities and fluctuations of the citta or mind-stuff. The ideal is not reached until all thoughts are suppressed. To the mind as such, yoga attaches no importance, regarding it as an obstacle or veil, so to say, that hides the true self. When the yogin succeeds in suppressing the activities of the mind by means of his mental exercises, then he is said to have realized himself. This is the "pure consciousness" untarnished by the modifications of the mind-stuff which usually result in sense-perception, reasoning, intellectual activities, etc.

Similarly, in a discussion of the various types of Zen practice, Yasutani, as quoted by Kapleau (1965, p. 45) has taught

> Shojo Zen provides the answer to this need. It has as its aim the stopping of all thoughts so that the mind becomes a complete blank and enters into a state called *mushinjo*, a condition in which all sense functions have been eliminated and the faculty of consciousness suspended.

Cerebral Laterality and Meditation   **399**

The aim of mindfulness in Indian Buddhist tradition also is directed towards the creation of a state in which no objects arise into consciousness. In addition, detachment or a release from emotional influences is sought as a major component of meditation and its aftereffects. Goleman (1972) has written of a summit state of insight meditation (*nirvana*):

> Insight is now on the verge of its culmination; noticing is keen, strong and lucid. All mental formations are instantly known to be impermanent, painful, or without self, just by seeing their dissolution. All formations are seen either as limited and circumscribed or as devoid of desirability, or as alien. Detachment from them is at a peak. Noticing no longer enters into or settles down on any formations at all. Then consciousness arises that takes as its object the 'signless, no-occurrence, no-formation': In nirvana, physical and mental phenomena cease entirely (pp. 23–4).

Finally, while tantric practice may systematically utilize visual imagery in the search for objectless awareness, the use of such a strategy is self-extinguishing. Blofeld (1974, p. 126) in summarizing the tantric path has stated

objectless awareness and pure attention

> The essence of this tantric method is to start with visualization of an appropriate being; the body, speech and mind of the adept must then be united with the Body, Speech and Mind of that which is visualized; then both adept and object are merged and finally 'banished' so that nothing is left but pure Mind resting in stillness.

It appears then, that in advanced stages of meditation, only the exercise of attention occupies the mind. Thus, whether the contents of consciousness be visual, verbal, sensory or emotional or whether they originate from the left or right cortical hemispheres, the eventual impact of meditation is the same. Inhibition of most functions in both hemispheres may underlie the higher meditative states of consciousness.

EXCITATORY PHENOMENA

Although successful practice of meditation may lead to functional inhibition and a reduction in cortical activity, excitatory phenomena in the form of visual hallucinations, spontaneous emotional feelings and somatic illusions are often reported. Experienced during the early and middle phases of meditation practice, these phenomena are reported by meditators using both concentration methods (Carrington, 1978; Deikman, 1963; Kapleau, 1965) and mindfulness techniques (Kornfield, 1979). Because similar phenomena may be induced primarily through electrical stimulation of the right hemisphere (Baldwin, 1970; Penfield & Perot, 1963) or after injury to this area

reports of excitatory phenomena

(Hecean & Badaraco, 1956), it is possible that meditation may lead to a condition in which the non-dominant lobe is disinhibited. However, while less frequently reported, verbal hallucinations may also be produced during this phase of practice (Serbida, 1975). Moreover, olfactory and gustatory hallucinations, verbal and motor perseverations and intense myogenic discharges may be induced, suggesting that wide areas of the cortex may be disinhibited (Carrington, 1978; Harris, 1975). One factor that may determine the types of phenomena experienced may be the nature of the meditation support. For example, hallucinations or distortions might tend to occur in the same modality as the perceived meditation object. Meditating on one's reflection, for example, may initially produce visual distortions, followed by archetypical hallucinations and eventually lead to the disruption of the sense of three-dimensional space (Luce, 1975).

complexity of factors and inadequacy of simple model

In the case of concentration on the breath, hallucinations may even be of a particular type (e. g. white light experience). However, this factor cannot explain why meditation on a visual image (kriya yoga) and a verbal mantram (T.M.) can produce the kundalini experience which has both visual and somatic components (Sannella, 1979). Knowing the type of meditation support also does not explain why some meditators report hallucinatory phenomena, while others do not. Finally, the nature of the meditation object probably does not explain why there is a disparity in the frequency of visual and verbal hallucinations. Given the complexity of these various factors, then, it seems unlikely that a simple model that identifies disinhibition of one area of the brain as the underlying cause, is an entirely adequate construct.

ATTENTION AND MEDITATION

the right hemisphere and control of attention

Perhaps the most compelling evidence for the right hemisphere theory of meditation is the growing amount of data suggesting that the control of attention may be a right hemisphere specific function. Mesulam & Geschwind (1978) have described the symptoms of a number of right hemisphere damaged individuals who show dramatic impairments of selective attention. These symptoms include inability to direct and maintain vigilance, distractibility, incoherent thought and an apathetic demeanor. The non-reactivity of right hemisphere lesioned patient, or the so-called "neglect syndrome," has been shown to be associated with a defect in the orienting response to sensory input (Critchley, 1949), a reduction in reaction time to auditory stimuli (Howes & Boller, 1975), and a lack of autonomic responsiveness to visual stimuli (Marrow, Urtrinski, Youngjai, & Boller, 1981). In studies of vigilance with commissurotomized epileptics, Dimond (1979) has reported that unlike performance with the left hand or right hemisphere, right hand performance showed a steep decrease in the detection of visually presented signals. Moreover, when signals were not detected, the number of additional signals needed to evoke a response was significantly higher when the right hand was responding in comparison to the left hand condition.

Assuming then that attention is controlled by the right hemisphere, it seems justifiable to conclude that the practice of meditation induces relative right hemisphere activation. However, similar to practice of mindfulness with regard to left hemisphere functioning, automatization of sustained attention most likely leads to decreased levels of activation. Presumably as sustained attention becomes effortless, subcortical mechanisms may begin to operate more efficiently in subserving this function. In the initial stages of meditation, however, relative right hemisphere activation might be expected.

MENTAL TASKS AND MEDITATION AFTEREFFECTS

Several investigators have claimed that as a consequence of meditation, cognitive task performance may improve, performance may become more stable, and susceptibility to stress may be reduced (Appelle & Oswald, 1974; Blasdell, 1973; Orme-Johnson, 1973). However, few studies of the aftereffects of meditation have included control procedures that would rule out the effects of self-selection in the ability examined, differences in the motivational level of meditators and control subjects, and experimenter bias. Those studies which have included such controls procedures have generally found that meditation does not lead to increased levels of performance (Frumkin, 1979; Yuille & Sereda, 1980).

after-effects of meditation

Nevertheless, some investigations of the effects of meditation on cognitive abilities have suggested that right hemisphere specific abilities may be facilitated. For example, several reports have demonstrated that meditators in comparison to control subjects show faster reaction times on simple visual reaction time tasks (Appelle & Oswald, 1974; Holt, Caruso, & Riley, 1978). Using a more powerful design, Pagano & Frumkin (1977) reported that on a right hemisphere specific musical task, experienced meditators performed significantly better than either a less experienced group or non-meditator

the impact on right hemisphere specific abilities

control group. Although no pre- to post-meditation effect was observed, the authors concluded that meditation-induced increments in ability might be too small to be detected over a short period of time. Recently, rather significant increases in perceptual ability have been observed as an immediate aftermath of meditation and after only two weeks of practice (Dillbeck, 1977). In contrast, other investigators have found that meditation (transcendental meditation) has no effect on pursuit rotor tasks (Williams & Herbert, 1976; Williams, Lodge, & Reddish, 1977), or mirror-tracing tasks (Williams, 1978), Raven's progressive matrices (Yuille & Sereda, 1980) or on iconic memory task (Frumkin & Pagano, 1979). Assuming that these tasks involve a right hemisphere component, it is apparent that if meditation does have an impact on right hemisphere abilities, it is undramatic and selective in character.

impact on left hemisphere activities

Studies of left hemisphere abilities and meditation have also yielded mixed results. While some studies have found that meditation has no effect on short- or long-term verbal memory (Yuille & Sereda, 1980), others have found that verbal memory may be facilitated (Abrams, 1977). Similarly, while verbal-analytic performance has been found to be actually lower in meditators than in controls (Schwartz, 1974), meditation has been reported to increase arithmetic performance (Miskinian, 1977). Because of the methodological problems mentioned previously, it is unclear how these data should be interpreted. It does seem clear, however, that no impact of meditation on hemisphere associated abilities is implied by the pattern of results.

ELECTROPHYSIOLOGICAL EVIDENCE

EEG Synchronization and Meditation

hemispheric synchronization

Perhaps the most distinguishing EEG characteristic of meditation is unusually high intra- and interhemispheric synchronization. While highly correlated bilateral activity has been observed in meditators during the initial meditation (Farrow, 1976), and as a meditation aftereffect (Levine, Herbert, Haynes, & Strobel, 1977), it appears to be associated with sustained concentration (Cazard, 1972; Fehmi, 1971), subjective state reports of "pure awareness" during transcendental meditation (Orme-Johnson, 1977) and to be much higher than during sleep or drowsiness (Banquet & Sailhan, 1974; Levine, 1975). Nevertheless, recent investigations of sleep EEG have indicated that higher values of synchronization or coherence are found during REM sleep in comparison to NREM sleep

(Dumermith & Lehmann, 1979; Levine, 1975). This finding suggests that there might be physiological similarities between REM sleep and meditation. Banquet, Haynes, Russel & Relier (1978) have even argued that the characteristics of REM sleep in transcendental meditators indicates that meditation may act as a substitute for this stage of sleep. The authors point out that meditation may reduce the number of REM periods experienced over the night, the average number of REMs for a REM period as well as time within the REM stage. Relevant to this hypothesis are other reports which have linked meditation to increases in dream vividness (Kornfield, 1979) and recall (Reed, 1978) and, of course, reports indicating that meditation itself may induce dream-like images and primary process thinking (Prince & Savage, 1966). Recently, electrophysiological and cerebral blood flow studies have indicated that the right hemisphere may be dominant during REM sleep (Goldstein, Stoltzfus & Gardocki, 1972; Hirshkowitz, Karacan, Meyer, Ware, & Saki, unpublished manuscript; Hirshkowitz, Ware & Karacan, 1979). Given the similarities between meditation and this sleep stage, it is possible that meditation may be mediated by the right hemisphere as well.

meditation and REM activity

However, in the classical literature of yoga, the summit state of awareness associated with meditation is described as a state similar to dreamless sleep or that sleep state in which no mental objects are perceived. Furthermore, a number of reports have suggested that unlike visual fantasy activity, meditation does not reduce the REM rebound effect after REM deprivation (Butters, 1976; Cartwright, Butters, Weinstein, & Kroeker, 1977). Since this paradigm has been the one most often used to assess whether particular types of cognitive activity can "substitute" for REM, it appears doubtful that the substitution hypothesis is correct. Finally, Banquet *et al.* (1978) also reported that meditation may have dramatic effects on NREM sleep as well as on REM sleep, suggesting that meditation may substitute for sleep, but is not specific to the sleep stage. In summary, then, these considerations do not justify indirect conclusions regarding REM, meditation and right hemisphere specialization. It is possible, however, that like REM dreams, meditation-induced visual hallucinations may be subserved by a disinhibition of the non-dominant lobe.

Other EEG reports of coherent activity during meditation tend to favor a bilateral hypothesis. High anterior-posterior coherence has been found in both hemispheres during meditation (Farrow, 1976; Levine, Herbert, Haynes, & Strobel, 1977), while in the performance of non-verbal spatial tasks, there is a tendency for synchronization to be higher in the right hemisphere than the left (Beaumont & Rugg, 1979; Shaw, Brooks,

other EEG reports

Colter, & O'Connor, 1979; Shaw, O'Connor, & Ongley, 1977). Although it is possible that differences in the dominant frequencies associated with meditation and cognitive task performance may invalidate any comparison between the two, the intrahemispheric data does not suggest a non-dominant lobe specialization for meditation.

EEG Amplitude, Frequency and Meditation

Greater support for the right hemisphere theory of meditation is found in EEG studies that have focused on the parameters of amplitude and frequency. Glueck and Strobel (1975), for example, reported that transcendental meditators at the beginning of their meditation exhibited an increase in alpha density (8–13 Hz) in the dominant hemisphere followed one to two minutes later by a spreading of activity to the non-dominant lobe. Similarly, when subjects were asked to meditate using their own style of meditation, Ehrlichman and Wiener (1980) found forty seconds of this activity was associated with greater alpha or slow wave (2–13 Hz) activity in the left hemisphere in comparison to the right. Furthermore, out of seventeen tasks involving the utilization of either verbal or visual strategies, the meditation condition produced the greatest mean asymmetry. Assuming an increase in alpha activity is indicative of lower arousal or activation, the data suggests that the initial stages of meditation are associated with greater deactivation of the left hemisphere than the right.

activation, deactivation and hemispheric dominance

In contrast to these reports, a number of authors have been unable to find asymmetry differences between meditation and resting baseline conditions (Bennett & Trinder, 1977; Brown, Fischer, Wagman, & Horrom, 1977–8; Earle, 1977) or left hemisphere specific tasks (Bennett & Trinder, 1977; Brown, Fischer, Wagman, & Horrom, 1977–8). Bennett and Trinder (1977), for example, reported no alpha asymmetry differences between a 20-minute transcendental meditation and left or right hemisphere specific tasks when asymmetry values were compared within subjects (N = 16). In addition, the authors reported that an across-subject comparison of meditation with a relaxation group produced no significant results. It is possible that some of these across-study discrepancies may be explained by differences in the time over which asymmetry was assessed during meditation. As was observed by Glueck and Stroebel, right hemisphere dominance during meditation appears to be transient; thus, using long periods of meditation to compute asymmetry ratios may obscure rapid changes in lateralization.

The transience of relative right hemisphere activation during meditation was examined in a study carried out by the author (Earle, 1977) using subjects trained in breath concentration.

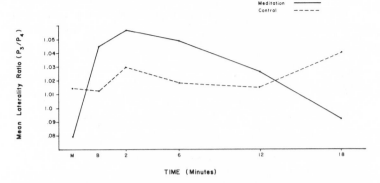

Figure 1. Mean left hemisphere (P_3) / right hemisphere (P_4) full wave (1–40 Hz.) power ratio during the mathematics (M), baseline (B), and experimental recording sessions for the meditation and control groups. For the meditation group— M<2; p<.05, M<B, 4; p<.06. Greater relative right hemisphere activation is up.

After two weeks of training or after completing 12 meditations of one hour in length, six meditators were asked to meditate for 18 minutes while parietal activity was recorded. In comparison with values associated with an arithmetic condition (successive subtraction of 7's from 200 for 2 minutes), meditation was associated with a higher left to right hemisphere ratio of full wave power (1–40Hz) during the initial six minutes of meditation (first 2 minutes p<.05; next 4 minutes, p<.06) but not during the last 12 minutes.

transience of relative right hemisphere activation

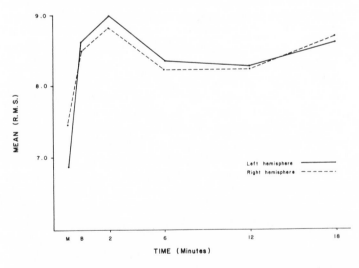

Figure 2. Mean full wave power (1–40 Hz.) for the left and right hemispheres (P_3, P_4) during the mathematics (M), baseline (B), and meditation period for the meditation group.

Physiology of Meditation

Inspection of power values at each electrode site revealed that in comparison to values associated with the arithmetic condition, full wave power increased more in the left hemisphere compared to the right during the first third of the meditation when alpha activity was prominent. This was not the case, however, during the rest of the meditation when slower activity was also found.

Even though the right hemisphere may be in ascendancy only during the initial stages of meditation, EEG amplitude data does suggest that meditation may have long-term effects on right hemisphere specific abilities. Bennett and Trinder (1977) found that as a group, meditators exhibited greater asymmetry differences between visual and verbal tasks. Similarly, the present author found that while an arithmetic condition was significantly left-lateralized from a baseline condition for a trained group of meditators, this was not true for an untrained group. Greater EEG asymmetry differences between verbal and visual tasks has been associated with spatial orientation and superior ability (Fiore, 1978). Thus, in concordance with Davidson's contention, it is possible that meditation may lead to greater right hemisphere specific abilities. Recently West-cott (1976) in an alpha asymmetry study of transcendental meditation, reported that meditators showed a higher degree of relative right hemisphere activation (lower right to left ratio of activity) in comparison to a group of control subjects. Because relative right hemisphere activation has been found to be correlated positively with performance on spatial tasks (Davidson, Taylor, & Saron, 1979; Furst, 1976), Westcott's findings add further support to the notion that meditators are spatially oriented. However, it must be pointed out that data does not directly confirm Davidson's hypothesis that meditation leads to greater right hemisphere abilities. Further research is necessary to determine if meditation is responsible for increases in spatial ability or if spatially oriented individuals are more attracted to meditation than individuals lacking this ability.

Finally, EEG investigations that have focused on the physiological correlates of meditation practiced by advanced or experienced meditators have found little evidence that amplitude asymmetry is associated with deep meditative states. Banquet (1973) did report a transient asymmetry in fast wave activity in association with "pure awareness," a deep state of transcendental meditation. Fast wave activity appeared initially in the left frontal region and then spread to more posterior and lateral regions of the cortex. Other researchers, however, have not reported such asymmetries (Brown, 1977; Das & Gastaut, 1957). With regard to slower frequencies that often dominate the record of advanced meditators, symmetry of activity is apparently quite noticeable. Cade & Coxhead (1979) have asserted that with increasing practice, alpha and theta activity increase both in amplitude and symmetry. In agreement with these results are the findings of Herbert and Lehmann (1977) who found that theta bursts were about equal amplitude in the records of some advanced T.M. meditators and in only two cases did gross asymmetries (>30%) favor one hemisphere or the other. Thus, it appears that meditation in its more advanced forms leads to a condition in which both hemispheres undergo similar changes.

Other Physiological Evidence

While the majority of laterality investigations of meditation have involved electrophysiological measures, a few reports utilizing other indices of lateralization have been carried out. *other* Similar to the EEG data, little evidence has been found in *indices of* support of the right hemisphere hypothesis. In contrast to the *lateralization* EEG amplitude asymmetry data (Westcott, 1976), meditators do not exhibit a bias towards leftward reflective eye movements (Spanos, Rivers, & Gottlieb, 1978). Because such a bias is associated with superior spatial ability (Tucker & Suib, 1978, a note; Harnad, 1972), the data indicating that meditation may facilitate right hemisphere specific abilities is not supported. In a study of regional cerebral blood flow changes during meditation, Jevning and Wilson (1981) have found bilateral increases in blood flow. This pattern of excitation can be contrasted to spatial task performance (Gur & Reivich, 1980; Risberg, Halsey, Wills, & Wilson, 1975) and REM sleep (Hirshkowitz, Ware, & Karacan, 1979) in which flow is higher in the right hemisphere in comparison to the left.

Finally, although no neuropsychological studies of meditation have been carried out, Dewhurst and Beard (1970) have studied a number of epileptic patients who have experienced mystical states as part of their auras. There is no indication from their report that the site of the lesion is an important variable in determining the character of their aura experience.

In conclusion and summary, it appears that the phenomenological and psychological data on meditation does not fully *conclusion* support the right hemisphere hypothesis. What it does seem to *and* suggest is that in the early stages of meditation, relative right *summary* hemisphere activation may be induced through the control of attention, the use of visual imagery and the inhibition of verbal-analytical thought. During the advanced stages of meditation, however, cognitive functions associated with each hemisphere are either automatized or inhibited, leading to a reduction in cortical activity or diminished cortical participation in the generation of mental phenomena. The degree of asymmetry exhibited by meditators in the early stages of meditation may vary according to the type of meditation they are engaged in, the particular object or objects of meditation they are utilizing and on individual differences. During the advanced stages of meditation, these factors probably become less important in the production of meditation experience.

REFERENCES

ABRAMS, A. I. Paired-associate learning and recall: A pilot study of the transcendental meditation program. In D. W. Orme-Johnson & J. T. Farrow (Eds.), *Scientific research on the transcendental meditation program: Collected papers.* 1977. 1.

APPELLE, S. & OSWALD, L. E. Simple reaction time as a function of alertness and prior mental activity. *Percept. Motor Skills*, 1974, *38*, 1263–68.

BAKAN, P. The eyes have it. *Psychol. Today*, April, 1971, 64–67.

BALDWIN, M. Neurological syndromes and hallucinations. In W. Kemp, (Ed.), *Origin and mechanisms of hallucinations*, New York: Plenum Press, 1970, 3–12.

BANQUET, J. P. Spectral analysis of the EEG in meditation. *Electroencephal. Clin. Neurophys.* 1973, 143–51.

BANQUET, J. P., HAYNES, C., RUSSEL, H. & RELIER, B. Analysis of sleep in altered states of consciousness by classical EEG and coherence spectra. *Waking and sleeping*, Society Proceedings, 1978, *2*, 250.

BANQUET, J. P. & SAILHAN, M. EEG analysis of spontaneous and induced states of consciousness, *Revue d' Electroencephal. Neurophysiol. Clin.*, 1974, *4*, 445–53.

BEAUMONT, J. G., & RUGG, M. D. The specificity of intrahemispheric EEG Alpha coherence asymmetry related to psychological task. *Biol. Psychol.*, 1979, *9*, 237–48.

BEHANAN, K. T. *Yoga: A scientific evaluation.* New York: Dover 1964, 214.

BENNETT, J. E. & TRINDER, J. Hemispheric laterality and cognitive style associated with transcendental meditation. *Psychophysiol.*, 1977, *14*, 293–6.

BLASDELL, K. S. The effects of the transcendental meditation technique upon a complex perceptual-motor task. In K. Kannelakos and J. Lucas, (Eds.), *The psychobiology of transcendental meditation: A literature review.* Menlo Park: Stanford Research Institute, 1973.

BLOFELD, J. *Beyond the gods: Buddhist and Taoist mysticism.* New York: Dutton 1974, 126.

BLOFELD, J. *Mantras: Sacred words of power*. New York: Dutton, 1977, 38.

BRAIN, R. Disorders of memory. In R. Brain & M. Wilkinson, (Eds.), *Recent advances in neurology and neuropsychiatry*. Boston: Little Brown, 1969.

BROWN, B. B. *Stress and the art of biofeedback*. New York: Harper and Row, 1977.

BROWN, B. C., FISHCHER, R., WAGMAN, A. M. I. & HORROM, H. The EEG in meditation and therapeutic touch healing. *J. Altered States Consc.*, 1977–8, *3*, 2, 169–80.

BUTTERS, E. The effects of divine light meditation on some electrophysiological indices of sleep. Paper presented to the Association for the Psychophysiological Study of Sleep, Cincinnati, 1976.

CADE, D. M., & COXHEAD, N. *The awakened mind*. New York: Dell Pub. 1979.

CARRINGTON. *Freedom in meditation*. Garden City, N.Y.: Anchor Doubleday, 1978.

CARTWRIGHT, E., BUTTERS, M., WEINSTEIN, & KROEKER, L. The effects of pre-sleep stimuli of different sources and types on REM sleep. *Psychophysiol.*, 1977, *14*, 4, 388–92.

CAZARD, P. Interhemispheric synchrony of parieto-occipital alpha rhythms attention and conscious experience. *Electroencephal. Clin. Neurophysiol.* 1972, *34*, 715.

CRITCHLEY, M. The phenomenon of tactile inattention with special reference to parietal lesions. *Brain.* 1949, *72*, 538.

DAS, N. N., & GASTAUT, H. Variations de l'activite electrique du cerveau du coeur et des muscles squelettiques au cours de la meditation et de l'extase yogique. *Electroencephal. Clin. Neurophysiol.*, 1957, supplement 6, 211–19.

DAVIDSON, J. M. The physiology of meditation and mystical states of consciousness. *Perspectives Biol. Med.*, 1976, *19*, 345–79.

DAVIDSON, R. J., TAYLOR, N. & SARON, C. Hemisphericity and styles of information processing: Individual differences in EEG asymmetry and their relationship to cognitive performance. *Psychophysiol.*, 1979, *16*, 197.

DEIKMAN, A. J. Experimental meditation. *J. Nerv. Ment. Dis.*, 1963, *136*, 329–43.

DEWHURST, K. & BEARD, A. W. Sudden religious conversions in temporal lobe epilepsy. *Brit. J. Psychiat.*, 1970, *117*, 497–507.

DILLBECK, M. C. The effects of the transcendental meditation technique on visual perception and verbal problem solving. *Diss. Abstr. Internat.*, 1977, *37 (10–B)*, 5319.

DIMOND, S. J. Vigilance and split-brain research. *Vigilance: Theory, operational performance, and physiological correlates*. New York: Plenum Press, 1979.

DUMERMITH, G. & LEHMAN, D. EEG power and coherence

during NREM, REM, and wakefulness. *Waking and Sleeping*, 1979, *3*, 83.

EARLE, J. Hemispheric specialization and the hypnogogic process in meditation: An EEG study. Masters Thesis, Tufts University, June, 1977.

EARLE, J. & PIKUS, A. The effect of sex and task difficulty on EEG, alpha activity in association with arithmetic. Unpublished manuscript, 1981.

EHRLICHMAN, H. & WIENER, M. S. EEG asymmetry during covert mental activity. *Psychophysiol.* 1980, *17*, 228–35.

FARROW, J. T. Physiological changes associated with transcendental consciousness. In D. W. Orme-Johnson & J. T. Farrow, (Eds.), *Scientific research on the transcendental meditation program: Collected papers*, 1976, *1*, 108–33.

FEHMI, L. G. Biofeedback of electroencephalographic parameters and related states of consciousness. Paper presented at the Annual American Psychological Association, Washington, D.C., 1971.

FIORE, J. Sex and occupation differences in EEG asymmetries and cognitive abilities. *Diss. Abstr. Internat.*, 1978, *39 (1B)*, 428.

FISCHER, R. Cartography of inner space. In R. Siegel and L. J. West. (Eds.), *Hallucinations: Behavior, experience, and theory*. New York: Wiley and Sons, 1975, 197–239.

FRUMKIN, L. R., & PAGANO, R. R. The effect of transcendental meditation on conic memory. *Biofeedback and self-regulation*. 1979, *4*, 4, 313–22.

FURST, C. G. EEG alpha asymmetry and visuospatial performance. *Nature* (London), 1976, *260*, 254–5.

GLUECK, B. C., & STROEBEL, C. F. Biofeedback and meditation in the treatment of psychiatric illnesses. *Comprehensive Psychiat.* 1975, *16*, 303–21.

GOLDSTEIN, N. W., STOLTZFUS, & GARDOCKI, J. F. Changes in interhemispheric amplitude relationships in EEG during sleep. *Physiol. Behav.* 1972, *8*, 811–15.

GOLEMAN, D. The buddha on meditation and states of consciousness, Part I: The teachings. *J. Transpersonal Psychol.*, 1972, *1*, 1, 1–44.

GUR, R. & REIVICH, M. Cognitive task effects on hemispheric blood flow in humans: Evidence for individual differences in hemispheric activation. *Brain and Language*, 1980, *9*, 78–92.

HARNAD, S. R. Creativity, lateral saccades and the non-dominant hemisphere. *Percept. Motor Skills*, 1972, *34*, 656–64.

HARRIS, J. C. Personal communication to Dr. Paul MacLean. Nov. 12, 1975.

HECEAN, H., & BADARACO, J. G. Semeiologie des hallucinations visuelles en clinique neurologigue. *Acta Neurol. Latin America*. 1956, *2*, 23–57.

HERBERT, R. & LEHMANN, D. Theta bursts: An EEG pattern in normal subjects practicing the transcendental meditation. *Electroencephal. Clin. Neurophysiol.*, 1977, *42*, 397–405.

HIRSHKOWITZ, M., KARACAN, I., MEYER, J. S., WARE, J. C. & SAKAI, F. Hemispheric asymmetry during sleep. Unpublished manuscript.

HIRSHKOWITZ, M. WARE, J. C., & KARACAN, I., Integrated EEG amplitude asymmetry during early and late REM and NREM periods, Poster presentation, *Neurosciences*, 1979.

HOLT, W. R., CARUSO, J. L., & RILEY, J. B. Transcendental meditation versus pseudo-meditation on visual choice reaction time. *Percept. Motor Skills*, 1978, *46*, 726.

HOWES, D., & BOLLER, F. Simple reaction time: Evidence for focal impairment from lesions of the right hemisphere. *Brain*, 1975, *98*, 317–32.

HUMPHREYS, C. *Concentration and meditation.* Baltimore, Md.: Penguin Books, 1968, 159.

JEVNING, R. & WILSON, A. F. Behavioral increase of cerebral blood flow. Unpublished abstract, September 28, 1981.

KAPLEAU, P. (Ed.)., *Three pillars of Zen.* New York: Beacon Press, 1965, 45.

KORNFIELD, J. Intensive insight meditation: A phenomenological study. *J. Transpersonal Psychol.*, 1979, *11*, 44–58.

LEVINE, P. H. The coherence spectral array (COSPAR) and its application to the study of spatial ordering in the EEG. Proceedings of the San Diego Bio-medical Symposium, 1975.

LEVINE, P. H. HERBERT, J. R. HAYNES, C. T. & STROBEL, U., EEG coherence during the transcendental meditation technique. In D. W. Orme-Johnson & J. T. Farrow (Eds.), *Collected papers*, 1977, *1*, 187–207.

LEZAK, M. D. *Neuropsychological assessment.* New York: Oxford Univ. Press, 1976.

LUCE, G. G. Western psychology meets Tibetan Buddhism. In T. Tulku (Ed.), *Reflections of mind.* Emeryville, Ca.: Dharma Pub., 1975, 20–40.

MARROW, L. URTRINSKI, P. B., YOUNGJAI, K. & BOLLER, R. Arousal responses to emotional stimuli and laterality of lesion. *Neuropsychol.*, 1981, *19*, 65–71.

MESULAM, M. & GESCHWIND, N. On the possible role of neo-cortex and its limbic connections in the process of attention and schizophrenia: Critical cases of inattention in man and experimental anatomy in monkey. *J. Psychiat. Research*, 1978, *14*, 249–59.

MISKINIAN, D. E. The effect of transcendental meditation on the organization of thinking and recall (secondary organization). In D. W. Orme-Johnson & J. T. Farrow (Eds.), *Scientific research of the Transcendental Meditation program: Collected Papers.* New York: MIU Press, 1977, *1*.

ORME-JOHNSON, D. W. Autonomic stability and transcendental meditation. *Psychosom. Med.*, 1973, *35*, 341–9.

ORME-JOHNSON, D. W. Higher states of consciousness: EEG coherence, creativity and experiences of the siddhis. *Electroencephal. Clin. Neurophysiol.*, 1977, *4*, 581.

ORNSTEIN, R. *The psychology of consciousness.* New York: Pelican Books, 1975.

PAGANO, R., & FRUMKIN, L. The effect of transcendental meditation on right hemispheric functioning. *Biofeedback Self-Regulation*, 1977, *2*, 407–15.

PENFIELD, W., & PEROT, P. The brain's record of auditory and visual experience. *Brain*, 1963, *84*, 4, 595–693.

PRINCE, R. Meditation: Some psychiatric speculations. *Psychiat. J. Univ. Ottawa*, 1979, *3*, 3, 202–9.

PRINCE, R. & SAVAGE, C. Mystical states and the concept of regression. *Psychedelic Rev.*, 1966, *8*, 59–81.

REED, H. Improved dream recall associated with meditation. *J. Clin. Psychol.*, 1978, *34*, 1, 151–8.

RISBERG, J., HALSEY, J., WILLS, E. L. & WILSON, E. M. Hemispheric specialization in normal man studied by bilateral measurements of the regional cerebral blood flow, a study with the 133-Xe inhalation technique. *Brain*, 1975, *98*, 511–24.

SANNELLA, L. Kundalini: Classical and clinical. In J. White (Ed.), *Kundalini evolution and enlightenment.* Garden City, N.Y.: Anchor Doubleday, 1979, 306–15.

SCHWARTZ, G. The facts on transcendental meditation. P. II: TM relaxes some people and makes them feel better. *Psychol. Today*, April 1974, 39–44.

SERBIDA, K. *Zen training.* New York: Weatherhill, 1975.

SHAW, J. C., BROOKS, S., COLTER, N., & O'CONNOR, K. P. A comparison of schizophrenic and neurotic patients using EEG power and coherence spectra. In J. Gruzelier & P. Flor-Henry, (Eds.), *Hemisphere asymmetries of function in psychopathology.* New York: Elsevier/North-Holland, Biomedical Press, 1979, 257–284.

SHAW, J. C., O'CONNOR, K. P., & ONGLEY, C. O. The EEG as a measure of cerebral function organization. *Brit. J. Psychiat.*, 1977, *130*, 1977, 260–4.

SPANOS, N. P., RIVERS, S. M., & GOTTLIEB, J. Hypnotic responsivity, meditation, and laterality of eye movements. *J. Abnorm. Psychol.*, 1978, *87*,5, 566–69.

TUCKER H. & SUIB, M. R. Conjugate lateral eye movement (C.L.E.M.) direction and its relationship to performance on verbal and visual spatial tasks. *Neuropsychol.*, 1978, *16*, 251–4 (a note).

WESTCOTT, M. Hemispheric symmetry of the EEG during the transcendental meditation technique. In D.W. Orme-Johnson & J. T. Farrow (Eds.), *Scientific research on the tran-*

scendental meditation program: Collected Papers, 1976, *I*, 160–4.

WILLIAMS, L. R. T. Transcendental meditation and mirror tracing skill. *Percept. Motor Skills*, 1978, *46*, 371–8.

WILLIAMS, L. R. T. & HERBERT, P. G., Transcendental meditation and fine perceptual-motor skill. *Percept. Motor Skills*, 1976, *43*, 303–09.

WILLIAMS, L. R. T., LODGE, B. & REDDISH, P. S. Effects of transcendental meditation on rotary pursuit skill. *Research Quart.*, 1977, *48*, 196–201.

YUILLE, J. & SEREDA, L. Postitive effects of meditation: A limited generalization? *J. Appl. Psychol.*, 1980, *65*,3, 333–40.

Requests for reprints to Jonathan B. B. Earle, 10 Farmington Rd., W. Newton, Mass. 02165.

B. General Metabolic and Autonomic Changes

This section presents two of the classical articles, one dealing with metabolic changes in meditation by Wallace *et al.* (29), and one showing the changes in galvanic skin response as a measure of autonomic stability by Orme-Johnson (30). The article by Fenwick (32) suggests that the metabolic changes Wallace, Benson, and Wilson found may not be unique to meditation. The article by Corby (31) highlights the importance of recognizing meditation as a diverse multidimensional technique, involving a variety of different parameters. Sometimes meditation brings about a state of quiescence and is a passive type of meditation; sometimes concentrative meditation may result in a very active physiological response. Finally, the article by Jevning and O'Halloran (33) presents a view which suggests that meditation is, in fact, a unique state of consciousness and that these unique qualities of meditation, phenomenologically, will eventually be found in physiological parameters. They present some of their research on blood flow and other metabolic activities which may be a promising area in which to look for finer changes which would differentiate meditation as a unique metabolic state.

Therefore, in this section we begin with two of the early and still classical articles which make claims for the uniqueness of meditation, both metabolically (Wallace, Benson, and Wilson) and autonomically (Orme-Johnson). Corby suggests that meditation cannot be seen as a unidimensional technique, and that even within a meditation at different times there may be many different physiological effects occurring. The articles by Fenwick *et al.* and Jevning and O'Halloran are useful in that they suggest differing views, Fenwick suggesting that there are no unique physiological or EEG mentation patterns in meditation, and Jevning and O'Halloran reporting on potentially unique metabolic changes within meditation and suggesting that with more research, other unique metabolic patterns will be found.

29

A WAKEFUL HYPOMETABOLIC
PHYSIOLOGIC STATE

Robert Keith Wallace, Herbert Benson, and
Archie F. Wilson

WALLACE, ROBERT KEITH, HERBERT BENSON, AND ARCHIE F. WILSON. *A wakeful hypometabolic physiologic state.* Am. J. Physiol. 221(3): 795–799. 1971.—Mental states can markedly alter physiologic function. Hypermetabolic physiologic states, with in creased oxygen consumption, accompany anticipated stressful situations. Hypometabolic physiologic changes, other than those occurring during sleep and hibernation, are more difficult to produce. The present investigation describes hypometabolic and other physiologic correlates of a specific technique of meditation known as "transcendental meditation." Thirty-six subjects were studied, each serving as his own control. During meditation, the respiratory changes consisted of decreased O_2 consumption, CO_2 elimination, respiratory rate and minute ventilation with no change in respiratory quotient. Arterial blood pH and base excess decreased slightly; interestingly, blood lactate also decreased. Skin resistance markedly increased, while systolic, diastolic, and mean arterial blood pressure, arterial P_{O_2} and P_{CO_2}, and rectal temperature remained unchanged. The electroencephalogram showed an increase in intensity of slow alpha waves and occasional theta-wave activity. The physiologic changes during meditation differ from those during sleep, hypnosis, autosuggestion, and characterize a wakeful hypometabolic physiologic state.

---

behavior; hypometabolism; O_2 consumption; CO_2 elimination; minute ventilation; respiratory quotient; blood pressure; pH; P_{O_2}; P_{CO_2}; base excess; blood lactate; heart rate; rectal temperature; skin resistance; electroencephalogram; meditation; respiratory rate

MENTAL STATES can markedly alter physiologic function. Hypermetabolic physiologic states, with associated increased oxygen consumption, accompany anticipated stressful situations (34, 61). Hypometabolic physiologic changes, other than those occurring during sleep and hibernation, are more difficult to produce, but may accompany meditational states.

Physiologic changes during meditation have been investigated, (1–4, 6, 11, 14, 15, 23, 29, 30, 38, 42–44, 46, 53, 55, 56, 58, 59), but interpretation of the results has been problematic because of difficulties of subject selection. It was difficult to evaluate which subjects were expert in the investigated technique and therefore could be expected to produce physiologic changes (4, 53); many so-called experts were located in geographic areas where adequate research facilities were not available; the magnitude of physiologic changes was sometimes dependent upon the length of time the subject had been practicing a particular technique and his personal aptitude for the specific discipline (30, 53). However, consistent physiologic changes have been observed during the practice of certain mental techniques of meditation (1–3, 30, 46, 53, 56). Oxygen consumption and respiratory rate have decreased markedly, while the electroencephalogram has shown increased alpha- and occasional theta-wave activity. The present study confirms and extends earlier physiologic observations during the practice of one of these techniques, taught by Maharishi Mahesh Yogi, known as "transcendental meditation" (56).

Transcendental meditation was investigated because: *1)* consistent, significant physiologic changes, characteristic of a rapidly produced wakeful hypometabolic state, were noted during its practice (2, 46, 56); *2)* the subjects found little difficulty in meditating during the experimental measurements; *3)* a large number of subjects were readily available who had received uniform instruction through an organization specializing in teaching this technique (Student's International Meditation Society, National Headquarters located at 1015 Gayley Avenue, Los Angeles, Calif. 90024). The technique comes from the Vedic tradition of India made practical for Western life (36). Instruction is given individually and the technique is allegedly easily learned, enjoyable, and requires no physical or mental control. The

Physiology of Meditation

individual is taught a systematic method of perceiving a "suitable" sound or thought without attempting to concentrate or contemplate specifically on the sound or thought. The subjects report the mind is allowed to experience a thought at a "finer or more creative level of thinking in an easy and natural manner." There is no belief, faith, or any type of autosuggestion involved in the practice (37). It involves no disciplines or changes in life style, other than the meditation period of 15 or 20 min twice a day when the practitioner sits in a comfortable position with eyes closed.

METHODS

Thirty-six subjects were studied with each serving as his own control. Informed consent was obtained from each. The subjects sat quietly in a chair with eyes open for 10–30 min prior to the precontrol measurements. During the precontrol period, all subjects continued to sit quietly with eyes open or closed for 10–30 min. The subjects were then instructed to start meditating. After 20–30 min of meditation, they were asked to stop. During the postcontrol period, they continued to sit quietly with eyes closed for 10 min and then with eyes open for another 10 min. Blood pressure, heart rate, rectal temperature, and skin resistance and electroencephalographic changes were measured continuously. Other measurements were made and samples taken every 10 min throughout the precontrol, meditation, and postcontrol periods. Mean values were calculated for each subject in each period. The data from the precontrol period were then compared to those during meditation by use of a paired t test (52).

Oxygen consumption was measured in five subjects by the closed- (7) and in 15 subjects by the open-circuit methods (13). In the open-circuit method, expired gas was collected in a Warren E. Collins, Inc. 120 l Tisot spirometer for 6- to 10-min periods. The expired gas was analyzed in triplicate for P_{O_2} and P_{CO_2} with a Beckman Instruments, Inc. physiological gas analyzer model 160. Oxygen consumption, CO_2 elimination, and respiratory quotient were calculated according to standard formulas (13). In all subjects tested by the closed-circuit method and in four subjects tested by the open-circuit method, a standard mouthpiece and nose clip were used. A tight-fitting face mask was made for use in 16 subjects. The face mask contained two one-way low-resistance inspiration valves (id 1.5 cm) in its sides and a one-way expiration valve (id 2.3 cm) in its front. The Tisot spirometer was weighted to ensure adequate collection, regardless of tidal volume or rate of respiration. Total ventilation was measured in the four subjects with the unweighted Tisot spirometer. Respiration rate was recorded during the closed-circuit method measurements.

Systemic arterial blood pressure was measured and arterial blood samples were obtained from a polyethylene or Teflon catheter inserted percutaneously via a no. 18 Cournand or a Becton, Dickinson & Co. Longwell 20-g 2-in catheter needle, respectively, after local anesthesia with 5–10 ml of 1% procaine HCl (novocaine; Winthrop Laboratories, Inc.) or 2% lidocaine HCl (Xylocaine, Astra Pharmaceutical Products, Inc.). The catheters were filled with a dilute heparin saline solution (5,000 USP units Na heparin per 1 0.9% NaCl) and connected to a Statham P23Db strain-gauge pressure transducer. Systolic and diastolic or mean arterial blood pressure were recorded on either a Hewlett-Packard Co. Sanborn recorder, model 964, or a Brush Instruments Division, Clevite Corp. Mark 240 polygraph. Mean pressures were obtained by low-pass filtering in the driver amplifier. Average values for mean and systolic and diastolic blood pressure were calculated using horizontal lines of best fit drawn through records every 100 sec. Arterial blood samples were taken in heparinized syringes for determination of pH, P_{CO_2}, and P_{O_2} with a Sanz pH glass microelectrode and Radiometer (Copenhagen), model pH M4; a Severinghaus P_{CO_2} electrode system (49); and a Clark P_{O_2} Instrumentation Laboratory, Inc. ultramicro system, model 113-S1, respectively. Base excess was calculated for each of the arterial blood samples (51). Blood lactate concentration was determined by enzymatic assay from unheparinized arterial blood samples (48). Lactate determinations for each sample were performed in duplicate and the results averaged.

Electrocardiograms were recorded with a Grass Instruments Co. polygraph, model 5, or the Hewlett-Packard

Sanborn recorder, model 964. Heart rate was calculated by counting the number of QRS electrocardiogram spikes occurring during two out of every five consecutive minutes. Rectal temperature was continuously measured with a Yellow Springs Instruments, Inc. telethermometer, model 44TA, utilizing a flexible probe inserted 2.5–3.0 cm into the rectum. The values for rectal temperature were recorded every min. Skin resistance was measured with Beckman Instrument, Inc. silver-silver chloride electrodes placed 0.5 cm apart on the left palm (40) and recorded continuously on the Grass Instrument Co. polygraph, model 5 at a current of 50 μa. Values for skin resistance were recorded every min.

Electroencephalograms (EEG) were recorded with a Grass Instrument Co. electroencephalograph model 6. The EEG traces were recorded with an Ampex Corp. tape recorder, model FR-1300. The skin electrodes were placed, according to the International 10–20 system, at Fpl, Cz, T3, P3, 01, 02, and A2 (26). Grass Instruments Co. gold-plated cup electrodes and EEG electrode cream were employed. Recordings were monopolar with A2 acting as the reference electrode, and the ground electrode was placed over the right mastoid bone. The EEG tracings were recorded as analog data on tape and then were converted to digital data by a Systems Data, Inc. SDS 930 computer with a nominal accuracy of one part in 2048, operating at 256 samples/sec on each channel. These digital data were subsequently processed by an IBM 360-91 computer with spectral analysis computed by the BMD X92 program (19), sampling 2 of every 15 sec of data with a resolution of 1 c/sec for 32 frequencies. Every 10 samples were averaged and displayed as a time history of intensity (mean square amplitude) for each frequency and as a contour map of time vs. frequency with a representation of intensity (57). The sampling of short periods of data was used to increase the likelihood of including temporary frequency changes which might have occurred during the meditation period. Eye movements (electro-oculograms), were recorded in five subjects with the electrodes placed at E1 and A1, and E2 and A1 (45).

The age of the subjects ranged from 17 to 41 years with a mean of 24.1 years. There were 28 males and eight females. The length of time practicing transcendental meditation ranged from 0.25 to 108.0 months, with a mean of 29.4 months. Oxygen consumption averaged 251.2 ml/min prior to meditation, with small variation between the two mean precontrol measurements (5.3 ml/min) (Table 1). During meditation, O_2 consumption decreased 17% to 211.4 ml/min, and gradually increased after meditation to 242.1 ml/min. Carbon dioxide elimination decreased from 218.7 ml/min during the precontrol period to 186.8 ml/min during meditation. Respiratory quotient prior to meditation was in the normal basal range (0.85) and did not change significantly thereafter. Minute ventilation decreased about 1 liter/min and respiratory rate decreased about three breaths per min during meditation.

Systolic, diastolic, and mean arterial blood pressure changed little during meditation (Table 1). Average systolic blood pressure before meditation was 106 mm Hg; average diastolic blood pressure 57 mm Hg; average mean blood pressure 75 mm Hg. The arterial pH decreased slightly in almost all subjects during meditation, while Pco_2 and Po_2 showed no consistent or significant changes during meditation. The average base excess decreased about 1 unit during meditation.

Mean blood lactate concentration decreased from the precontrol value of 11.4 to 8.0 mg/100 ml (Table 1). In the 10 min following meditation, lactate continued to decrease to 6.85 mg/100 ml, while in the next and final 10 min it increased to 8.16 mg/100 ml. During the 30-min precontrol period, there was a slow decrease in lactate concentration of 2.61 mg/100 ml per hr. At the onset of meditation, the rate of decrease markedly increased to 10.26 mg/100 ml per hr.

During meditation, the average heart rate decreased by 3 beats/min (Table 1). Rectal temperature remained essentially constant throughout the meditation period (Table 1). Skin resistance increased markedly at the onset of meditation, with a mean increase of about 140 kilohms (Table 1).

TABLE 1. *Physiologic changes before, during, and after meditation*

Measurement	No. of Subjects	Precontrol Period, mean ± SD	Meditation Period, mean ± SD	Postcontrol Period, mean ± SD
Oxygen consumption, ml/min	20	251.2 ±48.6	211.4 ±43.2*	242.1 ±45.4
CO_2 elimination, ml/min	15	218.7 ±41.5	186.8 ±35.7*	217.9 ±36.1
Respiratory quotient	15	0.85 ±0.03	0.87 ±0.04	0.86 ±0.05
Respiratory rate, breaths/min	5	13 ±3	11 ±3†	11 ±3
Minute ventilation, l/min	4	6.08 ±1.11	5.14 ±1.05†	5.94 ±1.50
Blood pressure, mm Hg				
Systolic	6	106 ±12	108 ±12	111 ±10
Diastolic	6	57 ±6	59 ±5	60 ±5
Mean	9	75 ±7	75 ±7	78 ±7
pH	10	7.421 ±0.022	7.413 ±0.024†	7.429 ±0.025
P_{CO_2}, mm Hg	10	35.7 ±3.7	35.3 ±3.7	34.0 ±2.9
P_{O_2}, mm Hg	10	103.9 ±6.4	102.8 ±6.2	105.3 ±6.3
Base excess	10	−0.5 ±1.5	−1.3 ±1.5*	−1.0 ±1.8
Blood lactate, mg/100 ml	8	11.4 ±4.1	8.0 ±2.6*	7.3 ±2.0
Heart rate, beats/min	13	70 ±8	67 ±7†	70 ±7
Rectal temperature, °C	5	37.5 ±0.4	37.4 ±0.3	37.3 ±0.2
Skin resistance, kilohms	15	90.9 ±46.1	234.6 ±58.5*	120.5 ±92.0

P is the probability of the mean value of the precontrol period being identical to the mean value of the meditation period. *$P < 0.005$.   †$P < 0.05$.

After meditation skin resistance decreased, but remained higher than before meditation.

The EEG pattern during transcendental meditation showed increased intensity (mean square amplitude) of 8–9 cycles/sec activity (slow alpha waves) in the central and frontal regions (Fig. 1). The change in intensity of 10–11 ˙cycles/sec alpha waves during meditation was

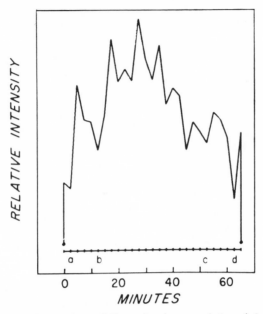

FIG. 1. Relative intensity of 9 cycles/sec activity (alpha-wave activity) in lead FP1 (see text) in a representative subject. *a-b:* premeditation control period with eyes closed. *b-c:* meditation period. *c-d:* postmeditation period with eyes closed. During meditation period, relative intensity of alpha-wave activity increased.

variable. In five subjects, the increased intensity of 8–9 cycles/sec activity was accompanied by occasional trains of 5–7 cycles/sec waves (theta waves) in the frontal channel (Fig. 2). Intensity of 12–14 cycles/sec waves and 2–4 cycles/sec waves either decreased or remained constant during meditation. In three subjects, who reported feeling tired and drowsy at the beginning of meditation, flattening of the alpha activity and low voltage mixed frequency waves with a prominence of 2–7 cycles/sec activity was noted. As meditation in these three subjects continued, the pattern was replaced by regular alpha activity. In the five subjects in whom electro-oculograms were recorded, no changes were observed.

Consistent and pronounced physiologic changes occurred during the practice of a mental technique called transcendental meditation (Table 1). The respiratory changes consisted of decreased O_2 consumption, CO_2 elimination, respiratory rate, and minute ventilation, with no change in respiratory quotient. Arterial blood pH and base excess decreased slightly; interestingly, blood lactate also decreased. Skin resistance markedly increased and the EEG showed an increase in the intensity of slow alpha waves with occasional theta-wave activity.

The physiologic changes during transcendental meditation differed from those reported during sleep. The EEG patterns which characterize sleep (high-voltage slow-wave activity, 12–14 cycles/sec sleep spindles and low-voltage mixed-frequency activity with or without rapid eye movements) (45), were not seen during transcendental meditation. After 6–7 hr of sleep, and during high-voltage slow-wave activity, O_2 consumption usually decreases about 15% (8, 10, 20, 33, 47). After only 5–10 min of meditation, alpha-wave activity predominated and O_2 consumption decreased about 17%. During sleep, arterial pH slightly decreases while P_{CO_2} increases significantly, indicating a respiratory acidosis (47). During meditation, arterial pH also decreased slightly. However, arterial P_{CO_2} remained constant while base excess decreased slightly, indicating a mild condition of metabolic acidosis. The skin-resistance changes during meditation were also different from those observed during sleep (22, 54). In sleep, skin resistance most commonly increases continuously, but the magnitude and rate of increase are generally less than that which occurred during meditation.

The consistent physiologic changes noted during transcendental meditation also differed from those reported during hypnosis or autosuggestion. During hypnosis, heart rate, blood pressure, skin resistance, and respiration either increase, decrease, or remain unchanged, approximating changes which normally occur during the states which have been suggested (5, 25, 32). During so-called hypnotic sleep, in which complete relaxation has been suggested, no

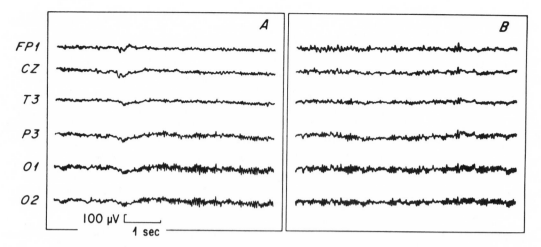

FIG. 2. EEG records of a subject with theta-wave activity during meditation. A: EEG record close to start of meditation period. B: EEG record during middle of meditation period. EEG leads are noted on vertical axis (see text). In A, alpha-wave activity is present as shown in leads P3, 01 and 02. In B, prominent theta-wave activity is present in lead FP1 simultaneous with alpha-wave activity in leads T3, P3, 01, and 02.

noticeable change in O_2 consumption occurs (5, 24, 60). EEG patterns occurring during hypnosis are usually similar to the suggested wakeful patterns and therefore differ greatly from those observed during meditation (32).

Operant conditioning procedures employing physiologic feedback can also alter autonomic nervous system functions and EEG patterns (9, 21, 28, 31, 39, 50). Animals can be trained to control autonomic functions, such as blood pressure, heart rate, and urine formation (9, 18, 39). Human subjects can alter their heart rate and blood pressure by use of operant conditioning techniques (31, 35, 50) and can be trained to increase alpha-wave activity through auditory and visual feedback (21, 28). However, the physiologic changes during transcendental meditation occurred simultaneously and without the use of specific feedback procedures.

The relative contribution of various tissues to lactate production has not been established, but muscle has been presumed to be a major source (16). The fall in blood lactate observed during meditation might be explained by increased skeletal muscle blood flow with consequent increased aerobic metabolism. Indeed, forearm blood flow increases 300% during meditation while finger blood flow remains unchanged (46). Patients with anxiety neurosis develop an excessive rise in blood lactate concentration with "stress" (12, 27). The infusion of lactate ion can sometimes produce anxiety symptoms in normal subjects and can regularly produce anxiety attacks in patients with anxiety neurosis (41). The decrease in lactate concentration during and after transcendental meditation may be related to the subjective feelings of wakeful relaxation before and after meditation. Further, essential and renal hypertensive patients have higher resting serum lactate levels than normotensive patients (17). The subjects practicing meditation had rather low resting systolic, diastolic, and mean blood pressures.

A consistent wakeful hypometabolic state accompanies the practice of the mental technique called transcendental meditation. Transcendental meditation can serve, at the present time, as one method of eliciting these physiologic changes. However, the possibility exists that these changes represent an integrated response that may well be induced by other means.

The authors thank Mr. Michael D. Garrett, Mr. Robert C. Boise, and Miss Barbara R. Marzetta for their competent technical assistance; Dr. Walter H. Abelmann and Dr. J. Alan Herd for their review of the manuscript; and Mrs. G. Shephard for typing the manuscript.

This investigation was supported by Public Health Service Grants HE 10539-04, SF 57-111, NIMH 2-T01, MH 06415-12, and RR-76 from the General Clinical Research Centers Program of the Division of Research Resources; the Council for Tobacco Research; and Hoffmann-LaRoche, Inc., Nutley, N. J. 07110.

Some of these data were submitted by R. K. Wallace in partial fulfillment of the requirements for the degree of Doctor of Philosophy in physiology at the University of California, Los Angeles. A preliminary report of another part of these experiments was presented at the April, 1971, meeting of the Federation of American Societies for Experimental Biology.

Received for publication 22 February 1971.

REFERENCES

1. Akishige, Y. A historical survey of the psychological studies in Zen. *Kyushu Psychol. Studies, V, Bull. Fac. Lit. Kyushu Univ.* 11: 1–56, 1968.

2. Allison, J. Respiration changes during transcendental meditation. *Lancet* 1: 833–834, 1970.

3. Anand, B. K., G. S. Chhina, and B. Singh. Some aspects of electroencephalographic studies in Yogis. *Electroencephalog. Clin. Neurophysiol.* 13: 452–456, 1961.

4. Bagchi, B. K., and M. A. Wenger. Electrophysiological correlates of some Yogi exercises. *Electroencephalog. Clin. Neurophysiol.* Suppl. 7: 132–149, 1957.

5. Barber, T. X. Physiological effects of "hypnosis." *Psychol. Bull.* 58: 390–419, 1961.

6. Behanan, K. T. *Yoga, a Scientific Evaluation.* New York: Macmillan, 1937.

7. Benedict, F. G., and C. G. Benedict. *Mental Effort in Relation to Gaseous Exchange, Heart Rate, and Mechanics of Respiration.* Washington, D.C.: Carnegie Inst. Washington, 1933, p. 29–39.

8. Benedict, F. G., and T. M. Carpenter. *The Metabolism and Energy Transformation of Healthy Man During Rest.* Washington, D.C.: Carnegie Inst. Washington, 1910, p. 179–187.

9. Benson, H., J. A. Herd, W. H. Morse, and R. T. Kelleher. Behavioral induction of arterial hypertension and its reversal. *Am. J Physiol.* 217: 30–34, 1969.

10. Brebbia, D. R., and K. Z. Altshuler. Oxygen consumption rate and electroencephalographic stage of sleep. *Science* 150: 1621–1623, 1965.

11. Brosse, T. A psycho-physiological study. *Main Currents Modern Thought* 4: 77–84, 1946.

12. Cohen, M. E., and P. D. White. Life situations, emotions and neurocirculatory asthenia (anxiety neurosis, neurasthenia, effort syndrome). *Res. Publ. Assoc. Res. Nervous Mental Disease* 29: 832–869, 1950.

13. Consolozio, F., R. E. Johnson, and L. J. Pecora. *Physiological Measurements of Metabolic Functions in Man.* New York: McGraw-Hill, 1965, p. 1–30.

14. Das, N. N., and H. Gastaut. Variations de l'activité electrique due cerveau, du coeur et des muscles squelletiques au cours de la meditation et de l'extase Yogique. *Electroencephalog. Clin. Neurophysiol.* Suppl. 6: 211–219, 1957.

15. Datey, K. K., S. N. Deshmukh, C. P. Dalvi, and S. L. Vinekar. "Shavasan": a yogic exercise in the management of hypertension. *Angiology* 20: 325–333, 1969.

16. Decker, D. G., and J. D. Rosenbaum. The distribution of lactic acid in human blood. *Am. J. Physiol.* 138: 7–11, 1942–43.

17. Demartini, F. E., P. J. Cannon, W. B. Stason, and J. H. Laragh. Lactic acid metabolism in hypertensive patients. *Science* 148: 1482–1484, 1965.

18. DiCara, L. V., and N. E. Miller. Instrumental learning of systolic blood pressure responses by curarized rats: dissociation of cardiac and vascular changes. *Psychosomat. Med.* 30: 489–494, 1968.

19. Dixon, W. J. (Editor). *BMD: Biomedical Computer Programs: X-Series Programs Supplement.* Los Angeles, Calif.: Univ. of California Press, 1969.

20. Grollman, A. Physiological variations in the cardiac output of man. *Am. J. Physiol.* 95: 274–284, 1930.

21. Hart, J. T. Autocontrol of EEG alpha. *Psychophysiology* 4: 506, 1968.

22. Hawkins, D. R., H. B. Puryeur, C. D. Wallacf, W. B. Deal, and E. S. Thomas. Basal skin resistance during sleep and "dreaming." *Science* 136: 321–322, 1962.

23. Hoenig, J. Medical research on Yoga. *Conf. Psychiat.* 11: 69–89, 1968.

24. Jana, H. Energy metabolism in hypnotic trance and sleep. *J. Appl. Physiol.* 20: 308–310, 1965.

25. Jana, H. Effect of hypnosis on circulation and respiration. *Indian J. Med. Res.* 55: 591–598, 1967.

26. Jasper, H. H. The ten twenty electrode system of the international federation. *Electroencephalog. Clin. Neurophysiol.* 10: 371–375, 1958.

27. Jones, M., and V. Mellersh. Comparison of exercise response in anxiety states and normal controls. *Psychosomat. Med.* 8: 180–187, 1946.

28. Kamiya, J. Operant control of the EEG alpha rhythm and some of its reported effects of consciousness. In: *Altered States of Consciousness*, edited by C. T. Tart. New York: Wiley, 1969, p. 507–517.

29. Karambelkar, P. V., S. L. Vinekar, and M. V. Bhole. Studies on human subjects staying in an airtight pit. *Indian J. Med. Res.* 56: 1282–1288, 1968.

30. Kasamatsu, A., and T. Hirai. An electroencephalographic study on the Zen mediation (Zazen). *Folia Psychiat. Neurol. Japon.* 20: 315–336, 1966.

31. Katkin, E. S., and E. N. Murray. Instrumental conditioning of autonomically mediated behavior: theoretical and methodological issues. *Psychol. Bull.* 70: 52–68, 1968.

32. Kleitman, N. *Sleep and Wakefulness.* Chicago: Univ. of Chicago Press, 1963, p. 329–330.

33. Kreider, M. B., and P. F. Iampietro. Oxygen consumption and body temperature during sleep in cold environments. *J. Appl. Physiol.* 14: 765–767, 1959.

34. Landis, C. Studies of emotional reactions IV. Metabolic rate. *Am. J. Physiol.* 74: 188–203, 1925.

35. Levene, H. I., B. T. Engel, and J. A. Pearson. Differential operant conditioning of heart rate. *Psychosomat. Med.* 30: 837–845, 1968.

36. Maharishi Mahesh Yogi. *Maharishi Mahesh Yogi on the Bhagavad*

Gita: A New Translation and Commentary. Baltimore: Penguin, 1969, p. 10–17.

37. MAHARISHI MAHESH YOGI. *The Science of Being and Art of Living.* London: Intern. SRM Publ. 1966, p. 50–59.

38. MILES, W. R. Oxygen consumption during three yoga-type breathing patterns. *J. Appl. Physiol.* 19: 75–82, 1964.

39. MILLER, N. E., AND L. V. DICARA. Instrumental learning of urine formation by rats; changes in renal blood flow. *Am. J. Physiol.* 215: 677–683, 1968.

40. O'CONNELL, D. N., AND B. TURSKY. Silver-silver chloride sponge electrodes for skin potential recording. *Am. J. Psychol.* 73: 302–306, 1960.

41. PITTS, F. N., JR., AND J. N. MCCLURE, JR. Lactate metabolism in anxiety neurosis. *New Engl. J. Med.* 277: 1329–1336, 1967.

42. RAO, S. Metabolic cost of head-stand posture. *J. Appl. Physiol.* 17: 117–118, 1962.

43. RAO, S. Cardiovascular responses to head-stand posture. *J. Appl. Physiol.* 18: 987–990, 1963.

44. RAO, S. Oxygen consumption during yoga-type breathing at altitudes of 520 m and 3800 m. *Indian J. Med. Res.* 56: 701–705, 1968.

45. RESCHTSCHAFFEN, A., AND A. KALES, R. J. BERGER, W. C. DE-MENT, A. JACOBSON, L. C. JOHNSON, M. JOUVET, L. J. MONROE, I. OSWALD, H. P. ROFFWARD, B. ROTH, AND R. D. WALTER. *A Manual of Standardized Terminology, Techniques and Scoring System for Sleep Stages of Human Subjects.* Washington, D. C.: U. S. Govt. Printing Office, 1968.

46. RIECHERT, H. Plethysmograpische Untersuchungen bei Konzentrations-und Meditationsübungen. *Ärztliche Forsch.* 21: 61–65, 1967.

47. ROBIN, E. D., R. D. WHALEY, C. H. CRUMP, AND D. M. TRAVIS. Alveolar gas tensions, pulmonary ventilation and blood pH during physiologic sleep in normal subjects. *J. Clin. Invest.* 37: 981–989, 1958.

48. SCHOLZ, R., H. SCHMITZ, T. BUCHLER, AND J. O. LAMPEN. Über die Wirkung von Nystatin auf Bäckerhefe. *Biochem, Z.* 331: 71–86, 1959.

49. SEVERINGHAUS, J. W., AND A. F. BRADLEY. Electrodes for blood P_{O_2} and P_{CO_2} determination. *J. Appl. Physiol.* 13: 515–520, 1958.

50. SHAPIRO, D., B. TURSKY, E. GERSHON, AND M. STERN. Effects of feedback and reinforcement on the control of human systolic blood pressure. *Science* 163: 588–590, 1969.

51. SIGGARD-ANDERSEN, O. *The Acid-Base Status of the Blood.* Baltimore: Williams & Wilkins, 1963.

52. SNEDECOR, G. W., AND W. G. COCHRAN. *Statistical Methods.* Ames, Iowa: Iowa State Univ. Press, 1960, p. 91–119.

53. SUGI, Y., AND K. AKUTSU. Studies on respiration and energy-metabolism during sitting in Zazen. *Res. J. Phys. Ed.* 12: 190–206, 1968.

54. TART, C. T. Patterns of basal skin resistance during sleep. *Psychophysiology* 4: 35–39, 1967.

55. VAKIL, R. J. Remarkable feat of endurance of a Yogi priest. *Lancet* 2: 871, 1950.
56. WALLACE, R. K. Physiological effects of transcendental meditation. *Science* 167: 1751–1754, 1970.
57. WALTER, D. O., J. M. RHODES, D. BROWN, AND W. R. ADEY. Comprehensive spectral analysis of human EEG generators in posterial cerebral regions. *Electroencephalog. Clin. Neurophysiol.* 20: 224–237, 1966.
58. WENGER, M. A., AND B. K. BAGCHI. Studies of autonomic functions in practitioners of Yoga in India. *Behavioral Sci.* 6: 312–323, 1961.
59. WENGER, M. A., B. K. BAGCHI, AND B. K. ANAND. Experiments in India on "voluntary" control of the heart and pulse. *Circulation* 24: 1319–1325, 1961.
60. WHITEHORN, J. C., H. LUNDHOLM, E. L. FOX, AND F. G. BENEDICT. The metabolic rate in "hypnotic sleep." *New Engl. J. Med.* 206: 777–781, 1932.
61. WHITEHORN, J. C., H. LUNDHOLM, AND G. E. GARDNER. The metabolic rate in emotional moods induced by suggestion in hypnosis. *Am. J. Psychiat.* 86: 661–666, 1929–30.

AUTONOMIC STABILITY AND
TRANSCENDENTAL MEDITATION

David W. Orme-Johnson

Physiological indices of stress were found to be lower in people who regularly practiced Transcendental Meditation *(N=*14) than in nonmeditating control subjects *(N=*16). During normal waking (eyes open) a noxious loud tone (100 db, 0.5 sec, 3000 Hz) was presented to subjects a mean of once every 53 sec at irregular intervals. The stress reaction to each tone, as indicated by the galvanic skin response (GSR), was compared for the two groups. Habituation of the GSR to tones was faster for meditators than for controls, and meditators made fewer multiple responses during habituation, indicating greater stability in response to stress. In two other experiments, meditators were found to make fewer spontaneous GSR's than control subjects, both during meditation, as compared with rest (eyes closed), and while out of meditation with eyes open. Thus meditators were found to be more stable than controls on three autonomic indices: rate of GSR habituation, multiple responses, and spontaneous GSR.

Transcendental Meditation (TM) is a mental technique of deep relaxation which was adapted for Westerners from the Vedic tradition of India by Maharishi Mahesh Yogi. TM has been shown to produce a physiologic state of restful alertness which is different from sleep, dreaming, hypnosis, or waking (1, 2, 3, 4). The regular experience of this state is reported to alleviate drug abuse (5, 6, 7, 8)

and a variety of psychosomatic disorders (1). Meditators typically report that they progressively acquire more emotional stability and less susceptibility to the debilitating effects of stress as a benefit of meditating (9, 10, 11, 12, 13). The present study is an initial investigation of the effects of TM on two indices of stress, spontaneous fluctuations in skin resistance (GSR or galvanic skin response) and GSR habituation.

Spontaneous GSR is defined as fluctuations in skin resistance which occur independently of ambient noise or movements by the subject. The frequency of spontaneous GSR is one way of defining the lability or stress level of an individual (14, 15, 16). When a person is angry or fearful the frequency rises (17), as it does when adrenaline and nonadrenaline levels increase (18). Stimulants (19) and environmental stresses of various kinds

From the Department of Psychology, The University of Texas at El Paso, El Paso, Texas

A modified version of this paper was presented at the Stanford Research Institute, Menlo Park, California, August 5, 1971, and at the Second International Symposium of the Science of Creative Intelligence, Humboldt State College, Arcata, California, August 22, 1971.

Received for publication December 16, 1971; final revision received December 20, 1972.

Address for reprint requests: David Orme-Johnson, Ph.D., Maharishi International University, 1015 Gayley Avenue, Los Angeles, California 90024.

also elevate the frequency of spontaneous GSR (18, 20, 21, 22, 23). Within a given situation, some individuals (stabiles) consistently show lower frequencies of spontaneous GSR than other individuals (labiles). Stabiles exhibit more effective behavior than labiles in a number of situations. For example, they are better able to withstand stresses (18, 23, 24) and they score higher on Barron's Ego Strength scale which measures general ability to cope with environmental pressures (25). Stabiles are less impulsive on motor tasks (26) and have quicker perceptions (Embedded Figures Test) (27). They also are less conditionable to aversive stimuli than labiles (16, 28, 29, 30). Thus, for stabiles, present behavior is less likely to be restricted by past conditioning.

The frequency of spontaneous GSR is also correlated with the rate of GSR habituation. When tones are repeatedly presented to subjects, stabiles habituate faster on the GSR than labiles (14, 15, 31, 32, 33). Rapid habituators tend to be more extroverted than introverted (34) and psychologically normal persons habituate more rapidly than schizophrenics (35). When schizophrenics were measured and then retested in five weeks, those who habituated faster on the second testing had better hospital discharge records than the slow habituators (36). This research indicates a correlation of rapid habituation with improved mental health. Furthermore, rapid habituation is characteristic of species higher on the philogenetic scale, and it may be considered as a more highly evolved form of adaptation than slow habituation (37). The present investigation compared the rate of GSR habituation between meditator and nonmeditator groups. Three weeks later, these two groups were compared on spontaneous GSR. The investigation of spontaneous GSR was then replicated using new groups of subjects.

METHOD

Subjects

The initial study of GSR habituation and spontaneous GSR (EXP I) was with eight subjects of college background in the meditator and nonmeditator groups. Both groups consisted of three females and five males and the mean age of the meditators was 24 years (range 19–33 years) and the mean age of nonmeditators was 28 years (range 19–40 years). The meditators were obtained through the University of Texas at El Paso Center of the Students International Meditation Society, and each had been instructed in meditation by a teacher qualified by Maharishi to teach Transcendental Meditation. All meditators regularly practiced TM (twice a day for 15–20 minutes each time), and they had been meditating from two to 36 months, with a mean of 15 months.

The second study (EXP II) of spontaneous GSR was of a different group of eight meditators (three females and five males) and eight nonmeditators (two females and six males) who planned to start the practice of TM in two weeks. Two of the meditators were not included in the final data analysis, one because he began meditation during a rest control period, and the other because she had a history of unwarned shocks in a psychological laboratory. This left six meditators, two females and four males, whose ages ranged 19–40, with a mean age of 24 years. The ages of nonmeditators in the second study ranged 13–40 years with a mean age of 23 years. The six meditators in the second experiment had been meditating regularly for a mean of 24 months (range 2–54 months). Of the 14 meditators, four had been in the experimental room before. Of the 16 nonmeditators, five had been in the experimental room before. The experimenter personally knew nine of the meditators before the experiment and seven of the nonmeditators.

Apparatus

The tone used in the habituation study was generated by a Maico Audiometer and delivered through earphones monaurally. The GSR was recorded on a Lafayette Polygraph which used the exosomatic (Féré) method of applied current. Silver-plated contoured electrodes, 4 x 6 cm on the palm and 1.5 x 2 cm on the middle finger, were used with Hewlett Packard Electrolyte Redux creme electrode paste. The experiment was conducted in a quiet room with a temperature thermostatically controlled at 72°F. Subjects were seated in a comfortable chair placed in front of and facing away from the table containing the audiometer and polygraph, so that subjects could not see the apparatus, but the experimenter, seated quietly at the table, could observe any movements made by the subject.

Procedure

Subjects were invited into the experimental room and asked to sit in the chair. The electrodes were attached and subjects were instructed, "I am going to measure your response to some loud tones played through these earphones. Please just sit comfortably until I indicate that we are finished." The earphones were then put on the subject and the experiment began.

The tone was 100 decibels SPL, 3000 Hz, 0.5 sec, and was presented an average of once every 53 sec, with a range 10–190 sec between stimulus presentations. The GSR was allowed to recover and/or stabilize before the next tone was presented. Tones were presented until three consecutive responses of an amplitude of less than 0.35 K ohms occurred, and this was the criterion for habituation. Response measures used were latency, or the time from the onset of the tone until the onset of the response, half-life, which is the time taken to recover half of the maximum deflection of the response, and amplitude or the maximum deflection of the responses. Half-life was determined by means of a transparent overlay described by Edelberg (38).

Spontaneous GSR, which has been shown to be relatively stabile over time (33), was measured three weeks later for the subjects from the habituation experiment. Seven subjects from each group were able to come back for this measure. Spontaneous GSR was measured during three periods, 10 min of rest, eyes open (all subjects); 10 min of rest, eyes closed (nonmeditators), or 10 min meditation; and 10 minutes of rest, eyes open (all subjects). Subjects were invited in and instructed, "I am going to take some physiological measures, GSR, while you are resting. Sit down; make yourself comfortable. All you have to do is rest for 30 minutes, then we will be finished. (Electrodes were attached.) I would like for you to rest with your eyes open for 10 minutes, then I will signal you to close your eyes for 10 minutes of rest (or meditation), then I will signal you again to open your eyes for 10 minutes. Sit comfortably. It's important not to move your hand, so make yourself comfortable. If you have to scratch or something, that's okay, go ahead and scratch. I'm going to start now, so just sit comfortably for 10 minutes with your eyes open." Basal resistance was measured before and after each 10 min period, and spontaneous GSR

was measured during each period. A spontaneous response was defined as a sudden decrease in resistance of 100 ohms or more followed by a recovery of resistance, and only responses which occurred independently of noise or movement were scored as "spontaneous." In the second spontaneous GSR study, the same procedure and instructions were used as in the above study.

RESULTS AND DISCUSSION

Habituation

For the first 11 trials, habituation was similar for meditators and nonmeditators. During this period the latency and recovery time of responses (half-life) did not differ significantly between the two groups. (See Table 1.) Neither did response amplitude for the first 11 trials; a chi square for goodness of fit between the mean amplitude curves for meditators and controls over the first 11 trials was not significant ($x^2 = 12.5$, $df = 10$, $0.3 > P > 0.2$). However, although habituation was initially similar for the two groups, meditators habituated in significantly fewer trials than nonmeditators.

These results are consistent with the findings of others that response amplitude is initially similar for fast and slow habituators (14). (See Table 1 and Figure 1.) The mean number of trials to criterion was 11.0 for meditators and 26.1 for nonmeditators. In addition, three of the nonmeditators never met criterion before

TABLE 1   Results of Habituation Study Latency and Half-Life for the First 11 Trials

	Latency (sec)		Half-Life (sec)		Trials to Criterion		Multiple Responses to First Tone	
	M	S	M	S	M	S	M	S
Meditators	2.26	0.31	11.9	10.22	11.0	4.81	1	0.92
Nonmeditators	2.70	0.68	17.5	9.74	26.1	12.8	2.25	1.28
t tests $df = 14$	$t = 1.6$, NS		$t = 1.12$, NS		$t = 3.13$, $P < 0.01$		$t = 2.23$ $P < 0.05$	
Randomization test [a]					$P < 0.01$			

[a]Siegel S: Nonparametric Statistics for the Behavioral Sciences. New York, McGraw-Hill, 1956, pp. 152–156

the session had to be terminated, whereas all meditators reached criterion.

Insert A in Figure 1 shows that meditators also made fewer multiple responses than controls. The difference between the two groups on the mean number of multiple reponses to the first tone was statistically significant (see Table 1), but the curves do not significantly differ otherwise. For both groups, the number of multiple responses decreased during habituation, indicating that the wave form of the GSR tends to stabilize as habituation progresses.

To summarize, when noxious tones were presented to the two groups, the GSR was initially more stable and habituated faster for meditators than for controls.

Spontaneous GSR Exp I, Subjects from the Habituation Study

with 18.25 per 10 minutes for controls during rest, eyes closed (see Figure 2 and Table 2). During the two periods of rest, eyes open, meditators made a mean of 8.71 responses per 10 minutes, compared with 21.0 per 10 minutes for control subjects. Thus, meditators were more stabile than control subjects out of meditation as well as during meditation.

The frequency of spontaneous GSR was significantly correlated with trials to criterion during habituation ($r=0.73$) for the combined data of the two groups. This result is consistent with several studies in the literature showing that stabile subjects habituate faster than labile subjects (14, 15, 31, 32, 33). The correlation between the frequency of spontaneous GSR measured in this experiment and number of

The mean basal resistance during rest, eyes open, did not differ significantly between the two groups in either EXP I or

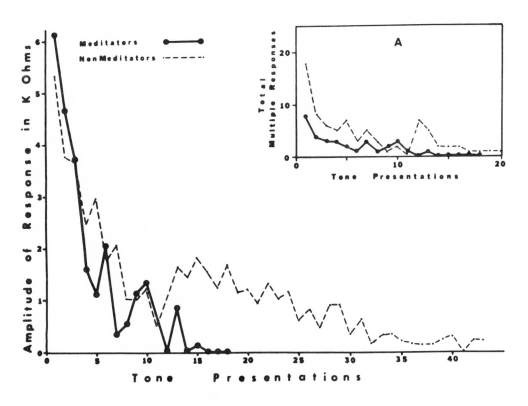

Fig. 1. This figure shows the mean response amplitude as a function of serial tone presentations for the meditator and nonmeditator groups. Insert A shows the total number of multiple responses for each group over tone presentations.

TABLE 2   100 ohm or Greater Spontaneous GSR/10 min

	Meditation or Rest, Eyes Closed		Rest, Eyes Open		Basal Resistance (in K ohms)	
Exp. I	M	S	M	S	M	S
Meditators	6.14	6.90	8.71	4.57	45.3	9.7
Nonmeditators	18.25	10.56	21.0	11.77	44.2	7.6
t test df = 12	t = 2.56, P < 0.05		t = 2.57 P < 0.05		NS	
Randomization test[a]	P < 0.05		P < 0.05			
Exp. II	M	S	M	S	M	S
Meditators	2.66	2.34	9.75	3.43	41.0	11.8
Nonmeditators	29.13	20.86	34.25	20.14	38.8	14.3
t test df = 12	t = 3.55, P<0.01		t = 3.37, P<0.01		NS	
Randomization test[a]	P<0.01		P<0.01			

[a]Siegel S: Nonparametric Statistics for the Behavioral Sciences. New York, McGraw-Hill, 1956, pp. 152–156

EXP II. (See Table 2.) Because basal resistances were equivalent for the two groups, the more convenient resistance measures were used to measure spontaneous GSR rather than conductance units.

Meditators were found to be more stabile as measured by a low frequency of spontaneous GSR than controls. During meditation, the mean rate of spontaneous GSR's was 6.14 per 10 min, compared multiple responses during habituation was also significant ($r=0.75$). Thus, a more stabile individual, as measured by spontaneous GSR, is also more stabile during habituation.

Spontaneous GSR, Exp II, Nonmeditators Who Planned to Start TM

The results of this experiment showed that subjects planning to start meditation made more spontaneous GSR than subjects already meditating. (See Figure 2 and Table 2.) Nonmeditators made a mean of 34.25 responses per 10 min during the two rest, eyes open periods, compared with 9.75 responses per 10 min for meditators.

There was a small but fairly consistent decrease in spontaneous GSR going from rest, eyes open, to meditation. Out of 13 measurements in the two experiments, spontaneous GSR decreased 10 times, increased twice, and stayed the same once during meditation ($p=0.038$, Sign test). For controls, closing the eyes didn't have any consistent effect on spontaneous GSR. It decreased six times out of 15.

Approximately 20% of the responses made in the two experiments were correlated with movement by the subject and were not included in the above data analysis. A rationale could be made that they should be included in the analysis because spontaneous GSR and movement-correlated GSR may have a common source. For example, an anxiety provoking thought may produce both spontaneous GSR and a shifting of posture. Therefore, an analysis was made of the total GSR fluctuations over 100 ohms; total GSR = spontaneous GSR + movement-correlated GSR. This inclusion of movement-correlated GSR in the analysis

Physiology of Meditation

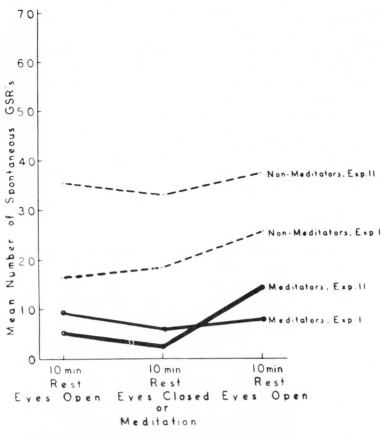

Fig. 2. The mean number of spontaneous GSRs for the various experimental conditions for the indicated groups is shown. "Exp. 1" refers to subjects from the habituation study, and "Exp. II" refers to the experiment in which the control group was composed of nonmeditators who plánned to start TM.

modified the interpretation of the results of EXP I, but does not change the interpretation of EXP II or the interpretation of combined results of the two experiments. Meditators and nonmeditators did not differ significantly on the mean number of movement-correlated responses in EXP I, and total GSR (15/10 min for meditators, 25/10 min for nonmeditators) did not show a significant difference. However, the interpretation of EXP II was essentially unchanged by including movement produced GSR in the analysis, and the combined data on total GSR for the two experiments was statistically different for the two groups (mean meditator = 14.17/10 min, mean

nonmeditator = 29.11/10 min: $t=3.03$, $df=26$, $p < 0.01$).

During meditation, basal resistance increased for 12 out of 13 individuals ($p=0.004$, Sign test) consistent with Wallace's (2) finding that basal resistance increases during meditation. During rest, eyes closed, for control subjects, basal resistance increased 7 out of 15 times, a nonsignificant change.

Familiarity with the experimental conditions (laboratory and experimenter) is an important determinant of autonomic arousal (39). In the present experiment, subjects from the two groups had a similar amount of prior exposure to the laboratory and acquaintance with the experimenter, with a slight advantage for meditators (see section on subjects). However, additional data on eight meditators attending a teacher training course at Humboldt State College supports the conclusion that the low resting levels of sympathetic activity by meditators seen in the present experiment is not just due to laboratory familiarity. Of the eight college age subjects at Humboldt, only one subject previously knew the experimenter or had been in the experimental room before. The resting levels of spontaneous GSR for this group were $M=7.15/10$ min, $S=5.9$, quite low when compared with the present control subject data. These results support the conclusion that the practice of Transcendental Meditation itself is responsible for the autonomic stability observed in meditators.

SUMMARY

Rapid GSR habituation and low levels of spontaneous GSR are reported in the literature to be correlated with physiological and behavioral characteristics associated with good mental health, e.g. behavioral and autonomic stability, less motor impulsivity, stronger ego, outgoingness, field independence, less susceptibility to a variety of stresses, and less susceptibility to acquiring conditioned stresses. In the present study rapid GSR habituation and low levels of spontaneous GSR were observed in practitioners of Transcendental Meditation. Eight meditators and eight nonmeditators were presented with 100 db, 0.5 sec, 3000 Hz tones at irregular intervals at a mean of once every 53 sec. Meditators habituated in a mean of 11 trials and nonmeditators in 26.1 trials, a statistically significant difference. In addition, meditators made fewer multiple responses in the recovery limb of the GSR to the first tone. In a second experiment three weeks later, meditators made fewer spontaneous GSR fluctuations (100 ohm or greater) than nonmeditators.

A third study showed that nonmeditators planning to begin TM made higher resting levels of spontaneous GSR than meditators. By three criteriá of autonomic stability: rate of habituation, number of multiple responses, and spontaneous GSR, meditators were more stabile than control subjects.

The author wishes to thank Richard Moore, Tom Rosell, and David Beaver for their assistance in the data analysis, Dr. John Bristol for his interest and support of the project, George Kavanagh for doing the photographic work, Mrs. Dorothy Alderman and Mrs. Carolyn Skriiko for typing the manuscript, and the Human Resources Research Organization, Division No. 5 for the use of their computer and photographic facilities.

REFERENCES

1. Wallace RK: The Physiological Effects of Transcendental Meditation: A Proposed Fourth Major State of Consciousness. Los Angeles, Herbert Herz Co., 1970
2. Wallace RK: Physiological Effects of Transcendental Meditation. Science 167:1751–1754, 1970
3. Wallace RK, Benson H, Wilson AF: A wakeful hypometabolic physiologic state. A J Physiol 221:795–799, 1971
4. Wallace RK, Benson H: The physiology of meditation. Sci Amer 226: 84–90, 1972
5. Benson H; Yoga for drug abuse. N Eng J Med, 281:20, 1969
6. Benson H, Wallace RK: Decreased drug abuse with Transcendental Meditation—a study of 1,862 subjects, in Drug Abuse, Proceedings of the International Conference. Philadelphia, Lea & Febiger, 1972 (edited by CJD Aarafonetis), pp. 369–376.
7. Otis L: Survey results presented in plates 15, 16, in Scientific Research on Transcendental Meditation. Los Angeles, MIU Press, 1972
8. Brautigam E: The effect of Transcendental Meditation on drug abuses. Unpublished research report, Dec 1971. (Copies may be obtained from SIMS, 2202 Pico, Santa Monica, Cal.)

9. Schultz T: What science is discovering about the potential benefits of Meditation. Today's Health 50 No. 4: April, 1972

10. Towards pinning down meditation. Hospital Times, May 1, 1970

11. Keil P: Pillar to post. California Business, January 4, 1971

12. Kanellakos DP: Voluntary Improvement of Individual Performance: Literature Survey. Menlo Park, Cal. Stanford Research Institute Report 24–29, 1970

13. Robbins J, Fisher D: Tranquility Without Pills, All About Transcendental Meditation. New York, Peter H. Wyden, 1972

14. Katkin ES, McCubbin RJ: Habituation of the orienting response as a function of individual differences in anxiety and autonomic lability. J. Abnorm Psychol 74:54–60, 1969

15. Mundy-Castle AC, McKiever BL: The psychophysiological significance of the galvanic skin response. J Exp psychol 46:15–24, 1953

16. Stern JA: Stability-lability of physiological response systems. Ann NY Acad Sci 134:1018–1027, 1966

17. Ax Af: The physiological differentiation between fear and anger in humans. Psychosom Med 15:433–442, 1953

18. Silverman AJ, Cohen SI, Shmavonian BM: Investigation of psychophysiologic relationships with skin resistance measures. J Psychosom Res 4:65–87, 1959

19. Greiner TH, Burch NR; Response of human GSR to drugs that influence the reticular formation of brain stem. Fed Proc 14: 346, 1955

20. Katkin ES: Relationship between manifest anxiety and two indices of autonomic response to stress. J Pers Soc Psychol 2: 324–333, 1965

21. Katkin ES: The relationship between a measure of transitory anxiety and spontaneous autonomic activity. J Abnorm Psychol 71:142–146, 1966

22. Rappaport H, Katkin ES: Relationship among manifest anxiety, response to stress and the perception of autonomic activity. Unpublished manuscript, State University of New York at Buffalo, Department of Psychology, 1967

23. Zuckerman M: Perceptual isolation as a stress situation. Arch Gen Psychiat 11:255–276, 1964

24. Burch GE, Cohn AE, Neuman C: A study by quantitative methods of spontaneous variations in volume of the fingertip, toe tip and posterio-superior portion of the pinna of resting, normal, white adults. Amer J Physiol 136:433–447, 1942

25. Alexander AA, Roessler R, Greenfield N: Ego strength and physiological responsivity. Arch Gen Psychiatry 9:142–145, 1963

26. Lacey JI, Lacey BC: The relationship of resting autonomic cyclic activity to motor impulsivity, in The Brain and Human Behavior. HC Solomon, Baltimore, Williams and Wilkins, 1958 (Edited by S Cobb and W Pennfield)

27. Hustmyer FE Jr., Karnes, E: Background autonomic activity and "analytic perception." J Abnorm and Soc Psychol 68:467–468, 1964

28. Stern JA, Stewart MA, Winokur G: An investigation of some relationships between various measures of galvanic skin response. J Psychosom Res 5:215–223, 1961

29. Martin J: Variations in skin resistance and their relationship to GSR conditioning. J. Ment Sci 106:281, 1960

30. Spence KW: A theory of emotionally based drive (D) and its relation to performance in simple learning situations. The Am Psychol 13:131–141, 1958

31. Geer JH: Effect of interstimulus intervals and rest-period length upon habituation of the orienting response. J Exp Psychol 72:617–619, 1966

32. Koepke JE, Pribram KH: Habituation of GSR as a function of stimulus duration and spontaneous activity. J Comp Physiol Psychol 61:442–448, 1966

33. Johnson LC: Some attributes of spontaneous autonomic activity. J Comp Physiol Psychol 56:415–422, 1963

34. Scott ED, Wilkinson D: Adaptation as related to the introversion-extroversion dimension. U. S. Public Health Service, National Institute of Mental Health Report, Grant M1106956-01, 1962

35. Israel NR: Individual differences in GSR orienting response and cognitive control. J Exp Res Person 1:244–248, 1966

36. Stern JA, Surphlis W, Koff E: Electrodermal responsiveness as related to psychiatric diagnosis and prognosis. Psychophysiology 2:51–61, 1965

37. Vedyayev FP, Karmanova IG: On the comparative physiology of the orienting reflex, in Orienting Reflex and Exploratory Behavior. Washington, D. C., American Institute of Biological Sciences, (Edited by LG Vororin, AN Leontiev, AR Luria, EN Sokolov, OS Vinogradova), 1965 pp. 261–265

38. Edelberg R: The information content of the recovery limb of the electrodermal response. Psychophysiology 6:527–539, 1970

39. Sternback RA: Principles of Psychophysiology. New York and London, Academic Press, 1966, pp. 111–138

Wakeful Hypometabolic State 439

31

PSYCHOPHYSIOLOGICAL CORRELATES OF THE PRACTICE OF TANTRIC YOGA MEDITATION

James C. Corby, Walton T. Roth,
Vincent P. Zarcone, Jr., and Bert S. Kopell

● Autonomic and electroencephalographic (EEG) correlates of Tantric Yoga meditation were studied in three groups of subjects as they progressed from normal consciousness into meditation. Groups differed in their level of meditation proficiency. Measures of skin resistance, heart rate, respiration, autonomic orienting response, resting EEG, EEG alpha and theta frequencies, sleep-scored EEG, averaged evoked responses, and subjective experience were employed.

Unlike most previously reported meditation studies, proficient meditators demonstrated increased autonomic activation during meditation while unexperienced meditators demonstrated autonomic relaxation. During meditation, proficient meditators demonstrated increased alpha and theta power, minimal evidence of EEG-defined sleep, and decreased autonomic orienting to external stimulation. An episode of sudden autonomic activation was observed that was characterized by the meditator as an approach to the Yogic ecstatic state of intense concentration. These findings challenge the current "relaxation" model of meditative states.

(Arch Gen Psychiatry 35:571-577, 1978)

Meditation research since 1970 has been almost exclusively concerned with studies of Transcendental Meditation (TM), which uses techniques drawn from the Vedic tradition in India. As presented to the American public, TM employs a single-stage meditation during which the subjects sits quietly with eyes closed for 20 minutes twice a day and mentally repeats a specifically chosen Sanskrit word or *mantra*. The simplicity and uniformity of the technique make it relatively easy to teach. No philosophic or religious commitment is required of the practitioner. The TM meditation technique appears to have been chosen for its particular relaxing qualities; the now volumi-

Accepted for publication Sept 12, 1977.
From the Psychiatry Service, Veterans Administration Hospital, Palo Alto, Calif, and the Department of Psychiatry and Behavioral Sciences, Stanford (Calif) University School of Medicine.
Reprint requests to Department of Psychiatry and Behavioral Sciences, Stanford University School of Medicine, Stanford, CA 94305 (Dr Corby).

nous research literature documents a physiological state of deep relaxation characterized by lowered autonomic nervous system arousal and by a relative deactivation of the electroencephalograph (EEG), resulting typically in a shift to the higher voltage, slower frequencies of alpha and theta.[1-3] High frequency beta activity has been occasionally observed,[3] but the bulk of the reported findings present an EEG picture similar to drowsiness or stage 1 sleep.

With the exception of two field studies of Yoga in India by Das and Gastaut[4] and Wenger and Bagchi,[5] all researched meditations including Zazen and Indian Yoga appear similar to TM since they tend to produce states of lowered autonomic arousal and EEG deactivation. This convergence of EEG and autonomic findings supports the contention that meditation is primarily a state of deep physiological relaxation. The major reviews of the meditation literature by Kanellakos and Lukas,[6] Woolfolk,[7] and Davidson[8] take this position.

However, the exceptions deserve further scrutiny. Das and Gastaut[4] studied the meditations of seven highly experienced Yogis during Krya Yoga meditation, and reported clear signs of autonomic arousal and EEG activation, most pronounced during the deepest meditations of the most experienced subjects. They concluded that the techniques studied represented a state of intense concentration of attention that was probably not attained in Western students of Yoga. Wenger and Bagchi[5] reported autonomic activation with increased heart rate and skin conductance during the meditation of four Yoga students and five older Yogis. The more advanced subjects demonstrated greater autonomic activation. The EEG results were unremarkable. They commented that meditation was an active process for the Yogis who demonstrated autonomic activation, not a passive relaxed contemplation. Taken together, these two studies characterize meditation in a distinctly different light than the relaxation model of meditation. They suggest that meditative techniques involving active concentration may produce physiological activation when performed by very experienced subjects. This is in contrast to the relaxation reported in studies of meditation techniques that are relatively more passive and that typically have been practiced by less experienced meditators.

It should be emphasized that there is a wide diversity in India among schools of Yoga and their various meditational techniques. Previous studies have failed to clearly define the nature of techniques under scrutiny. Often subjects appear to have been chosen on the basis of a global assessment of competence in "Yogic meditation." Thus, studies of Indian Yoga may have lumped together practitioners of techniques that produced distinctly different physiological changes. It is probably inadequate to conceptualize Indian "Yogic Meditation" as a unitary discipline such as Zazen or TM.

For the above reasons, we chose to study Tantric Yoga, a type of meditation that seemed to clearly involve intense concentration of attention and the subjective sense of an ongoing struggle to achieve the ultimate union with the object of concentration and total self-absorption (*Samādhi*). The Tantric tradition has ancient roots that may antedate Yoga, but it has now been incorporated into the *Bhakti* or devotional tradition in Yoga. The Tantric tradition emphasizes that all the energies of the organism are potentially capable of transformation into the spiritual energy of union with the object of devotion. It is probable that the Krya meditators studied by Das and Gastaut[4] were from the Tantric tradition since their techniques utilized Tantric concepts of *kundalini* (spinal energy source) and *chakras* (spinal energy sites).

This study investigates a type of Tantric meditation practiced by Ananda Marga, which characterizes itself as an international society dedicated to the achievement of both social and individual spiritual goals. A considerable personal commitment is expected of the members. There is an emphasis on the ongoing relationship between the meditator and the Guru, or spiritual master. Advanced students meditate several hours a day. There are six lessons of progressively more advanced meditational techniques taught by traveling teachers or *Acharias*. Anada Marga practitioners often report the subjective sense of energy discharges or "rushes" at times during these meditations. Ananda Marga is currently practiced in 50 countries and is active in India. There are an estimated 100,000 practitioners.

This study conceptualized meditation as a set of techniques designed to improved the meditator's ability to concentrate attention and to direct its focus either inward or outward. With extended practice of meditation, one could be expected to demonstrate increased control over these dimensions of attention. We compared three carefully balanced groups of subjects that differed only in their prior experience with Ananda Marga meditation techniques. This study is unique in that a relatively large number of extremely proficient meditators were employed, and its design required the control group to actually perform meditation techniques similar to the techniques used by the experienced meditators. This rigorous control allowed differences between groups that emerged during meditation to be attributed to the effects of prolonged practice of meditation, rather than to the effects of the meditation techniques per se.

METHODS

Three groups of ten experimentally naive subjects (four women and six men) were paid to participate in the study. College student controls (mean age, 22.9 years) had no previous experience with meditation or attention control training. Trainees (mean age, 23.7 years) were recruited from the Ananda Marga Regional Training Center. They had been meditating for an average of 2.1 years and were meditating an average of 3.1 hours a day when studied. Experts (mean age, 25.8 years) were chosen by Ananda Marga as the ten most proficient meditators in the San Francisco area. They had been meditating for an average of 4.4 years and were meditating for an average of 3.4 hours a day when studied. All had met the spiritual leader of Ananda Marga during visits to India, and had received the most advanced set of meditation techniques. All subjects attended a laboratory orientation prior to the recording session and were asked to not use any drugs during the three days before the recording session. Informed consent was obtained after the nature of the procedures was fully explained.

For the recording session, subjects sat alone in a dimly lit, sound-attenuated room. Meditators sat in the half-lotus posture. Controls sat upright in a comfortable chair. A device that produced white noise when tipped by 45° was attached to the subject's head to signal overt sleep during the session.

Each subject received three 20-minute tone sequences with different instructions for each sequence. Each sequence consisted of 55-dB, 100-msec tones with a 10-msec rise-fall time presented at 1-second intervals by an overhead speaker. Within the sequence, an infrequent different frequency tone randomly replaced the frequent background tones with a ratio of 1:15 and occurred at intervals of 10 to 20 seconds. Frequencies of background and infrequent tones were either 500 or 800 Hz, balanced for order across subjects. These tones were presented to elicit cortical evoked potentials. Also, four 70-dB, 400-msec, white noise bursts were presented at approximately four-minute intervals to elicit the autonomic orienting response. A continuous 40-dB white noise masked extraneous laboratory sounds.

The three instruction conditions were designed to induce three states of consciousness. Condition order was fixed. Condition 1 was a baseline state of relaxed normal consciousness. Subjects were told to relax and pay attention to the background tone sequence. Condition 2 was a "withdrawal condition," taught by Ananda Marga as a preparation for meditation. Subjects were told to ignore external stimuli and pay attention to their breathing. Condition 3 was the Ananda Marga meditative state. Subjects were told to ignore external stimuli, pay attention to their breathing, and silently repeat a two-syllable word in phase with their breathing. Controls chose their own word, while meditators used their *mantras*, Sanskrit words chosen for this purpose by their meditation teachers. Instructions were read over an intercom to the subject before each tone sequence. After the recording session, subjects filled out a questionnaire dealing with their subjective experience during the sessions. Meditators rated the quality of their meditation on a ten-point scale. Room temperature was measured and sessions were conducted at either 4 or 6 PM, balanced for order across groups.

The EEG was recorded with subdermal pins (C_z referenced to joined mastoids) for frequency, evoked response, and sleep stage analysis.[10] The EEG and electro-oculogram (EOG) were recorded and amplified as described in previous publications.[9] Heart rate was recorded with Ag-AgCl disk electrodes using a lead II configuration, and amplified for FM tape recording. Skin resistance was recorded with Ag-AgCl disk electrodes (thenar eminence referenced to the abraded ventral forearm). The signal was passed through a skin resistance coupler adjusted for a constant current density of 10 μamp/sq cm. A forehead disk electrode grounded the subject. Respiration rate and depth were recorded from a midthoracic strain gauge whose signal was passed through a strain gauge coupler. All signals were recorded on a multichannel FM tape recorder for subsequent analysis and printout on paper charts. Conductive electrolyte electrode paste was used except for the skin resistance measure in which water-soluble lubricating jelly was used.

Data Analysis

Galvanic skin response (GSR) data were scored from the output of a coupler that combined resistance base level and resistance response on a single channel. Base level was averaged for each five-minute period and expressed as $\log_{10}$ skin conductance. Spontaneous responses greater than 1 kohm (excluding responses occurring within one minute of the start of each condition or of the presentation of the orienting stimuli) were summed over each condition. The GSR orienting responses, defined as the maximum decrease in resistance within ten seconds of the orienting stimuli, were measured in kohms and expressed as a change $\log_{10}$ conductance score ($\log_{10}$ conductance$_{Max}$ $-\log_{10}$ conductance$_{Min}$). Respiratory rate and amplitude were determined by averaging one-minute samples from each five-minute epoch of each condition. Heart rate base level was determined by averaging the number of QRS complexes in a 60-second sample of each 90-second epoch of each condition. Heart rate orienting response was determined by subtracting the mean velocity of the three heart beats before the orienting stimulus from the velocity of each of nine beats following it. The resulting heart rate profiles for each of the four orienting stimuli were averaged, yielding a single profile for each subject in each condition. Theta and alpha frequencies of the EEG were quantified by passing the EEG signal through band-pass filters (effective dropoff, −48 dB per octave) centered at 6 and 11 Hz, and through resetting integrators to yield alpha and theta power. The EEG and EOG responses to 512 frequent and 80 infrequent tones were summed separately to yield averaged evoked responses (AER) as described previously.[9] Three components—P_1 (maximum positivity between 40 and 100 msec), N_1 (maximum negativity between 90 and 170 msec), and P_{2-3} (maximum positivity between 170 and 270 msec)—were visually identified and height above or below a prestimulus baseline calculated by hand. Analysis of variance (ANOVA) was applied to these data; where appropriate, further statistical tests were conducted.

RESULTS
Autonomic Measures

Table 1 presents means and standard errors for the measures not presented in graphic form. Unless otherwise noted, results of ANOVA failed to indicate significance.

The ANOVA for base skin conductance indicated a significant ($F(4,54) = 3.61$; $P < .05$) groups × conditions interaction. Meditators increased skin conductance relative to controls as they went from normal consciousness into meditation (Fig 1, top). A Kruskal-Wallis test on the skin conductance change score (meditation minus normal) indicated a significant ($P < .05$) difference between meditators and controls. Likewise, the ANOVA for skin resistance responses (Fig 1, bottom) indicated a significant ($F(4,54) = 2.54$; $P < .05$) groups × conditions interaction. Meditators increased skin resistance lability relative to controls as they went from normal consciousness into meditation. A significant ($F(2,54 = 18$; $P < .001$) condition effect indicated that skin resistance lability increased with meditation.

The ANOVA for basal heart rate (Table 1) failed to indicate significance. Meditators tended to increase heart rate relative to controls as they went into meditation.

The ANOVA for respiratory rate (Table 1) demonstrated rate slowing ($F(2,54) = 22.8$; $P < .001$) for all groups as they went into meditation. The ANOVA for respiratory amplitude (Table 1) indicated a significant ($F(2,54) = 11.1$; $P < .001$) condition effect. Across groups, respiratory amplitude increased with meditation. Surprisingly, controls achieved peak amplitude in the withdrawal condition, resulting in a significant ($F(4,54) = 3.60$; $P < .05$) groups × conditions interaction.

The ANOVA for heart rate orienting response indicated a significant ($F(36,486) = 1.60$; $P < .05$) groups × conditions interaction (Fig 2). Meditators showed a predominantly biphasic response during normal consciousness that became a predominantly acceleratory response during meditation. Controls showed a predominantly biphasic response during normal consciousness that became a predominantly deceleratory response during meditation. The ANOVA for skin conductance orienting response (Table 1) indicated a nonsignificant trend for meditators to have smaller skin conductance responses than controls for all conditions. The mean experimental temperature for the three groups was 25.2°C (control), 26.2°C (trainee), and 25.6°C (expert).

EEG Measures

The ANOVA for theta power (Fig 3) indicated significant ($F(2,27) = 3.61$; $P < .05$) group and ($F(2,54) = 5.21$; $P < .01$) condition effect. Meditators increased theta with meditation more than controls. A Kruskal-Wallis test showed the group difference in theta to be significant ($P < .05$) only during normal consciousness, with expert meditators showing greatest theta power. Three of 20 meditators failed to increase theta power (binomial test, $P < .05$, two-tailed); four of ten controls failed to increase theta power.

The ANOVA for alpha power (Table 1) failed to indicate significant effects. Alpha power tended ($F(2,54) = 3.07$; $P < .10$) to increase as subjects meditated. Meditators increased alpha power with meditation more than controls. Three of 20 meditators failed to increase alpha power (binomial test, $P < .05$, two-tailed); four of ten controls failed to increase alpha power.

The ANOVA on AER data failed to indicate significant group or groups × conditions interaction effects. The principle finding was a significant ($F(2,54) = 18.7$; $P < .001$) condition effect, reflecting a progressive decrease in the mean amplitudes of the N_1 AER component to the frequent and infrequent tones ($−7.4$ to $−4.9$ μV) as subjects went into meditation. Amplitude of the P_{2-3} AER component to the infrequent tones decreased (6.8 to 3.3 μV) as subjects went into meditation, whereas the same component of the AER to the frequent tones increased slightly (2.5 to 3.5 μV). This differential response of the P_{2-3} AER component to the frequent and infrequent tones was reflected in a significant ($F(2.54) = 8.27$; $P < .001$) tones × conditions interaction effect. The AER decrements observed are compatible with either an active withdrawal of attention from the tones, or with the known effects of habituation[11,12] on the AER. For this reason results will not be discussed further.

Table 1.—Means and Standard Errors of Autonomic Measures									
	Controls			**Trainees**			**Experts**		
Measure	C1	C2	C3	C1	C2	C3	C1	C2	C3
Basal heart rate, beats/min									
Mean	66.6	67.1	67.0	65.0	65.0	65.8	69.4	71.0	72.8
SE	4.3	4.1	4.2	2.9	3.3	2.9	3.3	3.2	3.1
Respiratory rate, cycles/min									
Mean	15.1	10.2	9.7	14.7	12.5	9.8	16.6	13.0	11.7
SE	1.5	1.7	1.9	1.1	1.4	1.4	1.5	2.1	2.2
Respiratory amplitude, mV									
Mean	739.8	1,274.3	1,049.7	518.2	661.7	868.8	682.7	774.0	777.6
SE	76.5	210.0	134.6	43.5	71.0	117.9	166.5	155.0	119.4
Skin conductance orienting responses, $\log_{10} \mu mV$									
Mean	0.1273	0.0986	0.1181	0.0409	0.0458	0.0209	0.0762	0.0887	0.0609
SE	0.0585	0.0445	0.0631	0.0113	0.0125	0.0060	0.0248	0.0304	0.0139
EEG alpha power relative units									
Mean	70.5	72.2	70.4	62.9	68.6	72.5	81.0	84.5	94.8
SE	7.9	5.4	4.6	5.2	6.8	6.9	8.8	9.1	13.3

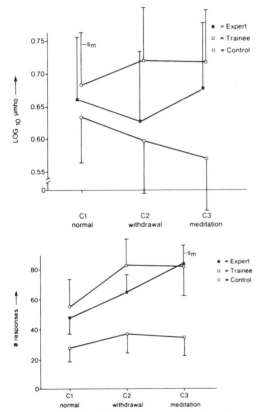

Fig 1.—Top, Base level skin conductance. Bottom, Spontaneous skin resistance responses.

Sleep-scored EEG data are presented in Table 2. Data are percentage of 30-second epochs in each sleep stage. All three subject groups spent less time in light sleep (stage 1 and 2) as they went into meditation. Controls spent 23% of normal consciousness time in light sleep and 8% of meditation time in light sleep. Meditators spent 19% of normal consciousness time in light sleep and 5% of meditation time in light sleep. Experts consistently slept less than trainees. No rapid eye movement, stage 3, or stage 4 epochs were seen. The ANOVA on the number of awake (stage 0) epochs failed to demonstrate a significant group or groups × conditions effect. A significant ($F(2,54) = 4.47$; $P < .05$) condition effect indicated that subjects slept less as they went into meditation.

One expert meditator reported the experience of "having my breathing taken over by the *mantra*" during the meditation condition, and felt it might represent what she termed a "near-*Samâdhi*" experience. The concurrent respiratory record (Fig 4, top) showed a pattern of respiratory acceleration with little change in respiratory amplitude followed by cessation of respiration for approximately 100 seconds. Figure 4, bottom, presents respiratory rate, heart rate, and skin resistance measures plotted for each ten-second interval during the event. A dramatic decrease in skin resistance of approximately 200 kohms preceded the respiratory acceleration.

Visual inspection of the meditation EEG record of this subject disclosed large amounts of high amplitude (up to 100 μV) alpha range frequencies and also large amounts of theta range frequencies (up to 150 μV). Occasionally there were discrete bursts of theta range frequencies of amplitudes up to 300 μV. No particular EEG changes were associated with the "near-*Samâdhi*" event.

Questionnaire Data

Subjects' questionnaire responses showed that all meditators thought they had been able to meditate. Experts' meditation ratings varied from fair to excellent, allowing

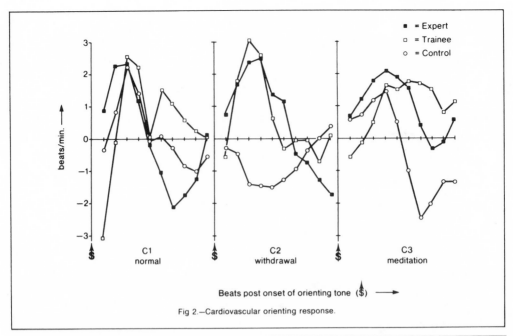

Fig 2.—Cardiovascular orienting response.

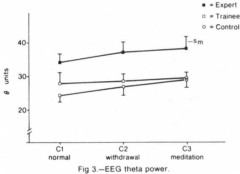

Fig 3.—EEG theta power.

Table 2.—Results of EEG Sleep Scoring for Groups in Each Condition

Condition	% of Subjects			
	Awake	Stage 1	Stage 2	Stage 3-4
Controls				
Normal (C1)	76	20	3	0
Withdrawal (C2)	80	14	5	0
Meditation (C3)	91	8	0	0
Trainees				
Normal (C1)	72	28	0	0
Withdrawal (C2)	85	14	1	0
Meditation (C3)	90	9	1	0
Experts				
Normal (C1)	90	10	0	0
Withdrawal (C2)	93	7	0	0
Meditation (C3)	100	0	0	0

the computation of a Spearman correlation between the physiological measures and the meditation ratings. There was a significant ($P < .01$) negative correlation between the experts' meditation ratings and their skin conductance levels. Values of p were -0.89, -0.80, and -0.85 for the three conditions, respectively. Corresponding correlations were not significant for the trainees, possibly due to the more uniform quality of their meditation ratings. Other correlations were not significant.

In general, the three subject groups were remarkably similar in their reports of subjective experience. No group reported significant restlessness or difficulty staying awake. All groups reported increased euphoria and a continued state of relaxation as they moved from normal consciousness into meditation.

COMMENT

Our results indicate that the meditators became physiologically activated during their meditations while the control subjects became relaxed. This differential change is evident in the significant groups × conditions interactions for the measures of basal skin conductance and frequency of spontaneous GSR responses. The heart rate of the meditators also increased during meditation relative to the control period, although the increase was not statistically significant. Controls demonstrated relaxation similar to that reported in previous studies of TM,[1,2,13] whereas meditators demonstrated activation similar to the previously cited field studies of Indian Yoga.[4,5] The one previous study of Ananda Marga meditation by Elson et al[14] used meditators with an average of 1.8 years' experi-

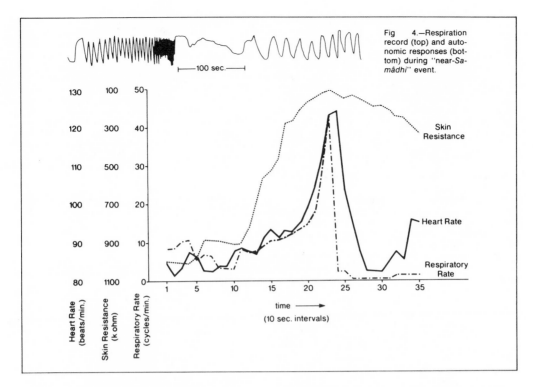

Fig 4.—Respiration record (top) and autonomic responses (bottom) during "near-*Samādhi*" event.

ence in Ananda Marga techniques. Their responses are similar to the responses of the controls in this study.

The general similarity of the respiratory responses of the controls and meditators in this study makes it unlikely that respiratory factors account for the differential autonomic activation of the meditators and controls. The significant decrease in respiratory rate has been reported for previously studied meditation techniques.[7]

The EEG sleep scoring confirmed the general picture of increased activation during the meditation of the meditators. As a group, the 20 meditators spent only 5% of their meditation time in light sleep. Controls spent 8% of their meditation time in light sleep. Meditation significantly decreased the incidence of sleep in the EEG records of the entire subject group. These findings contrast to sleep studies of TM[15,16] reporting that up to 40% of the meditation time of experienced TM meditators was spent in overt sleep (stages 2 through 4), and are in accord with the prior Ananda Marga study[14] in which none of the meditators were found to enter sleep stages 2 through 4 during meditation.

The EEG frequency analysis disclosed that 17 of the 20 meditators increased EEG alpha and theta power during meditation. Similar results have been reported for previously studied meditation techniques[7] and for the Elson et al[14] study. Like Elson and colleagues, we found more proficient subjects to have higher theta power in their EEG records. The significantly increased theta power

in the EEG of the experts during normal consciousness is particularly interesting since meditation practitioners assert that meditation changes the quality of normal consciousness. It appears possible that either subjects with a high EEG theta power selectively become expert meditators or that prolonged practice of this meditation technique results in increased EEG theta power even during normal consciousness.

Meditators had consistently smaller skin conductance orienting responses in each condition than did the controls. The heart rate response is reported to be biphasic in nature, with an early acceleration associated with the warning or threat value of the stimulus followed by a later deceleration associated with the subject orienting.[17,18] Meditators showed progressively less of the later (orienting) component as they went into meditation than did controls. Thus, the orienting response data from both skin conductance and heart rate measures suggest that meditators oriented less than controls. This observation is in general agreement with field studies of Indian Yogis demonstrating decreased responsiveness of meditators to external stimuli during states of profound meditation.[4,19]

The significant negative correlation in the expert group between meditation rating and skin conductance level suggests that although this group's meditation was associated with increased activation, within the group more relaxed subjects tended to have better meditations. Also, initially relaxed subjects tended to remain relaxed relative

Tantric Yoga Meditation

445

to their subject group throughout the study. Greater relaxation before meditation may facilitate access to a good meditation state even though the meditation produces a physiological activation.

We were extremely fortunate to have observed the "near-*Samâdhi*" event. *Samâdhi* is the Yogic term for the ecstatic state of complete concentration and self-absorption. Results of a detailed autonomic and respiratory analysis indicated that the skin resistance activation preceded respiratory and heart rate activation. Thus it is unlikely that the event merely represents a hyperventilation episode. These observations are similar to those reported by Wenger and Bagchi[5] in which profound meditation was associated with autonomic activation without EEG activation. Das and Gastaut[4] also observed autonomic activation during the Yogi ecstatic state, although they observed concomitant EEG activation.

In conclusion, this study reports the physiological correlates of a form of Tantric meditation as practiced by Ananda Marga. This study differs from previous studies of meditation in several respects. First, the meditators studied were unusually experienced with meditation techniques. As a group, their daily meditations of approximately three hours were much longer than the 20-minute, twice-a-day meditations of most other studies. Our expert group had been meditating an average of 4.4 years and was meditating an average of 3.4 hours a day when studied. Such expertise is unusual in meditation studies with the exception of the field studies conducted in India. Second, the design of this study required all subjects to practice meditation techniques. We were thus able to study the physiological characteristics of different levels of proficiency in meditation.

It appears that proficiency in this form of Tantric meditation is characterized by physiological activation by EEG and autonomic criteria. This activation is consistant with the Tantric emphasis on the struggle to achieve union with the object of concentration. The activation appears to be associated with proficiency rather than the techniques per se since the inexperienced control subjects tended to relax rather than become activated. The decreased orienting to external stimuli reflects the inward focus of attention characteristic of this meditation. These findings tend to discount the current assumption that meditation is indistinguishable from states of deep relaxation. Rather, they suggest that meditative techniques may give access to a variety of physiological and subjective states, depending on the technique and the proficiency of the meditator. It appears inadequate to conceptualize Yogic meditation as one unified technique.

The autonomic activation might be expected to prevent the intrusion of overt sleep into the meditation. We speculate that meditative techniques in general permit access to a state of consciousness in the borderline between sleep and wakefulness. Those techniques that employ longer meditations, such as Zazen and Anada Marga, would be expected to be accompanied by greater physiological activation than shorter meditation techniques such as TM. The activation may reflect progressive conditioning as subjects attempt to meditate without falling asleep, or it may also be a direct result of the meditation technique. For example, Zazen meditators keep their eyes open and focused in front of them during meditation. This technique would appear to maintain activation and prevent sleep.

Charlotte Whitaker Lewis and Charissa Hogeboom assisted in the data collection and data analysis of the study.

This investigation was supported in part by research training grant MH11028 from the National Institute of Mental Health and by the Veterans Administration.

References

1. Wallace RK: Physiological effects of Transcendental Meditation. *Science* 167:1751-1754, 1970.

2. Wallace RK, Benson H, Wilson AF: A wakeful hypometabolic physiological state. *Am J Physiol* 221:795-799, 1971.

3. Banquet JP: Spectra analysis of the EEG in meditation. *Electroencephalogr Clin Neurophysiol* 35:143-151, 1973.

4. Das NN, Gastaut H: Variations de l'activité electrique due cerveau, du coeur et des muscles squelletiques au cours de la meditation et de l'extase Yogique. *Electroencephalogr Clin Neurophysiol* 6(suppl):211-219, 1955.

5. Wenger MA, Bagchi BK: Studies of autonomic functions in practitioners of Yoga in India. *Behav Sci* 6:312-323, 1961.

6. Kanellakos DP, Lukas JS (eds): *The Psychobiology of Transcendental Meditation: A Literature Review.* Menlo Park, Calif, WA Benjamin Inc, 1974.

7. Woolfolk RL: Psychophysiological correlates of meditation. *Arch Gen Psychiatry* 32:1326-1333, 1975.

8. Davidson JM: The physiology of meditation and mystical states of consciousness. *Perspect Biol Med* 19(3):345-379, 1976.

9. Corby JC, Roth WT, Kopell BS: Prevalence and methods of control of the cephalic skin potential EEG artifact. *Psychophysiology* 11:350-360, 1974.

10. Rechtschaffen A, Kales A (eds): *A Manual of Standardized Terminology, Techniques and Scoring System for Sleep Stages of Human Subjects.* US Department of Health, Education and Welfare, Public Health Service, 1968.

11. Roth WT, Kopell BS: P$_{300}$: An orienting reaction in the human auditory evoked response. *Percept Mot Skills* 36:219-225, 1973.

12. Roth WT: Auditory evoked responses to unpredictable stimuli. *Psychophysiology* 10:125-138, 1973.

13. Orme-Johnson DW: Autonomic stability and Transcendental Meditation. *Psychosom Med* 35:341-349, 1973.

14. Elson BD, Hauri P, Cunis D: Physiological changes in Yoga meditation. *Psychophysiology* 14:52-57, 1977.

15. Younger J, Adriance W, Berger RJ: Sleep during Transcendental Meditation. *Percept Mot Skills* 40:953-954, 1975.

16. Pagano RR, Rose RM, Stivers RM, et al: Sleep during Transcendental Meditation. *Science* 191:308-310, 1976.

17. Lang PJ, Hnatiow M: Stimulus repetition and the heart rate response. *J Comp Physiol Psychol* 55:781-785, 1962.

18. Graham FK, Clifton RK: Heart-rate change as a component of the orienting response. *Psychol Bull* 65:305-320, 1966.

19. Anand BK, Chhina GS, Singh B: Some aspects of electroencephalographic studies in Yogis. *Electroencephalogr Clin Neurophysiol* 13:452-456, 1961.

Physiology of Meditation

32

METABOLIC AND EEG CHANGES DURING TRANSCENDENTAL MEDITATION: AN EXPLANATION

P. B. C. Fenwick, S. Donaldson, L. Gillis, J. Bushman,
G. W. Fenton, I. Perry, C. Tilsley, and H. Serafinowicz

Two experiments were conducted to measure the oxygen uptake (Experiment II) and the carbon dioxide production (Experiment I) during transcendental meditation. A control group of non-meditators and a few meditators listening to music was used for both experiments. In Experiment I, a control group of fasting meditators was also included. A drop in oxygen consumption and carbon dioxide production, found by previous authors during transcendental meditation, was confirmed. It was, however, possible to show that these drops were physiologically of small significance, and were of the magnitude to be expected from muscle relaxation. EEG recordings were taken during Experiment II in the meditating group. The EEG results showed transcendental meditation to be a method of holding the meditator's level of consciousness at stage 'onset' sleep. No evidence could be found to suggest that meditation produced a hypometabolic state beyond that produced by muscle relaxation and there was no evidence that the EEG changes were different from those observed in stage 'onset' sleep. No support was found for the idea that transcendental meditation is a fourth stage of consciousness.

1. Introduction

Transcendental Meditation (TM) is an effortless yoga-derived technique which is claimed to produce both a transient state of deep physical relaxation and beneficial long-term effects in both physiological and psychological functioning, (Wallace, Benson and Wilson, 1971; Maharishi Mahesh Yogi, 1966). The word 'meditation' in this paper will refer exclusively to the specific practice of TM.

Wallace et al. (1970, 1971 and 1972) have reported that TM produces a transient 'hypometabolic' state marked by dramatic falls in O_2 consumption (16%) and CO_2 output (14%), as well as by other physiological changes including increased skin resistance, decreased blood lactate levels, and decreased cardiac output. All these changes occurred during a twenty minute period of TM, after which most variables returned to control period levels. Because the arterial pO_2 remained within normal limits during the meditation period, the authors concluded that the subjects had reduced their O_2 requirements; they postulated the existence of a 'hypometabolic' state unique to TM, and suggested that TM represented a fourth major state of consciousness, along with waking, sleeping and dreaming. Dhanaraj el Mohan Singh (1973) and Corey (1974) have confirmed the previous authors' findings and have supported the idea of a 'hypometabolic' state specific to meditation.

The above studies, although suggestive of metabolic alterations during TM, did not take into account alternative and perhaps simpler explanations for the observed changes in metabolic rate. The 16% fall in O_2 consumption appears dramatic in comparison with the 8% drop occurring during sleep (Benedict and Carpenter, 1910; Brebbia and Altshuler, 1965; Kreider and Iampietro, 1959). However, it is trivial in comparison to the normal fluctuations which occur during the waking state, when changes can exceed 300% (Committee on Aviation Medicine, 1944; Astrand, 1954). The 16% drop is, therefore, only significant if it can be shown to have started from a true, relaxed basal level. Previous papers have not satisfactorily excluded the possibility that the initial level of O_2 consumption was artificially raised by muscular tension or bodily movements. Because the level of the first control period could have been artificially high, the observed fall in O_2 consumption and CO_2 production might have been caused entirely by nonspecific factors such as muscular relaxation, cessation of small body movements, and minor alterations of body posture. It will be shown that such factors are more than adequate to produce an effect of this magnitude.

Recent support for this view is confirmed by a paper from Beary and Benson (1974), who showed that subjects who had been given a relaxation method were able to drop their oxygen consumption (−13%) and CO_2 output (−12%) significantly more than by sitting with their eyes closed. Two important factors which were not controlled were the change in body posture and tone between the control and relaxation situation which in itself could account for the author's findings, and the difference in mental set between the two experimental conditions.

Because of the magnitude of the error which can be introduced by movements or other artefacts, the method of measurement of O_2 consumption must allow for the differentiation between long-term variation in metabolic rate and transient changes not related to the variables being investigated. A continuous method of measurement allows the detection of these short term changes. Changes in EEG rhythms have been observed during TM by two authors, Wallace et al. (1971a, 1971b) and Banquet, (1972, 1973). They describe the alpha rhythm spreading forward into the central and precentral regions, increasing in amplitude and slowing by one or two cycles per second. Later in meditation, medium voltage theta components are observed intermixed with the alpha activity, of highest voltage in the frontal and temporal areas. The alpha rhythm may disappear entirely, the record then being dominated by theta activity. Banquet described more specifically the difference between TM and light sleep, showing that in TM the alpha and theta rhythms coincided for prolonged periods, whereas in light sleep the two rhythms were never seen concurrently. He also described as specific to TM the occurrence of high voltage beta spindling in the frontal and central areas. He concluded, as did Wallace, that TM was a unique state of 'transcendental consciousness' separate from waking, sleeping or dreaming.

Like the metabolic findings, these phenomena may also be amenable to a simpler explanation. Although Banquet differentiated the EEG rhythms of TM from those of light sleep, he failed to distinguish TM from the early stages of drowsiness. The EEG rhythms of these two states are so similar that the EEG phenomena reported for meditation can be seen as a subset of accepted phenomena of drowsiness, (Reschtoschoffen et al., 1968). The EEG patterns of drowsiness are varied, but one constant feature is slow, rolling eyeball movements that are specific to the state. Wallace et al. (1971a) report that the electro-oculograms were only recorded in 5 of the 36 subjects studied and that no eye movements were found. This negative finding could be explained by the great variations in the depth of meditation produced by any group of meditators in a tense and complex experimental situation as shown in this paper. It should be shown that these movements do not occur during meditation in any of the subjects examined.

2. Method

2.1. Experiment 1: CO_2 production with fasting and music controls

The eleven subjects had all completed a formal course of instruction in TM organised by the Spiritual Regeneration Movement, and participated voluntarily in the study.

The equipment for measuring CO_2 production consisted of a transparent plastic helmet which rested lightly on the subject's shoulders, with an air inlet directly in front of the subject's nose and air outlets at the back of the helmet. Thirty-four litres of outside air were pumped into the helmet every minute, most of the air escaping around the bottom of the helmet. One litre of air per minute was continuously pumped out of the helmet and through a Hartmann and Braun CO_2 analyser, which gave a reading of percent CO_2 accurate to 0.01%. A continuous plot of CO_2 concentration was recorded on a Rikadenki potentiometric recorder. The records were scored at every minute and any artefacts were taken into account. This percentage was converted to CO_2 production in ml per minute by multiplying the total air flow supplied per minute to the helmet by the percentage concentration of CO_2 in the analysed sample. The problem of accurate mixing of the expired air within the helmet was investigated. Tests showed that proper mixing was maintained if the air supply played directly over the subject's nose after diffusion through a baffle: a reasonable degree of head movement was nonetheless possible. This arrangment also ensured that the subject was breathing the fresh air supplied and not the mixed gases. Most subjects reported that this equipment was comfortable and offered minimal distraction to the process of meditating.

Subjects entering the laboratory were allowed a period of relaxation and familiarization with the equipment before the experiment started. They were then asked to sit quietly in a hardbacked, armless chair with eyes closed for twenty minutes, but not to meditate, while a baseline level of CO_2 production was obtained. They then meditated for 20 minutes. After meditation they sat quietly with eyes closed for an additional 10 to 20 minutes. Any small voluntary movements were noted. During the entire procedure the experimenter remained silent except while giving prearranged instructions to the subject. Following the trial each subject completed a self-rating scale which allowed him to describe his meditation and rate the amount of distraction or tension introduced by the experimental situation.

Two control conditions were also studied. In the first, seven subjects (predominantly non-meditators) were tested exactly as in the original condition, but instead of meditating were asked to listen to classical music of their own choice for twenty minutes. In the second, eight meditating subjects were tested early in the morning, having fasted since the previous evening.

2.2. Experiment II: O_2 consumption and EEG

Ten subjects were chosen specifically as experienced meditators or teachers of TM, and participated voluntarily in the study.

Subjects were fitted with a light, flexible mask which covered the nose and mouth. The mask had a two-way valve attached; subjects inhaled room air through a Wright's respirometer, which was read every minute. Expired air entered a mixing bag, from which samples were drawn continuously for analysis. The sample of expired air was continuously pumped through an Instrumentation Laboratories 313 blood gas analyser, which was read at minute intervals. As a check, a Beckman paramagnetic O_2 analyser sampled the expired air every minute. (Appendix I). Subjects initially reported some discomfort in this situation, mostly due to airway resistance, but most were able to adapt during later sessions and reported 'average' meditations. EEG electrodes were applied according to the international 10—20 system, together with a standard eye movement channel. Eight bipolar channels were recorded, six EEG (F_2–F_4, F_4–C_4, C_4–P_4, P_4–O_2, C_3–P_3, P_3–O_1) and two eye movement channels. A portable SLE 8-channel EEG machine was used, with a time constant of 0.3 seconds. The EEG records were separated into control or meditation epochs, all distinguishing marks were removed. The records were rated by a consultant neurophysiologist who then allocated them to either control or meditation groups using as the criteria the changes which have already been published as occurring during meditation. These were increase in alpha amplitude, slowing of alpha amplitude, slowing of alpha frequency, spreading forwards of alpha activity and concurrent alpha and theta activity, and frontal and temporal theta bursts. If these occurred with the slow rolling eyeball movements of drowsiness they were rated as control records. Absence of eye movements and records which were not typical of drowsiness were rated as due to meditation. Records showing a continuous alert pattern were noted as controls. The records were also rated for level of alertness using the criteria of Loomis A, B and C (Loomis, Harvey and Hobart, 1937). Each ten second length of record was rated for level of alertness. Alert was given a score of 0, stage A a 1 and stage B a 2. The score for each 30 seconds during the experiment was then computed. The experiment was designed so that the results of the first trial for each subject were discarded as they were thought to be affected by the experimental situation (Chapman, 1974; Mendels and Hawkins, 1967). Subjects then returned for two more trials in two different conditions, the order of which was randomized. In one condition subjects were seated in an easy chair, providing support so that the subject rested with minimal muscle tone. The procedure in this condition was identical to that used in the CO_2 experiment. In the other condition, subjects were seated in an upright, hardback chair with no armrest, to maximise postural muscle tone. These trials lacked the final 20 minute control period, but were otherwise identical to the easy chair and CO_2 trials. A music control was included, similar to that in Experiment I with the subjects sitting in a soft chair.

3. Results

Table 1 shows ages, weight and meditation experience for all subjects in both experiments. There were no significant differences on a Student t test between the weights or heights between groups. It was therefore considered unneccessary to correct the metabolic values for subject size.

3.1. Experiment I

Eleven subjects, 10 male and 1 female, were tested in the meditation condition. Four subjects were tested twice, making a total of 15 trials. All trials have been grouped and analysed together. Eight subjects were tested in the fasting control condition, four males and four females. One subject was tested twice making a total of nine trials. In the music control group seven subjects were tested, six males and

Table 1
Mean age in years, weight in kilos, meditation experience in months for the groups in Experiment I and II. The final column is the number of meditation teachers in each group.

Groups		Age (years)	Weight (kilos)	Meditating experience (months)	Teachers of meditation
CO_2	Meditation	28.0	65.0	22.3	2
	Fasting meditators	35.1	63.5	54.7	3
	Music	31.3	73.3	–	–
O_2	Meditation	37.6	69.2	37.4	6
	Music	30.8	66.7	–	–

one female, a total of seven trials. Three were meditators and four non-meditators.

Figure 1 shows the mean CO_2 production for the three groups for each minute over the three periods, control, meditation, control with artefacts removed. The fifteen minutes scored for each period were: for the first control period, minutes 6–20; for the meditation period, minutes 3–17; and for the second control period, minutes 3–17. This scoring procedure eliminated the artefacts due to the arousal of

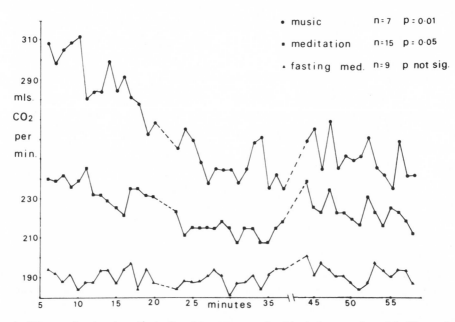

Fig. 1. CO_2 production in ml/min for three groups of subjects in experiment I. The period of meditation took place between the 20th and 40th minutes.

Physiology of Meditation

Table 2
Mean CO_2 production in ml/min for 15 min scored per period.

	Control I	Meditation	Control II	CI−M %	t-test p	CI−CII %
Meditation	236	211	220	−10	0.05	− 6
Fasting meditation	192	188	191	−2	n.s.	0
Music	289	247	247	−14	0.01	−14

Colums 5 and 7 represent the drop in CO_2 production as percent change between first control (CI) and Meditation (M) periods and the first and second (CII control) periods.

the subject at period junctures. Table 2 shows the means for each period for the three groups.

The CO_2 data were subjected to a multivariate analysis of variance using a program distributed by National Educational Resources Inc. (1972, version V), on the London University CDC 6600 computer, see table 3. The groups were tested for significant differences between the first and second periods with respects to both mean level of CO_2 production and linear trend. Inter-group differences were also tested with respect to mean starting level, linear trend, and difference in the amount of change between the control and meditation periods. Because differences in starting level were a significant variable, the transformation matrix was not orthonormalised as this procedure would have cancelled out this variable. A problem was presented by the presence in the series of more than one trial for some subjects: this duplication called into question the statistical independence of the trials involved and suggested that the degrees of freedom in the analysis should be reduced. However, separate trials from the same subject were generally different, and in later analyses trials were grouped according to variables which varied among trials for one subject, such as self-rating of depth of meditation: it was therefore considered legitimate to treat the trials as independent. A sample analysis was carried out using the reduced degrees of freedom with no appreciable change in the levels of significance.

For all three groups taken together there was a significant drop between the first and second periods ($p = 0.002$). The meditation group by itself showed a significant fall in CO_2 production ($p = 0.05$), as did the music group ($p = 0.01$) on a t-test. The fasting group, however, showed no significant change. A significant difference was found between the initial levels of CO_2 production of the music and meditation groups ($p = 0.04$), but there was no difference between the initial levels of the mediation group and the fasting meditators ($p = 0.09$). Multivariate analysis further established that the three groups taken together showed a significant downward linear trend throughout the first forty minutes ($p = 0.042$). There was no significant difference in the way the groups contributed towards this trend, although the contribution of the music group nearly reached significance in comparison with the

Metabolic and EEG Changes   453

Table 3
Results of the multivariate analysis of variance for means and linear trends for Experiment I and II

Experiment	Groups tested	N		% Change		p Values									
						Mean						Trend			
						A	B	C	D	E	F	G	H	I	J
Experiment I															
CO_2	Meditation/music	15	7	10.0	14.0	0.03 *	0.002 *	0.34	0.005 *	0.028 *	0.85	0.04 *	0.06	0.12	0.71
CO_2	Meditation/fasting meditation	15	9	10.0	2.0	0.09	0.002	0.139	0.005	(0.028)	0.62	(0.04 *)	0.39	0.12	0.62
CO_2	Relaxed/tense	7	7	6.1	14.9	0.75	0.05 *	0.376	0.05 *	0.12	0.42	0.49	0.70	0.15	0.02 *
CO_2	Good/bad	7	7	10.2	10.9	0.26	0.05 *	0.865	0.05 *	0.09	0.61	0.25	0.17	0.22	0.47
Experiment II															
O_2	Easy/hard chair	8	8	4.3	10.1	0.60	0.002 *	0.22	0.19	0.45	0.28	0.38	0.57	0.17	0.40
O_2	Relaxed/tense	9	10	2.0	12.0	0.57	0.002 *	0.01 *	0.19	0.49	0.27	0.38	0.37	0.17	0.37
O_2	Good/bad	9	10	4.6	10.0	0.467	0.002 *	0.19	0.22	0.49	0.27	0.38	0.32	0.17	0.54
O_2	Alert/drowsy	10	9	10.0	4.6	0.588	0.002 *	0.26	0.19	0.45	0.34	0.36	0.19	0.17	0.51
O_2	Alert-Drowsy/Drowsy-Alert	9	10	12.4	2.8	0.828	0.002 *	0.02 *	0.13	0.372	0.02 *	0.38	0.37	0.17	0.85

Column N is the number of trials in each group, the first figure refers to the 1st group of the pair. Percentage change is the mean % change in CO_2 production or O_2 consumption between the 1st control period and the meditation period; the 1st figure again refers to the first group. Columns A-J show the probability after comparing the control and meditation periods between and within groups.

(A) Difference in control periods between groups
(B) Drop between control and meditation periods both groups combined
(C) Difference in the drop from the control to the meditation periods between the groups
(D) Significance of the correlation coefficient between initial level of control period and the drop
(E) Control period covaried, drop within groups
(F) Difference in the drop between groups, the control period covaried
(G) Trend for combined groups
(H) Difference in trend between groups
(I) Both groups, difference in trend between periods
(J) Between groups, difference in trend, between periods
* = Significant at the 5% level.

The figures in brackets in columns F and G should be interpreted with caution as this level of significance was only seen in the three way analysis of the music, meditation and fasting groups and not in the meditation groups alone.

Physiology of Meditation

contribution of the other two groups ($p = 0.06$). For all three groups taken together there was a significant correlation between the initial level of CO_2 production and the amount of change between the two periods ($p = 0.05$).

In order to detect the presence of subgroups which might have contributed differently to the observed changes, the meditation group was split according to various criteria: (1) self-rating on the dimension 'physically relaxed vs. tense', (2) high vs. low initial level of CO_2 production and (3) self-rating on the dimension 'meditation better vs. worse than usual'. The analysis of the groups 'tense vs. relaxed' showed no significant differences between the groups in initial level or amount of change between the two periods; it did, however, reveal a significant difference in trend between periods between the two groups ($p = 0.03$). The division high vs. low initial level showed the expected difference in initial level, and also a trend towards significance in the amount each group contributed to the drop between periods, with the high initial group contributing more. The division along the dimension 'meditation better vs. worse than usual' showed no significant differences between the two groups.

3.2. Experiment II

The same multivariate analysis of variance that was used in Experiment I was used in Experiment II. The mean age, weight and meditation experience for each group of subjects are listed in table 1. Easy chair condition: nine subjects were tested, four males and five females, making a total of nine trials.

Straight chair condition: nine subjects were tested, four females and five males. One subject was tested twice, making a total of ten trials. Eight subjects were tested in both conditions.

Music condition in the easy chair: six subjects were tested, four females and two males. Two subjects were tested twice, making a total of eight trials. Five subjects were non-meditators, one was a meditator.

Table 4 shows the mean O_2 consumption for each 20-minute period for the

Table 4
Experiment II. Mean O_2 consumption in ml/min for the 20 min periods, control, mediation, control. Eight subjects tested in the easy chair and hard chair (matched pairs), six subjects tested in the music control.

Condition	Control	Meditation	Control	$(C_1-M)\%$	t-test p	$(C_1-C_2)\%$
Easy chair	254	243	236	-4.3	0.01	-7.1
Hard chair	246	220	–	-10.1	0.01	–
Music	236	225	–	-4.7	0.01	–

three groups and the percent change in O_2 consumption between periods. The multivariate analysis, table 3, showed a significant fall in O_2 consumption between the control and meditation periods for the two meditation conditions combined ($p = 0.002$). When the initial levels of O_2 consumption were covaried, however, the change between periods was no longer significant. The two conditions, easy chair vs. straight chair, were then compared, using the multivariate analysis: no significant differences were found. All the meditation trials were then combined, making a total of 19 trials. The trials were treated independently, for the reasons given above. The pooled meditation sample was divided according to various self rating and other scales.

The division according to the self-rating dimension 'physically tense vs. relaxed' yielded two groups showing no significant differences in initial level, but showing a significant difference in the drop in O_2 consumption between the control and meditation periods, with the 'tense' group showing more change ($p = 0.01$). This significant difference was still significant after the different rates of O_2 consumption during the control period were covaried ($p = 0.02$). The division of the sample according to whether the subjects were alert or drowsy during the control period, as indicated by EEG ratings (see below) showed no significant differences between the groups: However, when the sample was split according to the degree of change in alertness between the control and meditation periods, there was a significant difference between the groups in the fall in O_2 consumption between the two periods ($p = 0.02$). This difference remained significant after the levels of O_2 consumption

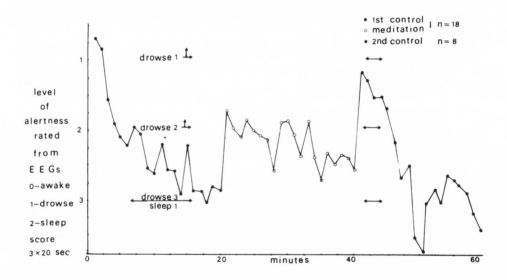

Fig. 2. The level of alertness rated from the EEG records as shown plotted against the control and meditation periods. The level of alertness was derived by rating each 20 sec of the EEG record according to the Classification of Loomis A and B, 0 = awake; 1 = drowsy; 2 = asleep; and summing the score for 3 × 20 sec epochs. Illustrated is the mean curve.

Table 5
The table shows the mean number of abnormal theta bursts during the Control and Meditation periods for four subjects, two trials each and the level of significance between the control and meditation periods.

	Control	Meditation
Mean	7.7	16.6
Standard deviation	4.7	10.7
Students t	Significant at the 1% level	

during the control period were covaried ($p = 0.02$). The division of the subjects according to their own rating of their meditation, 'better or worse than usual', showed no significant difference in the amount of change between periods. The music control group showed a drop of 4.7% in O_2 consumption between the control and music periods, as compared with 4.3% for the easy chair meditation group. This difference between groups was not significant. EEG records: The mean level of alertness for all meditation trials can be seen in figure 2.

A consultant clinical neurophysiologist allocated the coded EEG records of the meditators to two groups, meditation or control. Twenty-four subjects were so rated as described previously; this number includes subjects from a previous pilot study. In thirteen cases the meditation record was correctly identified; in the

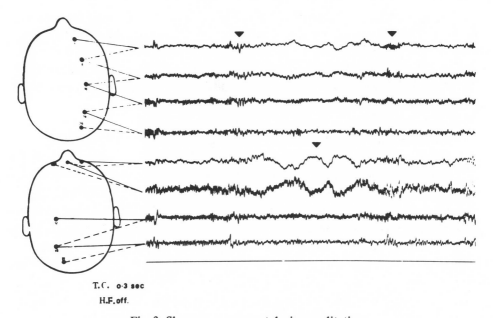

T.C. 0·3 sec
H.F. off.

Fig. 3. Slow eye movement during meditation.

Metabolic and EEG Changes 457

remaining eleven a control record was mistaken for a meditation. This score would have been expected by chance.

The EEGs of four subjects, two of these from a previous pilot study, were found to contain abnormal paroxysmal theta bursts. These bursts were counted for both periods and the number of bursts in each period is shown in table 5. Figure 3 shows an example of the characteristic eye movements of drowsiness which were observed in all but two of the meditation records.

4. Discussion

The main hypothesis of this paper is that the drop in metabolic rate observed by previous authors in meditating subjects is due not to a specific effect of meditation but to the contrast between a state of simple relaxation induced by meditation and a state of tension or restlessness induced during control periods by the experimental situation. These falls are of little physiological significance and no special hypothesis is required to account for them except small changes of body posture. Table 3 shows a comprehensive analysis of the data. Columns A-J show p values for various tests between a pair of subject subgroups, or between the control and meditation periods. The following important points are demonstrated.

Column A: All pairs of groups analysed were statistically comparable during the control period, except for the music-meditation pair in Experiment I. The higher starting level of the music group can be explained by the shorter time allowed this group for habituation to the experimental situation.

Column B: In both experiments, an analysis of all trials averaged together shows a significant difference between the control and meditation periods. This observation confirms the work of previous authors, (Corey, 1974; Dhanaraj el Mohan Singh, 1973; Wallace, 1970; Wallace et al., 1971; Wallace et al., 1972). The two separate values for Experiment I reflect the different N's in each analysis.

Column C: With only two exceptions, the two groups in each analysed pair showed similar changes between the control and meditation or music periods. In particular, the music group in Experiment I showed a change comparable to the meditation group; and in both experiments, groups reporting 'bad' meditations showed changes similar to those reporting 'good' meditations. The latter finding justified including trials in the analysis even when subjects felt they had not meditated successfully.

In Experiment II, the 'tense' group showed a significantly greater change than the 'relaxed' group; and the group which was alert during the control period and drowsy during the medition showed a greater change than the group which was drowsy during the control and alert during the meditation. These results suggest that the significant change between periods seen in the groups as a whole results not from meditation alone, but from the interaction between meditation and the initial level of relaxation of the individual subjects. Those who were already relaxed during the control period showed no further change in metabolic rate. A similar trend exists between the 'tense' and 'relaxed' groups in Experiment I, but is less marked. The experimental situation here provoked less anxiety than that in Experiment II, but also allowed a shorter time for habituation; consequently, the 'tense' group could have been relaxing progressively during the actual control period (see Column J), thus reducing the difference between the periods.

The initial-state hypothesis appears to contradict the results in Column A, which shows that groups were statistically similar during the control period. However, the individual variation in metabolic rate is so great that many more subjects would be needed to detect a statistically significant difference in starting levels: thus, it is still possible to hypothesize that control conditions were dissimilar for the two groups.

Column D: Supports this hypothesis for Experiment I, but not for Experiment II. It shows the significance of the correlation coefficient between the initial level of the control period, and the change produced during meditation or music. This correlation indicates that those individuals who started at a higher level tended to show more change between the two periods.

Column E: Highlights the fact that if the starting level is covaried, then no significant change between the periods occurred in Experiment II or among the meditators in Experiment I. This again indicates that the effect of meditation which has been demonstrated in Column B is due, not to the meditation procedure alone, but to the interaction of the meditation and the initial starting level of the subjects. The significant result of the meditation/fasting group reflects the high starting level of the music in the 3 way comparison and so should be interpreted with caution; particularly as the comparisons of the meditation alone do not show it.

Column F: This analysis is similar to that in Column C, but includes covariation of the control level. The disappearance of the difference between the 'tense' and 'relaxed' group in Experiment II suggests that the previously seen difference in the effect of the meditation was due to the higher starting level of the 'tense' subjects. This finding again supports the hypothesis that an artificially raised starting level contributes greatly to the observed drop in metabolic rate during meditation.

Column G: This column shows the results of analysis for a possible downward linear trend over both periods for all meditators combined. Such a trend would suggest a process of continuous relaxation throughout the experiment, which could produce a difference in the means of the two periods. No such trend was found except in the music group.

Columns H and I: Test for a difference in trend between the two groups at each pair (H) and for a difference in trend between control and meditation periods for the groups combined (I). No significant differences were found.

Column J: Tests for differences between the groups of each pair in the degree of difference in linear trend, for each group, between the control and meditation periods. In Experiment I, there is a significant difference between the 'tense' and 'relaxed' groups; this finding supports the suggestion made earlier, that the 'tense' group relaxed rapidly during the control period as the subjects adapted to the experimental situation.

In summary, these results indicate that the metabolic change which occurs during meditation is related to the initial metabolic level of the subject, and to the degree of subjective tension which the subjects are experiencing. Subjects in both experiments who were tense showed a more marked effect (figure 4) than did those who were relaxed. The fasting control condition, which was designed to reduce the level of tension and the metabolic rate to the lowest possible level, showed that under these circumstances meditation failed to produce any significant change in the metabolic rate. It was also found that non-specific techniques of relaxation such as listening to music were equally as effective as meditation. One significant point was that the changes which were produced by meditation and by listening to music were relatively trivial in physiological terms and were similar to the degree of change which occurs in a person sitting quietly, half raising and then relaxing his arm. It is thus not necessary to postulate the presence of a specific system to account for the minor changes found, as small alterations in body posture are sufficient in themselves. The following section suggests one mechanism which could account for the small falls in metabolic rate already found.

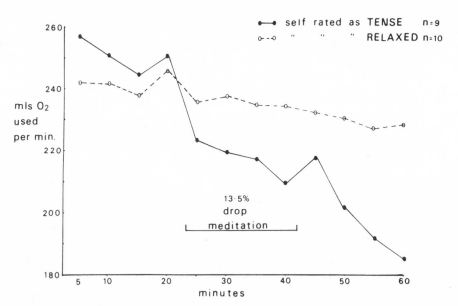

Fig. 4. Oxygen consumption in ml/min in two groups of subjects who rated themselves as 'tense' or 'relaxed' during the experimental session. Difference in the change in oxygen consumption between the two groups is at the 5% level of significance on a student *t*-test.

5. EEG changes and meditation

The phenomena previously described by Wallace et al. (1970, 1971, 1972) and Banquet (1972, 1973), were observed in the present study. These phenomena have been described as specific to meditation, and on this basis previous authors have suggested that TM represents a fourth major state of consciousness. A simpler explanation is, however, available. The reported changes have all been described as occurring during drowsiness. Moreover, pathognomic of the drowsy state are slow, rolling eyeball movements. These movements were not reported by previous authors, but they are apparent only in a channel specifically designed to monitor such movements. In all but two cases in the present study, the subjects showed these eye movements in the meditation period when the meditator balanced himself precisely between sleeping and waking without falling into sleep: the two who did not show them also did not show the other phenomena characteristic of drowsiness. Figure 2 bears out this hypothesis. In the control periods of Experiment II, subjects pass through the drowsy state and begin to fall asleep; during meditation, the level of alertness is held steady. The high incidence of drowsiness and sleep during the control periods is probably explained by the partial sensory deprivation induced by the experimental situation. The relaxation accompanying this induced drowsing has been an important factor in reducing the metabolic change observed during meditation. The few EEG recordings done on the music control group suggest that this state is not specific to meditation but can occur while listening to music. Both the physical and psychic phenomena of meditation are consistent with the subject being in a hypnagogic state: changes in body image, in emotional state and in mentation are all characteristic of the hypnagogic state as well as of meditation. Meditators deny that the experience of meditation resembles drowsiness and in fact describe TM as a state of 'restful alertness'. However, it was noted that several subjects whose EEG records showed them to be drowsy or frankly asleep during the control periods did not recognise this experience but insisted they had been wide awake.

It is predictable from the level of alertness seen in meditation that the subject's self-report systems will not be functioning effectively. Further evidence for the hypnagogic hypothesis is the observation that several meditators in both the present and pilot studies showed gross myoclonic jerks during meditation. Unlike those seen in normal drowsing, usually single stereotyped simple jerks, the jerks observed during meditation consist of repetitive, large, well organised bodily movements, usually confined to a limb or the trunk; as in normal drowsing, the jerks were accompanied by an alerting response in the EEG. Myoclonic jerks are characteristic of hypnagogic sleep, and their presence during meditation suggests that the two states have much in common and could well be identical. A possible explanation for the difference in frequency and character of the myoclonic jerks in meditation from those of drowsiness is that if the meditators' level of consciousness is held at the hypnagogic level then the jerks can become multiple rather than single, and, because of the increased cortical excitability known to occur at this level (Pompeiano, 1969) the jerks will increase in complexity. A further point in favour of the hypnagogic hypothesis is the increased incidence of abnormal paroxysmal theta bursts seen in some subjects during meditation. Such an increase in frequency of occurrence is normally associated with a decreased level of awareness (Pompeiano, 1969).

This hypothesis is dependant on a correlative logic which may not necessarily hold. Because the EEG phenomena are suggestive of a hypnagogic state it is not possible to be sure that the mental state of stage onset sleep is present. This area requires further investigation before it can be definitely stated that the unique mental state described by the meditators is not present.

6. Conclusions

No evidence has been found to support the hypothesis that TM produces a unique state of consciousness or metabolic functioning. Both the metabolic changes and the EEG phenomena observed during TM can be explained within the framework of accepted physiological mechanisms. Many of the other phenomena reported in past studies on TM, such as changes in skin resistance, blood lactate levels, or cardiac output, may well be explained by the same sort of mechanisms suggested in this paper: it is at any rate certain that their investigation is subject to the same pitfalls as the study of O_2 consumption or CO_2 production, with respect to questions of controls and baseline levels.

The findings of this study, or of any similar study, can have little to say about the ultimate significance to the individual of the practice of meditation. It is well known that slow-wave sleep and REM sleep are both necessary to efficient functioning in the waking state, and it is therefore entirely possible that the quality of the waking state may also be altered and improved by regular periods of hypnagogic sleep. At present science has no effective way of relating the short term physiological effects of TM to the possible long-term psychological effects for the sake of which it is practiced, and until more is known in this area the value of meditation must remain an open question.

Appendix I

A Beckman paramagnetic analyser, an I.L. oxygen polarographic electrode and Wrights mechanical respirometer were used in the second part of the project to measure the uptake of oxygen.

During calibration both gas analysers were set to zero while purged with pure nitrogen. The Beckman was set to read 20% while purged with room air and the I.L. was set to read 20% of the room's barometric pressure measured in mm of mercury.

Though this method of calibration failed to take water vapour into account, it was chosen as being the simplest method which would minimise the time taken for calibration before, during and between investigations. Both instruments continuously measured the average concentration of oxygen from a five litre bag into which passed all the gas expired from the patient before it escaped to atmosphere through a valve which was set so as to keep the bag partially filled.

Since the gas left the subject fully saturated with water vapour at body temperature, it reached the analysers fully saturated with water vapour at room temperature. Room temperature did not change more than $1°C$ during any one investigation, therefore the partial pressure of water vapour in the tubing remained constant. From the above it will be appreciated that though the amount of oxygen measured was not corrected to standard temperature and pressure, any changes in concentration observed were true changes originating from the subject and not from the circuit or apparatus. This hypothesis was confirmed by the agreement between the two instruments and periodic recalibration both against air and nitrogen during and following each study.

Appendix II

The actual volume of oxygen in the expired air was calculated by multiplying the volume of air inspired as measured with a Wrights spirometer by the percentage of oxygen as measured from the expiratory bag. The inspired volume was measured rather than the expired volume as this overcame the problems associated with the condensation of water vapour on the flow meter.

Leakage between the subject's face and the mask was prevented by using a mask of our own design which was sealed to the face with double-sided adhesive tape. This method was shown to resist leakage even when the pressure in the circuit was made artificially positive far above the pressures normally reached in the circuit.

The inspired volume measured was in fact fractionally less than the expired volume, the oxygen content of which was measured. This was because the expired volume was fully saturated with water vapour at room temperature. This small constant uptake made no difference to the percentage changes on which the conclusions in this paper are based.

Acknowledgements

The authors wish to thank the subjects who took part in the experiments, the Institute of Psychiatry and Professor Payne of the Research Department of Anaesthetics for the use of their facilities, Dr. J. Stevens for the use of his laboratory and equipment in the CO_2 production experiment, and also Mrs. A. Leech, Mrs. J. Fyfe and Miss D. Jackson for typing the manuscript.

References

Astrand, P.O., (1954). The respiratory activity in man exposed to prolonged hypoxia. Acta Physiology Scandinavia, 30, 343.

Banquet, J.P., (1972). EEG and meditation. Electroencephalography and Clinical Neurophysiology, 33, 454.

Banquet, J.P. (1973). Spectral analysis of the EEG in meditation. Electroencephalography and Clinical Neurophysiology, 35, 143–151.

Beary, J.F. and Benson, H. (1974). A simple psychophysiologic technique which elicits the hypometabolic changes of the relaxation response. Psychosomatic Medicine 36, No. 2.

Benedict, F.G. and Carpenter, T.M. (1910). The metabolism and energy transformation of healthy man during rest. Washington D.C. Carnegi Institute, Washington. 179–187.

Brebbia, D.R. and Altshuler, K.Z. (1965). Oxygen consumption rate and electroencephalographic stage of sleep. Science, 150, 1621–1623.

Chapman, A.J. (1974). An electrographic study of social facilitation: A test of the 'mere presence' hypothesis. British Journal of Psychology, 65, 123–128.

Corey, P.W. (1974). Airway conductance and oxygen changes in human subjectes via a wakeful hypometabolic technique. Science, In press.

Dhanaraj el Mohan Singh, (1973). Effects of yoga relaxation and TM as metabolic rate. (In p press). Paper presented to First Canadian Congress for Multi-Disciplinary Study of Sport and Physical Activity (Montreal).

Handbook of Respiratory Data in Aviation (1944). Committee on Aviation Medicine, Washington D.C.

Kreider, M.B. and Iampietro, P.F. (1959). Oxygen consumption and body temperature during sleep in cold environments. Journal of Applied Physiology, 14, 765–767.

Loomis, A.L., Harvey, E.N. and Hobart, G.A. (1937). Cerebral states during sleep as studied by human brain potentials. Journal of Experimental Psychology, 21, 127.

Maharishi Mahesh Yogi, (1966). The Science of Being and Art of Living. London International SRM Publications.

Mendels, J. and Hawkins, D. (1967). Sleep laboratory adaptation in normal and depressed patients (first night effect). Electroencephalography and Clinical Neurophysiology, 22, 558–562.

Pompeiano, O. (1969) Sleep Mechanisms. Basic Mechanisms of the Epilepsies. Ed. Jaspar, H.H., Ward, A.A., Pope, A. 453–473. Published Churchill, London.

Reschtoschoffen, A., Kales, A., Berger, R.J., Demont, W.C., Jacobson, A., Johnson, L.C., Jaurent, M., Monroe, L.J., Oswald, I., Roffward, H.P., Roth, B. and Walter, R.D. (1968). A Manual of Standardized Terminology, Techniques and Scoring System for Sleep Stages of Human Subjects. Washington D.C., U.S. Government Printing Office.

Wallace, R.K. (1970). Physiological effects of transcendental meditation. Science, 167, 1751–1754.

Wallace, R.K. (1970). The Physiological Effects of Transcendental Meditation. Ph. D. Thesis. Published by University of California Press, Los Angeles.

Wallace, R.K., Benson, H. and Wilson, A.F. (1971). A wakeful hypometabolic physiologic state. American Journal of Physiology, 221, 795–799.

Wallace, R.K. and Benson, H. (1972). The physiology of meditation. Scientific American, 226, 84–90.

33

METABOLIC EFFECTS OF
TRANSCENDENTAL MEDITATION:
TOWARD A NEW PARADIGM OF NEUROBIOLOGY

Ronald A. Jevning and James P. O'Halloran

Until recently "mystical states" were precisely that—by definition, lying outside the realm of neurobiology or scientific understanding in general. In spite of a vast literature reporting experience variously called "samadhi," "satori," yogic "ecstasy," with lasting and beneficial effects, a clear description of such behavior in Western scientific terminology had not been forthcoming. If, as some have said (Pribram, 1977), this is the era when "the soft sciences of today will become the core of the hard sciences of tomorrow," the understanding of "mystical" states will surely play a major role. Perhaps the greatest contribution to science made by Transcendental Meditation ("TM") study has been the enunciation of a clear paradigm for comprehending and investigating phenomena that had heretofore been only subjective, at best, and anecdotal, at worst.

Although as early as 1957 attempts at scientific study of "extraordinary" feats or phenomena in this area had been conducted on yogis in remote regions of India (Bagchi and Wenger, 1957) or on Zen monks in Japan (Kasumatsu and Hirai, 1966), little was learned due primarily to the lack of a uniform or even identifiable subject population, since "experts" had to be located, who were generally in remote areas and whose bent of expertise was a matter of conjecture. Even more restricting in these early studies was the lack of a coherent hypothesis to be tested.

It was therefore a major advance in the study of consciousness when Maharishi Mahesh Yogi proposed (1968, pp. 192–198) that the behavior or experience known as "samadhi" phenomenon, was simply a definite, although perhaps unfamiliar, physiological state, a fourth state—in addition to the three commonly experienced ones of waking, dreaming, and sleeping. He furthermore proposed that this state could be easily experienced by almost anyone through the technique of TM. The theoretical underpinnings of this position were entirely unique to the field of meditation, because, contrary to all previously described techniques, whether from yogic or zen tradition, no effort in meditation was prescribed and no special prerequisites to successful experience of samadhi were required.* Finally, this fourth state was described metabolically as being a rest state and psychologically as one of enhanced awareness; repeated elicitation was proposed to have major health benefits. While the existence of this paradigm does not necessarily imply its correctness, the numerous publications forthcoming since its announcement attests to the sore need for a meaningful paradigm in the study of human consciousness.

---

*Some authors have remarked that the technique of TM is really not unique, since it is a variety of "mantra" meditation. Mantra meditation, however, has in all previous traditions meant rote repetition of a "mantra" or sanskrit sound with attendant effort to continue this repetition. Emphasizing the difficulty of meditation, these traditions have prescribed special circumstances or requirements such as a reclusive way of life, special diet, and other austerities to enable "successful" meditation. In contrast TM is described by Maharishi as the spontaneous and effortless mental experience of the mantra, as easy as ordinary thinking. This effortlessness is attributed to the natural tendency of the mind to experience successively more charming levels of experience. As the most charming mental experience possible, samadhi is then automatically experienced; far from being difficult, this experience, the goal of meditation, is extraordinarily easy. So, there is an entirely different utilization of sanskrit sound or mantra in TM.

Since the introduction of this paradigm by Maharishi and its first utilization by Wallace *et al.* (1971) in scientific studies of meditation, its implications have been primary in the selection of subjects for study (uniformly trained meditators were now available in the West and were acceptable as research material). It has also determined research strategies and criticisms (in studies not only of TM but other practices; see Corby *et al.* 1978). In particular, because of the proposed nature of TM as a rest state, metabolism—metabolic rate—or closely allied parameters have become primary in research attempts to identify and describe meditation as well as suggesting health applications. We will discuss here some of these results and implications as well as ancillary questions such as: Is TM unique? How does it relate to sleep or sleep stages and to simple eyes-closed rest/relaxation and to other stylized practices such as the "relaxation response" (Beary and Benson, 1974)? Data other than metabolic or closely allied measurements will sometimes be adduced to the extent that they supplement our understanding of some of these issues.

Wallace *et al.* (1971) undertook the first detailed study of metabolic changes accompanying TM, seeking to test the hypothesis of decreased metabolic rate. They reported a significant decline of about 16% in O_2 consumption and CO_2 elimination during 20–30 minutes of TM compared to a 10- to 30-minute eyes open or closed premeditation control period. Associated findings were a significant decline of arterial lactate concentration, and a large increase in skin resistance. No change was noted in arterial P_{O_2} and P_{CO_2}. The decline of O_2 consumption and CO_2 elimination were interpreted as reflecting a decrease in oxygen utilization rather than any forced or artificial hypoventilation, since arterial P_{O_2} and P_{CO_2} remained constant and, indeed, arterial lactate declined inconsistent with anoxia. The basic finding of decreased O_2 consumption during TM has been verified many times (Benson *et al.* 1975; Treichel, 1973; Fenwick *et al.* 1977) even in studies critical of its precise interpretation (Fenwick *et al.* 1977). Therefore, Benson *et al.* (1975) in a continuous sampling technique found significant *average* declines of 5 and 6% in O_2 consumption and CO_2 elimination, respectively, during TM as compared with a premeditation control reading period. However, when the lowest O_2 consumption and CO_2 elimination rates during meditation were compared with the average premeditation levels (consistent with the discontinuous sampling method of Wallace), values of 15 and 12%, respectively, were reported, similar to those of Wallace.

Treichel *et al.* (1973) in an abstract also reported similar declines; however, these authors noted similar changes in a separate control rest group, thus introducing the question of the relationship of TM to other unstylized rest/relaxation states. In this respect, Benson *et al.* (1974) has also noted declines of 13 and 12% in O_2 consumption and CO_2 elimination during a "noncultic" relaxation method incorporating, he states, "the essential elements" of TM. Fenwick *et al.* (1977) in a detailed study addressing the status of TM as a fourth distinct state of consciousness (where it is clear below we will use "TM" interchangably as both the practice and the associated behavior), measured O_2 consumption and CO_2 elimination, verifying previous measurements. However, similar changes were observed in a music control group and Fenwick attributed the decline of metabolic rate in both groups to nonspecific "muscle relaxation." Based upon concomitant monitoring of the EEG, he also concluded that maintenance of a "hypnagogic state" during TM is a likely explanation of the metabolic and EEG characteristics of this behavior and that there was no basis for the proposed fourth state of consciousness. Therefore, with respect to metabolic measurements, TM appears to have been correctly identified as acute hypometabolic behavior. However, with respect to the paradigm's description of the behavior as a different state of consciousness from waking, dreaming, and sleeping, the studies of Benson, Treichel and especially Fenwick underscore the inadequacy of the metabolic measurements alone to answer this question. While the Fenwick study underscores this point, it does not, contrary to these authors' conclusions, present convincing evidence for a "simpler explanation" of the observed decrease in metabolic rates. Therefore, invocation of a "hypnagogic state," whose physiological characteristics are not in reality better identified than TM, does not constitute such an explanation. We will return to this important question of the relationships of TM to other rest behavior in what follows, reserving for the conclusion an attempt to bring the data of various studies together to bear on this point.

The early studies demonstrating the rapid decline of metabolic rate during TM were an important spur to investigating the efficacy of this practice and of others in helping to relieve disorders such as essential hypertension. This disorder is believed by many (Folkow and Neil, 1971) to be related to stress which is characterized by *hyper*metabolic activity (Hamburg, 1964). To date, it seems likely that the regular elicitation of TM behavior is associated with lower blood pressures in hypertensive patients (Blackwell *et al.*, 1976; Benson *et al.* 1974) and low normal blood pressure in normal individuals (Wallace *et al.* 1971), although one study was unable to demonstrate lowered blood pressures in a longitudinal design (Pollack *et al.*, 1977). Another yogic practice (Stone and Deleo, 1976) has also been found to be helpful in blood pressure reduction. In another probable stress-related disorder, bronchial asthma, TM has been found to be effective as an adjunct in therapy (Wilson *et al.,* 1975). We will only note here (Shafii *et al.,* 1975) the numerous positive evaluations of TM as an aid in drug abuse prevention or amelioration, as further examples of research that stemmed from the original paradigm and the early physiological investigations it encouraged.

We will now discuss some of our own and others' recent metabolic or closely allied studies of TM which were motivated by: (1) the desire for a greater in-depth physiological understanding of human rest states, in general, and (2) assessment of the relationships of TM hypometabolism to ordinary rest/relaxation and to sleep. These two goals are, of course, mutually supplementary—particularly in that the differentiation of the relationships among the various rest states is hampered by the relative lack of data (except perhaps for sleep). Therefore, it is not surprising that the question of uniqueness is a difficult one—few data on rest states exist and most of these data have been measurements of low "power" (i.e., unlikely to be specific enough in their relationships to underlying physiological events to be capable of distinguishing among different behaviors—metabolic measurements, which generally only reflect whole body metabolism, are an example). The situation prevailing here is precisely analogous to that which existed 20 years ago when the subjective experience of dreaming seemed to distinguish it clearly from either waking or sleeping—yet physiologically, only the states of sleep and wakefulness were acknowledged (Kleitman, 1963). Indeed, on the basis of brain wave pattern and metabolism alone one might conclude that dreaming, or what we now know as "REM" sleep, is a "hypnagogic state." Meditators' subjective experience similarly points toward TM as clearly distinct behavior (Kanellakos and Lukas, 1974).

Adrenocortical activity may be one parameter of sufficient power to help us understand the relationship of TM to sleep, and other rest/relaxation states, since, although the secretion of cortisol is closely related to the level of "stress" and anxiety (Hamburg, 1964; Rubin and Mandell, 1966), it is not apparently closely related to sleep or sleep state (Weitzman, *et al.,* 1974). Based upon the metabolic characteristics of TM and subjective reports of meditators, it is reasonable to ask whether stress or anxiety, as measured by plasma corticosteroid levels, decreases during this practice (Selye, 1950; Hamburg, 1964). With these points in view and because of the inherent importance that would attach to a drugless method of stress reduction, we, in collaboration with Julian Davidson at Stanford, have measured plasma cortisol levels during TM (Jevning *et al.,* 1978a).

Three groups of normal individuals were studied: controls studied before learning TM, where plasma cortisol levels were monitored before, during, and after 40 minutes of ordinary eyes closed rest/relaxation; these same individuals, after approximately 4 months of regular TM elicitation, before, during, and after 40 minutes of TM; and finally, a long-term practitioner group (consisting of TM instructors with 3 to 5 years of regular practice) before, during, and after 40 minutes of TM. (Assays were done blind.) A sharp and significant decline (25%) of cortisol level was noted in the long-term group with a small, nonsignificant decline in the 4-month meditators and no change in the control (rest) group. Although the magnitude of decline in the long-term group was small (*all* groups of subjects had very low cortisol levels before rest or TM), it was consistent with complete inhibition of cortisol secretion. This effect seemed to persist in the post-TM period. The most likely explanation of these results seems to be that long-term regular practice is associated with development of a psychophysiological response of decreased pituitary–adrenal activity during meditation. Testosterone level—also measured because of its responsiveness to stress (Kreuz *et al.,* 1972)—did not change in the groups. Concomitant monitoring of a unipolar EEG showed appreciable and almost identical amounts of stage 1 sleep in all three groups (about 20%) with no correlation between duration of sleep and cortisol changes.

These results suggest that it is unlikely that TM can be the same as sleep or accounted for as unstylized rest/relaxation. It is also unlikely that the beneficial effects of TM can be accounted for by the sleep that may occur during the practice, since the groups were not different in duration of sleep or sleep stage. The effects of TM on cortisol are apparently closely related to repeated elicitation. These data do not, of course, necessarily mean that *another* stylized practice repeated regularly might not result in similar effects. This may be mostly an academic point, since, other than the "relaxation response" (Beary and Benson, 1974), there are no examples of which the authors are aware, of known hypometabolic behavior that is regularly elicited in connection with a stylized practice. [A recent study of a variety of regular meditation practices associated with "tantric" yoga, reported *hyper*metabolic effects (Corby *et al.,* 1978).]

Another study related to possible effects of TM on stress, measured plasma catecholamines and lactate

Metabolic Effects of TM

467

during eyes-closed rest and TM (Michaels *et al.*, 1976). These authors reported general declines in the levels of these parameters in both groups, although the trends were not significant. This study is not necessarily inconsistent with the results of the cortisol measurements, since the secretion of cortisol and of catecholamines may be dissociated (Selye, 1950) and the duration of regular practice in Michaels' practitioner groups was not clearly specified. These authors concluded that biochemically, TM was not different from an unstylized eyes-closed rest state, a peculiar conclusion in that a significant effect on catecholamines or lactate was not demonstrated for *either* TM or eyes-closed rest. In our opinion, the study of Michaels simply demonstrated that plasma catecholamine concentration may not be a sufficiently responsive variable for assessment of the characteristics of rest states in man.

Other measurements of plasma constituents made in the authors' laboratory that were selected for their possible sensitivity and relationship to underlying specific neural and/or metabolic events in the study of TM and other rest states have included measurement of: (1) plasma amino acids (Jevning *et al.* 1977), (2) plasma prolactin and growth hormone (Jevning *et al.*, 1978), and (3) plasma insulin, glucose, fatty acids, and glycerol (unpublished data). These measurements were made in a protocol similar to that employed in the cortisol measurements discussed previously. Of thirteen amino acids measured, significant increases of phenylalanine* (with smaller and nonsignificant increases of leucine and tyrosine) were noted—again only in the long-term practice group. Once more, as in the case of cortisol secretion, the effect on phenylalanine levels persisted for sometime after the TM period. We hypothesized that this *specific* effect of TM on phenylalanine levels may be due to decreased hepatic hydroxylation of phenylalanine and/or to decreased brain uptake. It should be noted that, in this study also, the total amount of time slept and the time spent in each sleep stage was almost identical in the three groups.

Of the other hormones or plasma metabolites measured in our laboratory, the variation of plasma prolactin in relation to TM was most interesting (Jevning *et al.*, 1978b). This hormone was measured primarily because of its close relationship to sleep—the rise of plasma prolactin coincides closely with sleep onset and falls immediately upon awakening. This behavior of prolactin also occurs during nap sleep (Parker *et al.*, 1973, 1974). No change of plasma prolactin occurred during either rest or TM in our studies. However, *after* cessation of practice, plasma prolactin concentration rose sharply in both short- and long-term meditators. Levels were elevated at least 30 minutes after cessation of TM practice, at which time, unfortunately, blood sampling was terminated. Levels of prolactin in controls were unvarying. This increase of prolactin cannot be attributed to sleep, since the small total percentage sleep in the subjects was not different between the three groups and, most paradoxical for sleep explanation, plasma prolactin levels rose during the *eyes open* post-TM period! Several factors are currently believed to participate in the regulation of prolactin secretion (Zacur *et al.*, 1976). The observed increase in plasma prolactin levels during TM may be mediated by a decrease in dopamine activity and/or an increase in serotonin activity either on neurosecretory hypothalamic cells "indirectly" or on lactotrophs within the pituitary gland "directly."

The sensitivity, specificity, and interpretation of change of plasma metabolites in the study of acute behavior is compromised by: (1) the multiplicity of pathways that may be involved in the generation of a specific increase or decrease of a blood constituent, and (2) the often relatively slow time course of this class of effects. These facts motivated us to enlist a different set of measurements as supplementary and possibly more penetrating in the analysis of TM and ordinary eyes-closed rest behavior.

Circulation, especially in muscle and brain, is closely related to the metabolic requirements of those tissues (Guyton *et al.*, 1973). Furthermore, it is exquisitely sensitive and regular in its response to behavior (Figar 1965). These features and its nature as a dynamic measure recommended it to us in our studies of rest states. Total cardiac output, renal and hepatic blood flows, arterial lactate, and respiratory minute volume were measured in a blind study before, during, and after either 40 minutes of eyes-closed rest/relaxation or TM (Jevning *et al.*, 1978b). Unfortunately, in this study, the meditator group was not divided into long- and short-term meditators, with the mean period of regular TM practice being 1 year. The rest/relaxation group, as in previous studies, was a group of individuals studied prior to learning TM.

Our expectations of the sensitivity and regularity of blood flow response to behavior were borne out in

---

*Phenylalanine is an essential, aromatic amino acid and is a precursor of catecholamine neurotransmitters (i.e., dopamine, norepinephrine, and epinephrine) via conversion to tyrosine by phenylalanine hydroxylase. This hydroxylation occurs almost exclusively in the liver and is a necessary first step for subsequent utilization. Brain uptake of plasma phenylalanine exceeds that of most other plasma amino acids.

Physiology of Meditation

the results of this study. Sharp decline of renal blood flow accompanied both eyes-closed rest and TM compared with pre levels. Hepatic blood flow also declined in practitioners. Surprisingly, there was also a small but highly regular *increase* of cardiac output during meditation. Small significant declines of minute volume (the amount of air respired in one minute) and arterial lactate occurred in the TM group. Hepatic blood flow an arterial lactate remained low. The hepatic blood flow and arterial lactate changes during TM differed significantly from changes in controls. These changes of blood flow imply a marked redistribution of blood flow during TM and to a significantly lesser extent during eyes-closed rest. We have hypothesized that most of the redistributed circulation must be to either brain or skin, a hypothesis that has recently been supported by direct estimation of relative cerebral blood flow changes in our laboratory (unpublished data). The large increase in brain blood flow implied by our experiments have led us to surmise that cerebral blood flow may be a very distinctive parameter or marker for TM and may enable more meaningful future comparisons with other behaviors, although this promise needs further investigation.

The redistribution of blood flow and slight increase of cardiac output have interesting implications for the fine structure of metabolic changes elicited by TM. Although this behavior is hypometabolic overall, from these results it appears likely that there is an *increase* of metabolism in some specific tissue(s); we surmise that this tissue is probably brain. Could this be related to descriptions of samadhi as "ecstasy" (cf. Das and Gastaut, 1955)?

To summarize the results of our own and others' studies of the metabolic characteristics of TM and its relationship to sleep and unstylized eyes-closed rest/relaxation, it seems clear that a further evolution of sophistication of methodology and experimental design must occur to enable investigators to clearly relate these subjectively distinct behaviors. We have seen, in the course of research into these questions, a clearer delineation of the differences and similarities between TM and other hypometabolic states as more sophisticated studies involving more clearly specified subject groups and more powerful measures have been applied. At present, it seems unlikely that TM is sleep or that it is the same as simple eyes-closed rest. Whether physiological changes accompanying TM might be induced by other stylized means is at present a moot and, in our opinion, a probably unproductive question, in view of the dearth of other regularly practiced techniques. The "noncultic" relaxation response advocated by Benson *et al.* (1974), may deserve further investigation in this regard.

Also, the newer studies have made clearer the direction in which future studies might most productively proceed: it seems that, generally, longer-term practitioners demonstrate larger physiological changes (this has also been noted in EEG studies, cf., particularly, Levine, 1976) during TM. There also appears to be an admixture of behavior during TM—mostly wakefulness, but combined with some stage 1 and a small percentage of stage 2 sleep (Pagano *et al.,* 1976 have reported appreciable percentages of stages 2, 3, and 4 sleep during TM, but their findings seem unique in this regard. We will return to this question below.)

These results suggest the importance of selecting subject groups of uniform experience (preferably TM instructors who are numerous and are long-term practitioners) and restricting analyses to periods of meditation free of sleep as judged by standard EEG criteria. One may make the valid objection that the TM paradigm specifies no particular period of regular practice before its hypothesized fourth state is experienced. In fairness to the originator, however, it must be added that Maharishi Mahesh Yogi (1968, pp. 285–290) had specified certain "impediments" or inherent "stresses" that might temporarily disallow experience of this state. This is probably an academic point now in that practitioners of several years experience are readily available. Perhaps in these early stages we may also be allowed the license of discovering ideal conditions under which effects can be detected—a tradition frequently followed in the initial period of investigation of new and hypothetical phenomena. (We assume, of course, that the conditions discovered can be specified in a relatively simple, repeatable fashion.)

Assuming that the characteristics of such a state were specified in a group of sufficient experience, it would then be desirable to follow, longitudinally, a single group studied as their own controls, and then afterward, as they continued TM elicitation. This sort of study would enable evaluation of a possible (although unlikely) operation of self-selection as the determinant of the observed physiological changes in the advanced practitioner.

Last, but not least, an important feature that emerged in several of our own studies of TM was the clear persistence of TM-correlated changes *after* cessation of practice: this fact is consistent with repeated reports of persistence of EEG changes (cf. Banquet, 1973; Levine, 1976; Tebecis, 1975) and should encourage research into isolation of possible long-term effects of this behavior.

Relevant to the questions posed and addressed in the metabolic studies are some of the more recent conclusions based upon EEG measurements, which have reflected analogous development and application of more sophisticated measures and strategies. Therefore, while Wallace *et al.* (1971) and Banquet *et al.* (1973) made only nonquantitative observations regarding the topography and frequency distribution of the EEG during TM, subsequent studies have employed some combination of: (1) power spectrum analysis; (2) correlation or coherence analysis between separate derivations, (3) statistical comparisons of the EEG between eyes-closed rest and TM, and (4) study of long-term meditators who are also TM instructors (Banquet and Sailhan, 1974; Levine, 1976; Tebecis, 1975; Hebert and Lehmann, 1977). Parallel with the results of applying more sophisticated measures and sharper delineation of subject groups in the metabolic studies, clear and striking changes have been found to accompany TM. The most common finding has been an increase of spatial coherence or synchrony in the EEG recorded from separate derivations, especially in central and frontal regions (Banquet and Sailhan, 1974; Hebert and Lehmann, 1977; Levine, 1976). Both drowsiness and sleep have been found to be different in spectral composition from TM (Banquet and Sailhan, 1974), and sleep during TM has been found to be accompanied by the disappearance of spatial EEG coherence (Levine, 1976). This increase of spatial coherence or a related parameter, synchrony, has been repeatedly observed, even in earlier studies (cf. Banquet, 1973; Glueck and Stroebel, 1975).

Another feature common to many of the EEG studies (cf. Fenwick *et al.,* 1977; Banquet, 1973; Tebecis, 1975), and investigated in detail by Hebert and Lehmann (1977), has been the characteristic of prominent theta activity during TM. Of seventy-eight long-term meditators who had been meditating for periods ranging from 24 to 140 months, twenty-one demonstrated intermittent bursts of very high amplitude theta activity on the average of every 2 minutes during meditation. These periods of theta were accompanied by synchrony in all channels. Fifty-four nonmeditating controls exhibited no theta bursts either during relaxation or sleep onset.

In summary the electroencephalographic investigations and comparison of TM with other behaviors has, for the most part, become increasingly informative as techniques of greater power and resolution have been applied. Most of these studies have supported the attribution to TM of a physiology different from that of waking, dreaming, or sleeping. Notable exceptions to this conclusion have included the study of Pagano *et al.* (1976) and that of Fenwick *et al.* (1977). The former recorded a high percentage of sleep (stages 2, 3, 4) during TM, a result whose uniqueness among studies in the area suggest that it is not a representative sample of typical meditation experience. The latter interpreted the EEG of meditation as consistent with a "hypnagogic state;" this conclusion was based primarily on a general, nonqualitative characterization of the EEG. To our knowledge there have been no published reports of EEG activity (i.e., spatial coherence, synchrony, alpha "spreading") similar to that evoked by TM during biofeedback training, during any of the various relaxation techniques (i.e., "relaxation response") or during hypnosis. While many of these behaviors produce "alpha activity" they cannot, on the basis of present knowledge, be said to produce the same electroencephalographic effects as TM (Glueck and Stroebel, 1975, discuss these in depth). For the purpose of distinguishing various behaviors, presently applied methods of EEG analysis have established that "alpha activity" is too general and ambiguous for the purpose of distinguishing different behavioral states (see Glueck and Stroebel, 1975; Hebert and Lehmann, 1977; Levine, 1976).

The proposal of the existence of a unique or fourth state of consciousness with a basis in physiology (as suggested by Maharishi Mahesh Yogi, 1968 pp. 192–198) has been a major contribution to the study of human behavior. It has resulted in a myriad of scientific studies both basic and applied in an area heretofore reserved for "mysticism." While the answers to basic questions that have arisen as a consequence of this paradigm are not yet agreed upon, progress has been made in this difficult field. In our opinion, the main substance of this progress has consisted of: (1) an increase of the likelihood that TM is physiologically distinct from sleep or simple eyes-closed rest as evidenced by: electroencephalographic studies indicating a high degree of bilateral and unilateral synchrony (Banquet, 1973) and/or bilateral and unilateral spatial coherence (Levine, 1976); blood chemical changes unlike those known to accompany sleep or simple eyes-closed rest as discussed in the preceding pages) as well as the mental experiences of advanced practitioners, which are unlike those of sleep or simple relaxation; (2) development of more powerful chemical and electrophysiological armamentaria for future studies; and (3) better identification of subject groups in which changes can be most easily detected. We envision that continued research will reveal more clearly the distinctive physiological characteristics of TM and correlate them more precisely with subjects' judgments of "clear transcending" (clear experience during TM of the hypothesized fourth state—described by meditators as "restful alertness;" see Maharishi Mahesh Yogi, 1968; Kanellakos and

Lukas, 1974). Then, in retrospect, it will be seen that the problem of the uniqueness of TM has really been a pseudoproblem—a problem of methodology and research strategy—not one of the reality of a state, whose existence rests ultimately on the primary datum of the subjective reports of over one million practitioners of TM.

References

Bagchi, B. K., and Wenger, M. A. Electrophysiological correlates of some yogi exercises. *Electroencephalography clinical neurophysiology*, Suppl. 1957, **7**, 132–149.

Banquet, J. P. Spectral analysis of the EEG in meditation. *Electroencephalography clinical neurophysiology*, 1973, **35**, 143–151.

Banquet, J. P., and Sailhan, M. Analyse EEG d'etats de conscience induits et spontanes. *Revue d'electroencephalographie et de neurophysiologie clinique*, 1974, **4**, 445–453.

Beary, J. F., and Benson, H. A simple psychophysiologic technique which elicits the hypometabolic changes of the relaxation response. *Psychosomatic Medicine*, 1974, **36**, 115–120.

Benson, H., Rosner, B. A., Marzetta, B. R., *et al.* Decreased blood pressure in pharmacologically treated hypertensive patients who regularly elicited the relaxation response. *Lancet*, 1974, **1**, 289–291.

Benson, H., Steinert, R. F., Greenwood, M. M., Klemchuk, H. M., and Peterson, N. H. Continuous measurement of O_2 consumption and CO_2 elimination during a wakeful metabolic state. *Journal of human stress*, 1975, **1**, 37.

Blackwell, B., Bloomfield, S., Gartside, P., *et al.* Transcendental meditation in hypertension. Individual response patterns. *Lancet*, 1976, **1**(7953), 223–226.

Corby, J. C., Roth, W. T., Zarcone, Jr., V. P., and Kopell, B. S. Psychophysiological correlates of the practice of tantric yoga meditation. *Archives general psychiatry*, 1978, **35**, 571–580.

Das, N. N., and Gastaut, H. Variations de l'activite electrique due cerveau, du coeur et des muscles squelletiques au cours de la meditation et de l'extase Yogique. *Electroencephalography clinical neurophysiology*, Suppl. 1955, **6**, 211–219.

Fenwick, P. B., Donaldson, S., Gillis, L. *et al.* Metabolic and EEG changes during transcendental meditation: An explanation. *Biol. psychology*, 1977, **2**, 101–118.

Figar, S. Conditional circulatory responses in men and animals. In Handbook of Physiology, **3**, Section 2: Circulation, Chapt. 57. Washington, D.C.: American Physiological Society, 1965.

Folkow, B., and Neil, E. *Circulation*, Oxford: Oxford University Press, 1971.

Glueck, B. C., and Stroebel, C. F. Biofeedback and meditation in the treatment of psychiatric illnesses. *Comprehensive psychiatry*, 1975, **16**, 303–321.

Guyton, J. C., Jones, C. E., and Coleman, T. G. *Circulatory physiology: cardiac output and its regulation*, 1973, p. 60. 2nd Edition. Philadelphia: Saunders.

Hamburg, D. A. Plasma and urinary corticosteroid levels in natural stresses. In S. R. Korey (Ed.), *Ultrastructure and metabolism of the nervous system*. Association for Research in Nerves and Mental Diseases, Baltimore, Maryland: Williams and Wilkins, 1964.

Hebert, R., and Lehmann, D. Theta bursts: An EEG pattern in normal subjects practicing the transcendental meditation technique. *Electroencephalography clinical neurophysiology*, 1977, **42**, 397–405.

Jevning, R. A., Pirkle, H. C., and Wilson, A. F. Behavioral alteration of plasma phenylalanine concentration. *Physiological behavior*, 1977, **19**(5), 611–614.

Jevning, R. A., Wilson, A. F., and Davidson, J. M. Adrenocortical activity during meditation. *Hormones and behavior*, 1978, **10**(1), 54–60.

Jevning, R. A., Wilson, A. F., Smith, W. R., and Morton, M. E. Redistribution of blood flow in acute hypometabolic behavior. *American Journal of Physiology*, 1978, **235**(1), 200–210.

Jevning, R. A., Wilson, A. F., and Vanderlaan, E. F. Plasma prolactin and growth hormone during meditation. *Psychosomatic medicine*, 1978, **40**(4), 329–331.

Kanellakos, D. P., and Lukas, J. S. *The psychobiology of transcendental meditation: a literature review*. Menlo Park: Benjamin, 1974.

Kasamatsu, A., and Hirai, T. An electroencephalographic study on Zen meditation (Zazen). *Folia psychiatry neurology japonica*, 1966, **20**, 315–336.

Kleitman, N. *Sleep and wakefulness*. Chicago, Illinois: University of Chicago Press, 1963.

Kreuz, L. E., Rose, R. M., and Jennings, J. R. Suppression of plasma testosterone levels and psychological stress. A longitudinal study of young men in Officer Candidate School. *Archives general psychiatry*, 1972, **26**, 479–482.

Levine, P. H. The coherence spectral array (COSPAR) and its application to the studying of spatial ordering in the EEG. *Proceedings of the San Diego biomedical symposium*, 1976, **15**, 237–247.

Maharishi Mahesh Yogi. Transcendental Meditation 1963a pp. 192–198. The New American Library, Inc., 1968. New York: Signet Addition.

Michaels, R. R., Huber, M. J., and McCann, D. S. Evaluation of transcendental meditation as a method of reducing stress. *Science*, 1976, **192**, 1242–1244.

Pagano, R. R., Rose, R. M., Stivers, R. M., and Warrenburg, S. Sleep during transcendental meditation. *Science*, 1976, **191**, 308–310.

Parker, D. C., Rossman, L. G., and Vanderlaan, E. F. Sleep-related, nyctohemeral, and briefly episodic variation in human plasma prolactin concentration. *Journal clinical endocrinology metabolism*, 1973, **36**, 1119.

Parker, D. C., Rossman, L. G., and Vanderlaan, E. F. Relation of sleep-entrained human prolactin release to REM-nonREM cycles. *Journal of clinical endocrinology metabolism*, 1974, **38**, 646.

Pollack, A. A., Case, D. B., Weber, M. A., Laragh, J. H. Limitations of transcendental meditation in the treatment of essential hypertension. *Lancet*, 1977, **1**(8002), 71–3.

Pribram, K. H. Future to bring 'hard-nosed' work in 'soft sciences.' *Brain/Mind Bulletin*, 1977, **3**(3), 1–2.

Rubin, R. T., and Mandell, A. J. Adrenal cortical activity in pathological emotional states: A review. *American journal psychiatry*, 1966, **123**, 4.

Selye, H. *The physiology and pathology of exposure to stress: a treatise based on the concepts of the general-adaptation-syndrome and the diseases of adaptation*, Montreal: ACTA, 1950.

Shafii, M., Lavely, R. A., and Jaffe, R. D. Decreased drug abuse in practitioners of transcendental meditation. *American Journal of psychiatry*, 1975, **132**, 9.

Stone, R. A., and DeLeo, J. Psychotherapeutic control of hypertension. *New England journal of medicine*, 1976, **294**(2), 80–84.

Tebecis, A. K. A controlled study of the EEG during transcendental meditation: Comparison with hypnosis. *Folia Psychiatrica et Neurologica Japonica*, 1975, **29**, 305–313.

Treichel, M. Respiratory changes during transcendental meditation (abstr.). *The Physiologist*, 1973, **3**, 472.

Wallace, R. K., Benson, H., and Wilson, A. F. A wakeful hypometabolic physiologic state. *American journal of physiology*, 1971, **221**, 795–799.

Weitzman, E. D., Nogeire, C., Perlow, M., Fukushima, D., Sassin, J. F., and McGregor, P. Effects of a prolonged 3-hour sleep-wake cycle on sleep stages, plasma cortisol, growth hormone, and body temperature in man. *Journal of clinical endocrinology metabolism*, 1974, **38**, 1018–1030.

Wilson, A. F., Honsberger, R., Chiu, J. T., and Novey, H. S. Transcendental meditation and asthma. *Respiration*, 1975, **32**, 74–80.

Zacur, H. A., Foster, G. V. and Tyson, J. E. Multifactorial regulation of prolactin secretion. *Lancet*, 1976, **1**(7956), 410–413.

C. Electroencephalographic Changes

Some of the more interesting and promising initial findings in meditation research dealt with EEG mentation patterns. Two early classical studies, those by Anand (34) and his colleagues dealing with Raj Yogis, and by Kasamatsu and Hirai (35) dealing with Zen meditators, suggested that there could be quite different EEG patterns dependent upon the type of meditation utilized—concentrative meditation versus opening up meditation.

Banquet's study (36) shows the use of spectral analysis in analyzing EEG patterns, and Williams and West (37) suggest the way EEG may be utilized to measure sustained attention during the meditation process. The final three articles in this section, by Bennett and Trinder (38), Pagano and Frumpkin (39), and Glueck and Stroebel (40), deal with the question of hemispheric lateralization and synchronicity in meditation research. They provide competing hypotheses, different results, and reveal that the data is not yet conclusive on these issues. Glueck and Stroebel's work suggests that meditation involves a unique mentation pattern—syncronis EEG pattern both within and between hemispheres. Whereas Bennett and Trinder, in attempting to assess whether during meditation there is a shift such that the nondominant hemisphere in normal right-handed individuals is activated and the left dominant hemisphere shows a state of quiescence, found that there is asymmetry with respect to hemispheric function on both analytical and spacial task. Pagano's article suggests that meditation facilitates right hemispheric function.

The article by Earle at the beginning of the physiology section discusses this conflicting evidence. Earle makes the important distinction between research on hemispheric laterality occurring in short- versus long-term meditators. He notes that in the early stages of meditation, there may be "relative right hemisphere activation . . . induced through the control of attention, the use of visual imagery, and the inhibition of verbal-analytical thought." However, he suggests that in later stages of meditation, with more advanced meditators, there may be a deactivation of cognitive activity in both hemispheres.

SOME ASPECTS OF ELECTROENCEPHALOGRAPHIC STUDIES IN YOGIS

B. K. Anand, G. S. Chhina, and Baldev Singh

INTRODUCTION

Yogis practising *Raj Yoga* claim that during *samadhi* (meditation) they are oblivious to 'external' and 'internal' environmental stimuli although their higher nervous activity remains in a state of 'ecstasy' *(mahanand)*. Physiological and experimental studies have demonstrated that the basis of the conscious state of the brain is the activation of the reticular activating system through peripheral afferents (Magoun 1958), without which

samadhi. Some reports have already appeared on the subject (Das and Gastaut 1955; Bagchi and Wenger 1957), but the physiological mechanism of the state of *samadhi* still needs further elucidation.

EXPERIMENTAL SUBJECTS

Scalp EEG was used to study the brain activity of Yogis during *samadhi.* Two types of yoga practitioners, who volunteered for this study, were investigated.

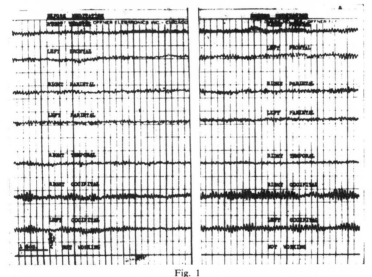

Fig. 1

Monopolar EEG scalp recordings of Shri Ramanand Yogi before meditation and during meditation. Reference electrodes on both ear lobes were joined together. During meditation there is a well marked increased amplitude modulation of alpha activity, especially in the occipital leads, where the amplitude increases from average to a maximum of 50–100 μV. The frequency was between $11\frac{1}{2}$ c/sec and 12 c/sec both before and during meditation.

higher nervous activity passes into the 'sleep' state. Studies were, therefore, undertaken to investigate electroencephalographically the activity of the brain during

[1] Aided by a grant from the Indian Council of Medical Research.

[2] Present address: *Tirath Ram Shah Charitable Hospital, Delhi (India).*

1. *Yogis practising meditation*

Four Yogis practising *samadhi* had their EEG recordings taken before as well as during meditation. Two of them were exposed to 'external' stimuli which were photic (strong light), auditory (loud banging noise), thermal (touching with hot glass tube) and vibration (tuning fork). The effect of these on the EEG activity was studied both before as well as during meditation. One

Yogi during *samadhi* also practised "pin-pointing of consciousness" (which means concentrating attention on different points of the vault of the skull).

2. *Yogis with raised pain threshold*

Two Yogis, who had developed increased pain threshold to cold water, were also investigated. They were able to keep their hand in water at 4°C for 45–55 min respectively without experiencing any discomfort. Their EEG records were obtained before and during the period when they kept their hand in cold water.

RESULTS

The changes observed in the EEG records of the Yogis investigated are presented below.

1. *Yogis practising meditation*

All these Yogis showed prominent alpha activity in their normal resting records. During the stage of *samadhi* all of them had persistent alpha activity with well marked increased amplitude modulation (Fig. 1). In addition one of them showed occasional hump activity in the parietal

2. *Yogis with raised pain threshold*

The EEG records of these two Yogis also showed persistent alpha activity, both before and during the period in which the hand was immersed in cold water (Fig. 5). No change in the electrical activity in the parietal leads was observed even when sensory afferents from the hand were expected to be projecting there.

3. EEG studies were also made on a number of beginners in the various yoga practices. It was observed that those who had a well marked alpha activity in their normal resting records showed greater aptitude and zeal for maintaining the practice of yoga.

DISCUSSION

In these experimental observations on Yogis, a persistent and well modulated alpha activity, more marked during *samadhi*, was observed. This alpha activity could not be blocked by various sensory stimuli when the Yogi was in *samadhi*, although it could easily be blocked when he was not meditating. Even during deep meditation when the Yogis appeared quite relaxed and in a sleep-like con-

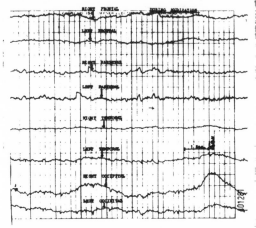

Fig. 2

Monopolar EEG scalp recording of one Yogi during meditation showing occasional hump activity in the parietal zones. For most of the remaining period of meditation he showed prominent alpha activity of 11–12 c/sec.

zones (Fig. 2), although he professed to remain awake throughout this period. In both the Yogis who were exposed to 'external' stimulation, all the stimuli blocked the alpha rhythm and changed it to a low voltage fast activity when the Yogis were not meditating. This blocking reaction did not show any adaptation to repetition of the same stimuli. On the other hand, none of these stimuli produced any blockage of alpha rhythm, when the Yogis were in meditation *(samadhi)* (Fig. 3). In the Yogi who concentrated attention on different points of the vertex ("pin-pointing of consciousness"), these attempts were accompanied by well marked 'blinking' responses recorded from the frontal electrodes (Fig. 4).

dition, the EEG record showed only prominent alpha activity. Only in one Yogi was occasional hump activity observed, the alpha rhythm persisting in the rest of the period. Bagchi and Wenger (1957) also found the normal alpha pattern, sometimes with good amplitude modulation, in the EEG records of some Yogis during meditation. Okuma *et al.* (1958) observed in *Zen* practitioners that the alpha waves of these subjects increased remarkably with the progress of their performance, even if their eyes were kept open. Das and Gastaut's (1955) observations on high amplitude fast waves in the EEG records of Yogis during meditation have not been confirmed.

The significance of prominent alpha activity observed

during meditation is not yet clear. Yogis generally claim that during *samadhi* they are oblivious to their external and internal environments, and in the present experiments their alpha rhythm could not be blocked by external beta rhythms are probably under the control of a sub-cortical pacemaker, or system of pacemakers. It is, there-fore, suggested that the brain activity of Yogis during the stage of *samadhi* has for its basis a type of consciousness

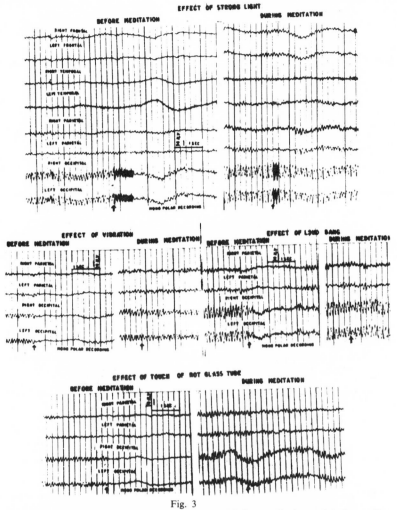

Fig. 3

Monopolar EEG scalp recordings of Shri Ramanand before meditation and during medita-tion. Photic, vibration, auditory, and thermal stimuli block the alpha rhythm when he is not in meditation. No blockage of the alpha rhythm occurs when he is in meditation.

stimuli. They also did not pass into delta activity. Al-though the reticular activating system (RAS) is activated by peripheral sensory inputs, it has also been reported that this system is capable probably of some spontaneous or autonomous discharge (Bremer 1954; Dell 1952). The alpha activity may be due to this discharge. Garoutte *et al.* (1958) have also observed that bilateral alpha and which probably depends upon mutual influences between the cephalic RAS and the cortex, and which does not depend upon the activation of RAS through external and internal afferents.

The two Yogis, who could keep their hand without discomfort in ice cold water for long periods, showed alpha activity during this practice. This suggests again

Electroencephalographic Studies 477

that these individuals were able to block the afferents from activating the RAS and thus remain in alpha activity.

Lastly the observation that those beginners who had a well marked alpha activity in their resting records, showed greater aptitude for maintaining the practice of yoga, is quite important and may have some bearing on the problem under discussion.

SUMMARY

Four Yogis who practised *samadhi* were investigated electroencephalographically. It was observed that their resting records showed persistent alpha activity with increased amplitude modulation during *samadhi*. The alpha activity could not be blocked by various sensory stimuli during meditation.

Two Yogis, who could keep their hand immersed in ice cold water for 45–55 min, also showed persistent alpha activity both before and during this practice.

The possible mechanism of these observations has been discussed.

The authors gratefully acknowledge the willing co-operation of the following Yogis for undergoing the various investigations reported in this paper: Shri Ramanand Yogi, Pandit Parkash Dev, Shri Rishi Ram, Shri N.S. Paintal, Shri Babu Ram Gupta and Shri Narain Chander Singh Ray.

REFERENCES

BAGCHI, B. K. and WENGER, M. A. Electrophysiological correlates of some Yogi exercises. *Electroenceph. clin. Neurophysiol.*, **1957**, *Suppl. 7*: 132–149.

BREMER, F. The neurophysiological problem of sleep. In *Symposium on brain mechanisms and consciousness.*

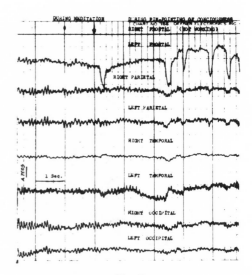

Fig. 4
Monopolar EEG scalp recording of Shri N.S. Paintal during meditation when he started concentrating his attention on different points of the vertex ("pin pointing of consciousness"). It shows a well marked blinking response from the frontal leads during this act.

Blackwell Scientific Publications, Oxford, **1954** pp., 137–162.

DAS, N. N. et GASTAUT, H. Variations de l'activité

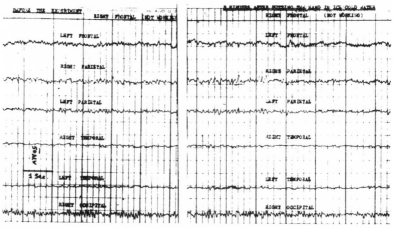

Fig. 5
Monopolar EEG scalp recordings of Shri Babu Ram Gupta who kept his right hand immersed in cold water at 4°C for 55 min. It shows records taken before the start of the experiment and 3 min after placing the hand in water. The alpha activity of 11 c/sec persisted throughout the whole period the hand was kept in water. No discomfort or pain was felt by him throughout this period.

électrique du cerveau, du coeur et des muscles squélettiques au cours de la méditation et de 'l'extase' yoguique. *Electroenceph. clin. Neurophysiol.*, **1955,** *Suppl. 6*: 211–219.

DELL, P. Corrélation entre le système végétatif et le système de la vie de relation, mésencéphale, diencéphale et cortex cérébrale. *J. Physiol. (Paris)*, **1952,** *44*: 471–557.

GAROUTTE, B. and AIRD, R. B. Studies on the cortical pacemakers. Synchrony and asynchrony of bilaterally recorded alpha and beta activity. *Electroenceph. clin. Neurophysiol.*, **1958,** *10*: 259–268.

MAGOUN, H. W. *The waking brain.* C. C. Thomas, Springfield, Ill., **1958,** 138 pp.

OKUMA, T., KOGU, E., IKEDA, K. and SUGIYAMA, H. The EEG of Yoga and Zen practitioners. *Electroenceph. clin. Neurophysiol.*, **1957,** *Suppl. 9*: 51

35

AN ELECTROENCEPHALOGRAPHIC
STUDY OF THE ZEN MEDITATION (ZAZEN)

Akira Kasamatsu and Tomio Hirai

INTRODUCTION

It is our common knowledge that EEG undergoes strikes changes in the transition from wakefulness to sleep, and has become one of the reliable ways to assess the state of wakefulness or sleep. In clinical practice, EEG often becomes a good neurophysiological method to find out the disturbance of consciousness. And many studies, both clinical and experimental, on the consciousness have been published during the past 30 years. In recent years electroencephalographic and neurophysiological studies on the consciousness are focused on an understanding of the relationship between the brain mechanisms and consciousness in general (Gastaut, in Adrian et al., Eds., 1954). These studies give rise to an attempt to relate the various electrographic findings with the psychological states and their behavioral correlates (Lindsley, 1952).

The authors have carried out the study on EEG changes during anoxia, epileptic seizures, the exogeneous disorders of the brain and other allied states from neurophysiological and psychological points of view (Kasamatsu & Shimazono, 1957). In the course of our study, it was revealed that a series of EEG changes was observed in the state of attentive awareness during Zen-sitting (Zazen. And what Zazen is like will be explained later, Hirai, 1960; Kasamatsu & Shimazono, 1957). These findings deserve further investigation because of understanding EEG pattern to corresponding psychological state and of interpreting the neurophysiological basis of consciousness. The subject of the present paper is to describe the results of our experiments in detail and to discuss some of the electrographic characteristics in which the mental state in Zen-sitting will be reflected.

Zazen—Zen meditation means the sitting meditation which is a kind of religious exercise in Zen-Buddhism. In Japan there are two Zen sects named Soto and Rinzai. Both sects regard Zazen as the most important training method of their disciples to enlighten their minds. Zen sitting is performed in two basic meditation forms: A full cross-legged sitting and a half cross-legged sitting. During the Zen sitting, the disciple's eyes must be open and look downward about one meter ahead, and his hands generally join. In a quiet room the disciple sits on a round cushion and practices the meditation for about 30 minutes. Sometimes the intensive Zen training is performed 8 to 10 times a day for about one week. This is called *Sesshin* in Zen Buddhism. The disciples do not engage in daily activities but live the religious life following a strict schedule (Hirai, 1960).

By practising Zen meditation it is said that man can become emancipated from the dualistic bondage of subjectivity and objectivity, of mind and body and of birth and death. And he can be free from lust and self-consciousness, and be awakened to his pure, serene and true-self.

This mental state (Satori or enlightenment) will often be misunderstood as trance or hypnosis. It is said that Satori is not an abnormal mental state but one's everyday mind in the Zen sense. Dr. Erich Fromm describes it, "If we would try to express enlightenment in psychological terms, I would say that it is a state in which the person is completely tuned to the reality outside and inside of him, a state in which he is fully aware of it and fully grasps it. *He* is aware of it—that is, not his brain, nor any other part of his organism, but *he*, the whole man. He is aware of *it*; not as of an object over there which he grasps with his thought, but *it*, the flower, the dog, the man, in its or his full reality. He who awakes is open and responsive to the world, and he can be open and responsive because he has given up holding on to himself as a thing, and thus has become empty and ready to receive. To be enlightened means 'the full awakening of the total personality to reality'" (Fromm, Suzuki & de Martino, 1960).

If one asks what this state of mind is concerned with in psychotherapy, it may be said that Zen meditation is the method through which we can communicate with the unconscious. In this context, however, the unconscious does not mean Freud's "unconsciousness." Rather the "unconscious" in Zen is closely related to the unconscious which is stated by Jung, C. G. (Suzuki, 1960) or Fromm, E. (Fromm, Suzuki & de Martino, 1960). In regard to this problem Dr. Daisetsu Suzuki states the meaning of it as "the Cosmic unconscious" (Suzuki, 1959).

At any rate the Zen meditation influences not only the mind but also the body as a whole organism. The authors want to investigate Zen meditation as a subject of psychophysiology, especially that of electroencephalography.

SUBJECTS AND METHODS

EEG was recorded continuously through all stages—before, during and after Zazen with opened eyes. All our EEG data were obtained in the eyes opened state.

As recording electrodes the silver-coated disc electrodes with thin (100μ to 200μ) copper wire in vinyl tube were used, and they were applied with collodion on the scalp of the frontal, central, parietal, and occipital regions in the middle line of the head. These electrodes did not disturb Zen meditation and long-lasting recordings were obtained.

Along with EEG, the pulse rate, respiration and GSR were polygraphically recorded on a San-ei 12 channel ink-writing electroencephalograph. The same experiments were performed for one week during Zen meditation's intensive training (Sessin). These results were useful to confirm the EEG changes in the whole course of Zen meditation.

In order to investigate the functional state of the brain, the responses to sensory stimuli with several modalities were examined. And the blocking time of alpha pattern to repeated click stimulations was measured.

Our experiments were made at the usual Zen-training hall with cooperations of the Zen priests and their disciples as our subjects. But the stimulation experiments were performed in the air-conditioned, sound-free shield room of our laboratory.

The cooperative 48 subjects were selected among the priests and disciples in both Soto and Rinzai sects. Their ages ranged from 24 to 72 years old. According to their experience in Zen training, these subjects could be classified into the following 3 groups:

Group I: 1 to 5 years experience (20 disciples).
Group II: 5 to 20 years experience (12 disciples).
Group III: over 20 years experience (16 priests).

As control subjects, we selected 18 research fellows (23 to 33 years of age) and 4 elderly men (54 to 60 years of age). They have had no experience in Zen meditation, and their EEGs were recorded under the same condition with opened eyes, as the Zen disciples.

RESULTS

1. EEG Changes of Zen-Masters during Zen Meditation

First we shall consider the typical EEG changes of a certain master in detail.* He is a priest with over 20 years' experience in Zen meditation. Before Zen meditation the activating pattern is predominant because his eyes are open (low voltage, fast activity). After Zen meditation has started, the well organized alpha waves of 40–50μV, 11–12/sec. appear within 50 seconds in all the regions and continue for several minutes in spite of opened eyes. After 8 minutes and 20 seconds, the amplitude of alpha waves reaches to 60–70 μV predominantly in the frontal and the central regions. Initially, these alpha waves alternate with the short runs of the activating pattern, but a fairly stable period of the persistent alpha waves ensues during the progress of Zen meditation. After 27 minutes and 10 seconds, rhythmical waves of 7–8/sec. appear for 1 or 2 seconds. And 20 seconds later rhythmical theta trains (6–7/sec., 70–100uV) begin to appear. However, it does not always occur. After the end of Zen meditation alpha waves are seen continuously and 2 minutes later alpha waves still persist. It seems to be the after-effect of Zen meditation.

In the control subjects, EEG changes are not observed; a control subject shows the long-lasting activating pattern of opened eyes. Another 2 control subjects of 58 and 60 years of age also show beta dominant type of EEG with short runs of small alpha waves. But neither increase of alpha amplitude nor decrease of alpha frequency are observed on their EEG of opened eyes. It is not likely that the aging process of the control subjects influences EEG changes during Zen meditation.

Sometimes the theta waves appear as Zen meditation progresses. These changes are clearly shown in the EEG of another Zen master of 60 years of age, large alpha waves with 70–100μV. in amplitude and 8–9/sec. in frequency appear after 24 minutes of his Zen meditation. And 30 seconds later, the rhythmical theta train (6–7/sec. 60–70μV.) begins to appear. The appearance of the theta train becomes distinct through the stable periods of large and slow alpha waves. From the above-mentioned results it is pointed out that a series of EEG changes in the course of Zen meditation are observed; the activating pattern (of opened eyes) before Zen meditation—appearance of alpha waves at initial stage—increase of alpha amplitude—decrease of alpha frequency—appearance of rhythmical theta train in later stage of Zen meditation.

This series of changes cannot always be observed in all Zen subjects. Some subjects only show the appearance of alpha waves through all the meditation

*Note: Figures illustrating the various EEG changes discussed in this paper have been deleted due to space limitations.—*Editor.*

period and others show the typical series of electrographic changes. But from our findings, the changes of electroencephalogram during Zen meditation are classified in the following four stages:

Stage I: a slight change which is characterized by the appearance of alpha waves in spite of opened eyes.
Stage II: the increase in amplitude of persistent alpha waves.
Stage III: the decrease of alpha frequency.
Stage IV: the appearance of the rhythmical theta train, which is the final change of EEG during Zen meditation but does not always occur.

2. EEG Changes and the Degree of Zen Training

In accordance with the subjects' years spent in Zen training, 23 Zen disciples were classified into 3 groups—within 5 years, 5–20 years and over 20 years. Also, the evaluation of the mental states in the Zen sense of these disciples were used and their Zen master divided them into 3 groups; low (L), middle (M) and high (H). This evaluation was made independently without regard to their EEG changes.

Then the authors attempted to relate these degrees of Zen training in the 4 stages (I, II, III and IV) of the EEG changes. Tables 1 and 2 show the results. In the vertical line the stages of EEG changes are plotted and the horizontal line shows the subjects' training years (Table 1). It is clear that the more years spent in Zen training, the more EEG changes are seen. The correlation of EEG changes with mental state, which was evaluated by the Zen master, is shown in Table 2. It shows the close relationship between the evaluation by the master and the degree of EEG changes. From these findings, it will be concluded that the degrees of EEG changes during Zen meditation are parallel with the disciples' proficiency in Zen training. The 4 stages of EEG changes reflect physiologically the mental state during Zen meditation. This will be discussed later.

3. EEG Changes during Zen Meditation and Hypnosis

The mental state in hypnosis is generally considered as "trance." Some may think that the mental state of Zen meditation will be a trance-like state. The authors compared the EEG changes in hypnotic trance with those of Zen meditation. In a hypnotized subject, a university student of 20 years, the catalepsy is manifested. Few alpha waves are seen, but the activating pattern is more prominent than EEG in Zen meditation. The series of EEG changes during Zen meditation is not observed in the course of hypnotic trance.

TABLE 1

Relationship between Degree of EEG Changes and Years Spent in Zazen Training

	Stage	0–5	6–20	21–40
Rhythmical theta waves	IV	0	0	3
Decrease in alpha frequency	III	3	2	3
Increased alpha amplitude	II	2	1	0
Alpha with eyes open	I	8	1	0

Years of Experience in Zazen

TABLE 2

Relationship between Degree of EEG Changes and Ratings of Disciples' Proficiency at Meditation by the Zen Master.

	Stage	Low	Medium	High
Rhythmical theta waves	IV	0	0	3
Decrease in alpha frequency	III	0	7	1
Increased alpha amplitude	II	2	1	0
Alpha with eyes open	I	5	4	0

Proficiency Rating

4. EEG Changes during Zen Meditation and Sleep

In the course of EEG recording during Zen training, the disciples some-times fall into a drowsy state, which becomes clear on the EEG pattern. At this time the click stimulus is given, then the drowsy pattern turns into the alpha pattern and alpha arousal reaction is observed. This electrographical change is usually accompanied with a floating consciousness from sleep to wakefulness, according to the disciple's introspection. This state is different from the mental state in Zen meditation. The sleepiness, which is called "Konchin," is suppressed in Zen training.

As mentioned before the rhythmical theta train appears in some Zen priests during their Zen meditation. The theta train is also seen in the sleep pattern. But the electrographical difference exists between the theta waves in sleep and the rhythmical theta train in Zen meditation. This difference is evident in the following example: A rhythmical theta train is clearly seen on EEG during a certain Zen master's meditation. At this time, the click stimulus is given. The rhythmical theta train is blocked by the stimulation and reappears spontaneously after several seconds later. The alpha arousal reaction, which is often seen by the stimulation in a drowsy state, is not observed. Therefore the rhythmical theta train in this instance has an "alpha activity" (Brazier, 1960) which is similar to the waking alpha rhythm.

Just before falling into sleep or in the hypnagogic stage, large alpha waves are often seen. These waves are similar to that of Zen meditation. But the large alpha waves seen in stage II or III of Zen meditation persist much longer than the pre-sleep pattern. This difference will be discussed later in detail.

5. EEG Response to Click Stimulation in Zen Meditation

In the preceding sections a series of EEG changes in Zen meditation was described. In this section, the authors will deal with the results of alpha blocking to the repetitive click stimuli with regular intervals.

The click stimulation was performed at the stage of long persisting alpha waves of a certain Zen master. To the first stimulus the alpha blocking occurs for 2 seconds. With the regular intervals of 15 seconds, the click stimuli are repeated 20 times, the alpha blocking is always observed for 2–3 seconds. On the other hand the same stimulation is performed in alpha pattern of control subjects with closed eyes. The more the stimulation repeats, the less the alpha blocking time. The same experiments were performed on 3 Zen masters and 4 control subjects and the alpha blocking time to each stimulation was measured. The measurement of the alpha blocking time leads to the following results: In control subjects, the alpha blocking time decreases rapidly, but in Zen masters, the alpha blocking time is fairly constant, though some random changes are seen.

From the above mentioned results it is concluded that there is almost no adaptation of alpha blocking during Zen meditation.

DISCUSSION

It has become apparent in our study that the electrographic changes of Zen meditation are the appearance of alpha waves without regard to opened eyes. These alpha waves increase amplitude and decrease frequency with the progress of Zen meditation. And sometimes the rhythmical theta train appears in the later stage of the meditation. These findings are also parallel with the degree of Zen disciples' mental states in the Zen sense and their years spent in Zen training.

It is common that the mental activities of concentration, mental calculation and efforts to perceive the objects elevate the level of consciousness accompanied by the activating pattern (Adrian & Matthews, 1934; Bartley, 1940; Callaway, 1962; Glass, 1964; Slater, 1960; Walter & Yeager, 1956; Walter, 1950). Thus the activating pattern indicates the augmentation of level of consciousness (Lindsley, 1952; Mundy-Castle, 1958).

Zen meditation is the concentrated regulation of inner mind. It will be, therefore, expected that Zen meditation will bring about the activating pattern. Nevertheless the lowering of cortical potentials is confirmed by our electrographic findings. This is rather paradoxical but is of prime interest to consider a relationship between the physiology of the brain and the level of consciousness.

According to the instructions of Zen meditation, the regulation of inner mind is strongly emphasized. And by obeying the rules of Zen training the well-achieved meditation has been completed. In the well-achieved meditation, it will be said that "concentration" without tension (that is the true concentration) is going on in the utmost inner world of psychic life.

From the electroencephalographic point of view, our results are coincident with EEG changes of lowered consciousness or vigilance. A. C. Mundy-Castle (1953, 1958) states that the persistent appearance of alpha waves indicates the brain function at the time of lowered vigilance. And many empirical observations of alpha waves point out its being not of action but of hypofunction of the brain (Dynes, 1947; Lindsley, 1952).

In attempting to relate the various stages of the EEG pattern to corresponding psychological states and the behavioral correlates, D. B. Lindsley (1952) states that during more or less continuous relaxed state of wakefulness, amplitude modulated alpha waves are characteristic. The same concept is stated by H. Jasper (1941; Jasper & Shagass, 1941) in his sleep-wakefulness continuum; he introduces the concept of the cortical excitatory states reflected on these EEG patterns. According to Jasper's suggestion, it is said that the amplitude modulated alpha waves reflect the lowered level of the cortical excitatory states.

On the other hand, many agents which affect nerve cell metabolism, are known to alter the EEG (Brazier & Finesinger, 1945; Grunthal & Bonkalo, 1940; Jung, 1953). A. Kasamatsu and Y. Shimazono (1957) report that the large and slow alpha waves are observed in the earlier stage of N_2 gas inhalation, just before the loss of consciousness. In this state, subjects experience relaxed consciousness or slightly elevated mood-changes. In the acute alcoholic intoxication the same effects are seen in both the EEG and consciousness (Kasamatsu & Shimazono, 1957). T. Hirai (1960) points out a decrease of the respiratory rate accompanied with the slowing of EEG pattern during Zen meditation. Y. Sugi et al. (1964) report the results of measurements of the respiratory rate, tidal volume and O_2 consumption during Zen meditation. They find a decrease of energy metabolism which is lower than basic metabolism. According to Sugi's suggestion, it may be due to the decrease of energy metabolism in the brain. It is possible that the decrease of energy metabolism also alters the electrographic pattern in Zen meditation.

From the foregoing surveys and discussions, EEG changes during Zen meditation seem to indicate that the cortical excitatory level will be gradually lowered even by the "concentration" of inner mind.

From a psychological point of view, both Zen meditation and hypnotic trance bring about the changes of consciousness. But the trance is called "Sanran" (confusion) and is strictly suppressed in Zen meditation. Therefore, some discussions will be needed about the difference of EEG changes between Zen meditation and hypnotic trance. The authors discovered that there are no definite changes of subjects' electroencephalograms in hypnotic trance. There are many reports concerning the EEG changes in hypnotic trance but many of these indicate that the pattern does not differ from the waking EEG (Kleitman, 1963; Loomis, Harvey, & Habart, 1936). There are no similarities of the pattern in hypnotic trance to EEG changes during Zen meditation.

Some scholars state that the sleep-like changes of EEG, more or less slight, are observed in hypnotic trance. Goldie et al. (Kleitman, 1963) elicited a paradoxical electrographic effect in a drowsy hypnotized subject— the alpha pattern appearing in the opened-eyes condition D. J. Frank (1950) reports that slow activity seen in deep sleep is recorded during the hypnosis. D. B. Lindsley (1952) points out that in accordance with general relaxation, which occurs during hypnotic episodes, there is sometimes an increase in alpha pattern if slight drowsiness supervenes.

K. Fujisawa (1960) studies EEG in the hypnotic state caused by sleep suggestion ("hypnotic sleep") (Baker & Burgwin, 1949; Dynes, 1947) and reveals the low voltage theta pattern which is similar to the drowsy pattern. He also points out that the drowsy-like pattern continues for a fairly long time as far as the rapport with the hypnotized subject is not lost and true sleep ensues if the rapport is lost. It is noticed that the slow rhythm in hypnotic sleep is more similar to the drowsy pattern than the rhythmical theta activity seen in Zen meditation.

Zen meditation is not a sleep from the disciples' introspections. But during Zen training, sometimes the slight drowsiness also can be supervened in a hypnosis. In the transitory state from wakefulness to drowsiness, large alpha waves are prominently seen and are prone to decrease in frequency just before the subject shows slight drowsiness (Oswald, 1959). It may be said, therefore, that the large and slow alpha pattern during Zen meditation is a foregoing pattern of the drowsiness. Perhaps there is the lower threshold in a sweep or span of consciousness during Zen meditation. But in actual sleep, alpha waves recede, spindles burst and slow waves appear, and consciousness is lost. Such a series of electrographic changes does not occur in Zen meditation and consciousness is not lost, since in Zen meditation there is no lack of awareness of things going on externally and internally.

Even in the later stage of Zen meditation, in which the rhythmical theta train is seen on EEG, the sensibility is not lost and in fact the rhythmical theta train shows the marked blocking to sensory stimulation. From these findings, we will show the difference between both schematically in Fig. 1. A series of EEG changes is common at a limit of alpha activities, but the sleep pattern diverges from this series in a downward curve, and turns to deep sleep.

From the foregoing discussions, it can be said that during Zen meditation the level of the cerebral excitatory state is gradually lowered in a way that is different from sleep.

Next we will discuss the alpha blocking in Zen meditation. As described before, each click stimulus brings about a fairly constant alpha blocking continued for several seconds, even though the stimulation is repeated 20 times at regular intervals. But in control groups with closed eyes, the alpha blocking time is longer at 1st and 2nd stimulations but rapidly decreases and almost diminishes after 3rd or 4th stimulation. So the habituation of alpha blocking is clearly recognized in this ordinary awakening state.

In Zen meditation the alpha blocking is less susceptible to habituation to sensory stimuli than in ordinary waking state. This fact is noteworthy to clarify the arousal state of consciousness in Zen meditation. During Zen meditation "concentration" without tension is maintained in the inner mind of the disciple while keeping the correct sitting form. These mental and physical conditions naturally lead to production of the certain constant

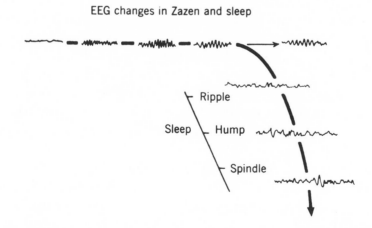

Figure 1 A schematical representation of the difference between EEG changes in Zen meditation and in sleep. A series of EEG changes is common at a limit of alpha activities but the sleep pattern diverges from above horizontal train in a downward curve and turns to deep sleep.

Electroencephalographic Study of Zen

experimental circumstances: A kind of concentration subserves the maintenance of a certain level of the consciousness on the one hand, and the sitting meditation form supports the centripetal sensory inflows at a certain level on the other. In these circumstances, it would be supposed that the alpha blocking becomes less susceptible to habituation.

These findings are also supported by the introspection of our subjects in this experiment. The Zen masters reported to us that they had more clearly perceived each stimulus than in their ordinary waking state. In this state of mind one cannot be affected by either external or internal stimulus, nevertheless he is able to respond to it. He perceives the object, responds to it, and yet is never disturbed by it. Each stimulus is accepted as stimulus itself and treated as such. One Zen master described such a state of mind as that of noticing every person one sees on the street but of not looking back with emotional curiosity.

However, it seems to be impossible to consider separately the continuous appearance of alpha waves and the alpha blocking, which is less susceptible to habituation in Zen meditation. The alpha blocking depends upon the cortical excitatory state, conversely the cortical excitatory state closely related to the centrifugal sensory impulses brought about alpha blocking.

Using the arousal reaction of EEG as a criterion response, S. Sharpless and H. Jasper (1956) studied a great variety of characteristics of the habituation. They classified two types of arousal reaction: a longer lasting one more susceptible to habituation and a shorter lasting one less susceptible. This finding, in agreement with other studies (Jung, 1953; Lindsley, 1952) suggests that a longer lasting arousal reaction corresponds to the tonic activation on the cerebral cortex and a shorter lasting one to the phasic activation.

According to Jasper's suggestion, the alpha blocking, which is less susceptible to habituation, seems to be decided by the equilibrium of the tonic and phasic activation on the cerebral cortex. The authors want to postulate that there is an optimal activation mediated by the equilibrium of cortical excitatory state in a broad sweep or span of the waking consciousness. And perhaps its underlying neurophysiological basis may be an interaction between the cerebral cortex and the reticular activation systems of the diencephalic and mesencephalic portions in the brain stem (Moruzzi & Magoun, 1949).

The optimal preparedness for incoming stimuli, which conversely maintains the optimal level of the cortical excitatory state, is well reflected in both the alpha blocking, which is less susceptible to habituation, and in the series of EEG changes, which directs to the slowing of the pattern.

These EEG findings persist for a fairly long time and are constant though slight fluctuation is observed. Also these persistant alpha waves can be often seen even after the end of Zen meditation. These findings suggest that in the awakening consciousness, there will be the special state of consciousness, in which the cortical excitatory level becomes lower than in ordinary wakefulness, but is not lowered as in sleep, and yet outer or inner stimulus is precisely perceived with steady responsiveness.

Zen meditation is purely a subjective experience completed by a concentration which holds the inner mind calm, pure and serene. And yet Zen meditation produces a special psychological state based on the changes in the electroencephalogram. Therefore, Zen meditation influences not only the psychic life but also the physiology of the brain. The authors call this state of mind the "relaxed awakening with steady responsiveness."

SUMMARY

Zen meditation (Zazen) is a spiritual exercise held in the Zen sect of Buddhism. Apart from its religious significance, the training of Zen meditation produces changes not only in the mind but also in the body—these influences are of interest to scientific studies, from the standpoint of psychology and physiology.

In the present study the EEG changes accompanied with Zen meditation have been revealed and described in detail. The authors discussed further these electrographic changes in relation to the consciousness with its underlying neurophysiological background, compared with that of the hypnotic trance and sleep.

In our study, 48 priests and disciples of Zen sects of Buddhism were selected as the subjects and their EEGs were continuously recorded before, during, and after Zen meditation. The following results were obtained:

1. The appearance of alpha waves were observed, without regard to opened eyes, within 50 seconds after the beginning of Zen meditation. These alpha waves continued to appear, and their amplitudes increased. And as Zen meditation progressed, the decrease of the alpha frequency was gradually manifested at the later stage. Further the rhythmical theta train with the amplitude modulated alpha-background was observed in some records of the priests. These EEG changes could be classified into 4 stages: the appearance of alpha waves (Stage I), an increase of alpha amplitude (Stage II), a decrease of alpha frequency (Stage III), and the appearance of rhythmical theta train (Stage IV).

2. These 4 stages of EEG changes were parallel with the disciples' mental states, which were evaluated by a Zen master, and disciples' years spent in Zen training.

3. These electrographic changes were also compared with that of the hypnotic trance and sleep. From the electroencephalographic point of view, the changes of Stages I, II and III could not be clearly differentiated from

those seen in hypnagogic state or the hypnotic sleep, though the changes during Zen meditation were more persistent and did not turn into a deeper sleep pattern. The rhythmical theta train is suppressed by click stimulation and turns into a desynchronized pattern, whereas the drowsy pattern turns into alpha waves (the alpha arousal reaction).

4. The alpha blocking to the repeated click stimuli with regular intervals was also examined in Zen meditation with opened eyes and the ordinary conditions of control subjects with closed eyes. The former showed a fairly constant blocking time (3–5 seconds) to every stimuli repeated 20 times and the habituation was not recognized. On the other hand, in control subjects the habituation of alpha waves occurred very quickly. This alpha blocking, which is less susceptible to habituation, is of importance in considering the neurophysiological basis of the mental state during Zen meditation.

These electroencephalographic findings lead to the following conclusions: In Zen meditation, the slowing of the EEG pattern is confirmed on the one hand, and the dehabituation of the alpha blocking on the other. These indicate the specific change of consciousness. The authors further discussed the state of mind during Zen meditation from the psychophysiological point of view.

References

Adrian, E., & Matthews, B. *Brain,* 1934, **57**, 355–385.
Baker, W., & Burgwin, S. *Arch. neurol. psychiat.,* 1949, **62**, 412–420.
Bartley, S. *J. exp. psychol.,* 1940, **27**, 627–639.
Brazier, M. *The electrical activity of the nervous system,* 2nd ed. London: 1960.
Brazier, M., & Finesinger, J. *Arch. neuro. psychiat.,* 1945, **53**, 51–58.
Callaway, E., III. *EEG clin. neurophysiol.,* 1961, **13**, 674–682.
Dynes, J. *Arch. neurol. psychiat.,* 1947, **57**, 84–93.
Frank, B. *Electroenceph. clin. neurophysiol.,* 1950, **2**, 107.
Fromm, E., Zuzuki, D., and de Martino, R. *Zen Buddhism and psychoanalysis.* London: Allen & Unwin, 1960.
Fujisawa, K. *Jap. psychol. res.,* 1960, **2**, 120–134.
Gastaut, H. In E. Adrian et al. (Eds.), *Brain mechanisms and consciousness.* Oxford: Blackwell, 1954.
Glass, A. *EEG clin. neurophysiol.,* 1964, **16**, 595–603.
Grunthal, E., & Bonkalo, A. *Arch. psychiat.,* 1940, **3**, 652–655.
Hirai, T. *Psychiat neurol. jap.,* 1960, **62**, 76–105.
Jasper, H., & Shagass, C. *J. exp. psychol.,* 1941, **28**, 503–508.
Jung, R. Neurophysiologische untersuchungmethode. In G. Bergmann (Ed.), *Handbuch d. inn. med, neurologie.* Berlin: Springer-Verlag, 1953.
Kasamatsu, A., & Shimazono, Y. *Psychiat. neuro. jap.,* 1957, **11**,969–999.
Kleitman, N. *Sleep and wakefulness,* 2nd ed. Chicago and London: University of Chicago Press, 1963.
Lindsley, D. *EEG clin. neurophysiol.,* 1952, **4**, 443–456.
Loomis, A., Harvey, E., & Hobart, G. *Science,* 1936, **83**, 239–241.
Moruzzi, G., & Magoun, H. *EEG clin. neurophysiol.,* 1949, **1**, 455–473.
Mundy-Castle, A. *Monogr. suppl.* No. 2 of *J. nat. Insti. f. personnel Res.,* 1958, 1–43.
Mundy-Castle, A. & McKiever, B. *J. exp. psychol.,* 1953, **45**, 15–24.
Slater, K. *EEG clin. neurophysiol.,* 1960, **12**, 851–859.
Sugi, Y., & Akutsu, K. *Science of Zazen-energy metabolism.* Tokyo, 1964.
Suzuki, D. *An introduction to Zen Buddhism.* New York: Arrow-Books, 1960.
Suzuki, D. *The training of the Zen Buddhist monk.* New York: University Books, 1959.
Walter, W. *J. ment. sci.,* 1950, **86**, 1–31.
Walter, R., & Yeager, C. *EEG clin. neurophysiol.,* 1956, **8**, 193–199.

36

SPECTRAL ANALYSIS OF THE
EEG IN MEDITATION[1]

J. P. Banquet[2]

Several investigators have reported changes in the EEG of normal adults induced by yoga meditation: Das and Gastaut (1957) recorded fast frequencies during deep states of meditation. Anand *et al.* (1961) pointed out the prominence of alpha activity associated with the absence of reaction to external stimuli. More recently Wallace (1970) remarked the appearance of theta waves in the frontal area during the practice of Transcendental Meditation (TM). The purpose of this study was to seek further evidence of EEG alterations to determine whether meditative states can be distinguished from other states of consciousness. To test this hypothesis we compared twelve subjects practising TM, as taught by Maharishi Mahesh Yogi (1966), with adequate controls. Methods of classical electroencephalography were combined with computerized spectral analysis and correlated with subjective data. The present work has been the subject of a preliminary presentation (Banquet 1972).

METHODS

Subjects

The study was carried out on twelve experimental subjects (9 males, 3 females) and a group of twelve matched controls who were about to learn TM. Three of the controls (2 males and 1 female) were also experimental subjects and were tested before and after starting meditation. All subjects volunteered and were obtained through the Students International Meditation Society, Cambridge Center. The method, de-

scribed as a mental repetition of a special sound or Mantra, was imparted individually to meditators. All of them had practised TM daily during two 30 min sessions over a period ranging from 9 months to 5 years with an average of 24 months. The group was composed of one undergraduate, six teachers of TM, three office workers and two college faculty members. The mean age was 30 with a range between 23 and 52. The control group consisted of two college faculty members, one undergraduate, one Ph. D., and eight office workers (mean age 29 years 9 months, range 18–58).

Procedure

The experiment was conducted in a sound-proof room, dimly lit for observation purposes. Subjects were seated comfortably. Records, with linked ears for reference electrode, were taken from electrodes F3,4 C3,4 P3,4 O1,2 of the 10–20 system. The time constant was 300 msec, the high pass limitation 60 c/sec, the EEG machine a Grass Model 78 polygraph. The EEG was recorded on paper and stored on tape (Ampex, 7-channels).

In 6 experimental subjects the EMG was recorded from a surface electrode applied below the chin with linked ears as reference electrode. The respiratory rate and amplitude were studied with a Grass TCT-IR thermocouple transducer fixed to the right nostril and linked to a polygraph DC driver amplifier.

A push-button with a code of 5 signals permitted the subjects to indicate the psychological events occurring during meditation or relaxation: body sensation, involuntary movement, visual imagery, deep meditation and

[1] This work was supported by a Fullbright and French Government Fellowship.
[2] Present address: Groupe d'Informatique Bio-Médicale C.R.T.S.–C.H.U. PURPAN, 31300 Toulouse, France.

Spectral Analysis of EEG

transcendence (deepest point of meditation). A phone dial at the disposal of the operator signalled the EEG segments of special interest on paper and tape.

The planning of the experiment was explained to the subjects as follows: (a) Rest 5 min with eyes open and 5 min with eyes closed. (b) Meditate for their usual time of meditation (about 30 min) or, for the controls, relax for 30 min with eyes closed. (c) Come progressively out of meditation or relaxation (3 min). (d) Concentrate on a thought or image with eyes closed for 5 min. (e) Open the eyes.

Once the experiment was over, an interviewer investigated the quality and the events of meditation and relaxation. The number of sessions ranged from 1 to 10.

Data analysis

The entire sequence of record from O1 (with 6 meditators and 6 controls, also from C3 and F3) was filtered by a band-pass filter (0–60 c/sec) and digitized at a rate of 200 points/sec (or 100/sec for the specific study of low frequencies). These data were stored on Dectapes of a PDP 7 general purpose computer.

The spectral analysis was performed by Fast Fourier Transform, in the band 0–50 c/sec. A program used the Fourier Transform to produce a succession of EEG spectra in time (Gabor 1946). Each line of the plot made by a Calcomp plotter represented the Fourier analysis of 128 data points, *i.e.* 1.28 or 0.64 sec for the sampling rates of respectively 100 and 200/sec. The separation of these curves along the time axis covering the entire duration of the experiment was either 0.5 or 1 sec. On the X axis are the different frequency bands, with a resolution of 1 c/sec (Fig. 1,5). The Y axis represents the relative voltages of the different frequencies. A second program computed the integration over the 4 frequency bands: delta 0–3, theta 4–7, alpha 8–14, beta and fast frequencies 15–50 c/sec.

RESULTS

The results are derived from the comparative interpretation of the conventional EEG and frequency spectrum arrays, for both control and experimental subjects.

Control group

These subjects can be divided in two subgroups: alpha minus and alpha plus groups.

Alpha minus group

Four subjects showed beta dominant mixed frequencies throughout, with muscle activity

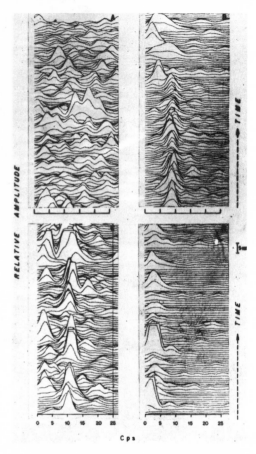

Fig. 1. Portions of spectral analysis plots from electrode O1 in four control subjects, during relaxation with eyes closed. *A*: Alpha-minus subject with beta dominant mixed frequencies and muscle artifacts. *B*: Alpha-plus subject with alpha rhythm at 9 c/sec shifting to theta and delta activity of drowsiness at the end of the period. *C*: Subject during drowsiness with mixed frequencies; short alternations of 10 c/sec alpha rhythm and delta frequencies at 2–3 c/sec. Notice the small amount of theta activity. *D*: Higher voltage delta activity and disappearance of alpha frequency. As a feature of the plotting program, the peaks were cut off when the amplitude reached a predetermined level.

Physiology of Meditation

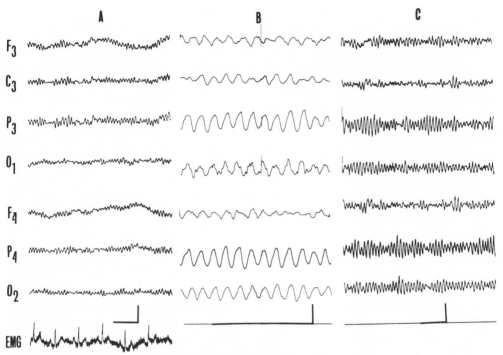

Fig. 2. Alpha frequencies at the beginning and the end of meditation in three subjects. In this and the following figure, vertical calibration = 50 μV, horizontal = 1 sec. A: First stage of meditation 10 min after the beginning. All the channels display a similar alpha rhythm at 9 c/sec, 30 μV. The EMG still presents some muscle activity. B: The recording speed at 60 mm/sec shows a slow alpha frequency at 8 c/sec, 30–60 μV, homogeneous in all channels at the end of stage 1. C: End of meditation. High voltage alpha waves at 9 c/sec, 60 μV maximum amplitude. In P and O channels the spindles are continuous and merging into one another.

superimposed on the spectrum. They did not develop a stable alpha rhythm during relaxation with eyes closed (Fig. 1,A).

Alpha plus group

Eight subjects developed an alpha rhythm at a constant frequency (Fig. 1,B).

(1) Four subjects of this group alternated posterior alpha waves with the previous pattern of beta dominant mixed frequencies. Muscle artifacts decreased or disappeared during the alpha periods. We could term this state a successful relaxation.

(2) The four remaining subjects associated alpha activity with slow theta and low voltage delta frequencies (Fig. 1,B, C) The paper record showed a relatively low voltage mixed frequency during this time, and drowsiness was reported. Two of the subjects presented periods of high

voltage delta waves of sleep, with disappearance of alpha activity (Fig. 1,D).

Meditators

Meditation was associated with changes in the different parameters characterizing the brain waves.

Amplitude and frequency changes

The general tendency was for an early shift from the basic alpha rhythm to slower frequencies and, in four subjects, the emergence of a stable rhythmic beta activity at 20 c/sec.

(1) Alpha activity around 10 c/sec and 50 μV was present in the resting record of all the meditators. This frequency became predominant at the beginning of meditation (Fig. 2,A). Its amplitude increased up to 70 μV; in 10 subjects, the frequency slowed down by 1 or 2 c/sec, first in

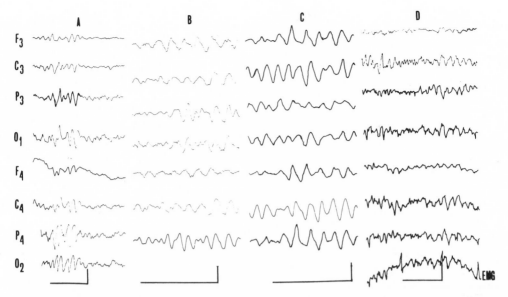

Fig. 3. Second stage of meditation. *A*: Theta burst at 7 c/sec and 80 μV recorded at 30 mm/sec. *B*: Transition phase from alpha to theta frequency. The recording speed of 60 mm/sec shows the theta waves at 6 c/sec appearing first in the frontal channels. *C*: Beginning of a theta train with simultaneous shift from alpha to theta frequency. *D*: Predominant theta frequency at 6 c/sec recorded at 30 mm/sec.

the frontal channels (Fig. 2,*B*). The pattern of this first stage of meditation was repeated at the end of TM with an even greater abundance of alpha waves, the spindles becoming continuous or merging into one another (Fig. 2,*C*).

(2) After the first stage there was a typical shift from dominant alpha to slower activity. If alpha waves appeared in this second phase they took the form of short bursts of a few seconds. A dominant theta pattern (unlike that of drowsiness) was observed in the second stage of meditation. Within 5–20 min after the beginning of meditation short bursts of high voltage (up to 100 μV) theta frequency at 5–7 c/sec occurred during 1 or 2 sec, simultaneous in all channels (Fig. 3*A*) or first in the frontal region (Fig. 3,*B*). Longer rhythmic theta trains (10 sec to several minutes) at 60–80 μV usually followed (Fig. 3*C,D* and 5,*C*). No further evolution in the meditation state happened in most subjects.

(3) In four of the meditators a third stage occurred, signalled with the push-button as being deep meditation or even transcendence. It was characterized by a pattern of generalized fast frequencies with a dominant beta rhythm

around 20 c/sec. Das and Gastaut found similar fast frequencies during Krya Yoga Meditation. On the ink-written record this fast activity appeared as beta periods at 20 and 40 c/sec. Intermittent spindle-like bursts alternated first with alpha or theta rhythms (Fig. 4,*A,B,C*). They showed a tendency to become continuous on a persistent background of slower activity (Fig. 4*E*). This amplitude-modulated activity reached a surprisingly high voltage (30–60 μV). It predominated in the anterior channels but was present and sometimes simultaneous in all of them (Fig. 4*B,C*).

In the spectral arrays, the beta peaks lay nearly on a straight line, *i.e.* at an almost constant frequency (Fig. 5,*D*), with a high voltage beta peak at 20 c/sec and small amplitude fast frequencies around 40 c/sec.

(4) These 3 phases of meditation were not individualized clearly. The change from one dominant frequency to another was progressive. Two major frequencies could appear simultaneously in the different transition periods: alpha and theta or slow and fast frequencies (Fig. 5,*B,D*). If meditation lasted longer than the average

Physiology of Meditation

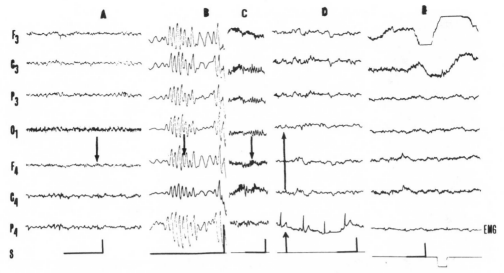

Fig. 4. Beta frequencies during meditation. *A, B, C*: The 3 arrows show the same pattern of spindle-like amplitude modulation recorded at 30, 60, 15 mm/sec. Notice in *B* and *C* the simultaneous occurrence of the spindles in the different channels. The frequency is around 20 c/sec. *D*: Disorganized pattern with beta rhythm at 20 c/sec on a background of mixed frequencies. Notice the absence of muscle activity in the EMG and compare with the EMG of Fig. 2,*A* from the same subject in stage 1 meditation. The ongoing pattern is not altered by the click stimulation indicated by the arrows. *E*: Fast frequency on a background of slower activity of small amplitude and absence of activity in the EMG. The subject indicates by the signal the deepest phase of meditation called transcendence. *A, C, E* come from the same subject.

30 min several cycles took place. The end of meditation was characterized by the return of alpha trains (Fig. 2,*C*). In advanced subjects alpha, and more rarely theta, waves persisted in the post-meditation period with eyes open. The concentration exercise after meditation produced alpha activity and brief periods of dominant beta frequencies (Fig. 6).

The changes observed during the different stages of meditation somewhat reduced the differences between the EEG channels, bringing about similar brain wave patterns in all of them.

Topographical changes in the EEG rhythms during meditation

Two kinds of topographical change could be observed: on the one hand, there was a constant tendency to synchronisation of the anterior and posterior derivations. Alpha rhythms spread from the occipito-parietal to the anterior channels, resulting in a possible gradient shift (Fig. 7,*A, B*). Theta and beta frequencies, which usually

appeared first in the frontal channels, diffused posteriorly. On the other hand, a transient asymmetry between right and left hemispheres could occur in the shifting phase from slow to fast frequencies. Beta dominant activity appeared first in the left hemisphere from frontal to occipital channels (Fig. 7,*C*). There were periods of uniformity of frequency, amplitude and wave form in all channels.

EEG response to stimulation

Meditation brought about particular responses to flash and click stimuli administered to seven subjects during different stages of the practice.

(1) In accordance with the findings of Anand *et al.* (1961), during the alpha periods there was usually no alpha blocking.

(2) Click stimulation blocked the rhythmic theta frequencies of meditation, but they reappeared spontaneously within a few seconds

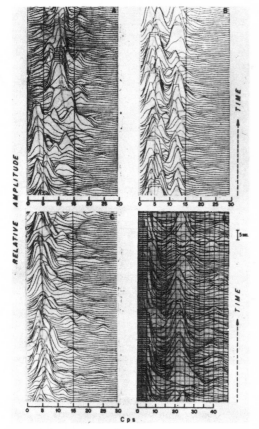

Muscle activity

Das and Gastaut (1957), using needle electrode recording of the tonic EMG, found complete disappearance of muscle activity during deep meditation. Our paper records from submental muscle areas showed the same trend, and muscle artifacts appearing like fast frequencies of large amplitude on the spectral arrays disappeared early during meditation.

Involuntary movements similar to those of early sleep could occur at the beginning of meditation, but disappeared in the deep phase. Eye movements recorded with the frontal electrodes varied in time: REMs of the beginning of meditation shifted early to slow eye movements. In deep meditation there was no eye movement. At the same time breathing became very slow and shallow. An occasional burst of rapid eye movements, similar to dream REMs, was related by the subjects to the occurrence of kaleidoscopic visual activity.

Voluntary movement (proper use of the signal) could be performed at any stage of meditation, testifying to the wakefulness of the subject. This performance did not alter the brain wave pattern of deep meditation (Fig. 4,E). The subjects could also answer any question readily and accurately.

DISCUSSION

The main EEG alterations must be compared with those of other states of consciousness in an attempt to individualize the meditative state.

(1) The dramatic increase in alpha abundance is not particular to meditation, since such techniques as operant control of the brain waves produce the same results (Kamiya 1969). More unusual is the ability of the meditators to maintain alpha activity after the end of meditation with eyes open, as well as the diffusion of large amplitude alpha waves to anterior regions.

(2) The strong propensity to slow frequencies in stage 2 of meditation must be differentiated from drowsiness and sleep. The main argument comes from the response to stimuli; the rhythmic theta trains of stage 2 were blocked by click stimuli but reappeared spontaneously within a few seconds. The usual drowsy pattern was changed into the alpha rhythm of an arousal reaction; therefore the rhythmic theta train of

Fig. 5. Spectral arrays from derivation O1 during meditation. *A, B, C* from the same meditator. *A*: The picture shows the end of a theta train, a transition period and the beginning of an alpha train of high voltage; the spectral array comes from the end of meditation. The alpha train at that beginning of meditation is similar, with usually smaller amplitude. *B*: Transition phase between first and second stages of meditation with simultaneous presence of alpha and theta frequencies. *C*: Second stage of meditation showing a long train of 5 c/sec theta rhythm. *D*: Third stage of meditation. The vertical calibration has been increased to make more apparent the 20–25 c/sec beta rhythm, associated with slow frequencies and fast activity around 40 c/sec.

less than 1–2 or 3 sec), whereas the drowsy pattern was displaced into the alpha activity of an arousal reaction.

(3) During the deep meditation stages of low mixed frequencies and fast frequencies, there was no change in the electrical pattern (Fig. 4,D).

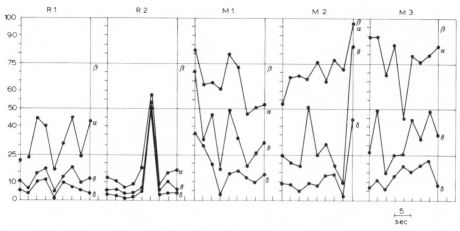

Fig. 6. Plots of the integrals of EEG amplitudes over the 4 different frequency bands: delta 0–3, theta 4–7, alpha 8–14, beta and fast frequencies 15–50 c/sec. X axis = time in 2.5 sec units. Y axis = relative abundance of each frequency band in % of the total. Each line is an upper boundary for the surface below and also the lower boundary for the area above. Delta and beta bands have the horizontal axis for outer boundaries. The areas between lines (not between lines and X axis) are the surface of integration of each frequency band, proportional to their abundance. R 1: Control subject during relaxation. The presence of alpha activity locates him in the alpha plus group. R 2: Control subject with almost no alpha activity. The isolated delta peak at the middle of the figure is rather an artefact (movement) than a period of drowsiness. M 1: Meditator in the relaxation phase just prior to meditation. Notice the greater amount of alpha and theta frequency than in the controls. M 2: Same subject during the first phase of meditation. The alpha band expands first, then slow activity increases dramatically and its beta band decreases. M 3: Same subject after meditation, during the concentration period. There is an important alpha remanence and a beta peak at the middle of the figure. The relative amounts of the different frequencies in meditators keep some stability during the change from meditation to other states of consciousness.

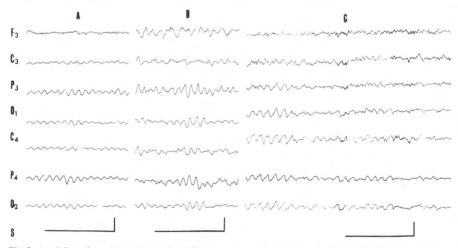

Fig. 7. A and B are from the same record at different moments of meditation. In B we see the increase of alpha amplitude in the different channels, and the appearance of alpha waves in F3. C represents the shift from alpha to beta dominant disorganized pattern. The change occurs successively in F3, C3, P3, O1 on the left and then on the right.

Spectral Analysis of EEG   499 meditation has a reactivity similar to the waking alpha rhythm (Brazier 1968). The spectral analysis showed a morphological difference: meditation theta rhythms are continuous trains of dominant theta activity at a constant frequency (Fig. 5,*B,C*). Drowsiness produces a mixture or alternation of alpha, low delta and discontinuous theta frequencies (Fig. 1,*B,C,D*). Finally, theta waves can persist in the post-meditation period, with eyes open. Short bursts of large amplitude delta waves identical to those of sleep stage 4 could occur during meditation. In advanced subjects a simultaneous alpha rhythm deeply indented the curves of the delta waves; and this same pattern was found during deep night sleep.

The third important distinction is between the activating pattern of low voltage fast activity of the awake subject and that of deep meditation. On the ink-written record the beta rhythm of deep meditation appears on a background of slow frequencies; it has a spindle-like amplitude modulation (Fig. 4,*A,B,C*). Spectral analysis shows rhythmic fast frequencies around 20 and 40 c/sec. The activation pattern of the control subjects consists of dominant fast frequencies without any rhythmicity or regularity (Fig. 1,*A*).

These self-induced changes during meditation are of special interest inasmuch as they are not produced by other techniques like autosuggestion and hypnosis (Kasamatsu and Hirai 1966). Their neurophysiological interpretation could be based on three consistent findings of the deep meditation state: absence or decrease of EEG reaction to stimulation, even if the subject perceives external and internal stimuli; simultaneous persistence of an alert state of consciousness, allowing the subject to memorize and answer questions; possibility of voluntary movement without any noticeable modification of the brain wave pattern of deep meditation. We must deduce, therefore, that the EEG changes of meditation are independent of the interaction between the subject and the outer world but produced by the specific mental activity of the practice. The initiation of a loop between cortex, thalamo-cortical coordinating system and subcortical rhythm generators (Andersen and Andersson 1968) could account for the different alterations.

SUMMARY

Classical EEG combined with spectral analysis was performed on a group of subjects during Transcendental Meditation (TM). The findings were compared with those obtained in a resting control group.

(1) Alpha rhythm increased in amplitude, slowed down in frequency and extended to anterior channels at the beginning of meditation.

(2) In a second stage, theta frequencies different from those of sleep diffused from frontal to posterior channels. They took the form of short theta periods or longer rhythmic theta trains.

(3) Rhythmic amplitude-modulated beta waves were present over the whole scalp in a third stage of deep meditation by advanced subjects.

(4) The most striking topographical alteration was the synchronisation of anterior and posterior channels.

Therefore EEG records from meditators practising TM distinguish the meditative state from other states of consciousness. The combination of sequential EEG changes in relation to topographical alterations produces a particular pattern.

RESUME

ANALYSE SPECTRALE DE L'EEG DE L'ETAT DE MEDITATION

Une étude électroencéphalographique classique combinée avec analyse spectrale a été réalisée sur un groupe de sujets pratiquant la Méditation Transcendentale (MT). Les résultats ont été comparés avec ceux d'un groupe de contrôle en état de relaxation.

(1) Le rythme alpha s'amplifia, diminua de fréquence et diffusa vers les dérivations antérieures en début de méditation.

(2) Dans une seconde phase des fréquences thêta différentes de celles observées dans le sommeil s'étendirent de la région frontale aux dérivations postérieures, sous la forme de courtes périodes thêta ou de long trains d'ondes rythmiques.

(3) Des fréquences bêta à amplitude modulée en fuseaux, de fréquence fixe étaient rencontrées sur tout le scalp dans une troisième phase de méditation profonde, chez les sujets avancés.

(4) Les modifications topographiques les plus frappantes constituaient un phénomène de synchronisation entre les dérivations antérieures et postérieures.

Ainsi l'EEG des sujets pratiquant MT permet d'individualiser un état différent des autres états de conscience. Des modifications séquentielles de l'EEG combinées à des changements liés à la topographie de l'enregistrement produisent un type particulier de tracé.

Thanks to F. Ervin, Warren E. Foote, Directors, and M. McGuire, Director of residential training, for their guidance and support. We also acknowledge the suggestions of Doctors Janice Stevens, John Barlow and Jacques Bouloux; the technical assistance of Paul Johnson, Jerome Holland, Joseph Withman, Mildred Riley, Thomas Busby, Jeffrey Modest, Frederick Dittman; the support of Charles Duffault, John Thomas, Andree Leonhard, Sally Peden and all the staff of Stanley Cobb Laboratories; the invaluable cooperation of all the subjects.

REFERENCES

ANAND, B. U., CHHINA, G. S. and SINGH, B. Some aspects of electroencephalographic studies in yogis. *Electroenceph. clin. Neurophysiol.*, **1961**, *13*: 452–456.

ANDERSEN, P. and ANDERSSON, S. A. *Physiological basis of the alpha rhythm*. Appleton–Century–Crofts, New York, **1968,** 235 p.

BANQUET, J. P. EEG and meditation. *Electroenceph. clin. Neurophysiol.*, **1972,** *33*: 454P.

BRAZIER, M. A. B. *The electrical activity of the nervous system*, 3rd ed. Williams and Wilkins, Baltimore, Md., **1968,** 317 p.

DAS, N. N. et GASTAUT, H. Variations de l'activité électrique du cerveau, du coeur et des muscles squelettiques au cours de la méditation et de l'extase yogique. *Electroenceph. clin. Neurophysiol.*, **1957,** *Suppl. 6*: 211–219.

GABOR, D. On the time-frequency relation in the signal analysis. *J. Inst. Elect. Eng.*, **1946, ** *3*: 429.

KAMIYA, J. Operant control of the EEG alpha rhythm and some of its reported effects on consciousness. In C. T. TART (Ed.), *Altered states of consciousness*. Wiley, New York, **1969,** 575 p.

KASAMATSU, A. and HIRAI, T. An electroencephalographic study on zen meditation (Zazen). *Folia psychiat. neurol. jap.*, **1966,** *20*: 315–316.

MAHARISHI MAHESH YOGI. *The science of being and the art of living*. Int. SRM Publ., London, **1966,** 335 p.

WALLACE, R. K. Physiological effects of transcendental meditation. *Science*, **1970,** *167*: 1751–1754.

EEG RESPONSES TO PHOTIC STIMULATION IN PERSONS EXPERIENCED AT MEDITATION

Paul Williams and Michael West

Transcendental meditation (TM) is a form of mantra meditation which is simple to learn and requires no adherence to any special philosophy. Subjects are taught by a teacher qualified by Maharishi Mahesh Yogi, and then meditate regularly for 15–20 min twice daily.

A number of EEG changes have been noted during TM itself, including a predominance of alpha activity (Wallace 1970; Wallace *et al.* 1971; Banquet 1973), an increase in amplitude and slowing in frequency of alpha activity (Banquet 1973), the occurrence of activity of alpha frequency in the frontal region (Brown *et al.* 1971; Wallace *et al.* 1971; Banquet 1973), and the occurrence of theta activity (Wallace *et al.* 1971; Banquet 1973). Fenwick (1974), whilst substantially confirming these findings, has demonstrated further that the EEG changes seen during TM are identical with those of drowsiness.

During TM also, the response of alpha rhythm to afferent stimulation is altered. Wallace (1970) reported that no habituation of the blocking effect of auditory and photic stimulation took place, whereas Banquet (1973) reported that there was "usually no alpha blocking". The findings of Wallace are similar to those of Kasamatsu and Hirai (1969) studying Zen meditation, but the findings of Banquet await replication.

It has also been claimed that regular practice of TM is associated with a number of physiological changes in the non-meditative state, *e.g.*, faster habituation of galvanic skin response to stimulation (Orme-Johnson 1973) and increased resting alpha abundance (Vassiliadis 1971).

The blocking response of alpha rhythm to stimulation is well known. Less attention has been paid to the alpha provocation, or induction response. This is contingent upon a pre-stimulus EEG background of slow or mixed frequencies, and consists of a burst of 8–13 c/sec activity within 2.5 sec of the stimulus (Morrell 1966). It has been observed in states of lowered arousal, *i.e.*, drowsiness (Blake and Gerard 1937, and many others since), when it has been interpreted as an arousal, or orienting response; during classical conditioning (Wells 1963) and during states of increased attention, *e.g.*, mental arithmetic (Kreitman and Shaw 1965), responding to stimuli (Morrell 1966), where it has been interpreted as a sign of increased internal inhibition.

Below are reported the results of an investigation into the EEG response patterns to photic stimulation in a group of meditators and a group of control subjects. This experiment extends earlier work on the EEG response to stimulation in two directions: (a) the occurrence of alpha induction, in addition to blocking, was examined; and (b) the subjects were not actively meditating (*i.e.*, not using the mantra) during the experiment.

METHOD

The experimental design and method of scoring was similar to that of Morrell (1966).

Subjects

There were 10 male subjects in the control (non-TM) group, mean age 27 years 9 months. All were volunteers drawn from the staff of the University Hospital of Wales.

There were 9 subjects in the experimental group (it proved impossible to obtain a tenth suitable subject). All were male, and the mean age was 28 years 5 months. These were obtained with the assistance of the Cardiff Transcendental Meditation Centre, and had been meditating on average for 31 months (range 10–72 months).

Apparatus

Silver/silver chloride scalp pad electrodes (SLE pattern) were used, placed in the O_1, O_2, P_3 and P_4 positions (10–20 system) and bipolar recordings were made of two channels (O_1–P_3, O_2–P_4), using a Beckmann type T-S007 electroencephalograph, with a time constant of 0.3 sec. An SLE photic stimulator was used, placed 30 cm in front of the subjects' eyes.

All recording apparatus was in a separate room from the subject, with two-way communication available at all times.

Procedure

The subject was instructed to rest quietly with eyes closed throughout the experimental period. The meditators were instructed not to meditate, *i.e.*, not to use the mantra. The electrodes were then attached, and the subject was seated in a comfortable chair in a sound-attenuated, darkened room. He was allowed a few minutes to adapt to the situation, whilst baseline recordings were taken.

Photic stimulation was then delivered aperiodically around a mean inter-stimulus interval of 10 sec (range 8–12 sec); stimulation was delivered without reference to the EEG pattern. The experiment ceased when 150 flashes had been delivered, and the subject was then asked to comment on his experience of the experiment.

All recordings were done in the afternoon, to minimize the effects of diurnal variation in arousal level.

Scoring of records

All records were scored by eye. For each trial (*i.e.*, stimulus), observations were recorded concerning the background activity and the response to stimulation.

a. *Background.* The 1 sec of EEG prior to each stimulus was classified into: (i) alpha—continuous 8–13 c/sec activity throughout the epoch; or (ii) non-alpha—either mixed frequencies or slow activity.

b. *Reactivity.* The post-signal EEG was classified as follows: (i) blocking—at least a 50 % decrease in voltage from the average of the three preceding waves, contingent upon a pre-stimulus background of alpha, with a maximum latency of 500 msec (Young and Fenton 1971); (ii) induction—the occurrence of 8–13 c/sec activity within 2.5 sec of the stimulus, contingent upon a background of "non-alpha"; (iii) no criterion change from the pre-stimulus pattern.

Where artefact (*e.g.*, gross body movement) or ambiguity

TABLE 1

Results analysed in blocks of thirty stimuli

Stimuli	Alpha pre-stim. background		Reactivity			
			Blocking		Induction	
	Mean	S.D.	Mean	S.D.	Mean	S.D.

a. CONTROL GROUP. N = 10. Total number of trials = 1500.

1– 30	20.2	6.09	18.2	7.09	2.5	2.67
31– 60	15.9	8.86	13.2	8.86	7.1	3.84
61– 90	12.3	8.76	10.1	8.37	9.9	5.18
91–120	10.6	7.86	8.3	7.45	10.0	3.71
121–150	8.8	8.06	5.7	5.37	10.6	2.59

b. MEDITATION GROUP. N = 9. Total number of trials = 1350.

1– 30	18.4	6.84	16.8	6.88	6.0	4.54
31– 60	15.4	6.26	12.6	4.36	9.6	4.00
61– 90	14.7	4.20	12.4	2.74	11.0	5.20
91–120	12.2	5.91	10.2	2.54	11.7	4.81
121–150	10.5	6.72	8.9	5.55	11.1	2.97

made it impossible to distinguish clearly the reactivity pattern, that trial was ignored (this happened for less than 2% of the data).

The results for all the subjects in each group were summed, and analysed in groups of 30 stimuli (*i.e.*, 5 blocks). Also, for part of the data, the method of analysis used by Morrell (1966) was employed. In this method, each record was scanned for the first stimulus which yielded alpha induction. The record was then analysed in two parts, "early trials" and "late trials", taking that stimulus as the point of division.

RESULTS (see Table I).

Pre-stimulus background

The pre-stimulus background was alpha in 45.1% of trials for the control group and 47.6% for the meditators ($X^2 = 2.28$, n.s.). Looking at the disappearance of alpha activity during the course of the experiment, a Student's t test showed no significant difference between the two groups ($t = 0.254$). However, using Morrell's method of analysis (see Table II), it can be seen that alpha activity as a pre-stimulus background during late trials was significantly less common in the control group than the meditator group ($X^2 = 5.52$, $P < 0.05$).

Alpha blocking

For trials with an appropriate pre-stimulus background, alpha blocking occurred in 81.9% and 83.5% for the controls and meditators respectively ($X^2 = 0.79$, n.s.). Looking at the disappearance of alpha blocking during the course of the experiment, a Student's t test revealed no significant difference between the two groups ($t = 0.408$). However, using Morrell's method of analysis (see Table II), it can be seen that alpha blocking during late trials was significantly less common in the control group than the meditator group ($X^2 = 4.32$, $P < 0.05$).

Alpha induction

Induction of alpha activity occurred earlier in the meditators than the controls—on average, after 18.4 and 28.1 stimuli respectively. Induction occurred as a response to 48.2% of all stimuli with a non-alpha background in the control group, and to 62.9% in the meditators ($X^2 = 30.73$, $P < 0.0001$).

Relationship between alpha induction and alpha blocking (see Table III).

For the meditators, trials yielding alpha blocking correlated significantly with trials yielding alpha induction (Spearman's rho = +0.62, one tail $P < 0.05$). For the control group, the correlation, whilst still positive, did not reach significance (Spearman's rho = +0.27, n.s.).

DISCUSSION

It is apparent that although the experimental group was not actively meditating (*i.e.*, they were not using the mantra), their EEG response patterns differ significantly from those of the control group.

The results from the control group indicate that they were becoming drowsy. Alpha activity became less common (being replaced by activity in the theta frequency), as did

TABLE II

Results analysed into "early trials" and "late trials" (after Morrell 1966)

		Early trials					Late trials					
	Total no.	Alpha bkgd.	%	Alpha block	%*	Total no.	Alpha bkgd.	%	Alpha block	%**	Alpha induction	%***
Controls	281	220	78.2	200	90.9	1219	458	37.4	355	77.6	401	52.7
Meditators	166	140	84.3	122	87.1	1184	503	42.5	417	82.9	445	65.3

* Expressed as a percentage of early trials with an alpha background.
** Expressed as a percentage of late trials with an alpha background.
*** Expressed as a percentage of late trials with a non-alpha background.

alpha blocking: alpha induction, a phenomenon known to occur in the drowsy state, was manifest. This view is supported by the verbal report of subjects.

The meditators, whilst exhibiting the same general pattern, demonstrated a smaller decrement in alpha activity and alpha blocking, with alpha induction occurring earlier and being more frequent. These findings are consistent with the view that they "shifted" less along the arousal continuum than did the control subjects.

Teachers of meditation express the view that experienced meditators spontaneously enter a quasi-meditative state on closing the eyes and, as discussed earlier, Fenwick (1974) has shown that from the physiological point of view, the meditative state is one of finely held prolonged drowsiness—non-meditators in a similar situation would be supposed to progress more towards sleep.

The results described here are consistent with that view

and support Fenwick's findings. The earlier occurrence of alpha induction in the meditators is also consistent with this —in the control subjects, there is a delay to the onset of drowsiness and thus induction, whereas the meditators enter their altered state of conciousness earlier. In 7 of the meditators, who all reported that they felt as if they had been meditating (despite non-use of the mantra) induction occurred on average after 8.9 stimuli (90 sec into the experiment). The remaining 2 subjects in this group reported feeling drowsy, and for them, induction occurred after 43 and 61 stimuli respectively (as compared with an average of 28.1 stimuli for the control, non-meditator group).

The more frequent occurrence of alpha induction in the meditation group also supports the findings of Fenwick. Induction is a phenomenon of lowered arousal, but disappears as the progression towards sleep takes place (Kiloh and Osselton 1966). Thus, the controls as a group would appear

TABLE III

Relationship between alpha blocking and alpha induction

	Controls		Meditators	
	Blocking % (of trials with alpha bkgd.)	Induction % (of trials with non-alpha bkgd.)	Blocking % (of trials with alpha bkgd.)	Induction % (of trials with non-alpha bkgd.)
S1	92.8	92.0	98.1	64.6
S2	92.2	91.2	96.4	69.1
S3	91.7	33.3	93.5	59.7
S4	89.7	58.5	90.9	80.4
S5	82.1	27.9	90.2	74.7
S6	80.0	45.8	83.1	56.1
S7	74.6	48.1	79.4	57.5
S8	71.8	60.8	71.7	41.4
S9	69.8	68.5	58.9	58.4
S10	63.3	44.6		

Spearman's rho = +0.27
n.s.

Spearman's rho = +0.62
one tail $P < 0.05$

to approach more nearly to sleep than the meditators.

If this interpretation is correct, than our findings do not support those of Banquet (1973) concerning alpha blocking during meditation.

Our findings are conducive of an alternative, or rather, complementary interpretation to that described above. Morrell (1966) using the same experimental design compared a group of subjects required to attend and respond to the stimuli, with a control group. She found that for the responders, there was a smaller decrement in alpha activity over time, induction occurred earlier and more frequently than for the control group. She interpreted these findings as supporting those of Kreitman and Shaw (1965), who demonstrated that alpha induction was a neurophysiological correlate of attention. Extrapolating from this, then the meditators exhibited the EEG response patterns of sustained attention. The correlation between alpha blocking and induction (Table III), both "attentional" events, supports this.

Meditation itself may be an attentional process, but this may also be explained in terms of the attitude of the subjects. The control group knew that they were a control group, and consequently had no vested interest in their performance. The meditators, however, knew that both meditation and they themselves were under test, and consequently would be more likely to maintain attention and be less likely to become drowsy.

Further research into meditation, and the process of learning to meditate, is necessary. However, it is important to specify adequately the experimental conditions; simply to ask subjects to "close the eyes and rest quietly", and then to assume that they are all in the same physiological state is insufficient.

SUMMARY

The EEG responses to intermittent photic stimulation were examined in a group of subjects experienced in meditation, and compared with those of a control group.

The meditators exhibited a significantly smaller decrement in alpha activity and alpha blocking over the course of the experiment than did the control group, and alpha induction occurred earlier and more frequently in the meditators.

These findings support the hypothesis that experienced meditators spontaneously enter the meditative state on closing the eyes, and also the view that physiologically the meditative state is one of prolonged drowsiness. An alternative interpretation, that meditation is a state of sustained attention, is discussed.

RESUME

REPONSES EEG A LA STIMULATION PHOTIQUE CHEZ DES SUJETS ENTRAINES A LA MEDITATION

Les réponses EEG à une stimulation photique intermittente ont été étudiées sur un groupe de sujets entraînés à la méditation et comparées à celles d'un groupe témoin.

Les sujets entraînés ont présenté des diminutions de l'activité alpha et du blocage alpha significativement plus faibles que le groupe témoin; de même l'induction alpha était réalisée plus précocément et plus fréquemment que dans le groupe témoin.

Ces résultats viennent à l'appui de l'hypothèse que de tels sujets entrent spontanément en méditation lorsqu'ils ferment les yeux; et que l'état de méditation correspond physiologiquement à une somnolence prolongée. On examine également une interprétation différente selon laquelle il s'agit d'un état d'attention soutenue.

Thanks are due to Mr. A. Gale (University of Wales Institute of Science and Technology) for his advice and helpful criticism, and to Mr. D. Care and Miss J. Gibbs (University Hospital of Wales) for their technical assistance and advice.

REFERENCES

BANQUET, J. P. Spectral analysis of the EEG in meditation. *Electroenceph. clin. Neurophysiol.*, **1973**, *35*: 143–151.

BLAKE, H. and GERARD, R. W. Brain potentials during sleep. *Amer. J. Physiol.*, **1937**, *119*: 692–703.

BROWN, F. M., STEWART, W. S. and BLODGETT, J. T. EEG kappa rhythms during transcendental meditation and possible perceptual changes following. Paper presented to the Kentucky Academy of Sciences, cited in D. P. KANELLAKOS and J. S. LUKAS (Eds.), *The psychobiology of transcendental meditation: a literature review.* Stanford Research Institute press, Calif. **1971**.

FENWICK, P. B. C. *Metabolic and EEG changes during transcendental meditation.* Paper read at conference "*Transcendental meditation–research and application.*" University of Wales Institute of Science and Technology, Cardiff, **1974**.

KASAMATSU, A. and HIRAI, T. An electroencephalographic study on the Zen meditation. In C. TART (Ed.), *Altered states of conciousness.* Wiley, New York, **1969**.

KILOH, L. and OSSELTON, J. W. *Clinical electroencephalography.* 2nd. ed. Butterworths, London, **1966**.

KREITMAN, N. and SHAW, J. C. Experimental enhancement of alpha activity. *Electroenceph. clin. Neurophysiol.*, **1965**, *18*: 147–155.

MORRELL, L. K. Some characteristics of stimulus provoked alpha activity. *Electroenceph. clin. Neurophysiol.*, **1966**, *21*: 552–561.

ORME-JOHNSON, D. W. Autonomic stability and transcendental meditation. *Psychosom. Med.*, **1973**, *35*: 341–349.

VASSILIADIS, A. Physiological effects of transcendental meditation. Unpublished report, cited in D. P. KANELLAKOS and J. S. LUKAS (Eds.), *The Psychobiology of transcendental meditation: a literature review.* Stanford Research Institute press, Calif., **1971**.

WALLACE, R. K. Physiological effects of transcendental meditation. *Science*, **1970**, *167*: 1751–1754.

WALLACE, R. K., BENSON, H. and WILSON, A. F. A wakeful, hypometabolic physiologic state. *Amer. J. Physiol.*, **1971**, *221*: 795–799.

WELLS, C. E. Electroencephalographic correlates of conditioned responses. In G. H. GLASER (Ed.), *EEG and behaviour.* Basic Books, New York, **1963**.

YOUNG, J. P. R. and FENTON, G. W. An investigation of the genetic aspects of the alpha attenuation response. *Psychol. Med.*, **1971**, *1*: 365–371.

38

HEMISPHERIC LATERALITY AND COGNITIVE STYLE ASSOCIATED WITH TRANSCENDENTAL MEDITATION

James E. Bennett and John Trinder

ABSTRACT

The hemispheres of the brain are thought to be specialized with respect to the manner in which they process information. In view of this it is possible to explore the way information is processed during the performance of a specified task by identifying the relative activity of the hemispheres. The hypothesis, that meditation is characterized by a gestalt, holistic and spacial cognitive style associated with the right hemisphere was tested. Sixteen Transcendental Meditators were compared to 16 control subjects with respect to the degree of lateral asymmetry during meditation-relaxation and the performance of two analytic and two spacial cognitive tasks. Lateral asymmetry was assessed by the relative distribution of alpha activity. The only difference between the two groups was that meditators showed a greater degree of lateral asymmetry on both analytical and spacial tasks. During both meditation and relaxation the hemispheres were found to be symmetrical with respect to the distribution of alpha activity, suggesting that neither analytical nor spacial processing was dominant during these exercises.

DESCRIPTORS: Hemispheric laterality, Cognitive style, Transcendental meditation, EEG.

Ornstein (1972) has proposed that meditation is characterized by a gestalt, holistic and spacial cognitive style which is identified with predominant right hemisphere activity. This hypothesis contains two elements. The first is that the right hemisphere processes gestalt, holistic and spacial information, as opposed to analytical, logical and verbal information which is processed by the left hemisphere. If it is assumed that this statement is correct, and there is now strong supportive evidence (Dimond, 1972; Galin & Ornstein, 1973; Gazzaniga, 1970; Ornstein, 1972), then it provides the basis for testing the second element: that meditation is characterized by a gestalt, holistic and spacial cognitive style.

A number of studies have measured the distribution of alpha activity as a means of determining the relationship between cognitive style and hemispheric laterality (Doyle, Ornstein, & Galin, 1974; Galin & Ornstein, 1972; McKee, Humphrey, & McAdam, 1973; Morgan, MacDonald, & Hilgard, 1974; Morgan, McDonald, & Mac Donald, 1971). During the performance of analytical and verbal tasks the level of alpha was found to be relatively greater in the right hemisphere, whereas during the

Address requests for reprints to John Trinder, who is now at the Department of Psychology, University of Tasmania, Hobart, Tasmania, Australia.

performance of spacial tasks the left hemisphere had relatively more alpha, thus supporting the relationship between cognitive style and hemispheric laterality. (Each of these studies assumed that the presence of alpha activity reflected inactivity of the brain at the recording site.)

This technique was selected for the present study to determine the nature of cognitive processing during meditation. The procedure adopted established lateral asymmetry indices for tasks which were thought to require cognitive activity representative of the two alternative cognitive styles and which were known to have hemispheric specialization. The index for meditation was then compared to these established values. The hypothesis tested was that meditation would be characterized by right hemisphere activity, and thus a gestalt, holistic or spacial style (Ornstein, 1972).

Method

Subjects

The subjects consisted of 16 Transcendental Meditators and 16 control subjects. The average age of the meditators and controls was 23.2 and 21.3 yrs respectively. There were 8 males and 8 females in each group. All subjects were volunteers from the university community, the meditators being contacted through the auspices of the local branch of the International Meditation Society. The meditators had been practicing from 14 to 70 months and, as far as it was possible to determine, were all meditating according to the procedure taught by the Transcendental Meditation Society. The mean practice period was 29.69 months. All subjects were required to be right-hand dominant.

Design

The two groups of subjects were tested under two conditions. The first was during the performance of the meditative exercise (in the case of the control group, subjects were instructed to close their eyes and relax) while the second was during a series of four tasks. The tasks, based on the work of Galin and Ornstein (1972), were designed to represent analytical (a letter writing and a mental arithmetic test) and spacial (Koh's blocks and a tonal awareness test) tasks. They also represented eyes closed-nonmotor (arithmetic and tonal awareness) and eyes open-motor (letter writing and Koh's blocks) tasks.

Each subject was tested twice, once on each of two non-consecutive days. On each day both conditions, meditation-relaxation and the four tasks, were run. The order was reversed from the first to the second day and counterbalanced across subjects. On each day the tasks were presented twice, with the second presentation of the four tasks in the inverse order. A 2 min rest period separated the two presentations of the four tasks. In addition, the order of tasks within a series was counterbalanced across subjects in a Latin Square design. The four orders of tasks and the two orders of conditions provided eight experimental sequences. Two subjects from each group (meditators and control) were tested in each sequence. The order of sequences was counterbalanced.

Apparatus

All recordings were made on a Grass Model 78 Polygraph. EEG electrode placements were determined by the International 10-20 system. Two temporal electrodes (EEG) were located bilaterally at T_3 and T_4. The selection of temporal sites was based on the work of Galin and Ornstein (1972). Each was referred to C_z in a bipolar connection.

Alpha activity was isolated using a bandpass filter with a central frequency margin of 8–12 Hz. The sensitivity of the filter was set at 10 μV. Thus alpha activity was defined as that activity between 8 and 12 Hz above a threshold of 10 μV.

Only one bandpass filter was available for this experiment. Consequently, the alpha activity was isolated on only one channel at a given time. For each task the recording time was divided into two 90 sec segments; one for each hemisphere. The length of the testing period for each task presentation was selected with this limitation in mind. The order of the alpha recording was counterbalanced in an ABBA manner over the four presentations of each task. The EEG channel for each hemisphere was continuously recorded. There was no evidence that this procedural variation unduly affected the results.

The tones were recorded from the Seashore Tonal Memory Test onto a Uher 5000 tape recorder. They were channelled into the sound attenuated experimental room via a separate speaker arrangement from the normal intercom system.

Procedure

Each subject was informed that the experiment was concerned with the relationship between brain wave activity and behavior, but not that the lateral asymmetry of the activity was important. Hand dominance information was determined by the subject's own account, but was not collected until the end of the experiment so as to eliminate any subject bias.

On each day, immediately preceding the presentation of the task sequence, the subject was given ample time to become familiar with each of the four tasks. The practice period was designed to eliminate novelty effects from the data recording sessions.

The subjects in the meditation condition were instructed to conduct their usual meditative exercise. This period was limited to 20 min and was terminated by the experimenter. The control subjects were instructed to close their eyes and relax, but not to move around excessively or to go to sleep. During all recordings, both the meditation-relaxation condition and the performance of the four tasks, the subjects sat in a straight back chair.

Lateral Asymmetry Index

The level of alpha activity was defined as the amount of time during which activity above 10 μV was present within each 90 sec recording period. Any 0.5 sec period in which movement was apparent in the EEG channels and in which artifacts appeared in the alpha channel, was discarded. The amount of alpha time was then expressed as a percentage of the remaining time (90 sec minus artifact time).

The lateral asymmetry for a given task presentation was then determined by comparing the alpha percentages for the left and right hemispheres. A laterality index was computed by dividing the difference between the two hemispheres by their sum and multiplying the result by 100.[1] This index is the same as that used by Morgan et al. (1974). The resulting values potentially ranged from 100, in those cases in which the left hemisphere had zero alpha activity, to −100, in those cases in which the right hemisphere had zero alpha activity. Thus lateral asymmetry indices ranging from 0 to 100 indicated relatively more information processing in the left hemisphere while indices ranging from 0 to −100 indicated relatively more information processing in the right hemisphere. An index of 0 indicated equivalent alpha activity in the two hemispheres.

An initial analysis of the data indicated that there was a positive and significant (.05 level) correlation between the magnitude of the difference between the two hemispheres and the overall level of alpha activity (defined as the average of the two hemispheres) computed over subjects, within each task (.44, .49, .58, .83, and .70 for meditation-relaxation tones, mental arithmetic, blocks, and letter respectively). These results are important because the lateral asymmetry index, which is a *ratio* of these two measures, requires that they be highly correlated. Benjamin (1967) has argued that in those cases in which response magnitude is related to the prestimulus level of

---

[1]Laterality Index = 100 × right hemisphere − left hemisphere/ right hemisphere + left hemisphere.

the response measure then analysis of covariance (ANA-COVA) is the appropriate method of data analysis since it takes account of the actual correlation between the two measures. While Benjamin's argument was made with reference to the Law of Initial Values it appears to generalize to the present case in which the magnitude of the difference between the two hemispheres is related to the average level. Thus an ANACOVA was also conducted in which the average alpha level was the covariate and the difference between the hemispheres was the variate.

Results and Discussion

Task Related Lateral Asymmetry

The lateral asymmetry associated with the performance of the tasks essentially replicated the results of previous studies (see Fig. 1) (Doyle et al., 1974; Galin & Ornstein, 1972; McKee et al., 1973; Morgan et al., 1974; Morgan et al., 1971). The data were analyzed using both a one between, two within ANOVA of the lateralization index and a similar ANACOVA of the difference between the two hemispheres. The between group variable contained meditators and controls; the first within variable involved analytical versus spacial cognitive tasks; and the second within variable consisted of two levels of motor-visual activity, motor-visual and nonmotor-nonvisual. As indicated, the effect of cognitive tasks (analytic-spacial) was statistically significant $(F(1/30)=62.54, MS_e=1328.6; F(1/29)=10.61, MS_e=56.90^2)$, thereby establishing the necessary framework for determining the nature of cognitive processes associated with meditation.

The main effect of groups (meditation and control) was not significant $(F(1/30)=.41, MS_e=3799.9; F(1/29)=2.48, MS_e=357.2)$. However the Group × Cognition interaction was statistically sig-

[2]In each case the ANOVA is reported first followed by the ANACOVA. Significance level was set at $p<.05$.

nificant $(F(1/30)=6.32, MS_e=1328.6; F(1/29)=7.09, MS_e=56.90)$. As Fig. 1 indicates, the meditators were found to have a greater degree of lateral asymmetry than the control group; the analytic tasks being more left hemisphere for meditators than the control group and the spacial tasks more right. This effect was unexpected and no other aspect of the data offered any clarification of the finding. It is interesting, though not particularly enlightening, to note that Galin and Ornstein (1973) reported a greater degree of task related lateral asymmetry for lawyers than ceramicists.

The main effect of motor-visual versus non-motor-nonvisual tasks was not significant $(F(1/30) = .001, MS_e=2699.3; F(1/29)=1.26, MS_e=290.6)$. However, the Motor-Visual × Cognition interation was significant $(F(1/30)=32.63, MS_e=1456.1)$ for the ANOVA analysis but not for the ANACOVA $(F(1/29)=2.74, MS_e=66.88)$. This finding, in the case of the lateralization index, replicates that of Doyle et al. (1974) though the ANACOVA analysis suggests that both results may be an artifact of the relationship between absolute alpha levels and the difference between the hemispheres; higher levels of alpha being associated with nonmotor-eyes closed conditions.

Hemispheric Lateral Asymmetry During the Performance of Meditation-Relaxation

The degree of asymmetry during meditation-relaxation was evaluated in two ways. They differed as to the method used to establish the index value indicative of balanced hemispheric activity (the neutral point). In the first method the neutral point was considered to be that value at which the recorded alpha activity of the hemispheres was balanced, that is, an index value of zero. The second identified the neutral point as the average value between analytic

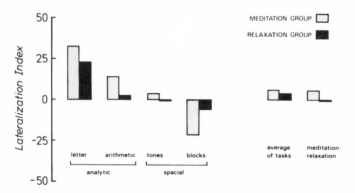

Fig. 1. Lateralization indices for each task, the average of these tasks and meditation-relaxation, for both meditation and control groups.

and spacial tasks. As indicated in Fig. 1 both methods gave the same result.

The degree of lateral asymmetry during meditation was not significantly different from that during relaxation ($t(30)=1.17$, $MS_e=5.01$), with both having indices approximately zero (meditation = 5.63, and relaxation $-.25$). Considering the neutral point to be an index value of zero, meditation and relaxation represented a state in which the hemispheres were equally active, or inactive. The same conclusion was reached when the conditions were compared to the average of the spacial and analytic tasks (see Fig. 1). The average index for all tasks for the meditation group was 6.0 and 3.2 for the control group. Comparisons of these averaged indices with the values obtained during meditation and relaxation did not produce statistically significant differences ($t(14)=0.35$, $MS_e=4.07$ for meditation and $t(14)=.58$, $MS_e=6.28$ for the control). Thus there was no support for the hypothesis that the performance of meditation is characterized by a predominance of right hemisphere activity.

While the two groups did not differ with respect to the degree of lateralization during meditation versus relaxation, it could be predicted that they would differ with respect to variances, in that the meditation condition presents a more structured situation than that of relaxation. In fact the between subject variability during relaxation for the control group was greater than that during meditation for the meditators. However this would appear to be a characteristic of meditators themselves, not the act of meditation, since the same relationship was found to be true of all the tasks. This finding is perhaps related to that reported above in which meditators are more laterally extreme than non-meditators during the performance of the tasks. In addition, it was possible to assess within task variability during the performance of the meditation and relaxation using consecutive 3 min periods as data points. Standard deviations, averaged over subjects, were greater for the control subjects during relaxation than for the meditation group during meditation (22.39 vs 14.80 for session one and 18.23 vs 12.48 for session two). However these differences were not statistically significant ($t(30)=1.75$, $MS_e=4.34$ and $t(29)=1.64$, $MS_e=3.51$ for sessions one and two respectively).

It should be added that a number of other analyses of the data were conducted. In several instances significant results were obtained using the lateralization index but these findings were not supported by the ANACOVA. In each case there were marked discrepancies between the conditions with respect to overall alpha level. (This being true also for the Motor-Visual × Cognition interaction reported above.) These results illustrate the difficulties associated with data analysis in this area and support the application of covariance techniques.

REFERENCES

Benjamin, L. S. Facts and artifacts in using analysis of covariance to undo the law of initial values. *Psychophysiology,* 1967, *4,* 187–206.

Dimond, S. *The double brain.* Edinburgh: Churchill Livingston, 1972.

Doyle, J. C., Ornstein, R., & Galin, D. Lateral specialization of cognitive mode: II. EEG frequency analysis. *Psychophysiology,* 1974, *11,* 567–578.

Galin, D., & Ornstein, R. Lateral specialization of cognitive mode: An EEG study. *Psychophysiology,* 1972, *9,* 412–418.

Galin, D., & Ornstein, R. E. Hemispheric specialization and the duality of consciousness. In H. Wildroe (Ed.), *Human behavior and brain function.* Springfield, Ill.: Charles C Thomas, 1973.

Gazzaniga, M. S. *The bisected brain.* New York: Appleton-Century-Crofts, 1970.

McKee, G., Humphrey, B., & McAdam, D. W. Scaled lateralization of alpha activity during linguistic and musical tones. *Psychophysiology,* 1973, *10,* 441–443.

Morgan, A. H., MacDonald, H., & Hilgard, E. R. EEG alpha: Lateral asymmetry related to task, and hypnotizability. *Psychophysiology,* 1974, *11,* 275–282.

Morgan, A. H., McDonald, P. J., & MacDonald, H. Differences in bilateral alpha activity as a function of experimental task, with a note on lateral eye movements and hypnotizability. *Neuropsychologia,* 1971, *9,* 459–469.

Ornstein, R. E. *The psychology of consciousness.* San Francisco: W. H. Freeman, 1972.

(Manuscript received November 4, 1974; revision received October 2, 1976; accepted for publication December 8, 1976)

39

THE EFFECT OF TRANSCENDENTAL MEDITATION ON RIGHT HEMISPHERIC FUNCTIONING[1]

Robert R. Pagano and Lynn R. Frumkin

This study reports two experiments investigating the effects of transcendental meditation on right hemispheric functioning. The task used in both experiments was the Seashore Tonal Memory Test. In the first experiment a nonmeditator group and an experienced meditator group were run. The design involved three periods: a pretest, a meditation or rest period, and then a posttest. The results showed the experienced meditators were significantly better in both pretest and posttest performance. There were no pretest–posttest differences. The second experiment was done to replicate the first experiment and to control for possible selection bias. The design was the same as the first experiment, except that an additional group of inexperienced meditators was included. The results again showed significantly superior performance for the experienced meditators compared to the nonmeditators. In addition, the experienced meditators were superior to the inexperienced meditators. There were no significant differences between the nonmeditators and the inexperienced meditators. These results support the hypothesis that meditation facilitates right hemispheric functioning. Alternative explanations, such as selection bias, are also discussed.

Within the last several years, research into hemispheric lateralization of function has shown that in man each cerebral hemisphere appears to specialize in a different mode of information processing. The left (major) hemisphere appears to be primarily responsible for verbal, mathematical, logical, sequential, and time-based analytic thinking. The right (minor) hemisphere, on the other hand, seems more important when dealing with

[1]The authors wish to thank Ms. Michelle Ellis and Ms. Bridget Carr for their assistance in conducting these experiments. We also wish to thank the Seattle SIMS for their cooperation in obtaining subjects.

spatial and musical relationships relating parts to whole, in a nonverbal, holistic manner based on direct perceptual experience (Galin, 1974; Nebes, 1974). In a discussion of this material, Ornstein (1972) raises the possibility that meditation may be a process that facilitates right hemisphere functioning. Although provocative, the evidence for this hypothesis is indirect and rests largely on the similarity between dreaming and meditation. During meditation, meditators report a subjective state that seems quite similar to dreaming both in the experience of time (nonlinear) and in information processing (Deikman, 1963). Although the data are far from conclusive, several studies have demonstrated that dreaming appears to involve right hemisphere dominance (Bogen, 1969; Galin, 1974; Humphrey & Zangwill, 1951).

We have begun a series of experiments designed to test the meditation–laterality hypothesis by evaluating the effects of meditation on tasks known to be right hemisphere dominant. In this article we report two experiments studying the effects of meditation on tonal memory. This task was chosen because the specialization of melody reception to the right hemisphere is well documented both clinically and experimentally (Gordon, 1970; Kimura, 1964; Luria, Tsvetkova, & Futer, 1965; Shankweiler, 1966). The test we employed was the Tonal Memory Subtest of the Seashore Music Battery. It has been used in several laterality studies with consistent results showing right hemisphere dominance (Chase, 1967; Doyle, Ornstein, & Galin, 1974; Milner, 1962).

EXPERIMENT 1

Method

Subjects

In this experiment we compared experienced transcendental meditators and nonmeditators. Seventeen subjects participated in the experiment. Eight meditators were drawn from available practitioners in the Seattle area. These subjects had meditated twice daily for a period of at least 1 year (range of 1.4 to 3 years). The remaining nine subjects came from an introductory psychology class at the University of Washington. All subjects were between 18 and 30 years of age and were right-handed. To ensure that subjects were musically "naive" and hence did not engage in analytical (and left hemisphere) processing, all subjects were required to have less than 1 year of instrumental or vocal training during the 8 years preceding the study (see Bever & Chiarello, 1974).

Materials

The tonal memory test was from the Seashore Measures of Musical Talents (Series B, 1939 revision). Two forms were constructed. Each form consisted of 30 pairs of tone sequences with four, five, or six notes in each sequence. The second sequence of each pair had one note changed in pitch.

Procedure

Each S was given a response grid and read the following instructions:

> The purpose of this experiment is to measure some aspect of your ability to hear sounds as they occur in music or in speech. There will be a $10 prize awarded to the highest scorer in the experiment. On each trial, you will hear a short series of tones which will be played through twice. For example, you might hear four tones, da-da-da-da followed by four tones again, da-da-da-*ta*. In the second tone series, one note was different from the first series. You are to listen to each pair of sequences and write down the number of the tone that was changed in the second sequence: either, 1, 2, 3, or 4. There are three parts to this experiment. In the first part, the two sequences will have four tones in each, the second part will consist of five tones per sequence, and the last part will have six tones in each sequence.

Subjects were tested in groups composed of one meditator and one nonmeditator. All subjects were run for 3 days to eliminate any practice effects. On Day 1 each subject was given a pretest, followed by a treatment period, followed by a posttest. One form of the Tonal Memory Test was given on the pretest and the other on the posttest. During the treatment period the meditators practiced their usual meditation for 20 minutes whereas the nonmeditators sat comfortably with eyes closed. On Days 2 and 3 the procedure was identical to Day 1, differing only in that the order of the two forms of Tonal Memory Tests were counterbalanced between groups and across the last 2 days.

All experimental sessions were conducted between 3:00 and 6:00 p.m. The experimenter had no knowledge of the subject's condition and data was scored "blind." To keep the experimenter unaware of the subject's condition, all subjects received the same instructions at the beginning of the treatment period. Each was told that if (s)he was a meditator, (s)he should meditate for 20 minutes; if a nonmeditator, (s)he should relax with eyes closed for 20 minutes. The subjects were then moved to separate rooms to meditate or relax.

Table I. Percentage Correct on Tonal Memory
Test – Experiment 1

	Meditators	Nonmeditators
Pretest	92.13	70.66
Posttest	91.50	69.10

Results

Table I shows the pre- and posttest percentage of correct responses for both groups on Day 3. The data were analyzed with a two-way analysis of variance. There were no significant pre–posttest main effects, $F(1,15) < 1$. However, there was a highly significant difference, $F(1,15) = 10.58$, $p < .005$, between the meditation and nonmeditation groups. Individual contrasts (t tests) showed that the meditators were superior to nonmeditators in tonal memory on both the pre- and posttest, $t(15) = 2.84$, $p < .01$; $t(15) = 3.19$, $p < .005$.

EXPERIMENT 2

The question arises as to whether the above results were due to selection factors, i.e., was the superior performance of the meditators on the tonal memory test the result of meditation or were the results due to meditation attracting individuals having superior tonal memory at the outset? Experiment 2 was designed to answer this question as well as to replicate Experiment 1.

Subjects and Procedure

A group of inexperienced transcendental meditators was added to the basic experiment to assess the selection bias. Twenty-eight new subjects were tested, 10 in the experienced meditator condition, and 9 each in the inexperienced meditator and nonmeditator conditions. The experienced meditators and nonmeditators were drawn from the same populations as in Experiment 1. The inexperienced meditators had been practicing meditation for less than 1 month prior to the beginning of the experiment. All subjects satisfied the selection criteria given in Experiment 1. The materials and procedure were also the same as in Experiment 1, differing only in that subjects were run in groups of three at a time (1 experienced meditator, 1 inexperienced meditator, and 1 nonmeditator in each group).

Table II. Percentage Correct on Tonal Memory Test – Experiment 2

	Experienced meditators	Inexperienced meditators	Nonmeditators
Pretest	89.00	70.50	74.00
Posttest	89.50	68.30	75.44

Results

Table II shows the pre- and posttest percentages of correct responses on the Tonal Memory Tests for all groups on Day 3. As can be seen, the results closely replicate those of Experiment 1. There were no significant pre–posttest main effects, $F(1,25) < 1$. There was, however, a highly significant groups effect, $F(2,25) = 6.74$, $p < .005$. As before, individual contrasts showed that the experienced meditators were superior to the nonmeditators in both pre- and posttest performance, $t(17) = 2.62$, $p < .01$; $t(17) = 3.48$, $p < .005$. In addition, experienced meditators were superior to the inexperienced meditators in pre- and posttest performance, $t(17) = 3.67$, $p < .005$; $t(17) = 3.87$, $p < .005$. There was no significant difference between nonmeditators and inexperienced meditators. For the pretest, $t(17) = .44$, $p < .20$; for the posttest, $t(17) = 1.03$, $p < .20$.

To assess the stability of the experienced meditator trait effect, we have plotted in Figure 1 the data from all 3 days of testing for both experi-

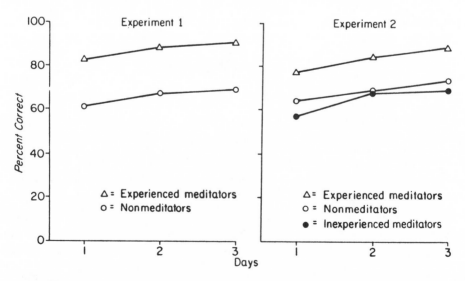

Fig. 1. Performance in experiments 1 and 2 for the 3 days of testing.

Physiology of Meditation

ments. Average values have been used for each subject's score on each day. As can be seen from the graphs, the superior performance of the experienced meditators was manifested on each day of testing.

DISCUSSION

The results of these two experiments support the hypothesis that the relatively long-term practice of TM facilitates right hemispheric functioning as assessed by performance on a task requiring right hemispheric specialization. However, these results should be interpreted cautiously, for several reasons.

First, while there is a good basis to believe that the Seashore Tonal Memory Test is a right hemisphere dominant task (Chase, 1967; Doyle et al., 1974; Milner, 1962), recent evidence indicates that various right hemisphere dominant tasks (melody reception, block design, and arc matching) do not correlate highly with each other (Jernigan, Sadalla, & Ahumada, 1976). Clearly more research is necessary using other tasks before we can properly generalize the present results to improved right hemispheric functioning.

Second, there is a discrepancy between the state and trait results of the present study. The data clearly establish an experienced meditator trait effect; experienced meditators are greatly superior to both nonmeditators and inexperienced meditators in performing this task. Furthermore, this superiority persists over 3 days of testing. Several other studies have also shown trait effects associated with practitioners of transcendental meditation (Ferguson & Gowan, 1974; Goleman & Schwartz, 1976; Orme-Johnson, 1973). While it is tempting to attribute the trait differences found in this study to the effects of meditation per se, it seems reasonable to have found a similar state effect (pre—posttest facilitation) if meditation per se is responsible for the trait superiority. No such state effects were found. A performance ceiling may have masked a state effect in experienced meditators, yet this would not explain the failure to find state effects in the inexperienced meditators. A more reasonable explanation is that the effects of meditation are cumulative and that one or two 20-minute meditations add such a small increment as to be undetected.

Third, it is possible that the superior performance of experienced meditators was due to motivational/attentional differences. Although possible, it seems unlikely that motivational or attentional differences produced the present results. First, we have shown in another series of experiments (manuscript in preparation) that experienced meditators do no better than nonmeditators in a perceptual task involving immediate recall of numbers shown tachistoscopically. This task probably involved left hemisphere dominance and required a high degree of attention for successful performance. Moreover, the task was run under conditions quite similar to the present study. If meditators are more motivated or pay closer attention than nonmeditators, it is difficult to understand why they didn't do better than nonmeditators on the numbers task as in the tonal memory task. In fact, the meditators did worse on each day's performance in the numbers task. The second reason for believing the results are not attributable to attentional or motivational differences is that a $10 prize for best performance was offered to maximize motivation and attention for both groups. Further, there is no reason to suspect a priori that beginning meditators would be less motivated than experienced meditators. It is also important to note that the nonmeditator and inexperienced meditator performance on the tonal memory task is not spuriously low but rather is in the normal range (see Milner, 1962, for a comparison of scores). It is the experienced meditator performance that is above average and that has produced the significant differences.

Finally, the last alternative explanation involves selection bias. It seems likely that the people who practice TM are not a random selection from the population at large. Therefore, it is possible that the individuals who choose to practice TM are better in tonal memory from the outset and that meditation per se has no effect on this ability. Certainly this explanation is consistent with the failure to find state effects. The fact that inexperienced meditators did no better than nonmeditators and did significantly worse than experienced meditators in Experiment 2 makes selection bias less plausible. However, it is still possible to explain these data on a selection bias basis due to a possible dropout of meditators over time. Unfortunately there are no published data on the dropout rate associated with TM, although an unpublished Stanford Research Institute study (Kanellakos & Lukas, 1973) has reported that 46% of the meditators were no longer regularly practicing meditation 6 months after onset. It is clear that only a longitudinal study can fully settle this issue. We do note, however, that even if we drop the lowest 44% of the inexperienced meditator scores, the significance between the groups still remains.

Despite the above cautions, these data are interesting because, to our knowledge, this is the first experimental study linking meditation with the nondominant hemisphere. The demonstration of such a link is consistent with a growing body of empirical research which associates the right hemisphere with techniques or processes that are capable of altering consciousness. Thus, greater hypnotizability has been related to right hemisphere dominance via the direction of lateral eye movements (Bakan, 1969; Gur & Gur, 1974; Gur & Reyher, 1973). In addition, there are several studies showing that hypnosis is related to those aspects of cognition which seem to be subserved by the right hemisphere (see Gur & Reyher, 1976, for a partial review). In the research connected with dreaming, Humphrey and Zangwill (1951) reported cessation of dreaming following damage to the visual pathways of the right hemisphere. Goldstein, Stoltzfus, and Gardocki (1972), employing a ratio of right–left hemispheric EEG activity as a measure of laterality, show greater right hemispheric involvement during shifts from slow wave sleep to REM activity in man, cats, and rabbits. The observation of Bogen (1969) that split-brain patients report the absence of dreams following commissurotomy further supports the dreaming–right hemisphere association. Finally, there is one known study relating hallucinogens to right hemispheric functioning (Goldstein & Stoltzfus, 1973).

In light of the foregoing, it seems reasonable that meditation, a technique capable of dramatically altering consciousness, also produces a differential effect on right hemisphere functioning. A more conclusive resolution regarding the meditation–right hemisphere facilitation hypothesis awaits the demonstration of generalizability of these results to other right hemisphere specialized tasks, as well as further research that eliminates alternative explanations, such as selection bias.

REFERENCES

Bakan, P. Hypnotizability, laterality of eye movements and functional brain asymmetry. *Perceptual and Motor Skills,* 1969, *28,* 927-932.

Bever, T. G., & Chiarello, R. J. Cerebral dominance in musicians and non-musicians. *Science,* 1974, *184,* 537-539.

Bogen, J. E. The other side of the brain: II. An appositional mind. *Bulletin of the Los Angeles Neurological Society,* 1969, *34,* 135-162.

Chase, R. A. The effect of temporal lobe lesion on some auditory information processing tasks in man. In F. L. Darley (Ed.), *Brain mechanisms underlying speech and language.* New York: Grune and Stratton, 1967.

Deikman, A. Experimental meditation. *Journal of Nervous and Mental Diseases,* 1963, *136,* 329-373.

Doyle, J. C., Ornstein, R., & Galin, D. Lateral specialization of cognitive mode: II EEG frequency analysis. *Psychophysiology,* 1974, *11,* 567-578.

Ferguson, P. C., & Gowan, J. The influence of transcendental meditation on anxiety, depression, aggression, neuroticism, and self-actualization. In D. P. Kannellakos & J. Lucas (Eds.), *The psychobiology of transcendental meditation: A literature review.* Menlo Park: W. A. Benjamin, 1974.

Galin, D. Implications for psychiatry of left and right cerebral specialization. *Archives of General Psychiatry,* 1974, *31,* 572-583.

Goldstein, L., & Stoltzfus, N. Psychoactive drug-induced changes of interhemispheric EEG amplitude relationships. *Agents and Action,* 1973, *3,* 124-132.

Goldstein, L., Stoltzfus, N., & Gardocki, G. Changes in interhemispheric amplitude relationships in the EEG during sleep. *Physiology and Behavior,* 1972, *8,* 811-815.

Goleman, D. J., & Schwartz, G. E. Meditation as an intervention in stress reactivity. *Journal of Consulting and Clinical Psychology,* 1976, *44,* 456-466.

Gordon, H. W. Hemispheric asymmetries in the perception of musical chords. *Cortex,* 1970, *6,* 387-398.

Gur, R. C., & Gur, R. E. Handedness, sex and eyedness as moderating variables in the relation between hypnotic susceptibility and functional brain asymmetry. *Journal of Abnormal Psychology,* 1974, *83,* 635-643.

Gur, R. C., & Reyher, J. Relationship between style of hypnotic induction and direction of lateral eye movements. *Journal of Abnormal Psychology,* 1973, *82,* 499-505.

Gur, R. C., & Reyher, G. R. Enhancement of creativity via free-imagery and hypnosis. *American Journal of Clinical Hypnosis,* 1976, *18*(4), 237-249.

Humphrey, M., & Zangwill, O. Cessation of dreaming after brain injury. *Journal of Neurology, Neurosurgery and Psychiatry,* 1951, *14,* 322-325.

Jernigan, T., Sadalla, E., & Ahumada, A. Relationship between "hemispherically localized" tasks. In D. O. Walter, L. Rogers, & J. M. Finzi-Fried (Eds.), *Conference on human brain function.* Los Angeles: Brain Information Service, 1976.

Kanellakos, D. P., & Lukas, J. S. *The psychobiology of transcendental meditation: A literature review* (IR & D 933535-AFB). Menlo Park, California: Stanford Research Institute, 1973.

Kimura, D. Left-right differences in the perception of melodies. *Quarterly Journal of Experimental Psychology,* 1964, *16,* 355-378.

Luria, A. R., Tsvetkova, L. S., & Futer, O. S. Aphasia in a composer. *Journal of Neurological Sciences,* 1965, *2,* 288-292.

Milner, B. Laterality effects in audition. In V. B. Mountcastle (Ed.), *Interhemispheric relations and cerebral dominance.* Baltimore: Johns Hopkins Press, 1962.

Nebes, R. D. Hemispheric specialization in commissurotomized man. *Psychological Bulletin,* 1974, *81,* 1-14.

Orme-Johnson, D. Autonomic stability and transcendental meditation. *Psychosomatic Medicine,* 1973, *35*(4), 341-349.

Ornstein, R. *The psychology of consciousness.* San Francisco: W. H. Freeman, 1972.

Shankweiler, D. Effects of temporal-lobe damage on perception of dichotically presented melodies. *Journal of Comparative and Physiological Psychology,* 1966, *2,* (1), 115-119.

(Revision received March 24, 1977)

*PSYCHOPHYSIOLOGICAL CORRELATES OF MEDITATION: EEG CHANGES DURING MEDITATION**

Bernard C. Glueck and Charles F. Stoebel

In looking at the various psychophysiologic parameters we found that those patients doing TM were showing the same physiological changes described by Wallace (1,2), e.g., slowing of the heart rate, respiration, and the GSR. The most consistent finding was a universal increase in the GSR in all subjects (up to 30% increase over baseline), although we never saw the extreme changes described by Wallace in his original studies (up to 400%). The same types of changes have been observed in subjects utilizing Benson's Relaxation Response, and in patients using the specifically targeted biofeedback procedures.

Each of the relaxation techniques we have studied produces augmentation of alpha density in subjects with significant alpha rhythm in the "eyes-closed" baseline condition. While subjects with minimal baseline alpha rhythm achieve very little EEG augmentation, they do report a comparable subjective "alpha state." We recognize that alpha density per se was probably only a portion of the physiological variance which was needed to clarify the possible psychophysiological differences among these techniques. However, more recent evaluation of EEG records in patients and subjects using these relaxation techniques reveals remarkable periods of intrahemispheric alpha and theta synchrony at times, even for inexperienced subjects. This observation has been confirmed by Banquet (3) and Levine (4) in their studies of intra- and interhemispheric synchrony in experienced meditators. We are currently using machine and Fortran language programs for our PDP-12, PDP-15, and 15-Graphics terminal configuration for analyzing monopolar and/or bipolar eight lead EEG's[†] for isometric power spectra using the fast Fourier transform, and associated measures of coherence and phase angle (for each cycle, 1–30 hertz), and also a measure of synchronicity expressed as a percentage of time that two electrode placements had a coherence greater than 0.8 and a phase angle within ±10° for whatever frequency is being measured.[‡]

In a TM meditator who has been meditating for more than 4 years, there occurs synchronous alpha activity upon closing the eyes, even before starting to meditate on the temporal, central, and occipital cortical areas (see Fig. 1). An increased amount of synchronization occurs upon meditating for the temporal and central areas (see Fig. 2).

This program is proving particularly useful in evaluating subjects who utilize different varieties of the relaxation techniques, and in our patients, because of its ability to give a precise analysis of the amount of energy in each frequency from 1 to 31 hertz, as well as giving averages for the various bands, such as theta

---

[*]*Editor's note:* This article is the second half of Glueck and Stoebel's chapter on Meditation in the Treatment of Psychiatric Illness, Article 14.

[†]International electrode placements: Fp1, left frontal; Fp2, right frontal; T3, left mid-temporal; T4, right mid-temporal; O1 left occipital; O2, right occipital; C3, left central; C4, right central. Reference electrodes are placed on the mastoid bone behind each ear, A1 and A2. The left ear is used for ground.

[‡]Documentation and calibration techniques for these programs is being published elsewhere, or, alternately, may be obtained at reproduction cost from the authors.

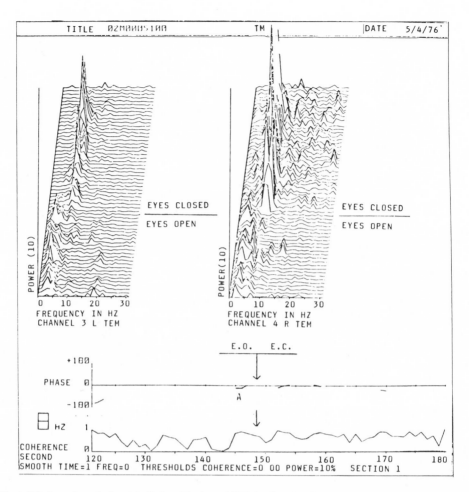

Fig. 1. This figure shows the isometric display of 1 minute of EEG data from the left (channel 3) and right (channel 4) temporal areas. Each line in the upper part of the display shows the distribution of the energy in each frequency from 1 to 31 hertz for 1 second of EEG recording. The bottom half of the display (24 seconds) is during the initial "eyes open," resting state. With eye closure, there is a prompt organization of high-amplitude alpha waves in the 8 to 10 hertz range. The bottom lines of the display show the phase angle and coherence between the two temporal leads for the same minute of the EEG recording. Phase angle is only shown (the intermittent lines, e.g., "A") when the coherence exceeds 0.8.

and alpha. Other authors have referred to synchrony primarily in terms of the amount of coherence between any two leads. We believe that adding in the phase angle relationship after coherence exceeds a certain threshold, in this example a coherence of 0.9, provides a much truer estimate of the amount of synchronization between any two cortical areas being analyzed. The high percentage of synchrony seen in the temporal and central cortical areas is more characteristic of the synchronization-relaxation effect produced by TM, as compared to the other techniques we have studied.

We have also found synchronization in the temporal and occipital cortex produced even quite early in the use of the TM technique. These are from a meditator who had been meditating just 4 weeks at the time that we ran his EEG patterns. While it is obvious that he does not show the marked degree of synchronization exhibited by the more experienced meditator, it is also obvious that he is showing a considerable degree of synchronization early on, more so than we see in naive subjects or in our psychiatric patients.

Using these techniques we are beginning to see some very interesting similarities and differences in the degree of synchronization produced by the various relaxation techniques. Figure 3 is an early estimate of the percentage of time synchrony in individuals using TM, the Benson Relaxation Response (RR), and thermal and EMG biofeedback (BF). Interhemispheric synchrony is shown in the upper panel, and

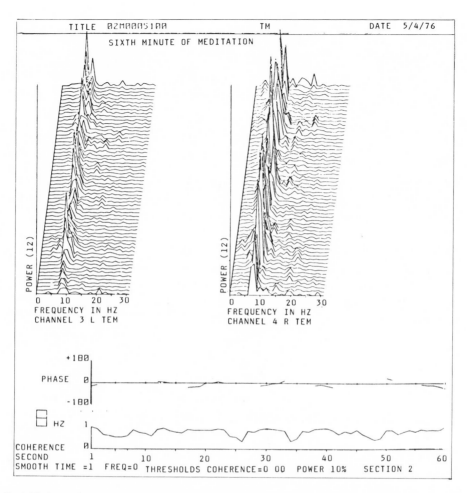

Fig. 2. The increase in the amount of synchronization during meditation is visible here in the increased amount of time that the phase angle relationships remain within the ±10° criterion. The left and right temporal areas are being compared during the sixth minute of meditation in an experienced (4-year) meditator.

intrahemispheric synchrony (dominant side only) in the lower panel for representative individuals in these three groups. Although sample sizes are still small, interesting differences in synchrony are emerging. The percentage of time that the synchrony measure was above criterion was obtained from a 20-minute sample of each technique with each subject sitting with eyes closed in a comfortable chair under dim ambient light conditions. Both TM and RR subjects demonstrate significant interhemispheric synchrony between the temporal placements, while BF subjects demonstrate virtually none. Compared to TM and BF conditions, RR subjects have virtually no occipital synchrony. In contrast to TM and RR subjects, the BF subjects demonstrate a relatively greater amount of intrahemispheric synchrony than do the meditating conditions. While none of the three techniques can be differentiated as yet on the basis of simple enhancement of the dominant alpha frequency, these data suggest that significant differences do exist for measures of synchrony (high coherence and low phase angle).

Studies presently underway with the Carrington technique, in which the beginning meditator self-selects a mantra most pleasing for him, may illuminate the issue of mantra uniqueness which is a central claim of the TM organization. Will certain mantras produce greater degrees of synchrony than others? By age to the nearest five years? Can multiple pattern biofeedback of synchrony, per se, be used to exactly replicate the synchrony patterns which develop with the meditation modalities (5)? Pending the outcome of these studies, we have several speculative hypotheses for interpreting the development of synchrony between the various cortical areas as described above.

EEG Changes During Meditation   521

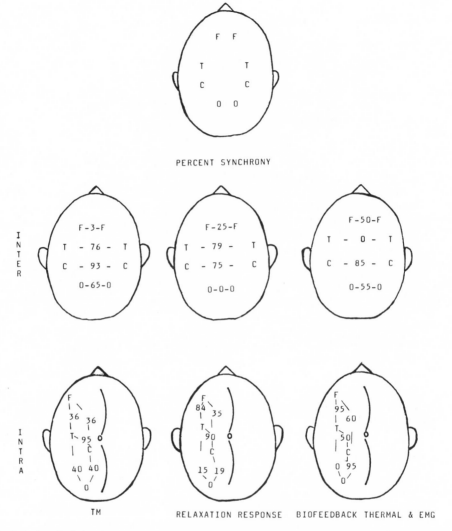

Fig. 3. A schematic display of the differences in synchrony percentages seen in three different relaxation techniques. The positions do not represent actual electrode placements and are given only as a schematic. The interhemispheric synchrony is presented in the top three displays, and the intrahemispheric synchrony for the dominant hemisphere is shown in the three bottom displays.

1. The mantra as a boring habituation stimulus. This hypothesis suggests that the language-logic functions of the dominant left temporal cortex predominate mental activity under conditions of beta rhythm activation (desynchronization) with a tendency for symbolic activation of the emergency response; that normalization of viscero-autonomic homeostasis, regulated by the normally unconscious right temporal cortex-limbic system, predominates under conditions of alpha-theta synchronous activity (schematically represented in Fig. 4); that "Type A" persons feel so much time pressure from depending on left cortical beta activation that they are in a state of relative deprivation of right cortical alpha activation; that the mantra is a boring stimulus lead to habituation of beta activation and augmentation of alpha-theta synchrony.

2. The mantra as a critical driver of synchronization. If the mantra is a key factor in achieving the kinds of psychophysiologic changes observed, it may represent an input stimulus to the central nervous system, most likely the limbic circuitry. We have been informed that analysis of the resonance frequencies of a number of mantras gives a value of 6–7 hertz, which is in the high theta EEG range and also approximates the optimal processing of the basic language unit, the phoneme, by the auditory system (6). Our current

speculation is as follows: Since the mantra is a series of sounds, the formation of the thought mantra, e.g., Oom, which is a common, well-known mantra, probably takes place, according to most neurophysiologists, in the ideational speech area in the temporal lobe. Penfield and Roberts (7) have mapped three areas involved in the ideational elaboration of speech—a large area in the posterior temporal lobe, an area in the posterior-inferior parietal region, and a small area in the posterior part of the third frontal convolution anterior to the motor-voice control area. They claim that the second two areas both can be destroyed and speech will return, so that the posterior temporal speech area is the fundamental locus for the formation of words.

They state that the ideational mechanism of speech is organized for function in one hemisphere only—usually the dominant hemisphere. Therefore, in thinking a mantra, a significant stimulus is introduced in the temporal lobe and probably directly into the series of cell clusters and fiber tracts that have come to be known as the limbic system. Since limbic system activity is fairly well accepted today as the origin of much emotionally based behavior, and since an increasing excitation in the limbic system through a series of feedback stimulatory mechanisms has been postulated to explain disturbed behavior (8), we are theorizing that introducing a driving mechanism with a dominant frequency of 6-7 hertz may act, with considerable rapidity, to dampen the limbic system activity and produce a relative quiescence in this critical subcortical area.

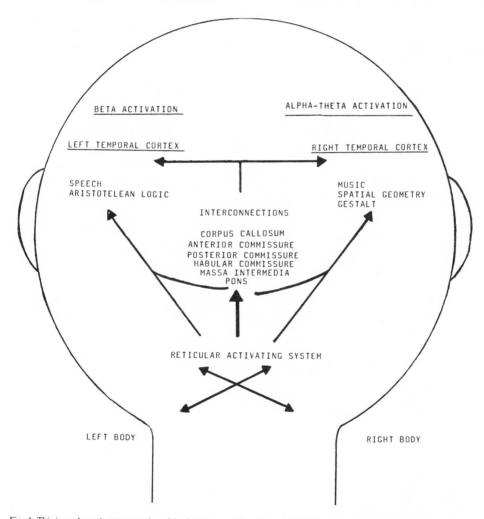

Fig. 4. This is a schematic representation of the functions usually attributed to the left and right temporal cortices, with some of the interconnecting pathways between them. Our speculations about the effect of the relaxation techniques upon these systems is discussed in the text.

EEG Changes During Meditation

Since there are extensive connections running from the thalamic structures to the cortex, quieting the limbic system activity might allow for the inhibition of cortical activation, with the disappearance of the usual range of frequencies and amplitudes ordinarily seen coming from the cortex, and with the imposition of the basic resting or idling rhythms as shown by the appearance of very dense, high-amplitude, alpha wave production.

Similarly, since the autonomic nervous system is controlled to a considerable extent by stimuli arising in the midbrain, the rapid changes observed in the peripheral autonomic nervous system, such as the GSR changes and the change in respiratory rate and heart rate, could be explained by the quieting of the limbic system activity.

Presumably, in sleep, limbic system activity diminishes, mediated perhaps by the reticular activating system. One of the theories about the appearance of dreams, especially about the ideational content in dreams, has to do with an increasing access to the nondominant hemisphere, where presumably repressed memories are stored. The weakening of the repression barrier that occurs in sleep and in other altered states of consciousness, such as free association during the process of psychoanalytic therapy, *may* be produced in a relatively simple fashion during TM meditation. This would offer an explanation of a phenomenon that has been reported by a number of investigators, and which we have seen repeatedly in our patients. During meditation, thoughts and ideas may appear that are ordinarily repressed, such as intense hostile-aggressive drives, murderous impulses, and, occasionally, libidinal ideation. An impressive aspect of this phenomenon is that, during the meditation, the intense emotional affect that would ordinarily accompany this ideation, e.g., when obtained by free association, seems to be markedly reduced or almost absent.

Our speculation is that, during passive meditation, the usual affective outflow from limbic structures is diminished with enhanced transmission of signals between the hemispheres, via the corpus callosum or other commissures, as shown schematically in Fig. 4.

We have been investigating a number of techniques that are claimed to have powerful potential for counteracting the stress responses to which we all are subject. The subjective reports of individuals practicing these various techniques tend, in general, to be quite enthusiastic. A major problem, however, is that of getting individuals, even those who have had relief from incapacitating symptoms, to continue practicing these techniques regularly in order to continue their effectiveness. The possible reasons for individuals discontinuing the techniques they are using are discussed, along with some potential psychodynamic interpretations. The objective evidence, especially that coming from electro-encephalographic studies, is presented in some detail, since this seems to provide the best "hard" data available for the evaluation of the impact of these techniques, over and above the subjective reports. Several possible explanations for the impact of these techniques, especially the passive mantra type meditations, are discussed and lines for further research suggested.

References

1. Wallace, R. K. *Physiological effects of transcendental meditation: a proposed fourth state of consciousness.* Ph.D. Thesis, Physiology Dept., University of California, Los Angeles, 1970.
2. Wallace, R. K. Physiological effects of Transcendental Meditation. *Science*, 1970, **167**, 1751–1754.
3. Banquet, J. P. Spectral analysis of th EEG in meditation. *Electroencephalography clinical neurophysiology*, 1973, **35**, 143–151.
4. Levine, P. H., Hebert, J. R., Haynes, C. T., and Strobel, U. *EEG coherence during the transcendental meditation technique.* Weggis, Switzerland: MERU Press, 1975.
5. Fehmi, L. In *Proceedings of the biofeedback research society.* Denver, Colorado, 1975. (Abstr.)
6. Lenneberg, E. H. *Biological foundation of language.* New York: John Wiley, 1967.
7. Penfield, W. and Roberts, L. *Speech and brain mechanisms.* New Jersey: Princeton University Press, 1959.
8. Monroe, R. R. *Episodic behavioral disorders.* Cambridge, Massachusetts: Harvard University Press, 1970.

D. Sleep

There are two different viewpoints and sets of data relating to meditation and sleep. The work of Pagano *et al.* (Article 41) suggests that meditators may be spending a large portion of the meditating time in sleep. This replicates the finding of Younger *et al.* (1975). However, another point of view suggests that these measures may not have been sensitive enough and that meditators are, in fact, not sleeping, but hovering at a state of low arousal.

It seems quite possible, even likely, that sleep may sometimes occur as an undesired side effect, particularly in beginning meditators. Classical texts note sleep and drowsiness as one of the five major "hindrances" which the beginning meditator must confront and overcome. However, to attribute all meditation effects to sleep may be a gross oversimplificaton. As was noted by Jevning and O'Halloran (Article 33), specific cerebral blood flow and blood hormone changed during meditation, which differed in patterning from those of sleep.

41

SLEEP DURING TRANSCENDENTAL MEDITATION

Robert R. Pagano, Richard M. Rose, Robert M. Stivers,
and Stephen Warrenburg

Abstract. *Five experienced practitioners of transcendental meditation spent appreciable parts of meditation sessions in sleep stages 2, 3, and 4. Time spent in each sleep stage varied both between sessions for a given subject and between subjects. In addition, we compare electroencephalogram records made during meditation with those made during naps taken at the same time of day. The range of states observed during meditation does not support the view that meditation produces a single, unique state of consciousness.*

In 1970, Wallace reported several physiological changes observed during transcendental meditation (TM) (*1*). His results were replicated and extended by Wallace, Benson, and Wilson (*2*) and they were subsequently made available to a wider audience (*3*). They found, in meditating subjects, reduced oxygen consumption, increased skin resistance, increased alpha activity in the electroencephalogram (EEG), decreased heart rate, and decreased blood lactate. Although many of these changes take place in ordinary relaxed wakefulness and in sleep, Wallace and his co-workers postulated that, during most of the meditation period, experienced practitioners of TM enter a single, unique state of consciousness, a "wakeful hypometabolic state," that differs from ordinary relaxed or sleep states.

The Stanford Research Institute estimates that, from a few hundred in 1965,

the number of practitioners of TM has increased to more than 240,000 as of June 1973. Estimates from the TM organization indicate that this number now exceeds 900,000 (*4*). The findings of Wallace and his co-workers are often cited to prospective meditators and may have played an important role in producing this increase.

We have found that meditators spend considerable time in sleep stages 2, 3, and 4 during meditation; their subjective reports of sleep confirm our analysis of the EEG records. Further, our data suggest that the meditation period is not spent in a single, unique, wakeful, hypometabolic state.

The five subjects we observed had at least 2.5 years of experience with TM, and four of them were teachers of the technique. All were male Caucasians between the ages of 20 and 30, accustomed to meditating for 40-minute periods twice each day, and not in the habit of napping. Subjects reported, on the average, 7.8 hours of sleep per night.

Psychophysiological measures were made on each subject during ten sessions, each of which lasted 40 minutes. During five of these sessions, the subjects were asked to meditate in their accustomed sitting position, and in the other five sessions, they were asked to nap lying down on a bed. The first nap and the first meditation were scheduled on the first observation day. The data collected on this day are not included for analysis here because initial unfamiliarity with the laboratory situation produces atypical sleeping patterns (5). On eight subsequent days, subjects were asked either to meditate or to nap. These sessions were all conducted in the afternoon within 2 hours of the same time each day. The order in which the two types of sessions were scheduled followed an irregular pattern, and subjects were not told whether they would be asked to meditate or to nap on a particular day until they arrived in the laboratory. If a subject reported that his previous night's sleep was more than 30 minutes shorter than normal, he did not take part on that day. Subjects were asked not to consume food, coffee, or tea for at least 2 hours before each session.

At the beginning of each session, electrodes were applied so that occipital, central, and frontal EEG responses, eye movements, submental (below the chin) muscle potentials, and skin resistance level could be measured (6). The subject then moved to the room where he was to meditate or nap. A 45-db white noise partially masked any disturbance from the adjoining apparatus room (7). The room in which the subject sat during meditation was dimly illuminated, but the room was dark when the subject lay down to nap. Once the recording was proceeding smoothly, the subject was asked to relax for 5 minutes with his eyes closed, and then a signal was given to begin meditation or napping. After 40 minutes, an identical signal required the subject to stop meditating or napping and to relax with his eyes closed for an additional 5 minutes before leaving the recording room. At the end of the session, the subject filled out a questionnaire on his subjective impressions of what had transpired and stated whether he had slept or become drowsy during the meditation or nap.

Table 1. Percentage of time spent in stages 2, 3, or 4 during each session.

Subject	Meditation session				Nap session			
	1	2	3	4	1	2	3	4
1	51	90	59	78	37	41	59	62
2	0	0	0	26	78	92	79	58
3	49	0	0	78	86	31	83	89
4	0	90	59	74	18	38	95	88
5	37	0	86	31	95	95	93	78

Table 2. Percentage of time spent in each stage, averaged over sessions.*

Subject	Meditation				Nap			
	W	1	2	3, 4	W	1	2	3, 4
1	19	12	42	27	32	17	40	10
2	44	46	6	0	7	14	62	14
3	53	15	16	15	15	12	31	41
4	37	6	28	27	31	8	51	9
5	43	17	23	15	1	7	54	36

*These percentages do not sum to 100 because some epochs were scored as movement time.

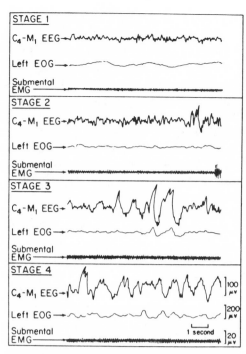

Fig. 1. Representative records from subject 5 during a meditation session. The time scale and channel gain are shown on the stage 4 record.

The most striking feature of our data is that meditators spent appreciable amounts of time in EEG sleep stages 2, 3, and 4 while they were meditating (Fig. 1). Averaged over meditation sessions, we found that 39 percent of the time was spent in wakefulness (stage W), 19 percent in stage 1, 23 percent in stage 2, and 17 percent in stages 3 or 4. More than a quarter of the meditation time was spent in stages 2, 3, or 4 in 13 out of the 20 meditation sessions (Table 1). It is customary to identify stages 2, 3, and 4 as sleep and stage 1 as drowsiness (8); according to these conventional designations, our subjects were asleep during, on the average, 40 percent of their meditation time.

Meditation might produce a dissociation between the EEG and consciousness that would permit a subject to be awake even though his EEG record indicated sleep (9). However, this does not appear to have occurred in our study, because our subjects reported having slept in 12 of the 13 medi-

tation sessions in which patterns of stages 2, 3, or 4 appeared. In addition, they reported feeling drowsy in 18 of the 19 sessions during which they spent more than 30 seconds in stage 1. The consistency of the reports with the EEG rcords indicates that the conventional EEG criteria defining sleep and drowsiness were applicable.

No rapid eye movement (REM) sleep was observed during either the meditations or the naps. This is probably because we conducted all sessions during the afternoon and limited each session to a length of 40 minutes; REM sleep does not normally occur during the first 40 minutes of an afternoon nap (10).

Although meditation in a laboratory might lead to a state different from that outside the laboratory, our subjects' ratings of their meditations indicated that in 7 of the 13 sessions in which stage 2 was observed, the subject rated his meditation as typical rather than atypical. Further, on a 7-point scale from 7 (very deep) to 1 (very light), the modal depth of meditation was 5, and there was no significant correlation between reported depth of meditation and the amount of time asleep. Thus, in several meditations described as typical and relatively deep, considerable amounts of sleep occurred. This corroborates reports that we have received from these and other meditators that they occasionally fall asleep while meditating in their normal settings.

If TM produces the wakeful state described by Wallace (1), one would expect to find less sleep during meditation than during a nap period. An analysis of variance of time spent in sleep stages 2, 3, or 4 revealed no significant differences between meditation and nap sessions ($F = 3.2$, $P > .1$). Because we obtained repeated measures over sessions for each subject, we also carried out individual t-tests on each subject's data. Only in subject 2 was there a significant difference ($t = 7.3$, $P < .01$) indicating fewer EEG sleep patterns during meditations than during naps. Because of the high variability in the states observed, we caution against the conclusion that meditation and napping produce identical distributions of EEG stages.

One of the striking features of our data was the variability in the time spent in the various EEG stages both for a single subject (from meditation to meditation) and between subjects (Tables 1 and 2). For example, subject 2 slept in only one of his four meditations, whereas subject 1 slept more than half the time in each of his four meditations. Subjects 3, 4, and 5 each had at least one meditation in which they did not sleep at all and another in which they slept for more than three-fourths of the session. What emerges from these EEG findings is that meditation is an activity that gives rise to quite different states both from day to day and from meditator to meditator.

Our data differ from the EEG responses reported by Wallace (1). Only 4 of his 15 subjects occasionally evidenced drowsiness, and he states, "The EEG pattern during meditation clearly distinguishes this state from the sleeping state. There are no slow (delta) waves or sleep spindles, but alpha-wave activity predominates." Several factors may account for the differences between Wallace's data and ours. He reported on records from just one session per subject, presumably the first experience for the subject in the laboratory. In addition, many of his subjects meditated while breathing through a mouthpiece or with arterial cannulae or rectal thermometers in place (1, 2). Both of these factors would probably tend to activate the EEG more

than would be expected in a normal meditation session outside the laboratory.

Wallace's subjects meditated for 20 to 30 minutes, whereas our sessions lasted 40 minutes; it could be argued that sleep was more likely to occur in our longer sessions. But when we examined the data from the first 20 minutes of each of our subject's meditations, the discrepancies remained: In the first 20 minutes, an average of 42.5 percent of the time was spent in sleep stages 2, 3, and 4.

In three other studies EEG responses were recorded during transcendental meditation: Younger et al. report that advanced meditators spent 41 percent of their meditations in sleep stages 1 and 2 (11); Wada and Hamm also found sleep stages 1 and 2 in the EEG records of both experienced and inexperienced meditators (12); Banquet recorded EEG responses during meditation but did not present an analysis by sleep stage (13). He did, however, mention the presence of "short bursts of large amplitude delta waves identical to those of sleep stage 4."

The results of Younger et al., of Wada and Hamm, and of this experiment raise the question of whether the beneficial effects reported for meditation (14) are due to the sleep that occurs during meditation or to some other feature of that process.

ROBERT R. PAGANO, RICHARD M. ROSE
ROBERT M. STIVERS
STEPHEN WARRENBURG

Department of Psychology, University of Washington, Seattle 98195

References and Notes

1. R. K. Wallace, Science 167, 1751 (1970).
2. _____, H. Benson, A. F. Wilson, Am. J. Physiol. 221, 795 (1971).
3. R. K. Wallace and H. Benson, Sci. Am. 226 (No. 2), 84 (1972).
4. D. P. Kanellakos and J. S. Lukas, The Psychobiology of Transcendental Meditation: A Literature Review (Stanford Research Institute, Menlo Park, 1973), p. iii; Fundamentals of Progress: Scientific Research on Transcendental Meditation (Maharishi International Univ. Press, New York, 1975).
5. See, for example, H. W. Agnew, Jr., W. B. Webb, R. L. Williams, Psychophysiology 2, 263 (1966).
6. Electrodes for the EEG were placed according to the international 10-20 system, and recordings were taken between each of leads O_2, C_4, and F_4 and a reference electrode on the opposite mastoid. A Beckman Dynograph (type RM) was used to record the data, and the records were scored according to the criteria of Rechtschaffen and Kales [A. Rechtschaffen and A. Kales, Eds., A Manual of Standardized Terminology, Techniques, and Scoring System for Sleep Stages of Human Sub-

jects (Public Health Service Publ. No. 204, Government Printing Office, Washington, D.C., 1968), pp. 8–15]. The scorers had no knowledge of the condition under which a record was made; the agreement between the two scorers averaged 93 percent.

7. In order to make additional comparisons between meditation and naps beyond those that we report here, a 45-db, 600-hertz tone of 0.5-second duration was presented on an irregular schedule averaging one presentation per minute. This tone was found to evoke EEG responses without disturbing the course of meditation, as judged by pilot subjects. In this report we present only the sleep stage and sleep report data. The galvanic skin responses and the responses to the tone have not yet been analyzed.

8. F. Snyder and J. Scott, in *Handbook of Psychophysiology*, N. S. Greenfield and R. A. Sternback, Eds. (Holt, Rinehart & Winston, New York, 1972), p. 645.

9. E. Green, in *Biofeedback and Self-Control 1972*, D. Shapiro *et al.*, Eds. (Aldine, Chicago, 1973), p. 164; A. Jus and K. Jus, in *Proceedings of the Third International Congress of Psychiatry*, B. Stoukis, Ed. (Montreal, 1961), pp. 473–482.

10. L. Maron, A. Rechtschaffen, E. A. Wolpert, *Arch. Gen. Psychiatry* **11**, 503 (1964); S. A. Lewis, *Br. J. Psychiatry* **115**, 107 (1969); I. Karacan, W. W. Finley, R. L. Williams, C. J. Hursch, *Biol. Psychiatry* **2**, 261 (1970).

11. J. Younger, W. Adriance, R. Berger, *Percept. Mot. Skills* **40**, 953 (1975).

12. J. A. Wada and A. E. Hamm, paper presented at the 27th annual meeting, American EEG Society, Boston, Mass., 15 and 16 June 1973.

13. J. P. Banquet, *Electroencephalogr. Clin. Neurophysiol.* **35**, 143 (1973).

14. See, for example, H. Benson and R. K. Wallace [in *Drug Abuse: Proceedings of the International Conference*, C. J. D. Zarafonetis, Ed. (Lea & Febiger, Philadelphia, 1972), p. 369]; S. Nidlich, W. Seeman, T. Dreskin [*J. Couns. Psychol.* **20**, 565 (1973)]; and J. Robbins and D. Fisher [*Tranquility Without Pills* (Wyden, New York, 1972)].

15. We thank A. Lubin, G. Chatrian, D. Barash, and A. Marlatt for constructive comments. We thank the Student International Meditation Society Seattle Center for their cooperation in helping us locate subjects.

17 June 1975; revised 12 November 1975.

IV

ADDITIONAL DEVELOPMENTS IN CLINICAL AND RESEARCH ASPECTS OF MEDITATION

An Introduction to Part IV:
Additional Developments in Clinical
and Research Aspects of Meditation

In this part we are going to look primarily at three different developments. Section A looks at studies which try to refine the independent variable and related ''confounding'' variables: expectation effects, demand characteristics, the effects of just sitting, and the role of concentration. Section B looks at which subject population meditation might work best with, and with which clinical problem? The third section compares meditation on both a theoretical and research level with other self-regulation strategies such as meditation, hypnosis, behavioral self-control, and other general relaxation strategies.

A. Refining the Independent Variable: Clinical Improvements

The first two articles in this section by Smith (42) and by Malec and Sipprelle (43) reveal some confusion in the literature between the issue of expectation effects and their interaction with demand characteristics. What Smith calls "expectation effects," that is, telling the subjects in the experiment what positive results they can expect, Malec and Sipprelle call "demand characteristics." The articles are important because they suggest the need for refining the components of meditation, as well as possible confounding variables. The article by Woolfolk (44) is included here for two different reasons. First, it illustrates an interesting addition to formal meditation of sitting twice daily, by combining it with what has been referred to later by Shapiro and Zifferblatt (48) as contingent informal meditation—that is, doing meditation contingent upon specified cues in the environment. Based on preliminary research, it seems that for certain clinical problems this may be a more effective strategy than meditation alone. The second reason the article is included is it presents a useful example of intensive design research.

Journal of Consulting and Clinical Psychology
1976, Vol. 44, No. 4, 630–637

42

PSYCHOTHERAPEUTIC EFFECTS OF TRANSCENDENTAL MEDITATION WITH CONTROLS FOR EXPECTATION OF RELIEF AND DAILY SITTING

Jonathan C. Smith

In 1959, Maharishi Mahesh Yogi introduced to America an exercise involving sitting quietly twice daily and passively attending to a special thought called a "mantra." This exercise is called transcendental meditation (TM) and has since been taught to at least 600,000 persons.

One possible reason for TM's popularity is Maharishi's (1968) claim that the technique is a "natural and effective cure for mental illness" (p. 191). TM promotional literature cites an impressive volume of studies that appear to support this claim. In my review of the literature (Smith, 1975), I concluded that research does "show the regular practice of meditation to be associated with decrements in psychopathology, particularly anxiety, over a period of time usually ranging from 4–10 weeks" (p. 562). However, I added this note of caution:

> The critical therapeutic variables underlying meditation could be something other than the meditation exercise. Two main possibilities not controlled for in the studies reviewed are (a) expectation of relief and (b) the regular practice of sitting quietly. (p. 562)

The present study consists of two experiments that focused on isolating the effects of the TM exercise from expectation of relief and daily sitting. The dependent variables were self-reported trait anxiety as measured by the State-Trait Anxiety Inventory (STAI) A-Trait Scale (Spielberger, Gorsuch, & Lushene, 1970) and anxiety symptoms of striated muscle tension and autonomic arousal as measured by the Epstein-Fenz Manifest Anxiety Scale (Fenz & Epstein, 1965). I chose trait anxiety because it was investigated in more than two-thirds of the studies I reviewed and is the most frequently investigated trait variable in meditation research (Smith, 1975).

In Experiment 1 the strategy was to compare the effects of TM (taught by the Student's International Meditation Society but with the $45 initiation fee waived) with a control treatment called "periodic somatic inactivity" (PSI). PSI was designed to match TM in every respect that might foster expectation of relief. However, unlike TM, PSI incorporated a daily exercise involving sitting with eyes closed and not meditating.

The rationale for this design is simple. If the effects of TM are due to the regular practice of the TM exercise, and not to expectation of relief or sitting daily with eyes closed, then TM should be more effective than PSI.

The strategy for Experiment 2 was somewhat different. Two treatments were compared, one incorporating a TM-like exercise, the other, an exercise designed to be the near antithesis of meditation. This exercise involved sitting with eyes closed and actively and deliberately generating as many positive thoughts as possible. In every other respect these two treatments were identical and were even given the same name, "cortically mediated stabilization" (CMS).

It was reasoned that if the effects of TM are due to the TM exercise, then the CMS treatment incorporating TM-like instructions should be more effective than the CMS treatment involving sitting with eyes closed and engaging in a presumably innocuous exercise nearly antithetical to meditation.

Experiment 1

Method

Subjects

Subjects were 139 (70 male and 69 female) Michigan State University students who attended an orientation lecture and 4 days of pretesting, were not receiving psychotherapy, and had at no time practiced meditation or yoga. Mean age was 22.

Procedure

Pretreatment orientation and assessment. Four hundred five persons responded to a campus-wide advertising campaign soliciting volunteers interested in receiving free treatments for reducing anxiety. Specific treatments involved were not named. These potential subjects attended an orientation lecture in which every effort was made to discourage participation by those who were not highly motivated.

Two hundred twenty-one subjects completed 4 days of pretreatment assessment. In addition to the STAI A-Trait Scale and the Epstein-Fenz Manifest Anxiety Scale, numerous supplementary measures were given, the most noteworthy being the 16 PF, Forms A and B (Cattell, Eber, & Tatsouka, 1970), the Tennessee Self-Concept Scale (Fitts, 1965), the Marlowe-Crowne Social Desirability Scale (Crowne & Marlowe, 1964), and a test of skin conductance reactivity. The supplementary measures were given for the purpose of selecting covariates for an analysis of covariance of posttest scores and for making exploratory post hoc comparisons (not reported here).

Subjects were randomly assigned using a random numbers table to two treatment conditions, TM and PSI, and to a third no-treatment condition.

Treatments. Forty-nine subjects were assigned to the TM group, 51 to the PSI group, and 39 agreed to be in the no-treatment condition. No-treatment subjects were told that they had been assigned to a "wait group" that would receive treatment in about 3 months. At no time during the experiment were subjects informed that several treatments were being compared.

TM was taught by two official TM instructors from the East Lansing, Michigan, Students' International Meditation Society. The traditional initiation fee was waived. The TM technique involves sitting twice daily for 15 to 20 minutes and passively and continuously attending to a special thought called a mantra. Complete TM instruction includes two introductory lectures that outline supporting theory and research, a 15-day drug-free fast, standardized individual initiation, 3 days of follow-up discussion, and monthly follow-up checking. In this experiment each TM subject was phoned once a month to schedule checking sessions, a departure from traditional TM procedure.

PSI was a control treatment specifically contrived to match every aspect of TM with one exception: Instead of sitting and meditating, the PSI technique involved simply sitting with eyes closed. Like TM, PSI instruction began with two introductory lectures that outlined a highly credible yet contrived theory explaining why sitting twice daily should be an immensely effective cure for most forms of psychopathology. In addition, bogus research was presented supporting the claims made. Between lectures subjects participated in a 15-day fast from illegal drugs. After the fast and the lectures, each subject was scheduled for technique initiation. During initiation each subject was ushered into a small quiet room and sat facing his instructor. After a few introductory remarks the instructor presented the PSI instructions summarized below:

Sit up straight in your chair. Place your feet flat on the floor. Place your arms in a position that is comfortable for you. If you are carrying a handbag or package, put it aside. Now, simply close your eyes and sit for the next 15 to 20 minutes. Remain physically inactive for this period of time; that is, sit still and avoid unnecessary movements. Let your mind do whatever it wants. Whatever you do mentally will have little or no impact on the effectiveness of the technique. The important thing is to remain physically inactive. Do not talk, walk around, or change chairs. You may engage in an occasional action such as shifting your position or making yourself more comfortable. And you may scratch. At the end of the session, open your eyes, breathe deeply a few times, and continue with your everyday activities.

Then the instructor left the room and let the subject practice. Fifteen minutes later he returned to discuss the session, present a "session experiences questionnaire," and answer questions.

Subjects were urged to attend three 1-hour follow-up discussion sessions devoted to answering questions and giving further instruction during the next 3 days. Finally, each month throughout the project, each subject was phoned and scheduled for a follow-up session. During follow-up sessions, each subject met alone with an instructor and practiced PSI. Subjects were given further instruction if it appeared they were practicing incorrectly.

Considerable effort was made to make PSI as credible as TM. Liberal use was made of "official" logos, sign-up books, questionnaires, contrived testimonials, professional-looking slides, and the like. PSI was taught by an undergraduate selected from 30 candidates for the degree to which he resembled the TM instructors. He was given the 71-page PSI instruction manual, which detailed all aspects of PSI theory, technique, and answers to "frequently asked questions." He practiced each aspect of instruction until he could proceed fluently without notes. The instructor was deliberately misinformed that PSI was highly effective and well researched and that the main purpose of the project was to determine if PSI is effective for different people for different reasons. He enthusiastically accepted this rationale and only months later began to suspect that other treatments were being compared. He never suspected that PSI was actually a control treatment. The PSI instructor had one assistant who knew, but kept secret, the control nature of PSI.

Posttreatment assessment. Three and one-half months later, no-treatment subjects were posttested and assigned to the treatments in Experiment 2, and 6 months later TM and PSI subjects were posttested. All subjects were given the tests used during pretesting assessment. In addition, numerous supplementary measures were given to TM and PSI subjects, including a frequency of practice questionnaire inquiring how many times PSI and TM were practiced each month; a questionnaire asking which therapeutic activities subjects participated in throughout the project; a drug-use questionnaire; and an extensive essay test asking subjects to evaluate the enjoyability, value, and overall impact of their treatments. At the end of assessment, all subjects who wanted to know and the PSI instructor were told what deceptions had been made and the design and results of the experiment. The experimenter offered to teach PSI, CMS_1, or CMS_2 (see Experiment 2) to any subject who wanted instruction.

Results

Twenty TM, 24 PSI, and 34 no-treatment subjects reported for posttesting. This represents an attrition rate of 59% for TM, 53% for PSI, and 13% for no-treatment controls.

Pretest and posttest means and standard deviations for TM, PSI, and no-treatment groups are presented in Table 1. Analyses of covariance comparing posttest scores for TM and PSI, TM and no treatment, and PSI and no treatment are presented in Table 2. Posttest scores were adjusted for their corresponding pretest scores, as well as for any variable that met all of the following criteria: (a) correlated significantly ($p <$ .01) with pretest-posttest difference scores or with posttest scores for those variables for which no pretests were given, (b) differed significantly among groups, (c) contributed significantly to the total variance for posttest scores when used with other covariates, and (d) made rational sense as a confounding variable.

Table 1. Pretest and Posttest Means and Standard Deviations for TM, PSI, and No-Treatment Groups[a]

| | | Variable | |
Statistic	A-Trait	Symptoms of striated muscle tension	Symptoms of autonomic arousal
TM			
Pretest			
M	47.00	28.84	37.16
SD	14.88	9.11	15.58
Posttest			
M	36.05	24.05	31.89
SD	14.28	9.41	11.98
PSI			
Pretest			
M	47.86	32.23	35.41
SD	9.26	8.25	6.43
Posttest			
M	38.05	27.18	31.77
SD	12.46	9.16	6.79
No treatment			
Pretest			
M	50.00	32.65	39.29
SD	11.13	7.90	10.26
Posttest			
M	48.88	31.74	38.12
SD	12.76	8.65	10.33

[a]TM = transcendental meditation; PSI = periodic somatic inactivity.

Table 2. Analyses of Covariance Comparing Posttest Scores for TM, PSI, and No-Treatment Groups[a]

Variable	*MS*	*df*	*F*	*p*
TM vs. PSI				
A-Trait[b]	11.42	1, 36	.13	>.715
SSMT[c]	3.85	1, 37	.12	>.726
SAA[c]	3.32	1, 37	.05	>.809
TM vs. no treatment				
A-Trait[d]	1,247.56	1, 50	18.88	<.0001
SSMT[d]	229.00	1, 50	7.86	<.008
SAA[d]	249.66	1, 50	4.64	<.036
PSI vs. no treatment				
A-Trait[d]	1,082.12	1, 53	12.75	<.0008
SSMT[d]	236.23	1, 53	6.75	<0.12
SAA[d]	140.66	1, 53	4.02	<.050

[a]For all comparisons complete data were available for 19 transcendental meditation (TM), 22 periodic somatic inactivity (PSI), and 34 no-treatment subjects. Abbreviations: SSMT = symptoms of striated muscle tension; SAA = symptoms of autonomic arousal.

[b]Covariates were pretest scores, total number of times subjects practiced throughout the project, and whether subjects discontinued practicing during the last full month of the project.

[c]Covariates were pretest scores and whether subjects discontinued practicing during the last full month of the project.

[d]Covariates were pretest scores.

TM and PSI groups did not differ significantly on STAI A-Trait scores, $F(1,36) = .13, p > .715$; on symptoms of striated muscle tension, $F(1,37) = .12, p > .726$; or on symptoms of autonomic arousal, $F(1,37) = .05, p > .809$. Both TM and PSI posttest means were significantly lower than no-treatment means on all dependent variables.

Experiment 2

Method

Subjects

Subjects consisted of 54 (27 male and 27 female) Michigan State University students with a mean age of 21.5 years. Of these, 9 males and 15 females were in the no-treatment condition in Experiment 1. The remaining responded to an extensive advertising campaign similar to that of Experiment 1 and were given the same orientation that subjects in Experiment 1 had.

Procedure

Pretreatment assessment. Over 3 days, all subjects were given the STAI A-Trait Scale and the Epstein-Fenz Manifest Anxiety Scale plus the following supplementary measures: the 16PF (Forms A and B), the Tennessee Self Concept Scale, and the Marlowe-Crowne Social Desirability Scale. For subjects in the no-treatment group in Experiment 1, posttreatment assessment in Experiment 1 served as pretreatment assessment in Experiment 2.

Subjects signed up for one of two treatment conditions. Treatments were identical except that one was at 7 and 9 and 7 and 9 P.M. on consecutive evenings and the other was at 9 and 7 and 9 and 7 P.M. on the same evenings. Subjects chose the treatment that best fit their schedules. Subjects who had no preference were randomly assigned to groups matched as closely as possible for sex and for ratio of no-treatment subjects to new recruits. Both treatment groups consisted of 27 subjects—one with 14 males and 13 females and the other with 13 males and 14 females.

Treatments. The two treatments were called CMS and were identical except that CMS_1 incorporated a TM-like exercise devised by the experimenter, and CMS_2, an "antimeditation" exercise. Subjects were not informed as to the relationship between the various treatments and meditation to reduce the possibility that claims made for meditation in the popular press would be generalized to the treatments.

Both treatments were taught by the experimenter. He carefully mastered each aspect of the instruction procedure and made an effort to appear credible and enthusiastic. In addition he misinformed subjects that he had practiced CMS for 5 years and had taught it for 2. The experimenter's expectation was that CMS_1 would be significantly more effective than CMS_2.

The first of the four training sessions for both groups incorporated the same introductory lecture. This lecture briefly outlined a plausible but contrived theory supporting the therapeutic potential of CMS. At the end of the first session, CMS was taught and practiced for 15 minutes by both the instructor and subjects and was then discussed. The CMS_1 group was instructed as follows:

CMS involves mental activity centered around a meaningless word, called a "focus." The focus we will use is the word "shanti." I will first read the instructions to acquaint you with them, and then I will reread them slowly and would like you to begin practicing as I read. We will then practice as a group for 15 minutes. Here are the instructions: Sit up straight in a comfortable position. Close your eyes. Give yourself a few minutes, about two, to settle down. Let the focal word repeat itself in your mind as effortlessly as possible; let it come to you and start on its own. If it won't repeat itself on its own, you may gently begin it, providing you do so with a minimum of effort. Whenever you notice you have been distracted or that your mind has wandered, let your mind return to the focal word as gently and effortlessly as possible. Let this happen easily, without making a big thing of it. Distractions, especially inner distractions, are an important part of the processes involved in CMS. They are normal and healthy. You are practicing CMS when they occur.

The CMS$_2$ group received the following instructions:

Here are the instructions for CMS. I will first read them to acquaint you with them, and then I will reread them slowly and would like you to begin practicing as I read. We will then practice as a group for 15 minutes. Here are the instructions: Sit up straight in a comfortable position. Close your eyes. Remain physically inactive. Shift your eyes back and forth, at a slow regular pace, about 15 times. Then deliberately pursue a sequence of cognitive activity that has a positive direction and is comprehensive. That is, simply engage in thought activity that you intend to be positive, that is, good, desirable, interesting, or anything the word "positive" means to you. There are three types of cognitive activity you may pursue: fantasy-daydream, storytelling, and listing. If you engage in fantasy-daydream, make it good. Make it have a good outcome. Put components in it that for you are positive—people you like, activities you like, your favorite possessions, places you like, colors you like, etc. If you engage in storytelling, tell yourself a story that has a positive ending. Put in details that are good and desirable for you. If you engage in listing, simply list the positive attributes of something. List all the good, desirable, and beneficial qualities of something. Whatever thoughts and feelings you have in addition to your deliberate sequence of cognitive activity are normal and healthy. They are part of the processes involved in CMS. As you may have gathered, the specific content of your positive cognitive activity is irrelevant. What is really important is that you engage in deliberate cognitive effort that is directed in a positive direction.

The remaining 3 days of instruction started out with a question and answer session. CMS instructions were briefly summarized, and the technique was practiced by everyone for 15 minutes. This was followed by 30 minutes of discussion and further instruction. Both groups were instructed that the effects of CMS are "gradual, accumulative, cyclical, and automatic." In addition, finer points of the meditation and antimeditation techniques were elaborated.

Once a month for the duration of the experiment each subject was phoned and scheduled for a group follow-up checking session. During these sessions instructions were reviewed, CMS was practiced, and questions were answered.

Posttreatment assessment. Eleven weeks after the onset of the project subjects took all posttests given in Experiment 1. Subjects who were interested were told what deceptions had been made and the design and results of the experiment. As in Experiment 1, the experimenter offered to teach PSI, CMS$_1$, or CMS$_2$ to any subject who wanted instruction.

Table 3. Pretest and Posttest Means and Standard Deviations for CMS$_1$ and CMS$_2$ Groups[a]

Statistic	A-Trait	Symptoms of striated muscle tension	Symptoms of autonomic arousal
CMS$_1$			
Pretest			
M	46.21	28.50	38.14
SD	12.51	9.09	10.13
Posttest			
M	41.14	26.42	34.07
SD	12.57	7.86	9.07
CMS$_2$			
Pretest			
M	52.78	36.44	41.00
SD	6.84	8.39	8.06
Posttest			
M	46.72	30.17	36.06
SD	8.37	8.89	7.26

[a]CMS = cortically mediated stabilization.

Results

Fourteen CMS_1 and 19 CMS_2 subjects reported for posttesting. This represents an attrition rate of 48% of CMS_1 and 30% for CMS_2.

Pretest and posttest means and standard deviations for CMS_1 and CMS_2 are presented in Table 3. Analyses of covariance comparing posttest scores for both groups are presented in Table 4. Posttest scores were adjusted for their corresponding pretest scores, as well as for any variable that met the criteria used in Experiment 1 for selecting covariates.

CMS_1 and CMS_2 groups did not differ significantly on STAI A-Trait scores, $F(1, 29) = .02, p > .871$; on symptoms of striated muscle tension, $F(1, 29) = .25, p > .617$; or on symptoms of autonomic arousal, $F(1, 29) = .005, p > .942$. The t tests of within-group differences are shown in Table 5 and reveal significant improvement on STAI A-Trait and symptoms of autonomic arousal ($p < .03$) for both groups.

Discussion

TM is no more effective in reducing trait anxiety than a parallel control treatment consisting of sitting without meditation. A treatment using a TM-like exercise is no more effective than a parallel control treatment using an exercise designed to be the near antithesis of meditation. These findings support the conclusion that the crucial therapeutic component of TM is not the TM exercise.

A critic might wonder if the degree of improvement displayed by our TM subjects is comparable to the degree of improvement displayed by persons who chose on their own to learn TM. Previous research

Table 4.   Analyses of Covariance Comparing CMS_1 and CMS_2 Groups[a]

Variable[b]	MS	F[c]	p>
A-Trait	1.39	.02	.871
Symptoms of striated muscle tension	10.85	.25	.617
Symptoms of autonomic arousal	.12	.005	.942

[a]CMS = cortically mediated stabilization. Complete data were available for 14 CMS_1 and 18 CMS_2 subjects.
[b]Pretest scores were covaried for all variables.
[c]$df = 1, 29$.

Table 5.   Mean Difference Scores and Significance of Difference Scores for CMS_1 and CMS_2 Groups[a]

Variable	M	t	df	p<
CMS_1				
A-Trait	5.07	2.43	13	.030
Symptoms of striated muscle tension	2.08	1.89	13	.081
Symptoms of autonomic arousal	4.07	3.19	13	.007
CMS_2				
A-Trait	6.06	3.88	17	.001
Symptoms of striated muscle tension	6.27	3.02	17	.008
Symptoms of autonomic arousal	4.94	3.84	17	.001

[a]CMS = cortically mediated stabilization.

Psychotherapeutic Effects of TM

supports an affirmative answer. Ferguson and Gowan (1973) gave the STAI A-Trait Inventory to 31 TM initiates before and 6 weeks after learning TM. Mean pretest and posttest scores were 42.90 and 32.87, an improvement of 10.03 points. Renshaw* tested 12 TM initiates on the same scale and found an improvement from 41.08 to 38.08, or 2 points, over 2 months. My TM subjects displayed a mean improvement of 10.95 points on the STAI A-Trait Scale. Although attrition among our TM subjects was relatively high (59%), there is some indication that attrition among persons who chose to learn TM on their own may be comparable (Otis, 1974).

Several legitimate questions can be raised with respect to my conclusion that the TM exercise is not the crucial therapeutic component of TM. The act of meditation is not a singular entity but can be seen as involving several components. Three important components of TM meditation (essentially the same as the CMS_1 meditation described earlier) are: (a) the sustained voluntary regulation of attention; (b) the deployment of attention toward a simple, limited stimulus; and (c) passivity. The first two components are usually seen as the defining characteristics of meditation (Benson, 1975; Deikman, 1963; Maupin, 1969; Naranjo & Ornstein, 1971; Smith, 1975). Although the TM exercise as an intact entity is apparently not essential for TM's therapeutic impact, perhaps some set of "nonmeditative" components is. Unfortunately, the results of this article can provide only tentative insight into this question. The main difference between TM and PSI is that TM involves the sustained voluntary regulation of attention, whereas PSI did not. That these groups did not differ suggests that the sustained voluntary regulation of attention is not a crucial therapeutic component of TM. Also, both CMS treatments involved the sustained voluntary regulation of attention. However, in CMS_1 the focus of attention was simple (the word shanti); in CMS_2 the focus was complex and varied, as many positive thoughts one could generate in a CMS session. A second difference between the techniques was that CMS_1, like TM, was passive, whereas CMS_2 was active. The finding that these groups did not differ suggests that a technique involving attending to a simple stimulus in a passive manner is as effective in reducing anxiety as a technique involving attending to a complex stimulus in an active manner. Of course, there are other combinations of regulation of attention, simplicity of focal stimulus, and passivity that were not compared in this study, and hence any further conclusions with respect to these components of meditation would be inappropriate.

It may be worthwhile to point out that the intended purpose of this study was to investigate *only* the extent to which the TM exercise contributes to changes displayed by subjects who participate in the TM program. I did not attempt to weigh the relative contribution of such variables as expectation of relief, daily sitting, passage of time, and repeated test administration. All of these variables were simply held constant while aspects of the meditation exercise were manipulated. However, I shall take the liberty of sharing my own opinions. I suspect expectation of relief contributed much to the effectiveness of all of our treatments. Numerous behavior modification studies (Borkovec, 1972; Lazarus, 1968; Leitenberg, Agras, Barlow, & Oliveau, 1969; Marcia, Rubin, & Efran, 1969; McReynolds, Barnes, Brooks, & Rehagen, 1973) show that an odd assortment of bogus treatments can be rendered effective in reducing fears and anxieties providing that some combination of the following several conditions is met: (a) The treatment is taught by a person who believes it is effective; (b) the treatment is complex and highly structured; (c) claims of effectiveness and a plausible and comprehensive theoretical rationale are supplied; and (d) the person receiving the treatment receives what he/she believes to be signs that the treatment is working for him/her. Although other factors undoubtedly contribute to expectation of relief, the above have actually been found, either separately or in combination, to increase bogus treatment effectiveness. All of these factors were present in the TM and PSI treatments. Both were enthusiastically taught by persons fully convinced of the treatments' effectiveness. Both incorporated equally complicated and sophisticated instruction rituals, including highly formalized personal initiation and follow-up checking sessions. For both, initiation was preceded by lectures outlining formidable claims and theoretical rationales. And finally, both TM and PSI subjects were reassured that they were practicing correctly virtually every time they had questions concerning things experienced while practicing their techniques; indeed, many reported experiences were described by the instructors as signs that the techniques were working effectively.

In addition I believe the improvements displayed by the treatment groups were not entirely due to the effects of repeated test administration and passage of time. Differences in attrition rate between the treatment groups (59% for TM) and the no-treatment group (13%) make it difficult to assess the contribution of these two variables. However, if one assumes that after attrition the treatment groups

*Personal communication, March 1975.

included only those subjects who displayed the most improvement, then it should be possible to artificially create a comparable no-treatment group consisting of an equal proportion of "most improved" subjects. Such a comparison was made. As reported earlier, 59% of the original TM group and 13% of the original no-treatment group failed to report for posttesting. The remaining no-treatment subjects were ranked according to degree of improvement and the 18 who displayed the least improvement were removed (making an artificial 59% attrition rate). The mean STAI A-trait change score of the artificial no-treatment group was 6.50, compared with 10.95 for the TM group. This somewhat contrived comparison lends informal support to my opinion that the treatment group changes were not entirely due to passage of time or repeated test administration.

Another limitation of this study is that the results are based on self-report data. We simply do not know if projective or objective test data would yield the same results. Also, the main focus of this project was psychopathology, particularly anxiety. It is conceivable that the TM exercise has an impact on traits other than anxiety, for example, traits related to perception.

Finally, numerous physiological studies (Wallace, 1970; Wallace, Benson, & Wilson, 1971) show changes in physiological state while a person is in meditation. These changes appear to reflect a state of restful alertness that is quite different from the state of anxiety. The results of the present study are not at all inconsistent with these findings. The focus of this study was trait anxiety, the enduring predisposition to behave anxiously; the focus was not transient or state anxiety. It is conceivable that TM may have a state-anxiety-reducing potential and have little potential for reducing the enduring predisposition to behave anxiously. TM may well be a tranquilizer but not a cure.

References

Benson, H. *The relaxation response*. New York: Morrow, 1975.

Borkovec, T. D. Effects of expectancy on the outcome of systematic desensitization and implosive treatments for analogue anxiety. *Behavior Therapy*, 1972, *3*, 29–40.

Cattell, R. B., Eber, H. W., & Tatsouka, M. M. *Handbook for the Sixteen Personality Factor Questionnaire*. Champaign, Ill.: Institute for Personality and Ability Testing, 1970.

Crowne, D. P., & Marlowe, D. *The approval motive: Studies in evaluative dependence*. New York: Wiley, 1964.

Deikman, A. J. Experimental meditation. *Journal of Nervous and Mental Disorders*, 1963, *136*, 329–373.

Fenz, W. D., & Epstein, S. Manifest anxiety: Unifactorial or multifactorial composition? *Perceptual and Motor Skills*, 1965, *20*, 773–780.

Ferguson, P. D., & Gowan, J. The influence of transcendental meditation on anxiety, depression, aggression, neuroticism, and self-actualization. In D. P. Kanellakos & P. C. Ferguson (Eds.), *The psychobiology of transcendental meditation*. Los Angeles: Maharishi International University Press, 1973. (Abstr.)

Fitts, W. H. *Tennessee Self-Concept Scale Manual*. Nashville: Counselor Recordings and Tests, 1965.

Lazarus, A. A. Behavior therapy and graded structure. In R. Porter (Ed.), *The role of learning in psychotherapy*. London: Churchill, 1968.

Leitenberg, H., Agras, W. S., Barlow, D. H., & Oliveau, D. C. Contribution of selective positive reinforcement and therapeutic instructions to systematic desensitization therapy. *Journal of Abnormal Psychology*, 1969, *74*, 113–118.

Maharishi Mahesh Yogi. *Transcendental meditation*. New York: Signet, 1968.

Marcia, J. E., Rubin, B. M., & Efran, J. S. Systematic desensitization: Expectancy change or counterconditioning? *Journal of Abnormal Psychology*, 1969, *74*, 382–387.

Maupin, E. W. On meditation. In C. Tart (Ed.), *Altered states of consciousness*. New York: Wiley, 1969.

McReynolds, W. T., Barnes, A. R., Brooks, S., & Rehagen, N. J. The role of attention-placebo influences in the efficacy of systematic desensitization. *Journal of Consulting and Clinical Psychology*, 1973, *41*, 86–92.

Naranjo, C., & Ornstein, R. E. *On the psychology of meditation*. New York: Viking Press, 1971.

Otis, L. S. If well-integrated but anxious, try TM. *Psychology Today*, April 1974, pp. 45–46.

Smith, J. C. Meditation as psychotherapy: A review of the literature. *Psychological Bulletin*, 1975, *82*, 558–564.

Spielberger, C. D., Gorsuch, R. L., & Lushene, R. E. *Manual for the State-Trait Anxiety Inventory*. Palo Alto, Calif.: Consulting Psychologists Press, 1970.

Wallace, R. K. Physiological effects of transcendental meditation. *Science*, 1970, *167*, 1751–1754.

Wallace, R. K., Benson, H., & Wilson, A. F. A wakeful hypometabolic physiologic state. *American journal of Physiology*, 1971, *221*, 795–799.

Journal of Consulting and Clinical Psychology
1977, Vol. 45, No. 2, 339–340

43

PHYSIOLOGICAL AND SUBJECTIVE EFFECTS OF ZEN MEDITATION AND DEMAND CHARACTERISTICS

James Malec and Carl N. Sipprelle

Forty male undergraduate volunteers were assigned to one of four groups. During the treatment period, the control group was asked to "just sit there." The deactivation demand, neutral demand, and activation demand groups were shown a videotape demonstrating the Zen meditation exercise "counting breaths" and modeling and suggesting relaxation outcome, no specific outcome, and arousal outcome for each group, respectively. A baseline period preceded and a recovery period followed treatment. Respiration rate and electromyogram decreased and heart rate increased, then gradually declined for the meditation groups during the treatment period. Differences among groups in self-reported mood were not statistically reliable. Results show that Zen meditation produces small physiological changes in naive, unpracticed subjects.

A Zen meditation exercise was studied under various demand conditions. Forty male undergraduate volunteers were assigned to one of four groups. During the 15-minute treatment period, the control group was asked to "just sit there." Three other groups were instructed to meditate after viewing a videotape demonstrating the Zen exercise "counting breaths" followed by (a) relaxation outcome, (b) no specific outcome, or (c) arousal outcome. A 15-minute baseline period preceded treatment, and a 15-minute recovery period followed treatment.

Heart and respiration rates were recorded on a Gilson polygraph (Model M5P). Electromyogram (EMG) was recorded from the frontalis by a Model 401 Feedback Myograph and integrated by a Model 215 Time-Period Integrator (Biofeedback Technology, Inc.). Averages for heart rate, respiration rate, and EMG were ob-

---

Requests for reprints and for an extended report of this study should be sent to Carl N. Sipprelle, Department of Psychology, University of South Dakota, Vermillion, South Dakota 57069.

tained for each period. Galvanic skin responses (GSRs) during each period were determined by a 58028 Dual Limit GSR unit and counted by a 5804 Data Recorder (Lafayette Instrument Co.). Subjects completed the Mehrabian-Russell mood scale after each period and, after the last period, wrote a verbal description of how they felt after the treatment period.

A profile analysis of average respiration rate revealed a significant interaction between treatment groups and periods, $F(6, 74) = 2.55$, $p < .05$. After being adjusted for baseline rate, respiration rate during the treatment period was lower for the combined meditation groups than for the control group according to Scheffé's test, $F(4, 35) = 8.55$, $p < .05$. This only shows that the meditation groups followed instructions, since the very act of counting breaths was expected to slow respiration. No significant effects were obtained in a profile analysis of average heart rate, although for the meditation groups, it increased at the beginning of the treatment period and then gradually decreased. Profile analysis of the EMG data revealed a significant interaction between treatment groups and periods, $F(2, 37) = 3.75$, p

< .05, when the meditation groups were combined and compared to the control group. Analysis of covariance confirmed that treatment EMG adjusted for baseline was lower for the combined meditation groups than for the control group, $F(1, 37) = 6.31$, $p < .05$. No significant differences were found for the GSR data.

The mood scale sampled three factors: pleasantness, activation, and dominance. Profile analysis did not reveal effects for treatment groups or for the interaction of groups and periods on any factor. However, for all treatment groups, pleasantness decreased across periods, $F(2, 35) = 3.58$, $p < .05$; activation increased, $F(2, 35) = 7.00$, $p < .005$; and dominance was lower after the treatment period than after the other periods, $F(2, 35) = 7.60$, $p < .005$. The verbal descriptions were ranked on the dimensions of pleasant-ness and activation, with nonparametric tests showing no significant effects.

The mediation exercise produced lowered muscle tension and respiration rate independent of type of demand. Heart rate could have been confounded by changes in respiration volume, which was not measured in this study. Other researchers may wish to include this measure.

Neither physiological changes nor self-report was related to varying conditions of demand. This study varied experimental demand but not the expectations that the subject brought to the experiment. The investigation of the interaction between demand characteristics and subjects' expectations and attitudes is a promising area for future research.

Received March 2, 1976 ∎

44

SELF-CONTROL MEDITATION AND THE TREATMENT OF CHRONIC ANGER

Robert L. Woolfolk

Introduction

The emotion of anger is central to many inter- and intrapersonal disorders. Anger is the emotional state which most often accompanies and facilitates aggressive behavior (Rule and Nesdale, 1976). Anger can also be viewed as one emotional pole of Cannon's (1932) fight-or-flight response, as one style of mobilizing the organism's resources to cope with stress. The evidence is mounting that chronic anger and aggressiveness are at the root of many physical diseases and of much personal unhappiness (Woolfolk and Richardson, 1978). Despite the fact that anger can be among the most destructive of human emotions, its clinical treatment, until recently, has received little systematic attention.

Reported work on the systematic treatment of anger has tended to focus either upon lowering arousal through counterconditioning or relaxation training or upon modifying the cognitions which promote anger. Some early case studies reported successful attempts to apply systematic desensitization to anger aroused by specific situations (Herrell, 1971; Rimm *et al.,* 1971). Novaco (1976) found that a training program which combined a version of self-instructional training (cf. Meichenbaum, 1975) and a modified form of progressive relaxation training to be significantly more effective than an attention placebo in reducing anger. When applied singly, self-instructional training and progressive relaxation training were intermediate in effectiveness between the combined treatment and the control condition.

Much research has demonstrated that meditation can serve to produce a lowered state of physiological arousal (Woofolk, 1975). In their recent review of the therapeutic applications of meditation, Shapiro and Giber (1978) cite numerous studies which have successfully employed meditation to reduce anxiety and to ameliorate other stress-related disorders. Although no research has examined the efficacy of meditation in anger reduction, the rationale for its use in the treatment of anger is quite straightforward. Anger is an emotion which is characterized by physiological arousal (Ax, 1953). Meditation commonly produces lowered arousal and has been effective in treating emotional disorders which are also characterized by physiological arousal.

Most previous therapeutic applications of meditation have restricted themselves to the traditional twice-a-day meditation regimen, but some exceptions to this trend are to be found in the literature. Shapiro and Zifferblatt (1976) in comparing Zen meditation with behavioral self-control techniques, described "contingent informal meditation," the making of detached self-awareness, contingent upon experiences associated with stress. Shapiro (1976) found this procedure in combination with twice-a-day formal meditation to be an effective treatment for a case of generalized anxiety. Based upon much clinical evidence, Carrington (1978) has advocated the use of brief sessions (1–3 minutes) of her mantra-based method of meditation. These "mini-meditations" are employed as a behavioral self-control skill in combating feelings of tension and anxiety.

Within the behavior therapy tradition progressive relaxation is often taught as a self-control skill. After initial training in progressive relaxation, clients often are taught either conditioned relaxation or relaxation by recall, both methods of which quickly achieve relaxation by focusing on cues associated with the relaxed state (Bernstein and Borkovec, 1973). The ability to achieve relaxation in a quick and expedient manner makes it then available as a device useful in coping with transitory fluctuations in tension and arousal.

The present study sought to apply meditation training to a case of chronic and debilitating anger. Using a reversal-type design, it was possible to contrast the relative effectiveness of baseline periods, standard twice-a-day meditation, and the standard practice pattern combined with the use of meditation as a self-control skill.

Case History

The client was a 26-year-old construction worker who had been referred because of chronic anger and outbursts of temper which had placed both his job and his significant social relationships in jeopardy. The client's job and home were the only two settings in which the anger and anger-related behavior seemed to be a serious problem. The client reported that he had experienced "temper problems" throughout his life and thought of himself as a "pretty uptight guy." The client had lost several jobs after getting into fistfights with co-workers and reported that one more such incident might result in his expulsion from his union.

The client reported that particularly severe anger problems occurred at home. He lived with a divorced 23-year-old woman and her 4-year-old son. Both his girlfriend and her son were frequent elicitors of intense anger from the client. Although his firmly held values prohibited a pattern of physical violence within the household, highly emotional arguments did occur with great frequency. Both the client's girlfriend and her son were the recipients of much verbal abuse. An interview with the girlfriend corroborated that they were on the verge of separation and very probably would separate if something could not be done to change the client's pattern of behavior.

After an assessment interview and an initial week of data collection, treatment was begun. During the first treatment session the client was trained in the method of meditation developed by the author (Woolfolk et al., 1976). This method of meditation incorporates features both of Yogic meditation and of Zazen. A breathing focus is combined with a mantra which serves to direct attention to the process of breathing. The client was instructed to meditate for 15 minutes, twice each day.

The second treatment session occurred at the end of the second week of data collection. During this session the client was instructed in self-control meditation. The client was taught to employ a brief meditation (1–2 minutes) whenever situational cues indicated that anger might be forthcoming or when he experienced the initial feelings of frustration or irritation which were a customary prelude to intense anger. The client was instructed to utilize whenever possible the regimen of a brief meditation contingent on the first stages of anger arousal. Given the difficulty of meditating with eyes closed in many social situations, the client was taught an eyes-open variation of the meditation procedures. This variation involves visual fixation on some distal object during breath and mantra focus. The client was also instructed during this session to continue standard twice-a-day meditation.

The third, fourth, and fifth treatment sessions were essentially evaluation and review sessions in which the therapist reviewed procedures with the client, discussed any problems of technique implementation which had arisen over the previous week, and made certain that the client was correctly employing the meditation procedures. During the fourth week a reversal phase was instituted. The client was instructed to suspend the use of both self-control meditation and standard meditation during the fourth week, thus instituting a second baseline phase. During the fifth week the client resumed twice-a-day meditation only. In the sixth week of the study the client returned to the practice of self-control meditation combined with standard meditation. This 6-week period completed the treatment phase of the study.

The client self-monitored his anger reactions throughout the study. Each day before retiring he rated for the preceding day: (1) the amount of anger experienced; (2) the amount of angry behavior displayed; and (3) the effectiveness of his anger management. Each rating was made on a 9-point Likert-type scale. The client also recorded the time he spent meditating. Convergent validation of the self-report measures was sought through obtaining ratings from significant others. Independent ratings were obtained from the client's girlfriend and from a co-worker whose participation was enlisted by the girlfriend. They rated the client on the same three scales. Each day during the study all daily ratings were mailed to a research assistant who kept their contents secret until the end of the study.

Follow-up data were gathered from the client and his girlfriend for a week 1 month after the treatment phase and for a week 3 months after treatment. Data from the co-worker were unavailable at follow-up. After the collection of the 3-month follow-up data, the client was brought in for an evaluation session and offered further therapy. He was seen for three more sessions, during which time he received a cognitively oriented therapy focused on enabling him to alter his appraisals of typical anger-provoking incidents.

Results

The overall pattern of results suggests that the client's ability to cope successfully with anger was unaffected by meditation practiced twice-a-day. When self-control meditation was added to the standard regimen, substantial alterations in the client's anger were recorded. He reported himself to be less angry and to have engaged in less angry behavior during self-control meditation as well as having been more able to cope effectively with anger-provoking situations. Independent ratings by the client's girlfriend and by a co-worker corroborated these findings.

An inspection of Tables 1 and 2 shows that both for amount of anger and amount of angry behavior during twice-a-day meditation (weeks 2 and 5) no change is observed from the preceding baseline week. During weeks in which the client practiced twice-a-day meditation combined with self-control meditation (weeks 3 and 6) substantial reductions on these anger variables were recorded by all three raters.

Table 1. Weekly Means of Amount of Anger Made by Client, Girlfriend, and Co-worker

	Week						Follow-up	
Rater	1	2	3	4	5	6	1-Month	3-Month
Client	6.43	5.57	3.00	6.29	5.71	2.14	2.57	2.86
Girlfriend	7.71	7.86	3.71	6.43	6.29	4.14	3.14	3.86
Co-worker	5.42	5.29	4.14	5.86	5.57	3.14	—	—

Table 2. Weekly Means of Ratings of Amount of Angry Behavior Made by Client, Girlfriend, and Co-worker

	Week						Follow-up	
Rater	1	2	3	4	5	6	1-Month	3-Month
Client	5.71	5.57	3.00	5.14	5.43	2.14	3.14	2.57
Girlfriend	6.86	6.43	3.86	7.14	6.29	3.29	2.86	2.14
Co-worker	5.00	4.57	3.14	5.14	5.57	3.57	—	—

Table 3. Weekly Means of Ratings of Effectiveness of Anger Management Made by Client, Girlfriend, and Co-worker

	Week						Follow-up	
Rater	1	2	3	4	5	6	1-Month	3-Month
Client	2.43	2.86	6.00	2.86	3.00	6.57	5.57	5.71
Girlfriend	1.86	2.00	4.57	2.57	3.14	5.14	4.86	5.86
Co-worker	3.14	3.86	6.00	4.29	5.29	7.71	—	—

The data for the effectiveness of anger management variable reflect the expected inverse relationship with the anger variables (see Table 3). Here again we see the pattern of change occurring on this variable only when self-control meditation is applied or withdrawn. The application of self-control meditation increased the effectiveness of anger management; the withdrawal of the combined program resulted in a return to pretreatment levels which were not altered by the subsequent application of twice-a-day meditation. The observed changes are not attributable to differential practice of standard meditation during weeks 2, 3, 5, and 6. Self-reported practice time was constant across these weeks.

The client reported that he faithfully practiced the self-control meditation plus standard meditation program during the follow-up period. The data collected from the client and his girlfriend at 1- and 3-month follow-up indicate that posttreatment changes were maintained. This was further verified in interviews with the client and his girlfriend at 3 months following treatment. At that time both indicated that they considered the client to be "greatly improved" relative to pretreatment.

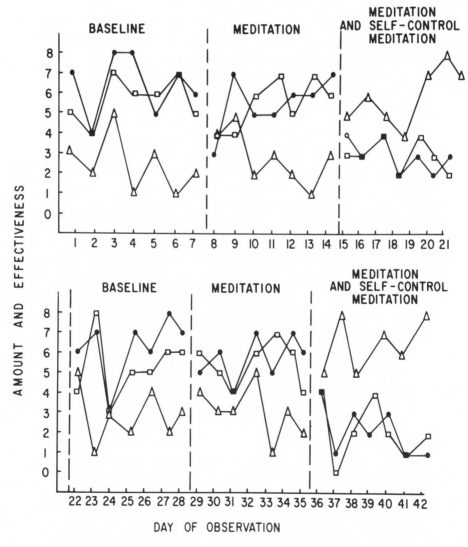

Fig. 1. Self-monitored ratings of amount of anger, amount of angry behavior, and effectiveness of anger management. ●—●, Amount of anger; □—□, amount of angry behavior; —, effectiveness of anger management.

Self-Control Meditation   553

Discussion

Great caution must be exercised in the interpretation of the results of a case study. Although the findings of a case study can never be definitive, they can have heuristic import by suggesting possible revisions in current theory and practice or in pointing directions for future research. The findings of the present study are suggestive in several ways.

The results of the present study cast further doubt on the ability of meditation, employed in the standard twice-a-day fashion, to alleviate stress-related disorders of significant duration and severity. The present study is consistent with the results of Girodo (1974), who found yoga treatment to be effective only with anxiety neurotics with short histories of dysfunction. For patients with longer histories of dysfunction, it was necessary to employ flooding to achieve symptom remission.

The findings of the present study suggest that brief meditation employed within a self-control framework may be of great clinical value. Within the present study self-control meditation was not examined except as it was practiced in conjunction with twice-a-day meditation. Whether self-control meditation practiced without standard meditation can be effective is a question which should be addressed by future studies. Within the present study self-control meditation was always instituted immediately following a week of standard meditation which always followed a baseline period. Although this ordering was thought to provide the most stringent test of the effects of self-control meditation, it is possible that this particular ordering may have interacted with treatments to produce the obtained results. It is probable also that the combined treatment had greater credibility in the second half of the treatment period because of its initial superior performance during the third week of treatment.

Further research is needed to document the effects of self-control meditation. Should that documentation be forthcoming, research should then address itself to questions concerning the effects of individual treatment components, treatment order, and treatment credibility upon outcome.

References

Ax, A. F. The physiological differentiation between fear and anger in humans. *Psychosomatic Medicine,* 1953, **15**, 433–442.

Bernstein, D. A., and Borkovec, T. D. *Progressive relaxation training: A manual for the helping professions.* Champaign, Illinois: Research Press, 1973.

Cannon, W. B. *The wisdom of the body.* New York: W. W. Norton, 1932.

Carrington, P. *Clinically standardized meditation.* Kendall Park, New Jersey: Pace Systems, 1978.

Girodo, M. Yoga meditation and flooding in the treatment of anxiety neurosis. *Journal of Behavior Therapy and Experimental Psychiatry,* 1974, **5**, 157–160.

Herrell, J. M. Use of systematic desensitization to eliminate inappropriate anger. *Proceedings of the 79th annual convention of the american psychological association,* 1971, **6**, 431–432.

Meichenbaum, D. A self-instructional approach to stress management: A proposal for stress inoculation training. In C. Spielberger and I. Sarason (Eds.), *Stress and Anxiety,* Vol. 2. New York: Wiley, 1975.

Novaco, R. W. The treatment of anger through cognitive and relaxation controls. *Journal of Consulting and Clinical Psychology,* 1976, **44**, 681.

Rimm, D. C., de Groot, J. C., Boord, P., Reiman, J., and Dillow, P. V. Systematic desensitization of an anger response. *Behaviour Research and Therapy,* 1971, **9**, 273–280.

Rule, B. G., and Nesdale, A. R. Emotional arousal and aggressive behavior. *Psychological Bulletin,* 1976, **83**, 851–863.

Shapiro, D. H. Zen meditation and behavioral self-control strategies applied to a case of generalized anxiety. *Psychologia,* 1976, **19**, 133–138.

Shapiro, D. H., and Giber, D. Meditation and psychotherapeutic effects: Self-regulation strategy and altered state of consciousness. *Archives of General Psychiatry,* 1978, **35**, 294–302.

Shapiro, D. H., and Zifferblatt, S. M. Zen meditation and behavioral self-control: Similarities, differences, and clinical applications. *American Psychologist,* 1976, **31**, 519–532.

Woolfolk, R. L. Psychophysiological correlates of meditation. *Archives of General Psychiatry,* 1975, **32**, 1326–1333.

Woolfolk, R. L., and Richardson, F. C. *Stress, sanity, and survival.* New York: Simon and Schuster, 1978.

Woolfolk, R. L., Carr-Kafashan, L., Lehrer, P. M., and McNulty, T. F. Meditation training as a treatment for insomnia. *Behavior Therapy,* 1976, **7**, 359–365.

B. Meditation: For Whom, Which Subject Population, and for Which Clinical Problem?

The first two articles in this section, by Smith (45) and by Beiman *et al.* (46) are the first efforts at beginning to determine the characteristics of those clients who will benefit from meditation. They provide an important step toward the matching of treatment with subject. The article by Schwartz, Davidson, and Goleman (47) illustrates the potential importance of refining the dependent variable more precisely (e.g., cognitive versus somatic anxiety), and matching treatment to dependent variable.

Therefore, in this section, we begin to see ways to match subject, clinical problem, and treatment modality.

Journal of Consulting and Clinical Psychology
1978, Vol. 46, No. 2, 272-279

45

PERSONALITY CORRELATES OF CONTINUATION AND OUTCOME IN MEDITATION AND ERECT SITTING CONTROL TREATMENTS

Jonathan C. Smith

In a 6-month double-blind study, 49 anxious college student volunteers were assigned to transcendental meditation (TM) and 51 to a control treatment, periodic somatic inactivity (PSI). The control treatment was carefully designed to match the form, complexity, and expectation-fostering aspects of TM, but it incorporated an exercise that involved sitting erect with eyes closed twice daily rather than sitting and meditating. For each treatment 30 demographic and pretest personality variables were correlated with continuation in treatment and outcome defined in terms of trait anxiety change scores. As predicted, the TM dropout was more disturbed and less self-critical than the person who continued meditating. For TM, outcome correlated significantly with anxiety, Sizothymia (16 Personality Factor Questionnaire, Factor A), and Autia (16 Personality Factor Questionnaire, Factor M). Contrary to what was predicted, there was virtually no overlap between the variables correlated with continuation and outcome for TM and for PSI. It is concluded that differing treatment rationales rendered the treatments appealing, credible, and effective for different types of individuals.

Meditation research seems destined to repeat the sins of a generation of psychotherapy outcome research. In both areas the tendency has been to ask "does it work?" As Bergin (1971) has chronicled, this amorphous question has littered the journals with controversial and ambiguous results. Instead, Paul (1967) suggested:

The question towards which all outcome research should ultimately be directed is the following: *What* treatment, by *whom*, is most effective for *this* individual with *that* specific problem, and under *which* set of circumstances? (p. 111)

Meditation researchers have tended to ignore such questions of specificity (Smith, Note 1).

A surplus of studies show that individuals generally display reductions in trait anxiety after learning meditation (Smith, 1975b). However, not everyone benefits, and up to half discontinue (Smith, 1976; Otis, Note 2). To date no one has systematically explored

the type of person who gains from meditation, and only one person, Otis (Note 2), has looked at the meditation dropout. On the basis of two questionnaire studies, Otis found that subjects who stop practicing transcendental meditation (TM) compared with those who continue feel "less positive about themselves," have "more serious problems," and are more "withdrawn, irritable, and anxiety ridden." In addition, he suggested that subjects who continue with TM are somewhat less disturbed, although they may admit to more problems; that is, they may be more self-critical.

The present study examined characteristics of subjects who drop out of TM and subjects who continue practicing for up to 6 months and who display significant reductions in trait anxiety. On the basis of Otis's findings, it was predicted that subjects who continue practicing TM, compared with those who discontinue, are at pretest less disturbed, less anxious, and less withdrawn but more self-critical. Also, a previous study based on the same subject sample used in the present study (Smith, 1976) concluded that TM and a yogalike treatment involving sitting erect are equally

Requests for reprints should be sent to Jonathan C. Smith, Department of Psychology, Roosevelt University, 430 South Michigan Avenue, Chicago, Illinois 60605.

psychotherapeutic, and that the therapeutic processes operating in both are the same—some combination of expectation of relief and daily sitting. For this reason it was predicted that the correlates of continuation and outcome are the same for TM and the treatment involving sitting erect.

Method

Procedure

The present study used data collected in a previous study (Smith, 1976) that compared the psychotherapeutic effects of TM and a control treatment, periodic somatic inactivity (PSI). Subjects were 100 (51 male, 49 female) Michigan State University students who were suffering from a high level of trait anxiety. All were carefully screened for motivation, were not involved in psychotherapy, and had at no time practiced meditation or yoga. Mean age was 22.

All subjects were pretested, and 49 were randomly assigned to TM and 51 to PSI. TM was taught by two official TM instructors from the Students' International Meditation Society and was identical to ordinary TM in every respect except that it was offered free. The TM technique involves sitting erect with feet flat on the floor and eyes closed while passively and continuously attending to a special thought called a "mantra." This is done for 15–20 minutes twice daily. Complete TM instruction includes two introductory lectures that outline supporting theory and research, a 15-day drug fast, standardized individual instruction, 3 days of follow-up instruction and discussion, and monthly follow-up checking.

PSI was designed to control for the potentially therapeutic effects of daily sitting and expectation of relief. Specifically, the treatment matched TM in every respect with one exception—instead of sitting and meditating, the instructions were to simply sit. Subjects were told that while in this position they could think about anything (even worry) and the technique would still work. Like TM, PSI instruction began with two introductory lectures that outlined a rationale explaining why sitting twice daily should be an immensely effective cure for most forms of psychopathology. In addition, bogus research was presented to support the claims made. Between lectures, subjects participated in a 15-day fast from illegal drugs. After the fast and lectures, subjects were individually initiated and met for 3 days of follow-up checking. PSI was taught double blind; both the subjects and the instructor were deceived into believing that the treatment was legitimate and widely researched and not a bogus control treatment.

One important feature of PSI was its rationale. Care was taken to construct a rationale that was credible and complex. To enhance credibility, actual psychological concepts and research were woven together in a superficially elegant manner. That not one component of PSI theory was false or deceptive (although supporting "process" and "outcome" research was faked) makes it unique among bogus treatment rationales. A summary of the rationale given to subjects is presented below (Smith, 1975a):

> Built into life are factors that disrupt inner calm and generate and maintain anxiety. Research has shown that one of these factors is the desynchronization of circadian rhythms, daily rhythmic changes in physiological functioning. PSI works to bring circadian rhythms into synchrony.
>
> The way PSI works is complex. All physical activity, no matter how small, generates a fatiguelike and stresslike nonspecific physiological by–product called *reactive inhibition*. Simple physical inactivity tends to trigger the automatic dissipation of reactive inhibition. Such dissipation appears physiologically as a decrease in physiological activity and as a small dip or signature in the constellation of circadian rhythms. PSI involves remaining physically inactive for 15 to 20 minutes at the same time each day. The result is that regular inactivity-induced signatures appear at and become classically conditioned to the same point in one's circadian rhythms each day. As one continues practicing PSI, conditioning continues, overlearning occurs, "dips become conditioned onto dips," and gradually, and automatically, the associated physiological changes become deeper and deeper.
>
> The regular appearance of inactivity-induced signatures in circadian rhythms serve as zeitgeber, stimuli that pull and keep circadian rhythms in synchrony. PSI thereby functions to pull and keep circadian rhythms in synchrony, and as a result reduces anxiety and increases psychological well-being.
>
> Periodic inactivity is the single commonality among a variety of highly effective growth and therapy techniques including progressive relaxation, biofeedback training, autogenic therapy, self-hypnosis, meditation, and yoga. However, since PSI incorporates only the essentials of these techniques, and does away with all the unnecessary and cumbersome extras associated with them, it is in fact more effective and efficient.

Both treatments continued for 6 months, after which subjects were posttested and debriefed. Twenty TM and 24 PSI subjects reported for posttesting. To this sample were added 2 TM and 3 PSI subjects who were not available for 6-month posttesting but who did take an abbreviated posttest after $3\frac{1}{2}$ months. These subjects were included to increase sample size, since there is strong evidence that 6 months of TM is no more therapeutic than $3\frac{1}{2}$ months (Smith, 1975a).

Outcome and Continuation Measures

Trait anxiety was selected as the main outcome variable, specifically pretest–posttest difference scores on the Anxiety Trait (A-Trait) scale of the State–Trait Anxiety Inventory (STAI; Spielberger, Gorsuch, & Lushene, 1970). Anxiety was selected because it is the most widely studied trait in meditation research (Smith,

1975b). Although proponents of TM claim that their technique has a desirable impact on other variables, notably self-esteem, psychosis, self-actualization, creativity, and even intelligence (Glueck & Stroebel, 1975; Kanellakos & Ferguson, 1973; Orme-Johnson, Domash, & Farrow, 1974), the supporting evidence is scanty. Indeed, TM subjects in the present study displayed no change on *any* of these variables (Smith, 1975a).

In addition, at posttest subjects were asked to estimate how often they had practiced each month throughout the project. Subjects were considered to have continued practicing if they practiced at least once during the last month.

Demographic and Pretest Personality Measures

Before the onset of the project, each subject was given the STAI A-Trait scale, the Epstein–Fenz Manifest Anxiety Scale (Fenz & Epstein, 1965), the 16 Personality Factor Questionnaire Forms A and B (16 PF; Cattell, Eber & Tatsuoka, 1970), the IPAT Neuroticism Scale Questionnaire (Scheier & Cattell, 1961), the Tennessee Self-Concept Scale (Fitts, 1965), and the Marlowe–Crowne Social Desirability Scale (Crowne & Marlowe, 1964). The Epstein–Fenz test was scored for symptoms of autonomic arousal and symptoms of striated muscle tension. The three Cattell tests were pooled to increase factor reliability and were scored for the 16 primary source traits. On the Tennessee scale, the Total Positive, Psychosis, Personality Disorder, Personality Integration, Defensive Positive, and Self-criticism scales were used. In addition subjects indicated their sex and age and stated if they had at any time prior to the project considered psychotherapy or meditation and yoga. In sum, outcome and continuation were correlated with 30 variables.

Results

Tables 1 and 2 show the correlations of demographic and pretest personality variables with outcome and continuation for TM and PSI subjects. For TM subjects, outcome correlated significantly ($r \geq .396$, $p \leq .047$) with (ranked in order of significance): not having considered psychotherapy prior to the onset of the project, Sizothymia (16 PF Factor A), Autia (Factor M), anxiety (STAI A-Trait), Weaker Superego Strength (Factor G), and lack of Personality Integration.

Continuation with TM correlated significantly ($r \geq .397$, $p \leq .034$) with a low degree of Psychoticism and a high degree of Self-criticism, as well as with having considered psychotherapy prior to the onset of the project.

For PSI the results were quite different. Outcome correlated significantly ($r \geq .462$, $p \leq .027$) with Shrewdness (Factor N). Con-

tinuation correlated significantly ($r \geq .338$, $p \leq .042$) with Alaxia (Factor L), Shrewdness (Factor N), Desurgency (Factor F), Untroubled Adequacy (Factor O), High Strength of Self-sentiment (Factor Q_3), and Ego Strength (Factor C).

Discussion

One must be extremely cautious when drawing conclusions from research involving many variables and few subjects. For this reason I chose to give particular credence only to those variables that correlated most highly with outcome and continuation and have in previous research displayed greatest validity, reliability, and immunity to the effects of motivational distortion.

An intriguing picture emerges of those individuals who continue with TM and display the greatest reduction in trait anxiety. Not only are they anxious, but they score high on 16 PF Factors Sizothymia and Autia. Cattell and his colleagues (Cattell, 1957; Cattell et al., 1970) describe Sizothmic individuals as "reserved, detached, critical, cool, aloof," and "stiff." Emotionally, they are "flat" or "cautious." They tend to be critical, precise, and skeptical, and like working alone with things or words rather than with people. In interpreting this factor, Cattell (1957) hypothesizes that it reflects a "steadiness in purpose and a high level of interest in symbolic and subjective activity...a secondary result of blocking of easy interaction with the changing external world" (p. 180). In light of the apparent introversion of those who benefit from TM, it is not surprising that they tend not to have considered psychotherapy as a treatment option.

Those who benefit from TM also score high on Autia. These individuals tend to be unconventional and interested in "art, theory, basic beliefs" and "spiritual matters." However, their most important characteristic is what Cattell variously describes as a tendency to be "imaginatively enthralled by inner creations," "charmed by works of the imagination," and "completely absorbed" in the momentum of their own thoughts, following them "wherever they lead, for their intrinsic attractiveness and with neglect of realistic considerations." Cattell speculated that fundamental to Autia may be a capacity to dissociate and engage in "autonomous, self-absorbed relaxation."

A quite different picture emerges of those who continue with and benefit from PSI. They tend to score high on 16 PF Factor N. Such individuals, according to Cattell, tend

Table 1

Demographic and Pretest Personality Correlates of A-Trait Change Scores for Transcendental Meditation (TM) and Periodic Somatic Inactivity (PSI)

Variable	TM			PSI		
	r	n	p	r	n	p
Sex[a]	.297	19	.109	.021	18	.467
Age	−.120	18	.317	.206	18	.206
Considered meditation[b]	.070	19	.388	.366	18	.067
Considered therapy[c]	−.546	19	.008	.387	18	.056
A-Trait	.488	19	.017	.359	18	.072
SSMT	−.136	19	.289	.086	18	.367
SAA	.021	19	.466	.106	18	.338
Factor A[d]	−.543	18	.010	.272	18	.138
Factor B	−.064	18	.400	.132	18	.301
Factor C	−.133	18	.300	−.013	18	.480
Factor E	−.305	18	.110	.104	18	.341
Factor F	−.395	18	.052	−.037	18	.443
Factor G	−.485	18	.021	.005	18	.492
Factor H	−.309	18	.106	.181	18	.236
Factor I	.378	18	.061	.296	18	.117
Factor L	.044	18	.431	.150	18	.276
Factor M	.519	18	.014	−.001	18	.499
Factor N	.286	18	.125	.462	18	.027
Factor O	.183	18	.234	−.197	18	.216
Factor Q_1	−.107	18	.336	−.345	18	.081
Factor Q_2	.288	18	.123	−.066	18	.397
Factor Q_3	−.001	18	.498	.009	18	.486
Factor Q_4	.148	18	.279	−.220	18	.190
Marlowe-Crowne	.208	19	.197	.262	18	.147
Defensive positive[e]	−.002	19	.497	.157	18	.267
Psychosis	.077	19	.378	.376	18	.062
Personality disorder	−.044	19	.429	.175	18	.243
Personality integration	−.396	19	.047	.117	18	.322
Self-criticism	−.361	19	.064	.034	18	.447
Total positive	−.044	19	.428	.187	18	.229

Note. A-Trait = Trait Anxiety scale of the State–Trait Anxiety Inventory; SSMT = symptoms of striated muscle tension; SAA = symptoms of autonomic arousal; Factor A = Sizothymia vs. Affectothymia; Factor B = Low Intelligence vs. High Intelligence; Factor C = Lower Ego Strength vs. Higher Ego Strength; Factor E = Submissiveness vs. Dominance; Factor F = Desurgency vs. Surgency; Factor G = Weaker Superego Strength vs. Stronger Superego Strength; Factor H = Threctia vs. Parmia; Factor I = Harria vs. Premsia; Factor L = Alaxia vs. Protension; Factor M = Praxernia vs. Autia; Factor N = Artlessness vs. Shrewdness; Factor O = Untroubled Adequacy vs. Guilt Proneness; Factor Q_1 = Conservatism of Temperament vs. Radicalism; Factor Q_2 = Group Adherence vs. Self-sufficiency; Factor Q_3 = Low Self-sentiment Integration vs. High Strength of Self-sentiment; Factor Q_4 = Low Ergic Tension vs. High Ergic Tension.
[a] Keyed so that 1 = male, 2 = female.
[b] Keyed so that 1 = did not consider meditation prior to the project, 2 = did consider meditation prior to the project.
[c] Keyed so that 1 = did not consider therapy, 2 = did consider therapy.
[d] 16 Personality Factor Questionnaire (16 PF) factors were obtained by pooling scores from Forms A and B of the 16 PF with scores from the Neuroticism Scale Questionnaire.
[e] This and the following variables were taken from the Tennessee Self-Concept Scale.

to have "exact calculating" minds and tend to be emotionally detached and disciplined, ambitious, and esthetically fastidious. They tend not to be gregarious or to get "warmly emotionally involved" with others.

My hypothesis that the TM dropout is disturbed, anxious, withdrawn, and somewhat lacking in self-criticism appears to be supported. Although only three dropouts reported

for posttesting, they had extremely high Psychoticism scores. Fitts (1965) reports the "normal limits" on Psychoticism to be from 34 to 54 and the average score of hospitalized psychotics to be 62. The average Psychoticism score of the TM dropout was 63 (SD = 4.58), whereas the average score of those who continued was 48.74 (SD = 6.46). In addition, the dropouts scored lower in Self-criticism.

Table 2
Demographic and Pretest Personality Correlates of Continuation[a] for Transcendental Meditation (TM) and Periodic Somatic Inactivity (PSI)

	TM			PSI		
Variable	r	n	p	r	n	p
Sex	.025	22	.456	−.158	27	.215
Age	.164	21	.239	.281	27	.078
Considered meditation	.208	22	.176	−.267	27	.090
Considered therapy	.397	22	.034	.158	27	.215
A-Trait	.180	22	.212	−.032	27	.436
SSMT	.021	22	.463	−.069	27	.367
SAA	.014	22	.476	−.039	27	.423
Factor A	.194	21	.200	−.310	27	.058
Factor B	−.170	21	.230	−.159	27	.214
Factor C	.012	21	.480	.338	27	.042
Factor E	−.094	21	.343	.003	27	.495
Factor F	.236	21	.152	−.440	27	.011
Factor G	−.028	21	.451	−.052	27	.398
Factor H	.056	21	.404	−.119	27	.278
Factor I	.211	21	.179	−.109	27	.294
Factor L	−.337	21	.067	−.548	27	.002
Factor M	.161	21	.243	.130	27	.260
Factor N	.038	21	.436	.455	27	.009
Factor O	.123	21	.297	−.377	27	.026
Factor Q_1	−.232	21	.156	.156	27	.219
Factor Q_2	−.329	21	.073	.267	27	.089
Factor Q_3	−.108	21	.320	.342	27	.040
Factor Q_4	.280	21	.109	−.298	27	.066
Marlowe-Crowne	−.034	22	.441	.093	27	.322
Defensive positive	−.105	22	.320	−.012	26	.476
Psychosis	−.586	22	.002	.039	26	.426
Personality disorder	−.054	22	.405	.135	26	.255
Personality integration	−.032	22	.443	−.044	26	.416
Self-criticism	.409	22	.029	−.193	26	.173
Total positive	.028	22	.450	.076	26	.357

Note. A-Trait = Trait Anxiety scale of the State–Trait Anxiety Inventory; SSMT = symptoms of striated muscle tension; SAA = symptoms of autonomic arousal; Factor A = Sizothymia vs. Affectothymia; Factor B = Low Intelligence vs. High Intelligence; Factor C = Lower Ego Strength vs. Higher Ego Strength; Factor E = Submissiveness vs. Dominance; Factor F = Desurgency vs. Surgency; Factor G = Weaker Superego Strength vs. Stronger Superego Strength; Factor H = Threctia vs. Parmia; Factor I = Harria vs. Premsia; Factor L = Alaxia vs. Protension; Factor M = Praxernia vs. Autia; Factor N = Artlessness vs. Shrewdness; Factor O = Untroubled Adequacy vs. Guilt Proneness; Factor Q_1 = Conservatism of Temperament vs. Radicalism; Factor Q_2 = Group Adherence vs. Self-sufficiency; Factor Q_3 = Low Self-sentiment Integration vs. High Strength of Self-sentiment; Factor Q_4 = Low Ergic Tension vs. High Ergic Tension.
[a] Keyed so that 1 = did not practice at least once during the last month of the project, 2 = did practice at least once during the last month of the project.

Again, a somewhat different picture emerges of those who stop PSI. Consistent with what was predicted, they score higher on 16 PF factors related to anxiety (Factors L, O, Q₃, and C). However, they do not score higher on Psychoticism or lower on Self-criticism. Tentatively, they appear to be suspecting and are prone to dwell on frustrations (Factor L), as well as being a bit naive and gregarious (Factors N and F).

Examining the overall pattern of these results, it appears that there is virtually *no* overlap between the variables correlated with continuation and outcome for TM and for PSI. Yet I had hypothesized that if the same therapeutic processes were operating in the two treatments, they should work for the same types of individuals. I propose that a key to interpreting this inconsistency can be found in the possible interaction between treatment rationale and treatment outcome.

The rationale given for a treatment is fast emerging as a variable that can mediate attention placebo and possibly actual treatment effects (Borkovec & Nau, 1972; McReynolds, Barnes, Brooks, & Rehagen, 1973; Rosen, 1975, 1976). A treatment with a rationale that lacks credibility can be less effective than a treatment with a credible rationale. A rationale that imparts the expectation that a set of procedures is not therapeutic, or does not constitute a treatment, can reduce the effectiveness of those procedures. In addition, different rationales might render treatments appealing, credible, and as a result, effective for different types of individuals. For example, Fish (1973) described a case in which a patient from the hippie counterculture responded to systematic desensitization when it was presented as a consciousness-raising technique, whereas an engineer responded to the same technique when it was explained in terms of reciprocal inhibition.

Following what is common procedure in outcome research using attention placebo controls, highly credible but *different* rationales were given for TM and PSI. These rationales may have rendered the treatments credible, appealing, and effective for different types of individuals. The TM rationale, a religious–philosophical system from Hindu Vedantic tradition, can be summarized briefly:[1]

The TM technique involves passively and continuously attending to a meaningless thought or word called a mantra. As this thought repeats in meditation, it is experienced at progressively earlier phases in its development as increasingly subtle, fine, and charming. This process is similar to following bubbles arising in an ocean to their source in the ocean bed.

As one attends to the mantra, distracting thoughts, images, and feelings spontaneously emerge. These are treated with detached acceptance; one simply favors the mantra as soon as he or she recognizes that attention has wandered. Such distractions are normal and indicate that stress is being released.

As a thought is experienced at developmentally earlier stages, relaxation increases, which, in turn, dissolves neurological knots of tension. One's mind becomes increasingly still, like a rippleless pond or the depths of an ocean. One approaches the source of thought, the eternal and absolute field of transcendental being, creative intelligence. All aspects of life are thereby enriched and improved.

It takes little imagination to see how the TM rationale may be highly appealing and credible to Sizothymic and Autic individuals. As described earlier, such people tend to be emotionally cool, steady, and detached, and might find the TM metaphors relating to stillness and detachment appealing. They tend to be "charmed" by "inner creations," a characteristic that aptly summarizes the gist

---

[1] The specific content of the rationale given in TM lectures and instruction is not available to the non-TM researcher. However, after interviewing two TM instructors and 15 practitioners, I concluded that much of the rationale is similar to accounts published in the popular press by TM instructors and advocates Maharishi Mahesh Yogi (1968) and Bloomfield, Cain, and Jaffe (1975). The rationale presented in this article is derived from the accounts of Maharishi and Bloomfield et al.

It should be noted that the TM program is shrouded with considerable secrecy. Not only are the specific content of lectures and instruction unavailable to the outside researcher, but TM practitioners are urged not to describe their technique or training to others. If psychologists wish to learn TM, they are asked to promise not to divulge the technique. Secrecy tends to be reinforced by the requirement that TM research proposals must first be approved by the TM organization. In my opinion, these restrictions pose serious ethical problems for the TM researcher. As exemplified in the present study, such secrecy limits the extent to which procedural components of the TM program can be isolated and investigated. At least one study on TM has been prematurely terminated partly because of the ethical difficulties associated with secrecy (White, 1976).

of the claimed TM process. And they tend to be unconventional and interested in art, theory, basic beliefs, and spiritual matters. The TM philosophy is blatantly spiritual and relies heavily on visual "artistic" metaphor.

In contrast to the TM rationale, the PSI rationale was highly intricate and mechanistic. The person who benefits from PSI was described as "shrewd, astute, exacting, calculating, ambitious," and having complex tastes. Such a person might well find the scientific-sounding precision and ambitious complexity of the PSI rationale highly credible and appealing.

Another interpretation of these findings is that the treatment processes basic to TM and PSI are in fact different and are effective for different types of individuals. Indeed, the act of meditation has frequently been claimed to have therapeutic properties (Smith, 1975b), and Pratap (1972) argues that sitting erect with eyes closed may in itself be therapeutic. However, if sitting and meditation are equally therapeutic for different individuals, then one would expect more people to benefit from TM than from PSI, since TM is done in a seated position. This was clearly not the case. The most direct way out of this inconsistency is to make the somewhat awkward assumption that something in TM, perhaps some undisclosed aspect of the TM rationale, suppresses the therapeutic impact of erect sitting.

However they may be interpreted, the findings of this experiment clearly show that personality characteristics are correlated with continuation and outcome in meditation. I propose that this finding underlines the importance of paying heed to questions of specificity. The trend in past research has been to speak of a global meditation response experienced to some degree by all meditators, with the same overall desirable effect. Meditation is quite likely a heterogeneous phenomenon, producing effects ranging from sleep to enlightenment, and incorporating such diverse processes as insight, desensitization, and suggestion. It is time that meditation researchers examine the question of *who* experiences *what* state and trait changes with *which* technique.

Reference Notes

1. Smith, J. C. *Problems in meditation and yoga research*. Paper presented at the International Yoga and Meditation Conference, Chicago, June 1976.
2. Otis, L. S. Meditation or simulated meditation by nonpredisposed volunteers: Some psychological changes. In E. Taub (Chair), *The psychobiology of meditation*. Symposium presented at the meeting of the American Psychological Association, Montreal, August 1973.

References

Bergin, A. E. The evaluation of therapeutic outcomes. In A. E. Bergin & S. L. Garfield (Eds.), *Handbook of psychotherapy and behavior change: An empirical analysis*. New York: Wiley, 1971.

Bloomfield, H. H., Cain, M. P., & Jaffe, D. T. *TM: Discovering inner energy and overcoming stress*. New York: Delacorte Press, 1975.

Borkovec, T. D., & Nau, S. D. Credibility of analogue therapy rationales. *Journal of Behavior Therapy and Experimental Psychiatry*, 1972, *3*, 257–260.

Cattell, R. B. *Personality and motivation structure and measurement*. New York: World Book, 1957.

Cattell, R. B., Eber, H. W., & Tatsuoka, M. M. *Handbook for the Sixteen Personality Factor Questionnaire*. Champaign, Ill.: Institute for Personality and Ability Testing, 1970.

Crowne, D. P., & Marlowe, D. *The approval motive: Studies in evaluative dependence*. New York: Wiley, 1964.

Fenz, W. D., & Epstein, S. Manifest anxiety: Unifactorial or multifactorial composition? *Perceptual and Motor Skills*, 1965, *20*, 773–780.

Fish, J. M. *Placebo therapy*. San Francisco: Jossey-Bass, 1973.

Fitts, W. H. *Tennessee Self-Concept Scale manual*. Nashville, Tenn.: Counselor Recordings and Tests, 1965.

Glueck, B. C., & Stroebel, C. F. Biofeedback and meditation in the treatment of psychiatric illnesses. *Comprehensive Psychiatry*, 1975, *16*, 303–321.

Kanellakos, D. P., & Ferguson, P. C. (Eds.) *The psychobiology of transcendental meditation*. Los Angeles: Maharishi International University Press, 1973.

Maharishi Mahesh Yogi. *Transcendental meditation*. New York: Signet, 1968.

McReynolds, W. T., Barnes, A. R., Brooks, S., & Rehagen, N. J. The role of attention-placebo influences in the efficacy of systematic desensitization. *Journal of Consulting and Clinical Psychology*, 1973, *41*, 86–92.

Orme-Johnson, D. W., Domash, L. H. & Farrow, J. T. (Eds.) *Scientific research on transcendental meditation: Collected papers*. Los Angeles: Maharishi International University Press, 1974.

Paul, G. L. Strategy of outcome research in psychotherapy. *Journal of Consulting Psychology*, 1967, *31*, 109–118.

Pratap, V. *Reactivity level in yogic and non-yogic sitting conditions* (Abstract guide of the XXth International Congress of Psychology). Tokyo: Sasaki, 1972.

Rosen, G. M. Subjects' initial therapeutic expectancies towards systematic desensitization as a function of varied instructional sets. *Behavior Therapy*, 1975, *6*, 230–237.

Rosen, G. M. Subjects' initial therapeutic expectancies and subjects' awareness of therapeutic goals in systematic desensitization: A review. *Behavior Therapy*, 1976, *7*, 14–27.

Scheier, I. H., & Cattell, R. B. *Handbook for the Neuroticism Scale Questionnaire*. Champaign, Ill.: Institute for Personality and Ability Testing, 1961.

Smith, J. C. Meditation as psychotherapy (Doctoral dissertation, Michigan State University, 1975). *Dissertation Abstracts International*, 1975, *36*, 3073B. (University Microfilms No. 75-27, 343). (a)

Smith, J. C. Meditation as psychotherapy: A review of the literature. *Psychological Bulletin*, 1975, *82*, 558–564. (b)

Smith, J. C. Psychotherapeutic effects of transcendental meditation with controls for expectation of relief and daily sitting. *Journal of Consulting and Clinical Psychology*, 1976, *44*, 630–637.

Spielberger, C. D., Gorsuch, R. L., & Lushene, R. E. *Manual for the State-Trait Anxiety Inventory*. Palo Alto, Calif.: Consulting Psychologists Press, 1970.

White, J. *Everything you want to know about TM—Including how to do it*. New York: Pocket Books, 1976.

Received May 11, 1977 ∎

46

THE RELATIONSHIP OF
CLIENT CHARACTERISTICS TO
OUTCOME FOR
TRANSCENDENTAL MEDITATION,
BEHAVIOR THERAPY,
AND SELF-RELAXATION

*Irving H. Beiman, Stephen A. Johnson, Antonio E. Puente,
Henry W. Majestic, and Lewis E. Graham*

Introduction

Considerable attention within the psychological literature has been devoted to anxiety as a clinical problem. Several procedures have been proposed for the treatment of problems related to general (nonphobic) anxiety: progressive relaxation training (Beiman, Israel, and Johnson, 1978); cognitive restructuring (Ellis, 1962; Goldfried and Davidson, 1976); self-relaxation (Benson, Greenwood & Klemchuk, 1975); and transcendental meditation (Maharishi Mahesh Yogi, 1973). These techniques have not previously been compared in the treatment of general or chronic tension and anxiety.

The present investigation combined progressive relaxation training and cognitive restructuring into one treatment package (behavior therapy). This package (BT) was compared to self-relaxation (SR), transcendental meditation (TM), and a waiting list control group (WL) on multiple self-report and psychophysiological measures using traditional statistical procedures for a treatment outcome investigation. In addition, the relationship of client characteristics to outcome was evaluated separately for each of the treatments via stepwise multiple regression analyses.

Method

Subjects

Participants were 18 males and 32 females who were selected from over 100 respondents to announcements of a research project involving tension reduction treatments for people who were generally tense and nervous. An initial screening interview was held: (1) to select participants who reported experiencing subjective discomfort due to general anxiety and tension (as opposed to a specific anxiety-provoking situation or phobia); and (2) to eliminate persons who were curiosity seekers, psychotic, experiencing serious medical problems, taking psychoactive medication regularly, or currently in therapy or had previously received one of the therapies being evaluated. Those selected were not told of the specific treatments being evaluated, and were randomly assigned via repeating latin square for each sex to one of the treatments with the following final n's for each condition: BT = 14, SR = 13, TM = 12, WL = 13.

Apparatus

Psychophysiological assessment was conducted in two adjoining sound-proof electrically shielded chambers. The control chamber contained a Grass Model 7 polygraph with standard preamplifier's except as described below. A Consol BSR/GSR preamplifier provided a constant current of 16 μamp with one channel for skin resistance level (SRL) and one for skin resistance response (SRR). This electrodermal response was recorded using Beckman silver-silver chloride electrodes 2 cm^2 in area with an electrolyte of saline solution in Unibase. Arterial pulse rate (HR) was recorded using a Grass photoelectric plethysmograph. Integrated frontalis muscle action potential (EMG) was recorded using standard Beckman electrodes and paste. Time from pre- to post-assessment was balanced for all four experimental conditions and averaged approximately 4 weeks.

Procedure

Pre- and Posttreatment Self-Report Measures

After the screening interview, participants signed a consent form and were then administered the following questionnaires: Internal-External Locus of Control (IE; Rotter, 1966); Repression-Sensitization (RS; Byrne, 1961); a modification of the Autonomic Perception Questionnaire (APQ; Mandler, Mandler and Uviller, 1958); Trait Anxiety Inventory (TAI; Spielberger, Gorsuch, and Lushene, 1969); and Fear Survey Schedule (FSS; Rubin, Lawlis, Tasto, and Namenck, 1969). These same questionnaires were also administered following the posttreatment psychophysiological assessment.

Pre- and Posttreatment Psychophysiological Measures

The participant was seated in a recliner chair and the transducers were attached to the following sites: electrodermal/left palm and forearm; HR/left earlobe; EMG/frontalis muscle. The participant was then asked to sit quietly with eyes open and not to consciously relax. This period of continuous physiological recording lasted for 15 minutes, with the final 3 minutes serving as the assessment of baseline physiological response. Immediately following this baseline assessment the participant was instructed to relax as much as possible with eyes closed. Physiological recording continued for 10 minutes with the final 3 minutes serving as the assessment of the participant's ability to relax.

Treatments

There were a total of seven treatment sessions for each treatment condition. BT involved two 1½ hour sessions per week of training in: (a) progressive relaxation (Bernstein and Borkovec, 1973) as modified by Beiman, Israel, and Johnson (1978); and (b) cognitive restructuring adapted from Ellis (1962) and Goldfried and Davison (1976). The therapists were two male graduate students in clinical psychology supervised by the senior author. TM involved six 1½ hour sessions spanning a period of 2 weeks and a seventh session approximately 2 weeks later. A *certified* trainer administered this procedure precisely according to the principles of Maharishi Mahesh Yogi (1973). SR involved two 1½ hour sessions per week of training in the procedure described by Beiman et al. (1978) and was patterned after Benson,

Greenwood, and Klemchuk (1975). Therapists for SR were two male graduate students in clinical psychology supervised by the senior author. Treatment manuals for each of the treatments are available upon request from the senior author.

Data Reduction

Raw quantification of all dependent variables was performed by paid research assistants blind to the experimental condition of each participant. For each of the baseline and relax periods of physiological recording, the raw and statistical quantification procedures were as follows. Raw SRL was sampled every 60 seconds, converted to micromhos by a reciprocal transformation and averaged. A SRR was defined as any decrease in resistance exceeding .1% of SRL; frequency was totalled for each period. HR was determined by counting blood volume pulses and converting to beats per minute. The amplitude of the integrated EMG in microvolts was sampled every 20 seconds and averaged. Physiological response during the baseline period was then subtracted from that during the relax period yielding a difference score representing the participant's self-control over tonic physiological arousal. The raw self-report and physiological data were first transferred to computer cards and all conversions, computations, and statistical analyses were performed via SOUPAC and BMD programs using the IBM 360 computer at the University of Georgia.

Results

Outcome

Four multivariate and seventeen univariate Groups × Pre/Post analyses of variance were performed on: (a) the five self-report measures (I-E, RS, APQ, TAI, & FSS); (b) the four baseline physiological measures (SRL, SRR, HR, EMG); (c) the four relax physiological measures; and (d) the four physiological difference score measures. In no case did the multivariate tests for differential treatment effects approach significance for the two-way interaction. Only one of the seventeen univariate two-way interactions was significant and this should be attributed to chance. Descriptively, the mean change from pre to post for each dependent variable generally favored the BT condition but the within group of error variance was so large in each case that the statistical test was nonsignificant (all $p > .20$).

Relationship of Subject Characteristics to Outcome

During the design of this investigation we became interested in the extent to which certain kinds of subject variables might predict a favorable therapeutic outcome for certain treatments. We were interested in whether such a predictive relationship could be determined and, if so, whether it might be different for each of the experimental conditions. Because of this interest, we included four self-report variables generally considered to be "trait" measures (I-E, R-S, APQ, and TAI) and conceptualized the participants' pretreatment scores on these measures as predictor variables. For this more specialized set of analyses, the predicted outcome or dependent variables selected were the change scores from pre- to posttreatment (post − pre = Δ) for the FSS and the four physiological difference score measures of self-control over tonic physiological arousal.

The predictability of the participants' response to each of the experimental conditions was tested by performing stepwise multiple regressions separately for each treatment using the I-E, R-S, APQ, and TAI as predictor variables and the FSS, SRL, SRR, HR, and EMG as dependent variables. Thus for each dependent variable in each of the four experimental conditions a stepwise multiple regression analysis was performed. Table 1 presents those predictor variables which significantly predicted ($p < .05$) a dependent variable in each experimental condition. The predictor variable accounting for the largest proportion of variance in a dependent variable is listed first. A second (and third) predictor variable is listed only if it predicted a significant ($p < .05$) additional portion of the variance independently of the first (and second) predictor variable listed. The proportion of variance independently accounted for by each significant predictor variable is listed in parentheses.

Also listed are the correlation coefficients for the relationship between a dependent variable and all four predictor variables. The sign of the coefficients has been set so that positive correlations indicate that the higher the score on the predictor variable prior to treatment, the greater the improvement (or reduction) in the dependent variable after treatment. Conversely, negative correlations indicate the lower the score on the predictor variable, the greater the improvement in the dependent variable. High scores on the I-E, R-S, APQ, and TAI indicate, respectively, external locus of control, sensitization, more autonomic perception, and more trait anxiety.

Transcendental Meditation

Inspection of Table 1 indicates three of the five dependent variables were significantly predicted by the trait measures. In each case the regression equation predicted more than 50% of the variance in the three dependent variables. Furthermore, in each case the I-E scale accounted for the largest proportion of the predicted variance. The more internal locus of control participants reported prior to treatment, the more they benefitted from TM, as measured by the FSS and the two electrodermal measures of autonomic arousal.

Self-Relaxation

Thirty percent of the FSS, SRR, and HR variance was predicted by the R-S, APQ, and IE scales, respectively, The more cognitive sensitization, the less autonomic perception and the more internal locus of control participants reported prior to treatment, the more they benefitted from SR.

Table 1. Significant Predictions From the Stepwise Multiple Regression Analyses for Each Treatment Condition and Correlations Between Predictor and Dependent Variables[a]

Dependent variable	Predictor variables	'IE	'RS	'APQ	'TAI
Transcendental meditation					
Δ FSS	IE RS (.430 + .092)	−.656	+.356	−.343	−.024
Δ SCL	IE RS TAI (.622 + .052 + .021)	−0.787	−0.164	−0.196	+.126
Δ SRR	IE RS TAI (.340 + .230 + .080)	−.587	−.439	−.131	+.153
Self-relaxation					
Δ	RS (.318)	+.059	+.564	+.321	+.300
Δ SRR	APQ (.306)	−0.134	+0.006	−.554	−.432
Δ HR	IE (.312)	−.559	−.124	−.210	−.370
Behavior therapy					
Δ HR	APQ TAI (.312 + .150)	+.174	+.439	+.558	+.479
Wait-list control					
Δ HR	TAI (.309)	+.215	+.431	+.510	+.556

[a]See text for full explanation of table. Proportion of variance independently accounted for by each significant predictor is listed below it in parentheses.

The APQ and TAI combined to predict 45% of the variance in HR. The more autonomic perception and trait anxiety participants reported prior to treatment, the more control over HR they exhibited after treatment.

Wait List Control

The TAI predicted 30% of the variance in HR with more trait anxiety associated with greater control over HR after treatment.

Discussion

The results of the stepwise multiple regression analyses presented in Table 1 indicate that participant characteristics prior to treatment predicted a surprisingly large proportion of the variance in the participants' response to treatment. The results suggest participant characteristics interacted with treatment in such a way as to produce differential outcomes within each of the treatments. This was particularly true for transcendental meditation and self-relaxation, although the pattern of results for TM was more consistent than that for SR.

For transcendental meditation, the Internal-External Locus of Control scale predicted 34–62% of the variance in three of the five dependent variables analyzed. Higher internal locus of control presumably reflecting greater psychological adjustment (Rotter, 1966) prior to training, was consistently associated with more improvement in the dependent variables after training in meditation. Conversely, the less well-adjusted participants benefitted less from meditation. This finding seems to have particularly important implications for the future use of TM as a psychotherapeutic technique. The present results, when considered with the review by Smith (1975), suggest the therapeutic potential of TM for clinical problems has not been established. This does not seem surprising given the standardization of training in TM, and thus the apparent absence of means by which meditation training could be tailored to the particular problems of a given client.

On the other hand, the present results provide empirical support for the view that TM leads to measurable adaptive benefits in individuals who perceive themselves as experiencing more internal than external control over events occurring in their world. This is consistent with the introductory lectures on TM which present it as promoting positive growth rather than the therapeutic remediation of psychological dysfunction (Maharishi Mahesh Yogi, 1973).

The finding that locus of control predicted self-report and physiological responses to meditation also has methodological implications for future research. This result suggests the IE scale should be considered a potential control variable in future meditation research. This could be accomplished by assuring equivalence of groups on locus of control measures prior to any experimental manipulation. An alternative would be to simply assess locus of control, randomly assign participants to various experimental conditions, and then use analysis of covariance (with locus of control as the covariate) to statistically remove any potential biasing of the results. Research designs which compare experienced versus nonexperienced meditators are potentially subject to the criticism that the groups may not have been equivalent on locus of control prior to training. This threat to internal validity may be particularly relevant if "internals" practice meditation more regularly than "externals" and consequently have a higher probability of being selected for inclusion in an experienced meditation group.

The results of the regression analyses for self-relaxation training were not as consistent as those for TM. Three different predictors individually accounted for 30% of the variance in three of the dependent variables such that a different predictor was associated with each dependent variable. Less perception of physiological cues and more internal locus of control were associated with more control over autonomic arousal as a result of SR training. This suggests that participants who did not rely on interoceptive physiological cues, but instead used a more global cognitive strategy were better able to develop control over their autonomic arousal. This is consistent with previous research (Bergman and Johnson, 1971; Ray

Client Characteristics vs. Outcome

and Lamb, 1974). SR has been proposed as an alternative clinical procedure to progressive relaxation training (Greenwood and Benson, 1977), although Beiman, Israel, and Johnson (1978) found PRT was superior to SR for training self-control over autonomic arousal. The Beiman *et al.* investigation employed the standard statistical analyses for an outcome study and did not evaluate the relationship of client characteristics to outcome. It is possible that SR could be equivalent to PRT for certain clients and this issue seems to deserve further investigation considering the relative efficiency afforded by SR training. The statistical analyses used in the present investigation would be appropriate for addressing such a question.

The regression analyses for behavior therapy indicated more autonomic perception and trait anxiety prior to training were associated with more control over autonomic arousal after training. This provides empirical support for Paul and Bernstein's (1973) speculation that perception of physiological cues may be important in developing relaxation skills via PRT and is consistent with a recent review of PRT research (Borkovec and Sides, 1978). Thus the present results suggest that progressive relaxation training and cognitive restructuring should be the treatment package of choice when clients have high general anxiety and are aware of interoceptive physiological indicants of tension. Because PRT promotes self-control over autonomic arousal, it has been recommended as a stress-reduction treatment for stress-mediated medical problems (Beiman, Israel and Johnson, 1978). Consistent with this view, Beiman, Graham, and Ciminero (1978) found PRT to be an effective nonpharmacological alternative treatment for stress-mediated hypertension. This line of behavioral medicine research seems to have considerable clinical promise.

Unfortunately, the large within-group variance prevented an adequate test of the differential effectiveness of the training procedures employed. This variance may have been a function of our heterogeneous client population, a state of affairs which is usually undesirable in an outcome study. This heterogeneity, however, probably facilitated the detection of relationships between client characteristics and differential response to each of the treatments. We, therefore, conclude that the research strategy of employing a moderate degree of subject heterogeneity in outcome investigations, and subsequently using regression techniques to isolate sources of variance attributable to subject characteristics, may have considerable potential for determining the optimal matching of clients with treatments in future research.

Summary

Male and female respondents ($n=52$) to an ad for anxiety-reduction therapy were randomly assigned to transcendental meditation, behavior therapy, self-relaxation, or a wait list control group. They were evaluated before and after treatment on multiple self-report and psychophysiological measures. The results of multivariate analyses of variance indicated there were no significant differential treatment effects. The results of stepwise multiple regression analyses performed separately for each experimental condition indicated client characteristics accounted for significant portions of the variance in one or more of the dependent variables for each treatment. Clients who reported perceiving more internal locus of control benefitted more from transcendental meditation than clients who reported greater external locus of control.

Acknowledgment

These data were presented at the annual meeting of the Association for the Advancement of Behavior Therapy, New York, December, 1976. Appreciation is expressed to the Students International Meditation Society for their cooperation and to Fred Atwood, the TM trainer, whose nonreimbursed participation made this investigation possible. Appreciation is also expressed to James Mullins who served as a therapist.

References

Beiman, I, Graham, L. E., and Ciminero, A. R. Self-control progressive relaxation training as an alternative nonpharmacological treatment for essential hypertension: Therapeutic effects in the natural environment. *Behaviour Research and Therapy*, 1978, **16**, 371–375.

Beiman, I., Israel, E., and Johnson, S. A. The during and posttraining effects of live and taped progressive relaxation, self-relaxation and electromyogram biofeedback. *Journal of Consulting and Clinical Psychology, 1978, 46, 314–321.*

Benson, H., Greenwood, M., and Klemchuk, H. The relaxation response: psychophysiological aspects and clinical applications. *International Journal of Psychiatry in Medicine, 1975, 6, 87–98.*

Bergman, J. S., and Johnson, H. J. The effects of instructional set and autonomic perception on cardiac output. *Psychophysiology, 1971, 8, 180–190.*

Bernstein, D. A., and Borkovec, T. D. *Progressive relaxation training: A manual for the helping professions.* Champaign, Illinois: Research Press, 1973.

Borkovec, T. and Sides, J. Critical procedural variables related to the physiological effects of progressive relaxation: A review. *Behavior Therapy, 1978.*

Byrne, D. The repression-sensitization scale: Rationale, reliability and validity. *Journal of Personality, 1961, 29, 334–349.*

Ellis, A. *Reason and emotion in psychotherapy.* New York: Lyle Stuart, 1962.

Goldfried, M. and Davison, G. *Clinical behavior therapy.* New York: Holt, Rinehart & Winston, 1976.

Greenwood, M. M., and Benson, H. The efficacy of progressive relaxation in systematic desensitization and a proposal for an alternative competitive response—the relaxation response. *Behavior Research and Therapy, 1977, 15, 337–343.*

Mahesh Yogi, Maharishi. *The science of being and the art of living.* Los Angeles: SRM publications, 1973.

Mandler, G., Mandler, J. M., and Uviller, E. T. Autonomic feedback: The perception of autonomic activity. *Journal of Abnormal and Social Psychology, 1958, 56, 367–363.*

Paul, G. L., and Bernstein, D. A. *Anxiety and clinical problems: Systematic desensitization and related techniques.* Morristown, New Jersey: General Learning Press, 1973.

Ray, W. J., and Lamb, S. B. Locus of control and the voluntary control of heart rate. *Psychosomatic Medicine, 1974, 36, 180–182.*

Rotter, J. B. Generalized expectancies for internal versus external control of reinforcement. *Psychological Monographs, 1966, 80* (Whole No. 609).

Rubin, S. E., Lawlis, G. F. Tasto, D. L., and Namenck, T. Factor analysis of the 122 item fear survey schedule. *Behaviour Research and Therapy, 1969, 7, 381–386.*

Smith, J. C. Meditation as psychotherapy: A review of the literature. *Psychological Bulletin, 1975, 82, 558–564.*

Spielberger, C., Gorsuch, R., and Lushene, R. *Manual for the self-evaluation questionnaire.* Palo Alto: Consulting Psychologists Press, 1969.

47

PATTERNING OF COGNITIVE AND SOMATIC PROCESSES IN THE SELF-REGULATION OF ANXIETY: EFFECTS OF MEDITATION VERSUS EXERCISE

Gary E. Schwartz, Richard J. Davidson,[†] and Daniel J. Goleman[‡]*

Davidson and Schwartz (1) have proposed a psychobiological analysis of anxiety that emphasizes the patterning of multiple processes in the generation and self-regulation of this state. The present article specifically reviews recent research on cognitive and somatic components of anxiety. A dual component scale which separately assesses cognitive and somatic trait anxiety is described and applied to the study of the differential effects of a somatic (physical exercise) and a cognitive (meditation) relaxation procedure. A total of 77 subjects was employed; 44 regularly practiced physical exercise and 33 regularly practiced meditation for comparable periods of time. As predicted, subjects practicing physical exercise reported relatively less somatic and more cognitive anxiety than meditators. These data suggest that specific subcomponents of anxiety may be differentially associated with relaxation techniques engaging primarily cognitive versus somatic subsystems. It is proposed that relaxation consists of (1) a generalized reduction in multiple physiological systems (termed the relaxation response by Benson) and (2) a more specific pattern of changes superimposed upon this general reduction, which is elicited by the particular technique employed. The data from this retrospective study need to be followed up by prospective studies to establish the precise mechanisms for these effects.

INTRODUCTION

A variety of recent evidence has begun to challenge long-held assumptions concerning hypothetical, relatively global internal states such as anxiety and depression, which presumably result in particular biobehavioral dysfunctions. These findings have implications for both the assessment and treatment of psychosomatically based disorders. It is our intention in this article to selectively review these data and to present the results of a preliminary study designed to explore the differential effectiveness of two types of relaxation procedures in differentially attenuating different components of anxiety.

A number of writers have recently commented upon the multidimensional nature of fear and anxiety (e.g., 2, 3). When anxiety is elicited in an individual in response to a stressful event, the quality of feelings aroused in one situation may be different than in another. In addition, some people may experience anxiety in one predominant mode, while others might become anxious in a differ-

*From the Department of Psychology, Yale University, New Haven, Connecticut 06520.

†From the Department of Psychology, State University of New York at Purchase, Purchase, New York 10577.

‡Boulder, Colorado.

Received for publication February 25, 1977; final revision received December 5, 1977.

Address reprint requests to: Gary E. Schwartz, Department of Psychology, Yale University, New Haven, Connecticut 06520.

0033-3174/78/0040-0321$01.25

ent manner. Unfortunately, most anxiety questionnaires provide but a single, global score reflecting an unknown mixture of typologically different forms of anxiety. The existence of these different dimensions of anxiety has been established psychometrically through factor-analytic studies of traditional anxiety questionnaires. For example, a number of investigators have uncovered partially independent, trait anxiety factors on the basis of factor analyzing the MAS (e.g., 4, 5). More recently, Barrett (6) has performed an item analysis of anxiety items from a large battery of commonly used scales. The analysis "indicated two major subsets: (1) awareness of somatic changes, for example, I blush often or I am often aware of my heart beating; (2) conscious awareness of unpleasant feelings about self or external stimuli, for example, I frequently find myself worrying about something ..." (6, p. 202). Two similar factors emerged from studies using psychiatric patients as subjects. In factor analyses of self-ratings, Hamilton (7) and Buss (8) found that two factors, labeled psychic and somatic anxiety, accounted for the major portion of the variance in test performance.

On the basis of the results described above as well as upon a series of interviews with patients suffering from anxiety, Schalling and her colleagues (9) developed a multicomponent anxiety inventory consisting of separate psychic and somatic subscales with 20 items each. Unfortunately, the face validity of item assignment to each of the two subscales is not immediately apparent. The somatic anxiety scale "included items concerning autonomic disturbances (N=9), disquietable and mental discomfort of a diffuse kind and panic attacks (N=9), concentration difficulties and dis-

tractability (N=2). ... The psychic anxiety scale included items referring to worrying and pronounced anticipatory reactions as well as prolonged post-stress reactions (N=10) and increased muscular tension (N=4), ... the remaining six items concerned nervousness and lack of self-confidence in social situations" (9, p. 611). The item content overlap apparent to the present authors is borne out in Schalling et al.'s (9) finding of a 0.81 correlation between subscale scores in a group of psychiatric patients. However, it should be noted that although subscale scores were highly correlated, a different pattern of correlation was obtained between each subscale score and the Eysenck Personality Inventory Neuroticism and Extraversion Scales. Schalling et al. (9) found that both psychic and somatic anxiety were highly positively correlated with neuroticism (0.70 and 0.90, respectively). However, psychic anxiety was inversely related to extraversion (−0.50) while somatic anxiety was unrelated to this construct. Thus, psychic anxiety appears to be more prominent in introverts versus extroverts.

On the basis of both logical and empirical analyses of the anxiety construct, Borkovec (10) has arrived at a similar distinction with some minor modifications. He operationally defines anxiety by the multiple measurement of three separate but interacting response components: cognitive, overt behavioral, and physiological. He further suggests that each of these systems may be separately influenced by different environmental conditions and that individuals may differ "in the intensity and/or functional importance of the response from each component in reaction to a particular feared stimulus" (10, p. 267). The fact that anxiety may be defined by the measurement of these three response components does not necessarily imply that an individual is capable of self-reporting on these separate systems. It rather appears that cognitive and behavioral symptoms, as well as more covert somatic ones such as perspiration, are most prominent in consciousness. Physiological parameters may be seen as providing independent measures sensitive to cognitive versus behavioral/somatic processes but not necessarily always a part of the phenomenology of anxiety.

The multidimensional nature of anxiety is also revealed in psychophysiological research on fear reduction. For example Hodgson and Rachman (3) have observed desynchrony in different physiological dependent measures which all have considerable face validity. In a study designed to explore the efficacy of learned control of alpha for reducing stress associated with an aversive stimulus, Orne and Paskewitz (11) observed significant psychophysiological fractionation and specificity. They found no significant decrement in learned control of occipital alpha presence when subjects were confronted with the possibility of receiving an electric shock, while heart rate and spontaneous skin conductance responses were elevated. Orne and Paskewitz conclude by suggesting that their data "demonstrate that it is possible for the subjects to report the experience of apprehension of fear as well as manifesting the autonomic concomitants of such experiences without associated changes in alpha density" (p. 460). Findings such as these raise important questions concerning the assumed undifferentiated nature of arousal, which was hypothesized to underlie such states as anxiety. Instead of assuming, as some activation theorists have occasionally

done (12), that such fractionation is indicative of poor validity for the measures in question or inadequacies in the measurement procedures, we can view data such as these as reflecting meaningful patterns of physiological processes that are associated with particular behavioral and experiential states.

A number of clinical researchers have suggested, on the basis of findings such as those reviewed above, that different subsystems involved in dysfunctional states may be separately manipulated (2). Lazarus (13) has recently proposed that therapeutic regimes be individually constructed to reduce troublesome symptoms in the specific modes and systems that have gone awry. Although data are currently available that indicate that different relaxation procedures elicit distinct patterns of autonomic activity (14), little systematic work has been performed in specifying which particular therapeutic interventions should attenuate specific subcomponents of anxiety (1). Based on the psychometric and psychophysiological research reviewed above, Davidson and Schwartz (1) have developed a psychobiological model of subcomponents involved in anxiety and its reduction. These authors began with the assumption of two relatively independent types of anxiety: cognitive (psychic) and somatic.[1] It was further suggested that different procedures utilized in the reduction of anxiety differ in the degree to which they affect the cognitive versus somatic system. For ex-

---

[1]It should be emphasized that this is the most basic of all splits. For example, somatic may be further subdivided into skeletal and autonomic and cognitive may be dissected into right versus left hemisphere mediated (1).

ample, while physical exercise has been found to reduce global anxiety under certain situations (15), it was hypothesized that such an activity would specifically lead to reductions primarily in somatic anxiety with less of an effect upon cognitive anxiety. Alternatively, a technique requiring the self-generation of cognitive versus somatic activity is suggested to specifically attenuate anxiety in the cognitive system.

These predictions were based on well-known principles of psychobiological specificity. If we conceptualize particular biobehavioral systems as having a finite amount of channel space, and if we further assume that cognitive or somatic anxiety, for example, represents a recycling of unwanted information in each of the respective systems, then further activity of a neutral nature in a particular system will compete with the ongoing behavioral sequence for channel space. This competition results in an attenuation of the ongoing behavior. In the nonclinical realm, this basic principle has been observed consistently in research on cognitive processes. Segal and her colleagues (16, 17) have explored whether the active generation of imagery in a given mode (e.g., visual versus auditory) will inhibit the perception of stimuli in that mode more than in an irrelevant mode. Subjects were asked to generate both auditory and visual images, and their task involved detecting both auditory and visual signals. It was reliably demonstrated that auditory images interfered more with detection of auditory signals, and visual images with the detection of visual signals. Similar data have been obtained in the area of hemispheric-specific competition (18, 19).

One way of assessing the utility of

subdividing anxiety into cognitive and somatic components is to examine the differential effects of relaxation procedures specifically hypothesized to reduce anxiety in one versus the other mode. Any such attempt necessitates a measuring instrument with separate cognitive and somatic subscales. Since the one existing scale of this nature has been found to consist of subscales that are highly correlated (9), one purpose of the present study was to develop an anxiety symptom checklist with separate cognitive and somatic scales. The second purpose was to determine the utility of such a dichotomy by assessing the efficacy of physical exercise (a somatic procedure) versus meditation (a cognitive procedure relative to physical exercise) (1) in the differential reduction of the cognitive and somatic components of anxiety.

METHODS

Subjects

A total of 77 persons was employed as subjects (Ss). Forty-four Ss were participants in a physical exercise class[2] and attended a mean of 3.56 one-hour sessions per week. Thirty-three Ss practiced cognitively based, passive meditation (1) at least once daily. The type of meditation practiced was primarily transcendental meditation (20) although a small number of Ss practiced other passive techniques such as attending to and counting breathing. All subjects were practicing either meditation or physical exercise for at least 1 month with the median duration of practice being approximately 6 months within each group.

The age and sex distributions of the two groups were beyond our control and hence not matched. The physical exercisers had a mean age of 27.36 years (SD = 6.03) while the meditators had a mean

---

[2]The exercise class was conducted by Maggie Letvin at MIT.

age of 20.86 years (SD = 2.74). The exercisers were predominantly female while the sex ratio of the meditators was approximately equal. However, since the findings for the total sample are observed in analyses based on smaller matched subgroups, it is likely that the age and sex differences are not responsible for the observed differences in patterns of cognitive and somatic anxiety. All subjects were solicited unpaid volunteers.

Cognitive-Somatic Anxiety Questionnaire (CSAQ)

A cognitive-somatic trait anxiety inventory was constructed by selecting items from well-known questionnaires that three independent judges unanimously agreed reflected cognitive or somatic anxiety. The 14 items comprising the inventory, half cognitive and half somatic, are presented in Table 1. Subjects were asked to "rate the degree to

TABLE 1. Item Content of the Cognitive-Somatic Anxiety Questionnaire (CSAQ) Separately for Cognitive and Somatic Items.

Cognitive	Somatic
I find it difficult to concentrate because of uncontrollable thoughts.	My heart beats faster.
I worry too much over something that doesn't really matter.	I feel jittery in my body.
I imagine terrifying scenes.	I get diarrhea.
I can't keep anxiety provoking pictures out of my mind.	I feel tense in my stomach.
Some unimportant thought runs through my mind and bothers me.	I nervously pace.
I feel like I am losing out on things because I can't make up my mind soon enough.	I become immobilized.
I can't keep anxiety provoking thoughts out of my mind.	I perspire.

which you generally or typically experience this symptom when you are feeling anxious" by circling a number from 1 through 5 with 1 representing "not at all" and 5 representing "very much so." The sums of the circled ratings were separately computed for the cognitive and somatic items and constituted the main dependent measures. The cognitive and somatic items appeared in random order.

To ascertain the validity of the CSAQ, correlations were computed between the latter test and a standard measure of trait anxiety. The Speilberger State-Trait Anxiety Inventory (STAI) (21) was administered in the trait form to a sample of 78 nonexercisers, and it was observed that separate correlations between the cognitive and somatic scales of the CSAQ with the STAI were both highly significant ($r = 0.67$ and 0.40, respectively, for both $P < 0.001$).

The correlation between the cognitive and somatic scales of the CSAQ for the entire sample was $r = 0.42$. This represents a substantially lower correlation than was obtained by Schalling (0.81) between the psychic and somatic subcomponents of her multicomponent anxiety inventory (9). These data indicate that the cognitive and somatic scales are modestly correlated, and that their shared variance is sufficiently low to allow for patterning of results as a function of different training techniques.

Procedure

Subjects were presented with the CSAQ in the context of a larger battery of tests. The subjects in the exercise group were asked to fill out the questionnaires at the end of a class while the remaining subjects were given the questionnaires in a classroom (at Harvard) and asked to complete them at home and return them the following day. All subjects were told that these questionnaires were part of a study on psychological concomitants of different forms of self-regulation techniques.

RESULTS

An analysis of variance with group (exercisers vs. meditators) as a between factor and mode of anxiety (cognitive vs. somatic) as a repeated factor revealed, as predicted, a significant interaction [F (1, 75) = 5.32, $P < 0.03$]. This interaction is illustrated in Fig. 1 and indicates that meditators report less cognitive and more somatic anxiety than exercisers and, conversely, exercisers report less somatic and more cognitive anxiety than meditators. Importantly, the main effect for group was not significant ($F < 1$), indicating that the two groups did not differ on overall anxiety but rather on the specific patterning of anxiety subsystems. Interestingly, the significant interaction is largely a function of the significantly higher cognitive versus somatic anxiety within the exercisers ($t = 2.32$, $df = 43$, $P < 0.05$). The meditators revealed no significant difference between the two anxiety modes.

DISCUSSION

The present findings support the general thesis that anxiety is not a diffuse, undifferentiated internal state, but rather

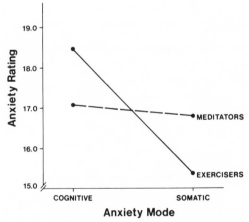

Fig. 1.   Mean anxiety rating on the separate cognitive and somatic scales of the Cognitive-Somatic Anxiety Questionnaire (CSAQ) by group. For exercisers, $N = 44$; for meditators, $N = 33$.

reflects a set of patterns of specific psychobiological processes having important implications for the assessment and treatment of affective disorders. Clearly, subdividing anxiety into its cognitive and somatic components as measured by the present questionnaire is itself an oversimplification (1), but it is a useful starting point for stimulating theory and research. In a recent study, which emerged from the present findings, it was found that cognitive and somatic anxiety could be reliably distinguished on the basis of the patterning of cardiovascular, electrodermal, and electromyographic measures (22). More sophisticated psychobiological subdivisions of anxiety would include examination of hemispheric asymmetry in emotion (23, 24) and differential patterning of fundamental emotions in anxiety and depression (25). The relevance of the latter concept to the psychophysiological assessment of depression and anxiety has been recently documented by measuring patterns of facial muscle activity in different affective states (26). The systematic assessment and self-regulation of psychophysiological patterning and specificity is rapidly becoming an important tool in the understanding and treatment of a variety of clinical dysfunctions (27, 28).

The data generated in this study and the body of literature reviewed in the introduction question the notion of a generalized, relaxation response as a complete description of the nature of relaxation. The present findings suggest that different techniques employed for the elicitation of relaxation may be associated with specific consequences, which in turn may be a function of the underlying systems directly affected by the procedure in question. Just as recent psychophysiological research has challenged the adequacy of concepts of generalized arousal (28), so too in the clinical domain, conceptions of undifferentiated relaxation and anxiety are incomplete. Importantly, however, the patterning of biobehavioral systems may be superimposed upon a more nonspecific continuum of relaxation and anxiety and assessment may be made of both the general level of relaxation and anxiety as well as their specific subcomponents. We would propose that relaxation consists of (1) a generalized reduction in multiple physiological systems (termed the relaxation response by Benson) and (2) a more specific pattern of changes superimposed upon this general reduction, which is elicited by the particular technique employed. The present line of reasoning highlights the importance of considering these components in any complete account of anxiety and its reduction.

The findings obtained in the present study are consistent with the hypothesis that the practice of meditation versus exercise may be associated with the differential patterning of cognitive and somatic symptoms of anxiety (1). The regular practice of physical exercise, a somatic relaxer, was associated with less somatic and more cognitive anxiety than the regular practice of meditation, a technique believed to be associated with cognitive relaxation (1, 30). However, a cautionary note should be raised in interpreting the present data. Although the subjects practicing either physical exercise or meditation had been doing so on a regular basis for a median duration of approximately 6 months, the present retrospective design does not rule out the possibility of predispositional (including expectation) contributions to the observed effects (31). It may be the case that individuals attracted to the practice of meditation versus physical relaxation differ in their patterning of cognitive and somatic anxiety. The influence of such predispositional variables may be unambiguously disentangled in the future with longitudinal, prospective designs that include appropriate behavioral and physiological measures.

This research was supported by an award to G. E. Schwartz from the Stress Grant program of the Roche Psychiatric Service Institute and by an NSF predoctoral fellowship to R. J. Davidson. The assistance of M. Finn in computer analysis and J. Siewe in administration of the questionnaire is gratefully acknowledged. Gerald C. Davison provided helpful comments on an earlier draft of the manuscript.

REFERENCES

1. Davidson RJ, Schwartz GE: The psychobiology of relaxation and related states: a multi-process theory, in Mostofsky, DI), Behavior Control and Modification of Physiological Activity. Englewood Cliffs, NJ, Prentice-Hall, 1976, pp. 399–442
2. Lang P: The mechanics of desensitization and the laboratory study of human fear, in Franks CM, Behavior Therapy: Appraisal and Status. New York, McGraw-Hill, 1969, pp. 160–191
3. Hodgson R, Rachman R: II. Desynchrony in measures of fear. Behav Res Ther 12:319–326, 1974
4. O'Connor JP, Lorr M, Stafford JW: Some patterns of manifest anxiety. J Clin Psychol 12:160–163, 1956
5. Fenz WD, Epstein S: Manifest anxiety: unifactorial or multi-factorial composition? Percept Mot Skills 20:773–780, 1965

6. Barrett ES: Anxiety and impulsiveness: toward a neuropsychological model, in Spielberger CD, Anxiety: Current Trends in Theory and Research (Vol. I). New York, Academic Press, 1972, pp. 195–222

7. Hamilton M: The assessment of anxiety states by rating. Br J Med Psychol 32:50–55, 1959

8. Buss AH: Two anxiety factors in psychiatric patients. J Abnorm Soc Psychol 65:426–427, 1962

9. Schalling D, Cronholm B, Asberg M: Components of state and trait anxiety as related to personality and arousal, in Levi L, Emotions: Their Parameters and Measurement. New York, Raven Press, 1975, pp. 603–617

10. Borkovec TD: Physiological and cognitive processes in the regulation of anxiety, in Schwartz GE and Shapiro D, Consciousness and Self-Regulation: Advances in Research (Vol. 1). New York, Plenum Press, 1976, pp. 261–312

11. Orne MT, Paskewitz DA: Aversive situational effects on alpha feedback training. Science 186:458–460, 1974

12. Duffy E: Activation, in Greenfield HS and Sternbach RA, Handbook of Psychophysiology. New York, Holt, Rinehart and Winston, 1972, pp. 577–622

13. Lazarus AA: Multimodal behavior therapy: treating the "basic id." J Nerv Ment Dis 156:404–411, 1973

14. Paul GL: Physiological effects of relaxation training and hypnotic suggestion. J Abnorm Psychol 74:425–437, 1969

15. Morgan WP, Roberts JA, Feinerman AD: Psychologic effect of acute physical exercise. Arch Phys Med Rehabil 52:422–425, 1971

16. Segal SJ: Processing of the stimulus in imagery and perception, in Segal SJ, Imagery: Current Cognitive Approaches. New York, Academic Press, 1971, pp. 69–100

17. Segal SJ, Fusella U: Influence of imaged pictures and sounds on detection of auditory and visual signals. J Exp Psychol 83:458–464, 1970

18. Kinsbourne M, Cook J: Generalized and lateralized effects of concurrent verbalization on a unimanual skill. Q J Exp Psychol 23:341–345, 1971

19. Hicks RE: Intrahemispheric response competition between vocal and unimanual performance in normal adult males. J Comp Physiol Psychol 89:50–60, 1975

20. Kanellakos DP, Lukas JJ: The Psychobiology of Transcendental Meditation: A Literature Review. Reading, Mass., W. A. Benjamin, 1974

21. Spielberger CD, Gorsuch RL, Lushene RE: Manual for the State-Trait Anxiety Inventory. Palo Alto, Calif., Consulting Psychologists Press, 1970

22. Davidson RJ, Davison GC, Freedland E: Psychophysiological specificity and the self-regulation of cognitive and somatic anxiety. Paper presented at the International Conference on Biofeedback and Self-Control, Tubingen, Germany, November 1977

23. Schwartz GE, Davidson RJ, Pugash E: Voluntary control of patterns of EEG parietal asymmetry: cognitive concomitants. Psychophysiology 13:498–504, 1976

24. Davidson RJ, Schwartz GE: Patterns of cerebral lateralization during cardiac biofeedback versus the self-regulation of emotion: sex differences. Psychophysiology 13:62–68, 1976

25. Izard CE: Patterns of Emotions. New York, Academic Press, 1972

26. Schwartz GE, Fair PL, Salt P, Mandel MR, Klerman GL: Facial muscle patterning to affective imagery in depressed and nondepressed subjects. Science 192:489–491, 1976

27. Schwartz GE: Biofeedback, self-regulation and the patterning of physiological processes. Am Sci 63:314–324, 1975

28. Davidson RJ: Specificity and patterning in biobehavioral systems: implications for behavior change American Psychologist, in press.

29. Benson H: The Relaxation Response. New York, William Morrow, 1975

30. Davidson RJ, Goleman DJ, Schwartz GE: Attentional and affective concomitants of meditation: a cross-sectional study. J Abnorm Psychol 85:235–238, 1976

31. Smith JC: Meditation as psychotherapy: a review of the literature. Psychol Bull 83:558–564, 1976

C. Comparison with Other Self-Regulation Strategies

This section is divided into two parts—theoretical and research comparisons, although, of course, the division is not always that clear-cut within articles. In the theoretical section (C1) we look at meditation and its relationship to behavioral self-control strategies, hypnosis, biofeedback, and relaxation strategies, in general. In the second section (C2) on research comparisons, we will look at specific research studies which have compared meditation with other self-regulation strategies.

One primary goal of these comparisons is to begin to determine which clinical self-regulation strategy may be most effective for which type of client with which type of treatment problem.

C1.   Theoretical Comparisons

Making descriptive comparisons between treatment strategies requires that an individual be conversant with what at times seem to be two different languages. It is important to learn both of the languages just to see where, in fact, differences do occur in the actual behavior of the treatments and where differences are merely semantic distinctions. The first article, by Shapiro and Zifferblatt (48), begins with a comparison of meditation and behavioral self-control strategies. The second, by Davidson and Goleman (49), looks at meditation and hypnosis. Stroebel and Glueck's article gives a fine comparison between passive meditation techniques and biofeedback. (For discussion of the EEG comparisons, the reader is referred to Article 40 by Glueck and Stroebel and for discussion of a specific research strategy, the reader is referred to Article 14 by Glueck and Stroebel.) Glueck and Stroebel have nicely laid out the parameters of biofeedback and a comparison of when biofeedback seems a useful strategy versus when passive meditation seems the treatment of choice. In addition, they compare the issue of adherence in a variety of different self-regulation strategies. The Davidson and Schwartz article (51) is an interesting model for the utility of various self-regulation strategies in the treatment of anxiety disorders. Some preliminary evidence for this was already presented earlier by Schwartz *et al*. (Article 47).

48

ZEN MEDITATION AND
BEHAVIORAL SELF-CONTROL:
SIMILARITIES, DIFFERENCES,
AND CLINICAL APPLICATIONS

Deane H. Shapiro, Jr. and Steven M. Zifferblatt

ABSTRACT: *An attempt is made to understand the behaviors involved in two different self-control strategies: Zen meditation and behavioral self-management. The first technique is derived from the Eastern "religious–philosophical" tradition of Zen Buddhism; the other technique is derived from Western laboratory and field settings and is based on social learning theory. Using tools of naturalistic observation and experimental analysis, Zen breath meditation is conceptualized as a sequence of behaviors involving certain cues and consequences, and thereby under explicit contingency arrangements. The same tools of experimental analysis are then applied to the behavioral self-management techniques, and a series of comparisons and contrasts are made between the two. After briefly reviewing the clinical outcome literature for both strategies, the article concludes with a discussion of the rehabilitative and preventive benefits that may be gained from a combination of the two techniques.*

Based on current biofeedback, meditation, and self-control research, a new paradigm of the person is emerging within the scientific community. This paradigm conceptualizes the healthy person as an individual who can pilot his or her own existential fate in the here-and-now environment, and who can have far greater self-regulatory control over his or her own body than heretofore imagined. Concomitant with this new paradigm is an attempt to develop and improve techniques by which people can self-observe their behavior, change it (if desired), and then continually modify and monitor it according to their needs.

This article compares self-control techniques developed within the Eastern "religion" of Zen Buddhism and the Western psychological framework of social learning theory. Because of seemingly different epistemological and cultural frameworks, it might at first appear an impossible task to bridge this gap between an Eastern religious technique, such as Zen meditation, and Western therapeutic

strategies, such as self-management skills. There is certainly no doubt that differences both in origin and goals do exist.

For example, formal Zen breath meditation (*Zazen*) is a single technique that was developed thousands of years ago as a method of attaining religious insight (Kapleau, 1967; Maupin, 1969; Weinpahl, 1964). Behavioral self-control techniques, on the other hand, involve a constellation of strategies tailored to specific problem areas, and are the product of recent empirical investigations derived from experimental research in Western laboratories and field settings (cf. Goldfried & Merbaum, 1973; Mahoney & Thoresen, 1974; Thoresen & Mahoney, 1974). In addition, Zen meditation is a technique within a religious–philosophical framework that has a view of man different from the philosophical view of man on which social learning theory rests (cf. Bandura, 1974a,

Part of the research involved in this article was funded by the National Institute of Education, U.S. Department of Health, Education, and Welfare (Contract Ne-C-00-300061). Certain sections of the article were presented by the first author at the Annual Awareness Symposium on Clinical Problems, at the Center for Research and Development in Teaching, Stanford University, 1973; at the annual meeting of the American Psychological Association, Montreal, August 1973; at the annual meeting of the American Educational Research Association, Washington, D.C., 1975; and at the National Symposium on Behavioral Counseling, Santa Barbara, California, 1975.

The first author is a member of the clinical faculty in the Department of Psychiatry and Behavioral Sciences, Stanford University, and a founding faculty member of the Pacific Graduate School of (Clinical) Psychology, Palo Alto, California. The second author is currently a visiting scholar at the National Heart and Lung Institute. Both authors want to express special thanks to Carl E. Thoresen and Johanna Shapiro for comments on previous drafts of the manuscript.

Requests for reprints should be sent to Deane H. Shapiro, Jr., P.O. Box 2084, Stanford, California 94305.

1974b; Hirari, 1974; Suzuki, 1960). Finally, based on current split-brain research (Galin, 1974), it may be argued that Zen meditation may primarily involve the right side of the brain (i.e., nonrational, nonanalytic, simultaneous integration of material), while behavioral self-control strategies may primarily involve the left side of the brain (i.e., analytical, rational, sequential processing of information).

Despite the fact that the techniques were developed in different eras, for different philosophical purposes, and with different assumptions about the nature of humankind, systematic investigation of the two techniques is fruitful for several reasons: (a) By looking closely at the *behaviors* involved in both techniques, it might be possible to determine when behavioral differences in fact exist between the two, and when the supposed differences are merely semantic distinctions. (b) Where behavioral differences do exist, further research might then document whether unique aspects of one could become profitable additions to the other. (c) Social learning theory employs a naturalistic observation technology to identify and measure behaviors and events (cf. Zifferblatt & Hendricks, 1974). By using these tools of experimental analysis (naturalistic observation), it is possible to gain an understanding of meditation as a series of behavioral events under explicit contingency arrangements. In this way, meditation is removed from the realm of "mystical practice" accessible only to the select few, and is redefined as a technique that, if useful, could be practiced and understood by many people.

Formal Zen Meditation: A Tentative Conceptualization

In this section of the article, a five-stage conceptualization of Zen breath meditation is suggested. The division of meditation into different steps is used here only as a heuristic device to help understand the "process" of meditation, and is not meant to give the impression that meditation consists of discrete, nonoverlapping steps. Further, the different steps discussed as follows should be considered only as plausible hypotheses until verified by additional research.

PREPARATION

The individual picks a quiet spot, either in a natural setting or in a room set aside for that purpose. If a room is selected, often incense is lit and the room is semidarkened. In formal Zen meditation, the person sits in a full- or half-lotus position, with his hands placed together in his lap. Although an awkward-looking posture, the lotus position is not intended as a demonstration of a person's ability to contort the body; rather, the lotus position is considered to be a posture of "physical centeredness," with the knees and buttocks forming the solid base of a triangle (Kapleau, 1967; Weinpahl, 1964). Akishige (1974) and his colleagues (cf. Ikegami, 1974) compared muscle tensions in the lotus position with other relaxed forms of sitting and found that muscle tensions in the lotus position are lower than in any other posture except that of lying down.

THE TARGET BEHAVIOR

Although the posture and environment are helpful prerequisites to proper meditation, they do not, in and of themselves, ensure its occurrence. For example, the studies of Ikegami have shown that it is the mental "attitude" of the meditator, and not his posture, that correlates with electroencephalograph changes. When the subject's "attitude was right" (i.e., when certain covert behaviors were engaged in, and certain others not engaged in), alpha rhythms appeared in both ordinary postures, such as sitting in a chair, as well as in the formal meditation posture. Without this attitude, there was no rise in alpha activity, even in the formal meditation posture (see Ikegami, 1974).

Essentially, the practice of Zen breath meditation may be conceptualized as a five-step process. The beginning meditator is told to breathe through the nose, letting the air come in by extending the diaphragm: "Don't draw it in, rather, let it come to you" (Lesh, 1970). The person is taught to count one number (e.g., 1, 2 . . . up to 10) after each exhalation, and to let the numbers "descend" into the abdominal region (cf. Shapiro, in press-b, for extended description).

Anecdotal data suggest that when the person is first asked to observe his or her breathing, there is often an alteration in this behavior. The person has difficulty letting the air "come," catches his breath, and breathes more quickly and shallowly than normal. Often the person complains about not getting enough air and of "drowning" (see Figure 1, Step 1; cf. Shapiro & Zifferblatt, in press).

Soon, however, the person who is meditating forgets about the task at hand, stops focusing on his

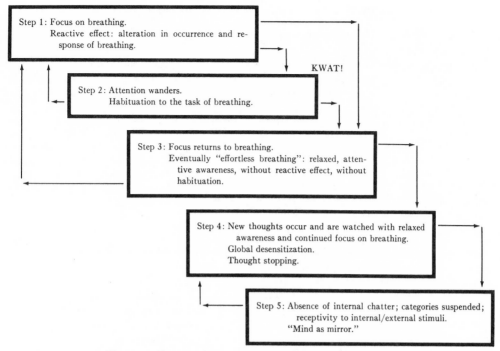

Figure 1. Process of Zen meditation (a behavioral analysis).

breath, and a variety of unrelated thoughts and images occur (Figure 1, Step 2).

In the third stage, the individual is taught to note every time his or her attention wanders from the task of breathing, and to turn the focus back to that task. "If images or thoughts come into awareness, do not follow them, do not try to expel them, but merely relax, let go, and focus on counting the inhalations and exhalations of your breath" (Figure 1, Step 3). With practice, the individual learns to focus on breathing without altering the behavior of breathing (the reactive effect of Step 1) and without habituating to the task (as in Step 2). This step may be described as "effortless breathing."

As new thoughts are self-observed, the meditator is able to take note of them and to continue focusing on breathing. Because he is in a relaxed, comfortable, and physically stable posture, he is able to self-observe with equanimity everything that comes into awareness: fears, thoughts, fantasies, guilts, decisions, and other covert events. No attempt is made to systematically structure the covert stimuli; rather, there occurs what may be referred to as a "global hierarchy" consisting of things that are currently "on a person's mind" (Goleman, 1971). In this way, the individual

learns to discriminate and observe all covert stimuli that come into awareness, without making any judgment, thereby desensitizing himself (unstressing) to those covert images and statements (Figure 1, Step 4).

Thus, at first, focus on breathing seems to reduce the aversiveness of the thoughts and images; then, focus on breathing becomes a competing response that eventually "empties the mind of internal chatter," that is, dispels covert thoughts and images. This reduction of thoughts and images (Figure 1, Step 5) seems to increase the receptivity of the individual to other covert stimuli typically ignored, which may be the reason Zen and Yoga masters "hear" their internal body signals so clearly; it further allows the individual to be more receptive to whatever stimuli are present in the external environment (Kasamatsu & Hirari, 1966; Lesh, 1970).

INFORMAL MEDITATION

In addition to formal meditation, an individual often is asked to practice Zen meditation informally throughout the day. This informal meditation requires that one be conscious of everything he or she does, to attend very closely to ordinary activities:

Be aware and mindful of whatever you do, physically or verbally, during the daily routine of work in your life. Whether you walk, stand, sit, lie down, or sleep, whether you stretch or bend your legs, whether you look around, whether you put your clothes on, whether you talk or keep silent, whether you eat or drink, whether you answer the calls of nature—in these and other activities you should be fully aware and mindful of the act performed at the moment, that is to say, that you should live in the present moment, in the present action. (Rahula, 1959, p. 7)

Thus, in informal meditation, the individual merely observes all actions that he or she performs throughout the day, without judging or evaluating. As Alan Watts noted, in discussing informal meditation: "Listen. Listen to the sound of your own complaint when the world gets you down, when you are angry, when you are filling out income tax forms. Above all, just listen" (Watts, 1972, p. 142). The "listening" without comment and without evaluation that occurs during informal meditation seems to be functionally similar to the detached observation (i.e., observation of covert stimuli with equanimity) that occurs in Step 4 of formal meditation.

SUMMARY

A descriptive analysis of formal Zen meditation suggests the following: When a person begins to focus on breathing, there is a "reactive effect": his breath comes faster, he feels as though he is not getting enough air and forces more air into himself (Step 1). Soon, his attention wanders from the task of breathing (habituates to the task, Step 2). The individual is taught to catch himself whenever his attention wanders, and to return to the task of breathing. This will either cause another reactive effect, or with practice the person will learn to breathe effortlessly (Step 3). At this point the person has learned to observe his or her breathing without a reactive effect and without habituation.

As new thoughts come into awareness, the individual is able to continue to focus on breathing while at the same time watching the thoughts with equanimity (Step 4). This process serves the dual function of (a) desensitizing the individual to the thoughts (i.e., detached observation of thoughts) and (b) eventually removing those thoughts by the continued focus on the competing response of breathing. In this way, the person feels relaxed, calm, and with a "mind emptied of internal chatter" (Step 5).

Breath meditation seems to serve several different functions. First, it is a type of relaxation training. The individual sits in a physically centered posture and breathes in a calm, effortless way. Second, the person learns to focus attention on one thing—his breath—and to do so in a relaxed, yet deliberate fashion. Third, the person learns to be self-conscious (i.e., to self-observe) without a reactive effect and without habituating to the task. Fourth, the individual is able to desensitize himself to whatever is on his mind: thoughts, fears, worries. And fifth, the meditator is able to eventually remove all covert thoughts and images, thereby allowing him to "let go" of cognitive labels, "reopen" the senses, and be more receptive to internal and external stimuli; or, in the words of the Zen master, the individual learns "To be able to see the flower the five hundredth time as he saw it the first time."

Behavioral Self-Control and Zen Meditation

In this section of the article the behavioral self-control literature is briefly reviewed, and a series of comparisons and contrasts are made with Zen meditation. In so doing, the foregoing descriptive analysis of Zen meditation should be clarified and interpreted more directly in terms of social learning theory.

BEHAVIORAL SELF-OBSERVATION

The concept of awareness, so predominant in the literature on meditation, is also critical to behavioral self-change strategies. In the behavioral literature, the means of attaining this awareness is called "self-observation." Self-observation is the initial step of a self-change strategy, and involves teaching a person how to monitor his or her own behavior (Kanfer & Phillips, 1966). Other behavior therapists (e.g., Ferster, 1972; Goldiamond, 1965; Thoresen & Mahoney, 1974) also stress the importance of a self-directed functional analysis of the environment as a prerequisite to behavior change. Ferster (1972) has referred to his functional analysis as "outsight therapy," noting that probably the most significant and difficult event to learn to observe is the functional relationship between one's own behavior and the elements of the environment that are controlling it. By learning to recognize what elements of the environment are controlling his or her behavior, the individual takes the necessary first step toward manipulating, rather than being manipulated by, the environment (Bandura, 1974b).

Self-observation strategies are not limited to the individual's interaction with the external environment, and may include monitoring of covert thoughts and feelings, such as physiological reactions, somatic complaints, and covert images (Cautela, 1967, 1971; Homme & Tosti, 1971; Jacobson, 1971; Kazdin, 1974; Thoresen & Mahoney, 1974; Meichenbaum, Note 1). After discriminating and labeling certain specified behaviors in the internal and/or external environment, the individual then examines the antecedents and consequences of the behaviors. In this way the individual learns to recognize antecedent or initiating stimuli; to recognize consequences maintaining the behavior; and to recognize the behavior itself: frequency, latency, duration, and intensity.

Zen meditation also focuses attention both on inner experiences (Maupin, 1965) and on the external environment (Kasamatsu & Hirari, 1966). In Zen, however, the goal is to remain aware of the "ongoing present" without dwelling on it. Therefore, in Zen meditation, unlike behavioral self-observation strategies, no attempt is made to plot data charts, use counting devices, or employ systematic and written evaluation of data gathered from the ongoing present. The contrast might be one of a relaxed awareness, a receptive "letting go" compared to an active focusing and dwelling on data (cf. Deikman, 1971). Furthermore, in Eastern self-observation strategies (cf. Rahula, 1959; Spiegelberg, 1962), the important factor is not what is observed (i.e., all behaviors experienced by the individual) but *how* it is observed (i.e., nonevaluative, without comment); in Western self-observation strategies, the important factor is the specific problem area observed, that is, the behavior to be changed or altered.

One of the consequences of behavioral self-observation is that the procedure serves both as a method of gathering data and also as a possible self-change technique. As Kanfer and Karoly (1972) pointed out, self-observation appears to be intimately linked with self-evaluation and self-reinforcement. And Homme and Tosti (1971) suggest that the "act of plotting on a graph serves as a positive consequence for self-management, and, once conditioned, the operation of a wrist counter appears to act as a reinforcer in its own right" (Book 4, p. 13). Several recent studies have attempted to verify this "reactive effect." Most indicate that self-observation of a behavior does influence the occurrence of that behavior, depending on such factors as the valence of the behavior, the timing of the self-observation, the nature of the response monitored, and the frequency of the observations (cf. Broden, Hall, & Mitts, 1971; Johnson & White, 1971; Kazdin, 1974; McFall, 1970; McFall & Hammen, 1971; Thoresen & Mahoney, 1974). It was noted earlier how a similar reactive effect takes place during Step 1 of Zen meditation, in which self-observation of the behavior of breathing influences its occurrence. However, the reactive effect in Zen seems to serve no therapeutic value, but rather causes a difficulty in breathing. Because the behavior of breathing is presumably nonvalenced, further research needs to clarify the exact nature and differences between the reactive effects that occur in behavioral self-observation and meditation.

Thus, in summary, although both behavioral self-control and meditation strategies involve the concept of awareness, there are differences in terms of the nature of what is observed, the method by which it is observed, and the types of reactive effects that occur as a result of observation.

SELF-EVALUATION AND GOAL SETTING

In a behavioral self-control strategy, after discriminating, labeling, recording, and charting the data, the individual evaluates the data and often sets a personal goal (e.g., Kanfer & Karoly, 1972; Kolb & Boyatzis, 1970).

The goal in Zen, on the other hand, is not to evaluate the effects of self-observation but rather to just self-observe. As Alan Watts (1972) put it: "Zen meditation is a trickily simple affair, for it consists only in watching everything that is happening, including your own thoughts and your breathing, without comment" (p. 220). Further, Zen also stresses the importance of living in the present without setting goals. For example, Suzuki (1960) discusses the dilemma of modern Western man, who is so busy striving after future accomplishments that he is unable to appreciate the day-to-day beauty right beside him.

However, there is a contradiction in the Zen explanation of nonevaluative self-observation. In fact, two goals are posited: One is the goal of "living in the moment" without self-evaluation, and the other is the goal of not having any goals. From a behavioral standpoint, a series of techniques are involved that represent a successive approximation toward the "goal of nongoals." For example, beginning meditators are taught, as noted earlier, to count from 1 to 10. More advanced meditators, however, are taught to just count "1" over and over again. This represents an attempt to focus the individual meditator more in the present, without striving after the goal of "reaching 10." Finally, there is a technique in the Soto Zen sect for the most advanced meditators called *Shikan-taza,* which means "just sitting" and involves neither focusing on counting nor breathing. Thus, rather than no goals in Zen, there are a series of subgoals designed to help the person reach the goal of being "goal free" and fully in the present.

A similar analysis could be made of the goal of no self-evaluation. In order for an individual to be able to observe himself without comment and without evaluation, he has to be able to discriminate, label, and evaluate those times when he in fact evaluates, for example: "I'm no longer focusing on breathing; I'm being too self-critical, I should stop being so critical and return to just observing myself." Thus, a behavioral analysis, although not denying that Zen in fact has a goal of nonevaluation, raises the question of whether that goal can be reached and maintained without the aid of evaluating the effects of one's progress. Seemingly, one must first learn how to evaluate before one can experience nonevaluation.

ENVIRONMENTAL PLANNING

Once the individual has become aware of the target behavior, several self-management strategies are available for him or her to use. The first of these strategies is environmental planning, which occurs *prior* to the execution of the target behavior. Examples of environmental planning include arranging antecedent or initiating stimuli (stimulus control), preprogramming certain punishments or reinforcements for specified actions (e.g., self-contract), self-regulated stimulus exposure (e.g., self-administered desensitization), and covert self-verbalizations and imagery (e.g., self-instructions) (cf. Mahoney & Thoresen, 1974; Thoresen & Mahoney, 1974).

Stimulus control. The development of stimulus control may be a prerequisite step in successfully implementing a behavioral self-management strategy. The individual must identify and plan changes in relevant situations: ones that will "cue" or set the occasion for self-change responses to occur. Stimulus control strategies may involve the association of desired responses with stimuli likely to

evoke them; examples of successfully implemented stimulus control procedures have been reported in the areas of weight control (Ferster, Nurnberger, & Levitt, 1962), obesity (Stuart, 1967; Stunkard, 1972), study skills (Beneke & Harris, 1972), and smoking (Bernard & Efran, 1972; Shapiro, Tursky, Schwartz, & Shnidman, 1971).

The uncluttered location of the meditation setting may be seen as a type of stimulus control in that the individual prearranges the physical environment to reduce unwanted distractions and thereby to help him or her focus attention on breathing. Similarly, the physical posture may be seen as a way of reducing unwanted proprioceptive feedback; incense may be a means to block out other smells; the dimness of the lighting as a method of reducing unwanted visual distractions. All of the above are examples of stimulus control, in that the individual is trying to prearrange the physical environment to set the occasion for the proper occurrence of meditative behavior.

Other examples of environmental planning include meditating with a group of people in order to ensure daily practice (i.e., using social reinforcement to encourage the performance of certain actions). Similarly, in formal Zen meditation, the use of the *Kwat,*[1] a slap by the master to a "nonconcentrating" student, represents a preprogramming of punishment to reduce "nonalert" behavior. These are examples of environmental programming because they occur *prior* to the execution of the target behavior of meditation, with the individual prearranging relevant environmental cues and social consequences to influence the occurrence of the behavior.

It is important to note, however, that although the meditator prearranges environmental cues, and may use social reinforcement and consequences to influence the occurrence and proper execution of meditative behavior, the long-term goal of meditation is eventually to eliminate the need for social consequences, environmental cues, or even covert

[1] In a Zen monastery, there is a special room set aside for the practice of meditation. During the act of formal meditation, the beginning meditator is aided by the Zen master, who walks around the meditation hall, literally carrying a big stick. He watches each of the meditators to make sure they are alert and receptive. Because sleepiness (*Kanchin*) is considered undesirable in Zen training, if the Zen master sees one of the students sagging or not concentrating, he will walk over to that student and bow. After the student bows back, the master raises the stick and gives a blow (*Kwat*), which "awakens" the student and brings him back to the ongoing present in a "nonverbal, nonreflective manner."

self-reinforcement. In the beginning, however, the need for these cues and consequences is both recognized and used.

Systematic desensitization. Wolpe (1958, 1969) borrowed from Jacobson's relaxation techniques and used them as the first step in his three-step process of systematic desensitization. Wolpe hypothesized on the basis of reciprocal inhibition that the presence of a phobic or stressful event would extinguish if it could symbolically occur in the presence of an incompatible response, such as relaxation. He had the patient construct elaborate hierarchies, labeling the items on the hierarchy in ascending order of subjective units of disturbance. He would then relax the subject using Jacobson's method, and once the subject was relaxed, have him visualize the lowest subjective units of disturbance anxiety-producing item on the hierarchy. If the subject began to feel tense, Wolpe would have him dismiss the image and continue to relax. If the subject felt no tension, the therapist would have him imagine the next highest tension-producing item.

Step 4 of formal meditation has several similarities to the Wolpe paradigm. First, Step 4 of formal meditation may be conceptualized as a type of counterconditioning (cf. Bandura, 1969; Davison, 1968b) in which responses incompatible with maladaptive behavior are practiced; that is, relaxation (Step 3: effortless breathing) precedes the feared image (Step 4). However, Step 4 of meditation is different from Wolpe's paradigm in that there is no structured hierarchy of anxiety-producing events, but rather a "global desensitization hierarchy" (Goleman, 1971).

There is still considerable debate, however, in the literature as to what exactly accounts for the success of systematic desensitization. Wolpe and others have argued on the basis on reciprocal inhibition: An incompatible response causes a counterconditioning to occur (Bandura, 1969; Davison, 1968b). Others have argued in favor of a cognitive refocusing model, suggesting that it is primarily the attention shifts that cause the effectiveness of systematic desensitization (Wilkins, 1971; Yulis et al., 1975).

Both of the above explanations would seem plausible alternatives for the effects that occur in Step 4 and Step 5 of formal meditation. A third explanation might involve the use of operant punishment, that is, behavioral thought stopping (Wolpe, 1969). In behavioral approaches to thought stopping, whenever the individual realizes the presence of an unwanted aversive thought, he or she covertly yells "Stop!" It is possible that a similar process occurs during meditation, in which the individual tells himself to stop focusing on thoughts and images and to return to the behavior of breathing.

BEHAVIORAL PROGRAMMING

The second of the behavioral self-management strategies is behavioral programming. In behavioral programming, the individual presents himself with consequences following the occurrence of a target behavior. These consequences can be either verbal, imaginal, or material self-reward (positive or negative, overt or covert) or verbal, imaginal, or material self-punishment (positive or negative, overt or covert) (Mahoney & Thoresen, 1974; Thoresen & Mahoney, 1974).

Although Zen does not espouse attachment to material possessions (i.e., material self-reward), Zen meditation does involve internal processes. Therefore, of particular interest to this discussion is the behavioral literature on covert events, both imaginal and verbal.

It is only within the last 10 years that behaviorists have actively begun to pay attention to covert events, finally entering the "lion's den of private events" (Cautela, 1967, 1971; Homme, 1965; Kanfer & Karoly, 1972; Mahoney, in press; Meichenbaum, Note 1). This expansion into the study of covert events has occurred for several reasons. First, improved scientific instrumentations have made it possible to study some internal processes (e.g., research on biofeedback: Barber et al., 1971; Shapiro et al., 1973; Stoyva et al., 1972). Second, animal studies (e.g., Miller, 1969) began to question the traditional distinctions of operant and classical conditioning, especially the interdependence of environmental–cognitive influence processes and the primary role of "symbolic processes" in behavior change. Third, the clinical experiences of clients and patients have almost invariably involved maladaptive cognitive problems.

As early as 1964, Skinner noted that internal events, even though self-reported and unobservable, are justified in a science of behavior if they delineate functional behavioral relationships. L. Homme (1965), in a seminal article entitled "Control of Coverants, the Operants of the Mind," hypothesized that a behavioral relationship existed between what a person said to himself covertly and his subsequent overt behavior. Several recent studies have attempted to show the relationship between

Zen Meditation and Self-Control

covert events and overt actions. Cautela (1967, 1971) has discussed the use of covert sensitization (covert imagery as punishment) as a technique for modifying maladaptive approach behavior such as alcoholism (cf. Ashem & Donner, 1968), sexual behavior (Barlow, Leitenberg, & Agras, 1969; Davison, 1968a), and obesity. Ferster (1965) has discussed the use of ultimate aversive consequences in which the individual (e.g., with a problem of smoking) imagines an aversive future consequence (e.g., lungs rotting, doctors talking over his decayed body) every time he begins to engage in the maladaptive behavior (e.g., lighting a cigarette). The individual thereby learns to modify his overt behavior by covertly summoning up aversive future consequences at the onset of his present maladaptive activity.

Other studies employing covert responses as examples of behavioral programming have been discussed by Cautela (1967, 1971) and Bandura (1974c). Both authors review studies suggesting that covert desensitization can be used to modify maladaptive avoidance responses, and that covert self-reinforcement, both positive and negative, can be used to modify maladaptive approach or avoidance behavior. Other studies have taken Homme's (1965) coverant control therapy paradigm, which is based on the Premack principle (Premack, 1965), and have successfully applied it to modifying covert thoughts: increasing positive self-thoughts and decreasing negative self-thoughts (Johnson, 1971; Mahoney, 1971). Further, it has been shown that covertly practicing the behavior (behavioral rehearsal) is a successive approximation of the overt act and increases the likelihood of its successful occurrence (Johnson, 1971).

Based on the recent research on covert events discussed above, several stress and tension management training packages have been developed (cf. Suinn & Richardson, 1971; Meichenbaum, Note 1). These training packages have altered the traditional Wolpe paradigm in both theory and practice. As noted earlier, Wolpe believed that relaxation should precede the fear-arousing imagery. In the new paradigm, the fear-arousing situation becomes a discriminative stimulus for relaxation. The two paradigms were recently compared in a group study involving acrophobics. One group practiced the passive paradigm (relaxation before phobic scene and avoidance of arousal), and one group practiced the active paradigm (fear arousal as a discriminative stimulus for active relaxation and positive imagery). On both self-report and actual performance tests of climbing and looking down from a 12-story building, subjects in the active "stress as a cue to relax" procedure did significantly better (Jacks, 1972). The latter technique first involves training in deep-muscle relaxation and then teaching the person to discriminate anxiety by imagining the fear-arousing situation and maintaining that situation in the imagination. While maintaining the tension, the person then practices controlling arousal by means of muscular relaxation, covert self-modeling (i.e., observing himself acting in a competent and successful fashion in the anxiety-arousing situation), and self-instructions to cope with the situation (e.g., "relax," "I am in control," "I can handle the situation") (cf. Goldfried, 1973; Jacks, 1972; Mahoney, in press; Suinn & Richardson, 1971; Meichenbaum, Note 1).

These training procedures involve practices quite different from both formal and informal meditation. For example, in informal meditation, the individual observes *all* actions and behaviors throughout the day. In the training package, the individual is instructed to discriminate certain specified "anxiety-arousing" situations, and then to use those situations as discriminative stimuli for engaging in relaxation, covert self-modeling, and self-instruction activities. In informal meditation, although all cues are observed, the individual is instructed to "merely observe, as a witness" and to take no specific action after recognizing any particular cue. In terms of formal meditation, although the beginning meditator may subvocalize such self-instructions as "relax; keep focused on your breathing; your attention has wandered, better return to breathing again," the goal of meditation is to remove these verbal cues eventually and have an "empty mind," that is, an absence of covert statements and images (Step 5).

A Clinical Combination of Zen Meditation and Behavioral Self-Control Techniques

The preceding discussion has attempted to suggest that there is a common ground between Zen meditation and behavioral self-management techniques. One of the more important clinical questions, however, still remains unexplored: Can these techniques complement each other to provide a more effective treatment strategy in combination than either strategy can when practiced alone? To date, there has been almost no research in this area. Therefore, the comments that follow are intended only as plausible hypotheses and must await further research for empirical documentation of their effectiveness.

INFORMAL MEDITATION PLUS BEHAVIORAL SELF-CONTROL TECHNIQUES: "CONTINGENT INFORMAL MEDITATION"

Current research suggests that the technique of informal meditation can be converted into a more powerful clinical intervention strategy [2] by making its performance contingent on certain antecedent cues, and by coupling it with covert self-imagery, covert self-statements, and focused breathing. In this model, the subject, in addition to observing all events and behaviors occurring throughout the day (informal meditation), also discriminates certain specified cues in the internal and external environment (e.g., tension, anger, anxiety, social events). Once the individual has discriminated those cues, he then self-observes in a "detached" nonevaluative manner, as in informal meditation. However, the individual also focuses on breathing and covertly initiates cues to relax, to feel in control, and imagines acting in a relaxed, competent fashion (cf. Boudreau, 1972; Shapiro, in press-c; Shapiro & Zifferblatt, in press).

The research thus far, though suggestive, is cursory and is based on case reports. Further replications are necessary; these replications should try to determine the variance of outcome effects attributable to various aspects of the treatment.

FORMAL MEDITATION PLUS BEHAVIORAL SELF-CONTROL TECHNIQUES

The acquisition of formal meditation behavior might possibly be facilitated by borrowing from certain behavioral self-management techniques. For

---

[2] It appears that making informal meditation contingent on certain cues and coupling it with covert self-modeling and self-instructions make informal meditation a more powerful clinical strategy for an immediate problem. However, this is in no way meant to suggest that the combination of informal meditation with behavioral self-control strategies makes informal meditation more effective for the goal for which it was originally intended: "ongoing awareness of all cues."

Similarly, from a Western perspective, formal Zen meditation is often seen merely as a technique that may be useful when applied to certain clinical problems. However, from an Eastern perspective, Zen meditation is a way of "being" in the world: a total awareness of oneself, of nature, of others. Thus, it is important to note that the technique of formal Zen meditation may be being used for goals other than those for which it was originally intended.

example, individuals have been given a wrist counter and instructed to punch the counter every time their attention wandered from the task of breathing. The punching of the wrist counter was then made a discriminative stimulus for returning attention to the task of breathing. Functionally, a tool used in behavioral self-observation (the wrist counter) took the place of the *Kwat* of the Zen monk (cf. Shapiro & Zifferblatt, in press; Van Nuys, 1971). It is possible that biofeedback techniques might also serve to facilitate the acquisition and proper performance of meditative behavior.

Conversely, certain aspects of formal meditation might help complement and facilitate behavioral self-control skills. For example, during formal meditation, the individual learns to unstress (desensitize) himself (Step 4, Figure 1) and to reduce the frequency and duration of covert chatter and images (Step 5, Figure 1). It is hypothesized that this ability to relax and have an "empty mind" gained during formal meditation will help an individual be more alert and responsive to stress situations occurring at other times, thus facilitating a person's performance of behavioral self-observation of internal and external cues throughout the day (Shapiro, in press-a, in press-c; Shapiro & Zifferblatt, in press).

Second, formal meditation seems to give the individual practice in noticing when his or her attention wanders from a task. At first, there is usually a long time period that elapses between the attention wandering and the realization that the attention has wandered. With practice, however, the person may learn to catch himself almost as soon as he stops focusing on breathing. Similarly, in behavioral self-control strategies, often several minutes or longer pass before the individual realizes that he is supposed to have discriminated a cue and subsequently interrupted the maladaptive behavioral chain. For example, the chronic smoker illustrates this lack of awareness (Premack, 1970) as does the heroin addict (Shapiro & Zifferblatt, in press). The practice of discriminating a stimulus (e.g., wandering attention) developed in meditation may generalize to situations involved in behavioral self-control strategies (e.g., reaching for a cigarette, the "need" for a fix). As such, the individual practicing meditation may be aided in eventually discriminating the stimulus as soon as it occurs, thereby placing the individual in a much better position to interrupt a maladaptive behavioral sequence.

The third way in which formal meditation might help behavioral self-control strategies involves the cognitive set that meditation can help give to the practitioner. Formal meditation allows the individual an opportunity for fixed reference points in the day during which he feels relaxed, calm, and in control. Therefore, when recognizing tension at subsequent points during the day, the individual should be able to say to himself, "I was relaxed, calm, and in control this morning," thereby attributing current stress to a specific situation rather than to an "anxious personality trait" (Mischel, 1968). In this way the person may learn to increase feelings of self-control and learn to perceive himself as a responsible individual who has the ability to control his own behavior and actions (Lefcourt, 1966; Rotter, 1966, 1969).

Fourth, although the physiological data are still equivocal (cf. Hirari, 1974), aspects of the technique of formal meditation may make it more powerful than other self-management techniques in certain respects. For example, other self-control techniques, such as autogenic training (Luthe, 1968), self-hypnosis (Paul, 1969), or relaxation with covert self-statements (Jacobson, 1971; Meichenbaum, Note 1), employ certain covert images and self-statements (e.g., "I'm feeling warm; my right arm feels heavy; I am feeling relaxed"). In formal Zen meditation, the individual does not say anything to himself, nor does he attempt to engage in positive covert images or thoughts. It is this absence of preprogrammed covert thoughts and images that seems to allow the meditator to observe and become desensitized to "what's on his own mind" (Step 4, Figure 1). Repetition of preprogrammed covert statements and images would seemingly interfere with this process and would also seem to prevent the "mind from becoming empty" (Figure 1, Step 5). This "empty mind" (i.e., an absence of verbal behaviors and images) may be important in certain externally oriented situations, such as the counseling setting (Lesh, 1970) and interpersonal relationships (Shapiro, in press-c). The empty mind may also be important for hearing certain internal cues, especially in clinical areas dealing with stress and tension, obesity, tachycardia, migraine, and hypertension.

Finally, because during meditation the individual seems to be able to step back from personal fears, concerns, and worries, and observe them in a detached, relaxed way (Shapiro, in press-a, in press-c; Shapiro & Zifferblatt, in press), it is possible to hypothesize that *after* meditation the individual should be able to think about the fears and evaluate how he or she wants to act without being overwhelmed or oppressed by them. Within Kanfer's behavioral model of self-management involving self-observation, self-evaluation, and self-reinforcement, this type of detached self-observation would presumably alter the subsequent self-evaluation by reducing the self-evaluative threat, that is, making the problem seem less intense; and by giving the person a sense of strength and control (from the firm, centered posture, and relaxed, focused breathing) so that he or she need not be afraid to self-evaluate at a subsequent time (Kanfer & Karoly, 1972). Thus, even though during the process of formal meditation there is ideally no thinking or evaluation, subsequent to meditation the individual may be well prepared to think and make decisions. In this way, meditation might help produce "self-observation conditions such that inner feedback for behavior change is optimal" (Goleman, 1971, p. 17).

Unanswered Questions: Concluding Remarks

The foregoing discussion leaves several questions unanswered, both with respect to the effectiveness of meditation as a complementary strategy with behavioral self-control skills and also with respect to the exact mechanism by which meditation works. The first set of unanswered questions include the following: Is formal Zen meditation a necessary part of the intervention? Is it sufficient by itself? Is it the relaxation component of meditation that makes the greatest contribution? Is meditation really different from, or more effective than, deep-muscle relaxation (Smith, in press), systematic desensitization, covert imagery, and covert self-statements? Further research is necessary to address these questions and to determine the variance of outcome effects attributable to various aspects of the treatment.

A different set of questions involves the role of breathing in formal Zen meditation. There is a paucity of empirical literature dealing with the effect of breathing. Timmons, Salamy, Kamiya, and Girton (1972) have compared different types of breathing in general, and Nakamizo (1974) and Matsumoto (1974) have researched Zen meditation breathing in particular. However, the question is still unanswered as to whether focusing on breathing is more clinically effective than other types of cognitive focusing techniques. The Eastern literature is replete with different examples of cognitive focusing techniques (cf. Ornstein, 1971; Shapiro,

Note 2). The "objects of focus" can be located in either the external or internal environments. Examples from the external environment (*tratakam* meditation) include the Taoist focus on the abdomen, the early Christian focus on the cross, focus on a vase (Deikman, 1969), a guru, a mandala. The meditator can also focus on internal visual images (*Kasina*) such as a fire in the hearth, the symbol of a guru, sexual mandalas (cf. Moorkerjee, 1966; Speigelberg, 1962), the third eye, or the vault of the skull (Raj Yogas). The meditator can also focus on words or phrases chanted aloud, such as the Sufi dervish call (cf. Ornstein, 1971) or a mantra (Mishra, 1959); or he or she can concentrate on internally generated unspoken sounds such as a bee humming (Mishra, 1959), a prayer, or a sentence (e.g., the Zen *Koan*); or the meditator can focus on internal bodily processes, for example, on the heart beating and on breathing (Datey, Deshmukh, Dalui, & Vinekar, 1969).

Although it is true that different types of meditation can produce different physiological and behavioral indexes *during* meditation (Anand, Chhina, & Singh, 1961; Kasamatsu & Hirari, 1966), it is not yet clear whether there are in fact any differences *after* the occurrence of different types of meditation. Although each school of focus seems to make claims and develops rationales for the use of its own particular technique, whether it be Zen's focus on breath (cf. Akishige, 1974; Hirari, 1974) or transcendental meditation's focus on an internal mantra (Bloomfield, Cain, & Jaffe, 1975; Kanellakos & Lukas, 1974), there has been almost no research comparing the clinical effectiveness of different types of cognitive focusing (cf. Yamaoka, 1974; Otis, Note 3).

Within the behavioral literature, there has also been an interest in different types of cognitive focusing, including work with delay of gratification (Mischel, Ebbesen, & Zeiss, 1972), the use of different types of imagery in therapy (Singer, 1974), and the use of cognitive focusing on external slides (Kanfer & Goldfoot, 1966) and on music (Yulis et al., 1975). Again, however, systematic comparison of different audiovisual techniques (both overt and covert) has not been undertaken. What truly seems needed is a convergence of several different schools and strategies, such as cognitive behavior modification (Mahoney, 1974), work on imagery (Singer, 1975), meditation research (cf. Hirari, 1974; Kanellakos & Lukas, 1974; Shapiro & Giber, Note 4), behavioral self-observation research (Kazdin, 1974), and biofeedback research (Blanchard &

Young, 1974; Schwartz, 1973), to deal with the common problems and issues involved in evaluating the clinical uses of covert processes. With this convergence of academic and clinical scholars, perhaps some of the unanswered questions will begin to be better understood.

This article has made an attempt to look at two clinical strategies: Zen meditation and behavioral self-control. Current research has suggested that either technique alone provides potentially effective self-directed attempts to control one's everyday life, thoughts, and feelings. Researchers have found meditation effective in reducing fear (Boudreau, 1972), curbing drug abuse (Benson & Wallace, 1971; Brautigam, Note 5), increasing empathy in counselors (Lesh, 1970), decreasing generalized anxiety (Girodo, 1974), decreasing test anxiety (Linden, 1973), and reducing blood pressure and hypertension (Datey et al., 1969; Wallace & Benson, 1972). The behavioral self-management literature suggests the effectiveness of social learning strategies applied to a variety of problems, such as weight reduction (Mahoney, Moura, & Wade, 1973; Jeffrey, Note 6), curbing smoking (Axelrod, Hall, Weis, & Rohrer, 1974; Premack, 1970), changing negative self-thoughts (Hannum, Thoresen, & Hubbard, 1974), reducing fears (Jacks, 1972), and in other clinical areas (cf. Bandura, 1969; Cautela, 1971; Goldfried & Merbaum, 1973; Meichenbaum & Cameron, 1974; Thoresen & Mahoney, 1974; Meichenbaum, Note 1).

The foregoing research suggests the clinical intervention effectiveness of the techniques of meditation and behavioral self-control strategies alone. Subsequent research should determine whether a combination of the two techniques will, in fact, be more powerful in dealing with applied clinical problems. To this end, pilot studies have applied a treatment package combining Zen meditation and behavioral self-management techniques to such clinical areas as drug abuse (Shapiro & Zifferblatt, in press) and stress and tension management (Shapiro, in press-c). Currently pilot studies are extending these investigations both to rehabilitative programs, such as coronary heart problems (Zifferblatt, Note 7), and to preventive and educational programs dealing with "positive mental health" (Shapiro, in press-a; Shapiro, Note 8). Although the results of these pilot studies combining behavioral self-control and Zen meditation techniques are tentative and need further replication, the continued exploration of the applied interface between Eastern disciplines and Western psychology promises to be an important and clinically useful area for further investigation.

REFERENCE NOTES

1. Meichenbaum, D. *Cognitive factors in behavior modification: Modifying what people say to themselves.* Paper presented at the meeting of the Association for the Advancement of Behavior Therapy, Washington, D.C., December 1971.
2. Shapiro, D. *Meditation: Theory, research, practice.* Paper presented at the meeting of the American Psychological Association, Montreal, August 1973.
3. Otis, L. *Meditation or simulated meditation by nonpredisposed volunteers: Some psychological changes.* Paper presented at the meeting of the American Psychological Association, Montreal, August 1973.
4. Shapiro, D., & Giber, D. *Meditation: A review of the clinical literature.* Manuscript in preparation, 1976. (Available from D. Shapiro, Department of Psychiatry and Behavioral Sciences, Stanford University, Stanford, California 94305.)
5. Brautigam, E. *The effects of transcendental meditation on drug abusers.* Unpublished manuscript, Malmo, Sweden, 1971.
6. Jeffrey, D. B. *Relative efficacy of external control and self-control in the production and maintenance of weight loss.* Paper presented at the meeting of the American Psychological Association, New Orleans, August 1974.
7. Zifferblatt, S. *Self-management training for stress and tension reduction in coronary heart disease patients.* Manuscript in preparation, 1976. (Available from the author, Department of Psychiatry and Behavioral Sciences, Stanford University, Stanford, California 94305.)
8. Shapiro, D. *Values, identity, and self-control: An East–West approach.* Grant proposal submitted to the National Science Foundation, 1975. (Available from the author, Department of Psychiatry and Behavioral Sciences, Stanford University, Stanford, California 94305.)

REFERENCES

Akishige, Y. A historical survey of the psychological studies on Zen. *Bulletin of the Faculty of Literature of Kyushu University,* 1974, *5,* 1–57.
Anand, B. K., Chhina, E. S., & Singh, B. Some aspects of electroencephalographic studies in yogis. *EEG Clinical Neurophysiology,* 1961, *13,* 452–456.
Ashem, B., & Donner, L. Covert sensitization with alcoholics: A controlled replication. *Behavior Research and Therapy,* 1968, *6,* 7–12.
Axelrod, S., Hall, V., Weis, L., & Rohrer, S. Use of self-imposed contingencies to reduce the frequency of smoking behavior. In M. J. Mahoney & C. E. Thoresen (Eds.), *Self-control: Power to the person.* Monterey, Calif.: Brooks/Cole, 1974.
Bandura, A. *Principles of behavior modification.* New York: Holt, Rinehart & Winston, 1969.
Bandura, A. Behavior theory and the models of man. *American Psychologist,* 1974, *29,* 859–869. (a)
Bandura, A. Foreward. In C. E. Thoresen & M. J. Mahoney (Eds.), *Behavioral self-control.* New York: Holt, Rinehart & Winston, 1974. (b)
Bandura, A. Self-reinforcement processes. In M. J. Mahoney & C. E. Thoresen (Eds.), *Self-control: Power to the person.* Monterey, Calif.: Brooks/Cole, 1974. (c)
Barber, T., DiCara, L. V., Kamiya, J., Miller, N. E., Shapiro, D., & Stoyva, J. (Eds.). *Biofeedback and self-control: An Aldine reader on the regulation of body processes and consciousness.* Chicago, Ill.: Aldine-Atherton, 1971.
Barlow, D. H., Leitenberg, H., & Agras, W. S. Experimental control of sexual deviation through manipulation of the noxious scene in covert sensitization. *Journal of Abnormal Psychology,* 1969, *4,* 597–601.
Beneke, W. M., & Harris, W. B. Teaching self-control of study behavior. *Behavior Research and Therapy,* 1972, *10,* 35–41.
Benson, H., & Wallace, R. K. *Decreased drug abuse with transcendental meditation: A study of 1862 subjects* (Congressional Record, Hearings Before the Select Committee on Crime, House of Representatives, 1971. Serial No. 92-1). Washington, D.C.: U.S. Government Printing Office, 1971.
Bernard, H. S., & Efran, J. S. Eliminating versus reducing smoking using pocket timers. *Behavior Research and Therapy,* 1972, *10,* 399–401.
Blanchard, E. B., & Young, L. D. Clinical applications of biofeedback training: A review of the evidence. *Archives of General Psychiatry,* 1974, *30,* 573–592.
Bloomfield, H. M., Cain, D. T., & Jaffe, D. T. *TM: Overcoming stress and developing inner energy.* New York: Delacorte, 1975.
Boudreau, L. Transcendental meditation and yoga as reciprocal inhibitors. *Journal of Behavior Therapy and Experimental Psychiatry,* 1972, *3,* 97–98.
Broden, M., Hall, R. V., & Mitts, B. The effects of self-recording on the classroom behavior of two eighth grade students. *Journal of Applied Behavioral Analysis,* 1971, *4,* 191–199.
Cautela, J. R. Covert sensitization. *Psychological Record,* 1967, *20,* 459–468.
Cautela, J. R. Covert conditioning. In A. Jacobs & L. B. Sachs (Eds.), *The psychology of private events: Perspectives on covert response systems.* New York: Academic Press, 1971.
Datey, K. K., Deshmukh, S. N., Dalui, C. P., & Vinekar, S. L. Shavasan, a yogic exercise in the management of hypertension. *Angiology,* 1969, *20,* 325–333.
Davison, G. C. Elimination of a sadistic fantasy by a client-controlled counterconditioning technique: A case study. *Journal of Abnormal Psychology,* 1968, *73,* 84–90. (a)
Davison, G. C. Systematic desensitization as a counterconditioning process. *Journal of Abnormal Psychology,* 1968, *73,* 91–99. (b)
Deikman, A. Experimental meditation. In C. Tart (Ed.), *Altered states of consciousness.* New York: Wiley, 1969.
Deikman, A. Bimodal consciousness. *Archives of General Psychiatry,* 1971, *25,* 481–489.
Ferster, C. B. Classification of behavior pathology. In L. Krasner & L. P. Ullman (Eds.), *Research in behavior modification.* New York: Holt, Rinehart & Winston, 1965.
Ferster, C. B. An experimental analysis of clinical phenomenon. *Psychological Record,* 1972, *22,* 1–16.
Ferster, C. B., Nurnberger, J. I., & Levitt, E. B. The control of eating. *Journal of Mathematics,* 1962, *1,* 87–109.
Galin, D. Implications for psychiatry of left and right cerebral specialization. *Archives of General Psychiatry,* 1974, *31,* 572–583.
Girodo, M. Yoga meditation and flooding in the treatment of anxiety neurosis. *Journal of Behavior Therapy and Experimental Psychiatry,* 1974, *5,* 157–160.
Goldfried, M. R. Reduction of generalized anxiety through a variant of systematic desensitization. In M. R. Goldfried & M. Merbaum (Eds.), *Behavior change through self-control.* New York: Holt, Rinehart & Winston, 1973.

Goldfried, M. R., & Merbaum, M. (Eds.). *Behavior change through self-control*. New York: Holt, Rinehart & Winston, 1973.

Goldiamond, I. Self-control procedures in personal behavior problems. *Psychological Reports*, 1965, *17*, 851–868.

Goleman, D. Meditation as metatherapy. *Journal of Transpersonal Psychology*, 1971, *3*, 1–25.

Hannum, J., Thoresen, C. E., & Hubbard, D. A behavioral study of self-esteem with elementary teachers. In M. J. Mahoney & C. E. Thoresen (Eds.), *Self-control: Power to the person*. Monterey, Calif.: Brooks/Cole, 1974.

Hirari, T. *Psychophysiology of Zen*. Tokyo: Igaku Shoin Ltd., 1974.

Homme, L. E. Perspectives in psychology: XXIV. Control of coverants, the operants of the mind. *Psychological Record*, 1965, *15*, 501–511.

Homme, L. E., & Tosti, D. *Behavior technology: Motivation and contingency management*. San Rafael, Calif.: Individual Learning Systems, 1971.

Ikegami, R. Psychological study of Zen posture. *Bulletin of the Faculty of Literature of Kyushu University*, 1974, *5*, 105–135.

Jacks, R. *Systematic desensitization compared with a self-management paradigm*. Unpublished doctoral dissertation, Stanford University, 1972.

Jacobson, E. The two methods of tension control and certain basic techniques in anxiety tension control. In J. Kamiya, T. Barber, L. V. DiCara, N. E. Miller, D. Shapiro, & J. Stoyva (Eds.), *Biofeedback and self-control: An Aldine annual on the regulation of body processes and consciousness*. Chicago, Ill.: Aldine-Atherton, 1971.

Johnson, S. M., & White, G. Self-observation as an agent of behavior change. *Behavior Therapy*, 1971, *2*, 488–497.

Johnson, W. G. Some applications of Homme's coverant control therapy: Two case reports. *Behavior Therapy*, 1971, *2*, 240–248.

Kamiya, J., Barber, T., DiCara, L. V., Miller, N. E., Shapiro, D., & Stoyva, J. (Eds.). *Biofeedback and self-control: An Aldine annual on the regulation of body processes and consciousness*. Chicago, Ill.: Aldine-Atherton, 1971.

Kanellakos, D. P., & Lukas, J. D. *The psychobiology of transcendental meditation: A literature review*. Menlo Park, Calif.: Benjamin, 1974.

Kanfer, F. H., & Goldfoot, D. A. Self-control and tolerance of noxious stimulation. *Psychological Reports*, 1966, *18*, 79–85.

Kanfer, F. M., & Karoly, P. Self-control: A behavioristic excursion into the lion's den. *Behavior Therapy*, 1972, *3*, 398–416.

Kanfer, F. M., & Phillips, J. S. Behavior therapy: A panacea for all ills or a passing fancy? *Archives of General Psychiatry*, 1966, *15*, 114–128.

Kapleau, A. *Three pillars of Zen*. Boston, Mass.: Beacon Press, 1967.

Kasamatsu, A., & Hirari, T. An electroencephalographic study of the Zen meditation (Zazen). *Folia Psychiatria et Neurologica Japonica*, 1966, *20*, 315–336.

Kazdin, A. E. Self-monitoring and behavior change. In M. J. Mahoney & C. E. Thoresen (Eds.), *Self-control: Power to the person*. Monterey, Calif.: Brooks/Cole, 1974.

Kolb, D. A., & Boyatzis, R. E. Goal setting and self-directed behavior change. *Human Relations*, 1970, *23*, 439–458.

Lefcourt, H. M. Internal versus external control of reinforcement: A review. *Psychological Bulletin*, 1966, *65*, 206–220.

Lesh, T. Zen meditation and the development of empathy in counselors. *Journal of Humanistic Psychology*, 1970, *10*, 39–74.

Linden, W. Practicing of meditation by school children and their levels of field dependence–independence, test anxiety, and reading achievement. *Journal of Consulting and Clinical Psychology*, 1973, *41*, 139–143.

Luthe, W. Autogenic training: Method, research, and applications in medicine. In C. Tart (Ed.), *Altered states of consciousness*. New York: Wiley, 1968.

Mahoney, M. The self-management of covert behavior: A case study. *Behavior Therapy*, 1971, *2*, 575–578.

Mahoney, M. J. *Cognitive behavior modification*. Boston, Mass.: Ballinger, 1974.

Mahoney, M. J., Moura, N. G. M., & Wade, T. C. The relative efficacy of self-reward, self-punishment, and self-monitoring techniques for weight loss. *Journal of Consulting and Clinical Psychology*, 1973, *40*, 404–407.

Mahoney, M. J., & Thoresen, C. E. *Self-control: Power to the person*. Monterey, Calif.: Brooks/Cole, 1974.

Matsumoto, H. A psychological study of the relation between respiratory function and emotion. *Bulletin of the Faculty of Literature of Kyushu University*, 1974, *5*, 167–207.

Maupin, E. Individual differences in response to a Zen meditation exercise. *Journal of Consulting Psychology*, 1965, *29*, 139–145.

Maupin, E. On meditation. In C. Tart (Ed.), *Altered states of consciousness*. New York: Wiley, 1969.

McFall, R. M. The effects of self-monitoring on normal smoking behavior. *Journal of Consulting and Clinical Psychology*, 1970, *35*, 135–142.

McFall, R. M., & Hammen, C. L. Motivation, structure, and self-monitoring: The role of nonspecific factors in smoking reduction. *Journal of Consulting and Clinical Psychology*, 1971, *37*, 80–86.

Meichenbaum, D., & Cameron, R. The clinical potential of modifying what clients say to themselves. In M. J. Mahoney & C. E. Thoresen (Eds.), *Self-control: Power to the person*. Monterey, Calif.: Brooks/Cole, 1974.

Miller, N. E. Learning of visceral and glandular responses. *Science*, 1969, *163*, 434–453.

Mischel, W. *Personality and assessment*. New York: Wiley, 1968.

Mischel, W., Ebbesen, E. B., & Zeiss, A. R. Cognitive and attentional mechanisms in delay of gratification. *Journal of Personality and Social Psychology*, 1972, *21*, 204–218.

Mishra, R. *Fundamentals of yoga*. New York: Julian Press, 1959.

Mookerjee, A. *Tantra art: Its philosophy and physics*. New Delhi, India: Ravi Kumar, 1966.

Nakamizo, S. Psycho-physiological studies on respiratory patterns. *Bulletin of the Faculty of Literature of Kyushu University*, 1974, *5*, 135–167.

Ornstein, R. The techniques of meditation and their implications for modern psychology. In C. Naranjo & R. Ornstein (Eds.), *The psychology of meditation*. New York: Esalen-Viking Press, 1971.

Paul, G. Physiological effects of relaxation training and hypnotic suggestion. *Journal of Abnormal Psychology*, 1969, *74*, 425–437.

Premack, D. Reinforcement theory. In D. Levine (Ed.), *Nebraska Symposium on Motivation* (Vol. 13). Lincoln: University of Nebraska Press, 1965.

Premack, D. Mechanisms of self-control. In W. Hunt (Ed.), *Learning and mechanisms of control in smoking*. Chicago, Ill.: Aldine, 1970.

Rahula, W. *What the Buddha taught*. New York: Grove Press, 1959.

Rotter, J. B. Generalized expectancies for internal versus external control of reinforcement. *Psychological Monographs*, 1966, *80*(1, Whole No. 609).

Rotter, J. B. Internal–external control scale. In J. Robinson & P. Shaver (Eds.), *Measures of social psychological attitudes*. Ann Arbor: University of Michigan Press, 1969.

Schwartz, G. E. Biofeedback as therapy: Some theoretical and practical issues. *American Psychologist*, 1973, *28*, 666–673.

Shapiro, D., Barber, T., DiCara, L. V., Kamiya, J., Miller, N. E., & Stoyva, J. (Eds.). *Biofeedback and self-control: An Aldine annual on the regulation of body processes and consciousness*. Chicago, Ill.: Aldine, 1973.

Shapiro, D., Tursky, B., Schwartz, G. E., & Shnidman, S. R. Smoking on cue: A behavioral approach to smoking reduction. *Journal of Health and Social Behavior*, 1971, *12*, 108–113.

Shapiro, D. H. Behavioral and attitudinal changes resulting from a Zen experience workshop and Zen meditation. *Journal of Humanistic Psychology*, in press. (a)

Shapiro, D. H. Instructions for a training package combining formal and informal meditation with behavioral self-control strategies. *Psychologia*, in press. (b)

Shapiro, D. H. Zen meditation and behavioral self-management applied to a case of generalized anxiety. *Psychologia*, in press. (c)

Shapiro, D. H., & Zifferblatt, S. M. An applied clinical combination of Zen meditation and behavioral self-control strategies: Reducing methadone dosage in drug abuse. *Behavior Therapy*, in press.

Singer, J. L. *Imagery and daydream methods in psychotherapy and behavior modification*. New York: Academic Press, 1974.

Singer, J. L. Navigating the stream of consciousness: Research in daydreaming and related inner experience. *American Psychologist*, 1975, *30*, 727–738.

Skinner, B. F. Behaviorism at fifty. In T. W. Wann (Ed.), *Behaviorism and phenomenology*. Chicago, Ill.: University of Chicago Press, 1964.

Smith, J. Meditation as psychotherapy. *Psychological Bulletin*, in press.

Spiegelberg, F. *Spiritual practices of India*. New York: Citadel Press, 1962.

Stoyva, J., Barber, T., DiCara, L. V., Kamiya, J., Miller, N. E., & Shapiro, D. (Eds.). *Biofeedback and self-control: An Aldine annual on the regulation of body processes and consciousness*. Chicago, Ill.: Aldine-Atherton, 1972.

Stuart, R. B. Behavioral control over eating. *Behavior Research and Therapy*, 1967, *5*, 357–365.

Stunkard, A. New therapies for the eating disorders: Behavior modification of obesity and anorexia nervosa. *Archives of General Psychiatry*, 1972, *26*, 391–398.

Suinn, R., & Richardson, R. Anxiety management training: A non-specific behavior therapy program for anxiety control. *Behavior Therapy*, 1971, *2*, 498–510.

Suzuki, D. T. Lectures in Zen Buddhism. In E. Fromm (Ed.), *Zen Buddhism and psychoanalysis*. New York: Harper-Collephon, 1960.

Thoresen, C. E., & Mahoney, M. J. *Behavioral self-control*. New York: Holt, Rinehart & Winston, 1974.

Timmons, B., Salamy, J., Kamiya, J., & Girton, D. Abdominal, thoracic respiratory movements and levels of arousal. *Psychonomic Science*, 1972, *27*, 173–175.

Van Nuys, D. A novel technique for studying attention during meditation. *Journal of Transpersonal Psychology*, 1971, *3*, 125–133.

Wallace, R., & Benson, H. The physiology of meditation. *Scientific American*, 1972, *226*, 84–90.

Watts, A. The sound of rain. *Playboy*, April 1972, p. 220.

Weinpahl, P. *The matter of Zen: A brief account of Zazen*. New York: New York University Press, 1964.

Wilkins, W. Desensitization: Social and cognitive factors underlying the effectiveness of Wolpe's procedure. *Psychological Bulletin*, 1971, *76*, 311–317.

Wolpe, J. *Psychotherapy by reciprocal inhibition*. Palo Alto, Calif.: Stanford University Press, 1958.

Wolpe, J. *The practice of behavior therapy*. New York: Pergamon Press, 1969.

Yamaoka, T. Psychological study of mental self-control. *Bulletin of the Faculty of Literature of Kyushu University*, 1974, *5*, 225–271.

Yulis, S., Brahm, G., Charnes, G., Jacard, L. M., Picota, E., & Rutman, F. The extinction of phobic behavior as a function of attention shifts. *Behavior Research and Therapy*, 1975, *13*, 173–176.

Zifferblatt, S., & Hendricks, C. G. Applied behavioral analysis of societal problems. *American Psychologist*, 1974, *29*, 750–761.

49

THE ROLE OF ATTENTION IN MEDITATION AND HYPNOSIS: A PSYCHOBIOLOGICAL PERSPECTIVE ON TRANSFORMATIONS OF CONSCIOUSNESS[1,2]

Richard J. Davidson and Daniel J. Goleman[3,4]

Abstract: A temporally based scheme for investigation of changes in consciousness, applicable to areas such as meditation and hypnosis, is proposed and is divided into 3 basic epochs: before – predispositional variables that affect response to consciousness altering techniques; during – the state effects of the particular technique; and after – the trait effects of the practice. Research is surveyed which indicates the role of attentional processes during each of these 3 basic epochs in both meditation and hypnosis. Attentional flexibility is a predispositional variable affecting response to both meditation and hypnosis. The state effects of concentrative meditation involve alterations in stimulus set while the state effects of hypnosis may reflect primarily response set. The trait effects elicited by meditation depend critically on the psychobiological systems which are called into play. Evidence is discussed which suggests that concentrative meditation shares with relaxation an autonomic quiescence, but in addition enhances some attentional skills. A mindfulness technique involving the adoption of a particular attentional stance toward all objects of awareness appears to enhance cortical specificity, but a

Manuscript submitted January 5, 1976; final revision received October 1, 1976.

[1] The research reported in this paper was supported in part by an NSF Predoctoral Fellowship to the first author. The data reported in this paper were collected while both authors were in the Department of Psychology and Social Relations, Harvard University.

[2] An earlier version of this paper was presented in Erika Fromm (Chm.), Altered states of consciousness and hypnosis. Symposium presented at the 27th Annual Meeting of the Society for Clinical and Experimental Hypnosis, Chicago, October 1975.

[3] The authors are grateful to Gary E. Schwartz for his assistance in various phases of the present research. R. J. D. now at the State University of New York at Purchase. D. J. G. now at *Psychology Today,* New York.

[4] Reprint requests should be addressed to Richard J. Davidson, Department of Psychology, State University of New York at Purchase, Purchase, New York 10577.

concentration technique does not. Some implications of attentional self-regulation are discussed.

In his classic chapter on attention in *Principles of Psychology*, William James (1890) proposed that

> The practical and theoretical life of whole species, as well as of individual beings, results from the selection which the habitual direction of their attention involves. . . . each of us literally *chooses*, by his ways of attending to things, what sort of a universe he shall appear to himself to inhabit [p. 424].

The direct implication of this suggestion is that changing one's habitual ways of attending should change both behavior and experience.

James (1890) was quite emphatic on a related point. He argued that "the brain is the one immediate bodily condition of the mental operations [p. 4]" and that any change in mental events necessarily implies a concomitant neural change. The application of this basic fact of psychobiology to the study of attentional processes has recently led to some significant advances in our understanding of the neural substrates of attention (e.g., Pribram & McGuinnes, 1975).

A growing body of data indicates that humans (as well as lower organisms) can acquire some degree of control over usually autonomous psychobiological processes through a variety of procedures, such as biofeedback. One of the oldest techniques for achieving such self-regulation, particularly of attention, is meditation. From research in this area, a model has emerged which helps us understand some basic principles in the self-regulation of consciousness. Though the present model uses meditation as a reference case, it is applicable to all voluntarily elicited altered states of consciousness.

A General Model of Transformations of Consciousness

The model which has emerged from the present authors' research starts with the three basic temporal epochs present in all changes in consciousness. These three periods may be simply labeled *before, during,* and *after. Before* refers to the psychobiological patterns of an individual prior to the experience of a particular altered state of consciousness. It is often referred to under the rubric of predispositional variables and encompasses the study of personality traits and other individual differences that enable one either to be receptive and open to the experience of particular altered states of consciousness or antagonistic and closed to the experience of such states. As such, it includes the genetic history of the individual, the psychobiological encoding of the individual's learning experience (including culturally conditioned learning), as well as the immediate social and interpersonal environment within which the individual experiences the altered state of consciousness. For example, some investigators, in controlled studies of long-term effects of LSD, have found that persons who emphasized "structure and control" in their cognitive style, respond minimally to the drug, while more intense reactions are seen in Ss preferring a more unstructured, spontaneous, inward-turning life (e.g., Barr, Langs, Holt, Goldberger, & Klein, 1972; McGlothlin, Cohen, & McGlothlin, 1967).

The next period, *during*, refers to the state effects of a particular vehicle or pathway (such as meditation or drugs). It is upon this period that the vast majority of research in the area of altered states has focused. State effects are a function of the interaction of the vehicle or pathway for altering consciousness with predispositional variables. For example, the state effects of hypnosis appear to be a function of the hypnotic procedures interacting with a broad range of predispositional and situational variables. Thus, we now have evidence that a portion of the variance in hypnotic susceptibility can be attributed to genetic factors (e.g., Morgan, 1973; Morgan, Hilgard, & Davert, 1970), which interact significantly with early history of the individual (see, J. R. Hilgard, 1972; Morgan, 1973), and with a variety of situational factors as well as specific aspects of the hypnotic induction which all have important influences on hypnotic responsiveness (e.g., Barber, 1969, 1970; Orne, 1959). More specifically, the effects of hypnotic suggestion differ between high and low susceptible Ss: many psychological and biological changes induced by hypnotic suggestion occur only in high susceptible Ss. These include analgesia, time distortion, and the self-regulation of some autonomic nervous system functions (Engstrom, 1975; Garrett, 1975; E. R. Hilgard, 1969). In sum, an altered state is an interactive product of what came before and the pathway or vehicle employed for consciousness alteration. That is, the before is a potent determinant of the during; predispositon shapes state effects.

It is this latter variable—the pathway or vehicle—which is suggested as a critical determinant of the third major temporal epoch in the present model: the *after*, or trait effects of the particular practice. As a person develops the requisite skills for entering particular states on command, the experiential and biological consequences of such control may become more persistent and enduring through learned control. If we assume that the patterning and structure of neural events reflect an organism's state of consciousness (see John, 1976), a tonic change in key psychobiological processes will result in a shift in information-processing mode and, consequently, can be termed an altered trait of consciousness. Whether such trait effects do in fact arise is hypothesized to be a function of the vehicle or pathway adopted, not of the state effects elicited. For example, an individual may have had a particularly profound experience following the ingestion of a psychedelic chemical. The available evidence, however, is inconclusive with regard to long-term carry over from psychedelic altered states (e.g., Barber, 1970; McGlothlin et al., 1967).

Finally, the remaining element in the present model is the feedback effects of trait changes on predispositional variables. For example, high anxiety is a predispositional variable which appears not to be conducive to the practice of meditation (Otis, 1973). One of the most reliable trait effects of meditation is a reduction of anxiety (e.g., Linden, 1973). And, we suggest, lowered anxiety further increases an individual's receptivity to meditation. This feedback process can be put simply as: the after is the before for the next during. In other words, the trait effects of a particular vehicle for altering consciousness change the predispositional matrix, which will in turn affect the state changes elicited by a subsequent utilization of the vehicle. However, this feedback process is hypothesized to occur only when a core biocognitive process such as attention is changed as a function of the learning which ensues upon practice of the particular vehicle. Thus, while attempts to modify hypnotizability through repeated exposure to hypnotic suggestions have been only partially successful (see review by Diamond, 1974),[5] training in processes closely related to selective attention has consistently been associated with increases in hypnotizability (Gur, 1974; Wickramasekera, 1973).

This temporal model of changes in consciousness organizes data on altered states and leads to specific predictions about the effects of different vehicles for altering consciousness. The remainder of this paper will illustrate the application of the model to meditation and hypnosis.

Before: Biocognitive Preparedness

What sort of person is attracted to and can be benefited by meditation? A number of converging lines of evidence suggest that Ss who are not highly anxious and who have some capacity to voluntarily self-regulate their attention are likely to experience subjectively positive effects from meditation.[6] Interestingly, facility at attentional

[5] It should be noted, however, that training programs designed to maximize motivational and attitudinal conditions have been associated with significant gains in hypnotizability (e.g., Burns, 1976; Sachs & Anderson, 1967). It may be, as Burns 81976) has suggested, that the change in attitude may have the effect of allowing S's "natural" level of hypnotizability to become expressed.

[6] While it may be tempting to classify the individual differences described here on existing dimensions or continua of arousal (e.g., Fischer, 1971), the underlying mechanisms appear to be much more complex and preclude analysis in terms of general arousal. Moreover, the question of the concept of general arousal has recently been called into question by contemporary research on psychophysiological specificity (e.g., Davidson, 1976; Davidson & Schwartz, 1976).

self-regulation is also associated with superior performance on standard tests of hypnotizability. A principle process indexed by standard tests of susceptibility is the capacity for sustained attentional involvement (e.g., Galbraith, Cooper, & London, 1972; Tellegen & Atkinson, 1974; Van Nuys, 1973). If tests of hypnotizability do in fact reflect attentional competence, then we might expect to find that people who are initially attracted to meditation are more highly susceptible before beginning their practice than a comparable control group. Although the necessary longitudinal data are lacking, preliminary findings support this prediction (Walrath & Hamilton, 1975). Van Nuys (1973) has approached this question from the opposite perspective and has found that those Ss who are better able to concentrate during meditation (operationally defined as fewer "thought intrusions") are more highly susceptible to hypnosis.

Based upon these initial findings, Davidson, Goleman, & Schwartz (1976) sought to more fully explore the personality patterns associated with the predisposition to meditate. This study emerged partially from a recent theory of the psychobiology of relaxation and related states proposed by Davidson and Schwartz (1976). These latter investigators have suggested that individuals differ with respect to the type and amount of ongoing intrusive or unwanted events, which for lack of a better term, has acquired the label "anxiety." Specifically, Davidson and Schwartz have proposed that anxiety occurs in two predominant modes—cognitive and somatic.[7] Cognitive symptoms include phenomena such as difficulty in concentration because of uncontrollable thoughts, excessive worry over something not objectively important, and anxiety over the inability to make decisions. Somatic symptoms, alternatively, include such things as feeling jittery in the body, symptoms of diarrhea, tension in the stomach, and excessive perspiration. Unfortunately, most standard anxiety inventories do not separate these different modes and consequently preclude the assessment of the specificity of particular techniques or vehicles in differentially affecting one versus the other type of anxiety. Davidson and Schwartz have hypothesized that certain configurations of anxiety will benefit by the practice of particular procedures which specifically block unwanted activity in a given mode. For example, these authors propose that a pattern consisting of high cognitive and low somatic anxiety (e.g., excessive rumination in the absence of somatic tension) will be maximally attenuated by a procedure which specifically blocks cognitive anxiety. In this case, it is predicted that activities which maximally engage the cognitive

[7] It should be noted that this distinction is at the most molar level. Somatic may be further subdivided into autonomic and skeletal components (see Borkojec, 1976), while cognitive may be separated into left versus right hemisphere mediated anxiety.

system, such as doing a crossword puzzle or playing chess, would result in the greatest reductions in cognitive anxiety. It is hypothesized that other procedures emphasizing somatic activation would result in greater decrements in somatic relative to cognitive anxiety. Some of these predictions have recently received empirical support (Davidson, Davison, & Freedland, 1977; Schwartz, Davidson, & Goleman, in press).

Davidson and Schwartz (1976) have additionally suggested that meditation will be undertaken by individuals who, on the average, show low cognitive and low somatic anxiety. This suggestion was based upon evidence which indicates that people with elevated levels of anxiety will not, at least initially, be benefited by meditation and will be less likely to persist in their practice. Thus, Otis (1973) has performed a longitudinal study of meditators and found that those initiates who practiced regularly for more than 12 months characterized themselves as less anxious, more calm and peaceful than those who dropped out before 12 months. These self-evaluations were made *before* either group had begun meditation. These data suggest that predispositional differences in global anxiety had significant effects on Ss' ability to persist in the practice of meditation.

In their study of predispositional variables associated with the practice of meditation, Davidson et al. (1976) found no significant differences in global trait anxiety as assessed by the State-Trait Anxiety Inventory (Spielberger, Gorsuch, & Lushene, 1970) between a group of Ss ($N = 14$) who had just begun the practice of meditation (who were practicing less than 1 month) and an age and education matched control group ($N = 11$). However, the means indicated that Ss beginning meditation had less anxiety than controls as assessed by this measure ($\bar{X}$ for beginners = 40.86; $\bar{X}$ for controls = 42.6). An additional anxiety questionnaire (Schwartz et al., in press) designed to separately assess cognitive and somatic components was also administered to these Ss. This questionnaire consisted of 14 symptoms, half cognitive and half somatic. The Ss were instructed to circle a number from 1–5 according to the degree to which they generally or typically experienced this symptom *when they are feeling anxious*. This questionnaire is therefore not sensitive to the absolute amount of anxiety experienced but rather reflects the modality in which anxiety is typically experienced when it occurs. The results obtained with this questionnaire indicated that there were no significant differences between controls and beginners in preponderance of cognitive anxiety ($\bar{X}$ for beginners = 20.64; $\bar{X}$ for controls = 19.82) while beginners reported significantly more somatic symptoms than controls ($\bar{X}$ for beginners = 18.9; $\bar{X}$ for controls = 16.2; $t = 2.16$, $d.f. = 23$;

$p < .05$).[8] Apparently, when they feel anxious, those Ss initially attracted to meditation experience more somatic symptoms than controls. The fact that such somatic processes are usually easily discriminable may have been influential in motivating these Ss to seek a means to greater relaxation. It may be that in the absence of any discriminable anxiety, individuals would not be motivated to begin meditation.

Davidson et al. (1976) have compared beginners to controls on a number of other measures in order to explore the pattern or configuration typically associated with a predisposition toward meditation, and many of these antecedent measures are also associated with hypnotizability. There was a highly significant difference between scores of beginners and of controls on the Tellegen Absorption Scale (Tellegen & Atkinson, 1974), ($\bar{X}$ for beginners = 26.1; $\bar{X}$ for controls = 21.6; $t = 3.02$, $d.f. = 23$; $p < .01$) which measures the capacity for sustained attentional involvement. For example, the following item from the scale, answered true, indicates capacity for absorption: "If I wish, I can imagine . . . some things so vividly that they hold my attention in the way a good movie or story does [p. 270]."

These results suggest that individuals, who are interested enough in meditation to have begun to practice, report more instances of spontaneous, total attentional involvements than a comparable control group. In addition, there is a non-significant trend suggestive of less overall anxiety among the beginners, who at the same time report that they do experience anxiety more in the somatic mode than did the controls. These findings replicate and extend prior work in this area (e.g., Lesh, 1970; Maupin, 1965; Walrath & Hamilton, 1975).

During: Some State Effects of Meditation and Hypnosis

Comparing the state effects of meditation and hypnosis highlights some important differences between these procedures and allows for the development of a model, based partially on signal detection theory (Green & Swets, 1966), for understanding their differential consequences.

It is important to take into account the different forms of meditation when considering their state effects (e.g., Goleman, 1972). The two basic types which have been identified consistently in the classical literature on meditation are *mindfulness* — the maintenance of a particular attentional stance toward all objects of awareness, and *concentration* — the focusing of attention on a single-target percept. These two different forms of meditation have stable, differential,

---

[8] All statistics employed in this paper are based upon two-tailed tests.

experiential, and psychobiological consequences (see, Goleman, 1972).

One of the frequently reported state effects of *concentrative* meditation is a decreased reactivity to the external environment (e.g., Anand, Chhina, & Singh, 1961; Prabhavananda & Isherwood, 1953). In their classic study of yogi's in *samādhi*, Anand et al., (1961) observed no alpha blocking to a variety of sensory stimuli including strong light and a hot test tube. Banquet (1973) has replicated this effect in practitioners of Transcendental Meditation (also a concentrative practice) during periods of alpha abundance in addition to demonstrating nonresponsiveness of raw EEG during the "deep" stages of meditation associated with fast (20 to 40 Hz.) frequency activity. Although these findings are preliminary and lack the necessary quantitative evaluation, they do suggest that during periods of intense concentration in meditation, sensory information may become attenuated below the level of the cortex.

These state effects differ from those typically observed during hypnosis. One of the most interesting recent developments in evaluating state effects during hypnosis is the resurrection by E. R. Hilgard (1973, 1974, 1976) of a very old and neglected procedure for assessing information at levels below conscious awareness. This procedure involves hypnotically induced automatic writing or its equivalent to gain access to normally unreported information. Hilgard has used this procedure to explore a consistent paradoxical finding in experiments on pain reduction in hypnosis. When cold pressor pain is reduced through hypnotically suggested analgesia, the concomitant cardiovascular changes remain essentially unchanged. When, through "automatic writing" or "automatic talking," the S is queried about his experience, he reports the pain just as in the normal nonhypnotic state. The experience of suffering (the affective component) may be reduced but the sensory experience of pain is not significantly different during automatic writing versus the normal state.

These findings are consistent with a growing body of literature suggesting that, in the area of pain reduction, hypnosis as well as placebos function primarily by altering S's criterion for reporting pain (β), but have no significant effects on sensitivity (d') (e.g., Clark, 1969, 1974).[9] This model of hypnotic state effects also applies to situations other than suggested analgesia. For example, when suggestions are given for deafness or blindness, the bulk of the available

[9] There is one report, however, which may be interpreted as indicating that for highly susceptible Ss, hypnotic analgesia may significantly affect pain sensitivity (McGlashan et al., 1969). However, signal detection methodology was not employed in that report, thus precluding an unambiguous interpretation (see also, Hilgard & Hilgard, 1975).

evidence indicates that the early component of the scalp recorded evoked responses (which primarily reflect the physical characteristics of the stimulus) to stimuli in the relevant modalities are not affected compared with control conditions during which no suggestion was given (e.g., Beck & Barolin, 1965; Beck, Dustman, & Beir, 1966; Halliday & Mason, 1964).[10] Interestingly, other states closely resembling hypnosis — such as hysteria — have also been found, using signal detection and other psychophysical methods, primarily to affect the individual's criterion for reporting various sensations but not the person's sensitivity to these events (e.g., Theodor & Mandelcorn, 1973; Zimmerman & Grosz, 1966). Thus, it appears that procedures based upon suggestion act primarily on the output side of the organism and alter the person's response set while other altered states appear to exert consequential effects on the input or afferent side and alter the person's stimulus set (see Broadbent, 1970). As we have previously seen, advanced stages of concentrative meditation appear to affect the practitioner's stimulus set as do certain pharmacological agents (e.g., Chapman, Murphy, & Butler, 1973). It remains to be determined by future research whether very highly hypnotizable individuals show alterations in stimulus set (sensitivity) during certain types of hypnotic suggestions. It may be that the interaction of certain procedures with Ss who are highly susceptible would result in the type of attentional change characteristic of concentrative meditation (McGlashan, Evans, & Orne, 1969).

A comparison of the state effects of mindfulness meditation with hypnosis is not yet warranted due to the paucity of relevant data. One unique state effect of such meditation is the lack of habituation to simple, repetitive stimuli (Kasamatsu & Hirai, 1966) as well as the lack of differential responsiveness to affective versus nonaffective stimuli (Hirai, 1974). Such a pattern, in contrast to that found for concentrative meditation, is suggestive of sustained cortical responsiveness to sensory events in conjunction with attenuated affective (limbic) influences on perception. While, based upon the available knowledge, there is little reason to believe that hypnosis would elicit similar changes, no systematic studies have been performed to explore these questions.

To briefly summarize, the available evidence suggests that techniques utilizing a strategy which require the sustained focusing of attention on a single-target percept result in state effects of a stimulus set variety. These procedures result in modifications of afferent input which may, in certain instances, take place below the cortical level. The existence of this specific form of neuronal plasticity has

[10] However, Clynes, Kohn, and Lifshitz (1964) found that hypnotic suggestion of blindness did result in a reduced visual evoked response in one of two Ss studied.

been suggested in evoked potential studies of selective attention in humans (Harter & Salmon, 1972) and is consistent with recent neurophysiological data on modulation of afferent input at sensory-specific thalamic relay stations (Doty, Wilson, Bartlett, & Pecci-Saavedra, 1973; Pribram, 1973; Spinelli & Pribram, 1967).

After: Altered Traits of Consciousness

The after affects or the more enduring consequences of the practice of particular procedures is dependent on the nature of the technique in question. This basic principle is illustrated in a recent study performed by Schwartz et al. (in press) on the differential effects of meditation and exercise in the reduction of cognitive and somatic anxiety. In this study, individuals who had been regularly attending a weekly class in physical exercise as well as practicing by themselves daily, were compared with a group of meditators on a cognitive-somatic anxiety questionnaire.[11] Since one of the consistent claims made by practitioners of meditation is a reduction of cognitive intrusions (see Goleman, 1972), we specifically hypothesized that long-term practice (for approximately six months) of meditation would lead to significant reductions in cognitive symptoms of anxiety, while long-term training in physical exercise would result in reductions in somatic anxiety. The results indicated that the regular practice of meditation led to a greater reduction in cognitive anxiety than did the regular practice of physical exercise (for the same period of time) while the opposite was true for somatic anxiety. Thus, meditators had less cognitive and more somatic anxiety than exercisers. The latter group, in turn, had less somatic and more cognitive anxiety than meditators. These findings illustrate the need to consider the specificity of effects elicited by different self-regulation techniques and specifically suggest that the systems primarily engaged by a particular vehicle are also those that are most enduringly affected.

The neural concomitants of the specificity of trait effects are illustrated in a recent experiment by Schwartz, Davidson, and Margolin.[12] In this study, the authors were interested in exploring differences in the voluntary control of attention among practitioners of two different forms of meditation. Three groups of 10 Ss each were employed. Group 1 comprised teachers of Transcendental Meditation—a passive procedure consisting of the subvocal repetition of a phrase and concomitant attentional focusing upon this stimulus. All Ss in

[11] Copies of the Cognitive-Somatic Anxiety Questionnaire (CSAQ) may be obtained from the senior author.

[12] Schwartz, G. E., Davidson, R. J., & Margolin, R. A. Meditation and the self-regulation of attention: Intrahemispheric EEG changes. (in preparation)

this group were teachers of meditation who had been practicing for at least 2 years.

Group 2 (the Sherbourne group) consisted of practitioners of a Gurdjieffian form of meditation who were all trained in a standard 10-month course in Sherbourne, England. The type of meditation practiced by these Ss was an active form of attentional self-regulation whose object was ongoing proprioceptive or exteroceptive stimuli. These Ss also practiced a variety of exercises emphasizing the self-regulation of somatic and motoric processes. All persons in this group had been practicing the meditation daily for at least 2 years. A description of one form of meditation regularly practiced by this group was offered by a student of this technique:

> A man lies on his back on the floor. Trying to relax all his muscles, he then concentrates his attention on trying to sense his nose. When he begins to sense his nose the man then transfers his attention and tries to sense his ear; when this is achieved he transfers his attention to the right foot. From the right foot to the left; . . . then to the left ear and back again to the nose, and so on [Ouspensky, 1949; p. 351].

Group 3 was a control group interested in, but not practicing, meditation.

Schwartz et al.[13] predicted that all Ss would show specificity in cortical activation as a function of the modality of the stimulus to be attended and that the Sherbourne meditators would show greater cortical specificity during such a task than either the Transcendental Meditation or control group. This hypothesis was based upon the specific training in the voluntary control of attention undergone by the Sherbourne group in comparison with the Transcendental Meditation group.

All Ss were required to attend to either a visual or a kinesthetic stimulus. The visual stimulus was a photograph of a person sitting in the psychophysiology lab; while during kinesthetic conditions, Ss were required to attend to kinesthetic sensations in their right hand.

In order to assess the cortical concomitants of mode-specific attention, we recorded monopolar EEG from areas known to be actively involved with visual and kinesthetic information-processing: the occipital (01) and the sensory-motor regions (C3). The output of each EEG channel was filtered for alpha and quantified on line. The results revealed that during kinesthetic attention the ratio of occipital to sensory-motor alpha was significantly higher (indicative of relative C3 activation) than during visual attention for each group indicating relatively greater occipital activation during the latter versus the former task. Importantly, the difference in this EEG ratio for kinesthetic versus visual trials was significantly greater for the

---

[13] See footnote 12.

Sherbourne group than for the Transcendental Meditation or the control group.

One limitation of this study should be recognized and must necessarily temper the conclusions which are drawn. Since the study was entirely between groups, the contributions of self-selection and predispositional influences could not be assessed (see Smith, 1975). Recent research (Davidson, Schwartz, & Rothman, 1976) on Ss scoring in the upper and lower extremes of the distribution on the Tellegen Absorption Scale (Tellegen & Atkinson, 1974) indicates that the groups differ significantly on EEG concomitants of mode-specific selective attention in a task similar to that employed by Schwartz et al.[14]

These findings, however, highlight an important principle of the present model; the vehicle or technique for altering consciousness is a critical determinant of the trait effects elicited. Specifically, different meditation techniques may lead to the cultivation of different attentional skills which are reflected in a particular patterning of neural processes. The Ss in the Sherbourne group all had been trained in the active, voluntary control of attention to a restricted range of somatic and other stimuli. The findings of greater cortical specificity in the Sherbourne Ss compared to the Transcendental Meditation and control Ss seems consistent with the techniques practiced by the former group.

While different meditation techniques lead to differential task-specific cortical patterning, they do share a number of common components among themselves and with other relaxation techniques, including hynotically suggested relaxation (see Davidson & Schwartz, 1976; Walrath & Hamilton, 1975). At the core of these commonalities is a reduction in self-reported anxiety. Both training in relaxation and meditation have been found to result in decrements in self-reported anxiety (Davidson, Goleman, & Schwartz, 1976; Davidson & Schwartz, 1976; Hjelle, 1974). In addition, Goleman and Schwartz (1976) have found that, compared to nonmeditating control Ss, meditators show improved recovery on autonomic variables (SCR and HR) following arousal by a stressful stimulus. Others have found that hypnotic suggestions of relaxation as well as other relaxation procedures lead to decrements in a variety of autonomic measures (e.g., Damaser, Shor, & Orne, 1963; Luthe, 1970; Walrath & Hamilton, 1975) and preliminary data exists suggesting that such changes may be more persistent and enduring in Ss practicing meditation (e.g., Goleman & Schwartz, 1976) though the veracity of this claim must await further research.

[14] See footnote 12.

The consideration of the feedback effects of learned trait changes raises the issue of whether repeated practice of a particular technique results simply in a subsequent decreased latency to induce the particular altered state of consciousness or whether, in fact, the depth of the state is enhanced. Unfortunately, this distinction has not been systematically addressed in the existing literature. However, the available evidence does tentatively suggest that if a particular vehicle results in a change in a core biocognitive process (i.e., the mechanisms of attention) then one consequence of the learned (trait) effects will be an enhanced "depth" of experience upon subsequent utilization of the vehicle. Hirai (1974) has reported a positive correlation between length and quality (assessed by teacher ratings) of meditation practice and electrophysiological parameters reflecting depth of state (percent-time theta, responsiveness of the EEG to external stimuli). Whether the analogous situation applies to experience with hypnosis must await further research.

In summary, a temporal-developmental scheme was outlined and employed to organize data on changes in consciousness arising from the practice of meditation and the induction of hypnosis. The first epoch, before, refers to predispositional variables that influence S's response to a particular technique. It was here suggested that both meditation and hypnosis share a number of common variables associated with a positive response to the experience. These parameters have to do with attentional flexibility and the capacity to engage sustained attention. In addition, low anxiety was identified as being associated with the inclination to persist in the practice of meditation. The relevance of the anxiety dimension to hypnosis is less clear (e.g., Orne, 1974).

Some state effects of meditation and hypnosis were reviewed in the context of research on selective attention and signal detection theory. The effects of concentrative meditation and hypnotic suggestions of analgesia were compared on measures of responsiveness to painful stimuli. It was suggested that concentrative meditation involves alterations in attention of the stimulus set variety while hypnotic suggestions of analgesia result in shifts in response set, except possibly in highly susceptible Ss (McGlashan et al., 1969).

The trait effects of particular types of interventions were seen to depend critically on the patterning of underlying processes activated by the technique. This notion was illustrated in the studies comparing the trait effects of different types of meditation and relaxation on both psychometric and psychophysiological, dependent measures. Meditation techniques emphasizing active, attentional self-regulation were found to be associated with enhanced specificity of cortical activation during selective attention tasks, compared with more passive meditation procedures. In addition, a number of trait effects (learned changes) common to most meditative practices and relaxation procedures, including hypnotically suggested relaxation, were identified. These effects were all concerned with decrements in self-reported anxiety, accompanied by enhanced "limbic quiescence" as indexed by decreases in various autonomic indicators of stress.

While the review of the meditation and hypnosis literature is necessarily selective in such a brief overview, a number of themes have been identified which warrant further study. These issues concern the nature and structure of the attentional mechanisms which influence S's initial response to meditation and hypnosis, the type of attentional change associated with the induction of meditative versus hypnotic altered states and, finally, the learned transformations in attentional competence that are associated with the practice of these techniques.

REFERENCES

ANAND, B. K., CHHINA, G. S., & SINGH, B. Some aspects of electroencephalographic studies in yogis. *Electroenceph. clin. Neurophysiol.*, 1961, *13*, 452–456.

BANQUET, J. P. Spectral analysis of the EEG in meditation. *Electroenceph. clin. Neurophysiol.*, 1973, *35*, 143–151.

BARBER, T. X. *Hypnosis: A scientific approach*. New York: Van Nostrand Reinhold, 1969.

BARBER, T. X. *LSD, marihuana, Yoga, and hypnosis*. Chicago: Aldine, 1970.

BARR, H. L., LANGS, R. J., HOLT, R. R., GOLDBERGER, L., & KLEIN, G. S. *LSD: Personality and experience*. New York: Wiley-Interscience, 1972.

BECK, E. C., & BAROLIN, G. S. Effect of hypnotic suggestions on evoked potentials. *J. nerv. ment. Dis.*, 1965, *140*, 154–161.

BECK, E. C., DUSTMAN, R. E., & BEIR, E. G. Hypnotic suggestions and visually evoked potentials. *Electroenceph. clin. Neurophysiol.*, 1966, *20*, 397–400.

BORKOVEC, T. D. Physiological and cognitive processes in the regulation of anxiety. In G. E. Schwartz and D. Shapiro (Eds.), *Consciousness and self-regulation: Advances in research*. (Vol. 1) New York: Plenum, 1976. Pp. 261–312.

BROADBENT, D. E. Stimulus set and response set: Two kinds of selective attention. In D. I. Mostofsky (Ed.), *Attention: Contemporary theory and analysis*. New York: Appleton-Century-Crofts, 1970. Pp. 51–60.

BURNS, A. Changes in hypnotizability following experience. *Int. J. clin. exp. Hypnosis*, 1976, *24*, 269–280.

CHAPMAN, C. R., MURPHY, T. M., & BUTLER, S. H. Analgesic strength of 33 percent nitrous oxide: A signal detection theory evaluation. *Science*, 1973, *179*, 1246–1248.

CLARK, W. C. Sensory-decision theory analysis of the placebo effect on the criterion for pain and thermal sensitivity (d'). *J. abnorm. Psychol.*, 1969, *74*, 363–371.

CLARK, W. C. Pain sensitivity and the report of pain: An introduction to sensory decision theory. *Anesthesiology*, 1974, *40*, 272–287.

CLYNES, M., KOHN, M., & LIFSHITZ, K. Dynamics and spatial behavior of light evoked potentials, their modification under hypnosis, and on-line correlation in relation to rhythmic components. *Ann. N. Y. Acad. Sci.*, 1964, *112*, 468–508.

DAMASER, E. C., SHOR, R. E., & ORNE, M. T. Physiological effects during hypnotically requested emotions. *Psychosom. Med.*, 1963, *25*, 334–343.

DAVIDSON, R. J. On the psychobiology of attention and awareness: Scalp topography of averaged evoked responses to visual and auditory unconscious and conscious stimuli under varying attentional demands. Unpublished doctoral dissertation, Harvard Univer., 1976.

DAVIDSON, R. J., DAVISON, G. C., & FREEDLAND, E. Psychophysiological specificity and the self-regulation of cognitive and somatic anxiety. Paper to be presented at the International Meeting on Biofeedback and Self-Control. Tubingen, Germany, November 1977.

DAVIDSON, R. J., GOLEMAN, D. J., & SCHWARTZ, G. E. Attentional and affective concomitants of meditation: A cross-sectional study. *J. abnorm. Psychol.*, 1976, *85*, 235–238.

DAVIDSON, R. J., & SCHWARTZ, G. E. The psychobiology of relaxation and related states: A multi-process theory. In D. I. Mostofsky (Ed.), *Behavior control and modification of physiological activity*. Englewood Cliffs, N. J.: Prentice-Hall, 1976. Pp. 399–442.

DAVIDSON, R. J., SCHWARTZ, G. E., & ROTHMAN, L. P. Attentional style and the self-regulation of mode-specific attention: An electroencephalographic study. *J. abnorm. Psychol.*, 1976, *85*, 611–621.

DIAMOND, M. J. Modification of hypnotizability: A review. *Psychol. Bull.*, 1974, *81*, 180–198.

DOTY, R. W., WILSON, P. D., BARTLETT, J. R., & PECCI-SAAVEDRA, J. Mesencephalic control of lateral geniculate nucleus in primates. I. Electrophysiology. *Exp. Brain Res.*, 1973, *18*, 189–203.

ENGSTROM, D. R. Hypnosis versus biofeedback among hypnotizable and unhypnotizable subjects. Paper presented at the meeting of the American Psychological Association, Chicago, September 1975.

FISCHER, R. A cartography of the ecstatic and meditative states: The experimental and experiential feature of a perception-hallucination continuum are considered. *Science*, 1971, *174*, 897–904.

GALBRAITH, G. C., COOPER, L. M., & LONDON, P. Hypnotic susceptibility and the sensory evoked response. *J. comp. physiol. Psychol.*, 1972, *80*, 509–514.

GARRETT, J. B. Effect of hypnotic time distortion upon embedded figures test performance. Paper presented at the meeting of the American Psychological Association, Chicago, September 1975.

GOLEMAN, D. The Buddha on meditation and states of consciousness. Part I: The teachings. *J. transpers. Psychol.*, 1972, *4*, 1–44.

GOLEMAN, D. J., & SCHWARTZ, G. E. Meditation as an intervention in stress reactivity. *J. consult. clin. Psychol.*, 1976, *44*, 456–466.

GREEN, D. M., & SWETS, J. A. *Signal detection theory and psychophysics*. New York: Wiley & Sons, 1966.

GUR, R. C. An attention-controlled operant procedure for enhancing hypnotic susceptibility. *J. abnorm. Psychol.*, 1974, *83*, 644–650.

HALLIDAY, A. M., & MASON, A. A. Cortical evoked potentials during hypnotic anaesthesia. *Electroenceph. clin. Neurophysiol.*, 1964, *16*, 314. (Abstract)

HARTER, M. R., & SALMON, L. E. Intra-modality selective attention and evoked cortical potentials to randomly presented patterns. *Electroenceph. clin. Neurophysiol.*, 1972, *32*, 605–613.

HILGARD, E. R. Pain as a puzzle for psychology and physiology. *Amer. Psychologist*, 1969, *24*, 103–113.

HILGARD, E. R. A neodissociation interpretation of pain reduction in hypnosis. *Psychol. Rev.*, 1973, *80*, 396–411.

HILGARD, E. R. Toward a neo-dissociation theory: Multiple cognitive controls in human functioning. *Perspect. Biol. Med.*, 1974, *17*, 301–316.

HILGARD, E. R. Neodissociation theory of multiple cognitive control systems. In G. E. Schwartz & D. Shapiro (Eds.), *Consciousness and self-regulation: Advances in research* (Vol. 1). New York: Plenum Press, 1976. Pp. 137–171.

HILGARD, E. R., & HILGARD, J. R. *Hypnosis in the relief of pain*. Los Altos, Calif.: Kaufman, 1975.

HILGARD, J. R. Evidence for a developmental-interactive theory of hypnotic susceptibility. In E. Fromm & R. E. Shor (Eds.), *Hypnosis: Research developments and perspectives*. Chicago: Aldine-Atherton, 1972. Pp. 387–397.

HIRAI, T. *Psychophysiology of Zen*. Tokyo: Igaku Shoin, 1974.

HJELLE, L. A. Transcendental meditation and psychological health. *Percept. mot. Skills*, 1974, *39*, 623–628.

JAMES, W. *The principles of psychology* (Vol. 1). New York: Dover, 1950. (Orig. Publ. 1890.)

JOHN, E. R. A model of consciousness. In G. E. Schwartz & D. Shapiro (Eds.), *Consciousness and self-regulation: Advances in research* (Vol. 1). New York: Plenum Press, 1976. Pp. 1–50.

KASAMATSU, A., & HIRAI, T. An electroencephalographic study on the Zen meditation (Zazen). *Folia psychiat. neurol. jap.*, 1966, *20*, 315–336.

LESH, T. V. Zen meditation and the development of empathy in counselors. *J. human. Psychol.*, 1970, *10*, 39–74.

LINDEN, W. Practicing of meditation by school children and their levels of field dependence-independence, test anxiety, and reading achievement. *J. consult. clin. Psychol.*, 1973, *41*, 139–143.

LUTHE, W. (Ed.) *Autogenic therapy. Volume IV. Research and theory*. (W. Luthe, Auth.) New York: Grune & Stratton, 1970.

MAUPIN, E. W. Individual differences in response to a Zen meditation exercise. *J. consult. Psychol.*, 1965, *29*, 139–145.

McGLASHAN, T. H., EVANS, F. J., & ORNE, M. T. The nature of hypnotic analgesia and placebo response to experimental pain. *Psychosom. Med.*, 1969, *31*, 227–246.

McGLOTHLIN, W., COHEN, S., & McGLOTHLIN, M. S. Long lasting effects of LSD on normals. *Arch. gen. Psychiat.*, 1967, *17*, 521–532.

MORGAN, A. H. The heritability of hypnotic susceptibility in twins. *J. abnorm. Psychol.*, 1973, *82*, 55–61.

MORGAN, A. H., HILGARD, E. R., & DAVERT, E. C. The heritabiliy of hypnotic susceptibility of twins: A preliminary report. *Behav. Genet.*, 1970, *1*, 213–224.

ORNE, M. T. The nature of hypnosis: Artifact and essence. *J. abnorm. soc. Psychol.*, 1959, *58*, 277–299.

ORNE, M. T. Pain suppression by hypnosis and related phenomena. In J. J. Bonica (Ed.), *Advances in neurology. Vol. 4. Pain*. New York: Raven Press, 1974. Pp. 563–572.

OTIS, L. S. Meditation or simulated meditation by nonpredisposed volunteers: Some psychological changes. In E. Taub (Chm.), The psychobiology of meditation. Symposium presented at the American Psychological Association, Montréal, August 1973.

OUSPENSKY, P. D. *In search of the miraculous: Fragments of an unknown teaching*. New York: Harcourt, Brace & World, 1949.

PRABHAVANANDA, S., & ISHERWOOD, C. (Trans.) *How to know God: The yoga aphorisms of Patanjali*. Hollywood: Vedanta Press, 1953.

PRIBRAM, K. H. The primate frontal cortex – Executive of the brain. In K. H. Pribram & A. R. Luria (Eds.), *Psychophysiology of the frontal lobes*. New York: Academic Press, 1973. Pp. 293–314.

PRIBRAM, K. H., & McGUINNESS, D. Arousal, activation, and effort in the control of attention. *Psychol. Rev.*, 1975, *82*, 116–149.

SACHS, L. B., & ANDERSON, W. L. Modification of hypnotic susceptibility. *Int. J. clin. exp. Hypnosis*, 1967, *15*, 172–180.

SCHWARTZ, G. E., DAVIDSON, R. J., & GOLEMAN, D. J. Patterning of cognitive and somatic processes in the self-regulation of anxiety. *Psychosom. Med.*, in press.

SMITH, J. C. Meditation as psychotherapy: A review of the literature. *Psychol. Bull.*, 1975, *82*, 558–564.

SPIELBERGER, C. D., GORSUCH, R. L., & LUSHENE, R. E. *Manual for the State-Trait Anxiety Inventory ("Self-Evaluation Questionnaire")*. Palo Alto, Calif.: Consulting Psychologists Press, 1970.

SPINELLI, D. N., & Pribram, K. H. Changes in visual recovery functions and unit activity produced by frontal and temporal cortex stimulation. *Electroenceph. clin. Neurophysiol.*, 1967, *22*, 143–149.

TELLEGEN, A., & ATKINSON, G. Openness to absorbing and self-altering experiences ("absorption"), a trait related to hypnotic susceptibility. *J. abnorm. Psychol.*, 1974, *83*, 268–277.

THEODOR, L. H., & MANDELCORN, M. S. Hysterical blindness: A case report and study using a modern psychophysical technique. *J. abnorm. Psychol.*, 1973, *82*, 552–553.

VAN NUYS, D. Meditation, attention, and hypnotic susceptibility: A correlational study. *Int. J. clin. exp. Hypnosis*, 1973, *21*, 59–69.

WALRATH, L. C., & HAMILTON, D. W. Autonomic correlates of meditation and hypnosis. *Amer. J. clin. Hypnosis*, 1975, *17*, 190–197.

WICKRAMASEKERA, I. Effects of electromyographic feedback on hypnotic susceptibility: More preliminary data. *J. abnorm. Psychol.*, 1973, *82*, 74–77.

ZIMMERMAN, J., & GROSZ, H. J. "Visual" performance of a functionally blind person. *Behav. Res. Ther.*, 1966, *4*, 119–134.

50

PASSIVE MEDITATION:
SUBJECTIVE, CLINCAL COMPARISON
WITH BIOFEEDBACK

Charles F. Stroebel and Bernard C. Glueck

Prior to the introduction of the concept of biofeedback, Western scientists lacked a meaningful model for studying the voluntary self-regulation of visceroautonomic body functions achieved via hypnosis and/or Eastern meditation techniques. In fact, until recently, psychologists taught that it was impossible to condition the autonomic nervous system, smooth muscles, and glands by other than classic Pavlovian techniques. This was in contrast to the very complex types of operant conditioning procedures employed in the behavioral laboratory which enabled investigators to teach a wide range of mammals intricate skeletal muscle performance tasks. In 1960, Kimmel and Hill demonstrated the possibility of instrumental conditioning of the galvanic skin response (GSR) (Kimmmel and Hill, 1960). Since then, there have been reports of learned control of a wide range of autonomic nervous system responses, including the GSR (Shapiro, 1964; Fowler and Kimmel, 1962), heart rate (Engel and Chism, 1967; Engel and Hansen, 1966), blood pressure (Dicara and Miller, 1968), salivation (Delse and Feather, 1968), and the relaxation of striated muscle (Budzynski, Stoyva, and Adler, 1970).

Biofeedback provided a comparative scientific model for operational examination of altered states of consciousness and visceroautonomic self-regulation achieved by whatever means—yoga, hypnosis, or drugs. In contrast to our conscious awareness of the five senses, and the extensive kinesthetic-position feedback from the striate musculature, functional reporting at the conscious level from smooth muscles, glands, and the gamma efferent regulation of striate muscle tension is meager, except under conditions of malfunction. The major sensation with malfunction of the latter systems is the relatively crude sensation of pain, sometimes referred to a distant dermatome. In other words, we are relatively unaware of blood pressure, of gastrointestinal peristaltic activity, of cardiac mechanics, of vasomotor regulation—the "involuntary" inner machinery of the body—except when significant malfunction occurs. While the adaptive regulation of inner machinery under conditions of normalcy indicates that relatively precise proprioception of its functioning does occur, this reporting is largely at an unconscious level, probably not ascending above the limbic system and is not normally under "voluntary" control.

The basic psychophysiological principle of biofeedback is the provision of *parallel external proprioception* via an external biofeedback loop, so that an inner machinery function becomes observable at the conscious level. This is accomplished with suitable sensors (electrical, thermal, pressure, etc.), electronics, and audio, visual, or tactile feedback signals. Considerable experimental controversy currently exists as to how animals and man use this parallel external proprioception to gain voluntary control of the inner machinery function in question (e.g., operant conditioning, mediation, suggestion, and placebo effect) (Stroebel and Glueck, 1973). However, voluntary control has now been demonstrated for many physiological systems under relatively passive learning conditions (i.e., voluntary control is difficult to demonstrate if the subject "tries too hard").

Procedures for self-regulation with biofeedback may be operationally specified, permitting laboratory scrutiny of relevant variables. For example, once a subject has acquired voluntary control over a visceral effector mechanism, it is possible to measure reaction times as has been traditionally done with striate

Function	Median reaction time (seconds)
EEG alpha blocking	.03
EEG alpha enhancement	0.75
Heart rate change	1
Hand warming	2
Foot warming	3
Electrodermal response	3
Colonic motility change	6–9

[a]Pilot study data. $n=5$.

motor responses in psychology laboratories. Upon presentation of a stimulus, the subject is instructed to alter visceral functioning in a specific direction. The measured stimulus-response interval is the reaction time, as shown for seven variables in Table 1.

Parallel proprioception probably should not be instantaneous; instead, a time lag should be introduced into the extrinsic feedback circuit which is suitable for the function in question. This hypothesis has been tested in irritable colon patients where fastest learning of control of colonic motility occurs when biofeedback signals correlated with colonic activity lag by 6–9 seconds. We surmise that the intrinsic proprioceptive report of colonic activity requires 6–9 seconds to reach the unconscious brain via relatively slowly conducting general visceral afferent neurons.

In addition to its applicability in treating a wide variety of psychosomatic conditions, biofeedback has provided psychophysiologists with an exciting new research strategy. Namely, biofeedback can be used to create a physiological steady state, that is, making some aspect of the physiological state a constant, permitting examination of the associated state of consciousness, both mentation and feelings. Normally, psychophysiologists must deal with a complicated mixture of additive and multiplicative factors as shown in Fig. 1. Psychophysiologic variance may be divided into components assignable to physiology (P), behavior (B) and their interaction (I). In analyzing a psychophysiological outcome the effect of the last term (I), is crucial in interpreting the other two. For, when the interaction is zero, the physiological and behavioral components are related to psychophysiological variance in a simple additive fashion, but, when nonzero, vastly more complicated *multiplicative* relationships must be considered as well.

To take advantage of the simplicity of the additive relationship, neurophysiologists classically study the effects of drugs on nervous system functioning with immobilized (curarized or anesthetized) animal preparations with the environment held constant; this familiar black environment experiment holds interactive effects relatively constant. Similarly, pharmacologists study the effect of drugs on some aspect of physiological functioning in situations in which the environment is clearly limited, such as with isolated gut or isolated nerve preparations. Using comparable logic but a different strategy, experimental psychologists have studied the effects of drugs on the behavior of inbred animals with similar genetic constitutions, where P is relatively constant; this is the familiar black box experiment. In either the black box or the black environment experiments, the complexities of interpreting the multiplicative effects (exponential, logarithmic, rank reversal, or other) ascribable to interaction variance are minimized.

$$\begin{array}{lllllll}
 & \sigma^2_{pp} & = & \sigma^2_{physiology} & + & \sigma^2_{behavioral} & + & \sigma^2_p \times \sigma_b \\
 & \text{Psychophysiological} & & & & & & \text{interaction} \\
 & \text{Variance} & & & & & &
\end{array}$$

Black Box Model $\quad \sigma^2_{pp} = k^2 + \sigma^2_b + k \times \sigma_b$

Black Environment Model $\quad \sigma^2_{pp} = \sigma^2_p + k^2 + \sigma_{p \times k}$

Fig. 1. Schematic paradigm showing physiological, behavioral and interactive components of psychophysiological (psychosomatic) variance. In the black box model, the physiological component is held constant. In the black environment model, the behavior component is held constant.

Passive Meditation

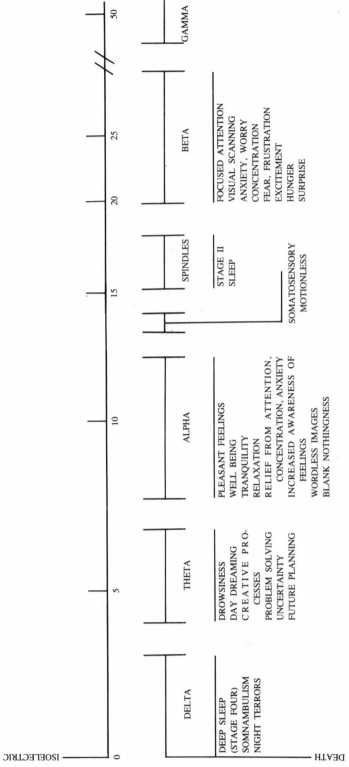

Fig. 2. Emotions and behavioral states associated with various bands within the spectrum of EEG activity stabilized as steady states using EEG biofeedback.

618

Psychophysiologists, on the other hand, favor more realistic designs approximating real life in which both behavioral and physiological factors may vary; this situation is more like that faced by the clinician, who is confronted with a sick patient who needs help now, despite the presence of many complicating nonadditive factors.

Biofeedback then, has enhanced the psychophysiologists research armamentarium by permitting him to create a variety of relative physiological steady states in subjects under a variety of conditions. An analogy would be the mathematician's use of asymptotes and intercept crossings to analyze boundary properties of a mathematical function.

An example covering an area relative to this chapter may make this point clearer. Brown (1970), and Stroebel and Glueck (1973) created electroencephalographic steady states by setting filters to provide biofeedback signals for three classically defined bands of EEG activity: theta, 4–7.5 hertz; alpha 8–12 hertz; and beta 20–35 hertz. Once a subject had achieved criterion levels of enhancement of activity in a given band, he was asked to describe his mental activity at the time (1) subjectively and (2) more objectively, using a variant of the Clyde Mood Scale (Clyde, 1963) adjective checklist. The results are tabulated in rank order along a spectrum of electroencephalographic activity in Fig. 2.

Once an altered steady physiological state has been achieved, psychological factors determine how the altered physiological state is subjectively interpreted. Orne (1962) has described some of these psychological factors as the "demand characteristics" of the situation; e.g., the subject's expectations of a possible alteration in mood, or "high," from the experience, or implicit/explicit suggestions or cues provided by the experimenter (Stroebel and Glueck, 1973).

It is a distinct possibility that certain of the EEG states (theta and alpha) may make subjects especially prone to suggestion and/or uncritical of primary process thoughts, conceivably enhancing hypnotic phenomena and/or free association in psychoanalytic psychotherapy.

An alternative explanation for variations in subjects' mood reports correlated with a specific band of EEG activity would be the dissociation of EEG patterns and behavioral arousal that has been demonstrated pharmacologically and in sensory deprivation experiments (Bradley, 1958; Mathews, 1971; Zubek, 1969). For example, Lynch and Paskewitz (1971) have suggested that alpha biofeedback has certain similarities to sensory deprivation, including elimination of patterned external stimulation and unfocusing of attention. The important point is that all these many possible sources of variation may be manipulated systematically in the context of a relatively steady state achieved through biofeedback. This powerful new experimental procedure will likely serve as the basis for many doctoral dissertations in years ahead, including the manipulation of other independent variables, such as, drug states and illness states.

Schwartz (1975) has extended this model, providing biofeedback for patterns of response for multiple variables. His work has emphasized that, since variables such as blood pressure are multiply determined, some form of patterned biofeedback will probably be optimal in treating conditions like essential (idiopathic) hypertension. This will likely be the case for other psychosomatic illnesses as well.

As noted in Fig. 2, most subjects report positive kinds of feelings, such as relaxed, floating, peaceful, very pleasant, and free from anxiety as the main subjective awareness at the time that alpha frequencies are occurring. An occasional subject may report some feeling of discomfort from the detachment of dissociative feelings that arise at this time (Brown, 1970; Lynch and Paskewitz, 1971; Stroebel and Glueck, 1973). Experience in our Psychophysiology Clinic, as well as in many other centers, strongly indicates that a combination of EMG frontal biofeedback to lower the set point of the gamma efferent system of striate muscle tension, and thermal feedback, where handwarming is accomplished by a lessening of vasoconstriction of smooth muscle in arteries, is an optimal strategy in enabling patients to produce a relaxed state correlated with enhanced alpha density. Further, that with practice (4–6 months) the biofeedback state of reduced striate and smooth muscle tension can be achieved with a latency of several seconds, even with eyes open while carrying on fairly normal "Type A" behavior. This is in marked contrast to passive meditation procedures which require two 15-minute quiet periods each day. We suspect that guilt over failing to adhere to this schedule is a major reason why people stop meditating.

This raises the issue of long-term compliance with self-responsibility relaxation-alpha state techniques. For general relaxation purposes we have observed the following rank order of attrition rate with compliance from high to low at 3-month follow-up: TM, (80%) > Carrington's CSM, (60%) > Benson Relaxation Response, (25%) > EMG-thermal biofeedback (10%). We are currently investigating the roles of personality style, perceptual orienting style, hypnotic suggestability, and the demand characteristics of each technique (very high for TM with its secrets and mystique, very low for biofeedback for general

Table 2. Potential Applications of Biofeedback: General Stress Reduction and Specific Treatment Objectives

General	Specific
Objectives	Objectives
1. Relaxation	1. To regulate or lower the activiation of a target organ
2. Lowering of tension	symptom
3. States incompatible with emergency fight-or-flight response	Thermal (smooth muscle relaxation)
	Classic migraine—vascular headache (rapid)
	Common migraine—vascular headache (slow)
EEG alpha	Raynaud's disease
	Irritable colon syndrome
EEG theta	Essential hypertension
	Angina pectoris
Frontalis EMG	
	Frontalis EMG
	Tension—muscular contraction headache
Non-Biofeedback modalities	Bruxism
Passive Meditation—TM	TMJ syndrome
Benson relaxation response	
Autogenic training	Lumbar-sacral EMG
Progressive relaxation	Muscular back pain
	EKG
	Cardiac dysrhythmias
	GSR and thermal
	Hypertension
	Stress aspect of eczematous conditions

relaxation). In contrast, compliance is very high for EMG-thermal biofeedback applied to *specific* psychosomatic problems where symptom relief is self-reinforcing as in reduction of headache pain; compliance is much lower for conditions with relatively "silent" symptoms such as hypertension.

Based on compliance and the self-reinforcing aspect of specific symptom relief, we have differentiated potential applications of biofeedback into two categories, general stress reduction and specific treatment objectives, as shown in Table 2. Non-biofeedback modalities with best compliance are probably the techniques of choice for general stress reduction unless a fundamental change in attitude toward preventive medicine occurs; i.e., reducing insurance premiums for individuals who demonstrate continuing complicance with a self-responsibility relaxation technique.

Acknowledgment

The support of the Fannie E. Rippel Foundation in creating the computer programs used in this study is gratefully acknowledged.

References

Bradley, P. B. Central action of certain drugs in relation to the reticular formation of the brain. In H. H. Jasper (Ed.), *The reticular formation of the brain*. Boston: Little, Brown, 1958.

Brown, B. Recognition of aspects of consciousness through association with EEG alpha activity represented by a light signal. *Psychophysiology,* 1970, **6**, 442.

Budzynski, T., Stoyva, J., and Adler, C. Feedback induced muscle relaxation: Application to tension headache. *Journal of Behavioral and Experimental Psychiatry,* 1970, **1**, 205.

Clyde, D. J. The Clyde Mood Scale, Biometrics Laboratory, University of Miami, 1963.

Delse, C., and Feather, R. The effect of augmented sensory feedback on control of salivation. *Psychophysiology,* 1968, **5**, 15–21.

Dicara, L., and Miller, N. Instrumental learning of systolic blood pressure responses by curarized rats: Dissociation of cardiac and vascular changes, *Psychosomatic Medicine,* 1968, **30,** 489–494.

Engel, B., and Chism, R. Operant conditioning of heart rate speeding. *Psychophysiology,* 1967, **3,** 418–428.

Engel, B., and Hansen, S. Operant conditioning of heart rate slowing. *Psychophysiology,* 1966, **3,** 563–567.

Fowler, R., and Kimmel, H. Operant conditioning of GSR. *Journal of Experimental Psychology,* 1962, **63,** 536–567.

Kimmel, E., and Hill, R. Operant conditioning of the GSR. *Psychological Reports,* 1960, **7,** 555–562.

Lynch, J. J., and Paskewitz, D. A. On the mechanisms of the feedback control of human brain wave activity. *Biofeedback and self control.* Chicago: Aldine, 1971.

Mathews, A. M. Psychophysiological approaches to the investigation of desensitization and related procedures. *Psychological Bulletin,* 1971, **76,** 73.

Orne, M. T. On the social psychology of the psychological experiment: With particular reference to demand characteristics and their implications. *American Psychologist,* 1962, **17,** 776.

Schwartz, G. E. Biofeedback, self-regulation and the patterning of physiologic process. *American Scientist,* 1975, **3,** 314–324.

Stroebel, C. F., and Glueck, B. C. Biofeedback treatment in medicine and psychiatry: An ultimate placebo? *Seminars in Psychiatry,* 1973, **5,** 379–393.

Zubek, J. P. Physiology and biochemical effects. *Sensory deprivation: Fifteen years of research.* New York: Appleton-Century, 1969.

Passive Meditation

51

MATCHING RELAXATION THERAPIES
TO TYPES OF ANXIETY:
A PATTERNING APPROACH

Richard J. Davidson and Gary E. Schwartz

A number of authors have recently commented upon the multi-dimensional nature of fear and anxiety (e.g. Hodgson & Rachman, 1974; Lang, 1969). When anxiety is elicited in an individual in response to a stressful event, the quality of feelings aroused in one situation may be different than in another. In addition, some people may experience anxiety in one predominant way, while others might become anxious in a different manner. For example, it is not uncommon for a person who is physically tired and somatically relaxed to lie down, unable to fall asleep because his "mind is racing." This individual is manifesting *cognitive* symptoms of anxiety. On the other hand, *somatic* anxiety is characteristic of the person who complains of bodily tension and autonomic stress without accompanying cognitive symptoms.

Given that these two general forms of anxiety exist,[1] is one relaxation technique more effective than others for alleviating cognitive versus somatic anxiety, and vice versa? A number of clinicians have recently proposed that therapeutic regiments should be tailored to particular symptom configurations or response patterns (e.g. Lazarus, 1973). Such a suggestion is based upon the fact that different therapeutic procedures affect different psychobiological systems. We have proposed that the analogous situation prevails in the analysis of the varieties of relaxation procedures (Davidson and Schwartz, 1976). Specifically, relaxation techniques differ in the degree to which they affect the cognitive versus the somatic system. Furthermore, it is hypothesized that those relaxation procedures which affect primarily somatic processes will be maximally effective in the reduction of somatic anxiety while techniques resulting in changes in cognitive events will most effectively attenuate cognitive anxiety. Insofar as different physiological measures reflect predominantly cognitive versus somatic processes, such measures should be changed predictably by the practice of one versus another type of relaxation. By assessing the specific patterning of physiological processes (cf. Schwartz, 1975) in response to different relaxation techniques, the underlying mechanisms of such practices may be elucidated. The following sections will present a brief description of some commonly employed relaxation techniques which will be followed by a discussion of research illustrating the differences in effects elicited by such practices. Finally, a typology of anxiety will be presented and relaxation techniques hypothesized to be maximally effective in reducing particular configurations of anxiety will be discussed.

Some Common Relaxation Techniques:
A Search for their Underlying Mechanisms

Progressive Relaxation (PR)

PR (see Jacobson, 1938) is probably the most extensively used relaxation technique today. Despite the fact that few researchers or clinicians administer this training for as long as Jacobson (1938) prescribed (up

---

[1]It should be noted that such a split is at the most basic of levels. Further subdivisions have recently been made (see Davidson and Schwartz, in press) and will ultimately be necessary in any complete account of the nature of anxiety.

to 200 sessions), the effectiveness of even brief training is well established. This relaxation technique entails the systematic focus of attention on the various gross muscle groups throughout the body. The subject is first instructed to actively tense each group for a few seconds after which he is told to release his muscles and relax. Paul (1969) captures the essence of the technique in his instructions to subjects. He explains, "When I say 'relax,' I want you to immediately let go—to stop tensing—and merely focus your attention on what those muscles feel like as relaxation takes place" (p. 427). This sequence, i.e., tension, release, and attention is systematically applied to the following gross muscle groups: dominant hand and forearm, dominant upper arm, nondominant hand and forearm, nondominant upper arm, forehead, eyes and nose, cheeks and mouth, neck and throat, chest, back, and respiratory muscles, abdomen, dominant upper leg, calf, foot, nondominant upper leg, calf, and foot. Progression to each new muscle group is contingent upon complete relaxation of the prior group. The major emphasis of this technique is on *somatic* relaxation. The tensing of each major muscle group increases the saliency of somatic cues, enabling subjects to passively attend to specific body parts, thus facilitating complete somatic relaxation.

Hypnotic Suggestion

Hypnotic suggestions of relaxation are commonly employed to reduce anxiety (e.g., Barber & Hahn, 1963; Paul, 1969). Hypnotic suggestions of relaxation typically involve the active generation of cognitive behavior. For example, a clinician may suggest to a hypnotized patient that he imagine a calm beach with waves gently rolling on the shore. A number of authors (e.g., Shor, 1959, 1962; Orne, 1959) have postulated that the successful completion of a hypnotic suggestion usually involves an alteration of cognitive orientation. This change primarily involves a shift in attention from the external environment to internally generated *cognitive* activity. In a discussion of the effects of hypnotic suggestion, Spanos (1971) explains that "these suggestions often ask subjects to shift their perspective from the natural attitude to the attitude of fantasizing and then to construct in fantasy or imagination a situation which, if it objectively transpired, would result in the behavorial act performed by the subject when he 'passes' the suggestion" (p. 87). The latter situation may be illustrated by the wording of various standard test suggestions. Rather than simply asking subjects to lower their arms, Form C of the Standard Hypnotic Susceptibility Scale (SHSS) suggests arm heaviness in the following manner: "*Imagine* you are holding something heavy in hour hand . . . Now the hand and arm *feel* heavy as if the (imagined) weight were pressing down . . . " (Weitzenhoffer and Hilgard, 1962, p. 17, italics added). It therefore seems evident that an important component in the execution of a hypnotic suggestion is the active generation of imagery with occasional attention to somatic processes. Recent research by other investigators (e.g., Spanos, 1971) confirms the important of this type of cognitive activity in hypnotic suggestion. It should be noted that such a relaxation technique, emphasizing active cognitive self-regulation, will elicit subjective and physiological changes which are different from those following the practice of a somatic procedure.

One might suppose, given the important role of imagery in the hypnotic suggestion process, that individual differences in vividness of imagery should co-vary with hypnotic susceptibility. Sutcliffe, Perry and Sheehan (1970) examined this relationship and found that vividness of imagery (as assessed by a modified form of the Betts Questionnaire Upon Mental Imagery, Sheehan, 1967) was, in fact, significantly related to hypnotizability (as assessed by SHSS Form C, Weitzenhoffer and Hilgard, 1962), especially for males, although the veracity of this relationship has recently been questioned (Perry, 1973).

Autogenic Training

This relaxation technique was developed in the early 1900's by J. H. Schultz, a Berlin neuropsychiatrist (Schultz & Lutke, 1959). The core of the procedure is passive somatic attention. Autogenic training typically involves the subject leaning back in an armchair with his eyes closed in a quiet room. Verbal formulae are introduced (e.g., my right arm is heavy) and the subject is specifically instructed to "passively concentrate" on its repetition. The formulae, which consist of verbal somatic suggestions, are intended to facilitate concentration upon and "mental contact" with the part of the body indicated by the formula (e.g., the right arm). The training begins with the theme of heaviness and the first formula is "My right arm is heavy.'' The heaviness training is then continued for each extremity. The next group of formulae involve warmth and begin with ''My right arm is warm.'' Following warmth training in all the limbs, the trainee continues with passive concentration on cardiac activity by using the formula ''Heartbeat calm and regular.'' Then follows the respiratory mechanism with ''It breathes me,'' and warmth in the abdominal region ''My solar plexus is warm.'' Finally the last formula, ''My forehead is cool,'' is introduced. It is claimed that between four and ten months are usually needed to establish these exercises effectively (Luthe, 1963).

Since the primary emphasis of autogenic training is upon somatic attention and relaxation, one would predict that its effects would be similar to progressive relaxation and different from hypnotic suggestion. Specifically such a technique should exert its greatest effects upon measures of somatic processes which in turn should not be as greatly affected by hypnotic suggestions of relaxation.

Meditation

Although meditative practices were not originally designed as relaxation techniques, the experience of relaxation is a by-product of most such techniques (e.g., Davidson & Goleman, in press). Although there are important differences among the various meditative traditions (see Goleman, 1972), most forms of meditation share a number of common components, including some form of attentional self-regulation and the production of general autonomic quiescence (see Davidson & Goleman, 1975; in press). In the context of the present paper, what concerns us most is the object of attention during meditation. We propose that meditation involving the generation of cognitive events (such as a mantra in Transcendental Meditation) should elicit greater changes on measures of cognitive processing than meditation upon somatic events (such as attention to breathing or attention to the movements of the belly during breathing). Conversely, somatic meditation should result in greater changes on measures of somatic activation than cognitive meditation.

The mechanisms underlying the relaxation techniques discussed above are further revealed by a consideration of some relevant research. The laboratory findings which have emerged in the study of relaxation provide some empirical support for the classification scheme adopted above. Furthermore, the physiological studies on the nature of relaxation have never been guided by any systematic theoretical structure and various anomalies and unexplained findings may be parsimoniously interpreted within the above outlined scheme.

Relaxation Research: Some Core Physiological Findings

Due to the absence of a theoretical foundation, most investigators studying relaxation have rather haphazardly manipulated various treatment parameters and have looked for changes in physiological and subjective measures. The lack of uniformity sometimes observed in the effects of a procedure on a variety of different parameters does not necessarily indicate the lack of validity of those measures. Rather, it is often indicative of the specificity of effects of particular treatments. For example, one relaxation technique may result in heart rate decrements twice as large as another procedure practiced for the same length of time. Such an observation may indicate that the former procedure is a somatically based technique relative to the latter, since heart rate is a good index of overall somatic activity (see Obrist, Webb, Sutterer, & Howard, 1970). As we will see in the next section, such a somatically based technique may be optimally effective in the reduction of somatic anxiety while a cognitively based technique should result in greater change in cognitive anxiety.

Paul (1969) performed a comparative study of the physiological and subjective effects of progressive relaxation and hypnotic suggestion. Sixty subjects participated in two 1-hour sessions held 1 week apart. They were randomly assigned to one of three conditions: (a) brief progressive relaxation; (b) hypnotic suggestion (of relaxation); and (c) self-relaxation control. Forearm EMG, heart rate, skin conductance level, and respiration rate were employed as the physiological dependent measures. To examine subjective effects, subjects were administered the Anxiety Differential (Husek and Alexander, 1963). The data for each session were separately examined.

During session 1, relaxation training produced significant reduction as compared with controls on the Anxiety Differential (AD), EMG, heart rate, and respiration rate. Hypnotic suggestion versus controls produced significant decreases on the Anxiety Differential and respiration rate. Progressive relaxation produced significantly greater reductions than hypnosis in heart rate, and EMG. Eighty-five percent of the subjects in the progressive relaxation condition demonstrated significant reductions in the relaxed direction on the AD, EMG, heart rate, and respiration rate while only 30% of the hypnotic suggestion subjects manifested this change. The results for session 2 again indicate that progressive relaxation produced significant reductions as compared with controls on the Anxiety Differential, EMG, heart rate, and respiration rate. When the hypnosis group was compared with controls, significant reductions were noted on the Anxiety Differential, EMG, heart rate, and respiration rate. Again, progressive relaxation was significantly better than hypnotic suggestion in reducing heart rate and EMG. On the other hand, the results for the skin conductance measure were all nonsignificant in both sessions. In session 2, 70% of the relaxation subjects evidenced significant reduction in the four measures, while only 25% of the hypnotic suggestion subjects evidenced the same degree of change.

It can be inferred from the findings of this study that there are components of the relaxation procedure, absent in hypnotic suggestion, which are responsible for the superior performance of the former group. Paul (1969) suggests that:

> Restricted attention, narrow and monotonous stimulus input, and suggested ease of response were . . . factors common to both relaxation training and hypnotic conditions. The results obtained on the Anxiety Differential suggests that the latter factors in combination with either direct or indirect suggestions of relaxation, are sufficient to alter the *cognitive* experience of distress, while the results on physiological measures suggest that the differential content of stimulus input and attentional focus were of prime importance in the alteration of *somatic* responses (p. 435) (italics added).

Paul correctly implicates differences in stimulus input and attentional focus as being important factors underlying the differential consequences of progressive relaxation versus hypnotic relaxation. The question that now can be posed concerns the nature of these differences. What are the underlying processes in progressive relaxation and hypnotic suggestion that can account for the observed results?

In addition, it is also important to examine the nature of the dependent variables to determine the modality most represented by each measure. Hypnotic suggestion, as previously argued, involves the active generation of imagery. In his instructions to subjects, Paul (1969) explained that the hypnotic procedure utilizes imagery to induce a state of deep relaxation. He further suggested to subjects that during hypnosis, they are to "systematically focus your attention on a visual image of yourself" (p. 428).

Progressive relaxation, on the other hand, is precisely antithetical in its process to hypnotic suggestion. As was previously suggested, this technique involves a somatic attentional focus. Subjects are first instructed to tense a specific group of muscles, followed by letting go, relaxing and passively attending to the results of the procedure. It should be emphasized that subjects in the progressive relaxation procedure do not actively generate relaxation, but rather relaxation "takes place" and they just passively attend to how it feels. There is a reduction in efferent commands which allows the subject to more fully attend to the specific body part to be relaxed, free from the distractions of the former processes. In summary, then, one can state that hypnotic suggestion is an active cognitive process while progressive relaxation is a passive somatic process.

The dependent measures chosen by Paul may also be classified into primarily somatic-sensitive or cognitive-sensitive variables as was outlined in the previous section. Forearm EMG, respiration, and heart rate (Obrist, Webb, Sutterer, and Howard, 1970) are all somatic measures, while skin conductance level (Kilpatrick, 1972) and the Anxiety Differential may reflect more cognitive processes. Since the goal of both relaxation techniques is to effect changes in the somatic system, one's attention must be focused there. Because this was true for the progressive relaxation subjects, one would expect greater changes in the direction of relaxation for this group versus the hypnosis group on somatic dependent measures. In both sessions, progressive relaxation led to greater decrements in heart rate and forearm EMG than hypnotic suggestions, although decrements in respiration rate and on the Anxiety Differential were not significantly different in either session. While not statistically significant, there was a greater decrement in respiration rate for the progressive relaxation versus the hypnosis group in both sessions. Both the progressive relaxation and hypnotic suggestion groups and the control group all manifested decrements in skin conductance level with no significant differences between the three groups. Therefore, it is evident that a relaxation technique that requires somatic attention will result in a greater degree of relaxation when assessed by somatic measures than a technique that requires cognitive attention.

It is important to note that the two variables reflecting primarily cognitive activity did not differentiate between the two relaxation techniques. One might ask why progressive relaxation, a somatic procedure, also led to increases in cognitive relaxation. It is probable that the phenomenon in question is multiply-determined and more than one explanation is possible. A number of tentative hypotheses, none mutually exclusive, may be offered. To begin with, neither the Anxiety Differential nor skin conductance level are "pure" cognitive measures. The Anxiety Differential has some items which are somatic in nature, although there are a greater number of cognitive items. Although recent research on electrodermal activity suggests that skin conductance level (as distinct from skin conductance responses) primarily reflects cognitive activity (Kilpatrick, 1972) these data are by no means conclusive. Therefore, the first hypothesis is that these measures could have reflected changes in both cognitive *and* somatic behavior, so that it is possible for the somatic changes induced by progressive relaxation to be reflected in the Anxiety Differential and skin conductance. The second, and probably more tenable hypothesis, is that *processes occurring in a given mode strongly affect that same mode, although they also influence other modes to a lesser degree.* In other words, if an individual employs a somatic relaxation technique and becomes very relaxed, this relaxation will partially generalize to the cognitive sphere as well.

A number of other investigators have performed comparative studies of the physiological concomitants of different relaxation procedures. For example, Langen (1969) found that autogenic training elicited greater increases than hypnotic suggestion in heat conveyance, which is a measure of peripheral vasodilatation. Langen's data are clearly in agreement with those obtained by Paul (1969). Both studies compared hypnotic suggestion—an active cognitive process—with techniques that require passive somatic attention. Both experiments revealed that the active generation of internal cognitive behavior was not as effective as passive somatic attention in altering cardiovascular processes. The Paul (1969) study did demonstrate, however, that there were no differences between progressive relaxation and hypnotic suggestion in the alteration of cognitive behavior.

There exist numerous additional findings in areas other than relaxation per se which have bearing on the basic cognitive-somatic distinction discussed herein (e.g., Bell and Schwartz, 1973; Kurie and Mordkoff, 1970). These studies suggest, not surprisingly, that when subjects are asked to self-regulate somatic activity, greater changes are seen on dependent measures which reflect somatic processes (e.g. heart rate) than on other types of measures and vice versa. It should be emphasized that such a distinction (i.e., cognitive versus somatic) is at the most molar level of behavior and further, more refined subdivisions may be made within each of the two larger modes. For example, the general class of imagery may be differentiated into its modality-specific components, i.e., visual imagery, auditory imagery, etc. Importantly, research suggests that the generation of imagery in a particular modality will inhibit the perception of stimuli in that modality more than in others (e.g. Segal and Fusella, 1970). These data have bearing on the mode-specific treatment of anxiety which will be described below.

Cognitive and Somatic Anxiety and Relaxation Mode

A number of writers have recently commented upon cognitive and somatic distinctions in anxiety (e.g., Corah, 1964; Eysenck, 1961; Barratt, 1972). For example, Barratt (1972) performed an item analysis of anxiety items from a large battery of popular scales. This analysis "indicated two major subsets: (1) awareness of somatic changes, for example, I blush often or I am often aware of my heart beating; (2) conscious awareness of unpleasant feelings about self or external stimuli, for example, I frequently find myself worrying about something . . . " (Barratt, 1972, p. 202). The latter factor clearly represents the cognitive symptoms of anxiety. These two distinct manifestations of anxiety may also be represented quantitatively by a ratio of cognitive/somatic symptoms or other similar ratios. For example, Corah (1964) has computed a "proportion of somatic anxiety score" which was obtained for each patient by subtracting the number of cognitive symptoms from the number of somatic symptoms and dividing by the total number of symptoms.

If we conceive of cognitive and somatic anxiety as reflecting mode-specific intraorganismic states, it follows, in the context of the principles previously developed, that different relaxation techniques, i.e., cognitive vs. somatic, will be more effective in reducing same mode vs. other mode anxiety. As an illustration, let us return to an example offered in the introduction. An extreme case of high cognitive-low somatic anxiety occurs when an individual is somatically tired and lying down, but can't fall asleep because his mind is "racing." Assuming that this individual's body is relatively relaxed, it is clear that a cognitive/somatic anxiety ratio would yield a result greater than 1. In this situation, the most efficient type of relaxation would be a cognitive procedure which would reduce *unwanted* cognitive activity (hence the age-old procedure of visualizing and counting sheep).

Table 1 presents a 2 × 2 table with the following four combinations of anxiety represented in each cell: (a) low cognitive-low somatic; (b) low cognitive-high somatic; (c) high cognitive-low somatic; and (d) high cognitive-high somatic. Within each cell, a number of techniques and/or activities are presented which theoretically should be maximally effective in eliciting "relaxation" for the particular configuration of anxiety represented by each cell. A number of general characteristics of this table will first be discussed, followed by a more detailed explanation of the hypothesized relationships.

The low cognitive anxiety column subjectively represents a lack of unwanted cognitive intrusions. Because of this absence, attention is not distracted by activity in the cognitive sphere. Hence, every activity and technique in this column has the following important characteristic in common: none requires sustained active generation of cognitive behavior. In other words, since the cognitive mode is already relatively quiescent, it is not necessary to utilize a technique which directly inhibits cognitive intrusions.

The high cognitive anxiety column represents, on the other hand, an abundance of unwanted cognitive activity which requires a relaxation technique that will directly inhibit these cognitive distractions. All of the techniques and activities in the high cognitive anxiety column require the active generation of cognitive behavior or, in the case of television, the total engagement and involvement of the entire perceptual-cognitive system. According to the principle outlined in the previous section, it can be argued that *active* cognitive generation, either predominantly self-initiated as in chess, or predominantly externally initiated as in television, will most effectively inhibit cognitive intrusions.

A parallel analysis can be applied to the rows. In the low somatic anxiety row, every activity and technique requires little or no active somatic generation, while in the high somatic anxiety row, every technique and activity requires the active generation of somatic behavior.

A closer inspection of Table 1 reveals a number of more specific hypotheses concerning anxiety-relaxation relationships. The low cognitive-low somatic anxiety cell suggests that only those individuals, at those moments experiencing generally low anxiety in both modes, will choose meditation as a form of relaxation. Additionally, one can deduce that these techniques (e.g., TM and Zen) would not be totally effective for *generally* anxious individuals (i.e., those manifesting high cognitive and high somatic anxiety).

We have placed meditation in this cell because of evidence which suggests that people with elevated levels of anxiety will not, at least initially, be benefitted by meditation and will be less likely to persist in their practice. Otis (1973) has performed a longitudinal study of meditators and found that those initiates who practiced regularly for more than 12 months characterized themselves as less anxious, more calm and peaceful than those who dropped out before 12 months, *before* either group had begun meditation.

Table 1. Cognitive and Somatic Components of Anxiety and Associated Relaxation Techniques Hypothesized to Reduce such Anxiety

| | | Somatic anxiety | |
		Low	High
Cognitive Anxiety	Low	Meditation	Progressive relaxation Hatha Yoga
	High	Reading Watching Television Playing Chess	Walking Dancing Active sports (e.g., tennis, football)

The low cognitive-high somatic anxiety cell indicates that techniques demanding somatic attention with little or no cognitive generation are effective in reducing this pattern of anxiety. A curious clinical observation is worth noting here. Many teachers and practitioners of meditation have commented upon the importance of relaxing the body and reducing somatic anxiety (usually through the practice of hatha yoga) *before* commencing intensive meditation (e.g., Satchidananda, 1970). Due to the relative passivity of most meditation procedures, distracting cognitive and somatic anxiety must first be reduced through the utilization of more active, mode-specific techniques.

The procedures included in the high cognitive-low somatic cell all require active cognitive generation with little somatic attention. It is hypothesized that these complex behaviors demand the active generation of cognitive events which serve to inhibit ongoing unwanted cognitive activity, i.e., cognitive anxiety (see Csikszenthmihalyi, 1974; 1975). It is particularly intriguing that most of these activities are among those most frequently reported as being related to increased susceptibility to hypnosis (J. Hilgard, 1970, 1972). Hilgard (1970) has found that involvement in reading and drama is significantly related to hypnotizability. These activities and procedures all have the same common theme at their core: the sustained involvement in active generation of cognitive behavior.

Finally, the last cell—high cognitive-high somatic—includes activities that require both active cognitive and somatic generation. These activities are among the most attentionally demanding behaviors in which individuals typically engage. A lapse of attention in either mode in a game of tennis, for example, will have detrimental consequences. One may question how intensive physical activity can be relaxing, particularly in light of Pitts' (Pitts and McClure, 1967; Pitts, 1969; Pitts, 1971) suggestion that lactate, an exercise metabolite, can provoke anxiety symptoms and attacks in anxiety neurotics and in normal persons under stress. Pitts' theorizing and data have been recently criticized by a number of investigators (e.g., Ackerman and Sacher, 1974; Grosz and Farmer, 1969; Levitt, 1972; Morgan, 1973). Grosz and Farmer (1969) present convincing evidence suggesting that the anxiety producing substance is not lactate, but rather sodium bicarbonate. However, perhaps most damaging is a series of studies by Morgan and his colleagues (Morgan, 1973; Morgan, Roberts, Brand and Feinerman, 1970; Morgan, Roberts and Feinerman, 1971) which convincingly demonstrated that physical exercise consistently led to significant decrements in state anxiety among both normal and high anxious subjects. These data lend empirical support to the general hypothesis that intensive physical exercise can lead to decrements in anxiety, probably by inhibiting unwanted cognitive and somatic behavior, plus producing a fatigue state which further reduced such behavior (Grim, 1972).

Summary and Conclusions

A process-oriented patterning conception of relaxation and related states was presented. It was argued that different relaxation techniques activate different major modes or systems and it was suggested that the effects of particular relaxation techniques can be meaningfully understood only after determining the type of dependent variable employed (i.e., is it more sensitive to cognitive or somatic processes?). The utilization of these principles in the examination of some core findings in the empirical literature on relaxation rendered a number of anomalous findings understandable. Data were presented demonstrating that progressive relaxation—a somatic technique—was significantly superior to hypnotic relaxation—a cognitive technique—on a number of somatic measures, while the results on a cognitive measure yielded no significant differences. Similar results for other relaxation procedures were also described. Finally, the principles that were previously developed were applied to an examination of anxiety. It was demonstrated that the congitive and somatic contributions to anxiety can be meaningfully separated and a model was presented which matched specific relaxation techniques to specific anxiety patterns on the basis of their underlying processes. Clearly additional research is needed to test and clarify the numerous hypotheses presented.

A number of empirical and practical conclusions emerge from this kind of analysis. On the empirical side, it is suggested that various meditative and relaxation practices can be understood and investigated by careful analysis of the underlying cognitive, somatic, and attentional processes that are brought into play. Current theories of emotion (e.g., Schacter, 1970) and self-regulation of consciousness (e.g., Schwartz, 1975) and recent research on delay of gratification (e.g., Mischel, 1974) utilize a multi-process or pattern approach. This conceptual scheme emphasizing *interactions* of factors is consistent with present neurophysiological theories of perception (Pribram, 1971), memory (John, 1972), and consciousness (Shallice, 1972; Sperry, 1969). Although we have emphasized cognitive and somatic factors as two general modes, this broad classification by definition is an oversimplication since each can be meaningfully broken into subcomponents (e.g., visual, auditory, and kinesthetic imagery). Nonetheless, we believe that two general principles pertaining to relaxation and anxiety reduction will still apply: (1) that self-regulation of behavior (including voluntary focusing of attention) in a given mode will reduce (or inhibit) unwanted activity in that specific mode, and (2) that self-regulation of behavior in a given mode may, to a lesser degree, reduce unwanted activity in other modes.[2]

The importance of considering patterns of underlying processes must be underscored. The theory suggests that the age-proven procedure of visualizing *and* counting sheep to fall asleep when one's mind is racing succeeds because it effectively blocks both unwanted visual *and* auditory imagery at the same time. Similarly, it may be hypothesized that forms of Zen meditation which require that the person count his breaths or say a mantra in synchrony with breathing are particularly effective because they simultaneously attenuate both cognitive and somatic components of anxiety. If follows that a 2×2 classification representing high and low cognitive and somatic anxiety is also an oversimplification, for it represents only a first-order breakdown. For example, the present theory suggests that within the low cognitive-low somatic category, a meditation procedure based upon the self-generation of cognition (e.g., a mantra technique such as Transcendental Meditation) will be relatively more effective for reducing cognitive components of anxiety than a meditation practice based upon the passive attentional focusing upon somatic events, which should be relatively more effective for reducing the somatic components of anxiety.

From a clinical point of view, it would seem valuable to assess anxiety in a more systematic way so as to uncover the specific modes in which the unwanted behavior is occurring. The theory implies that then, and only then, will it be possible to determine which relaxation technique [i.e., which mode-specific tactic(s)] should be most effective in reducing anxiety for a given patient in a given state. Although clearly in need of additional experimental tests, this general hypothesis must be tempered by the fact that also important is the patient's motivation to faithfully practice any given technique (e.g., Schwartz, 1973). As in all forms of psychological and medical treatment, isolating the most powerful procedure is not enough; the procedure must also be acceptable to the patient if it is going to be used most effectively. It might also be mentioned that a new direction in therapy may be to teach people to recognize in themselves when they are experiencing what kinds of anxiety, and how best to eliminate it, since it is conceivable that people differ in their ability to best fit a type of relaxation to the bio-behavioral need (e.g., how does one learn to select a slow, quieting passage to listen to versus a fast, loud passage which activates foot-tapping and dancing?).

In a review of laboratory studies on desensitization, Lang (1969) once described fear as a "loosely woven fabric or responses, with many edges where an unravelling process may be initiated" (p. 190). We would suggest that the same applies to the concept of relaxation as used in every-day language. Central to any concept of relaxation is the attempt at eliminating unwanted behavior; what the behavior is and how the person goes about avoiding or eliminating it can vary greatly. However, it is possible to consider what relaxation would be if it occurred in all modes simultaneously. This, we suggest, is what the final end point of many (but not all) eastern and western relaxation techniques is—a reduction in self-generated cognitive, somatic and attentional behavior (i.e., attentional receptivity rather than active focusing of attention). It seems likely that only under such circumstances is it possible for the deep, integrated "hypometabolic" state described by Wallace and Benson (1972) and renamed "the relaxation response" (Benson, 1975) to occur.

Acknowledgment

The preparation of this paper was supported in part by the Advanced Research Projects Agency of the Department of Defense and monitored by the Office of Naval Research under Contract N00014-70-C-0350

[2]The converse of this principle is that reductions in self-generated behavior in one mode may result in an increase in (or release of) spontaneous behavior in another mode. Hence, deep muscle relaxation with biofeedback may be accompanied by increases in spontaneous thoughts and imagery (e.g., Green, Walters, Green and Murphy, 1969; Stoyva, 1973). This phenomenon of spontaneous release of cognitive events concomitant with reductions in somatic activity has been recognized by investigators of autogenic training and has been termed "autogenic discharge" (Gorton, 1959; Luthe, 1963).

to the San Diego State University Foundation to GES and by National Science Foundation predoctoral fellowship to RJD. This paper is a revised and abridged version of the paper by Davidson and Schwartz noted in the references.

References

Ackerman, S. H. and Sacher, R. J. The lactate theory of anxiety: A review and reevaluation. *Psychosomatic Medicine,* 1974, *36,* 69–81.

Barber, T. X., and Han, K. W. Hypnotic induction and "relaxation": An experimental study. *Archives of General Psychiatry,* 1963, *8,* 295–300.

Barrett, E. S. Anxiety and impulsiveness: Toward a neuropsychological model. In C. D. Spielberger (Ed.), *Anxiety: Current Trends in Theory and Research, Vol. 1.* New York: Academic Press, 1972.

Bell, I. R., and Schwartz, G. E. Cognitive and somatic mechanisms in voluntary control of heart rate. In Shapiro, T. X. Barber, L. V. DiCara, J. Kamiya, N. E. Miller and J. Stoyva (Eds.), *Biofeedback and Self-Control, 1972.* Chicago: Aldine, 1972 (Abstract).

Benson, H. *The Relaxation Response.* New York: William Morrow, 1975.

Corah, N. L. Neuroticism and extraversion in the MMPI: Empirical validation and exploration. *British Journal of Social and Clinical Psychology,* 1964, *3,* 168–174.

Czikszenthmihalyi, M. *Flow: Studies of Enjoyment.* Unpublished PHS Grant Report, 1974.

Czikszenthmihalyi, M. *Beyond Boredom and Anxiety.* San Francisco: Jossey-Bass, 1975.

Davidson, R. J. and Goleman, D. J. The role of attention in meditation and hypnosis: A psychobiological model of transformations of consciousness. Paper presented at the Society for Clinical and Experimental Hypnosis, Chicago, October, 1975.

Davidson, R. J. and Goleman, D. J. Attentional and affective concomitants of meditation: A cross-sectional study. *Journal of Abnormal Psychology,* in press.

Davidson, R. J. and Schwartz, G. E. The psychobiology of relaxation and related states: A multi-process theory. In D. I. Mostofsky (Ed.) *Behavior Control and the Modification of Physiological Processes.* New York: Prentice-Hall, in press.

Eysenck, H. J. Classification and the problems of diagnosis. In H. J. Eysenck (Ed.), *Handbook of Abnormal Psychology.* New York: Basic Books, 1961.

Goleman, D. The Buddha on meditation and states of consciousness, Part II: a typology of meditation techniques. *Journal of Transpersonal Psychology,* 1972, *4,* 151–210.

Green, E. E., Walters, D. E., Green, A. M., and Murphy, G. Feedback technique for deep relaxation. *Psychophysiology,* 1969, *6,* 371–377.

Grim, P. F. Relaxation therapies and neurosis: A central fatigue interpretation. *Psychosomatics,* 1972, *13,* 363–370.

Grosz, H. J., and Farmer, B. B. Blood lactate in the development of anxiety symptoms: A critical examination of Pitts and McClure's hypothesis and experimental study. *Archives of General Psychiatry,* 1969, *21,* 611–619.

Hilgard, J. R. *Personality and Hypnosis: A Study of Imaginative Involvement.* Chicago: University of Chicago Press, 1970.

Hilgard, J. R. Evidence for a development-interactive theory of hypnotic susceptibility. In E. Fromm and R. E. Shor (Eds.), *Hypnosis: Research Developments and Perspectives.* Chicago: Aldine, 1972.

Hodgson, R. and Rachman, R. II. Desynchrony in measures of fear. *Behavior Research and Therapy,* 1974, *12,* 319–326.

Husek, T. R., and Alyxander, S. The effectiveness of the Anxiety Differential in examination situations. *Educational and Psychological Measurement,* 1963, *23,* 309–318.

Jacobson, E. *Progressive Relaxation.* Chicago: University of Chicago Press, 1938. (2nd edition).

John, E. R. Switchboard versus statistical theories of learning and memory. *Science,* 1972, *177,* 850–864.

Kilpatrick, D. G. Differential responsiveness of two electrodermal indices to psychological stress and performance of a complex cognitive task. *Psychophysiology,* 1972, *9,* 218–226.

Kurie, G. D. and Mordkoff, A. M. Effects of brief sensory deprivation and somatic concentration on two measures of field dependence. *Perceptual and Motor Skills,* 1970, *31,* 683–687.

Lang, P. The mechanics of desensitization and the laboratory study of human fear. In C. M. Franks (Ed.), *Behavior Therapy: Appraisal and Status.* New York: McGraw-Hill, 1969.

Langen, D. Peripheral changes in blood circulation during autogenic training and hypnosis (Results of experimental research). In L. Chertok (Ed.), *Psychophysiological Mechanisms of Hypnosis.* Berlin: Springer-Verlag, 1969.

Lazarus, A. A. Multimodal behavior therapy: Treating the "basic id." *Journal of Nervous and Mental Disease,* 1973, *156,* 404–411.

Levitt, E. E. A brief commentary on the "psychiatric breakthrough" with emphasis on the hematology of anxiety. In C. D. Spielberger (Ed.), *Anxiety: Current Trends in Theory and Research. Volume 1.* New York: Academic Press, 1972.

Luthe, W. Autogenic training: Method, research and application in medicine. *American Journal of Psychotherapy,* 1963, *17,* 174–195.

Mischel, W. Processes in delay of gratification. In L. Berkowitz (Ed.), *Advances in Social Psychology. Volume 7.* New York: Academic Press, 1974, 249–292.

Morgan, W. P. Influence of acute physical activity on state anxiety. Paper presented at the Annual Meeting of the National College Physical Education Association for Men, January 9, 1973.

Morgan, W. P., Roberts, J. A., and Feinerman, A. D. Psychologic Psychological effect of chronic physical activity. *Medicine and Science in Sports,* 1970, *2,* 213–217.

Morgan, W. P., Robert, J. A., and Feinerman, A. D. Psychologic effect of acute physical exercise. *Archives of Physical Medicine and Rehabilitation,* 1971, *52,* 422–425.

Obrist, P. A., Webb, R. A., Sutterer, J. R., and Howard, J. L. The cardio-somatic relationship: Some reformulations. *Psychophysiology,* 1970, *6,* 569–587.

Orne, M. T. The nature of hypnosis: Artifact and essence. *Journal of Abnormal and Social Psychology,* 1959, *58,* 277–299.

Otis, L. S. The psychobiology of meditation: Some psychological changes. Paper presented at the 81st annual meeting of the American Psychological Association, Montreal, August, 1973.

Paul, G. L. Physiological effects of relation training and hypnotic suggestion. *Journal of Abnormal Psychology*, 1969, *74*, 425–437.

Perry, C. Imagery, fantasy and hypnotic susceptibility: A multidimensional approach. *Journal of Personality and Social Psychology*, 1973, *26*, 217–221.

Pitts, F. N., Jr. The biochemistry of anxiety. *Scientific American*, 1969, *220*, 69–75.

Pitts, F. J., Jr. Biochemical factors in anxiety neurosis. *Behavioral Sciences*, 1971, *16*, 82–91.

Pitts, F. N., Jr., and McClure, J. N., Jr. Lactate metabolism in anxiety neurosis. *New England Journal of Medicine*, 1967, *277*, 1329–1336.

Pribram, K. H. *Languages of the Brain*. Englewood Cliffs, New Jersey: Prentice-Hall, 1971.

Satchidananda, Y. S. S. *Integral Yoga Hatha*. New York: Holt, Rinehart and Winston, 1970.

Schachter, S. The assumption of identity and peripheralist-centralist controversies in motivation and emotion. In M. Arnold (Ed.), *Feelings and Emotions*. New York: Academic Press, 1970.

Schultz, J. H., and Luthe, W. *Autogenic Training: A Psychophysiological Approach to Psychotherapy*. New York: Grune and Stratton, 1959.

Schwartz, G. E. Biofeedback as therapy: Some theoretical and practical issues. *American Psychologist*, 1973, *28*, 666–673.

Schwartz, G. E. Biofeedback, self-regulation and the patterning of physiological processes. *American Scientist*, 1975, *63*, 314–324.

Segal, S. J., and Fusella, V. Influence of imaged pictures and sounds on detection of auditory and visual signals. *Journal of Experimental Psychology*, 1970, *83*, 458–464.

Shallice, T. Dual functions of consciousness. *Psychological Review*, 1972, *79*, 383–393.

Sheehan, P. W. A shortened form of Betts' Questionnaire Upon Mental Imagery. *Journal of Clinical Psychology*, 1967, *23*, 386–389.

Shor, R. E. Hypnosis and the concept of the generalized reality-orientation. *American Journal of Psychotherapy*, 1959, *13*, 582–602.

Shor, R. E. Three dimensions of hypnotic depth. *International Journal of Clinical and Experimental Hypnosis*, 1962, *10*, 23–38.

Spanos, N. P. Goal-directed fantasy and the performance of hypnotic test suggestions. *Psychiatry*, 1971, *34*, 86–96.

Sperry, R. W. A modified concept of consciousness. *Psychological Review*, 1969, *76*, 532–536.

Stoyva, J. Biofeedback techniques and the conditions for hallucinatory activity. In F. J. McGuigan and R. A. Schoonover (Eds.), *The Psychophysiology of Thinking*. New York: Academic Press, 1973.

Sutcliffe, J. P., Perry C. W., and Sheehan, P. W. Relation of some aspects of imagery and fantasy to hypnotic susceptibility. *Journal of Abnormal Psychology*, 1970, *76*, 279–287.

Wallace, R. K., and Benson, H. The physiology of meditation. *Scientific American*, 1972, *226*, 84–90.

Weitzenhoffer, A. M., and Hilgard, E. R. *Stanford Hypnotic Susceptibility Scale, Form C*. Palo Alto, California: Consulting Psychologists Press, 1962.

C2. Research Comparisons

In this subsection we present two of the most elegant, "cleanly" designed studies comparing meditation with other self-regulation strategies. In the Walrath and Hamilton study (52), based on certain autonomic variables, like heart rate, respiration, and GSR, no significant differences between meditation, hypnosis, and instructional relaxation were found, with the exception of heart rate. This is one of the first studies to contradict the initial findings of Wallace, Benson, and Wilson (article 29). The second article (53) by Morse *et al.* is a well-designed study comparing meditation, hypnosis, and relaxation. Except for muscle activity, again no differences were found between experimental groups on the variables monitored (respiration rate, pulse rate, blood pressure, skin resistance, EEG activity, and muscle activity). The accompanying table is included here as a reference, which details studies comparing mediation with different self-regulation strategies.

Table 7. Summary of Studies Comparing Meditation with Other Self-Regulation Strategies: Physiological Measures[a]

Reference	Type of Meditation	Amount of Meditation	Changes During Meditation	Type of Design	Quality of Control Procedures
Walrath & Hamilton, 1975	TM	> 6 months practice	Meditators, autohypnotizers and controls all showed decreases in heart and respiration rates and GSR activity but did not differ between groups.	Between-subjects	Adequate except for equal amounts of practice for meditators and hypnosis subjects.
Curtis & Wessburg, 1975/76	TM	~ 2 years practice	No effects across trials or between meditation, progressive relaxation and controls, in GSR, heart or respiration rate.	Between-subjects	Adequate
Cauthen & Prymak, 1977	TM	7 days, 14 months, or 5 years	2 more experienced groups of meditators showed heart rate during meditation. Relaxers and least experienced meditators showed skin temperature.	Between-subjects	Adequate. Controls focused on a word.
Travis, Kondo, & Knott, 1977	TM	5–30 months	No differences between meditators and relaxation controls on EEG, alpha, heart rate and frontal EMG. Both groups showed alpha activity. Meditators showed less EEG sleep patterns than relaxation controls.	Between-subjects	Adequate.
Morse et al. 1977	TM	2 months–8 years	Measures of pulse rate, respiratory rate, blood pressure, GSR, EEG and muscle activity all suggested significantly greater relaxation in experimental subjects trained in TM, self-hypnosis or both, than in controls. However experimental groups did not differ between themselves except for lower muscle activity in TM.	Between-subjects	Good design and statistical analysis.

634

Reference	Type	Subjects	Results	Design	Evaluation
Pagano et al., (Note 14)	TM	Experienced average = 3.4 years	Both TM and progressive muscle relaxation subjects showed similar small (2–5%) decrements in O_2 consumption from a resting baseline, which did not differ from eyes-closed controls.	Between-subjects	Adequate. Good statistical analysis.
Glueck & Stroebel, 1977	TM	Intermediate	Showed heart and respiration rates ↓ GSR, ↑ EEG alpha. Intrahemispheric alpha and theta synchrony even in inexperienced meditators. Greater intrahemispheric synchrony in thermal and EMG biofeedback subjects than in TM or relaxation response subjects. Evidence of interhemispheric synchrony in TM and relaxation response subjects but not in biofeedback subjects.	Between and within subjects	Adequate.
Boswell & Murray, 1979	Zen	2 weeks	No significant differences between groups in Spiegelberger Trait-State Anxiety inventory, GSR, skin conductance, and heart rate.	Between-subjects	Good. Three control groups: Relaxation, placebo, and no treatment
Beiman et al., 1980	TM	Seven 1½ hour sessions	No significant differences in effectiveness of TM, behavior therapy, or self-relaxation, were detected for self-report measures (locus of control, regression sensitization, autonomic perception, trait anxiety, or fear survey schedule), or physiological measures (skin resistance, skin response, pulse rate, EMG). Locus of control accounted for a major proportion of variance in the response to TM.	Between-subjects	Adequate. Good use of multivariate analyses, especially multiple regression to determine amounts of variance accounted for by subject variables.

[a]Data compiled by Roger N. Walsh.

52

AUTONOMIC CORRELATES OF MEDITATION AND HYPNOSIS[1]

Larry C. Walrath[2] and David W. Hamilton

Peripheral autonomic responses during meditation and autohypnosis are compared with controls. HR, Resp, and GSR were assessed during a meditation/hypnosis period and compared to both pre- and post-baseline conditions for three groups of 10 Ss each: Transcendental Meditators, Ss trained in autohypnosis, and control Ss. All Ss were selected for high susceptibility to hypnosis. There were no significant differences between groups on any initial baseline measures. All groups showed a marked reduction of all autonomic measures during the experimental period. Meditators showed a more persistent reduction of HR extending into the post-baseline condition. The results suggest that, at least for the measures investigated, meditation and hypnosis do not differ markedly from each other nor from instructed relaxation.

In recent years there has been increasing interest in psychophysiological indices of changing states of awareness. Notable among these are investigations into autonomic changes associated with meditation, which indicate that this state is distinguishable from other states such as waking, sleeping, and dreaming. The present study constitutes a partial replication of pioneer work in the field and a comparison between the autonomic effects of meditation and autohypnosis.

Wallace (1970b) conducted the first major investigation into the psychophysiology of meditation. Earlier studies had indicated decreased autonomic reactivity in at least a few response systems, for both Zen (*e.g.*, Akishige, 1968) and Yogic

(*e.g.*, Anand, Chhina & Singh, 1961; Wenger & Bagchi, 1961) forms of mediation. Extensive research in this country has, however, been hampered by the unavailability of a sufficient number of Ss systematically trained in any one technique and willing to volunteer for physiological experiments. Wallace overcame this difficulty by selecting Ss trained in the techniques of Transcendental Meditation (TM) as taught by Maharishi Mahesh Yogi (See Mahesh, 1966, 1969). Practitioners of TM are available to serve as subjects on most college and university campuses.

Wallace (1970b) found consistent reductions in autonomic functions for meditators during meditation compared to nonmeditation base rate recordings: reduced heart rate (HR); reduced respiration rate (Resp); increased basal skin resistance (GSR); and increased evidence of alpha rhythms in the electroencephalogram (EEG) with a reduction in dominant frequency of alpha. Banquet (1973) observed an increase in both slow ($\simeq$ 20 Hz) and fast

[1] We wish to acknowledge critical reading of the manuscript by T. W. Pyle, L. R. Beideman and J. A. Stern.

[2] Requests for reprints should be sent to Larry C. Walrath, Washington University Behavior Research Laboratory, 1420 Grattan Street, St. Louis, Mo. 63104.

($\simeq$ 40 Hz) EEG beta activity superimposed on the slow wave pattern during the period of deepest meditation. Further research indicates that during meditation, oxygen consumption is reduced by as much as 20% (Wallace, 1970a), while the blood lactate level drops precipitously, indicating oxidative anabolism progressing at a rate three-to-four times higher than normal resting rates (Wallace & Benson, 1972). These findings, coupled with subjective experiences reported by the Ss, led Wallace (1970a, b) to propose that the meditative state is a unique state characterized by hypometabolic functioning, decreased sympathetic activity, and a characteristic EEG pattern accompanied by reports of "transcendent" subjective experiences and distinguishable physiologically from the other major states: waking, sleeping, and dreaming. More recent findings (Beary & Benson, 1974) indicate that the hypometabolic functioning observed in meditation may be produced by relaxation instructions combined with a mental "trick" similar to meditative methods.

Wallace and Benson (1972) specifically exclude hypnosis from inclusion in the meditative state on the basis of greater variability of autonomic functioning during hypnosis. Kroger (1963), however, reports a physiological trend toward reduced autonomic functioning during hypnosis, and Tart (1963) found that verbal reports of depth of hypnotic trance correspond directly with basal GSR. Although EEG patterns following hypnotic induction are often highly variable, depending in part on the instructions given Ss, Ulett, Akpinar, and Itil (1972) report increases in alpha and slow (20–26 Hz) beta activity during trance induction and testing. An increase in fast beta (40- over 50 Hz) was observed in the best hypnotic subjects. Morgan, Mac-Donald, and Hilgard (1974) found that lateral asymmetry of alpha (a measure of relative amplitudes of alpha in left and right hemispheres) was greater during hypnosis than during eyes-open baseline recording. The amount of asymmetry during hypnosis corresponded to that observed when the same Ss were engaged in spatial imagery, as opposed to analytical tasks, in a non-hypnotized eyes-closed condition. Much of this current evidence supports the contention that hypnosis is a state different from normal waking.

A relationship between patterns of EEG activity and hypnotic susceptibility has also been observed. Duration of alpha rhythms in the waking state is highly correlated with susceptibility (London, Hart & Leibovitz, 1968; Howlis & Rhead, 1968), and more recent evidence (Galbraith, London, Leibovitz, Cooper & Hart, 1970) suggests that low frequency (5-8 Hz) rhythms are even better predictors of hypnotic susceptibility. Morgan *et al.* (1974) conclude that hypnosis *per se* is not a unitary generalized state, but that hypnotic susceptibility may be characterized by a characteristic pattern of cognitive function.

Subjective reports from Ss who have had experience in both meditation and hypnosis indicate numerous similarities. Experiences common to both include: dissociation of the mind from the body, dizziness, withdrawal from external reality with some awareness of external stimuli, and visual blackness (Tart, 1970). The subjective similarities together with the indication of similar autonomic changes and EEG patterns for hypnosis and meditation make salient more direct concurrent investigations of the two phenomena.

In addition, Beary and Benson's (1974) findings pursuant to O_2 consumption and CO_2 production (indicators of hypometabolic functioning), suggest that results purporting to demonstrate the unique effects of meditative technique may reflect more general processes. A comparison of meditation with other techniques of relaxation on measures of autonomic arousal is in order.

The present study utilizes both autohypnosis and instructed relaxation for comparison with meditation. Autohypnosis is, like meditation, an individual experience rather than an *E*-directed social experience. Autohypnosis allows *S* to achieve greater involvement in internal events and greater absorption in thought than standard instructed hypnosis. Instructed relaxation includes meditation-like instruction to view both thoughts and external events nonevaluatively.

Autonomic activity is assessed during two baseline periods and one treatment period for meditators, *S*s trained in autohypnosis, and control *S*s. Response systems monitored are HR, GSR, and Resp.

METHOD

Subjects

Three groups of 10 *S*s were drawn from the student population of Eastern Washington State College. Because one group was to be trained in autohypnosis, it was desirable to select those *S*s on the basis on high susceptibility to hypnosis. Accordingly, *all S*s were screened by individual administration of the *Stanford Hypnotic Susceptibility Scale, Form A* (Weitzenhoffer & Hilgard, 1959). Criterion for inclusion in the study was a score of at least 10 on the 12 point scale. All hypnosis sessions, both testing and training, took place in a partially darkened, relatively quiet room, different from the experimental chamber used during the recording session.

Non meditation *S*s were randomly assigned to either the control group (Group C) or the hypnosis group (Group H). *S*s in Group C were given an appointment to return approximately two weeks after the susceptibility screening. *S*s in Group H received preliminary instructions for autohypnosis immediately following the screening procedure and returned on two occasions (approximately one day and seven days later) for additional training in autohypnosis. Instructions were based on a standardized format adapted from a method outlined by Slater (1941). Each *S* was hypnotized and given the posthypnotic suggestion that he would find it easy to hypnotize himself, and was instructed in the use of visual and auditory images to deepen trance. *S*s were asked to practice autohypnosis daily from the first screening procedure until the conclusion of the study, approximately two weeks.

Members of Students' International Meditation Society were screened for inclusion in the meditation group (Group M). These *S*s had all received standard personalized instruction in the techniques of TM by teachers trained by Maharishi Mahesh Yogi. They regularly (two 20-minute periods daily) practiced a form of contemplative meditation which is not impaired by experimental recording apparatus or laboratory context. Each *S* in this group had at least six months experience in meditation.

Group M contained six males and four females. Group H contained four males and six females. Group C contained six males and four females. All *S*s were Caucasians between the ages of 18 and 23.

Apparatus

HR, Resp, and GSR were recorded on an E & M Instrument Company six-channel physiograph. HR was measured by a cardiotach triggered by a photo-electric transducer attached to the index finger of *S*'s preferred hand. Zinc/zinc-sulfate GSR electrodes, placed on the first and third fingers of the non-preferred hand, were used to record GSR. Resp was recorded from a bellows-type pneumonocuff strapped diagonally across *S*'s chest. *S*s were seated in a comfortable chair in a sound-attenuated chamber with constant, low ambient lighting during the recording session. An intercom permitted communication between S and E.

Procedure

After each S was conducted to the experimental chamber, electrodes were attached and the experimental sequence was described. S was given instructions specific to his group. The experimental session consisted of three 10-minute measurement periods.

The first period was a relaxed base rate period (B1). S was asked to relax and sit quietly, but to remain awake during B1. Five to 10 minutes after E left the chamber, timing was begun. The delay gave S an opportunity to become accustomed to the experimental setting and allowed the response systems time to stabilize.

Instructions for the meditation-hypnosis period (MH) were similar for all groups. All Ss were instructed to "reduce autonomic functioning, relax as much as possible, ignore or render neutral all external stimuli and let thoughts come as they may." (These instructions are similar to those received by meditators during TM training.) Additional instruction for Ss in Group M were "go into meditation," and for Ss in Group H "hypnotize yourself." Timing of this period began five minutes after the signal was given to S to allow time for stabilization of response systems.

The final measurement period (B2), was a post-experimental base rate to assess the persistence of treatment effects. Ss were again instructed to relax and remain still, but to stay awake. Several minutes were allowed to give adequate time for meditators to complete their meditation and response systems to stabilize before the timing of the measurement period was begun.

The signal to mark the change from one measurement period to the next was a click generated by the switch on the intercom.

Measurement

A single score was derived for each of four response measures for each subject in each 10 minute measurement period. HR was assessed at 10 second intervals and the average HR, in bpm, computed for the entire 10 minute period. The Resp score was computed by counting the total number of breaths taken during each period and dividing the count by 10 to obtain average number of breaths per minute. Basal GSR was computed by averaging obtained resistance, sampled at 30 second intervals, for each period. Resistance scores were transformed to log conductance measures in order to normalize the distribution for analysis and 3 was added to the transformed score to increase ease of analysis. Discrete GSR responses, defined as any reduction of 250 ohms or greater, were simply counted throughout each period.

RESULTS

Heart rate.

Differences in mean HR during B1 and MH were evaluated using a Groups x Trials analysis of variance. The Trials effect was significant (F (1, 27) = 5.33, $p < .05$), indicating that the observed reduction (see Figure 1a) in HR from B1 to MH is a reliable phenomenon. Neither the main effect for Groups nor the Groups x Trial interaction approached significance ($F < 1.0$ in both cases). Although there was no overall difference between groups, the possibility of some initial difference remained. Accordingly Group M was compared to both Group C and Group H by means of t tests. These initial differences also proved to be non-significant (t (18) = .251, $p > .50$; .316, $p < .25$, respectively).

The persistence of the observed HR reduction was evaluated by applying the Groups x Trials analysis to MH and B2 means. Again, the Trials effect was significant (F (1, 27) = 182.131, $p < .01$) in-

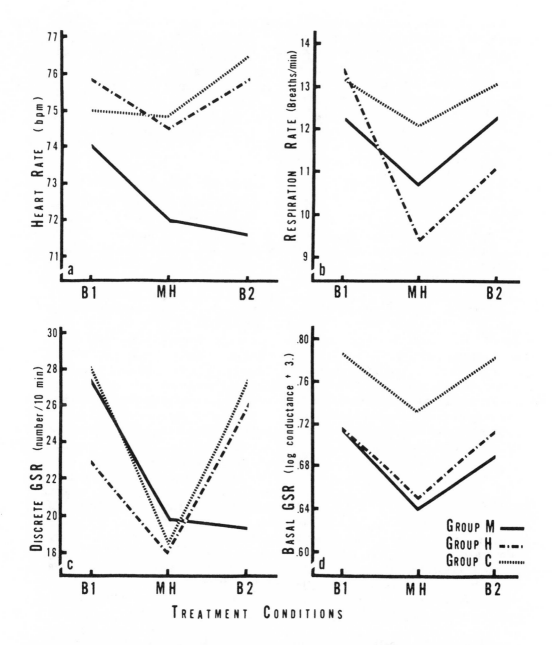

Fig. Group averages for each of the four responses assessed: (a) heart rate, (b) respiration, (c) discrete GSR responses, (d) basal level of the GSR. B1 and B2 represent pre- and post-base rate recording, re-spectively. MH denotes the experimental condition; meditation (Group M), autohypnosis (Group H), or relaxation (Group C).

dicating a reliable overall return to B1 levels. The differences between groups were not reliable ($F < 1.$), but the Groups x Trials interaction was significant ($F (2, 27) = 8.093, p < .01$). In subsequent t tests, none of the comparisons between groups proved to be significant. However, HR increased in Groups H and C ($t (9) = 1.383, 1.484$, respectively, $p < .10$) from MH to B2 and decreased insignificantly in Group M ($t (9) = .374, p > .25$).

Respiration.

Groups x Trials analysis of B1 and MH data showed the reduction in Resp (Fig. 1b) across trials to be significant ($F (1, 27) = 9.059, p < .01$). Neither the Groups effect ($F < 1.$) nor the Groups x Trials interaction ($F (2, 27) = 1.896, p > .10$) was significant. Closer inspection of B1 data using t tests revealed no initial differences in rate between groups.

Evaluation of MH and B2 means found a significant Trials effect ($F (1, 27) = 8.261; p < .01$) corresponding to an increase in rate following the conclusion of the MH period. Neither the main effect for groups nor the interaction approached significance ($F (2, 27) = 1.987, 1.037$, respectively; $p > .10$).

Discrete GSR.

The reduction in the number of discrete GSR responses from B1 to MH (Figure 1c) proved to be significant ($F (1, 27) = 5.399, p < .05$) in the analysis of variance. Neither the Groups nor the Groups x Trials effect was significant (both $F < 1.0$). Further, no specific comparison between groups on B1 data was significant.

Analysis of MH and B1 data similarly indicated a significant trials effect ($F (1, 27) = 5.063, p < .05$) but no reliable differences due to group membership ($F < 1.$) or to the Groups x Trials interaction ($F (2, 27) = 1.475, p > .10$).

Basal GSR.

Analysis of basal GSR levels (Figure 1d) found no significant difference between groups during B1. The two analyses of variance showed significant trials effects ($F (2, 27) = 23.542, 28.387, p < .01$ for B1 to MH and MH to B2, respectively). The Fs for all other comparisons were less than 1.

DISCUSSION

For all three procedures investigated, meditation, instructed self-hypnosis, and instructed relaxation, the instructions led to a period of markedly reduced autonomic arousal in all response measures studied. Contrary to expectations predicated on prior work (Wallace & Benson, 1972), the extent of the reduction did not differ among the three procedures investigated. These results are, however, congruent with the more recent findings of Benson (1974) that ''TM-like'' instructions can be used to induce a hypometabolic state with a minimum of practice using the technique.

In none of the measures studied was there a difference among the groups on initial baseline levels. Prior work indicated that meditators should show lower base HR (Wallace, 1970b) and fewer discrete GSR responses (Orme-Johnson, 1973) than nonmeditators. One possible explanation for the discrepancy between earlier findings and those of the present study is the highly select population from which the present Ss were selected. All Ss were highly susceptible to hypnosis. One can posit that autonomic response levels reflect hypnotic susceptibility, or perhaps the cognitive style which characterizes hypnotic-susceptible Ss (Morgan, et al. 1974) rather than the practice of some particular technique. There is some indication that TM is related to hypnotic susceptibility. In the present study, although only 44% of the non-TM volunteer Ss were rated highly susceptible (scores of 10 or higher), 100% of the TM practitioners received scores of 11 or 12 on the Stanford Scale. Either the practice of TM increases susceptibility to hypnosis or, alternatively, only highly susceptible *S*s find sufficient reinforcement in the technique to continue its practice for long periods of time.

There is some indication in the data that the reduction in autonomic functioning is more persistent following meditation, although this proved reliable only for the HR measures. This may reflect an intrinsic difference between meditation and the other techniques employed here, or it may simply represent the results of additional practice. The meditators had been practicing for at least six months, the other *S*s for only two weeks.

In general, autohypnosis and meditation produce similar effects on autonomic arousal, and the effects do not differ from those observed in an instructed relaxation control group. The relationship between hypnotic susceptibility and meditation bears further exploration.

Results of earlier studies attributing unique hypometabolic functioning to the practice of meditative techniques must be interpreted with caution. Earlier studies are contaminated by the lack of control procedures or an inappropriately selected control group. The results of the present study, together with that by Beary and Benson (1974), indicate that many of the effects of meditation can be replicated by simple instruction without the benefit of extended practice, at least in certain subjects.

REFERENCES

AKISHIGE, Y. *Psychological studies of Zen.* Bulletin of the Faculty of Literature of Kyushu University, 1968, 11. Cited by Wallace (1970a, b).

ANAND, B. K., CHHINA, G. S. & SINGH, B. B. Some aspects of EEG studies in Yogis. *Elec-troencephalography and Clinical Neurophysiology*, 1961, 13, 452–456.

BANQUET, J. P. Spectral analysis of the EEG in meditation. *Electroencephalography and Clinical Neurophysiology*, 1973, 35, 143–151.

BEARY, J. F. & BENSON, H. A simple psychophysiologic technique which elicits the hypometabolic changes of the relaxation responses. *Psychosomatic Medicine*, 1974, 36, 115–120.

GALBRAITH, G. C., LONDON, P., LEIBOVITZ, M. P., COOPER, L. M., & HART, J. T. EEG and hypnotic susceptibility. *Journal of Comparative and Physiological Psychology*, 1970, 72, 125–131.

KROGER, W. S. *Clinical and experimental hypnosis.* Philadelphia: Lippincott, 1963.

LONDON, P., HART, J. T., & LEIBOVITZ, M. P. EEG alpha rhythms and susceptibility to hypnosis. *Nature*, 1968, 219, 71–72.

MAHESH, M. Y. *The science of being and the art of living.* London: International SRM Publications, 1966.

MAHESH, M. Y. *Maharishi Mahesh Yogi on the Bhagavda-Gita: A new translation and commentary.* Baltimore: Penguin Books, 1969.

MORGAN, A. H., MACDONALD, H. & HILGARD, E. R. EEG alpha: Lateral asymmetry related to task, and hypnotizability. *Psychophysiology*, 1974, 11, 275–282.

NOWLIS, D. P., & RHEAD, J. C. Relation of eyes-closed resting EEG alpha activity to hypnotic susceptibility. *Perceptual Motor Skills*, 1968, 27, 1047–1050.

ORME-JOHNSON, D. W. Autonomic stability and transcendental meditation. *Psychosomatic Medicine*, 1973, 35, 341–349.

SLATER, A. Three methods of autohypnosis. *Journal of General Psychology*, 1941, 24, 423–438.

TART, C. T. Hypnotic depth and basal skin resistance. *The International Journal of Clinical and Experimental Hypnosis*, 1963, 11, 81–92.

TART, C. T. Transpersonal potentialities of deep hypnosis. *Journal of Transpersonal Psychology*, 1970, 2, 27–40.

ULETT, G. A., AKPINAR, S. & ITIL, T. M. Hypnosis: Physiological, pharmacological reality. *American Journal of Psychiatry*, 1972, 128, 799–805.

WALLACE, R. K. Physiological effects of transcendental meditation. *Science*, 1970a, 167, 1751–1754.

WALLACE, R. K. *The physiological effects of Transcendental Meditation: A proposed fourth major state of consciousness.* Los Angeles: Students' International Meditation Society, 1970b.

WALLACE, R. K., & BENSON, H. The physiology of meditation. *Scientific American*, 1972, 226, 85–90.

WEITZENHOFFER, A. M., & HILGARD, E. R. *Stanford hypnotic susceptibility scale: Forms A & B.* Palo Alto: Consulting Psychologists Press, 1959.

WENGER, M., & BAGCHI, B. Studies of autonomic function in practitioners of Yoga in India. *Behavior Science*, 1961, 6, 312–323.

53

A PHYSIOLOGICAL AND SUBJECTIVE EVALUATION OF MEDITATION, HYPNOSIS, AND RELAXATION

Donald R. Morse, John S. Martin, Merrick L. Furst,
and Louis L. Dubin

Ss were monitored for respiratory rate, pulse rate, blood pressure, skin resistance, EEG activity, and muscle activity. They were monitored during the alert state, meditation (TM or simple word type), hypnosis (relaxation and task types), and relaxation. Ss gave a verbal comparative evaluation of each state. The results showed significantly better relaxation responses for the relaxation states (relaxation, relaxation-hypnosis, meditation) than for the alert state. There were no significant differences between the relaxation states except for the measure "muscle activity" in which meditation was significantly better than the other relaxation states. Overall, there were significant differences between task-hypnosis and relaxation-hypnosis. No significant differences were found between TM and simple word meditation. For the subjective measures, relaxation-hypnosis and meditation were significantly better than relaxation, but no significant differences were found between meditation and relaxation-hypnosis.

INTRODUCTION AND LITERATURE REVIEW

Transcendental Meditation (TM) is a progressive relaxation technique and philosophy that has recently been introduced into Western culture. Its rapid

*Associate Professor, Department of Endodontology, Temple University School of Dentistry, Philadelphia, Pennsylvania 19140.

**Assistant Professor, Department of Physiology and Biophysics.

†Associate Professor, Department of Community Dentistry.

‡Clinical Associate Professor, Department of Community Dentistry, Temple University School of Dentistry.

A preliminary report based on this study was given at the 28th annual meeting of the Society for Clinical and Experimental Hypnosis, Philadelphia, Pennsylvania, June, 1976.

Address reprint requests to: Donald R. Morse, DDS, MA, Department of Endodontology, Temple University School of Dentistry, 3223 North Broad Street, Philadelphia, Pennsylvania 19140.

Received for publication July 19, 1976; final revision received April 21, 1977.

popularity is based on the technique's simplicity and apparent effectiveness for deep relaxation. TM is a passive meditation in which the subject sits quietly, silently repeats a mystical Sanskrit sound (mantra), concentrates on nothing, and lets his "mind" drift. The subject receives his personal mantra (one of a select number used in TM) from a TM teacher during a semireligious initiating ceremony. Selection of the mantra is purportedly based on the TM teacher's learned ability to match mantra with subject (1).

Regular practice of TM has been reported to yield unique physiological, psychological, medical, and sociological benefits (2). The physiological findings showed changes suggestive of deep relaxation (3–6). The specific changes found during meditation, as compared to the alert or relaxed states, were significant decreases in heart rate, respiratory rate, O_2 consumption, CO_2 elimination, and blood lactate level

(3,4,6). Blood pressure did not decrease significantly (3), but a subsequent investigation showed that with hypertensives who meditated regularly for several months, blood pressure did decrease measurably (7). During meditation, as compared to the alert and relaxed states, there were marked increases in skin resistance (3,6) and slow alpha and theta EEG patterns (3,5,6). Synchronization of slow alpha and theta EEG activity in various cortical areas occurred only during meditation (5,6). Other findings peculiar to meditation were the absence of changes in alpha activity when external stimuli were presented (no alpha blocking) and persistence of alpha activity at the end of meditation (3,5).

TM practice also resulted in improved ability to manage stress according to skin resistance measures (8). During the awake state, meditators and controls were presented a loud tone at irregular intervals. The stress reaction to the tone was compared by an examination of the galvanic skin response (GSR). Meditators showed habituation to the tones quicker than nonmeditators and made fewer multiple responses in skin resistance during habituation. Meditators also made fewer spontaneous GSR's (fluctuations in skin resistance independent of subject movement or ambient noise) than did controls.

Psychological, medical, and sociological benefits reported from the practice of TM include faster reaction time for TM Ss than for nonmeditators (9), better auditory discrimination for TM practitioners than for reading controls (10), superior psychological health for TM meditators than for nonmeditators (11), greater self-sufficiency, stability, and happiness for TM Ss than for controls (12), and TM practitioners showed decreases in smoking, alleviation of alcohol and drug abuse, improved study habits, better interpersonal relationships, increased productivity, improvement in mental health, decreases in tension and anxiety, and alleviation of asthma (2,13,14).

On the metaphysical level, continued practice of TM supposedly can lead to an expansion of consciousness or the attainment of "cosmic" or "unity" consciousness (1,2).

These various findings related to TM have been considered to be of such magnitude that TM has been proposed as a fourth state of consciousness, distinct from the awake state, sleep, dreaming, and hypnosis (1,2,3,15). However, there are at least two possible explanations for the apparent uniqueness of TM. First TM practitioners are highly motivated because of the positive presentations given at their courses and the subsequent regular feedback. Relaxing control Ss are generally not well motivated for the relaxation procedure. Therefore, motivation could account for some of the significant results with the previous studies. Second, many of the previous studies were uncontrolled or poorly controlled and findings could be questioned. Nevertheless, until 1974 the results of most studies were favorable for TM. However, recent findings have cast doubt on those prior resuts.

Meditating Ss using the word "one" (instead of a TM mantra) were compared with alert controls in the first study (16). O_2 consumption, CO_2 elimination, and respiratory rate were measured and all three were significantly decreased as compared to controls.

The results of two other studies indicate that TM practice is not the only means to achieve marked decreases in O_2 consumption (17). In the first study, Ss lying still while listening to soothing music had an O_2 consumption decrease equivalent to that of TM Ss. In the second study, it was observed that if prolonged periods of rest preceded testing of TM, then there was no significant decrease in O_2 consumption from the control period. Only when the Ss meditated from a relatively alert state was there a pronounced decrease in O_2 consumption.

Although TM practice can reduce blood pressure for hypertensives (7), a recent study has shown that simple word meditation is also effective in that regard (18).

Catecholamine (epinephrine, norepinephrine) levels increase during stress and decrease during relaxation (19). To evaluate TM as a stress-reducing method, TM Ss were compared with relaxing controls (20). There were no significant differences found between the two groups on reduction in catecholamine levels.

Blood lactate levels increase during stress and decrease during relaxation (15). Although previous reports showed that lactate levels decreased significantly better during meditation than relaxation (3,15), a current study showed no significant differences in lactate levels between the two states (20).

Skin resistance levels decrease during stress and increase during relaxation (21). Although previous findings indicate that skin resistance results are significantly better with TM than with relaxation (3,8,15), results of two recent studies showed no significant difference in skin resistance levels between TM Ss and resting controls (22,23).

TM practice may reduce anxiety (13), but it is not unique in that regard according to two studies by Smith (24). In the first study, TM Ss were compared with an eyes-closed relaxation group that received TM-like indoctrination (strong, positive suggestions of the method's effectiveness). In the second study, a group taught a TM-like method (received a mantra) was compared with an eyes-closed group taught an "anti-meditation" method (told to concentrate on as many positive thoughts as possible). After several months, anxiety level measurement tests were given to all Ss in both studies. The test results were compared with test results obtained from Ss not participating in the studies. Analysis showed significantly better results for Ss in all four groups as compared to nonparticipating Ss. However, there were no significant differences among the four groups. Sitting quietly with eyes closed, regardless of the mental activity, was equally effective for all four groups.

EEG alpha levels had been thought to increase during relaxation and decrease during stress (25). Although prior results showed significantly more alpha production during meditation than relaxation (3,5,6,15), a recent study showed no significant difference in alpha levels between the two states (22). However, the importance of alpha EEG is now open to question. Newer findings show that there are large individual variations in base level alpha that are related to genetic and early environmental influences (26). Individuals have optimal levels of alpha (usually observed under quiet conditions with eyes closed) and these levels cannot be significantly increased (27,28). One method used to reach optimal alpha is upward rotation of the eyeballs followed by eye closure (29). Alpha activity is at its maximum only when the eyes are closed (27,28,30). Alpha training does not appear to be effective in the control of anxiety (31). Alpha level was also shown not to be related to muscular relaxation as it was maintained even during vigorous muscle tension (29,32). Therefore, the high alpha levels found in previous studies during TM practice (3,5,6,15) could have been related to the use of Ss with naturally high alpha levels given optimal conditions for alpha production.

The original EEG findings showed that TM was unrelated to sleep (3,5,6,15). However, a recent EEG study of experienced TM Ss showed that 40% of meditation time is spent in sleep (33).

TM has also been considered distinct from hypnosis (2,3,15). Studies on physiological parameters of hypnosis have shown no responses that separated hypnosis from the alert state (21,28,34–38). This was partly related to the different conditions induced under hypnosis. According to the results of a recent study, when Ss practicing autohypnosis-relaxation type were compared to TM Ss on the parameters of heart rate, respiratory rate, and GSR, no significant differences were found between the two groups (23). The Ss were examined for hypnotic susceptibility and all the TM Ss showed high susceptibility. It has also been reported that good hypnotic Ss meditate better than poor hypnotic Ss (39). In a clinical study, meditation (TM and simple word type) was shown to be a rapid, effective method for hypnotic induction (40). Hypnosis has been used for anxiety control, tension reduction, and analgesia (41) and in a recent study TM was used effectively for the same purposes (42). Patients who used both hypnosis and meditation reported that the subjective sensations were similar for the two states (40,42). It has also been shown that hypnosis practice can result in psychological, medical, and sociological

benefits similar to those reported for TM practice (9–14,43,44). Therefore, there appears to be similarities between TM and relaxation-hypnosis.

Considering the contradictory findings concerning TM as compared to simple word meditation, relaxation, and hypnosis, it was decided to conduct an extensive, well-controlled physiological and subjective evaluation of those four states.

METHODS

In preliminary examination, it was found that there were marked differences between Ss in slow alpha EEG activity, base-line skin resistance levels, and changes in skin resistance in response to stimuli. Some Ss produced less than 1% slow alpha while others had over 50%. With base-line skin resistance levels (S alert but quiet), some Ss had a mean skin resistance of less than 10 kilohms (K=ohms), while others had over 100 K=ohms. When retesting those Ss several weeks later, the mean skin resistance levels remained relatively constant. In response to stimuli, we found, as did others (8,45), that there were underresponders (stabiles) and overresponders (labiles). The underresponders showed approximately no changes in skin resistance, while the overresponders had marked changes. Based on this marked variability, it was decided to use Ss as their own controls.

The total population was 48 Ss including 37 males and 11 females, with a mean age of 29. Thirty-nine were health care professionals and the others had varied occupations. Ss were not paid; the incentive given was that the individual's results would be shown at the session's conclusion.

Ss were monitored for respiratory rate, pulse rate, blood pressure, skin resistance, and EEG activity from four cortical areas (frontal, temporal, parietal, occipital) and scalp muscle activity from the same four sites.[1]

There were four experimental groups with 12 Ss

---

[1]It was decided that invasive measuring techniques, such as those used for O_2 consumption, would not be done to avoid undue stress on the Ss.

per group. The groups were (1) $\overline{\text{H}}$/M-Ss trained in TM, training varied from 2 months to 5 years, median 1.3 years; (2) H/$\overline{\text{M}}$-Ss trained in autohypnosis, training varied from 3 months to 10 years, median 1 year; (3) H/M-Ss trained in both, TM training varied from 6 months to 8 years, median 3.8 years, hypnosis training varied from 1 month to 4 years, median 1.3 years; (4) $\overline{\text{H}}$/$\overline{\text{M}}$-Ss trained in neither.

At the session's initiation, if Ss had no previous hypnotic training, they were taught auto-hypnosis. Ss with no TM training were taught simple word meditation. Ss untrained in both techniques were taught both. Prior to hypnosis, all Ss were tested for hypnotic susceptibility by the Spiegel Eye-Roll Method (46) and found to be in the moderate to high range (2–4).

Ss were monitored under six conditions, alert state (A), relaxation (R), hetero-hypnosis-relaxation type (H-R), hetero-hypnosis-task type (H-T), auto-hypnosis-relaxation type (A-R), and meditation [M, either TM or simple word type (SM)].

Instructions for R were, "Close your eyes and relax, do not meditate, do not use hypnosis." The technique for H-R was eye fixation, progressive relaxation, "descending elevator" deepening method, and suggestions of a mental trip to a relaxing destination. A-R was similar, except the Ss induced themselves. To prevent anticipation, Ss were not told that a task would be given under hypnosis. The task, attainment of "glove" anesthesia of the right hand (H-T), was given immediately following H-R. Glove anesthesia was verified at the conclusion of the hypnotic session by verbal discussion with the Ss. Testing for anesthesia was not done during the procedure to prevent interference with the monitoring. Glove anesthesia was used (1) as a contrast to relaxation-hypnosis to ascertain if significant differences could be found between the types and (2) as an indicator of the hypnotic state (47).

For M, the TM Ss used their personal mantras. Other Ss chose one of the following words, "one," "om," "flower," "garden," "river," and "sail." Ss were told to relax, close their eyes, and silently repeat the word at any pace. Intruding thoughts could be completed, but they were told to return to repetition of the word (as is done in TM).

To reduce expectancy effects (48,49), Ss were informed that no differences had been found to date between hypnosis, meditation, and relaxation. Instructions for A were, "Open your eyes, become wide awake, do not move your head." The alert breaks were used for the following four purposes: (1) as a control period for comparison with the experimental states; (2) as a means of verifying whether the Ss were practicing the mental task requested. Other studies have shown that TM Ss can go into meditation automatically with eye closure and that they may stay in meditation after they are requested to stop meditating (3,15). Ss in the present study reported that they only did the mental technique requested; (3) as a means to try to control for interactive effects among the experimental states; (4) to allow the Ss to evaluate their subjective feelings during the previous experimental state. The Ss were not told about their physiological results when they were questioned about their subjective evaluation. Ss were asked to compare the states on the basis of "euphoria," "dissociation," "depth," and "most effortless induction."

Ss were kept in each experimental state for 6-8 min with a 3-4-min alert break between the experimental states.[2]

For each S in the four groups, one of four orders was followed. Order alteration was used as another means to try to control for interactive effects between the experimental states. The orders were (a)

A-R-A-H-R-A-A-R-A-M;		A-
M-A-A-R-A-H-R-H-T-A-R-A;	(b)	A-
R-A-M-A-H-R-A-A-R;		A-
A-R-A-H-R-H-T-A-M-A-R-A;	(c)	A-
H-R-A-A-R-A-M-A-R;		A-
R-A-M-A-A-R-A-H-R-H-T-A;	(d)	A-
M-A-H-R-A-A-R-A-R;		A-
R-A-A-R-A-H-R-H-T-A-M-A.		

Testing was done in a quiet, darkened, temperature controlled (70°F) room at about the same time and day for each S. The senior author was the hypnotist. All Ss completed medical and personality inventory questionnaires. Results showed no extreme personality conditions or medical disorders.

Prior to the recordings, Ss remained seated and inactive for a 30-min preparatory time. The basic equipment used was two Grass Ink Writing Polygraphs, Model 7.

Respiratory rate (RR) was recorded with a pneumograph and a preamplifier Model 7P1A. RR was counted per minute and a mean value entered for each state. Pulse rate (PR) was recorded by the use of a photocell plethysmograph placed on the

---

[2] The experimental time period produced no S irritability and previous findings showed that most physiological changes with TM occurred within the first few minutes (3,6,15).

left earlobe and a preamplifier Model 7P1A. PR was counted per minute and a mean value entered per state.

Systolic and diastolic blood pressure (SBP, DBP) was measured with a sphygmomanometer previously calibrated before each session with a mercury manometer and recorded with a preamplifier Model 7P8B. Blood pressure was taken during the midperiod of each state. It was used for two purposes: to record blood pressure levels and to act as a stressor during the various states. This was evaluated by monitoring of changes in skin resistance during blood pressure detection (SR/BP).

Skin resistance levels (SR) and nonspecific fluctuations (NSF) were recorded by the use of a preamplifier Model 7P1A with set input on PGR. Two silver-silver chloride electrodes were placed with electrode jelly (Electrogel) 5 cm apart upon the palm of the left hand (3). SR was recorded in kilohms of resistance with each millimeter pen deflection equivalent to 2 K-ohms of resistance. SR was counted at 1-min intervals and a mean value entered per state. An NSF was considered to be a change of 0.5 K-ohms or more within a period of 5 sec or less.[3] The lower limit of 0.5 K-ohms was chosen to have a minimally discernible visual change on the Grass Chart Paper. The NSF were counted per minute and a mean value entered per state.

EEG activities were recorded with wide band AC preamplifier and integrator Model 7P3A that had been calibrated for 50 μv equivalent to 0.5-cm pen deflection. Recordings were taken from the right frontal, parietal, temporal, and occipital cortex with the use of four preamplifiers and paired plate electrodes. The reference electrode was placed in the occipital region. Using Electrogel, the electrodes were positioned with an electrode headband. The standard machine speed was run at 25 mm/min. Records for evaluation were made at a speed of 25 mm/sec at stated intervals for each state.[4] Slow alpha activity (8-10 cps) was counted and tabulated

as percent of total EEG activity in the four cortical areas and a mean value was entered per state.

Synchronous slow alpha activity (SSA) was evaluated as $(-)$ =absent; $(\pm)$=questionable, present in any area less than 10% of the time; $(\,)$ =slight, present in two cortical areas for 10% of the time or more; $(\,\,)$ =moderate, present in three cortical areas for 10% of the time or more; $(\,\,\,)$ =definite, present in four cortical areas for 10% of the time or more (Fig. 1).

Biofeedback studies indicate that frontalis and temporalis muscle activities are good indicators of tension (29). As muscle activity apparently diminishes during TM practice (2,15), it was decided to evaluate muscle activity during the various states. A pilot study revealed that muscle artifacts occurred in EEG records when Ss concentrated and disappeared when Ss relaxed (Fig. 2). Electromyogram recordings from the EEG sites would have interfered with the EEG recordings. Therefore, filters were not used to remove muscle artifacts during the EEG recordings. This then gave a means to determine if there were differences in muscle activity during the various states. Muscle artifacts (MA) were counted and a mean value entered per state.

A blind evaluation of the records was done by physiology department members who were not involved in the study.

The data for the four experimental groups and four orders under six conditions were subjected to a repeated measures analysis of variance (ANOV) for each of the 10 objective measures. Statistical significance was set at the 0.05 level. Nonparametric sign test analysis was used for the subjective measures with significance set at the 0.05 level.

RESULTS

Skin resistance is believed to be a measure of sweat gland activity and it is an important monitor of the sympathetic nervous system. As such, it can be used as a relatively accurate measure of Ss stress and relaxation responses (8,21,45). Of the 10 objective measures, SR was found to be the most sensitive. Therefore, a complete set of results for SR is given.

SR—Main Results

A summary of mean SR in kilohms for

---

[3]With a sensitivity of 2 mV/cm, 0.5 K-ohms is equivalent to a 0.25-mm change recorded on the Grass Chart Paper.

[4]During each alert state, two recordings of 24 sec each were run at the start of the first minute and during the last minute. During each of the experimental states, three 24-sec recordings were run; the first at the start of the first minute, the second at the start of the third minute, the third during the last minute.

Clinical and Research Aspects in Meditation

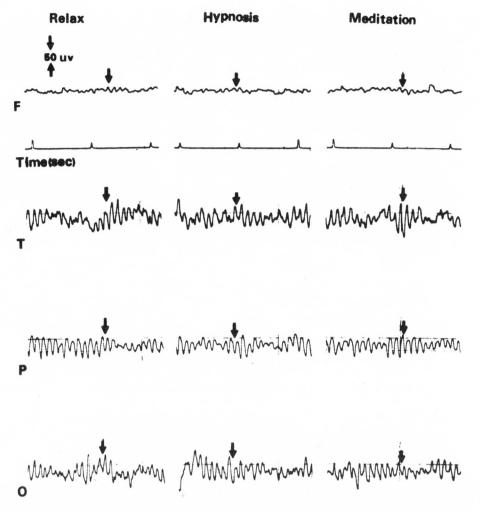

Fig. 1. Synchronous slow alpha EEG activity is shown. ↓=areas of synchronous slow alpha activity. F=frontal, T=temporal, P=parietal, O=occipital.

the four experimental groups and four orders under six conditions is presented in Table 1 (Groups) and Table 2 (Orders). Also given are combined means for the four relaxation conditions (R, A-R, H-R, M) and percent increases from alert means to relaxation means. A summary of ANOV for mean SR is presented in Table 3. A statistically significant main effect was found for the Groups factor ($F=4.35$; $df=3,32$; $P < 0.05$). Referring to Table 1, it is noted that the mean Groups

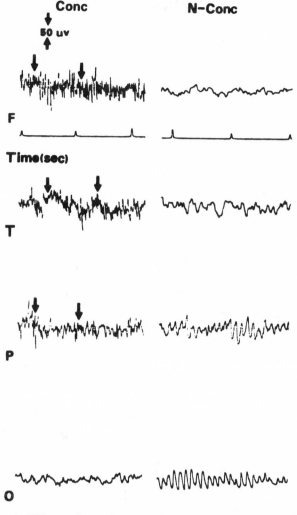

Fig. 2. Muscle artifacts in EEG records are shown. Conc=subject concentrated, N-Conc=subject relaxed, ↓=muscle artifacts, F=frontal, T=temporal, P=parietal, O=occipital.

values are as follows: H/M (44.0 K-ohms), H/$\overline{M}$ (57.2 K-ohms), $\overline{H}$/M (61.5 K-ohms, and $\overline{H}$/$\overline{M}$ (97.1 K-ohms). Trained Ss had a mean of 54.2 K-ohms and untrained Ss had a mean of 97.1 K-ohms. Percent change from the alert means to the relaxation means showed increases as follows: H/M (17.8), $\overline{H}$/$\overline{M}$ (21.7), H/$\overline{M}$ (22.2), and $\overline{H}$/M (26.4). Trained Ss had a percent increase of 22.1 and untrained Ss had a 21.7% increase.

A highly significant main effect was

TABLE 1
Summary of Mean Skin Resistance Levels in Kilohms for Four Groups under Six Conditions

Groups	Conditions									
	A	R	H-R	A-R	M	R Mn[a]	H-T	T Mn	N In	% In
H/M	37.6	42.9	45.3	43.5	45.3	44.3	49.2	44.0	6.7	17.8
H/M̄	50.3	62.3	59.1	66.3	66.5	63.6	64.2	61.5	13.3	26.4
H̄/M	48.2	58.5	58.8	59.3	58.8	58.9	59.8	57.2	10.7	22.2
H̄/M̄	82.4	102.7	95.8	101.3	101.3	100.3	99.1	97.1	17.9	21.7
Mean	54.6	66.6	64.8	67.6	68.0	66.8	68.0	64.9	12.2	22.0

[a] Definitions of symbols not defined in the text are: R Mn = mean of combined relaxation states; T Mn = total mean of six conditions; N In = numerical increase from A mean to R Mn; % In = percent increase from A mean to R Mn.

TABLE 2
Summary of Mean Skin Resistance Levels in Kilohms for the Four Orders and Six Conditions

Orders	Conditions									
	A[a]	R	H-R	A-R	M	R Mn	H-T	TMn	N In	% In
A	50.7	66.1	61.8	64.7	64.3	64.2	60.1	61.3	13.5	26.6
B	85.6	103.8	101.6	103.9	108.2	104.4	112.6	102.6	18.8	22.0
C	38.6	44.7	45.0	46.7	48.3	46.2	45.5	44.8	7.6	19.7
D	43.7	51.9	50.6	55.2	51.0	52.2	54.0	51.1	8.5	19.5
Mean	54.6	66.6	64.8	67.6	68.0	67.0	68.0	64.9	12.1	22.0

[a] See text for explanation of symbols.

TABLE 3
Summary of Repeated-Measures ANOV for Four Groups under Four Orders and Six Conditions in Terms of Mean Skin Resistance Levels in Kilohms

Source	ss	df	MS	F
Between Ss	618,663.21	47		
Groups (G)	111,350.07	3	37,116.69	4.35[a]
Orders (O)	146,222.80	3	48,740.93	5.71[b]
G×O	88,084.90	9	9,787.21	1.15
Error	273,005.44	32	8,531.42	
Within Ss	36,215.67	240		
Conditions (C)	6,493.00	5	1,298.60	8.96[b]
G×C	697.97	15	46.53	0.32
O×C	5,125.50	15	341.70	2.36[b]
G×O×C	697.97	45	15.51	0.11
Error	23,201.23	160	145.01	

[a] F.95 (3;32) = 2.93; F.95 (5;160) = 2.27.

[b] F.99 (3;32) = 4.50; F.99 (5;160) = 3.13; F.99 (15;160) = 2.18.

found for the Orders factor ($F = 5.71$; $df = 3,32$; $P < 0.01$). Referring to Table 2, it is noted that the mean Orders values are as follows: C (44.8 K-ohms), D (51.1 K-ohms), A (61.3 K-ohms), and B (102.6 K-ohms). With hypnosis (C) or meditation (D) as the first state, the combined Order mean (C,D) was 49.2 K-ohms. When relaxation preceded either hypnosis or meditation, the combined Order mean was 82.0 K-ohms. Percent change from the alert means to the relaxation means showed increases as follows: D (19.5), C (19.7), B (22.0), and A (26.6). With hypnosis or meditation as the first state, the combined Order mean percent increase was 19.6. When relaxation preceded either hypnosis or meditation, the

Physiological and Subjective Evaluations

combined Order mean percent increase was 24.3.

No significance was found for the interaction between Groups and Orders factors (P>0.05). A highly significant main effect was found for the Conditions factor ($F=8.96$); $df=5,160$; $P<0.01$). The results of tests for differences between the means for Conditions using a Newman-Keuls procedure are presented in Table 4. Significant differences were found between the alert condition and the experimental conditions, but not among the experimental conditions.

No significance was found for the interaction between Groups and Conditions factors and for the interaction among Groups, Orders, and Conditions factors (P>0.05).

A highly significant interaction effect was found between the Orders and Conditions factor ($F=2.36$; $df=15,160$; $P<0.01$). A graphical representation is shown in Fig. 3. The apparent main effects difference is between the alert condition and all the other experimental conditions. None of the other conditions seem to be different among themselves. The significant interaction between Orders and Conditions may be attributed to the H-T condition, particularly for Order B, which seems to be elevated in contrast to the other orders.

SR for H-R and H-T Conditions

The four groups were compared under the limited conditions of H-R-last 2 min (H-R-2) and H-T-first 2 min (H-T-2) as H-T followed immediately after H-R with no intervening alert state.

Significant main effects were found for the Groups factor ($F=2.87$; $df=3,44$; $P<0.05$). The mean Groups values were as follows: H/M (43.2 K-ohms), H/$\overline{M}$ (62.0 K-ohms), $\overline{H}$M (66.2 K-ohms), and $\overline{H}$/$\overline{M}$ (103.3 K-ohms). Trained Ss had a mean of 57.1 K-ohms and untrained Ss had a mean of 103.3 K-ohms. Percent changes from the H-R-2 means to the H-T-2 means were as follows: H/M (0), H/$\overline{M}$ (-2.8), $\overline{H}$/$\overline{M}$ (-8.8), and $\overline{H}$/M (-12.4). Trained Ss had a percent change of -5.1 and untrained Ss had a percent change of -8.8. Ss trained in hypnosis (H/M, H/$\overline{M}$) had the lowest percent change (-1.4).

Highly significant main effects were found for the Conditions factor ($F=22.12$; $df=1,44$; $P<0.01$) and for the interaction between Groups and Conditions factors ($F=11.71$; $df=3,44$; $P<0.01$). A graphical representation is shown in Fig. 4. The significance of both the main effects and the interaction is mainly accounted for by the $\overline{H}$/$\overline{M}$ and $\overline{H}$/M groups in that the mean SR values decrease going from H-R-2 to H-T-2.

SR for TM and SM Groups

A summary of the mean SR for the TM

TABLE 4
Results of Tests for Differences between the Means for Six Conditions in Terms of Skin Resistance Levels Using a Newman-Keuls Procedure

	Conditions					
	A[a]	H-R	R	A-R	M	H-T
Ordered means	54.6	64.8	66.6	67.6	68.0	68.0
A	—	10.2[b]	12.0[c]	13.0[c]	13.4[b]	13.4
H-R		—	1.8	2.8	3.2	3.2
R			—	1.0	3.4	3.4
A-R				—	0.4	0.4
M					—	0.0

[a] See text for definition of symbols.
[b] $P < 0.05$.
[c] $P < 0.01$.

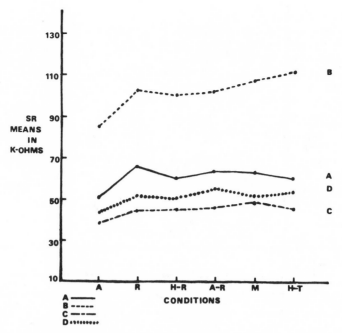

Fig. 3. Mean skin resistance levels in kilohms for six conditions sequenced in four orders. See text for explanation of symbols.

group and the SM group under the conditions of A and M is presented in Table 5. Also given are percent increases from A to M. A summary of ANOV for the mean SR is presented in Table 6.

No significant main effects were found for the Groups factor ($P > 0.05$), although large mean SR differences were present (TM = 50.0 K-ohms, SM = 72.7 K-ohms). Percent changes from the A mean to the

TABLE 5

Summary of Mean Skin Resistance Levels in Kilohms for Groups Trained and Untrained in TM under the Conditions of Alert and Meditation

Groups	Conditions				
	A[a]	M	Mean	N In	% In
TM	44.0	55.9	50.0	11.9	27.0
SM	65.3	80.0	72.7	14.7	22.5
Mean	54.6	68.0	61.3	13.3	24.8

[a] See text for explanation of symbols.

TABLE 6

Summary of Repeated-Measures ANOV for Groups Trained and Untrained in TM under the Conditions of Alert and Meditation in Terms of Mean Skin Resistance Levels in Kilohms

Source	SS	df	MS	F
Between Ss	185,120.74	47		
Groups (G)	9,421.26	1	9,421.26	2.47
Error	175,699.48	46	3,819.55	
Within Ss	10,439.50	48		
Conditions (C)	4,280.01	1	4,280.01	62.79[a]
G×C	3,024.26	1	3,024.26	44.37[a]
Error	3,135.23	46	68.16[a]	

[a] F.99 (1;46) = 7.25.

Physiological and Subjective Evaluations

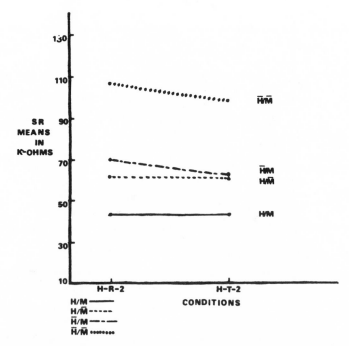

Fig. 4. Mean skin resistance levels in kilohms for four groups under relaxation-hypnosis and task-hypnosis. See text for explanation of symbols.

M mean showed an increase of 22.5% (SM) and 27.0% (TM).

Highly significant main effects were found for the Conditions factor ($F = 62.71$; $df = 1,46$; $P < 0.01$). Referring to Table 5, it is noted that the mean SR is greater for M than for A (68.0 vs. 54.6 K-ohms).

A highly significant interaction effect was found between the Groups and Conditions factors ($F = 44.37$; $df = 1,46$; $P < 0.01$). A graphical representation is shown in Fig. 5.

Other Objective Measures

The results of the repeated measures ANOV for all 10 objective measures were generally similar. As a complete analysis is given for SR, only a summary of mean values across groups (i.e., 48 Ss) and relaxation means are presented for the other objective measures (see Table 7). Note that the alert means (column 1) tend to be different from the relaxation means (column 8), although the actual differences are generally small. No significant differences were found between the relaxation states except for the measure MA. For that measure, M was significantly better than R and A-R (means 25.1 vs. 49.0 and 41.7; $F = 35.79$; $df = 1,235$; $P < 0.01$).

Subjective Measures

A summary of the sign test analysis for the four subjective measures comparing the conditions R, A-R, and M is pre-

Clinical and Research Aspects in Meditation

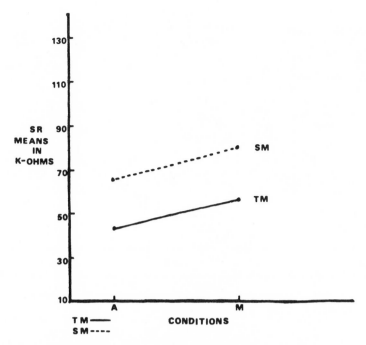

Fig. 5. Mean skin resistance levels in kilohms for Ss trained and untrained in TM under the alert and meditation conditions. See text for explanation of symbols.

sented in Table 8. The first two values given for each measure are the total number of plus signs found in comparing one condition with another for each S under study. The third (decimal) value is the probability associated with a given result, with "ties" not entering into the statistical analysis.

The summary of the logical rankings of the three self-induced states based on the statistically significant results using the sign test is presented in Table 9. Note that for all four subjective measures, both M and A-R were ranked "best" as compared to R ($P<0.001$). There was no statistically significant difference between M and A-R ($P>0.05$), although the trend was toward "better" responses with A-R.

A summary of the sign test analysis results for the four subjective measures comparing TM and SM is presented in Table 10. A-R was found significantly "better" than SM for the mental measures (best dissociation, best euphoria, greatest depth). TM showed a trend toward "better" responses than A-R, but it was not statistically significant ($P>0.05$). For "most effortless induction," TM was significantly "better" than A-R ($P<0.001$), while there was a trend toward "better" responses with A-R as compared to SM, but it was not statistically significant ($P>0.05$).

Although not statistically analyzed, Ss were asked to describe their sensations during "dissociation" and "depth." Usually, absence of thoughts was correlated

Physiological and Subjective Evaluations 657

TABLE 7
Summary of Mean Values of 10 Objective Measures for the 48 Ss Under Eight Conditions

Measures	A [a]	R	H-R	A-R	TM	SM	M	R Mn	H-T	T Mn
PR/min	75.5	72.0	70.0	72.0	73.0	69.5	71.3	71.3	72.0	72.1
RR/min	17.5	15.0	14.5	14.0	14.0	13.5	13.8	14.3	17.5	15.4
Systolic BP	120.5	118.5	118.0	118.0	118.0	119.0	118.5	118.3	122.5	119.3
Diastolic BP	71.0	69.5	69.0	68.5	67.5	70.0	68.8	69.0	72.0	69.8
MA in %	92.0	49.0	42.7	41.7	31.3	18.8	25.1	39.3	42.2	48.6
SA in %	7.0	19.0	25.0	20.5	20.5	23.5	22.0	21.6	20.5	19.0
SSA in +	0	1.5	1.5	1.5	1.5	2.0	1.8	1.6	1.5	1.3
SR in K-ohms	54.6	66.6	64.8	67.6	55.9	80.0	68.0	66.8	68.0	64.9
NSF/min	3.5	1.0	0.5	0.5	0.5	0.5	0.5	0.5	1.5	1.3
SR/BP in K-ohms	3.5	3.0	1.5	1.5	1.5	3.0	2.3	2.1	2.5	2.4

[a] See text for explanation of symbols.

TABLE 8
Sign Test Comparison of Relaxation, Auto-Hypnosis-Relaxation Type, and Meditation for Four Subjective Measures

Measures	R vs. A-R			R vs. M			A-R vs. M		
	R	A-R	P	R	M	P	A-R	M	P
Best dissociation	0	37	<0.001 [a]	0	37	<0.001 [a]	18	9	0.062
Best euphoria	0	34	<0.001 [a]	0	34	<0.001 [a]	14	10	0.271
Greatest depth	0	44	<0.001 [a]	0	44	<0.001 [a]	20	14	0.195
Most effectless induction	0	48	<0.001 [a]	0	48	<0.001 [a]	15	25	0.248

[a] $P < 0.001$.

TABLE 9
Logical Rankings of Relaxation, Auto-Hypnosis-Relaxation Type, and Meditation for Best Relaxation Response Based on the Significant Subjective Measures Results

Measures	Logical rankings
Best dissociation	M, A-R > R
Best euphoria	M, A-R > R
Greatest depth	M, A-R > R
Most effortless induction	M, A-R > R

with high alpha production, but some Ss reported that their minds were active, yet their EEG patterns showed prominent alpha activity (Fig. 6). Other Ss reported "blank" minds but had high beta EEG activity.

DISCUSSION

The inferences drawn in this article are based on (1) the objective data subjected to the repeated measures ANOV, which seeks to establish differences among the

TABLE 10
Sign Test Comparison of Meditation and Auto-Hypnosis-Relaxation Type for Ss Trained and Not Trained in
TM on Four Subjective Measures

Measures	Conditions					
	A-R vs. TM			A-R vs. SM		
	A-R	TM	P	A-R	SM	P
Best dissociation	5	8	0.250	13	1	0.002[b]
Best euphoria	4	9	0.134	9	1	0.004[b]
Greatest depth	5	9	0.212	16	4	0.007[b]
Most effortless induction	2	19	<0.001[a]	13	6	0.084

[a] $P < 0.001$.
[b] $P < 0.01$.

various conditions for the several groups and (2) the subjective data subjected to the nonparametric sign test analysis, which seeks to establish which relaxation states were perceived as "better."

Complete analysis was done of the SR measure. Studies have shown that skin resistance levels decrease with stressful stimuli and increase with relaxing stimuli (21). In the present study, large individual variations in base-line skin resistance levels are apparent in examination of the mean SR findings. Ss who were untrained in either hypnosis or meditation had a mean SR of 97.1 K-ohms, while trained Ss had a mean SR of 54.2 K-ohms. With only these results considered it might be concluded that (1) people who take up meditation or hypnosis are more stressed or (2) training causes a decrease in skin resistance. However, it has been found that base-line skin resistance levels are highly variable, relatively constant over time, and may not be affected by training. Orme-Johnson (8) found that mean basal skin resistance was not significantly different between TM Ss and relaxation controls. The more sensitive indication is changes

in skin resistance to stimuli (3,8,21). In considering changes in skin resistance level from the base-line alert condition to the mean of the relaxation states, it was found that untrained (U) and trained (T) Ss had similar percent increases (U=21.7, T=22.1). Therefore, these findings indicate that training in either TM or hypnosis does not lead to greater ability to relax than does the absence of training.

Order definitely appears to be a factor in the end result. When Ss began the sessions with meditation or hypnosis as the first experimental state, the mean SR and the percent increase from the alert state to the relaxation mean was much lower than when the sessions began with relaxation (49.2 vs. 82.0 K-ohms, 19.6% vs. 24.3%). Order effect could have accounted for the large increases found in skin resistance with the original TM studies (3,15). In those studies, relaxation always preceded meditation.

All the relaxation states (RS) were significantly different from the alert state (A mean=54.6 K-ohms, RS mean=67.0 K-ohms). However, there were no significant differences between relaxa-

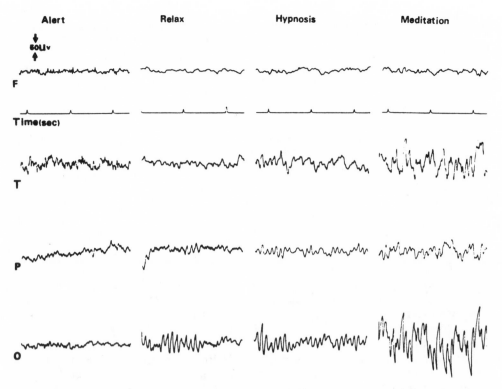

Fig. 6. High alpha EEG in a subject with active thoughts. F=frontal, T=temporal, P=parietal, O=occipital.

tion, hypnosis, and meditation. This result is contrary to the findings in the original TM studies (3,6,8,15) but similar to the results in a more recent investigation (23).

In comparing relaxation-hypnosis with task-hypnosis, it was again found that untrained Ss had a higher mean SR than did trained Ss (U mean=103.3 K-ohms, T mean=57.1 K-ohms). Untrained Ss also were more reactive showing a greater percent decrease in resistance from relaxation-hypnosis to task-hypnosis (U=8.8, T=5.1). It appears that untrained Ss react excessively to hypnotic task suggestions, while trained Ss, being more

accustomed to hypnotic-like suggestions, react less. This was especially true for Ss trained in hypnosis (% decrease=1.4). However, overall there were significant decreases in SR when Ss went from relaxation-hypnosis to task-hypnosis. This reinforces the contention that the prior results showing great variability in physiological changes of hypnosis were related to the different conditions induced under hypnosis (21,28,34–38).

In comparing TM Ss with Ss taught simple word meditation, it is once more apparent that untrained Ss had a higher mean SR (SM=72.7 K-ohns, TM=50.0 K-ohms). The SM Ss had a larger numerical increase than the TM Ss in going from the alert condition mean to the meditation mean (SM = 14.7 K-ohms, TM = 11.9 K-ohms), but in percent increase the TM Ss did somewhat better (TM = 27, SM = 22.5). Therefore, the results of SR findings confirm the previous conclusion that the practice of TM and simple word meditation yield similar physiological results (16).

As the results of eight of the nine objective measures were similar to those found for SR, it appears that relaxation, meditation, and relaxation-hypnosis yield similar physiological responses, suggestive of deep relaxation. Two possible reasons for the good results with simple relaxation were (1) motivation was increased because Ss were informed that previous Ss did well with all three relaxation states and (2) as the principal investigator was known by the Ss to be the hypnotist, the simple suggestion to relax may have had a greater effect than had the Ss tried to relax themselves.

The results of some of the specific measures are of interest. It was found that slow alpha production was similar in all three relaxation states. This is contrary to the findings in the original TM studies (3,5,6,15) but similar to a more recent finding (22). Unlike previous reports (5,6), synchronization of slow alpha was not found to be unique to TM. When present, it was found in all the relaxation states (Fig. 1).

There were no significant differences among the relaxation states on skin resistance changes induced by blood pressure detection. However, there was a trend toward better responses with both TM and relaxation-hypnosis as compared to relaxation and simple word meditation (means TM = 1.5, A-R = 1.5, R = 3.0, SM = 3.0). This shows that, in agreement with previous conclusions (8), TM tends to be superior to relaxation and simple word meditation as a means of coping with stressful stimuli. However, TM does not seem to be better than relaxation-hypnosis.

Muscle activity was more frequent with relaxation and hypnosis than with meditation, and simple word meditators tend to perform better than TM Ss on this measure (means R = 49.0, A-R = 41.7, M = 25.1, SM = 18.8, TM = 31.3). Muscle activity occurred primarily in the frontal and temporal regions [previously indicated to be good monitors of tension (29) and generally within the first few minutes. It appeared to be related to the greater concentration accompanying eye-fixation hypnotic induction and the difficulty of Ss completely relaxing their muscles when instructed to relax. Had a non-eye-fixation hypnotic induction method been used, it is probable that no difference would have been found between meditation and hypnosis in muscle activity. Nevertheless, meditation appears to be an effective means of muscle relaxation.

All the physiological findings showed that physiological responses found under task-hypnosis were opposite in effect to those found in relaxation-hypnosis and generally similar to those responses observed during the alert state. However, slow alpha and synchronous alpha were higher in both types of hypnosis than they were in the alert state.

The findings of all the objective measures confirmed the SR results that physiological responses under TM and simple word meditation are similar. It also appears that training in either hypnosis or meditation does not yield deeper relaxation responses.

Although physiologically meditation, relaxation-hypnosis, and relaxation were not readily discernible, the analysis of the subjective results showed that, regardless of their training, Ss reported that the "mental" effects and "most effortless induction" for meditation and relaxation-hypnosis were vastly superior to those for simple relaxation. However, Ss did not agree on whether relaxation-hypnosis or meditation was better, although more favored relaxation-hypnosis. TM Ss found difficulties in differentiating between TM and relaxation-hypnosis on the "mental" measures, although more of them believed TM to be "better." Contrariwise, Ss using simple word meditation found the distinction more apparent, with many more considering relaxation-hypnosis to be "mentally" superior. Therefore, relaxation-hypnosis and meditation can be considered similar on both physiological and subjective levels.

TM Ss are repeatedly told about the effortlessness of their technique. This was verified in the results with most TM Ss finding TM to be much "better" than relaxation-hypnosis in the measure, "most effortless induction." However, simple word meditators, who had no prior indoctrination, did not find meditation to be a more effortless procedure than relaxation-hypnosis. Most of them found the opposite to be the case. It is possible that the use of TM mantras along with regular practice allow for a more effortless induction than can be obtained from the use of simple words.

The results with some Ss related to the negative correlation of subjective interpretation of "euphoria" and "depth" with alpha levels tend to reinforce previous findings (26–31). The absence of correlation in some Ss between subjective evaluation of "blank mind" and alpha production shows that mental relaxation doesn't have to elicit alpha activity. The finding that high alpha could be present while Ss were concentrating (physically and mentally) to achieve "glove" anesthesia shows that alpha may not be related to relaxation. This also confirms previous findings (29,32).

As physiological responses failed to show significant differences between the three relaxation states and subjective evaluation did show significance, Tart's (21) remark seems appropriate for the results of this study: "A Ss own estimate of his behavior and internal state is a rich and promising source of data, which some Es tend to ignore in their passionate search for 'objectivity.'"

Finally, from the results of this study, it can be concluded that TM does no better than other forms of relaxation.

SUMMARY

Forty-eight Ss were monitored during the alert state, relaxation-hypnosis, task-hypnosis, meditation (TM or simple word type), and relaxation. Parameters used were pulse rate, respiratory rate, blood pressure, skin resistance, EEG activity, and muscle activity. Subjective verbal evaluation was given of comparisons between the experimental states. Analysis using the repeated measures ANOV for the objective measures showed that physiological changes suggestive of deep relaxation were significantly better for the relaxation states (relaxation, relaxation-hypnosis, meditation) than for the alert state. However, there were no significant differences between the relaxation states except that there was significantly less muscle activity during meditation than during relaxation or relaxation-hypnosis. Ss trained in hypnosis or TM did not have significantly better results than Ss untrained in either modality. Relative to order, significantly better results were found when relaxation preceded either hypnosis or meditation than when hypnosis or meditation was the first experimental state. Overall, there were significant differences between task-hypnosis and relaxation-hypnosis. There were no significant differences between TM Ss and Ss practicing simple word meditation. Sign test analysis of the subjective data showed that Ss found the "mental effects" and "most effortless induction" to be significantly "better" for hypnosis and meditation than for relaxation.

No significant differences were found for the "mental" measures between relaxation-hypnosis and meditation. With the parameter "most effortless induction," TM Ss found meditation significantly "better" than relaxation-hypnosis, while Ss using simple word meditation did not find meditation "better" than relaxation-hypnosis for that measure.

The authors thank Drs. Samuel Seltzer, Martin Tansy, Richard Mumma, and Dale Roeck for their cooperation; Drs. Dave Innes, Jack Zabara, and Frank Hohenleitner for their review of the data; Alex V. Mucha for the photographic reproductions; and Harold Perrong for technical assistance.

REFERENCES

1. Course in Transcendental Meditation. Presented at the Westmont branch, International Meditation Society, Westmont, N.J., Sept. 1974
2. Bloomfield HH, Cain MP, Jaffe DT: TM: Discovering Inner Energy and Overcoming Stress. New York, Delacorte Press, 1975
3. Wallace RK: Physiological effects of transcendental meditation. Science 167:1751–1754, 1970
4. Allison J: Respiratory changes during transcendental meditation. Lancet 1:833–834, 1970
5. Banquet JP: Spectral analysis of the EEG in meditation. Electroencephalogr Clin Neurophysiol 35:143–151, 1973
6. Glueck BC, Stroebel CF: Biofeedback and meditation in the treatment of psychiatric illnesses. Comp Psychiatry 16:303–321, 1975
7. Benson H, Rosner BA, Marzetta BR: Decreased systolic blood pressure in hypertensive subjects who practiced meditation. J Clin Invest 52:8a, 1973
8. Orme-Johnson DW: Autonomic stability and transcendental meditation. Psychosom Med 35:341–349, 1973
9. Shaw R, Kolb D: One-point reaction time involving meditators and non-meditators, cited in The Psychobiology of Transcendental Meditation. Los Angeles, Maharishi International University, 1973
10. Graham J: Auditory discrimination in meditators, cited in The Psychobiology of Transcendental Meditation. Los Angeles, Maharishi International University, 1973
11. Nidich S, Seeman W, Dreskin T: Influence of transcendental meditation: a replication. J Counsel Psychol 20:565–566, 1973
12. Shelly MW: The theory of happiness as it relates to transcendental meditation, cited in The Psychobiology of Transcendental Meditation. Los Angeles, Maharishi International University, 1973
13. Cox SB: Transcendental meditation and the criminal justice system. Kent Law J 60:2, 1971–1972
14. Wilson AF, Honsberger R: The effects of transcendental meditation upon bronchial asthma. Clin Res (in press)

15. Wallace RK, Benson H: The physiology of meditation. Sci Am 226:85–90, 1972
16. Beary JF, Benson H: A simple psychophysiologic technique which elicits the hypometabolic changes of the relaxation response. Psychosom Med 36:115–120, 1974
17. Nova: Meditation. Presented on the Public Education Television Network. Channel 12, Philadelphia, 1976
18. Stone RA, DeLeo J: Psychotherapeutic control of hypertension. N Engl J Med 294:80–84, 1976
19. Goodman LS, Gilman A: The Pharmacological Basis of Therapeutics, ed. 5. New York, Macmillan, 1975, pp. 477–513
20. Michaels RR, Huber MJ, McCann DS: Evaluation of transcendental meditation as a method of reducing stress. Science 192:1242–1244, 1976
21. Tart CT: Hypnotic depth and basal skin resistance. Int J Clin Exp Hypn 11:81–92, 1963
22. Schwartz GE: Pros and cons of meditation. Current findings on physiology and anxiety control, drug abuse and creativity. Paper presented at the 81st annual APA convention, 1973, cited in RL Woolfolk: Psychophysiological correlation of meditation. Arch Gen Psychiatry 32:1326–1333, 1975
23. Walrath LC, Hamilton DW: Autonomic correlates of meditation and hypnosis. Am J Clin Hypn 17:190–196, 1975
24. White J: Everything You Want to Know About TM Including How to Do It. New York, Pocket Books, 1976
25. Benson H, Beary JF, Carol MP: The relaxation response. Psychiatry 37:37–46, 1974
26. Paskewitz DA: EEG alpha activity and its relationship to altered states of consciousness. Paper presented at the Conference on Conceptual and Investigative Approaches to Hypnosis and Hypnotic Phenomena of the New York Academy of Sciences, New York, 1977
27. Orne MT, Wilson SK: Biofeedback control of alpha wave activity, cited in Alpha rhythms: back to baselines. Sci News 109:148, 1976
28. Edmonston Jr WE, Grotevant WR: Hypnosis and alpha density. Am J Clin Hypn 17:221–232, 1975
29. Owen A: How to handle stress in modern society. Paper presented to the annual Greater Long Island Dental Meeting, New York, 1976
30. Paskewitz DA, Orne MT: Visual effects on alpha feedback training. Science 181:360–363, 1973
31. Orne MT, Paskewitz DA: Alpha training and anxiety control, cited in Alpha waves and anxiety—no link? Sci News 107:294, 1974
32. Brown BB: Awareness of EEG subjective activity relationships detected within a closed feedback system. Psychophysiology 7:451–464, 1971
33. Pagano RP, Rose RM, Warrenburg S: Sleep during transcendental meditation. Science 191:306–309, 1976
34. Crasilneck HB, Hall JA: Physiological changes associated with hypnosis: a review of the literature since 1948. Int J Clin Exp Hypn 7:9–49, 1959
35. Edmonston Jr WE: Hypnosis and electrodermal responses. Am J Clin Hypn 11:16–25, 1968
36. Peter JE, Stern RM: Peripheral skin temperature and vasomotor responses during hypnotic induction. Int J Clin Exp Hypn 21:102–108, 1973
37. Tebécis AK, Provius KA, Farnback RW, Pentony P: Hypnosis and the EEG: a quantitative investigation. J Nerv Ment Dis 161:1–17, 1975
38. Roberts AH, Schuler P, Bacon J, Zimmerman R, Patterson R: Individual differences and autonomic control: absorption, hypnotic susceptibility and the unilateral control of skin temperature. J Abnorm Psychol 84:272–279, 1975
39. Evans FJ: Hypnosis and sleep: the control of altered states of awareness. Paper presented at the Conference on Conceptual and Investigative Approaches to Hypnosis and Hypnotic Phenomena of the New York Academy of Sciences, New York, 1977
40. Morse DR: Use of a meditative state for hypnotic induction in the practice of endodontics. Oral Surg 41:664–672, 1976
41. Morse DR: Hypnosis in the practice of endodontics. J Am Soc Psychosom Dent Med 22:17–22, 1975
42. Morse DR, Hildebrand CN: Case report: use of TM in periodontal therapy. Dent Surv 52(11):36–39, 1976
43. Deabler HL, Fidel E, Dillenkoffer RL, Elder ST: The use of relaxation and hypnosis in lowering high blood pressure. Am J Clin Hypn 16:75–83, 1973

44. Kroger WS, Fezler WD: Hypnosis and Behavior Modification: Imagery Conditioning. Philadelphia, J. B. Lippincott, 1976

45. Toomin MK, Toomin H: GSR biofeedback in psychotherapy: some clinical observations. Psychother Theory Res Practice 12:33–38, 1975

46. Spiegel H: An eye-roll test for hypnotizability. Am J Clin Hypn 15:25–28, 1972

47. Orne MT: Research in hypnosis—implications for clinical practice. Paper presented to the Philadelphia Society of Clinical Hypnosis, Philadelphia, 1975

48. Shor RE, Orne MT: The Nature of Hypnosis. New York, Holt, Rinehart and Winston, 1965

49. Young LD, Langford HG, Blanchard EG: Effect of operant conditioning of heart rate on plasma renin activity. Psychosom Med 38:278–281, 1976

V

VIEWS OF THE
STATE-OF-THE-ART

An Introduction to Part V:
Views of the State-of-the-Art

As one way of placing meditation in the context of western science and as a way of assessing how different respected individuals in the field view meditation, we wrote to several individuals who are experts, either in the field of meditation or in related fields, to invite their comments. A subjective view of meditation by the scientific community is important. For, as much as we would like science to be a pure, academic, objective discipline, often it is not. It is influenced both by the people who study it, the general *zeitgeist* surrounding it, which in turn either attracts, or makes a field less attractive for subsequent researchers. Also the study of any particular field is often influenced by sociocultural and political variables, which determine which topics are of general and pressing interest for funding resources. It is an interesting cycle in that the funding resources that are available, in part, determine what types of studies are researched, which determines what information is disseminated, which determines the general interest and level of individuals in a field.

These following comments run an interesting gamut. They range from the view that meditation may be an important contribution to western therapeutic practice, if the spiritual element can be removed from it [e.g., Ellis (Article 54) and Woolfolk and Franks (Article 55)] to the view that meditation will only be of use if the spiritual component can be maintained (Deikman, Article 57), and that selfless preparation is needed for "right effects" of meditation (Akishige, Article 59).

The article by Smith (56) is interesting in that it gives a first-hand account of some of the views of a meditation researcher, including his own development and relationship to the study of meditation. Finally, Globus's article (58) nicely suggests some of the philosophical principles underlying the mind-brain dilemma and the utility of meditation in researching some of those issues. The comments by Arnold Lazarus (60) are important because they suggest, as we have tried to emphasize throughout the book, that there is no one unimodal technique which is effective in all cases. Lazarus presents a well-reasoned comment suggesting that meditation may be a treatment of choice in some cases and not in others and that we must be careful not to blind ourselves by belief in a particular technique. As Abraham Maslow once noted "if the only tool you have is a hammer, everything begins to look like a nail."

Some additional brief comments which may be of interest include the following. Joseph Wolpe notes

> I have frequently made use of the emotional state obtained by subjects who have had previous training in transcendental meditation for purposes of systematic desensitization as a substitute for progressive relaxation. As far as I can see, its effects and those of progressive relaxation are much the same.

Wolpe's comments are interesting in that, from his clinical viewpoint, meditation seems to be similar to progressive relaxation in its effects.

Jerome Singer notes,

> On the relationship between meditation and daydreaming, I do believe that meditation bears a close relationship to many aspects of normal daydreaming. Many individuals use daydreaming, whether of wishful fantasy or merely of picturing pleasant or enjoyable scenes, as a means of distracting themselves during the tension of long waits, with the boredom of the drive or train ride. The state of absorption in day dreaming, especially of the more positive type, leads to considerable relaxation and to many similar physiological reactions as meditation. Daydreaming, thus, for many people becomes a useful form of self-regulation—of avoiding undue stress while often playfully probing future possibilities.

Singer's comment illustrates a common view of meditation. However, it is interesting because, beginning meditators are told, when they begin to daydream or to have fantasies, to return their attention to the object of meditation and not to indulge in probing fantasies further. Yet, in the study by Smith (see Article 56), no differences were found between individuals who focused in a relative, random, daydream like fashion on positive self-images and thoughts, and a group which focused on a specific object of meditation.

Finally, Meyer Friedman's comments suggest the difficulty of any treatment being effective in which generalization is not built in. He notes that,

> I don't think I've had a sufficient experience with people indulging under my direction in meditation. But from what I have seen of various colleagues, I believe that it is almost worthless in the amelioration of Type A behavior. I doubt very much whether any 20 or 30 minute exercise, even done three times a day, if it's proceeded and followed by the driving, compulsive, hostile behavior of most Type A's can be expected to do much good. . . . I should add that some Type A patients, when they have attempted transcendental meditation, very frequently fall asleep.

54

THE PLACE OF MEDITATION IN COGNITIVE-BEHAVIOR THERAPY AND RATIONAL-EMOTIVE THERAPY

Albert Ellis

Cognitive or cognitive-behavior therapy is probably the fastest growing field of the vast general area of behavior therapy today and in some ways is taking over this field (Beck, 1976; Meichenbaum, 1977; Thoresen and Coates, 1978). Rational-emotive therapy (RET) in its general form is synonymous with cognitive-behavior therapy (CBT), and in its more elegant or specific form provides a comprehensive theory of personality change (Ellis, 1977a, b; Ellis and Grieger, 1977). What place does meditation play in CBT and RET? Let me briefly attempt to answer this question by giving the answers to several more specific questions regarding meditation and its place in psychotherapy, in general, and CBT and RET, in particular.

Is Meditation a Form of Psychotherapy?

Yes, it definitely is. It can legitimately be seen as one of the many cognitive-behavioral methods that are sometimes employed in CBT and RET. Largely, it is mainly a mode of cognitive distraction or diversion—just as muscular relaxation, Yoga, studying, window shopping, TV viewing, sports, and many other methods of concentrating on something other than worrying or rating oneself are modes of cognitive distraction (even when they seem to be "physical" techniques). The human mind usually focuses on one major thing at a time; and consequently, when you concentrate on meditating you cannot simultaneously concentrate on how badly you are performing at something or what a worm you are for performing this badly. You focus, instead, on *what* you are doing rather than *how* you are doing; at least temporarily, you find it almost impossible to worry.

As you meditate, moreover, and as you temporarily interfere with your anxiety, self-damning, depression, or hostility by this powerful form of cognitive distraction, you often (consciously or unconsciously) make a philosophic change as well. You tell yourself, for example, "I now have a technique of controlling or changing my disturbed feelings; and I therefore *can* function more effectively. This philosophic change, or the belief that meditation works and that you *can* help distinctly yourself by its use, may be even more important and longlasting than the temporary cognitive distraction that meditation provides. Consequently, it may be profoundly therapeutic.

Is Meditation a Self-Regulation Strategy?

Yes—and often a strong one. Cognitive-behavior therapy and rational-emotive therapy especially emphasize self-control or self-management procedures and emphasize cognitive (and other modes) homework. Meditation usually requires a great deal of self-training, especially cognitive self-regulation through homework. It is a distinct form of self-discipline, and by doing it, you again *perceive* that you have self-control and *tell yourself* important ideas about the virtues of this kind of control. It can, therefore, be a powerful self-regulation strategy.

Is Meditation a Form of Spiritual Discipline or Therapy?

Unfortunately, it often or usually is. Meditative techniques, per se, are not necessarily spiritual—which the dictionary defines as "of the spirit or soul, often in a religious or moral aspect, as distinguished from the body; not corporeal; sacred, devotional, or ecclesiastical; spiritualistic or supernatural." Today's most popular form of meditation, Transcendental Meditation or TM, is mainly a special kind of meditative technique that, for many of its adherents, is highly untranscendental and unspiritual. But, partly for historical reasons, many meditative methods stem from and are integrally allied with Eastern modes of religion or philosophy that emphasize spiritual, noncorporeal, or sacred outlooks. They are not only "religious," in the philosophic or general sense of the term, but include "religiosity" or an attitude of devoutness, anti-intellectualism, and anti-scientificness. The goal of the religious or spiritual devotee of "transcendental" meditation is to achieve "higher" consciousness, unity with all things, or superhumanness.

This is most probably an illusory, highly disturbed goal since humans are essentially human, or fallible, and there is little likelihood of their ever becoming godlike or superhuman. Ideal mental health, therefore, seems to include the full acceptance of themselves as fallible, screwed-up creatures; and the rejection of all dogmatic, anti-scientific, spiritual, holier-than-thou aspirations. Meditation completely divorced from "transcendentalism" or "religiosity" may be a productive, although probably always limited, form of psychotherapy. Combined with mysticism and magic, as it often is, it includes highly dangerous, anti-therapeutic elements.

Does Meditation Produce Harmful Results?

All known methods of psychotherapy, including meditation, probably produce harmful results when used with some of the people some of the time. Meditation may well be more potentially harmful than many other techniques largely for the reason just given: its common tie-up with spirituality and antiscience. It also encourages some individuals, though probably a small number, to become even more obsessive-compulsive than they usually are and to dwell in a ruminative manner on trivia or nonessentials. A few of my own clients have gone into dissociative semi-trance states and upset themselves considerably by meditating.

Perhaps the greatest potential danger of meditation, however, which it again shares with many other therapy procedures, is the highly undramatic one of diverting people from doing the "right" or "more efficient" thing in overcoming their disturbances by encouraging them to focus on this "effective" but highly palliative procedure. Perhaps most of what we call psychotherapy today consists, at bottom, of diversionary methods that help people to feel better but rarely get better—including such techniques as empathic listening, abreaction of feeling, the establishment of a warm relationship between the therapist and the clients, and even skill training. In RET, we usually attempt to help clients get better—that is, make a profound philosophic change in themselves so that they can meet present and future "disturbing" situations in a healthy manner. I would guess that in the great majority of instances, meditation only helps its devotees to feel better and perhaps sabotages their acquiring a basically health, non-*must*urbatory outlook.

Is Meditation Self-Actualizing?

Yes, it often, though not necessarily, is. It adds a technique of human thinking and self-control that requires training and practice, and once you have this method at your disposal you have an additional means of coping with some of your problems and actualizing your potential for enjoyment. It also, as noted above, may lead to a more optimistic philosophy of coping with life that may help you actualize yourself. On the other hand, it can be used (as, of course, can other effective methods of psychotherapy) in a rigid, restrictive manner; and can be resorted to so frequently and compulsively that it actually helps you constrict and deactualize your existence. A life that overemphasizes meditation—and, of course, "spirituality"—may result in the needless and foolish sacrifice of many potentially fulfilling experiences.

How Can Meditation Best Be Used in CBT and RET?

Mainly as *one* specific thought-distracting method that can effectively relax and divert people from some of their overwhelming anxieties and dysfunctional obsessions and compulsions. I find it best, with my own clients, to explain to them what meditation really is, from a cognitive-behavioral standpoint, how it helps, and what its limitations are. Like tranquilizers, it may have both good and bad effects— especially, the harmful result of encouraging people to look away from some of their central problems, and to refrain from actively disputing and surrendering their disturbance-creating beliefs. It may also be perniciously used to enhance self-rating or "ego-strength," so that people end up by believing, "I am a great meditator and *therefore* am a good and noble person!" I therefore recommend meditation, just as I recommend the use of Jacobsen's relaxation method or other focusing and relaxing techniques, as a palliative, distraction method, and advise most of my clients to use it with discretion and not to take it too seriously or view it as a general therapeutic method. Thus used, it can be a useful *part* of cognitive-behavior or rational-emotive therapy.

What Will Be the Real, Enduring Value of Meditation to Western Psychology and Psychiatry?

I believe that two forms of meditation are now in use and will continue to be employed: scientific and antiscientific meditation. Scientific meditation consists of a number of focusing or cognitive concentration techniques that work in their own right and that have been shown in many cases to have therapeutic effectiveness (LeShan, 1975; Lind, 1977; Smith, 1975; Shapiro, 1976; Shapiro and Giber, 1978). Antiscientific meditation consists of the same kind of focusing or cognitive concentration techniques plus a mystically oriented philosophy that is not empirically verifiable, that leads its devotees away from coping with themselves or reality, and that usually does much more therapeutic harm than good. I believe that for the present both these forms of meditation will persist and achieve greater popularity but that eventually the antiscientific form will die out. One of the goals of Western psychology and psychiatry can well be that of aiding scientific and unmasking antiscientific meditation.

References

Beck, A. T. *Cognitive therapy and the emotional disorders.* New York: International Universities Press, 1976.

Ellis, A. Rational-emotive therapy: research data that supports the clinical and personality hypotheses of RET and other modes of cognitive-behavior therapy. *Counseling psychologist,* 1977a, **7**(1), 2–42.

Ellis, A. Elegant and inelegant RET. *Counseling psychologist,* 1977b, **7**(1), 73–82.

Ellis, A., and Grieger, R. *Handbook of rational-emotive therapy.* New York: Springer, 1977.

LeShan, L. *How to meditate.* New York: Bantam, 1975.

Lind, T. P. *Behavioral changes through meditation techniques.* M.A. Thesis, California Western University, January, 1977.

Meichenbaum, D. *Cognitive behavior modification.* New York: Plenum, 1977.

Shapiro, D. Zen meditation and behavioral self-control. *American psychologist,* 1976, **31**, 519–532.

Shapiro, D., and Giber, D. Meditation and psychotherapeutic effects. *Archives of General Psychiatry,* 1978.

Smith, J. Meditation as Psychotherapy: a review of the literature. *Psychological bulletin,* 1975, **32**, 553–564.

Thoresen, C. E., and Coates, T. J. What does it mean to be a behavior therapist? *Counseling psychologist,* 1978.

55

MEDITATION AND BEHAVIOR THERAPY

Robert L. Woolfolk and Cyril M. Franks

The analysis of relationships between behavior therapy and meditation is best preceded by a clarification of our understanding of these two terms. Let us begin with behavior therapy. Although commonly identified with principles and methods derived from operant and classical conditioning, there is no necessary restrictive conceptual linkage between conditioning per se and behavior therapy. Behavior therapy is neither a school or theory of psychotherapy nor a set of therapeutic techniques. It is a set of metatheoretical assumptions leading to an approach to the understanding and modification of behavior in social learning theory terms from which a variety of therapeutic models and specific techniques can be generated. It is also a methodological approach and as such it need not be wedded to any overriding theoretical substrate or set of techniques (Franks and Wilson, 1977). Conditioning, although very much an integral component of much of current behavior therapy practice, is neither necessary nor sufficient as a conceptual cornerstone.

Meditation, as we will use the term, refers to a body of techniques, and the research data and theories which explain them, derived from the practices of various Eastern "ways of liberation." Among these, those which had their origin in Mantram Yoga and Zen Buddhism are the most popular and extensively researched. The field of meditation is defined by its allegiance to a specific area of investigation rather than any group of methodological or theoretical assumptions.

It follows from the above that to compare meditation with behavior therapy is a different order of undertaking from a comparison of meditation with a clearly delineated school of therapy, such as psychoanalysis or gestalt therapy. While it is legitimate, and perhaps useful, to compare techniques of meditation with techniques employed by contemporary behavior therapists (e.g., Shapiro and Zifferblatt, 1976), the more fundamental comparison involves a determination of the degree to which the field of meditation has employed or could employ the methodologial assumptions and investigatory practices of behavior therapy (cf. Shapiro, 1978).

Behavior therapy may also be defined as the application of the methods of scientific investigation to clinical practice (Yates, 1975). The methodology of behavior theory involves a commitment to rigor, objectivity, replicability, specificity, and testability. By and large, existing schools of psychotherapy are based upon unsystematic, subjective data and upon theories which are conceptually loose and untestable in terms of the criteria of the behavior therapist. Behavior therapy arose as part of a general dissatisfaction with therapy "schools" and with behavior change efforts based on such foundations. Parenthetically, it might be noted that this contrast between behavior therapy and psychotherapy implies no absolute value judgment on our part. Rather, it is a statement about differing viewpoints as to what constitute "data" and their acceptability.

With certain additions stemming from the intricacies of interpersonal relationships and the limiting constraints of clinical exigency, as conceptualized by the behavior therapist is analogous to the domain of research which confronts the experimental psychologist. The actions of the therapist are analogous to the independent variables of the psychology experiment. The behavior of the client is analogous to the dependent variables of the experimental situation. Changes in the client's behavior are hypothesized to be, in part, a function of actions on the part of the therapist. In both behavioral clinical practice and the psychology experiment, the goal is an understanding of relationships between independent and dependent variables. The specification and refinement of variables, and the determination of precise empirical

State-of-the-Art

relationships among them, are as much essential features of the behavior therapy approach as of the laboratory experiment. This, of course, is the ideal toward which we strive. In practice, it has to be tempered by the realities of patient needs, but always with a sense of humility and a recognition of our limitations, rather than a flaunting of our speculative intervention (Franks, 1969).

The affinity between behavior therapy and the experimentally based psychology of learning is methodological rather than axiomatic. The fact that many current techniques in behavior therapy are inspired by basic research in operant and classical conditioning does not stem from any definitive identification of behavior therapy with the principles of conditioning. Any branch of experimental psychology which bears some systematic relationship to behavior change processes, and which possesses adequate conceptual rigor, could, in principle, be incorporated into one or another of the many behavior therapy models. This is equally true of the field of meditation and there is no reason, in principle, why techniques of meditation could not one day become regular features of the behavior therapist's clinical armamentarium along with systematic desensitization, reinforcement methods, and other procedures. For this to occur, however, several key requirements would have to be met:

1. *Independent variables must be specified.*To subject meditation procedures to adequate empirical scrutiny, we must first know what it is that we are testing. The procedures must be explicit and replicable. Meditation is not often practiced within a complex framework of philosophical/spiritual commitment and social influence. (Woolfolk, 1975). Because the techniques of meditation have been embedded within this unspecified, but potentially influential, matrix of variables, it is virtually impossible in many studies to infer what it is about meditation that is important or efficacious. Without specification and standardization of meditation procedures, these variables can not be subjected to the experimental control and manipulation necessary for the generation of precise causal relationships. So called "nonspecific factors," such as credibility of procedures and client motivation, need to be identified. This kind of specificity is required for meaningful comparisons of findings from different laboratories and for effective sharing of information.

2. *Dependent variables must be specified.* The efficacy of a techniques is never established in a vacuum. We must be able to state which problems of living are favorably (or unfavorably) influenced by a particular intervention. Systematic assessment of presenting problems is the hallmark of behavioral research and therapy. Such assessment is a necessary ingredient of any research strategy leading to systematic relationships between therapy and outcome.

In the case of meditation, it is desirable to move away from the kind of research that provides no clearer rationale for the selection of dependent variables than some vague assumption about meditation being "good for people." Additional methodological improvements include the more extensive use of multiple dependent measures (behavioral, phenomenological, and physiological) rather than the customary reliance upon one kind of dependent measure.

3. *Functional relationships between independent and dependent variables must be empirically documented.* Once independent and dependent variables are appropriately specified, the inference of precise causal relationships among variables becomes possible. Empirical test is the *sine qua non* of behavioral strategy. Such tests can be of the most rudimentary variety. For example, a methodologically adequate study showing that a standardized Zen meditation exercise reduces behavioral, affective, and physiological components of social anxiety would lend support to the use by behavior therapists of that particular meditation technique in treating this problem. In addition to evaluating specific techniques, it is desirable to conduct studies which contribute to the theoretical understanding of the mechanisms mediating change. Systematic dismantling of treatment techniques in a search for active ingredients together with an examination of such mediators as client expectation, are of great potential utility. Scientifically based therapy is clearly benefitted by systematic evaluations of treatment and the establishment of effective therapeutic techniques. However, over the long term, a theoretical explanation of the various phenomena under investigation may be of even greater importance.

In the preceding pages we have presented an understanding of the behavior therapy approach and its relevance to the field of meditation. We have offered also a methodological prescription for the field of meditation which flows from the metatheoretical assumptions of behavior therapy rather than the spiritual/philosophical underpinnings which have characterized the study of meditation in the past. It is encouraging to report that many of our recommendations are currently being followed by investigators in the meditation area. Attempts to produce standardized, easily replicable meditation procedure are beginning to appear (Benson, 1974; Woolfolk, Carr-Kaffashan, Lehrer, and McNulty, 1976). Smith's

(1976) study is a promising attempt to tease apart the active and inactive components of the practice of meditation. More investigations of this sort are needed.

The potential for cross-fertilization between behavior therapy research and meditation research is great. A respect for scientific method and a predilection for rigorous experiment have characterized behavior therapy since its inception. Now, most encouragingly, the recent history of meditation is beginning to reflect a similar tradition. There is good evidence that many investigators of meditation are finally seeing the necessity to divest the *scientific* study of meditation from the shrouds of mystery that are part of its noble origin. The complete removal of meditation from the realm of the arcane will require careful attention to the recommendations mentioned above. Such a development could create not only a field of meditation, which is methodologically related to behavior therapy, but one which might even become an integral part of behavior therapy.

References

Beary, J. F. and Benson, H. A simple psychophysiologic technique which elicits the hypometabolic changes of the relaxation response. *Psychosomatic Medicine,* 1974, **36**, 115–120.

Franks, C. M. The practitioner as behavioral scientist—myth, wishful thinking or reality? *New Jersey Psychologist,* 1969, **19**, 4–8.

Franks, C. M., and Wilson, G. I. (Eds.) *Annual review of behavior therapy: theory and practice,* 1977, New York: Brunner/Magel, 1977.

Shapiro, D. *Precision nirvana.* Englewood Cliffs, New Jersey: Prentice Hall, 1978.

Shapiro, D. and Zifferblatt, S. Zen meditatation and behavioral self-control: similarities, differences, clinical applications. *American Psychologist,* 1976, **31**, 519–532.

Smith, J. C. Psychotherapeutic effects of transcendental meditation with controls for expectation of relief and daily sitting. *Journal of Consulting and Clinical Psychology,* 1976, **44**, 630–637.

Woolfolk, R. L. Psychophysiological correlates of meditation. *Archives of General Psychiatry,* 1975, **32**, 1326–1333.

Woolfolk, R. L., Carr-Kaffashan, L., Lehrer, P. M., and McNulty, T. F. Meditation training as a treatment for insomnia. *Behavior Therapy,* 1976, **7**, 359–365.

Yates, A. M. *Theory and practice in behavior therapy.* New York: Wiley, 1975.

56

MEDITATION RESEARCH: THREE OBSERVATIONS ON THE STATE-OF-THE-ART

Jonathan C. Smith

At this point in the young history of meditation research some trends are beginning to appear. These trends concern not the content of specific findings, but the types of questions and methodologies that are proving to be most productive.

The Decline of Messianic Research

The most conspicuous trend is that messianic research appears to be on the decline. In the early 1970's meditation research tended to be conducted by new meditation converts who at times seemed more committed to furthering their cause than to objective research. However, rather than point fingers, I would like to share some experiences I have had while first learning the ways of science. In 1973, I was no less enthusiastic than my fellow researchers about the possibilities of meditation. However, I realized that the rest of the scientific community would remain skeptical until rigorous double-blind placebo-control research was done. I decided to attempt such a study, and show once and for all that meditation is, as Maharhishi Yogi once said, "a natural and effective cure for mental illness."

The design for this study involved comparing transcendental meditation (TM) to no treatment and to a control treatment carefully constructed to match the form, complexity, and expectation-fostering aspects of TM. To control for the potentially therapeutic effects of daily sitting, the control treatment incorporated an exercise that involved just sitting (and not meditating). To make the treatment complete, I decided to provide bogus supporting research, theory, and testimonials. I even invented an impressive sounding name for the treatment—"Periodic Somatic Inactivity," or "PSI." I was filled with excitement about the study I had designed, and decided to spend an extra year in graduate school to complete the research.

After obtaining help from the TM organization, I began the study. The original design called for running the experiment for 3 months. However, after 3 months I made an unexpected and disturbing discovery. The TM subjects appeared to be doing no better than the controls. I reasoned that perhaps my subjects did not meditate for a sufficient period of time (although virtually all previous longitudinal research on meditation had involved even shorter periods of time). So I decided to revise the study and continue the treatments for an additional 3 months. However, 3 months later there were still no differences between the treatments. I was unwilling to believe the results, and decided to run a second experiment, one that would be even more sensitive to the assumed effects of meditation. In it I compared meditation to a treatment that involved what I reasoned should be the near antithesis of meditation—actively and effortly generating thoughts. The results were the same. For over thirty variables, meditation was no more therapeutic than PSI or "anti-meditation." I finally had to conclude that perhaps my assumptions about meditation were a bit grandiose and egocentric. I had learned a valuable lesson about objectivity and the scientific method.

I share this example not to make a point about what meditation may or may not be, but to show the lengths an enthusiastic pro-meditation researcher may go to find empirical support for his or her beliefs. Examples of such experimenter bias are common in early meditation research, and include one-sided literature reviews, outcome studies without controls, and interpretations of results that make no mention of likely alternative explanations that do not appear favorable to meditation. Fortunately, research now tends to be better, as evidenced by the fact that meditation studies are finding their way into a diverse range of high-caliber journals.

The Standardization and Operationalization of Meditation

A second trend in meditation research is a move away from vague and often secret techniques bound to religious and philosophical traditions. Meditation instructions are now openly described in journal articles and are even beginning to appear in introductory psychology texts (as well as in newspaper Sunday supplements). Although this trend is welcome, it has two risks. The first is that meditation may be viewed as a simple technique that can be mastered in a single session or after reading a page or two of instructions. My own research suggests that meditation is a subtle and elusive skill that takes time and preparation to develop. In fact, most time-honored traditions precede meditation with a variety of preparatory exercises and disciplines. This, by the way, is an important commonality among meditation tradition that Herbert Benson misses in his much-quoted discussion of "relaxation response" techniques.

The second risk is that completely severing meditation from an existential or spiritual context (even to the point of calling it something else, like "self-relaxation") eliminates something important and unique. I feel that meditation as a technique always contains a possibility for self-discovery, for changing or enriching oneself. Treating meditation as just one more relaxation technique does violence to this potential. This brings me to my concluding point—that there is more to meditation than may be first apparent.

Meditation as a Complex Phenomenon

In many respects meditation is proving to be a complex and heterogeneous phenomenon. For example, early meditation research, like early psychotherapy research, devoted much time and effort to the question "does it work?" It is now apparent that not everyone benefits, and those who do, often benefit in different ways. In addition, the early notion that meditation produces a homogeneous "hypometabolic state" now appears to be oversimplified. Meditation may well be as complex as sleep, and involve various stages within and across sessions. Finally, early researchers tended to think of meditation as involving a single process, for example, "self-paced densitization," psychodynamic insight, or even self-suggestion. There now appears to be a good chance that all of these are involved. In sum, meditation appears to be more complex than many first imagined.

Conclusion

These are the most prominent trends I see in meditation research today. One may wonder why I have not commented on specific findings, such as the relationship between meditation and EEG synchrony, creativity, stress, and the like. The topics of current meditation research are indeed filled with exciting possibilities, as can be seen from the selections in this volume. However, it is too early to draw firm conclusions from this research. As in any area of study, it will take much time, replication, and refinement of design before we can begin to say something definite about meditation.

57

THE STATE-OF-THE-ART OF MEDITATION

Arthur J. Deikman

In the past 10 years, meditation has become acceptable to Western culture and a subject of increasing interest to scientists. It has been studied in university laboratories, adapted to statistical analysis, and translated into various physiological dimensions, all of which has yielded data of increasing refinement. Through these procedures, meditation has been demonstrated to have "real" effects. However, there is a problem in the way it is being put to use. As meditation has become approved, it has been employed for personal benefit, for better health or increased power. That is not surprising, for the power of meditation makes such benefits appear likely. In fact, increased calmness, creativity, concentration, and endurance are reported to accompany meditation practice and it has been suggested as a remedy for stress-related illnesses such as hypertension and for problems of chronic anxiety. In more esoteric circles, psychic abilities, healing powers, and "enlightenment" are promised.

What could be the problem with all that? The problem is the acquisitive, self-centered attitude that lies behind such usage, for that attitude affects the outcome of meditation. This issue has been overlooked, perhaps because dealing with it is quite difficult and its implications are ones that we do not wish to face. Whatever the reason may be, it is hard to find a single research paper in this field that mentions: (1) the importance of the context within which classical meditation was developed and practiced and, (2) the instructions in the classical meditation literature that specify the need for humility, service, and sincerity. Ironically, although the power of meditation to affect physiological and psychological functions has been substantiated in many different laboratories, we have paid little attention to what the originators of meditation have said about its intended purpose and the requirements for its appropriate use.

Meditation was developed as part of a teaching system whose purpose was spiritual growth. "Spiritual growth" is an awkward goal for the scientific community to embrace—it sounds religious. It would appear however, that mystics have had as little interest in formal religion as Western science does now. What mystics meant by "spiritual growth" was the development of an inherent intuitive capacity to perceive the reality that underlies the world of appearances. That goal was said to be the supreme task and the greatest benefit of human life.

The sages who invented the powerful techniques of meditation apparently knew what they were doing. Shouldn't we give careful consideration to what they said and respect the instructions that accompany their technical inventions? Those instructions are rather specific. They deal, first, with the necessity for "purifying the heart"—developing a *selfless* orientation—before acquiring special powers. "Purifying the heart" was evidently a difficult process in every spiritual tradition, requiring years of effort and the right attitude. It would be fair to say that such correctly attuned effort is practically nonexistent among most Westerners who practice meditation. Second, they emphasize that meditation function as only one component of an integrated, individualized teaching system requiring the supervision of a Teacher, someone whose own perceptual capacity has been developed and thus knows how to prescribe meditation according to the specific needs of the student.

Focusing primarily on the experiences and bodily effects of meditation is like collecting oyster shells and discarding the pearls. Such "spiritual materialism" inevitably interferes with the real potential of

Meditation   **679**

meditation. The remedy is take *motivational* dimensions as seriously as those we measure with the EEG, the EMG, and the GSR. Unless we do we will continue to select only what attracts us from the technology of mysticism and discard the rest.

What is the state of the art of meditation? It is about what it has been for over 3000 years—except in the Western world where there appears to be a real danger that it is deteriorating. If we wish to practice meditation and contribute to the art, perhaps we should first master its fundamental requirements, whether they appeal to us or not.

58

POTENTIAL CONTRIBUTIONS OF
MEDITATION TO NEUROSCIENCE

Gordon G. Globus

The conjunction of neuroscientific investigation and meditation generally has been in the area of the neural correlates of meditation. I shall take a different tack here. First, I support the plausibility of the claim that disciplined acquaintance with consciousness might contribute to neuroscience, and then discuss the level of neuroscientific knowledge at which this contribution might occur.

Whether or not it seems plausible that meditation could contribute to neuroscience is very much a function of *a priori* philosophical views on the mind/body (or consciousness/brain) problems. (I say "problems" advisedly, since there is a tangle of mind/body problems and pseudoproblems, which are more complex than can be adequately dealt with here.) For a crass materialist, meditation is without promise for neuroscience, for consciousness is an illusion. For a dualist [like J. C. Eccles (1976)] or an emergentist [like R. Sperry (1976)], on the other hand, consciousness really is different from brain, so meditation would be at best an indirect path to knowledge of brain.

In contrast, from the viewpoint of the "psychoneural identity thesis" [Schlick, 1974 (1925); Feigl, 1967)] which holds that consciousness is "identical with" brain, it could seem a plausible strategy to study brain via meditation, since consciousness and brain (at some level) are—in a sense to be explained—"the same thing." However, this identity thesis has been subject to severe criticism by philosophers, and is by no means widely accepted (O'Connor, 1969; Borst, 1970; Rosenthal, 1971). Let us first formulate this thesis more precisely, attend to its defects, and consider how these defects might be elided.

As presented by Feigl (1967), the identity thesis claims that mental and neural terms have different connotations but the same denotation, just as the "Morning Star" and the "Evening Star" differ in meaning but have the same referent (Venus). In addition, the kind of knowledge claim made with respect to the referents of mental and neural terms are categorically different. Mental terms entail knowledge immediately given to our "direct acquaintance," whereas neural terms entail indirect knowledge by "description," which is inferred from that given to direct acquaintance (just as we might infer the presence of particles from our direct acquaintance with tracks in a cloud chamber.)[1] Philosophical criticism of this thesis has attempted to show that the referents of mental and neural are at the least not *strictly* identical, i.e., do not have all properties in common.

One especially vexing and illuminating criticism is the "grain objection" (Sellars, 1963) which holds that consciousness is essentially homogeneous, whereas brain is essentially nonhomogeneous ("grainy"). According to Sellars,

> . . . colour expanses in the manifest world consist of regions which are themselves colour expanses, and these consist in their turn of regions which are colour expanses, and so on; whereas the state of a group of neurons, though it has regions which are also states of groups of neurons, has ultimate regions which are *not* states of groups of neurons but rather states of single neurons. And the same is true if we move to the finer grained level of biochemical process.

[1]The distinction between knowledge by description and by acquaintance (Russell, 1948) is often not appreciated due to the error of naive realism. We do not apprehend reality per se, although it seems that way to us. The brain which is the true object of neuroscientific knowledge is not the "phenomenal" brain that we perceive. The "real" brain is not perceivable, but only inferred from the phenomenal brain we do perceive.

Since the referents of mental and neural terms do not have all properties in common, being, respectively, homogeneous and grainy, it appears that the strict identity thesis fails.

To rescue the identity thesis, a complementarity principle is required (Globus, 1973). Mental and neural terms refer not to the same thing but to the same *structure*, where the embodiments of that structure are complements as a function of mutually exclusive perspectives. This thesis of the structural identity of complements (Globus, 1976; Globus and Franklin, 1979) is supported by the following (telescoped) argument.

Consider two world addresses, A and B, where signals representing the state of affairs at A are carried to B. B can support an "extrinsic" perspective on A, whereas A can support an "intrinsic" perspective on A. Now suppose there are nervous systems occupying these addresses.

Consider the case of an observer coextensive with the nervous system at A, (i.e., the intrinsic perspective on A). Now, events in a nervous system represent input to the system but contain no information as to *their own* neural embodiments.[2] From the perspective of the whole system, those events just are the case, as disembodied events per se. Such pure events cannot be grainy, because graininess implies discrete embodied events; they are instead continuous (wavelike).

On the other hand, the extrinsic perspective on A must find these events to be embodied, hence grainy, and ultimately particlelike. Whereas the intrinsic perspective is certain events, the extrinsic perspective knows those events indirectly via their representation, which largely conserves the structure (order) of those events.

We are so accustomed to taking an extrinsic perspective on dynamic systems, which we find to consist of interrelated physically embodied events (such as digital devises in a computer) that it is difficult to "intuit" an intrinsic perspective. (Indeed, there is only one dynamic system with respect to which we ever can succeed in truly adopting an intrinsic perspective, and that system—according to the extrinsic perspective—is our own brain.) If we can imagine ourselves to be coextensive with some dynamic system—no more and no less than that whole system—then the events of that system would be our case. We—the totality of ourselves as conscious beings—would be the actual happenings in that system, happenings which an extrinsic perspective would find sustained by physical embodiments but which on our intrinsic perspective would be pure happenings as such.

In principle, then, there is no impediment to inferring from the direct knowledge of the consciousness at B to the order at A. However from B, the order at A must be inferred to be embodied—grainy—whereas from the intrinsic perspective of A itself, this same order cannot be embodied, but is the case of the pure events which are consciousness.[3]

Since extrinsic and intrinsic perspectives are mutually exclusive (for one observer), provide incompatible accounts (grainy particlelike versus continuous wavelike) events at A, yet these events have the same order, we may say that mental and neural terms refer to an identical structure in complementary forms. From the extrinsic perspective, and speaking metaphorically, there is no Cheshire grin without the embodying cat, but from the mutually exclusive intrinsic perspective of the whole cat, a complementary pure disembodied Cheshire grin per se is the case.

An adequate presentation and defense of this view cannot be attempted here. Let us assume for the purpose of discussion that this thesis, or some modification of it, is largely correct. It follows that the order of consciousness (by acquaintance) is in principle the order of brain (by description). Meditation is *de facto* structural brain investigation, and meditators, as the ultimate connoisseurs of consciousness, ought to be consulted in this regard.

There are serious methodological problems which immediately arise, since it appears that the kind of "objectivity" (public accessibility) required by science cannot be maintained for data acquired through meditation, which is given privately to each person for himself. Mystics tend to scoff at this objection and claim that the proof of the objective pudding is in the subjective eating; if we but meditate properly, then knowledge will be attained.

This seems to be essentially correct. Nevertheless, both the practical and conceptual issues of "phenomenological coreflection" remain to be worked out. (Matters have not been helped by some of the rasher claims of certain contemporary mystics.) I suspect that what the methodological issues finally come

---

[2]The exception is that unique circumstance in which there are *mirroring* devices, such that these neural embodiments can be reflected back as input into the brain. I have discussed the intricacies of this situation elsewhere (Globus, 19730.

[3]Of course, for the intrinsic perspective on B there is the case of a *different* set of pure events which are consciousness.

down to is this: We follow over time a repetitive sequence of comeditating and then talking together. We are interested in and attentive to meditation and then talking, *without expectation or attachment as to outcome*. [See Zaner (1970) for an illuminating discussion of "phenomenological co-meditation."]

We have considered the plausibility of the claim that disciplined acquaintance with consciousness (i.e., meditation) might contribute to neuroscience. But just what level of neuroscience is meant here? Surely meditation tells us nothing about the chemical structure of neurotransmitters, or the event structure of neurons, or of spinal cord reflexes.

The levels of neuroscience at which structure can be studied through meditation are the higher (richer) levels of nervous system functioning.[4] It is precisely at the level of these higher systems that neuroscience falters, due to the enormous complexity. At the level of neurons and on down, a series of brilliant achievements have been accomplished by neuroscientists in the last 25 years; but next to nothing is known of the system properties of even such well-defined subsystems as the various sensory cortices.

At the enormous complexity of this systems level, it is impractical (and perhaps impossible) to comprehend emergent neural organizations *qua* physical systems, so many and such complex interacting components are involved. But it is eminently practical to comprehend emergent consciousness, especially through the discipline of meditation. At the least, meditation is of heuristic value in directing neuroscientific inquiry.

By way of brief illustration, consider the following claims which are suggested by meditation. Although presented in declarative form, it is properly appreciated as an "invitation to comeditate" (Zaner, 1970) with the understanding that these claims are open to modification by virtue of this comeditation.

Awareness bifurcates into two phases, which I shall term "pure awareness" and "conscious experiencing." Pure awareness is the phase of awareness in which there is no distinguishing (*meaning*) whatsoever. Accordingly, it is the case of an unbounded continuous whole which supports nothing particular, not even "here and there," "now and then," "this and that," and so on.

Conscious experiencing, in contrast, supports distinguishing. There is the primary distinction between subject and object, and the secondary distinctions between the various objects, which taken together comprise the world.[5] Thus, the action of distinguishing "constitutes," as Husserl says, the world.[6]

What of the relations between the two phases of awareness and "reality," which relations have much exercised philosophers? For most neuroscientists, some form of representational realism seems inevitable (and philosophical disputations in their regard seem precious.) There is a reality, and energetic signals from this reality (the "fact" of reality) impinge on the brain and set up neural representation which carry the order of the fact. On the intrinsic perspective, this order is given to direct acquaintance. Reality can be inferred ("known by description") from this directly known order.

Thus, the world in conscious experiencing is not constituted whole-cloth by the action of meaning, but by action on the fact. The world results from the convolution of the fact and meaning.[7]

During pure awareness, when there is no action, the whole fact configures pure awareness. To use a Tibetan metaphor, pure awareness is a "crystal mirror" which veridically (without distortion) and indelibly (without trace of past impressions) reflects the undivided fact of reality.

---

[4]This view is, in one respect, similar to that of Sperry (1969) who emphasizes that consciousness is a dynamic "emergent property" of higher neural systems. But Sperry sees consciousness directly emergent from physical brain and further, having causal efficacy with respect to that brain. For the present account, there is on the extrinsic perspective a physical organization emergent from (sustained by) higher neural systems, which on the intrinsic perspective is emergent consciousness itself. No question of causality is involved for there is "merely" a shift in perspective on the properties of a functionally whole system.

In any case, it appears that Sperry begs the question. What emerges from interacting physical parts—say, two hydrogen and one oxygen atom—is the physical emergent we call "water." Indeed, all interacting physical components which we know about sustain an emergent physical organization. Why should interacting neural parts, which are typically physical, instead sustain an emergent but anomalous nonphysical consciousness? This is certainly conceivable, but we are owed an account of just why we should conceive an anomalous nonphysical emergent. Sperry elides the very problem and just tells us that this is the case.

[5]It is tempting to construe "the one, the two, and the ten thousand things" of Taoism as pure awareness, subject/object, and world, respectively.

[6]So far these three features of conscious experiencing have been emphasized: subject, objects, and the action of meaning. These features can be collapsed to two by strictly identifying the subject with meaning, i.e., "I" am the action which constitutes the world (Globus, 1979).

[7]It is often claimed by mystics that the world (*samsara*) is an "illusion;" there is no "fact of realiy," for this idealism. In contrast, I would hold that the world is "illusory" in a much more limited sense. The world collapses unless it is sustained by the action of meaning, where the grammar for this action is mainly learned, in significant ways arbitrary and a function of social consensus. "Illusion" implies only the relativity of an ordinary description of the world and the possibility of world collapse.

Potential Contributions to Neuroscience

Now, given this phenomenological reflection in the context of representational realism, what is implied about those higher neural systems which are of such enormous complexity that we have difficulty in encompassing them neuroscientifically? The phase of pure awareness tells us that there is an extraordinary neural state characterized by profound interconnectivity. We usually think of the brain as partitioned into a number of interacting but rather distinct subsystems, the visual cortex, auditory cortex, limbic system, etc. The phase of pure awareness achieved in meditation indicates a functional interrelatedness such that there is in effect *but one whole system*, i.e., a "holistic brain."[8]

Furthermore, recalling the veridical and indelible "crystal mirror," this "holistic brain" is freely modulated by input without constraint from the past. This is to say that *it is possible to disengage from a functional nervous system what previously has been learned,* while at the same time maintaining full (indeed, enhanced) awareness. Any adequate neurophysiology of learning will have to acknowledge this truly remarkable state of affairs.

The phase of conscious experiencing, on the other hand, tells us that there is a neural action which interfaces with the interconnectivity (functional interrelatedness) characterizing the "holistic brain," and serves to *segregate* both between and within neural subsystems. This action (which can be most easily construed as inhibitory) is rule governed and presumably has both innate and learned components. A complete neuroscience must identify the neural systems which subserve this distinguishing action and their convolution with representations of input.

In summary we have seen that the foundations for a contribution of meditation to neuroscience require a viable version of the consciousness/brain identity thesis. A "structural identify of complements" solution has been described. It was also noted that certain methodological issues relating to objectivity (verifiability) arise with respect to meditation.

On the assumption that these conceptual and methodological problems can be resolved, let us review how meditation, as a method for disciplined acquaintance with consciousness, might contribute to neuroscience. It is at the higher levels of brain functioning that meditation becomes relevant. Scientific techniques—even those of a utopian neuroscience—may not be able to encompass the extraordinary richness of higher level neural systems. The path of meditation, although arduous in its own right, is well trodden, with many signposts dating back to antiquity.

Of course, meditation can tell us nothing about the embodiment of those events whose varying degrees of functional interrelatedness comprise the system. Obviously, meditation can tell us nothing about neurotransmitters or neurons as such. But the structural (informational) and functional characteristics of whole neural systems of a certain richness are in principle open to the direct acquaintance of meditators. Indeed, it may turn out that a complete neuroscience will require the disciplined acquaintance with consciousness provided by meditation.

References

Borst, C. Introduction. In E. Borst (Ed.), *The mind/brain identity theory*. London: MacMillan, 1970.

Eccles, J. E. Brain and free will. In G. Globus, G. Maxwell, and I. Savodnik (Eds.), *Consciousness and the brain: a scientific and philosophical inquiry*. New York: Plenum Press, 1976.

Feigl, H. *The Mental and the physical*. Minneapolis, Minnesota: Univ. of Minnesota Press, 1967.

Globus, G. Unexpected symmetries in the 'World Knot.' *Science*, 1973, **180**, 1129–1135.

Globus, G. Mind, structure, and contradiction. In G. Globus, G. Maxwell, and I. Savodnik (Eds.), *Consciousness and the brain: a scientific and philosophical inquiry*. New York: Plenum Press, 1976.

Globus, G. *A formal epitome of some mystical philosophy*, in preparation.

Globus, G. and Franklin, S. Prospects for the scientific observer of perceptual consciousness. In J. M. Davidson and R. J. Davidson (Eds.) *The psychobiology of consciousness*. New York: Plenum Press, 1979.

O'Connor, J. (Ed.) *Modern materialism: readings on mind/body identity*. New York: Harcourt, Brace & World, 1969.

---

[8]Mystics are wont to believe that in the phase of pure awareness they somehow fuse with the totality, i.e., become literally interconnected with and absorbed into everything else, rather than remaining singular. In a certain sense, we are *always* interconnected with the whole, according to quantum physical conceptions, but this participation is quite independent of which phase of awareness we happen to assume. Although it is claimed that this cosmic fusion is experienced as such, it would be more proper to say that there is a certain peculiar kind of experience—which is the way it is—that may be interpreted as a fusion with the whole.

An alternative interpretation is as follows. The profound interconnectivity of the "holistic brain" reiterates the interconnectivity of the cosmic whole. No literal fusion occurs. Instead, an internal, seamless unity is achieved which mirrors the undivided cosmic whole.

Rosenthal, D. (Ed.) *Materialism and the mind/body problem*. Englewood Cliffs, New Jersey: Prentice-Hall, 1971.

Russell, B. *Human knowledge: Its scope and limits*. New York: Simon and Schuster, 1948.

Schlick, M. *General theory of knowledge*. A. E. Blumberg (Trans.). Vienna: Springer-Verlag, 1974. (Original 1918, revised 1925.)

Sellars, W. *Science, perception and reality*. London: Routledge & Kegan Paul, 1963.

Sperry, R. W. A modified concept of consciousness. *Psychological Review*, 1969, **76**. 532–536.

Sperry, R. W. Mental phenomena as causal determinants in brain function. In G. Globus, G. Maxwell and I. Savodnik (Eds.), *Consciousness and the brain: a scientific and philosophical inquiry*. New York: Plenum Press, 1976.

Zaner, R. *The way of phenomenology: criticism as a philosophical discipline*. New York: Pegasus, 1970.

59

THE PRINCIPLES OF PSYCHOLOGY OF ZEN

Yoshiharu Akishige

Zen Buddhism is primarily a religion, but it also possesses an intimate relationship with numerous aspects of human life. In conclusion, I would like to offer a few thoughts on this relationship.

If the most desirable constancy of self can be reached through Zen, it should be possible to utilize this principle in the wider sense of psychotherapy. In actuality psychologists and psychiatrists in Japan and other countries have in various forms carried out treatment through Zen. One of these is the internationally known Morita therapy. Respiratory treatment widely practiced in such countries as India and China can probably be seen as one aspect of respiratory regulation which has been singled out and made independent. I have for convenience's sake termed as "Zen therapy" the several treatments carried out applying the principles of Zen to counselling and psychotherapy in the narrow sense. I will here refrain from introducing these treatments one by one, and take up only the commonly held features of Zen therapy.

Zen Buddhism is derived from the two main stems of hearing the teachings and zazen. The former may be considered as corresponding to personality theory of psychotherapy, while the latter is applicable to the actual practice of treatment. We will first take up the theoretical side.

The world view and human view as seen from the standpoint of Zen is learned through hearing the teachings of Zen Buddhism. Zen Buddhism teaches two kinds of selflessness. One is the selflessness of the human "self," and the other is the selflessness of "phenomena" of all things outside of humans. In the first and second chapters were taken up the subjects of selflessness of the human "self" and the selflessness of "things" of the perceptual world surrounding humans. It was stated that "self" and "things" are created as prescribed by a reference system, and that they are primarily empty things which of themselves do not possess invariant substance. The selflessness of "phenomena" is not limited to "things." Good phenomena, bad phenomena, right phenomena, and wrong phenomena all are essentially empty. They do not have their own natural quality.

People must divorce themselves from evil and wrong acts. All acts defiled by desire, beginning with evil and wrong acts, are called evil passions (*bonnō*) in Buddhism. All of these evil passions must be denied. However, this denial does not signify the eradication of the existence of these evil passions. To the extent that humans exist, the eradication of evil passions is impossible. To deny and separate from evil passions is to deny and separate from the relative interpretation of considering diverse evil passion as evil or wrong.

People should progress toward doing good and correct acts. However, if these good and correct acts become simply acts of relative good or correctness which are defined by attachments, they too become evil passions which ought to be denied and separated from. If the world of relative evil and wrong actions is the world of the devil, that of relative good and correct acts is likewise a devil's world.

Men must escape this devil's world, the world of delusion, and enter the world of enlightenment. In enlightenment evil acts, wrong acts, good acts, and correct acts all exist. However, they are separated from the relative distinctions of good, evil, right, and wrong, and are all grasped as empty quantities which do not arouse the least attachment. This world separates from all relative distinctions and attachments which take one thing as bad or wrong and another as good or right. In the world of enlightenment even if acts like evil passion occur, if they are completely liberated from egoistic attachment they will no longer be evil passion as such. This is the concept expressed in the statement that evil passions and Buddhahood are identical.

In the world of enlightenment the phenomena and action before one's eyes are released from and free from relative distinction and egoistic attachments. But this liberation and freedom is not limited only to present phenomena. In the same way it is possible for memories of past events to be released from relative distinctions and egoistic attachments and set free. According to modern psychology, memory traces of the past are not accumulated as fixed quantities. In those instances when memories of the past reappear in the consciousness, they are invested with significance in correspondence with the internal and external situation of the person at the time in which they reappear. In other words, the significance a memory possessed when it comes to life in the consciousness is determined by the condition of the time of its appearance. The original experience which may have been objectionable or painful at the time it was imbedded in the mind often becomes for us a nostalgic experience when it returns to our senses as a memory. Buddhism calls karmic existence (*gō*) the disposition left in the organism by all experiences. Thus it is said that men as a result of evil acts will be born into the evil worlds which are the manifestation of bad karmic existence, the world of hell, hungry spirits, and beasts. However, these fearful evil worlds are extinguished through the powers of zazen. Let us quote one passage of the *Zazen Wasan (Zazen Hymns of Praise)* of Priest Hakuin (1685–1768), which clearly and simply relates the circumstances of this process,

> All sentient beings are by nature the Buddha,
> Just as with water and ice,
> Where apart from water there is no ice,
> Apart from sentient beings there is no Buddha.
> Oh, the emptiness of mankind, seeking that which is far away,
> Without knowing what is close at hand.
> It is just as the man who
> In the midst of water cries from thirst.
> It is no different from the child of a rich household
> Who goes astray in some poor village.
> The cause of the transmigration of the six evil worlds
> Is that the self follows the dark road of foolishness.
> While treading dark road after dark road,
> When can they ever leave *Saṃsāra*!
> For this the Samadhi of Zen
> Goes beyond all praise.
> The man who gains the merits of one sitting
> Wipes out the innumerable sins that he has built up,
> Where are these evil worlds now?
> The Pure Land is not far away. . . . .
> At this time what ought we to seek?
> In that Nirvana is right before our eyes,
> This very place is a lotus garden,
> This very body is a Buddha.

Priest Hakuin teaches us that the innumerable sins accumulated in the past disappear with only one sitting of zazen. He asks what has happened to the evil worlds which are the manifestation of bad karmic existence, the worlds of hell, hungry spirits, and beasts. They have been extinguished with the appearance of the world of nirvana, and for that reason man is now in the Pure Land where lotus flower blooms and where he lives peacefully as the Buddha.

The power to extinguish the innumerable sins accumulated in the past transform evil worlds into the Pure Land, and change the common man into Buddha, is contained in the meditation of zazen. It is not easy for the person who does not practice zazen to believe in such a power. There is thus reason why we must here explain the belief of the original enlightenment. The belief of original enlightenment signifies that the self is by nature the Buddha. The *Wasan* tells how the rich man wanders aimlessly through the caverns of the poor because he is completely ignorant of his own origins. In the same way people who have lost the true path are completely incognizant and unconscious of the fact of their natural Buddhahood. They doubt the words of the man who tells them of this fact and to the very end believe themselves to be children of the poor. It is just as the insane man thinks that his present condition is correct and is entirely unconscious of his truly correct self. That which wakes man to the belief in original enlightenment is training, in other words zazen. Because training and enlightenment are the same thing, it is through training that the belief in original enlightenment flowers and becomes the belief permeating the whole body. Thus belief, training, and enlightenment are not three different things but are all one and the same. This is one characteristic of Zen Buddhism.

General phenomena outside of the self—the free good, evil, right, and wrong released from egoistic attachments—appear in consequence of the manifestation of the free self or selflessness released from egoistic attachments. They come into being simultaneously. As frequently stated, it is zazen which makes possible the appearance of the free self and free general phenomena.

Zazen is, together with hearing the teachings, a main pillar of Zen Buddhism. The process does not call for contemplating any specific images, or following free thought associations, or conceiving some unknown quantity, or reconstructing memories of the past. On the contrary, it ends all distinguishing between good and evil and right and wrong, stops all observations, stops thought associations, does not pursue memory, and does not think of the future. It discards all human judgments and becomes no-contrivance. The practice of zazen in this respect holds the notable feature of moving in a diametrically opposite direction from various other forms of psychotherapy practiced up to now.

The selflessness theory of Zen Buddhism which corresponds to personality theories of psychotherapy teaches human selflessness and phenomenal selflessness and emphasizes the emptiness of all existence. If traditional psychotherapy is seen from the position of being, then Zen is in the position of emptiness. While the former considers that the deep level self is a weak thing suppressed by the unconscious, the latter thinks that the essential self is the Buddha.

Thus the task allotted to Zen therapy will be to put into practical use the principles of Zen Buddhism which contain these remarkable features concerning theories of the self and training practices, and to contribute to the cultivation and development of a new field of psychotherapy.

A few thoughts should also be said about how Zen thought can contribute to world peace.

It is the logic of logos, the base and support of Western thought, that has given birth to today's civilization of great scientific advancements. This logic is prescribed by the three laws of identity, contradiction, and the excluded middle, with all judgments being either positive or negative. That which is neither positive nor negative is not recognized in that it violates the law of excluded middle.

According to dialectical logic, thesis is broken down by antithesis, and synthesis is formed when the two opposites are joined. But the synthesis also becomes its own thesis and finally calls out another antithesis to act in opposition to it. In this manner things develop in an endless repetition of breakdown and union. To the extent that there is opposition and contradiction between affirmation and negation, struggles will always occur. And if the resolution of problems emerges only from such destruction, it has to be said that there is nothing so sorry as human society which must suffer through these constant confrontations of affirmation and negation.

Fortunately, however, all logic is not based on logos. Man is also able to live in the world controlled by the logic of lemma. The logic of the world of enlightenment in Zen comes from the logic of lamma. In lemma-logic, the absolute negative which denies both the affirmative and the negative is in that very form transformed into an absolute affirmative which affirms both the affirmative and the negative. In the world of absolute affirmation those things which are in contradiction and opposition mutually take the other as a necessary condition for their own coming into being and form a relationship of negative mutual dependence. The nature of this system is fundamentally different from dialectical logic, where because of the sublation of contradiction and opposition those things which stand in opposition must be thoroughly broken down.

Isolated phenomenon do not exist in the world of enlightenment. Because each and every phenomenon stands as a necessary condition for all others in the twofold sense of mutual identity and mutual entry, it is not possible for isolation to occur. Whether temporal or spatial phenomenon, each individually stands as a necessary condition for all others. In this way the individual phenomenon has included within it the whole, and a world is constructed in which all is in harmony with all. The logic of Zen is thus not that of essential breakdown and struggle, but one of peace.

The special concept of time in Zen is also a contributing factor. History is usually considered merely as a straight line continuing from the past to the future, but that is not necessarily correct. That history has circularity has been pointed out by various historians and philosophers in the past. The practicer of Zen is not always well versed in history and philosophy and has not particularly studied historical circularity. However, he does in a very basic sense know that the historical present which bears the past and conceives the future forms a complete circle. He also knows that the historical present appears only "here and now" and does not exist in any other place or time. He knows that the human life from birth to death is merely the chain of non-contingent circles of life which are born one moment and perish the next.

The special nature of the historical present where the enlightened person lives in the "here and now" is that is is not merely characterized by closed circularity of momentary life and death. The content of the historical present he is actually experiencing is in each moment changing in a thousand and ten thousand ways, stopping not for an instant. Yet no matter how much the content changes, the historical present possessing the features of the world of enlightenment neither increases nor decreases, is neither pure nor defiled, right nor wrong, and neither life nor death. Invariant self-identity and constancy are always maintained, and this invariance and constancy is the state of nirvana and emptiness.

The world of the enlightened person may at times be the world of hell, of hungry spirits, or of beasts. These various worlds are permeated by contradiction, opposition, struggle, and suffering. However, for the enlightened person, at the same time that they are the spheres of hell, hungry spirits, and beasts, they are also worlds of tranquil nirvana and peace. The enlightened person does not possess any existence particular only to him outside of these worlds.

If this is the case, for the enlightened person the peaceful world of no contradiction, opposition, and struggle is not only a dream of the future, but has already been attained in the present. It is in a grammatical sense not future tense but past perfect tense. On the contrary, if we vainly wait for the appearance of this peaceful world in some future date while at the same time maintaining a sense of discrimination between self and other, we will very likely never see its arrival. This is because to the extent that mankind continues to exist, there will never be a time when contradiction, opposition, and struggle completely disappear.

At this point the following must not be forgotten: There is no greater mistake than to think that in the world of peace there is already no necessity to work to eliminate contradiction, opposition, and struggle. In this peaceful world, acts of good, no matter how small, must be performed. Acts of evil, no matter how small, must be avoided. We must strive ceaselessly until the end of our lives to lessen to a small extent contradiction, opposition, and struggle in order that mankind can live a more happy and fortunate life. Yet this striving is for the purpose of making more peaceful the world of nirvana already achieved, and is not in order to bring about a peaceful world which has not yet been arrived at.

As stated before, the world of nirvana is one of no increase, no decrease. No matter how much the content of the world increases, decreases, and changes, the nirvana quality and self-identity of that world does not change in the slightest. There is nothing in the nature of development. However, this lack of development does not mean that there is no change in the content of the world or that the world is in a fixed state. The world maintains at all times its constancy while ceaselessly changing and advancing. Our theme in the future may be to form a new view of history differing from previously established views and based on the logic of Zen.

References

1. Akishige, Y. Perceptual constancy and the law of conservation of perceptual information. *Bull. Fac. Lit. Kyushu Univ.*, 1965, 9.
2. Akishige, Y. Mind-body monism on the base of the theory of perceptual constancy. *Bull. Fac. Lit. Kyushu Univ.*, 1967, 10.
3. Akishige, Y.(Ed.), *The constancy of the perceptual world* I–V. Tokyo: Risesha, 1970–1972.
4. Cassirer, E. The concept of group and the theory of perception. *Philosopy and Phenomenologial Research.* 1944, 5.
5. Dōgen, K. *Shōbōgenzō* (written 1233–1253). In Ōkubo D. (Ed.), *The collections of Dōgen.* Tokyo: Shunjū-sha, 1970.
6. Dōgen, K. *Fukanzazengi* (written 1227). ditto.
7. Dōgen, K. *Gakudōyōjinshū* (written 1234). ditto.
8. Doen, K. *Shōbōgenzō Zazenshin* (written 1242).ditto.
9. Dōgen, K. *Shōbōgenzō 37 Bodai bunpō* (written 1244). ditto.
10. Dōgen, K. *Shōbōagenzō Zanmai ōzanmai* (written 1244). ditto.
11. Dōgen, K. *Bendōhō* (written 1245). ditto.
12. Hakuin, E., *Zazen Wasan.* In *The collections of Hakuin.* Tokyo: Ryūgin-sha, 1934.
13. Harada, T. Psychological study on the mind-body relation. In Y.Akishige (Eg.), Psychological studies on Zen. *Bull. FAc. Lit. Kyushu Univ.*, 1968, 11.
14. Kajō, K. *Sanron Genri. Taishō-shinshū-daizō-kō*, Bd. 4.
15. Kishizawa, I. *Goi Kenketsu Genjikyaku Kattōshū* I–XI. Shizuoka: Kyokudenin, 1960.
16. Sōzan, H. *Goi Kunshin Shiketsu.* In *Sōzan Goroku, Taishō-shinshū-daizō-kyō*, Bd. 47, 1987 A.B.
17. Tōzan, R. *Goi Kenketsu, Goiju.* In *Tōzan Goroku, Taislō-shinshū-daizō-kyō*, Bd. 47, 1968 A.B.

Articles

60

MEDITATION: THE PROBLEMS OF
ANY UNIMODAL TECHNIQUE

Arnold A. Lazarus

In this brief article, I should like to present my views and ideas about the practice of meditation. First, on the negative side, I published a brief report in *Psychological Reports* (Lazarus, 1976) in which I emphasized that casualties can and do result from meditation, especially TM. On the positive side, I see the value of meditation in terms of the profound levels of general relaxation that can ensue, plus the impact of an altered state of consciousness. There are data that show how "self-talk" and "images of personal mastery" tend to make a deeper and more profound impression when one is relaxed, with one's eyes closed, and in a semi-drowsy state (presumably emitting alpha waves). These identical methods of "cognitive restructuring" are often much less potent when administered or self-administered in ordinary waking states.

Clinically, I continually come across people who prefer deep muscle relaxation to meditation (i.e., the mantra tends to act as an interference) and vice versa. Similarly, I find that formal hypnosis proves far superior to ordinary relaxation and/or meditation in others. Thus, my point is that meditation is no panacea—it is strongly indicated in some cases, mildly in others, and clearly contraindicated in others. The precise guidelines for these discriminations have yet to be worked out.

The upshot of my observation in that a good clinician will not limit him or herself to a specific technique. The pundits of meditation are just as limited, rigid, and misguided as the people who carry a torch for hypnosis, or relaxation, or any other unimodal method. Flexibility in acquiring a repertoire of effective procedures is the main requirement. A young women who was a compulsive vomiter failed to respond to relaxation, hypnosis, aversion therapy, drug treatment, and insight-oriented methods; she consulted one of my associates who used meditation. It proved effective almost immediately. As Gordon Paul (1967) put it: What treatment, by whom, is most effective with this individual, with that specific problem, and under which set of circumstances? Let us not forget that some people may be highly "allergic" to meditation!

References

Lazarus, A. A. Psychiatric problems precipitated by transcendental meditation. *Psychological Reports*, 1976, **39**, 601–602.
Paul, G. L. Strategy of outcome research in psychotherapy. *Journal of Consulting Psychology*, 1967, **31**, 109–118.

VI

EPILOGUE

EPILOGUE

Deane H. Shapiro, Jr. and Roger N. Walsh

> He looked at de Gier, but de Gier was still studying the display.
>
> There were several small cartons filled with incense and a gilded Buddhist statue sitting on a pedestal, staring and smiling, with the headgear tapering off into a sharp point.
>
> "A pointed head," Grijpstra said. "Is that what you get when you meditate?
>
> "That isn't known as a pointed head," said de Geir, using the voice of his lecture evening, once a month when he taught young constables at the emergency squad the art of crime detection.
>
> "Not a pointed head," de Gier repeated, "But a heaven head. The point points at heaven. Heaven is the goal of meditation. Heaven is thin air. Heaven is upstairs."
>
> "Ah," said Grijpstra. "Are you sure?"
>
> "No," said de Gier.
>
> *Outsider in Amsterdam*
> Janwillem von de Watering

This collection of readings was intended for scientists, scholars, and academicians. By gathering in one source the major seminal articles on meditation theory, research, and practice, it is our hope to begin to develop a true science of meditation. Clearly, as is true of the beginning of any new field of inquiry, questions seem to beget questions, and simple hopes give way to complex multiple interpretations.

As a spiritual discipline, meditation is an ancient and revered practice, and its most outstanding practitioners have been ranked among the wisest people in history. Unfortunately, that history and tradition is sometimes lost and/or forgotten by those who unquestioningly and evangelically embrace a particular meditation technique or path, and try to convince all around them of its absolute truth. On the other hand, it may also be lost to us as Western scientists if we are not careful of our own biases and views as we study meditation. What seems needed on both sides, is an openmindedness and willingness to explore, as unencumbered as possible by rigid preconceptions. This exploration may include not only the content of the technique itself, but also an openness to the process by which this exploration might be undertaken—including not only the use of highly sophisticated technological equipment, but also experiential practice and understanding. Although this throwback to the "introspectionistic" school of the late 19th century may seem distasteful to some, at this point in the state of our art, we should allow ourselves the freedom to keep an openness to as many approaches as possible.

Reflecting this is the statement by SanSaNein, patariarch of Zen in Korea who, in somewhat broken English, extols his Western students to practice their Zen and meditation as intensively as possible and to "keep don't know mind, only keep don't know mind":

One day as the Rabbi was crossing his village square to go to the temple to pray he was accosted by the village Cossack. "Where are you going." "Don't know," said the Rabbi.

"What do you mean you don't know," exploded the Cossack. "For 20 years every morning you've gotten up and crossed this square to go to the temple and now you're telling me you don't know where you're going." So saying he grabbed the Rabbi and hauled him off to the village jail and just as he was about to throw him into the cell the Rabbi turned to him and said, "See you just don't know!"

Although we as Western scientists bring with us highly sophisticated technologies of a like never before applied to meditation, in many ways, as we begin to investigate meditation, we need to acknowledge that we just do not know. Within the meditation traditions such recognition of one's ignorance and a corresponding humility are recognized as essential prerequisites for learning.

With our equipment we are capable of investigating phenomena associated with meditation which were not even known to exist only a few years ago. Clearly there is the potential for exploring vast new realms of knowledge associated with the meditative discipline. But what we scientists have only recently come to recognize, and what is important for us to remember as we begin this exploration of meditation, is that any and every method of investigation, any concept, hypothesis, or theory, only affords us a partial and elective picture of reality. From the vastness of "what is," our chosen technologies and concepts dissect nature along corresponding lines and provide a selective and limited perspective on the whole. Thus what we observe is ultimately a function not only of the reality we wish to know, but of the tools and concepts by which we seek to know it, and ultimately ourselves. No where is this recognition more important than in the investigation of meditation which, as a discipline, traditionally aimed at the deepest and most fundamental types of knowing. This knowing aims at developing greater and greater degrees of experiential sensitivity to more and more subtle realms called perception, consciousness, and being. Therefore, the scientist who expects that the corresponding psychobiological changes should be large and easily detectable may be disappointed.

In addition the meditative disciplines recognize a range of states of consciousness which is far broader than that of traditional Western psychology. The latter views our usual state as "normal" and optimal and views others as limited in number and usually necessarily dysfunctional, psychosis, delirium, etc. For the meditator the states recognized by Western psychology are complimented by a range of functionally specific states, so called "higher" states. What may often be involved here is no less than a paradigm clash and as with any paradigm clash there is a grave danger of misunderstanding and miscommunication between the two camps. Thus, for the traditionally Western trained scientist whose paradigm contains no "higher" states such claims must necessarily sound nonsensical, and the fact that subtle shifts in consciousness do not register on his/her instrument will seem to add support to this belief.

Thus there is a real danger that if we as Western scientists coming out of our own paradigm, employing physical empirical approaches and cartographic knowledge (by inference), do not recognize the possibility of other types and modes of knowledge, states of consciousness and heightened subtlety than we are likely to end up with an (unknown to us) reductionistic and nihilistic picture of reality which denies the possibility of the picture obtained by the meditator and misses the opportunity for a broader complimentary prospective.

We therefore may need to be aware not only of our own research methods and literature, but also the experiential knowledge and wisdom of a classical literature which describes those aspects of meditation for which our current paradigms and technologies are least designed to examine. Ideally both the scientist and meditator might wish to combine the goals and aims of both disciplines: (a) employing rigorous relevant problem-oriented experiments which are designed with an awareness of the complex multidimensional interactional nature of meditative outcome; and (b) combining this with a service oriented, sensitive, intuitive, open wisdom which looks without preconception freshly on each experience and finding. The ultimate aim of both approaches and of this complimentary approach is the same, namely as is stated in the meditative disciplines, "to see things just as they are."

Whether we utilize meditation as a spiritual path, consciousness discipline, therapeutic tool, clinical self-regulation strategy, or research interest, it is clear that it can be approached by many different paths, modes, and types of knowledge each of which is necessarily partial but may also be complimentary. Whatever our viewpoint, our contributions and personal gains may be greater the more multifaceted our approach. And, as in the story of the Rabbi, if we can also "only keep don't know mind," we may soon develop a truly, broad, encompassing, precise, rigorous, and integrated science of meditation. This approach, drawing from the best wisdom of both classic and contemporary perspectives of meditation, may ultimately provide the greatest scientific contribution, as well as the greatest contribution to the betterment of our human species.

BIBLIOGRAPHY

BIBLIOGRAPHY ON MEDITATION AND RELATED ARTICLES*

Aaronson, B. S. The hypnotic induction of the void. *Journal of the American Society of Psychosomatic Dentistry and Medicine.* 1944, **26**(1), 22–30.

Abrams, A. I. Paired associate learning and recall. In D. Orme-Johnson and J. Farrow (Eds.), *Scientific research on the transcendental meditation program.* Vol. I, 2nd Ed. Maharishi European Research University Press, 1977.

Abrams, A. I. and Siegal, L. M. The transcendental meditation program and rehabilitation at Folsom state prison: a cross-validation study. *Criminal Justice and Behavior.* 1978, **5**(1), 3–20.

Akers, T. K., Tucker, D. M., Roth, Randy S., and Vidiloff, J. S., Personality correlates of EGG change during meditation. *Psychology Reports,* 1977, **40**, 439–442.

Akishige, Y. (Ed.) Psychological Studies on Zen. Kyushu Psychological Studies. *Bulletin of the Faculty of Literature of Kyushu University,* Fukuoka, Japan, 1968, No. 5.

Akishige, Y. (Ed.) *Psychological studies on Zen.* Tokyo: Zen Institute of the Komazawa University, 1970.

Akishige, Y. A historical survey of the psychological studies on Zen. *Bulletin of the Faculty of Literature of Kyushu University,* 1974, **5**, 1–57.

Akishige, Y. The principle of psychology of Zen. This volume.

Albert, I. B., & McNeece, B. The reported sleep characteristics of meditators and nonmeditators. *Bulletin of the Psychonomic Society,* 1974, **3**(1B), 73–74.

Alexander, F. Buddhistic training as an artificial catatonia. *Psychoanalytic Review,* 1931, **18**, 129–45.

Allen D. TM at Folsom Prison: A critique of Abrams and Siegel. *Criminal Justice & Behavior,* 1979, **6**(1), 9–12.

Allison, J. Respiratory change during transcendental meditation. *Lancet,* 1970, **1**, 833–834.

American Psychiatric Association. Position statement on meditation. *American Journal of Psychiatry,* 1977, **134**, (6), 720.

Anand, B. K. and Chhina, G. Investigations on yogis claiming to stop their heart beats. *Indian Journal of Medical Research,* 1961, **49**, 90–94.

Anand, B. K., Chhina, G. S., and Singh B. Some aspects of electroencephalographic studies in Yogis. *Electroencephalography and Clinical Neurophysiology,* 1961, **13**, 452–456.

Anand, B. K., Chhina, G. S., and Singh B. Studies of Shri Ramanand Yogi during his stay in an air-tight box. *Indian Journal of Medical Research,* 1961, **49**, 82–89.

Anderson, D. J. Transcendental meditation as an alternative to heroin abuse in servicemen. *American Journal of Psychiatry,* 1977, **134**(11), 1308–1309.

Aron, A. and Aron, E. N. The transcendental meditation program's effect on addictive behavior. *Addictive Behaviors,* 1980, **5**(1), 3–12.

Aron, A., Orme-Johnson, D. W., & Brubaker, P. The TM program in the college curriculum. A 4-year longitudinal study of effects of cognitive & affective functioning. *College Student Journal,* 1981, **15**(2), 140–146.

Aron, E. N. and Aron, A. The Transcendental Meditation program for the reduction of stress related conditions. *Journal of Chronic Diseases and Therapeutic Research,* 1979, **3**(9), 11–21.

Avila, D., and Nummela, R. Transcendental Meditation: A psychological interpretation. *Journal of Clinical Psychology,* 1977, **33**(3), 842–844.

Bagchi, B. K. Mental hygiene and the Hindu doctrine of relaxation. *Mental Hygiene,* 1936, **20**, 424–40.

Bagchi, B. K. and Wenger, M. Electrophysiological correlates of some yogi exercises. *Electroencephalography and Clinical Neurophysiology,* 1957, Suppl. No. 7, 132–149.

Bagchi, B. K. and Wenger, M. A. Simultaneous EEG and other recordings during some yogic practices. *Electroencephalography & Clinical Neurophysiology,* 1958, **10**, 193.

Bahrke, M. S. Exercise, meditation and anxiety reduction: a review. *American Corrective Therapy Journal,* 1979, **32**(2), 41–44.

Bahrke, M. S. and Morgan, W. P. Anxiety reduction following exercise and meditation. *Cognitive Therapy and Research, 1978,* **2**(4), 323–333.

Bakker, R. Decreased respiratory rate during the Transcendental Meditation technique: A replication. In D. Orme-Johnson and J. Farrow (Eds.), *Scientific research on the Transcendental Meditation program.* Vol. I, 2nd Ed. Maharishi European Research University Press, 1977.

Banquet, J. P. EEG and meditation. *Electroencephalography and Clinical Neurophysiology,* 1972, **33**, 449–458.

Banquet, J. P. Spectral analysis of the EEG in meditation. *Electroencephalography and Clinical Neurophysiology,* 1973, **35**, 143–151.

*Based on Dr. Robert R. Pagano, D. Giber, and S. Carrere.

Banquet, J. P. and Silhan, M. EEG analysis of spontaneous and induced states of consciousness. *Revue d'Electroencephalographie Neurophysiologie Clinque*, 1974, **4**, 445–453. Reprinted in D. Orme-Johnson & J. Farrow (Eds.), *Scientific research on the Transcendental Meditation program*. Vol. I, 2nd Ed. Maharishi European Research University Press, 1977.

Banquet, J. P. and Silhan, M. Quantified EEG spectral analysis of sleep and Transcendental Meditation. In D. Orme-Johnson and J. Farrow (Eds.), *Scientific research on the Transcendental Meditation program*. Vol. I, 2nd Ed. Maharishi European Research University Press, 1977.

Barber, T. (Ed.) *Advances in altered states of consciousness and human potentialities*, Vol. I. NY: Psychological Dimensions, 1976.

Barber, T., DiCara, L. V., Kamiya, J., Miller, N. E., Shapiro, D., and Stoyva, J. (Eds.) *Biofeedback and self-control: An Aldine reader on the regulation of body processes and consciousness*. Chicago, Ill.: Aldine-Atherton, 1971.

Barmark, S. M. and Gaunitz, S. Transcendental meditation and heterohypnosis as altered states of consciousness. *International Journal of Clinical and Experimental Hypnosis*, 1979, **27**(3), 227–239.

Barwood, T. J., Empson, J. A. D., Lister, S. G., and Tilley, A. J. Auditory evoked potentials and transcendental meditation. *Electroencephalography and Clinical Neurophysiology*, 1978, **45**(5), 671–673.

Beary, J. F. and Benson, H. A simple psychophysiologic technique which elicits the hypometabolic changes of the relaxation response. *Psychosomatic Medicine*, 1974, **36**, 115–120.

Becker, D. and Shapiro, David. Physiological response to clicks during Zen meditation. *Biofeedback Society of America Proceedings, 10th, Feb., 1979*, Denver: B.S.A., 1979.

Becker, E. The central psychologic role of the trance in Zen therapy. *American Journal of Psychotherapy*, 1961, **15**(4), 645–651.

Beiman, I., Majestic, H., Johnson, S. A., Puente, A., and Graham, L. E. Transcendental meditation versus behavior therapy: A controlled investigation. Paper presented at the annual meeting of the Association for the Advancement of Behavior Therapy, New York, December, 1976.

Bieman, I. H., *et al.* Client characteristics and success in TM. This volume.

Bennett, J. and Trinder, J. Hemispheric laterality and cognitive style associated with TM. *Psychophysiology*, 1977, **14**(3), 293–6.

Benson, H. Yoga for drug abuse. *New England Journal of Medicine*, 1969, **281**(20), 1133.

Benson, H. *The relaxation response*. New York: William Morrow & Co., 1975.

Benson, H. Reply to Muchlman. *New England Journal of Medicine*, 1977, **297**(9), 513.

Benson, H. and Wallace, R. Decreased blood pressure in hypertensive subjects who practice meditation. *Circulation*, 1972a, Suppl. No. 2, 516.

Benson, H. and Wallace, R. Decreased drug abuse with transcendental meditation: A study of 1862 subjects. In C. J. Zarafonetis (Ed.), *Drug abuse: Proceedings of the international conference*. Phil: Lea & Febiger, 1972b.

Benson, H., Malvea, B. P., and Graham, J. R. Physiologic correlates of meditation and their clinical effects in headache: An ongoing investigation. *Headache*, 1973a, **13**, 23–24.

Benson, H., Rosner, B. A., and Marzetta, B. R. Decreased systolic blood pressure in hypertensive subjects who practiced meditation. *Journal of Clinical Investigation*, 1973b, **52**, 8a.

Benson, H., Beary, J. F., and Carol, M. P. The relaxation response. *Psychiatry*, 1974a, **37**, 37–46.

Benson, H., Rosner, B., Marzetta, B., and Klemchuck, H.M. Decreased blood pressure in borderline hypertensive subjects who practiced meditation. *Journal of Chronic Diseases*, 1974b, **27**, 163–169.

Benson, H., Marzetta, B. R., Rosner, B. A., and Klemchuck, H. M. Decreased blood pressure in pharmacologically treated hypertensive patients who regularly elicited the relaxation response. *Lancet*, 1974c, (7852), 289–91.

Benson, H., Klemchuk, H. P., & Graham, J. R. The usefulness of the relaxation response in the therapy of headache. *Headache*, 1974d, **14**, 49–52.

Benson, H., Steinert, R. F., Greenwood, M. M., Klemchuk, H. M., and Peterson, N. H. Continuous measurement of O_2 consumption and CO_2 elimination during a wakeful, hypometabolic state. *Journal of Human Stress*, 1975, **1**, 37–44.

Benson, H. *et al.* Treatment of anxiety: A comparison of the usefulness of self-hypnosis and a meditational relaxation technique: An overview. *Psychotherapy and Psychosomatics*, 1978, **30**, 229–242.

Benson, H., Lehmann, J. W., Malhotra, M. S., Goodman, R. F., Hopkins, J., & Epstein, M. D. Body temperature changes during the practice of g-tum-mo yoga. *Nature (London)*, 1982, **295**, 234–236.

Berker, E. Stability of skin resistance responses one week after instruction in the transcendental meditation technique. In D. Orme-Johnson and J. Farrow (Eds.), *Scientific research on the Transcendental Meditation program*. Maharishi European Research University Press, 1977.

Berwick, P. and Oziel, L. J. The use of meditation as a behavioral technique. *Behavior Therapy*, 1973, **4**, 743–745.

Blackwell, B., Bloomfield, S., Gantside, P., Robinson, A., Hanenson, I., Magenheim, H., Nidich, S., and Zigler, R. Transcendental meditation in hypertension. *Lancet*, 1976, **31**(1), 223–226.

Blasdell, K. The effect of transcendental meditation on a perceptual motor task. In D. Kanellakos (Comp.) *The psychobiology of transcendental meditation: A literature review*. Menlo Park, CA: W. A. Benjamin, 1974.

Block, B. Transcendental Meditation as a reciprocal inhibitor in psychotherapy. *Journal of Contemporary Psychology*, 1977, **9**(1), 78–82.

Bloomfield, H., Cain, M., and Jaffe, R. *Transcendental meditation: Discovering inner energy and overcoming stress*. NY: Delacorte, 1975.

Boals, G. Toward a cognitive reconceptualization of meditation. *Journal of Transpersonal Psychology*, 1978, **10**(2), 143–182.

Boese and Berger. In D. Kanellakos (Comp.) *The psychobiology of transcendental meditation: A literature review*. Menlo Park, CA: W. A. Benjamin, 1974.

Bono, J. Psychological assessment of transcendental meditation. This volume.

Borkovec, T. D. Physiological and cognitive processes in the regulation of anxiety. In G. E. Schwartz and D. Shapiro (Eds.), *Consciousness and self-regulation: Advances in research*. Vol. 1. New York: Plenum, 1976.

Boswell, P. C. and Murray, G. J. Effects of meditation on psychological and physiological measures of anxiety. *Journal of Consulting and Clinical Psychology*, 1979, **47**(3), 606–607.

Boudreau, L. Transcendental meditation and yoga as reciprocal inhibitors. *Journal of Behavior Therapy and Experimental Psychiatry,* 1972, **3**, 97–8.

Brautigam, E. The effect of transcendental meditation on drug abusers. Research Report, City Hospital of Malmo, Sweden, 1971.

Brosse, T. A psychophysiological study. *Main Currents in Modern Thought,* 1946, **4**, 77–84.

Brown, C., Fischer, R., Wagman, A., & Horrom, B. The EEG in meditation and therapeutic touch healing. *Journal of Altered States of Consciousness,* 1977–78, **3**(2), 169–180.

Brown, D. A model for the levels of concentrative meditation. *International Journal of Clinical and Experimental Hypnosis.* 1977, **25**, 236–273.

Brown, D. P. and Engler, J. The stages of mindfulness meditation: a validation study. *Journal of Transpersonal Psychology,* 1980, **12**(2), 143–192.

Brown, D. and Engler, J. A Rorschach study of the stages of mindfulness meditation. This volume.

Brown, F., Stuart, W., and Blodgett, J. EEG kappa rhythms during transcendental meditation and possible perceptual threshold changes following. In D. Kunellakos (Ed.). *The psychobiology of transcendental meditation.* Menlo Park, CA: W. A. Benjamin, 1974.

Bujatti, M., & Riederer, P. Serotonin, noradrenaline, dopamine metabolites in transcendental meditation. *Journal of Neural Transmission,* 1976, **39**(3), 257–267.

Burns, D. and Ohayv, R. J. Psychological changes in meditating western monks in Thailand. *Journal of Transpersonal Psychology,* 1980, **12**(1), 11–24.

Candelent, T. and Candelent, G. Teaching transcendental meditation in a psychiatric setting. *Hospital and Community Psychiatry,* 1975, **26**(3), 156–159.

Cannon, W. B. *The wisdom of the body.* New York: Norton, 1932.

Capra, R. *Tao of physics.* Berkeley, CA: Shambhalla, 1976.

Carpenter, J. T. Meditation, esoteric traditions—contributions to psychotherapy. *American Journal of Psychotherapy,* 1977, **31**(3), 394–404.

Carr, K. and Woolfolk, F. Active and placebo effects in treatment of moderate and severe insomnia. *Journal of Consulting and Clinical Psychology,* 1979, **47**(6), 1072–1080.

Carrington, P. *Freedom in meditation.* New York: Anchor/Doubleday, 1978.

Carrington, P. and Ephron, H. Meditation as an adjunct to psychotherapy. In S. Arieti & G. Chrzanowski (Eds.), *The world biennial of psychotherapy and psychiatry (III).* New York: Wiley, 1975a.

Carrington, P. and Ephron, H. S. Meditation and psychoanalysis. *Journal of the American Academy of Psychoanalysis,* 1975b, **3**, 43–57.

Carrington, P., & Ephron, H. S. Clinical use of meditation. *Current Psychiatric Theories,* 1975c, **15**, 101–108.

Carruthers, M. E. Voluntary control of the involuntary nervous system: Comparison of autogenic training and siggha meditation. *Experimental & Clinical Psychology,* 1981, **6**, 171–181.

Carsello, C. and Creaser, J. Does TM training affect grades? *Journal of Applied Psychology,* 1978, **63**(5), 644–5.

Cartwright, R. *et al. Night life: explorations in dreaming.* Englewood Cliffs, N.J.: Prentice-Hall, 1977.

Cassel, R. M. Basic fundamentals of mind control and transcendental meditation. *Psychology,* 1974, **11**(2), 28–33.

Cassel, R. M. Fostering transcendental meditation using biofeedback eliminates hoax and restores creditability to art. *Psychology,* 1976, **13**(2), 58–64.

Cassell, R. M. Fundamentals involved in the scientific process of transcendental meditation. *Journal of Instructional Psychology,* 1976, **3**(3), 2–11.

Cauthen, N. and Prymak, C. Meditation versus relaxation. *Journal of Consulting and Clinical Psychology,* 1977, **45**(3), 496–7.

Chang, S. The psychology of consciousness. *American Journal of Psychotherapy,* 1978, **32**(1), 105–16.

Chihara, T. Psychological studies on Zen meditation and time-experience. In Y. Akishige (Ed.). *Psychological studies on Zen.* Tokyo: Zen Institute of Komazawa University, 1977.

Clark, F. V. Transpersonal perspectives in psychotherapy. *Journal of Humanistic Psychology,* 1977, **17**(2), 69–81.

Cohen, W. Spatial and textural characteristics of the ganzfeld, *American Journal of Psychology,* 1957, **70**, 403–410.

Connor, W. H. Effects of brief relaxation training on automatic response to anxiety-evoking stimuli. *Psychophysiology,* 1974, **11**(5), 591–99.

Cooper, M. J., & Aygen, M. M. Effect of meditation on serum cholesterol & blood pressure. *Journal of the Israel Medical Association,* 1978, **95**(1), 1–2.

Cooper, M. J. and Aygen, M. M. A relaxation technique in the management of hypercholesterolemia. *Journal of Human Stress,* 1979, **5**(4), 24–27.

Conze, E. *Buddhist meditation,* New York: Harper & Row, 1969.

Corby, J. C., Roth, W. T., Zarcone, V. P., and Kopell, B. S. Psychophysiological correlates of the practice of Tantric Yoga meditation. *Archives of General Psychiatry,* 1978, **35**, 571–580.

Cox, D. J., Freundlich, A., & Meyer, R. G. Differential effectiveness of feedback, verbal relaxation instructions & meditation placebo for tension headaches. *Journal of Consulting & Clinical Psychology,* 1975, **43**, 892–898.

Credidio, S. G. Comparative effectiveness of patterned biofeedback vs meditation training on EMG and skin temperature changes. *Behavior Research & Therapy,* 1982, **20**(3), 233–241.

Crick, B. Meditation on socialism and 9 theories. *Political Quarterly,* 1980, **51**(1), 84–97.

Curtis, W. D. and Wessberg, H. W. A comparison of heart rate, respiration, and galvanic skin response among meditators, relaxers, and controls. *Journal of Altered States of Consciousness,* 1975/6, **2**, 319–24.

Cuthbert, B., Kristeller, J., Simons, R., Hodes, R., & Lang, P. J. Strategies of arousal control: Biofeedback, Meditation & Motivation. *Journal of Experimental Psychology—General,* 1981, **110**(4), 518–546.

Dalal, A. and Barber, T. Yoga, "yogic feats," and hypnosis in the light of empirical research. *American Journal of Clinical Hypnosis,* 1969, **11**, 155–166.

Bibliography 701

Daniels, L. Treatment of psychophysiological disorders and severe anxiety by behavior therapy, hypnosis and transcendental meditation. *American Journal of Clinical Hypnosis,* 1975, **17**(4), 267–70.

Das, J. Yoga and hypnosis. *International Journal of Clinical and Experimental Hypnosis,* 1963, **11**, 31–37.

Das, H. and Gastaut, H. Variations de l'activité electrique du cerveau, et du couer et des muscles squelettiques au cours de la meditation et de l' extase yogique. *Electroencephalography and Clinical Neurophysiology,* 1955, Suppl. No. 6, 211–19.

Datey, K. K., Deshmukh, S. N., Dalvi, C. P., and Vinekar, S. L. "Shavasan": a yogic exercise in the management of hypertension. *Angiology,* 1969, **20**, 325–333.

Davidson, J. Physiology of meditation and mystical states of consciousness. *Perspectives in Biology and Medicine,* 1976, **19**, 345–80.

Davidson, R. and Goleman, D. The role of attention in meditation and hypnosis: A psychobiological perspective on transformation of consciousness. *International Journal of Clinical and Experimental Hypnosis,* 1977, **25**(4), 291–308

Davidson, R. and Schwartz, G. The psychobiology of relaxation and related states: A multi-process theory. In D.I. Mostofsky (Ed.), *Behavior control and the modification of physiological activity.* New York: Prentice-Hall, 1976.

Davidson, R., Goleman, D. and Schwartz, G. Attentional and affective concomitants of meditation: A cross-sectional study. *Journal of Abnormal Psychology,* 1976, **85**, 235–308.

Davidson, R., Schwartz, D., and Rothman, L. Attentional style under self-regulation of mode specific attention: An electroencephalographic study. *Journal of Abnormal Psychology.* 1976, **85**, 611–21.

Davies, J. The transcendental meditation program and progressive relaxation: Comparative effects on trait anxiety and self-actualization. In D. Orme-Johnson and J. Farrow (Eds.), *Scientific research on the transcendental meditation program.* Vol. 1, 2nd Ed. Maharishi European University, 1977.

Deathridge, G. The clinical use of mindfulness meditation techniques in short-term psychotherapy. *Journal of Transpersonal Psychology,* 1975, **7**(2), 133–43.

DeBont, H. G. Transcendental meditation: a critical view. *Tijdschrift voor Psychotherapie,* 1980, **6**(1), 1–11.

deGrace, G. Effect of meditation on personality and values. *Journal of Clinical Psychology,* 1976, **32**(4), 809–13.

Deikman, A. J. Experimental meditation. *Journal of Nervous and Mental Diseases,* 1963, **136**, 329–373.

Deikman, A. J. Deautomatization and the mystic experience. *Psychiatry,* 1966, **29**, 324–38.

Deikman, A. J. Implications of experimentally produced contemplative meditation. *Journal of Nervous and Mental Disease,* 1966, **142**, 101–16.

Deikman, A. J. Bimodal consciousness. *Archives of General Psychiatry,* 1971, **25**, 481–489.

Deikman, A. J. The state-of-the art of meditation. This volume.

Deliz, A. J. Meditation, protein, diet, and megavitamins in the treatment of a progressive, iatrogenic cardiac psychotic condition. *Journal of Orthomolecular Psychiatry,,* 1977, **6**(1), 44–49.

Delmonte, M. M. Pilot study of conditioned relaxation during simulated meditation. *Psychological Reports,* 1979, **45**, 169–170.

Delmonte, M. M. Personality characteristics and regularity of meditation. *Psychological Reports,* 1980, **46**(3, part 1), 703–712.

Delmonte, M. M. Expectation & meditation. *Psychological Reports,* 1981a, **49**(3), 699–709.

Delmonte, M. M. Suggestibility & meditation. *Psychological Reports,* 1981b, **48**(3), 727–737.

Dhammapada. English. *The Dhammapada.* Tr. Byrom. 1st Ed. New York: Knopf, 1976.

Dhanaraj, H. and Singh, M. Reduction in metabolic rate during the practice of the TM technique. In D. Orme-Johnson and J. Farrow (Eds.), *Scientific research on the transcendental meditation program.* Vol. 1, 2nd Ed. Maharishi European University Press, 1977.

DiGiusto, G. L. and Bond, N. W. Imagery and the autonomic nervous system: Some methodological issues. *Perceptual and Motor Skills,* 1979, **48**, 427–438.

Dillbeck, M. The effect of the transcendental meditation technique on anxiety level. *Journal of Clinical Psychology,* 1977, **33**(11), 1076–1078.

Dillbeck, M. C., & Bronson, E. C. Short-term longitudinal effects on the Transcendental Meditation technique on EEG power & coherence. *International Journal of Neuroscience,* 1981, **14**, 147–151.

Dillbeck, M. C., Aron, A. P., and Dillbeck, S. L. Transcendental meditation program as an educational technology research and applications. *Educational Technology,* 1979, **19**(11), 7–13.

Dillbeck, M. C., Orme-Johnson, D. W., and Wallace, R. K. Frontal EEG coherence, H-reflect recovery, concept learning and the TM-Sidhi program. *International Journal of Neuroscience,* 1981, **15**, 151–157.

Di Nardo, P. and Raymond, J. Locus of control and attention during meditation. *Journal of Consulting and Clinical Psychology,* 1979, **47**(6), 1136–1137.

Doi, M. Psychological study of the relation between respiratory function and mental self-control. In Y. Akishige (Ed.), *Psychological studies in Zen.* Tokyo: Zen Institute of Komazawa University, 1977.

Domino, G. Transcendental Meditation & creativity: An empirical investigation. *Journal of Applied Psychology,* 1977, **62**(3), 358–362.

Don, N. Transformation of conscious experience and its EEG correlates. *Journal of Altered States of Consciousness,* 1977–8, **3**(2), 147–68.

Dostalek, C. *et al.* Meditational yoga exercises in EEG and EMG. *Ceskoslovenska Psychologie,* 1979, **23**(1), 61–65.

Dostalek, C., Faber, J., Krasa, H., Roldan, E., and Vele, F. Yoga meditation effect on the EEG and EMG activity. *Activitas Nervosa Superior,* 1979, **21**(1), 41.

Dostalek, C., Roldan, E., and Lepicovska, V. EEG changes in the course of hatha-yogic exercises intended for meditation. *Activitas Nervos Superior,* 1980, **22**(2). 123–124.

Dukhan, H. and Rao, K. Meditation and ESP scoring. In M. and J. Morris (Eds.), *Research in parapsychology.* Metuchen, NJ: Scarecrow, 1973.

Dwivedi, K. N., Gupta, V. M., & Udupa, K. N. A preliminary report on some physiological changes due to Vipashyana meditation. *Indian Journal of Medical Science,* 1977, **31**(3), 51–54.

Earle, J. B. Cerebral laterality and meditation: A review of the literature. *Journal of Transpersonal Psychology,* 1981, **13**(2), 155–173.

Editorial: meditation or methyldopa? *British Medical Journal,* 1976, **1**(6023), 1421–1422.

Ehrlich, M. P. Family meditation. *Journal of Family Counseling,* 1976, **4**(2), 40–45.

Elkins, D., Anchor, K. N., and Sandler, H. M. Relaxation training and braver behavior as tension reduction techniques. *Behavioral Engineering*, 1979, **5**(3), 81–87.

Ellis, A. The place of meditation in cognitive and rational emotive therapy. This volume.

Elson, B. Ananda-Marga meditation. *Archives of General Psychiatry*, 1979, **36**(5), 605–606.

Elson, B., Hauri, P., and Cunis, D. Physiological changes in yoga meditation. *Psychophysiology*, 1977, **14**, 52–7.

Emerson, V. Can belief systems influence neurophysiology? Some implications of research on meditation. In T. Barber (Ed.), *Advances in altered states of consciousness and human potentialities*. NY: Psychological Dimensions, 1976.

Epstein, M. D., & Lieff, J. D. Psychiatric complications of meditation practice. *Journal of Transpersonal Psychology*, 1981, **13**(2), 137–147.

Eyerman, J. Transcendental meditation and mental retardation. *Journal of Clinical Psychiatry*, 1981, **42**(1), 35–36.

Faber, P. A., Saayman, G. S., and Touyz, W. Meditation and archetypal content of nocturnal dreams. *Journal of Analytic Psychology*, 1978, **23**(1), 1–22.

Fahmy, J. A. and Fledulisu, H. Yoga-induced attacks of acute glaucoma. *Acta Opthalmologica*, 1973, **51**, 80–84.

Farge, E. J., Hartung, G. H., and Borland, C. M. Runners and meditators: a comparison of personality profiles. *Journal of Personality assessment*, 1979, **43**(5), 501–503.

Farrow, J. Physiological changes associated with transcendental consciousness. In D. Orme-Johnson and J. Farrow (Eds.), *Scientific research on the transcendental meditation program*. Vol. 1, 2nd Ed. Maharishi European Research University Press, 1977.

Farrow, J. T., & Hebert, J. R. Breath suspension during the Transcendental Meditation technique. *Psychosomatic Medicine*, 1982, **44**(2), 133–153.

Fee, R. A. and Girdano, D. A. The relative effectiveness of three techniques to induce the trophotrophic response. *Biofeedback and Self-Regulation*, 1978, **3**(2), 145–157.

Fehr, T. Longitudinal study of the effect of the transcendental meditation program on changes in personality. In D. Orme-Johnson and J. Farrow (Eds.), *Scientific research on the transcendental meditation program*. Vol. I, 2nd Ed. Maharishi European Research University Press, 1977.

Fehr, T., Nerstheimer, U., and Torber, S. Study of changes resulting from the transcendental meditation program. In D. Orme-Johnson and J. Farrow (Eds.), *Scientific research on the transcendental meditation program*. Vol. I, 2nd Ed. Maharishi European Research University Press, 1977.

Fenwick, P. B., Donaldson, S., Gillis, L., Bushman, J., Fenton, G. W., Perry, I., Tilsley, C., & Serafinowicz, H. Metabolic and EEG changes during Transcendental Meditation: An explanation. *Biological Psychology*, 1977a, **5**(2), 101–118.

Fenwick, P. B. C., Donaldson, S., Gillis, L., Bushman, J., Fenton, G. W., Perry, I., Tilsley, C., and Serafinowicz, H. Metabolic and EEG changes during transcendental meditation: an explanation. *Biological Psychology*, 1977b, **5**, 101–118.

Fenz, W. D. and Plapp, J. M. Voluntary control of heart rate in a practitioner of yoga: Negative findings. *Perceptual and Motor Skills*, 1970, **30**, 493–494.

Ferguson, P. Psychobiology of TM: A review. *Journal of Altered States of Consciousness*, 1975, **2**(1), 15–36.

Ferguson, P. TM and its potential application in the field of special education. *Journal of Special Education*, 1976, **10**(2), 211–20.

Ferguson, P. O. and Gowan, J. C. Transcendental meditation: Some preliminary findings. *Journal of Humanistic Psychology*, 1976, **16**(3), 51–60.

Fiebert, M. S. Responsiveness to an introductory meditation method. *Perceptual and Motor Skills*, 1977, **45**(3, part 1), 849–50.

Fiebert, M. S., & Mead, T. M. Meditation and academic performance. *Perceptual & Motor Skills*, 1981, **53**(2), 447–450.

Fischer, R. Transformations of consciousness: A cartography. II: The perception-meditation continuum. *Confina Psychiatrica*, 1976, **19**(1), 1–23.

Fischer, R. A. cartography of the ecstatic and meditative states. *Science*, 1971, **174**, 897–904.

Fling, S., Thomas A., & Gallaher, M. Participant characteristics & the effects of two types of meditation vs. quiet sitting. *Journal of Clinical Psychology*, 1981, **37**(4), 748–790.

Frank, J. D. Nature and functions of belief systems: Humanism and transcendental religion. *American Psychologist*, 1977, **32**(7), 555–9.

Frankel, B. L. TM & Hypertension. *Lancet*, 1976, **1**(7959), 589.

Franks, J. *Persuasion and healing*. New York: Schocken Books, 1963.

French, A. P. and Tupin, J. Therapeutic application of a simple relaxation method. *American Journal of Psychotherapy*, 1974, **28**(2), 282–287.

French, A. P., Smid, A. C., and Ingalls, E. Transcendental Meditation, altered reality testing and behavioral change: A case report. *Journal of Nervous and Mental Disease*, 1975, **161**, 55–58.

Frew, D. Transcendental meditation and productivity. *Academy of Management Journal*, 1974, **17**, 362–368.

Fromm, E. *Zen Buddhism and psychoanalysis*. NY: Harper & Row, 1960.

Frumkin, L. R. and Pagano, R. R. The effect of transcendental meditation on iconic memory. *Biofeedback and Self-regulation*, 1979, **4**(4), 313–322.

Fujisawa, K., Koga, E., and Toyoda, G. The polygraphical study on the psychogenic changes of consciousness (1). *Electroencephalography and Clinical Neurophysiology*, 1959, Suppl. No. 18, 51.

Galanter, M. and Buckley, P. Evangelic religion and meditation: Psychotherapeutic effects. *Journal of Nervous and Mental Disease*, 1978, **166**(10), 685–691.

Galin, D. Implications for psychiatry of left and right cerebral specialization. *Archives of General Psychiatry*, 1974, **31**, 572–83.

Gash, A. and Karliner, J. S. No effect of transcendental meditation on left ventricular function. *Annals of Internal Medicine*, 1978, **88**(2), 215–216.

Gellhorn, E. and Kiely, W. Mystical states of consciousness. *Journal of Nervous and Mental Disease*, 1972, **154**, 399–405.

Gersten, D. J. Meditation as an adjunct to medical and psychiatric treatment. *American Journal of Psychiatry*, 1978, **135**(5), 598–599.

Ghista, D. N., Mukherji, A., Nandagopal, D., Srinivasan, T. M., Ramanurthi, B., & Das, A. Psychological characteristics of the "meditative state" during intuitional practice (the Ananda Marga system of meditation) & its therapeutic value. *Medical & Biological Engineering*, 1976, **14**(2), 209–213.

Bibliography

Ghosh, H. K. Anxiety, fear and meditation. *Medical Journal of Australia*, 1981, **1**(7), 375.

Gilbert, G. S., Parker, J. C., and Claiborn, C. D. Differential mood changes in alcoholics as a function of anxiety management strategies. *Journal of Clinical Psychology*, 1978, **34**(11), 229–232.

Girodo, M. Yoga meditation and flooding in the treatment of anxiety neurosis. *Journal of Behavior Therapy and Experimental Psychiatry*, 1974, **5**, 157–60.

Glueck, B. and Stroebel, C. Biofeedback and meditation in the treatment of psychiatric illness. *Comprehensive Psychiatry*, 1975, **16**(4), 303–21.

Goldman, B. L., Domitor, P. J., and Murray, E. J. Effects of Zen meditation on anxiety reduction and perceptual functioning. *Journal of Consulting and Clinical Psychology*, 1979, **47**(3), 551–56.

Goldstein, J. *Experience of insight: A natural unfolding*. Santa Cruz, CA: Unity Press, 1976.

Goleman, D. Meditation as meta-therapy: Hypotheses toward a proposed fifth state of consciousness. *Journal of Transpersonal Psychology*, 1971, **3**(1), 1–25.

Goleman, D. The Buddha on meditation and states of consciousness, Part I: The teachings, *The Journal of Transpersonal Psychology*, 1972, **4**(1), 1–43.

Goleman, D. The Buddha on meditation and states of consciousness, Part II: A typology of meditation techniques. *Journal of Transpersonal Psychology*, 1972, **4**(2), 151–210.

Goleman, D. Meditation & consciousness: An Asian approach to mental health. *American Journal of Psychotherapy*, 1976, **30**(1), 41–54.

Goleman, D. *The varieties of the meditative experience*. New York: E. P. Dutton, 1977.

Goleman, D. A taxonomy of meditation-specific altered states. *Journal of Altered States of Consciousness*, 1979, **4**(2), 203–213.

Goleman, D. and Schwartz, G. Meditation as an intervention in stress reactivity. *Journal of Consulting and Clinical Psychology*, 1976, **44**, 456–466.

Gowan, J. C. The facilitation of creativity through meditational procedures. *Journal of Creative Behavior*, 1978, **12**(3), 156–160.

Goyeche, J., Chihara, T., and Shimizu, H. Two concentration methods: A preliminary comparison. *Psychologia*, 1972, **15**, 110–111.

Grace, G. D. Effects of meditaton on personality and values. *Journal of Clinical Psychology*, 1976, **32**(4), 809–813.

Graham, J. Effects of transcendental meditation upon auditory thresholds, In D. Johnson, L. Domash, J. Farrow (Eds.). *Scientific Research on the Transcendental Meditation Program*. Switzerland: MIU Press, 175, Vol. 1.

Green, E. and Green, A. *Beyond Biofeedback*. New York: Delacorte, 1977.

Green, E., Green, A., and Walters, E. Voluntary control of internal states: Psychological and physiological. *Journal of Transpersonal Psychology*, 1970, **2**, 1–26.

Griffith, F. Meditation research: Its personal and social implications. In J. White (Ed.), *Frontiers of consciousness*. New York: Julian, 1974.

Grim, P. F. Relaxation, meditation, and insight. *Psychologia, 1975*, **18**, 125–33.

Group for the Advancement of Psychiatry. *Mysticism: Spiritual quest or psychic disorder?* Washington, D.C.: Group for the Advancement of Psychiatry, 1977.

Gruber, L. Simple techniques to relieve anxiety. *Journal of Family Practice*, 1977, **5**(4), 641–644.

Gundu, Rao, H. V., Krishnaswamy, N., Narasimhaiya, R. L., Hoenig, J., and Gouindaswamy, M. V. Some experiments on a Yogi in controlled states. *Pratibha, Journal of the All India Institute for Mental Health*, 1958, **1**, 99–106.

Hager, J. L. and Surwit, R. S. Hypertension self-control with a portable feedback unit or meditation-relaxation. *Biofeedback and Self-Regulation*, 1978, **3**(3), 269–275.

Haimes, N. Zen Buddism and psychoanalysis. *Psychologia*, 1972, **15**, 22–30.

Hanley, C. and Spates, J. Transcendental meditation and social psychological attitudes. *Journal of Psychology*, 1978, **99** (part II), 121–127.

Hastings, A., Fadiman, J., and Gordon, J. S. (Eds.) *Holistic medicine*. Rockville, MD: NIMH, 1980.

Hardt, J. V. et al. Studying power. Zen meditation. *Biofeedback and Self-Regulation*, 1976, **1**, 362–63.

Haynes, C. Psychophysiology of advanced participants in the transcendental meditation program. In D. Orme-Johnson and J. Farrow (Eds.), *Scientific research on the transcendental meditation program*. Vol. I, 2nd Ed. Maharishi European Research University Press, 1977.

Heaton, D. and Orme-Johnson, D. W. The transcendental meditation program and academic achievement. In D. Orme-Johnson and J. Farrow (Eds.), *Scientific research on the transcendental meditation program*. Vol. I, 2nd Ed. Maharishi European Research University Press, 1977.

Heide, F. J. Habituation of alpha blocking during meditation. *Psychophysiology*, 1979, **16**(2), 198.

Heide, F. J., Wadlington, W. L., and Lundy, R. M. Hypnotic responsivity as a predictor of outcome in meditation, *International Journal of Clinical and Experimental Hypnosis*, 1980, **28**(4), 358–366.

Hendlin, S. J. T'ai Chi Chaun and gestalt therapy. *Journal of Contemporary Psychotherapy,*1978, **10**(1), 25–31.

Hendricks, C. G. Meditation as discrimination training. *Journal of Transpersonal Psychology*, 1975, **7**(2), 144–6.

Herbert, R. and Lehmann, D. Theta bursts: An EGG pattern in normal subjects practicing the transcendental meditation technique. *Electroencephalography and Clinical Neurophysiology*, 1977, **42**, 387–405.

Herrigel, E. *Zen in the art of archery*. NY: McGraw Hill, 1953. (Now entitled *Method of Zen*.)

Hesse, H. *Siddhartha*. New York: New Directions Books, 1951.

Hewitt, J., & Miller, R. Relative effects of meditation vs. other activities on ratings of relaxation and enjoyment of others. *Psychological Reports*, 1981, **48**(2), 395–398.

Hirai, T. Electroencephalographic study on Zen meditation (Zazen): EEG changes during the concentrated relaxation). *Psychiatria Neurologia Japonica*, 1960, **62**(1), 76–105. (Jap.)

Hirai, T. *Psychophysiology of Zen*. Tokyo: Igaku Shin Ltd., 1974.

Hirai, T. *Zen meditation therapy*. Tokyo: Japan Publications, 1975.

Hirai, T. *Zen and the mind: scientific approach to Zen practice*. Tokyo: Japan Publications, 1978.

Hirai, T. and Watanabe, T. Biofeedback and electrodermal self-regulation in a Zen meditator. *Psychophysiology, 1977,* **14,** 103 (Abstr.).

Hirai, T., Izawa, S., and Koga, E. EEG and Zen Buddhism: EEG changes in the course of meditation. *Electroencephalography and Clinical Neurophysiology, 1959,* Suppl. No. 18, 52–53.

Hjelle, L. A. Transcendental meditation and psychological health. *Perceptual and Motor Skills, 1974,* **39,** 623–8.

Hoenig, I. Medical research on yoga. *Confinia Psychiatrica (Basel), 1968,* **11,** 69–89.

Holeman, R. and Seiler, G. Effects of sensitivity training and transcendental meditation on the perceptions of others. *Perceptual and Motor Skills, 1979,* **49**(1), 270.

Holt, R. R., Imagery: The return of the ostracized. *American Psychologist, 1964,* **19,** 254–264.

Holt, W. R., Caruso, J. L., and Riley, J. B. Transcendental meditation vs. pseudo-meditation on visual choice reaction time. *Perceptual and Motor Skills, 1978,* **46,** 726.

Honsberger, R. and Wilson, A. P. Transcendental meditation in treating asthma. *Respiratory Therapy: Journal of Inhalation Technology, 1973,* **3,** 79–81

Horowitz, M. J. *Image formation and cognition.* New York: Appleton-Century-Crofts, 1970.

Ikegami, R. Psychological study of Zen posture. *Bulletin of the Faculty of Literature of Kyushu University, 1968,* **5,** 105–35.

Jacobs, R. G., Kraemer, H. C., and Agras, W. S. Relaxation therapy in the treatment of hypertension: A Review. *Archives of General Psychiatry, 1977,* **34,** 1417–1427.

Jacobson, E. The two methods of tension control and certain basic techniques in anxiety tension control. In J. Kamiya, T. Barber, L. V. DiCara, N. E. Miller, D. Shapiro, and J. Stoyva (Eds.). *Biofeedback and self-control: An Aldine annual on the regulation of body processes and consciousness.* Chicago, Ill.: Aldine-Atherton, 1971.

Jacobson, E. *Progressive relaxation.* Chicago: University of Chicago Press, 1929.

James, W. *The varieties of religious experience.* New York: Longmans, 1901.

Janby, J. Immediate effects of the transcendental meditation technique: increased skin resistance during the first meditation after instruction. In D. Orme-Johnson and J. Farrow (Eds.), *Scientific research on the transcendental meditation program.* Vol. I. 2nd Ed. Maharishi European Research University Press, 1977.

Jevning, R., et al. Alterations in blood flow during transcendental meditation. *Psychophysiology, 1976,* **13**(2), 168. [Abstr.]

Jevning, R. and Halloran, J. P. Metabolic effects of transcendental meditation: Toward a new paradigm of neurobiology. This volume.

Jevning, R. and Wilson, A. F. Altered red cell metabolism in transcendental meditation. *Psychophysiology, 1977,* **14**(1), 94. (Abstr.)

Jevning, R., Wilson, A., Vanderloan, E. & Levine, S. Plasma prolactin and cortisol during transcendental meditation. *The Endocrine Society Program 57th Annual Meeting, 1975,* 257. (Abstr.)

Jevning, R., Wilson, A., and Smith, W. Plasma amino acids during the transcendental meditation technique: Comparison to sleep. In D. Orme-Johnson and J. Farrow (Eds.), *Scientific research on the transcendental meditation program.* Vol. I. 2nd Ed. Maharishi European Research University Press, 1977.

Jevning, R., Wilson, A., and Vanderlaan, E. Plasma prolactin and growth hormone during meditation. *Psychosomatic Medicine, 1978,* **40**(4), 329–33.

Jevning, R. I., Wilson, A. F., and Davidson, J. M. Adrenocortical activity during meditation. *Hormones and Behavior. 1978,* **10**(1), 54–60.

Jevning, R., Wilson, A. F., and Smith, W. R. The transcendental technique, adrenocortical activity, and implications for stress. *Experientia 1978,* **34**(5), 618–619.

Jung, C. (1947) Foreword. In D. T. Suzuki. *Introduction to Zen.* New York: Random House, 1964.

Kabat-Zinn, J. An outpatient program in behavioral medicine for chronic pain patients based on the practice of mindfulness meditation, theoretical considerations & preliminary results. *General Hospital Psychiatry, 1982,* **4,** 33–47.

Kaivalyadhama Shreeman Madhava Yoga Mandira Samiti. Experiments on Pranayama: Bhastrika Pranayama. Effect on urinary acid excretion and pH. *Yoga-Mimamsa, 1956,* **6,** 9–18

Kaivalyadhama Shreeman Madhava Yoga Mandira Samiti. Studies in alveolar air, I: carbon dioxide concentration in different parts of the alveolar air samples. *Yoga-Mimamsa, 1956,* **6,** 99–105.

Kaivalyadhama Shreeman Madhava Yoga Mandira Samiti. Studies in alveolar air, II: variation in composition of different parts of resting alveolar air. *Yoga-Mimamsa, 1957,* **7,** 9–17.

Kaivalyadhama Shreeman Madhava Yoga Mandira Samiti. Studies in alveolar air, III: carbon dioxide concentration in resting alveolar air. *Yoga-Mimamsa, 1957,* **7,** 79–86.

Kaivalyadhama Shreeman Madhava Yoga Mandira Samiti. Studies in alveolar air at the end of two minutes Kapalabhati. *Yoga-Maimamsa, 1957,* **7,** 18–25.

Kaivalyadhama Shreeman Madhava Yoga Mandira Samiti. Studies in alveolar air in Kapalabhati, II: alveolar air at the end of five minutes Kapalabhati. *Yoga-Mimamsa, 1957,* **7,** 87–94.

Kambe, T., Sato, K., and Naggua, K. Medical and psychological studies on Zen. *Proceedings of 25th Convention of J.P.A. 1961,* p. 287.

Kamiya, J. Conscious control of brain waves. *Psychology Today, 1968,* **1**(1), 57-60.

Kamiya, J. A fourth dimension of consciousness. *Experimental Medicine and Surgery, 1969,* **27,** 13–18.

Kamiya, J. Autoregulation of the EEG alpha rhythm: A program for the study of consciousness. In M. H. Chase (Ed.), *Operant control of brain activity.* LA: Brain Information Service, Brain Research Institute, U.C.L.A., 1974.

Kamiya, J. Operant control of the EEG alpha rhythm . . . consciousness. In C. Tart (Ed.), *Altered States of Consciousness.* NY: Julian, 1969.

Kanas, N. and Horowitz, M. Reactions of TMers and non-meditators to stress films. *Archives of General Psychiatry, 1977,* **34**(12), 1431–36.

Kanellakos, D. P., and Lukas, J. D. *The psychobiology of transcendental meditation: A literature review.* Menlo Park, Calif.: Benjamin, 1974.

Kaplan, S. An appraisal of a psychological approach to meditation. zygon. *Journal of Religion and Science, 1978,* **13**(1), 83–101.

Bibliography

Kapleau, A. *Three pillars of Zen*. Boston, MA: Beacon Press, 1967.

Karambelkar, P., Vinekar, S., and Bhole, M. Studies on human subjects staying in an air-tight pit. *Indian Journal of Medical Research*, 1968, **56**, 1282–88.

Karambelkar, P., Bhole, M., and Gharotte, M. Effect of yogic asanas on uropepsin excretion. *Indian Journal of Medical Research*, 1969, **57**, 944–947.

Karambelkar, P., Bhole, M., and Gharotte, M. Muscle activity in some asanas. *Yoga-Mimamsa*, 1969, **12**, 1–13.

Kasamatsu, A. and Hirai, T. Science of Zazen. *Psychologia*, 1963, **6**, 86–91.

Kasamatsu, A. and Hirai, T. An electroencephalographic study on the Zen meditation (zazen). *Psychologia*, 1969, **12**, 205–25.

Kasamatsu, A., Okuma, T., Takenaka, S., Koga, E., Ikada, K., and Sugiyama, H. The EEG of 'Zen' and 'Yoga' practitioners. *Electroencephalography and Clinical Neurophysiology*, 1957, Suppl. No. 9, 51–2.

Kasamatsu, A., Hirai, T., and Ando, N. EEG responses to click stimulation in Zen meditation. *Proceedings of the Japanese EEG Society*, 1962, pp. 77–78.

Kasamatsu, A., Hirai, T., and Izawa, H. Medical and psychological studies on Zen. *Proceedings of the 26th Convention of J.P.A.*, 1962.

Keefe, T. Meditation and the psychotherapist. *American Journal of Orthopsychiatry*, 1975, **45**(3), 484–9.

Keutzer, C. Whatever turns you on: Triggers to transcendent experiences, *Journal of Humanistic Psychology*, 1978, **18**(3), 77–80.

Kiefer, D. EEG alpha feedback and subjective states of consciousness. In C. White (Ed.), *Frontiers of consciousness*, NY: Julian, 1974.

Kielly, W. F. Critique of mystical states: A reply. *Journal of Nervous & Mental Diseases*, 1974, **159**(3), 196–197.

Kim, Y. M. Meditation and behavioral therapy. *Interciencia*, 1980, **5**(3), 157–158.

Kindler, H. S. The influence of a meditation relaxation technique on group problem solving effectiveness. *Journal of Applied Behavioral Science*, 1979, **15**(4), 527–533.

Kirkland, K. and Hollandsworth, J. G. Effective test taking: skills acquisition versus anxiety reduction techniques. *Journal of Consulting and Clinical Psychology*, 1980, **48**(4), 431–439.

Kirsch, I. and Henry, I. Self-desensitization and meditation in the reduction of public speaking anxiety. *Journal of Consulting and Clinical Psychology*, 1979, **47**(3), 536–41.

Kline, K. S., Docherty, E. M., & Farley, F. H. TM, self-actualization & global personality. *Journal of General Psychology*, 1982, **106**(1), 3–8.

Kobal, G., Wandohoefer, A., & Plattig, K. H. EEG power spectra and auditory evoked potentials in transcendental meditation. *Pflueger's Archiv.*, 1975, **359**, R96.

Kohr, E. Dimensionality in the meditative experience: A replication. *Journal of Transpersonal Psychology*. 1977, **9**(2), 193–203.

Kohr, R. L. Changes in subjective meditation experience during a short term meditation project. *Journal of Altered States of Consciousness*, 1977–8, **3**(3), 221–234.

Kolsawalla, M. B. An experimental investigation into the effectiveness of some yogic variables as a mechanism of change in the value attitude system. *Journal of Indian Psychology*, 1978, **1**(1), 59–68.

Kondo, A. Zen in psychotherapy. *Chicago Review*, 1958, **12**, 57–64.

Kornfield, J. Meditation: Aspects of research and practice. *Journal of Transpersonal Psychology*, 1978, **2**, 122–124.

Kornfield, J. Intensive insight meditation: A phenomenological study. *Journal of Transpersonal Psychology*, 1979, **11**, 41–58.

Kothari, L. K., Bordia, A., and Gupta, O. P. The yogic claim of voluntary control over the heart beat: An unusual demonstration. *American Heart Journal*, 1973, **86**, 282–284.

Krahne, W., & Tenoli, G. EEG and Transcendental Meditation. *Pflueger's Archiv.*, 1975, **359**, R93.

Kras, D. Transcendental meditation technique and EEG alpha activity. In D. Orme-Johnson and J. Farrow (Eds.), *Scientific research on the transcendental meditation program*. Vol. I, 2nd Ed. Maharishi European Research University Press, 1977.

Kretschmer, W. Meditative techniques in psychotherapy. In C. Tart (Ed.), *Altered states of consciousness*. New York: Wiley, 1969.

Krippner, S. and Maliszewski, M. Meditation and the creative process. *Journal of Indian Psychology*, 1978, **1**, 40–58.

Krishnamurti, J. *Commentaries on living: Third series*. Ed. D. Rajagopal. Wheaton: Theosophical, 1967.

Krishnamurti, J. *The only revolution*. NY: Harper & Row, 1970.

Krishnamurti, J. *Meditation*. Ojai, CA: Krishnamurti Foundation, 1979.

Kristeller, J. L. Heart rate slowing: biofeedback vs. meditation. In Oborne, D. (Ed.), *Research in psychology and medicine*. London, Academic Press, 1979, Vol. I, 486 pp.

Kubose, S. K. An experimental investigation of psychological aspects of meditaton. *Psychologia*, 1976, **19**(1), 1–10.

Lang, R., Dehof, K., Meurer, K. A., and Kaufman, W. Sympathetic activity and transcendental meditation. *Journal of Neural Transmission*, 1979, **44**, 117–135.

Lao-tzu. *Tao Te Ching*. (Transl. G. Feng and J. English). New York: Vintage, 1973.

Laubry, C. and Brosse, T. Data gathered in India on a yogi with simultaneous registration of the pulse, respiration, and electocardiogram. *Presse Medicale*, 1963, **44**, 1601–1604. (Fr.)

Laurie, G. An investigation into the changes in skin resistance during the transcendental meditation technique. In D. Orme-Johnson and J. Farrow (Eds.), *Scientific research on the transcendental meditation program*. Vol. I, 2nd Ed. Maharishi European Research University Press, 1977.

Lazar, Z., Farwell, L., and Farrow, J. Effects of transcendental meditation program on anxiety, drug abuse, cigarette smoking and alcohol consumption. In D. Orme-Johnson and J. Farrow (Eds.), *Scientific Research on the Transcendental Meditation program*. Vol. I, 2nd Ed. Maharishi European Research University Press, 1977.

Lazarus, A. A. Psychiatric problems precipitated by transcendental meditation. *Psychological Reports*, 1976, **10**, 39–74.

Lazarus, A. Meditation: The problem of any unimodal technique. This volume.

Lefcourt, H. M. Internal versus external control of reinforcement: A review. *Psychological Bulletin*, 1966, **65**, 206–220.

Lefcourt, H. M. Belief in personal control. *Journal of Individual Psychology*, 1966, **22**(2), 185–95.

Legrand, P., Toubol, M., Barrabino, J., Darcourt, G., and Fadeuilhe, A. Contingent negative variation in meditation. *Electroencephalography and Clinical Neurophysiology*, 1977, **43**, 532–533. (Abstr.)

Lehmann, D. *et al.* Changes in patterns of the human EEG during fluctuations of perception of stabilized retinal images. *Electroencephalography and Clinical Neurophysiology,* 1965, **19**, 336–43.

Lehmann, D. *et al.* EEG responses during the observation of stabilized and normal retinal images. *Electroencephalography and Clinical Neurophysiology,* 1967, **22**, 136–42.

Lehrer, P. M., Schoicket, S., Carrington, P., and Woolfolk, R. L. Psychophysiological and cognitive responses to stressful stimuli in subjects practicing progressive relaxation and clinically standardized meditation. *Behavior Research and Therapy,*, 1980, **18**(4), 293–303.

Lesh, T. Zen meditation and the development of empathy in counselors. *Journal of Humanistic Psychology,* 1970, **10**(1), 39–74.

Lesh, T. V. Zen and psychotherapy: A partially annotated bibliography. *Journal of Humanistic Psychology,* 1970, **10**, 75–83.

Leung, P. Comparative effects of training in external and internal concentration on two counseling behaviors. *Journal of Counseling Psychology,* 1973, **20**, 227–34.

Levander, V. L., Benson, H., Wheeler, R. C., and Wallace, R. K. Increased forearm blood flow during a wakeful hypometabolic state. *Federation Proceedings,* 1972, **31**, 405 (Abstr.)

Levine, Paul *et al.* EEG coherence during the TM technique. In D. Orme-Johnson and J. Farrow (Eds.), *Scientific research on the transcendental meditation program.* Vol. I, 2nd Ed. Maharishi European Research University Press, 1977.

Linden, W. The relationship between the practice of meditation by schoolchildren and their levels of field dependence-independence, test anxiety, and reading achievement. *Journal of Consulting and Clinical Psychology,* 1973, **41**, 139–43.

Lingis, A. Face to face phenomenological meditation. *International Philosophical Quarterly,* 1979, **19**(2), 151–163.

Lintel, A. G. Physiological anxiety responses in transcendental meditators and nonmeditators. *Perceptual and Motor Skills,* 1980, **50**(1), 295–300.

Lowrison, M. Transcendental meditation vs. relaxation therapy. *Bulletin of the British Psychological Society,* 1979, **32**, 39.

Luthe, W. Autogenic training: Method, research, and applications in medicine. In C. Tart (Ed.), *Altered states of consciousness.* New York: Wiley, 1968.

Luthe, W. *Autogenic training: Research and theory.* New York: Grune & Stratton, 1970.

Magarey, C. J. Anxiety, fear, and meditation. *Medical Journal of Australia,* 1981, **1**(7), 375.

Malec, J. and Sipprelle, C. Physiological and subjective effects of Zen meditation and demand characteristics. *Journal of Consulting and Clinical Psychology.* 1977, **44**, 339–340.

Malhotra, J. C. Yoga and psychiatry: A review. *Journal of Neuropsychiatry,* 1963, **4**, 375–385.

Maliszewski, M., Twemlow, S. W., Brown, D. P. & Engler, J. M. A phenomenological typology of intensive meditation: A suggested methodology using the questionnaire approach. *ReVision,* 1981, **4**(2), 3–27.

Marcus, J. B. Transcendental meditation: Consciousness expansion as a rehabilitation technique. *Journal of Psychedelic Drugs,* 1975, **7**(2), 169–79.

Marlatt, G. A. *et al.* Effects of meditation and relaxation training upon alcohol use in male social drinkers. This volume.

Maupin, E. W. Zen Buddhism: A psychological review. *Journal of Consulting Psychology,* 1962, **26**, 362–378.

Maupin, E. Individual differences in response to a Zen meditation exercise. *Journal of Consulting Psychology,* 1965, **29**, 139–45.

Maupin, E. Meditation. In H. Otto and J. Mann (Eds.), *Ways of growth.* New York: Viking, 1968.

Maupin, E. On meditation. In C. Tart (Ed.), *Altered states of consciousness.* New York: Wiley, 1969.

McCuvig, L. W. Salivary electrolytes, protein, and pH during transcendental meditation. *Experientia,* 1974, **30**(9), 988–989.

McDonagh, J. and Egenes, T. Transcendental meditation technique and temperature homeostasis. In D. Orme-Johnson and J. Farrow (Eds.), *Scientific research on the transcendental meditation program.* Vol. I, 2nd Ed., Maharishi European Research University Press, 1977.

McEvoy, T. M., Frumkin, L. R. and Harkins, S. W. Effects of meditation on brain stem auditory evoked potentials. *International Journal of Neuroscience,* 1980, **10**(2–3), 165–170.

McLeod, J. The social psychology of meditation. *Bulletin of the British Psychological Society,* 1979, **32**, 219.

Maquet, J. Meditation in contemporary Sri Lanka. *Journal of Transpersonal Psychology,* 1975, **7**(2), 182–196.

Maris, L., & Maris, M. Mechanics of Stress Release—the TM program and occupational stress. *Police Stress,* 1979, **1**(2), 29–36.

Martinetti, P. Influence of transcendental meditation on perceptual illusion. *Perceptual and Motor Skills,* 1976, **43**(3, pt. 1), 822.

Martinetti, R. F. Influence of Transcendental Meditation on perceptual illusion: A pilot study. *Perceptual & Motor Skills,*, 1976, **43**(3Pt. I), 822.

Meares, A. Regression of cancer after intensive meditation *Medical Journal of Australia,* 1976a, **2**(5), 184.

Meares, A. The relief of anxiety through relaxing meditation. *Australian Family Physician,* 1976b, **5**(7), 906–910.

Meares, A. Vivid visualization and dim visual awareness in the regression of cancer in meditation. *Journal of the American Society of Psychosomatic Dentistry and Medicine,* 1978, **25**(3), 85–88.

Meares, A. The quality of meditation effective in the regression of cancer. *Journal of the American Society of Psychosomatic Dentistry and Medicine,* 1978, **25**(4), 129–132.

Meares, A. Meditation—psychological approach to cancer treatment. *Practitioner,* 1979, **222**(1327), 119–122.

Meares, A. Remission of massive metastatis from undifferentiated carcinoma of the lung associated with intensive meditation. *Journal of the American Society of Psychosomatic Dentistry and Medicine,* 1980, **27**(2), 40–41.

Meserve, H. C. Meditation and health. *Journal of Religion and Health,* 1980, **19**(1), 3–6.

Meuhlman, M. Transcendental meditation. *New England Journal of Medicine,* 1977, **297**(9), 513.

Michaels, R., Huber, M., and McCann, D. Evaluation of transcendental meditation as a method of reducing stress. *Science,* 1976, **192**(4245), 1242–4.

Michaels, R. R., Parra, J., McCann, D. S., and Vander, A. J. Renin, cortisol, and aldosterone during transcendental meditation. *Psychosomatic Medicine,* 1979, **41**(1), 50–54.

Miike, D. Psychological study on the individual differences of Electroencephalography. In: Akishige (Ed.), *Psychological Studies on Zen.* Tokyo: Komazawa University, 1973.

Miles, W. Oxygen consumption during three yoga-type breathing patterns. *Journal of Applied Physiology,* 1964, **19**, 75–82.

Bibliography

Miller, N. Learning of visceral and glandular responses. *Science,* 1969, **163**(3866), 434–445.

Mills, W. W. and Farrow, J. T. The transcendental meditation technique and acute experimental pain. *Psychosomatic Medicine,* 1981, **43**(2), 157–164.

Mishra, R. *Fundamentals of Yoga.* New York: Julian, 1959.

Miskman, D. Effect of the transcendental meditation program on compensatory paradoxical sleep. In D. Orme-Johnson and J. Farrow (Eds.), *Scientific research on the transcendental meditation program.* Vol. I, 2nd Ed. Maharishi European Research University Press, 1977.

Miskiman, D. Effects of the transcendental meditation program on the organization of thinking and recall. In D. Orme-Johnson and J. Farrow (Eds.), *Scientific research on the transcendental meditation program.* Vol. I, 2nd Ed. Maharishi European Research University Press, 1977.

Monahan, R. J. Secondary prevention of drug dependence through the Transcendental Meditation program in metropolitan Philadelphia. *International Journal of the Addictions,* 1977, **12**(6), 729–754.

Mookerjee, A. *Tantra art.* New York: Ravi Kumar, 1966.

Morse, D. R. Meditation in dentistry. *General Dentistry,* 1976a, **24**(5), 57–59.

Morse, D. R. Use of a meditative state for hypnotic induction in the practice of endodontics. *Oral Surgery, Oral Medicine, Oral Pathology,* 1976b, **41**, 664–672.

Morse, D. R. An exploratory study of the use of meditation alone & in combination w/hypnosis in clinical dentistry. *Journal of the American Society of Psychosomatic Dentistry & Medicine,* 1977a, **24**(4), 113–120.

Morse, D. R. Overcoming practice stress via meditation and hypnosis. *Dental Survey,* 1977b, **53**(7), 32–36.

Morse, D. R. Variety, exercise, meditation can relieve practice stress. *Dental Studies,* 1977, **53**(7), 26–29.

Morse, D. R. and Wilcko, J. M. Nonsurgical endodontic therapy for a vital tooth with meditation hypnosis as the sole anesthetic: a case report. *American Journal of Clinical Hypnosis,* 1979, **21**(4), 258–262.

Morse, D. R., Martin, J. S., Furst, M. L., and Dubin, L. L. A physiological and subjective evaluation of neutral and emotionally charged words for meditation. *Journal of the American Society of Psychosomatic Dentistry and Medicine,* 1979, **26**(1), 31–38.

Morse, D. R., Martin, J. S., Furst, M. L., and Dubin, L. L. A physiological and subjective evaluation of neutral and emotionally charged words for meditation. Part II. *Journal of the American Society of Psychosomatic Dentistry and Medicine.* 1979, **26**(2), 56–62.

Morse, D. R., Martin, J. S., Furst, M. L., and Dubin, L. L. A physiological and subjective evaluation of neutral and emotionally charged words for meditation. *Journal of the American Society for Psychosomatic Dentistry and Medicine,* 1979, **26**(3), 106–112.

Muchlman, M. Transcendental meditation. *New England Journal of Medicine,* 1977, **297**(9), 513.

Murdock, M. H. Meditation with young children. *Journal of Transpersonal Psychology,* 1978, **10**(1), 29–44,

Nakamizo, S. Psychophysiological studies on respiratory patterns. *Bulletin of the Faculty of Literature of Kyushu University,* 1974, **5**, 135–67.

Naranjo, C. Meditation: Its spirit and techniques. In C. Naranjo and R. Ornstein. *On the psychology of meditation,* New York: Viking, 1971.

Naranjo, C. and Ornstein, R. *On the psychology of meditation.* New York: Viking, 1971.

Nash, C. B. Hypnosis and Transcendental Meditation as inducers of ESP. *Parapsychology,* 1982, **13**(1), 19–20.

Needleman, J. *et al.* Psychology, science, and spiritual paths: Contemporary issues, *Journal of Transpersonal Psychology,* 1978, **10**(2), 93–112.

Neki, J. Guru-chela: The possibility of a therapeutic paradigm. *American Journal of Orthopsychiatry,* 1973, **43**(5).

Nideffer, R. Alpha and the development of human potential. *Biofeedback and Self-Control,* 1972, 167–88.

Nidich, S., Seeman, W., and Dreskin, T. Influence of transcendental meditation on a measure of self-actualization: A replication. *Journal of Counseling Psychology,* 1973a, **20**, 565–6.

Nidich, S., Seeman, W., & Dreskin, T. Influence of Transcendental Meditation: A replication. *Journal of Counseling Psychology,* 1973b, **20**(6), 565–566.

Nidich, S., Seeman, W., and Seibert, M. Influence of the transcendental meditation program on state anxiety. In D. Orme-Johnson and J. Farrow (Eds.), *Scientific research on the transcendental meditation program.* Vol. I, 2nd Ed., Maharishi European Research University Press, 1977.

Nixon, P. G. F. Meditation or methyldopa? *British Medical Journal,* 1976, **2**(6034), 525.

Nurnberg, H. Meditation and psychotherapy. *World Journal of Psychosynthesis,* 1978, **10**(1), 37–40.

Nystul, M. S., & Garde, M. Comparison of self-concepts of Transcendental Meditators & non-meditators. *Psychological Reports,* 1977, **41**(1), 303–306.

Nystul, M. S. and Garde, M. The self-concepts of regular transcendental meditators, dropout meditators, and nonmeditators. *Journal of Psychology,* 1979, **103**(1), 15–18.

O'Haire, T. D. & Marcia, J. E. Some personality characteristics associated with Ananda Marga meditators: A pilot study. *Perceptual & Motor Skills,* 1980, **51**(2), 447–452.

Onda, A. Autogenic training and Zen. In W. Luthe (Ed.), *Autogenic Training.* New York: Grune & Stratton, 1965.

Onda, A. Zen autogenic training, and hypnotism. *Psychologia,* 1967, **10**, 133–136.

Orme-Johnson, D. W. Autonomic stability and transcendental meditation. *Psychosomatic Medicine,* 1973, **20**, 565–566.

Orme-Johnson, D. W., Kolb, D., and Hebert, J. R. An experimental analysis of the effects of the transcendental meditation technique on reaction time. In D. Orme-Johnson and J. Farrow (Eds.), *Scientific research on the transcendental meditation program.* Vol. I, 2nd Ed. Maharishi European Research University Press, 1977.

Orme-Johnson, D. W. *et al.* Transcendental meditation and drug abuse counselors. In D. Orme-Johnson and J. Farrow (Eds.), *Scientific research on the transcendental meditation program.* Vol. I, 2nd Ed. Maharishi European Research University Press, 1977.

Orme-Johnson, D. and Farrow, J. (Eds.), *Scientific Research on the Transcendental Meditation Program.* Vol. I, 2nd edition. Maharishi European Research University Press, 1977.

Ornstein, R. The techniques of meditation and their implications for modern psychology. In C. Naranjo and R. Ornstein. *On the psychology of meditation.* New York: Viking, 1971.

Ornstein, R. *The psychology of consciousness.* San Fransisco: W. H. Freeman, 1972.

Osis, K., Bokert, E., Carlson, M. L. Dimensions of the meditative experience. *Journal of Transpersonal Psychology,* 1973, **5**(1), 109–135.

Otis, L. S. If well-integrated but anxious, try transcendental meditation. *Psychology Today,* 1974, **7**, 45–46.

Otis, L. S. Adverse effects of transcendental meditation. This volume.

Otis, L. S., Kanellakos, D. P., and Lukas, J. S. *et al.* The psychophysiology of transcendental meditation: A pilot study, in Kanellakos, D. S. and Lukas, J. S. (Eds.), *The Psychobiology of Transcendental Meditation: A Literature Review.* Menlo Park, Calif.: Benjamin, 1974.

Oudshoorn, M. and Ransijn, P. Transcendental meditation and dianetics, (two sections) 2 ways of confronting comments. *Sedrag Tijdschrift Voor Psychologie,* 1979, **7**(4), 255–259.

Pagano, R. R., Rose, R. M., Stivers, R. M., and Warrenburg, S. Sleep during transcendental meditation. *Science,* 1976, **191**, 308–310.

Pagano, R. R. and Frumpkin, L. R. Effects of transcendental meditation in right hemispheric functioning. *Biofeedback and Self-Regulation,* 1977, **2**, 407–415.

Palmer, D. K. Inspired analgesia through TM. *New Zealand Dentistry Journal,* 1980, **76**, 61–63.

Palmer, J., Khamashta, K., & Israelson, K. An ESP ganzfeld experiment with Transcendental Meditators. *Journal of American Society of Psychical Research,* 1979, **73**(4), 333–348.

Parker, J. C., Gilbert, A. S., Thoreson, R. W. Reduction of autonomic arousal in alcoholics. *Journal of Consulting and Clinical Psychology,* 1978, **46**(5), 879–886.

Parulkar, V. G. *et al.* Observations on some physiological effects of transcendental meditation. *Indian Journal Medical Science,* 1974, **28**(3), 156–8.

Patel, C. Yoga and biofeedback in the management of hypertension. *Lancet,* 1973, **2**, 1053–55.

Patel, C. H. 12-month follow-up of yoga and biofeedback in the management of hypertension. *Lancet,* 1975, **1**, 62–65.

Patel, C. H. Randomized control trial of yoga and biofeedback in management of hypertension. *Lancet,* 1975, **11**, 93–94.

Patel, C. TM and hypertension. *Lancet,* 1976, **1**(7958), 539.

Patel, C. H. Biofeedback-aided relaxation and meditation in the management of hypertension. *Biofeedback and Self-Regulation,* 1977, **2**, 1–41.

Patel, C., & Carruthers, M. Coronary risk factor reduction through biofeedback-aided relaxation and meditation. *Journal of the Royal College of General Practitioners,* 1977, **27**(180), 401–405.

Patel, C. H. and North, W. R. S. Randomized controlled trial of yoga and biofeedback in management of hypertension. *Lancet,* 1975, **2**, 93–95.

Patey, J., Vincent, J. D., & Faure, J. M. A. CNV studies during meditation. *Electroencephalography & Clinical Neurophysiology,* 1977, **43**, 540.

Paul, G. Physiological effects of relaxation timing and hypnotic suggestion. *Journal of Abnormal Psychology,* 1969, **74**, 425–37.

Pelletier, K. Influence of transcendental meditation upon autokinetic perception. *Perceptual and Motor Skills,* 1974, **39**, 1031–1034.

Pelletier, K. *Mind as Healer: Mind as Slayer.* NY: Delacorte, 1977.

Pelletier, K. and Pepper, E. The Chutzpah factor in altered states of consciousness, *Journal of Humanistic Psychology,* 1977, **17**(1), 6373.

Peper, E. and Ancoli, S. The two endpoints of an EEG continuum of meditation. . . . *Biofeedback and Self-Regulation,* 1977, **2**, 289–90.

Piggins, D. and Morgan D. Note upon steady visual fixation and repeated auditory stimulation in meditation and the lab. *Perceptual and Motor Skills,* 1977, **44**(2), 357–8.

Piggins, D. and Morgan, D. Perceptual phenomena resulting from steady visual fixation and repeated auditory input under experimental conditions, and in meditation. *Journal of Altered States of Consciousness,* 1977–1978, **3**(3), 197–203.

Pirot, M. The effects of the transcendental meditation technique on auditory discrimination. In D. Orme-Johnson, L. Domash, and J. Farrow, (Eds.),*Scientific research on the transcendental meditation program, collected papers.* Switzerland: MIU Press, 1975, Vol. I.

Pollack, A. A., Weber, M. A., Case, D. B. and Laragh, J. H. Limitations of transcendental meditation in the treatment of essential hypertension. *Lancet,* 1977, **8**, 71–73.

Puente, A. E. and Beiman, I. The effects of behavior therapy, self-relaxation, and transcendental meditation on cardiovascular stress response. *Journal of Clinical Psychology,* 1980, **36**(1), 291–295.

Peunte, A. E. Psychophysiological investigations on Transcendental Meditation. *Biofeedback & Self Regulation,* 1981, **6**(3), 327–342.

Puente, A. E., & Beiman, I. The effects of behavior therapy, self-relaxation, and Transcendental Meditation on cardiovascular stress response. *Journal of Clinical Psychology,* 1980, **1**, 291–295.

Puryear, H. B., Cayce, C. T., & Thurston, M. A. Anxiety reduction associated with meditation: Home study. *Perceptual & Motor Skills,* 1976, **43**(2), 527–531.

Rachman, A. W. Clinical Meditation in groups. *Psychotherapy: Theory, Research & Practice,* 1981, **18**(2), 252–258.

Rahav, G. Transcendental meditation programs in prison. TM and rehabilitation: another view. *Criminal Justice and Behavior,* 1980, **7**(1), 11–17.

Ram Dass, Baba, Ram Dass lecture at Maryland Psychiatric Research Center. *Journal of Transpersonal Psychology,* 1973, **5**(1), 75–103.

Rao, K. R. and Puri, I. Subsensory perception (SSP), extrasensory perception (ESP) and transcendental meditation (TM). *Journal of Indian Psychology,* 1978, **1**(1), 69–74.

Rao, K. R., Dukhan, H. and Rao, P. V. K. Yogic meditation and PSI scoring in forced-choice and free-response tests. *Journal of Indian Psychology,* 1978, **1**, 160–175.

Rao, S. Metabolic cost of head-stand posture. *Journal of Applied Physiology,* 1962, **17**, 117–118.

Bibliography   **709**

Rao, S. Cardiovascular response to headstand posture. *Journal of Applied Physiology*, 1963, **18**, 987–990.

Rao, S. Oxygen consumption during yoga-type breathing at altitudes of 520 m. and 3800 m. *Indian Journal of Medical Research*, 1968, **56**, 701–705.

Raskin, M., Bali, L. R., and Peeke, H. V. Muscle biofeedback and transcendental meditation: a controlled evaluation of efficacy in the treatment of chronic anxiety. *Archives of General Psychiatry*, 1980, **37**(1), 93–97.

Redfering, D. L., & Bowman, M. J. Effects of a meditative-relaxation exercise on non-attending behaviors of behaviorally disturbed children. *Journal of Cinical Child Psychology*, 1981, **10**(2), 126–127.

Redmond, D. P. Meditation and medicine: combined strategies for treating hypertension. *Behavioral Medicine*, 1980, **7**(6), 14–18.

Reed, H. Improved dream recall associated with meditation. *Journal of Clinical Psychology*, 1978, **34**(1). 150–156.

Rieckert, H. Plethysmographic studies in concentration and meditation exercises. *Aerztliche Forschung*, 1976, **21**, 61–65 (Ger.)

Rimol, A. Transcendental meditation technique and effects on sensory-motor performance. In D. Orme-Johnson and J. Farrow (Eds.), *Scientific research on the transcendental meditation program*. Vol. I, 2nd Ed. Maharishi European Research University Press, 1977.

Rivers, S. M., & Spanos, N. P. Personal variables predicting voluntary participation in & attrition from a meditation program. *Psychological Reports*, 1981, **49**(3), 795–801.

Roll, W. G., Solfvin, G. F., and Krieger, J. Meditation and ESP: an overview of four studies. *Journal of Parapsychology*, 1979, **43**(1), 44–45.

Roll, W. G., Solfvin, F. G., Krieger, J., Ray, D., and Younts, L. Group ESP scores, mood, and meditation. *Journal of Parapsychology*, 1980, **44**(1), 74–75.

Routt, T. Low-normal heart and respiratory rates in individuals practicing the transcendental meditation technique. In D. Orme-Johnson and J. Farrow (Eds.), *Scientific research on the transcendental meditation program*. Vol. I, 2nd Ed. Maharishi European Research University Press, 1977.

Rubottem, A. Transcendental Meditation and its potential uses for schools. *Social Education*, 1972, **36**(8).

Russell, W. R. Yoga and the vertebral arteries. *British Medical Journal*, 1972, **1**, 685.

Sabel, B. A. Transcendental meditation in psychology, psychiatry and psychotherapy. *Medizinische Klinik*, 1979, **74**(47), 1779–1784.

Sabel, B. A. Transcendental meditation and concentration ability. *Perceptual and Motor Skills*, 1980, **50**(3, part 1), 799–802.

Sacks, H. L. The effect of spiritual exercises on the integration of self-system. *Journal for the Scientific Study of Religion*, 1979, **18**(1), 46–50.

Sallis, J. F. Meditation and self-actualization: A theoretical comparison. *Psychologia: International Journal of Psychology in the Orient*, 1982, **25**(1), 59–64.

Schacter, S. and Singer, J. Cognitive, social, and physiological determinants of emotional state. *Psychological Review*, 1962, **69**(5), 379–99.

Scharfetter, C. and Benedetti, G. Meditation conceptual field, sifting of findings application in psychotherapy. *Psychotherapie Medizinische Psychologie*, 1979, **29**(3), 78–95.

Schechter, H. The transcendental meditation program in the classroom: A psychological evaluation. In D. Orme-Johnson, L. Domash, and J. Farrow, (Eds.), *Scientific research on the transcendental meditation program, collected papers*. Switzerland: MIU press, 1975, Vol. 1.

Schilling, P. Effect of the regular practice of the transcendental meditation technique on behavior and personality. In D. Orme-Johnson and J. Farrow (Eds.), *Scientific research on the transcendental meditation program*. Vol. I, 2nd Ed. Maharishi European Research University Press, 1977.

Schuster, R. Empathy and mindfulness. *Journal of Humanistic Psychology*, 1979, **19**(1), 71–7.

Schwartz, G., and Weiss, S. What is behavioral medicine? *Psychosomatic Medicine*, 1977, **36**, 377–381.

Schwartz, G. E. Biofeedback as therapy: Some theoretical and practical issues. *American Psychologist*, 1973, **28**, 666–673.

Schwartz, G. Biofeedback, self-regulation, and the patterning of physiological processes. *American Scientist*, 1975, **63**, 314–25.

Schwartz, G., Davidson, R., and Goleman, D. Patterning of cognitive and somatic processes in the self-regulation of anxiety: Effects of medication versus exercise. *Psychosomatic Medicine*, 1978, **40**, 321–8

Seeman, W., Nidich, S., and Banta, T. Influence of TM on a measure of self-actualization. *Journal of Counseling Psychology*, 1972, **19**(3), 184–7.

Seer, P. Psychological control of essential hypertension: review of the literature and methodological critique. *Psychological Bulletin*, 1979, **86**(5), 1015–1043.

Seer, P. and Raeburn, L. M. Meditation training and essential hypertension: a methodological study. *Journal of Behavioral Medicine*, 1979, **3**(1), 59–71.

Seiler, G. and Seiler, V. The effects of transcendental meditation on periodontal tissue. *Journal of the American Society of Psychosomatic Dentistry and Medicine*, 1979, **26**(1), 8–12.

Selye, H. *The stress of life*. New York: McGraw-Hill, 1956.

Shafii, M. Adaptive and therapeutic aspects of meditation. *International Journal of Psychoanalytic Psychotherapy*, 1973, **2**(3). 364–382.

Shafii, M. Silence in the service of ego: Psychoanalytic study of meditation. *International Journal of Psychoanalysis*, 1973, **54**(4), 431–43.

Shafii, M., Lavely, R., and Jaffe, R. Meditation and Marijuana. *American Journal of Psychiatry*, 1974, **131**, 60–3.

Shafii, M., Lavely, R., and Jaffe, R. Meditation and the prevention of alcohol abuse. *American Journal of Psychiatry*, 1975, **132**, 942–45.

Shapiro, D., Tursky, B., and Schwartz, G. Differentiation of heart rate and systolic blood pressure in man by operant conditioning. *Psychosomatic Medicine*, 1970, **32**(4), 417–23.

Shapiro, D., Tursky, B., Schwartz, G. E., and Shnidman, S. R. Smoking on cue: A behavioral approach to smoking reduction. *Journal of Health and Social Behavior*, 1971, **12**, 108–113.

Shapiro, D., Barber, T., DiCara, L. V., Kamiya, J., Miller, N. E., and Stoyva, J. (Eds.), *Biofeedback and self-control: An Aldine annual on the regulation of body processes and consciousness*. Chicago, Ill.: Aldine, 1973.

Shapiro, D. H. A combined personal self-management and environmental consultation strategy. In J. P. Krumboltz and C. E. Thoreson (Eds.). *Counseling methods.* New York: Holt, Rinehart & Winston, 1976a.

Shapiro, D. H. Zen meditation and behavioral self-management applied to a case of generalized anxiety. *Psychologia,* 1976b, **19**(3), 134–8.

Shapiro, D. H. Behavioral and attitudinal changes resulting from a Zen experience workshop in Zen meditation. *Journal of Humanistic Psychology,* 1978a, **18**(3), 21–9.

Shapiro, D. H. *Precision nirvana.* Englewood Cliffs, NJ: Prentice-Hall, 1978b.

Shapiro, D. H. Instructions for a training package combining Zen meditation and behavioral self-management strategies. *Psychologia,* 1978, **21**(2), 70–76.

Shapiro, D. H. Meditation and holistic medicine. In A. Hastings, J. Fadiman, and J. Gordon (Eds.). *Holistic medicine.* Rockville, MD: NIMH, 1980.

Shapiro, D. H. Meditation: Clinical and health related applications. *Western Journal of Medicine,* 1981, **134**, 141–142.

Shapiro, D. H. Overview: Clinical & physiological comparison of meditation and other self-control strategies. *American Journal of Psychiatry,* 1982, **139**(3), 267–274.

Shapiro, D. H. A content analysis of views of self-control: Relation to positive and negative values and implications for a working definition. *Biofeedback and Self Regulation.* 1983, **8**(1), 73–86.

Shapiro, D. H. Meditation as an altered state of consciousness: Empirical contributions of Western behavioral science. *Journal of Transpersonal Psychology,* 1983, **15**(1), 61–81.

Shapiro, D. H. Meditation and behavioral medicine: Use of a self-regulation strategy in anxiety reduction. In S. Burchfield (Ed.), *A comprehensive approach to the treatment of anxiety.* New York: Wiley, in press.

Shapiro, D. H. and Giber, D. Meditation and psychotherapeutic effects. *Archives of General Psychiatry,* 1978, **35**, 294–302.

Shapiro, D. H. and Zifferblatt, S. M. An applied clinical combination of Zen meditation and behavioral self-management techniques: Reducing methadone dosage in drug addiction. *Behavior Therapy,* 1976a, **7**, 694–5.

Shapiro, D. H. and Zifferblatt, S. M. Zen meditation and behavioral self-control: Similarities, differences and clinical applications. *American Psychologist,* 1976b, **31**, 519–32.

Shapiro, D. H. *Meditation: Self-Regulation Strategy and Altered States of Consciousness.* New York: Aldine Press, 1980.

Shapiro, D. H., Shapiro, J., Walsh, R. N., Brown, D. The effects of intensive meditation on sex role identification: Implications for a control model of psychological health. *Psychological Reports,* 1982, **51**, 44–46.

Shapiro, J. and Shapiro, D. H. The psychology of responsibility. *New England Journal of Medicine,* 1979, **301**(4), 211–212.

Shaw, R. and Kolb, D. Improved reaction time following transcendental meditation. In D. Orme-Johnson and J. Farrow (Eds.), *Scientific research on the transcendental meditation program.* Vol. I, 2nd Ed. Maharishi European Research University Press, 1977.

Shelley, 1971. In D. Kanellakos (Comp.) *The psychobiology of transcendental meditation.* Menlo Park, CA: Benjamin, 1974.

Shimano, E. T. and Douglas, R. B. On research in Zen. *American Journal of Psychiatry,* 1975, **132**, 9–12, 1300–02.

Simpson, D., Dansereau, D., and Giles, G. A preliminary evaluation of physiological and behavioral effects of self-directed relaxation. *Catalog of Selected Documents in Psychology,* 1972, Spring, **2**(59).

Singer, J. L. Navigating the stream of consciousness: Research in daydreaming and related inner experience. *American Psychologist,* 1975, **30**, 727–38.

Singer, J. L. *Imagery and daydream methods in psychotherapy and behavior modification.* New York: Academic Press, 1974.

Sinha, S. N., Prasad, S. D. and Sharma, K. N. An experimental study of cognitive control and arousal processes during meditation. *Psychologia (Kyoto),* 1978, **21**(4), 227–230.

Shiomi, K. Respirator and EEG changes by cotention of Trigant Burrow. *Psychologia,* 1969, **12**, 24–43.

Sisley, D. Transcendental meditation and TM Sidhi program—ongoing psychometric evaluation. *New Zealand Psychologist,* 1979, **8**, 49.

Smith, J. Meditation and psychotherapy: A review of the literature, *Psychological Bulletin,* 1975, **32**(4), 553–64.

Smith, J. Psychotherapeutic effects of TM with controls for expectations of relief and daily sitting. *Journal of Consulting and Clinical Psychology,* 1976, **44**(4), 630–7.

Smith, J. Personality correlates of continuation and outcome in meditation and erect sitting control treatments. *Journal of Consulting and Clinical Psychology,* 1978, **46**(2), 272–9.

Smith, J. Meditation research: Three observations on the state of the art. This volume.

Smith, T. The transcendental meditation technique and skin resistance response to loud tones. In D. Orme-Johnson and J. Farrow (Eds.), *Scientific research on the transcendental meditation program.* Vol. I, 2nd Ed. Maharishi European Research University Press, 1977.

Solomon, G. G., and Bumpus, A. K. The running meditation response: An adjunct to psychotherapy. *American Journal of Psychotherapy,* 1978, **32**(4), 583–592.

Soskis, D. A. Teaching meditation to medical students. *Journal of Religion and Health,* 1979, **17**(2), 136–143.

Spanos, N. P., Rivers, S. M., and Gottlieb, J. Hypnotic responsivity, meditation, and laterality of eye movements. *Journal of Abnormal Psychology,* 1978, **87**(5), 566–569.

Spanos, N. P., Steggles, S., Radtke-Bodorik, H. L., and Rivers, S. M. Nonanalytic attending, hypnotic susceptibility, and psychological well-being in trained meditators and nonmeditators. *Journal of Abnormal Psychology,* 1979, **88**(1), 85–87.

Spanos, N. P., Stam, H. J., Rivers, S. M., and Radtke, H. L. Meditation, expectation and performance on indexes of nonanalytic attending. *International Journal of Clinical and Experimental Hypnosis,* 1980, **28**(3), 244–251.

Spanos, N. P., Gottlieb, J. and Rivers, S. H. The effects of short-term meditation practice on hypnotic responsivity. *Psychological Record,* 1980, **30**(3), 343–348.

Sperry, R. A revised concept of consciousness. *Psychological Review,* 1969, **76**, 532–6.

Speigelberg, F. *Spiritual practices of India.* New York: Citadel, 1962.

Stace, W. T. *Mysticism & philosophy.* 1st Ed. Phil.: Lippincott, 1960.

Stek, R. and Bass, B. Personal adjustment and perceived locus of control among students interested in meditation. *Psychological Reports,* 1973, **32**, 1019–22.

Bibliography

Stern, M. Effects of the transcendental meditation program on trait anxiety. In D. Orme-Johnson and J. Farrow (Eds.), *Scientific research on the transcendental meditation program*. Vol. I, 2nd Ed. Maharishi European University Research Press, 1977.

Stewart, R. A. C. Self-realization as the basis of psychotherapy: A look at two Eastern-based practices, Transcendental Meditation and alpha brainwave biofeedback. *Social Behavior & Personality*, 1974, **2**(2), 191–200.

Stigsby, B., Rodenburg, J. C., & Moth, H. B. Electroencephalographic findings during mantra meditation (Transcendental Meditation)—A controlled, quantitative study of experienced meditators. *Electroencephalography & Clinical Neurophysiology*, 1981, **51**(4), 434–442.

Stone, R. and DeLeo, J. Psychotherapeutic control of hypertension. *The New England Journal of Medicine,*, 1976, **294**(2), 80–84.

Stoyva, J., Barber, T., DiCara, L. V., Kamiya, J., Miller, N. E., and Shapiro, D. H., (Eds.). *Biofeedback and self-control: An Aldine annual on the regulation of body processes and consciousness*. Chicago, Ill.: Aldine-Atherton, 1972.

Stroebel, C. and Glueck, B. Passive meditation: Subjective and clinical comparison with biofeedback. In G. Schwartz & D. Shapiro (Eds.), *Consciousness and self-regulation*. New York: Plenum, 1977.

Stunkard, A. Interpersonal aspects of an Oriental religion. *Psychiatry*, 1951, **14**, 419–31.

Subrahmanyam, S., & Porkodi, K. Neurohumoral correlates of TM. *Journal of Biomedicine*, 1980, **1**, 73–88.

Sugi, Y. and Akutsu, K. Studies on respiration and energy metabolism during sitting in Zazen. *Research Journal Physical Education*, 1968, **12**(3), 190–206.

Sugi, Y., & Akutsu, K. Studies on respiration & energy—metabolism during sitting in Zazen. *Research Journal of Physiology*, 1968, **12**, 190–206.

Suinn, R. and Richardson, F. Anxiety management training: A nonspecific behavior therapy program for anxiety control. *Behavior Therapy*, 1971, **2**(4), 498–510.

Surwillo, W. W., & Hobson, D. P. Brain electrical activity during prayer. *Psychological Reports*, 1978, **43**(1), 135–143.

Surwit, R. S., Shapiro, D., and Good, M. I. Comparison of cardiovascular biofeedback, neuromuscular feedback, and meditation in the treatment of borderline hypertension. *Journal of Consulting and Clinical Psychology*, 1976, **46**(2), 252–263.

Suzuki, D. T. Lectures in Zen Buddhism. In E. Fromm (Ed.), *Zen Buddhism and psychoanalysis*. New York: Harper-Colophon 1960.

Suzuki, D. T. *Manual of Zen Buddhism*. London: Rider, 1956.

Takeda, S. A psychological study on 'Zenjo' and breath regulation. In Y. Akishige (Ed.), *Psychological studies in Zen*. Tokyo: Zen Institute of the Komazawa University, 1977.

Tart, C. (Ed.) *Altered states of consciousness*. New York: Wiley, 1969.

Tart, C. A psychologist's experience with T.M. *Journal of Transpersonal Psychology*, 1971, **3**(2), 135–40.

Tart, C. States of consciousness and state-specific sciences. *Science*, 1972, **186**, 1203–10.

Tart, C. *Transpersonal psychologies*. New York: Harper & Row. 1975.

Tebecis, A. A controlled study of the EEG during transcendental meditation: comparison with hypnosis. *Folia Psychiatrica et Neurologica Japonica*, 1975, **29**, 305–313.

Tebecis, A. K. Eye movements during transcendental meditation. *Folia Psychiatrica et Neurologica Japonica*, 1976, **30**(4), 487–493.

Tellegen, A. and Atkinson, G. Openness to absorbing and self-altering experiences. *Journal of Abnormal Psychology*, 1974, **83**(3), 268–77.

Thomas, D. and Abbas, K. A. Comparison of transcendental meditation and progressive relaxation in reducing anxiety. *British Medical Journal*, 1978, **2**(6154), 1749.

Throll, D. A. Transcendental Meditation and progressive relaxation: Their physiological effects. *Journal of Clinical Psychology*, 1982, **38**(3), 522–530.

Timmons, B. and Kamiya, J. The psychology and physiology of meditation and phenomena: A bibliography. *Journal of Transpersonal Psychology*. pp. 1–59.

Timmons, B. and Kanellakos, D. P. The psychology and physiology of meditation and related phenomena: A bibliography. II. *Journal of Transpersonal Psychology*, 1974, **6**, 32–38.

Timmons, B., Salamy, J., Kamiya, J., and Girton, D. Abdominal thoracic respiratory movements and levels of arousal. *Psychonomic Science*, 27, 173–175.

Tjoa, A. Increased intelligence and reduced neuroticism through the transcendental meditation program. In D. Orme-Johnson and J. Farrow (Eds.), *Scientific research on the transcendental meditation program*. Vol. I, 2nd Ed. Maharishi European Research University Press, 1977.

Todd, C. Meditation, mystical and therapeutic. *Bulletin of the British Psychological Society*, 1981, **34**, 101–102.

Travis, F. The transcendental meditation technique and creativity: a longitudinal study of Cornell University graduates. *Journal of Creative Behavior*, 1979, **13**(3), 169–180.

Travis, T., Kondo, C., and Knott, J. Subjective aspects of alpha enhancement. *British Journal of Psychiatry*, 1975, **127**, 122–6,

Travis, T., Kondo, C., and Knott, J. Heart rate, muscle tension, and alpha production of transcendental meditation and relaxation controls. *Biofeedback and self-regulation*. 1976, **1**(4), 387–94.

Traynham, R. The effects of experimental meditation, feedback, and relaxation training on electromyograph and self-report measures of relaxation and altered states of consciousness. *Biofeedback and self-regulation*, 1978, **3**(2), 187.

Treichel, M., Clinch, N., and Cran. M. The metabolic effects of transcendental meditation. *The Physiologist*, 1973, **16**, 472. (Abstr.).

Tulpule, T. Yogic exercises in the management of ischemic heart disease. *Indian Heart Journal*, 1971, **23**, 259–64.

Turnball, M. J., & Norris, H. Effects of TM on self-identity indices & personality. *British Journal of Psychology*, 1982, **73**(1), 57–68.

Udupa, K. N. The scientific basis of yoga. *Journal of the American Medical Association*, 1972, **220**, 1365.

Udupa, K. N. *et al.* Comparative biochemical studies on meditation. *Indian Journal Medical Research*, 1975, **63**(12), 1676–9.

Udupa, K. N., Singh, R. H., and Yadav, R. A. Certain studies on psychological and biochemical responses to the practice of Hatha Yoga in young normal volunteers. *Indian Journal of Medical Research*, 1973, **61** 237–44.

Vahia, H. S., Doengaji, D. R., and Jeste, D. V. *et al.* A deconditioning therapy based upon concepts of Patanjali. *International Journal of Social Psychiatry*, 1972, **18**(1), 61–66.

Vahia, N. S., Doengaji, D. R., Jeste, D. V., Ravindranath, S., Kapoor, S. N., and Ardhapurkar, I. Psychophysiologic therapy based on the concepts of Patanjali. *American Journal of Psychotherapy*, 1973, **27**, 557–565.

Vahia, N. S., Doengaji, D. R., Jeste, D. V., Kapoor, S. N., Ardhapurkar, I. and Ravindranath, S. Further experiences with therapy based on concepts of Patanjali in the treatment of psychiatric disorders. *Indian Journal of Psychiatry*, 1973, **15**, 32–37.

Vakil, R. Remarkable feat of endurance by a Yogi Priest. *Lancet*, 1950, **259**(2), 871.

Valle, R. Chisholm, R., and DeGood, D. The relation of . . . personality factors to alpha. . . . Paper presented at meeting of Biofeedback Research Society, 6th Annual, Monterey, CA, 1975.

Van denBerg, W. P. and Mulder, B. Psychological research on the effects of the transcendental meditation technique on a number of personality variables. In D. Orme-Johnson and J. Farrow (Eds.), *Scientific research on the transcendental meditation program*. Vol. I, 2nd Ed. Maharishi European Research University Press, 1977.

Van Der Lans, J. Religious experience and meditation (Religieuze ervaring en meditatie.) *Psychology*, 1979, **14**, 154–164.

Van Nyus, D. A novel technique for studying attention during meditation. *Journal of Transpersonal Psychology*, 1971, **3**, 125–133.

Van Nuys, D. Meditation, attention and hypnotic susceptibility: A correlational study. *International Journal of Clinical and Experimental Hypnosis*, 1973, **21**, 59–69.

Vanselow, K. Meditative exercises to eliminate the effects of stress. *Hippokrates*, 1968, **39**, 462–465 (Ger.).

Varni, J. W. Self-regulation techniques in the management of chronic arthritic pain in hemophilia. *Behavior Therapy*, 1981, **12**(2), 185–194.

Vattano, A. Self management procedures for coping with stress. *Social Work*, 1978, **23**(2), 113–119.

Waalmanning, H. J. and Jenkins, D. A. Systolic blood-pressure and pulse-rate during transcendental meditation. *Proceedings of the University of Otago Medical School*, 1979, **57**(3), 75–76.

Wachsmuth, D., Dolce, T., & Offenloch, K. Computerized analysis of the EEG during Transcendental Meditation and sleep. *Electroencephalography and Clinical Neurophysiology*, 1980, **48**(3), 39.

Wada, J. A. and Hamm, A. E. Electrographic glimpse of meditative state. *Electroencephalography and Clinical Neurophysiology*, 1974, **37**, 201.

Wallace, R. The physiological effects of transcendental meditation. *Science*, 1970, **167**, 1751–4.

Wallace, R., Benson, H., and Wilson, A. A wakeful hypometabolic physiologic state. *American Journal of Physiology*, 1971, **221**(3), 795–99.

Wallace, R. K., Benson, H., Wilson, A. F., and Garrett, M. D. Decreased blood lactate during transcendental meditation. *Federation Proceedings*, 1971, **30**, 376 (Abstr.).

Wallace, R. K. and Benson, H. The physiology of meditation. *Scientific American*, 1972, **226**(2), 84–90.

Wallace, R. K., Harrington, B., Jacobe, E., and Wagoner, D. The effects of the transcendental meditation and transcendental meditation sidhi programs on the aging process. *Gerontologist*, 1980, **20**(5), 219.

Walrath, L. C. and Hamilton, D. W. Autonomic corelates of meditation and hypnosis. *American Journal of Clinical Hypnosis*, 1975, **17**(3), 190–197.

Walsh, R. Initial meditative experiences: Part I. *Journal of Transpersonal Psychology*, 1977, **9**(2), 151–92.

Walsh, R. Initial meditative experiences: Part II. *Journal of Transpersonal Psychology*, 1978, **10**(1), 1–28.

Walsh, R. Meditation research: An introduction & review. *Journal of Transpersonal Psychology*, 1979, **11**(2), 161–174.

Walsh, R. The consciousness disciplines and the behavioral sciences: questions of comparison and assessment. *American Journal of Psychiatry*, 1980, **137**(6), 663–673.

Walsh, R. A model for viewing meditation research. *Journal of Transpersonal Psychology*, 1982, **14**(1), 69–84.

Walsh, R. N. An evolutionary model of meditation research. This volume.

Walsh, R. N., Goleman, D., Kornfield, J., Pensa, C., and Shapiro, D. Meditation: aspects of research and practice. *Journal of Transpersonal Psychology*, 1978, **10**(2), 113–133.

Walsh, R. and Rauche, L. The precipitation of acute psychoses by intensive meditation in individuals with a history of schizophrenia. *American Journal of Psychiatry*, 1979, **138**(8), 1085–6.

Walsh, R. and Vaughan, R. *Beyond ego: Readings in transpersonal psychology*. Los Angeles: J. B. Tarcher, in press.

Walsh, R. and Shapiro, D. H. (Eds.). *Beyond health and normality: Explorations of extreme psychological well-being*. New York: Van Nostrand, 1983.

Wandhoefer, A., and Platting, K. H. Stimulus-linked DC-shift and auditory evoked potentials in transcendental meditation. *Pfluegers Archiv*, 1973, **343**, R79. (Abstr.).

Warrenburg, S., Pagano, R. R., Woods, M., and Hlastala, M. Oxygen consumption, HR., EMG, and EEG during progressive muscle relaxation (PMR) and transcendental meditation. *Biofeedback and self-regulation*, 1977, **2**, 321 (Abstr.).

Warrenburg, S., Pagano, R. R., Woods, M., and Hlastala, M. A comparison of somatic relaxation and EEG activity in classical progressive relaxation and transcendental meditation. *Journal of Behavioral Medicine*, 1980, **3**(1), 73–93.

Warshal, D. Effects of the transcendental meditation technique on normal and jendrassik reflex time. *Perceptual and Motor Skills*, 1980, **50**(3), 1103–1106.

Washburn, M. Observation relevant to a unified theory of meditation. *Journal of Transpersonal Psychology*, 1978, **10**(1), 45–66.

Watanabe, T., Shapiro, D., and Schwartz, G. Meditation as an anoxic state: A critical review and theory. *Psychophysiologia*, 1972, **2**, 279.

Waxman, J. A finite state model for meditation phenomena. *Perceptual and Motor Skills*, 1979, **49**(1), 123–127.

Weide, T. Varieties of transpersonal therapy. *Journal of Transpersonal Psychology*, 1973, **5**(1), 7–14.

Weinpahl, P. *Matter of Zen*. New York: University Press, 1964.

Welwood, J. Meditation and the unconscious. *Journal of Transpersonal Psychology*, 1977, **9**(1), 1–26.

Welwood, J. Self knowledge as a basis for an integrative psychology. *Journal of Transpersonal Psychology*, 1979, **11**(1), 23–40.

Welwood, J. Befriending emotion: self-knowledge and transformation. *Journal of Transpersonal Psychology*, 1979, **11**(2), 141–160.

Welwood, J. Reflections on psychotherapy, focusing, and meditation. *Journal of Transpersonal Psychology*, 1980, **12**(2), 127–141.

Bibliography

Wenger, M. and Bagchi, B. Studies of autonomic functions in practitioners of Yoga in India. *Behavioral Science*, 1961, **6**, 312–23.

Wenger, M., Bagchi, B., and Anand, B. Experiments in India on "voluntary" control of the heart and pulse. *Circulation*, 1961, **24**, 1319–1325.

Wenger, M., Bagchi, B., and Anand, B. "Voluntary" heart and pulse control by yoga methods. *International Journal of Parapsychology*, 1963, **5**, 25–41.

West, L. J. Transcendental meditation and other nonprofessional psychotherapies. In A. Freedman, H. I. Kaplan, and B. J. Sadock (Ed.), *Comprehensive textbook of psychiatry*, Vol. 2, Baltimore: Williams & Wilkins Co., 1975.

West, M. Transcendental meditation vs. relaxation therapy. *Bulletin of the British Psychological Society*, 1979, **32**, 39–40.

West, M. Meditation, personality, and arousal. *Bulletin of the British Psychological Society (London)*, 1979, **32**, 28.

West, M. Meditation. *British Journal of Psychiatry*, 1979, **135**, 457–467.

West, M. A. Physiological effects of meditation: A longitudinal study. *British Journal of Social and Clinical Psychology*, 1979, **18**, 219–226.

West, M. A. Meditation, personality and arousal. *Personality & Individual Differences*, 1980, **1**(2), 135–142.

West, M. A. The psychosomatics of meditation. *Journal of Psychosomatic Research,*, 1980, **24**(5), 265–273.

West, M. A. Meditation and the EEG. *Psychological Medicine*, 1980, **10**, 369–375.

Westcott, M. Hemispheric symmetry of the EEG during the transcendental meditation technique. In D. Orme-Johnson and J. Farrow (Eds.), *Scientific research on the transcendental meditation program*. Vol. I, 2nd Ed. Maharishi European Research University Press, 1977.

White, K. D. Salivation: The significance of imagery in its voluntary control. *Psychophysiology*, 1978, **15**(3), 196–203.

Wilbur, K. *Spectrum of consciousness*. Wheaton, Illinois: Theosophical Publishing House, 1977.

Wilcox, G. Autonomic functioning in subjects practicing the transcendental meditation technique. In D. Orme-Johnson and J. Farrow (Eds.), *Scientific research on the transcendental meditation program*. Vol. I, 2nd Ed. Maharishi European Research University Press, 1977.

Williams, L. R. and Herbert, P. G. Transcendental meditation and fine perceptual-motor skill. *Perceptual and Motor Skills*, 1976, **43**(1), 303–9.

Williams, L. R. and Vickerman, B. L. Effects of transcendental meditation on fine motor skill. *Perceptual and Motor Skills*, 1976, **43**(2), 607–13.

Williams, L. R. *et al.* Effects of transcendental meditation on rotary pursuit skill. *Research Quarterly*, 1977, **48**(1), 196–201.

Williams, L. R. T. Transcendental meditation and mirror tracing skills. *Perceptual and Motor Skills*, 1978, **46**, 371–378.

Williams, P. and West, M. EEG responses to photic stimulation in persons experienced at meditation. *Electroencephalography and Clinical Neurophysiology*, 1975, **39**(5), 519–22.

Williams, P., Francis, A., & Durham, R. Personality & Meditation. *Perceptual & Motor Skills*, 1976, **43**(3 Pt. I), 787.

Willis, R. J. Meditation to fit the person: Psychology and the meditative way. *Journal of Religion and Health*, 1979, **18**(2), 93–119.

Wilson, A. F. and Honsberger, R. The effects of Transcendental Meditation upon bronchial asthma. *Clinical Research*, 1973, **21**, 278. (Abstr.).

Wilson, A., Honsberger, R., Chiu, J., and Novey, H. Transcendental Meditation and asthma. *Respiration*, 1975, **32**, 74–80.

Winters, T. H. and Kabatzinn, J. Awareness meditation for patients who have anxiety and chronic pain in the primary care unit. *Clinical Research*, 1981, **29**(2), 642.

Woolfolk, R. Psychophysiological correlates of meditation. *Archives of General Psychiatry*, 1975, **32**(1)), 1326–33.

Woolfolk, R., Carr-Kaffeshan, L., and McNulty, T. F. Meditation training as a treatment for insomnia. *Behavior Therapy*, 1976, **7**(3), 359–65.

Woolfolk, R. Self-control, meditation and the treatment of chronic anger. This volume.

Woolfolk, R. and Franks, C. Meditation and behavior therapy. This volume.

Wuthnow, R. Peak experiences: Some empirical tests. *Journal of Humanistic Psychology*, 1978, **18**(3), 59–75.

Yamaoka, T. Psychological study of mental self-control. *Bulletin of the Faculty of Literature of Kyushu University*, 1974, **5**, 225–271.

Yamaoka, T. Psychological study of self control. In Y. Akishige (Ed.), *Psychological studies on Zen*. Tokyo: Zen Inst. of Komazawa University, 1973.

Younger, J., Adrianne, W., and Berger, R. Sleep during transcendental meditation. *Perceptual and Motor Skills*, 1975, **40**, 953–4.

Yuille, J. and Sereda, L. Positive effects of meditation: a limited generalization. *Journal of Applied Psychology*, 1980, **65**(3), 333–340.

Yulis, S., Brahm, G., Charnes, G., Jacard, L. M., Piccta, E., and Retman, F. The extinction of phobic behavior as a function of attention shifts. *Behavior Research and Therapy*, 1975, **13**, 173–76.

Zaichkowsky, L. D. and Kamen, R. Biofeedback and meditation: Effects on muscle tension and locus of control. *Perceptual and Motor Skills,*, 1978, **46**, 955–958.

Zuroff, D. and Schwartz, J. Effects of TM and muscle relaxation on trait anxiety, maladjustment, locus of control, and drug use. *Journal of Consulting and Clinical Psychology*, 1978, **46**(2), 264–71.

Zuroff, D. and Schwartz, J. Transcendental meditation versus muscle relaxation: a two-year follow-up of a controlled experiment. *American Journal of Psychiatry*, 1980, **137**(10), 1229–1231.

INDEX

INDEX